# BRIEF CONTENTS

## PART ONE  FRAMEWORK, THEORY AND REGULATION

## PART TWO  ANNUAL FINANCIAL STATEMENTS

## PART THREE CONSOLIDATED ACCOUNTS AND THE MULTINATIONAL

## PART FOUR FINANCIAL ANALYSIS

# CONTENTS

# PART TWO ANNUAL FINANCIAL STATEMENTS

# PREFACE

## WHY THIS BOOK?

Financial reporting is changing. Accounting has always been a reactive service, changing and developing to meet the practical needs created by the environment in which it operates. This process of change can be illustrated by both time considerations and place considerations. In particular, in the days when most business operations were largely organized within national boundaries, accounting thought, practices and regulation grew up in significantly different ways in different countries, consistent with national environments and characteristics, a process discussed in more detail in Chapter 2.

Now, however, big business is international, and the process and its implications are moving at a very fast rate. Big business is global in its operations; the demand for finance is global and the supply of finance is global. The provision of information, the oil which lubricates any working market, is global in its reach and instantaneous in its transmission. Financial reporting must of necessity be global too. From slow beginnings, the International Accounting Standards Board (IASB) is now poised to become the generally accepted regulator at this international level. From 2005, every listed EU company (and also in Australia) has been required to produce its group financial statements in accordance with International Accounting Standards (IAS) and International Financial Reporting Standards (IFRS). Many countries followed this example and now require IFRS compliance for their listed companies (e.g. Argentina, Brazil, Canada, South Korea). Other countries, as diverse as the USA and China, are seeking close convergence, at minimum, with IASB requirements. The USA allows IFRS accounts without reconciliations for US stock exchange listing for foreign registrants.

The effects on accounting and reporting for business entities operating at a national or local level, many of them of the small and medium-sized enterprises (SME) size, are unclear, and are likely to differ in different places. Two points are very clear to us, however. First, national needs, characteristics and ways of thinking will remain significant at the SME level. Second, the application of agreed IAS, a subjective process of necessity, will continue to be influenced by the context and environment in which the application takes place.

This book is written to reflect this situation and its implications. A knowledge of the requirements of the IFRS is now essential to anyone studying financial accounting and reporting, whether the aim is the preparer focus implied by a desire to enter the accounting professions or the user focus implied by finance, business or MBA-type programmes aimed at management or the educated public.

But, of course, knowledge is not enough. A critical understanding of issues and alternatives, of the whys and wherefores, is also required. The author team has been carefully constructed to contain significant academic, pedagogic and writing experience and to reflect the diversity of European and international thought and experience. Our approach is to expose the reader to the issues by a carefully developed sequence of exposition, student-centred activity and constructive feedback. This process provides a framework with which the reader can assimilate, understand and appraise the exposition of international requirements that follows. Only with such an overall understanding, enhancing both depth and breadth, will the reader be able to follow, and hopefully to take an active part in, the future development of financial accounting and reporting as the process of international change continues.

It is important to be clear that our emphasis is on the IASB requirements, and on a full understanding thereof. How those requirements will actually be applied in detailed practice in the many different countries and cultures involved has to be largely outside our scope. As already indicated, we certainly believe that there will continue to be material differences in the practical interpretation and application of international standards. We give a full justification and explanation of that belief, and provide a framework for analyzing its implications. Nevertheless, it has to be up to the individual reader and/or teacher, situated in a 'local' context, to explore what the implications of that local context may be.

The discussion of all standards has been updated for this sixth edition and brought in line with the latest developments in the IFRS standard-setting programme of the IASB. This implies that at the time of writing, attention has been paid to current evolutions and possible changes in the standards taking place in the near future. For this new edition we have included extracts from company reports from a variety of international corporations to provide students with real-life insight into financial accounting and have introduced a new chapter (Chapter 8) on fair value accounting.

## STRUCTURE AND PEDAGOGY

The broad structure of the book is as follows: Part One provides the essential conceptual and contextual background. Parts Two and Three explore the detailed issues and problems of financial reporting both in general and through the specific regulatory requirements of the International Accounting Standards Board – for individual company issues in Part Two and for group and multinational issues in Part Three. Part Four provides a summation by an in-depth consideration of financial statement analysis within a dynamic international context.

Each chapter follows a similar pattern in terms of pedagogic structure. Learning objectives set out what the student should be aiming to achieve, with an introduction to put the chapter in context. There are frequent activities throughout the chapter, with immediate feedback so that students can work through practical examples and reflect on the points being made. The chapter closes with a summary and exercises. Answers to some of the exercises can be found on our dedicated CourseMate, the remainder on the Instructor online support resources.

## SUPPLEMENTARY MATERIALS

Students have access to the following resources on Cengage's interactive 'Course-Mate' platform via the printed access card in the front of the book, which contains access details and a unique access code:

- Answers to students' exercises (at end of chapters)
- Sample chapter – Chapter 24 on Statements of cash flows
- Online chapters on industry-specific IFRSs – mineral resources exploration and agriculture
- A glossary of Accounting and Finance definitions
- Related links

Instructors have access to the following additional resources (via specific login details which they can request from the Cengage sales representative after adoption of the book):

- Answers to students' exercises
- Answers to instructors' exercises
- PowerPoint slides
- Online chapters on industry-specific IFRSs – mineral resources exploration and agriculture

## TARGET AUDIENCE

This is not a book for those with no prior exposure to accounting. A one-year introductory course in accounting and a basic understanding of the principles of double-entry, or some practical business exposure, are assumed. However, we recognize that such earlier work may have taken any of a wide variety of different forms, have approached the subject from any of several different directions, and indeed may well not have been studied in the English language. The book will be particularly suitable for the middle and advanced years of undergraduate three- or four-year degree programmes, for post-graduate programmes requiring an internationalization of prior studies of a national system and for MBA-type programmes where a true understanding of the issues and the implication of accounting subjectivity and diversity is required.

## LIST OF REVIEWERS

The publishers would like to thank the following academics for their insightful feedback and suggestions which helped shape the sixth edition:

Simon Brook,  Sheffield Hallam University, UK
Stefano de Cesaris,  City University, UK
Jing Li,  University of Bradford, UK
T.A. Marra,  Groningen University, The Netherlands
Wendy Mason Burdon,  Northumbria University, UK
Dirk Swagerman,  Groningen University, The Netherlands

## OFFICIAL EXAM QUESTIONS

We are grateful to the Association of Chartered Certified Accountants (ACCA) for permission to reproduce past examination questions. The suggested solutions in the exam answer bank have been prepared by us, unless otherwise stated.

We are also grateful to the Chartered Institute of Management Accountants (CIMA) for granting permission to reproduce past examination questions and answers.

# ACKNOWLEDGEMENTS

We are grateful for constructive help and support from several quarters. First of all the authors are indebted to Christoph Muller (Air Lingus, formerly CEO Sabena) for the assistance given and the insight into the airline industry derived from discussion with him. Further, the authors want to thank Leo van der Tas (Tilburg University and Ernst & Young) for his comments on Chapter 2. We are especially grateful to Karel van Hulle for providing many helpful comments to us regarding earlier editions. For the 6th edition we are grateful to George Georgiou for contributing Chapter 29 to this edition. Five spouses and their offspring have coped with the conflicting demands on our time and thoughts. Now, perhaps, it is your turn to help us, or to help us to help you. Suggestions for further development and improvement would be gratefully received by authors or publisher.

Finally, to come back to where we started, we hope that you, the reader, will be interested and stimulated. The internationalization of accounting is an unstoppable force, which will create new and demanding challenges. We believe that participation in this process will be a fascinating and rewarding experience. We hope that you will agree when you have finished studying this book.

David Alexander, University of Birmingham
Anne Britton, Formerly of Leeds Metropolitan University
Ann Jorissen, University of Antwerp
Martin Hoogendoorn, Erasmus University Rotterdam
Carien Van Mourik, Open University – United Kingdom

# WALK THROUGH TOUR

**Learning Objectives** These appear at the start of each chapter to help you monitor your understanding and progress through each chapter. Learning objectives are followed by an introduction which puts the chapter's content in context.

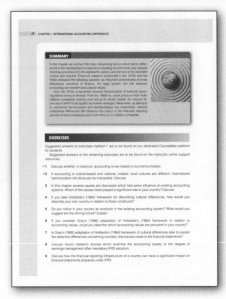

**Chapter Summary** Each chapter ends with a comprehensive summary that provides a thorough re-cap of the issues in each chapter, helping you to assess your understanding and revise key content.

**Activity (and Activity Feedback)** With immediate feedback, these activities provide an opportunity to work through practical examples and reflect on the points being made.

**Annual Reports** Extracts from company reports from a variety of international corporations provide students with real-life insight into financial accounting.

**Illustrations and Real World Illustrations** Providing an example of a detailed, practical application, the illustrations work through core concepts to aid understanding.

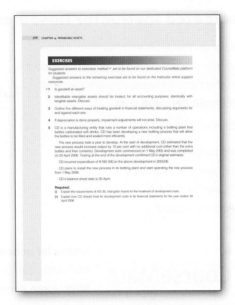

**Exercises** Appearing at the end of each chapter, these help reinforce and test your knowledge and understanding, and provide a basis for group discussions and activities. Answers to questions marked with ✓ are available in the students' area of CourseMate and the remainder in the instructors' area.

**REFERENCES**

**Figures** Throughout the chapters, figures and tables help explain the subject by giving a visual representation of key concepts or data.

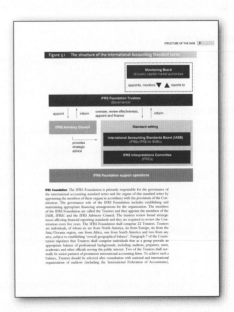

**References** Comprehensive references at the end of the book allow you to explore the subject further, and act as a starting point for projects and assignments.

# DIGITAL SUPPORT RESOURCES

## Dedicated Instructor Resources

To discover the dedicated instructor online support resources accompanying this textbook, instructors should register here for access:
**http://login.cengage.com**

Resources include:

- Instructor's Manual
- Solutions to Exercises
- PowerPoint slides
- Additional chapter

**Instructor access**

Instructors can access CourseMate by registering at **http://login.cengage.com** or by speaking to their local Cengage Learning EMEA representative.

**Instructor resources**

Instructors can use the integrated Engagement Tracker in CourseMate to track students' preparation and engagement. The tracking tool can be used to monitor progress of the class as a whole or for individual students.

**Student access**

Students can access CourseMate using the unique personal access card included in the front of the book.

**Student resources**

CourseMate offers a range of interactive learning tools tailored to the sixth edition of *International Financial Reporting and Analysis*, including:

- Solutions to selected exercises
- Interactive eBook
- A glossary of Accounting and Finance definitions
- Links to useful websites

# PART ONE

# FRAMEWORK, THEORY AND REGULATION

In this first part we look at what financial reporting is all about – what it is trying to achieve and how the accountant sets about achieving it. We explore the international context, reasons for national differences in accounting practice and tradition and the developing international regulatory system designed to achieve greater harmonization.

# BASICS OF FINANCIAL REPORTING

**1**

**OBJECTIVES** After studying this chapter you should be able to:

- explain and discuss the scope of accounting in general and of financial reporting in particular

- describe the major types of users of published financial information and discuss the implications of their different needs

- list and discuss the characteristics of accounting information that are likely to maximize its usefulness

- describe and apply the traditional conventions applied in financial reporting

- discuss and illustrate the internal coherence or inconsistency of these conventions.

## INTRODUCTION

At its simplest level, accounting is about the provision of figures to people about their resources. It is to tell them such things as:

1 what they have got
2 what they used to have
3 the change in what they have got
4 what they may get in the future.

You may have done quite a lot of 'accounting' already. In many cases this will have consisted largely of technical manipulation – writing up ledger accounts, preparing profit and loss accounts and balance sheets, and so on. Much of the emphasis is likely to have been on 'doing things with numbers'. Given a figure to start with, you can probably record it in a proper double-entry manner and see its effect through onto a balance sheet that actually balances.

But this is only part of the story. Suppose you are not 'given a figure'. Suppose you are given, or have available, a whole variety of figures all related to a particular item or transaction. Which figure or figures should you actually put into the double-entry system? More fundamentally, *how* are you going to decide which ones to put in? In very general terms, we can answer this question by going back to our original simple definition of accounting. Namely, that it concerns the provision of figures to people about their resources. Presumably, therefore, the figures that we as accountants should provide to people are the figures that they need to know for their own particular purpose.

So the key question is: What do people want to know about their resources? Or, what use do they wish to make of the figures we as accountants provide? Once we have answered this question, we can go on to say that the figure we should put into our double-entry system is the one likely to be *most useful to the user of our accounting reports.*

Accounting therefore needs:

- an effective and efficient data handling and recording system
- the ability to use that system to provide something useful to somebody.

This book is essentially concerned with the second of these needs. We have to consider three fundamental issues:

1 Who are the users of accounting statements?
2 What is the purpose for which each particular type of user requires the information?
3 How can we provide the user with the information best suited to their needs?

However, we have also to remember that the accountant and the user themselves have to operate within, and under the control of, the community at large. There is, therefore, an element of *regulation* that has to be taken into account.

## USERS OF FINANCIAL REPORTS

As readers will be aware, accounting can be divided into management accounting and financial accounting. Very broadly, management accounting is designed for the management user, i.e. for internal decision making, and financial accounting is designed for all other users. The theoretical distinction is that management, by definition, can obtain whatever information it needs from within the organization. External users, however, have to rely on negotiation or regulation in order to obtain information. Financial reporting is only concerned with external users and so is this book.

## ACTIVITY 1.1

Nine user groups can be suggested for financial reporting, as follows:

1 The equity investor group, including existing and potential shareholders and holders of convertible securities, options or warrants.

2 The loan creditor group, including existing and potential holders of debentures and loan stock and providers of short-term secured and unsecured loans and finance.

3 The employee group, including existing, potential and past employees.

4 The analyst-adviser group, including financial analysts and journalists, economists, statisticians, researchers, trade unions, stockbrokers and other providers of advisory services, such as credit-rating agencies.

5 Suppliers and trade creditors – past, present and potential.

6 Customers – also past, present and potential.

7 Competitors and business rivals.

8 The government, including tax authorities, departments and agencies concerned with the supervision of commerce and industry, and local authorities.

9 The public, including taxpayers, consumers and other community and special interest groups, such as political parties, consumer and environmental protection societies and regional pressure groups.

Taking each of these groups one at a time, consider first the sorts of decisions that they are likely to wish to make using accounting information and, second, the implications from this as to what information they might need.

### Activity feedback
### The equity investor group
Essentially, this group consists of existing and potential shareholders. This group is considering whether or not to invest in a business: to buy shares or to buy more shares; or, alternatively, whether or not to disinvest, to sell shares in the business. Equity investors look for one or a combination of two things: income, a money return by way of dividend, or capital gain, a money return by way of selling shares at more than their purchase price. It should be apparent that these two are closely related. Indeed, the only difference is the timescale. However, the simple theory is made immensely more complex in practice by the effects on share prices of other equity investors' expectations.

For example, share prices for a company may rise because higher dividends are expected to be announced by the company. Alternatively they may rise because other people believe dividends will increase. A buys some shares in expectation of 'good news'. This causes prices to rise. B then buys some shares in expectation of the price rise continuing. This causes the price to rise again – a self-fulfilling prophecy – which brings in C as a buyer too. The original hope of 'good news' is soon forgotten. If, however, at a later date the news arrives and turns out to be bad, everyone involved – A, B and C – may want to sell and the price will come crashing down.

The motivational and psychological arguments involved here are well beyond the scope of this book. It is the information requirements that concern us. If the investor is taking a short-term view then current dividends may be a major factor. As the time horizon of our investor lengthens, then future dividends become more important and future dividends are affected crucially by present and future earnings. The focus then is on profits, which both determine future dividends and influence the share price.

One obvious point is that investors, both existing and potential, need information about future profits. The emphasis in published accounting information is almost wholly on past or more or less present profits. These may or may not be a good guide to the future. The need to make the past results useful for estimating (guessing) the future is an important influence on some of the detailed disclosure requirements we shall explore later. The general trend is to make reported accounting statements as suitable as possible for investors to make their own estimations. We should note an alternative possibility, however. This is that the company itself – through either the management or possibly through the auditors – should make a forecast. After all, the management and the

(Continued)

## ACTIVITY 1.1    *(Continued)*

auditor have a much greater insight into possibilities and risks than the external shareholder.

### The loan creditor group

This group consists of long-, medium- or short-term lenders of money. The crucial question an existing or potential loan creditor wishes to consider is obvious: Will he or she get their money back? A short-term loan creditor will primarily be interested, therefore, in the amount of cash a business has got or will very soon get. As a safeguard, they will also be interested in the net realizable value (NRV) of all the assets and the priority of the various claims, other than their own, on the available resources. Longer-term lenders will clearly need a correspondingly longer-term view of the firm's future cash position. Their needs are thus similar to the needs of the equity investor group – they need to estimate the overall strength and position of the business some way into the future.

### The employee group

Employees or their representatives need financial information about the business for two main reasons:

1  fair and open collective bargaining (i.e. wage negotiations)
2  assessment of present and future job security.

In these respects they also need to be able to assess the economic stability and vulnerability of the business into the future.

The employees, actual or potential, will also have additional requirements, however:

1  They will often need detailed information at 'local' level, i.e. about one particular part of the business or one particular factory.
2  They will need information in a clear and simple non-technical way.
3  They will need other information that is inherently non-financial. They will want to know, for instance, about management attitudes to staff involvement in decision making, about 'conditions of service' generally, promotion prospects and so on. It can thus be seen that the employee group may require particular statements for its own use and that it may require information not traditionally regarded as 'financial' at all.

### The analyst-adviser group

In one sense this is not a separate group. It is a collection of experts who advise other groups. Stockbrokers and investment analysts will advise shareholders, trade union advisers will advise employees, government statisticians will advise the government and so on. The needs of the analyst-adviser group are obviously essentially the needs of the particular group they are advising. However, being advisers, and presumably experts, they will need more detail and more sophistication in the information presented to them.

### Suppliers and trade creditors

Suppliers and trade creditors need similar information to that required by short-term loan creditors. But they will also need to form a longer-term impression of the business's future. Regular suppliers are often dependent on the continuation of the relationship. They may wish to consider increasing capacity specifically for one particular purchaser. They will therefore need to appraise the future of their potential customers both in terms of financial viability and in terms of sales volume and market share.

### Customers

Customers will wish to assess the reliability of the business both in the short-term sense (will I get my goods on time and in good condition?) and in the long-term sense (can I be sure of after-sales service and an effective guarantee?). Where long-term contracts are involved, the customer will need to be particularly on his or her guard to ensure that the business appears able to complete the contract successfully.

### Competitors

Competitors and business rivals will wish to increase their own effectiveness and efficiency by finding out as much as possible about the financial, technical and marketing structure of the business. The business itself will naturally not be keen for this information to become generally available within the industry and it is generally recognized that businesses have a reasonable right to keep the causes of their own competitive advantage secret. Competitors may also wish to consider a merger or an amalgamation or a straight takeover bid. For this purpose they need all this information, plus the information required by the equity investor group. They also need information about what they – the bidders – could do with the business. In other words, they need to be able to form an opinion on both:

- what the existing management is likely to achieve
- and what new management could achieve with different policies.

*(Continued)*

## ACTIVITY 1.1    (Continued)

### The government

Everybody is aware that governments require financial information for purposes of taxation. This may be the most obviously apparent use by governments, but it is not necessarily the most important. Governments also need information for decision-making purposes. Governments today take many decisions affecting particular firms or particular industries, both in a control sense and in its capacity as purchaser or creditor. Also, governments need information on which to base their economic decisions regarding the economy as a whole. This information is likely to need to be very detailed and to go well beyond the normal historic information included in the usual published accounting reports. Again, there is an obvious need for future-oriented information.

### The public

Economic entities, i.e. businesses in the broadest and most general sense, do not exist in isolation. They are part of society at large and they react and interact with society at every level. At the local level, there will be concern at such things as employment, pollution, and health and safety. At the wider level, there may be interest in, for example, pollution and 'green' issues, energy usage, effective use of subsidies, dealings with foreign governments and contributions to charities in money or kind. Much of this information is non-financial. Indeed, some of it cannot be effectively measured at all. Whether it is accounting information is an open question. But it is certainly useful information about businesses.

## Summary of user needs

Several general points emerge from the preceding discussion:

1 Many, although not all, of the information requirements are essentially forward looking.

2 Different users, with different purposes, may require *different* information about the *same* items.

3 Different users will require (and be able to understand) different degrees of complexity and depth.

4 Not all the information required is likely to be included in financial accounts.

## CHARACTERISTICS OF USEFUL INFORMATION

## ACTIVITY 1.2

Make a list of the desirable attributes or characteristics (such as relevance, for example) that financial information should have if it is likely to be useful.

### Activity feedback

Seven general ideas occur to us, as follows.

### Relevance

This sounds obvious, but on reflection it is difficult to define and therefore to achieve. A report must give the user what he or she wants. As already indicated, this presupposes that we, the accountants preparing the report, know:

1 who the user is

2 what their purpose is

3 what information he or she requires for this purpose.

Clearly these requirements may change as time progresses.

### Understandability

Different users will obviously have different levels of ability as regards understanding accounting information. Understandability does not necessarily mean simplicity. It means that the reports must be geared to the abilities and knowledge of the users concerned. Complex economic

(Continued)

## ACTIVITY 1.2 *(Continued)*

activities being reported to an expert user may well require extremely complicated reports. Simple aspects being reported to users with little or no background knowledge will need to be very simple. The problems really arise when we have the task of reporting on complex activities to the non-expert user.

### Reliability
The user should be able to have a high degree of confidence in the information presented to him or her. This does not necessarily mean that the information has to be factually correct, but it should be as credible, as believable, as possible. Preferably it should be independently verified, for example by an independent, qualified auditor. However, unverified – or unverifiable – information may be better than no information at all.

### Completeness
The user should be given a total picture of the reporting business as far as possible. This is a tall order. It implies large and complex collections of information. It may also imply problems of understandability.

### Objectivity
The information presented should be objective or unbiased in that it should meet all proper user needs, and be neutral in that the perception of the measurer should not be biased towards the interest of any one user group. Objectivity is a confused notion, with several different possible meanings. We shall consider the problems in more detail later. The present proposition is that reports should not be biased by the personal perception, the personal opinion, of the preparer of those reports. The stated need is not for reports with no personal opinion, but for reports with unbiased *personal opinion*.

### Timeliness
Essentially, this means that information should be provided to the user in time for use to be made of it. Information presented should be as up to date as possible. Approximate information, made available in time to assist with some decision or action, is likely to be more useful than precise and accurate information presented after the decision has already been made.

### Comparability
Information about any one business for any one period should be presented so that:

1 it can be easily compared with information about the same business for a different period

2 it can be easily compared with information about a different business for the same, or even a different, period.

Clearly, consistency of treatment is very important here – the application of generally accepted standards (and generally accepted regulatory standards).

## NEED FOR COMMUNICATION

So we have some idea of the various characteristics of useful information. But, more fundamentally, what is information? Remember our earlier suggestion that accounting is about the 'provision of useful figures to people about their resources'. The accountant has to provide figures to the user. But 'provide' does not just mean 'send'. It is not enough to send, to deliver, sheets of paper or electronic documents with words and figures. There has to be *communication*, there has to be *understanding* by the user. The point about communication, the point about information, is that the receiver is genuinely informed. He or she must become mentally and personally aware.

If effective communication is to take place, the language used must be such that the signs employed evoke in others the same response as if those others were to see the object represented instead of the signs. This is, of course, an idealistic position. A television news film can never really put the viewer in the same position in every respect as if they were physically present at the actual event filmed. Even less successful is a verbal description by 'someone who was present'. In accounting, the means of communication is essentially a few numbers, usually prepared by someone who was not actually involved in the financial events supposedly being portrayed anyway. But it is a useful idea to bear in mind, however impossible to achieve.

Another problem is the likely ignorance of the intended receiver of the information. Accounting 'signs' are highly 'coded'. The accountant knows what he or she means, but does anybody else? And how is the user requiring the information to specify exactly what is wanted from the accountant if they cannot 'speak the language'? Clearly, when we think about it, the accountant has to communicate the main features of the reports in non-accounting terms.

## Financial accounting conventions

We have looked at some of the possible things that financial accountants could do in order to provide useful figures to people about their resources. We have looked at who the users are and what sort of information they might need. In this and the following chapters we look at what accountants usually *do* do. Many different words are used in textbooks, articles and statements to describe these ideas – concepts, conventions, assumptions, postulates, for example. Some of them are described as being more 'fundamental' than the others. In this chapter we shall simply refer to all of them as 'conventions'. Later we shall look at how international bodies define and divide them, but here we concentrate on the ideas themselves.

We shall consider 12 separate conventions, as follows: business entity, duality, monetary measurement, cost, accounting period, continuity (going concern), conservatism (prudence), consistency, materiality, objectivity, realization of revenue and matching.

## Business entity

This states that the business has an identity and existence distinct from its owners. To the accountant, whatever the legal position, the business and the owner(s) are considered completely separately. Thus the accountant can always speak of the business owing the owner money, borrowing money from the owner, owing profits to the owner and so on. Think of the basic business balance sheet:

| | |
|---|---|
| Non-current assets | Capital |
| Current assets | Liabilities |
| Total | Total |

As we know, a properly prepared balance sheet can always be relied on to balance. Why is this? The simple answer is because capital is the balancing figure. Capital is the amount of wealth invested in the business by the owner, the amount of money borrowed by the business from the owner or the amount the business owes the owner. None of these three statements could be made unless the accountant is treating the business as separate from, and distinct from, the owner. The accountant usually prepares the accounts of, i.e. the balance sheet of, the business. Transactions of the business are recorded as they affect the business, not as they affect the owner. In principle, another balance sheet always exists, namely for the owner as an individual. This will contain the owner's investment in the business, shown as one of his or her assets.

## Duality

This may be regarded as a formalization of the basis of double-entry. It states that in relation to any one economic event, two aspects are recorded in the accounts, namely:

1 the source of wealth

2 the form it takes (i.e. its application).

In the simplest of terms, 1 is 'where it comes from' and 2 is 'what we have done with it'. The source it came from will have a claim back on it. Thus, again in balance sheet terms, we can say that the balance sheet shows the array of resources at a point in time (assets) and the claims on those resources (liabilities); it shows the application of what was available (assets) and the source of what is available (liabilities or claims).

## Monetary measurement

Accountants regard their job as dealing with financial information. This convention states that the accountant only records those facts that are expressed in money terms. Any facts, however relevant they may be to the user of the information, are ignored by the accountant if they cannot conveniently be expressed in money terms. It is often said that the greatest asset an effective and efficient business possesses is its workforce. So why does the workforce never appear on a business balance sheet? The short answer is that it would be extremely difficult to 'put a figure on' the workforce, i.e. to express this asset, this resource, in money terms. So the accountant does not even bother to try. Facts and outcomes that cannot be expressed in money terms are ignored. This convention and its limitations are sometimes queried.

## Cost

This convention states simply that resources acquired by the business are recorded at their original purchase price. It follows on from the previous convention in that it tells us how that item is actually to be measured. This is the well-known historical cost (HC) convention. It does not now receive the near universal support of earlier years.

## Accounting period

This very simple convention recognizes that profit occurs over time and we cannot usefully speak of the profit 'for a period' until we define the length of the period. The maximum length of period normally used is one year. This is supported by legislation normally requiring the preparation of full audited accounts annually. This does not, of course, preclude the preparation of accounts for shorter periods as well. But the formal 'published accounts' period is nearly always one year.

## Continuity (going concern)

This important convention states that in the absence of evidence to the contrary it is assumed that the business will continue into the indefinite future. This convention has a major influence on the assumptions made when evaluating particular items in the balance sheet. For example, the convention allows us to assume that inventory will eventually be sold in the normal course of business, i.e. at normal selling prices. Perhaps even more obviously it allows for the principle of depreciation. If we depreciate an item of plant over ten years, then we are assuming that the plant will have a useful life to the business (not necessarily a useful total *physical* life) of ten years. This assumption can only be made if we are first assuming that the business will continue – or keep going – for at least ten years. Notice, incidentally, that the going concern assumption does not say that the business is going to keep being profitable into the indefinite future. It merely assumes that the business will manage not to collapse altogether.

## Conservatism (prudence)

This convention refers to the accounting practice of recognizing all possible losses, but not anticipating possible gains. This will tend to lead to an understatement of profits – to an understatement of asset values with no corresponding understatement of liability.

The accounts are in essence trying to give an indication of the current position (the balance sheet) and of the degree of success achieved through the accounting period (the profit and loss (P&L) account). This convention requires the accountant to attempt to ensure that the position or the degree of success is not overstated. Recognizing that absolute accuracy is not possible, the accountants, according to this convention, should ensure the avoidance of overstatement by deliberately setting out to achieve a degree of understatement. This requires that similar items, some of which are favourable and some of which are unfavourable, should not be treated identically or symmetrically.

---

### ACTIVITY 1.3

Give some examples of regular non-symmetrical treatment of favourable and unfavourable aspects of otherwise similar items.

*Activity feedback*
There are many examples to choose from. Two examples are:

1  *the treatment of inventory, which is usually shown at cost or NRV if lower (but not at NRV if higher) – see Chapter 17*

2  *the whole approach to contingent items – see Chapter 20.*

---

## Consistency

This is the practice of applying the same accounting rules, methods or procedures in each similar case. This convention should:

1  avoid short-term manipulation of reported results
2  facilitate comparisons within the firm over different accounting periods (intra-firm comparisons)
3  facilitate comparison between different entities (inter-firm comparisons).

Consistency can, of course, never overrule the requirements of proper and useful reporting. But the convention does certainly support the argument that where several alternative treatments or approaches are acceptable, the business should make a decision and then stick to it year by year for all similar items.

## Materiality

This is a statistical concept that, in its application to accounting, implies that insignificant items should not be given the same emphasis as significant items. The insignificant items are, by definition, unlikely to influence decisions or provide useful information to decision makers, but they may well cause complication and confusion to the user of accounts. Their detailed treatment may also involve a great deal of time and effort – and therefore of money – for no useful purpose. Many firms, for example, treat smallish items that fulfil all the theoretical requirements of the definition of fixed assets, but cost below a defined minimum amount, as simple current expenses. This is not done because it is correct. It is done because it is easier and because it is 'good enough' for practical purposes and for users' informational needs.

## Objectivity

This convention refers to an attribute or characteristic of accounting information generally regarded as desirable. This is that accounting measurements and information should permit qualified individuals working independently to develop similar measures or conclusions from the same evidence. In a nutshell, accounting information should be verifiable. Two schools of thought seem to have arisen in recent years over the full implications of this. One argues that the desire for objectivity implies as much factual content as possible. Facts, for example the actual cost figure specified in a contract, are easily verifiable. This idea surely corresponds with the everyday meaning of objectivity, i.e. the avoidance of subjectivity, the avoidance of personal opinion.

The second school of thought seems to argue that the degree of objectivity can be indicated not by the amount of formal (factual) verifiability, but by the degree of consensus achieved by several independent opinions. The question of whether a young woman is pretty or a young man is handsome clearly depends on the person giving the opinion ('beauty is in the eye of the beholder'). But this second school of thought would presumably argue that if, say, six people all say that they agree with such a statement, it becomes objective, becomes a fact ('the majority is always right'). You, the reader, must make your own mind up. But what is clear in any event is the convention that verifiability is a desirable element in accounting.

## Realization of revenue

We have just established the convention that an asset acquired by the business is usually recorded at the original purchase price. It is thus based on a market transaction. It is obvious that, at the latest, when the asset is disposed of by the business, we must record the actual disposal price. So if we buy inventory for €30, €30 has to be recorded as having gone and inventory (of €30, cost convention) has to be recorded as being present. If we then sell the inventory for €50, we must record €50 as being present and inventory has to be removed from the accounts. Thus an asset of €30 has been replaced by an asset of €50, giving a profit of €20. Once the €50 is physically in, there is no other possibility than to record an asset of €50. But is there no possibility of recognizing an asset of €50 before, i.e. earlier than, the physical arrival of the money? Suppose we sell the inventory on 1 December and receive the money on 10 December. When did assets of €30 turn into assets of €50? Was it 10 December when we received the money? Or was it 1 December, when we acquired the expectation – indeed the right – to receive the money?

More importantly perhaps, what criteria are we going to use to answer this question? On what grounds should we decide when the total asset figure increased, i.e. when the profit was made? This is a very complicated matter. We can first of all state the usual conventional answer: revenue is recognized as soon as, and is allocated to the period in which:

1 it is capable of objective measurement, and
2 the asset value receivable in exchange is reasonably certain.

But this is really rather simplistic and we need to explore the area in more detail (see Chapter 19).

Before we do that, we should complete our overview by seeing how the revenue recognition question leads on to the calculation of profit. Since profit is revenue less expenses, we must explore the idea of matching expenses and revenues together.

## Matching

Looking back over the conventions we have discussed so far, we have:

1 decided on the basic characteristics of the recording system (business entity and duality)
2 decided on how we are going to record items entering the business's control (monetary measurement and cost)
3 decided on how to record the proceeds from the disposal of such items (revenue recognition).

The essential item missing is clearly the mechanism for recording the actual loss of the item – its removal from the financial statements about the business. The earlier question was: 'When did assets of €30 turn into assets of €50?' It is intuitively clear that whenever this did happen (and the revenue recognition convention tells us when), a profit of €20 was made. Thus, if the revenue – the benefit – is €50, then the expense – the amount used or lost – is €30. The matching convention covers this final stage in the process of profit calculation. It states that:

> Income (or profit) determination is a process of matching against revenue the expenses incurred in earning that revenue.

When an asset gets used, it becomes an expense. The question in effect is: At precisely what point does the accountant regard an asset as being 'used'? The answer is: At the point when the related revenue is recognized, so the process of profit calculation can be summarized as follows. First, we determine the point at which the revenue is to be recognized, the time when the proceeds are 'made'. Second, we match the expense against the revenue, i.e. we regard the expense as occurring at the same time as the revenue. So if the revenue from selling an item of inventory is recognized on 28 December as €50 then the expense of €30 is also recognized on 28 December. Accounts prepared on 31 December will include profit of €20 and an asset of €50 (debtors or cash). But if the revenue from selling an item of inventory is recognized on 2 January, then the expense will also be recognized on 2 January. Accounts prepared on 31 December will include an asset of €30 (inventory), no revenue and no expense, and therefore no profit or loss from this transaction.

The **matching convention** is often referred to as the **accruals convention**, although some writers distinguish between them. The accruals convention should be contrasted with the ideas of cash flow accounting (Chapter 24). The essence of the accruals convention is that the time when an item of benefit should be recognized and recorded by the accountant is determined by the reasonably ascertainable generation of the benefit – not by the date of the actual (cash) receipt of the benefit. Similarly, the time when an item of expense should be recognized and recorded as such by the accountant is determined by the usage of the item, not by the date of the acquisition of the item or of the payment for the item. The accruals convention is therefore another way of saying that the process of profit calculation consists of relating (matching) together the revenues with the expenses. It is not directly concerned with cash receipts and cash payments.

## COHERENT FRAMEWORK

Thus far we have considered, separately, 12 conventions. How do they relate together? The idea of an all-embracing framework is discussed more fully in Chapter 9. What we can usefully do at this stage is to look at the 12 conventions to consider whether they are 'coherent' or consistent with each other.

One of the most problematic conventions is that of prudence or conservatism. At its most basic this derives from the obviously sensible belief that it is important not to encourage the users of accounts to spend money or to consume resources they do not have. Consideration of this convention, together with several of the other conventions, gives rise to certain difficulties.

## ACTIVITY 1.4

Suggest pairs of conventions that we have already discussed, which are, or may be, contradictory or in opposition to each other, and illustrate the possible problems between them.

### Activity feedback
Here are some possibilities we thought of:

1  **Prudence** and **going concern**. The going concern convention argues that the firm will 'keep going', for example that it will not be forced out of business by competition or bankruptcy. This may be a likely and rational assumption, but it is not necessarily prudent – in certain circumstances it could be decidedly risky.

2  **Prudence** and **matching**. The matching convention, building on the going concern convention, allows us to carry forward assets into future periods on the grounds that they will be used profitably later. This obviously makes major assumptions about the future that may not be at all prudent. The contradiction between these two conventions is one of the major problems of accounting practice. Should we, when in doubt, emphasize prudence or matching? Should we ensure that we never overstate the position or should we do our professional best to 'tell it like it is'? Should we report the worst possible position (prudence) or the most likely position (matching)?

3  **Prudence** and **objectivity**. Objectivity implies certainty and precision. It implies freedom from personal opinion, freedom from bias. Prudence, quite explicitly, implies that we should bias the information we choose to report in a certain direction. If accounting information could be genuinely objective, then prudence would be irrelevant by definition, because any bias would be impossible. In practice, of course, since accounting always has to make assumptions about future events, objectivity can never be completely achieved.

4  **Prudence** and the **cost concept**. This is a particularly interesting pairing of ideas. The cost concept is supported by objectivity (not on the grounds that it is objective, but on the grounds that it usually has a greater objective element than alternative valuation concepts) and is often regarded as being supported by prudence and, in some respects, it is.

Prudence suggests that in areas of valid choice, lower asset figures should be incorporated in accounts. In times of rising prices, use of replacement costs (RCs) could therefore be seen as imprudent, as compared with use of HCs. But consider the effect on reported profits of using an RC basis rather than HCs (Chapter 5). This splits up the HC profit into operating profit and holding gain, enabling the 'genuine', and therefore safely distributable, operating profit to be distinguished. Nothing could be more imprudent than to distribute resources needed to maintain the business and HC accounting can easily permit this to happen. Now try the following activity.

## ACTIVITY 1.5

On 20 December 20X7 your client paid €10 000 for an advertising campaign. The advertisements will be heard on local radio stations between 1 January and 31 January 20X8. Your client believes that, as a result, sales will increase by 60 per cent in 20X8 (over 20X7 levels) and by 40 per cent in 20X9 (over 20X7 levels). There will be no further benefits.

**Required**

Write a memorandum to your client explaining your views on how this item should be treated in the accounts for the three years 20X7 to 20X9. Your answer should include explicit reference to at least three relevant traditional accounting conventions and to the requirements of two classes of user of published financial accounts.

### Activity feedback

*To: Client*
*From: Accountant*
*Treatment of advertising costs*
*There are a number of possible treatments:*

- *Write off the whole amount in 20X7. This could be justified on the grounds of prudence – any return being highly speculative.*

- *Write off the amount in strict proportion to the expected benefits. This would be supported by the matching convention, i.e. to allocate the expenses over the period of benefit in proportion to that benefit. This would imply expenses of €0 in 20X7 (as benefit does not commence in 20X7), €6000 in 20X8 and €4000 in 20X9.*

- *The conflict between prudence and matching is usually resolved through compromise, although in areas of real doubt and difficulty prudence should prevail and be given greater emphasis. A reasonable compromise in this case might well be to charge all the €10 000 as an expense in 20X8 – any returns in 20X9 being much more speculative than those expected in 20X8.*

- *The validity of this suggestion would depend on the particular circumstances, advice of advertising and industry experts, your earlier treatment of similar items (consistency is an important accounting convention) and also on the materiality of the amounts concerned. If the amounts concerned are small in relation to your results as a whole, then it is pointless to spend my time (and your money!) in a lengthy and detailed investigation.*

- *We should perhaps also consider the users of your accounting reports. For example, a trade creditor will be particularly interested in your assets and liability position. From this point of view, an asset that exists because of the speculative expectation of higher sales next year is not exactly a safe 'near-cash' security. Contrariwise, a shareholder will be concerned with the future trend of profits, and application of the matching convention is arguably an essential requirement for showing a fair indication of present profit and current and future trends.*

The general conclusion from Activity 1.5 should be clear. A great deal of choice and subjectivity is involved in trying to produce useful financial information.

## INTERNATIONAL DIMENSION

This introductory chapter has discussed basic and general ideas. We have not been at all concerned with what is likely to happen in any particular country or any particular jurisdiction. Historically, accounting and reporting grew up largely independently, and often very differently, in different countries. Practice, regulation and, indeed, the mode and volume of regulation, differed, often very greatly.

With the global economy, instant communication and a global finance market, this situation has changed sharply and this process of change is continuing. The historical developments, and the reasons for them, are discussed in Chapter 2. The institutional and regulatory developments in the ongoing process of increasing harmonization, involving the European Union (EU) and the International Accounting Standards

Board (IASB) in particular are discussed in Chapter 3. The speed of this process has increased sharply in recent years; all listed (quoted) companies within the EU are using International Accounting Standards (IASs) for their consolidated financial statements for year-ends beginning on or after 1 January 2005. Australia switched to International Financial Reporting Standards (IFRS) from the same date, China has adopted something closely related to IFRS in text if not in spirit, and many other countries are moving closer towards IFRS requirements. The situation regarding the USA is more complex. There has been a history over the last decade of public commitments to 'convergence', including the intention to produce common standards. By the end of 2012 it became clear, with formal recognition by both the American Financial Accounting Standards Board (FASB) and IASB, that full 'convergence' was not going to happen. In Europe at the individual country level, i.e. in relation to entities not obligated to use IFRS as mentioned above, reactions against the usage of 'full' IFRS can often now be seen, although the influence remains strong.

The international dimension is explored more fully in Chapter 3. The whole process is both fascinating and fluid, and it is necessary to keep up to date. Whatever the 'local' scenario in the country of individual readers, the international dimension is of major influence and importance. The international approach of this book is now essential to understand the accounting process.

## TERMINOLOGY AND THE ENGLISH LANGUAGE

Many readers of this book will be trying not only to master a subject new to them but also doing so in a language that is not their first. One added difficulty is that there are several forms of the English language, particularly for accounting terms. UK terms and US terms are extensively different. Some examples are shown in the first two columns of Table 1.1. At this stage, you are not expected to understand all these terms; they will be introduced later, as they are needed.

**TABLE 1.1  Some examples of UK, US and IASB terms**

| UK | US | IASB |
|---|---|---|
| Stock | Inventory | Inventory |
| Shares | Stock | Shares |
| Own shares | Treasury stock | Treasury shares |
| Debtors | Receivables | Receivables |
| Creditors | Payables | Payables |
| Finance lease | Capital lease | Finance lease |
| Turnover | Sales (or revenue) | Sales (or revenue) |
| Acquisition | Purchase | Acquisition |
| Merger | Uniting of interests | Uniting of interests |
| Fixed assets | Non-current assets | Non-current assets |
| Profit and loss account | Income statement | Income statement |
| Balance sheet | Balance sheet/Statement of financial position | Statement of financial position |

The IASB operates and publishes its Standards in English, although there are approved translations in several languages. The IASB uses a mixture of UK and US terms, as shown in the third column of Table 1.1. On the whole, this book uses IASB terms, but UK terms tend to be used in the Fourth EU Directive. Familiarity with both is essential.

## SUMMARY

Financial reporting is concerned with the provision of information about business organizations to people outside the management function. We have thought about the various users of financial reporting, and the type and characteristics of information they might need. Finally we have explored the accountant's traditional approach to meeting these needs, i.e. the traditional underlying conventions of accounting. It can be demonstrated that they are often not mutually consistent. As we shall see in Chapter 2, different national traditions have sharply differing views on which conventions should be given priority.

## EXERCISES

*Suggested answers to exercises marked ✓ are to be found on our dedicated CourseMate platform for students.*

*Suggested answers to the remaining exercises are to be found on the Instructor online support resources.*

✓ **1**  Look up as many definitions of accounting as you can find, noting the source, country, original language and date of publication. Note and try to explain their differences.

✓ **2**  Consider the relative benefits to users of financial statements of:

- information about the past
- information about the present
- information about the future.

✓ **3**  Do you think that a single set of financial statements can be prepared that will be reasonably adequate for all major external users and their needs?

**4**  Which of the suggested conventions do you regard as most important? Why?

**5**  Which of the suggested conventions do you regard as most useful? Why?

**6**  Explain the differences, if any, between your answers to questions 4 and 5.

✓ **7**  How objective is the traditional HC balance sheet?

8   Completeness is not compatible with the monetary measurement convention. Discuss.

9   A firm spends €10 000 developing a new product and €5000 on an advertising campaign for it. Which conventions will help you in deciding on the appropriate accounting treatment and what do they imply?

10   Which conventions underlie the usual accounting treatment of inventory and work in progress?

11   HC accounts are neither objective nor useful. Discuss.

12   The normal accounting practice of revenue recognition proves that accountants are prudent. Discuss.

13   How do accountants decide when to recognize revenue?

14   When do accountants usually recognize revenue?

15   Do your answers to questions 13 and 14 satisfy the objectivity convention?

16   Explain the relationship between revenue recognition and asset valuation.

17   A local group collects subscriptions from its members, and also has to pay 60 per cent of them to central funds. In the year to 31 December 20X8 the group receives:

| for 20X7 | €20 |
| for 20X8 | €60 |
| for 20X9 | €10 |

It pays to central funds in that year:

| for 20X7 | €12 |
| for 20X8 | €30 |
| for 20X9 | nil |

**Required:**
(a)  Produce a summary of the subscription position for the group for the year 20X8, on:
   (i)    a receipts and payments basis
   (ii)   a revenue and expenses basis.

(b)  Outline the advantages and disadvantages of each basis with reference to appropriate accounting conventions. Give the group leader your recommended method, with reasons. Discuss also any difficult decisions you have to make in deciding your answer to (a) above.

(ACCA – adapted)

# INTERNATIONAL ACCOUNTING DIFFERENCES

# 2

**OBJECTIVES** After studying this chapter you should be able to:

- describe and explain how the following factors influenced the development of financial reporting and the existing accounting systems in a country:

  – provision of finance

  – the legal system

  – the system of taxation

  – cultural values

- explain and appraise the influence of cultural values on accounting values

- explain how different systems of accounting regulation could develop

- describe the purpose of country classification exercises

- appraise whether country influences are still relevant today.

# INTRODUCTION

Chapter 1 introduced you to the subject of accounting and why accounting matters. It also touched on the importance of international harmonization with respect to financial reporting. In this chapter we will focus on why accounting and financial reporting systems developed differently in different countries. At the end of this chapter we will pay attention to research approaches which try to explain, with the help of these national characteristics, the differences in the degree of accounting quality observed between various countries, even after these countries switched to mandatory compliance with IFRS for listed groups.

In Activity 2.1 we take another look at the main issues of Chapter 1.

## ACTIVITY 2.1

Try to formulate in your own words the subject of accounting, especially financial reporting. Why does international harmonization matter?

### Activity feedback
A company draws up its financial statements to reflect the effects of transactions and events within and outside the company on its assets and liabilities, financial position and income. As such a company communicates its financial situation to all stakeholders involved through financial reporting. Whether and in what way events and transactions are reflected in the financial report depends on the accounting policies chosen by the company's management. For every kind of transaction and event, management must decide, either explicitly or implicitly, whether and how to reflect it in the financial statements. The methods of recognition and measurement, consolidation and presentation must be chosen and decisions made as to what data to disclose in what degree of detail. Within limits, these choices are at the management's discretion. The limits of these choices are determined by the diverse national regulations (today their scope is in most countries limited to the non-listed companies). Since stakeholders use the information conveyed through the financial reports for decision-making purposes, stakeholders must be able to compare the information communicated through the financial reports of companies originating from different countries. Therefore international harmonization does matter.

The limits mentioned in Activity 2.1 are set by standard setters in different countries or international standard setters such as the IASB, which promulgate the methods of recognition and measurement, consolidation presentation and disclosure that the company must comply with. Some standard setters allow many options with regard to those issues. Other standard setters are strict and prescribe, for example, one specific measurement method for a specific asset. Companies located in countries where standard setters allow many choices with regard to recognition and measurement issues have much more accounting flexibility in the presentation and valuation of their assets, liabilities, earnings and financial position. As a result, users of financial statements of companies located in countries with accounting flexibility will face more problems comparing the performance of different companies with one another, than users of annual accounts of companies located in countries with very little accounting flexibility. However, less accounting flexibility might also hamper the communication of real economic performance. A discussion of the influence of accounting flexibility on financial analysis can be found in Chapter 31. Since these differences in flexibility hinder cross-border and within-borders comparison of financial information, many jurisdictions switched to mandatory compliance with IFRS for listed groups. Harmonization or convergence between accounting standards from different jurisdictions increases the comparability of financial information and creates more transparency for the users of financial information. As a result, the information asymmetry between stakeholders and the companies decreases. The transparency on the financial situation of a company increases as a result and therefore stakeholders can make much better informed decisions about the company. This increased transparency results in a lower cost of capital for companies (see, for example, Leuz and Verrecchia, 2000; Botosan and Plumlee, 2002) and an increase in market liquidity since more stakeholders will include the company in their portfolio of firms to consider and as a result the number of shares offered and demanded increases (Lambert *et al.*, 2007; Daske *et al.*, 2008). Today the comparability of financial information published by listed groups might have been improved, but the situation for the large majority of non-listed companies (often small and medium-sized enterprises – SMEs) has not improved yet.

## ACTIVITY 2.2

Remember the contents of Chapter 1 and list again a number of users of financial information and for what purpose they will use the information.

### Activity feedback

*From Chapter 1 we know that different external stakeholders of financial statements exist and that they use the information of the annual accounts in their own decision-making process.*

Shareholders: *They use information from the financial statements in order to determine whether or not they are going to invest or disinvest in a company.*

Creditors: *On the basis of the financial statements, creditors will assess the capability of a company to repay its debt in the long-term. Based on the results of that analysis, credit will be granted or denied and the conditions will be negotiated.*

Suppliers: *They will assess the capability of the firm to repay their invoices in the short-term before they decide to grant short-term credit.*

Workforce: *Employees will use financial statement data to get an idea of the financial health of their company.*

Government: *Governments use financial statements for several purposes, including for determining taxable income, controlling compliance with regulation or making decisions about government grants to certain industries.*

All over the world stakeholders use the information provided by financial statements in their decision-making process for the purposes enumerated earlier. Although the use of the information is more or less the same worldwide, the communication of that information can differ according to the types of accounting standards used or other influencing factors (e.g. legal system, development of the capital market, enforcement of accounting standards, governance regulations, culture).

Information from the annual accounts becomes useful for decision making if it can be compared to a certain benchmark. Very often data taken from the financial statements of other companies are used as a benchmark. However, the performance and the financial position of another company is only a yardstick for evaluation if comparability is not jeopardized by accounting flexibility, which is to a large extent determined by the type of accounting standards used or other factors (e.g. legal system, the degree of enforcement of accounting standards, the risk of litigation, culture, the reporting incentives of management – for the latter, see Part Four of this textbook). Comparing two financial reports that are based on different accounting policies is like comparing two lengths without knowing that one is in centimetres and the other in inches.

So if readers want to compare financial reports which are the reflections of transactions and events as recorded under a particular accounting policy, it is important that the accounting policies do not differ to such an extent that the comparison of financial reports is meaningless. The accounting policies or accounting decisions of a company were, and still are to a large extent, influenced by the national environment. Evidence from empirical studies analyzing the impact on accounting quality of the mandatory switch to IFRS for listed groups reveals that the benefits differ between countries. Differences in institutional characteristics are responsible for these results (Daske *et al.*, 2008; Barth *et al.*, 2008; Armstrong *et al.*, 2010; Landsman *et al.*, 2011; Kvaal and Nobes, 2011; Christensen *et al.*, 2012; Florou and Pope, 2012; Tarca, 2012 ). In a period where international harmonization or even standardization seems to be almost realized, national differences still play a role. Therefore we focus in this chapter on the differences between national accounting practices and standards and national accounting environments.

## ORIGIN OF NATIONAL DIFFERENCES

Financial reporting in general can be viewed as part of a communication process. The report is a medium through which information is transferred by a sender to a receiver.

The nature and functions of reporting with respect to organizations differ depending on the nature of the sender and the receiver as well as on the nature of the information transferred. The sender and the receiver form an integral part of their environment, which at the time that financial reporting developed in the past centuries was merely a national environment.

Financial reporting was, to start with, mainly internal reporting. Early financial reports can hardly be called external; they were a means by which the owners could get an insight into their income and capital. The owners of the company were usually also the managers of the company and one could hardly distinguish between internal and external financial reports. From the early 1800s on, the increasing scale of companies resulted in finance problems and the need for a disconnection of management and capital supply. Private capital alone was insufficient to finance business activities, so capital was gathered from people outside the company.

This separation of ownership and management makes it possible to have the company managed by people specializing in management. The owners delegate control and the evaluation of the management to the board of directors (Fama and Jensen, 1983). The board of directors also has the power to hire and fire top management and to approve any strategic decisions. The directors, by way of contrast, are accountable to the owners for their deeds, decisions and policy. The external financial report provides a means of rendering account of this authority. Besides the functions of profit and capital determination already mentioned, the financial report now also serves a stewardship role. So financial reporting evolved from internal to external reporting, but for a long time external reporting meant providing information within the borders of a specific country. Because national environments have different characteristics, standard setters and accounting bodies have chosen different alternatives for recognition, measurement and presentation of assets, liabilities, equity, revenue and expenses. They have chosen those recognition, measurement, consolidation, presentation and disclosure policies that best fitted their national environments. In each country annual accounts provide information on the financial position of a company and its result. Although the general mission is similar in most countries, many differences between countries occur. In each country there was, and still is, a different mix of influences on financial reporting. These differences result from different environmental, institutional and cultural influences in the individual countries. We now focus on the most important environmental, institutional and cultural differences that shaped financial reporting in

## TABLE 2.1    Shareholder-oriented versus credit-oriented countries

| Shareholder-oriented countries | Credit/family/state-oriented countries |
|---|---|
| United States | Germany |
| United Kingdom | France |
| The Netherlands | Belgium |
| Sweden | Italy |
| Australia | Spain |
| Canada | Portugal |

Source: Adapted from Alexander and Nobes (2004), Nobes and Parker (2003) and Ordelheide and KPMG (2001).

the individual countries: provision of finance; the existing legal system; the link between accounting and taxation; and cultural differences between societies. These elements still influence accounting practices, even after mandatory compliance with IFRS is installed in many jurisdictions.

## Provision of finance

According to Nobes and Parker (2003, p. 21) 'This difference in providers of finance (creditors) versus (equity) is the key cause of international differences in financial reporting.' We saw earlier in this chapter that through the increasing scale of companies two centuries ago, firms had to find extra capital to finance their growth. Companies in different countries responded differently to this increased need for funds. In countries such as Germany, France, Italy and Belgium, banks became the major supplier of extra funds. Companies in these countries relied more on debt to finance their activities than on equity. In contrast, in the UK and USA the extra funds tend to be provided by shareholders, often by many shareholders for small amounts. Companies in these countries rely more on equity for the financing of their activities. In these countries an active stock exchange was and still is present.

Table 2.1 presents some examples of countries in which companies are more shareholder-oriented and countries in which companies are more credit/family/state-oriented. This divide represents the situation in the twentieth century. To a large extent, it is still representative for today's situation, especially for non-listed groups and SMEs.

## ACTIVITY 2.3

Could you argue why the difference between credit versus equity has an impact especially on financial reporting?

### Activity feedback
Insiders or parties that have a power relation towards a company are in a position to ask for internal data about the financial position of the firm towards which they exercise power. The power relation of outsiders is much weaker: they are not in a position to ask for extra information and have to rely on public information. Especially in countries where widespread shareholdership exists, the power of the individual shareholder to get financial information is limited. Although the power of the individual shareholder is weak, in those countries where companies rely on the capital market for extra funding there is a strong incentive towards high-quality external financial reporting. Through financial reports, companies communicate their financial situation to existing and potential shareholders.

So in countries where companies are largely financed through equity, financial statements will have an investor or shareholder orientation. This means that financial statements must provide the kind of information that will enable a potential shareholder to make the best investment decision. Financial information which communicates the underlying economic performance of the firm in a timely manner enables investors to make those investment decisions and is called 'high-quality' accounting information. Earnings are of higher accounting quality if they enable the users of accounting information to assess current performance as well as future performance (Chaney *et al.*, 2011). Empirical research on the 'quality of accounting earnings' has indicated that in those countries with a strong capital market influence, the quality of accounting earnings is higher than in countries with a creditor orientation (see the discussion of today's role of national differences later in this chapter). In countries where companies rely more on debt financing, the financial statements have a creditor orientation. In these countries information provided through the annual accounts must be useful to judge whether a company is able to repay its debt. Creditor protection becomes important in this respect and accounting practices will become more conservative.

## ACTIVITY 2.4

If you were to compare the financial risk between companies on the basis of the debt/equity ratio calculated from the published annual accounts, in which countries would you come across firms with the highest ratio?

### Activity feedback

If we exclude the impact of other influencing factors on the debt/equity ratio (e.g. type of industry, profit distribution versus reservation) and take into account only these national differences, then you would find, for example in Germany and France, companies with higher debt/equity ratios than in companies in the USA or in the UK. This difference is then due solely to national differences with regard to the way in which companies are financed.

These differences in financing are worth bearing in mind when companies from different countries are compared with each other for financial analysis purposes. (See Chapters 31 and 32.)

## Existing legal system

Over the years in the Western world two types of legal system have developed: the so-called common law system and the code law system. Both legal systems were exported in the twentieth century to different parts of the world. The common law system originated in England and is developed from case law. The legal system in most Commonwealth countries is the common law system. Common law is characterized as a legal system that is developed case by case and does not prescribe general rules that could be applied to several cases. In a common law situation accounting rules are not a part of the law. In common law countries accounting regulation is in the hands of professional organizations of the private sector. Company law in these countries is kept to a minimum. Detailed accounting regulation is produced by the private standard setter, as we will discuss later when we look at accounting regulation.

The code law system originated in Roman law and has developed in continental Europe. It is characterized by a wide set of rules that try to give guidance in all situations. In code law countries the company law is very detailed and accounting standards

## TABLE 2.2 Common law versus code law countries

| Common law countries | Code law countries |
|---|---|
| England and Wales | Scotland |
| United States | France |
| Australia | Germany |
| Canada | Belgium |
| Ireland | The Netherlands |
| New Zealand | Portugal |
| Singapore | Spain |
|  | Japan |

*Source:* Adapted from Alexander and Nobes (2004), Nobes and Parker (2003) and Ordelheide and KPMG (2001).

are often embodied in the company law. Accounting regulation in code law countries is in the hands of the government and financial reporting is in those circumstances often reduced to complying with a set of very detailed legal rules.

Table 2.2 gives some examples of code law and common law countries. (See also La Porta *et al.*, 1997, 1998.)

Related to the legal system is the degree of enforcement of the legal rules or standards by the judicial authorities or a supervising body. Research evidence reveals that very often in common law countries the degree of enforcement and the mechanisms for investor protection are much stricter than in code law countries (Bushman and Piotroski, 2006; Jackson and Roe, 2009; Leuz, 2010). Recent research shows that in countries with stricter enforcement, accounting information is of higher quality (see section 'National differences: do they still play a role in an era of globalized accounting' further in this chapter).

## Link between accounting and taxation

In some countries the fiscal authorities use information provided in the financial statements in order to determine taxable income. In a number of continental European countries expenses are tax deductible only if they are also recognized in the profit and loss account. As a result, financial reporting becomes tax influenced or even tax biased. In this respect, Germany is well known for its *Massgeblichkeitsprinzip*, which stands for the fact that the tax accounts (*Steuerbilanz*) should be identical to the accounts published for external stakeholders (*Handelsbilanz*). This link between financial reporting and taxation is often found in those countries that do not have an explicit investor approach in their financial reporting orientation.

In countries like the USA, the UK and the Netherlands the link between taxable income and accounting income is much weaker. Separate accounts are filed for tax purposes. The measurement and recognition rules and estimates used in the tax accounts can differ from the valuation rules used in the preparation of the financial statements published for all external stakeholders.

Table 2.3 shows the general relationship between accounting and taxation using some examples based on the situation in the 1990s.

This relationship between accounting income and tax income can vary over time. For example, Spain was for a long time in the column of dependence, which implies that there

| TABLE 2.3 General relationship between accounting and taxation | |
| --- | --- |
| *Independence* | *Dependence* |
| Denmark | Germany |
| Ireland | France |
| United Kingdom | Belgium |
| The Netherlands | Italy |
| Czech Republic | Sweden |
| Poland | Norway |

*Source:* Adapted from Alexander and Nobes (2004), Nobes and Parker (2003) and Ordelheide and KPMG (2001).

was a strong link between the accounting income and the tax income; with the reform of 1989, however, the link between taxable income and accounting income became less strong and they are now moving towards independence. The introduction of IFRS will have an impact on the relation between accounting and taxation in those countries characterized by a dependence relationship, especially when SMEs will start to use IFRS for private entities in the near future.

## Cultural differences

Research indicates that another cause of variation between national accounting systems is cultural differences. Cultural differences between nations are identified as an important influencing factor on reporting and disclosure behaviour with regard to financial statements. One of the prominent researchers on cultural differences is Hofstede (1984). Initially he used four constructs to classify countries according to the cultural differences he observed in his empirical research. The constructs resulted from empirical survey-based research in one multinational (IBM; survey population 100 000 employees in 39 countries, 1984). Hofstede labelled his constructs as follows: individualism, power distance, uncertainty avoidance and masculinity. According to Hofstede, these labels describe the following characteristics of a society.

**Individualism versus collectivism** Individualism stands for the preference for a loosely knit social framework in society wherein individuals are supposed to take care of themselves and their immediate families only. Collectivism describes the preference for a tightly knit social framework in which individuals expect their relatives, clan or other in-group to look after them in exchange for unquestioning loyalty. The fundamental issue addressed by this dimension is the degree of interdependence a society maintains among individuals. This difference relates to the people's self-concept: 'I' or 'we'.

**Large versus small power distance** Power distance is the extent to which the members of a society accept that power in institutions and organizations is distributed unequally. People in larger power distance societies accept a hierarchical order in which everybody has a place that needs no further justification. In small power distance societies there is less hierarchy and power is distributed more evenly. The fundamental issue addressed by this dimension is how a society handles inequalities among people when they occur.

**Strong versus weak uncertainty avoidance** Uncertainty avoidance is the degree to which the members of a society feel uncomfortable with uncertainty and ambiguity. This feeling leads them to beliefs promising certainty and to maintain institutions protecting conformity. Strong uncertainty avoidance societies maintain rigid codes of belief and behaviour and are intolerant of deviant people and ideas. Weak uncertainty avoidance societies maintain a more relaxed atmosphere in which practice counts more than principles and deviance is more easily tolerated.

**Masculinity versus femininity** Masculinity stands for the preference in society for achievement, heroism, assertiveness and material success. Its opposite, femininity, stands for the preference for relationships, modesty, caring for the weak and the quality of life.

More recently Hofstede added a fifth component, namely long-term orientation.

Based on Hofstede's classification scheme, Gray (1988) defined 'accounting values' that can be linked to the different cultural values as follows:

- professionalism versus statutory control
- uniformity versus flexibility
- conservatism versus optimism
- secrecy versus transparency.

**Professionalism versus statutory control** The accounting value professionalism links to individualism. Professionalism is consistent with a society where the emphasis is on 'I' rather than 'we'. Professionalism also goes together with a society with small power distance. Statutory control is observed in the opposite situation, namely in societies with large power distance. In relation to the accounting profession, professionalism implies self-regulation by the accounting profession itself, as in the USA and the UK and much less in continental Europe. Statutory control implies control by the government. Statutory control could also be linked to strong uncertainty avoidance.

**Uniformity versus flexibility** First of all, uniformity can be linked to strong uncertainty avoidance. Uniformity leads to detailed regulations embedded in the law and adherence to consistency (e.g. in Belgium, France and Spain uniform accounting plans were imposed on companies by law). Uniformity is therefore also associated with large power distance societies and societies in which the emphasis is on 'we' rather than 'I'. Flexibility, however, can be associated with weak uncertainty avoidance, small power distance and individualism.

**Conservatism versus optimism** Conservatism could be linked to uncertainty avoidance. In these societies one is more conservative with regard to profit recognition and asset measurement. Conservatism is an important value for accountants, especially in continental Europe where financial reporting is more creditor-oriented and where there is a strong link between accounting income and taxable income. Less conservatism in the accounts is applied in the UK, the USA and the Netherlands in comparison to France, Switzerland and Germany.

**Secrecy versus transparency** Secrecy implies a preference for confidentiality. Secrecy can be linked to uncertainty avoidance, but also to societies with large power distances. Information asymmetry will then reinforce inequalities and power relations between the different parties. Secrecy will have a direct impact on the level of information disclosure by companies. In Japan and continental Europe lower levels of information disclosure are observed in comparison to disclosure levels in the USA and the UK.

The most important economic and cultural elements cited in the literature as causes for differences between national accounting systems have now been discussed. Other factors also listed in the literature as contributors to those differences are, for example, the level of economic development in a country, the degree of industrialization, inflation levels, the adherence to accounting theory (e.g. in the Netherlands income determination and valuation is inspired by the theory of Limperg (Mey, 1966); financial reporting in Germany was inspired by the theory of Schmalenbach (1927)).

---

## ACTIVITY 2.5

Consider again the cultural values described by Hofstede. How do they link with the accounting value dimensions defined by Gray? Is there a direct link or an indirect link?

*Activity feedback*
*Between some variables there is a direct relationship; between other characteristics and values the relationship*

*is rather indirect. For example, one can distinguish a relation between uncertainty avoidance and conservatism or large power distribution and secrecy versus short power distribution and transparency.*

---

In the next part of the chapter we will analyse how the different economic and cultural factors, discussed above, shaped financial reporting practices and standards in each individual country. The causes for differentiation had an influence on the existing accounting system and on the implementation of IFRS in a country.

## DIFFERENCES IN ACCOUNTING SYSTEMS

Since accounting responds to its environment, different environments produce different accounting systems, while similar environments produce similar accounting systems.

In this section we focus on these differences in accounting systems. In the next section the emphasis lies on the different sets of domestic generally accepted accounting principles (GAAP), which still exist for large numbers of non-listed entities worldwide. Under the heading of accounting systems we discuss two elements that characterize accounting systems, namely the organization of accounting regulation and the organization of the accounting profession.

### Types of accounting regulation

We can distinguish between two types of accounting regulation, namely private sector accounting standard setting or public sector accounting standard setting. When shareholders are the main providers of capital we expect them to have great interest in the way in which companies communicate their financial information. The shareholders will definitely want to have a hand in the communication process, including the financial reporting process. The shareholders are mainly trying to achieve this objective by hiring professional accountants who check on their behalf the communication process and its outcome within a company. In order to be able to fulfil their task properly, preparers together with the accountants started to play a major role in the standard-setting process of those countries characterized by active capital markets.

We observe that in countries with a code law system and a creditor orientation, the government sets the accounting standards and often makes use of financial reporting for its own purposes. First of all, in those countries the annual accounts are often used for tax purposes which serves the government. Second, the financial statements may be used for specific information needs of the government. In Belgium, for example, the social balance sheet – a document containing employment statistics, e.g. number of employees, breakdown into different categories, change in the workforce, use of government incentives for the creation of employment – must be included in the financial statements by Royal Decree of 1996. It mainly serves the need of the government for information with regard to employment in order to evaluate the effectiveness of their governmental employment policies. Financial reporting in those countries essentially comes down to compliance with legal requirements and tax laws.

## ACTIVITY 2.6

Consider Tables 2.1 and 2.2 which provide information on the different sources of finance in each country and the existing legal system. What kind of accounting regulation would you expect in those countries?

### Activity feedback

If we consider Tables 2.1 and 2.2 again, we observe to a certain extent a correlation between the provision of finance (debt versus equity) and the legal system in place (code law/common law). In most countries with active equity markets, the legal system is the common law system. This is in favour of the private sector developing financial reporting rules or standards. In countries in which companies are financed to a large extent through debt, the code law system is present as the legal system. In those countries creditor protection is high on the agenda. Because large creditors, such as banks, are able to obtain inside information from the companies, they are less in need of financial information published by these companies. In these countries accounting regulation is in the hands of the government.

So there are two types of accounting regulation, each of which is embedded in a different economic and legal environment. First of all, there are countries in which accounting regulation is in the hands of the private sector: the UK, the USA, Australia and the Netherlands. In these countries private standard setting goes together with a shareholder orientation of the financial information published and, in most countries, a common law system. Second, there are countries in which the government plays a major part in accounting regulation. This system is observed in many continental European countries. In those countries detailed accounting rules are embodied in the law, normally the company law. Financial information has mainly a creditor orientation in those countries and they are further characterized by a code law system. These two types of accounting regulation still apply for the time being to non-listed groups and small and medium-size entities. With the compulsory introduction of the IFRS, a substantial number of countries with diverse backgrounds now operate in a similar setting with regard to accounting regulation. This implies that UK and USA constituents are much more familiar with a due process of private standard setting than European continental preparers who originate from a public sector standard-setting environment.

## Differences in the organization of the accounting profession

When companies are financed by equity capital and if this equity capital is in the hands of a widespread group of small shareholders, these shareholders are in need of a well-organized control system with regard to the quality and reliability of the information provided by the financial statements. The strength and size of the accounting profession is directly influenced by the need for the external control mechanisms or audit of the published financial information. Table 2.4 illustrates that in those countries with

| TABLE 2.4 | Dates of establishment of professional accountancy bodies | |
|---|---|---|
| Country | Professional body | Founding date (founding date of predecessor) |
| Belgium | Instituut der Bedrijfsrevisoren/Institut des Reviseurs d'Entreprises | 1953 |
| England and Wales | Institute of Chartered Accountants in England and Wales | 1880 (1870) |
| Denmark | Foreningen af Statsautoriserede Revisorer | 1912 |
| Finland | KHT-yhdistys | 1925 (1911) |
| France | Ordre des Experts Comptables | 1942 |
| Germany | Institut der Wirtschaftsprüfer | 1932 |
| Ireland | Institute of Chartered Accountants of Ireland | 1888 |
| Italy | Consiglio Nazionale dei Dottori Commercialisti | 1924 |
| | Collegio dei Ragionieri e Periti Commerciali | 1906 |
| Japan | Japanese Institute of Certified Public Accountants | 1948 (1927) |
| Norway | Den norske Revisorforening | 1999 (1930) |
| Portugal | Sociedade Portuguesa de Contabilidade | 1930 |
| Scotland | Institute of Chartered Accountants of Scotland | 1951 (1854) |
| Spain | Institute of Sworn Auditors of Accounts | 1943 |
| Sweden | Foreningen Auktoriserade Revisorer (FAR) | 1923 |
| | Svenska Revisorsamfundet (SRS) | 1899 |
| The Netherlands | Nederlands Instituut voor Registeraccountants | 1967(1895) |
| New Zealand | New Zealand Society of Accountants | 1909(1894) |
| United States | American Institute of Certified Public Accountants | 1887 |

*Source:* Alexander and Nobes (2004), Nobes and Parker (2003) and Ordelheide and KPMG (2001).

active capital markets the profession developed earlier than in countries where companies are more financed by debt.

In countries with a well-organized accounting profession we observe that the influence of that profession on local accounting practices and on national GAAP is larger than in countries with smaller and later developed professional organizations.

## CHARACTERISTICS AND DIFFERENCES IN NATIONAL GAAP

All these different factors, discussed at the start of this chapter, lead to differences in accounting systems (e.g. regulation). These accounting systems produce different national or domestic accounting standards. The following points illustrate several differences in financial reporting characteristics. Although they are presented as separate items, they are linked together.

### Shareholder orientation versus stakeholder orientation

In countries with widespread ownership there is a need for high-quality published financial information. As companies have to rely to a large extent on the capital market, information disclosure becomes extremely important because existing and potential shareholders do not have access to internal information in order to assess the financial situation of the company they might want to invest in or increase their investment in. In those countries the pressure for disclosure is much greater than in countries where providers of finance have the power to obtain internal information. Besides the need for more disclosure and more auditing, the debt versus equity orientation also has a direct influence on valuation issues.

In equity-oriented countries financial reporting is aimed at communicating the performance and efficiency of the business to existing and potential shareholders. Profit measurement is very important and reported data on earnings, financial position and cash flow will be used to make predictions about the future recurring stream of earnings, cash flow and the financial position of the company. In countries where companies are financed through debt, financial statements serve the information needs of many different stakeholders, especially creditors, and also the government. Their information needs are concerned with the value of underlying assets of the company as collateral and the determination of taxable income. The debt/equity orientation lies at the origin of the different reporting and principles described next.

## Fairness versus legality

In common law countries the aim of financial reporting is a fair representation of the financial situation of the company. In the UK this is translated into the 'true and fair view' concept. In code law countries financial reporting is focused on compliance with the legal requirements and tax laws. In code law countries the 'legal form' often dominates 'the substance'. The most cited example in this respect is the accounting treatment of a lease contract. In countries with strong shareholder orientation and emphasis on fairness, lease contracts are accounted for on the balance sheet although the company is not the legal owner of the assets (e.g. the UK and USA). In countries where the legal form prevails, these assets used by the company are often kept off balance sheet as the company is not the legal owner (e.g., until recently, France).

## Conservatism

In countries in which financial reporting is more creditor-oriented and used for tax purposes, valuation rules will be more conservative or prudent than in countries with a shareholder orientation. Adherence to conservatism will lead to a different choice in valuation rules and accounting practices. For example, with regard to depreciation, the declining balance method will be used more often than the straight line method, if conservatism is an important characteristic in financial reporting. Further, more use will be made of provisions in these countries, especially when provisions are tax deductible. Conservative accounting is often regarded as a system in which lower profits are reported than under a system driven by accrual accounting. However, with the use of extensive depreciation and creation of provisions, those companies are also able to increase results in periods with weak economic performance.

Much research is undertaken with regard to the quality of earnings reported under conservative accounting. With quality of accounting information, one refers to the use of accounting data for the prediction of future performance (value relevance of accounting information). The results of these studies reveal that information provided under conservative accounting practices is less value relevant for decision-making purposes (e.g. buying and selling shares) (see Basu, 1997; Pope and Walker, 1999; Penman and Zhang, 2002). For stewardship purposes, however, some authors argue (e.g. Lambert and Larcker, 1987) that conservative accounts are more useful for evaluating managers.

## Uniformity, accounting plans and formats

In code law countries we observe that the regulator attaches importance to uniformity. Compliance with prescribed accounting plans (France, Spain and Belgium) and detailed formats for the balance sheet and the profit and loss account are a result of this drive for uniformity. When regulation is in the hands of the government, the layout of the balance sheet, profit and loss accounts and notes are much more detailed. The schemes for balance sheet and profit and loss account put forward by the Fourth and Seventh Directives of the EU are more detailed than the layout presented by the IASB (see Chapter 10). On the other hand, the level of detail in the notes to the balance sheet and profit and loss account is much higher when accounts in compliance with IFRS are prepared.

## Consolidated accounts

In countries where financial reporting has a strong shareholder orientation, the practice of preparing and publishing consolidated financial statements emerged much earlier. Preparing consolidated financial statements was already common practice at the beginning of the twentieth century in the USA (in the 1920s). In the UK and the Netherlands consolidation became common practice in the 1930s. In typical creditor orientation countries, which are usually also code law countries, consolidation was introduced by law. This was done in the late second half of the twentieth century (Germany, 1965, *Aktiengesetz* for public companies; France, 1985, a law which obliged listed companies to publish consolidated accounts; Belgium, the Royal Decree of March 1990; in Italy consolidation became compulsory in the early 1990s).

## Deferred taxation

In countries with no direct link between tax income and accounting income the practice of recording deferred taxes on the balance sheet is well-established and common practice. For countries in which there is a strong link between accounting income and tax income, the practice of recording and calculating deferred taxes is relatively new. Further, in the individual accounts of companies in those countries the amounts recorded under deferred taxes will be rather small.

## COUNTRY CLASSIFICATION

Research into the possible causes to explain the observed differences in national accounting practices reveals several influencing factors (e.g. providers of finance, legal system, cultural differences and taxation). These factors shape the existing accounting systems in the different countries (accounting regulation and organization of the profession), accounting values and financial reporting practices.

These different factors are used by researchers as cluster variables in order to classify different countries into separate more homogeneous groups according to their characteristics. These classification exercises were very popular in the 1970s and 1980s. Examples can be found in the following publications: Hatfield (1966); Mueller (1967); Seidler (1967); American Accounting Association (1977); da Costa *et al.* (1978); Frank (1979); and Nair and Frank (1980). The most cited classification pattern of countries is that of Nobes (1980) (see Figure 2.1).

**Figure 2.1    Suggested classification of 'accounting systems' in some developed countries**

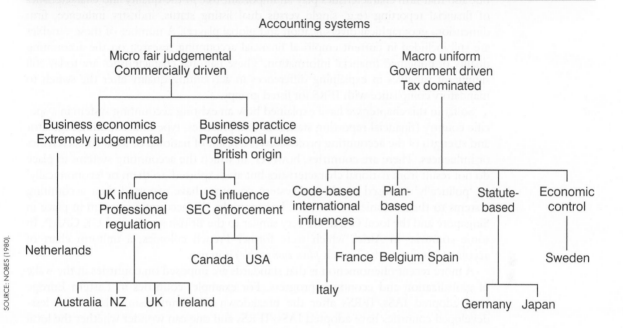

SOURCE: NOBES (1980).

To illustrate these country classification exercises, we now look at the classification system of Nobes. The popularity of classification attempts based purely on observed differences dropped in the 1990s, although Nobes' classification scheme still figures in many textbooks.

Nobes based his classification research on the financial reporting practices of public companies in the Western world. The date of classification was 1980, that is, before the enactments in EU countries of the Fourth Directive on company law and before the emergence of IAS. Nobes selected the following nine discriminating variables for the classification of countries in more homogeneous groups:

1  type of user of the published accounts of listed companies
2  degree to which law or standards prescribe in detail and exclude judgement
3  importance of tax rules in measurement
4  conservatism/prudence
5  strictness of application of historical cost
6  susceptibility to replacement cost adjustments in main or supplementary accounts
7  consolidation practices
8  ability to be generous with provisions and to smooth income
9  uniformity between companies in application of rules.

In the 1990s classification attempts were carried out, but they were becoming less popular. The classification exercises that were undertaken in the 1990s (e.g. d'Arcy, 2001), show us that clusters are moving towards each other and that more countries are now clustered into one group, especially when group accounting is considered. The clustering research of d'Arcy, which is based on data from the second half of the 1990s, shows not only that national differences matter in explaining financial reporting, but also that firm characteristics play an important role in the quality and characteristics of financial reporting (e.g. single versus dual listing status, industry influence, firm dimension, geographical diversification and global player). A number of these variables are still included in current empirical financial accounting research on the accounting quality of published financial information. These national characteristics are today still significant variables in explaining differences in accounting quality after the switch to mandatory compliance with IFRS for listed groups.

So far in this chapter we have explained how an existing accounting system in a specific country (financial reporting standards and practices, type of accounting regulator and strength of the accounting profession) is a result of national or local characteristics or influences. There are countries, however, in which the accounting systems in place do not result from national characteristics but are 'exported' to them or 'economically' or 'politically' imposed on them. Western countries have exported their accounting systems to their colonies in the past. For example, the accounting system in place in Singapore and the local GAAP are very similar to the British system and UK GAAP. In some countries in Africa which were former French colonies, a uniform chart of accounts (similar to the French *plan comptable*) is in use.

A more recent phenomenon is that standards are imposed on countries in the wake of globalization and economic progress. For example, countries in Eastern Europe have adopted IASs/IFRSs after the breakdown of communism. Also, some less-developed countries have adopted IASs/IFRSs and one can wonder whether the local economies are in need of a set of such technical accounting standards.

## NATIONAL DIFFERENCES: EVOLUTIONS AT THE END OF THE TWENTIETH CENTURY

As mentioned earlier in this chapter, classification exercises that attempted to cluster countries in homogeneous groups became less popular in the 1990s. In the 1980s through the enactment of the Fourth Directive in EU countries, and in the 1990s under the pressure of the globalization of capital markets, national accounting practices started slowly to move towards each other. This development is still going on and some differences have already become less noticeable or have almost disappeared for certain categories of companies or for certain financial statement items. From the late 1980s on, more and more companies sought dual listings. In the early 1990s, many European multinationals went to capital markets abroad, especially to the USA. In Germany, for example, Daimler-Benz started to publish two sets of annual accounts – annual accounts presented according to German GAAP and annual accounts presented according to US GAAP. At that time the differences between equity and earnings presented according to US GAAP and the equity and earnings presented according to German GAAP surprised many. Figure 2.2 became world famous.

Figure 2.2 provides clear evidence of the impact of conservative accounting practices on the reported result. In 1993, the US GAAP result of Daimler-Benz is much lower: conservative accounting leads to a kind of smoothing. Through conservative valuation rules earnings are decreased in 'good' years, but at times of weak economic performance results can be increased.

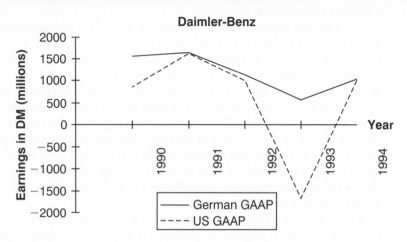

**Figure 2.2    Earnings evolution of Daimler-Benz, 1989–1994**

SOURCE: ANNUAL REPORTS OF DAIMLER-BENZ (1989–1994)

Many Swiss, German and Scandinavian multinationals switched to IAS in the second half of the 1990s. In France, a number of listed companies prepared their consolidated accounts using US GAAP (e.g. Total Fina, Suez) or IAS (e.g. Eutelsat, Rémy Cointreau, Renault). Academics started to study the reaction of the capital market to these voluntary switches of companies from 'conservative or low-quality' accounting standards to a set of 'higher-quality' accounting standards (IAS or US GAAP). Empirical research results showed that capital markets reacted positively to the voluntary switch, since capital markets perceived the switch as a reduction in information asymmetry between firms and investors. As a result, the cost of capital dropped for these companies (e.g. see Leuz and Verrecchia, 2000). The switch of large European global players from national GAAP to IAS or US GAAP was one of the major triggers for the EU to review its accounting harmonization policy (see Chapter 3).

The switch of the European global players resulted in the emergence of two groups of companies in most countries. This dichotomy still exists today. The first group consists of companies that made an appeal to the international capital market for funds and subsequently started to apply accounting rules that would lead to an increase of comparability of their financial information worldwide. This group started to use 'high-quality' accounting standards such as IAS/IFRS, US GAAP and UK GAAP, whereby 'high-quality' standards are defined as follows: 'Financial reporting quality relates to the usefulness of financial statements for contracting, monitoring, valuation and other decision making by investors, creditors, managers and all other parties contracting with the firm' (Ball and Shivakumar, 2002). Nowadays in more than 100 jurisdictions, listed groups have to comply on a mandatory basis with IFRS. The second group consists of non-listed domestic companies, predominantly small and medium-sized, who continue to apply national GAAP so far.

## NATIONAL DIFFERENCES: DO THEY STILL PLAY A ROLE IN AN ERA OF GLOBALIZED ACCOUNTING?

Even when all companies comply with US GAAP or IAS/IFRS, academic research provides evidence that national influences still affect the quality of financial reporting in the different countries. Empirical research provides us with evidence of this influence, and this is another reason why we have paid so much attention to such national variables in this chapter.

The variables pointed out by researchers in the 1970s and 1980s as causes that might explain and have led to differences in national accounting systems and national GAAP, are now used in empirical multi-country studies in which different aspects of the financial reporting practices of companies are researched. These studies focus on, among other things, the value relevance of accounting information, earnings management practices and characteristics of the audit market and audit process. A few examples of these empirical studies will be presented here together with their research results. In the first decade of the twenty-first century, most empirical studies analyzed either the quality of the accounting information of firms that adopted IFRS or US GAAP on a voluntary basis, or the quality of accounting information from companies subject to similar types of accounting standards, but different institutional regimes (e.g. risk of litigation, degree of enforcement, degree of investor protection, ...).

Ali and Hwang (2000) found that the value relevance of accounting information is lower for countries with bank-oriented (as opposed to market-oriented) financial systems. Value relevance was specified in terms of explanatory power of accounting variables (earnings and book value of equity) for security returns. Their results indicate further that value relevance of accounting income is lower for countries where private sector bodies are not involved in the standard-setting process. Ball *et al.* (2000) investigated two properties of accounting income (conservatism and timeliness) and the influence of international institutional factors on accounting income. The property timeliness is defined as the extent to which current period accounting income incorporates current period economic income. Conservatism has been used in this study using the definition of Basu (1997), which regards conservatism as the extent to which current period income asymmetrically incorporates economic losses relative to economic gains. Their central result is that accounting income in common law countries is significantly more timely than in code law countries, due entirely to quicker incorporation of economic losses which implies also more income conservatism at the same time.

Guenther and Young (2000) investigated how cross-country differences in legal systems, differences in legal protection for external shareholders and differences in the degree of tax conformity, affect the relation between financial accounting earnings and real economic value-relevant events that underlie those earnings. The results provide evidence that the association between financial accounting earnings and real economic activity in a country is related in predictable ways to the legal and economic systems that underlie financial accounting standard setting and the demand for financial accounting standards. The high association for the UK and the USA and the low association for France and Germany are consistent with expectations that accounting earnings in common law countries, countries with legal systems that protect external shareholder rights, countries with market-oriented (rather than bank-oriented) capital markets, and countries where financial accounting rules are independent of tax rules, better reflect underlying economic activity. Not only do the traditional elements of differentiation (provision of capital, legal system, link with taxation) seem to be relevant, but also elements such as risk of litigation, investor protection and enforcement of accounting rules are important factors that explain differences in reporting behaviour.

Leuz *et al.* (2003) found that the quality of financial reports increased in countries where investor protection is stronger. Their findings suggest an important link between legal institutions and the quality of financial information provided. The legal rights accorded to outside investors, especially minority investors, and the quality of their enforcement are both associated with the properties of firms' accounting earnings. Their study indicated further that a switch to high-quality standards alone was not a guarantee for high-quality financial information. Other academics had also put forward this issue. For example, Schipper (2000) stated that: 'Reporting quality is not only a function of the set of standards applied. High-quality standards implemented in a defective manner will not result in high-quality financial reports.' Without adequate enforcement, even the best accounting standards will be inconsequential. Hope (2003a, 2003b) constructed an enforcement index which took into account judicial efficiency, rule of law, anti-director rights, audit firm type, audit spending, stock exchange listings and insider trading. Hope found evidence that the enforcement score varied widely among countries. Therefore, accounting quality will still differ among countries even if they apply the same set of accounting standards. Research paying attention to non-listed companies confirms to a large extent the results found in relation to listed companies (Burghstahler et al., 2006).

The research results in the articles cited above are based on financial information published by companies that complied on a voluntary basis with IFRS. The mandatory compliance with IFRS since 2005 for listed companies in many jurisdictions (EU, Australia, New Zealand, South Africa and more recently Argentina, South Korea, Canada, Brazil, Mexico, Turkey and Russia) stimulated a stream of research trying to find out whether accounting quality has improved, and whether comparability of these IFRS accounts has improved after the mandatory country adoptions of IFRS. Many studies find evidence of an increase in accounting quality after the change to IFRS (Beuselinck et al., 2009, 2010; Byard et al., 2011; Horton et al., 2012; Jiao et al., 2012). However a large number of these studies also provide evidence that the beneficial impact of the mandatory compliance with IFRS differs upon the characteristics of the institutional environment in which a company operates and upon a company's reporting incentives (Daske et al., 2008; Barth et al., 2008; Armstrong et al., 2010; Landsman et al., 2011; Gebhardt and Novotny-Farkas, 2011; Florou and Pope, 2012; Christensen et al., 2012; (for an overview see Pope and McLeay, 2011 and Tarca, 2012)). These studies show that the benefits of adopting IFRS with respect to an increase in accounting quality are linked to the extent to which prior national GAAP and IFRS differ and are dependent on the quality of enforcement in the individual countries. Studies focusing on whether or not the mandatory adoption of IFRS increases the comparability of accounting information find similar results. Kvaal and Nobes (2010, 2012) find that pre-IFRS policy choices still influence the choices in the IFRS accounts. Lang et al. (2010) come to similar conclusions when they analyse earnings comovement and accounting comparability. Based on the results of these studies we might state that those national differences which shaped the development of national accounting systems in the twentieth century, are today's drivers of the variation in quality of the global comparable accounting information.

## SUMMARY

In this chapter we outlined the major influencing factors which led to differences in the development of national accounting environments and national reporting practices from the eighteenth century until the end of the twentieth century and beyond. Empirical research conducted in the 1970s and the 1980s indicated the following variables as important determinants of those differences: provision of finance, the legal system, the link between accounting and taxation and cultural values.

From the 1970s, a movement towards harmonization of financial reporting started slowly to emerge. From the 1990s on, under pressure from multinational companies seeking dual listings to attract capital, the request for one set of GAAP to be applied worldwide emerged. Meanwhile, as attempts for worldwide harmonization and standardization are undertaken, national institutional differences still influence the output of the financial reporting process of listed companies and even more so of unlisted companies.

## EXERCISES

*Suggested answers to exercises marked ✓ are to be found on our dedicated CourseMate platform for students.*

*Suggested answers to the remaining exercises are to be found on the Instructor online support resources.*

✓**1**  Discuss whether, in essence, accounting is law-based or economics-based.

✓**2**  If accounting is culture-based and national, indeed, local cultures are different, international harmonization will obviously be impossible. Discuss.

**3**  In this chapter several causes are discussed which had some influence on existing accounting systems. Which of the causes listed played a significant role in your country? Discuss.

**4**  If you take Hofstede's (1984) framework for describing cultural differences, how would you describe your own country in relation to these constructs?

**5**  Do you notice in your country an evolution in the existing accounting system? What would you suggest are the driving forces? Explain.

**6**  If you consider Gray's (1988) adaptation of Hofstede's (1984) framework in relation to accounting values, could you describe which accounting values are prevalent in your country?

**7**  Is Gray's (1988) adaptation of Hofstede's (1984) framework of cultural differences able to explain the observed differences concerning voluntary disclosures made to the financial statements?

**8**  Discuss recent research articles which examine the accounting quality or the degree of earnings management after mandatory IFRS adoption.

**9**  Discuss how the financial reporting infrastructure of a country can have a significant impact on financial statements prepared under IFRS.

# THE PROCESS OF HARMONIZATION

**3**

## OBJECTIVES  After studying this chapter you should be able to:

- outline the role of the EU in the development of accounting harmonization

- describe in your own words the meaning of endorsement of IFRS in the EU

- outline the history and changing role of the International Accounting Standards Committee/Board in the development of accounting harmonization

- describe in your own words the different steps in the due process of standard setting of the IASB

- understand current developments and their implications (developments are current when you read the chapter!).

## INTRODUCTION

Chapter 2 gave some idea of the very real historical differences between accounting thinking and practice across the world. Since accounting is essentially a communication process, such differences are not helpful in the context of multinational and international business. Either reporting entities need to prepare multiple sets of financial statements under different bases, or users have to familiarize themselves with and understand a variety of different accounting preparation systems. Both alternatives are time consuming and costly, and can easily lead to confusion and error.

Reduction in such differences, and ideally the elimination of such differences, is desirable. This process is also difficult because of the deep-seated causes discussed in Chapter 2. However, for listed companies the harmonization process on a global scale is well under way. We provide in this chapter an overview of harmonization processes undertaken in the past decades and recently. A number of attempts have been made on a regional basis – of which that of the EU is perhaps the most significant – to reduce country differences. The International Accounting Standards Board (IASB) and its predecessor, the International Accounting Standards Committee (IASC), pursue harmonization at the global level. In the early years, the EU had a much greater effect than the IASC; now, however, its influence relative to the IASB has declined. In this chapter we discuss first the EU efforts towards harmonization and later we pay attention to the international harmonization on a global level.

Before we discuss this process of harmonization, we pay attention to the terminology which can be very confusing. 'Harmonization' is a process of increasing the compatibility of accounting practices by setting bounds to their degree of variation. 'Standardization' appears to imply the imposition of a more rigid and narrow set of rules. However, within accounting these two words have almost become technical terms and one cannot rely on the normal difference in their meanings. Harmonization is a word that tends to be associated with the supranational legislation promulgated in the EU, while standardization is a word often associated with the IASB and its predecessor (the IASC). In practice, the words are often used interchangeably. In the twenty-first century the word 'convergence' was introduced by the international accounting standard setter. Convergence refers to the elimination of differences between two sets of accounting standards (e.g. IFRS and US GAAP). The objective of the convergence process is making accounting information published in annual reports in compliance with two different sets of accounting standards more comparable through the convergence of the underlying standards applied in the reports.

Further, one can distinguish between de jure harmonization (that of rules, standards, etc.) and de facto harmonization (that of corporate financial reporting practices). For any particular topic or set of countries, it is possible to have one of these two forms of harmonization without the other. For example, countries or companies may ignore the harmonized rules of standard setters or even lawmakers. By contrast, market forces persuade many companies in France or Switzerland to produce English-language financial reports that approximately follow Anglo-American practice.

## EU DIRECTIVES

For many years the major method of engendering change across the EU has been by means of Directives. Once agreed (a process that can take and has taken over 20 years), a Directive is a binding agreement by all the Member States of the EU that they will introduce the principles set out in the Directives into national legislation. It is important to clarify precisely what this means and what it does not mean. It does mean that all Member States are required to implement the Directives. It does not mean that citizens or institutions within a Member State are required to follow the Directive, unless and until the contents of the Directive are enacted by legislation within the state. Another important point is that each Directive exists not merely in one language version, but in each of the official EU languages. It is the language version applicable to a particular Member State that is to be enacted into the law of that country. There may not be perfect semantic equivalence between different language versions of the Directives. Furthermore, where the contents of the national legislation following from a Directive differ from that Directive (either by restricting allowed options or by going against the terms of the Directive itself), only European legal procedures can be used to enforce the Directive requirements.

The fundamental EU Directive relating to financial reporting is the Fourth Company Law Directive of 25 July 1978. This relates to the annual accounts of limited companies. It was followed by the Seventh Company Law Directive of 13 June 1983, which extended the principles of the Fourth Directive to the preparation of consolidated (group) accounts. The Fourth Directive seeks to provide a minimum of coordination of national provisions for the content and presentation of annual financial accounts and reports, of the valuation methods used within them and of the rules for publication. It applies to 'certain companies with limited liability' – broadly, all those above defined minimum size criteria – and aims to ensure that annual accounts disclose comparable and equivalent information.

It is important to place the Fourth Directive into its historical context. It was drafted and debated over a period of some ten years, beginning when the EU had six members and ending when it had ten. The pre-Directive national characteristics of the accounting practices of the Member States were significantly different, both in degree of sophistication and in direction. When appraising the success (or otherwise) of this Directive we must measure its achievements against those, at times, startlingly diverse existing practices.

Crucial to the content of the Fourth Directive is the requirement that published accounts should show a 'true and fair view'. The implications and origin of the phrase are discussed in some detail in Chapter 9. Briefly, however, this is a classic example of the cultural divide between the common law tradition and the tradition of codified law. In the former, definitions of such concepts are typically provided by courts in relation to specific situations rather than by legislative texts intended to apply to many different situations. In the latter, the converse is true: the courts have a role of interpretation and clarification of legislative texts, but not of providing situationally appropriate legal definitions. Thus, the tradition of economic liberalism of the English-speaking countries, the faith in markets and the suspicion of technocracy, go hand in hand with an essentially pragmatic common law tradition and a belief that the accounting profession can largely lay down its own rules in the form of 'generally accepted accounting principles'. By contrast, the countries of continental Europe have less historical attachment to economic liberalism, more faith in technocracy and a preference for explicit legal texts, which extends to the framing of accounting rules. Harmonization of accounting within the EU has involved bringing these two traditions into some degree of harmony and it is in this respect that the inclusion of the 'true and fair' requirement in the Fourth Directive was both crucial and controversial.

The Fourth Directive contained many options with regard to recognition and measurement of a substantial number of balance sheet items and profit and loss items. Analyzing the different national implementations of the Fourth Directive in the EU Member States revealed that huge differences still existed with regard to the individual financial statements published in the different Member States. The Seventh Directive, which was developed in the 1980s, contained fewer options than the Fourth Directive. The latter was due to the fact that consolidation practices were less developed in a number of EU Member States (see Chapter 2), therefore fewer national practices and interests had to be defended during the development of the Seventh Directive.

By the early 1990s it had become clear, even to the European Commission, that Directives were too cumbersome and slow to achieve further useful harmonization. The Fourth Directive, agreed in 1978, did not cover several topics and it had been too complicated to amend it often. Furthermore, global harmonization had become more relevant than regional harmonization.

It had also become clear that, for large European companies, voluntary harmonization might focus on US rules over which the European Commission and other Europeans have no influence. Consequently, from the middle of the 1990s the European Commission began to support the increasingly important efforts of the IASC.

In 1995 the European Commission developed its new 'Accounting Strategy'. Within the frame of that new strategy, the contact committee on Accounting Directives analyzed the degree of conformity between the IASs and the content of the European Accounting Directives. With the results of this analysis, the individual EU Member States could decide whether or not they would allow national companies to comply with IAS instead of the domestic GAAP.

In May 1999 the European Commission agreed on the Financial Services Action Plan. One of the objectives of this Plan is to create a single large capital market within the EU. To facilitate this creation of a large single capital market, the European Commission proposed in 2000 that all listed companies should use one set of accounting standards for financial reporting purposes. The International Accounting Standards (IAS) was chosen to be that set of accounting standards. In 2002, Regulation (EC) No. 1606/2002 on the application of IAS was approved by the European Parliament.

Unlike an EU Directive, the Regulation has the force of law and no further action is required by Member States before the Regulation comes into effect. The Regulation applies in all EU Member States plus Iceland, Norway and Lichtenstein.

The Regulation requires all listed companies within the EU and the European Economic Area to publish IAS consolidated financial statements for accounting periods beginning on or after 1 January 2005. The term IAS encompasses all standards and interpretations issued or adopted by the IASB.

## The enforcement of IASs and IFRSs and their interpretations in the EU

Although the Regulation requires the publication of IAS/IFRS consolidated financial statements, this does not imply that when the IASB issues standards and interpretations they become immediately applicable in the EU. The European Commission is required to decide on the applicability of individual IASs/IFRSs and Interpretations within the EU. The latter implies that it may adopt an IAS only if:

- it is not contrary to the principles of the EU Fourth and Seventh Directives
- it is conducive to the European public good
- it meets the criteria of understandability, relevance, reliability and comparability required of financial information needed for making economic decisions and assessing stewardship of management.

The EU decision on applicability of standards and interpretations issued by the IASB in the EU is called the enforcement process. The European Commission is assisted in its decision on the applicability of the IAS/IFRS and Standards Interpretations Committee (SIC)/IFRICs in the EU by three different committees. First, a group called the European Financial Reporting Advisory Group (EFRAG) advises the European Commission in this endorsement process. The EFRAG is a private institution, set up in 2001 by organizations active in the area of financial reporting. Its activities are:

- providing proactive advice to the IASB
- advising the European Commission on the acceptability of IFRSs for endorsement in Europe
- advising the European Commission on any resulting changes to be made to the Accounting Directives and related topics.

Within EFRAG a 12-member Technical Experts Group considers each standard and each interpretation for its acceptability for endorsement in the EU. Based on the advice of its Technical Expert Group, EFRAG will provide advice to the Commission. Since EFRAG is not defined in the EU Regulation on the adoption of IFRSs, the Commission has no regulatory obligation to listen to EFRAG.

In 2006, the European Commission added another player to this endorsement process (Commission Decision No. 2006/505/EC). The Standards Advice Review Group (SARG) was created. This group consists of seven independent experts. This group is expected to give advice to the Commission that is not influenced by governments (unlike the Accounting Regulatory Committee (ARC)) or by audit firms, companies, users or other stakeholders (unlike EFRAG). The SARG issues its opinion whether EFRAG's endorsement advice is well-balanced and objective. Third, there is the Accounting Regulatory Committee (ARC). The ARC consists of representatives from Member States and its function is to provide an opinion to the Commission on proposals to adopt (endorse) an IAS. The governments of Member States try to influence this endorsement process through ARC.

Based on the advice of EFRAG and the opinion of SARG, the Commission prepares a draft endorsement Regulation. The adoption of the Regulation follows a regulatory comitology procedure. This means in practice that the ARC votes on the Commission proposal. The qualified majority rule applies. If the vote is favourable, the European Parliament and the Council of the EU have three months to oppose the adoption of the draft Regulation by the Commission. If the European Parliament and the Council give their favourable opinion on the adoption, or the three months elapse without opposition from their side, the Commission adopts the draft Regulation. After adoption, it is published in the Official Journal and enters into force on the day laid down in the Regulation itself.

Since the establishment of this endorsement process, the original text of all standards (IAS/IFRS) and interpretations (SIC/IFRIC) of the IASB have been endorsed in full except for IAS 39 and a few IFRICs. IAS 39 has been endorsed with a number of exceptions (carve-outs) and the debated IFRICs have been withdrawn by the IASB.

## ACTIVITY 3.1

Go to the website of EFRAG and check the endorsement processes of standards and interpretations issued by the IASB recently (www.efrag.org/ – see 'Endorsement Status' section).

its way. The comment letters EFRAG receives from European constituents with regard to the standards and interpretations to be endorsed can also be found on EFRAG's website.

### Activity feedback
On EFRAG's website you will find a list of standards and interpretations for which the endorsement process is on

As soon as a standard or interpretation (SIC/IFRIC) is endorsed, it is translated into the official languages of the EU. When companies do prepare financial statements using IAS, they have to declare that their financial statements are in compliance with IAS/IFRS as endorsed by the EU. If a company uses carve-outs foreseen through the endorsement process of the EU, this company complies with IAS/IFRS as endorsed by the EU, but it does not comply with the IAS/IFRS as issued by the IASB. The latter element is important for the recognition of accounts in compliance with the international standards outside the EU (e.g. in the USA, as we will see later in this chapter). Companies will communicate with which versions of IAS they comply. We include here as an illustration an extract of the annual accounts of Unilever 2009.

## ILLUSTRATION

### Opinion on financial statements

In our opinion the Group financial statements:

- give a true and fair view of the state of the Group's affairs as at 31 December 2009 and of its profit and cash flows for the year ended
- have been properly prepared in accordance with IFRSs as adopted by the EU, and
- have been prepared in accordance with the requirements of the Companies Act 2006 and Article 4 of the IAS Regulation.

### Separate opinion in relation to IFRS as issued by the IASB

As explained in note 1 to the consolidated financial statements, the Group – in addition to complying with its legal obligation to apply IFRSs as adopted by the EU – has also applied IFRSs as issued by the International Accounting Standards Board (IASB). In our opinion, the Group financial statements comply with IFRSs as issued by the IASB.

After the endorsement of the IASs, IFRSs and their Interpretations, the texts of the standards and the interpretations are translated in the different official EU languages. These translations are the standards EU-listed groups have to comply with on EU stock markets. As enforcement of these standards is still a national issue, the different Courts of the Member States will judge whether the financial statements are in compliance with the official EU translation of IAS, IFRS or an Interpretation. So, in order to have comparable information, it is crucial that the translations of IAS in the different EU languages embed the same concepts and substance. In order to stimulate consistent application of IFRS in the EU, the European Security and Markets Authority (ESMA) oversees and stimulates the European Enforcement Coordination Sessions (EECS). A key function of these EECS is the analysis and discussion of decisions taken by independent EU National Enforcers in respect of financial statements published by issuers with securities traded on a regulated market and who prepare their financial statements in accordance with IFRS. Decisions taken by Enforcers do not provide generally acceptable interpretations of IFRS, which remains the role of the International Financial Reporting Standards Interpretations Committee. The publication of the enforcement decisions, however, will inform market participants about which accounting treatments EU National Enforcers may consider as complying with IFRS; that is, whether the treatments are considered as being within the accepted range of those permitted by the standards or IFRIC interpretations. Such publication, together with the rationale behind these decisions, will contribute to a consistent application of IFRS in the EU.

## ACTIVITY 3.2

Check ESMA's website on pronouncements with regard to application of certain international standards and interpretations (www.esma.europa.eu).

### Activity feedback

On ESMA's website you will find pronouncements with regard to problems of application of a number of stand- ards and interpretations. After deliberations, ESMA formulates an opinion on application problems and bundles these decisions into a report. If you review all the decisions published so far, one notices that most decisions had to be taken with regard to fair value measurements of financial instruments and issues related to all kinds of business combinations.

Member States have the option of extending the application of the Regulation to unlisted companies and to legal entity, rather than consolidated financial statements. A number of Member States in the EU have already extended this compulsory application of IAS to financial institutions, group accounts of unlisted companies and even individual accounts (e.g. Czech Republic, Estonia, Malta, Lithuania). In other Member States companies are allowed to prepare their group accounts or individual accounts according to IAS/IFRS on a voluntary basis. These statements then replace the statements which would have been prepared according to national GAAP. Only a few Member States still prohibit companies from preparing their individual accounts in compliance with IAS/IFRS (e.g. Austria, Belgium, France, Spain and Sweden). The reason for this prohibition is that in those countries there is a strong link between the accounting profit and the taxable profit (see also Chapter 2, 'Link between accounting and taxation').

## The future of EU accounting regulation

The EU updated in 2003 the Fourth and Seventh Directives to make them more receptive to the international standards. Major amendments include to:

- empower Member States to allow or require a cash flow statement
- bring the definition of parent and subsidiary fully into line with IAS 27 (see Chapter 27)
- require the consolidation of all subsidiaries, even those with dissimilar activities
- achieve consistency between the formal requirements for the financial statements and IAS requirements
- allow for likely IAS requirements on performance reporting
- allow the revaluation of intangible assets and any other class of assets
- allow the application of the fair value
- extend the disclosures about environmental and social aspects of a business
- modify the format and content of the audit report to reflect current best practice and achieve harmonization.

The EU continuously works on the modernization and simplification of the Fourth and Seventh Directives in which the EU consulted stakeholders several times through the publication of consultation papers. In a Discussion Paper for the Stakeholders' meeting on 12 June 2009, the European Commission stated that stakeholders support that the Directives should continue to be based on a 'minimum harmonization approach'. Regarding the future role of the Directives, different views exist. On one side, some prefer that the Directives only constitute a high level legal framework and general principles according to which Member States determine their own accounting requirements in conformity with the principle of subsidiarity. On the other side, other stakeholders believe that the Directives should continue to provide detailed accounting requirements for all European limited liability companies, tailored to the specific needs of Europe. The revision of the Fourth and Seventh EU Directives currently in progress (winter 2013) aims to limit the administrative burden for SMEs in the EU, which is linked to the current reporting requirements driven by the Fourth and Seventh EU Directives on financial reporting. In the light of the publication of IFRS for SMEs, stakeholders suggest that the Directives should provide Member States with the possibility to make use of IFRS for SMEs – at least to certain categories of companies. However the EU did not opt for that route. As a consequence, individual Member States in the EU could choose whether they adapted their national GAAP for SMEs in accordance with IFRS for SMEs, as long as the IFRSs were not in contradiction with the EU Directives, or whether they developed national GAAP further in line with the EU Directives. As a consequence of the non-adoption of IFRS for SMEs by the EU, national differences in financial reporting for non-listed companies will still persist for a long time within the EU.

After the discussion of harmonization efforts in the EU, we now focus on the worldwide harmonization efforts of the IASB and its predecessor the IASC.

## INTERNATIONAL ACCOUNTING STANDARDS

### The IASC and the start of international harmonization

The IASC was created in 1973. Its creation was related to that of the International Federation of Accountants (IFAC), which is the worldwide umbrella organization of accountancy bodies. It is independent of government or pseudo-government control. Its stated purpose is to develop and enhance a coordinated worldwide accountancy profession with harmonized standards. All members of the IFAC were, under the old IASC constitution, automatically members of the IASC.

IASC's description of itself as an 'independent private sector body' is accurate and revealing. It was, in essence, a private club with no formal authority. This is in contrast to national regulatory or standard-setting bodies, which operate within a national jurisdiction and some form of legal and governmental framework that delineates, defines and provides a level of authority. The IASC, however, operated throughout its existence in the knowledge that, in the last resort, it and its standards had no formal authority. It therefore always had to rely on persuasion and the quality of its analysis and argument. This can be seen to have had two major effects. First, the quality of logic and discussion in its publications was generally high and its conclusions were – if sometimes debatable – feasible and clearly articulated. Second, however, the conclusions and recommendations of many of the earlier published IAS documents often had to accommodate two or more alternative acceptable treatments, simply because both or all were already being practised in countries that were members of IASC and were too significant to be ignored.

The disadvantages of this state of affairs are obvious and were well recognized by the IASC itself. Towards the end of the 1980s the IASC decided it would attempt a more proactive approach and early in 1989 it published an exposure draft (E32) on the comparability of financial statements. This proposed the elimination of certain treatments permitted by particular IASs and the expression of a clear preference for one particular treatment, even where two alternatives were still to be regarded as acceptable.

This 'comparability project' led to a large number of revised standards operative from the mid-1990s, which did indeed considerably narrow the degree of optionality compared with the earlier versions of the standards issued in the 1970s and 1980s. The comparability project, therefore, can be said to have made the set of IAS more meaningful and significant. Of course, it did nothing to increase the formal authority of the IASC.

## Towards acceptance of IAS by IOSCO

In 1995, as the next stage in its development, IASC entered into an agreement with the International Organization of Securities Commissions (IOSCO) to complete a 'core set' of IAS by 1999. With regard to the agreement, the IOSCO's Technical Committee stated that completion of 'comprehensive core standards acceptable to the Technical Committee' would allow it to 'recommend endorsement' of those standards for 'cross-border capital raising in all global markets'. The significance of this agreement is great. It would mean that one set of financial statements, properly prepared in accordance with IAS GAAP, would automatically be acceptable for listing purposes without amendment and without any reconciliation to national (i.e. local) GAAP on each and all of the world's important stock exchanges. This would save huge resources at the international and multinational level, both for preparers and for users and analysts. The role of national standard setters – except, arguably, for small and medium-sized entities – would simply disappear, if enforcement were left to bodies other than the standard setter.

From the IAS viewpoint, successful implementation of this process would provide the de facto authority that it needed. With regard to enforcement, however, the IASB is still dependent on securities regulators and other bodies with the power to impose de-listing and other sanctions and on a mechanism for bringing breaches of IASs to the attention of such bodies.

In December 1998 the then IASC completed its 'core standards' programme with the approval of IAS 39, *Financial Instruments Recognition and Measurement*. In late 1999, following the publication of the report *Recommendations on Shaping IASC for the Future* of IASC's Strategic Working Party, the board of IASC approved proposals to make significant changes to IASC's structure, in order to prepare it for an enhanced role as a global accounting standard setter.

Following these proposals for changes, the year 2000 was a momentous one for IASC. In May the proposed structural changes were approved by IASC's membership. (The results of these changes are outlined in the following section.) Also, in May the IOSCO formally accepted the IASC's 'core standards' as a basis for cross-border securities-listing purposes worldwide (although for certain countries, notably the USA, reconciliations of items such as earnings and stockholders' equity to national GAAP would still be required up until 2007). In June, the European Commission issued a Communication proposing that all listed companies in the EU would be required to prepare their consolidated financial statements using IASs, a proposal that has since been adopted.

## International Accounting Standards: From voluntary adoption to compulsory adoption

Up until 2005, companies complied with IASs and IFRSs on a voluntary basis. From 2005 onwards, not only did EU listed groups have to comply with IFRS on a mandatory basis, also Australian listed groups were now subject to mandatory compliance with IFRS. New Zealand followed this Australian and EU example, and from 2007 onwards listed companies in New Zealand have to prepare their group accounts according to IFRS.

Since then, worldwide use of IASs/IFRSs is increasing. Regulatory authorities in a number of countries have decided to move towards compulsory application of IFRS for listed groups. The following is a list of these decisions. We notice that IFRS adoption has increased in Asia as well as in the Americas. Korea decided that from 2009 any company could choose to apply IFRS, with the use of IFRS becoming mandatory for all listed companies from 2011. China announced that its central-level state-owned enterprises and large- to mid-scale companies would adopt China's new accounting standards that comply with IFRSs by the end of 2009. In Brazil banks had to comply with IFRSs from 2009 onwards and listed companies from 2010 onwards. Canada has implemented IFRS in 2011. In 2008 Israel, Malaysia and Mexico decided to adopt IFRS for listed groups.

Further, we are able to distinguish a number of countries in which the domestic GAAP are identical to the IAS/IFRS. These countries are South Africa, Singapore, the Philippines and the jurisdiction Hong Kong. There is always a period of time which elapses between the issuance of a new international standard (IAS/IFRS) or interpretation (SIC/IFRIC) and the moment it is translated into these national GAAP rules. Auditors, when certifying these accounts, state that the financial statements are in compliance with the national GAAP, although the national GAAP is similar to IAS.

Next we observe countries which stopped developing their own national GAAP and have substituted their national GAAP with IASs. We find this situation in Bahrain, the Emirates, Croatia, the Dominican Republic, Kenya, Haiti, Nepal and Venezuela. In these countries, international accounting standards receive a national label.

One global set of accounting standards or worldwide use of IASs/IFRSs will only be achieved if the American Securities and Exchange Commission (SEC) accepts international accounting standards for listing purposes for all firms listed on US stock exchanges. Up until now IFRS is only accepted on US stock markets for foreign listed firms only. In the next section we provide some insights on that process.

## The process of acceptance of IAS/IFRS in the USA

The Securities and Exchange Commission approved in November 2007 that for 'foreign private issuers' (a corporation or other organization incorporated or organized under the laws of any foreign country) financial statements prepared in accordance 'with IFRS as issued by the IASB' would be accepted on American stock exchanges without reconciliation to US GAAP. This new regulation applies to financial statements covering years ended after 15 November 2007. Shortly after the decision to allow foreign registrants to file annual accounts in compliance with IFRS for listing in the US, the SEC announced that it would decide in 2011 whether it would also allow US issuers to prepare financial statements in accordance with IFRS for listing on US stock exchanges. The change in attitude of the SEC dates back to the turn of the century. The collapse of Enron and subsequent further 'scandals' have shaken the complacency of American regulation to the core. At almost the same time as the Enron collapse, a new chairman was appointed to the US Financial Accounting Standards Board (FASB) – Robert Herz. Herz was one of the two half-time appointments to the new IASB, was an active supporter of convergence between the USA and IAS, and was of a more principles-based, than rules-based, approach for US standards, which would obviously make such convergence easier. However the positive momentum towards IFRS did not continue, the decision to be taken in 2011 was postponed.

Finally on 13 July 2012 the staff of the SEC published a report on IFRS (SEC Final Staff Report – Work plan for the consideration of incorporating IFRS into the financial reporting system for US issuers). The SEC Staff Report was designed to inform the SEC commissioners when they would come to decide whether, and if so, how, IFRS should be applied in the US. It is understood that the next step in this process is the development by the SEC Staff of a recommendation to commissioners on the possible adoption of IFRS for US companies listing in the US. However, so far (winter 2013), no timetable has been disclosed for completing this work.

Despite this evolution, the convergence process between the standards issued by the IASB and the FASB still continues. This process of convergence between the IASB and the FASB started in September 2002 when, after a joint meeting by the two bodies, the 'Norwalk Agreement' was issued in which both parties acknowledged their commitment to the development of high-quality, compatible accounting standards that could be used for both domestic and cross-border financial reporting. On 27 February 2006, a Memorandum of Understanding (MoU) between the FASB and the IASB was issued. The title of the MoU was 'A Roadmap for Convergence between IFRSs and US GAAP: 2006–2008'. The FASB and the IASB agreed on the following guidelines regarding their approach to the convergence programme:

- Convergence of accounting standards can best be achieved through the development of high-quality, common standards over time.

- Trying to eliminate differences between two standards that are in need of significant improvement is not the best use of the FASB's and the IASB's resources – instead, a new common standard should be developed that improves the financial information reported to investors.

- Serving the needs of investors means that the boards should seek convergence by replacing weaker standards with stronger standards.

The IASB and the FASB agreed on a convergence programme 2006–2008 after discussions with the representatives of the European Commission and the American Securities and Exchange Commission. The convergence process can in fact be divided into two distinct groups of projects. On the one hand, there is the short-term convergence project whereby a limited list of topics is on the agenda of both organizations to remove the differences before 2008. In 2009, in the wake of the financial crisis, the Group of 20 Leaders (G20) called for standard setters to redouble their efforts to complete convergence in global accounting standards by June 2011. Following this request, in November 2009 the IASB and the FASB published a progress report *FASB and IASB Reaffirm Commitment to Memorandum of Understanding,* describing an intensification of their work programme, including the hosting of monthly joint board meetings and providing quarterly updates on their progress on convergence projects. In their joint statement, they explicitly underlined 'we aim to complete each major project by the end of June 2011, consistent with the milestones established by the 2008 update of the MoU'.

If we consult the update of the IASB on the convergence project with the FASB, we learn that convergence has been reached on the following items (April 2013): share-based payments, segment reporting, inventory accounting, non-monetary assets, accounting changes, fair value option, borrowing costs, research and development, non-controlling interests and joint ventures. On the other hand, there were projects with a longer timeframe where practices were studied in order to find out how the current standards could be improved. With regard to these longer-term projects, the following projects have been completed: business combinations, derecognition, consolidated financial statements, fair value measurement post-employment benefits and financial statement presentation – other comprehensive income. In Part Two and Part Three of this book you will therefore witness the introduction of a substantial number of new IFRSs released in the last years. Many of these new IFRSs result from the discussions and the work under the convergence project. Projects not yet finished under the convergence agreement are leasing, revenue recognition and financial instruments. Under the convergence project the IASB and the FASB also try to come to a joint conceptual framework of accounting (see Chapter 9 for more information on the development of the conceptual framework).

## ACTIVITY 3.3

Go to the website of the IASB (www.ifrs.org) and check the status of the convergence project of the IASB with the FASB.

*Activity feedback*
*On the website of the IASB under the heading standards development, you will find the information on the*

*Memorandum of Understanding with the FASB and its current status. List the items they are still working on at the time when you consult the website. See if there is any progress compared to the situation mentioned in this book.*

## STRUCTURE OF THE IASB

In order to become a world leader in standard setting, it was necessary to change the structure of the IASC at the turn of the century. This happened in 2001. We discuss below the structure of the IASB and subsequently we pay attention to its due process of standard setting. Like the Financial Accounting Standards Board (FASB) in 1972 and the UK Accounting Standards Board in 1990, which replaced the APB and the ASC respectively, the IASB differs from its predecessor by having a two-tier structure, based on an organ of governance not involved in standard setting (the trustees) and a standard-setting board. The change to the two-tier structure was proposed in the Strategic Working Party's November 1999 report, *Recommendations on Shaping IASC for the Future*. This structure was articulated in the IASC Foundation Constitution on 24 May 2000. In the aftermath of the financial crisis, this structure was changed into a three-tier structure. Next to the governance organ and the standard-setting board, a monitoring board was introduced. According to Clause 3 of the Constitution (governance of the IASC Foundation, December 2010):

> The governance of the IFRS Foundation shall primarily rest with the Trustees and such other governing organs as may be appointed by the Trustees in accordance with the provisions of this Constitution. A Monitoring Board shall provide a formal link between the Trustees and public authorities. The Trustees shall use their best endeavours to ensure that the requirements of this Constitution are observed; however, they are empowered to make minor variations [in the Constitution] in the interest of feasibility of operation if such variations are agreed by 75 per cent of all the Trustees.

The Constitution has been adapted several times since 2000. The current structure of the IASB can be found in Figure 3.1. The role of each of the organs listed in Figure 3.1 will now be discussed.

## Figure 3.1    The structure of the International Accounting Standard Setter

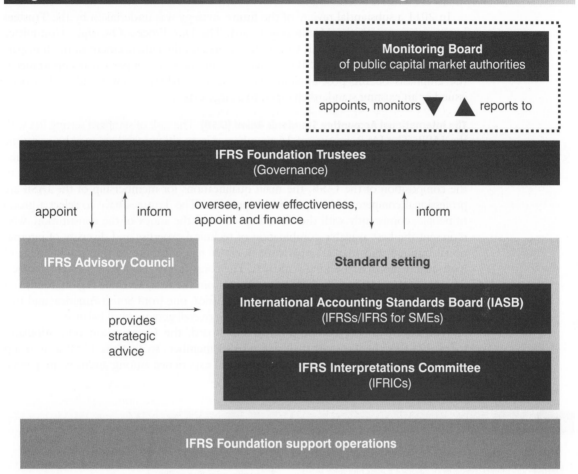

**IFRS Foundation** The IFRS Foundation is primarily responsible for the governance of the international accounting standard setter and the organs of this standard setter by appointing the members of these organs in accordance with the provisions of the Constitution. The governance role of the IFRS Foundation includes establishing and maintaining appropriate financing arrangements for the organization. The members of the IFRS Foundation are called the Trustees and they appoint the members of the IASB, IFRIC and the IFRS Advisory Council. The trustees review broad strategic issues affecting financial reporting standards and they are required to review the Constitution every five years. The IFRS Foundation shall comprise 22 Trustees. Trustees are individuals, of whom six are from North America, six from Europe, six from the Asia/Oceania region, one from Africa, one from South America and two from any area, subject to establishing 'overall geographical balance'. Paragraph 7 of the Constitution stipulates that Trustees shall comprise individuals that as a group provide an appropriate balance of professional backgrounds, including auditors, preparers, users, academics and other officials serving the public interest. Two of the Trustees shall normally be senior partners of prominent international accounting firms. To achieve such a balance, Trustees should be selected after consultation with national and international organizations of auditors (including the International Federation of Accountants), preparers, users and academics. Trustees are appointed for a three-year term, with a possibility for renewal once.

In 2011 a substantial review of the future strategy was undertaken by the Trustees in cooperation with the Monitoring Board. The Due Process Oversight Committee (DPOC) was established. This Committee works on the enhancement of the transparency and oversight of the IASB's standard-setting process. Of particular importance is the emphasis on the post-implementation reviews when a new standard has been issued or an existing standard changed to a large extent.

**The International Accounting Standards Board (IASB)** The task of standard setting lies with the IASB. The IASB consists of 16 members. Up to three members may be part-time members. The expression 'part-time members' means that the members concerned commit most of their time in paid employment to the IASC foundation. With regard to the composition of the IASB, the main qualifications for membership of the IASB are professional competence and practical experience. The Trustees have to select a group of people, consistently with the criteria specified in the annex of the constitution, who represent the best available combination of technical expertise and diversity of international business and market experience in order to contribute to the development of high-quality global accounting standards. The constitution also foresees in geographical diversity of these 16 members (four members from the Asia/Oceania region, four from Europe, four from North America, one from Africa, one from South America, and two appointed from any area, subject to maintaining overall geographical balance).

With regard to the composition of the Board, the Constitution now stipulates (para. 27) that the Trustees shall select IASB members so that the IASB as a group provides an appropriate mix of recent practical experience among auditors, preparers, users and academics.

## ACTIVITY 3.4

Go to the website of the IASB (www.ifrs.org) and look for the IFRS Foundation Constitution. Check for the criteria for IASB members in the Appendix to the Constitution. What are these criteria?

### Activity feedback
*You will find that eight criteria are found to be of importance to become a member of the IASB.*

*1  demonstrate technical competency and knowledge of financial accounting and reporting*

*2  ability to analyze*

*3  communication skills*

*4  judicious decision making*

*5  awareness of the financial reporting environment*

*6  ability to work in a collegial atmosphere*

*7  integrity, objectivity and discipline*

*8  commitment to the IASC Foundation's Mission and Public Interest.*

Each member has one vote. On both technical and other matters, proxy voting shall not be permitted, nor shall members of the IASB be entitled to appoint alternates to attend meetings. The publication of an exposure draft on final IAS or final interpretation of the Standing Interpretations Committee, requires approval by at least ten of the 16 members of the IASB (by nine if there are fewer than 16 members). Other decisions of the IASB, including the publication of a discussion paper, shall require a simple majority of the members of the IASB present at a meeting that is attended by at least 60 per cent of the members of the IASB, in person or by telecommunications.

**The Monitoring Board** On 21 July 2008 the IASCF (the predecessor of the IFRS Foundation) communicated an important change in the structure of the standard setter in a document *Review of the Constitution: Public Accountability and the Composition of the IASB – Proposals for Change*: the creation of a new organ in the structure of the international accounting standard setter, namely the Monitoring Board. The role of the Monitoring Board is to provide a formal link between the Trustees and public authorities. This relationship seeks to replicate, on an international basis, the link between accounting standard setters and those public authorities that have generally overseen accounting standard setters.

The Monitoring Group will consist of public authorities outside the IFRS Foundation's organizational framework. The Monitoring Board shall comprise the responsible member of the European Commission, the chair of the IOSCO Emerging Markets Committee, the chair of the IOSCO Technical Committee, the commissioner of the Japan Financial Services Agency, the chairman of the US Securities and Exchange Commission, and, as an observer, chairman of the Basel Committee on Banking. The Monitoring Group shall participate in the process for appointing the Trustees and approve the appointment of the Trustees. The Trustees report to the Monitoring Group regularly to enable it to address whether and how the Trustees are fulfilling their role as set out in the Constitution.

**The International Financial Reporting Standards Interpretations Committee** Next to the Trustees and to the Board, the structure of the international accounting standard setter includes an Interpretations Committee named the International Financial Reporting Standards Interpretations Committee. Since 1997, a committee which issues interpretations to the IASs exists. At that time the name of the committee was the Standards Interpretations Committee (SIC); the SIC's name was changed to the International Financial Reporting Interpretations Committee (IFRIC) in 2001 with the change in structure of the IASB. Recently the name changed again to the International Financial Reporting Standards Interpretations Committee. The Committee consists of 14 members, who are appointed by the Trustees. The Trustees have the task of selecting members of the Committee so that it comprises a group of people representing, within that group, the best available combination of technical expertise and diversity of international business and market experience in the practical application of IFRSs and analysis of financial statements prepared in accordance with IFRSs. The task of this Committee, according to the Constitution, is to interpret the application of IASs and IFRSs and to provide timely guidance on financial reporting issues not specifically addressed in IASs and IFRSs, in the context of the IASB framework, and to undertake other tasks at the request of the IASB. In carrying out this work, IFRIC needs to work together with national standard setters to bring about convergence and to reach high-quality solutions.

**The International Financial Reporting Standards Advisory Council** This Council (formerly named the Standards Advisory Council) with 30 or more members, provides a forum for participation by organizations and individuals with an interest in international financial reporting and having diverse geographic and functional backgrounds. The IFRS Advisory Council gives advice to the Board on agenda decisions and priorities and informs the Board of the view of members of the Council on major standard-setting projects. The Council shall be consulted by the IASB in advance of IASB decisions on major projects, and by the Trustees in advance of any proposed changes in the Constitution. The Chairman of the Council is appointed by the Trustees and shall not be a member of the IASB or its staff.

## The objectives of the IASB

When the IASC was established in the 1970s its mission statement was:

- to formulate and publish in the public interest accounting standards to be observed in the presentation of financial statements and to promote their world-wide acceptance and observance; and
- to work generally for the improvement and harmonization of regulations, accounting standards and procedures relating to the presentation of financial statements.

In this mission statement the emphasis lies on the harmonization of financial reporting and promoting worldwide acceptance of these standards. In order to gain this worldwide acceptance, the IASC allowed many options in the standards it promulgated in the early years.

Together with the reorganization of the IASC, in 2001 its mission was reformulated. In the Constitution of the International Accounting Standards Committee Foundation the mission statement includes the following objectives:

The objectives of the IASC Foundation are:

**(a)** to develop, in the public interest, a single set of high quality, understandable and enforceable global standards that require high quality, transparent and comparable information in financial statements and other financial reporting to help participants in the world's capital markets and other users make economic decisions

**(b)** to promote the use and rigorous application of those standards

**(c)** in fulfilling the objectives associated with (a) and (b), to take account of, as appropriate, the needs of a range of sizes and types of entities in diverse economic settings

**(d)** to promote and facilitate the adoption of International Financial Reporting Standards (IFRSs), being the standards and interpretations issued by the IASB, through the convergence of national accounting standards and IFRSs.

We do observe an evolution in the objectives of the IASC; the focus lies now on developing one single set of high-quality and enforceable standards. The role of the IASB has evolved towards the role of a global standard setter. This implies, however, that the IASB will issue standards that have to be applied in a variety of different legal and cultural contexts. This will require the use of IFRS by companies that vary considerably in size, ownership structure, capital structure, political jurisdiction and financial reporting sophistication (Schipper, 2005). Financial reports must be comprehensible across countries, across jurisdictions and across cultures. This universality of IAS application is increasingly being questioned, especially as the direction of USA and EU influence is likely to push IASs further towards a large enterprise multinational focus. The relevance of this focus to SMEs or to developing economies is debatable. The latter has come to the attention of the IASB which has issued IFRS for SMEs. Recently the IASB formed an Emerging Economies Group consisting of members from: Argentina, Brazil, China, India, Indonesia, Korea, Malaysia, Mexico, Russia, Saudi Arabia, South Africa and Turkey.

It is important to emphasize that the IASB has no authority with regard to the enforcement of its standards in the different jurisdictions. The enforcement of the IAS or IFRS is still a national matter. There is a real need, again strongly expressed from the USA, for visible enforcement and adequately uniform application of international standards. The people applying those standards come from many different countries with many different native languages. Their attitudes are inevitably influenced by all the historical and cultural baggage inherent in our discussion in Chapter 2. In this respect, academic research plays a major role by providing evidence that differences in enforcement quality across the different jurisdictions impede the global objective of comparable high-quality financial information (see Chapter 2).

## The IASB's due process of standard setting

In order to achieve its objectives, it was necessary for the IASB to develop accounting standards along a transparent process in which the different constituent parties could have their voices heard. This transparency and accountability was highly criticized during the financial crisis in 2008 and 2009. The IASB communicated several times in the wake of the financial crisis that 'they aim to provide a high degree of accountability through appropriate due process, including wide engagement with stakeholders, and oversight conducted in the public interest' (IASB and FASB – joint statement – 9 November 2009). The standards promulgated by the IASB are developed through a formal due process in which opportunities for broad international consultation – which involves accountants, financial analysts and other users of financial statements, the business community, stock exchanges, regulatory and legal authorities, academics and other interested individuals – are foreseen.

The IASB's due process of standard setting involves six stages (see the IASB's Due Process Handbook – February 2012) which we will briefly enumerate here.

---

### ACTIVITY 3.5

While you are reading the different stages of the standard-setting process, it is interesting to look at the website of the IASB (www.ifrs.org) and consult its timetable of projects.

#### Activity feedback
You will find a timetable of the IASB's agenda for the future. This agenda lists the standards, the exposure drafts of standards, the discussion documents and the research projects the IASB is working on in the coming years. A projected timetable of the IASB workplan is posted on the website. A distinction is drawn in their active agenda between new standards, major projects, amendments to standards, the conceptual framework and research projects. Except for the text of a standard which is going to be approved, you will find the texts of all the other documents (exposure drafts, discussion papers, research reports) on the IASB website. Besides the texts of these documents you are able to consult the comment letters sent by the constituent parties in relation to exposure drafts and discussion documents. Looking at the website helps you better understand the process described below.

---

**Stage 1: Setting the agenda** The IASB will set the agenda for the future by taking into account the users' needs in relation to high-quality accounting standards. The IASB will evaluate the merits of adding a potential item to its agenda mainly by reference to the needs of investors. According to the IASB, their needs will also meet most needs of other users such as employees, lenders, suppliers and other trade creditors, customers, government and their agencies and the public. Whether the latter is true is an issue of debate, certainly in Europe.

When deciding whether a proposed agenda item will address users' needs, the IASB considers:

(a) the relevance to users of the information and the reliability of information that could be provided

    **(b)**  existing guidance available

    **(c)**  the possibility of increasing convergence

    **(d)**  the quality of the standard to be developed

    **(e)**  resource constraints.

When the IASB considers potential agenda items, it may decide that some issues require additional research before it can take a decision on whether to add the item to its active agenda. Such issues may be addressed as research projects on the IASB's research agenda. A research project may be undertaken by the IASB or by another standard setter. The IASB discusses potential agenda items with the IFRS Advisory Council, IFRIC, other standard setters and other interested parties.

**Stage 2: Project planning** When adding an item to its active agenda, the IASB also decides whether to conduct the project alone, or jointly with another standard setter. The due process of standard setting is similar under both approaches. After considering the nature of the issues and the level of interest among constituents, the IASB may establish a working group at this stage.

**Stage 3: Development and publication of a discussion paper** Although a discussion paper is not a mandatory step in its due process, the IASB normally publishes a discussion paper as its first publication on any major new topic as a vehicle to explain the issue and solicit early comment from constituents. If the IASB decides to omit this step, it will state its reasons.

Typically, a discussion paper includes a comprehensive overview of the issue, possible approaches in addressing the issue, the preliminary views of its authors or the IASB, and an invitation to comment. This approach may differ if another accounting standard setter develops the research paper. The IASB normally allows a period of 120 days for comment on a discussion paper, but may allow a longer period on major projects (which are those projects involving pervasive or difficult conceptual or practical issues).

**Stage 4: Development and publication of an exposure draft** Publication of an exposure draft is a mandatory step in due process. Irrespective of whether the IASB has published a discussion paper, an exposure draft is the IASB's main vehicle for consulting the public. Unlike a discussion paper, an exposure draft sets out a specific proposal in the form of a proposed standard (or amendment to an existing standard). The development of an exposure draft begins with the IASB considering issues on the basis of staff research and recommendations, as well as comments received on any discussion paper, and suggestions made by the IFRS Advisory Council, working groups and accounting standard setters and arising from public education sessions.

An exposure draft contains an invitation to comment on a draft standard, or amendment to a standard, that proposes requirements on recognition, measurement and disclosures. The draft may also include mandatory application guidance and implementation guidance, and will be accompanied by a basis for conclusions on the proposals and the alternative views of dissenting IASB members (if any). The IASB normally allows a period of 120 days for comment on an exposure draft. However, this period can be extended if the standard deals with a major issue or the period can be shortened to 30 days if there is already broad consensus on the topic.

**Stage 5: Development and publication of an IFRS** The development of an IFRS is carried out during IASB meetings, when the IASB considers the comments received on the exposure draft. Changes from the exposure draft are posted on the website. After resolving issues arising from the exposure draft, the IASB considers whether it should expose its revised proposals for public comment, for example by publishing a second exposure draft.

When the IASB is satisfied that it has reached a conclusion on the issues arising from the exposure draft, it instructs the staff to draft the IFRS. A pre-ballot draft is usually subject to external review, normally by the IFRIC. Shortly before the IASB ballots the standard, a near-final draft is posted on its limited access website for paying subscribers. Finally, after the due process is completed, all outstanding issues are resolved and the IASB members have balloted in favour of publication, the IFRS is issued.

**Stage 6: Procedures after an IFRS is issued** After an IFRS is issued, the staff and the IASB members hold regular meetings with interested parties, including other standard-setting bodies, to help understand unanticipated issues related to the practical implementation and potential impact of its proposals. For each new IFRS or major amendment of existing IFRSs, a post-implementation review (PIR) is carried out. The first major post-implementation review that the IASB undertakes is the PIR of IFRS 8 'Operating Segments'.

The aim of this elaborate due process of standard setting is that all constituent parties from the different regions of the world do participate in this process. Whether or not this goal is achieved is not that easy to observe. Constituent parties often meet with members of the IASB or its staff to discuss items. No tracks are left of this kind of lobbying activity. Lobbying activities which are traceable are the comment letters sent by constituent parties in response to discussion documents and exposure drafts of standards.

Figure 3.2 presents a graphical overview of the IASB's due process of standard setting.

During the financial crisis, the due process of the IASB was not always respected. Political pressure from governments forced the IASB to bypass its own due process when making amendments to standards in relation to financial instruments. Due to the sharp drop in the stock markets in the late summer and autumn of 2008, a number of financial institutions in Europe, which had large amounts of debt securities classified as 'trading', wanted to avoid having to report huge losses on their holdings in their quarterly figures at the end of September 2008. The financial sector, supported by the French Government, asked the European Commission to pressure the IASB to approve an amendment of IAS 39 which would allow those financial institutions to reclassify their holdings as 'held to maturity' back-dated. If the IASB would issue this amendment, the financial institutions would not have to report huge losses for their third quarter of 2008. At the beginning of October 2008, the European Commission threatened the IASB that the IFRS would no longer be the accounting standards to comply with by listed companies in EU markets, unless the IASB would approve the amendment of IAS 39 the Commission asked for. The IASB asked permission to the IASC Foundation Trustees to override its own due process. By mid-October 2008 the IASB approved an amendment to IAS39 to enable the re-classification, with the backdating to 1 July 2008.

In order to avoid this breach of the due process in the future, an accelerated due process – to be applied only in exceptional circumstances – is now elaborated. Since receiving input from a diverse range of constituents from diverse professional backgrounds and geographical backgrounds is important for the deliberative process of the IASB, the standard setter now employs much more mechanisms besides the traditional comment letters to be informed on the view of its constituents. On a regular basis, public hearings, field tests and field visits are carried out.

## Figure 3.2    The IASB's due process of standard setting

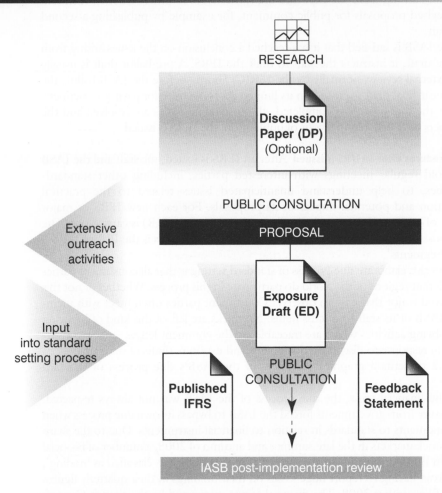

### IFRS FOR SMALL AND MEDIUM-SIZED ENTERPRISES (SMES)

After a long due process, starting in 2003, which included all possible steps of the due process (e.g. discussion papers, round tables, extensive field testing), the IASB published in 2009 IFRS for SMEs. These IFRS for SMEs are separate from the numbered IASs or IFRSs, which are now called 'full' IFRS. The IFRSs for SMEs are simplified IFRS, but built on an IFRS foundation. These IFRSs are aimed at non-publicly accountable entities that must produce general purpose financial statements. Since the large majority of companies worldwide are private, there is a large market for these new-track standards promulgated by the IASB. If we consult the website of the IASB, it seems that 'emerging' countries show a great deal of interest in these IFRSs for SMEs and are planning to adopt them (e.g. Cambodia, Ethiopia). These IFRSs for SMEs allow the IASB to fulfil its third objective, namely to take account of the special needs of SMEs and emerging countries. At the Trustees meeting in January 2010, an SME Implementation Group (SMEIG) was set up. The SMEIG has a dual role. First, it needs to consider implementation questions raised by users of IFRS for SMEs. Second, it needs to consider and make recommendations to the IASB on amendments for IFRS for SMEs. The IASB remains the standard-setting body for both groups of standards, namely the 'full' IFRS and the IFRS for SMEs. IFRS for SMEs are stand-alone standards; the only 'fallback' option to full IFRS is the option to use IAS 39 instead of the financial instruments section of IFRS for SMEs. In fact, IFRS for SMEs are simplifications from full IFRS and they contain only 230 pages, whereas full IFRS take up 2855 pages.

The simplification is achieved in many ways:

1 By the omission of topics not relevant for SMEs (e.g. segment reporting, interim reporting, earnings per share, insurance, assets held for sale).

2 When IFRS have options, only the simpler option is retained and the more complex options are omitted (e.g. financial instruments options including: available for sale, held to maturity, fair value option; proportionate consolidation; revaluation of property, plant and equipment; revaluation of intangibles; free choice on investment property; various options for government grants).

3 Recognition and measurement principles simplified (e.g. goodwill impairment – indicator approach, expense all R&D, cost method for associates and joint ventures, financial instruments: two classifications instead of four; expense all borrowing costs, defined benefit plans: no corridor or deferrals).

4 The number of disclosures is reduced. Whereas full IFRS has more than 3000 items in the disclosure checklist, IFRS for SME has about 300 disclosures. Disclosures that are kept in IFRS for SMEs are disclosures about short-term cash flow, liquidity, solvency, measurement uncertainties and accounting policy choices.

The IASB is currently reviewing IFRS for SMEs. This comprehensive review is undertaken by the SME Implementation Group (SMEIG). They plan to have the revisions finished by 2015.

## THE FUTURE?

Listed companies in more than 100 countries in the world prepare their financial accounts in compliance with IFRS. Whether IFRSs will truly become 'the' global accounting standards will depend on the attitude of the SEC and other US stakeholders involved. However, for their decision no timeline has even been proposed yet. The future agenda of the IASB will still be dominated by a number of convergence projects with the FASB but also by projects on financial instruments in the wake of the financial crisis (see Chapter 18 on accounting for financial instruments). Besides the convergence project with the FASB, the IASB also embarked on a convergence project with the Japanese standard setter. Along with these large projects on convergence, the IASB also started a review of its conceptual framework.

## ACTIVITY 3.6

By means of the IASB website (www.ifrs.org), websites of regulatory and professional accounting organizations in your own country and any other convenient sources, update this chapter for yourself. The chapter was written in January 2013.

*Activity feedback*
*Up to you, of course. Think about the political dimension as well as about the pure accounting issues.*

## SUMMARY

This chapter has provided a background of history and understanding behind current international accounting developments with an emphasis on the increasing importance of the IASB. Thirty years ago the EU started with the harmonization of financial reporting. The EU changed its accounting strategy in the mid-1990s and started to back the efforts of the IASC, and later on the IASB. The new accounting strategy of the EU, the acceptance by IOSCO of IASs for listing purposes and the change in the structure of the international standard setter in 2001 paved the way for the IASB to become a global standard setter. It seems that the final steps towards this status will be taken in the very near future.

## EXERCISES

*Suggested answers to exercises marked ✓ are to be found on our dedicated CourseMate platform for students.*

*Suggested answers to the remaining exercises are to be found on the Instructor online support resources.*

✓1   The European Commission has handed over accounting regulation in Europe to the IASB. Discuss.

2    Global accounting ignores the needs of developing economies. Discuss.

3    Enumerate which of the steps of the due process of standard setting are necessary in issuing standard.

4    The International Financial Reporting Standards Foundation oversees a number of other international committees, two of which are the IFRS Advisory Council and the International Financial Reporting Interpretations Committee (IFRIC).

   Explain the role of the IFRS Advisory Council and IFRIC in assisting with developing and implementing International Financial Reporting Standards.

(CIMA P7 – November 2008)

5    Explain the role of the Monitoring Board in the governance structure of the International Accounting Standard Setter.

# ECONOMIC VALUATION CONCEPTS

# 4

**OBJECTIVES** After studying this chapter you should be able to:

- provide an overview and context of the asset valuation debate

- explain definitions and interrelationships of income, capital and value

- describe the variety of alternatives that need to be explored within the parameters of the valuation debate

- outline the concepts of income developed by Fisher (1930) and Hicks (1946)

- contrast *ex ante* and *ex post* economic income

- outline the scope of economic thinking in this area.

## INTRODUCTION

This chapter is the first of a series that explores the whole area of asset valuation and income measurement. A number of separated research traditions have grown up, some over several centuries, often associated with particular individuals. There is a tendency in the English-speaking world to think that most of the important ideas involved were invented by Anglo-Saxons, but this is far from the truth.

Nevertheless, since, as we have shown in Chapter 2, IASB capital market-driven accounting has largely developed from Anglo-Saxon thinking (very broadly defined), it is suitable to present the analysis in something of what in the old nationalistic days would have been regarded as an Anglo-Saxon context. We briefly relate the ideas to a number of other research traditions at the end of Chapter 7. It is also important to realize that the principles underlying much of this theoretical debate are directly applicable to regulatory issues and debates considered in Parts Two and Three.

More pertinently, it is important to accept that we are here concerned with theoretical analysis, i.e. with what could be done, and what appear to be the advantages and disadvantages of doing it. Practical traditions are, again, outlined at the end of Chapter 7.

## THE BASIC EQUATION

We have already established that a well-behaved balance sheet does not balance just because accountants are good at adding up. It balances because it is defined in such a way that it must balance. Following from the business entity convention, capital is the balancing figure. Capital is the liability of the business entity to the ownership entity. The business owns a collection of assets, and owes a collection of borrowings to lenders and unpaid suppliers of goods and services. Deducting these borrowings from the assets enables us to say that the business owns a collection of net assets. So the owners own the business and the business owns the net assets. Therefore the owners' investment in the business – i.e. the capital – must equal the net assets.

That much is couched in static terms. But we can easily modify the wording to allow for profit or income. To avoid possible confusion, we will for the moment use profit and income as, in the accounting context, completely synonymous terms. Profit (income) means the positive difference between revenues and expenses for a given period. If a business makes a profit then money or money's worth received or to be received increases by more than money or money's worth consumed. This is a complicated way of saying that its net assets go up by the amount of the profit. But in logic and in bookkeeping profit represents an increase in capital. Profit is attributable to owners, is owned by owners and is therefore owed by the business to the owners.

So the amount of profit equals the amount of the increase in the net assets, which, in turn, equals the amount of the increase in the capital. In practice, drawings or dividends are likely to occur. These obviously represent a withdrawal of money or money's worth and therefore a reduction in net assets. They also mean that the business has paid the owners some of what is owed to them. There is therefore a reduction in what remains owing to them, i.e. a reduction in capital. If drawings in a period equal profits for the period, then capital (and net assets) is maintained at its original level. If profit exceeds drawings in a period, capital (and net assets) increases.

This can usefully be summarized schematically. Let $W_1$ be the opening wealth (net assets of the business) and $W_2$ be the closing net assets. Let $P$ be the profit for the period and $D$ be the (net) drawings. Then:

$$W_1 + P - D = W_2$$

Or in more purely accounting terms: Opening capital plus profit minus drawings equals closing capital.

It is obvious that the $W_1 + P - D = W_2$ equation fits our traditional accounting model. But it is in no way restricted to that model. It is expressed in the most general of terms. It can be reduced to:

What you had
+ What you've added to it
− What you've removed from it
= What you've got

This is a truism, mere tautology. The unit of measurement could be absolutely anything. But in accounting we take a particular view. First, we measure the elements in money terms. Second, we traditionally measure the sums of money in a particular way, following the concepts we considered in Chapter 1. We record assets using the historical cost convention and we recognize revenue and net asset increases following the realization and accrual conventions. We are so used to this procedure that we tend to do it automatically, without considering the alternatives. We tend to accept normal practice out of sheer habit. Such acceptance will not do.

## INCOME AND CAPITAL

A useful starting point is the work of the economist Irving Fisher (1930). He defines capital thus: 'Capital is a stock of wealth at an instant in time'. In contrast to this, we can say that: Income is a flow of benefits or services arising through time. This is quite consistent with our earlier tautological equation. What you had (capital, stock) plus additions (income, flow) less withdrawals equals what you have got.

Capital is a stock of wealth that generates income. Income is the enjoyment from the use of capital. These seem like circular, and therefore inadequate, definitions. The way around this difficulty is to distinguish between *capital* on the one hand, and *the value of capital* on the other. *Capital* is a stock of assets capable of generating future services. *The value of capital* is dependent on the value of those future services. For example, a field is a stock of wealth, a field is capital. The value of the field, the value of the capital, is dependent on the (net) value of crops to be grown on the field, i.e. on the income.

All this makes income and the value of capital sound like forward-looking concepts. Perhaps they are!

## ACTIVITY 4.1

Go to a library and look up the words 'income' (or 'profit') and 'capital' in: (a) a number of accounting texts, (b) a number of economics texts, (c) general dictionaries and encyclopaedias. Record book titles under these three subheadings and summarize the definitions given. Record book titles that fail to include definitions of either concept (you may wish to avoid these in the future). Does a clear consensus and a clear understanding emerge?

*Activity feedback*
*You may have more luck than we did, but likely conclusions are:*

1 *The terms have a wide variety of different meanings.*
2 *Clear definition is extremely difficult.*
3 *Many accounting texts evade the difficulties by talking in purely bookkeeping terms.*

## WEALTH AND VALUE

It should be clear by now that we can talk about evaluating the assets of an entity, we can talk about evaluating the wealth of an entity and we can talk about evaluating the capital of an entity. Each of these descriptions amounts to exactly the same thing.

It amounts to an evaluation of what the entity 'has got'. Whichever way we look at this problem, whichever word we wish to use, the key point is the obvious need for evaluation. We noticed earlier that any measuring unit will do. But there must be a measuring unit – certainly a generally understandable one and preferably one generally accepted as a means of exchange (i.e. acceptable as 'money'). You are already familiar with the ways in which accountants usually evaluate different assets in a balance sheet. You are familiar, at least intuitively, with the ideas of 'A is better off than B', or 'this car is worth more than that one' variety. Try the next activity – it may be both more fun and more productive if you try it in a group, but, if this is not possible, think it over for half an hour while doing something else and then summarize your ideas.

## ACTIVITY 4.2

We have an asset, for example a briefcase, and we wish to evaluate it, to attach a monetary value to it. List and describe all the possible ways of doing this you can think of. Illustrate each possible way by making up some simple figures. Which is the best method?

### Activity feedback

One of the purposes of this activity is simply the realization that there is a very large number of possible answers. Here are some possibilities:

1  We could take as our basic figure the amount of money we originally paid for the briefcase:

   (a) We could simply use this base figure as being our 'value'.

   (b) We could reduce it according to the life of the item. Thus, if the briefcase cost €10, is expected to last for ten years and is now eight years old, we could retain the figure of €10 as giving the 'value', but it arguably makes more sense to say that since the briefcase is eight-tenths 'used up', then eight-tenths of the €10 has been 'used up' and therefore the remaining 'value' is €2.

2  We could take as our basic figure the amount of money we would now have to pay to buy the briefcase. Again there are several specific possibilities arising from this basis:

   (a) We could take the cost, today, of buying a new briefcase.

   (b) We could take the cost, today, of buying a second-hand briefcase in this particular condition.

   (c) We could take the cost, today, of buying a new briefcase and reduce it according to the life of our briefcase. Thus, if a new briefcase

costs €20, the second-hand cost of an old one is €3 and other information is as before, the alternative figures under this basis would be (a) €20; (b) €3; (c) eight-tenths of €20, i.e. €4.

A variant of this basis is not to consider the cost of replacing the asset, but rather to consider the cost of replacing its function. Thus, in our example, we would consider the cost of enabling me to carry my bits and pieces if my briefcase were lost, rather than the cost of replacing my briefcase. In situations of rapid technology change, this variant may be the only practical possibility, as the original assets are no longer available.

3  We could take as our basic figure the amount of money we would get if we sold the briefcase in its existing condition – say, €1. This should be the net figure after deducting any selling expenses.

4  We could take as our basic figure an evaluation of the future usefulness to us of the briefcase if we keep it and use it. We might say that the value of the use we shall get from the briefcase in the two final years of its life is €3 and €2, respectively. This does not mean that our basic figure would be 3 + 2 = €5. The question is not: What is the sum of the valuations of the usefulness in each year over the remaining life of the briefcase? But it is rather: What is the value today of the receipts of usefulness expected in the future? Thus, in our example, we need to find the value today of receiving a benefit of €3 in one year's time and a further €2 in two year's time. (Strictly, this assumes that the whole of a year's benefit or usefulness occurs on the last day of the year.)

The essence of this problem can be considered as follows. Suppose I owe you €80. If I say, 'Would you prefer €80 now or €90 in one year?', you would probably

(Continued)

## ACTIVITY 4.2    (Continued)

say you would take €80 now. If I were to say, 'Would you prefer €80 now or €150 in one year?', however, you would probably prefer the €150 in one year.

There will be some point between €80 and €150 at which you are completely indifferent as between the €80 and the higher figure in one year. If that point occurs at €100 (i.e. you are completely indifferent between €80 now and €100 in one year), then the rate of discount is:

25% (25% × 80 = 20; 100 – 20 = 80). This enables us to say that €100 expense in one year is the equivalent of €80 expense today and, equally, that €100 benefit in one year is only 'worth' €80 benefit today.

Suppose a project involves expenses of €100 pa for three years, and then benefits of €200 for a further two years. At a 25 per cent discount rate, the present 'value' of this project is found as follows:

| End year | | | | |
|---|---|---|---|---|
| 1 – 100 × 80% = | | | | −80 |
| 2 – 100 × 80% = | 80 × 80% = | | | −64 |
| 3 – 100 × 80% = | 80 × 80% = | 64 × 80% = | | −51 |
| 4 + 200 × 80% = | 160 × 80% = | 128 × 80% = | | |
| | | 102 × 80% = | | +80 |
| 5 + 200 × 80% = | 160 × 80% = | 128 × 80% = | | |
| | | 102 × 80% = | | |
| | | 80 × 80% = | | +64 |
| | | | | € −51 |

Therefore, the project, involving net cash inflow of €100 (2 × 200) – (3 × 100), has a net present 'value' (discounted value) of −51 and is not worth pursuing (unless all available alternatives give even greater negative present values).

The problem, of course, is finding the rate of discount, which is influenced by alternative uses of the resource (e.g. interest on money) and by future expectations, which are of necessity subjective. Even if a discount rate as of now can be found, the implied assumption used here, that the rate remains constant, is almost certainly false.

If we take the same 25 per cent discount factor as in the example, then €3 in one year will be evaluated at 80 per cent of €3 today, i.e. €2.40, and €2 in two years will be evaluated at 80 per cent of 80 per cent of €2, i.e. €1.28. Thus, the value today of the future usefulness to us of the briefcase would, under these assumptions, be €2.40 + €1.28 = €3.68.

We can label these four evaluation approaches:

1 historical cost

2 replacement cost

3 net realizable value

4 net present value or economic value.

You may, of course, have thought of other ideas or other combinations. Our suggestions are restricted in at least two ways. First, we have thought purely in monetary terms. Second, we have assumed that money is a perfectly acceptable measuring unit – that we know exactly what one euro means. Both these assumptions require critical consideration.

## ACTIVITY 4.3

Analyze and summarize the thought process that made you decide this book was worth buying.

### Activity feedback

These suggestions make the assumption, not necessarily valid, that you did actually buy it. Whatever the price you paid, we can logically deduce that you considered having the book was worth more to you than having the money. But you do not want the book in order to have the book. You bought the book in order to read it, to learn from it, to enjoy and savour its every word. This cannot be precisely evaluated. Equally, if you had not bought the book it would not be because you wanted to have the money. It would be because you wanted to spend the money on something else even more advantageous than ownership of your own copy. This also would not mean that you had evaluated the benefits of this alternative with any precision. There is no need to evaluate the benefits of these alternative courses of action, merely to rank them. So in order to take this significant investment decision it is not obvious that we can necessarily restrict our thinking to the financially quantifiable. This idea is further explored in Chapter 11.

## ACTIVITY 4.4

Obtain a pencil, a measuring rule and an elastic band. Now attempt to measure the length of the pencil: (a) with the rule; and (b) with the elastic band.

### Activity feedback

*Quite! Stupid, isn't it? A centimetre is a precisely defined concept. But the idea of measuring a length with an elastic band is nonsensical because, of course, we do not know how far we have stretched it – it is continually changing by unknown amounts.*

*But a euro is as elastic a concept as an elastic band! In relative terms, for example in relation to the US dollar, the euro keeps changing, as published exchange rates tell us. Even more importantly, the euro keeps changing in absolute terms – indeed, is undefinable in absolute terms – as published inflation rates confirm. The value of a euro is neither clearly defined nor constant. Yet accountants use it as if it were both. This is another idea requiring detailed analysis and we return to it in Chapter 7.*

## AN ARRAY OF VALUE CONCEPTS

A fuller explanation of some possible value concepts is given in a book that every accounting student should read – Edwards and Bell (1961). We are asked to consider a semi-finished asset, i.e. part-way through the production process, to enumerate the various dimensions through which we can describe this asset and thus to calculate and define all possible permutations arising from this multidimensional consideration. Three dimensions are suggested:

1 the form (and place) of the thing being valued
2 the date of the price used in valuation
3 the market from which the price is obtained.

The form can be of three types. First, the asset could be described and valued in its present form, for example a frame for a chair. Second, it could be described and valued in terms of the list of inputs – wood, labour and so on; its initial form. Third, it could be described and valued as the expected output, less the additional inputs necessary to reach that stage – a chair less a padded seat, for example; its ultimate form.

The date of the price used in valuation when applied to any of these three forms gives rise to three possibilities – past, current and future. We can talk about past costs, current costs or future costs of the initial inputs. We can talk about past costs of the present form (i.e. what we could have bought it for in the past as bought-in work in progress), about current costs of the present form, or about future costs of the present form. Finally, the prices assigned to the asset in its ultimate form (and to the inputs which must be deducted) could also bear past, current or future dates.

This now yields nine possible alternatives for our asset. But we have still to consider the third dimension – the market from which the price is obtained. Two basic types of market need to be distinguished: the market in which the firm could buy the asset in its specified form at the specified time, giving entry prices; and the market in which the firm could sell the asset in its specified form at the specified time, giving exit prices. Adding this third dimension with its two possibilities leads to a total of 18 possible alternatives for the asset. Edwards and Bell (1961) summarize this in Table 4.1.

## TABLE 4.1    An array of value concepts

| Value date, market | Form and place of asset | | |
| --- | --- | --- | --- |
| | Initial inputs | Present form | Ultimate form |
| Past, entry | Historical costs | Discarded alternatives | Irrelevant |
| Past, exit | Discarded alternatives | Discarded alternatives | Irrelevant |
| Current, entry | Current costs | Present costs | Irrelevant |
| Current, exit | Irrelevant | Opportunity costs | Current values |
| Future, entry | Possible replacement costs | Possible replacement costs | Irrelevant |
| Future, exit | Irrelevant | Possible selling values | Expected values |

## ACTIVITY 4.5

Articulate and explain the meaning of each of the 18 alternatives shown in Table 4.1.

### Activity feedback

*Your words will undoubtedly be different from ours, but your ideas should be somewhat on the following lines.*

*Initial inputs*

| | |
| --- | --- |
| Past, entry | original costs of raw inputs |
| Past, exit | past selling prices of those raw inputs in their raw form |
| Current, entry | cost of those raw inputs today |
| Current, exit | today's potential selling price of those raw inputs, if still in their original form (which they are not) |
| Future, entry | expected future costs of those same raw inputs in their original form |
| Future, exit | the expected future selling price of those raw inputs, if still in their original form (which they are not) |

*Present form*

| | |
| --- | --- |
| Past, entry | the past cost at which the product could have been purchased in its present partially completed form (it was not) |
| Past, exit | past selling prices at which the product could have been sold in its present partially completed form (but it was not) |
| Current, entry | the cost at the present time of buying the asset in its present partially completed form |
| Current, exit | today's selling price of the product in its present partially completed form |
| Future, entry | the expected future cost of buying the asset directly from a supplier in its present partially completed form |
| Future, exit | the expected future selling price of the product in its present partially completed form |

*Ultimate form*

| | |
| --- | --- |
| Past, entry | the past cost at which the product could have been purchased directly from a supplier in its final fully completed form (but it was not) |
| Past, exit | the past selling price at which the product could have been sold in its final fully completed form (if we had had the product in that form, which we did not) |
| Current, entry | the cost at the present time of buying the product in its final fully completed form (which we did not) |
| Current, exit | today's selling price of the product in its final fully completed form |
| Future, entry | the expected future cost of buying the product directly from a supplier in its final fully completed form |
| Future, exit | the expected future selling price of the product in its final fully completed form |

## ACTIVITY 4.6

You may have found Activity 4.5 rather mind-bending! It is a good example of the type of mental flexibility required if we are going to analyze from first principles without being influenced by prior experience. Now a rather easier task. Select the six alternatives from the total of 18 that you think are most likely to lead to the provision of useful information.

### Activity feedback

The six as selected and defined by Edwards and Bell (1961) themselves are shown in Table 4.2. It is clear from the feedback to Activity 4.5 that not all the other tasks are totally irrelevant (although some of them obviously are). So you may have included one or two different ones. Satisfy yourself, however, that you at least agree that the six alternatives selected in Table 4.2 will indeed provide useful information for decision-making purposes. These six ideas, as developed by later thinking, are all explored in subsequent chapters.

### TABLE 4.2    Edwards and Bell's useful valuation possibilities

**Exit values**

1  *Expected values* (ultimate, future, exit) – values expected to be received in the future for output sold according to the firm's planned course of action.
2  *Current values* (ultimate, current, exit) – values actually realized during the current period for goods or services sold.
3  *Opportunity costs* (present, current, exit) – values that could currently be realized if assets (whether finished goods, semi-finished goods or raw materials) were sold (without further processing) outside the firm at the best prices immediately obtainable.

**Entry values**

1  *Present costs* (present, current, entry) – the cost currently of acquiring the asset being valued.
2  *Current cost* (initial, current, entry) – the cost currently of acquiring the inputs which the firm used to produce the asset being valued.
3  *Historic cost* (initial, past, entry) – the cost at time of acquisition of the inputs which the firm in fact used to produce the asset being valued.

## ECONOMIC VALUE

We have already met the idea of this in Activity 4.2. It is mentioned again here in order to point out that the Edwards and Bell (1961) exposition of the array of value concepts is clearly incomplete in that it excludes the economic value possibility. To extend their own illustration, one possible course of action with a partly completed chair is to complete it and hire it out for rental or use it oneself by sitting on it, in either case producing returns over a number of periods capable of being evaluated using the discounting process.

## CAPITAL MAINTENANCE

We established with our tautology that profit is an increase in capital. Turning the argument around, we can suggest that profit is the increase in the closing capital after having maintained the original capital. This provides a different, but often useful, way of looking at problems of income measurement. For each and every value concept that we can define, with its corresponding income concept, there is also a clearly definable capital maintenance concept.

## ACTIVITY 4.7

Under traditional accounting conventions, based on historical cost, what precisely is the definition of capital that has to be maintained before a profit is reported?

### Activity feedback
*Traditionally, profit is the numerical quantity of money units generated by the business for the owners over a period. If opening money capital is €100 and closing money capital €103, then (ignoring dividends and capital infusions) profit is €3. Profit is the excess after having maintained the original €100, so it is the original money capital, the number of euros originally invested, which has to be maintained under this traditional thinking. If the €100 were in 1898 and the €103 in 2014, this statement still applies!*

*We shall return to the idea of capital maintenance for each of the methods we consider in detail. It will help considerably in appraising the usefulness of the various alternatives. It is also an important element in the IASB conceptual framework discussed in Chapter 9.*

## CRITERIA FOR APPRAISING ALTERNATIVE VALUATION CONCEPTS

We discussed the definition and role of accounting together with suggested characteristics of useful information. In essence, accounting communicates useful information for decision making. We need to analyze each valuation concept to be considered so as to understand in detail the meaning and significance of the information it gives. Different users face different decisions. Users are asking a number of questions. An array of valuation bases are providing a number of answers. If we can match up question with answer then we are being useful. Many valuation bases may be useful, but for different purposes. The question is generally not 'which is the best valuation concept?', but 'which is the best valuation concept to answer this question or help this decision?' Appraisal is a way of analyzing and a way of thinking, never an absolute.

## ACTIVITY 4.8

What are the questions, what are the decisions, for which traditional historical cost accounting (as outlined in Chapter 1) appears to provide the relevant answers?

### Activity feedback
*One safe answer, following on from our discussion on capital maintenance, is that it tells us our gain, our profit, after ensuring the retention of the number of euros we originally invested. It does not seem obvious, however, that this is very useful information. Investment and expansion decisions as regards future activity require projections into the future based on today's euros. Reports on past activity related to euros of the day the business started seem a pretty illogical substitute. But you may, of course, have other ideas!*

## FISHER AND PSYCHIC INCOME

The implication of Activity 4.3 was that people buy something, not because of the object itself, but because of what they can do with it. This idea leads us into Fisher's concept of psychic income. People do things because of the satisfaction they derive from so doing. Satisfaction is a mental occurrence, an event of the mind. It is a psychic rather than a physical happening. People act, and make decisions about actions, so as to maximize their personal, mental or psychic satisfaction. Fisher (1930) puts the argument as follows:

> For each individual only those events which come within the purview of his experience are of direct concern. It is these events – the psychic experiences of the individual mind – which constitute ultimate income for that individual. The outside events have significance for that individual only in so far as they are the means to these inner events of the mind. The human nervous system is, like a radio, a great receiving instrument. Our brains serve to transform into the stream of our psychic life those outside events which happen to us and stimulate our nervous system.
>
> Directors and managers providing income for thousands of people sometimes think of their corporation merely as a great money-making machine. In their eyes its one purpose is to earn money dividends for the stock-holders, money interest for the bond-holders, money wages and money salaries for the employees. What happens after these payments are made seems too private a matter to concern them. Yet that is the nub of the whole arrangement. It is only what we carry out of the market place into our homes and our private lives which really counts. Money is of no use to us until it is spent. The ultimate wages are not paid in terms of money but in the enjoyments it buys. The dividend cheque becomes income in the ultimate sense only when we eat the food, wear the clothes, or ride in the automobile which are bought with the cheque.

The essence of this proposition seems to us to be obviously correct. How do we decide whether to work overtime and earn an extra €20 or to go for a walk in the sunshine? We shall take the decision that, we believe (possibly wrongly, of course), will lead to the greater pleasure. Clearly, the pleasure to be derived from spending the €20 is relevant in this equation. Equally obviously, such pleasure or satisfaction – enjoyment income as Fisher terms it – cannot be measured directly or objectively. He proposes a series of approximations. The first approximation he calls real income. This involves physical events and material things. A litre of milk and a daily newspaper are both examples of real income. Real income consists of:

> those final physical events in the outer world which give us our inner enjoyments. This real income includes the shelter of a house, the music of a radio, the use of clothes, the eating of food.

In one sense, real income is measurable – litre is an objective term (although 'milk' is less so!). But there is no additivity – no standard measuring unit or common denominator. To achieve this we need to move to a second approximation, which Fisher calls the cost of living. This consists of the money paid to obtain the real income – the cost of the litre of milk and the daily newspaper. Fisher's exposition of the argument has something of a period flavour:

> So, just as we went behind an individual's enjoyment income to his real income, we now go behind his real income, or his living, to his cost of living, the money measure of real income. You cannot measure in dollars either the inner event of your enjoyment while eating your dinner or the outer event of eating it, but you can find out definitely how much money that dinner cost you. In the same way, you

cannot measure your enjoyment at the cinema, but you do know what your house shelter is really worth to you, you can tell how much you pay for your rent, or what is a fair equivalent for your rent if you happen to live in your own house. You cannot measure what it is worth to wear an evening suit, but you can find out what it costs to hire one, or a fair equivalent of its hire if, perchance, the suit belongs to you. Deducing such equivalents is an accountant's job.

The total cost of living, in the sense of money payments, is a negative item, being outgo rather than income; but it is our best practical measure of the positive items of real income for which those payments are made.

The problem with this, as Fisher himself recognizes, is that money paid out (outgo) does not seem to make much sense as a measure of income in money terms. We therefore move to a third approximation, that of money income:

All money received and readily available and intended to be used for spending is money income.

We can illustrate Fisher's arguments by considering eating a meal. If we wish to eat, we have to go out and earn some money. This means that we have a money income – in this case, wages. This money income, of course, is the idea that corresponds to the everyday use of the words 'income' or 'earnings'. Having some money, we go out to a restaurant where we eat, and pay for, a meal. Here we have real income. We have the 'final physical event', namely the actual eating of the food. This is approximately measured by the 'cost of living', i.e. by the cost of the meal – the amount we pay the restaurant. This idea of taking a cost-based approach is clearly not a new one to an accountant.

But this is not the end of the story. Fisher argues further. We did not eat a meal for the sake of it, we ate a meal to receive the satisfaction, the pleasure of having eaten (or to avoid the unpleasantness, the pain, of feeling hungry). This satisfaction, this pleasure, is the 'enjoyment' or 'psychic' income. It may be unmeasurable, at least in a manner that can be recorded, but it is still, argues Fisher, the most important. After all, if it did not exist we would have had no reason to buy the meal. And without a reason to buy the meal, we have no reason to earn the wages.

Fisher thus distinguishes three successive stages, or aspects, of a person's income:

1 *enjoyment* or psychic income, consisting of agreeable sensations and experiences
2 *real income*, 'measured' by the cost of living
3 *money income*, consisting of the money received by someone for meeting their costs of living.

The last – money income – is most commonly called income; and the first – enjoyment income – is the most fundamental. But for accounting purposes real income, as measured by the cost of living, is the most practical.

This last statement may seem surprising. Fisher dismisses money income as being unimportant (enjoyment income is the most important, the cost of living is the most practical).

Notice again the definition he gives of money income, emphasis now added:

All money received and readily available and *intended* to be used for spending is money income.

So if we receive a salary of $10 000 (Fisher's figures, writing in 1930!), save $4000 and put $6000 as available for spending, the significant figure to Fisher is the $6000, not the $10 000. Real income, as measured by the cost of living, may be more or less than money income. Real income is a closer approximation to ultimate reality (i.e. psychic satisfaction) than money income, so real income is the preferable concept:

> A definition of income which satisfies both theory and practice, in both economics and accountancy, must reckon as income in the most basic sense all those uses, services, or living for which the cost of living is expended even though such expenditure may exceed the money income.

What this all boils down to is that Fisher's definitions of income *do not involve a concept of capital maintenance*. It is this point that distinguishes Fisher's ideas from the mainstream of both accounting and economic thinking. Fisher's measure of income is really a measure of *consumption*.

## HICKS AND CAPITAL MAINTENANCE

We have already seen (Activity 4.2) that, in very general terms, economic value is based on a current evaluation of future streams of (net) receipts. It is also obvious that, in our earlier equation $W_1 + P - D = W_2$, capital maintenance requires that $W_2$ is at least equal to $W_1$. Another way of putting this is that $D$ (= drawing or consumption) cannot exceed $P$ (= profit or income). The classic analysis of the implications of this thinking is by Hicks (1946). The opening of the following quote makes it clear just how fundamental he feels capital maintenance to be:

> The purpose of income calculations in practical affairs is to give people an indication of the amount which they can consume without impoverishing themselves. Following out this idea, it would seem that we ought to define a man's income as the maximum value which he can consume during a week, and still expect to be as well off at the end of the week as he was at the beginning. Thus, when a person saves, he plans to be better off in the future; when he lives beyond his income, he plans to be worse off. Remembering that the practical purpose of income is to serve as a guide for prudent conduct, I think it is fairly clear that this is what the central meaning must be.
>
> However, business men and economists alike are usually content to employ one or other of a series of approximations to the central meaning. Let us consider some of these approximations in turn.

Hicks moves on to attempt to operationalize this 'central meaning'. Like Fisher, Hicks is obviously adopting a forward-looking approach to valuation and income measurement. We have seen in Activity 4.2 that we can operationalize such an approach (once we have invented the raw figures!) by calculating net present value figures for expected receipts. Putting these two ideas together, we can regard capital, wealth, 'well-offness' as being the net present value of expected receipts. If we put this notion into the original definition in place of the vague 'as well off', we arrive at a first approximation:

> Income No. 1 is thus the maximum amount which can be spent during a period if there is to be an expectation of maintaining intact the capital value of prospective receipts (in money terms). This is probably the definition which most people do implicitly use in their private affairs; but it is far from being in all circumstances a good approximation to the central concept.

## ACTIVITY 4.9

Suppose that at the beginning of the week our individual possesses property worth €10 010 and no other source of income. If the rate of interest were one-tenth per cent per week, income would be €10 for the week. For, if €10 were spent, €10 000 would be left to be reinvested; and in one week this would have accumulated to €10 010 – the original sum. This is income No. 1. But suppose that the rate of interest per week for a loan of one week is one-tenth per cent, that the corresponding rate expected to rule in the second week from now is one-fifth per cent and that this higher rate is expected to continue indefinitely afterwards. What is the individual's income for: (a) week 1, (b) week 2?

### Activity feedback

At the beginning of week 1 the individual is bound to spend no more than €10 in the current week, if he is to expect to have €10 010 again at his disposal at the end of the week; however if he desires to have the same sum available at the end of the second week, he will be able to spend nearly €20 in the second week, not €10 only. The same sum (€10 010) available at the beginning of the first week makes possible a stream of expenditures:

€10, €20, €20, €20, . . .

while if it is available at the beginning of the second week it makes possible a stream:

€20, €20, €20, €20, . . .

It is obvious that these two alternative possible expenditure streams do not give equal well-offness. One is worth more than the other. If we put the income as €10 for week 1 and €20 for week 2, then we are not 'maintaining intact the capital value of prospective receipts (in money terms)'. The amount the individual can spend each week while still maintaining well-offness intact **must**, under these conditions, be the same in week 1 and in week 2 (and subsequent weeks):

This leads us to the definition of Income No. 2. We now define income as the maximum amount the individual can spend this week, and still expect to be able to spend the same amount in each ensuing week. So long as the rate of interest is not expected to change, this definition comes to the same thing as the first; but when the rate of interest is expected to change, they cease to be identical. Income No. 2 is then a closer approximation to the central concept than Income No. 1 is.

(Hicks, 1946)

There are several problems with this as an operational concept. First, interest rates may change. Second, prices may be expected to change. In principle we can deal with this easily by a small addition to the wording:

Income No. 3 must be defined as the maximum amount of money which the individual can spend this week, and still expect to be able to spend the same amount in real terms in each ensuing week. If prices are expected to rise, then an individual who plans to spend €10 in the present and each ensuing week must expect to be less well off at the end of the week than he is at the beginning. At each date he can look forward to the opportunity of spending €10 in each future week; but at the first date one of the €10s will be spent in a week when prices are relatively low. An opportunity of spending on favourable terms is present in the first case, but absent in the second.

(Hicks, 1946)

Thus, if €10 is to be his income for this week, according to definition No. 3 he will have to expect to be able to spend in each future week not €10, but a sum greater or less than €10 by the extent to which prices have risen or fallen in that week above or below their level in the first week.

In practice, of course, the apparent simplicity of this change is false. We need expectations of price changes for every individual for every commodity of projected purchase for every need of each anticipated expenditure!

In addition to this practical difficulty, Income No. 3 also has the problem of how to deal with long-term assets, i.e. fixed assets or 'durable consumption goods':

Strictly speaking, saving is not the difference between income and expenditure; it is the difference between income and consumption. Income is not the maximum amount the individual can spend while expecting to be as well off as before at the end of the week; it is the maximum amount he can consume. If some part of his expenditure goes on durable consumption goods, that will tend to make his expenditure exceed his consumption. If some part of his consumption is consumption of durable consumption goods, already bought in the past, that tends to make consumption exceed expenditure.

(Hicks, 1946)

It should be noted that we have now come full circle back to an emphasis on consumption. But Hicks is concerned with consumption and capital maintenance, whereas Fisher is only concerned with consumption. We

(Continued)

## ACTIVITY 4.9    *(Continued)*

*can summarize the basic difference between Fisher and Hicks by realizing that while Fisher is concerned with consumption, Hicks is concerned with the capacity to consume. This is clearly a long-run concept. To take an obvious example, consider the farmer's seed corn. This is the basis of next year's crops. It is available now and it could be eaten (consumed). But if it is eaten now there will be no crop next year and therefore no possibility of consumption next year. Therefore, if we wish to maintain the capacity to consume next year, the seed corn must not be consumed now. In other words, it must be saved. This is, to put it mildly, useful information.*

## CALCULATION OF ECONOMIC INCOME

One way of summarizing what we have just looked at is to say that for Fisher:

$$\text{Income} = \text{Consumption}$$

But for Hicks:

$$\text{Income} = \text{Consumption and Saving}$$

which can be expressed as:

$$Y = C + S$$

Savings can be expressed as $(K_e - K_s)$ where:

$$K_e = \text{value of capital at the end of a period}$$
$$K_s = \text{value of capital at the start of a period}$$

Thus:

$$Y = C + (K_e - K_s)$$

For example, if income = €100, capital at the end of the period = €280 and capital at the beginning of the period was €300, then: €100 = 120 + (280 – 300).

This tells us that consumption has exceeded income by €20 because of dis-saving of €20. 'Well-offness' has not been maintained.

In the business world rather than the personal consumption world, $C$ is redefined as the realized cash flows of the period. We will illustrate this as simply as possible.

## ACTIVITY 4.10

An investment on 1 January year 1 has expected receipts on 31 December each year of €1000 for three years. The discount rate to reflect the time value of money is 10 per cent. Calculate the capital as at 1 January for each of the years 1, 2 and 3.

### Activity feedback

On 1 January year 1 the expected receipt on 31 December year 1 needs to be discounted back by one year, the expected receipt on 31 December year 2 needs to be discounted back by two years and the expected receipt on 31 December year 3 needs to be discounted back by three years.

Thus, capital at 1 January year 1 is:

$$\frac{1000}{1.1} + \frac{1000}{(1.1)^2} + \frac{1000}{(1.1)^3} = 909 + 826 + 751 = €2486$$

*(Continued)*

## ACTIVITY 4.10 (Continued)

On 1 January year 2 the receipt on 31 December year 1 is now irrelevant. The expected receipt on 31 December year 2 now needs to be discounted back to 1 January year 2, i.e. by one year and the expected receipt on 31 December year 3 also needs to be discounted back to 1 January year 2, i.e. by two years. Similarly, on 1 January year 3 only the expected receipt on 31 December year 3 is of any relevance and this needs to be discounted back to 1 January year 3, i.e. by one year. Thus, capital at 1 January year 2 is:

$$\frac{1000}{1.1} + \frac{1000}{(1.1)^2}$$
$$= 909 + 826 = €1735$$

and capital at 1 January year 3 is:

$$\frac{1000}{1.1} = €909$$

## ACTIVITY 4.11

Considering the investment in the previous activity, now suppose that the actual cost of the investment on 1 January year 1 is €2486. According to the Hicksian way of thinking, what is the income for each year?

### Activity feedback

Our formula was:

$$Y = C + (K_e - K_s)$$

So in year 1:

$$Y = 1000 + (1735 - 2486)$$
$$= 1000 - 751$$
$$= €249$$

In year 2:

$$Y = 1000 + (909 - 1735)$$
$$= 1000 - 826$$
$$= €174$$

In year 3:

$$Y = 1000 + (0 - 909)$$
$$= 1000 - 909$$
$$= €91$$

In year 1, the cash receipts are €1000, but the income is stated as €249. The difference (€751) needs to be reinvested (saved) in order to facilitate future spending. This reinvestment of €751 on 1 January year 2 will by itself earn 10 per cent in the year 2, i.e. €75. So, total income in year 2 is €174, from the original investment, plus €75 from the reinvestment, i.e. again €249.

In year 2, the cash receipts from the original investment are €1000, but the income is stated as €174. The difference (€826) again needs to be reinvested. This investment of €826 will itself earn €83 in year 3, giving total cash receipts in that year of €91 from the original investment, €75 from the first reinvestment and €83 from the second reinvestment, i.e. €249 once again. Similarly in year 3, cash receipts will be €1000, but the income is stated as €91. The difference (€909) will be reinvested at 10 per cent, earning itself €91 in each year. Total cash receipts in year 4, all from reinvestments, will therefore be 75 + 83 + 91 = €249 and similarly in year 5 onwards. This of course satisfies our original conditions. The income of year 1 is the amount 'that can be spent while still enabling the income of all future periods to be the same amount'. This has been shown to be €249 under the given assumptions. These results are summarized in Table 4.3.

The present value of an annual income stream of €249, to infinity, at a 10 per cent discount rate is €2490. This, allowing for rounding errors, gives us our original 'capital' figure of €2486, which of course is what it should do. So the answer may possibly have come as no surprise. But you should still make sure you understand all the logic involved.

(Continued)

## ACTIVITY 4.11    (*Continued*)

### TABLE 4.3    Hicks' economic income model

| | 1 | 2 | 3 | 4 | 5 | 6 | 7 | 8 | 9 |
|---|---|---|---|---|---|---|---|---|---|
| Year | C | $K_e$ | $K_s$ | Y | Reinvestment | Cumulative reinvestment | Total reinvestment | Income from reinvestment | Total economic income |
| 0 | 0 | 2 486 | 0 | 0 | 0 | 0 | 2 486 | 0 | 0 |
| 1 | 1 000 | 1 735 | 2 486 | 249 | 751 | 751 | 2 486 | 0 | 249 |
| 2 | 1 000 | 909 | 1 735 | 174 | 826 | 1 577 | 2 486 | 75 | 249 |
| 3 | 1 000 | 0 | 909 | 91 | 909 | 2 486 | 2 486 | 158 | 249 |
| 4 | 0 | 0 | 0 | 0 | 0 | 2 486 | 2 486 | 249 | 249 |

Notes: $4 = 1 + 2 - 3$
$5 = 1 - 4$
$7 = 2 + 6$
$9 = 4 + 8$

## INCOME *EX ANTE* AND INCOME *EX POST*

We have assumed that we are in a world of perfect knowledge and perfect foresight, an ideal world in fact. The economic income devised under these assumptions is known as ideal income. It is obviously an unreal oversimplification. We can, however, extend our analysis to allow for estimates of future events and this leads to two further models: income *ex ante* and income *ex post*. Income *ex ante* means income measured before the event; income *ex post* means income measured after the event.

Two possibilities for changes exist: in the timing and/or amount of forecast cash flow and in the appropriate discount rate. Formally, income *ex ante* can be expressed as:

$$Y = C_1 + (K_e^1 - K_s)$$

where $C_1$ is the expected realized cash flow for the period anticipated at the beginning of the period, $K_c^1$ is the closing capital as measured (estimated) at the beginning of the period, and $K_s$ is the capital at the beginning of the period as measured (estimated) at the beginning of the period.

## ACTIVITY 4.12

Assume the same original information as in the previous two activities. Now suppose that, at the end of year 2, the expected return from the investment in year 3 increases to €1100. Using an *ex ante* approach, consider the effects on the calculations for each of the years.

### Activity feedback

Using an ex ante *approach the effects will be:*

*Year 1 – No change.*

*Year 2 – Still no change. The calculations for year 2 are based on expectations as at the beginning of the year 2 and they had not altered at that time.*

*Year 3 – The opening capital $K_s$ will no longer be the same as the closing capital $K_e$ at the end of year 2. It will now be:*

(*Continued*)

## ACTIVITY 4.12     *(Continued)*

$$K_s = \frac{1100}{1.1} = €1000$$

This compares with the corresponding figure of €909 for $K_s$ in year 3 under the ideal income calculations. There is therefore a windfall gain of €91 appearing under the ex ante *way of thinking* in year 3.

Income ex post *can be expressed correspondingly, as:*

$$Y = C + (K_e^1 - K_s^1)$$

*where C is the actual realized cash flow of the period, $K_e^1$ is the closing capital measured (estimated) at the end of the period, and $K_s^1$ is the opening capital measured (estimated) at the end of the period.*

## ACTIVITY 4.13

Given all the information of the previous Activity, reconsider the effects of the change in expectations which occurs at the end of year 2.

### Activity feedback

Again there will be no change in year 1 but, using an ex post *approach, there will be a change in the calculations for year 2, because at the end of year 2 our expectations had already altered. Capital at 1 January year 2, based on expectations as at the end of year 2, is:*

$$\frac{1000}{1.1} + \frac{1100}{(1.1)^2}$$
$$K_s = 909 + 909 = €1818$$

This compares with the corresponding figure of €1735 for $K_s$ in year 2 under the ideal income calculations, giving rise to a windfall gain of €83 appearing in year 2. For present purposes, it is not considered necessary to pursue the calculations any further as regards recalculation of reinvestment amounts and so on. However, several points should be noted:

**1** Income ex post *is measured after the event, but it is still based on expectations of the future; income* ex post *for year 2 is derived from the expectations held as at the end of year 2, but these expectations relate to years 3, 4 and so on to infinity. Economic income* ex post *is therefore just as subjective as economic income* ex ante.

**2** Is the windfall gain realized? This is relatively straightforward. The gain becomes realized as the cash flow whose estimation gave rise to it is actually received.

**3** Is the windfall gain income or capital, i.e. should it be saved (reinvested) or can it be spent? This is not so clear-cut, as it depends on where we

consider our starting point to be. Taking our original example, if our original, and permanent, intention is to maintain the capacity to consume €249 each year to infinity, then it is clear that we have already achieved that requirement without taking account of the windfall gain. The gain is, therefore, 'spare', it need not be reinvested and so it is available for immediate consumption. Notice carefully that the windfall gain is available for consumption as soon as it is recognized, whether or not it has been realized, i.e. in year 2 under the ex post *method and in year 3 under the* ex ante *method. Thus, the windfall gain could be regarded as a simple one-off increase in possible consumption (do not forget it could be a windfall loss, leading to a one-off decrease in possible consumption).*

However, the change in expectations might cause us to amend the permanent annual consumption requirement in some way. We might, for example, wish to redo the complete calculations taking year 2 as a new starting point, giving 2 years of cash flow only. Here the windfall gain would not, or not necessarily, be spendable at all (even if it is already realized!).

It is, of course, possible, taking the original ideal income scenario as our starting point, to consider an almost infinite number of changes in expectations, variable as to timing of the change in expectations, changes in the expected timing of receipts, changes in the expected amounts of receipts and changes in discount rates. In every case, under both ex ante *and* ex post *thinking, we need to establish whether the effect of the change is on income or on capital before we can attempt to rework all the calculations and this depends entirely on the intentions of the decision maker concerned. If these intentions remain unaltered despite the change in expectations, then the windfall will be income.*

*(Continued)*

## ACTIVITY 4.13    (Continued)

Refer back to Hicks' Income No. 3 definition: the maximum amount of money the individual can spend this week and still expect to be able to spend the same amount in real terms in each ensuing week. If 'this week' is, and remains, week 1, then the windfall is income. But if 'this week' means 'the current week', for example the week when expectations change, then the windfall affects capital and requires that a new permanently spendable weekly consumption be calculated.

## SUMMARY

Income, capital and value are interrelated concepts. Value can be defined and enumerated in a variety of ways and detailed description, analysis and appraisal of the alternatives is required.

It is suggested that the economic ideas outlined in this chapter are:

1   theoretically sound and logically sensible
2   highly subjective in application as regards:

   **(a)**   size of future cash flows
   **(b)**   timing of future cash flows
   **(c)**   discount rate to apply to future cash flows
3   problematic as regards windfall gains and losses
4   and therefore, as far as accounting is concerned, they probably represent an unattainable ideal.

## EXERCISES

*Suggested answers to exercises marked ✓ are to be found on our dedicated CourseMate platform for students.*

*Suggested answers to the remaining exercises are to be found on the Instructor online support resources.*

1   Obtain three sets of published accounts of quoted companies. Look carefully at the consolidated balance sheets and notes thereto and read the 'accounting policies'. Taking each item in the balance sheet separately, describe how the item is evaluated. Are these evaluations consistent? i.e. in mathematical terms, do we have genuine additivity?

✓2   Two retail businesses, *A* and *B,* run a similar trade from similar shops in similar areas. *A* bought its shop in 1950 for €5000 and *B* bought its shop in 1990 for €105 000. Both businesses consistently prepare their accounts on historical cost principles and they have identical operating profits. To what extent do the resulting accounts give a true (and fair) representation of the relative performance of the two businesses?

✓3   It is never possible to define capital or income, only to define capital and income. Do you agree?

4   (a)  Outline Fisher's thinking on the concept of income.

    (b)  Outline Hicks' thinking on this topic.

    (c)  Relate and compare the two.

5   Explain the principles of economic income, carefully distinguishing income *ex ante* and income *ex post.*

6   'Economic income is an unattainable ideal.' Consider and discuss.

7   Spock purchased a space invader entertainment machine at the beginning of year 1 for €1000. He expects to receive at annual intervals the following receipts: at the end of year 1 €400; end of year 2 €500; end of year 3 €600. At the end of year 3 he expects to sell the machine for €400.

    Spock could receive a return of 10 per cent on the next best investment. The present value of €1 receivable at the end of a period discounted at 10 per cent is as follows:

| | |
|---|---|
| End of year 1 | 0.909 |
| End of year 2 | 0.826 |
| End of year 3 | 0.751 |

**Required:**

Calculate the ideal economic income, ignoring taxation, and working to the nearest whole euro. Your answer should show that Spock's capital is maintained throughout the period and that his income is constant.

(ACCA – adapted)

# CURRENT ENTRY VALUE 5

## INTRODUCTION

The ideas of the previous chapter are of fundamental importance. But they are inherently highly subjective to apply. Of crucial importance from the point of view of accounting thinking, they are far removed from the marketplace. All 18 of the value concepts considered by Edwards and Bell (1961) (see Chapter 4) relate directly to actual or expected market values. One of these, past entry values, i.e. the historical cost (HC) of the initial inputs, is the traditional process which we summarized in Chapter 1.

Four of the remaining five are current values, two being current entry values and two current exit values. We look first at current entry values. Remember that entry values represent a market buying price, i.e. current entry values represent a cost-based process (but not a historical cost-based process).

## BACK TO BASICS

## ACTIVITY 5.1

On 1 January, Mr Jones starts off in business with 100 cents. His transactions are as follows:

| | |
|---|---|
| 2 January | Buys one bag of sugar for 40c |
| 4 January | Sells one bag of sugar for 50c |
| 5 January | Buys one bag of sugar for 44c |

Prepare balance sheets on 2 January and on 6 January, and a P&L account for the intervening period.

### Activity feedback

*This should not present major problems.*

**Balance sheet 2 January**

| | | | |
|---|---|---|---|
| Inventory | 40 | Capital | 100 |
| Cash | 60 | | |
| | 100c | | 100c |

**Balance sheet 6 January**

| | | | |
|---|---|---|---|
| Inventory | 44 | Capital | 110 |
| Cash | 66 | | |
| | 110c | | 110c |

**Profit and loss**

| | |
|---|---|
| Sales | 50 |
| Cost of sales | 40 |
| | 10c |

*In terms of our very general equation, $W_1 + P - D = W_2$:*

$$100 + 10 - 0 = 110$$

So Jones has made a profit of 10c. This, of course, is the usual accounting approach. But it is important to notice that there are really two stages in the progress from 2 January to 6 January. Between 2 January and the evening of 4 January, after the sale was made, Jones has turned 100c into 110c. On 4 January he actually has physically 110c and nothing else. Then, between the evening of 4 January and 6 January he has changed 110c plus nothing into 66c plus a bag of sugar. Since the second bag of sugar cost 44c and we are recording all our resources at original, or historical, cost, it necessarily follows that we show total resources of 110c on both 4 January and 6 January. The 4 January balance sheet was as follows:

**Balance sheet 4 January**

| | | | |
|---|---|---|---|
| Cash | 110 | Capital | 110 |
| | 110c | | 110c |

Comparing this 4 January position with the 2 January and 6 January balance sheets confirms that:

**1** A profit of 10c was made between 2 January and 4 January.

**2** No profit or loss at all was made between 4 January and 6 January.

Jones, of course, is running a business. He also has to live. So he decides to withdraw the business profit for his own spending purposes.

If he takes 10c out then, by the accountant's definition, he has still left in all the money originally put in. This 10c must therefore be genuine gain, so it can obviously be withdrawn from the business without in any way reducing the resources of the business. So we can rewrite our 6 January sheet, after the withdrawal, as follows:

**Balance sheet 6 January**

| | | | |
|---|---|---|---|
| Inventory | 44 | Capital | 100 |
| Cash | 56 | | |
| | 100c | | 100c |

Our equation now becomes:

$$100 + 10 - 10 = 100$$

## ACTIVITY 5.2

Compare the physical possessions of Jones' business on 2 January with those on 5 January, assuming still that Jones withdraws his 10c profit.

### Activity feedback

*In physical terms the business possesses: On 2 January:*

**1** one bag of sugar

**2** a pile of 60 shiny bright 1c pieces.

On 6 January:

**1** one bag of sugar

**2** a pile of 56 shiny bright 1c pieces.

Now, by simple subtraction, we can compare the physical position between 2 January and 6 January in terms both of sugar and of shiny bright 1c pieces. In terms of sugar, we are comparing one bag with one bag.

*(Continued)*

## ACTIVITY 5.2    (Continued)

*There is no difference. In terms of bags of sugar, the business is exactly the same size as it was before. In terms of shiny bright 1c pieces, the business had 60 on 2 January, and 56 on 6 January. There is therefore a reduction of four shiny bright 1c pieces. In terms of shiny bright 1c pieces the business has got smaller by four pieces.*

*Something must be wrong somewhere. The accountant has shown us that there is a 'genuine gain' of 10c over and above the original 100c capital put in. Jones has therefore withdrawn the 10c, and yet the result is not that the business is 'back where it started'. The result is that the business has got smaller to the tune of 4c.*

*Surely, either the physical comparison is wrong or the profit and loss statement prepared in Activity 5.1 is wrong. If the physical comparison is correct (try it yourself) then the 'genuine gain' of 10 per cent mentioned is quite simply not genuine! Further thinking is needed. On 4 January we had, in physical terms, as we have already seen, a pile of 110 shiny bright 1c pieces. We have also already seen that the profit of 10c was made by 4 January. It therefore follows that the accountant's statement at 4 January is identical with the actual physical position at that date. The accountant says cash is 110c and profit is 10c. The physical position shows a pile of 110 shiny bright 1c pieces. It is obvious that since the physical position and the accounting position were identical as at 4 January the divergence, the difference between the two, must have occurred after 4 January. But only one event has happened after 4 January. This was the purchase of the second bag of sugar on 5 January. So the problem must be something to do with the accounting treatment of the second bag.*

*Question: Why did Jones have to buy a second bag of sugar for 44c? The answer is because he has sold the first bag of sugar (for 50c). He would not have bought the second bag of sugar had he not sold the first one. It seems, therefore, that the selling of the first bag of sugar and the buying of the second bag of sugar are really two parts of one complete action. If he does not sell the first bag of sugar and does not buy the second bag of sugar, he obviously ends up with the same amount of cash on 6 January as he had on 2 January, i.e. 60c. If he does sell the first bag of sugar for 50c and does buy the second bag of sugar for 44c, he will end up with 6c more cash on 6 January than he had on 2 January. So the result of selling bag 1 and buying bag 2, as compared with doing neither, is a gain of 6c.*

*We can show this as follows:*

| | |
|---|---|
| Sales | 50c |
| Costs incurred as a direct result of making sale | 44c |
| Profit | 6c |

*We are now suggesting a profit of 6c, as compared with the earlier suggestion of 10c. This will presumably reduce the maximum drawing payable by 10c − 6c = 4c. And remember, we argued earlier that the error, the difference between the original accountant's calculations and physical reality, the amount by which Jones' business had unintentionally 'got smaller', was 4c. We seem to have corrected the error exactly. We have produced an accounting calculation that agrees with actual physical events:*

$$W_1 + P - D = W_2$$
$$100 + 6 - 6 = 100$$

## THE BUSINESS ITSELF

It is essential to remember the purpose and nature of Jones' business. It is a sugar-selling business. The essence of our conclusion is a very simple one. It is that the cost of sales figure that we should relate to any particular sale should be calculated as equal to the *cost of the resulting replacement*, assuming that the replacement occurs immediately. The cost of sales figure should not be related to the cost of the item actually sold. This raises a difficulty. In order to be able to transfer this higher replacement figure out of the balance sheet and into the profit and loss calculation, the higher replacement figure must obviously first be recorded in the balance sheet. The complete picture is most easily seen by a series of balance sheets:

**1 January**

| | | | |
|---|---|---|---|
| Cash | 100 | Capital | 100 |
| | 100c | | 100c |

**2 January**

| | | | |
|---|---|---|---|
| Sugar | 40 | Capital | 100 |
| Cash | 60 | | |
| | 100c | | 100c |

**3 January**

| | | | |
|---|---|---|---|
| Sugar (1st bag) | 44 | Capital | 100 |
| Cash | 60 | Gain | 4 |
| | 104c | | 104c |

**4 January**

| | | | |
|---|---|---|---|
| Cash | 110 | Capital | 100 |
| | | Gain | 4 |
| | | Profit | 6 |
| | 110c | | 110c |

**5 January**

| | | | |
|---|---|---|---|
| Sugar (2nd bag) | 44 | Capital | 100 |
| | | Gain | 4 |
| Cash | 66 | Profit | 6 |
| | 110c | | 110c |

Now, we must choose our words carefully. It is perfectly correct to say that Jones began his business on 1 January with 100c. But that is not the point. The point is that Jones began the business on 1 January with *60c plus the capacity to buy a bag of sugar*. Jones is setting up in business for the purpose of acquiring and selling bags of sugar. Therefore, we need to evaluate his position at any time in terms of his capacity, his ability, to carry out his purpose. In other words, his capacity to acquire and sell sugar.

So on 1 January, Jones had the capacity to buy one bag of sugar (for 40c) plus also 60c. On 4 January, Jones had 110c. More usefully, we can say that on 4 January, Jones had the capacity to buy one bag of sugar (for 44c), plus also 66c. Comparing the 4 January position with the 1 January position clearly shows that Jones has:

1 maintained his capacity to buy one bag of sugar, and

2 gained six shiny bright 1c pieces.

This calculation agrees with the real physical events. Jones has:

1 six more shiny bright 1c pieces, and

2 a statement from his accountant giving a figure for profit of 6c.

## ACTIVITY 5.3

Open individual accounts to reflect Jones' balance sheet on 2 January (as before). Record in these and any other necessary accounts the increase in inventory figure leading to the 3 January balance sheet, then the full effect of the sales transaction on 4 January.

### Activity feedback

We have on 2 January, the inventory T account shows a debit of 40c and on 3 January, a total debit of 44c.

*In full we have on 2 January:*

| Inventory | Cash | Capital |
|---|---|---|
| 40 | 60 | 100 |

*On 3 January, we increase the inventory so as to bring the recorded figure up to the current level of replacement cost (RC). Thus there is a debit of 4c to inventory and a credit of 4c somewhere else. This credit cannot be to cash, neither can it be to capital, so it must be to a new*

*(Continued)*

## ACTIVITY 5.3    *(Continued)*

*T account. Now this 4c represents a gain that has arisen as a result of holding our inventory over a period of time. We did not sell it, but we held it over a period during which the replacement cost rose. We shall more formally refer to this gain as a holding gain. So on 3 January:*

| Inventory | | | Cash | |
|---|---|---|---|---|
| Bal b/f | 40 | | Bal b/f 60 | |
| Holding gain | 4 | 44 Bal c/d | | |
| | 44 | 44 | | |
| Bal b/f | 44 | | | |

| Capital | Holding gain |
|---|---|
| 100 Bal b/f | 4 Inventory |

*This enables us to show on 4 January:*

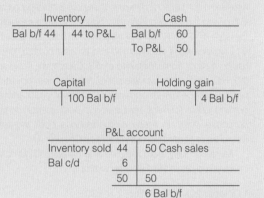

| Inventory | | Cash | |
|---|---|---|---|
| Bal b/f 44 | 44 to P&L | Bal b/f | 60 |
| | | To P&L | 50 |

| Capital | Holding gain |
|---|---|
| 100 Bal b/f | 4 Bal b/f |

| P&L account | | |
|---|---|---|
| Inventory sold | 44 | 50 Cash sales |
| Bal c/d | 6 | |
| | 50 | 50 |
| | | 6 Bal b/f |

On the assumptions that Jones wishes to carry on selling and buying bags of sugar, this is obviously the correct answer.

We have solved a major problem. We have shown the accountant how to produce a profit figure that actually makes physical sense and that Jones can actually believe. But we have created another difficulty. The statement from the accountant showed not only a *profit* of 6c, but also a separate, different *gain* of 4c. This gain of 4c occurred earlier than the profit. The gain was included in the balance sheet of 3 January and the profit did not appear until 4 January. We know that this 'gain' is not the same as profit – the whole point of all this is that the 'total' profit, i.e. the total increase in the capacity of the business to do things, is only 6c. So if the 'gain' is not profit, what on earth is it?

In the most simple of terms it is the double-entry for an increase in the recorded figure for an item of inventory.

## CAPITAL MAINTENANCE

Given that we are considering a different profit concept from the traditional historical profit, we are necessarily implying also a different capital maintenance concept from that discussed in Activity 4.7.

## ACTIVITY 5.4

Define clearly the capital maintenance concept implied by the T account calculations just examined.

### Activity feedback

*Profit could here be defined as the amount generated by the business over and above that necessary to replace the assets. The capital maintenance concept*

*could therefore be said to be the maintenance of the capacity to replace the resources of the business.*

### A more rigorous analysis

*If an item of inventory is bought for €10, held until its buying price increases to €12, and then sold for €15, then the HC profit is €15 − €10 = €5. But we know from the previous discussion that this can be split into two parts as follows.*

*(Continued)*

## ACTIVITY 5.4 (Continued)

During the time the inventory is held, the cost price rises from €10 to €12. There is therefore a holding gain of €2, giving a recorded inventory figure immediately before the sale of €12. When the inventory is sold, an asset of €12 (inventory) is transformed into an asset (cash) giving rise to a profit from operating of €3. Clearly we have split the HC profit into two elements, namely the operating profit (revenue minus current replacement cost) and the holding gain (current replacement cost minus original purchase cost). In these circumstances both elements would be regarded as 'realized' (see Chapter 1).

More normally, both realized and unrealized gains will be involved, as in the following example:

| 1 October 20X1 | Buy 2 at €30 |
| 1 November 20X1 | Sell 1 at €50, when RC is €35 |
| 31 December 20X1 | RC is €38 |
| 31 January 20X2 | Sell 1 at €60, when RC is €40 |

The HC profits are:

| Year 1 | 50 − 30 = €20 |
| Year 2 | 60 − 30 = €30 |

A fuller analysis gives the following:

**1** Between 1 October and 1 November there has been a holding gain of:

$$2 \times (35 - 30) = €10.$$

**2** On 1 November one of the items is sold; therefore on 1 November:

(a) half of the holding gain becomes realized (i.e. $1 \times [35 - 30]$), as the item to which it relates has been sold

(b) there is a (realized) operating profit of $50 - 35 = €15$.

**3** On 31 December there is an additional holding gain of $38 - 35 = €3$. This will be unrealized as the item is still unsold. Between 31 December 20X1 and 31 January 20X2 there has been a holding gain of $40 - 38 = €2$.

**4** On 31 January the second item is sold and therefore:

(a) there is a (realized) operating gain of $60 - 40 = €20$

(b) all the unrealized holding gain related to the second item becomes realized.

To summarize, for year 1 we have:

| Operating profit | €15 |
| Realized holding gain | €5 |
| Unrealized holding gain | €8 (5 + 3 or 38 − 30) |

For year 2 we have:

| Operating profit | €20 |
| Realized holding gain | €10 |
| Unrealized holding gain | € 0 |

Note carefully that the €10 holding gain realized in the year 2 includes the €8 holding gain that was recognized and recorded in year 1, but which had not become realized in year 1, as well as the €2 of holding gain recognized in year 2.

These figures demonstrate that the HC profit consists of two of the three elements involved:

HC profit = Operating profit + Realized holding gains

| In year 1 | €20 = 15 + 5 |
| In year 2 | €30 = 20 + 10 |

Notice that we include all the holding gains realized in the year, whether or not they have been recognized and recorded (as unrealized) in earlier years. Edwards and Bell (1961) referred to the reported results under an RC system as business income, which they defined as follows:

$$\text{Business income} = \begin{cases} \text{Operating profit} + \text{Realized holding} \\ \text{recognized in the period} + \\ \text{Unrealized holding gains} \\ \text{recognized in the period} \end{cases}$$

Thus business income in year 1 is:

$$15 + 15 + 8 = €28$$

And in year 2 is:

$$20 + 2 = €22$$

Observe that the proportion of the realized holding gain in year 2 which had already been included in business income of year 1 (as an unrealized holding gain) is not included in year 2. To do so would, of course, involve double counting.

Examination will show that the differences between accounting (HC) income and business income are caused by different elements of the holding gains being included.

## ACTIVITY 5.5

Derive the formal relationship between accounting income and business income and apply it to the preceding situation.

### Activity feedback
Accounting income includes:

1 Realized holding gains of the period recognized in the period; plus

2 Realized holding gains of the period recognized in previous periods.

Business income includes:

3 Realized holding gains of the period recognized in the period; plus

4 Unrealized holding gains recognized in the period.

Since 1 and 3 are the same, it follows that:

Accounting income – 2 = Business income – 4

or:

Accounting income = Business income – 4 + 2
(as defined earlier)

For the year 1            €20 = 28 – 8 + 0
For the year 2            €30 = 22 – 0 + 8

The important thing about all this analysis is that it enables us to discuss and decide which elements we wish to include in our own preferred definition of income. Edwards and Bell, arguing in favour of a current entry (RC) approach, include all the holding gains recognized in the period as being included in income. This has been criticized on two grounds. First, it is suggested that no unrealized gains should be included, as this would lack prudence. Second, and more importantly, it is suggested that all the holding gains, whether realized or unrealized, need to be retained in the business in order to enable it to replace resources as they are used. Using the terminology we developed earlier, the operating profit is the gain after having retained sufficient resources to enable us to do those things that we originally had the capacity to do. If we ask the question: 'How much profit can I remove without impairing the substance, the operating capability of the business?' then the answer is the operating profit. Only the operating profit should be regarded and reported as income. Holding gains, whether realized or not, should be excluded. This objection to the Edwards and Bell conclusion is generally regarded as a valid one, and most authors argue that the central profit figure under a current entry value system should consist of the operating profit alone.

Remember the capital maintenance concept as we defined it in Activity 5.4, i.e. the maintenance of the capacity to replace the resources of the business. The holding gains represent reserves – i.e. ownership claims on resources – corresponding to the resources which will have to be used in addition to replace existing assets if they are replaced at current prices. Income, within this capital maintenance requirement, therefore excludes all such holding gains.

In practice, the changes in cost levels are likely to be approximated to by the use of appropriate price indices. Activity 5.6 provides an example of the application of this mechanism to the principles already discussed. Study the activity carefully and try to at least rough out a solution before you work through the feedback which follows.

## ACTIVITY 5.6

Chaplin Ltd's balance sheet on 31 December year 1, after one year's trading was as follows:

| | € | | € | € |
|---|---|---|---|---|
| Capital – €1 | | Land and buildings at cost | | 110 000 |
| Ordinary shares | 200 000 | Plant and equipment at cost | 40 000 | |
| Profit | 26 000 | less Depreciation | 4 000 | 36 000 |
| | 226 000 | | | 146 000 |
| Creditors | 50 000 | Inventory | 90 000 | |
| Loan | 50 000 | Debtors | 90 000 | |
| | | | | 180 000 |
| | 326 000 | | | 326 000 |

(Continued)

## ACTIVITY 5.6 *(Continued)*

**1** The capital and loan had been contributed in cash and the land and buildings, plant and equipment and opening inventory of €60 000 had been purchased on 1 January.

**2** Transactions took place evenly during the year. The situation may therefore be treated as if all opening balances were held from 1 January until 30 June, as if all transactions took place on 30 June and as if all closing balances were held from 30 June until 31 December.

**3** Price indices were as follows:

|  | General inflation | Plant | Inventory |
|---|---|---|---|
| 1 January | 100 | 100 | 100 |
| 30 June | 110 | 105 | 115 |
| 31 December | 120 | 110 | 130 |

**4** The land and buildings were professionally valued at 31 December at €135 000.

Prepare a closing balance sheet on RC lines.

### Activity feedback

*Chaplin Ltd RC solution HC profit less Adjustments:*

| | | | |
|---|---|---|---|
| Depreciation | $4\,000 \times \dfrac{(110 - 100)}{100}$ | 400 | 26 000 |
| Inventory | $60\,000 \times \dfrac{(115 - 100)}{100}$ | 9 000 | 9 400 |
| Current operating profit add holding gains: | | | 16 600 |
| Inventory: realized as previously | | 9 000 | |
| unrealized | $90\,000 \times \dfrac{(130 - 115)}{115}$ | 11 740 | |
| Plant and equipment: realized as previously | | 400 | |
| unrealized | $40\,000 \times \dfrac{(110 - 100)}{100} - 400$ | 3·600 | |
| Land and buildings: Unrealized | $135\,000 - 110\,000$ | 25 000 | 49 740 |
| | | | €66 300 |

### Business income

The general view today is that the holding gains should be shown separately as holding gains, rather than combining all gains of every sort as 'business income'. This leads to the following balance sheet:

| | | € | € |
|---|---|---|---|
| Land and building | | | 135 000 |
| Plant and equipment | $40\,000 \times \dfrac{110}{100}$ | 44 000 | |
| less Depreciation | $4\,000 \times \dfrac{110}{100}$ | 4 400 | 39 600 |
| | | | 174 600 |
| Current assets | | € | € |
| Inventory | $90\,000 \times \dfrac{130}{110}$ | 101 740 | |
| Debtors | | 90 000 | 191 740 |
| | | | €366 340 |

| | € | € |
|---|---|---|
| Share capital | | 200 000 |
| Holding gain reserve | | 49 740 |
| P&L account | | 16 600 |
| | | 266 340 |
| Loan | | 50 000 |
| Creditors | | 50 000 |
| | | €366 340 |

In checking through Activity 5.6, note the treatment of the inventory gains; it is assumed that the opening inventory was all sold on 30 June, so the relevant holding gain is realized, the €90 000 closing inventory is treated as being purchased on 30 June and held ever since. Check that you understand the usage of all the index adjustments (and note the irrelevance of the general inflation index here). As regards the distinction between realized and unrealized holding gains, note that only the current operating profit can be distributed without impairing the ability to replace physical assets.

# REPLACEMENT COST ACCOUNTING AND DEPRECIATION

## ACTIVITY 5.7

There is one particular problem with replacement cost (RC) accounting and depreciation that is not revealed by the Chaplin illustration. Consider the following:

A fixed asset costs €100, has an expected useful life of four years, with zero scrap value and the RC of a new asset rises by €20 each year. Calculate the profit and loss (P&L) account charge and show the balance sheet position, for each of the first two years, under RC.

### Activity feedback

*The year 1 position is simple enough. We have:*

| | |
|---|---|
| Cost (RC) | € 120 |
| Depreciation (25%) (in P&L a/c) | 30 |
| Balance sheet | € 90 |

*But year 2 is problematic. From a P&L account viewpoint we have an RC figure of €140 and we have had 25 per cent of the benefit, therefore we should have an expense to match of 25 per cent of 140 = €35. This leaves total accumulated depreciation of €65 and a balance sheet figure of €75 (140 − 65). But taking a balance sheet view, we have an asset with an RC of €140 that is exactly half used up. Therefore, again following the matching convention, we should have accumulated depreciation of exactly half of €140, leaving a balance sheet figure also of exactly half of €140 to carry forward for future matching. This implies an expense figure in year 2 of €40 (closing depreciation balance €70, opening balance €30, therefore necessary charge for this year €40).*

*We are obviously in trouble. In year 2 we need a €35 charge in the P&L account (25% of 140) and at the same time a deduction of €40 (70 − 30) in the balance sheet. From a double-entry viewpoint this is somewhat disturbing. This problem is usually solved by the idea of backlog*

*depreciation. The year 2 balance sheet deduction is regarded as consisting of two elements:*

1 *The proper annual charge (€35).*
2 *The extra figure necessary to bring the accumulated depreciation at the beginning of year 2 up to what it would have been if the current (end of year 2) RC had been prevailing earlier (€5).*

*Thus we have a credit of €40 to depreciation provision, a debit of €35 to P&L account and a debit of €5 to – well, where?*

*Since the €5 relates in effect to the correction of what we now know with hindsight to have been under-depreciation in earlier years, one possibility would seem to be to reduce the accumulated revenue reserves figure brought forward – like a prior year adjustment. By the same token, the earlier years' accounts were certainly correct at that time with the matching convention properly applied in the then current circumstances. It could be argued that the problem of this backlog adjustment is covered by the existence and recording of holdings gains. Therefore, the €5 could be 'charged to' holding gain account. This last argument is usually followed. This would give year 2 balance sheet entries as follows in our example:*

| | | | |
|---|---|---|---|
| Fixed asset | RC | | 140 |
| | Depreciation | | 70 |
| | (Net book value) NBV | | 70 |
| Holding gain reserve | b/f | 20 | |
| | Add | 20 | |
| | Less | 5 | 35 |

# CURRENT ENTRY VALUES: PRELIMINARY APPRAISAL

## ACTIVITY 5.8

Prepare a list, in point form, of advantages and disadvantages which you think could reasonably be said to apply to current entry value accounting.

### Activity feedback

*Possible, but not necessarily exhaustive, suggestions are as follows:*

*(Continued)*

## ACTIVITY 5.8    (*Continued*)

### Advantages

1  It provides more information in that it splits the total profit into holding gains and operating profit. This permits better appraisal of earlier actions and provides more useful data for decision-making purposes.

2  By permitting holding gains to be excluded from reported profit, it allows for a proper maintenance of operating capacity – the 'business substance'.

3  It provides a balance sheet based on current value, on figures relevant to the date of the balance sheet.

4  It is consistent with accounting concepts – if holding gains are excluded from reported profit it is more prudent than HC.

5  Holding gains are recognized and reported when they occur.

6  Comparisons over time, and performance analysis, are more valid and meaningful.

7  It is practicable, it has been shown to be feasible in practical application.

### Disadvantages

1  It requires more subjectivity (or arbitrary choice between different available indices). It is therefore less 'auditable'.

2  It requires the use of replacement cost figures for assets that the firm does not intend, or perhaps could not possibly, replace.

3  It still fails to give an indication either of the current market value of most assets in their present state or of the business as a whole.

4  It fails to take account of general inflation, of changes in the purchasing power of money.

You may recall from the array of value concepts analyzed by Edwards and Bell that they suggested that two different concepts of current entry value were worthy of more detailed consideration. They named and defined these as:

1  *Present cost* – the cost currently of acquiring the asset being valued.

2  *Current cost* – the cost currently of acquiring the inputs which the firm used to produce the asset being valued.

So far in this chapter we have ignored this distinction. We would suggest, broadly following the thinking of Edwards and Bell themselves, that the route to making a rational choice between them lies in remembering the underlying arguments for using current entry values in the first place. As we saw in Activity 5.4, we are seeking the maintenance of the capacity to replace the resources of the business. We are therefore seeking to ensure the continued long-run operation of the business. The approach we need to adopt, therefore, is that which accords with the expected operations of the firm in the ordinary course of its business. Given that the going concern convention applies, and given that the firm is going to continue operations in the long run, it is clear that current cost rather than present cost (both as defined earlier) will better reflect the reality of transactions and economic events in most cases. To a firm in business to manufacture motor cars and aiming for long-run operations as a manufacturer of motor cars, it is the cost of the replacement inputs which it needs to manufacture motor cars which is the relevant datum to ensure the maintenance of operating capacity. The cost to a manufacturer of motor cars of buying in complete motor cars (at present cost) is not normally an operationally relevant figure.

So it is argued that current cost is normally the appropriate current entry value to use, on the grounds of its relevance to normal ongoing business operations. It follows, however, that where this justification ceases to be true, because, for example, the inputs are no longer available, then the conclusion may well no longer be correct. If the firm *would* as a matter of expected action (not merely *should* as a matter of efficient management) replace an asset in a more complete state than with the previous raw components, then the appropriate present cost should be used instead.

It could be suggested that in arguing for the relevance of current cost as a useful entry value measure leading to the practical maintenance of operational capability, we are failing to follow properly the logic of the arguments put forward. The essence of the whole thinking is that a firm should charge as an expense the costs of replacing the resources used or consumed. Past (historical) costs are useless for this purpose. But what is theoretically needed is obviously the amount that *will* have to be paid for the replacement items at the time when they are replaced. The *current* cost may or may not be identical to the actual cost when replacement eventually occurs. In many cases current cost will be the same as expected actual cost. But if it is not, should we make some adjustment?

Theoretically, at least from the viewpoint of the income statement and capital main-tenance in the operating sense, the answer seems to be yes. But there are at least two arguments against this. The first is the essentially practical one that a considerably greater degree of subjectivity is introduced which may more than outweigh the theo-retical advantages. The second argument is that there are perhaps implications for the matching principle and the balance sheet. A current entry value balance sheet can be argued as being consistent within itself, giving proper additivity in the mathematical sense. But a future entry value balance sheet, with the timing implications of the word future being different for different items, is of more suspect validity. And since today's asset figure affects next period's results there are possible implications for future peri-ods too.

## SUMMARY

In this chapter we have explored the logic of using current entry values for the preparation of accounting results, analyzed the effects and usefulness of the additional information derived, related the approach to capital mainte-nance and prepared and interpreted current entry value information.

The main advantages of current entry value accounting lie in its effects on the profit and loss account information given. It can be argued as giving more effective application of the matching and accruals conventions (*rent* costs against current revenues) and, through its long-run economically rational capital maintenance concept, of the going concern convention. It provides important information, at minimum, about those elements of histori-cal cost profit which do not represent increases in economic wealth (given continuing operation). As regards the balance sheet it gives figures based on up-to-date market numbers. However, the approach is still clearly to determine profit and loss figures and then to 'stick what is left' in the balance sheet. The balance sheet is still essentially a statement of unexpired expenses, not a list of marketable assets at valuation.

## EXERCISES

*Suggested answers to exercises marked ✓ are to be found on our dedicated CourseMate platform for students.*

*Suggested answers to the remaining exercises are to be found on the Instructor online support resources.*

1   Explain and demonstrate how replacement cost accounting affects reported profit as compared with historical cost accounting.

✓2   Is replacement cost accounting more or less prudent than historical cost accounting?

3   Under a replacement cost accounting system, which holding gains should be reported as:
   (a) realized
   (b) part of profit
   (c) distributable? Why?

4   In general, replacement cost accounting produces reported profit figures which are a better indication of long-run future performance than historical cost accounting does. Discuss.

5   A replacement cost balance sheet is just as useless as a historical cost balance sheet. Discuss.

✓6   I.M. Confused, computer dealer.
   From the following information compute
   (a) Profit and loss accounts and closing balance sheets for each of the years 20X1 and 20X2 under historical cost principles.
   (b) Profit and loss accounts and closing balance sheets for each of the years 20X1 and 20X2 under current replacement cost principles.
   Comment briefly on the significance of the results.

| Date | Event relating to trading in computers | 'Wealth' Computers | € cash |
|---|---|---|---|
| 01/01/X1 | Set up business with €10 000 in the bank | | 10 000 |
| 02/01/X1 | Buy six computers for €1 000 each | 6 | 4 000 |
| 01/05/X1 | Sell two for €1 500 each (RC = €1 100) | 4 | 7 000 |
| 01/09/X1 | Buy two computers for €1 200 each | 6 | 4 600 |
| 01/10/X1 | Pay annual rent of €600 | 6 | 4 000 |
| 31/12/X1 | Financial year-end. Pay tax of €200 | 6 | 3 800 |
| 03/03/X2 | Sell two computers for €1 800 each (RC = €1 300) | 4 | 7 400 |
| 01/10/X2 | Pay annual rent €700 | 4 | 6 700 |
| 01/11/X2 | Buy two computers for €1 400 each | 6 | 3 900 |
| 31/12/X2 | Financial year-end. Pay tax €450 | 6 | 3 450 |

7   Mallard Co. was formed on 1 January 20X1 with 10 000 issued €1 ordinary shares. The same day they obtained a 12 per cent loan of €8 000 and bought fixed assets for €9 000. During 20X1 their purchases and sales of widgets were as follows:

|  | Purchases | |  | Sales | |
|---|---|---|---|---|---|
| 3 January | 100 at €80 | 8 000 |  |  |  |
| 1 February |  |  |  | 60 at €120 | 7 200 |
| 1 April | 110 at €75 | 8 250 |  |  |  |
| 1 May |  |  |  | 90 at €120 | 10 800 |
| 1 July | 100 at €85 | 8 500 |  |  |  |
| 1 August |  |  |  | 130 at €120 | 15 600 |
| 1 October | 120 at €90 | 10 800 |  |  |  |
| 1 November |  |  |  | 110 at €130 | 14 300 |

(a)  Purchases and sales were all paid for in cash.

(b)  The loan interest was paid early in the following year (20X2).

(c)  The buying price of widgets changed on 1 March, 1 June, 1 September and on 1 December (when it was €100).

(d)  The fixed assets are to be depreciated at 10 per cent p.a. At 31 December 20X1 their buying price was €12 600.

(e)  General expenses during the year were €13 200.

    (i)   Prepare a balance sheet as at 31 December, 20X1 together with a trading profit and loss account for the year to 31 December 20X1, on replacement cost lines.

    (ii)  What are holding gains? In what circumstances are they distributable?

**8    L and H**

On 1 January, L and H each started a business by investing €100 in cash, and then immediately purchasing one widget.

    L sold her widget on 3 March for €110, but on 1 April discovered that she needed to pay this to buy another, which she did.

    On 30 June this was sold for €120, and a new one bought in July for €120.

    On 29 September this was sold for €130, and a replacement purchased on 30 September for €130.

    H had been less active and had merely kept his first widget and read the newspaper. Both have decided to adopt 30 September as their accounting date, and come to you for accounting services.

(a)  How would the above appear under:

    (i)    historical cost

    (ii)   replacement cost.

(b)  Which results make more sense, and why?

# CURRENT EXIT VALUE AND MIXED VALUES

# 6

OBJECTIVES  After studying this chapter you should be able to:

- explain the effects and implications of using current exit values to record the possession and usage of economic resources

- outline the implications of using an ad hoc mixture of valuation methods

- define and explain the effects and implications of deprival values as the basis of recording the possession and usage of economic resources

- discuss the overall relevance of current values.

## INTRODUCTION

In this chapter we look first of all at remaining current values worthy of consideration, current output or exit values. We then explore the possibility of using a combination of different valuation methods in preparing financial reports and, in particular, the concept of deprival value. In each case, as in earlier chapters, we seek to investigate both the techniques and logic of calculation and the meaning and usefulness of the resulting information.

## CURRENT EXIT VALUE ACCOUNTING

Edwards and Bell (1961) suggested two current exit value concepts as worthy of consideration (see p. 66). These were current values and opportunity costs.

Current values they defined as 'values actually realized during the current period for goods or services sold'. On reflection, however, it quickly becomes apparent that the idea of substituting current values so defined into our basic equation of $W_1 + P - D = W_2$ does not make a great deal of sense. Values actually realized for goods and services already sold cannot obviously be argued as relevant to resources still possessed at the date or dates under consideration. Rather, of course, these realized values are the basis of revenue flows.

It is the second concept, that of opportunity costs, which we need to develop. Edwards and Bell defined this as 'values that could currently be realized if assets were sold ... (without further processing) outside the firm at the best prices immediately obtainable'. This is certainly a concept relevant to the resources possessed at the date under consideration. It shows the amount of money we could derive immediately (currently) from the resources held, or to take the alternative viewpoint, it shows the amount of money we choose not to derive immediately if we retain the resources for any reason. We can adapt the application of the definition slightly to allow for further unavoidable processing or expenses of disposal and consider the concept of net realizable value (NRV), i.e. the proceeds after deducting these additional unavoidable expenses of disposal. These ideas are explored further in this chapter.

We intend to base our valuation figure on the current market selling price, more precisely, on NRV. So if an asset could be sold for €250, but the sale would involve €10 of selling expenses, the NRV is €240. The income under this method is based on the difference between the NRV of all resources at the two chosen dates. Following Edwards and Bell, it is often referred to as realizable income. It can be defined as follows:

$$Y_r = D + (R_e - R_s)$$

where $Y_r$ is the exit value income, $D$ is the distributions (less new capital inputs), $R_e$ is the NRV of the assets at the end of the period and $R_s$ is the NRV of the assets at the start of the period.

In practice, several possibilities exist as to exactly what we mean by NRV.

## ACTIVITY 6.1

Consider an item of work in progress that has an NRV today of €10 in its existing state. The finished product (which would require a further €4 of expenses) has an NRV today of €20, but by the time the actual item of current work in progress is finished and sold, it is expected to have an NRV of €22. On a forced sale (e.g. if all the assets have to be sold off at once by a liquidator), the item in its existing state would realize €6.

Suggest possible figures for the exit value and which one of these you would normally find most useful.

### Activity feedback

*Possible figures for the exit value would seem to include €6, €10, €(20 – 4) and €(22 – 4). It is generally agreed that exit values should refer to assets in their existing state, on the assumption that they are sold in an orderly manner, i.e. in the normal course of business. Thus, in our example, the exit value for the work in progress would be €10.*

*It is clear that the exit value capital (R) at any particular date shows the amount of money that the business*

*(Continued)*

## ACTIVITY 6.1    (*Continued*)

*could obtain from its assets as on that date. Turning this around, exit value is seen as an opportunity cost concept – it shows the amount of cash that the business could obtain if it did not keep the asset. The opportunity cost of having an asset is the amount of cash the business sacrifices by retaining the asset instead. Advocates of exit value accounting argue that it is necessary to know the cash resources tied up in a business in order to measure efficiency. The amount of cash potentially available – the 'current cash equivalent' of the resources of a business – also provides a genuinely common measuring unit when comparing different businesses.*

*It is often argued – indeed often merely stated – that exit value accounting does not conform to the going concern convention. Its advocates argue that it is not intended to show what will happen, rather it is intended to show the results of what could happen, in order to assist decision making and internal appraisal.*

*We can usefully divide the exit value income (Y$_r$) into four elements:*

$$Y_r = \text{realized operating gains} \left. \begin{array}{l} \\ + \text{ unrealized operating} \\ \text{gains} \end{array} \right\} \begin{array}{l} \text{i.e. on assets held for} \\ \text{resale} \end{array}$$

$$\left. \begin{array}{l} + \text{ realized non-operating} \\ \text{gains} \\ + \text{ unrealized non-operating} \\ \text{gains} \end{array} \right\} \begin{array}{l} \text{i.e. on assets held for} \\ \text{use} \end{array}$$

*Before looking at an example, it is important to understand the effect of exit value accounting on the P&L account. Since the opening and closing balance sheets are now value based and not cost based, it necessarily follows that the P&L account is also value based and not cost based. For example, 'depreciation' is no longer a process of cost allocation under the matching convention. It simply becomes the loss in value of the asset in the period.*

*Now work through the following example. Remember particularly that an unrealized gain in year 1, reported as such, will become a realized gain in a later year and will need to be reported as a realized gain. Care is needed to ensure that gains are not reported twice: as both unrealized and realized. This of course would be double counting.*

## Example

A company commences business with capital in cash of €15 000. It buys a fixed asset for €10 000. The following information is available:

|  | Year 1 | | Year 2 | |
|---|---|---|---|---|
|  | € | | € | |
| NRV of fixed asset | 6 000 | | 4 000 | |
| Sales | 20 000 | | 25 000 | |
| Cost of sales | 11 000 | | 12 000 | |
| Closing inventory: cost | 2 000 | | 3 000 | |
| NRV | 2 500 | | 3 800 | |
| *Exit value revenue statements* | | | | |
| Sales | 20 000 | | 25 000 | |
| Cost of sales | 11 000 | | 12 000 | |
|  | 9 000 | | 13 000 | |
| 'Depreciation' | 4 000 | (1) | 2 000 | (2) |
|  | 5 000 | | 11 000 | |
| *less* Operating gain included in previous year | – | | 500 | (3) |
|  | 5 000 | | 10 500 | |
| *add* Unrealized operating gain | 500 | (4) | 800 | (5) |
| Realizable income | 5 500 | | 11 300 | |

|  | Year 1 € | Year 2 € |
|---|---|---|
| *Exit value balance sheets* | | |
| Fixed assets | 6 000 | 4 000 |
| Inventory | 2 500 | 3 800 |
| Cash | 12 000   (6) | 24 000   (7) |
|  | 20 500 | 31 800 |
| Capital | 15 000 | 15 000 |
| Realizable income | 5 500 | 16 800 |
|  | 20 500 | 31 800 |

Notes:
1   10 000 – 6000
2   6000 – 4000
3   Included as realized in the 11 000, but already included, as unrealized, in the 5500 for year 1.
4   2500 – 2000
5   3800 – 3000
6   15 000 – 10 000 + 20 000 – (11 000 + 2000)
7   12 000 + 25 000 – (12 000 + 1000)

The unrealized gain on inventory is here calculated on an annual basis, inventory during the year being left at cost. It would be possible, although more complicated, to record such unrealized gains more frequently – even daily if desired. Care must be taken, however, to ensure that a previously recorded unrealized gain is not again added into 'realizable income' when it is realized.

Now try the following activity, making a proper attempt before looking at the feedback which follows.

## ACTIVITY 6.2

Bonds plc commenced business on 1 January year 7. Let us assume all transactions are by cheque and no credit is given or taken and that Bonds plc deals only in one type of item of inventory.

**1 January Year 7**

Introduced capital of €25 000 and purchased a machine for €9 000

Purchased 500 items of inventory for €15 each.

**31 December Year 7**

Sold 300 items of inventory for €30 each

Paid rent for the year of €1 000

Paid other expenses for the year of €1 000.

**1 January Year 8**

Purchased 400 items of inventory for €17 each.

**31 December Year 8**

Sold 500 items of inventory for €33 each

Paid rent for the year of €1 100

Paid expenses for the year of €1 200.

The following information relates to the machine:

|  | 31.12.7 € | 31.12.8 € |
|---|---|---|
| Replacement cost | 10 000 | 12 000 |
| Realizable value | 8 000 | 6 000 |
| Cost of realization | 1 000 | 1 000 |

*Required:*
Produce a set of realizable value accounts for years 7 and 8.

*Activity feedback*
*Bonds plc Trading and P&L account for the year ended 31 December.*

|  | 31.12.7 € | | 31.12.8 € | |
|---|---|---|---|---|
| Sales | | 9 000 | | 16 500 |
| Less cost of sales | | (4 500) | | (8 100) |
| Gross profit | | 4 500 | | 8 400 |
| Rent | 1 000 | | 1 100 | |
| Expenses | 1 000 | | 1 200 | |

*(Continued)*

## ACTIVITY 6.2    (Continued)

|  | 31.12.7 € |  | 31.12.8 € |
|---|---|---|---|
| Depreciation |  |  |  |
| (note 2) | 2 000 |  | 2 000 |
|  | (4 000) |  | (4 300) |
| Gross profit | 500 |  | 4 100 |
| Holding gain |  |  |  |
| (note 3) | 3 000 |  | (1 400) |
|  | 3 500 |  | 2 700 |

*Balance sheet as at 31 December*

|  | 31.12.7 € |  | 31.12.8 € |
|---|---|---|---|
| Fixed assets |  |  |  |
| Machine at NRV | 7 000 |  | 5 000 |
| Current assets |  |  |  |
| Inventory at |  |  |  |
| NRV (note 1) 6 000 |  | 3 300 |  |
| Bank 15 500 |  | 22 900 |  |
|  | 21 500 |  | 26 200 |
|  | 28 500 |  | 31 200 |
| Share capital | 25 000 |  | 25 000 |
| Profit | 3 500 |  | 6 200 |
|  | 28 500 |  | 31 200 |

*Notes:*

**1** *The inventory is also brought into the balance sheet at the end of each year at its net realizable value.*

    31.12.8    200 units × €30 = €6 000
    31.12.7    100 units × €33 = €3 300

**2** Depreciation. *The depreciation is the difference between the NRV of the asset at the end of each year less the NRV of the asset at the beginning of the year. Note that the NRV is after deducting the costs of realizing the asset.*

    Year 1    €7 000 – €9 000
    Year 2    €5 000 – €7 000

**3** Holding gain. *In year 7 the holding gain is the unrealized holding gain on the closing inventory:*

    200 units × €15 (i.e. €30 – €15) = €3 000

*In year 8 the holding gain of year 7 has now been realized (and therefore included in the trading account for year 8) while there is an unrealized holding gain on the closing stock of:*

    100 units × €16 (i.e. €33 – €17) = €1 600

*Therefore, in year 8 the holding gain (loss) is:*

|  | € |
|---|---|
| Unrealized holding gain in year 8 | 1 600 |
| *less* Unrealized holding gain from |  |
| year 7 now realized in year 8 | 3 000 |
|  | (1 400) |

*In effect we have a holding loss.*

# CURRENT EXIT VALUES: PRELIMINARY APPRAISAL

## ACTIVITY 6.3

Prepare a list, in point form, of advantages and disadvantages which you think could reasonably be said to apply to current exit value accounting.

### Activity feedback

#### Advantages

**1** *It follows the economic 'opportunity cost' principle. It reveals the money sacrifice being made by keeping an asset. This permits rational decision making on the alternative uses of resources.*

**2** *Exit values facilitate comparisons. They provide a genuinely common measure for the value of assets – cash or current cash equivalent.*

**3** *The concept of realizable value is easy for the non-accountant to understand.*

**4** *Useful information about assets is provided to outsiders, e.g. creditors.*

**5** *It is already widely used, e.g. debtors, inventory at lower of HC and NRV, revaluation of land and buildings.*

#### Disadvantages

**1** *It is highly subjective. Arguably more so than replacement cost (RC) accounting.*

**2** *It fails to follow the going concern assumption, fails to recognize that firms do not usually sell all*
(Continued)

## ACTIVITY 6.3    *(Continued)*

their assets (the proponents of exit value accounting explicitly deny this charge, arguing that it makes no assumptions either way, it merely provides useful information).

3  It fails to concentrate attention on long-run operational effectiveness.

4  It fails to give realistic information about the internal usefulness of assets – particularly of highly specialized assets that could have a very low NRV on the general market.

You may, of course, have some slightly different views. One point we should certainly consider is the possible relevance of expected values, which Edwards and Bell (1961) suggested to be a concept worth further exploration. They defined expected values (see Table 4.2) as 'values expected to be received in the future for output sold according to the firm's planned course of action'. Expected values are therefore a future exit rather than a current exit way of thinking. Expected values defined in this way certainly give useful information. In fact they form the raw material for the preparation of both cash and revenue budget statements. However, our essential purpose here is to prepare statements of current position and similar arguments apply to those already considered in relation to future entry values. To use future exit values would introduce greater subjectivity, greater possible inconsistency of evaluation and could be argued as failing to reflect current reality. Current exit values are suggested as a more useful concept.

It is essential to remember that exit value NRV accounting tends to focus on the balance sheet to a considerably greater extent than current entry value RC accounting. Profit or gain is very much determined by a consideration of changes in output values of resources. The balance sheet under NRV can be regarded as a consistent statement, with all figures on the same basis and as at the same date. This balance sheet is not just a list of 'balances left over' in the sense that a current entry value balance sheet is (see Chapter 5). However, it follows from this that it is the profit and loss calculation which in a sense picks up and contains 'the figures lying around'. Current exit value is essentially a short-run concept. It provides valuable information about market values of business resources and therefore about short-term alternatives and possibilities. This is clearly seen in the capital maintenance concept associated with NRV. This could be expressed as: the maintenance of the NRV, the current cash equivalent, of the resources of the business. But exit value accounting information does not provide us with the information necessary for management to seek to ensure the long-run operational capability of the business.

## MIXED VALUES – AD HOC METHODS

As we shall see in detail later on, companies following IAS, and also some national systems, may have a great deal of flexibility in practice as regards the valuation policy they wish to adopt. There is no requirement for any consistency of approach as between one asset and another. It is in fact extremely common for businesses that broadly follow historical cost accounting principles to revalue some of their fixed assets at intervals (not necessarily annually), sometimes then depreciating on the revalued figure, sometimes not depreciating at all. This may well lead to the provision of more useful information as regards particular resources. For example, a current or recent valuation of land or factory is surely more useful than a 50-year-old cost figure. But, of course, it further increases the inconsistencies within the accounting reports as a whole, making the balance sheet as a statement of resources and the sources thereof ever more difficult to understand, usually influencing the size of expense figures charged and certainly influencing any interpretational ratios relating return with the source base being employed.

## MIXED VALUES – DEPRIVAL VALUE

A much more theoretically defensible approach to the idea of using different valuation bases for different assets – or more accurately for using different valuation bases for assets in different circumstances – is the concept of deprival value.

Assume that a business owns an asset. What is that asset 'worth' to the business? The deprival value (DV) approach says that the DV of an asset is the loss that the rational businessman or businesswoman would suffer if he or she were deprived of the asset. This loss will depend on what would rationally have been done with the asset if he or she had not lost (been deprived of) it.

## ACTIVITY 6.4

Six people, A to F, are possessors and owners of six assets, U to Z, respectively. The various monetary evaluations (in €) of each asset by its owner are shown in the following table.

| Person | Asset | HC | RC | NRV | EV |
|--------|-------|----|----|-----|----|
| A | U | 1 | 2 | 3 | 4 |
| B | V | 5 | 6 | 8 | 7 |
| C | W | 9 | 12 | 10 | 11 |
| D | X | 16 | 15 | 14 | 13 |
| E | Y | 17 | 19 | 20 | 18 |
| F | Z | 23 | 22 | 21 | 24 |

All six people signed a contract with an insurance agent, Miss Prue Dential, under which they shall be reimbursed, in the event of loss of their assets, by 'the amount of money a rationally acting person will actually have lost as a result of losing the asset'.

Put yourself in the position of the rationally acting person, decide what action you would take in each circumstance and then calculate the net effect on your monetary position.

### Activity feedback

*In each situation the first question to ask is: Would the rationally acting businessman or businesswoman replace the asset or not? He or she will replace it if the proceeds of either selling it (NRV) or using it (economic value, EV) are higher than the costs of replacing it. If it is going to be replaced, then the loss suffered is clearly the cost of replacement. Thus, in situations where the rationally acting businessman or businesswoman would replace the asset, DV is RC. If he or she would not replace it, the loss suffered is given by the value of the benefits that would have derived from the asset but*

*which he or she will now never receive. Being rational, the intention must have been to act so as to derive the highest possible return, i.e. the higher of NRV and economic value (EV). Therefore, in situations where the rationally acting businessman or businesswoman would not replace the asset if deprived of it, DV is the higher of NRV and EV. This last element – the higher of NRV and EV – is known as the 'recoverable amount'.*

*So we can formally state that DV is the lower of RC and recoverable amount, where recoverable amount is the higher of NRV and EV (see Figure 6.1). Given three different concepts (RC, NRV and EV), there are in fact only six possible different rankings:*

| EV | > | NRV | > | RC |
|----|---|-----|---|-----|
| NRV | > | EV | > | RC |
| RC | > | EV | > | NRV |
| RC | > | NRV | > | EV |
| NRV | > | RC | > | EV |
| EV | > | RC | > | NRV |

*The example contains all six of these alternatives. The DV in each situation is as follows:*

| Person | DV | Reason |
|--------|----|--------|
| A | 2 | Cost of replacement |
| B | 6 | Cost of replacement |
| C | 11 | EV not received |
| D | 14 | Realizable value not received |
| E | 19 | Cost of replacement |
| F | 22 | Cost of replacement |

*Make sure that you understand why, in the context of the logic of the DV definition (and notice the irrelevance of the HC figures).*

*(Continued)*

## ACTIVITY 6.4    (*Continued*)

### Figure 6.1    Relationship between DV, RC, NRV and EV

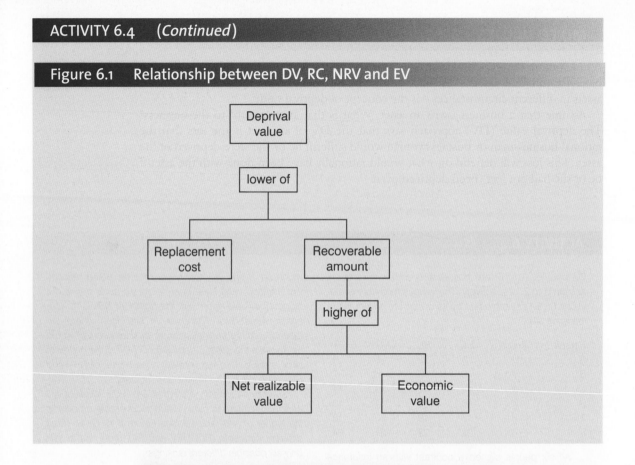

## DEPRIVAL VALUE: APPRAISAL

Deprival value (DV) has a clearly definable concept of capital maintenance. Profit is here being regarded as the excess after maintaining the 'value to the business' of its assets. The value to the business is clearly seen to be related to actual operations (what the business would do). Following from this, we can say that DV seeks to maintain the business's capacity to do things, usually expressed as the *operating capacity or operating capability*. We saw earlier that in four of the six possible rankings, DV equals RC. In the practical business situation, the chances of replacement cost being higher than both NRV and EV will generally be relatively small, so the other two rankings will in practice not occur frequently. This means that, in a practical business context, DV usually comes back to RC.

Theoretically, therefore, it can be suggested that deprival value provides an improvement and refinement on current replacement cost accounting. It reduces itself to replacement cost when the economically logical action is to replace and uses the more relevant benefit foregone figure in those situations where replacement would logically not occur. Notice, of course, that it is not strictly a completely current concept at all, as the EV possibility is a future orientation. Another way to look at the implications of the previous discussions would be to take the more practical line of arguing that deprival value shows that replacement cost is relevant most of the time. In other words, deprival value thinking positively explores the possibilities of refining replacement cost thinking and shows that in most situations the refinements introduce difficulty and subjectivity for very little benefit in terms of extra relevance of information.

As a final thought, what about additivity? Is deprival value a separate concept, leading to a balance sheet consistently valued in deprival terms? Or is deprival value merely a formula for choosing which of the three (RC, NRV, EV) valuation bases to use in any particular situation? Under the latter way of thinking, deprival value obviously leads to a variety of bases in the balance sheet and therefore to a lack of additivity.

---

## ACTIVITY 6.5

Prepare a list, in point form, of advantages and disadvantages which you think could reasonably be said to apply to deprival value accounting.

### Activity feedback

### Advantages

1 All the advantages of RC accounting can be claimed here also.

2 As a 'mixed value' system it is more realistic and relevant than either RC or NRV. It values resources at RC if it is profitable to replace them and at the expected proceeds if they would not be replaced.

### Disadvantages

1 Disadvantages 1, 3 and 4 of RC accounting can be claimed here too.

2 It is more subjective than RC.

3 If the balance sheet is expressed in 'mixed values', what do the asset and capital employed totals mean? Can mixed values be validly added at all?

4 Firms are not in practice being continually deprived of their assets.

---

The concept of fair value seems to have become popular in recent years. It is certainly a form of current value, but its precise nature and meaning has been a matter of considerable controversy, and indeed confusion. It is now important enough, with a new standard (IFRS 13) recently issued, to warrant a chapter by itself. We therefore defer consideration of fair value to Chapter 8.

## SUMMARY

In this chapter we have analyzed the logic and implications of current exit value accounting and prepared accounting statements on a current exit (NRV) basis. We then explored the possibility of ad hoc mixtures within the framework of traditional accounting reports and analyzed the logic and implications of deprival value accounting.

## EXERCISES

*Suggested answers to exercises marked ✓ are to be found on our dedicated CourseMate platform for students.*

*Suggested answers to the remaining exercises are to be found on the Instructor online support resources.*

1  Explain the principles of exit value accounting, providing a simple made-up illustration.

2  Explain the principles of deprival value accounting, providing a simple made-up illustration.

✓3  Discuss the proposition that businesses should be required to publish their P&L statement on replacement cost lines and their balance sheet on net realizable value lines.

4  Deprival value removes significant disadvantages of replacement cost, while retaining its advantages. Discuss.

5  **(a)** Provide a definition of the deprival value of an asset.

  **(b)** For a particular asset, suppose the three bases of valuation relevant to the calculation of its deprival value are (in thousands of euros): €12, €10 and €8. Construct a matrix of columns and rows showing all the possible alternative situations and, in each case, indicate the appropriate deprival value.

  **(c)** Justify the use of deprival value as a method of asset valuation, using the matrix in (b) to illustrate your answer.

✓6  Steward plc commences business on 1 January year 1. Let us assume all transactions are by cheque and no credit is given nor taken and that Steward deals only in one type of item of inventory.

  **1 January Year 1**
  Introduced capital of €30 000.
  Purchased machine for €10 000.
  Purchased 1000 items of inventory for €10 each.

  **31 December Year 1**
  Sold 800 items of inventory for €15 each.
  Paid expenses for the year of €1000.
  The NRV of the machine is €9000.

  **1 January Year 2**
  Purchased 800 items of inventory for €13 each.

  **31 December Year 2**
  Sold 500 items of inventory for €20 each.
  Paid expenses for the year of €1200.
  The NRV of the machine is €8000.
  Produce profit and loss accounts and balance sheets relating to years 1 and 2 using NRV accounting.

**7** On 1 January, Stan and Oliver each started a business by investing €100 in cash, and then immediately purchased one widget, which at that date could have been resold for €120.

Stan sold his widget on 31 March for €130, but on 1 April discovered that he needed to pay €115 to buy another, which he did. On 30 June this was sold for €140, and a new one bought on 1 July for €125.

On 29 September this was sold for €150, and a replacement purchased on 30 September for €130, on which date the new one could have been sold for €160.

Oliver had been less active and had merely kept his first widget and read the newspaper.

Both have decided to adopt 30 September as their accounting date, and come to you for accounting services.

All widgets are identical.

Replacement costs changed on 31 March, 30 June, 29 September. How would the above appear under:

**(a)** historical cost

**(b)** replacement cost

**(c)** net realizable value.

You may find it helpful to do this by using a table with each date on the left and columns for Cash, Inventory, Profit, Holding gains, etc. across the top.

# CURRENT PURCHASING POWER ACCOUNTING

# 7

## OBJECTIVES  After studying this chapter you should be able to:

- explain the concept of general inflation and its implications for accounting measurement

- explain the mechanisms for taking account of general inflation in financial reporting, especially, but not exclusively, in the context of historical cost accounting

- discuss theoretical arguments, and practical considerations, for and against current purchasing power accounting

- outline present attitudes to the whole changing prices and inflation debate.

## INTRODUCTION

In our discussion so far we have considered various methods of 'putting a monetary figure on something'. There are many ways of deriving a figure with a € sign in front that we must consider and appraise. But we have not yet stopped to consider what we mean by the € sign. What is a euro? It is a unit of money – and money is of no use by itself. Money has no intrinsic value. Its value is related to what we can get with it, what we can do with it. When most prices are rising, then we can obtain gradually less and less with any given number of euros. This means that if, under any particular valuation basis, we have maintained our capital appropriately defined in terms of numbers of euros, we have not necessarily maintained our capital in terms of the purchasing power of those euros. *Current purchasing power* (CPP) accounting attempts to take account of this.

## THE MEASURING UNIT PROBLEM

There are many examples of difficulties with measuring units. Litres and gallons or inches and centimetres are classic examples. In these cases the use of different measuring units may be a nuisance, but the problems are capable of rapid and objective solutions. An inch has a precise or standard specification. A centimetre has a precise or standard specification. It follows, of course, that the relationship between the two also has a precise or standard specification. We can very exactly convert one to the other and, even more significantly, the conversion factor is fixed and constant between different people, between different places and between different times.

None of this is true of money as a measuring unit. A unit of money is an artificial construct. It is related to spending power and spending patterns, and these are personal and individual. It follows that a unit of money is not fixed as between different people, is not fixed between different places and, crucially for accounting, it is not fixed between different times. We need a conversion factor between our altering measuring units. But since our units (euros) are not fixed in inherent valuation, it follows that the conversion factor cannot be fixed either. The solution (or evasion) which current purchasing power provides to this problem is to use averages as an approximate surrogate for the theoretically unique conversion factor required. The euro is converted, or adjusted, by means of general indices.

## CURRENT PURCHASING POWER

It is vital to understand that current purchasing power (CPP) is a general purchasing power concept. We are concerned with general inflation, usually expressed as the average rise in the cost of living, i.e. with inflation in the politicians' sense. If inflation in the last year is 10 per cent, then €100 last year has the same general (i.e. average) purchasing power as €110 this year. This means that in order to know what we are talking about we have to 'date' all our euros. Euros at different dates can no longer be regarded as the same, as a common measuring unit. In order to return to the position, essential for proper comparison, of having a common measuring unit, we have to convert euros of one date's purchasing power into euros of the other date's purchasing power. This needs illustrating!

Basic figures (all at 31 December) are:

20.1   €200
20.2   €250

The general inflation index stood at 300 in 20.1 and 330 in 20.2 (i.e. inflation in the year was 10 per cent). Over the year $200_{20.1}$ euros have been changed into $250_{20.2}$ euros. How much better off are we?

The description 'basic figure' is deliberately vague. The idea of CPP adjustments can be superimposed on any valuation basis. The practical proposals made in recent years for the introduction of CPP have generally assumed an HC basis and for the present we will discuss and illustrate the ideas under this assumption.

## ACTIVITY 7.1

Well. How much better off are we?

### Activity feedback

To answer this, we need to calculate the equivalent in $€_{20.2}$, of $€_{20.1}$ 200. In terms of general purchasing power this will be:

$$200 \times \frac{330}{300} = €_{20.2}\ 220$$

So in terms of a common measuring unit ($€_{20.2}$) we have an increase in well-offness of $250 - 220 = €_{20.2}\ 230$.

It is important to distinguish, when considering CPP accounting, between monetary and non-monetary items. Monetary items are items fixed by contract, custom or statute in terms of numbers of euros, regardless of changes in the general price level and the purchasing power of the euros. Examples are cash, debtors and creditors and longer-term loans. Non-monetary items are all items not so fixed in terms of number of euros, for example land, buildings, plant, inventory and shares held as investments.

Suppose I held a monetary asset in 20.1 of €200 (i.e. $€_{20.1}$ 200). If I still hold this asset, untouched and unchanged, a year later, it will be worth €200. It might even be a pile of 200 physical € coins, although it could equally be a debtor or a loan. But in 20.2 what sort of euro is it worth 200 of? The answer is 20.2 euros. By definition the item is fixed in terms of number of euros. So I have turned $€_{20.1}$ 200 into $€_{20.2}$ 200. But we know that in terms of general purchasing power $€_{20.2}$ is worth less than $€_{20.1}$ was. Therefore, in maintaining my position in terms of the number of euros of my monetary asset, I have failed to maintain my position in terms of purchasing power.

Contrariwise, suppose we borrow €100 in 20.1 and repay the loan, €100, one year later. We have borrowed $€_{20.1}$ 100 and repaid $€_{20.2}$ 100. We have repaid the same number of euros that we borrowed, but each euro is of lower purchasing power. Therefore, in terms of (general) purchasing power we have repaid less than we borrowed, so we have gained. (We shall also have to pay interest of course, which may have attempted to take account of the effects of inflation.) These gains and losses on monetary items are an important part of the argument in favour of CPP accounting – it is suggested that such gains and losses should be calculated and reported.

With monetary items, then, when considering two sets of accounts at different dates, no *adjustment* to the € figure reported is needed, but care must be taken in interpretation. However, when *comparing two* sets of accounts of the same business at different dates it is necessary to adjust all the contents of one balance sheet into the measuring unit (dated euro) of that of the other. The question may be: what is the current (today) purchasing power of the €100 I held one year ago (and still hold)? The answer is 100 of today's euros. But the question might be: If I have €200 today and I had €100 one year ago, how much better off am I in terms of purchasing power? The answer, in terms of today's euros is:

$$200 - 100 \times \frac{\text{(RPI today)}}{\text{(RPI 1 year ago)}}$$

For example:

$$200 - 100 \times \frac{(330)}{(300)}$$
$$= 200 - 110$$
$$= \text{€ today } 90$$

This process leads to a good deal of confusion. Study the following example carefully.

## Example

*Given:* All the information of Chaplin Ltd, as on pp. 87–88. Prepare: A closing balance sheet under CPP principles.

*Chaplin Ltd – CPP solution*

|  |  | € | € |
|---|---|---|---|
| Capital | $200\,000 \times \frac{120}{100}$ |  | 240 000 |
| Operating profit |  |  | 21 382 |
|  |  |  | 261 382 |
| Gain on net monetary liabilities |  |  | 2 000 |
|  |  |  | 263 382 |
| Loan |  |  | 50 000 |
| Creditors |  |  | 50 000 |
|  |  |  | 363 382 |
| Land and buildings | $110\,000 \times \frac{120}{100}$ |  | 132 000 |
| Plant and equipment: cost | $40\,000 \times \frac{120}{100}$ | 48 000 |  |
| Depreciation | $4000 \times \frac{120}{100}$ | 4 800 | 43 200 |
|  |  |  | 175 200 |
| Inventory | $90\,000 \times \frac{120}{110}$ | 98 182 |  |
| Debtors |  | 90 000 |  |
|  |  |  | 188 182 |
|  |  |  | 363 382 |

Notes

**1** *Operating profit. Balancing figure or provable as follows:*

|  |  |  |  |
|---|---|---|---|
| Per HC results |  |  | 26 000 |
| *less* Depreciation adj. | $4\,000 \times \frac{110 - 100}{100}$ |  | 400 |
|  |  |  |  |
| Inventory sold adj. | $60\,000 \times \frac{110 - 100}{100}$ |  | 6 000 |
| Adjusted profit at *30 June prices* |  |  | 19 600 |
| Adjusted profit at 31 December prices | $19\,600 \times \frac{120}{110}$ |  | € 21 382 |

**2** *Gain on net monetary liabilities.*

**(a)** In total, this is easily provable as follows:

Net monetary liabilities 1 January €10 000 (loan 50 000 less cash 40 000).

Net monetary liabilities 31 December €10 000 (loan 50 000 plus creditors 50 000 less debtors 90 000).

Therefore, the gain is $10\,000\left(1 - \dfrac{120}{100}\right) = €2000$ (at 31 December prices).

(b) More generally, however, the figures should be considered individually:

Debtors – arose on 30 June, remained until 31 December:

$$90\,000\left(1 - \frac{120}{100}\right) = \text{Loss} \qquad\qquad €8181$$

Creditors – arose on 30 June, remained until 31 December:

$$50\,000\left(1 - \frac{120}{100}\right) = \text{Gain} \qquad\qquad €4545$$

Loan – arose on 1 January, remained until 31 December:

$$50\,000\left(1 - \frac{120}{100}\right) = \text{Gain} \qquad\qquad €10\,000$$

Cash – arose on 1 January, remained until 30 June:

$$40\,000\left(1 - \frac{110}{100}\right) = \text{Loss} \qquad\qquad 4000$$

But this loss on holding cash is expressed in 30 June euros. This figure must be converted to 31 December euros, i.e.:

$$40\,000 \times \frac{120}{110} = \text{Loss} \qquad\qquad €4364$$

So in summary, we have:

| | |
|---|---|
| Losses of 8181 + 4364 | € 12 545 |
| Gains of 4545 + 10 000 | € 14 545 |
| Giving a net gain on net monetary liabilities of: | € 2 000 |

Is this €2000 gain distributable? Is it realized? In fact, as the practical businessman or businesswoman might say, where is it?

3 *Indices used*. Study carefully which index number is used where and make sure you see why. Remember the simplifying assumption that all sales, purchases and associated payments occurred on 30 June and also that monetary items need no adjustment for balance sheet purposes. Note the irrelevance of the plant and inventory indices.

4 *Complexity*. This example is highly simplified yet the numbers and, more importantly, the logic, are not at all easy.

5 *Comparatives*. Next year this balance sheet will be used as a comparative for next year's results. For this purpose it will need, next year, to be multiplied by:

$$\frac{\text{(RPI at 31 December next year)}}{120}$$

This will need to be done to every figure, whether monetary or non-monetary. Thus, for example, the loan figure at the end of the year 2 will be 50 000 year 2 euros. If the RPI is then 150, then the comparative figure from year 1, as updated to year 2 euros, will be:

$$50\,000 \times \frac{150}{120} = €62\,500$$

This cannot, of course, mean that the loan has been reduced in monetary amount by €12 500. What it does mean is that the loan has reduced in value in terms of year 2 euros (i.e. there has been another gain on monetary liabilities).

Now try the following activity. Our solution follows, but we strongly suggest that you make a serious attempt at your own solution first.

## ACTIVITY 7.2

Mushroom Ltd was established on 1 January 20X4. Its opening balance sheet (on this date) was as follows:

| | € |
|---|---|
| Land | 6 000 |
| Equipment | 4 000 |
| Inventory | 2 000 |
| Equity | 12 000 |

During 20X4, the company made the following transactions:

(a) Purchased extra inventory €10 000.

(b) Sold inventory for €11 000 cash, which had an historical cost value of €9000.

(c) Closing inventory on 31 December 20X4 had an historical cost of €3000 and was bought when the RPI index was 115 (average).

(d) The equipment has an expected life of four years and nil residual value. The straight line method of depreciation is used.

(e) The general price index stood at:

100 on 1 January 20X4

110 on 30 June 20X4

120 on 31 December 20X4

You should assume that purchases and receipts occur evenly throughout the year. There are no debtors or creditors.

**Required**

Calculate the CPP profit for 20X4 and prepare the CPP balance sheet as at 31 December 20X4.

*Activity feedback*

| | | €CPP | €CPP |
|---|---|---|---|
| Sales | 11 000 × 120/110 | | 12 000 |
| Opening inventory | 2000 × 120/100 | 2 400 | |
| Add purchases | 10 000 × 120/110 | 10 909 | |
| | | 13 309 | |
| *less* Closing inventory | (3000 × 120/115) | 3 130 | |
| | | | 10 179 |
| | | | 1 821 |
| Less Depreciation | | | 1 200 |
| | | | 621 |
| Loss on holding monetary assets (cash)* | | | 91 |
| CPP profit | | | 530 |

*If cash accrues evenly over the year, the loss is €(1000 × 120/110) − €1000 = €91

The historical cost profit (€11 000 − €9000 − €1000 for depreciation = €1000) and the CPP profit can be reconciled as follows:

*(Continued)*

## ACTIVITY 7.2    (*Continued*)

| | | |
|---|---|---|
| Historical cost profit | 1000 | |
| *Inventory* | | |
| Additional charge based on restating the cost of inventory at the beginning and end of the year in euros of current purchasing power, thus taking the inflationary element out of the profit on the sale of inventory. Opening inventory + 400 – closing Inventory – 130 | (270) | |
| *Depreciation* | | |
| Additional depreciation based on cost, measured in euros of current purchasing power of fixed assets €1200 – €1000 | (200) | |
| *Monetary items* | | |
| Net loss in purchasing power resulting from the effects of inflation on the company's net monetary assets | (91) | |
| Sales, purchases and all other costs* | | |
| These are increased by the change in the index between the average date at which they occurred and the end of the year. This adjustment increases profit as sales exceed the costs included in this heading | 91 | |
| *CPP profit* | 530 | |

*The historical cost profit is based on:

| | € | €$_{CPP}$ | € |
|---|---|---|---|
| Sales | 11 000 | 12 000 | 1 000 |
| Purchases | 10 000 | 10 909 | (909) |
| Net difference | | | 91 |

*Calculation of balance sheet items, and reconciliation of profit figure with balance sheet:*

| | | |
|---|---|---|
| 1 Value of equity, 1 January 20X4 | € | 12 000 |
| Revalued in terms of €$_{CPP}$ at 31 December 20X4 (€12 000 × 120/100) | €$_{CPP}$ | 14 400 |

2 Mushroom Ltd
CPP balance sheet as at 31 December 20X4

| | | €$_{CPP}$ | €$_{CPP}$ |
|---|---|---|---|
| Land | 6000 × 120/100 | | 7 200 |
| Equipment | 4000 × 120/100 | 4 800 | |
| *less* Depreciation | 1000 × 120/100 | 1 200 | |
| | | | 3 600 |
| | | | 10 800 |
| Inventory | 3000 × 120/115 | 3 130 | |
| Cash | (11 000 – 10 000) | 1 000 | |
| | | | 4 130 |
| | | | 14 930 |
| Financed by equity and reserves | | | 14 930 |
| CPP profit – ECPP (14 930 – 14 400) = | | €$_{CPP}$ | 530 |

## COMBINATION OF METHODS

As already stated, CPP thinking can be applied to any valuation basis, not just historical costs. It is often suggested that CPP adjustments could and indeed should be applied to replacement cost calculations. It is important to remember that:

1  RC accounting deals with specific price rises only
2  CPP accounting deals with general price rises only
3  both types of change are in fact occurring at the same time.

Thus, to take the simplest of examples, if HC = 10 and a year later RC = 13, there is a holding gain of €3. But if the GI has increased by 10 per cent, then $(10 \times 110/100) = €1$ of that holding gain of 3 (closing date) euros is not 'real' because it cannot be translated into increased purchasing power. The 'real' holding gain is arguably only 2 (3 – 1) (closing date) euros. This combined approach, known as *stabilized accounting*, is shown for Chaplin Ltd in the following example.

## Example

*Chaplin Ltd – stabilized (RC plus CPP) solution*

|  | € |
|---|---|
| Capital (per CPP answer) | 240 000 |
| Operating profit | 18 328 |
|  | 258 328 |
| Real holding gain | 8 012 |
|  | 266 340 |
| Loan | 50 000 |
| Creditors | 50 000 |
|  | 366 340 |
| Land and building (per RC answer) | 135 000 |
| Plant and equipment (per RC answer) | 39 600 |
| Inventory (per RC answer) | 101 740 |
| Debtors | 90 000 |
|  | 366 340 |

Notes:

**1** *Operating profit*

Per HC answer $\qquad 26\,000 \times \dfrac{120}{110} = 28\,364$

| Depreciation RC 30 June | 4 200 |
|---|---|
| Depreciation *less* HC | 4 000 |

$\qquad\qquad\qquad 200 \times \dfrac{120}{110} = \quad (218)$

Cost of sales
(per RC answer) $\qquad 9\,000 \times \dfrac{120}{110} = (9\,818)$

$\qquad\qquad\qquad\qquad\qquad\qquad\qquad 18\,328$

**2** *Real holding gain*

Gain on net monetary items (per CPP answer) $\qquad\qquad 2\,000$

Land and buildings $\qquad 110\,000 \times \left(\dfrac{135}{110} - \dfrac{120}{100}\right) = \qquad 3\,000$

Plant and equipment:
Cost $\qquad\qquad\quad 40\,000 \times \left(\dfrac{110}{100} - \dfrac{120}{100}\right) = (4\,000)$

Depreciation $\qquad \left(400 \times \dfrac{105}{100}\right) \times \left(\dfrac{110}{105} - \dfrac{120}{100}\right) = \quad 182 \quad (3\,818)$

$\qquad\qquad\qquad\qquad\qquad\qquad\qquad\qquad\qquad\qquad\qquad\qquad 1\,181$

Cost of sales:
Opening inventory $\qquad \left(60\,000 \times \left(\dfrac{115}{110} - \dfrac{110}{100}\right)\right) \times \dfrac{120}{110} = 3\,273$

Closing inventory $\qquad \left(90\,000 \times \left(\dfrac{130}{115} - \dfrac{120}{110}\right)\right) = 3\,557 \quad 6\,830$

$\qquad\qquad\qquad\qquad\qquad\qquad\qquad\qquad\qquad\qquad\qquad\qquad €8\,012$

# CURRENT PURCHASING POWER – WHAT DOES IT REALLY MEAN?

It is most important when thinking about CPP accounting to be fully aware of exactly what it is doing and what it is not doing. The crucial point is that it is not producing a current valuation of the term concerned in any sense. What it is doing, in general terms, is to re-express, in terms of current euros, the figures as originally calculated under the original measurement basis, whatever that was. It does not alter the basis of valuation. It alters the measuring unit which is being applied to the original basis of valuation.

## ACTIVITY 7.3

Look at the figure of €132 000 for land and buildings shown in the Chaplin Ltd example (p. 110) and think about it carefully. What does it mean?

### Activity feedback
We would suggest it means something like: the number of current euros that would have to be spent today to buy the land and buildings if all economic circumstances were exactly unaltered from when the original purchase was made. Since all economic circumstances will most certainly not be unaltered from when the original purchase was made, it is not obvious that this is particularly useful information.

The other point that could be made concerns the assumption that a general adjustment to purchasing power is of relevance even when viewed in measuring unit terms to the particular user of the particular set of accounts of the particular business being considered. Can the spending or purchasing power of one euro be equated as between a retail shop and a chemical manufacturer? Can the spending or purchasing power of one euro be equated as between a non-smoking pensioner and a smoking teenager? Is general purchasing power so general that it is not really relevant to any particular user?

# SOME INTERNATIONAL PRACTICES AND TRADITIONS

No attempt is made here to replicate a full coverage of either national research traditions or of national practices. Readers wishing to investigate the story as it applies in their own country should look elsewhere. We merely present a brief sketch and overview.

A significant starting point is the publication of a French *ordinance* (law) in 1673 and an authorized (by Royal Decree) commentary on it published in 1675 by Jacques Savary. Savary argued that an annual inventory – which we would now call balance sheet – had two functions. The first function is to give an indication of the position of the business as a performing (and continuing) operation. This function logically requires that assets are measured on a cost basis if not yet sold. The second function is an indication of debt coverage, i.e. to give an indication of the risk of bankruptcy. This function logically requires that assets are measured on a net realizable value basis.

## ACTIVITY 7.4

Prepare a list, in point form, of advantages and disadvantages which you think could reasonably be said to apply to current purchasing power accounting.

### Activity feedback
### Advantages
1 All necessary figures are stated or restated in terms of a common measuring unit (CPP units). This facilitates proper comparison.

2 It distinguishes between gains or losses on monetary liabilities and assets, on the one hand, and 'real' gains or losses through trading activities, on the other.

3 It requires only a simple objective adjustment to HC accounts. Easily auditable.

(Continued)

ACTIVITY 7.4 *(Continued)*

*Disadvantages*

1 *It is not clear what CPP units are. They are not the same as monetary units.*

2 *General purchasing power, by definition, has no direct relevance to any particular person or situation.*

3 *When CPP is applied to HC-based accounts, the resulting figures necessarily contain all*

*the disadvantages of the original HC accounts.*

4 *It fails to give any sort of meaningful 'value' to balance sheet items, although it gives the impression to non-accountants that it has done precisely that.*

5 *It is extremely difficult to understand and interpret.*

These two functions, and the resulting balance sheets, later became known as dynamic and static respectively. These are the terms used in the German tradition, developed to considerable sophistication by theorists in the early years of the twentieth century. Schmalenbach wrote *Dynamische Bilanz*, in several editions to 1926 (also available in English (1959)), which argues for a reporting system based on historical costs together with general indexation adjustment. This is in contrast with Schmidt, who, in various writings, supported the essentially static view (in the sense already described) that current values should be used, actually current entry (replacement cost) figures under his proposals.

The Dutch academic Theodor Limperg broadly followed and developed the Schmidt approach in the years to 1940 (e.g. see Mey (1966)). The essential argument is that replacement cost is the sacrificed value for production resources used. Distributable income is then logically defined as the difference between revenue and the value sacrificed in order to obtain that revenue, i.e. profit is revenue less replacement cost of consumption.

A connection into the English-speaking world was made through the publication by Sweeney of *Stabilized Accounting* (1936). Sweeney had access to the German literature and was strongly influenced by Schmidt. Sweeney went further, however, demonstrating in detail the feasibility of a full-scale combination of replacement cost measurement in combination with general indication, i.e. RC and CPP at the same time.

The 'resources sacrificed' approach, essentially an opportunity cost philosophy, can be traced to *The Valuation of Property*, by Bonbright, published in the USA in 1937. It was this book that provided the foundations for the development of the concept of deprival value, already discussed.

Practice since the middle of the twentieth century bears little resemblance to the earlier research developments. The general middle European practical approach, influenced by the factors discussed in Chapter 2, has been a strict adherence to historical costs. The same is true in the USA, although perhaps more for reasons of objectivity (and fear of the power of lawyers) than for reasons of prudence. The UK (and also the Netherlands) have adopted a more flexible approach, both in law and in practice. The large Dutch company, Philips, used a broadly Limpergian reporting system for several decades.

In the 1970s the UK experimented with a compulsory supplementary *Current Purchasing Power System* (SSAP 7, 1974). Following the government-sponsored (and influenced) Sandilands Report (1975), an expanded (and excessively complicated) development of deprival value, known as *Current Cost Accounting* (SSAP 16, 1980) was required (without general indexation). Neither lasted very long. Moves along similar lines were made over this period in a number of other countries, including the USA, which briefly introduced additional note disclosures using both specific and general adjustments. But the timing of these events strongly influenced the content and wording of the Fourth European Directive on the accounts of limited companies, published in 1978 and still very much with us today. This Directive allows a very wide variety of different approaches.

In terms of the future, general inflation adjustments are regularly employed in hyperinflationary economies, such as some South American countries and supported by requirements in IAS 29, discussed in Chapter 23. Specific price change adjustments are not generally in fashion at present. But as trends of price rise tend to increase, then the debate is likely to return.

## SUMMARY

In this chapter we have explored the concept of general inflation and current purchasing power adjustments and seen how the figures are calculated. Finally, we attempted to consider the meaning and usefulness of the resulting accounts and statements and to outline some practical developments.

## EXERCISES

*Suggested answers to exercises marked ✓ are to be found on our dedicated CourseMate platform for students.*

*Suggested answers to the remaining exercises are to be found on the Instructor online support resources.*

✓**1**  What do CPP adjustments do and how do they do it?

**2**  Are general indices more or less useful in financial reporting than specific price changes?

**3**  Look at the figure of €240 000 for capital shown in the Chaplin CPP example (p. 114) and think about it carefully. What does it mean?

**4**  To what extent do current purchasing power adjustments to historical cost figures lead to up-to-date valuations in a balance sheet?

**5**  Current purchasing power adjustments are simple to apply, but hard to explain and interpret. Discuss.

**6**   From the following historical cost accounts of Page plc, prepare a set of CPP accounts for the
year ended 31.12.8.

|  | 31.12.7 €000 | | 31.12.8 €000 | |
| --- | --- | --- | --- | --- |
| Fixed assets | | | | |
| Cost (purchased 1.1.5) | | 500 | | 500 |
| less depreciation | | 300 | | 400 |
| | | 200 | | 100 |
| Current assets | | | | |
| Inventory (purchased 31.10) | 100 | | 150 | |
| Debtors | 200 | | 300 | |
| Bank | 150 | | 350 | |
| | 450 | | 800 | |
| less Current liabilities | 300 | | 400 | |
| | | 150 | | 400 |
| | | 350 | | 500 |
| Share capital | | 100 | | 100 |
| Reserves | | 250 | | 400 |
| | | 350 | | 500 |

Profit and loss account for the year ended 31 December year 8:

|  | | € 000 |
| --- | --- | --- |
| Sales | | 1 850 |
| Cost of goods sold | | |
| Opening inventory | 100 | |
| Purchases | 1 350 | |
| | 1 450 | |
| Less Closing inventory | 150 | |
| | | 1 300 |
| Gross profit | | 550 |
| Expenses | 300 | |
| Depreciation | 100 | |
| | | 400 |
| Net profit | | 150 |

The movement on the retail price index has been as follows:

| | |
| --- | --- |
| 1 January year 5 | 180 |
| 1 January year 7 | 200 |
| Average for year 7 | 210 |
| 31 October year 7 | 215 |
| 31 December year 7 | 220 |
| Average for year 8 | 230 |
| 31 October year 8 | 235 |
| 31 December year 8 | 240 |

Assume all sales, purchases and expenses accrue evenly throughout the year.

7    You are the management accountant of a manufacturing company where production is capital-intensive, using machinery that is estimated to have a five-year life. The present machinery is now approximately three years old. Whilst raw material stocks have a low turnover due to supply problems, finished goods are turned over rapidly and there is minimal work-in-progress at any one time. The technology incorporated in the means of production is thought to be stable.

In recent years, it has not been possible to increase the price of the company's outputs beyond the rate of general inflation without diminishing market share, due to keen competition in this sector. The company does not consider that it has cash-flow problems. The company is all equity financed. Although a bank overdraft is a permanent feature of the balance sheet, this is primarily due to customers being given a 60-day credit period, whilst most suppliers are paid within 30 days. There is always a positive balance of short-term monetary assets.

In the previous financial year, net profit after taxation on a strict historical cost basis was considered very healthy, and the directors felt that they could prudently distribute a major portion of this by way of dividend. The directors are considering whether, and if so how, to reflect price-level changes in their financial statements. They are concerned that this would affect their profit figure and therefore the amount they could distribute as dividend.

The following price-level changes have been brought to the attention of the directors:

|  | Retail price index | Index for company's machinery | Raw materials stock index |
|---|---|---|---|
| 3 years previously | 100 | 100 | 100 |
| 2 years previously | 104 | 116 | 102 |
| 1 year previously | 107 | 125 | 108 |
| Present | 112 | 140 | 120 |

You are required to prepare a report for your directors setting out in general terms how to explain to the shareholders the likely impact on the historical cost profit of possible methods of accounting for price-level changes.

(CIMA – adapted)

# FAIR VALUES

> **OBJECTIVES** After studying this chapter you should be able to:
>
> - explain and discuss the concept of fair value
>
> - describe and appraise the requirements of IFRS 13, *Fair Value Measurement*
>
> - discuss the arguments for and against the usage of fair value
>
> - articulate your own views on the various valuation methods considered in Chapters 4, 5, 6 and 7.

## INTRODUCTION

The notion of fair value has a long and complicated history. It emerged gradually in a number of IASs from the early 1980s. However the term, without a clear definition, could be found rather earlier in the US. Generally the (limited) extent to which fair value has a coherent theoretical basis has grown up in a rather ad hoc way. For many years the formal IASB definition of fair value was 'the amount by which an asset could be exchanged, or a liability settled, between knowledgeable willing parties in an arm's length transaction'. This definition was used in a number of specific standards by both IASB and the American FASB. The definition has the obvious characteristic, since an exchange must by definition involve a buyer (with therefore an entry (cost) value) and a seller (with therefore a selling price (exit value), of avoiding, or defining away, the problem of exactly what kind of concept and number is represented by fair value. Since it is gross of transaction costs, it is necessarily the same number, under this definition, for both buyer and seller, so was arguably an entry and an exit concept at the same time. It is certainly a current value, being updated for each reporting date, but exactly what kind of current value, in the context of the exposition in the previous four chapters, is not so obvious.

In 2006 the FASB, at the same time as officially professing a desire for convergence with the IASB, issued a new standard, then numbered FAS 157, with a new and different definition, which changed fair value to an explicitly exit value concept. Eventually the IASB accepted this new definition, and issued a completely new standard relating to the definition and operationalization of fair value.

## IFRS 13, *FAIR VALUE MEASUREMENT*

IFRS 13, *Fair Value Measurement*, issued in May 2011, does not impose fair value (FV) measurement as a requirement. Instead, it:

- defines FV
- sets out:
  - a framework for measuring FV, including the 'Fair Value Hierarchy'
  - requirements for disclosures when FV measurement is used.

In other words, it specifies *how* an entity should measure FV and disclose information about FV measurement, but not *when* FV measurement should be used. When it should or may be used is a matter for individual standards, as discussed extensively in Parts Two and Three of this book.

FV is now defined as 'the price that would be received to sell an asset or paid to transfer a liability in an orderly transaction between market participants at the measurement date'. It is therefore now a market-based exit price. Before we go into details, try the following activity, to put the general idea of fair value into context.

## ACTIVITY 8.1

S takes a product to market, incurring transaction costs of €2 and exchanges it with B, in an arm's length (i.e. independent) transaction at an agreed exchange price of €30. B takes the product to his own entity, incurring transaction costs of €3. Calculate each of the following within the limits of the given data:

(a) S's selling price

(b) S's net realizable value

(c) B's buying price

(d) B's historical cost

(e) B's current replacement cost

(f) Fair value to S before the sale

(g) Fair value to B after the sale.

### Activity feedback

Answers would seem to be as follows:

| | | |
|---|---|---|
| (a) | S's selling price | €30 |
| (b) | S's net realizable value | €28 |
| (c) | B's buying price | €30 |
| (d) | B's historical cost | €33 |
| (e) | B's current replacement cost | €33 |
| (f) | Fair value to S before sale | €30 |
| (g) | Fair value to B after purchase | €30 |

A number of points emerge: (a) and (c) are necessarily equal, (f) and (g) are necessarily equal at least instantaneously before and after the transaction. Further, (a), (c), (f) and (g) are all necessarily equal. Third, (b) < (c) < (e), i.e. in the general case where disposal and acquisition costs are not nil:

NRV < Fair value < CRC

Both practically and conceptually, FV measurement is problematic insofar as it requires assumptions about 'an orderly transaction between market participants' in situations where there is in fact no active market. These assumptions relate among other things to prices, market characteristics, characteristics of market participants, assumed uses and accounting choices. The IASB has insisted that FV measurement is both feasible and meaningful in such circumstances. Its response is the 'Fair Value Hierarchy' of inputs into the FV measurement process. In this three-level hierarchy (passages in quotation marks below are from the text of IFRS 13):

- The unproblematic Level 1 inputs are 'quoted prices in active markets for identical assets or liabilities that the entity can access at the measurement date'.

- The Level 2 inputs are those which, while not being quoted prices as in Level 1, are observable, such as quoted prices for similar assets in active markets, or in markets that are not active, or are not quoted prices but are valuation-relevant information such as interest rates and yield curves, etc., or are market-corroborated data derived from or corroborated by observable market data by correlation or other means.

- The Level 3 inputs are to be used in the absence of Level 1 or Level 2 inputs (or in some cases to adjust Level 2 inputs) and are unobservable inputs which are 'used to measure FV to the extent that relevant observable inputs are not available, … [but which] reflect the assumptions that market participants would use when pricing the asset or liability, including assumptions about risk. [Such inputs] might include the entity's own data'. Nevertheless, the IASB insists that FV is not an entity-specific value such as net present value or net realizable value, but a market-based value.

It will be clear that it is FV measurement based on Level 3 inputs which is particularly problematic. IFRS 13 seeks to mitigate this problem by means of disclosure. For both Level 2 and Level 3 inputs, where so-called 'marking to model' is involved, IFRS 13 requires a description of the valuation technique and the inputs used, while for Level 3 inputs assumptions about risk and much more extensive disclosures are required, including the sensitivity of the FV measurement to changes in unobservable inputs. The application of this hierarchy is discussed in more detail later in this chapter.

Whether or not market information from observable market transactions is available, the objective of FV measurement under IFRS 13 is the same: to estimate the price at which an orderly transaction to sell the asset or transfer the liability would take place between market participants at the measurement date under current market conditions, i.e. an exit price from the standpoint of a market participant holding the asset or owing the liability. Because FV is a market-base measurement, the measurement takes place based on the assumptions that market participants would use when pricing the asset or liability, including assumptions about risk. Thus, in such measurement an entity's intention to hold or dispose of an asset, or settle or fulfil a liability, is irrelevant. As well as being applied to assets and liabilities, IFRS 13 is to be applied to an entity's own equity instruments. (IFRS 13, paras 1–4).

IFRS 13 applies, in both initial and subsequent measurement, when another IFRS requires or permits FV measurements or requires disclosures about such measurements or measurements based on FV, with the following exceptions:

1 Share-based payment transactions within the scope of IFRS 2, 'Share-based payments' (see Chapter 22);

**2** Leasing transactions within the scope of IAS 27, *Leases* (see Chapter 16);

**3** Measurements that have some similarities to FV but are not FV, such as net realizable value in IAS 2, *Inventories*, or value in use in IAS 36, *Impairment of Assets* (see Chapters 17 and 15).

In the first two cases, the relevant standards both state, surely bizarrely, that the earlier 'exchange price' definition continues to apply.

Further, the disclosure requirements of IFRS 13 do not apply to:

**4** Plan assets measured at FV in accordance with IAS 19, *Employee Benefits* (see Chapter 22);

**5** Retirement benefit plan investments measured at FV in accordance with IAS 26, *Accounting and Reporting by Retirement Benefit Plans* (see Chapter 22);

**6** Assets for which recoverable amount is FV less costs of disposal in accordance with IAS 36 (see Chapter 15).

On the other hand, the measurement requirements (and the disclosure requirements) apply when FV measurements are disclosed by an entity even if they are not used in the entity's financial statements, for example being disclosed only in the Notes (IFRS 13, paras 5–8).

FV measurement applies to a particular asset or liability (or a particular interest in an entity's own equity instruments, e.g. an equity interest issued or transferred in a business combination). Depending on its unit of account, an asset or liability measured at FV may be either:

- a stand-alone asset or liability such as a financial instrument
- a group of assets or a group of liabilities, which function together
- a group of assets and liabilities which necessarily function together, such as a business or a cash-generating unit.

The unit of account is determined based on the IFRS in accordance with which the FV measurement is being applied, except where otherwise stated in IFRS 13.

## APPLYING THE STANDARD

As noted above, a FV measurement assumes that the asset or liability (or interest in the entity's own equity instruments) is exchanged in an orderly transaction between market participants to sell the asset or transfer the liability or own equity instrument at the measurement date under current market conditions. The market should be either the principal market for the asset, liability or equity interest, or, in the absence of a principal market, the most advantageous market. The reporting entity must have access to the market in question, i.e. the practical ability to trade in the market, at the measurement date. The FV measurement represents the price in that market, whether directly observable or estimated using another valuation technique. Even when the FV measurement is entirely dependent on Level 3 inputs, a FV measurement assumes that a transaction takes place on that date considered from the perspective of a market participant that holds the asset or owes the liability (or transfers the equity instrument). That assumed transaction creates the basis for estimating the price to sell the asset or transfer the liability (IFRS 13, paras 13–21). Extensive guidance is provided in the

Standard on how to carry out FV measurements of assets based on Level 3 inputs and for liabilities and an entity's own equity instruments.

The price in the principal or most advantageous market is not to be adjusted for transactions costs, which should be accounted for in accordance with other IFRSs. Transactions costs are not considered to be a characteristic of an asset or liability, as they are specific to a transaction and may vary depending on how the transaction is entered into. In other words transaction costs are entity specific rather than market specific. Although fair value measurement is gross of transaction costs, thereby confirming our earlier proposition that FV is greater than NRV, transport costs are specifically excluded from transaction costs. Transport costs as regards IFRS 13 are defined as 'the costs that would be incurred to transport an asset from its current location to its principle (or most advantageous) market'. In contrast to transaction costs, transport costs may be a characteristic of an asset as they reflect a change in one of its attributes (its location). Hence, in making a FV measurement, a downwards adjustment to the hypothetical price should be made for any transport costs that would be necessary to transport an asset from its current location to the principal or most advantageous market (IFRS 13, paras 22–26).

## ACTIVITY 8.2

Does the distinction between transaction costs and transport costs make sense?

### Activity feedback

We find it hard to be positive here! The origin of the distinction seems to be the determination to maintain the position that fair value is defined in relation to a market and not in relation to an entity. Cows live in fields or barns owned by particular farmers/entities, but are sold in (physical) markets, so their location has to be changed (hence requiring transport costs) before they can be considered as market-related. The commission to the auctioneer is integral to the market, not to the farmer, and presumably is part of transaction costs since it is related to the market and not related to the entity itself.

But we have difficulty with all this. If you wish to sell a cow, or you do sell a cow, there is a selling price. But in order to sell, you have to both transport the cow, and pay the auctioneer. Gross selling (or exchange of course) price has a clear economic meaning. Net realizable value has a clear economic meaning. Fair value, as defined and applied here, is in the general case in-between. What precisely is its economic meaning or message? To whom and for what is it useful? We find these questions difficult to answer.

Apart from the IFRSs dealing with financial assets and liabilities, several IFRSs require or permit measurement at FV for non-financial assets. These include IAS 16, *Property, Plant and Equipment* (see Chapter 13), IAS 38, *Intangible Assets* (see Chapter 14), IAS 40, *Investment Property* (see Chapter 13), IAS 41, 'Agriculture' (see CourseMate) and a number of IFRICs.

A FV measurement of a non-financial asset takes into account a market participant's ability to generate economic benefits by using the asset in its 'highest and best use' or by selling it to another market participant that would do so. Highest and best use (HBU) is a valuation concept used to value many non-financial assets such as real estate. The concept is not relevant to items other than non-financial assets since they do not have an alternative use without being changed and therefore ceasing to be the same asset or liability.

The HBU of a non-financial asset must be physically possible, financially feasible and legally permissible. Financial feasibility takes into account whether a physically possible and legally permissible use would generate adequate income or cash flows to produce an investment return that market participants would require, and any costs of converting the asset to that use.

The HBU is determined from the perspective of market participants, even if the reporting entity has a different use in mind. Nevertheless, the entity's current use of a non-financial asset is presumed to be its HBU unless market or other considerations suggest otherwise (e.g. in the case of an intangible asset that the entity plans to use defensively so as to prevent others from using it).

The HBU establishes the valuation premise used to measure FV for a non-financial asset which might be used in combination with other assets as a group, or with other assets and liabilities as a business or business unit, as follows:

- If the HBU is the use of the asset in combination with a group of other assets or other assets and liabilities, the FV of the asset is the price that would be received in a current transaction to sell the asset assuming that it would be used with that group of other assets or assets and liabilities (its complementary assets and any associated liabilities) and that these would be available to market participants.

- Associated liabilities for this purpose include those that fund working capital but not those that fund assets other than those within the group of complementary assets.

- Assumptions about the HBU must be consistent for all the assets included in the group of complementary assets for which HBU is relevant.

- The HBU might provide maximum value to market participants when the asset is used on a stand-alone basis. In that case, the FV of the asset is the price that would be received on the assumption that the buyer would use it on a stand-alone basis.

A FV measurement of a financial or non-financial liability or an entity's own equity instrument (e.g. as issued as consideration in a business combination) assumes that:

- The instrument is transferred to a market participant at the measurement date.

- A liability would remain outstanding and the transferee would be required to fulfil the obligation which would not be settled with the counterparty or otherwise extinguished on the measurement date.

- An entity's own equity instrument would remain outstanding and the transferee would take on the rights and responsibilities associated with the instrument which would not be cancelled or otherwise extinguished at the measurement date.

Even when there is no observable market to provide pricing information about such a transfer (for example, because transfer is prevented by contractual or other legal restrictions), if such items are held by other parties as assets this may result in an observable market. In all cases, to meet the objective of FV measurement, which remember is to estimate the price at which an orderly transaction to transfer the item would take place between market participants under current market conditions at the measurement date, an entity maximizes the use of relevant observable inputs and minimizes the use of unobservable inputs.

When a quoted price is not available, and an identical item is held by another party as an asset, the FV is measured from the perspective of a market participant that holds the item as an asset at the measurement date, according to the FV hierarchy (see below).

When a quoted price is not available, and an identical item is not held by another party as an asset, the FV of the item is measured using a valuation technique from the perspective of a market participant that owes the liability or has issued the equity instrument.

The FV of a liability reflects the effect of the risk that the entity that owes it may not fulfil that obligation, i.e. non-performance risk, which includes, but is not limited to, the entity's own credit risk. Hence, when measuring the FV of a liability, an entity takes into account the effects of its own credit risk as well as other factors that may affect the likelihood that the obligation will be fulfilled. Non-performance risk related to a liability is assumed to be the same before and after the transfer of the liability, for various reasons:

- A market participant taking on the obligation would not enter into a transaction that changed the non-performance risk associated with it without reflecting that change in the price.

- Creditors would not knowingly agree to a transfer to a transferee with a lower credit standing.

- Those who might hold the liability as an asset would consider, when pricing those assets, the effects of the entity's own credit risk as well as other factors that may affect the likelihood that the obligation will be fulfilled.

## THE MEASUREMENT PROCESS

When an asset is acquired or a liability is assumed in an exchange transaction, the transaction price is an *entry* price, whereas FV is defined as an *exit* price. Nevertheless, in many cases the transaction price will be equal to FV, for example when on the transaction date the transaction to buy the asset takes place in the market in which the asset would be sold (remember that transaction costs are not taken into consideration). When this is not the case, the difference (gain or loss) between FV and the transaction price is recognized in profit or loss for the period unless the applicable IFRS specifies otherwise.

There are some cases where the transaction price will differ from FV:

- The transaction is between related parties, although the transaction price may be used as an input where the entity has evidence that the transaction was entered into at market terms.

- The transaction takes place under duress or in a forced sale (e.g. in financial distress of the seller).

- There is a difference in the units of account between the buyer and the seller, for example in a business combination where the transaction includes unstated rights and privileges that are to be measured separately or the transaction price includes transactions costs.

- The market in which the transaction takes place is not the principal or most advantageous market. This might be the case if the entity is a dealer that enters into transactions in the retail market, whereas the principal or most advantageous market is with other dealers in the wholesale market. If the entity is a dealer, the entry price it will pay for items in the retail market will be lower than the exit price for the same items in the principal or most advantageous market, namely the wholesale market (IFRS 13, paras 57–60).

The objective of using a valuation technique is to *estimate* the price at which an orderly transaction to sell the asset or transfer the liability takes place between market participants at the measurement date under current market conditions. Valuation techniques that are used should maximize the use of observable inputs and minimize the use of unobservable inputs. They include the market approach (a current transaction price), the cost approach (a historical cost) and the income approach (a present value calculation), all of which have been discussed at length in previous chapters. If a transaction price is used to measure FV on initial recognition, and a valuation technique that uses unobservable inputs is used to measure FV in subsequent periods, that valuation technique needs to be calibrated so that if applied at initial recognition it would result in the transaction price.

The FV hierarchy was originally included in IFRS 7 (see Chapter 18), but has now been transferred to IFRS 13. It classifies the inputs to valuation techniques used to measure FV into three levels. The FV hierarchy prioritizes inputs to valuation techniques, not the techniques themselves. Where a combination of inputs from different levels is used, the combined input is classified at the level of the lowest of the inputs. For example, if an observable input requires an adjustment using an unobservable input and the resulting adjustment is of a significant amount, then the resulting measurement is a Level 3 measurement. Hence, the FV hierarchy is also applied to FV measurements based on the lowest level of the inputs used in a particular FV measurement. This then leads to disclosure requirements which are somewhat more onerous for Level 2 measurements than for those at Level 1, and substantially more onerous for Level 3 measurements. The formal definitions are as follows.

Level 1 inputs are unadjusted quoted prices in active markets for identical assets or liabilities that the entity can access at the measurement date. These prices typically provide the most reliable indication of FV and should be used to measure FV whenever available.

Level 2 inputs are all inputs other than quoted prices included in Level 1 that are observable, either directly or indirectly, for the asset or liability, such as quoted prices for similar assets in active markets, or in markets that are not active, or are not quoted prices but are valuation-relevant information such as interest rates and yield curves, credit spreads, etc., or are market-corroborated data derived from or corroborated by observable market data by correlation or other means. Such inputs are substantially less subjective than Level 3 inputs.

Adjustments to Level 2 inputs will vary depending on various factors including the following:

- The condition or location of the asset (for non-financial assets).
- The extent to which inputs relate to items that are comparable to the asset or liability. There may be differences in characteristics such as credit quality or the unit of account.
- The volume or level of activity in the markets within which the inputs are observed.

Level 3 inputs are unobservable inputs to be used to measure FV (or in some cases to adjust Level 2 inputs) to the extent that relevant observable inputs are not available, which reflect the assumptions that market participants would use when pricing the asset or liability, including assumptions about risk. Such inputs might include the entity's own data. Nevertheless, as emphasized earlier, FV is not an entity-specific value, but a market-based value.

Assumptions about risk include the risk inherent in a particular valuation technique used to measure FV, such as a pricing model, and the risk inherent in the inputs to the valuation technique. A measurement that does not include an adjustment for risk would not be a FV measurement if market participants would include such an adjustment when pricing the asset or liability. For example, an adjustment might be called for when there is significant measurement uncertainty. This might be the case when there has been a significant decrease in the volume or level of activity when compared to normal market activity for the asset or liability (or similar assets or liabilities) and the entity has determined that a transaction or quoted price does not, as such, represent FV (for example, there might be transactions that are not orderly such as forced or distressed sales).

Where a Level 3 input is used to adjust a Level 2 input and the adjustment is significant, the result is a Level 3 measurement (IFRS 13, paras 67–90).

## DISCLOSURE

The disclosures required by IFRS 13 are onerous, especially for FV measurements based on Level 3 inputs. This is intended to mitigate the acknowledged uncertainty and subjectivity of such measurements. Much information is required about the assumptions which underpin the actual measurement process. The detailed disclosure requirements can be found in the standard itself (paras 91–99).

## TOWARDS AN APPRAISAL OF FAIR VALUE

There is no doubt that the fair value concept is controversial. One of the major issues is the insistence that it is, and should be, a market-specific value and not an entity-specific value. In a comment letter published in 2006 on an earlier discussion draft concerning the concept of fair value, EFRAG included the following paragraph:

> We think that a number of important statements the paper makes are neither generally accepted nor justified in the paper. We are also not convinced by the reasoning underlying a number of important conclusions. For example – and probably most important of all – we are not convinced by the arguments advanced in the paper in support of the statements that (a) the market value measurement objective provides superior information to entity-specific measurement objectives, at least on initial recognition (paragraph 60) and (b) fair value is more relevant than measurement bases that depend on entity-specific expectations (paragraph 102). If the arguments in the paper are the only arguments in favour that exist and have been expressed in the paper in the best way possible, we do not understand how the paper could have reached the conclusions it has.

We tend to be supportive of current values, regard fair value as a valid contender for an appropriate current value, but, like EFRAG, are not at all convinced by the apparent determination to avoid entity-specific measurements. If a user of financial statements is making a detailed comparison of, say, Daimler-Benz and Peugeot-Citroën, surely figures related to Daimler-Benz and Peugeot-Citroën are likely to be more relevant than figures related to the world markets for steel, rubber, cars and so on. Let the debate continue!

Parallel to the theoretical uncertainty of what fair value actually implies in terms of real-life calculation, there is great political uncertainty regarding the future of, and desirability of, the use of fair values. As a general and oversimplified comment, we suggest that the greater the emphasis by users of published financial reports on the estimation of long-run cash flows, and therefore on long-run profitability, the greater the support for fair values in some form is likely to be. It follows from the discussions on user needs in Chapter 1, and on international differences in Chapter 2, that those countries and traditions tending to take a common law economic focus are likely to be more receptive to fair values than those taking a code law legislation focus. It further follows within any given tradition that, other things equal, companies whose shares are actually traded are likely to be relatively favourable towards fair values, whereas companies where the only users in practice are creditors/bankers and taxation authorities are likely to be critical. The implications of these tensions and differences are nowhere near resolution amongst legal and regulatory authorities.

A further point of contention is the possible relationship between the use of fair value reporting and the financial crisis which began around 2008. In essence, fair value as applied to impairment of financial assets (of which bank receivables are a prime example) removes the possibility of income smoothing and secrecy about performance, and these are exactly the attributes which bankers, and banking regulators, wish to preserve. For consideration of this, and for other specific applications of the fair value concept in relation to particular standards, see the relevant chapters in Parts Two and Three of this book.

## VALUATION AND INCOME MEASUREMENT – SOME OVERALL CONSIDERATIONS

We have spent a long time and many pages exploring a variety of bases for the evaluation of assets and liabilities, and therefore for different measures of performance over time. In Chapter 1 we revised and developed the traditional historical cost model. This is backwards looking and relatively objective (remember the relatively!). In Chapter 4 we considered the thinking of important economists in this area, the psychic theories of Fisher – unmeasurable in money terms by very definition but properly recognizing that only human beings take decisions and that they are the ultimate consumers – and the more quantifiable work of Hicks with its important capital maintenance implications. These economic-based ideas are properly forward looking and logically relevant to the decision-making process, but they are highly subjective. Current values lie in the middle of this spectrum, both in terms of their time relationship (in between past and future) and in terms of their degrees of objectivity/subjectivity. In this sense they are clearly worth exploring as a compromise between relevance and verifiability.

There are stronger claims that can be made, however. The usual financial reporting statements essentially claim to report on the position at a (current) date and on the results ending on that date. Current values can properly claim to provide information consistent with this approach. The question follows, of course, which current value? The discussions in this and previous chapters suggest that each of the suggested bases has particular merits. All provide useful information. All give good and relevant answers to some questions. One obvious suggestion to follow from this is that the preferable method in any situation depends on the particular situation itself – in other words, the abstract question 'Which is the best method?' has no answer and indeed is simply a silly question. We should be prepared to use different valuation methods and different reporting methods for different purposes.

A second suggestion is an idea for you to take away and think about. The practice and application of double-entry channel us unthinkingly into the assumption that the balance sheet and the income statement are two elements in the same system and that they therefore have to be fully compatible with each other. But our basic purpose is to produce meaningful reports and there is no logical reason why they should be in any way constrained by data-recording systems. Perhaps we should consider producing smaller more ad hoc statements, using *combinations* of valuation bases depending on the purpose of each statement, or producing several different versions of a (loosely defined) income statement and a (loosely defined) statement of financial position, so that users can choose between them for their own particular purposes. Would the increased costs of preparation, and the increased complexity of published documents, be justified by the increased usefulness?

Here is an activity, deliberately in two major parts. We suggest you answer them quite independently of each other.

## ACTIVITY 8.3

First, suggest, with reasons, which method (or methods) seems likely to produce the most useful measurement of performance (revenues and expenses and therefore income).

Second, suggest, with reasons, which method (or methods) seems likely to produce the most useful measurement of financial position (assets and liabilities and therefore equity).

If the answers are not compatible, consider the implications.

### Activity feedback

In a sense, this is the ultimate accounting question. It can be approached in many different ways, and we make no attempt to suggest a definitive answer. It is in the end your own opinions that matter. The qualitative characteristics outlined in Chapter 1 could well point in different directions, depending on which characteristics are given more or less importance. But we suggest that the best starting point is the users and user needs. One argument which we find persuasive is derived from the Hicks emphasis on long-run repetitive performance, i.e. on the permanent maintenance of operating capability. This supports the removal of holding gains from the performance (earnings) measure, and therefore current replacement cost. This not only gives an important indicator for management, and for government economic and taxation policy, but also gives current and potential investors a meaningful approximation to long-run cash flows.

But the resulting balance sheet numbers, for both carrying value of assets and for the reserves section of equity, are more difficult either to explain precisely, or to defend in terms of usefulness. If there are no global investors to consider, i.e. the main or only likely users of the financial statements are groups such as banking lenders, tax authorities and lawyers, then some kind of meaningful estimate of asset valuations seems particularly relevant, perhaps either net realizable value or fair value, logically an entity-specific figure being preferable. But of course these ideas taken together do indeed mean the usage of multiple bases, which is both relatively costly in preparation and relatively difficult in comprehension. Note also that our discussion takes no account at all of the issue of general inflation, of the decline in value over time of the currency measuring unit in terms of spending power, and the only reason for holding currency is for what it can be exchanged for in terms of further investment or for consumption.

As a general and perhaps evasive conclusion, user needs, and the relevant culture (whether national or international) are likely to significantly affect preferences and desirabilities.

## SUMMARY

In this chapter we have explored the concept of fair value both in itself and through IFRS 13. We have considered its characteristics and usefulness, noting that there are uncertainties both conceptually and in terms of practical usage and application. We have also briefly considered the overall 'set' of valuation methods explored so far. It would be good to consider this appraisal again after reading and working through the rest of this book!

## EXERCISES

*Suggested answers to exercises marked ✓ are to be found on our dedicated CourseMate platform for students.*

*Suggested answers to the remaining exercises are to be found on the Instructor online support resources.*

✓**1**   What is 'fair value'? Is it a good idea?

**2**   Investors need an up-to-date forward-looking indication of annual performance, implying a focus on the income statement, and lenders need an up-to-date indication of asset values, implying a focus on the balance sheet. Discuss.

**3**   In the end, for most practical purposes, historical cost is best. Discuss.

**4**   The following extract is taken from the 'Accounting Policies' section of the 31 December 2011 Consolidated Annual Report of the Dutch firm Philips.

'The fair value of financial instruments that are not traded in an active market is determined by using valuation techniques. The Company uses its judgment to select from a variety of common valuation methods including the discounted cash flow method and option valuation models and to make assumptions that are mainly based on market conditions existing at each balance sheet date.'

Does this policy seem likely to provide data which are sufficiently reliable to be useful?

# ACCOUNTING THEORY AND CONCEPTUAL FRAMEWORKS

# 9

**OBJECTIVES** After studying this chapter you should be able to:

- explain the difference between accounting theory and a comprehensive theory of accounting

- describe the main attempts at constructing accounting theory

- appraise current developments in the area

- describe and discuss the contents of the IASB Framework

- appraise the quality and usefulness of the IASB Framework in the context of its self-declared purposes

- describe and discuss the parts of IAS 1 relating to accounting concepts and policies

- appraise the overall effect of the Framework and comparable parts of IAS 1

- describe and appraise the requirements of IAS 8 relating to accounting policies

- outline the requirements of IFRS 1 relating to first-time adoption of IFRS.

## INTRODUCTION

This chapter discusses accounting theory and the possibility of a comprehensive theory of accounting, as well as different approaches to formulating accounting theories. It then discusses the IASB Framework and its accounting principles and concepts, before moving on to IAS 1, IAS 8 and IFRS 1 to talk about the adoption and disclosure of accounting policies, accounting policy changes, and the first time adoption of IFRSs.

## ACCOUNTING THEORY AND A COMPREHENSIVE THEORY OF ACCOUNTING

According to Eldon S. Hendriksen in *Accounting Theory* (1977):

Theory as it applies to accounting is the coherent set of hypothetical, conceptual and pragmatic principles forming the general frame of reference for a field of inquiry. Thus accounting theory may be defined as logical reasoning in the form of a set of broad principles that:

1 Provide a general frame of reference by which accounting practices can be evaluated; and

2 Guide the development of new practices and procedures.

Accounting theory may also be used to explain existing practices to obtain a better understanding of them. But the most important goal of accounting theory should be to provide a coherent set of logical principles that form the general frame of reference for the evaluation and development of sound accounting practices.

Let us compare this with the IASB's *Conceptual Framework for Financial Reporting* issued in 2010. Among others, this Framework purports to:

1 assist the board of IASB in the development of standards and review of existing standards

2 provide a basis for reducing the number of permitted alternative accounting treatments

3 assist preparers in applying IFRSs and in dealing with topics that have yet to form the subject of a standard.

## ACTIVITY 9.1

Do you think that the quote from Hendriksen (1977) is about accounting theory or about a comprehensive theory of accounting? Do you think that the IASB Framework is intended to be a comprehensive theory of accounting?

### Activity feedback
Hendriksen appears to be talking about a comprehensive theory of accounting as he mentions that it serves as a general frame of reference. In other words, it has a scope that is broad enough to be comprehensive. He mentions logical reasoning in the form of a set of broad principles, which indicates that the set of principles that constitutes the theory must be coherent and internally consistent. In other words, on the basis of these principles, we would be able to explain and predict which accounting practices and rules are better for a certain specified purpose.

(Continued)

## ACTIVITY 9.1    *(Continued)*

*The IASB Conceptual Framework certainly sounds like a comprehensive accounting theory as defined by Hendriksen. But if it is, what is the certain specified purpose for which accounting practices and rules are developed? How was it determined and who determined it? If there was agreement on the general purpose of financial accounting, would it be the case that this theory would clearly determine how we should provide information to users, and different practices would not prevail? Such agreement may exist on an abstract level. For example, we probably agree that accounting information must be useful. However, at a detailed level, agreement is highly unlikely because accounting is an interested activity and the financial interests of most stakeholders are in conflict with one another. Historically, the FASB Conceptual Framework was called conceptual rather than theoretical because it consisted of generally agreed concepts rather than a coherent set of theoretical principles. The IASC modelled its 1989 Framework on that of the FASB and the IASB adopted the same in 2001. However, the IASB has a different mandate than the IASC and the FASB did.*

## ACTIVITY 9.2

In what ways did the IASB in 2001 (and today) have a different mandate than the IASC in 1989 or the FASB at any time?

### Activity feedback

*The FASB's mandate is to set accounting standards in the USA in the public interest of the people and businesses in the USA. The IASC was not an accounting standard setter. It was a private organization consisting of representatives of the accounting firms and professional bodies in a number of countries. When the IASC was reorganized into the IASB in 2001, it became a private accounting standard setter committed to act in the international public interest, but the IASB Conceptual Framework then and now is still based on the basic concepts that were agreed upon by the FASB in the American public interest.*

In sum, accounting theory as it is described in the textbooks, consists of many different theories for different purposes. Some are larger in scope, and others are smaller in scope. A comprehensive theory of accounting is not impossible, but it is not likely any time soon.

## APPROACHES TO THE FORMULATION OF ACCOUNTING THEORY

How do we approach the development of theories in accounting? Approaches to the development of theories in accounting are similar to approaches to theory development in other social sciences.

Non-theoretical approaches are concerned with developing accounting techniques and principles that will be useful to users, particularly decision makers. They may lead to the description of generally accepted principles and practices being regarded as a body of theory. These approach can be developed in a pragmatic or authoritarian way. In essence, in the past the accounting profession adopted a non-theoretical approach to formulating accounting theory. It is fairly apparent that this approach did not lead to the resolution of conflict in accounting practices or principles. An example is the regulatory approach.

**Regulatory approach** Many would regard this as the approach we currently have to accounting theory. They hold this view because to them it does not appear that standards, even those of the IASB (in spite of its Conceptual Framework), are based on a coherent set of broad, relevant theories, but are developed as solutions to current conflicts that emerge in our attempts to provide useful information to users. These solutions are sometimes influenced by the politics of standard setting and by political lobbying by interest groups. Indeed, some might argue that new standards are only developed when a particular user complains about misinformation or non-information. But there are ideological questions to consider if we do adopt this approach to the development of accounting theory. In the main, these questions centre on whether we should adopt a free market approach to the regulation, a private sector regulatory approach, or a public sector regulatory approach. This regulatory approach is also one that tends to identify solutions to difficulties that have occurred in our reporting, rather than providing us with a theory that anticipates the issues.

Apart from the non-theoretical pragmatic process to the development of an accounting theory from a basic methodological perspective we can distinguish deductive, inductive, or mixed processes.

**Deductive approach** This approach involves developing a theory from basic propositions, premises and assumptions that results in accounting principles that are logical conclusions about the subject. The theory is tested by determining whether its results are acceptable in practice. Edwards and Bell (1961) are deductive theorists (Chapter 4) and historical cost accounting was also derived from a deductive approach. This approach is sometimes considered 'normative' because the propositions, premises and assumptions are a priori truths. That is, you cannot prove them, other than in a circular manner. In other words, they are based on beliefs, values and accepted truths, and are supported by deductive logic. An example of such a theory is the Decision-usefulness Theory developed by Staubus (1959, 1961) which, as will be discussed later in this chapter, still forms the basis of the FASB and IASB conceptual frameworks today.

**Inductive approach** The inductive approach stems from the natural sciences, where theories often take the form of law-like generalizations. It starts with observed phenomena on the basis of which researchers form hypotheses about causal explanations. The approach requires empirical testing of the hypotheses, i.e. the theory must be supported by sufficient instances/observations that support the validity of the derived conclusions about which variable causes, an observed phenomenon and hence might explain it. Generalized conclusions about causality are made on the basis of inference, and must be interpreted with reference to the statistical likelihood that the same results will be obtained in the future. Some question whether the inductive approach is suitable for the social sciences, which include economics and accounting. Quite often the deductive and inductive approaches are mixed as researchers use their knowledge of accounting practices, or they may not be aware of the subjectivity with which they interpret their own observations.

**Mixed approaches** These attempt to use both conceptual reasoning and empirical observations to formulate and verify a paradigm from which to approach developing and testing an accounting theory. In the social sciences, approaches to doing research and formulating theories can, very roughly, be categorized as those based on positivist, interpretivist and critical methodological assumptions. Positivist assumptions include the belief that social scientists must use the same methods used in the natural sciences, and the belief that researchers can and must base their hypotheses and theories solely on purely objective empirical observations. On this view, the function of theory is to explain presently observed phenomena in terms of causality, which subsequently enables the prediction of behaviour, events and other phenomena in the future. Examples of paradigms based on the methodological assumptions of positivism include:

- the informational paradigm
- positive accounting theory (PAT)
- behavioural paradigm
- new institutional paradigm.

**The informational paradigm** This theoretical paradigm is rooted in neo-classical economics. It started with Ball and Brown (1968) and Beaver (1968) which introduced empirical methods based on the assumptions of economic general equilibrium models into accounting research. The aim is to demonstrate how accounting information influences investment decisions. Capital-markets-based accounting research is perhaps still the most popular and prolific form of positivist research in accounting.

**Positive accounting theory (PAT)** This theoretical paradigm was developed in the 1970s. Its best known proponents are Watts and Zimmerman (1978, 1979) and Jensen and Meckling (1976). The approach aims to develop a positive theory of accounting which will explain why accounting is what it is and why accountants do what they do, and predict what effects accounting choices have on people and the allocation and utilization of resources.

The assumption in neo-classical economics (micro-economics, also called positive economics) is that, as long as certain initial conditions are met, individuals freely pursuing their own interests will lead to the greatest economic benefit and happiness for all. PAT is based on the assumptions of positive economics, which includes the proposition that managers, shareholders and regulators are rational, self-interested and that they attempt to maximize their utility. PAT holds that, on aggregate, individual behaviour is predictably rational. Ideally, PAT would not lead to prescriptions of the accounting procedures and policies to be implemented, however, agency theory (Jensen and Meckling, through the anticipation of predictably rational behaviour, has a big impact on corporate governance and indirectly on accounting as well).

**Behavioural paradigm** The behavioural paradigm in economics and finance was developed on the basis of evidence in studies done by psychologists indicating that individuals are not necessarily always predictably rational or self-serving in their decision making. See for example, Kahneman and Tversky (1972, 1973, 1979), Odean (1998), Shefrin (2000), Simon (1979), Statman and Shefrin (1985), Shiller (2000, 2003), Shleifer (2000) and Thaler (1999). Hence, this approach attempts to take into account human behaviour as it relates to decision making in accounting. In many behaviourist theories in economics, finance and accounting, the assumption is that individuals are predictably irrational.

**New institutional paradigm** The new institutional approach in accounting is based on the new institutional approach in economics. The latter was developed by researchers doing comparative economic history because they realized that institutions influence economic growth and development. What is rational in one institutional environment is not necessarily rational in another. Researchers in comparative financial and accounting systems came to the conclusion that, particularly, legal and financial institutions matter to the development of accounting systems (e.g., La Porta *et al.*, 1997; Nobes, 1998). The gradual progression of the internationalization of capital markets and the increasing number of countries where IFRSs have been adopted has focused attention on the importance of differences in institutional environment between countries (e.g., Leuz, 2010; Hail *et al.*, 2010). It is important to understand the difference between the new and the old institutional paradigms in economics in order to appreciate the impact on accounting research. The old institutional paradigm grew out of political economy, which was later split up into political economy and economics. In the old institutional paradigm, importance is attached to the influence of political, economic and military power. If institutions matter so much to economic development and the development of accounting and financial systems, research questions will focus on who has the power to determine what the economic, legal and other institutions are. On the other hand, the new institutional accounting paradigm shares the assumption with neoclassical economic theory, that there is no single person or group or country which has the power to shape the development of institutions to their/its own benefit.

**Interpretive paradigm**  Interpretivist research and theories are based on the belief that it is not always possible for researchers to provide entirely objective interpretations of observed social phenomena (such as accounting practices and rules). In other words, they realize that some a priori truths are actually dependent on context and perspective, and that because of this it is difficult to judge our own ability to be objective about social phenomena. One implication is that these approaches to the formulation of accounting theory do not focus on predicting behaviour and events. They rather focus on explaining and interpreting the meaning of acts and actions from the perspective of the individuals involved. This paradigm is perhaps more popular in managerial than in financial accounting research. On the basis of data collected in case studies and interviews etc., researchers try to understand motivations behind and the meaning of behaviour and individual acts. They will then form hypotheses, for example about how workers can be motivated by sharing responsibility for setting performance targets as well as their realization.

**Critical paradigm**  The critical approach to accounting theory formulation originates in political economy, neo-Marxism and sociology, and focuses on theories about the distributional consequences of financial reporting. Critical researchers try to expose certain accepted truths as false or unfair, and point to how fairness and justice can be improved. In accounting, this approach has led to theories about the social responsibility of managers of large companies, or about the need to report on the social, economic and ecological sustainability or the operations of large companies. The critical paradigm may lead to ethical approaches that centre on social welfare. In other words, accounting principles and techniques are evaluated for acceptance after considering all effects on all groups in society. Writers/researchers in this area include Scott (1940), Yu (1976) and Williams (2002, 2006). Within this approach we would need to be able to account for a business entity's effect on its social environment.

Finally, there are two more approaches to the formulation of accounting theory that need to be mentioned here:

- economic approach
- eclectic approach.

**Economic approach**  A macro-economic approach focuses on the economic consequences of accounting policies and standards on general economic welfare. Thus accounting principles and techniques are evaluated for acceptance depending on their impact on the national economy. Sweden, in its national GAAP, uses an economic approach to its development. Theories about macro-economic consequences of accounting policies often relate to taxation and investment fixed capital formation. From a positivist perspective, theories about economic consequences may focus on the effects on businesses or on investor behaviour. From a critical perspective, they might focus on the effect of accounting policies on employment and wage levels. Traditionally, accounting standards have been set without considering economic consequences, but lobby pressures from groups who perceive themselves as being affected can be strong. The IASB in developing its standards does tend to take an economic approach into account. For example, the current discussion on accounting for leases focuses on the effect that a standard requiring the capitalization of all leases, whether finance or operating, might have on the economy or business in general.

**Eclectic approach** Here we have a combination of all the approaches already identified appearing in our accounting theory. This approach has come about more by accident than as a deliberate attempt due to the interference in the development of accounting theory by professionals, governmental bodies (including the EU) and individuals.

## ACTIVITY 9.3

Explain, with reference to the concepts of predictable rationality and bounded rationality, how PAT and behavioural accounting theory might consider disclosing information on the face of the financial statements or in the notes to the financial statements.

### Activity feedback
The assumption of rationality under PAT means that it does not matter what form the disclosure of information takes. Users of financial statements will be able to see through any attempt to manipulate their decisions. Behavioural theory probably takes into consideration the fact that most investors do not study the financial statements in great detail. Hence they might miss or discard information that is not presented on the face of the financial statements.

## The future of financial accounting theory

This section has merely listed the main approaches to the development of accounting theories that exist in the literature. For different overviews of this area, please refer to Smith (2011, Ch. 1) or Riahi-Belkaoui (2004). Van Mourik (2014a) presents an overview of methodology in financial accounting research and Van Mourik (2014b) outlines different types of issues in financial accounting theory. Other sources for information about accounting research methodology and methods include Ryan *et al.* (2002) and Smith (2011). Over the past 40 years or so, financial accounting theories have primarily been based on the assumptions of the positive approach and were aimed at explanation and prediction of preparers' and investors' actions and accounting phenomena. Most of the accounting theories developed by financial accounting researchers during this period have been of a relatively small scope. Some regard the IASB Conceptual Framework as the most promising avenue for the development of a comprehensive theory of financial accounting. A more cynical view held by others is that any conceptual framework is primarily an attempt to legitimize the authority of accounting standard setters and regulators. Yet others regard a conceptual framework as a possible means for private accounting standard setters (such as the IASB) to keep political interference from national regulators at bay. In essence, the IASB's conceptual framework is the result of a pragmatic regulatory approach to the determination of accounting principles which comprises an eclectic mixture of deductive, inductive and political elements. As the Framework and the IFRSs are applied in many different institutional environments, it will be interesting to see what theoretical contributions the old and new institutional paradigms will provide to the field of international accounting theory.

## THE IASB CONCEPTUAL FRAMEWORK

A number of attempts have been made since the 1970s to create some form of coherent conceptual framework. In 1978, the Financial Accounting Standards Board (FASB) of the USA issued its framework. In 1989, the International Accounting Standards Committee (IASC), the predecessor of the IASB, issued the *Framework for the Preparation and Presentation of Financial Statements*. Both belong to the family of conceptual frameworks for financial reporting that have been developed by accounting standard setters in a number of countries where accounting standard setting is carried out by a private sector body. On one level, such conceptual frameworks may be considered attempts to assemble a body of accounting theory (or interrelated concepts) as a guide to standard setting, so that standards are (as far as possible) formulated on a consistent basis and not in an ad hoc manner. On another, but complementary, level, they may be thought of as devices to confer legitimacy and authority on a private sector standard setter that lacks the legal authority of a public body. The IASB, as a private sector standard setter, shares these reasons for developing a conceptual framework.

In 2001, the EU announced its adoption of IFRSs for listed companies from 2005. Soon afterwards, the IASB and the FASB entered into a Memorandum of Understanding for the purpose of convergence and in 2004 started a joint project for convergence between the two conceptual frameworks. It was supposed to happen in different phases. The first phase involved the objectives of general purpose financial statements and the qualitative characteristics of information that are useful for making investment and other economic decisions. In September 2010, the IASB issued its revised framework: *The Conceptual Framework for Financial Reporting*.

As a result of completion of the first phase, the objectives and qualitative characteristics have now been converged with the FASB Conceptual Framework. Work on this project had stalled because the 2007/2008 financial crisis required the IASB to work on standards related to financial instruments. In the meantime, the USA still had not adopted IFRS. In 2011, the IFRS Foundation's Strategy Review revealed that the public opinion in those countries where IFRS had already been adopted, was against the privileged position of the FASB in the determination of the IASB Conceptual Framework and the IFRSs. However, most respondents had also indicated to attach great importance to the completion of the Framework. Hence, in late 2012, the IASB announced that it would resume work on its Conceptual Framework. This time, it will not be as part of a convergence project with the FASB. Although the IASB does not appear to see the need to revisit Chapters 1 and 3, at least it now recognizes that it is better to work on the Framework as a whole because its elements are interconnected. The IASB expects to issue the completed Conceptual Framework sometime in 2015.

### The Conceptual Framework for Financial Reporting (2010)

As of September 2010, the IASB Conceptual Framework consists of an introduction (remaining from the 1989 version) and four chapters:

Chapter 1. The objective of general purpose financial statements

Chapter 2. The Reporting Entity (does not yet have any content)

Chapter 3. Qualitative characteristics of useful information

Chapter 4. The Framework (1989): the remaining text

   Underlying assumption

   The elements of financial statements

   Recognition of the elements of financial statements

   Measurement of the elements of financial statements

   Concepts of capital and capital maintenance.

## The Conceptual Framework for Financial Reporting (2010): Introduction

The Conceptual Framework does not have the status of an IFRS, does not override any specific IFRS and, in case of conflict between the Framework and an IFRS, the latter prevails (Introduction: Purpose and Status). The purpose of the Conceptual Framework is stated as follows (Introduction: Purpose and Status):

1 To assist the Board of IASB in the development of future IFRSs and in its review of existing IFRSs.

2 To assist the Board of IASB in promoting harmonization of regulations, accounting standards and procedures relating to the presentation of financial statements by providing a basis for reducing the number of alternative accounting treatments permitted by FRSs.

3 To assist national standard-setting bodies in developing national standards.

4 To assist preparers of financial statements in applying FRSs and in dealing with topics that have yet to form the subject of an IFRS.

5 To assist auditors in forming an opinion as to whether financial statements conform with IFRSs.

6 To assist users of financial statements in interpreting the information contained in financial statements prepared in conformity with FRSs.

7 To provide those who are interested in the work of the IASB with information about its approach to the formulation of accounting standards.

The Conceptual Framework deals with (Introduction: Scope):

1 the objective of financial reporting

2 the qualitative characteristics of useful financial information

3 the definition, recognition and measurement of the elements from which financial statements are constructed; and

4 concepts of capital and capital maintenance.

## The Conceptual Framework for Financial Reporting (2010): Chapter 1

The 2010 Conceptual Framework states that '(t)he objective of general purpose financial reporting forms the foundation of the *Conceptual Framework*. Other aspects of the *Conceptual Framework* – a reporting entity concept, the qualitative characteristics of, and the constraint on, useful financial information, elements of financial statements, recognition, measurement, presentation and disclosure – flow logically from the objective' (OB1). It then continues: The objective of general purpose financial reporting is to provide information that is useful to existing and potential investors, lenders and other creditors in making decisions about providing resources to the entity. Those decisions involve buying, selling or holding equity and debt instruments, and providing or settling loans and other forms of credit' (OB2). Conform Decision-usefulness Theory (Staubus, 1959, 1961), OB3, states that 'existing and potential investors, lenders and other creditors need information to help them assess the prospects for future net cash inflows to the entity'. This includes information about 'the resources of the entity, the claims against the entity, and how efficiently and effectively the entity's management and governing board have discharged their responsibilities to use the entity's resources' (OB3).

The 2010 IASB Conceptual Framework then defines the primary users of general purpose financial reports 'existing and potential investors, lenders and other creditors (who) cannot require reporting entity's to provide information directly to them and must rely on general purpose financial reports for much of the information they need' (OB5). The information in general purpose financial reports includes information about economic resources and claims (i.e. the balance sheet or statement of financial position) (OB13 and OB14), changes in economic resources and claims (i.e. the income statement, the statement of comprehensive income, or the statement of financial performance) (OB14 and OB16). Financial performance is to be measured as the difference in the entity's resources (i.e. assets) and claims (i.e. liabilities) during a period on an accruals basis because this provides a better basis for assessing past and future performance than information about cash receipts and payments alone (OB17). However, financial performance does not include additional resources directly obtained from investors and creditors (OB18). Furthermore, according to OB19, financial performance includes 'the extent to which events such as changes in market prices or interests rates have increased or decreased the entity's economic resources and claims, thereby affecting the entity's ability to generate net cash inflows.' OB20 explains that a cash flow statement helps users assess the entity's ability to generate further cash flows in the future, and assess the entity's operating, financing and investing activities. Finally, OB21 indicates that it is important to be able to assess the changes in an entity's economic resources and claims that are not the consequence of financial performance. This is then the function of a statement of changes in shareholders' equity.

## ACTIVITY 9.4

What do you think is the logic according to which the rest of the IASB Conceptual Framework flows from the objective of general purpose financial reporting? As the IASB and the FASB conceptual frameworks share the same objective of general purpose financial reporting, if OB1 is correct, should we expect both frameworks to be (more or less) identical?

### Activity feedback
Although the idea expressed in OB1 is intuitively appealing, when you start thinking about the logic, it is actually not so straightforward. Unfortunately, the logic and its source have not been explained in the Framework. The objective outlined in OB2 is, in all likelihood, based on Decision-usefulness Theory (Staubus, 1959, 1961) as Staubus was involved in the development of the 1978 FASB Conceptual Framework. Decision-usefulness Theory regards assets and liabilities as net cash inflow potential and defines the qualitative characteristics of useful financial reporting information with reference to its relevance to economic decision making. One problem is that the same information is not necessarily relevant to

*(Continued)*

## ACTIVITY 9.4    *(Continued)*

economic decision making by different types of share-holders (i.e. long-term, speculative, majority or minority shareholders) or holders of debt securities or other types of debt. Short-term investors would find forward-looking information based on managers' expectations regarding future cash flows and the market value of net assets relevant to their decision whether or not to buy, hold or sell

their securities. Long-term lenders might prefer independently verifiable information based on the actual transactions and recordable events. The 1989 version of the Framework mentioned a trade-off between the qualitative characteristics of relevance and reliability. As you will see below, in the 2010 Conceptual Framework, the focus is squarely on relevance at the expense of reliability.

## The Conceptual Framework for Financial Reporting (2010): Chapter 3

Qualitative characteristics help identify the types of financial information that are likely to be most useful to existing and potential investors, lenders and other creditors for making economic decisions about the reporting entity (QC1). The 2010 Conceptual Framework states: 'If financial information is to be useful, it must be relevant and faithfully represent what it purports to represent. The usefulness of financial information is enhanced if it is comparable, verifiable, timely and understandable' (QC4).

## The fundamental qualitative characteristics

'The fundamental qualitative characteristics are *relevance* and *faithful representation*' (QC5). Applying the fundamental characteristics requires the identification of an economic phenomenon, information about which is potentially useful to users of the financial reports. It then requires identification of the type of information that would make it relevant and can be faithfully represented. Finally, determine if that information is available or can be produced (QC18).

## Relevance

This is defined as 'capable of making a difference in the decisions made by users' (QC6). 'Financial information is capable of making a difference in decisions if it has predictive value, confirmatory value or both' (QC7). Predictive value consists of the capability of being used as an input in processes or models used to predict future outcomes (QC8). Confirmatory value exists when the information provides feedback about earlier estimations. The information will either confirm or change previous estimations (QC9). 'Information is material if omitting or misstating it could influence decisions that users make on the basis of financial information about a specific reporting entity' (QC10). However, because materiality is an entity-specific aspect of relevance, it is difficult to specify a uniform quantitative threshold.

## Faithful representation

To be a perfectly faithful representation of an economic phenomenon, a depiction would be *complete*, *neutral* and *free from error* (QC12). Completeness means that the depiction will include all the information, including descriptions and explanations, necessary for a user to understand the phenomenon (QC13). Neutrality is obtained when a depiction is without bias in the selection or presentation of financial information. In other words, it is not manipulated in order to present a favourable or unfavourable depiction of an economic phenomenon (QC14). 'Faithful representation does not mean accurate in all respects. Free from error means that there are no errors or omissions in the description of the phenomenon, and the process used to produce the reported information has been selected and applied with no errors in the process' (QC15).

## Enhancing qualitative characteristics

As mentioned above, these include comparability, verifiability, timeliness and understandability. The enhancing characteristics enhance the usefulness of information that is relevant and faithfully represented, and may help decide on the best way to represent an economic phenomenon (QC19). 'Applying the enhancing qualitative characteristics is an iterative process that does not follow a prescribed order' (QC34).

**Comparability**  This relates to information of an entity that can be compared with other entities as well as with information about the same entity at another time (QC20). Interestingly, QC21 to QC25 discuss what comparability is not, such as consistency or uniformity.

**Verifiability**  This helps users to have confidence in the faithful representation of the economic phenomenon. Different knowledgeable and independent observers could reach consensus, although not necessarily agreement, about the faithful representation of a depiction (QC26). Direct verification is verification through observation. Indirect verification means checking the inputs to a model, formula or other estimation technique (QC27). When some forward-looking financial information cannot be verified indirectly, at least the underlying assumptions and estimation methods must be disclosed (QC28).

**Timeliness**  This is defined with reference to financial information being in time to be capable of influencing decisions (QC29).

**Understandability**  'Classifying, characterizing and presenting information clearly and concisely makes it understandable' (QC30). Inherently complex phenomena may not be made easy to understand, but this information must be included in the financial reports because otherwise they would be misleading (Q31). Users of financial reports are expected to have a reasonable knowledge of business and economic activities, but even well-informed users may occasionally need to seek the aid of a professional adviser (QC32).

## The cost constraint on useful financial reporting

Cost is a pervasive constraint on the information that can be provided by financial reporting (QC35). The providers of information directly bear the costs of producing the information, and the users of this information directly bear the costs of analyzing and interpreting the information (QC36). The idea is that financial reporting helps users make decisions with more confidence, capital markets become more efficient and costs of capital to become lower, which is assumed to benefit the international economy as a whole (QC37). As applying the cost constraint is inherently subjective, the IASB seeks to consider costs and benefits generally, and not in relation to individual reporting entities (QC38–QC39).

## The Conceptual Framework for Financial Reporting (2010): Chapter 4

As mentioned above, Chapter 4 contains the remaining text of the 1989 Framework. It discusses going concern as an underlying assumption, defines the elements of financial statements, discusses recognition and measurement of the elements of the financial statements and concepts of capital and capital maintenance. The IASB is currently working on revising Chapter 4.

## Underlying assumption: Going concern

'The financial statements are normally prepared on the assumption that an entity is a going concern and will continue in operation for the foreseeable future. Hence, it is assumed that the entity has neither the intention nor the need to liquidate or curtail materially the scale of its operations; if such an intention or need exists, the financial statement may have to be prepared on a different basis and, if so, the basis used is disclosed' (para. 4.1).

## The elements of financial statements

The section of the Framework concerning the elements of financial statements (paras 4.2–4.36) consists essentially of definitions of the elements of financial statements as identified by the Framework. The definitions given in this section, and especially those of assets and liabilities, are the core of the Framework as a prescriptive basis for standard setting. The section on 'Recognition of Elements' (paras 4.37–4.53) acts to reinforce this core. In particular:

1  The Framework defines income and expenses in terms of increases and decreases in economic benefits that are equated with changes in assets and liabilities.

2  The latter are defined in terms of 'resources controlled' and 'present obligations' to exclude some of the types of items that have been recognized as assets or liabilities (accruals and deferrals) in the name of 'matching' expenses and revenues.

In other words, the definitions of assets and liability are the starting point for the entire edifice, putting the focus on balance sheet items, not on profit (revenue and expense) calculation.

The elements considered to be 'directly related to the measurement of financial position' are assets, liabilities and equity, which are defined as follows (para. 4.4):

1  An asset is a resource

   **(a)** controlled by the entity

   **(b)** as a result of past events; and

   **(c)** from which future economic benefits are expected to flow to the entity.

   Recognition as an asset thus requires that all three components of the definition, (a), (b) and (c), be satisfied.

2  A liability is

   **(a)** a present obligation of the entity

   **(b)** arising out of past events

   **(c)** the settlement of which is expected to result in an outflow from the entity of resources embodying economic benefits.

Recognition as a liability thus requires that all three components of the definition, (a), (b) and (c), be satisfied.

**3** Equity is defined as the residual interest in the assets of the entity after deducting all its liabilities.

Merely satisfying these definitions does not entail recognition, since the recognition criteria must also be satisfied. In the 1989 Framework, also the principle of 'economic substance over legal form' had to be respected. For example, this principle requires non-current assets held under finance leases to be recognized by the lessee as non-current assets (with corresponding leasing liabilities), while the lessor recognizes a financial asset. In the 2010 IASB Conceptual Framework, 'substance over form' is assumed to be included in the qualitative characteristic called 'faithful representation' (BC3.26).

**Assets** The 'future economic benefit embodied in an asset' is defined as 'the potential to contribute, directly or indirectly, to the flow of cash and cash equivalents to the entity', including 'a capability to reduce cash outflows'. In case that definition should leave the status of cash itself as an asset unclear, it is stated that cash satisfies this definition, because it 'renders a service to the entity because of its command over other resources'. Assets embody future economic benefits that may flow to the entity by having one or more of the following capabilities:

- being exchanged for other assets
- being used to settle a liability
- being distributed to the entity's owners.

Cash conspicuously possesses these three capabilities, as well as that of being used singly or in combination with other assets in the production of goods and services to be sold by the entity (paras 4.8–4.10).

Neither having physical form nor being the object of a right of ownership is an essential attribute of an asset. Intangible items, such as patents and copyrights, may satisfy the definition of an asset, as may a fixed asset held under a finance lease (by virtue of which it is a resource controlled although not owned by the entity and from which future benefits are expected to flow). Moreover, knowledge obtained from development activity may meet the definition of an asset (capitalized development costs) even though neither physical form nor legal ownership is involved, provided there is de facto control such that, by keeping the knowledge secret, the entity controls the benefits that are expected to flow from it (paras 4.11–4.12).

Assets may result from various types of past transactions and other past events. Normally, these are purchase transactions and the events associated with production, but they may include donation (for example, by way of a government grant) or discovery (as in the case of mineral deposits). Expected future transactions or events do not give rise to assets; for example, a binding contract by an entity to purchase inventory does not cause the inventory in question to meet the definition of an asset of that entity until the purchase transaction that fulfils the contract has occurred. While expenditure is a common way to acquire or generate an asset, expenditure undertaken with a view to generating future economic benefits may fail to result in an asset, for example if the intended economic benefits cannot be expected or are not controlled by the entity (paras 4.13–4.14).

## ACTIVITY 9.5

Consider whether each of the following are assets, giving reasons for your answers.

1  A heap of rusty metal worth €10 as scrap but costing €20 to transport to the scrap dealer.

2  A municipal or trade union social or welfare centre outside the factory that substantially improves the overall working conditions of a firm's employees.

3  The benefits derived from next year's sales.

### Activity feedback
*None of these is an asset because it:*

*1  has no probable future benefit*

*2  is not possessed or controlled by the business*

*3  contains no earlier transaction or event.*

---

Assets are always divided into *non-current (or fixed) assets* and *current assets*. The definition of non-current assets is often misunderstood. A non-current asset is not an asset with a long life. The essential criterion is the *intention* of the owner, the intended use of the asset. A non-current asset is an asset that the firm intends to use within the business, over an extended period, in order to assist its daily operating activities. A current asset, by way of contrast, is usually defined in terms of time. A current asset is an asset likely to change its form, i.e. likely to undergo some transaction, usually within 12 months. Consider two firms, A and B. Firm A is a motor trader. It possesses some motor vehicles that it is attempting to sell, and it also possesses some desks used by the sales staff, management and so on. Firm B is a furniture dealer. It possesses some desks that it is attempting to sell and it also possesses some motor vehicles used by the sales staff and for delivery purposes. In the accounts of A, the motor vehicles are current assets and the desks are non-current assets. In the accounts of B, the motor vehicles are non-current assets and the desks are current assets. Note incidentally that a non-current asset, which, after several years' use, is about to be sold for scrap, remains in the non-current asset part of the accounts even though it is about to change its form.

These two definitions, because they are based on different criteria (one on use and one on time), are not mutually exclusive. It is possible to think of assets that do not conveniently appear to be either fixed or current; investments, for example, or goodwill.

**Liabilities** An essential characteristic of (or necessary condition for) a liability is that the entity should have a 'present obligation'. An obligation is 'a duty or responsibility to act or perform in a certain way'. The duty or responsibility may arise from the law, for example the law of contract; or it may arise from normal business practice, which leads to legitimate expectations that the entity will act or perform in a certain way (that is, a constructive obligation). An example of the latter is a constructive obligation to extend the benefits of a warranty for some period beyond the contractual warranty period, because this is an established practice (para. 4.15).

A present obligation (in the relevant sense) is not the same as a future commitment. An entity may have a commitment to purchase an asset in the future at an agreed price; however this does not entail a net outflow of resources. The commitment does not give rise to a liability, which arises only when the purchase has actually taken place and title in the asset has passed to the entity, leaving the latter with an obligation to pay for it. (In the case of a cash transaction, no liability would arise (para. 4.16).)

There are a number of ways in which a liability may be settled or discharged, which include replacement by another obligation, conversion into equity and the creditor waiving or forfeiting his rights. There are also various types of 'past transactions or past events' from which liabilities may result (paras 4.17–4.18). If a provision involves a present obligation and satisfies the rest of the definition of a liability given in the Framework, it is a liability even if the amount has to be estimated (para. 4.19). Paragraph 4.18 does not emphasize the equally important point that a provision that fails to satisfy the criterion of being an *obligation* arising from a past transaction or past event is not a liability. This point, however, was crucial in arriving at the requirements for recognition of provisions in IAS 22, *Business Combinations* (now IFRS 3), and IAS 37, *Provisions, Contingent Liabilities and Contingent Assets*.

**Equity** Paragraphs 4.20–4.23 are concerned with equity. The fact that equity is defined as a residual interest (assets minus liabilities) does not mean that it cannot be meaningfully divided into sub-classifications that are shown separately in the balance sheet. Examples are the difference among the following:

- paid-in capital (capital stock and paid-in surplus)
- reserves representing appropriations of retained earnings
- reserves representing the amounts required to be retained in order to maintain 'real' capital, that is, either real financial capital or (real) physical capital (para. 4.20).

There are various legal, tax and valuation considerations that affect equity, such as requirements for legal reserves and whether or not the entity is incorporated. It is emphasized that transfers to legal, statutory and tax reserves are appropriations of retained earnings and not expenses. (Likewise, releases from such reserves are credits to retained earnings and not income, but this is not spelled out.) The rather obvious point is made that the amount at which equity is shown in the balance sheet is not intended to be a measure of the market value of the entity, either as a going concern or in a piecemeal disposal. It is stated that the definition and treatment of equity in the Framework are appropriate for unincorporated entities, even if the legal considerations are different.

## Performance

Paragraphs 4.24–4.36 contain the section of the Framework in which definitions of the financial statement elements relating to performance are given. 'Profit is frequently used as a measure of performance or as the basis for other measures, such as return on investment and earnings per share' (para. 4.24). However, this section of the Framework does not discuss the relationship between the elements of performance and the profit measure, except to say that 'the recognition and measurement of income and expenses, and hence profit, depends in part on the concepts of capital and capital maintenance used by the entity in preparing its financial statements'. The determination of profit and related issues are discussed in a later section of the Framework (paras 4.59–4.65). The elements of income and expenses are defined as follows:

1  Income is increases in economic benefits during the accounting period in the form of inflows or enhancements of assets or decreases of liabilities that result in increases in equity, other than those relating to contributions from equity participants.

2  Expenses are decreases in economic benefits during the accounting period in the form of outflows or depletions of assets or incurrences of liabilities that result in decreases in equity, other than those relating to distributions to equity participants (para. 4.25).

These definitions identify the essential features of income and expenses but do not attempt to specify their recognition criteria (para. 4.26). The definition makes it clear that the Framework's approach treats the definitions of assets and liabilities as logically prior to those of income and expenses. This is sometimes characterized as a 'balance sheet approach' to the relationship between financial statements. This term is potentially misleading, however. The Framework's approach should certainly not be understood as implying the subordination of the income statements to the balance sheet from an *informational* perspective.

**Income**  The Framework's definition of income encompasses both revenue and gains. Revenue is described as arising in the course of the ordinary activities of an entity and includes sales, fees, interest, royalties and rent. Gains may or may not arise in the course of ordinary activities. Gains may arise on the disposal of non-current assets and also include unrealized gains, such as those arising on the revaluation of marketable securities and from increases in the carrying amount of long-term assets. Gains, when recognized in the income statements, are usually displayed separately because their economic significance tends to differ from that of revenue, and they are often reported net of related expenses (paras 4.29–4.31).

The counterpart entry corresponding to a credit for income may be to various asset accounts (not only cash or receivables) or to a liability account such as when a loan is discharged by the provision of goods or services (para. 4.32).

**Expenses**  The Framework's definition of expenses encompasses losses as well as expenses that arise in the course of the ordinary activities of the entity. Examples given of expenses that arise in the course of ordinary activities are cost of sales, wages and depreciation. They usually take the form (that is, are the accounting counterpart) of an outflow or depletion of assets such as cash and cash equivalents, inventory, property or plant and equipment (para. 4.33).

Losses represent items that may or may not arise in the course of ordinary activities. They include those that result from such disasters as fire or flood, as well as those arising on the disposal of non-current assets and also encompass unrealized losses, such as those arising from the effects of adverse currency exchange rate movements on financial assets or liabilities. Losses, when recognized in the income statement, are usually displayed separately because their economic significance tends to differ from that of other expenses and they are often reported net of related income (paras 4.34–4.35).

## Recognition of the elements of financial statements

Recognition issues are dealt with in paras 4.37–4.53. Recognition is described as 'the process of incorporating in the balance sheet or [the] income statement an item that meets the definition of an element and satisfies the criteria for recognition set out in paragraph 83'. (The statement of changes in financial position is not mentioned because its elements consist of those that are also elements of financial position or performance.) Failure to recognize *in the main financial statements* items that satisfy the relevant definition and recognition criteria is not rectified by disclosure of the accounting policies used or by use of notes or other explanatory material.

The recognition criteria, set out in para. 4.38, are that an item that meets the definition of an element should be recognized if:

1  it is probable that any future economic benefit associated with the item will flow to or from the entity

2  the item has a cost or value that can be measured with reliability.

Recognition is subject to materiality. Accounting interrelationships are also significant, since recognition in the financial statements of an item that meets the definition and recognition criteria for a particular element, for example an asset, entails the recognition of another (counterpart) element, such as income or a liability (para. 4.39). (This refers, strictly speaking, to the initial recognition of an item. However, a similar point could be made about the implications of re-measurement or valuation adjustments.)

**Probability of future economic benefit**  The concept of *probability* is used in the recognition criteria 'to refer to the degree of uncertainty [as to whether] the future economic benefits associated with the time will flow to or from the entity ... in keeping with the uncertainty that characterizes the environment in which an entity operates'. Assessments of such uncertainty are made on the basis of the evidence available when the financial statements are prepared. In regard to receivables, for example, for a large population of accounts, some statistical evidence will usually be available regarding collectibility (para. 4.40).

**Reliability of measurement**  Reliability, the second recognition criterion, was discussed earlier in the section on qualitative characteristics of financial statements. If an item does not possess a cost or value that can be measured with reliability (so that the information has that qualitative characteristic), then it is not appropriate to recognize it. However, in many cases, cost or (more particularly) value must be estimated; indeed, the use of reasonable estimates is an essential part of the financial reporting process and need not undermine reliability. In cases where an item satisfied the definition of an element but not the recognition criteria, it will not be recognized in the financial statements themselves, but its relevance is likely to require its disclosure in the notes to the financial statements or in other supplementary disclosures. This applies when the item meets the probability criterion of recognition but not the reliability criterion, but may also apply to an item that meets the definition of an element when neither recognition criterion is met. The key issue here is whether the item is considered to be relevant to the evaluation of financial position, performance or changes in financial position. An item that does not satisfy the recognition criteria for an asset or a liability at one time may do so later, if more information relevant to estimating its probability, cost or value becomes available (paras 4.41–4.43).

It is important to note that 'probable' and 'reliability' are both relative and subjective concepts. The Framework does not pretend otherwise. Professional judgement is required in the context of the particular situation in which the entity concerned operates.

**Recognition of assets**  An asset is recognized in the balance sheet when it is probable that future economic benefits will flow to the entity (as a result of its control of the asset) and the asset's cost or value can be measured reliably. When expenditure has been incurred but it is not considered probable that economic benefits will flow to the entity beyond the current accounting period, this expenditure will be recognized as an expense, not as an asset. The intention of management in undertaking the expenditure is irrelevant (paras 4.44–4.45).

**Recognition of liabilities**  A liability is recognized in the balance sheet when it is probable that an outflow of resources embodying economic benefits will result from the settlement of a present obligation and the amount of that settlement can be measured reliably. Obligations under executory contracts – that is, non-cancellable contracts that are equally proportionately unperformed (such as the amount that will be a liability when inventory ordered and awaiting delivery is received) – are not generally recognized as liabilities in the balance sheet, neither are the related assets recognized in the balance sheet. In some cases, however, recognition may be required (para. 4.46).

**Recognition of income** Recognition of income occurs simultaneously with the recognition of increases in assets or decreases in liabilities (or a combination of the two). The normal recognition procedures used in practice are applications of the Framework's recognition criteria. An example is the requirement that revenue should be earned (that is, it should be associated with a simultaneous increase in assets or decrease in liabilities). These procedures are concerned with restricting the recognition of income to items that, in effect, meet the Framework's recognition criteria of probability (a sufficient degree of certainty that an economic benefit has flowed or will flow to the entity) and reliability of measurement (paras 4.47–4.48).

**Recognition of expenses** Recognition of expenses occurs simultaneously with the recognition of an increase in liabilities or a decrease in assets (or a combination of the two). Expenses are commonly recognized in the income statement on the basis of an association (matching) between the incurrence of costs and the earning of specific items of revenue, that result directly and jointly from the same transactions or other events. An example is the matching of the cost of goods sold with the associated sales revenue. However, the Framework does not permit the application of the matching procedure to result in the recognition of items in the balance sheet that do not meet the definition of assets or liabilities (paras 4.49–4.53).

## Measurement of the elements of the financial statements

Paragraphs 4.54–4.56 deal with measurement issues, insofar as these are covered in the Framework. The treatment here is descriptive and avoids being prescriptive. Measurement is described as 'the process of determining the monetary amounts at which the elements of the financial statements are to be recognized and carried in the balance sheet and income statement'. It involves the selection of a particular basis of measurement.

Four different measurement bases are specifically mentioned and described (without any claim to exhaustiveness): historical cost, current cost (of replacement or settlement), realizable or (for liabilities) settlement value and present value. Historical cost is mentioned as the measurement basis most commonly adopted by entities in preparing their financial statements, usually in combination with other measurement bases. An example of the latter is the carrying of inventories at the lower of historical cost and net realizable value. Marketable securities may be carried at market value and pension liabilities are carried at their present value. Current cost may be used as a means of taking account of the effects of changing prices of non-monetary assets.

## Concepts of capital and capital maintenance

**Concepts of capital** The Framework identifies two main concepts of capital: the financial concept and the physical concept. The financial concept of capital may take two forms: invested money (nominal financial) capital or invested purchasing power (real financial) capital. In either case, capital is identified with the equity of the entity (in either nominal or real financial terms) and with its net assets measured in those terms. The physical concept of capital is based on the notion of the productive capacity or operating capability of the entity, as embodied in its net assets. Most entities adopt a financial concept of capital, normally (in the absence of severe inflation) nominal financial capital (paras 4.57–4.58).

**Capital maintenance and the determination of profit** Choice of a concept of capital is related to the concept of capital maintenance that is most meaningful, given the implications of the choice for profit measurement and the needs of the users of the financial statements in that regard, as follows:

- *Maintenance of nominal financial capital.* Under this concept a profit is earned only if the money amount of the net assets at the end of the period exceeds the money amount of the net assets at the beginning of the period, after excluding any distributions to, and contributions from, equity owners during the period (para. 4.59 (a)).

- *Maintenance of real financial capital.* Under this concept a profit is earned only if the money amount of the net assets at the end of the period exceeds the money amount of the net assets at the beginning of the period, restated in units of the same purchasing power, after excluding distributions to, and contributions from, owners. Normally, the units of purchasing power employed are those of the currency at the end of the period, into which the net assets at the beginning of the period are restated (para. 4.59 (a)).

- *Maintenance of physical capital.* Under this concept a profit is earned only if the operating capability embodied in the net assets at the end of the period exceeds the operating capability embodied in the net assets at the beginning of the period, after excluding distributions to, and contributions from, owners. Operating capability embodied in assets may, in principle, be measured by employing the current cost basis of measurement (para. 4.59 (b)).

The main difference among the three concepts of capital maintenance is the treatment of the effects of changes in the carrying amounts of the entity's assets and liabilities. Under nominal financial capital maintenance, increases in the money-carrying amounts of assets held over the period (to the extent that they are recognized as gains) are part of profit.

Under real financial capital maintenance, such increases are part of profit only if they are 'real' increases; that is, increases that remain after money-carrying amounts have been restated in units of the same purchasing power. The total amount of the restatement is known as a 'capital maintenance adjustment' and is transferred to a capital maintenance reserve, which is part of equity (but not of retained profits). Real financial capital maintenance may be used in conjunction with historical cost as a measurement basis but would more normally be used in conjunction with the current cost basis.

## ILLUSTRATION

Let us assume that a company begins with capital stock of €100 and cash of €100. At the beginning of the year, one item of inventory is bought for €100. The item of inventory is sold at the end of the year for €150, its replacement cost at that time is €120 and general inflation throughout the year is 10 per cent. Profit measured using each of the capital maintenance concepts mentioned earlier would be as shown:

|  | Nominal financial capital maintenance | Real financial capital maintenance | Real physical capital maintenance |
|---|---|---|---|
| Sales | € 150 | € 150 | € 150 |
| *less* Cost of sales | (100) | (100) | (120) |
| Operating profit | 50 | 50 | 30 |
| *less* Inflation adjustment | – | (10) | – |
| Total gain | € 50 | € 40 | € 30 |
| Capital maintenance adjustment | € 0 | € 10 | € 20 |

(Continued)

## ILLUSTRATION   (*Continued*)

Column 1 shows the gain after ensuring the maintenance of the stockholders' opening capital measured as a sum of money. Column 2 shows the gain after ensuring the maintenance of the stockholders' opening capital measured as a block of purchasing power. Both of these are concerned, under different definitions, with the maintenance of financial capital – in terms either of its money amount or of its general purchasing power. Column 3 shows the gain after ensuring the maintenance of the company's initial operating capacity and is therefore of a completely different nature.

Under real physical capital maintenance, changes in the money prices at current costs of assets and liabilities held over the period are considered not to affect the amount of operating capability embodied in those items and therefore the total amount of those changes is treated as a capital maintenance adjustment and excluded from profit.

Different combinations of measurement bases and capital maintenance concepts provide different accounting models, between which management should choose, taking into account relevance and reliability. Readers should be very familiar with the concepts underlying these alternatives, which have been fully discussed in Chapters 4–8.

## IAS 1, *PRESENTATION OF FINANCIAL STATEMENTS*

IAS 1, *Presentation of Financial Statements*, covers some of the topics discussed in the Framework. It was originally issued by the IASC in 1997 and adopted by the IASB in 2001. It was revised in 2003 and has subsequently been amended in 2007 and 2011. Minor amendments were made as a consequence of changes in standards in 2004, 2005, 2008, 2009 and 2010, particularly those relating to financial instruments. It is the 2011 version that we discuss here.

*Presentation of Financial Statements* represents an attempt to cover several important aspects, some of which are also covered in the Framework. As a full Standard, IAS 1 automatically takes priority over the Framework where there is any overlap or conflict. In 2010, the IASB issued a revised Conceptual Framework and a further revision is expected in 2015.

The objective of the Standard is to prescribe the basis for presentation of general purpose financial statements, in order to ensure comparability both with the entity's own financial statements of previous periods and with the financial statements of other entities. To achieve this objective, the Standard sets out overall considerations for the presentation of financial statements, guidelines for their structure and minimum requirements for the content of financial statements (para. 1).

In principle, therefore, IAS 1 applies to all aspects of all businesses. Many aspects of financial reporting are covered additionally by other more specific IASs and IFRSs, as detailed elsewhere in this volume. However, some other aspects are not further developed and IAS 1 therefore comprises the IAS GAAP in those respects. For example, disclosure of non-current assets is discussed in IAS 16, *Property Plant and Equipment* (see Chapter 13), but disclosure of current assets has no additional Standard, except for component parts such as inventories, covered by IAS 2, *Inventories* (see Chapter 17).

Broadly speaking, IAS 1 consists of two parts. Part 1 discusses a number of 'overall considerations' consisting of general principles, conventions and requirements. Much of Part 1 is a restatement of aspects of the Framework, as discussed already. Part 2 discusses in some detail the required contents of general purpose financial statements. It is worth noting that most national accounting standards operate, and are designed to operate, within the context of national legislation, especially for corporations. There is, of course, no single international company or corporation statute. To some extent, IAS 1 provides a minimal filling in of this lacuna.

Consistent with our chapter structure in this book, the first part of IAS 1 is discussed here. Part 2 is covered in Chapter 10.

## SCOPE OF IAS 1

The scope and applicability of IAS 1 is very wide. It should be applied in the presentation of all general purpose financial statements prepared and presented in accordance with International Financial Reporting Standards (IFRSs) (para. 2).

General purpose financial statements are those intended to meet the needs of users who are not in a position to demand reports tailored to meet their specific information needs. They include statements presented separately or those within another public document such as an annual report or prospectus.

IAS 1 does not apply to condensed interim financial information, but it must be applied in full to all general purpose statements as already described which claim to be in accordance with IFRSs. Not-for-profit organizations can also apply the Standard (and IFRSs generally) by amending item descriptions in the financial statements as appropriate.

IAS 1 repeats the objective of general purpose financial statements from the Framework, as being to provide information about the financial position, performance, and cash flows of an entity that is useful to a wide range of users in making economic decisions. Financial statements also show the results of management's stewardship of the resources entrusted to it. Financial statements provide information about an entity's (para. 9):

1  assets

2  liabilities

3  equity

4  income and expenses, including gains and losses

5  contributions by and distributions to owners in their capacity as owners, and

6  cash flows.

A complete set of financial statements, therefore, includes the following components (para. 10):

**(a)** a statement of financial position as at the end of the period

**(b)** a statement of profit or loss and other comprehensive income for the period

**(c)** a statement of changes in equity for the period

**(d)** a statement of cash flows for the period

**(e)** notes, comprising a summary of significant accounting policies and other explanatory information, and

**(f)** a statement of financial position as at the beginning of the earliest comparative period when an entity applies an accounting policy retrospectively or makes a retrospective restatement of items in its financial statements, or when it reclassifies items in its financial statements.

An entity may use titles for the statements other than those used in this Standard.

An entity shall present with equal prominence all of the financial statements in a complete set of financial statements. The implications of this are discussed and illustrated in more detail in Chapter 10.

IAS 1 encourages, but does not require, the additional presentation, 'outside the financial statements', of a management report about the financial performance and financial position of the enterprise, and about its environment, risks and uncertainties.

Brief suggestions as to coverage are made in paragraph 8, but none of the suggestions are mandatory. Further additional statements and reports – for example, on environmental matters – are also encouraged.

## FAIR PRESENTATION AND COMPLIANCE WITH IFRSs

The first substantive part of IAS 1 concerns the vexed question of, what in the UK is called the 'true and fair override'. The issue at stake is whether or not the detailed regulations – i.e. the IFRSs in this case – are always and automatically both necessary and sufficient conditions for the preparation of adequate financial statements, or whether some more fundamental overriding criterion – such as the provision of a true and fair view, a requirement to present fairly or a requirement not to mislead users – is, when a clash occurs, the determining requirement (hence 'overriding' the IFRSs). IAS 1 recognizes that compliance with the IFRSs may be insufficient or inadequate 'in extremely rare circumstances'.

Entities whose financial statements comply with IFRSs should make an unreserved statement of such compliance in the notes (para. 16). The appropriate application of IFRS, with additional disclosure when necessary, results, in 'virtually all circumstances', in financial statements that achieve a fair presentation (para. 17).

'In the extremely rare circumstances when management concludes that compliance with a requirement in an IFRS would be so misleading that it would conflict with the objective of financial statements set out in the Framework, the entity shall depart from that requirement set out in paragraph 20 if the relevant regulatory framework requires, or otherwise does not prohibit, such a departure' (para. 19).

When an entity departs from a requirement of a Standard or an interpretation, it shall disclose (para. 20):

**(a)** that management has concluded that the financial statements present fairly the entity's financial position, financial performance and cash flows;

**(b)** that it has complied with applicable Standards and Interpretations, except that it has departed from a particular requirement to achieve a fair presentation;

**(c)** the title of the IFRS from which the entity has departed, the nature of the departure, including the treatment that the IFRS would require, the reason why that treatment would be so misleading in the circumstances that it would conflict with the objective of financial statements set out in the Framework, and the treatment adopted; and

**(d)** for each period presented, the financial effect of the departure on each item in the financial statements that would have been reported in complying with the requirement.

The question of terminology and national positions here is both important and potentially confusing. The US requirement to present fairly in accordance with (US) GAAP means to follow GAAP, at least as far as accounting standards are concerned, although the situation is slightly less clear as regards US auditing standards. The UK requirement to give a true and fair view equally clearly means to follow standards

**TABLE 9.1  Terminology versus philosophy**

| Jurisdiction | Terminology | Overriding |
|---|---|---|
| UK | True and fair view | Yes |
| EU | True and fair view | Yes |
| USA | Fair presentation | No |
| IASB | Fair presentation | Yes |

where suitable, but to depart from them if a true and fair view requires it. The UK position in essence found its way into the EU Fourth Directive and hence, subject to varying degrees of bastardization, into other European countries. IAS 1 follows the US wording but the UK/EU philosophy. Table 9.1 makes this clear.

This is not to imply that the override is likely to be used in similar ways or in similar volumes in the various jurisdictions where it exists. We predict that its usage under the IASB will indeed be rare. But an important issue of principle is at stake. Can the qualitative characteristics required of financial reporting be ensured by compliance with a set of (static) rules, or is some professional judgement involved which may, in principle, entail departure from one or more rules?

Although no attempt to define 'fair presentation' is provided (rightly in our view), the presumption 'in virtually all circumstances' is that a fair presentation is achieved by compliance in all material respects with applicable IFRSs. A fair presentation requires (para. 17):

1 selecting and applying accounting policies in accordance with IAS 8 (described later)

2 presenting information, including accounting policies, in a manner which provides relevant, reliable, comparable and understandable information

3 providing additional disclosures when the specific requirements in IFRSs are insufficient to enable users to understand the impact of particular transactions or events on the entity's financial position and financial performance.

In extremely rare circumstances, application of a specific requirement in an International Accounting Standard might result in misleading financial statements. In such circumstances departure from the Standard is required. IASB is at pains to minimize the likelihood of this happening. The override can only be applied when following the Standard plus providing additional information would not give a fair presentation (i.e. presumably, would mislead). The existence of national regulations which conflict with IASB Standards is not an adequate reason for departing from an International Standard. IAS 1 requires in addition, as detailed earlier, if the override is employed, that full details of the departure are given in the financial statements, sufficient to enable users to make an informed judgement on whether the departure is necessary and to calculate the adjustments that would be required to comply with the Standard.

## Accounting policies

The actual process of selecting accounting policies by a particular entity was discussed in the 1997 version of IAS 1, but in 2004 was transferred to the new version of IAS 8. This is discussed below. However, IAS 1 proceeds to incorporate and discuss some, but not all, of the assumptions and qualitative characteristics of financial statements included in the 2010 IASB Conceptual Framework. The two 'underlying assumptions' in IAS 1 are going concern and the accrual basis of accounting. The going concern assumption means that it is assumed that the entity will continue in operation for the foreseeable future. Financial statements should be prepared on a going concern basis unless management either intends to liquidate the entity or to cease trading or has no realistic alternative but to do so. When management is aware, in making its assessment, of material uncertainties related to events or conditions which may cast significant doubt on the entity's ability to continue as a going concern, those uncertainties should be disclosed. When the financial statements are not prepared on a going concern basis, that fact should be disclosed, together with the basis on which the financial statements are prepared and the reason why the entity is not considered to be a going concern (para. 25). When the financial statements are prepared on the going concern basis it is not necessary to say so. Judgement, and in uncertain cases detailed investigation, may be required.

The accrual basis of accounting (except for cash flow statements) is also an automatic assumption that need not be explicitly stated (para. 27). Under the accrual basis of accounting, transactions and events are recognized when they occur (and not as cash or its equivalent is received or paid) and they are recorded in the accounting records and reported in the financial statements of the periods to which they relate.

Paragraph 28 indicates that, under the accruals basis of accounting, the elements in the financial statements must satisfy their definitions as well as their recognition criteria as set out in the Conceptual Framework.

The Framework states, however, that financial statements may include items not falling within these definitions if specific IFRSs require their recognition. Some other Standards do so require, for example with regard to the deferral of government grants (IAS 20, see Chapter 13) and the deferral of income and expenses relating to operating leases (IAS 17, Chapter 16). Although there seems to be conflict between the Framework and IAS 1 on this point, IFRSs explicitly override the Framework.

IAS 1 (para. 45) requires consistency of presentation and classification of items in the financial statement. A change in presentation and classification of items in financial statements between one period and another is permitted only when, following a significant change in the entity's operations or a review of the financial statements, another presentation or classification would be more appropriate according to the selection criteria in IAS 8 or is required by a specific IFRS.

The issue of materiality and aggregation raises some important considerations. Paragraph 29 states that each material class of similar items should be presented separately in the financial statements. Immaterial amounts should be aggregated with amounts of a similar nature or function and need not be presented separately (para. 30). In this context, information is material if its nondisclosure could influence the economic decisions of users taken on the basis of the financial statements. Materiality depends on the size and nature of the item judged in the particular circumstances of its omission. In deciding whether an item or an aggregate of items is material, the nature and the size of the item are evaluated together. Depending on the circumstances, either the nature or the size of the item could be the determining factor. For example, evidence of breaking the law causing a fine could be significant in principle, even if the amount is small. But similar items should be aggregated together however large they, or the resulting total, are in relation to the entity as a whole.

It is important that both assets and liabilities, and income and expenses, when material, are reported separately. Offsetting in either the income statement or the balance sheet, except when offsetting reflects the substance of the transaction or event, would detract from the ability of users to understand the transactions undertaken and to assess the future cash flows of the entity. Assets and liabilities, and income and expenses, should not be offset except when offsetting is required or permitted by an IFRS (para. 32).

It is often not fully appreciated that the prevention of offsetting between assets and liabilities and between income and expenses is not at all the same thing as the prevention of netting out between debits and credits in a bookkeeping sense. Receipts and payments in relation to the purchase of one asset, for example, involve the netting out of debits and credits and are not examples of offsetting as discussed in IAS 1.

It should also be noted that there are several examples where IFRSs do 'require or permit' offsetting. One such example is IAS 11 (see Chapter 17), where contract costs plus recognized profits less losses are offset against progress billings to give a net figure of amount due from customers.

Paragraph 35 states that gains and losses arising from a similar group of transactions, such as foreign exchange gains and losses, or gains and losses arising on financial instruments held for trading, may be presented on a net basis. However, if they are materials, they must be presented separately.

The 'presentation' section of IAS 1 concludes with requirements about comparative figures. Unless an IFRS permits or requires otherwise, comparative information should be disclosed in respect of the previous period for all numerical information in the financial statements. Comparative narrative and descriptive information should be included when it is relevant to an understanding of the current period's financial statements (para. 38).

Comparative information should be restated if necessary if the presentation or classification of items in the current financial statements is altered, unless it is impractical to do so, in which case the reason for not reclassifying should be disclosed together with 'the nature of the adjustments that would have been made if the amounts had been reclassified' (para. 42). Five- or ten-year summaries should logically be changed as well, although IAS 1 does not consider this point.

It should be noted that IAS 8, *Accounting Policies, Changes in Accounting Estimates and Errors*, applies if changes constitute a change in accounting policy as discussed in that Standard.

By now we have mentioned several times that financial statements serve as a means for communicating the economic health of a company to external parties. For a proper assessment of the performance and the financial status of a company, external stakeholders need a benchmark with which to compare the financial accounting information. This will be discussed and illustrated extensively in Part Four of this textbook. Data taken from the financial statements of other companies are often used for benchmarking purposes. In this respect, comparability of financial accounting information is extremely important. Comparability refers not only to inter-firm comparability, but also to the comparability over time of company data of the same enterprise. Techniques for inter-firm comparisons and within firm comparisons over time are presented in Part Four of this textbook.

As already indicated, the remainder of IAS 1 relates to the structure and content of published financial statements, which is dealt with in the next chapter.

## IAS 8, *ACCOUNTING POLICY CHANGES, CHANGES IN ESTIMATES AND ERRORS*

The objective of IAS 8 is to enhance comparability of financial statement data over time within the same firm and between firms. In order to improve comparability, IAS 8 focuses on the criteria for selecting accounting policies, the accounting treatment and disclosure of changes in accounting policies, changes in accounting estimates and errors. The purpose of the Standard is to ensure that entities prepare and present their financial statements on a consistent basis. IAS 8 shall be applied in selecting and applying accounting policies and accounting for changes in accounting policies, changes in accounting estimates and corrections of prior period errors. The tax effects of corrections of prior period errors and retrospective adjustments made to apply changes in accounting policies are accounted for and disclosed in accordance with IAS 12, *Income Taxes.*

The first part of IAS 8, which deals with accounting policies, determines first how to select and apply accounting policies (see paras 7–13). Accounting policies are defined as specific principles, bases, conventions, rules and practices adopted by an entity in preparing and presenting financial statements (para. 5). The selection process for an accounting policy starts with determining if there is a specific IFRS that deals with the transaction or event that has to be reported.

IAS 8 (para. 7) states that when an IFRS specifically applies to a transaction, other event or condition, the accounting policy or policies applied to that item shall be determined by applying the IFRS and considering the integral guidance to assist entities in applying the IFRS requirements (para. 9).

In the absence of an IFRS that specifically applies to an item in the financial statements, management shall use its judgement in developing and applying an accounting policy that results in information that is (para. 10):

- relevant to the decision-making needs of users; and reliable in that the financial statements:
  - represent faithfully the results and financial position of the entity
  - reflect the economic substance of transactions and other events, and not merely the legal form
  - are neutral, i.e. free from bias
  - are prudent
  - are complete in all material respects.

In making the judgement described in para. 10, management shall consider the following sources in descending order:

- the requirements and guidance in Standards and Interpretations of Standards, dealing with similar and related issues
- the definitions, recognition criteria and measurement concepts for assets, liabilities, income and expenses set out in the *Conceptual Framework for Financial Reporting* (para. 11).
- the most recent pronouncements of other standard-setting bodies that use a similar conceptual framework to develop accounting standards, other accounting literature and accepted industry practices, to the extent, but only to the extent, that these are consistent with the first two points of this paragraph (para. 12).

IAS 8 states explicitly that accounting policies should be applied consistently for similar transactions, other events and conditions, unless a Standard or an Interpretation specifically requires or permits categorization of items for which different policies may be appropriate. If an IFRS requires or permits such categorization, an appropriate accounting policy shall be selected and applied consistently to each category (para. 13).

## Accounting policy changes

Once an accounting policy is chosen it needs to be applied on a consistent basis over the years. Although consistency is the rule, changes in accounting policies are permitted if the change:

**(a)** is required by an IFRS, or

**(b)** results in the financial statements providing reliable and more relevant information about the effects of transactions, other events or conditions on the entity's financial position, financial performance or cash flows (para. 14).

---

### ACTIVITY 9.6

Can you think of events or elements which might induce a voluntary change in accounting policies?

*Activity feedback*
- *Company A becomes a subsidiary of company B; subsequently the accounting policies within company A should be harmonized with the accounting policies of company B.*

- *All changes between benchmark treatments and allowable treatments prescribed in the IAS/IFRS, for example a switch from capitalizing borrowing costs to expensing them, due to changes in the finance policy of a company.*

---

IAS 8 addresses changes of accounting policy arising from three sources:

**1** initial application (including early application) of an IFRS containing specific transitional provisions

**2** initial application of a IFRS which does not contain specific transitional provisions

**3** voluntary changes in accounting policy.

Policy changes under 1 should be accounted for in accordance with the specific transitional provisions of that IFRS.

A change of accounting policy under 2 or 3 should be applied retrospectively, that is applied to transactions, other events and conditions as if it had always been applied (paras 5–19). The Standard goes on to explain that retrospective application requires adjustment of the opening balance of each affected component of equity for the earliest prior period presented and the other comparative amounts disclosed for each prior period presented as if the new accounting policy had always been applied (para. 22). The Standard observes that the amount of the resulting adjustment relating to periods before those presented in the financial statements (which is made to the opening balance of each affected component of equity of the earliest prior period presented) will usually be made to retained earnings. However, it goes on to note that the adjustment may be made to another component of equity (for example, to comply with an IFRS). IAS 8 also makes clear that any other information about prior periods, such as historical summaries of financial data, should also be adjusted (para. 26).

It will frequently be straightforward to apply a change in accounting policy retrospectively. However, the Standard accepts that sometimes it may be impractical to do so. Accordingly, retrospective application of a change in accounting policy is not required to the extent that it is impracticable to determine either the period-specific effects or the cumulative effect of the change (para. 23). The concept 'impracticable' occurs also in relation to the accounting treatment of prior period errors (paras 43–48 and 50–53). As noted above, in the absence of a specifically applicable IFRS an entity may apply an accounting policy from the most recent pronouncements of another standard-setting body that uses a similar conceptual framework. The Standard makes clear that a change in accounting policy reflecting a change in such a pronouncement is a voluntary change in accounting policy which should be accounted for and disclosed as such (para. 21).

We have noticed that the IASB introduced the concept of impracticability in relation to the retrospective application of accounting policy changes. Since this concept can be used to circumvent the retrospective application of an accounting policy change, the Standard devotes a considerable amount of guidance to discussing what 'impracticable' means for these purposes, i.e. the limitations on retrospective application (paras 23–27).

The Standard states that applying a requirement is impracticable when an entity cannot apply it after making every reasonable effort to do so. It goes on to note that, for a particular prior period, it is impracticable to apply a change in an accounting policy retrospectively or to make a retrospective restatement to correct an error if:

1 the effects of the retrospective application or retrospective restatement are not determinable

2 the retrospective application or retrospective restatement requires assumptions about what management's intent would have been in that period

3 or the retrospective application or retrospective restatement requires significant estimates of amounts and it is impossible to distinguish objectively information about those estimates that:

   **(a)** provides evidence of circumstances that existed on the date(s) as at which those amounts are to be recognized, measured or disclosed

   **(b)** would have been available when the financial statements for that prior period were authorized for issue, from other information.

IAS 8 observes that it is frequently necessary to make estimates in applying an accounting policy and that estimation is inherently subjective and that estimates may be developed after the balance sheet date. But developing estimates is potentially more difficult when retrospectively applying an accounting policy or making a retrospective restatement to correct a prior period error, because of the longer period of time that might have passed since the affected transaction, other event or condition occurred.

However, the objective of estimates related to prior periods remains the same as for estimates made in the current period, namely, for the estimate to reflect the circumstances that existed when the transaction, other event or condition occurred. Hindsight should not be used when applying a new accounting policy to, or correcting amounts for, a prior period, either in making assumptions about what management's intentions would have been in a prior period or estimating the amounts recognized, measured or disclosed in a prior period. For example, if an entity corrects a prior period error in measuring financial assets previously classified as held-to-maturity investments in accordance with IAS 39, it should not change their basis of measurement for that period if management decided later not to hold them to maturity.

Therefore, retrospectively applying a new accounting policy or correcting a prior period error requires distinguishing information that:

**(a)** provides evidence of circumstances that existed on the date(s) as at which the transaction, other event or condition occurred, and

**(b)** would have been available when the financial statements for that prior period were authorized for issue from other information.

The Standard states that for some types of estimate (e.g. an estimate of fair value not based on an observable price or observable inputs) it is impracticable to distinguish these types of information. When retrospective application or retrospective restatement would require making a significant estimate for which it is impossible to distinguish these two types of information, it is impracticable to apply the new accounting policy or correct the prior period error retrospectively.

The concept of impracticability introduces limitations to the retrospective application of accounting policy changes. The future will tell us if this concept of impracticability will be used to avoid the retrospective application of accounting policy changes.

Although IAS 8 and similar standards of other GAAP systems require all these types of disclosure, we do observe in practice a difference in the quality of disclosure relating to changes in accounting policy or accounting methods. Less quality implies that external parties are hindered in comparing financial data from subsequent years or between firms. If accounting changes are used, for example, for earnings management purposes, then there is an incentive to drop the quality level of these disclosures. As disclosure requirements concerning these accounting method changes have become stricter over the years, accounting method changes are now less used for annual accounts' management purposes. The stricter disclosure requirements allow external parties to 'undo' the effect of the change and to detect the 'real' underlying economic performance.

The issue of accounting quality will be discussed further in Chapter 31.

## Changes in accounting estimates

IAS 8 defines a change in accounting estimates as an adjustment of the carrying amount of an asset or a liability, or the amount of the periodic consumption of an asset, that results from the assessment of the present status of and expected future benefits and obligations associated with assets and liabilities. Changes in accounting estimates result from new information or new developments and, accordingly, are not corrections for errors.

### ACTIVITY 9.7

Think of some balance sheet or profit and loss account elements in which estimates are needed for valuation purposes.

- inventory obsolescence
- determination of the fair value of assets
- determination of the useful life of an asset.

*Activity feedback*
*Estimates are required, for example, in the valuation of:*

- *allowances for bad debts*

*Indeed, it is difficult to think of elements that do not include estimations.*

Valuing balance sheet and profit and loss account items often involves making estimates. The use of reasonable estimates is an essential part of the preparation of financial statements. However, estimates may need to be revised over the years in light of new or changing information. The revision of an estimate does not affect the original classification of the transaction. As changes of accounting estimates imply in most circumstances elements of judgement, the IASB states explicitly in IAS 8 that the change of the estimate should not undermine the reliability of the financial statements.

IAS 8 requires that changes in estimate be accounted for prospectively; defined as recognizing the effect of the change in the accounting estimate in the current and future periods affected by the change (paras 36–38). The Standard goes on to explain that this will mean (as appropriate):

- adjusting the carrying amount of an asset, liability or item of equity in the balance sheet in the period of change
- recognizing the change by including it in profit and loss in:
  - the period of change, if it affects that period only (e.g. a change in estimate of bad debts), or
  - the period of change and future periods, if it affects both (e.g. a change in estimated useful life of a depreciable asset or the expected pattern of consumption of the economic benefits embodied in it).

## ACTIVITY 9.8

Think of an example of a change in an accounting estimate which affects only the current period. Then think of an example which might affect the current period as well as subsequent periods.

### Activity feedback

For example, a change in the estimate of the amount of bad debts affects only the current period and is therefore recognized in the current period. However, a change in the estimated useful life of or the expected pattern of consumption of the future economic benefits embodied in a depreciable asset affects depreciation expense for the remainder of the current period and for each future period during the asset's remaining useful life. In both cases, the effect of the change relating to the current period is recognized as income or expense in the current period. The effect, if any, on future periods is recognized in future periods.

An entity shall disclose the nature and amount of a change in an accounting estimate that has an effect in the current period or is expected to have an effect in future periods, except for the disclosure of the effect on future periods when it is impracticable to estimate that effect (para. 39).

Further, IAS 8 states explicitly that a change in an accounting estimate does not result from a change in the measurement basis or method applied, which is a change in an accounting policy. When it is difficult to distinguish between a change in an accounting policy and a change in an accounting estimate, the change is treated as a change in an accounting estimate, with appropriate disclosure.

Prospective recognition of the effect of a change in an accounting estimate means that the change is applied to transactions, other events and circumstances from the date of the change to estimate. A change in an accounting estimate may affect the current period only or both the current period and future periods.

So a change in an accounting estimate involves less administrative work and is somehow less visible than a change in accounting policy or method. The latter is applied retrospectively, and therefore prior year comparative data need to be restated as well. All these changes will probably catch the eye of the user of the annual accounts sooner or later. Empirical evidence exists (this will be discussed in Chapter 31) that changes in accounting estimates are now more popular for earnings management purposes than accounting policy changes as they are less costly and less visible.

## Errors

IAS 8 also deals with the treatment of prior period errors. Prior period errors are omissions from, and misstatements in, the entity's financial statements for one or more prior periods arising from a failure to use, or misuse of, reliable information that:

- was available when financial statements for those periods were authorized for issue
- could reasonably be expected to have been obtained and taken into account in the preparation and presentation of those financial statements.

Such errors include the effects of mathematical mistakes, mistakes in applying accounting policies, oversights or misinterpretations of facts, and fraud.

Paragraph 42 stipulates that the correction of the error has to be accounted for in a retrospective way in the first set of financial statements authorized for issue after their discovery, by:

- restating the comparative amounts for the prior period(s) in which the error occurred, or,
- if the error occurred before the earliest prior period presented, restating the opening balances of assets, liabilities and equity for the earliest prior period presented.

In this way the financial statements are presented as if the error had never occurred.

Also in the case of prior period errors, comparative information presented for a particular prior period need not be restated if restating the information would be impracticable (paras 43–45).

If the amount of the effect in future periods is not disclosed because estimating it is impracticable, an entity shall disclose that fact (para. 40).

Special disclosure requirements apply in relation to such prior period errors (para. 49):

**(a)** the nature of the prior period error

**(b)** for each prior period presented, to the extent practicable, the amount of the correction:

　**(i)** for each financial statement line item affected, and

　**(ii)** if IAS 33 applies to the entity, for basic and diluted earnings per share.

**(c)** the amount of the correction at the beginning of the earliest prior period presented, and

**(d)** if retrospective restatement is impracticable for a particular period, the circumstances that led to the existence of that condition and a description of how and from when the error has been corrected.

Financial statements of subsequent periods need not repeat these disclosures.

## ACTIVITY 9.9

During 20X2, company A discovered that certain products which had been sold during 20X1 were incorrectly included in inventory at 31 December 20X1 at €3250.

Company A's accounting records for 20X2 show sales of €52 000, cost of goods sold of €43 250 (including €3250 for error in opening inventory), and income taxes of €2625.

In 20X1, company A reported:

| | |
|---|---|
| Sales | 36 750 |
| Cost of goods sold | 26 750 |
| Profit from ordinary activities before income taxes | 10 000 |
| Income taxes | (3 000) |
| Net profit | 7 000 |

20X1 opening retained earnings were €10 000 and closing retained earnings were €17 000. Company A's income tax rate was 30 per cent for 20X2 and 20X1.

Show the necessary disclosures in the financial statements for the year 20X2.

### Activity feedback

Company A – an extract from the income statement

| | 20X2 | 20X1 (restated) |
|---|---|---|
| Sales | 52 000 | 36 750 |
| Cost of goods sold | 40 000 | 30 000 |
| Profit from ordinary activities before income taxes | 12 000 | 6 750 |

| | 20X2 | 20X1 (restated) |
|---|---|---|
| Income taxes | 3 600 | 2 025 |
| Net profit | 8 400 | 4 725 |

Company A

Statement of retained earnings

| | 20X2 | 20X1 (restated) |
|---|---|---|
| Opening retained earnings as previously reported | 17 000 | 10 000 |
| Correction of fundamental error (Net of income taxes of €975) (note 1) | 2 275 | – |
| Opening retained earnings as restated | 14 725 | 10 000 |
| Net profit | 8 400 | 4 725 |
| Closing retained earnings | 23 152 | 14 725 |

Extract from notes to the financial statements:

**1** Certain products that had been sold in 20X1 were incorrectly included in inventory at 31 December, 20X1 at €3250. The financial statement of 20X1 has been restated to correct this error.

Once again, we notice that the restatement is made on the judgement of the management whether or not the restatement is impracticable.

## IFRS 1, *FIRST-TIME ADOPTION OF IFRS*

When a company changes from its domestic GAAP to IFRSs, this change does not belong to the scope of IAS 8. IFRS 1, *First-time Adoption of IFRS*, provides guidance for all companies which change either compulsorily or voluntarily to IAS/IFRS Standards.

Paragraph 3 states that an entity's first IFRS financial statements are the first annual financial statements in which the entity adopts IFRSs, by an explicit and unreserved statement in those financial statements of compliance with IFRSs. Financial statements under IFRSs are an entity's first financial statements if, for example, the entity:

(a) presented its most recent previous financial statements:

(i) under national requirements that are not consistent with IFRSs in all respects

(ii) in conformity with IFRSs in all respects, except that the financial statements did not contain an explicit and unreserved statement that they complied with IFRSs

**(iii)** containing an explicit statement of compliance with some, but not all, IFRSs

**(iv)** under national requirements inconsistent with IFRSs, using some individual IFRSs to account for items which national requirements did not exist, or

**(v)** under national requirements, with a reconciliation of some amounts to the amounts determined under IFRSs.

**(b)** prepared financial statements under IFRSs for internal use only, without making them available to the entity's owners or any other external users

**(c)** prepared a reporting package under IFRSs for consolidation purposes without preparing a complete set of financial statements as defined in IAS 1, *Presentation of Financial Statements,* or

**(d)** did not present financial statements for previous periods.

If a company presents its financial figures for a particular financial year, these figures are usually accompanied by prior year figures. For the sake of comparability these figures should be prepared using the same GAAP. This implies that the prior year figures in an entity's first IFRS financial statements should also be prepared with the use of IAS/IFRS. If we apply this principle to the compulsory change to IAS/IFRS for listed companies in the EU we obtain the following situation.

The reporting date for entity A's first IFRS financial statements is 31 December 2005. If entity A decides to present comparative information in those financial statements for one year only, the date of transition to IFRSs is the beginning of business on 1 January 2004 (or, equivalently, close of business on 31 December 2003). Entity A will have presented financial statements under its previous GAAP annually to 31 December each year up to and including 31 December 2004. In this case entity A is required to apply the IFRSs effective for periods ending on 31 December 2005 in:

- preparing its opening IFRS balance sheet at 1 January 2004, and
- preparing and presenting its balance sheet for 31 December 2005 (including comparative amounts for 2004), income statement, statement of changes in equity and cash flow statement for the year to 31 December 2005 (including comparative amounts for 2004) and disclosures (including comparative information for 2004).

If a new IFRS is not yet mandatory but permits early application, entity A is permitted, but not required, to apply that IFRS in its first IFRS financial statements. For many preparers which present their first IFRS financial statements the main question is: 'Which accounting policies need to be applied for the recognition and measurement of the items of the financial statements?' The main rule is that an entity shall use the same accounting policies in its opening IFRS balance sheet and throughout all periods presented in its first IFRS financial statements. Those accounting policies shall comply with each IFRS effective at the reporting date for its first IFRS financial statements. This general rule implies that an entity shall not apply different versions of IFRSs that were effective at earlier dates.

In its opening IFRS balance sheet an entity shall (para. 10):

**(a)** recognize all assets and liabilities whose recognition is required by IFRSs

**(b)** not recognize items as assets or liabilities if IFRSs do not permit such recognition

**(c)** reclassify items that it recognized under previous GAAP as one type of asset, liability or component of equity, but are a different type of asset, liability or component of equity under IFRSs, and

**(d)** apply IFRSs in measuring all recognized assets and liabilities.

The accounting policies that an entity uses in its opening IFRS balance sheet may differ from those that it used for the same date using its previous GAAP. The resulting adjustments arise from events and transactions before the date of transition to IFRSs. Therefore, an entity shall recognize those adjustments directly in retained earnings (or, if appropriate, another category of equity) at the date of transition to IFRSs (para. 11).

In essence, companies have to use all IFRSs that are effective at reporting date for all the information included in the annual accounts. However, there are two categories of exception. First, IFRS 1 specifies a number of optional exemptions from retrospective application (paras 13–25). First-time adopters can elect to apply all, some or none of these optional exemptions. Second, IFRS 1 foresees mandatory exceptions from retrospective application.

The switch from a previous GAAP system to IFRS will have an impact on the published figures of a company. IFRS 1 requires that in the notes to the accounts the impact of the transition from the previous GAAP to IAS/IFRS on the financial position, the financial performance and the cash flow should be explained.

Observing reporting practices of companies that have switched to IAS/IFRS, we notice that there is an enormous difference with regard to the level of detail that is presented to users of financial statements in relation to the impact of the switch on a form's financial position. Some companies provide several pages of explanation with regard to the impact on the company's equity; other companies just disclose a few lines.

A number of companies divided the impact of the IAS/IFRS transition over a number of years. Some companies started complying with International Accounting Standards which have a favourable impact on equity in the financial years before the 'official' financial transition year. Compliance with International Accounting Standards that have an unfavourable impact on equity takes place in the 'official' transition year.

## SUMMARY

This chapter began with an outline of 'theories about theories' in the accounting context. We then looked at the nearest that accounting seems to have got to a generally agreed theory, as illustrated by the IASB Framework and relevant parts of IAS 1. These documents, however, seem far removed from theory in a scientific sense. We also discussed changes in accounting policies (IAS 8) and the first-time adoption of IFRS (IFRS 1).

## EXERCISES

*Suggested answers to exercises marked ✓ are to be found on our dedicated CourseMate platform for students.*

*Suggested answers to the remaining exercises are to be found on the Instructor online support resources.*

✓1    To what extent is financial reporting a suitable subject for theorizing about?

✓2    Positive research is a necessary starting point on the road to normative thinking, but it can never be enough by itself. Discuss.

3    Is the IASB Framework useful in its present form? How could it be improved?

4    Accounting standards and regulations should aim to state how to deal with all situations. Discuss.

5    Rework question 9 from Chapter 1, specifically by applying the IASB Framework. Does it alter or improve your original answer? Does IAS 1 make any difference?

# STRUCTURE OF PUBLISHED FINANCIAL STATEMENTS

# 10

## OBJECTIVES   After studying this chapter you should be able to:

- discuss the two fundamental conceptual issues concerning the presentation of information in the financial statements

- describe and apply the format and disclosure requirements of IAS 1

- describe and apply the format requirements of the EU Fourth Directive

- discuss the adequacy of the disclosure requirements of IAS 1 and the EU Fourth Directive and suggest and appraise possible alterations thereto.

## INTRODUCTION

There has been an increasing tendency over recent decades to regulate not only the contents of published financial statements, but also the precise layout and format in which those contents must be presented. Former country traditions in this respect varied considerably, as Chapter 2 should have made you expect. Traditionally, the degree of precise specification in the UK and US was low because the idea was that managers know best how to present the information that the users of their particular company's financial statements need. In countries at the other end of the spectrum, for example Japan, the formats of the financial statements, the notes to the financial statements and the supporting schedules to be submitted to the Ministry of Finance and the Tokyo Stock Exchange are standardized. Here the idea is that standardization makes information easier to find and compare.

There are two non-nationalistic influences of importance on the structure and contents of published financial statements. The first one chronologically, and in some ways the most detailed, is the Fourth Directive of the EU (Fourth Council Directive 78/660/EEC of 25 July 1978). This obviously only directly affects those countries that are members of the EU, and also those trying to join. The more recent influence, and the more general one, but becoming the more pervasive, is the IASB, as represented by IAS 1, *Presentation of Financial Statements*, issued in its current form in 2007 with further amendments in 2011.

This chapter first discusses the presentation and disclosure requirements from IAS 1. It starts with the balance sheet or statement of financial position, continues with the statement of profit or loss and other comprehensive income, moves on to the statement of changes in equity, briefly mentions the statement of cash flows which fall under IAS 7, and finishes with the notes (required by IAS 1, para. 10). IAS 1 presents (non-mandatory) illustrations of the financial statements, of which we reproduce extracts in this chapter. Note that we omit all comparatives, which of course must be included in practice, and notes.

Subsequently, it discusses the requirements under the Fourth Directive which include the balance sheet, the income statement (or profit and loss account) and the notes. However, before it turns to the financial statements, it introduces two important conceptual issues in the presentation and disclosure of a set of financial statements.

## CONCEPTUAL ISSUES IN THE PRESENTATION OF FINANCIAL STATEMENTS

Issues such as aggregation and materiality and other topics covered by IAS 1 have already been discussed in the previous chapter. Here, we briefly look at two other conceptual issues that are not explicitly discussed in the IASB Conceptual Framework, IAS 1 or the Fourth Directive, but that do find expression in the requirements. The first is the articulation of financial statements, and the second is different views on the presentation of performance and equity.

### The articulation of financial statements

As you know, the balance sheet presents the entity's financial position at a point in time. In its nature it is a stock statement because it shows the stock of asset, liability and equity line items which comprise the stock of wealth of the entity. On the other hand, the income statement, statement of changes in equity and cash flow statement present the respective flows generated by the entity during a period. If the statements have been prepared under the same set of rules, they will articulate. That is, a flow statement reconciles the difference between its corresponding account in the balance sheet at one point in time, with that in the balance sheet at the next point in time. See Table 10.1.

For example, the income statement (or statement of profit or loss) presents information about how the increase or decrease in the retained earnings account in the equity section of the balance sheet came about. The statement of changes in equity shows to

| TABLE 10.1    Stocks and flows | | |
|---|---|---|
| **Stocks in the balance sheet on 1 January** | →→ **Flows** →→ | **Stocks in the balance sheet on 31 December** |
| Cash and cash equivalents | Cash flow statement | Cash and cash equivalents |
| Retained earnings | Statement of profit or loss | Retained earnings |
| Shareholders' equity | Statement of changes in equity | Shareholders' equity |

what extent the net increase or decrease in equity was due to a change in retained earnings, gains or losses on the revaluation of property, other comprehensive income in the form of gains or losses on available for sale financial assets, or perhaps due to new share issues. Similarly, the cash flow statement shows how the change in cash came about and what part of the net cash inflow or outflow was due to operating, investing or financing cash flows. In sum, the flow statements reconcile (i.e. present the details of the changes in) certain stock accounts from one point in time to the next. Furthermore, the income statement can be reconciled with the cash flow statement by removing the accruals (or vice versa). This is what you do when you prepare a cash flow statement using the indirect method, starting with net profit and ending with net change in cash.

Most accountants think it important that the balance sheet, the income statement and the statement of changes in equity are prepared under the same set of rules so that they can be reconciled with each other and ultimately with the net cash inflow or outflow. Others believe that there is no need for articulation. As we will see below, depending on future developments, the statement of comprehensive income could represent a step towards abandoning articulation as we now know it.

## Different views on the presentation of performance and equity

Historically, accounting theorists have debated whether performance is best presented as an all-inclusive profit number or as a profit number that excludes non-recurrent and extraordinary items and the consequences of events that are outside of managers' control. Advocates of the all-inclusive approach think that it is in the owners' interests that elements of performance must not be hidden in the equity section of the balance sheet. Comprehensive income under a current values measurement system is the ultimate all-inclusive concept of performance because it includes the consequences of changes in market prices that have not been realized yet and may not be realized in the foreseeable future.

On the other hand, those who believe that performance must present only the effects of events that are under managers' control advocate presenting the other effects in equity. In other words, they do not object to presenting equity including a dirty-surplus. Currently, the statement of changes in equity presents the transfer of other comprehensive income to the retained earnings account and shows a revaluation reserve for unrealized gains or losses on property revaluations. Those who believe that comprehensive income is the best indicator of performance are likely to believe that equity must be presented on a clean-surplus basis. That is, equity must be represented by paid-in capital, paid-in surplus and retained earnings. A problem then is how to treat unrealised gains or losses under a current values measurement system.

## ACTIVITY 10.1

Do you think that performance measurement should be all-inclusive or an indication of current operating performance?

### Activity feedback

It depends on the nature of the reporting entity and its business model. In the case of a company producing goods or delivering services, it is perhaps better to use a current operating performance measure because the financing aspect is not the core of the model. However, if it is a financial services entity or an entity that invests in property, the success of the business is clearly dependent on the movements of market prices rather than a production process where assets are being converted into other goods for sale or used up to provide a service.

The introduction of the comprehensive income statement by IAS 1 in 2009 meant that the all-inclusive side was winning. However, as you will see below, the conceptual problem was the issue of recycling or not recycling other comprehensive income upon realization. To those who regard net income as the main performance measure, not recycling would mean abandoning the realization concept for the elements of other comprehensive income. To those who regard comprehensive income as the main measure of performance, recycling would mean double counting some elements of other comprehensive income upon realization. Hence, the 2011 version of IAS 1 is the consequence of an attempt to reconcile the two views as the IASB has not yet settled on a performance concept.

## STATEMENT OF FINANCIAL POSITION UNDER IAS 1

It should be noted that IAS 1 does not prescribe any particular balance sheet format. The so-called horizontal and vertical formats are equally acceptable. The descriptions used and the ordering of items may be amended according to the nature of the enterprise and its transactions, to provide information that is necessary for an overall understanding of the enterprise's financial position. For example, a financial institution amends the above descriptions in order to apply the more specific relevant requirements of financial institutions. Other amendments not prescribed by promulgated IFRSs may be necessary in other industrial or commercial situations.

However, as a minimum, the face of the balance sheet (i.e. not the notes to the balance sheet) should include separate line items that present the following amounts (para. 54):

1 property, plant and equipment
2 investment property
3 intangible assets
4 financial assets (excluding amounts shown under 5, 8 and 9)
5 investments accounted for using the equity method
6 biological assets
7 inventories
8 trade and other receivables
9 cash and cash equivalents

**10** the total of assets classified as held for sale and assets included in disposal groups classified as held for sale in accordance with IFRS 5, *Non-current Assets Held for Sale and Discontinued Operations*

**11** trade and other payables

**12** provisions

**13** financial liabilities (excluding amounts shown under 11 and 12)

**14** liabilities and assets for current tax, as defined in IAS 12, *Income Taxes*

**15** deferred tax liabilities and deferred tax assets, as defined in IAS 12

**16** liabilities included in disposal groups classified as held for sale in accordance with IFRS 5

**17** non-controlling interests, presented within equity

**18** issued capital and reserves attributable to owners of the parent.

Additional line items, headings and subtotals should be presented on the face of the balance sheet when their presentation is relevant to an understanding of the entity's financial position (para. 55). When an entity presents current and non-current assets and current and non-current liabilities, as separate classifications on the face of its balance sheet, it must not classify deferred tax assets (liabilities) as current assets (liabilities) (para. 56). Amounts included in line items in relation to IFRS 5 should not be also included elsewhere.

The necessity or otherwise of additional line items is obviously a subjective matter. Judgement on this should be based on: assessment of the nature and liquidity of assets; the function of assets within the entity; and the amounts, nature and timing of liabilities.

## The current/non-current distinction

It is usual in Europe (and required by the Fourth Directive even though not at present by IAS 1) for a balance sheet to present current and non-current assets and current and non-current liabilities as separate classifications on the face of the balance sheet. When an entity chooses not to make this analysis, assets and liabilities should still be presented broadly in order of their liquidity, although this alternative is only allowed when it would lead to information that is 'reliable and more relevant'. In such circumstances, IAS 1 does not specify 'which way up' the liquidity analysis should go. For example, it is European practice for assets to end with cash (which is required by the Directive), whereas it is North American, Japanese and Australian practice to start with cash. Whichever method of presentation is adopted, an entity should disclose the amounts included in each item that are expected to be recovered or settled before and after 12 months.

Where, as is usually the case, the current/non-current classification is followed, then IAS 1 specifies the distinctions as now described. IAS 1 deals with assets first, by defining a current asset.

An asset should be classified as a current asset when (para. 66):

**1** it expects to realize the asset, or intends to sell or consume it, in its normal operating cycle

**2** it holds the asset primarily for the purpose of trading

**3** it expects to realize the asset within 12 months after the reporting period, or

**4** the asset is cash or a cash equivalent unless the asset is restricted from being exchanged or used to settle a liability for at least 12 months after the reporting period.

All other assets should be classified as non-current assets.

This definition of a current asset requires careful consideration. Only one of the conditions needs to be met for classification as a current asset to be required. Thus, an asset which meets condition 1 in a business which has a two-year operating cycle is a current asset, even if it is not expected to be realized within 12 months.

Although the wording on the matter is perhaps not as clear as it might be, a non-current asset remains non-current throughout its useful life to the entity, as it is not held primarily for trading purposes. It does not eventually become 'current' merely because its expected disposal is within less than 12 months. The IASB definition also implies that the currently due portion of a long-term non-trading receivable is similarly not to be reclassified as current.

The classification of liabilities, when undertaken by the reporting entity, must follow a comparable distinction. A liability should be classified as current when it satisfies any of the following criteria (para. 69):

1  it is expected to be settled in the entity's normal operating cycle

2  it is held primarily for the purpose of being traded

3  it is due to be settled within 12 months after the balance sheet date

4  the entity does not have an unconditional right to defer settlement of the liability for at least 12 months after the balance sheet date.

All other liabilities shall be classified as non-current.

Again, only one of these criteria needs to apply, so a long operating cycle could lead to the classification as current liabilities of items due to be settled in more than 12 months. The 'current' (i.e. due within 12 months) portion of long-term interest-bearing liabilities is to be classified as 'current' in most cases.

It is common for loan agreements to contain clauses such that, in the event of defined undertakings by the borrower not being satisfied (e.g. maintenance of an agreed maximum leverage ratio), the liability becomes payable on demand. If this happens, then the liability would in general immediately become 'current' under IAS 1. The liability would continue to be classified as non-current, however, if the lender has agreed, before the approval of the financial statements, not to demand payment within 12 months of the balance sheet date.

## Further subclassifications

IAS 1 (para. 59) states that the use of different measurement bases for different classes of assets suggests that their nature or function differs and, therefore, that they should be presented as separate line items. It gives as an example the carrying of certain classes of property, plant and equipment at cost, and other classes at revalued amounts, under IAS 16, *Property, Plant and Equipment* (see Chapter 13).

It seems to us that the above proposition, or at least the example given, is not logical. The recording of different subsets of property, plant and machinery under different valuation bases does not necessarily suggest any difference in nature or function. Further disclosure in the notes may well be desirable, as discussed below, but that is a separate matter. A more logical example might be the different treatments allowed for investment properties (see Chapter 13), where the function of the property may affect the accounting treatment.

Further subclassifications of the line items should be presented, either on the face of the balance sheet or in the notes, classified in a manner appropriate to the enterprise's operations (para. 77). The detail provided in subclassifications, either on the face of the balance sheet or in the notes, depends on the requirements of specific IFRSs and the size, nature and function of the amounts involved (para. 78). In some cases, other IFRSs provide requirements (subject always to the materiality consideration). Tangible assets, for example, are classified by class as required by IAS 16, *Property, Plant and Equipment* (see Chapter 13), and inventories are subclassified in accordance with IAS 2, *Inventories* (see Chapter 17). Other applications will be more subjective. For example, IAS 1 states that receivables are analyzed between amounts receivable from trade customers, receivables from related parties, prepayments and other amounts, and that provisions are analyzed showing separately provisions for employee benefit costs and any other items.

## Equity

Paragraph 79 requires extensive detailed disclosure regarding owner's equity. This must be provided either on the face of the balance sheet, the statement of changes in equity or in the notes, as follows (para. 79):

**1** For each class of share capital:

    **(a)** the number of shares authorized

    **(b)** the number of shares issued and fully paid and issued but not fully paid

    **(c)** par value per share or that the shares have no par value

    **(d)** a reconciliation of the number of shares outstanding at the beginning and at the end of the period

    **(e)** the rights, preferences and restrictions attaching to that class, including restrictions on the distribution of dividends and the repayment of the capital

    **(f)** shares in the entity, held by the entity or by its subsidiaries or associates, and

    **(g)** shares reserved for issue under options and sales contracts, including the terms and amounts.

**2** A description of the nature and purpose of each reserve within equity.

Entities without share capital are required to present equivalent information showing details and movements of each category of equity interest (para. 80).

Below is an extract of the illustration of the statement of financial position provided by IAS 1. We omit all comparatives, which of course must be included in practice, and notes.

### XYZ Group – Statement of financial position as at 31 December 20X7

*(in thousands of currency units) as at 31 December 20X7*

| | |
|---|---:|
| **ASSETS** | |
| **Non-current assets** | |
|     Property, plant and equipment | 350 700 |
|     Goodwill | 80 800 |
|     Other intangible assets | 227 470 |
|     Investments in associates | 100 150 |
|     Investments in equity instruments | 142 500 |
| | 901 620 |
| **Current assets** | |
| Inventories | 135 230 |
| Trade receivables | 91 600 |

*(in thousands of currency units) as at 31 December 20X7*

| | |
|---|---|
| Other current assets | 25 650 |
| Cash and cash equivalents | 312 400 |
| | 564 880 |
| Total assets | 1 466 500 |

**EQUITY AND LIABILITIES**

Equity attributable to the owners of the parent

| | |
|---|---|
| Share capital | 650 000 |
| Retained earnings | 243 500 |
| Other components of equity | 10 200 |
| | 903 700 |
| Non-controlling interests | 70 050 |
| Total equity | 973 750 |

Non-current liabilities

| | |
|---|---|
| Long-term borrowings | 120 000 |
| Deferred tax | 22 800 |
| Long-term provisions | 28 850 |
| Total non-current liabilities | 177 650 |

Current liabilities

| | |
|---|---|
| Trade and other payables | 115 100 |
| Short-term borrowings | 150 000 |
| Current portion of long-term borrowings | 10 000 |
| Current tax payable | 35 000 |
| Short-term provisions | 5 000 |
| Total current liabilities | 315 100 |
| Total liabilities | 492 750 |
| Total equity and liabilities | 1 466 500 |

*Source:* adapted from IAS 1's illustrative presentation of financial statements (Red Book, Part B, 2013).

## STATEMENT OF PROFIT OR LOSS AND OTHER COMPREHENSIVE INCOME UNDER IAS 1

The requirement to report comprehensive income, mandatory from 1 January 2009, has made major changes regarding the reporting of performance over the period (and the corresponding comparatives). In 2011, the IAS 1 requirements regarding presentation were amended again to further specify the separate disclosure of reclassification adjustments relating to the components of other comprehensive income.

The statement of profit or loss and other comprehensive income (or statement of comprehensive income) shall present profit or loss, total other comprehensive income and comprehensive income for the period (para. 81A). Although the IASB preferred a single statement of comprehensive income, the comments to the Exposure Draft made it clear that many did not agree. 'They argued that there would be undue focus on the bottom line in the single statement' (BC 52). Hence IAS 1 requires that an entity shall present all items of income and expense recognized in a period:

(a) in a single statement of profit or loss and other comprehensive income, or

(b) in two statements: a separate profit or loss statement (separate income statement); and a second statement beginning with profit or loss and displaying components of other comprehensive income (separate comprehensive income statement).

## Information to be presented in the profit or loss section or the statement of profit or loss

In addition to items required by other IFRSs, the profit or loss section or the statement of profit or loss shall include line items that present the following amounts for the period (para. 82):

(a) revenue

   (aa) gains and losses arising from the derecognition of financial assets at amortized cost

(b) finance costs

(c) share of the profit or loss of associates and joint ventures accounted for using the equity method

   (ca) if a financial asset is reclassified so that it is measured at fair value, any gain or loss arising from a difference between the previous carrying amount and its fair value at the reclassification date (as defined in IFRS 9)

(d) tax expense

(e) a single amount for the total of discontinued operations (see IFRS 5).

An entity shall recognize all items of income and expense in a period in profit or loss unless an IFRS requires or permits otherwise (para. 88). Some IFRSs specify circumstances where an entity recognizes particular items outside profit or loss in the current period. For example, IAS 8 specifies the correction of errors and the effect of changes in accounting policies (IAS 1, para. 89).

## Information to be presented in the other comprehensive income section

Paragraph 82A states that the other comprehensive income section shall present line items for amounts of other comprehensive income in the period, classified by nature (including share of the other comprehensive income of associates and joint ventures accounted for using the equity method) and grouped into those that, in accordance with other IFRSs:

(a) will not be reclassified subsequently to profit or loss, and

(b) will be reclassified subsequently to profit or loss when specific conditions are met.

An entity shall disclose the amount of income tax relating to each component of other comprehensive income, including reclassification adjustments, either in the statement of profit or loss and other comprehensive income or in the notes (para. 90). An entity may present items of other comprehensive income either (a) net of related tax effects, or (b) before related tax effects with one amount showing the aggregate amount of tax relating to these items (para. 92). If an entity selects alternative (b), it must show the allocation of the tax between items that will not be reclassified (recycled) to profit or loss and items that may subsequently be reclassified to the profit or loss section. This is the option shown in the illustration below.

## Information on allocations of profit or loss and of total comprehensive income

Furthermore, an entity shall disclose the following items in addition to the profit or loss and other comprehensive income sections, as allocation of profit or loss and other comprehensive income for the period (para. 81B):

**(a)** profit or loss for the period attributable to:

   **(i)** non-controlling interests, and

   **(ii)** owners of the parent.

**(b)** total comprehensive income for the period attributable to:

   **(i)** non-controlling interests, and

   **(ii)** owners of the parent.

If an entity chooses to present two separate statements it must present each allocation in the corresponding statement. As you will see below, this requirement is also reflected in the statement of changes in equity. It stems from the view that the controlling shareholders are the owners of the consolidated entity. On this view the minority shareholders are treated, for accounting purposes, as liability holders. This view on the reporting entity is based on Proprietary Theory, which will be briefly explained in the next chapter in relation to corporate governance. An alternative treatment would be not to make such a sharp distinction between controlling and minority shareholders, but to treat holders of equity securities and debt securities as providers of long-term funding, which differ in terms of the seniority of their claims. This view of the reporting entity is based on the Entity Theory and results in financial statement requirements such as those by the Fourth Directive, shown later in this chapter.

An entity is required to present additional line items, headings and subtotals in the statement(s) presenting profit or loss and other comprehensive income, when such presentation is relevant to an understanding of the entity's financial performance (para. 85).

## Reclassification (recycling) of components of other comprehensive income

An entity shall disclose reclassification adjustments relating to components of other comprehensive income (para. 92). These reclassification adjustments may be presented in the statement(s) of profit or loss and other comprehensive income or in the notes. If they are presented in the notes, the items of other comprehensive income must be presented after any related reclassification adjustments (para. 94). Suppose that an amount was recognized as an unrealized in gain in other comprehensive income in one period, and it becomes a realized gain in the next. If it is an item that needs to be reclassified into profit or loss, it needs to be deducted from other comprehensive income in the second period so as to avoid including it in comprehensive income twice (para. 93).

Although the IASB fully embraced comprehensive income in 2009, as the quick revision in 2011 indicates, it is a somewhat controversial concept. The reason is that there are two ways to look at total comprehensive income. One can either regard comprehensive as the main performance concept, in which case profit or loss (i.e. realized net income) becomes a secondary measure of performance. Proponents of this approach do not object to abandoning the realization convention and the articulation of financial statements. Hence, they regard the reclassification of components of other comprehensive income to profit or loss upon their realization into cash as double counting these components. Others regard realized profit or loss as the main performance measure, to which the components of other comprehensive income provide additional information. Proponents of this view, which Cearns *et al.* (1999) called 'the holding tank approach' attach great importance to the realization convention and the articulation of financial statements because this 'anchors' profit or loss to net cash inflow or outflow via accruals. Therefore, they require components of other comprehensive income to be reclassified into the profit or loss section in the period that they are realized (recycling). The comprehensive income statement under IAS 1 is not fully based on either approach. This is because some IFRSs require recycling (e.g., unrealized gains or losses on available-for-sale financial assets under IAS 39 *Financial Instruments: Recognition and Measurement*) and others explicitly forbid it (e.g., unrealized gains or losses on investments in equity instruments under IFRS 9, *Financial Instruments*). Another example is IAS 16, *Property, Plant and Equipment*, which requires in para. 41 that a transfer from revaluation surplus to retained earnings, on realization, 'is not made through the profit or loss' (see Chapter 13). Many people have asked the IASB to clarify the theoretical (or conceptual) basis on which some components of other comprehensive income may be recycled and others may not be recycled. However, the IASB would first need to decide which it chooses as the main performance concept.

## Other requirements related to the presentation of performance

Unlike previously in IAS 1, there is no longer a requirement to present the result of operating activities because IAS 1 does not define 'operating activities'. Presenting operating results is not expressly forbidden. However, an entity shall not present any items of income or expense as extraordinary items, in the statement(s) presenting profit or loss and other comprehensive income or in the notes (para. 87). It is important to note that no line item for 'extraordinary items' is allowed. This is the result of an amendment in 2002, and contrasts with the requirements of the Fourth Directive. The reasons for the amendment are twofold. First, '(t)he Board decided that items treated as extraordinary result from the normal business risks faced by an entity' (BC 63) and second, the Board decided that the distinction between ordinary and extraordinary was too arbitrary (BC 64). IAS 33, *Earnings per Share*, requires the disclosure of earnings per share data on the face of the statement of profit or loss (see Chapter 25).

IAS 1 explicitly accepts that considerations of materiality and the nature of an entity's operations may require addition to, deletions from, or amendments of descriptions within, the list. The ordering of items may be changed from that given 'when this is necessary to explain the elements of performance' (which seems likely to occur only very rarely).

Finally, an entity should present, either on the face of the income statement which is encouraged but not obligatory, or in the notes to the income statement – an analysis of expenses using a classification based on either the nature of expenses or their function within the entity (para. 99). Entity's may choose because one or the other is more prevalent in certain industries and countries. However, an entity classifying expenses by function shall disclose additional information on the nature of expenses, including depreciation, amortization and employee benefits expenses (para. 104). The argument is that an analysis by nature is useful in predicting future cash flows (para. 105).

Below are two illustrations adapted from the (non-mandatory) illustrations presented by IAS 1. We omit all comparatives, which of course must be included in practice, and notes. The first illustrates a single statement of profit or loss and other comprehensive income. The profit or loss part analyzes expenses by function, and the other comprehensive income part is based on application of IAS 39 and includes tax. The second is an illustration of a separate statement of profit or loss, a separate comprehensive income statement based on application of IFRS 9 which shows tax separately in a note.

### XYZ Group – Statement of profit or loss and other comprehensive income
### for the year ended 31 December 20X7
### (analysis by function, application of IAS 39, and OCI including tax)

|  | (in thousands of currency units) 20X7 |
|---|---|
| Revenue | 390 000 |
| Cost of sales | (245 000) |
| Gross profit | 145 000 |
| Other income | 20 667 |
| Distribution costs | (9 000) |
| Administrative expenses | (20 000) |
| Other expenses | (2 100) |
| Finance costs | (8 000) |
| Share of profit of associates | 35 100 |
| Profit before tax | 161 667 |
| Income tax expense | (40 417) |
| Profit for the year from continuing operations | 121 250 |
| Loss for the year from discontinued operations | – |
| PROFIT FOR THE YEAR | 121 250 |
| Other comprehensive income: |  |
| Items that will not be reclassified to profit or loss |  |
| Gains on property revaluation | 933 |
| Remeasurements of defined benefit pension plans | (667) |
| Share of gain (loss) on property revaluation of associates | 400 |
| Income tax relating to items that will not be reclassified* | (166) |
|  | 500 |
| Items that may be reclassified subsequently to profit and loss |  |
| Exchange differences on translating foreign operations | 5 334 |
| Available-for-sale financial assets** | (24 000) |
| Cash flow hedges | (667) |
| Income tax relating to items that may be reclassified*** | 4 833 |
|  | (14 500) |

*(in thousands of currency units) 20X7*

| | |
|---|---:|
| Other comprehensive income for the year, net of tax | (14 000) |
| TOTAL COMPREHENSIVE INCOME FOR THE YEAR | 107 250 |
| Profit attributable to: | |
| Owners of the parent | 97 000 |
| Non-controlling interests | 24 250 |
| | 121 250 |
| Total comprehensive income attributable to: | |
| Owners of the parent | 85 800 |
| Non-controlling interests | 21 450 |
| | 107 250 |
| Earnings per share (in currency units): | |
| Basic and diluted | 0.46 |

*As a consequence, if IFRS 9 is applied, income tax relating to items that will not be reclassified will amount to 5 834 000 currency units.

**If IFRS 9 is applied, the unrealized loss on available-for-sale financial assets will have to be presented under items that will not be reclassified as profit or loss.

***As a consequence, if IFRS 9 is applied, income tax relating to items that may be reclassified will amount to −1 167 000 currency units.

*Source:* adapted from IAS 1's illustrative presentation of financial statements (Red Book, Part B, 2013).

### XYZ Group – Statement of profit or loss for the year ended 31 December 20X7 (analysis by nature)

*Statement of profit or loss (in thousands of currency units)*

| | |
|---|---:|
| Revenue | 390 000 |
| Other income | 20 667 |
| Changes in inventories of finished goods and works in progress | (115 100) |
| Work performed by the entity and capitalized | 16 000 |
| Raw material and consumables used | (96 000) |
| Employee benefits expense | (45 000) |
| Depreciation and amortization expense | (19 000) |
| Impairment of property, plant and equipment | (4000) |
| Other expenses | (6 000) |
| Finance costs | (15 000) |
| Share of profit of associates | 35 100 |
| Profit before tax | 161 667 |
| Income tax expense | (40 417) |
| Profit for the year from continuing operations | 121 250 |
| Loss for the year from discontinued operations | – |
| PROFIT FOR THE YEAR | 121 250 |
| Profit attributable to: | |
| Owners of the parent | 97 000 |
| Non-controlling interests | 24 250 |
| | 121 250 |
| Earnings per share (in current units): | |
| Basic and diluted | 0.46 |

*Source:* adapted from IAS 1's illustrative presentation of financial statements (Red Book, Part B, 2013).

### XYZ Group – Separate statement of comprehensive income for the year ended 31 December 20X7
### *(application of IFRS 9, OCI excluding tax)*

*(in thousands of currency units)*

| | |
|---|---:|
| PROFIT FOR THE YEAR | 121 250 |
| Other comprehensive income: | |
| Items that will not be reclassified to profit or loss | |
| Gains on property revaluation | 600 |
| Investments in equity instruments | (18 000) |
| Remeasurements of defined benefit pension plans | (500) |
| Share of gain (loss) on property revaluation of associates | 400 |
| | 17 500 |
| Items that may be reclassified subsequently to profit and loss | |
| Exchange differences on translating foreign operations | 4 000 |
| Cash flow hedges | (500) |
| | (3 500) |
| Other comprehensive income for the year, net of tax* | (14 000) |
| TOTAL COMPREHENSIVE INCOME FOR THE YEAR | 107 250 |
| | |
| Total comprehensive income attributable to: | |
| Owners of the parent | 85 800 |
| Non-controlling interests | 21 450 |
| | 107 250 |

*The income tax related to each component of other comprehensive income is disclosed in the notes.

*Source:* adapted from IAS 1's illustrative presentation of financial statements (Red Book, Part B, 2013).

### XYZ Group – Disclosure of tax effects relating to each component of other comprehensive income – Notes – Year ended 31 December 20X7

*(in thousands of currency units) 20X7*

| | Before-tax amount | Tax (expense) benefit | Net-of-tax amount |
|---|---:|---:|---:|
| Exchange differences on translating foreign operations | 5 334 | (1 334) | 4 000 |
| Available-for-sale financial assets | (24 000) | 6 000 | (18 000) |
| Cash flow hedges | (667) | 167 | (500) |
| Gains on property revaluation | 933 | (333) | 600 |
| Actuarial gains (losses) on defined benefit pension plans | (667) | 167 | (500) |
| Share of other comprehensive income of associates | 400 | | 400 |
| Other comprehensive income | (18 667) | 4 667 | (14 000) |

*Source:* adapted from IAS 1's illustrative presentation of financial statements (Red Book, Part B, 2013).

## STATEMENT OF CHANGES IN EQUITY UNDER IAS 1

An entity shall present a statement of changes in equity (para. 10) showing in the statement (para. 106):

total comprehensive income for the period, showing separately the total amounts attributable to owners of the parent and to non-controlling interests:

- for each component of equity, the effects of retrospective application or retrospective restatement recognized in accordance with IAS 8 (i.e., the effects of the correction of errors and changes in accounting policies), and
- for each component of equity, a reconciliation between the carrying amount at the beginning and the end of the period, separately disclosing changes resulting from:

  **(i)** profit or loss

  **(ii)** each item of other comprehensive income, and

  **(iii)** transactions with owners in their capacity as owners, showing separately contributions by and distributions to owners and changes in ownership interests in subsidiaries that do not result in a loss of control.

An entity shall present, either in the statement of changes in equity or in the notes, the following:

an analysis of other comprehensive income by item (para. 106A);
the amount of dividends recognized as distributions to owners during the period, and the related amount of dividends per share (para. 107).

### XYZ Group – Statement of changes in equity for the year ended 31 December 20X7

*(in thousands of currency units)*

|  | Share capital | Retained earnings | Translation of foreign operations | Investments in equity instruments | Cash flow hedges | Revaluation surplus | Total | Minority interest | Total equity |
|---|---|---|---|---|---|---|---|---|---|
| Balance at 1 January 20X7 | 600 000 | 161 700 | 2 400 | 17 600 | (400) | 1 600 | 782 900 | 48 600 | 831 500 |
| Issue of share capital | 50 000 |  |  |  |  |  | 50 000 |  | 50 000 |
| Dividends |  | (15 000) |  |  |  |  | (15 000) |  | (15 000) |
| Total comprehensive income for the year |  | 96 900 | 3 200 | (14 400) | (400) | 800 | 85 800 | 21 450 | 107 250 |
| Transfer to retained earnings |  | 200 |  |  |  | (200) |  |  |  |
| Bal. at 31 December 20X7 | 650 000 | 243 500 | 5 600 | 3 200 | (800) | 2 200 | 903 700 | 70 050 | 973 750 |

*Source:* adapted from IAS 1's illustrative presentation of financial statements (Red Book, Part B, 2013).

## STATEMENT OF CASH FLOWS UNDER IAS 1

The widespread inclusion of cash flow statements in annual financial reporting packages is a relatively recent phenomenon in some countries. There was no mention at all in the EU Directives of the possibility or need to provide such statements. This formal regulatory position as regards the reporting of cash flows may seem rather surprising given the demonstrable importance of cash availability and cash flows in the management of an entity. This is presumably because at the time of the creation of the directives there was no general practice of any such thing in the major countries involved. The effect was that when national governments came to enact national legislation derived from the directives, there was usually still no mention of any such statement.

Nevertheless the rise of the cash flow statement as a necessary part of a comprehensive reporting package has been rapid. Something like it became a standard requirement in the UK in 1975, in IASs in 1977 and eventually in German law, for listed companies, in 1998. There have been a number of developments in the format – and, indeed, in the underlying principles – of such statements and there have been two different versions of an International Accounting Standard in the area, IAS 7. This is dealt with in full in Chapter 24.

## NOTES TO THE FINANCIAL STATEMENTS UNDER IAS 1

In one sense, the notes to the financial statements are 'where everything else goes'. IAS 1 summarizes the functions of the notes as being to (para. 112):

1 Present information about the basis of preparation of the financial statements and the specific accounting policies selected and applied for significant transactions and events.

2 Disclose the information required by IFRSs that is not presented elsewhere in the financial statements.

3 Provide additional information which is not presented on the face of the financial statements but that is relevant to an understanding of those statements.

Notes to the financial statements should be presented in a systematic manner. Each item on the face of the balance sheet, income statement and cash flow statement should be cross-referenced to any related information in the notes (para. 113).

The Standard suggests that notes 'are normally' presented in the following order (para. 114):

1 a statement of compliance with IFRSs

2 a summary of significant accounting policies applied

3 supporting information for items presented on the face of the balance sheet, income statement, statement of changes in equity and cash flow statement, in the order in which each statement and each line item is presented

4 other disclosures, including:

   (a) contingent liabilities (see IAS 37, Chapter 20) and unrecognized contractual commitments

   (b) non-financial disclosures, such as the entity's financial risk management objectives and policies (see IFRS 7, Chapter 18).

An entity must disclose the following:

- *In the summary of significant accounting policies* – the measurement basis or bases used in preparing the financial statements and the other accounting policies used that are relevant to an understanding of the financial statements (para. 117).

- *In the summary of significant accounting policies or other notes* – the judgements, apart from those involving estimations (see below), management has made in the process of applying the entity's accounting policies that have the most significant effect on the amounts recognized in the financial statements (para. 122).

- *In the notes* – information about the key assumptions concerning the future, and other key sources of estimation uncertainty at the balance sheet date, that have a significant risk of causing a material adjustment to the carrying amounts of assets and liabilities within the next financial year. In respect of those assets and liabilities, the notes shall include details of their nature and their carrying amount as at the balance sheet date (para. 125).

- *In the notes* – the amount of dividends proposed or declared before the financial statements were authorized for issue but not recognized as a distribution to equity holders during the period, and the related amount per share; and the amount of any cumulative preference dividends not recognized (para. 137).

- *In information published with the financial statements (if not disclosed elsewhere):*
  - the domicile and legal form of the entity, its country of incorporation, and the address of its registered office (or principal place of business, if different from the registered office)
  - a description of the nature of the entity's operations and its principal activities
  - the name of the parent and the ultimate parent of the group
  - if it is a limited life entity, information regarding the length of its life (para. 138).

An entity shall disclose information that enables users of its financial statements to evaluate the entity's objectives, policies and processes for managing capital (para. 134). Therefore, to comply with para. 134, the entity must disclose the following:

1 Qualitative information about its objectives, policies and processes for managing capital, including (but not limited to):

  **(a)** a description of what it manages as capital

  **(b)** when an entity is subject to externally imposed capital requirements, the nature of those requirements and how those requirements are incorporated into the management of capital

  **(c)** how it is meeting its objectives for managing capital.

2 Summary quantitative data about what it manages as capital. Some entities regard some financial liabilities (e.g. some forms of subordinated debt) as part of capital; other entities regard capital as excluding some components of equity (e.g. components arising from cash flow hedges).

3 Any changes in items 1 and 2 from the previous period.

4 Whether, during the period, it complied with any externally imposed capital requirements to which it is subject.

5 When the entity has not complied with such externally imposed capital requirements, the consequences of such non-compliance.

These disclosures shall be based on the information provided internally to the entity's key management personnel.

Recent practical examples of the major statements are given in Appendix II to Chapter 32, pages 826–833.

## THE BALANCE SHEET UNDER THE FOURTH DIRECTIVE

The Fourth Directive sets out considerably more detail in its specifications regarding balance sheets. It requires that all Member States should prescribe one or both of the layouts specified by its Articles 9 and 10. Article 9, reproduced in Table 10.2, gives a 'horizontal' format with the debits on one side and the credits on the other, following the general continental European tradition. Article 10, reproduced in Table 10.3, gives a 'vertical' format of the type more traditional in the UK. Companies are required to show the items in these tables in the order specified, except that the headings preceded by Arabic numbers may be combined or taken to the notes.

In the EU, companies that fall below a given size limit, which is updated as circumstances change, may be permitted by the laws of Member States to produce abridged accounts. As far as the balance sheet is concerned, these would consist of only those items preceded by letters and roman numerals in Table 10.2 and Table 10.3.

## TABLE 10.2 Fourth Directive: Horizontal balance sheet format

*Assets*

A. **Subscribed capital unpaid**
B. **Formation expenses**
C. **Fixed assets**
   I. *Intangible assets*
     1. Costs of research and development
     2. Concessions, patents, licences, trademarks and similar rights and assets
     3. Goodwill, to the extent that it was acquired for valuable consideration
     4. Payments on account.
   II. *Tangible assets*
     1. Land and buildings
     2. Plant and machinery
     3. Other fixtures and fittings, tools and equipment
     4. Payments on account and tangible assets in course of construction.
   III. *Financial assets*
     1. Shares in affiliated undertakings
     2. Loans in affiliated undertakings
     3. Participating interests
     4. Loans to undertakings with which the company is linked by virtue of participating interests
     5. Investments held as fixed assets
     6. Other loans
     7. Own shares.
D. **Current assets**
   I. *Stocks*
     1. Raw materials and consumables
     2. Work in progress
     3. Finished goods and goods for resale
     4. Payments on account.
   II. *Debtors*
   (Amounts becoming due and payable after more than one year must be shown separately for each item.)
     1. Trade debtors
     2. Amounts owed by affiliated undertakings

*(Continued)*

## TABLE 10.2    (*Continued*)

      3. Amounts owed by undertakings with which the company is linked by virtue of participating interests
      4. Other debtors
      5. Subscribed capital called but not paid
      6. Prepayments and accrued income.
  III. *Investments*
      1. Shares in affiliated undertakings
      2. Own shares
      3. Other investments.
  IV. *Cash at bank and in hand*
**E. Prepayments and accrued income**
**F. Loss for the financial year**

*Liabilities*

**A. Capital and reserves**
  I. *Subscribed capital*
  II. *Share premium account*
  III. *Revaluation reserve*
  IV. *Reserves*
      1. Legal reserve
      2. Reserve for own shares
      3. Reserves provided for by the articles of association
      4. Other reserves.
  V. *Profit or loss brought forward*
  VI. *Profit or loss for the financial year*
**B. Provisions for liabilities and charges**
      1. Provisions for pensions and similar obligations
      2. Provisions for taxation
      3. Other provisions.
**C. Creditors**
**(Amounts becoming due and payable within one year, and amounts becoming due and payable after more than one year, must be shown separately for each item and for the aggregate of these items.)**
      1. Debenture loans, showing convertible loans separately
      2. Amounts owed to credit institutions
      3. Payments received on account of orders insofar as they are now shown separately as deductions from stocks
      4. Trade creditors
      5. Bills of exchange payable
      6. Amounts owed to affiliated undertakings
      7. Amounts owed to undertakings with which the company is linked by virtue of participating interests
      8. Other creditors including tax and social security
      9. Accruals and deferred income.
**D. Accruals and deferred income**
**E. Profit for the financial year**
    a. share of the profit or loss of associates and joint ventures accounted for using the equity method
    b. tax expense
    c. a single amount comprising the total of:
      i. the post-tax profit or loss of discontinued operations, and
      ii. the post-tax gain or loss recognized on the measurement to fair value less costs to sell or on the disposal of the assets or disposal group(s) constituting the discontinued operation.
    d. profit or loss

## TABLE 10.3   Fourth Directive: Vertical balance sheet format

**A. Subscribed capital unpaid**
**B. Formation expenses**
**C. Fixed assets**
  I. *Intangible assets*
    1. Costs of research and development
    2. Concessions, patents, licences, trademarks and similar rights and assets
    3. Goodwill, to the extent that it was acquired for valuable consideration
    4. Payments on account.
  II. *Tangible assets*
    1. Land and buildings
    2. Plant and machinery
    3. Other fixtures and fittings, tools and equipment
    4. Payments on account and tangible assets in course of construction.
  III. *Financial assets*
    1. Shares in affiliated undertakings
    2. Loans to affiliated undertakings
    3. Participating interests
    4. Loans to undertakings with which the company is linked by virtue of participating interests
    5. Investments held as fixed assets
    6. Other loans
    7. Own shares.
**D. Current assets**
  I. *Stocks*
    1. Raw materials and consumables
    2. Work in progress
    3. Finished goods and goods for resale
    4. Payments on account.
  II. *Debtors*
    (Amounts becoming due and payable after more than one year must be shown separately for each item.)
    1. Trade debtors
    2. Amounts owed by affiliated undertakings
    3. Amounts owed by undertakings with which the company is linked by virtue of participating interests
    4. Other debtors
    5. Subscribed capital called but not paid
    6. Prepayments and accrued income.
  III. *Investments*
    1. Shares in affiliated undertakings
    2. Own shares
    3. Other investments.
  IV. *Cash at bank and in hand*
**E. Prepayments and accrued income**
**F. Creditors: amounts becoming due and payable within one year**
    1. Debenture loans, showing convertible loans separately
    2. Amounts owed to credit institutions
    3. Payments received on account of orders insofar as they are not shown separately as deductions from stocks
    4. Trade creditors
    5. Bills of exchange payable
    6. Amounts owed to affiliated undertakings

*(Continued)*

## TABLE 10.3    *(Continued)*

    7.  Amounts owed to undertakings with which the company is linked by virtue of participating interests

    8.  Other creditors including tax and social security

    9.  Accrual and deferred income.

**G.  Net current assets/liabilities**

**H.  Total assets less current liabilities**

**I.  Creditors: amounts becoming due and payable after more than one year**

    1.  Debenture loans, showing convertible loans separately

    2.  Amounts owed to credit institutions

    3.  Payments received on account of orders in so far as they are not shown separately as deductions from stocks

    4.  Trade creditors

    5.  Bills of exchange payable

    6.  Amounts owed to affiliated undertakings

    7.  Amounts owed to undertakings with which the company is linked by virtue of participating interests

    8.  Other creditors including tax and social security

    9.  Accruals and deferred income.

**J.  Provisions for liabilities and charges**

    1.  Provisions for pensions and similar obligations

    2.  Provisions for taxation

    3.  Other provisions

**K.  Accruals and deferred income**

**L.  Capital and reserves**

    I.  *Subscribed capital*

    II.  *Share premium account*

    III.  *Revaluation reserve*

    IV.  *Reserves*

        1.  Legal reserve

        2.  Reserve for own shares

        3.  Reserves provided for by the articles of association

        4.  Other reserves

    V.  *Profit or loss brought forward*

    VI.  *Profit or loss for the financial year*

## THE INCOME STATEMENT UNDER THE FOURTH DIRECTIVE

The implications of this distinction between classification by nature and classification by function are conveniently illustrated by turning to the Fourth Directive's specifications for the income statement. The Directive requires that Member States allow one or more of the four layouts in its Articles 23 to 26.

These four layouts are necessary to accommodate the possibility of following either an analysis by nature or an analysis by function combined with either a horizontal-type presentation or a vertical-type presentation. Table 10.4 classifies the expense items by nature showing, for example, staff costs as a single separate figure. Table 10.5 classifies by function. Thus, for example, staff costs as a total are not shown, being split up between the various functional heads related to staff activity, such as distribution and administration.

The formats in Tables 10.4 and 10.5 are vertical in style, treating the revenues (credits) as pluses and the expenses (debits) as minuses. However, the Directive allows a horizontal double-entry style of income statement. Table 10.6 shows the horizontal version of the by nature format, i.e. a rearrangement of Table 10.4. Although the Directive also allows a horizontal by function format this is not used in practice and is not illustrated here.

## TABLE 10.4   Fourth Directive: Vertical profit and loss account by nature

| Item | Description |
|------|-------------|
| 1 | Net turnover |
| 2 | Variation in stocks of finished goods and in work in progress |
| 3 | Work performed by the undertaking for its own purposes and capitalized |
| 4 | Other operating income |
| 5 | a.  Raw materials and consumables<br>b.  Other external charges |
| 6 | *Staff costs*<br>a.  Wages and salaries<br>b.  Social security costs with a separate indication of those relating to pensions |
| 7 | a.  Value adjustments in respect of formation expenses and of tangible and intangible fixed assets<br>b.  Value adjustments in respect of current assets, to the extent that they exceed the amount of value adjustments which are normal in the undertaking concerned |
| 8 | Other operating charges |
| 9 | Income from participating interests, with a separate indication of that derived from affiliated undertakings |
| 10 | Income from other investments and loans forming part of the fixed assets, with a separate indication of that derived from affiliated undertakings |
| 11 | Other interest receivable and similar income, with a separate indication of that derived from affiliated undertakings |
| 12 | Value adjustments in respect of financial assets and of investments held as current assets |
| 13 | Interest payable and similar charges, with a separate indication of those concerning affiliated undertakings |
| 14 | Tax on profit or loss on ordinary activities |
| 15 | Profit or loss on ordinary activities after taxation |
| 16 | Extraordinary income |
| 17 | Extraordinary charges |
| 18 | Extraordinary profit or loss |
| 19 | Tax on extraordinary profit or loss |
| 20 | Other taxes not shown under the above items |
| 21 | Profit or loss for the financial year |

## TABLE 10.5   Fourth Directive: Vertical profit and loss account by function

| Item | Description |
|---|---|
| 1 | Net turnover |
| 2 | Cost of sales (including value adjustments) |
| 3 | Gross profit or loss |
| 4 | Distribution costs (including value adjustments) |
| 5 | Administrative expenses (including value adjustments) |
| 6 | Other operating income |
| 7 | Income from participating interests, with a separate indication of that derived from affiliated undertakings |
| 8 | Income from other investments and loans forming part of the fixed assets, with a separate indication of that derived from affiliated undertakings |
| 9 | Other interest receivable and similar income, with a separate indication of that derived from affiliated undertakings |
| 10 | Value adjustments in respect of financial assets and of investments held as current assets |
| 11 | Interest payable and similar charges, with a separate indication of those concerning affiliated undertakings |
| 12 | Tax on profit or loss on ordinary activities |
| 13 | Profit or loss on ordinary activities after taxation |
| 14 | Extraordinary income |
| 15 | Extraordinary charges |
| 16 | Extraordinary profit or loss |
| 17 | Tax on extraordinary profit or loss |
| 18 | Other taxes not shown under the above items |
| 19 | Profit or loss for the financial year |

## TABLE 10.6   Fourth Directive: Horizontal profit and loss account by nature

| Item | Description |
|---|---|
| A | **Charges** |

1. Reduction in stocks of finished goods and in work in progress
2. a. Raw materials and consumables
   b. Other external charges
3. *Staff costs*
   a. wages and salaries
   b. social security costs with a separate indication of those relating to pensions
4. a. Value adjustments in respect of formation expenses and of tangible and intangible fixed assets
   b. Value adjustments in respect of current assets, to the extent that they exceed the amount of value adjustments which are normal in the undertaking concerned.
5. Other operating charges
6. Value adjustments in respect of financial assets and of investments held as current assets

*(Continued)*

## TABLE 10.6 *(Continued)*

7. Interest payable and similar charges, with a separate indication of those concerning affiliated undertakings
8. Tax on profit or loss on ordinary activities
9. Profit or loss on ordinary activities after taxation
10. Extraordinary charges
11. Tax on extraordinary profit or loss
12. Other taxes not shown under the above items
13. Profit or loss for the financial year

**B    Income**

1. Net turnover
2. Increase in stocks of finished goods and in work in progress
3. Work performed by the undertaking for its own purposes and capitalized
4. Other operating income
5. Income from participating interests, with a separate indication of that derived from affiliated undertakings
6. Income from other investments and loans forming part of the fixed assets, with a separate indication of that derived from affiliated undertakings
7. Other interest receivable and similar income, with a separate indication of that derived from affiliated undertakings
8. Profit or loss on ordinary activities after taxation
9. Extraordinary income
10. Profit or loss for the financial year

## ACTIVITY 10.2

Consider the relative advantages and usefulness of the four Directive formats for the income statement.

### Activity feedback

As regards the financial reports of large listed entities, there is no doubt that the vertical presentations are increasingly predominant. As between the by nature and by function classification, both methods have advantages. Showing expenses by nature requires less analysis and less judgement, but is arguably less informative. It shows the amount incurred on production for the period, but does not highlight the total expenses under the accruals convention. It fails to reveal the cost of sales, and therefore the gross profit and it has the logical disadvantage that it might seem to imply (see Tables 10.4 or 10.6) that changes in inventory are an expense or a revenue in their own right, which they are not. They are logically an adjustment to purchases.

However, because information on the nature of expenses is regarded as useful in predicting future cash flows, IAS 1 and the Directive require additional disclosure on the nature of expenses, including depreciation and amortization expenses and staff costs, when the by function classification is used.

## SUMMARY

This chapter has described and discussed the requirements of IAS 1 and the EU Fourth Directive in relation to the structure of published financial statements. The major revisions to performance reporting introduced from 1 January 2009 have as their fundamental purpose the prevention of information being 'hidden away' outside the essential statement of performance, now designated the statement of comprehensive income. The word 'comprehensive' is precisely the point. All adjustments and events should be clearly reported in vision. The success of this policy remains to be seen.

## EXERCISES

*Suggested answers to exercises marked ✓ are to be found on our dedicated CourseMate platform for students.*

*Suggested answers to the remaining exercises are to be found on the Instructor online support resources.*

1   Are fixed formats for the key financial statements a good thing? If they are, why are several different ones allowed?

✓2  It is important that revenues as determined under the realization convention are reported in a separate statement from any other gains and asset increases. Discuss.

3   The accountant is entitled to assume that readers of financial statements will read and understand all the notes to the accounts. Discuss.

4   The latest formats of reporting comprehensive income, required by the latest version of IAS 1 and described in this chapter, will now be in regular use. Obtain two sets of consolidated IAS accounts for groups based in different countries. Consider whether these recent requirements:

(a)  increase comparability

(b)  increase the information content of the reports.

# CORPORATE GOVERNANCE, CORPORATE SOCIAL RESPONSIBILITY AND ETHICS

**11**

**OBJECTIVES**  After studying this chapter you should be able to:

- explain what corporate governance is, why it is important to shareholders and other stakeholders as well as the general public, and roughly what the two main views on corporate governance are

- describe the main corporate governance mechanisms and problems that they are meant to address

- describe the relation between corporate governance and financial reporting

- outline, and comment on the importance of, a variety of possible additional statements and reports which could be included in a reporting package

- explain corporate social responsibility (CSR) and describe the main ideas behind CSR reporting

- consider ethics and the professional accountant.

## INTRODUCTION

This chapter will first consider the definition of corporate governance in the *OECD Principles of Corporate Governance* and *The UK Corporate Governance Code*. Furthermore, it discusses the reasons why effective corporate governance is important for sustainable economic development and functioning of capital markets. The chapter then describes the main causes of corporate governance failures and the mechanisms that have been devised to address these problems. Subsequently, it introduces the main elements of the *OECD Principles of Corporate Governance, The UK Corporate Governance Code* and *The UK Stewardship Code*. It then discusses additional statements that a company could prepare in addition to its financial statements to provide contextual information for the interpretation of the financial statements or to meet the information needs of its stakeholders in a broader sense. From there the chapter moves on to the question of what is corporate social responsibility (CSR) and the main concepts underlying CSR reporting and discusses recent developments of guidelines for reporting on corporate strategies and performance with a view to achieving and maintaining economic, social and environmental sustainability. Finally, it discusses ethics and professional accountants.

## CORPORATE GOVERNANCE

### What is corporate governance and why is it important?

Many definitions on corporate governance exist. Below we will cite two definitions. The first is by the Organization for Economic Co-operation and Development (OECD) and the second by the Financial Reporting Council in *The UK Corporate Governance Code* (September 2012).

> Corporate governance is the system by which business corporations are directed and controlled. The corporate governance structure specifies the distribution of rights and responsibilities among different participants in the corporation, such as the board, managers, shareholders and other stakeholders, and spells out the rules and procedures for making decisions on corporate affairs. By doing this, it also provides the structure through which the company objectives are set, and the means of attaining those objectives and monitoring performance.
>
> (OECD, 1999)

> Corporate governance is the system by which companies are directed and controlled. Boards of directors are responsible for the governance of their companies. The shareholders' role in governance is to appoint the directors and the auditors and to satisfy that an appropriate governance structure is in place. The responsibilities of the board include setting the company's strategic aims, providing the leadership to put them into effect, supervising the management of the business and reporting to shareholders on their stewardship. The board's actions are subject to laws, regulations and the shareholders in the general meeting.
>
> (FRC, 2012, para. 2, or, originally, FRC, 1992, para. 2.5)

Although corporate governance is as old as the corporate legal form, since the millennium corporate scandals involving Enron, WorldCom and Parmalat have refocused attention on governance, accountability and disclosure and we, as accountants, must reconsider our role in it. The consequences of the financial crisis in 2007 and 2008, the credit crunch, and the ensuing sovereign debt crisis which is partly the consequence of having bailed out the financial institutions that were too big to fail, have made it clear that getting (corporate) governance wrong could potentially cause the (international) financial system to break down and leave national economies in ruins.

The OECD recognizes corporate governance as one important element in improving economic efficiency and growth as well as enhancing investor confidence. Good corporate governance should provide proper incentives for the board and management to pursue objectives that are in the interests of the company and its shareholders and should facilitate effective monitoring. The presence of an effective corporate governance system, within an individual company and across an economy as a whole, helps to provide a degree of confidence that is necessary for the proper functioning of a market economy (OECD, 2004, 11).

## ACTIVITY 11.1

Comparing the two definitions of corporate governance above, can you find a very important difference between them?

### Activity feedback

Both definitions regard corporate governance as the systems by which corporations are directed and controlled. However, the OECD definition regards the corporate governance structure as a system that clarifies the rights and responsibilities with respect to decision making among all the participants in the corporation. The OECD definition is more representative of a stakeholder perspective on corporate governance. Like Entity Theory in accounting, the stakeholder perspective regards corporations as

institutions in their own right, the managers of which must be responsible to their shareholders as well as the wider stakeholder community. The FRC definition sees the corporate governance structure as a matter between the board of directors and the shareholders. The board of directors monitors whether the managers fulfil their stewardship obligations in the best interests of the shareholders, and the shareholders monitor the board of directors. This FRC definition is more representative of a shareholder perspective on corporate governance. Like Proprietary Theory in accounting, the shareholder perspective regards corporations as the private property of its shareholders. Hence the managers are responsible to the owners of the firm.

## ACTIVITY 11.2

From the above discussion on the OECD's view on corporate governance, what do you think is the essential problem and how does this relate to financial reporting?

### Activity feedback

The above discussion is about economic efficiency and investor confidence. Corporate governance mechanisms are meant to support the functioning of capital markets and the market economy in general. Without investor

confidence in the economy in general and the liquidity of markets for equity and debt securities, corporations are not able to raise the capital they need for their operations. The discussion is also about incentives and monitoring. Providing the (independently audited) information on the basis of providing incentives and monitoring performance and operations is where financial reporting plays its part in corporate governance.

## Corporate governance mechanisms and the problems they are meant to address

Why does the governance of publicly held corporations present such challenges? What structures or mechanisms have been developed to meet these challenges? Corporate governance is not new – it has been around for as long as corporate entities, but the study of corporate governance is relatively new. Governance issues arise as soon as we separate ownership from management. Adam Smith *(The Wealth of Nations,* 1776) already understood the concept of governance: 'The directors of companies being managers of other people's money than their own, it cannot well be expected that they should watch over it with the same anxious vigilance with which the partners in a private copartnery frequently watch over their own.' The separation of ownership and control introduces the principal-agent (or agency) problem which creates the need for managers to discharge their stewardship obligations and for shareholders to monitor the managers. The economic opportunities are expanded but the corporate governance problems are compounded by attaching limited liability to shares, and making them freely tradable in liquid markets. When companies become very large and influential, they may become more powerful than local governments. Particularly when they become multinationals and are able to engage in regulatory arbitrage (for example, basing the company in a country with lenient company laws or in a tax haven) the need to monitor management becomes very acute. In sum, the need for corporate governance mechanisms must be sought in the characteristics of corporations, particularly large, multinational, publicly held corporations. These characteristics developed over time and include:

- the separation of the ownership of the company and the control of its resources
- limited liability
- the ability of shareholders to sell their shares at will
- large size and complexity
- global reach and structure.

## A brief history of corporations and corporate governance mechanisms

**Early history until 1930** The corporation finds its origin in the Middle Ages. Corporations were often established for a specific social purpose so that churches, universities, etc. could have a life beyond those who operated them. In the sixteenth and seventeenth centuries, at a time when the market economy was only germinating, they were used to raise capital for ventures of a limited period, such as sea voyages to the East. The VOC and East India Companies extended the corporate form again to make these ventures last beyond single voyages. Later, corporations were established for the purpose of building capital-intensive canals and railways, without which the Industrial Revolution would have been difficult, if not impossible. The concept of limited liability was developed to enable projects on an ever increasing scale to be realized. Limited liability makes investing in companies less risky for shareholders and hence more attractive. This was at the time a very controversial concept because it meant doing away with unlimited liability, which is one of the fundamental elements attached to the institution of private property. Public limited corporations listed on stock exchanges made markets more liquid and investment more flexible and thus even more attractive. However, limited liability also limits the incentives for shareholders to perform their monitoring task and, in combination with the ability to sell their shares at will, reduces shareholders' incentives to monitor managers even further, particularly when they invest in portfolios which they regularly adjust. By the third quarter of the nineteenth century, especially in the UK and the USA, corporations had lost their social purpose and were primarily regarded as vehicles for individual investors to increase their wealth. With a view to promoting shareholder democratization, ever smaller par value denominations enabled more and more ordinary people to invest in shares. During this period, Proprietary Theory, which holds that accounting for corporations must be done from the viewpoint of the owners, was based on the idea that the company is the private property of the shareholders and that they are, indeed, the effective owners of the company.

**1930 to 1960** The stock market crash in the USA in 1929 indicated a problem with corporate governance. The consequences of the crash reverberated around the world. Berle and Means (1932) found that the separation of ownership of the company and control of its assets caused a fundamental alteration in the institution of private property rights. They suggested solutions such as voting rights for all shareholders and greater transparency and accountability. The Securities and Exchange Laws (1932 and 1933) included a serious attempt at the regulation of financial reporting disclosure. In other words, this was the start of an increased role for financial reporting in corporate governance. During this period, the Entity Theory was developed. The Entity perspective on the corporation is based on the idea that it is not effectively owned by the shareholders and that therefore, the accounting must be done from the perspective of the reporting entity itself. World War II may have contributed to the development of the stakeholder perspective on corporate governance because it forced the introduction of greater equality in many societies in the post-war period.

**1960 to 1990** Developed in the 1960s and 1970s, Agency Theory focused solutions to the 'Principal/Agent' (or agency) problem on aligning the incentives of managers with those of the owners. The agency problem concerns potential conflicts of interests arising between the owners (principals) and boards of directors (agents) who have effective control over the company. Bonuses and other incentives became increasingly popular and these are often based, at least partially, on financial reporting information. Later, it became more common to also include market indicators, such as stock price, in the bonus calculations.

The 1970s also saw an emphasis on independent outside directors, audit committees and the establishment of two-tier boards in companies because it became apparent that if the relation between senior management and the board of directors is too close, it will pervert the monitoring function of the board. The EEC in its fifth draft directive 1972 advocated two-tier board governance as seen in Germany and Holland. In the USA the same problem caused litigation to increase as shareholders of failed companies sought recompense from directors and so on.

Owing to the gigantic size of some corporations, the 1970s also saw a growth in the idea that public companies, in addition to their duty to shareholders (owners) also had responsibilities to other stakeholders such as employees, customers, suppliers, lenders, community and government.

During the 1980s, action on corporate governance was minimal and more company collapses and questionable practices were seen throughout the world, attributed by many to the power of executive directors who had no checks or balances upon them. In particular, the combination of the chief executive officer and chairman role was questioned, as was the lack of power of non-executive directors.

**1990 to 2008** Until the early 1990s, the assumption was often that ownership of companies was widely dispersed, so that shareholders were often unable to influence management decisions unless they found ways to unite. However, the 1990s saw the growth in power of major institutional investors. In the UK the issue was brought to the fore by the *Cadbury Report* (Cadbury Committee, 1992) and the establishment of the Cadbury Code that focused on the financial aspects of corporate governance, corporate behaviour and ethics and led to improved boardroom practice. In 1995, the *Greenbury Report* (Greenbury Committee, 1995) added Principles on the Remuneration of Executive Directors in an attempt to curb CEO salaries. These two reports were brought together by the *Hampel Report* of 1998 and formed the first Combined Code. The following year, 1999, saw the publication of the *Turnbull Report* which concentrated on risk management and internal controls. All of these reports were as a result of shareholder disquiet as regards corporate performance and to avoid the threat of government legislation if such codes were not developed voluntarily by the business sector. The *Cadbury Report* had great influence around the world and several other countries published their own corporate governance reports in the 1990s. All of these reports were concerned with the abuse of corporate power and recommended wider use of audit committees, outside non-executive directors, remuneration committees composed of independent outside directors to advise on director remuneration and separation of the chairman and CEO role.

Starting in the 1980s, the 1990s also saw the use of (sometimes hostile) takeovers as an effective means to bring managers to heel. From then on, the takeover market was deemed an external corporate governance mechanism to help focus managers on the financial interests of shareholders. Particularly in the Anglophone countries, renewed shareholder power reversed the idea that shareholders were not effectively the owners of the company. During this period, there was a swing back from the Entity perspective on the corporation towards the Proprietary perspective. This can also be observed in the IASB Conceptual Framework and the IFRSs. This trend had started earlier in the USA, probably because the influence of Agency Theory, institutional investors and the takeover market had started earlier there. In 1998, the OECD proposed the development of global guidelines for corporate governance and emphasized the difference between the strong external investment culture of the USA and UK with the firm corporate governance practices in Japan, France and Germany where employees had more influence and investors seemed to take a longer-term view.

The turn of the century saw the growth in global corporate structures with vast networks of subsidiaries, strategic alliances and related parties. For better or worse, directors of major entities now wield extensive power and companies have a pervasive influence on communities.

The FRC in the UK took the *Higgs Report* forward together with the *Smith Report* on Audit Committees to publish its *Combined Code of Corporate Governance* in July 2003. This was further revised by the Turnbull Review Group and a revised code issued by the FRC in 2005. About this time the European Commission also issued its *Corporate Governance and Company Law Action Plan* covering disclosure requirements, exercise of voting rights, cross-border voting, disclosure by institutional investors and responsibilities of board members.

**From 2008 onwards** The events of 2008 have shown us that bankers, traders and financial institutions around the world wield extensive power and for all the reports, codes, action plans and publications on corporate governance it still remains an issue. James Wolfensohn, President of the World Bank, stated in 2008: 'The governance of companies is more important for world economic growth than the government of countries.' However, a potentially socially costly danger is multinational corporations engaging in regulatory arbitrage. This enables them to cherry-pick the countries with the most advantageous rules and regulations. Think, for example, of the news in November 2012 that Starbucks, Amazon and Google had not paid corporation tax in the UK for years because ingenious constructions allow them to legally show no profit. Under pressure of public opinion, Starbucks voluntarily decided to pay £10 million. How is it possible that Starbucks can decide how much tax it is going to pay? Since economic and financial globalization has progressed much faster than political globalization, it may not be so easy for governments of countries to effectively do anything about the problems of tax evasion and regulatory arbitrage.

Since 2008, many codes worldwide have been adapted or are in the process of adaptation, implying that new articles are added or that elements are being transferred to the law. The OECD did not reform its 2004 Code (the principles of which will be outlined below), but issued recommendations in three documents entitled: *Corporate Governance Lessons from the Financial Crisis* (January 2009), *Corporate Governance and the Financial Crisis: Key Findings and Main Messages* (June 2009), and *Conclusions and Emerging Good Practices to Enhance Implementation of the Principles* (February 2010). In the UK, the FRC revised its Code in 2010 and issued a new edition in 2012, when it also issued *The UK Stewardship Code* (both of which will be discussed below).

## ACTIVITY 11.3

Identify the main corporate governance mechanisms discussed above and indicate what problems they are meant to address. Can you think of any others?

### Activity feedback

*Corporate governance mechanisms discussed above include the following:*

| Corporate governance mechanism | Problem it is meant to address |
|---|---|
| Governance structure of the company | Specifies the distribution of rights and responsibilities among different participants in the corporation |
| Incentives for executive directors and other senior managers | Align the interests of the executive directors and senior managers with those of the company's shareholders in order to mitigate the agency problem |
| The audited annual and interim financial statements | To enable the discharge of managers' stewardship and responsibilities to the shareholders and provide accountability to the other stakeholders |
| Shareholder participation in the AGM | Monitor and influence the managers' decisions in the interest of long-term shareholders |
| Corporate takeover market | Discipline the managers to act in the best interests of short-term shareholders |

A mechanism that has not been discussed above is monitoring by creditors and lenders. Creditors will make use of financial statements to impose discipline on companies by demanding certain restrictions on ratios or demanding cash or liquidity ratios to not fall below a certain level. Credit rating agencies also perform a monitoring function by imposing discipline through lowering the credit rating based on ratios and other financial indicators (and hence making it more expensive for the company to issue debt or borrow from a bank). Customers also perform a role in the corporate governance. By not buying the company's products or complaining about its activities, the general public can force managers of companies to change their policies and behaviour.

## Broad comparison of the OECD and UK corporate governance principles

As mentioned before, the OECD views corporate governance from a stakeholder perspective whereas the FRC views corporate governance from a shareholder perspective. Unsurprisingly, this difference is also clear when we look at Table 11.1 below.

**TABLE 11.1    The elements of the OECD and the FRC principles of corporate governance**

| OECD Principles of Corporate Governance *(2004)* | FRC: The UK Corporate Governance Code and The UK Stewardship Code* *(2012)* |
| --- | --- |
| I. Ensuring the Basis for an Effective Corporate Governance Framework | |
| II. The Rights of Shareholders and Key Ownership Functions | E. Relations with Shareholders<br>*Seven principles of effective monitoring and managing conflicts of interest by institutional investors |
| III. The Equitable Treatment of Shareholders | |
| IV. The Role of Stakeholders in Corporate Governance | |
| V. Disclosure and Transparency | C. Accountability |
| VI. The Responsibilities of the Board | A. Leadership<br>B. Effectiveness<br>D. Remuneration |

The first of the OECD principles state that '(t)he corporate governance framework should promote transparent and efficient markets, be consistent with the rule of law and clearly articulate the division of responsibilities among different supervisory, regulatory and enforcement authorities' (Principle I). Of course, this is true for the UK as well, but because the FRC is only concerned with the UK, the FRC may assume this principle as given.

The second of the OECD principles sets out the basic rights of shareholders in the participation of decision making and voting at the annual general meeting (AGM), the authorization of additional shares and the sale of the company. Section III discusses the equitable treatment of all types of shareholders and the protection of minority shareholders' rights. Section E of the UK Code stipulates that the board must make sure that a satisfactory dialogue with shareholders takes place and that shareholders must be encouraged to participate in the AGM. Following the financial turmoil of 2008, since 2012, *The UK Stewardship Code* sets out principles which help institutional investors such as pension funds, insurance companies, investment trusts and other collective investment vehicles to fulfil their responsibilities to the companies they invest in as well as their stewardship obligations for those whose funds they invest.

Section IV of the OECD Principles discusses the role and rights of other stakeholders, such as employees (and their representative bodies), lenders and creditors in corporate governance. In contrast, there is no equivalent in the UK Code.

Section V of the OECD Principles discusses disclosure and transparency regarding the financial and operating results, company objectives, major share ownership and voting rights, remuneration policy for the board of directors and key executives, related party transactions, foreseeable risk factors, issues regarding employees and other stakeholders, and corporate governance issues. Section C of the UK Code also requires the presentation of the company's financial position and prospects, maintaining sound risk management and internal control systems.

Section VI of the OECD Principles sets out the responsibilities of the board of directors. These include reviewing and guiding strategy; plans of action; risk policy; annual budgets and business plans; overseeing major capital expenditures, acquisitions and divestitures; monitoring governance; selection, compensating and monitoring executives; aligning executive and board remuneration with the interests of the company and its stakeholders; monitoring and managing potential conflicts of interest of management, board members and shareholders; ensuring the integrity of the financial reporting system and the independent audit; and overseeing disclosure and communications. Sufficient non-executive board members must ensure independent judgement. *The UK Corporate Governance Code* as a whole is meant to identify principles that underpin an effective board of directors. Three of its five main principles, i.e. A. Leadership, B. Effectiveness, and D. Remuneration, are entirely dedicated to the functioning of the board. It stresses the collective responsibility of the board for the long-term success of the company and the chairman's responsibility for leadership of the board. Also, C. Accountability, and E. Relations with Shareholders, are presented as functions of the board. The UK Codes are not a rigid set of rules and do recognize that non-compliance may be justified in particular circumstances if good governance can be achieved by other means. The reasons for non-compliance should, however, be explained to shareholders. Thus, the UK Codes rely on a 'comply or explain approach'.

You can of course access the *OECD Principles of Corporate Governance* on the website: www.oecd.org and *The UK Corporate Governance Code* and *The UK Stewardship Code* on the FRC website: www.frc.org.uk.

## Corporate governance in the EU

Corporate governance codes are adapted to the needs of society. In the EU, the distribution of governance-related principles between law and codes in each Member State depends on a number of factors, including legal tradition, ownership structures and the maturity of the corporate governance tradition. In 2006, the European Commission issued Directive 2006/46/EC, introducing the comply-or-explain principle for the first time in European Law. According to *The Study on Monitoring and Enforcement Practices in Corporate Governance in the EU Member States* (23 September 2009 – contract no. ETD/2008/IM/F2/126) some topics are in most instances regulated by law, often following European legislation: general board organization, audit committees, statutory audit, as well as procedural shareholder rights. Other topics are more often treated in codes: board members' independence, remuneration and nomination committees, or internal control and risk management. Certain topics can also evolve from code-based norms to regulated rules, as the recent takeover by regulators of the remuneration issue shows in some Member States.

Since the comply-or-explain principle is an important feature of the EU approach to corporate governance, disclosure on the application of this principle by individual companies is of utmost importance. Users of financial information need to know whether a company followed the principles of the code or whether they followed firm specific rules. In the latter case, they need to explain why they do so. Paragraph 4 of the Preamble to the Dutch corporate governance code states that departures from best practice provisions may be justified in certain instances. However, '(s)hareholders (…) should carefully assess the reason for each and every departure from the Code's provisions.' The Dutch corporate governance code is part of a system based on national and international best practice integrated with Dutch and European legislation and case law on corporate governance, which must be viewed in its entirety. It is also an example of a corporate governance code that lies inbetween the OECD and FRC codes discussed above. See: www.commissiecorporategovernance.nl/monitoring-committee (accessed 1 May 2013).

## FINANCIAL REPORTING AND CORPORATE GOVERNANCE

### ACTIVITY 11.4

Identify the role of financial reporting within corporate governance.

#### Activity feedback

Financial reporting is about providing useful information to users to enable them to make informed decisions regarding stewardship and the future. Information on whether or not a company complies with the principles of the governance code is of key importance to judge the governance of the firm. In case of non-compliance, a transparent explanation should be provided why the company choose not to comply.

*The UK Corporate Governance Code* is quite pertinent as an example of the board of directors' responsibilities in respect of accountability and audit, and we reproduce it below.

## C.1 Financial Reporting

**Main principle** The board should present a balanced and understandable assessment of the company's position and prospects.

**Supporting principle** The board's responsibility to present a balanced and understandable assessment extends to interim and other price-sensitive public reports and reports to regulators as well as to information required to be presented by statutory requirements. The board should establish arrangements that will enable it to ensure that the information presented is fair, balanced and understandable.

# Code provisions

C.1.1   The directors should explain in the annual report their responsibility for preparing the accounts and there should be a statement by the auditors about their reporting responsibilities.

C.1.2   The directors should include in the annual report an explanation of the basis on which the company generates or preserves value over the longer term (the business model) and the strategy for delivering the objectives of the company.

C.1.3   The directors should report in annual and half-yearly statements that the business is a going concern, with supporting assumptions or qualifications as necessary.

## C.2 Risk management and internal control

**Main principle** The board is responsible for determining the nature and extent of the significant risks it is willing to take in achieving its strategic objectives. The board should maintain a sound risk management and internal control systems.

# Code provision

C.2.1   The board should, at least annually, conduct a review of the company's risk management and internal control systems and should report to shareholders that they have done so. The review should cover all material controls, including financial, operational and compliance controls.

## C.3 Audit committee and auditors

**Main principle** The board should establish formal and transparent arrangements for considering how they should apply the financial reporting and internal control principles and for maintaining an appropriate relationship with the company's auditors.

# Code provisions

C.3.1   The board should establish an audit committee of at least three, or in the case of smaller companies two, independent non-executive directors. In smaller companies the company chairman may be a member, but not chair, of the committee in addition to the independent non-executive directors, provided he or she was considered independent on appointment as chairman. The board should satisfy itself that at least one member of the audit committee has recent and relevant financial experience.

C.3.2   The main role and responsibilities of the audit committee should be set out in written terms of reference and should include:

• to monitor the integrity of the financial statements of the company, and any formal announcements relating to the company's financial performance, reviewing significant financial reporting judgements contained in them;

• to review the company's internal financial controls and, unless expressly addressed by a separate board risk committee composed of independent directors, or by the board itself, to review the company's internal control and risk management systems;

- to monitor and review the effectiveness of the company's internal audit function;
- to make recommendations to the board, for it to put to the shareholders for their approval in general meeting, in relation to the appointment, re-appointment and removal of the external auditor and to approve the remuneration and terms of engagement of the external auditor;
- to review and monitor the external auditor's independence and objectivity and the effectiveness of the audit process, taking into consideration relevant UK professional and regulatory requirements;
- to develop and implement policy on the engagement of the external auditor to supply non-audit services, taking into account relevant ethical guidance regarding the provision of non-audit services by the external audit firm; and to report to the board, identifying any matters in respect of which it considers that action or improvement is needed and making recommendations as to the steps to be taken; and
- to report to the board on how it has discharged its responsibilities.

C.3.3    The terms of reference of the audit committee, including its role and the authority delegated to it by the board, should be made available. A separate section of the annual report should describe the work of the committee in discharging those responsibilities.

C.3.4    Where requested by the board, the audit committee should provide advice on whether the annual report and accounts, taken as a whole, is fair, balanced and understandable and provides the information necessary for shareholders to assess the company's performance, business model and strategy.

C.3.5    The audit committee should review arrangements by which staff of the company may, in confidence, raise concerns about possible improprieties in matters of financial reporting or other matters. The audit committee's objective should be to ensure that arrangements are in place for the proportionate and independent investigation of such matters and for appropriate follow-up action.

C.3.6    The audit committee should monitor and review the effectiveness of the internal audit activities. Where there is no internal audit function, the audit committee should consider annually whether there is a need for an internal audit function and make a recommendation to the board, and the reasons for the absence of such a function should be explained in the relevant section of the annual report.

C.3.7    The audit committee should have primary responsibility for making a recommendation on the appointment, reappointment and removal of the external auditors. FTSE 350 companies should put the external audit contract out to tender at least every ten years. If the board does not accept the audit committee's recommendation, it should include in the annual report, and in any papers recommending appointment or re-appointment, a statement from the audit committee explaining the recommendation and should set out reasons why the board has taken a different position.

C.3.8    A separate section of the annual report should describe the work of the committee in discharging its responsibilities. The report should include:

- The significant issues that the committee considered in relation to the financial statements, and how these issues were addressed;

- An explanation of how it has assessed the effectiveness of the external audit process and the approach taken to the appointment or reappointment of the external auditor, and information on the length of tenure of the current audit firm and when a tender was last conducted; and

- if the auditor provides non-audit services, an explanation of how auditor objectivity and independence is safeguarded.

On the website www.frc.org.uk, you can find the latest version of the UK Corporate Governance Code. For an overview of codes of corporate governance worldwide, you can go to the website of the European Corporate Governance Institute: www.ecgi.org/codes/all_codes.php.

## ACTIVITY 11.5

What other information might investors and other stakeholders be interested in that is not provided in the published financial statements? You might check the 'investor relations' sections of a few websites of listed companies in order to find out what kind of additional information is provided most frequently.

### Activity feedback
You may find many different types of additional report, some of which are meant to give investors more informa-tion which helps them to better understand the entity's financial performance, such as a management commentary. Other statements will give more information about the entity's corporate governance structure, such as a corporate governance charter. Yet other statements will give information about the entity's relations with the broader stakeholder community in addition to the relations with its shareholders.

## ADDITIONAL STATEMENTS FOR EXTERNAL REPORTING

When doing Activity 11.4 you may have come across many types of reports including a management commentary and other information in the annual report as well as information that is often presented outside of the annual report.

### Management commentary

In December 2010, the IASB issued IFRS Practice Statement *Management Commentary*. The Practice Statement is not an IFRS. This means that entities applying IFRS do not have to comply with its recommendations unless specifically required to do so by their jurisdiction (IN2). The IASB has also issued a guidance document.

The IASB's definition of management commentary is as follows: A narrative report that provides a context within which to interpret the financial position, financial performance and cash flows of an entity. It also provides management with an opportunity to explain its strategic objectives and its strategies for achieving those objectives (IN3). When management commentary relates to financial statements, the commentary must make the financial statements available with the commentary or identify in the commentary to which financial statement it relates (IN5). However, management should clearly identify what it is presenting as management commentary and distinguish it from other information (IN6). Companies have to clarify to what extent they have followed the recommendations in the Practice Statement (IN7).

The principles underpinning useful management commentary are (para. 12):

**(a)** it provides management's view of the entity's performance, position and progress;

**(b)** supplements and complements information presented in the financial statements; and

**(c)** should include forward-looking information which possesses the qualitative characteristics described in the *Conceptual Framework for Financial Reporting*.

The elements of management commentary include (para. 24):

**(a)** The nature of the business

**(b)** Management's objectives and its strategies for meeting these objectives

**(c)** The entity's most significant resources, risks and relationships

**(d)** The results of operations and prospects

**(e)** The critical performance measures and indicators that management uses to evaluate the entity's performance against stated objectives.

The management commentary can be one comprehensive report or include a separate statement of corporate objectives, future prospects and risks, but it could include other information as well.

**A statement of corporate objectives** shows management policy and medium-term strategic targets. This statement will assist users to evaluate managerial performance, efficiency and objectives. It can be argued that the objectives being pursued by a business need to be publicised for two reasons. First, so that users can see the extent to which management objectives differ from their own and, second, so that management's ability to achieve the stated objectives can be assessed. Of course, there is a distinct danger that management will declare objectives that it feels it can be almost certain of achieving.

**A statement of future prospects** which shows forecasts of future profit, employment and investment levels. This statement will assist users to evaluate the future prospects of the entity and assess managerial performance. It may also include information in respect of innovations in the organization that will develop tangible and intangible capital/assets in the future. Many users want to assess an entity's future prospects. However, any such assessment of future prospects involves a high degree of uncertainty. Forecasts of future prospects do not predict the future, but they do set out in a logical and systematic manner the future implications of past and present known facts adjusted by reference to estimates of likely future developments. These projections will have different degrees of probability attached to them that the user will need to judge. It is the certainty of uncertainty that makes entities unwilling to make public projections, although all those acquainted with such exercises are perfectly familiar with the limits on reliability that are inherent in them. However, such forecasts are certainly desired by users and competitors and, in general, management and accountants are likely to be able to make better and more rational projections that can then be reported than the external users can make for themselves.

**A statement on the risks inherent in the entity** which provides information on the potential risks associated with an entity's activities may enable users to assess the possible consequence of materialization of that risk and whether suitable measures have been taken to mitigate it.

## ACTIVITY 11.6

Identify three objections to publishing a statement of future prospects.

### Activity feedback

- Forecasts are concerned with the future and are therefore inherently uncertain. Unless carefully presented, users may regard forecasts as presenting facts rather than best estimates.

- Management will be judged by how well it has met its forecasts and may be encouraged to lower its targets by publishing only conservative forecasts it knows are wholly attainable and to accept results that meet those forecasts.

- The provision of forecasts by entities suffering from financial difficulties may result in the withdrawal of support and thus precipitate an otherwise avoidable collapse.

It should be remembered that these forecasts will be highly subjective and based on various management assumptions.

## Other information aimed at investors

Many entities provide information in their annual reports that they believe investors will find useful. Such information covers:

- Stock data where share prices, market capitalizations, number of shares traded in a period and dividends are tracked for a number of years.

- Balance sheet ratios where the traditional ratios of return on capital employed, etc. are tracked.

- Financial highlights where the entity identifies key changes from one to the next in such items as sales, capital expenditure, personnel expenses, research and development expenses, etc.

- Ten-year summary information of sales, assets, financial obligations, etc.

Risk management issues where entities report, as part of best practice within corporate governance, on the potential risks associated with their activities, the assessment of the possible consequences of their materialization and measures available to mitigate them.

## Other information aimed at the broader group of stakeholders

Below are discussed the employment report, the statement of money exchanges with government, the value added statement and sustainability reports.

**An employment report** is a report which enables users of annual reports to assess the performance of the entity in relation to employees. Employees are obviously closely involved in business. They have to make many important decisions for themselves that will be heavily influenced by the activities, actions and prospects of business organizations. It could be argued that they have much more to lose than many shareholders or lenders, particularly as they are unable to spread their risk. Employees almost always have to put their faith in one business; they cannot involve themselves with large numbers, as investors or lenders can.

Employees certainly need some indication of future profitability, as do other users, but they also need additional information. Some of this may be financial – for example relating to the profitability of their own particular plant – but much of it will not be best presented in financial terms at all. In spite of this, many accountants would regard the provision of information useful to employees as being a necessary component of the total reporting package.

Employment reports could contain the following information:

- total workforce with breakdown by employment type, employment contract and gender
- employee wages and benefits with breakdown by employment type and gender
- total number and rate of employee turnover broken down by employment type, employment contract and gender (plus broad reasons for changes in the numbers employed)
- age, distribution, sex and functions of employees
- geographical location of major employment centres
- major plant and site closures, disposals and acquisitions during the period
- hours scheduled and worked by employees, giving as much detail as possible concerning the differences between groups of employees
- costs and benefits associated with pension schemes and the ability of such schemes to meet future commitments
- cost and time involved in training
- percentage of employees covered by collective agreements (plus the names of unions recognized by the entity for the purpose of collective bargaining and membership figures where available, or the fact that this information has not been made available by the unions concerned)
- information concerning safety and health including the frequency and severity of accidents and occupational diseases
- selected ratios relating to employment.

**A statement of money exchanges with government** will enable users of financial reports to assess the relationship between the entity and the state. Thus a statement of money exchanges with government will assist users to assess the economic function of the entity in relation to society.

**A value added statement** shows how the benefits of the efforts of an entity are shared between employees, providers of capital, the state and reinvestment. This statement will assist users to evaluate the economic performance of the entity from a more social perspective.

## ACTIVITY 11.7

Identify information in the value added statement in Table 11.2 that is not provided in the published financial statements.

### Activity feedback
Rather difficult to do as a value added statement does not give any information that is not already in traditional published accounts. What it does do is to rearrange the information and present it from a different perspective. The emphasis on shareholders inherent in the income

statement is removed and instead attention is focused on the wealth created by the business as a whole and on how that created wealth has been split up for various subgroups of the community. It is therefore arguable that a much more rounded picture is presented both of the business as a whole and of the interrelationships between the various essential inputs that make the business operations possible. Note that depreciation is not shown as providing for the maintenance of assets as retained profit does, but is shown as a deduction from

*(Continued)*

## ACTIVITY 11.7   (Continued)

turnover. Thus the value added shown is an indicator of wealth created over and above that required for current maintenance. In most countries, there are no formal requirements to include a value added statement in the reporting package, but in spite of this many entities do publish a statement of this type.

### TABLE 11.2   Value added by continuing operations

| Source | | | Distribution | | |
|---|---|---|---|---|---|
| Million euros | 2001 | Change in % | Million euros | 2001 | Share in % |
| Net sales | 28 938 | +1.1 | Stockholders | 657 | 6.7 |
| Other income | 701 | −22.5 | Employees | 7 576 | 77.1 |
| Total operating | | | Governments | 826 | 8.4 |
| Performance | 29 639 | +0.4 | | | |
| Cost of materials | 11 057 | +10.1 | Lenders | 463 | 4.7 |
| Depreciation | 2 403 | +20.8 | Earnings retention | 304 | 3.1 |
| Other expenses | 6 353 | +0.5 | | | |
| Value added | 9 826 | −10.1 | Value added | 9 826 | |

Data source: Bayer's Financial Report 2001

A **sustainability report** enables the general public to assess the social and environmental impact of the entity on the society surrounding it. The investor relations (IR) page on companies' websites will often have a corporate social responsibility section which may comprise several reports and statements.

## XBRL AND ELECTRONIC DISSEMINATION

Information, to be useful, requires the characteristic of timeliness. One means of ensuring timely information is to place financial statements and other information on the Internet. Many countries now facilitate this further by permitting electronic filing of statutory reports. Almost all large entities have their own website and provide not only the financial statements, but also environmental statements and CSR reports. However, not all financial information posted on the Internet is verified by auditors, and users need to beware.

In addition, new digital languages are being developed to speed up and increase transparency of reporting to users. XBRL – extensible business reporting language – is one example and many believe that it will revolutionize financial reporting. However, it will also bring its own problems of verification of information and we will need to ensure that XBRL information is relevant, reliable, understandable and comparable, and free from interference. Failure to do so will undermine corporate governance. XBRL could, if not closely governed, become the next 'creative accounting arena'.

## CORPORATE SOCIAL RESPONSIBILITY (CSR) AND CSR REPORTING

### What is corporate social responsibility?

#From the stakeholder perspective on corporate governance, it is not such a large jump to the idea of corporate social responsibility (CSR). CSR can be defined in many ways. In *A Renewed EU Strategy EU 2011–14 for Corporate Social Responsibility*, the European Commission defines CSR as 'the responsibility of enterprises for their impacts on society'. 'To fully meet their corporate social responsibility, enterprises should have in place a process to integrate social, environmental, ethical, human rights and consumer concerns into their business operations and core strategy in close collaboration with their stakeholders, with the aim of:

- Maximizing the creation of shared value for their owners/shareholders and for their other stakeholders and society at large;
- Identifying, preventing and mitigating their possible adverse impacts. (European Commission Communication COM (2011) 681 final, p. 6).

Many organizations have issued guidance for companies seeking a formal approach to CSR, including the United Nations Global Compact's ten principles, the ISO 26000 *Guidance Standard on Social Responsibility*, the ILO *Tri-partite Declaration of Principles Concerning Multinational Enterprises and Social Policy*, the OECD *Guidelines for Multinational Enterprises*, and the United Nations *Guiding Principles on Business and Human Rights* (European Commission Communication COM (2011) 681 final, p. 6). You will be able to find documents from these organizations on their respective websites. Here we will take a closer look at the United Nations Global Compact's ten principles and the ISO 26000 *Guidance on Social Responsibility*.

**The United Nations Global Compact's ten principles** – 'The UN Global Compact is a strategic policy initiative for businesses that are committed to aligning their operations and strategies with ten universally accepted principles in the area of human rights, labour, environment and anti-corruption. By doing so, business as a primary driver of globalization can help ensure that markets, commerce, technology and finance advance in ways that benefit economies and societies everywhere' (www.unglobalcompact.org/AboutTheGC/index.html). The ten principles are as follows.

*Human rights*
Principle 1: Business should support and respect the production of internationally proclaimed human rights; and
Principle 2: make sure that they are not complicit in human rights abuses.

*Labour*
Principle 3: Businesses should uphold the freedom of association and the effective recognition of the right to collective bargaining;
Principle 4: the elimination of all forms of forced and compulsory labour;
Principle 5: the effective abolition of child labour; and
Principle 6: the elimination of discrimination in respect of employment and occupation.

*Environment*
Principle 7: Businesses should support a precautionary approach to environmental challenges;

Principle 8: undertake initiatives to promote greater environmental responsibility; and Principle 9: encourage the development and diffusion of environmentally friendly techniques.

### Anti-corruption

Principle 10: Businesses should work against corruption in all its forms, including extortion and bribery (www.unglobalcompact.org/AboutTheGC/TheTenPrinciples/index.html).

**ISO 26000: 2010, Guidance on Social Responsibility** – At the end of September 2010, the International Organization for Standardization (ISO) had a membership of 163 national standard setters from countries all over the world. Unlike many other ISO standards, ISO 26000 is not a management system standard and is not for certification or regulatory purposes.

ISO 26000 describes the following core subjects in social responsibility: organizational governance; human rights; labour practices; the environment; fair operating practices (including fair competition, respect for property rights, and promoting social responsibility in the value chain, etc.); consumer issues (including fair marketing, sustainable consumption and protecting consumers' health and safety, etc.); and finally, community involvement and development.

In addition, it defines the following principles of social responsibility: accountability; transparency; ethical behaviour; respect for stakeholder interests; respect for the rule of law; respect for international norms of behaviour; and respect for human rights.

## What is CSR reporting?

If you accept the proposition that managers of a large publicly held corporation have wider responsibilities than the financial interests of their shareholders, the need arises to report on more than its financial position and its profit or loss and other comprehensive income or its cash flows. CSR reporting is also called social reporting or sustainability reporting. According to O'Rourke (2004, vii and 26) in a report for the World Bank, current CSR reporting initiatives disclose information on:

### Corporate governance

- Internal accountability procedures;
- Composition of the board;
- Management compensation;
- Disclosure of potential conflicts of interest.

### Forward-looking information

- Scenario planning to avoid specific problems;
- Plans for dealing with future risks.

### Environmental performance

- Compliance with environmental laws (rates of non-compliance, fines, legal proceedings, etc.);
- Emissions of toxic chemicals to air, water and land;
- Emissions of greenhouse gases;

- Material flows – energy, raw materials, water, land, etc.;
- Product life-cycle assessment;
- Environmental management systems (e.g. ISO 14000);
- Disclosure of environmental risks to local community members.

*Respect for labour rights*

- Policies on freedom of association, collective bargaining, non-discrimination, child labour, and forced labour;
- Facilitation of freedom of association and rates of unionization;
- Formal agreements with independent trade unions;
- Wages (comparable to industry average, prevailing wage, or 'living wage');
- Employee benefits provided;
- Working hours.

*Health and safety practices*

- Rates of occupational injuries, diseases, and fatalities;
- Lost time from injuries;
- Hazard communication programs;
- Training on health and safety;
- Joint employee-management health and safety committees.

*Community economic development and social impacts*

- Percentage of profits reinvested in community from which profits earned;
- Percentage of profits paid into a local community development trust;
- Impacts on local development patterns of investments/suppliers.

*Respect for human rights*

- Countries of operation with problematic human rights records;
- Role of government or military in factory operations;
- Political and economic rights guaranteed to employees.

*Corporate payments to governments*

- Payments for contracts or concessions;
- Corporate taxes and royalty payments;
- Donations to candidates for political office or political parties.

*Stakeholder engagement*

- Policies and procedures for engagement;
- Frequency and forms of engagement;
- Information that is accessible and understandable to stakeholders.

*Supply chain management*

- Locations of factories/farms/mines in supply chain;
- Number of workers in supply chain;
- Code implementation and monitoring program;

- Systems for measuring and monitoring performance;
- Compliance staff numbers and budgets;
- Process for verification of reported data.

Some of this information is provided in the type of reports discussed in the previous sections on corporate governance and additional statement for external reporting.

## ACTIVITY 11.8

Traditionally, accounting was based around the concepts of money measurement, going concern and accruals. Identify whether environmental issues are taken into account in the application of these concepts to a business and, if not, why not.

### Activity feedback

Money measurement requires that only those facts that can be recorded in monetary terms with some objectivity are taken into account even if other facts are extremely relevant. Environmental factors are very difficult to measure in monetary terms. How, for example, do you place a monetary measure on the damage being done to the environment through car exhaust emissions of employees travelling to work?

The going concern convention requires that, in the absence of evidence to the contrary, it is assumed that the entity will continue into the future. This concept is principally concerned with solvency and financial performance, not with the impact of environmental factors.

Accrual accounting requires a matching of expenses used up in generating revenues. However, entities make no assessment of the expense of environmental factors such as their contribution to global warming through the emission of carbon dioxide or to acid rain from the emission of sulphur and nitrogen oxides. Through legislation, society is imposing duties on entities to comply with anti-pollution, safety and health and other socially beneficial requirements. Legislation of this type will continue to increase in the future. Such legislation imposes costs on entities that were previously borne by the community at large and there is therefore good reason to require such expenditure, both compulsory and voluntary expenditure, to be reported. If entities do disclose information on their impact on social and environmental effects then we will, of course, need generally agreed measurement and recognition criteria for such impacts. And surely, this information will need to be verified and audited.

Thus far, the IASB has argued that financial reports governed by IFRSs are not the place for information on the economic, social and ecological sustainability of the operations of corporations. As a consequence, CSR reporting by companies and multinational corporations is voluntary unless it is required by regulators within a jurisdiction. In 2011, the European Commission made a commitment to 'present a legislative proposal on the transparency of the social and environmental information provided by companies in all sectors' (Single Market Act, SEC (2011) 467). To this purpose there has been a study of *CSR Reporting Practices of EU Companies*. This study finds that the needs of information users are best met when reporting is regulated, CSR reporting is integrated with financial reporting, and stakeholders are more involved in reporting.

There are several organizations that are working on establishing guidelines for CSR reporting. Here, we will briefly discuss the Global Reporting Initiative (GRI) and the International Integrated Reporting Council (IIRC). On 1 February 2013, the GRI and the IIRC signed a Memorandum of Understanding to cement their association. In Article II of this Memorandum of Understanding, the GRI acknowledges that the IIRC's main role is to develop and maintain an International IR Framework, and the IIRC acknowledges that the GRI's primary role is to develop and maintain sustainability reporting guidelines and standards.

**Global Reporting Inititative (GRI)** – The GRI has issued guidelines on sustainability reporting and recommends disclosure of the company's:

- vision on strategy on managing economic, social and environmental challenges in the short, medium and longer term
- organizational profile, the parameters
- scope and boundaries of the report
- governance, commitments and stakeholder engagement.

Furthermore, the guidelines list sustainability performance indicators that companies would need to report on in the categories: economic, environmental and social. The social category is further broken down into subcategories: labour, human rights, society and product responsibility. See GRI website at: www.globalreporting.org/Pages/default.aspx.

**International Integrated Reporting Council (IIRC)** – The IIRC is a global coalition of regulators, investors, companies, standard setters, the accounting profession and NGOs aiming to create a global framework for Integrated Reporting (IR). Integrated Reporting is a process that results in a periodic integrated report. According to the IIRC's website at www.theiirc.org/ an integrated report shows how an organization's strategy, governance, performance and prospects lead to the creation of value over the short, medium and long-term, and should be prepared in accordance with the International Framework. The IIRC plans to issue the International IR Framework in December of 2013.

## ACTIVITY 11.9

Identify key criteria for CSR in order for it to be useful to users.

### Activity feedback

- *Continuity – in that the same methods and metrics are used year after year.*
- *Comparability – to allow for benchmarking and assessing progress.*
- *Credibility – to ensure that the information provides a 'true and fair' picture of the company's environmental performance.*

*You could, of course, also have listed understandability, relevance and reliability just as easily. The ACCA identify the following principles on which social accounting should be based:*

- *complete*
- *comparable – to aid comparison with previous years and others*
- *embedded – integration of CSR into everything that the company does*
- *externally verifiable*
- *continuous improvement – to work up to and beyond the minimum.*

*Several worldwide companies produce CSR reports and make these freely available on their websites.*

## ACTIVITY 11.10

Look at the IIRC's website to see how far it has progressed with the International Framework. Are the concepts and criteria comparable to the ones outlined above?

### Activity feedback

*The draft issued in April 2013, for which the comment period is 90 days, sets out fundamental concepts related to:*

1 *the stock and flow of financial, intellectual, human and other types of capital*
2 *the business model, i.e. how the business aims to create value over the short, medium and long-term through the convention of inputs and business activities into outcomes*

*(Continued)*

## ACTIVITY 11.10    (Continued)

**3** value creation, i.e. the meaning of value for providers of financial capital and other stakeholders, and the value drivers that affect the organization's ability to create value.

It sets out six guiding principles underpinning the preparation of an integrated report pertaining to:

(a) strategic focus and future orientation

(b) connectivity of information

(c) stakeholder responsiveness

(d) materiality and conciseness

(e) reliability and completeness

(f) consistency and comparability.

The draft suggests that an integrated report contains the following elements:

(a) organizational overview and external environment

(b) governance

(c) opportunities and risks

(d) strategy and resource allocation

(e) business model

(f) performance

(g) future outlook.

Finally, it discusses topics related to the preparation, presentation and frequency of the reporting.

Hence, it looks like the fundamental concepts are unique to the IR framework (at least in its draft form), but the guiding principles and the elements may be similar.

## ACTIVITY 11.11

Identify reasons why corporations should take CSR reporting seriously.

### Activity feedback
The list is probably endless and we identify only a few here.

- The growth of SRI means entities will have to report on their social and environmental impact or risk losing investors.

- Environmental disasters caused by entities are now widely reported through the global media,

and entities are thus under greater scrutiny and pressure to disclose information.

- An entity's value in the market can be damaged if it does not take on board social and environmental risk factors. Its brand and reputation are likely to be damaged.

- An entity's reputation as a good 'corporate citizen' can have a positive effect on employee recruitment and retention.

- Good corporate citizenship can also generate customers and forge better links with suppliers.

# Perspectives on CSR and CSR reporting

According to Carroll (1991)'s pyramid, companies have four types of responsibility including:

**1** the economic responsibility to be profitable in order to be able to survive and fulfill its other responsibilities

**2** the legal responsibility to play by the rules and obey the law in the jurisdictions where it operates

**3** the ethical responsibility to do what is right, just and fair and to avoid doing harm

**4** the philanthropic responsibility to contribute to the community and be a good corporate citizen.

Not everybody recognizes each of these responsibilities. Some only recognize the first two and claim that trying to be ethical and contributing to the community may do more harm than good; for example, Milton Friedman (1970) in 'The social responsibility of business is to increase its profits'. In politics we may find some who emphasize how externally imposed measures to protect the environment or safeguard the rights of workers impose unfair costs on businesses and make it difficult for them to remain profitable. It is also possible to regard CSR is a voluntary set of activities in which a corporation engages to support social, economic and environmental causes. This view stresses that these activities are not legal, fiduciary or corporate governance requirements. In other words, this view holds that CSR is limited to philanthropic responsibilities. Others regard the philanthropic responsibility as a strategic opportunity for companies (Freeman, 1984). CSR can be very profitable. Think for example of fair trade coffee. A cynical perspective is to regard CSR as nothing more than a public relations exercise. This is particularly easy to understand in the case of the so-called 'sin industries', including tobacco, alcohol and fast food.

## ACTIVITY 11.12

If you want to find out if there is merit to the cynical perspective, take a look at the IR page of the websites of companies in 'sin industries' such as McDonald's and Heineken. What areas do they focus on in their CSR policies? Do you find the reports credible?

### Activity feedback
McDonald's, in its 2012 report, focuses on five areas: nutrition and well-being; sustainable supply chain; environmental responsibility; employee experience; and community.

Heineken, in its Sustainability Report 2011, focuses on seven areas: green brewing; green commerce; engaging employees; care about people and environment; promoting responsible alcohol consumption; partnerships to prevent alcohol abuse; and enabling sustainability through planning and incentives. For each of these focus areas, Heineken presents an overview of what they said they would do (the measurable targets set in the previous period) and what they have actually done (the extent to which the targets have been reached).

The issue of credibility is a personal one. It is clear that both companies have given sustainability a lot of thought, and the effect is probably more positive than when they did not have these focus areas and policies.

## Metrics and assurance challenges for CSR reporting

We briefly return to Hicks (1946) and his theory of capital maintenance discussed in Chapter 4. Remember the quote: 'The purpose of income calculations in practical affairs is to give people an indication of the amount which they can consume without impoverishing themselves.' This can be applied to the environment because if we continue to consume the environment, we will impoverish perhaps not ourselves but certainly future generations. Economic activity affects the environment as natural resources are depleted or polluted through, for example, usage, the effects of global warming and acid rain.

However, the indicators of environmental performance and ecological sustainability can be technical, and often there is disagreement between those who take an economic perspective on the environment and those who take an ecological perspective (or anything in-between). The concept of ecological sustainability, but also that of economic and social sustainability, is not straightforward. Standards, regulations and policies depend on facts, but also on the interpretation of data and facts, which is often based on personal values, interests, ideology and a sense of urgency. So if deciding on standards and measurement is difficult to agree on (let alone get right), reliable assurance and verification may be hard to realize.

Accountancy firms provide assurance for many of the CSR reports. In 2003, a British think tank and consultancy firm called AccountAbility (www.accountability.org/) issued its AA1000 Assurance Standard, which it revised in 2008. It is part of the AA1000 Series which is comprised of three standards:

- AA1000APS (2008) AccountAbility Principles
- AA1000AS (2008) Assurance Standard
- AA1000SES (2011) Stakeholder Engagement Standard.

AccountAbility's Assurance Standard distinguishes between two types of sustainability assurance engagement. Type 1 is intended to give stakeholders assurance on the way an organization manages sustainability performance, and how it communicates this in its sustainability reporting, without verifying the reliability of the reported information. Type 2 is intended to give stakeholders the Type 1 assurance and provide an evaluation and verification of the specified sustainability performance indicators. Furthermore, the standard distinguishes between providing a high level of assurance and a moderate level of assurance. In para. 4.3, the standard says that the assurance report must provide at a minimum:

1 intended users of the assurance statement;
2 the responsibility of the reporting organization and of the assurance provider;
3 assurance standard(s) used, including reference to the AA1000AS (2008);
4 description of the scope, including the type of assurance provided;
5 description of disclosures covered;
6 description of methodology;
7 any limitations;
8 reference to criteria used;
9 statement of level of assurance;
10 findings and conclusions concerning adherence to the AA1000 AccountAbility Principles of inclusivity, materiality and responsiveness (in all instances);
11 findings and conclusions concerning the reliability of specified performance information (for Type 2 assurance only);
12 observations and/or recommendations;
13 notes on competencies and independence of the assurance provider;
14 name of the assurance provider, and date and place.

With respect to the competence of the assurance provider, the standard requires the individual assurance practitioners and the team to be demonstrably competent in the following areas as a minimum (para. 3.3.1): the AccountAbility Principles, the application of reporting and assurance practices and standards, the sustainability subject matter (including the specific subject matter of the engagement), and stakeholder engagement.

## An example of CSR reporting

From Shell's Sustainability Report 2011 (http://reports.shell.com/sustainability-report/2011/servicepages/downloads/files/entire_shell_sr11.pdf):

> Shell is a global group of energy and petrochemical companies employing 90 000 people in more than 80 countries. Our aim is to help meet society's need for energy in economically, environmentally and socially responsible ways.

The report first outlines its approach to:

- building a sustainable energy future
- sustainable development and business strategy
- safety
- communities
- climate change
- environment
- living by Shell's principles.

It follows by outlining its activities aimed to support sustainable development, key projects, and delivering energy responsibly and delivering more sustainable products. The report presents Shell's economic, environmental and social performance indicators, and also an explanation of where the data comes from and how it has been assured by Lloyd's. The following are extracts from the 2011 report:

### Economic

> Our income in 2011 was $30.9 billion and we announced dividends of more than $10 billion for our shareholders. Our capital investment of over $31 billion will help to build and sustain our business for the future. We also spent $1.1 billion on our research and development programme. We continued to focus our efforts on those markets where we see the best potential for growth. A number of major projects started production in 2011: the Pearl GTL (gas-to-liquids) plant (Shell interest 100 per cent) in Qatar that can produce 140 000 barrels of oil equivalent (BOE) a day of synthetic oil products and 120 000 BOE a day of condensates, liquid petroleum gas and ethane; the 7.8 million tonnes-a-year Qatargas 4 LNG facility (Shell interest 30 per cent) also in Qatar; the final phase of the 100 000 BOE-a-day Athabasca Oil Sands Project expansion (Shell interest 60 per cent) in Canada; and enhanced oil recovery projects at Qarn Alam (Shell interest 34 per cent) in Oman and Schoonebeek (Shell interest 30 per cent) in the Netherlands. We also launched Raízen (Shell interest 50 per cent) that produces the lowest-$CO_2$ biofuel commercially available today, ethanol from sugar cane in Brazil. In 2011, Shell's oil and gas production was 3.2 million BOE a day, slightly down from 2010. We increased our sales of liquefied natural gas (LNG) by 12 per cent to 19 million tonnes. We had seven notable oil and gas discoveries, and we replaced 99 per cent of our production with additions to our proved reserves.

### Shell scorecard

> In 2011, sustainable development continued to account for 20 per cent of the company scorecard, which helps determine the annual bonus levels for all our

employees, including members of the Shell Executive Committee (EC). For the EC in 2011, sustainable development measures were split evenly between Shell's safety performance and targeted measures covering operational spills, energy efficiency and use of fresh water.

## Royal Dutch Shell plc Sustainability Report 2011

Environmental Data

| | 2011 | 2010 | 2009 | 2008 | 2007 | 2006 | 2005 | 2004 | 2003 | 2002 |
|---|---|---|---|---|---|---|---|---|---|---|
| **Greenhouse gas emissions (GHGs)** | | | | | | | | | | |
| Direct total GHGs (million tonnes $CO_2$ equivalent) [A] | 74 | 76 | 69 | 75 | 82 | 88 | 93 | 101 | 102 | 96 |
| Carbon dioxide ($CO_2$) (million tonnes) | 71 | 72 | 66 | 72 | 79 | 85 | 89 | 96 | 97 | 92 |
| Methane ($CH_4$) (thousand tonnes) | 133 | 128 | 127 | 126 | 119 | 124 | 173 | 192 | 187 | 196 |
| Nitrous oxide ($N_2O$) (thousand tonnes) | 1 | 2 | 2 | 2 | 2 | 2 | 2 | 2 | 3 | 4 |
| Hydrofluorocarbons (HFCs) (tonnes) | 22 | 23 | 25 | 23 | 28 | 24 | 20 | 13 | 9 | 11 |
| Indirect total GHGs (million tonnes $CO_2$ equivalent) | 10 | 10 | 9 | n/c | n/c | n/c | n/c | n/c | n/c | n/c |
| **Flaring [B]** | | | | | | | | | | |
| Flaring (Upstream) (million tonnes $CO_2$ equivalent) | 10.0 | 10.4 | 7.8 | 8.8 | 9.7 | 14.3 | 20.8 | 24.6 | 24.1 | 20.6 |
| Flaring (Upstream) (million tonnes hydrocarbon flared) | 3.4 | 3.6 | 2.6 | 2.8 | 3.4 | 4.8 | 7.0 | 8.1 | 8.1 | 6.8 |
| Nigeria [C] | 2.0 | 2.4 | 1.9 | 2.3 | 2.5 | 3.7 | 5.8 | 6.6 | 6.4 | 5.2 |
| Rest of world [D] | 1.4 | 1.2 | 0.7 | 0.5 | 0.9 | 1.1 | 1.2 | 1.5 | 1.7 | 1.6 |
| **Energy intensity** | | | | | | | | | | |
| Upstream excl. Oil Sands and GTL (gigajoules per tonne production) [E] | 0.75 | 0.74 | 0.76 | 0.74 | 0.78 | 0.78 | 0.71 | 0.69 | 0.69 | 0.73 |
| Oil Sands (gigajoules per tonne production) [F] | 7.4 | 7.2 | 7.0 | 7.0 | 5.7 | 5.3 | 5.2 | 5.8 | 10.0 | n/c |
| Refineries: Refinery Energy Index [G] | 100.8 | 101.8 | 102.2 | 98.9 | 98.6 | 98.4 | 98.0 | 96.7 | 97.8 | 100.0 |
| Chemical plants: Chemicals Energy Index | 90.8 | 89.3 | 92.0 | 93.0 | 92.6 | 92.5 | 95.8 | 93.3 | 98.3 | 99.7 |
| **Acid gases and VOCs** | | | | | | | | | | |
| Sulphur oxides (SOx) (thousand tonnes $SO_2$) | 136 | 139 | 141 | 175 | 212 | 233 | 226 | 247 | 257 | 240 |
| Nitrogen oxides (NO) (thousand tonnes $NO_2$) | 146 | 159 | 142 | 150 | 145 | 154 | 157 | 172 | 193 | 195 |
| Volatile organic compounds (VOCs) (thousand tonnes) | 111 | 133 | 126 | 130 | 148 | 185 | 199 | 213 | 226 | 324 |
| **Ozone-depleting emissions** | | | | | | | | | | |
| CFCs/halons/trichloroethane (tonnes) | 0.0 | 0.0 | 0.4 | 1.4 | 0.6 | 0.3 | 0.8 | 2.3 | 3.0 | 7.7 |
| Hydrochlorofluorocarbons (HCFCs) (tonnes) [H] | 11 | 21 | 24 | 26 | 27 | 35 | 35 | 42 | 44 | 57 |
| **Spills and discharges [I] [J]** | | | | | | | | | | |
| Sabotage spills – volume (thousand tonnes) [K] | 1.6 | 3.0 | 14.0 | 6.5 | 3.4 | 1.9 | 1.5 | 1.1 | 0.9 | 2.5 |
| Sabotage spills – number [K] | 118 | 112 | 95 | 115 | 197 | 123 | 111 | 101 | 105 | 128 |
| Operational spills – volume (thousand tonnes) [L] | 6.0 | 2.9 | 1.4 | 8.8 | 3.5 | 3.9 | 3.4 | 3.4 | 5.0 | 4.2 |
| Nigeria | 5.3 | 0.7 | 0.3 | 7.1 | 1.6 | 1.4 | 0.1 | 0.0 | 0.4 | 0.2 |
| Rest of world | 0.7 | 2.2 | 1.1 | 1.7 | 1.9 | 2.5 | 3.3 | 3.4 | 4.6 | 4.0 |
| Operational spills – number [M] | 208 | 195 | 275 | 275 | 392 | 465 | 560 | 711 | 678 | 784 |
| Nigeria [N] | 64 | 32 | 37 | 42 | 52 | 41 | 63 | 48 | 48 | 66 |
| Rest of world | 144 | 163 | 238 | 233 | 340 | 424 | 497 | 663 | 630 | 718 |
| Hurricane spills – volume (thousand tonnes) | 0.0 | 0.0 | 0.0 | 0.0 | 0.0 | 0.0 | 0.0 | 2.9 | 1.0 | 0.0 |
| Oil in effluents to surface environment (thousand tonnes) | 1.3 | 1.6 | 1.5 | 1.7 | 1.6 | 1.8 | 2.3 | 2.1 | 2.3 | 2.4 |
| **Water** | | | | | | | | | | |
| Fresh water withdrawn (million cubic metres) | 209 | 202 | 198 | 224 | 235 | n/c | n/c | n/c | n/c | n/c |
| **Waste disposal** | | | | | | | | | | |
| Hazardous (thousand tonnes) | 740 | 921 | 962 | 688 | 907 | 716 | 631 | 714 | 675 | 781 |
| Non-hazardous (thousand tonnes) [O] | 1737 | 1079 | 1139 | 996 | 1899 | 1154 | 632 | 421 | 443 | 480 |
| Total waste (thousand tonnes) | 2477 | 2000 | 2101 | 1684 | 2806 | 1870 | 1263 | 1135 | 1118 | 1261 |

# Royal Dutch Shell plc Sustainability Report 2011

Social Data

| | 2011 | 2010 | 2009 | 2008 | 2007 | 2006 | 2005 | 2004 | 2003 | 2002 |
|---|---|---|---|---|---|---|---|---|---|---|
| **Fatalities** | | | | | | | | | | |
| Total number | 6 | 12 | 20 | 26 | 21 | 37 | 34 | 31 | 45 | 51 |
| Employees | 1 | 0 | 1 | 2 | 1 | 2 | 3 | 2 | 5 | 8 |
| Contractors | 5 | 12 | 19 | 24 | 20 | 35 | 31 | 29 | 40 | 43 |
| Fatal accident rate (FAR) | 0.96 | 1.56 | 2.3 | 3.4 | 3.1 | 5.6 | 5.0 | 4.6 | 6.1 | 6.8 |
| Fatalities per 100 million working hours (employees and contractors) | | | | | | | | | | |
| **Injuries** | | | | | | | | | | |
| Total recordable case frequency (TRCF) | 1.24 | 1.23 | 1.4 | 1.8 | 1.9 | 2.1 | 2.5 | 2.6 | 2.6 | 2.5 |
| Injuries per million working hours (employees and contractors) | | | | | | | | | | |
| Lost time injury frequency (LTIF) | 0.36 | 0.35 | 0.4 | 0.6 | 0.7 | 0.8 | 1.0 | 1.1 | 1.1 | 1.1 |
| Lost time injuries per million working hours (employees and contractors) | | | | | | | | | | |
| **Illnesses** | | | | | | | | | | |
| Total recordable occupational illness frequency (TROIF) | 0.66 | 0.76 | 0.6 | 1.2 | 1.5 | 1.8 | 2.0 | 2.1 | 2.0 | 2.0 |
| Illnesses per million working hours (employees only) | | | | | | | | | | |
| S **Security** | | | | | | | | | | |
| Using armed security (% of countries) | 14 | 9 | 17 | 17 | 16 | 15 | 19 | 18 | 22 | 16 |
| Using armed company security (% of countries) | 1 | 1 | 1 | 1 | 2 | 2 | 2 | 2 | 2 | 1 |
| Using armed contractor security (% of countries) | 9 | 6 | 10 | 9 | 12 | 9 | 11 | 11 | 22 | 12 |
| **Gender diversity [A]** | | | | | | | | | | |
| In supervisory/professional positions (% women) | 27.3 | 26.3 | 26.4 | 24.7 | 24.6 | 23.2 | 21.8 | 20.7 | 19.5 | 18.9 |
| In management positions (% women) | 17.6 | 17.0 | 16.1 | 15.3 | 17.7 | 16.2 | 12.9 | 12.2 | 11.3 | 9.2 |
| In senior leadership positions (% women) | 16.6 | 15.3 | 14.0 | 13.6 | 12.9 | 11.6 | 9.9 | 9.6 | 9.6 | 8.8 |
| **Regional diversity [A]** | | | | | | | | | | |
| % countries with majority of local nationals in senior leadership positions | 34 | 36 | 37 | 32 | 33 | 25 | 36 | n/c | n/c | n/c |
| S **Staff forums and grievance procedures** | | | | | | | | | | |
| % countries with staff access to staff forum, grievance procedure or other support system | 99 | 100 | 99 | 100 | 100 | 99 | 100 | 100 | 100 | 100 |
| S **Child labour (% countries with specific procedures in place)** | | | | | | | | | | |
| Own operations | 100 | 99 | 98 | 100 | 99 | 95 | 88 | 83 | 78 | 86 |
| Contractors | | | | | 98 | 89 | 69 | 61 | 57 | 56 |
| Suppliers | 97 | 96 | 97 | 99 | 96 | 82 | 62 | 63 | 50 | 42 |
| S **Forced labour (% countries with specific procedures in place)** | | | | | | | | | | |
| Own operations | 100 | 99 | 98 | n/c | n/c | n/c | n/c | n/c | n/c | n/c |
| Contractors and suppliers | 99 | 95 | 89 | n/c | n/c | n/c | n/c | n/c | n/c | n/c |
| **Integrity** | | | | | | | | | | |
| Code of Conduct violations [B] | 226 | 205 | 165 | 204 | 361 | n/c | n/c | n/c | n/c | n/c |
| S Contracts cancelled due to incompatibility with Business Principles | 11 | 40 | 24 | 49 | 35 | 41 | 63 | 64 | 49 | 54 |
| S Joint ventures divested due to incompatibility with Business Principles | 0 | 0 | 0 | 0 | 0 | 0 | 0 | 0 | 1 | 0 |
| $ **Contracting and procurement** | | | | | | | | | | |
| Estimated expenditure on goods and services from locally owned companies in lower-income countries ($ billion) [C] | 12 | 13 | 12 | 12 | 13 | 10 | 9 | 6 | 5 | n/c |
| **Social investment [D]** | | | | | | | | | | |
| $ Estimated voluntary social investment (equity share) ($ million) | 125 | 121 | 132 | 148 | 170 | 140 | 127 | 106 | 102 | 96 |
| $ Estimated social investment spend (equity share) in lower-income countries ($ million) [E] | 45 | 61 | 54 | 61 | 65 | n/c | n/c | n/c | n/c | n/c |

## About our Data

There are inherent limitations to the accuracy of environmental and social data. We recognize that our environmental and social data will be affected by these limitations and continue to improve the integrity of our data by strengthening our internal controls. All non-financial data in this report are reported on a 100 per cent basis for companies and joint ventures where we are the operator. Environmental data are for our direct emissions unless otherwise stated. We report in this way, in line with industry practice, because these are the data we can directly manage and affect through operational improvements. Operations acquired or disposed of during the year are included only for the period we had ownership. Other data are collected from external sources, staff surveys and other internal sources as indicated. We only include data in this report that have been confirmed by the end of March 2012. If incidents are reclassified or confirmed, or if significant data changes occur after preparation of this report, they will be updated in the following year's publication. Data marked in the social data table come from an internal survey completed by the senior Shell representative in each country. The accuracy of environmental and social data may be lower than that of data obtained through our financial systems. Data provided are subject to internal controls. Lloyd's Register Quality Assurance Ltd has provided limited assurance of our direct and indirect greenhouse gas (GHG) emissions data for 2011. Limited assurance means nothing has come to the auditor's attention that would indicate that the data are not correct. For GHG emissions we provide more detailed data on our website. www.shell.com/ghg Conversions into US dollars are based on the average exchange rates for 2011.

## ACTIVITY 11.13

Which type of assurance does Shell's Sustainability Report have attached to it?

### Activity feedback

It looks like it is only Type 1 assurance. A quick look on the LRQA website (www.lrqa.co.uk/standards-and-schemes/environment-and-energy/csr.aspx?id=1&zoom_highlight=sustainability+report) would seem to confirm this as there it says: 'We were closely involved in helping develop the principles for the AA1000 Assurance Standard and our experts have participated in GRI's working groups. We were part of the materiality working group whose output produced GRI's Technical Protocol. This publication was created to provide process guidance on how to define the content of a sustainability report. This includes deciding on the Scope of a report, the range of topics covered, each topic's relative reporting priority and level of coverage, and what to disclose in the report about the process for defining its content.'

## ETHICS IN ACCOUNTING

### Introduction

As financial accounting information forms the basis for decisions that have consequences for the allocation of resources and the distribution of the income generated by reporting entities, it provides positive incentives to work productively and efficiently, but it also provides incentives and opportunities to be self-seeking at the expense of the interests of others. Users of financial reports expect the accountants who have prepared and audited them to have carried out their duties in a true and fair manner. Professional accountants, and particularly those in public service (i.e. auditors) within all their dealings must act with honesty, integrity and reliability if they expect public trust to be placed in them. The accounting profession and the associated professional bodies have established peer groups that oversee the discipline of members if their behaviour is not as expected. Penalties imposed by these professional bodies cover suspension of practising licences, fines and termination of membership. In addition, accountants are also of course subject to the law of the country in which they practice.

## IESBA and ethics

The International Federation of Accountants (IFAC) 'is the global organization for the accounting profession dedicated to serving the public interest by strengthening the profession and contributing to the development of strong international economies' (IFAC website, accessed 2 March 2013). It comprises the International Auditing and Assurance Standards Board (IAASB), the International Accounting Education Standards Board (IAESB), the International Public Sector Accounting Standards Board (IPSASB) and the International Ethics Standards Board for Accountants (IESBA).

You can find the IESBA Code of Ethics for Professional Accountants in the Handbook of the Code of Ethics for Professional Accountants on the IFAC website. At the time of writing the latest edition of the IESBA Code and Handbook is from 2012. The fundamental principles of the Code remain the same as those of the old IFAC Code of Ethics, which are (para. 100.5):

- Integrity – a professional accountant should be straightforward and honest in performing professional services.
- Objectivity – a professional accountant should not allow bias, conflict of interest or undue influence of others to override professional or business judgements.
- Professional competence and due care – a professional accountant has a continuing duty to maintain professional knowledge and skill at the level required to ensure that a client or employer receives competent professional service based on current developments. A professional accountant should act diligently and in accordance with applicable technical and professional standards when providing professional services. From the above it is apparent that accountants will need to commit to continuing professional development.
- Confidentiality – a professional accountant should respect the confidentiality of information acquired as a result of professional and business relationships and should not disclose any such information to third parties without proper and specific authority unless there is a legal or professional right or duty to disclose. Confidential information acquired as a result of professional and business relationships should not be used for the personal advantage of the professional accountant or third parties.
- Professional behaviour – a professional accountant should comply with relevant laws and regulations and should avoid any action that discredits the profession.

**Threats to adherence to the Code** The Code, as much else in accounting, is principles-based not rules-based, and therefore does not provide an extensive set of rules to follow. It considers how threats such as self-interest, self-review, advocacy, familiarity and intimidation create the conditions in which people might be tempted to act contrary to the principles and invites the application of safeguards in the form of institutional procedural frameworks and personal responses to overcome them. Part B of the Code deals with such threats in the case of accountants in public practice and Part C of the Code deals with professional accountants in business.

## ACTIVITY 11.14

The Code states that:

- Self-interest threats can occur as a result of the financial or other interests of an accountant or of an immediate or close family member.

- Intimidation can occur when a professional accountant may be deterred from acting objectively by threats, actual or perceived.

Give examples of self-interest threats and intimidation threats for both accountants in public practice and in business.

### Activity feedback
*Self-interest threats could be:*

- *a financial interest in a client or jointly holding a financial interest with a client*

- *undue dependence on total fees from a client*

- *concern about the possibility of losing a client*

- *having a close business relationship with a client*

- *potential employment with a client*

- *contingent fees relating to an assurance engagement*

- *financial interest, loans or guarantees in the business*

- *incentive compensation arrangements, e.g. bonuses*

- *inappropriate personal use of corporate assets*

- *concern over employment security*

- *commercial pressure from outside the employing organization.*

*Intimidation threats could be:*

- *threat of dismissal or replacement*

- *threat of litigation*

- *pressure to reduce inappropriately the extent of the work performed to reduce costs*

- *threat of dismissal or replacement of the professional accountant in business or a close or immediate family member over a disagreement about the application of an accounting principle or the way in which financial information is to be reported*

- *a dominant personality attempting to influence the decision-making process, e.g. with regard to the awarding of contracts or the application of an accounting principle.*

## ACTIVITY 11.15

Identify safeguards to guard against the threats to professional accountants that could be employed in the workplace.

### Activity feedback
*The safeguard examples given by the Code are:*

- *the employing organization's systems of corporate oversight or other oversight structures*

- *the employing organization's ethics and conduct programmes*

- *recruitment procedures in the employing organization emphasizing the importance of employing high calibre competent staff*

- *strong internal controls*

- *appropriate disciplinary processes*

- *leadership that stresses the importance of ethical behaviour and the expectation*

*(Continued)*

## ACTIVITY 11.15    *(Continued)*

*that employees will act in an ethical manner*

- *policies and procedures to implement and monitor the quality of employee performance*
- *timely communication of the employing organization's policies and procedures, including any changes to them, to all employees and appropriate training and education on such policies and procedures*
- *policies and procedures to empower and encourage employees to communicate to senior levels within the employing organization any ethical issues that concern them without fear of retribution*
- *consultation with another appropriate professional accountant. (Several professional accountancy bodies provide networks to facilitate this.)*

*The Code also includes what might be regarded as the final safeguard:*

*In circumstances where a professional accountant in business believes that unethical behaviour or actions by others will continue to occur within the employing organization, the professional accountant in business should consider seeking legal advice. In those extreme situations where all available safeguards have been exhausted and it is not possible to reduce the threat to an acceptable level a professional accountant in business may conclude that it is appropriate to resign from the employing organization.*

**Safeguards to such threats** The Code advocates the employment of safeguards to eliminate or reduce the threats to the professional accountant. These safeguards can be created by the profession, legislation or regulation or can be created within the workplace.

**Acting with sufficient expertise** The Introduction outlined the fundamental principles of the Code. One of these – acting with sufficient expertise – we would like to consider in a little more detail. This principle requires that the accountant only undertakes significant tasks for which he/she has, or can obtain, sufficient specific training or experience. Within the workplace there can be many potential threats to the maintenance of this principle by the accountant.

## ACTIVITY 11.16

Identify circumstances that could exist within the workplace that would threaten the ability of the accountant to perform his duties within his given level of expertise. In addition, identify safeguards that the accountant could employ to ensure he/she maintains this fundamental principle.

### Activity feedback
The Code gives the following threats:

- *insufficient time for properly performing or completing the relevant duties*
- *incomplete, restricted or otherwise inadequate information for performing the duties properly*
- *insufficient experience, training and/or education*
- *inadequate resources for the proper performance of the duties.*

*Safeguards that may be considered are:*

- *obtaining additional advice or training*
- *ensuring that there is adequate time available for performing the relevant duties*
- *obtaining assistance from someone with the necessary expertise*
- *consulting where appropriate, with superiors, independent experts, and a relevant professional body.*

*The final safeguard is, of course, to refuse to perform the task/duties but remember to communicate to your superiors the reasons for the refusal.*

## ACTIVITY 11.17

### Brief case study

You are a second-year trainee accountant about to go on study leave. Your manager asks you to complete some complicated reconciliation work before your study leave commences as your senior colleague who was due to do the work is on long-term sick leave. You feel the deadline given for the complicated task is unrealistic. You also do not feel sufficiently experienced to complete the work. You have asked your manager for additional supervision to complete the work but this has been refused. Your manager reiterates that he expects the work to be completed before you can take your study leave.

State which principles of the Ethical Code you think the above scenario brings into question, what threats exist and the action you would take to resolve the issue.

### Activity feedback

*The fundamental principles involved in this scenario are integrity, professional competence and due care, and professional behaviour.*

*The threat is intimidation.*

*A suitable course of action would be to explain, politely, to your manager that you do not have sufficient time to complete the work before your study leave; that if you do undertake the work you will need suitable supervision; and that you will of course complete the work when you return from study leave. If this action does not resolve the issue you must obtain advice from a senior colleague or from your professional body.*

*(Adapted – CIPFA ethics code case studies)*

## SUMMARY

We have considered the issue of corporate governance within this chapter and identified that the principles of corporate governance are evolutionary and will need to be reviewed in the light of significant changes in worldwide financial markets. As the OECD (2004) states in its *Principles of Corporate Governance*:

> To remain competitive in a changing world, corporations must innovate and adapt their corporate governance practices so that they can meet new demands and grasp new opportunities. Similarly, governments have an important responsibility for shaping an effective regulatory framework that provides for sufficient flexibility to allow markets to function effectively and to respond to expectations of shareholders and other stakeholders.

There is a school of thought that more information is always, provided it is properly presented, a good thing. The list of possibilities is almost endless as we have hopefully indicated in this chapter. But there is a danger that the purpose of the whole operation becomes lost. We need to provide information that is useful to the typical user. What evidence there is tends to suggest that many users are not able to understand the information they are already getting. It could be argued that the priority for accountants should be to improve their ability to communicate understanding, rather than to increase the detail and complexity of their reports. Is the graph or the pie chart more useful than the beautifully balanced balance sheet? Is the 'chatty' chairman's statement of more use than the precisely detailed and carefully audited accounts and voluminous notes? Is the CSR report of more use than the segmental report even if it does lack a degree of reliability? And how can we audit this CSR report? How will we verify information on the Internet and that provided through the use of new digital languages? These are all questions that the accounting profession will need to answer.

In this chapter we have outlined a wide variety of possible developments and extensions to the accounting framework and reporting practice. All involve additional effort and therefore additional cost. But if the advantages to some users or potential users outweigh those costs, then we should perhaps produce them.

Whatever additional statements accountants become involved in preparing or verifying, they will need to be trusted by all users and our ethical behaviour will become a powerful means of creating confidence in the business world. It is essential that you as a student of financial reporting understand and are guided by the fundamental principles of the IESBA Code of Ethics so that the accountant retains a position of trust within society.

## EXERCISES

*Suggested answers to exercises marked ✓ are to be found on our dedicated CourseMate platform for students.*

*Suggested answers to the remaining exercises are to be found on the Instructor online support resources.*

1 Using the annual report of any entity of your choice, discuss whether the information provided therein is of use to users.

2 For the same entity identify what, if any, additional information you as a potential shareholder would have wished to be available and what use you would make of the information.

3 Using the information given in Activity 11.7 in respect of Bayer's value added statement, identify possible conclusions that could be drawn in respect of Bayer's performance for the year and any caveats you would place on these conclusions.

4 Using the management report from any entity of your choice, identify all information it contains relevant to employees and discuss the importance of this information to the employees of the entity.

5 Critically appraise the following statement: 'All information provided by an entity in addition to that required by country law is potentially misleading to users.'

✓ 6 Discuss the need for entities to provide additional information to users.

✓ 7 Identify the potential drawbacks of entities providing additional information and suggest possible means of overcoming these drawbacks.

8 In the last analysis, financial reporting is about numbers. Discuss.

9 'When users are asked what they want from corporate environmental statements, there appears to be the usual mix of that which is deliverable, that which would be nice if only the accountants could find a way of delivering it, and that which will never be deliverable – available or not – because of commercial sensitivity' (Adams, 1994, 16). Is this pessimistic or realistic today? Discuss and illustrate.

10 Appraise the development of corporate governance in meeting the needs of business and its stakeholders in the twenty-first century.

11 Identify the recent developments in corporate social reporting and evaluate the effect such reporting has on alleviating social and environmental problems.

12 Identify the fundamental ethical principles that professional accountants must abide by and the threats they may be subject to in their working environment.

# BASICS OF INTERPRETATION OF FINANCIAL STATEMENTS

# 12

**OBJECTIVES**  After studying this chapter you should be able to:

- identify the needs of users wishing to make use of accounting information

- explain the technique of ratio analysis and calculate appropriate ratios

- explain what each of the ratios means and discuss their limitations

- identify additional information that users may require to aid their analysis.

## INTRODUCTION

We will be concerned in Parts Two and Three of this book with the provision of financial information to users which presents a true and fair view of the entity. Users will use this information to gain some insight as to the reporting entity's stability, performance, future prospects and/or whatever else may interest them.

In this chapter we will introduce the basic instruments of financial statement analysis. The presentation of these topics will enable you to understand the discussion on financial statement analysis in Part Four of this book. If you have already mastered the basics of ratio analysis and interpretation of financial statements, you can skip this chapter and continue on to Part Two of the book.

## ACCOUNTING INFORMATION AND USERS

Financial statements provide valuable information for both the owners of the business and any potential owners/investors, and for other stakeholders of the company. In Chapter 1 we identified the users of accounting information and their differing needs (see Activity 1.1).

### ACTIVITY 12.1

In its preface to the conceptual framework, the IASB gives a list of examples of different economic decisions which are made by users on the basis of the financial statements of a company. Consider the following list of examples of economic decisions. Try to figure out which group of users will be especially interested in each economic decision:

(a) deciding when to buy, hold or sell an equity investment

(b) assessing the stewardship or accountability of management

(c) assessing the ability of the entity to pay and provide other benefits to its employees

(d) assessing the security for amounts lent to the entity

(e) determining taxation policies

(f) determining distributable profits and dividends

(g) preparing and using national income statistics, or

(h) regulating the activities of entities.

*Activity feedback*

*The decisions listed in (a) and (b) will be taken by owners of the company and potential owners. Among the owners of the company we can distinguish different groups of owners, such as shareholders with small amounts of shares, or large institutional investors such as pension funds.*

*The decision listed in (c) will be an issue of concern to owners, but also to the creditors of the company and the employees. In a number of countries, including France, Germany and Belgium, the law prescribes that financial information should be provided in specific formats to the workforce. To make sure that the information is reliable, auditors have to certify the economics and financial information provided to the employees by corporate management. Decision (d) will concern especially the suppliers of long-term credit to the company. Decision (e) is important for owners as well as for the government. Owners try to establish the most favourable tax regime for their operations. Decisions (f), (g) and (h) refer to governmental decisions or decisions of regulatory authorities. These governmental or regulatory bodies can be national or supranational.*

Financial statement data serve as an input to these economic decisions of the different stakeholders of the company. The financial statements provide information on the financial position, the changes in the financial position and the performance of the company. These financial data are more appropriate for certain economic decisions than for others. For example, regulatory authorities will probably have to combine financial statement data with other data for their decision-making process. Regulatory authorities overseeing the competition in certain industries will also need to collect data on market shares or pricing policies of the different companies. So financial as well as non-financial data from other sources will be added to financial statement data in order to make decisions.

The analysis of the economic decisions carried out in Activity 12.1 indicates that it is possible to identify three general areas of interest in which users' needs and objectives may lie.

Although all the information needs of users cannot be met solely by financial statement data, there are needs that are common to all interested parties. The first two items below might interest a wide group of users. The third need relates to owners and potential owners:

- *Financial status* – Can the business pay its way in the short-term as well as in the long-term, so is it in fact *liquid* and *solvent*?

- *Performance* – How successful is the business? Is it making a reasonable profit? Is it utilizing its assets to the fullest? Is it in fact *profitable* and *efficient*?

- *Investment* – Is the business a suitable investment for shareholders, or would returns be greater if they invested elsewhere? Is it a good *investment*?

# BENCHMARKING

These three general areas of interest require answers to questions which are subjective in nature, not objective. For instance, how do we judge whether a profit is reasonable? We could do so by comparing current profit or income to profit or income made in previous years or to profit or income made by other businesses. In other words, we use benchmarks against which we compare current performance, financial status and investment potential. However, we need to take great care in carrying out this benchmarking so that we do not invalidate the results. Consider, for example, your opinion of the disco you attended last night. You may think it was the best disco you have ever attended; your friend may think it was the worst night out he or she ever had. This is because the experiences/benchmarks you each have are different and you are making a subjective judgement on how the current disco compares with those you previously attended. Thus, in setting benchmarks against which we can compare a company, we must be aware of the limitations of this comparison.

First we need to identify benchmarks/indicators we can use; then we need to consider their limitations. Four possible benchmarks are:

- past period achievements
- budgeted achievements
- other businesses' achievements
- averages of businesses' achievements in the same area.

## ACTIVITY 12.2

Identify for each indicator above its uses and limitations.

### Activity feedback

- *Past periods*

  Uses – *To identify whether current activity is better or worse than previous periods.*

  Limitations – *External factors may have influenced activity levels, e.g. public awareness of environmental issues may have necessitated a change in manufacturing process leading to increased costs.*

- *Budgets*

  Uses – *Has current activity matched planned activity?*

  Limitations – *The budget may not be a valid standard of performance, e.g. underlying assumptions may have been unrealistic or set at too high a level.*

- *Other businesses*

  Uses – *Is our business performing as well?*

  Limitations – *Businesses may not be truly comparable with regard to size and type, e.g. grocery sole trader compared to supermarket; manufacturer compared to retailer.*

  *External factors may affect one business, e.g. lengthy strike.*

  *Accounting policies and bases on which accounting information is prepared may be different, e.g. stock valuations, depreciation, historical cost or revalued amount, treatment of research and development, treatment of goodwill.*

- *Industry averages have uses and limitations very similar to those of other businesses. Additionally, an average is simply that – an average which takes account of the best and the worst.*

Each of the four benchmarks identified are commonly used in assessing business status, performance and potential, but interpretation of accounts is highly subjective and requires skilled judgement, bearing in mind the limitations of these benchmarks.

In Part Four of this book we will discuss further the pitfalls in the interpretation of the information included in the annual accounts of a company. We will also study the techniques of industry analysis and horizontal and vertical analysis (= trend analysis and common size analysis). In this chapter we will concentrate on the techniques of analysis which can be applied to financial statements without elaborating further on the issues of the benchmarks.

## TECHNIQUE OF RATIO ANALYSIS

Financial statements identify for us a multitude of figures, for example profit or income before tax, gross profit, total of fixed assets and net current assets. However, these figures do not mean very much unless we can compare them to something else. For example, looking at a set of financial statements for a high street retailer may tell us that profit before tax is £3 million, but will not tell us if this is a good profit. It will probably be more than the profit of a sole trader in the same industry, but does it mean that the high street retailer is performing better? Now look at Activity 12.3.

## ACTIVITY 12.3

You have £1150 to invest and discover that type 1 investment will provide interest of £68 per annum and type 2 investment will provide a single interest payment of £341 after five years. Which investment would you choose, assuming no compound interest and no change in the value of the pound?

*Activity feedback*
Investment 1 provides a return of 68/1150 = 5.91 per cent per annum. Investment 2 provides a return of 68.2/

1150 = 5.93 per cent per annum. Thus, investment 2 provides the highest return. In the above example we compared the return with the amount invested and expressed the figures in the same units – percentage per annum. We were then able to identify which investment provided the better return.

What we did in Activity 12.3 was calculate a ratio. We will illustrate in the remainder of this chapter how different ratios can be calculated in order to help solve the three information needs mentioned above and facilitate the decision-making process of the different stakeholders of the company.

The next section identifies which figures in a set of financial statements it would be useful to compare to evaluate financial status, performance and investment potential of a business. The financial statements used are those of Serendipity plc, which are reproduced below.

The layout and format of these financial statements is not the layout put forward in IAS 1. Note for simplicity of illustration the format below does not prescribe to IAS 1. The information provided in relation to the company Serendipity relates to the components which determine the profit or loss of the period. We will not include elements of other comprehensive income for the period in this example.

## Serendipity income statement

|  | Year-ended 31.12.X4 | | Year-ended 31.12.X5 | |
|---|---|---|---|---|
|  | £000 | £000 | £000 | £000 |
| Sales |  | 584 |  | 972 |
| Opening inventory | 31 |  | 47 |  |
| Purchases | 405 |  | 700 |  |
|  | 436 |  | 747 |  |
| Closing inventory | 47 |  | 62 |  |
| Cost of goods sold |  | 389 |  | 685 |
| *Gross profit* |  | 195 |  | 287 |
| Wages and salaries | 78 |  | 101 |  |
| Depreciation | 16 |  | 31 |  |
| Debenture interest | – |  | 8 |  |
| Other expenses | 54 | 148 | 62 | 202 |
| Net profit before tax |  | 47 |  | 85 |
| Taxation |  | 16 |  | 39 |
| Net profit after tax |  | 31 |  | 46 |
| Proposed dividend |  | 16 |  | 23 |
| Retained profit for year |  | 15 |  | 23 |

## Serendipity Statement of Financial Position

|  | 31.12.X4 | | 31.12.X5 | |
|---|---|---|---|---|
|  | £000 | £000 | £000 | £000 |
| Assets |  |  |  |  |
| Non-current assets |  | 280 |  | 428 |
| Current assets |  |  |  |  |
| Inventories | 47 |  | 62 |  |
| Debtors | 70 |  | 156 |  |
| Bank | 39 |  | 16 |  |
| Total current assets |  | 156 |  | 234 |
| Total assets |  | 436 |  | 662 |
| Equity |  | 365 |  | 411 |
| Share capital | 272 |  | 295 |  |
| Retained earnings | 93 |  | 116 |  |
| Non-current liabilities |  | – |  | 80 |
| 10% debentures | – |  | 80 |  |
| Current liabilities |  |  |  |  |
| Creditors | 39 |  | 109 |  |
| Taxation | 16 |  | 39 |  |
| Proposed dividends | 16 |  | 23 |  |
| Total current liabilities |  | 71 |  | 171 |
| Total equity and liabilities |  | 436 |  | 662 |

Strictly speaking in IAS jargon, current and non-current refers to the fact whether or not an asset will be expected to be realized in, or is intended for sale or consumption in, the entity's normal operation cycle (IAS 1, para. 66 (a)) and a liability is expected to be settled in the entity's normal operating cycle or due to be settled within 12 months (IAS 1, para. 69 (a) and (c)). Net current assets are current assets minus current liabilities.

In the format of the previous statement of financial position, total assets and total equity and liabilities are presented separately.

With regard to the income statement, the information on the changes in inventory levels and purchases will be provided in the notes to the accounts. On the face of an IAS income statement itself, you might only find the costs of goods sold which is calculated by combining the changes in inventory levels together with the purchases.

The ratios which will be introduced to you in the following sections are calculated with information found either on the face of the statement of financial position or on the face of the income statement or in the notes to the accounts.

Before beginning any ratio analysis it is useful to look at the accounts and identify any changes from one year to the next (see Activity 12.4).

## ACTIVITY 12.4

Compare and contrast each item on the statement of financial position and the income statement of Serendipity plc with the figure for the previous year. Note five points of interest from this comparison.

### Activity feedback
You should have identified five from the following:

- sales have increased in X5
- cost of sales has increased
- expenses have increased
- profit after tax has increased by 50 per cent
- fixed assets have increased substantially
- net current assets have reduced
- shares and debentures have been increased in X5.

Having identified various points of interest in Activity 12.4 we are now ready to carry out the ratio analysis. We will start with those ratios that are helpful in deciding whether or not a business is successful and whether or not it is operated in an efficient way.

## Performance

The first ratio to be considered in this respect is 'return on capital employed' (ROCE):

$$\text{ROCE} = \frac{\text{Profit before taxation and long-term loan interest}}{\text{Net assets (Equity + Long-term debt)}}$$

This ratio identifies how much profit the business has made from the capital invested in it and answers the question: Would the owners be better off selling the business and placing the proceeds in a bank deposit account?

In fact this ratio measures the return on investment. The question, however, is: What amount do we need to consider as invested capital? In the ROCE ratio above, net assets or equity with long-term debt is used as denominator. One could also use the total assets instead of net assets as a denominator. In the latter ratio we assume that all assets contribute to the profit of the company. Further, the ratio 'return on assets' (ROA) is not influenced by the financial structure of the company, whereas the ROCE ratio is to a certain extent, namely the trade-off between short-term and long-term financing. In the literature and in practice both ratios are used (ROA and ROCE).

$$\text{ROA} = \frac{\text{Profit before taxation + Interest}}{\text{Total assets}}$$

## ACTIVITY 12.5

Calculate the ROCE and ROA for Serendipity plc for X4 and X5.

*This ratio has increased from X4 to X5 indicating an increase in profitability of the business.*

### Activity feedback

|  | X4 | X5 |
|---|---|---|
| ROCE | 47/365 = 12.87% | 93/491 = 18.9% |
| ROA | 47/436 = 10.77% | 93/662 = 14.04% |

But where has this increased profitability come from? Is it because the business has increased sale prices or reduced expenses – that is, increased net profit margins – or is it because the business has increased the volume of trade compared to the capital employed?

In the following we continue with the ROCE ratio; the sub-analysis of the ROA ratio proceeds in exactly the same way and the interpretations are similar. The only difference is that capital employed is substituted by total assets, and in those circumstances, where one needs to take into account the interest expense, interest expense on short-term liabilities should be added to the interest expense which relates to long-term liabilities.

These two questions can be expressed as ratios as follows:

$$\text{Net profit margin} = \frac{\text{Profit before tax and Long-term interest}}{\text{Sales}}$$

$$\text{Volume of trade} = \frac{\text{Sales}}{\text{Capital employed}}$$

Calculating these two ratios for Serendipity plc we have:

|  | X4 | X5 |
|---|---|---|
| Net profit margin | 47/584 = 8% | 93/972 = 9.6% |

Net profit margin has increased indicating benefit gained from control of expenses or increased sale prices. An answer to that question will be given later on, with the help of other ratios:

|  | X4 | X5 |
|---|---|---|
| Volume of trade | 584/365 = 1.6 times | 972/491 = 1.98 times |

This indicates that Serendipity plc is earning more sales per pound of net assets or capital employed in X5 than X4.

The three ratios we have looked at so far have the following relationship:

$$\text{ROCE} = \text{Margin} \times \text{Volume}$$

$$\frac{\text{Profit}}{\text{Capital employed}} = \frac{\text{Profit}}{\text{Sales}} \times \frac{\text{Sales}}{\text{Capital employed}}$$

This relationship can be shown as a family tree:

ROCE

(Profit before tax + Long-term interest)/Sales        Sales/Capital employed

This family tree can be expanded and will provide a framework for the analysis of the performance and efficiency of the company. For example:

$$\text{Net profit/Sales} = \text{Gross profit/Sales} - \text{Expenses/Sales}$$

whereby,

$$\text{Gross profit} = \text{Sales} - \text{Cost of goods sold}$$

or, in brief:

$$\frac{GP}{S} - \frac{E}{S}$$

Sales/capital employed can be inverted to capital employed/sales, which is the value of assets held per pound of sales, and then expanded to:

$$\text{Fixed assets/Sales} + \text{Net current assets/Sales}$$

or, in brief:

$$\frac{FA}{S} + \frac{NCA}{S}$$

## ACTIVITY 12.6

Calculate these four further ratios for Serendipity plc and interpret them.

### Activity feedback

|  | X4 | X5 |
|---|---|---|
| Gross profit margin | 195/584 = 33.3% | 287/972 = 29.5% |

This demonstrates a reduction in gross profit.

This could be due to several reasons. First of all, we observe an increase in the relative cost of goods sold/sales. This percentage has increased from X4 to X5:

|  | X4 | X5 |
|---|---|---|
| Cost of good sold/ sales | 389/584 = 66% | 685/972 = 70% |

This could point at an inflation in the price of purchased goods or less efficient negotiations from the purchase department.

Another element could be that there is a decrease in sale prices which has generated more sales and a resulting increase in cost of goods sold:

|  | X4 | X5 |
|---|---|---|
| Expenses/sales | 148/584 = 25.3% | 194/972 = 20% |

This has decreased from X4 to X5 indicating a better control of all other expenses:

|  |  |  |
|---|---|---|
| FA/S | 280/584 = 0.48 | 428/972 = 0.44 |

If we invert the above, then for X4 we have 2.08 and for X5 2.27; that is, fixed assets have generated 2.08 times their value in sales in X4 and 2.27 times their value in sales in X5.

Fixed assets are earning more sales or are operated in a much more efficient way:

|  |  |  |
|---|---|---|
| NCA/S | 85/584 = 0.15 | 63/972 = 0.06 |

Inverting gives X4 6.87 and X5 15.4.

Net current assets are also earning more sales in X5 than X4.

So, all assets are used more efficiently in X5. Thus, we observe that the overall increase in profitability is positively influenced by the efficient use of the fixed assets and net current assets in X5, and the control of all expense except the cost of goods sold. The profitability was negatively influenced by the decrease in the gross profit margin.

The family tree of ratios, or pyramid, now looks like this:

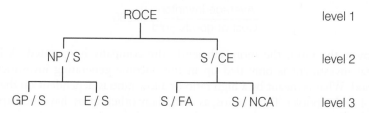

The pyramid can be extended to level 4 by comparing individual expenses to sales and breaking down the fixed assets and net current assets into their constituent parts:

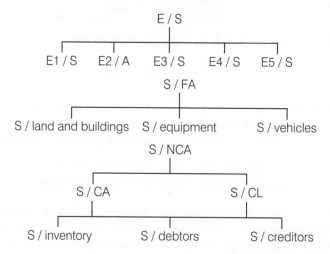

However, as inventory is recorded at cost, not selling price, then a more appropriate ratio than sale/inventory would be cost of goods sold/inventory, and as creditors relates to goods purchased on credit it would be better to look at credit purchases/creditors. Lastly sales/debtors would be more appropriate to credit sales/debtors.

Illustration 1 demonstrates the calculation and interpretation of these level 4 ratios.

## ILLUSTRATION

The following information is provided for TAX Ltd as at 31 December 20X4:

|  | £000 |
|---|---|
| Cost of goods sold | 220 |
| Average inventory for the year | 50 |
| Trade creditors | 86 |
| Credit purchases | 216 |
| Trade debtors | 96 |
| Credit sales | 284 |

Cost of goods sold/inventory = 220/50 = 4.4; that is, 4.4 times the average inventory level has been used in cost of goods sold for the year. This could be written more simply as: inventory is turned over every 83 days, i.e. 365/4.4 = 83 days.

The ratio is therefore:

$$\frac{\text{Average inventory}}{\text{Cost of goods sold}} \times 365$$

The lower the ratio, the more efficiently the company is operated. A low ratio means that investment is only tied up in non-income-generating investments for a short period. What is meant by a high ratio or a low ratio is dependent on the industry (see Part 4 of this book). These ratios, as with many other ratios, have industry-specific outcomes. Inventory days will be much higher in the steel industry than in industries which sell perishable goods.

The debtors' and creditors' ratios are written as:

$$\frac{\text{Trade debtors}}{\text{Credit sales}} \times 365$$

which will tell us on average how long it takes debtors to pay:

$$\frac{\text{Trade creditors}}{\text{Credit purchases}} \times 365$$

which will tell us how long on average it takes the business to pay its creditors.

The information provided above does not give a figure for credit sales or credit purchases, therefore we will have to use total sales and total purchases as an approximation:

$$\text{Debtors' period} = 96 \times 365/284 = 123 \text{ days}$$
$$\text{Creditors' period} = 86 \times 365/216 = 145 \text{ days}$$

Whether or not these level 4 ratios should be calculated when carrying out a ratio analysis will depend upon the information produced at previous levels. For example, when considering Serendipity plc we noted a marked improvement in the efficiency of net current assets; therefore, calculating the fourth level ratios may tell us where this improvement came from (see Activity 12.7).

## ACTIVITY 12.7

Calculate inventory, debtor and creditor turnover periods for Serendipity plc and interpret them.

### Activity feedback

|  | X4 | X5 |
|---|---|---|
| Inventory turnover | $(31 + 47)/2 \times$ 365/389 | $(47 + 62)/2 \times$ 365/685 |
| Number of inventory days | 36.6 days | 29 days |

Thus, inventory is being turned over quicker in X5, demonstrating greater efficiency.

| Debtors' turnover period | $70/584 \times 365$ | $156/972 \times 365$ |
|---|---|---|
|  | 44 days | 58 days |

Thus, debtors have been allowed (or have taken) 14 more days on average in X5 than X4 in which to pay their debts to the business. This could possibly indicate that Serendipity plc is losing control of its debtor collection, or that it has purposely allowed debtors more time to pay so as to encourage more sales.

| Creditors' turnover period | $39/405 \times 365$ | $109/700 \times 365$ |
|---|---|---|
|  | 35 days | 57 days |

(Note that cost of goods sold could be used as a substitute for purchases, if the financial statements do not provide a figure for purchases.) This indicates that Serendipity plc is taking longer to pay its suppliers – 22 days longer. This may damage relations with suppliers if Serendipity does not take care, but also demonstrates how Serendipity is using creditors to finance its business operations. A balance has to be struck within this dichotomy.

Within the analysis of Serendipity plc at level 3 there was also a benefit gained from control of expenses. Therefore fourth level analysis here would also be beneficial (see Activity 12.8).

---

## ACTIVITY 12.8

Calculate ratios of wages, depreciation and other expenses to sales and interpret them for Serendipity plc.

### Activity feedback

|  | X4 | X5 |
|---|---|---|
| Wages/sales | 78/584 = 13.3% | 101/972 = 10.4% |

This indicates that the amount of wages expended to generate £1 of sales has been reduced.

Depreciation/sales    16/584 = 2.7%    31/972 = 3.2%

*Depreciation has marginally increased as a proportion of sales. This may be due to an increase in assets.*

Other expenses/Sales  54/584 = 9.3%    62/972 = 6.4%

---

Other expenses have also been controlled as a percentage of sales. These three ratios, as we saw earlier, when combined gave an increase in profit margin – increased profitability. The pyramid also demonstrates that the ratios on the left-hand side show profitability and those on the right-hand side show efficiency in the use of assets. Before moving on to consider financial status within ratio analysis, we need to take another look at the first ratio on the pyramid – ROCE. Capital employed consists of shareholder funds – that is share capital and reserves – and long-term debt, for example debentures. In the example of Serendipity plc ROCE was:

|  |  |
|---|---|
| X4 | 12.87% |
| X5 | 18.9% |

However, the debentures in X5 only required a return to be paid to the holders of 10 per cent, even though the capital invested (£10 000) earned 18.9 per cent. The earnings over and above the 10 per cent will then accrue to the shareholders and their return will be increased beyond the 18.9 per cent that the total capital earned. This phenomenon can be demonstrated by calculating the ratio of return on equity:

$$\text{ROE} = \frac{\text{Profit before tax, but after interest}}{\text{Shareholders' equity (or owners' equity)}}$$

| X4 | X5 |
|---|---|
| $47/365 = 12.88\%$ | $85/411 = 20.68\%$ |

The shareholders have increased their earnings in the business partly due to the benefit gained by borrowing at a lower rate of return than the business is earning. However, the converse can also occur! Note that ROCE and ROE were both the same in X4 as there was no long-term debt.

Whereas ROCE or ROA provides an answer to the question of whether the business is worthwhile to invest in, the ROE ratio takes the perspective of the shareholder and tries to answer the question of whether the investment in the share capital of the company is beneficial for the owners of the shares.

## ACTIVITY 12.9

Given the following information, calculate ROCE and ROE for Knight Ltd for X4 and X5.

|  | X4 | X5 |
|---|---|---|
|  | £ | £ |
| Profit before tax | 80 | 85 |
| Interest charged | 10 | 10 |
| Capital employed | 1 250 | 1 280 |
| Long-term debt | 100 | 100 |

*Activity feedback*

| | | |
|---|---|---|
| ROCE | 90/1250 = 7.2% | 95/1280 = 7.4% |
| ROE | 80/1150 = 7% | 85/1180 = 7.2% |

*The return on capital employed made in each year is 7.2 per cent and 7.4 per cent, but the return payable to the long-term debt holders is 10 per cent in both years. Therefore the return available to the shareholders reduces to 7 per cent and 7.2 per cent.*

This is the opposite of the Serendipity case. Attracting external funds on which interest needs to be paid irrespective of the result of the company might be beneficial for the shareholders if ROA is higher than the interest rate paid by the firm on its debt. It is detrimental for the shareholders if ROA is lower than the interest rate paid by the firm on its debt. We need to compare ROCE with the interest paid on long-term debt.

After the discussion of the ratios which could help in determining whether or not a company is successful and operated in an efficient way, we turn our attention to the information needs in relation to the financial status of the company. The following questions will be asked by the interested parties:

1  Can the business pay its way? Is it liquid?

2  Has the company the ability to repay its debt? What is the security for the amounts lent to the company?

## FINANCIAL STATUS

It is essential for a business to be able to pay its debts as and when they fall due, otherwise its chances of remaining in operation become remote. Thus, there is a need to analyze the assets available to meet liabilities. This can be done in the short-, medium- and long-term since some debt will have to be repaid on short notice and other amounts will only fall due in the distant future.

Within the group of ratios which analyze the financial structure of the company, we distinguish on the one hand the liquidity ratios which are used to assess the company's ability to meet its short-term obligations. On the other we have the group of solvency ratios which concentrate on the question whether or not a company will repay its debt in the long-term.

### Liquidity ratios

Liquidity refers to the capacity of a company to generate liquidity from its current operations to repay its current debt. Therefore, ratios concentrating on the liquidity question will focus on the current assets or short-term assets and the current or short-term liabilities of the firm. The first liquidity ratio is the current ratio:

$$\frac{\text{Current assets}}{\text{Current liabilities}}$$

In most industries this ratio needs to be higher than one in order to indicate that no liquidity problem will arise. However, within the current assets there are items which might not be realizable in the very short-term, for example inventory items that are damaged. Therefore, there is a second liquidity ratio, the quick ratio or the acid test ratio:

$$\frac{\text{Current assets} - \text{Inventory}}{\text{Current liabilities}}$$

The acid test is often called the short-term liquidity test and the current ratio the medium-term liquidity test.

## Solvency

Solvency ratios try to measure the risk involved in the repayment of debt and the ability of a company to meet its debt in the long-run. A key element in this respect is the capital structure of the firm. Companies have two main resources of funds, namely debt and equity. Each has different well-known characteristics (e.g. fixed versus variable rewards, fixed repayment schedules versus repayment when the company liquidates). The financial risk or financial strength of a company is measured by ratios which relate debt to equity. The most commonly used ratio worldwide in this respect is the debt/equity ratio. A high debt/equity ratio implies higher financial risk, since a higher ratio points at higher interest charges and a wider exposure to possible interest changes. Further, debt needs to be repaid often at a fixed date irrespective of whether or not the company has sufficient funds available. Several alterations can be made to the numerator and the denominator of this ratio in relation to the focus of the analysis, for example:

$$\frac{\text{Debt}}{\text{Equity}} \quad \text{or} \quad \frac{\text{Long-term debt}}{\text{Equity}}$$

The ratios mentioned above are often called gearing ratios.

$$\frac{\text{Debt}}{\text{Equity} + \text{Debt}} \quad \text{or} \quad \frac{\text{Equity}}{\text{Equity} + \text{Debt}}$$

The interest cover ratio is a ratio which indicates the safety margin between profits generated and interest charges and is calculated as follows:

$$\frac{\text{Net profit before interest and taxes}}{\text{Total interest charges}}$$

Whether or not a company is able to repay its debt in the long-term depends on the ability of the company to generate cash flow from operations, from the disposal of assets or from external funding. The future cash flow generating capacity of a company can be estimated on the basis of the current cash flow. Whether or not a company will dispose of its assets depends on its strategy and the role of these assets in implementing the strategy. The possibility to attract external funds will depend on the appreciation of the company by the capital markets and the suppliers of the long-term and short-term credit. These items will be explained further in Part Four of this book.

## ACTIVITY 12.10

Calculate the two liquidity ratios, the gearing ratio, the interest cover ratio, the debt/equity ratio and the debt/(equity + debt) ratio for Serendipity plc and interpret them.

### Activity feedback

| | X4 | X5 |
|---|---|---|
| Acid test | $\dfrac{156 - 47}{71} = \dfrac{109}{71}$ | $\dfrac{234 - 62}{171} = \dfrac{172}{171}$ |
| expressed as, | 1.5:1 | 1:1 |

The ratio has decreased from X4 to X5 quite considerably, but there are still plenty of liquid assets. The ratio will need careful monitoring to control this downward trend.

Current ratio   156/71 = 2.2:1   234/171 = 1.4:1

Again, this ratio has been substantially reduced but still appears adequate. Monitoring of this downward trend is again required.

Gearing ratio   not relevant   80/411 = 19.5%

This is low and we would consider this company low geared. If a company is high geared, then it may have difficulty meeting the required interest payments. However, this needs to be interpreted not only within the specific industry context, but also within the national environment (more on these items in Part Four).

| | | |
|---|---|---|
| Debt/Equity | 71/365 = 19.45% | 251/411 = 61.07% |
| Debt/Equity + Debt | 71/436 = 16.28% | 251/662 = 37.91% |

We notice a deterioration of the financial structure.

Interest cover   not relevant   $(85 + 8)/8 = 12$

In X5 the profit covered the required interest payment 12 times, indicating no immediate problem for Serendipity plc. Notice how consideration of all four ratios helped to build up a picture of the financial status of Serendipity plc.

---

The last grouping of ratios we will discuss in this chapter relate specifically to the information needs of current and potential shareholders. This group is especially interested in finding out whether or not the investment they make, or intend to make, in a company is a profitable investment compared to other investment possibilities they have (e.g. buying shares in other companies subscribing to debentures or putting their money into a savings account).

## Investment potential

Before looking in detail at investment ratios, it is useful to carry out some practical research.

## ACTIVITY 12.11

Obtain a fairly recent copy of a financial newspaper (e.g. The Wall Street Journal or The Financial Times, or the equivalent in your own country). Look up the share information service and make a note of the data provided for each company. Also read the 'company news section' either in a financial newspaper or any other quality newspaper, and note down any ratios or indicators used to evaluate the companies.

### Activity feedback
Your list possibly includes the following:

- book value per share compared with market value per share
- net dividend
- dividend cover
- earnings per share (EPS)
- gross dividend yield
- price/earnings ratio.

We will look at each of these ratios in turn.

**Book value per share** This is the ordinary shareholders' equity/number of shares. This book value is the value each share would have if the company's assets and liabilities were sold at their balance sheet or statement of financial position (book) value. The market value is the price a potential shareholder is willing to pay to acquire a share in the company. Comparing these two values identifies whether the market values the company at more or less than its book value.

**Net dividend** This is the amount of dividend declared in any one year per share which equals paid and proposed dividends divided by the number of shares. People invest in shares for one of two reasons: either to earn dividends or to earn capital growth in the value of the share, or both. The level of dividend and its comparison with previous years is generally regarded as an important indicator of future expectations. However, one danger with this comparison is that dividends are not necessarily just paid out of the current year's earnings, but can be paid out of retained earnings. It is, therefore, important to look at dividend cover in any one year.

**Dividend cover**

$$\frac{\text{Net profit available to ordinary shareholders}}{\text{Total ordinary dividend}}$$

## ACTIVITY 12.12

The following information is available in respect of Kit plc:

|  | X4 £ | X5 £ |
|---|---|---|
| Ordinary shares issued £1 | 1 875 000 | 1 875 000 |
| 8% preference shares £1 | 660 000 | 660 000 |
| Dividend ordinary shares | 225 000 | 187 500 |
| Net profit after tax | 257 500 | 231 900 |

Calculate dividend per share in pence for both preference and ordinary shares, and dividend cover.

### Activity feedback

| Dividend per preference share | 8p | 8p |
|---|---|---|
| Dividend per ordinary share | 12p | 10p |
| Dividend cover | 257 500/277 800 | 231 900/240 300 |
|  | 0.93 | 0.97 |

Thus the dividend per share has reduced from X4 to X5, but the dividend cover has improved. However, this dividend cover is less than one which indicates that the company is not earning enough in either year to pay the dividend, and is therefore using past earnings retained to fund the dividend payment. This may be a danger sign for potential investors.

**Earnings per share** This is another indicator used widely by the investment community. It represents the amount of profit available to ordinary shareholders the company has earned during the year for each ordinary share. We will provide more information on this ratio when we discuss IAS 33 'Earnings per share' in Chapter 25.

For the example of Kit plc (see Activity 12.12), the/in X4 is 204 700/1 875 000 = 10.9p and in X5 is 179 100/1 875 000 = 9.6p.

**Gross dividend yield** This is calculated using the formula:

$$\frac{\text{Gross dividend}}{\text{Market price of ordinary share}}$$

Shareholders may be willing to accept a low gross dividend yield if there is a greater than average capital growth in share value expected or if the company is a safe investment. Gross dividend is calculated by grossing up the dividend declared in the accounts for basic rate taxation as dividends are always declared and paid net of basic income tax.

For example, in the case of Kit plc if the basic rate of tax is 20 per cent, then the gross dividend is:

|  | X4 | X5 |
|---|---|---|
|  | 225 000/80% | 187 500/80% |
|  | 281 250 | 234 375 |
| or per share, | 15p | 12.5p |

If the market value per share for Kit was £1.75 in X4 and £1.82 in X5, then the gross dividend yield is:

|  | X4 | X5 |
|---|---|---|
|  | 15/175 | 12.5/182 |
|  | 8.6% | 6.9% |

**Price/Earnings (PE) Ratio** The formula for this is:

$$\frac{\text{Market price per share}}{\text{Earnings per share}}$$

For Kit this is:

| 175/10.9 | 182/9.6 |
|---|---|
| 16.1 | 19 |

Like the dividend yield, the PE ratio will change as the market price per share changes. It represents the market's view of the growth potential of the company, its dividend policy and the degree of risk involved in the investment. In general, a high PE indicates that the market has a high/good opinion of these factors, a low PE a low/poor opinion. Another way of looking at the PE is that it represents the number of years' earnings it is necessary to have at the current rate to recover the price paid for the share. For Kit plc this was 19 years at the X5 rate of earnings.

In the discussion of the ratios we have covered the three principal areas in which users need information to make economic decisions (profitability, financial status and investment potential). More ratios and evaluation concepts (like economic value added and total shareholder return) are introduced in Chapter 32 'Techniques of Financial Analysis'. Although financial statement data represent an important source of information, they have to be interpreted with caution and must be combined with additional information to make sound business decisions. The pitfalls in ratio analysis will be discussed further in Part Four of this book, as well as an analysis of the additional information needed. To provide an idea on this additional information, see Activity 12.13.

## ADDITIONAL INFORMATION

Ratio analysis is a tool that aids the user in building up an overall picture of the condition/state of a business entity. Other information can help to fill in more of this picture.

## ACTIVITY 12.13

Identify additional information that you would like when undertaking a ratio analysis of a company.

### Activity feedback

- *Inflation effects on the company.*
- *Does the statement of financial position represent the position of the business throughout the year or just at the year-end?*
- *Cash flow throughout the year.*

- *Forecast business plans in the form of budgets and cash flows.*
- *Information in respect of the quality of goods and services and other factors affecting the assessment of goodwill in the business.*
- *Industrial averages of ratios.*
- *Differences in accounting policies between businesses.*

Much of the information in Activity 12.13 will not be available to all users. For example, it would be very difficult, probably impossible, for a potential investor to obtain detailed information in respect of future plans of the business apart from that disclosed in the directors' report in the financial statements.

## SUMMARY

This chapter has considered the users of the financial statements and their needs. We identified a tool – ratio analysis – in an attempt to meet these needs. We have illustrated how individual components of the statement of financial position, the income statement and the notes can be used in ratio analysis in order to provide useful data for economic decision making. In this chapter the illustrations of performance, liquidity, solvency and investment ratios only allowed us to judge whether or not the position of Serendipity had improved from year X4 to year X5. To make sound business decisions, however, we need to compare the outcomes of the ratios not only over a longer time span than just two years, but we also need to compare with the outcomes of other companies. This will be elaborated further in Part Four of this book. We continue in Part Two and Part Three with the analysis of the definition, recognition and measurement of the individual components of the statement of financial position and the income statement. We will also pay attention to the disclosures in the notes. The choices made in these domains of definition, recognition and measurement will without doubt influence the outcome of the ratios and subsequently influence the appreciation of the stakeholders of the company with regard to the company's efficiency, success and financial position.

## EXERCISES

*Suggested answers to exercises marked ✓ are to be found on our dedicated CourseMate platform for students.*

*Suggested answers to the remaining exercises are to be found on the Instructor online support resources.*

✓1   The following are extracts from an industrial performance analysis for two groups, Alpha Group plc and Omega Group plc.

The two groups operate in different industrial sectors and have accordingly adopted different operating and financial strategies.

| *Alpha Group plc* | *20X3* *£000* | *20X2* *£000* | *20X1* *£000* |
|---|---|---|---|
| Income data | | | |
| Turnover | 20 915 | 19 036 | 16 929 |
| Operating profit | 1 386 | 1 189 | 943 |
| Depreciation | 299 | 264 | 214 |
| Income from investments | 23 | 20 | 14 |
| Interest payable | 95 | 66 | 60 |
| Statement of financial position data | | | |
| Intangible fixed assets | 636 | 660 | 484 |
| Tangible fixed assets | 7 213 | 5 605 | 4 654 |
| Investments | 234 | 201 | 148 |
| | 8 083 | 6 466 | 5 286 |
| Stocks | 1 405 | 1 312 | 1 217 |
| Trade debtors | 65 | 54 | 57 |
| Cash | 97 | 62 | 43 |
| Other current assets | 1 000 | 550 | 700 |
| Total current assets | 2 567 | 1 978 | 2 017 |
| Trade creditors | 1 651 | 1 521 | 1 381 |
| Overdraft | 150 | – | 160 |
| Short-term loans | 300 | 151 | 200 |
| Other current liabilities | 1 371 | 1 271 | 1 008 |
| Total current liabilities | 3 472 | 2 943 | 2 749 |
| Total assets less current liabilities | 7 178 | 5 501 | 4 554 |
| Creditors: amounts falling due after more than 1 year | 904 | 604 | 239 |
| Provisions for liabilities and charges | 180 | 159 | 158 |
| Minority interests | 150 | 132 | 130 |
| | 5 944 | 4 606 | 4 027 |
| Ordinary shares | 3 000 | 3 000 | 3 000 |
| Preference shares, redeemable 20X6 | 2 000 | – | – |
| Reserves | 944 | 1 606 | 1 027 |
| | 5 944 | 4 606 | 4 027 |

| *Omega Group plc* | *20X3* | *20X2* | *20X1* |
|---|---|---|---|
| | *£000* | *£000* | *£000* |
| Income data | | | |
| Turnover | 19 540 | 15 260 | 16 320 |
| Operating profit | 620 | 340 | 220 |
| Depreciation | 240 | 220 | 220 |
| Income from investments | 20 | 20 | 20 |
| Interest payable | 720 | 660 | 720 |
| Statement of financial position data | | | |
| Intangible fixed assets | – | – | – |
| Tangible fixed assets | 1 620 | 1 360 | 1 360 |
| Investments | 220 | 280 | 240 |
| | 1 840 | 1 640 | 1 600 |
| Stocks | 3 870 | 2 540 | 2 040 |
| Trade debtors | 2 660 | 1 920 | 2 040 |
| Cash | 800 | 480 | 400 |
| Other current assets | 4 000 | 4 000 | 3 580 |
| Total current assets | 11 330 | 8 940 | 8 060 |
| Trade creditors | 2 700 | 1 620 | 1 020 |
| Overdraft | 60 | 180 | – |
| Short-term loans | 1 800 | 1 200 | 1 820 |
| Other current liabilities | 1 140 | 840 | 740 |
| Total current liabilities | 5 700 | 3 840 | 3 580 |
| Total assets less current liabilities | 7 380 | 6 740 | 6 080 |
| Creditors: amounts falling due after more than 1 year | 5 400 | 5 100 | 4 660 |
| Provisions for liabilities and charges | 260 | 300 | 360 |
| Minority interests | 200 | 180 | 200 |
| | 1 520 | 1 160 | 860 |
| Ordinary shares | 600 | 600 | 600 |
| Preference shares, redeemable 20X6 | 200 | 200 | 200 |
| Reserves | 720 | 360 | 60 |
| | 1 520 | 1 160 | 860 |

**Required:**

(a) A set of five key ratios of use in monitoring the operational performance of the two groups over three years. Show clearly your workings and justify the definitions of the inputs to your ratio calculations.

(b) A set of three key ratios of use in monitoring the financial structure of the two groups over three years. Show clearly your workings and justify the definitions of the inputs to your ratio calculations.

(c) Identify the contrasting operating and financing strategies of the two groups as revealed by your ratio analysis.

(d) For each group suggest an industrial sector for which such a strategy would give a best fit. Give reasons for your suggestions.

(e) List five ways in which financial statements could be improved in order to make them more useful as the basis for input to ratio analysis. Identify the constraints on implementation of these improvements.

(ACCA)

2  Obtain a set of accounts for a supermarket and a manufacturer. You can do this by accessing the website of the company and searching for the annual report, probably under the information heading 'investor relations'. Compare and contrast the nature of the current assets and liabilities of your two companies.

3  You are given the following information in relation to Olivet Ltd.

| Income statement | 20X4 | 20X5 |
|---|---|---|
| Sales | 100 000 | 100 000 |
| Cost of sales | 50 000 | 60 000 |
| | 50 000 | 40 000 |
| Expenses | 30 000 | 30 000 |
| | 20 000 | 10 000 |
| Dividends | 10 000 | 10 000 |
| | 10 000 | – |
| Balance b/d | 2 500 | 12 500 |
| | 12 500 | 12 500 |

| Statement of financial position at | 20X4 | 20X5 |
|---|---|---|
| Land | 31 500 | 31 500 |
| Buildings | 20 000 | 39 500 |
| Equipment | 3 000 | 3 000 |
| | 44 500 | 74 000 |
| Investments at cost | 25 000 | 40 000 |
| Stock | 2 500 | 32 500 |
| Debtors | 20 000 | 25 000 |
| Bank | 1 500 | – |
| | 118 500 | 171 500 |
| Ordinary £1 shares | 20 000 | 25 000 |
| Share premium | 6 000 | 7 000 |
| Revaluation reserve | – | 10 000 |
| Profit and loss | 12 500 | 12 500 |
| Debentures 10% | 50 000 | 75 000 |
| Creditors | 20 000 | 30 000 |
| Proposed dividend | 10 000 | 10 000 |
| Bank | – | 2 000 |
| | 118 500 | 171 500 |

**Required:**
You are required to comment on the financial position of Olivet Ltd as at 20X5. Calculate any ratios you feel necessary.

4    You are given the attached information about Fred plc, comprising summarized income statements, summarized statements of financial position and some suggested ratio calculations. You should note that there may be alternative ways of calculating some of these ratios. The holders of a small number of the ordinary shares in the business have come to you for help and advice. There are a number of things they do not properly understand, and a friend of theirs who is an accountancy student has suggested that some of the ratios show a distinctly unsatisfactory position, and that holders should sell their shares as quickly as possible.

**Required:**

Write a report to the shareholders commenting on the apparent position and prospects of Fred plc, as far as the information permits. Your report should include reference to liquidity and profitability aspects, and should advise whether, in your view, the shares should indeed be sold as soon as possible.

**Fred plc**

**Some possible ratio calculations (which can be taken as arithmetically correct).**

|  | 20X2 | 20X1 |
|---|---|---|
| Current ratio | 54/147 = 36.7% | 56/172 = 32.6% |
| Acid test ratio | 12/147 = 8.2% | 15/172 = 8.7% |
| ROCE | 57/249 = 22.9% | 41/161 = 25.5% |
| EPS | 31/190 = 16.3p | 22/190 = 11.6p |
| Trade debtors' turnover | 4/910 × 365 = 2 days | 4/775 × 365 = 2 days |
| Trade creditors' turnover | 60/730 × 365 = 30 days | 60/633 × 365 = 35 days |
| Gross profit % | 180/910 = 19.8% | 142/775=18.3% |
| Operating profit % | 57/910 = 6.3p | 41/775 = 5.3% |
| Stock turnover | 42/730 × 365 = 21 days | 41/633 × 365 = 24 days |
| Gearing | 61/188 = 32.4% | 1/160 = 0.6% |

**Fred plc**

**Summarized statements of financial position at year-end (£m)**

|  |  | 20X2 |  | 20X1 |
|---|---|---|---|---|
| Fixed assets |  |  |  |  |
| Tangible – not yet in use |  | 49 |  | 41 |
| – in use |  | 295 |  | 237 |
|  |  | 344 |  | 278 |
| Investments |  | 1 |  | 1 |
| Loan redemption fund |  | 1 |  | 1 |
|  |  |  | 346 |  | 280 |
| Current assets |  |  |  |  |
| Stocks |  | 42 |  | 41 |
| Debtors – trade | 4 |  | 4 |  |
| – other | 4 |  | 4 |  |
|  |  | 8 |  | 8 |
| Bank |  | 2 |  | 5 |
| Cash |  | 2 |  | 2 |
|  |  | 54 |  | 56 |

(*Continued*)

| | | |
|---|---:|---:|
| Creditors – due within 1 year | | |
| – trade | 60 | 60 |
| – other | 87 | 112 |
| | 147 | 172 |
| Net current liabilities | 93 | 116 |
| Total assets less current liabilities | 253 | 164 |
| Creditors – due between one and five years | 61 | 1 |
| Provision for liabilities and charges | 4 | 3 |
| Net assets | 188 | 160 |
| Capital and reserves | | |
| Ordinary shares of 10p each | 19 | 19 |
| Preference shares of £1 each | 46 | 46 |
| Share premium | 1 | 1 |
| Profit and loss account | 122 | 94 |
| | 188 | 160 |

**Fred plc**
**Summarized income statements for the year (£m)**

| | 20X2 | 20X2 | 20X1 | 20X1 |
|---|---:|---:|---:|---:|
| Sales | | 910 | | 775 |
| Raw materials and consumables | | 730 | | 633 |
| | | 180 | | 142 |
| Staff costs | 77 | | 64 | |
| Depreciation of tangible fixed assets | 12 | | 10 | |
| Other operating charges | 38 | | 30 | |
| | | 127 | | 104 |
| | | 53 | | 38 |
| Other operating income | | 4 | | 3 |
| | | 57 | | 41 |
| Net interest payable | | 5 | | 4 |
| | | 52 | | 37 |
| Profit sharing – employees | | 2 | | 1 |
| | | 50 | | 36 |
| Taxation | | 17 | | 12 |
| | | 33 | | 24 |
| Preference dividends | | 2 | | 2 |
| | | 31 | | 22 |
| Ordinary dividends | | 3 | | 2 |
| | | 28 | | 20 |

Note:
Net interest payable:

| | | |
|---|---:|---:|
| interest payable | 12 | 9 |
| interest receivable | (1) | (1) |
| interest capitalized | (6) | (4) |
| | 5 | 4 |

5   You are given summarized results of an electrical engineering business, as follows. All figures are in £000.

**Income statement**

|  | year-ended | |
| --- | --- | --- |
|  | *31.12.20X1* | *31.12.20X0* |
| Turnover | 60 000 | 50 000 |
| Cost of sales | 42 000 | 34 000 |
| Gross profit | 18 000 | 16 000 |
| Operating expenses | 15 500 | 13 000 |
|  | 2 500 | 3 000 |
| Interest payable | 2 200 | 1 300 |
| Profit before taxation | 300 | 1 700 |
| Taxation | 350 | 600 |
| (Loss) profit after taxation | (50) | 1 100 |
| Dividends | 600 | 600 |
| Transfer (from) to reserves | (650) | 500 |

*Statement of financial position*

| Fixed assets | | |
| --- | --- | --- |
| Intangible | 500 | – |
| Tangible | 12 000 | 11 000 |
|  | 12 500 | 11 000 |
| Current assets | | |
| Stock | 14 000 | 13 000 |
| Debtors | 16 000 | 15 000 |
| Bank and cash | 500 | 500 |
|  | 30 500 | 28 500 |
| Creditors due within 1 year | 24 000 | 20 000 |
| Net current assets | 6 500 | 8 500 |
| Total assets less current liabilities | 19 500 | 19 500 |
| Creditors due after 1 year | 6 000 | 5 500 |
|  | 13 000 | 14 000 |
| Capital and reserves | | |
| Share capital | 1 300 | 1 300 |
| Share premium | 3 300 | 3 300 |
| Revaluation reserve | 2 000 | 2 000 |
| Profit and loss | 6 400 | 7 400 |
|  | 13 000 | 14 000 |

**Required:**

(a) Prepare a table of the following 11 ratios, calculated for both years, clearly showing the figures used in the calculations:

current ratio

quick assets ratio

stock turnover in days

debtors' turnover in days

creditors' turnover in days

gross profit %

net profit % (before taxation)

interest cover

dividend cover

ROCE

gearing.

(b) Making full use of the information given in the question, your table of ratios and your common sense, comment on the apparent position of the business and on the actions of the management.

# PART TWO

# ANNUAL FINANCIAL STATEMENTS

In this part we look in detail at the international rules that accountants have created for themselves to govern financial reporting. In each case, we explore the underlying issues involved, applying the principles developed in Part One, and consider the International Standards requirements. Do these Standards achieve what they are setting out to do when considered individually? Do they make sense when looked at as a whole? As with Part One, you are invited to form your own opinion on 'the story so far'.

# FIXED (NON-CURRENT) TANGIBLE ASSETS

# 13

**OBJECTIVES**  After studying this chapter you should be able to:

- discuss and apply the principles, concepts and major methods of providing for depreciation

- explain what depreciation does and does not do

- explain the issues involved in determining appropriate treatments for government grants

- describe, apply and appraise the requirements of IAS 20 relating to government grants

- explain the issues involved in determining appropriate treatments for borrowing costs

- describe, apply and appraise the requirements of IAS 23 relating to borrowing costs

- describe, apply and appraise the requirements of IAS 16, *Property, Plant and Equipment*

- discuss alternative treatments for investment properties

- describe, apply and appraise the requirements of IAS 40 related to investment properties.

## INTRODUCTION

Assets have been defined (in Chapter 9) as follows (Framework, para. 4.4):

> An asset is a resource controlled by the entity as a result of past events and from which future economic benefits are expected to flow.

Assets are divided into fixed assets and current assets. The IAS terms are non-current assets and current assets respectively. The distinction is formally defined in IAS 1 (para. 66), discussed in more detail in Chapter 10.

An asset should be classified as a current asset when it is:

1 expected to be realized in, or is intended for sale or consumption in, the normal course of the entity's operating cycle

2 held primarily for the purpose of being traded

3 expected to be realized within 12 months after the balance sheet date reporting period

4 cash or cash equivalent (as defined by IAS 7, see Chapter 24), unless it is restricted from being exchanged or used to settle a liability for at least 12 months after the reporting period.

All other assets should be classified as non-current assets.

The definition of non-current assets is often misunderstood. A non-current asset is not an asset with a long life. The essential criterion is the intention of the owner – the intended use of the asset. A non-current asset is an asset that the firm intends to use within the business over an extended period in order to assist its daily operating activities. A current asset, by way of contrast, is usually defined in terms of time. A current asset is an asset likely to change its form, i.e. likely to undergo some transaction within 12 months.

## ACTIVITY 13.1

Consider two firms, A and B. Firm A is a motor trader. It possesses some motor vehicles that it is attempting to sell and it also possesses some desks used by the sales staff, management, and so on. Firm B is a furniture dealer. It possesses some desks that it is attempting to sell and it also possesses some motor vehicles used by the sales staff and for delivery purposes. How are these items treated in each case?

### Activity feedback

*In the accounts of A, the motor vehicles are current assets and the desks are non-current assets. In the accounts of B, the motor vehicles are non-current assets and the desks are current assets. Note, incidentally, that a fixed asset which, after several years' use, is about to be sold for scrap remains in the fixed asset part of the accounts even though it is about to change its form.*

## PRINCIPLES OF ACCOUNTING FOR DEPRECIATION

The first major problem with depreciation, perhaps surprisingly, is to agree on what it is and what it is for. The generally agreed view nowadays is that it is in essence a straightforward application of the matching, or accruals, convention. With a non-current asset the benefit from the asset is spread over several years. The matching convention requires that the corresponding expense be matched with the benefit in each accounting period. This does not simply mean that the total expense for the asset's life is spread over the total beneficial life. It means, more specifically, that the total expense for the asset's life is spread over the total beneficial life *in proportion to the pattern of benefit*. Thus, to take a simple example, if a non-current asset gives half of its benefit, or usefulness, in year 1, one-third in year 2 and one-sixth in year 3 and the total expenses arising are €1200, then the matching convention requires the charging of €600 in year 1, €400 in year 2 and €200 in year 3, in the annual profit calculation. This charge is known as the *depreciation charge*.

In order to calculate a figure for this charge it is necessary to answer four basic questions:

1 What is the cost of the asset?
2 What is the estimated useful life of the asset to the business? (This may be equal to, or may be considerably less than, its technical or physical useful life.)
3 What is the estimated residual selling value ('scrap value') of the asset at the end of the useful life as estimated?
4 What is the pattern of benefit or usefulness derived from the asset likely to be (not the amount of the benefit)?

It is perfectly obvious that the second, third and fourth of these involve a good deal of uncertainty and subjectivity. The 'appropriate' figures are all dependent on future plans and future actions. It is important to realize that even if the first figure – the cost of the fixed asset – is known precisely and objectively, the basis of the depreciation calculation as a whole is always uncertain, estimated and subjective.

The estimates should, as usual, be reasonable, fair and prudent (whatever precisely this implies!). But the first figure is often not at all precise and objective, for several reasons.

## ACTIVITY 13.2

Suggest reasons why the cost of a particular fixed asset may be difficult to determine with precision.

### Activity feedback
Possible reasons include the following:

1 Incidental expenses associated with making the asset workable should be included, e.g. installation costs carried out by the business's own staff, probably including some overhead costs.

2 The non-current asset may be constructed within the business by its own workforce, giving rise to all the usual costing problems of overhead definition and overhead allocation.

3 Depending on the accounting policies used by the firm generally, the 'basic' figure for the fixed asset may be revalued periodically. Additionally, if land is not depreciated but the building on the land is, then this requires a split of the total cost (or value) figure for the land and buildings together into two possibly somewhat arbitrary parts.

4 Major alterations/improvements may be made to the asset part way through its life. If these appear to increase the benefit from the asset over the remaining useful life and perhaps also to increase the number of years of the remaining useful life, and are material, then the costs of these improvements should also be capitalized (i.e. treated as part of the non-current asset from then on). However, maintenance costs, including a major overhaul that does not occur frequently, are 'running' expenses and should be charged to the income statement as incurred. In practice, this distinction can be difficult to make.

5 Accounting policies in relation to government grants receivable and to capitalization of borrowing costs may influence the figures. These two issues are the subjects of separate International Standards. They are considered later in the chapter.

The total figure to be depreciated, known as the *depreciable amount*, will consist of the cost of the asset less the scrap value. This depreciable amount needs to be spread over the useful life in proportion to the pattern of benefit. Once the depreciable amount has been found, with revision if necessary to take account of material improvements, several recognized methods exist for spreading, or allocating, this amount to the various years concerned. The more important possibilities are outlined next. It is essential to understand the implicit assumption that each method makes about the pattern of benefit arising, and therefore about the appropriate pattern of expense allocation.

## Methods of calculating depreciation

**Straight line method**  The depreciable amount is allocated on a straight line basis, i.e. an equal amount is allocated to each year of the useful life. If an asset is revalued or materially improved then the new depreciable amount will be allocated equally over the remaining, possibly extended, useful life (see Activity 13.3).

### ACTIVITY 13.3

Using the straight line method, calculate the annual depreciation charge from the following data:

| | |
|---|---|
| Cost ('basic' value figure) | € 12 000 |
| Useful life | 4 years |
| Scrap value | € 2 000 |

*Activity feedback*

$$\text{Annual charge} = \frac{€12\,000 - €2\,000}{4}$$

$$= €2\,500$$

*This is by far the most common method. It is the easiest to apply and also the preparation of periodic (e.g. monthly) accounts for internal purposes is facilitated. This method assumes, within the limits of materiality, that the asset is equally useful, or beneficial, each year. Whether this assumption is as frequently justified as the common usage of the method suggests, is an open question.*

**Reducing balance method**  Under this method, depreciation each year is calculated by applying a constant percentage to the net book value (NBV) brought forward from the previous year. (Note that this percentage is based on the cost less depreciation to date.) Given the cost (or valuation) starting figure and the useful life and 'scrap' value figures, the appropriate percentage needed to make the NBV at the end of the useful life exactly equal to the scrap value can be found from a formula:

$$d = 1 - \sqrt[n]{S/C}$$

where $d$ is the depreciation percentage, $n$ is the life in years, $S$ is the scrap value and $C$ is the cost (or basic value).

This formula is rarely used. In practice, when this method is used a standard 'round' figure is usually taken, shown by experience to be vaguely satisfactory for the particular type of asset under consideration. Notice, incidentally, that the formula fails to work when the scrap value is zero and produces an extreme and possibly distorted allocation of expense when the scrap value is very small.

A particular variant found in practice in some countries is known as the double-declining balance method. This involves calculating the appropriate 'straight line' depreciation percentage, then doubling it and applying the resulting percentage on the reducing balance basis.

## ACTIVITY 13.4

Using the data from the previous activity and assuming a depreciation percentage of 40 per cent, calculate the depreciation charge for each of the four years using the reducing balance method.

### Activity feedback

| Year 1 | Cost | €12 000 |
|---|---|---|
| | Depreciation 40% | 4 800 |
| Year 2 | NBV | 7 200 |
| | Depreciation 40% | 2 880 |
| Year 3 | NBV | 4 320 |
| | Depreciation 40% | 1 728 |
| Year 4 | NBV | 2 592 |
| | Depreciation 40% | 1 037 |
| | NBV | € 1 555 |

If the estimated scrap value turns out to be correct, then a 'profit' on disposal of €445 would be recorded also in year 4. This is an example of a reducing charge method or of an accelerated depreciation method. The charge is highest in the first year and gradually reduces over the asset's life.

## ACTIVITY 13.5

Suggest, and critically appraise, arguments in favour of using the reducing balance method rather than the straight line method.

### Activity feedback

**1** It better reflects the typical benefit pattern, at least of some assets.

**2** It could be argued that, where the pattern of benefit is assumed to be effectively constant, the appropriate 'expense', which needs to be correspondingly evenly matched, is not the pure depreciation element, but the sum of:

(a) the pure depreciation element, and

(b) the maintenance and repair costs.

Because (b) will tend to increase as the asset gets older, it is necessary for (a) to be reduced as the asset gets older in the hope that the total of the two will remain more or less constant. This may be a valid argument in the most general of terms, but of course there is no reason why an arbitrary percentage applied in one direction should even approximately compensate for flexible and 'chancy' repair costs in the other.

**3** It better reflects the probable fact that the value (i.e. the market or resale value) of the asset falls more sharply in the earlier years. This argument, often advanced, is questionable in principle. Depreciation is concerned with appropriate allocation of expense, applying the matching convention. It is not concerned with an annual revaluation of the fixed assets, so whether or not a particular method is good or bad from this viewpoint is, or should be, irrelevant. So long as the original estimate of future benefit is still valid, the fact that current market value is small, at an intermediate time, is not of concern.

**4** Since it frontloads the depreciation expense charge in the earlier years of the useful life, it is consistent with the prudence principle. It is indeed true that prudence can be said to support the reducing balance method rather than the straight line method. What is not clear is whether this is a valid advantage. This is a particular example of the general debate concerning the relative importance of prudence, on the one hand, and a genuine attempt to apply the matching principle, on the other.

**Sum of the digits method** This is another example of a reducing charge method. It is based on a convenient 'rule of thumb' and produces a pattern of depreciation charge somewhat similar to the reducing balance method.

Using the same figures as before, we give the four years weights of 4, 3, 2 and 1, respectively and sum the total weights. In general terms, we give the $n$ years weights of $n$, $n-1$, ..., 1 respectively, and sum the total weights, the sum being $n(n+1)/2$. The depreciable amount is then allocated over the years in the proportion that each year's weighting bears to the total.

## ACTIVITY 13.6

Use the sum of the digits method to calculate annual depreciation charges for the data in the previous activities.

### Activity feedback

**1** $4 + 3 + 2 + 1 = 10$ (the 'sum' of the 'digits')

**2** Depreciable amount = €12 000 − €2 000

   = €10 000

*Depreciation charges are:*

| | |
|---|---|
| Year 1 | $4/100 \times 10\ 000 = €4\ 000$ |
| Year 2 | $3/10 \times 10\ 000 = €3\ 000$ |
| Year 3 | $2/10 \times 10\ 000 = €2\ 000$ |
| Year 4 | $1/10 \times 10\ 000 = €1\ 000$ |

*This gives NBV figures in the balance sheet of €8000, €5000, €3000 and €2000 for year-ends 1–4, respectively.*

**Output or usage method** This is particularly suitable for assets where the rate of usage or rate of output can be easily measured. For example, a motor vehicle might be regarded as having a life of 100 000 miles, rather than a life of four years. The depreciable amount can then be allocated to each year in proportion to the recorded mileage; for example, if 30 000 miles are covered in year 1, then 3/10 of the depreciable amount will be charged in year 1. The life of a machine could be defined in terms of machine hours. The annual charge would then be:

$$\text{Depreciable amount} \times \frac{\text{Machine hours used in the year}}{\text{Total estimated life in machine hours}}$$

**Revaluation or arbitrary valuation** This approach is occasionally used with minor items such as loose tools. An estimated or perhaps purely arbitrary figure for the value of the items (in total) is chosen at the end of each year. Depreciation is then the difference between this figure and the figure from the previous year. Strictly, of course, this is not a method of depreciation at all, but a lazy alternative to it.

All these methods can be criticized on the grounds that they ignore the fact that the resources 'tied up' in the fixed asset concerned have an actual cost to the business in terms of interest paid or an implied (opportunity) cost in terms of interest foregone. This could well be regarded as an essential expense that should be matched appropriately against the benefit from the asset. The 'actuarial' methods that attempt to take account of interest expense are complicated to apply and in financial accounting are hardly ever used.

## Some misconceptions underlined

The process of depreciation calculation is not designed to produce balance sheet numbers that are either particularly meaningful or particularly useful as measurements of value; in fact, they are measurements of unexpired costs.

It must be remembered that depreciation is a process of matching expenses in proportion to benefits. Given that the depreciable amount has been agreed, the annual charge is based on actual or implied assumptions as to the pattern of benefit being derived and nothing else. In simple bookkeeping terms, all that is happening is that a transfer is being made from the non-current assets section in the balance sheet to the expenses section in the income statement. And it is the expense that is being positively calculated, not the reduction in the asset figure. It follows from this that:

1 The asset figure for an intermediate year has no very obvious or useful meaning. It can only be defined in a roundabout way. For example, under historical cost (HC) accounting, it is the amount of the original cost not yet deemed to have been used, or not yet allocated. This intermediate figure is often called 'net book value' (NBV), but it is not a value at all within the proper meaning of the word.

2 Depreciation has nothing to do with ensuring that the business can 'afford' to buy another asset when the first one becomes useless. This is true even if we ignore the likelihood of rising price levels. Depreciation does not increase the amount of any particular asset, cash or otherwise.

3 However, depreciation, like any other expense figure, does have the effect of retaining *resources* (or total assets) in the business. By reducing profit we reduce the maximum dividend payable (which would reduce resources) and therefore increase the 'minimum resources remaining' figure. This is, in fact, a particular illustration of the idea of capital maintenance discussed in Chapter 4.

## DETERMINING THE COST OF A FIXED ASSET

In the following sections we look at two particular problem areas regarding cost determination, i.e. government grants and borrowing costs. Before that, as a check on your understanding of general principles, try Activity 13.7.

## ACTIVITY 13.7

In the year to 31 December, Hans bought a new fixed asset and made the following payments in relation to it:

|  | € | € |
| --- | --- | --- |
| Cost as per supplier's list | 12 000 | |
| *less* Agreed discount | 1 000 | 11 000 |
| Delivery charge | | 100 |
| Erection charge | | 200 |
| Maintenance charge | | 300 |
| Additional component to increase capacity | | 400 |
| Replacement parts | | 250 |

### Required

1 State and justify the cost figure which should be used as the basis for depreciation.

2 What does depreciation do and why is it necessary?

3 Briefly explain, without numerical illustration, how the straight line and reducing balance methods of depreciation work. What different assumptions does each method make?

4 Explain the term 'objectivity' as used by accountants. To what extent is depreciation objective?

5 It has been common practice in published accounts of individual entities in Germany to use the reducing balance method for a fixed asset in the early years of its life, and then to change to the straight line method as soon as this would give a higher annual charge. What do you think of this practice? Refer to relevant accounting conventions in your answer.

### Activity feedback

1 This figure should be the total cost of making the fixed asset usable, excluding all costs of actually using it. Therefore:

11 000 + 100 + 200 + 400 = €11 700

*(Continued)*

## ACTIVITY 13.7   (Continued)

The additional component is the cost of machine as it enhances the revenue earning capacity of the asset but the replacement parts are cost of using machine – hence the difference in treatment between the two. Maintenance is obviously a cost of usage.

2  Depreciation spreads the cost (or value) of an item over its useful life, in appropriate proportion to the benefit (usefulness). It is necessary in accordance with the matching convention – allocating expense against corresponding benefit, as part of the profit calculation.

3  The straight line method charges a constant percentage of the cost (or value) each year. The reducing balance method charges a constant percentage of the NBV (cost less accumulated depreciation brought forward). Thus, the straight line method has a constant charge but the reducing balance method has a charge reducing each year of the asset life. The two methods therefore make different assumptions about the

usefulness, the trend or pattern of benefit, of the fixed asset concerned.

4  Objectivity implies lack of bias. It removes the need for and the possibility of subjectivity, of personal opinion. For an accounting figure to be objective, it must be expected that all accountants would arrive at the same figure. Clearly, the figure stated on an invoice has a high degree of objectivity. However, the calculation of depreciation is based on estimates of future life and future usefulness and is therefore highly subjective.

5  This practice can claim the advantage of greater prudence, as the expense is always the higher of the two possibilities. However, it seems to lack consistency. Perhaps more importantly, it obviously fails to attempt to follow the matching convention. It makes no attempt to make the trend of expenses consistent with the trend of benefit or usefulness.

## GOVERNMENT GRANTS

Entities which receive a material amount of assistance from government or state sources are clearly in a different economic position from otherwise comparable entities which receive no such assistance. In order to allow proper appraisal of the results of the entity activities and to facilitate comparisons, disclosure of this government assistance in as much detail as practicable is necessary.

More specifically, government grants are usually easily quantifiable and the general principle of transparency requires that they are both properly accounted for and clearly disclosed. Government grants typically represent a reduction in net cash outflows and, therefore, at least ultimately, an increase in entity earnings.

Suppose a government grant is paid to an entity because, and under the condition that, the entity purchases a depreciable non-current asset. The figures concerned are as follows:

| | |
|---|---|
| Purchase price of asset | €12 000 |
| Expected useful life | 4 years |
| Expected residual value | Nil |
| Government grant | €2 000 |
| Annual profits before depreciation, and grants relating to the asset | €20 000 |

It is possible to suggest at least four possible different ways of treating the grant:

1  To credit the total amount of the grant immediately to the income statement.

2  To credit the amount of the grant to a non-distributable reserve.

3 To credit the amount of the grant to revenue over the useful life of the asset by:

(a) reducing the cost of the acquisition of the non-current asset by the amount of the grant, or

(b) treating the amount of the grant as a deferred credit, a portion of which is transferred to revenue annually.

## ACTIVITY 13.8

Which of these methods do you prefer? Give reasons.

### Activity feedback

The first two methods may be rejected on the grounds that they provide no correlation between the accounting treatment of the grant and the accounting treatment of the expenditure to which the grant relates. The first method would increase the profits in the first year by the entire amount of the grant, failing to associate the grant with the useful life of the asset. It thus ignores both the

prudence convention and the matching convention. The second method means that the grant will never affect the profit figure. It therefore also ignores the matching convention and, additionally, leaves the 'non-distributable reserve' in the balance sheet, presumably for ever, i.e. it is treated as paid-in surplus.

The third and fourth methods both follow and apply the matching convention. They both have exactly the same effect on reported annual profits, the differences only being concerned with balance sheet presentation.

## Illustration of different accounting treatments

Using the data just given, the two 'acceptable' methods give the following results.

| Method 3(a) | € | € | € | € |
|---|---|---|---|---|
| Profit before depreciation, etc. | 20 000 | 20 000 | 20 000 | 20 000 |
| Depreciation | (2 500) | (2 500) | (2 500) | (2 500) |
| Profit | 17 500 | 17 500 | 17 500 | 17 500 |
| Balance sheet extract at year-end | | | | |
| Non-current asset at (net) cost | 10 000 | 10 000 | 10 000 | 10 000 |
| Depreciation | 2 500 | 5 000 | 7 500 | 10 000 |
| Carrying amount | 7 500 | 5 000 | 2 500 | 0 |
| **Method 3(b)** | | | | |
| Profit before depreciation, etc. | 20 000 | 20 000 | 20 000 | 20 000 |
| Depreciation | (3 000) | (3 000) | (3 000) | (3 000) |
| Grant released | 500 | 500 | 500 | 500 |
| Profit | 17 500 | 17 500 | 17 500 | 17 500 |
| Balance sheet extract at year-end | | | | |
| Non-current asset at (net) cost | 12 000 | 12 000 | 12 000 | 12 000 |
| Depreciation | 3 000 | 6 000 | 9 000 | 12 000 |
| Carrying amount | 9 000 | 6 000 | 3 000 | 0 |
| Deferred credit | | | | |
| Government grant | 1 500 | 1 000 | 500 | 0 |

Thus method (a) shows assets of 7500, 5000, 2500 and 0 over the four years and method (b) shows assets of 9000, 6000, 3000 and 0 together with 'liabilities' of 1500, 1000, 500 and 0.

From a pragmatic point of view, method (a) has the obvious advantage of simplicity. No entries and no thought are required in the second and subsequent years. However, method (b) has the advantage that assets acquired at different times and locations are recorded on a uniform basis, regardless of changes in governmental policy. But what is the cost of the asset? Is it 12 000 or is it 10 000? IAS 16, *Property, Plant and Equipment* (see later) states that cost is the amount of cash or cash equivalents paid, net of any trade discounts and rebates. This statement does not seem to categorically resolve the question. The government grant is not a trade discount. It is not a trade rebate, but it is a rebate. This would seem to imply that the cost in the sense of IAS 16 is 10 000. This is surely the net outflow arising because of the purchase. Yet IAS 20, as discussed in detail shortly, allows both methods.

A difficult conceptual problem arises with the deferred credit under method (b), for example the 1500 at the end of year 1. We described it earlier as a 'liability'. As discussed in Chapter 9, IASB defines a liability as a present obligation of the entity arising from past events, the settlement of which is expected to result in an outflow of resources embodying economic benefits. On the assumption that the grant cannot be reclaimed by the governmental body concerned (the usual situation), the 1500 is clearly not a liability as no outflow of resources is foreseeable. It is more logically either a reserve (not yet realized) or a contra-asset. It could be suggested that this leads to a different possible treatment, i.e. regular inclusion in the balance sheet as a visible contra-asset, i.e. included as a negative balance among the 'assets' instead of as a positive balance among the liabilities. This would raise its own problems – not least the lack of user friendliness involved in the concept of a negative asset. Such conceptual difficulties do not appear to worry either IASB or other national regulators.

The IASB requirements relating to government grants are contained in IAS 20, effective since 1984. The full title of IAS 20 is *Accounting for Government Grants and Disclosure of Government Assistance*. Its coverage therefore extends beyond the area of fixed assets, but for completeness we deal with all aspects of IAS 20 here. Where IAS 41, *Agriculture*, applies, government grants are to be treated under IAS 41 (see Appendix), not under IAS 20. Key concepts introduced in IAS 20 are as follows.

*Government assistance* is action by government designed to provide an economic benefit specific to an entity or range of entities qualifying under certain criteria. Government assistance for the purpose of this Standard does not include benefits provided only indirectly through action affecting general trading conditions, such as the provision of infrastructure in development areas or the imposition of trading constraints on competitors.

A specific subset of government assistance is government grants. *Government grants* are assistance by government in the form of transfers of resources to an entity in return for past or future compliance with certain conditions relating to the operating activities of the entity. They exclude those forms of government assistance that cannot reasonably have a value placed on them and transactions with government that cannot be distinguished from the normal trading transactions of the entity.

The notion of government is to be interpreted broadly. *Government* refers to government, government agencies and similar bodies whether local, national or international.

Government grants may be related to revenue/expense items, such as repayment of 10 per cent of the wages bill, or to capital/asset items, such as repayment of 10 per cent of the cost of a machine. These two types are formally distinguished by IAS 20:

- *Grants related to assets* are government grants whose primary condition is that an entity qualifying for them should purchase, construct or otherwise acquire long-term assets. Subsidiary conditions may also be attached restricting the type or location of the assets or the periods during which they are to be acquired or held.

- *Grants related to income* are government grants other than those related to assets. The Standard gives two other definitions, including the familiar fair value.

- *Forgivable loans* are loans that the lender undertakes to waive repayment of under certain prescribed conditions.
- *Fair value* is the price that would be received to sell an asset or paid to transfer a liability in an orderly transaction between market participants at the measurement date.

## Government assistance

Despite the inclusion of government assistance in the title of IAS 20, the statements about it are brief and rather obscure. The definitions given suggest in effect that government grants are government assistance that is distinguishable and quantifiable. Turning this round, references to government assistance in the Standard are to government activities that cannot be quantified or clearly distinguished. It follows, of course, that government assistance in this sense cannot be included numerically in the financial statements.

Examples of assistance that cannot reasonably have a value placed on it are free technical or marketing advice and the provision of guarantees. An example of assistance that cannot be distinguished from the normal trading transactions of the entity is a government procurement policy that is responsible for a portion of the entity's sales. The existence of the benefit might be unquestioned, but any attempt to segregate the trading activities from government assistance could well be arbitrary.

The significance of the benefit in the examples just presented may be such that disclosure of the nature, extent and duration of the assistance is necessary in order that the financial statements may not be misleading (para. 36). The Standard explicitly stated (para. 37) that while loans at nil or low interest rates are a form of government assistance, the 'benefit is not quantified by the imputation of interest'. This was reversed with effect from 1 January 2009 (see below) by a newly inserted para. 10A.

The disclosure requirement implied in this seems rather weakly stated. Non-quantified government support need not be disclosed at all unless its omission would be so serious as to be 'misleading'.

## Treatment of government grants

The major portion of IAS 20 is concerned with the treatment of government grants. The first issue to deal with is the timing of recognition. The IAS requirement (para. 7) is that government grants, including non-monetary grants at fair value, should not be recognized until there is reasonable assurance that the entity will comply with the conditions attaching to them and that the grants will be received. Receipt of a grant does not of itself provide conclusive evidence that the conditions attaching to the grant have been or will be fulfilled.

'Reasonable assurance' is not, of course, definable or defined, but it is clearly less rigorous or demanding than, for example, 'virtual certainty' or 'beyond all reasonable doubt'. The Standard confirms (para. 10) that a forgivable loan (as defined above) is treated as a government grant when there is reasonable assurance that the entity will meet the terms for forgiveness of the loan. Once a government grant is recognized, any related contingency would be treated in accordance with IAS 37, *Provisions, Contingent Liabilities and Contingent Assets* (see Chapter 20).

The benefit of a government loan at a below-market rate of interest is treated as a government grant. The loan shall be recognized and measured in accordance with IAS 39, *Financial Instruments: Recognition and Measurement*. The benefit of the below-market rate of interest shall be measured as the difference between the initial carrying value of the loan determined in accordance with IAS 39 and the proceeds received. The benefit is accounted for in accordance with the Standard. The entry shall consider the conditions and obligations that have been, or must be, met when identifying the costs for which the benefit of the loan is intended to compensate (para. 10A).

The key requirement of the Standard (para. 12) is that government grants should be recognized as income over the periods necessary to match them with the related costs they are intended to compensate, on a systematic basis, i.e. following method 3(a) or (b) as discussed at the beginning of this chapter. They should not be credited directly to shareholders' interests. SIC 10, *Government Assistance – No Specific Relation to Operating Activities*, effective from 1 August 1998, has confirmed that government assistance to entities is a grant under IAS 20, even if granted generally to all entities within certain regions or industry sectors.

The matching principle will usually be simple to apply, as illustrated earlier in this chapter. Grants related to non-depreciable assets may also require the fulfilment of certain obligations and would then be recognized as income over the periods that bear the cost of meeting the obligations. As an example, a grant of land may be conditional on the erection of a building on the site and it may be appropriate to recognize it as income over the life of the building. A government grant that becomes receivable as compensation for expenses or losses already incurred or for the purpose of giving immediate financial support to the entity with no future related costs should be recognized as income of the period in which it becomes receivable. Separate disclosure and explanation may be required.

Usually, a careful reading of the contract with the governmental body will determine the appropriate accounting treatment, although an intelligent appraisal of the in-substance thrust of the contract may be required. For example, a grant towards building a factory, stipulating that the factory must remain operating and employing at least 30 people for at least three years, is clearly in essence a grant towards building a factory, not a revenue grant towards reducing net wage costs. However, where a grant clearly relates in material terms to both specific capital and specific revenue items, the Standard is silent on appropriate treatment. Accounting common sense obviously requires an apportionment in such cases.

The Standard is surprisingly vague about non-monetary government grants, such as land donated by a government. IAS 20 merely notes (para. 23) that:

> It is usual to assess the fair value of the non-monetary asset and to account for both grant and asset at that fair value. An alternative course that is sometimes followed is to record both asset and grant at a nominal amount.

This is worded as a description, not as a requirement, although the preference is clear enough. Our view is that merely to record the event at nominal amount lacks transparency to an unacceptable degree. Also, it is not consistent with the substance over form principle and would lead to an inconsistent treatment of assets affecting both inter-entity and intra-entity comparisons.

## Presentation of government grants

Regarding the presentation of grants related to assets, IAS 20 allows both methods (a) and (b) as discussed and illustrated earlier. Thus, government grants related to assets, including non-monetary grants at fair value, should (paras 24–28) be presented in the balance sheet either by setting up the grant as deferred income or by deducting the grant in arriving at the carrying amount of the asset. The Standard spells out that separate disclosure of the gross cash flows in the cash flow statement is likely to be necessary, whatever treatment is followed in the balance sheet. IAS 7, *Cash Flow Statements* (see Chapter 24), is more explicit in making this grossing up of cash flows a requirement.

Regarding the presentation of grants related to income, the Standard again accepts either of two alternatives (paras 29–31). It states, with approval, that grants related to income are sometimes presented as a credit in the income statement, either separately or under a general heading such as 'Other income'; alternatively, they are deducted in reporting the related expense.

A proper understanding of the financial statements may require separate disclosure of the grant and its effects on particular items of income or expense.

## Repayment of government grants

A grant to which conditions were attached may have been properly recognized under the 'reasonable assurance' criterion discussed earlier. However, it may still become repayable in whole or in part if, in fact, the conditions are not met. IAS 20 requires (para. 32) that such a grant, as soon as the repayment becomes foreseeable (which might be significantly earlier than when the repayment actually occurs), should be accounted for as a revision to an accounting estimate, under IAS 8, *Accounting Policies, Changes in Accounting Estimates and Errors* (see Chapter 9). This essentially requires that the entries be made in the financial statements of the year concerned. Repayment of a grant related to income should be applied first against any unamortized deferred credit set up in respect of the grant. To the extent that the repayment exceeds any such deferred credit, or where no deferred credit exists, the repayment should be recognized immediately as an expense. Repayment of a grant related to an asset should be recorded by increasing the carrying amount of the asset or reducing the deferred balance by the amount repayable. The cumulative additional depreciation that would have been recognized to date as an expense in the absence of the grant should be recognized immediately as an expense. Circumstances giving rise to repayment of a grant related to an asset may require consideration to be given to the possible impairment of the new carrying amount of the asset (see IAS 36, *Impairment of Assets*, discussed in Chapter 15).

## Disclosure

Key disclosure requirements are as follows:

- the accounting policy adopted for government grants, including the methods of presentation adopted in the financial statements
- the nature and extent of government grants recognized in the financial statements and an indication of other forms of government assistance from which the entity has directly benefited
- unfulfilled conditions and other contingencies attaching to government assistance that has been recognized.

## BORROWING COSTS

The second particular problem area related to the cost of fixed assets is that of interest costs. In the general case, interest cost is a straightforward periodic expense; it should be charged against revenues in proportion to the benefit received, i.e. on a time basis.

This is a normal application of the matching principle. The benefit is the existence of the loan and the expense is the interest cost, allocated proportionate to the size of the borrowing.

However, there are circumstances in which accounting theory seems to rationalize an alternative argument. We pointed out in our feedback to Activity 13.2 that 'cost of an asset' includes any item which is necessary to obtain the asset and make it workable. Suppose a loan is necessary in order to obtain the funds without which the asset cannot be obtained. Can it be argued that the cost of the loan (i.e. the interest) is part of the 'cost of the asset'? Clearly, once the asset is workable, i.e. able to function and generate revenues, then there can be no question of this argument justifying non-expensing of interest. But can interest be capitalized as part of the cost of an asset during the period of its creation or construction (see Activity 13.9)?

## ACTIVITY 13.9

From your knowledge of accounting principles, what do you think the answer to the above question should be?

### Activity feedback

As far as it goes, the logic of the 'cost' argument seems inescapable. With a typical self-constructed asset, all direct costs, and in some circumstances some allocable indirect costs, are properly regarded as part of the total historical cost. It follows that any borrowing costs that can be directly linked to the financing of the asset concerned are also logically part of the total historical cost, as an application of the matching principle.

However, it is not difficult to find arguments which point in a different direction. It is clearly not very prudent to avoid the immediate expensing of interest payments that undeniably relate to periodic costs of the accounting period in question. Further, is not the economic argument, i.e. that the cost of necessary finance is part of the cost of production, true, *whether or not* a separate source of finance related to the particular asset can be distinguished? If it is true, as we would certainly suggest that it is, then an imputed interest charge should be included even if not supported by any payments or external documentation. This arguably departs much too far from the traditional function of accounting as the recording of transactions. A problem of consistency in asset cost calculations thus arises if some interest costs are capitalized (relatable to specific loans) and others are not.

## IAS 23, *Capitalisation of Borrowing Costs*

IASB GAAP on the treatment of borrowing costs are set out in IAS 23, *Borrowing Costs*. The original 1984 version of the Standard permitted a free choice between systematically expensing costs and capitalizing them when certain conditions were met. In its comparability project in the early 1990s, the IASC proposed in E32 that a 'benchmark' treatment should be for borrowing costs to be expensed, with capitalization as an alternative treatment when certain conditions were met. The responses to E32 were divided on this issue; however, the IASC then issued E39, according to which capitalization would be required if certain conditions were met, and expensing would be required otherwise. This position is similar to that in US GAAP (FAS 34). Again, responses to E39 were mixed. In particular, there is the argument that capital structure would lead to different carrying values of 'qualifying assets.' Hence, IAS 23, *Capitalisation of Borrowing Costs*, issued in 1994, restored the choice between expensing and capitalization subject to certain conditions being met, but expensing became the 'benchmark treatment', and capitalization the 'alternative treatment'.

In March 2007, as part of the programme of convergence between IASB GAAP and US GAAP, a revised IAS 23, *Borrowing Costs*, was issued which reverted to the position proposed in ED 39. In fact, IASB GAAP on 'Borrowing Costs' now align in this respect with US GAAP, with the result that capitalization is required if certain conditions are met, and expensing is required otherwise.

The 'core principle' of the revised IAS 23 is that borrowing costs that are directly attributable to the acquisition, construction or production of a qualifying asset form part of the cost of that asset (i.e. are capitalized). Other borrowing costs are recognized as an expense (IAS 23, para. 1).

IAS 23 is to be applied in accounting for borrowing costs. It does not deal with the actual or imputed cost of equity, including that of preferred capital not classified as a liability. Borrowing costs are not required to be capitalized in the case of qualifying assets that are: (1) measured at fair value (e.g. biological assets), or (2) inventories manufactured or otherwise produced in large quantities on a repetitive basis (IAS 23, paras 2–4). The exclusion of (1) qualifying assets measured at fair value from the scope of IAS 23 is logical in that, as such assets are not measured on the basis of cost, the cost of borrowings is irrelevant to their measurement. The exclusion of (2) inventories manufactured or otherwise produced in large quantities on a repetitive basis is based on pragmatic reasons.

*Qualifying assets* are assets that necessarily take a substantial period of time to prepare for their intended use or sale, and depending on the circumstances may include:

- certain inventories (e.g. construction work-in-process)
- manufacturing plants
- power generation facilities
- intangible assets (e.g. patents)
- investment properties.

Qualifying assets do not include:

- financial assets
- inventories that are manufactured or otherwise produced over a short period of time
- assets that are ready for their intended use or sale when they are acquired.

(IAS 23, paras 5–7)

Borrowing costs that are directly attributable to the acquisition, construction or production of a qualifying asset are those borrowing costs that would have been avoided if the expenditure on the qualifying asset had not been made.

When funds are borrowed specifically for the purpose of obtaining a particular qualifying asset, it is clear that these funds are easily identified as directly attributable borrowing costs. If such borrowings are temporarily invested before being expended for the purpose of obtaining the asset, it is likewise clear that any investment income earned is to be deducted from the cost of the borrowings.

In other circumstances, identifying a direct relationship between particular borrowings and a qualifying asset, and determining the borrowings that would otherwise have been avoided, may be difficult and judgement may have to be exercised. To the extent that funds that have been borrowed for general purposes are used for obtaining a qualifying asset, the amount of borrowing costs that are eligible for capitalization should be determined by applying a capitalization rate to the expenditures on that asset. This capitalization rate is calculated as the weighted average of the borrowing costs applicable to the borrowings that are outstanding during the period, excluding any borrowings made specifically for the purpose of obtaining the particular qualifying asset or any other qualifying asset. The amount of borrowing costs capitalized by an entity during a period must not exceed the total amount of borrowing costs that it incurred during that period.

The commencement date for capitalization is that date on which the entity first meets all of the following three conditions:

1  expenditures on the qualifying assets are being incurred
2  borrowing costs are being incurred
3  activities that are necessary to prepare the asset for its intended use or sale are in progress.

Expenditures on the qualifying asset should include only those that have resulted in payments of cash, transfers of other assets, or the assumption of interest-bearing liabilities. They are reduced by any progress payments received (for work-in-process) and grants received in connection with the asset. For the application of the capitalization rate, a reasonable approximation of the balance of expenditures to which it should be applied for a period is given by the average carrying amount of the asset during that period, including all borrowing costs capitalized in prior periods.

Activities necessary to prepare the asset for its intended use or sale include technical and administrative work prior to the start of physical construction. However, the mere holding of the asset in the absence of such work does not count as an activity, and borrowing costs incurred during such a period of inactivity (e.g. when land acquired for building purposes is held without any associated development activity) do not qualify for capitalization (IAS 23, paras 17–19).

Moreover, capitalization of borrowing costs is suspended during extended periods in which active development of a qualifying asset is discontinued and no substantial technical or administrative work is carried out, except in the case of a temporary delay that is a necessary part of the process of preparing the asset for its intended use or sale (e.g. suspension of the building of a bridge during an extended period of high water levels) (IAS 23, paras 20–21).

Capitalization of borrowing costs should cease when substantially all of the activities necessary to prepare the qualifying asset for its intended use or sale are complete.

When a qualifying asset is completed in parts, and each part is capable of being sold or used while work continues on the others (e.g. in the case of a business park comprising several buildings), the capitalization of borrowing costs on a substantially completed part should cease.

An asset is normally considered as 'ready for its intended use or sale' when its physical construction is complete, even though: (1) some routine administrative work may still continue, or (2) minor modifications, such as the decoration of the property to the purchaser's or user's specification, may still be outstanding (IAS 23, paras 22–25).

An entity should disclose in the notes to its financial statements:

• the amount of borrowings capitalized during the period
• the capitalization rate used to determine the amount of borrowing costs eligible for capitalization (IAS 23, para. 26).

# PROPERTY, PLANT AND EQUIPMENT

We are now, at last, in a position to look at the central requirements of IAS GAAP in relation to accounting for fixed assets. Even now, four different aspects and four different IASs need to be considered, i.e. property, plant and equipment (PPE); investment properties; intangibles; and, finally, the whole question of impairment of fixed assets. Although there are relationships and interlinking between all of these, it will aid understanding to explore them separately. We begin with *Property, Plant and Equipment*, IAS 16, which is the general Standard regarding the treatment of fixed (non-current) assets. We deal only with the latest version of IAS 16, as revised in 2004, applicable from 1 January 2005, with further minor amendments effective from various years up to 2011.

The Standard notes that the general definition and recognition criteria for an asset, given in the Framework for the Preparation and Presentation of Financial Statements (discussed in Chapter 10), must be satisfied before IAS 16 applies. Subject to that, IAS 16 applies to accounting for all PPE, except when another IAS requires or permits a different accounting treatment (para. 2).

There are in fact a number of exclusions. It is explicitly stated (para. 2) that IAS 16 does not apply to biological assets related to agricultural activity (to which IAS 41 applies – see Appendix), and the recognition and measurement of exploration and evaluation assets (to which IFRS 6 applies – see Appendix). However, it does apply to PPE used to develop or maintain these activities or assets, but separable from those activities or assets. IAS 16 also does not apply to PPE classified as held for sale in accordance with IFRS 5, *Non-current Assets Held for Sale and Discontinued Operations* (see Chapter 15).

An entity applies IAS 40, *Investment Property*, rather than IAS 16, to its investment property (see below). With effect from 1 January 2009, IAS 40 applies to property being constructed or developed for future use as an investment property. IAS 40 also applies to existing investment property being redeveloped for future continued use as investment property.

If any other IAS permits a particular approach to the initial recognition of the carrying amount of PPE, then that Standard will prevail as regards this initial carrying value, but IAS 16 would then apply to all other aspects including depreciation. An example of this would be IFRS 3, *Business Combinations*, which requires PPE acquired in a business combination to be measured initially at fair value (see Chapter 26). The Standard then gives a number of key definitions as follows:

- *Property, plant and equipment* are tangible items that:
  - **(a)** are held for use in the production or supply of goods or services, for rental to others or for administrative purposes, and
  - **(b)** are expected to be used during more than one period.
- *Depreciation* is the systematic allocation of the depreciable amount of an asset over its useful life.
- *Depreciable amount* is the cost of an asset, or other amount substituted for cost, less its residual value.
- *Useful life* is:
  - **(a)** the period of time over which an asset is expected to be used by an entity, or
  - **(b)** the number of production or similar units expected to be obtained from the asset by an entity.

- *Cost is* the amount of cash or cash equivalents paid or the fair value of the other consideration given to acquire an asset at the time of its acquisition or construction or, where applicable, the amount attributed to that asset when initially recognized in accordance with the specific requirements of other IFRSs, e.g. IFRS 2, *Share-based Payment*.
- The *residual value* of an asset is the estimated amount that an entity would currently obtain from disposal of the asset after deducting the estimated costs of disposal, if the asset were already of the age and in the condition expected at the end of its useful life.
- *Entity-specific value* is the present value of the cash flows an entity expects to arise from the continuing use of an asset and from its disposal at the end of its useful life, or expects to incur when settling liability.
- *Recoverable amount* is the higher of an asset's fair value less costs to sell and its value in use.
- *Fair value* is the price that would be received to sell an asset or paid to transfer a liability in an orderly transaction between market participants at the measurement date.
- An *impairment loss* is the amount by which the carrying amount of an asset exceeds its recoverable amount.
- *Carrying amount* is the amount at which an asset is recognized after deducting any accumulated depreciation and accumulated impairment losses.

These definitions contain no real surprises and confirm the general earnings calculation focus of the depreciation process. The first issue to deal with is the issue of when an item of PPE should be recorded, i.e. *recognized*, in the financial statements.

An item of PPE should be recognized (para. 7) as an asset if, and only if:

1 it is probable that future economic benefits associated with the item will flow to the entity, and

2 the cost of the item to the entity can be measured reliably.

In determining whether an item satisfies the first criterion for recognition, an entity needs to assess the degree of certainty attaching to the flow of future economic benefits on the basis of the available evidence at the time of initial recognition. Existence of sufficient certainty that the future economic benefits will flow to the entity necessitates an assurance that the entity will receive the rewards attaching to the asset and will undertake the associated risks. The second criterion for recognition is usually readily satisfied because the exchange transaction evidencing the purchase of the asset identifies its cost.

IAS 16 allows for the aggregation of items which may individually be insignificant (para. 9), giving 'moulds, tools and dyes' as an example. The aggregation is then treated as 'an asset', if the recognition criteria are met. Conversely, when it is clear that, although an asset may initially be acquired as a whole, significant components of it will have significantly different useful lives, then the expenditure on the asset should be allocated to the component parts and each part should be accounted for as a separate item. An aircraft and its engines are given as a likely example. This separate treatment allows depreciation figures to properly reflect the different consumption patterns of the various components.

## Subsequent costs

The first and obvious point is that costs of day-to-day servicing of an item of PPE, often described as 'repairs and maintenance', are expenses, not additions to costs.

However, major parts of some items of PPE may require replacement at regular intervals. For example, a furnace may require relining after a specified number of hours of use; aircraft interiors such as seats and galleys may require replacement several times during the life of the airframe. Items of PPE may also be acquired to make a less frequently recurring replacement, such as replacing the interior walls of a building or to make a non-recurring replacement. Under the recognition principle in para. 7, an entity recognizes in the carrying amount of an item of PPE the cost of replacing such a part of an item when that cost is incurred if the recognition criteria are met. The carrying amount of those parts that are replaced is derecognized in accordance with the derecognition provisions of the Standard.

Note that in order to facilitate this, the component parts of the original item need to have been accounted for separately in the first place.

A major inspection or refit, even if it does not 'improve' the original item, may logically be treated the same way. Thus, para. 14 notes that a condition of continuing to operate an item of PPE (e.g. an aircraft) may be performing regular major inspections for faults regardless of whether parts of the item are replaced. When each major inspection is performed, its cost is recognized in the carrying amount of the item of PPE as a replacement if the recognition criteria are satisfied. Any remaining carrying amount of the cost of the previous inspection (as distinct from physical parts) is derecognized. This occurs regardless of whether the cost of the previous inspection was identified in the transaction in which the item was acquired or constructed. If necessary, the estimated cost of a future similar inspection may be used as an indication of what the cost of the existing inspection component was when the item was acquired or constructed.

Once the criteria for recognition have been met, the issue of measurement arises. This is considered in two stages: initial measurement and subsequent re-measurement.

## Initial measurement

The essential requirement is straightforward and can be simply stated (para. 15). An item of PPE that qualifies for recognition as an asset should initially be measured at its cost. The cost of an item of PPE comprises its purchase price, including import duties and non-refundable purchase taxes and any directly attributable costs of bringing the asset to working condition for its intended use; any trade discounts and rebates are deducted in arriving at the purchase price. Examples of directly attributable costs are:

- cost of site preparation
- initial delivery and handling costs
- installation costs
- professional fees such as for architects and engineers
- the estimated cost of dismantling and removing the asset and restoring the site, to the extent that it is recognized as a provision under IAS 37, *Provisions, Contingent Liabilities and Contingent Assets* (see Chapter 20).

In practice, however, a number of complications are likely to arise. The Standard goes into some detail about several aspects (paras 18–28). It notes that in cases where payment is deferred beyond normal credit terms, defined or imputed interest must be removed from the total of the payments, thus reducing the cost to the cash purchase price equivalent. General and administration overheads are not likely to be 'directly attributable costs' as the term was used earlier, but, for example, pension costs of direct labour could be.

The question of what is an essential cost of 'bringing the asset to working condition' is likely to be difficult and subjective.

The basic principle is that recognition of costs in the carrying amount of an item of PPE ceases when the item is in the location and condition necessary for it to be capable of operating in the manner intended by management. For example, the following costs are not included in the carrying amount of an item of PPE:

- costs incurred while an item capable of operating in the manner intended by management has yet to be brought into use or is operated at less than full capacity
- initial operating losses, such as those incurred while demand for the item's output builds up
- costs of relocating or reorganizing part or all of an entity's operations
- costs of opening a new facility
- costs of introducing a new product or service (including costs of advertising and promotional activities)
- costs of conducting business in a new location or with a new class of customer (including costs of staff training)
- administration and other general overhead costs.

## Measurement subsequent to initial recognition

The IASB has always operated on the basis that a strict adherence to historical cost is not required and, indeed, has recognized the possibility of rejecting historical cost accounting as the normal basis (see Chapter 9). Consistent with this approach, two alternative approaches to subsequent measurement are allowed under IAS 16 (paras 30 and 31). The first is described as the cost model and is simply stated:

After recognition as an asset, an item of property, plant and equipment shall be carried at its cost less any accumulated depreciation and any accumulated impairment losses.

The second is the revaluation model:

After recognition as an asset, an item of property, plant and equipment whose fair value can be measured reliably shall be carried at a revalued amount, being its fair value at the date of revaluation less any subsequent accumulated depreciation and subsequent accumulated impairment losses. Revaluations shall be made with sufficient regularity to ensure that the carrying amount does not differ materially from that which would be determined using fair value at the balance sheet date.

In the previous version of IAS 16, these were presented as the benchmark treatment and the alternative treatment, respectively. However, they are now presented simply as two alternatives.

IAS 16, paragraph 35 discusses the treatment of accumulated depreciation. The wording is obscure and we quote the paragraph in full:

When an item of property, plant and equipment is revalued, any accumulated depreciation at the date of the revaluation is treated in one of the following ways:

(a) restated proportionately with the change in the gross carrying amount of the asset so that the carrying amount of the asset after revaluation equals its revalued amount. This method is often used when an asset is revalued by means of an index to its depreciated replacement cost; or

(b) eliminated against the gross carrying amount of the asset and the net amount restated to the revalued amount of the asset. This method is often used for buildings.

The amount of the adjustment arising on the restatement or elimination of accumulated depreciation forms part of the increase or decrease in carrying amount that is accounted for in accordance with paras 39 and 40.

If an asset's carrying amount is increased as a result of a revaluation, the increase shall be recognized in other comprehensive income and accumulated in equity under the heading of revaluation surplus. However, the increase shall be recognized in profit or loss to the extent that it reverses a revaluation decrease of the same asset previously recognized in profit or loss.

## ACTIVITY 13.10

Suppose we have an asset to which IAS 16 applies, cost 10 000, useful life 5 years, estimated residual value nil, now 3 years old. The asset is then revalued to a new gross figure of 15 000, that is the new 'cost' is 15 000, for the purpose of treatment (a). Alternatively, the asset is now revalued to a current fair value *in its existing state of* 6000, for the purpose of treatment (b). Show the implications of each of these two treatments.

### Activity feedback

Treatment (a) suggests the following:

| Cost | Depreciation | Carrying amount |
|---|---|---|
| 10 000 | 6 000 | 4 000 |

The asset is now revalued, by index or otherwise, to a new gross figure of 15 000, i.e. the new 'cost' is 15 000. The depreciation is now 'restated proportionately', i.e. it is also increased by 50 per cent. We thus end up with:

| Gross revaluation | Depreciation | Carrying amount |
|---|---|---|
| 15 000 | 9 000 | 6 000 |

This increase in carrying amount of 2000 is then dealt with as discussed later.

Treatment (b) suggests a different sequence. Suppose the asset is again recorded before revaluation:

| Cost | Depreciation | Carrying amount |
|---|---|---|
| 10 000 | 6 000 | 4 000 |

The new carrying value is to be 6000. Other balances will need to be altered or eliminated as shown.

Asset revaluation Account

| | | | |
|---|---|---|---|
| Transfer of cost | 10 000 | 6 000 | Transfer of depreciation |
| Surplus (calculated) | 2 000 | 6 000 | New carrying value (given) |
| | 12 000 | 12 000 | |

If an asset's carrying amount is decreased as a result of a revaluation, the decrease shall be recognized in profit or loss. However, the decrease shall be recognized in other comprehensive income to the extent of any credit balance existing in the revaluation surplus in respect of that asset. The decrease recognized in other comprehensive income reduces the amount accumulated in equity under the heading of revaluation surplus.

Such a revaluation surplus reserve is not 'realized', and is therefore not 'earned' and not available for dividend. However, it is likely to become realized over time. Such revaluation surplus included in equity may be transferred directly to retained earnings when the surplus is realized. The whole surplus may be realized on the retirement or disposal of the asset. However, some of the surplus may be realized as the asset is used by the entity; in such a case, the amount of the surplus realized is the difference between depreciation based on the revalued carrying amount of the asset and depreciation based on the asset's original cost.

It is noteworthy that the word 'may' is used three times in the last three sentences. The increase in carrying amount may be transferred to retained earnings eventually when the asset is disposed of or gradually over the remaining useful life – thus, in effect, offsetting in the retained earnings balance the effect of 'extra' depreciation. Note that in neither case is there any effect on the income statement for any year; this will be charged in full with the new depreciation expense. Alternatively, it appears that the increase could be left in revaluation surplus forever. Under a historical cost accounting philosophy, this last possibility seems illogical, although under a current cost philosophy it would be logically correct (see Chapter 7).

The Interpretations Committee issued IFRIC 1 in May 2004, effective for annual periods beginning on or after 1 September 2004, earlier application being encouraged. IFRIC 1, *Changes in Existing Decommissioning, Restoration and Similar Liabilities*, provides guidance on how to account for the effect of changes in the measurement of such liabilities. The details of IFRIC 1 are complicated, pedantic and common sense.

## Depreciation

The formal requirement of IAS 16 for the calculation of depreciation should by now have a familiar ring (para. 50). The depreciable amount of an item of PPE should be allocated on a systematic basis over its useful life. The depreciation method used should reflect the pattern in which the asset's economic benefits are consumed by the entity. The depreciation charge for each period should be recognized as an expense unless it is included in the carrying amount of another asset (e.g. as part of the manufacturing cost of inventories).

The Standard goes into detail about a number of aspects. The residual value and the useful life of an asset shall be reviewed at least at each financial year-end and, if expectations differ from previous estimates, the change(s) shall be accounted for as a change in an accounting estimate in accordance with IAS 8, *Accounting Policies, Changes in Accounting Estimates and Errors*.

Depreciation is recognized even if the fair value of the asset exceeds its carrying amount, as long as the asset's residual value does not exceed its carrying amount. Repair and maintenance of an asset do not negate the need to depreciate it. The depreciable amount of an asset is determined after deducting its residual value. In practice, the residual value of an asset is often insignificant and therefore immaterial in the calculation of the depreciable amount. The residual value of an asset may increase to an amount equal to or greater than the asset's carrying amount. If it does, the asset's depreciation charge is zero unless and until its residual value subsequently decreases to an amount below the asset's carrying amount. This last point is rather significant. It recognizes and confirms that, while a depreciation charge is *required* for all items of PPE, the correctly calculated charge may well be zero.

Land and buildings are separable assets with different accounting characteristics and should be considered separately, even if acquired as a single purchase.

The Standard mentions three depreciation methods by name: straight line, reducing (or diminishing) balance, and the units of production (usage) method (para. 62).

This list is neither exhaustive nor in order of preference. The method used for an asset is selected based on the expected pattern of economic benefits and is consistently applied from period to period unless there is a change in the expected pattern of economic benefits from that asset. This implies that for any particular asset, with its own particular expected pattern of economic benefits, there is one particular appropriate method. Once the method has been chosen, consistency is required. Now look at Activity 13.11.

## ACTIVITY 13.11

It is sometimes argued, for example in the case of hotels, that depreciation of the building is not necessary on the grounds that its fair value is being maintained by the incurrence of expensive maintenance costs which are being charged as expenses. To charge depreciation as well could appear to be 'double-counting'. What do you think of this argument?

### Activity feedback

Standard setters generally are at pains to counter this argument. It is not valid to argue that maintenance increases residual value at the end of economic life, so in principle the proposition is invalid, although maintenance is certainly a factor in determining the length of the economic life. However, the useful life could, it must be remembered, be significantly shorter than the economic life. It certainly seems theoretically valid for a hotel owner to argue that expected residual value at the end of the expected useful life (to him) is equal to or greater than the initial carrying value. This would suggest that, while depreciation needs to be provided, the 'correct' figure will be nil! Auditors may be suspicious of this argument although, as discussed earlier, IAS 16 now recognizes its possible legitimacy.

The depreciation method applied to an asset shall be reviewed at least at each financial year-end and, if there has been a significant change in the expected pattern of consumption of the future economic benefits embodied in the asset, the method shall be changed to reflect the changed pattern. Such a change shall be accounted for as a change in an accounting estimate in accordance with IAS 8.

It is necessary to determine whether or not an item of PPE has become impaired. This area is covered by IAS 36, Impairment of Assets (see Chapter 15). Impairments or losses of items of PPE related claims for or payments of compensation from third parties and any subsequent purchase or construction of replacement assets, are separate economic events and are accounted for separately as follows:

- Impairments of items of PPE are recognized in accordance with IAS 36.

- Derecognition of items of PPE retired or disposed of is determined in accordance with IAS 16.

- Compensation from third parties for items of PPE that were impaired, lost or given up is included in determining profit or loss when it becomes receivable.

- The cost of items of PPE restored, purchased or constructed as replacements is determined in accordance with IAS 16.

## Derecognition

The carrying amount of an item of PPE shall be derecognized:

- on disposal, or
- when no future economic benefits are expected from its use or disposal.

The gain or loss arising from the derecognition of an item of PPE shall be determined as the difference between the net disposal proceeds, if any, and the carrying amount of the item. The gain or loss is to be included in profit or loss when the item is derecognized (unless IAS 17 requires otherwise on a sale and leaseback). Gains shall not be classified as revenue.

This confirms that any element of revaluation reserve relating to the item will not pass through the income statement.

However, an entity that, in the course of its ordinary activities, routinely sells items of PPE that it has held for rental to others shall transfer such assets to inventories at their carrying amount when they cease to be rented and become held for sale. The proceeds from the sale of such assets shall be recognized as revenue in accordance with IAS 18, *Revenue*. IFRS 5 does not apply when assets that are held for sale in the ordinary course of business are transferred to inventories (para. 68A inserted in 2008).

The disposal of an item of PPE may occur in a variety of ways (e.g. by sale, by entering into a finance lease or by donations). In determining the date of disposal of an item, an entity applies the criteria in IAS 18, *Revenue*, for recognizing revenue from the sale of goods. IAS 17 applies to disposal by a sale and leaseback.

## Disclosure

The disclosure requirements under IAS 16 are lengthy and incapable of effective summarization. In general, full details and reconciliations of movements concerning additions, disposals, impairments and revaluations are required. Have a look yourself at a recent real example.

## ACCOUNTING FOR INVESTMENT PROPERTIES

## Principles and definitions

The classic perception of a non-current asset is that of a long-term resource that is necessary to support the day-to-day operational activities of a business. It is used in production or administration, but is not itself sold. It generally wears out, as its use value or service potential is consumed, in recognition of which depreciation is charged in the annual profit calculation. The classic perception of an investment is that of an asset held so that the asset itself will earn positive returns, either through regular inflows such as interest, dividend, or rent or through capital appreciation. With an investment, the key issue is impairment or capital appreciation, rather than consumption of use value or service potential.

The specific problem with properties is that they can be held for either purpose or for both purposes at different times. Because of a general tendency, over the long term, for property prices to rise significantly in nominal terms, the distinction in practice is often particularly significant.

Until at least the 1970s, property held as an investment was generally treated for accounting purposes like any other property, with or without the possibility of revaluation and with or without the possibility of non-depreciation, depending on the jurisdiction. This approach began to be challenged, notably in the UK. It was argued that if a property is held as an investment then:

1 the matching convention is arguably not relevant as no service potential is being used up

2 the current values of such investments and any change therein are of prime importance and relevance.

## ACTIVITY 13.12

We have seen that, under IAS, a non-current asset is any asset other than a current asset, where a current asset is an asset which (IAS 1, para. 66) is:

1 expected to be realized in, or is intended for sale or consumption in, the entity's normal operating cycle

2 held primarily for the purpose of being traded

3 expected to be realigned within 12 months after the balance sheet date

4 cash or cash equivalent (as defined by IAS 7, see Chapter 24), unless it is restricted from being exchanged or used to settle a liability for at least 12 months after the balance sheet date.

If an entity owns a property which it intends to hire out in the short to medium term and eventually sell or possibly to sell in the short-to-medium term, consider:

(i) whether it is a non-current or current asset

(ii) whether the economic substance of the situation implies a need for annual depreciation.

### Activity feedback
The answer to (i) seems to depend on the particular situation. If the entity is actually trading in properties as an operating activity, then the property does seem to be a current asset. In this case, the question of depreciation does not arise, either logically under the matching principle, or in legal or regulatory terms under EC Directives or IAS GAAP.

If the entity is intending to hold the property for a number of accounting periods, for rental and/or capital gain, then the current/non-current distinction is less clear, although perhaps non-current better reflects the substance. However, the property is still not being consumed in supporting the operating activities of the entity. Further, the key information of relevance to stakeholders should accord with the expected future outcomes, i.e. some kind of rental income and an eventual profitable disposal, not the wearing out of the asset. Arguably, therefore, depreciation is neither logical nor relevant, although this can raise legal and regulatory issues. This whole area needs separate discussion.

IAS 25, *Accounting for Investments*, effective from 1 January 1987 until 31 December 2000, was constructed to allow, but not to require, the treatment of an investment property as a long-term investment under IAS 25, rather than as property under IAS 16, *Property, Plant and Equipment*. Even under IAS 25, such a property could be carried at either cost or revalued amount. Thus there was a great deal of choice involved.

The IASB issued an exposure draft on investment properties, E64, in July 1999. This proposed a mandatory fair value model for investment properties. However, in the resulting debate, IAS was forced to backtrack and the Standard, IAS 40, gives a choice.

Investment property, as defined later, can be treated in either of two ways. Entities can choose between a fair value model and a cost model. The fair value model is the model proposed in E64: investment property should be measured at fair value and changes in fair value should be recognized in the income statement.

The cost model is as defined in IAS 16, *Property, Plant and Equipment*: investment property should be measured at depreciated cost (less any accumulated impairment losses). An entity that chooses the cost model should additionally disclose the fair value of its investment property in the notes to the financial statements.

IAS 40 gives the following key definitions:

- *Investment property* is property (land or a building or part of a building, or both) held (by the owner or by the lessee under a finance lease) to earn rentals or for capital appreciation or both, rather than for:
  - use in the production or supply of goods or services or for administrative purposes, or
  - sale in the ordinary course of business.

- *Owner-occupied property* is property held (by the owner or by the lessee under a finance lease) for use in the production or supply of goods or services or for administrative purposes.

It follows from the definition of investment property that an investment property will generate cash flows 'largely independently' of other assets held by an entity. It is this which distinguishes investment property from owner-occupied property, as owner-occupied property only generates cash flows in conjunction with other operating assets necessary for the production or supply process.

An investment property within the definition should be recognized as an asset when, and only when:

1 it is probable that the future economic benefits that are associated with the investment property will flow to the entity

2 the cost of the investment property can be measured reliably.

Figure 13.1 summarizes the various alternatives for treating a property under IAS GAAP (based on a figure in the Appendix to the 2000 version of IAS 40).

Note that in marginal cases, judgement will be needed in distinguishing investment properties from owner-occupied properties. For example, an owner-managed hotel is essentially concerned with the provision of services to guests, so it is not an investment property. However, the owner of a building which is managed as a hotel by a third party is in the position of holding an investment, with 'largely independent' cash flows arising, hence creating an investment property. In complex intermediate situations, the substance of the situation and the balance of emphasis should be followed. Disclosure of the criteria used is required when classification is difficult.

## ACTIVITY 13.13

Consider each of the assets described in (a) to (i) (below) and indicate whether they are or are not investment properties as defined in IAS 40.

(a) Land held for long-term capital appreciation rather than for short-term sale in the ordinary course of business.

(b) Land held for a currently undetermined future use.

(c) Property that is being constructed or developed for future use as investment property.

(d) A building owned by the entity (or held by the entity under a finance lease) and leased out under one or more operating leases.

(e) A building that is vacant but is held to be leased out under one or more operating leases.

(f) Property intended for sale in the ordinary course of business, e.g. property held for trading by property traders or for development and resale by property developers.

(g) Property being constructed for third parties.

(h) Owner-occupied property.

(i) Property that is leased to another entity under a finance lease.

### Activity feedback
(a), (d), and (e) are clearly held for investment purposes and are investment properties. (b) cannot really be regarded as other than a speculative purchase at the time it was acquired and so is an investment property unless and until, presumably, it eventually becomes part of an owner-occupied property. (c), however, does not at present meet the definition; it is property under construction, and IAS 16 would apply. None of the final four is an investment property and IAS 40 would not apply to them: (f) would be dealt with as inventory under IAS 2 (see Chapter 17), (g) as a construction contract under IAS 11 (see Chapter 17), (h) and (i) as property PPE under IAS 16.

## Figure 13.1    Decision tree for treatment of most property under IAS GAAP

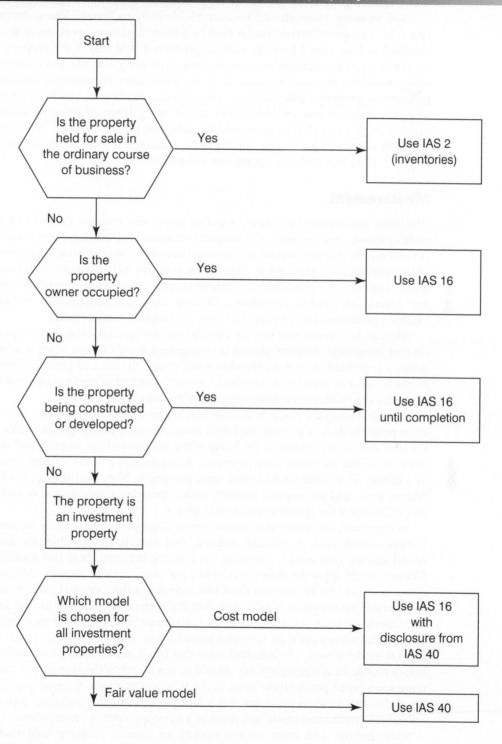

A new introduction in the 2004 version of IAS 40 concerns property interests under operating leases. It was widely suggested that, in substance, given the long life of most property, these should be treatable similarly to finance leases. Accordingly (para. 6), a property interest that is held by a lessee under an operating lease may be classified and accounted for as investment property if, and only if, the property would otherwise meet the definition of an investment property and the lessee uses the fair value model for the asset recognized. This classification alternative is available on a property-by-property basis. However, once this classification alternative is selected for one such property interest held under an operating lease, all property classified as investment property shall be accounted for using the fair value model. When this classification alternative is selected, any interest so classified is included in the disclosures required. Note that this is an option, not a requirement.

## Measurement

The initial measurement of a newly acquired investment property under IAS 40 is reasonably simple, but the issue of subsequent measurement is much more complicated. An investment property should be measured initially at its cost, which is the fair value of the consideration given for it. Transaction costs are included in the initial measurement. The cost of a purchased investment property comprises its purchase price and any directly attributable expenditure. Directly attributable expenditure includes, for example, professional fees for legal services and property transfer taxes.

When an investment property has already been recognized, subsequent expenditure on that investment property should be recognized as an expense when it is incurred unless it is probable that this expenditure will enable the asset to generate future economic benefits in excess of its originally assessed standard of performance and the expenditure can be measured and attributed to the asset reliably.

The initial cost of a property interest held under a lease and classified as an investment property shall be as prescribed for a finance lease by paragraph 20 of IAS 17, i.e. the asset shall be recognized at the lower of the fair value of the property and the present value of the minimum lease payments. An equivalent amount shall be recognized as a liability in accordance with that same paragraph. Note that this applies both to finance leases and to property interests under operating leases treated as investment properties under the option introduced in para. 6.

As suggested, the question of measurement subsequent to the initial measurement is more complicated. As already outlined, two models are available: the fair value model and the cost model. An entity has a choice between these two models under IAS and should apply the chosen model to all of its investment property. Although the choice given in IAS 40 between these two models is a free one, and there is no stated 'benchmark' treatment, it is very clear that the preference indicated in E64 for a fair value model remains. Fair value has to be determined in *all* cases – for measurement in the financial statements if the fair value model is used and for disclosure in the notes if the cost model is used. The Standard notes that IAS 8 (see Chapter 9) states that a voluntary change in accounting policy should be made only if the change will result in a more appropriate presentation of events or transactions in the financial statements of the entity. IAS 40 explicitly states that it is highly unlikely that a change from the fair value model to the cost model will result in a more appropriate presentation.

Some insurers and other entities operate an internal property fund that issues notional units, with some units held by investors in linked contracts and others held by the entity. A newly-introduced paragraph (32A) states that an entity may:

**(a)** choose either the fair value model or the cost model for all investment property backing liabilities that pay a return linked directly to the fair value of, or returns from, specified assets including that investment property, and

**(b)** choose either the fair value model or the cost model for all other investment property, regardless of the choice made in (a).

After initial recognition, an entity that chooses the cost model should measure all its investment property using the cost-based treatment in IAS 16; that is at cost less any accumulated depreciation and any accumulated impairment losses. In other words, if choosing the cost model, an entity proceeds in measurement (but not disclosure) terms to follow IAS 16 as if IAS 40 did not exist.

However, investment properties that meet the criteria to be classified as held for sale (or are included in a disposal group that is classified as held for sale) shall be measured in accordance with IFRS 5 (see Chapter 15).

There is a rebuttable presumption that an entity will be able to determine the fair value of an investment property reliably on a continuing basis. After initial recognition, an entity that chooses the fair value model should measure all its investment property at its fair value, unless this presumption is not valid.

A gain or loss arising from a change in the fair value of investment property should be included in net profit or loss for the period in which it arises. The Standard makes it absolutely explicit that changes in fair value are to be taken directly to earnings and not taken to or from reserves.

We have discussed the concept of fair value elsewhere (see Chapter 8). Fair value is the price that would be received to sell an asset or paid to transfer a liability in an orderly transaction between market participants at the measurement date. With the introduction of IFRS 13 a number of detailed explanatory paragraphs about the practicalities of calculating fair value (then using the previous definition of fair value of course, see Chapter 8 and revise this area if necessary) have been eliminated. By implication it is automatically assumed in IAS 40 as it stands from 2013 that IFRS 13 is rigorously and properly applied to the relevant investment properties. IAS 40 does note that, as a generality, the various inputs to fair value estimations reflect the assumptions market participants would or do actually make under the market conditions at the relevant time.

In the rare situations in which fair value measurement proves impossible for a particular property, the entity should measure that investment property using the cost model treatment in IAS 16. The residual value of the investment property should be assumed to be zero. The entity should continue to apply IAS 16 until the disposal of the investment property. In such circumstances, the entity measures all its other investment properties at fair value. IAS 40 requires that once an entity has begun measuring an investment property at fair value, it should continue to do so, even if the measurements subsequently become less reliable.

## Transfers and disposals

Under IAS 40, transfers to or from investment property should be made only when there is a clearly evidenced change of use. When the cost model is being used for investment properties, transfers between investment property, owner-occupied property and inventories do not change the carrying amount of the property transferred and they do not change the cost of that property for measurement or disclosure purposes. The Standard does not remind us, but we should note that the fair value of investment properties measured under the cost model has to be disclosed in the notes, a requirement that does not extend to owner-occupied property or to inventory.

A transfer to or from investment properties which are being carried at fair value obviously has potentially very significant effects on the measurement process and the carrying amount of an asset. If an investment property carried at fair value becomes an owner-occupied property or is transferred to inventory, then the property's cost for subsequent accounting purposes is its fair value as at the date of the change in use.

If an owner-occupied property becomes an investment property carried at fair value, then IAS 16 should be applied up to the date of the change of use, i.e. the entity continues to depreciate the property and to recognize any impairment losses. A difference between the carrying amount of the asset under IAS 16 at the date of the change of use and the fair value at that date is dealt with in the same way as a revaluation under IAS 16.

If a property classed as inventory is transferred to become an investment property carried at fair value, then the treatment is consistent with that of a sale of inventory under IAS 2. A difference between the fair value of the property at that date and its previous carrying amount is therefore part of net profit or loss for the period. Similarly, a self-constructed investment property that will be carried at fair value will give rise, on completion, to an effect on reported net profit or loss for the period equal to the difference between the fair value on the completion date and its previous (cost-based) carrying amount.

## ACTIVITY 13.14

Read the immediately preceding paragraph again. Does it meet the requirement in IAS 1 and the underlying concept in the IAS Framework to be prudent?

### Activity feedback
There is, certainly in comparison with what many would regard as normal, an apparent lack of prudence, and of strict adherence to the realization principle, inherent in the previous paragraph. However, this is the whole point of the fair value concept. There is, by definition, reliable evidence to determine fair value, which is a market-based concept and it therefore follows logically and consistently with a true sale, that a gain relating to operating processes has been 'made'. Anybody who regards only a completed transaction as providing adequate evidence for fair value should reject the whole notion of fair value accounting.

An investment property should be eliminated from the balance sheet (derecognized) on disposal. The disposal of an investment property may occur by sale or by entering into a finance lease. In determining the date of disposal for investment property, an entity applies the criteria in IAS 18, for recognizing revenue from the sale of goods (see Chapter 19). IAS 17 applies on a disposal by entering into a finance lease or by a sale and leaseback (see Chapter 16). An investment property must also be derecognized when it is permanently withdrawn from use and no further economic benefits are expected from its disposal. Gains and losses arising on derecognition, i.e. the difference between the net disposal proceeds and the carrying amount, are recognized as income or expense in the income statement, unless IAS 17 requires otherwise in the case of a sale and leaseback. This is, of course, consistent with the treatment of annual changes in fair value of a retained investment property, which are likewise taken directly to the income statement.

IAS 40 gives extensive and detailed disclosure requirements. The crucial point to remember is that if the cost model is used, then disclosure of fair values, by way of note, is still required.

## Some national considerations

Broadly speaking, the treatment of investment properties in important accounting jurisdictions mirrors the general characteristics of those jurisdictions, as discussed in

Chapter 2. It may be suggested that the attitude to investment properties often illustrates these characteristics quite strongly. It is generally argued that the Fourth EU Directive, as agreed in 1978, does not allow non-depreciation of property, although of course the true and fair override in Article 2 can be used to justify departure from this, at least in those countries that believe in the override anyway. National practice in 'continental' European countries would be, at least up to the present, to use the cost model.

The so-called Anglo-Saxons are clearly split on the matter. At the time of writing, UK Standards *require* investment properties to be evaluated on a broadly fair value basis in SSAP 19. US GAAP, as currently constituted (ARB 43, APB 6), require that investment properties be treated the same way as any other properties and are, therefore, squarely inconsistent with the original E64 proposals and with the UK requirements.

It is important to note, however, that although at first sight IAS 40 seems to be a compromise in that it allows both the UK to use fair values and the US to forbid them, this is over-simplistic. There is in fact a major difference between the UK and IAS. SSAP 19 in the UK, at para. 13, requires that changes in the market value of investment properties should not be taken to the income statements but should be taken to the statement of total recognized gains and losses (being a movement on an investment revaluation reserve), unless a deficit (or its reversal) on an individual property is expected to be permanent, in which case it should be charged (or credited) in the profit and loss account of the period.

This is in sharp contrast to the IAS 40 requirements, which, as discussed earlier, generally require such changes in market value to be taken directly to annual reported earnings. As regards the important concept of reported earnings, therefore, current UK GAAP is significantly more prudent than the requirements of the fair value alternative in IAS GAAP.

It should also be noted that IAS 40 has gone out of its way to give the impression that it is a stepping stone towards an eventual compulsory fair value model for investment properties. Time will tell.

## ACTIVITY 13.15

An extract from the financial statements of the British Land Company plc for the year to 31 March 2008 is shown below. Briefly explain how the group measures its properties, and what has happened during the year in relation to them.

At 31 March 2008, the Group book value of properties of £10 469m (2007: £14 047m) comprises freeholds of £9357m (2007: £13 118m); virtual freeholds of £303m (2007: £106m); long leaseholds of £802m (2007: £820m) and short leaseholds of £7m (2007: £3m). The historical cost of properties was £7315m (2007: £8897m).

At 31 March 2008, the book value of owner-occupied property is £53m (2007: £50m) after charging £nil (2007: £nil) depreciation to the income statement for the year.

The property valuation does not include any investment properties held under operating leases (2007: nil).

The property valued at £7162m (2007: £9194m) was subject to a security interest and other properties of non-recourse companies amounted to £2m (2007: £128m).

Cumulative interest capitalized in investment and development properties amounts to £33m and £84m (2007: £28m and £46m) respectively.

*(Continued)*

## ACTIVITY 13.15    *(Continued)*

### Financial statements of British Land plc for the year-ended 31 March 2008

|  | Investment £m | Development £m | Owner occupied £m | Total £m |
|---|---|---|---|---|
| Carrying value at 1 April 2007 | 12 891 | 1 106 | 50 | 14 047 |
| Additions – property purchases | 115 |  |  | 115 |
| Other capital expenditure | 253 | 292 |  | 545 |
| Disposals | (2 694) | (24) |  | (2 718) |
| Reclassifications | 360 | (360) |  |  |
| Revaluations: in income statement | (1 569) | (19) |  | (1 588) |
| in statement of recognized income and expense |  | 57 | 3 | 60 |
| Increase in tenant incentives and guaranteed rent uplift balances | 33 | 10 |  | 43 |
| Carrying value at 31 March 2008 | 9 389 | 1 062 | 53 | 10 504 |
| Head lease liabilities |  |  |  | (35) |
| Total Group property portfolio valuation 31 March 2008 |  |  |  | 10 469 |

### Activity feedback

*Most of the group properties are held as investments, with a significant minority under development. They are generally held at fair value. During the year there has been little acquisition of properties and significant disposals. In addition, a sizeable downward revaluation has been recorded, taken directly to reported earnings. The absolute historical cost of the properties has therefore fallen, as has the excess of valuation over historical cost for those remaining. Note also that most of the properties are pledged as security against group borrowings. The quality of disclosure and transparency seems quite high.*

Recent practical examples of the major statements are given in Chapter 32.

## SUMMARY

In this long chapter we have explored a number of aspects of IAS thinking in relation to the accounting treatment of fixed (non-current) assets. We looked at problems of cost determination, in particular IAS 20 on government grants and IAS 23 on borrowing costs and on the recognition and measurement of *Property, Plant and Equipment* (IAS 16), including alternative methods of depreciation calculation. We also exposed alternative views on the treatment of investment properties, and the IAS requirements on this in IAS 40.

## EXERCISES

*Suggested answers to exercises marked ✓ are to be found on our dedicated CourseMate platform for students.*

*Suggested answers to the remaining exercises are to be found on the Instructor online support resources.*

1  What are fixed (non-current) assets?

2  Outline four different depreciation methods and appraise them in the context of the definition and objectives of depreciation.

3  Are government grants related to the purchase of fixed assets by an entity, a reduction in cost of acquisition?

4  Can the receipt of a government grant create a liability?

5  In what circumstances, if at all, should borrowing costs be capitalized, in your opinion?

✓ 6  Should land be allowed to be, or required to be, revalued?

✓ 7  Should buildings be allowed to be, or required to be, revalued?

8  In what circumstances, if any, do you think that regulation should allow the non-depreciation of owned buildings?

9  IAS 40 gives a choice of accounting policy in relation to investment properties. Is a choice acceptable? If not, how should IAS 40 be altered?

✓10  The following is an extract of Errsea's balances of property, plant and equipment and related government grants at 1 April 2006.

|  | Cost $000 | Accumulated depreciation $000 | Carrying amount $000 |
|---|---|---|---|
| Property, plant and equipment | 240 | 180 | 60 |
| Non-current liabilities |  |  |  |
| Government grants |  |  | 30 |
| Current liabilities |  |  | 10 |
| Government grants |  |  |  |

Details including purchases and disposals of plant and related government grants during the year are:

(i)  Included in the above figures is an item of plant that was disposed of on 1 April 2006 for $12 000 which had cost $90 000 on 1 April 2003. The plant was being depreciated on a straight line basis over four years assuming a residual value of $10 000. A government grant was received on its purchase and was being recognized in the income statement in equal amounts over four years. In accordance with the terms of the grant, Errsea repaid $3000 of the grant on the disposal of the related plant.

(ii) An item of plant was acquired on 1 July 2006 with the following costs:

|  | $ |
|---|---|
| Base cost | 192 000 |
| Modifications specified by Errsea | 12 000 |
| Transport and installation | 6 000 |

The plant qualified for a government grant of 25 per cent of the base cost of the plant, but it had not been received by 31 March 2007. The plant is to be depreciated on a straight line basis over three years with a nil estimated residual value.

(iii) All other plant is depreciated by 15 per cent per annum on cost.

(iv) $11 000 of the $30 000 non-current liability for government grants at 1 April 2006 should be reclassified as a current liability as at 31 March 2007.

(v) Depreciation is calculated on a time apportioned basis.

**Required:**

Prepare extracts of Errsea's income statement and balance sheet in respect of the property, plant and equipment and government grants for the year ended 31 March 2007. Note: disclosure notes are not required.

(ACCA – June 2007)

✓11 Omega is an entity that owns three properties. All three properties were purchased on 1 October 2004. Details of the purchase price and market values of the properties are as follows:

|  | Property 1 $000 | Property 2 $000 | Property 3 $000 |
|---|---|---|---|
| Purchase price | 15 000 | 10 000 | 12 000 |
| Market value 30 September 2005 | 16 000 | 11 000 | 13 500 |
| Market value 30 September 2006 | 17 000 | 9 000 | 14 500 |

Properties 1 and 2 are used by Omega as factories whilst property 3 is let to a non-related third party at a commercial rent. Omega does not depreciate any of the properties on the basis that they are valued at market values that are generally expected to increase over time.

**Required:**

(a) Assess whether Omega's policy of non-depreciation of properties 1, 2 and 3 is in accordance with international financial reporting standards.

(b) Show how the movements in the carrying amount of each property will be reflected in the financial statements of Omega for the years ended 30 September 2005 and 2006. You can assume that any relevant depreciation is immaterial.

Where necessary you should justify your treatment with reference to appropriate international financial reporting standards. Where more than one treatment is permitted under international financial reporting standards you should show the impact of both treatments.

(ACCA – December 2006)

✓12 Omega prepares financial statements under International Financial Reporting Standards. In the year ended 31 March 2007 the following transactions occurred:

**Transaction 1**

On 1 April 2006 Omega began the construction of a new production line. Costs relating to the line are as follows:

| Details | Amount $000 |
|---|---|
| Costs of the basic materials (list price $12.5 million less a 20 per cent trade discount) | 10 000 |
| Recoverable sales taxes incurred not included in the purchase cost | 1 000 |
| Employment costs of the construction staff for the three months to 30 June 2006 (note 1) | 1 200 |
| Other overheads directly related to the construction (note 2) | 900 |
| Payments to external advisers relating to the construction | 500 |
| Expected dismantling and restoration costs (note 3) | 2 000 |

*Note 1*

The production line took two months to make ready for use and was brought into use on 31 May 2006.

*Note 2*

The other overheads were incurred in the two months ended 31 May 2006. They included an abnormal cost of $300 000 caused by a major electrical fault.

*Note 3*

The production line is expected to have a useful economic life of eight years. At the end of that time, Omega is legally required to dismantle the plant in a specified manner and restore its location to an acceptable standard. The figure of $2 million included in the cost estimates is the amount that is expected to be incurred at the end of the useful life of the production plant. The appropriate rate to use in any discounting calculations is 5 per cent. The present value of $1 payable in eight years at a discount rate of 5 per cent is approximately $0.68.

*Note 4*

Four years after being brought into use, the production line will require a major overhaul to ensure that it generates economic benefits for the second half of its useful life. The estimated cost of the overhaul, at current prices, is $3 million.

*Note 5*

Omega computes its depreciation charge on a monthly basis.

*Note 6*

No impairment of the plant had occurred by 31 March 2007.

**Transaction 2**

On 31 December 2006 the directors decided to dispose of a property that was surplus to requirements. They instructed selling agents to find a suitable purchaser and advertised the property at a commercially realistic price.

The property was being measured under the revaluation model and had been revalued at $15 million on 31 March 2006. The depreciable element of the property was estimated as $8 million at 31 March 2006 and the useful economic life of the depreciable element was estimated as 25 years from that date.

On 31 December 2006 the directors estimated that the market value of the property was $16 million, and that the costs incurred in selling the property would be $500 000. The property was sold on 30 April 2007 for $16.1 million. Omega incurred selling costs of $550 000. The actual selling price and costs to sell were consistent with estimated amounts as at 31 March 2007.

The financial statements for the year ended 31 March 2007 were authorized for issue on 15 May 2007.

**Required:**

Show the impact of the above transactions on the income statement of Omega for the year ended 31 March 2007, and on its balance sheet as at 31 March 2007. You should state where in the income statement and the balance sheet relevant balances will be shown.

(ACCA – June 2007)

13  (i)  Discuss the arguments in favour of, and those against, the capitalization of borrowing costs as part of the cost of an asset.

On 1 April 20X2, Webster commenced the construction of a large development consisting of several separate retail premises. It had a policy of capitalizing borrowing costs under IAS 23. At 31 March 20X3 the amount of expenditure on the development totalled $12 million. These expenditures can be taken to have been incurred evenly throughout the year. The development is being financed from funds generally borrowed for the construction of similar development projects. Webster's cost of capital on these funds can be calculated from the following:

$2 million overdraft at 15 per cent per annum

$3 million 5 year secured 8 per cent loan note

$5 million 5 year unsecured 10 per cent loan note

Construction of the development was halted twice during the accounting period to 31 March 20X3. The first occasion, for a two-week period, was due to the discovery of ancient artefacts unearthed during excavation work. The second, an extended period of two months, was due to an industrial relations dispute.

(ii)  Calculate the amount of finance costs that Webster should capitalize for the period to 31 March 20X3.

(ACCA – June 2003 adapted)

# INTANGIBLE ASSETS

## 14

INTANGIBLE ASSETS

14

**OBJECTIVES** After studying this chapter you should be able to:

- define and distinguish intangible assets and goodwill

- describe, apply and appraise the requirements of IAS 38 relating to intangible assets

- discuss alternative possible treatments for purchased goodwill

- describe, apply and appraise the requirements of IFRS 3 relating to purchased goodwill.

## INTRODUCTION

The accounting treatment of goodwill and intangible assets has caused great difficulty and confusion over the years. Part of the trouble was a failure to distinguish clearly between the two. In the 'bad old days', goodwill was often very loosely regarded as a conglomerate figure for all unrecorded net asset values. In other words, if a business was bought for €1 million and the recorded net assets had 'book values' of €600 000, then the difference of €400 000 was considered to be goodwill. This adherence to book values, which are by definition largely meaningless in market terms, is now generally unacceptable. IASB defines goodwill (IFRS 3, Appendix A) as follows:

Future economic benefits arising from assets that are not capable of being individually identified and separately recognized.

In principle, goodwill is in existence all the time. Its value is difficult to define and is constantly changing. Its value can, of course, be negative. But goodwill is always there; it is inherent in the business. This is often referred to as *inherent goodwill, non-purchased goodwill* or *internally generated goodwill*. It is contrasted with purchased goodwill. This contrast is not for reasons of principle, but purely for the practical reason that purchased goodwill has a convenient cost figure. There has been a transaction, the cost convention can be applied, we have a figure capable of being audited. If we buy a business for €100 000 and the net separable assets have fair value of €60 000 then we can certainly say that goodwill is, or at least at that instant was, worth €40 000.

The accounting treatment for purchased goodwill is regarded as an aspect of accounting for business combinations. IASB covers this in IFRS 3 and we discuss purchased goodwill separately in the next section. We first consider in detail the problems of accounting for intangibles other than purchased goodwill; this is covered by IAS 38, *Intangible Assets*.

## INTANGIBLE ASSETS

In IAS GAAP, an intangible asset is defined as an '*identifiable* non-monetary asset without physical substance'. This excludes goodwill which is by definition non-identifiable.

Identifiability in IAS GAAP does not equal separability, since an asset of an entity is defined as 'a *resource* [that is] (a) *controlled* by the entity as a result of past events; and (b) from which future economic benefits are expected to flow to the entity'. For an intangible asset to be recognized, the future economic benefits must be 'probable' and it must be possible to measure the cost of the asset reliably. 'Control' encompasses both the right to obtain the benefits and the ability to restrict access to them by others. It is not necessarily considered to imply the ability to sell the item separately from other assets of the entity. These criteria thus permit the recognition as assets, in appropriate circumstances, of non-separable items such as development costs that have not been converted into (separable) patents. They do not permit the recognition of internally generated goodwill.

At the original creation of IAS 38 in 1998 the IASB decided to include the requirements on research and development (R&D) costs, originally separately stated in IAS 9, with those on other intangibles because R&D costs are intangible in nature; any value attributable to them being due to the know-how embodied in them rather than to physical items such as prototypes. The IASB was concerned to achieve, as far as possible, uniformity of treatment for all long-term non-financial assets, whether tangible or intangible, and for intangibles whether internally generated or acquired. This concern is manifested in IAS 38 in the following ways:

- Many of the paragraphs of IAS 38 are similar in wording, and in places virtually identical, to paragraphs of IAS 16, *Property, Plant and Equipment*.
- The recognition as assets of internally generated intangibles is allowed, subject to stringent and cumbersome criteria.

Although the principle is that any intangibles that meet the asset recognition criteria should be recognized (except in the case of the 'alternative treatment' discussed later), it remains to be seen whether the effect of these criteria acts as a deterrent to a reporting entity from so doing, in the absence of a powerful reason.

The treatment of R&D costs has been the subject of particular controversy internationally. While there is general but not universal agreement (e.g. Norwegian law explicitly states the opposite), that research does not give rise to intangible values that can be recognized as assets, there is disagreement as to whether development may do so, subject to certain criteria. In its 1993 revision of IAS 9, *Research and Development Costs*, the IASB had changed its preferred (benchmark) treatment from that proposed in its Exposure Drafts E32 and E47, namely, the immediate expensing of all development costs, to capitalization (i.e. recognition as an asset), provided certain criteria were met. It was thought that this was more consistent with the concept of an asset as set out in the IASB's Framework. In IAS 38, capitalization is maintained, but the criteria for recognition have been tightened up; immediate expensing is not allowed as an alternative treatment if these criteria are met.

The new version of IAS 38, applicable from 1 January 2005, made various amendments and clarifications and, in a major development, requires the non-depreciation of intangible assets with indefinite lines, as defined, requiring regular impairment tests instead. There have been further minor revisions.

## Scope of IAS 38

The scope of IAS 38 is clarified in paras 2 and 3 by stating which categories of item are not included, namely:

(a) intangible assets that are within the scope of another Standard

(b) financial assets (as defined in IAS 39, *Financial Instruments: Recognition and Measurement*)

(c) the recognition and measurement of exploration and evaluation assets (covered by IFRS 6), and

(d) expenditure on the development and estimation of minerals, oil, natural gas and similar non-regenerative resources.

If another Standard prescribes the accounting for a specific type of intangible asset, an entity applies that Standard instead of IAS 38. For example:

(a) intangible assets held by an entity for sale in the ordinary course of business (see IAS 2, *Inventories*, and IAS 11, *Construction Contracts*)

(b) deferred tax assets (see IAS 12, *Income Taxes*)

(c) leases that are within the scope of IAS 17, *Leases*

(d) assets arising from employee benefits (see IAS 19, *Employee Benefits*)

(e) financial assets as defined in IAS 32; recognition and measurement of some financial assets are covered by IFRS 10 *Consolidated Financial Statements,* IAS 27, *Separate Financial Statements,* IAS 28, *Investments in Associates and Joint Ventures*

(f) goodwill acquired in a business combination (see IFRS 3, *Business Combinations*)

(g) deferred acquisition costs and intangible assets, arising from an insurer's contractual rights under insurance contracts within the scope of IFRS 4, *Insurance Contracts*

(h) non-current intangible assets classified as held for sale (or included in a disposal group that is classified as held for sale) in accordance with IFRS 5, *Non-current Assets Held for Sale and Discontinued Operations.*

The term *intangible assets* raises the major issue of which intangible items should be recognized as assets and which should not. Hence, IAS 38 mentions numerous items of expenditure on what may be termed *intangible resources,* many of which do not meet its asset recognition criteria. Such intangible resources include expenditure on advertising, training, start-up, R&D activities and computer software, patents, copyrights or motion picture films. A good number of these do not qualify for recognition as assets in terms of the criteria set out in the IASB's Framework and one of the main purposes of IAS 38 is to distinguish between those that do and those that do not. Examples of expenditure that do not meet these criteria, essentially on the grounds of a lack of any demonstrable connection between expense and desired benefit, are start-ups, research, training, advertising and/or promotion, and relocation or reorganization. Paragraph 63 adds internally generated brands, mastheads, publishing titles, customer lists and items similar in substance as items not qualifying for recognition as assets.

According to IAS 38, para. 6, an intangible asset held by a lessee under a finance lease is considered, after initial recognition, to be an asset falling within the scope of IAS 38.

## Recognition under IAS 38

Three criteria need to be satisfied before an item should be recognized as an intangible asset under IAS 38. These are identifiability, control and reliable measurability.

*Identifiability* (IAS 38, paras 11–12) is necessary in order to distinguish an intangible asset from goodwill. Separability is a sufficient condition for identifiability, but in IAS GAAP not a necessary one. An asset is separable if the entity could rent, sell, exchange or distribute the specific future economic benefits attributable to the asset without also disposing of other assets or future economic benefits that flow from them. (Future economic benefits include both revenues and cost savings.)

An entity, however, may be able to identify an intangible asset in some other way. If an intangible asset is acquired together with a set of other assets, it may be separately identifiable by virtue of separate legal rights attaching to it. An internally generated intangible asset may also result from an internal project that gives rise to legal rights for the entity. Nevertheless, usually legal rights are transferable so that such assets are separable (an exception is rights resulting from a legal duty on employees to maintain confidentiality). But identifiability in IAS GAAP can be achieved even if an asset generates future economic benefits only in combination with other assets; that is, it is not separable, provided the entity can identify the future economic benefits that will flow from the asset. In that case, however, the second criterion, control, is particularly crucial.

*Control* (IAS 38, paras 13–16) is exercised by an entity over an asset if the entity:

- has the power to obtain the future economic benefits flowing from the underlying resource
- can also restrict the access of others to such benefits.

The resource itself is not recognizable as an asset unless the criterion of control (as well as that of identifiability) is met. Control will generally result from legal rights enforceable in law and such rights provide a sufficient condition for control. IAS GAAP do not exclude the possibility that control over the future economic benefits could be exercised in some other way, but give no examples of this.

In the case of such intangible resources as benefits arising from a team of skilled staff and from training, even if the identifiability criterion can be satisfied, the criterion of controllability will most likely not be met in the absence of protection by legal rights. The same is true for customer lists or market shares. Such intangible resources, therefore, do not usually qualify for recognition as intangible assets.

*Reliable measurability* is also a necessary precondition for the recognition of intangible assets. IAS 38, paras 21 and 24, state that an intangible asset (that has met the other recognition criteria) should be recognized only if its cost can be measured reliably and that it should be measured initially at that cost.

For the purpose of determining cost, four different modes of acquisition are considered (paras 25–47): separate acquisition; acquisition as part of a business combination; acquisition by way of a government grant; and acquisition by exchange of assets. Little needs to be said in explanation of this.

In the case of separate acquisition, the rules for determining cost are the same as those for assets generally, discussed in Chapter 13. The rules for determining cost in the case of acquisition as part of a business combination are given in IFRS 3 (see Chapter 26). In the case of acquisition by way of a government grant, the rules in IAS 20 are applicable (see Chapter 13).

In general, exchanges of assets are accounted for at fair value; the fair value of the asset given being treated as the cost of the asset acquired, subject to any necessary adjustments for any other partial consideration such as cash. In the case of an intangible asset that is exchanged for an equity interest in a similar asset (such as a share in a R&D joint venture), the cost of the new asset is the carrying amount of the asset given up, with no gain or loss being recognized on the transaction, unless the fair value of the asset received is less than the carrying amount of the asset given up.

## Internally generated intangible assets

Note that internally generated goodwill cannot be an intangible asset within the terms of IAS 38 and so cannot be capitalized. In order to assess whether an internally generated intangible resource meets the criteria for recognition as an asset, IAS 38 sets out the following methodology (paras 51–64).

The entity first classifies the internal project resulting in the generation of the resource into two phases: a research phase and a development phase. If this distinction cannot be made for the internal project, then the entire project should be considered as a research phase.

Research is defined as original and planned investigation undertaken with the prospect of gaining new scientific or technical knowledge and understanding. Development is the application of research findings or other knowledge to a plan or design for the production of new or substantially improved materials, devices, products, processes, systems or services before the start of commercial production or use (IAS 38, para. 8).

It is worth pausing at this point to remind ourselves about the general principles involved here. It is obvious that the management of an entity will authorize the expenditure of money and resources on either research or development only if there is in some sense or other an expectation of benefit to the entity. It can be argued that an expectation of future benefit from a past event automatically creates the expectation of an asset now. However, the IAS definition of an asset needs to be remembered in full, i.e. an asset is a resource:

* controlled by an entity as a result of past events, and
* from which future economic benefits are expected to flow.

## ACTIVITY 14.1

From your knowledge of the IASB Framework and general accounting concepts, suggest briefly, with justification, how expenditure in the research and development phases should be treated.

### Activity feedback

*In essence, the matching convention argues in favour of capitalization now, in order to permit expensing later against resulting benefit. The asset figure will need to be charged to the P&L account over the period of benefits, in approximate proportion to the benefit pattern. In effect, we would have a fixed asset that would require depreciating. And since there is likely to be a gap, perhaps of several years, between expenditure and eventual benefit in terms of production and sales, it follows that the expense or depreciation may be zero for one or more accounting periods. If the benefit has not begun to appear yet, then under the matching convention we should not yet begin to write-off the asset as an expense. It can be suggested that this treatment is inconsistent with the prudence convention. Research and development expenditure is by definition speculative and, particularly with more basic investigation, the outcome is highly uncertain. It is perhaps difficult to argue that the existence of future benefit, of greater amount than the expenditure, can be established with 'reasonable certainty'. It is even harder to argue that the relationship to the revenue or benefit in any particular future period can be established with 'reasonable certainty'. It must also be remembered that a successful profitable outcome is crucially dependent on the validity of the going concern convention.*

There is clearly a tension regarding research and development expenditure between matching and prudence. Whatever detailed views an individual holds, it is obvious that research is significantly more speculative than development and that development expenditure becomes less speculative and more reasonably predictable in its outcome, as actual production and sale of the product comes nearer. The IASB solution is to forbid the capitalization of all research and development expenditure, except for development phase items which meet specified conditions, in which case they are required (not just permitted) to be capitalized.

Thus, under IAS 38, no intangible asset should be recognized as resulting from research or from the research phase of an internal project. Expenditure on research should be recognized as an expense when incurred.

An intangible resource arising from development (or from the development phase of an internal project) should be recognized as an intangible asset if, and only if, an entity can demonstrate all the following:

- The technical feasibility of completing the intangible asset so that it will be available for use or sale.
- Its intention to complete the intangible asset and use or sell it.
- Its ability to use or sell it.
- How the intangible asset will generate probable future economic benefits. Among other things, the following should be demonstrated: the existence of a market for the intangible asset or its output or, if it is to be used internally, its usefulness to the entity.
- The availability of adequate technical, financial and other resources to complete the development and to use or sell the intangible asset, which may be demonstrated by an appropriate business plan.
- The entity's ability to measure reliably the expenditure attributable to the intangible asset during its development, e.g. by means of the entity's costing system.

To demonstrate how an intangible asset will generate probable future economic benefits, the principles set out in IAS 36, *Impairment of Assets*, especially paras 30–57 on value in use, should be applied. If the asset will generate economic benefits only in combination with other assets, the principles for 'cash-generating units' set out in IAS 36 should be followed (IAS 36 is discussed in Chapter 15).

As discussed above, under the heading 'Scope of IAS 38', IAS 38 names a number of items that do not meet these criteria.

The cost of an internally generated asset is the sum of the expenditure incurred from the date when the intangible asset first meets the recognition criteria set out earlier. Cost includes all expenditure that is either directly attributable to generating the asset or has been allocated on a reasonable and consistent basis to the activity of generating it. Allocations of overheads should follow the principles set out in IAS 2, *Inventories* (see Chapter 17). With regard to the recognition of interest as a cost, IAS 23, *Borrowing Costs* (see Chapter 13), sets out the applicable principles.

Expenditure that is not part of the cost of the intangible asset includes that on selling, administration and training staff to operate the asset. Expenditure on an intangible resource that was initially recognized as an expense in previous financial statements or reports (e.g. expenditure during the 'research phase' of an internal project) should not be recognized as part of the cost of an intangible asset at a later date (IAS 38, para. 71).

Any expenditure that is not part of the cost of an intangible asset properly recognizable as defined and discussed earlier is, naturally, to be recognized as an expense when incurred (unless the expenditure is part of the cost of a business acquisition, when IFRS 3 applies as already stated).

## Subsequent expenditure

The view taken in IAS 38 is that only rarely will expenditure incurred after the initial recognition of a purchased intangible asset or after the completion of an internally generated intangible asset result in an addition to the amount of its capitalized cost. This is because it is generally difficult:

- to attribute such expenditure to a particular intangible asset rather than to the business as a whole, and
- (even when that difficulty does not arise) to determine whether such expenditure will enhance, rather than merely maintain, the probable economic benefits that will flow from the asset.

Consequently, subsequent expenditure should be recognized as an expense, except in the rare cases where:

- probable enhancement of the economic benefits that will flow from the asset can be demonstrated, and
- the expenditure can be measured and attributed to the asset reliably (IAS 38, paras 18–20).

## Measurement subsequent to initial recognition

Two treatments are available: the cost model and the revaluation model. In the 1998 version of IAS 38 these were characterized as 'benchmark' and 'alternative' treatments, respectively. These terms have been removed and IAS 38 now gives the two alternatives ostensibly equal weighting.

The cost model is that an intangible asset should be carried at cost less any accumulated depreciation and (if any) accumulated impairment losses (IAS 38, para. 74).

The revaluation model is to carry the intangible asset at a revalued amount. The revalued amount should be the fair value of the asset at the date of revaluation less any subsequent accumulated depreciation and (if any) subsequent accumulated impairment losses (IAS 38, para. 75). Fair value, in the context of this standard, should be measured by reference to an active market. This revaluation treatment can only be applied after initial recognition, i.e. all the conditions and requirements stated earlier must previously have been fully satisfied.

If an intangible asset is revalued, revaluation of all the other assets in its class should also be carried out (i.e. those of similar nature and use within the entity's operations), except those for which there is no active market, which should be carried at cost less accumulated amortization and impairment losses.

Fair value should be determined by reference to an active market within the requirements of IFRS 13 (see Chapter 8), and revaluations should be made with sufficient regularity so that the carrying amount does not diverge materially from the fair value at the balance sheet date.

It is considered unlikely that such an active market would exist for an intangible asset (IAS 38, para. 78), although there may be exceptions to this generalization; for example, there may be active markets in freely transferable taxi licences, fishing licences, production quotas or airport take-off and landing 'slots'. If an active market is not available, the revaluation model cannot be used.

The revaluation model cannot apply to initial recognition, which should be at cost, or to intangible resources that were not previously recognized as assets. However, if only part of the cost of an intangible resource was recognized as an asset because it did not meet the criteria for recognition until part of the way through an internal project, the revaluation treatment may be applied to the whole of the asset and not just to that proportion of it that would be represented by the amount recognized as its cost. The revaluation treatment may also be applied to an intangible asset received by way of a government grant and initially recognized at a nominal amount (IAS 38, para. 77).

An active market that has existed for an intangible asset may cease to exist. In that case, if the asset has been accounted for by using the alternative treatment, then its carrying amount should be its revalued amount at the date of the last revaluation by reference to the formerly active market less any accumulated depreciation and impairment losses. The cessation of the active market may be an indication of possible impairment of the asset's value and this should be tested in accordance with IAS 36, *Impairment of Assets* (see Chapter 15). If, at a subsequent measurement date, an active market is available again so that the fair value of the asset can be determined, the asset should be revalued at its fair value as of that date.

## Recognition of revaluation gains and losses

The usual prudence and realization conventions prevail. Increases in an intangible asset's carrying amount (gains) should be credited to other comprehensive income, and accumulated in equity under the heading of revaluation surplus, except to the extent that the increase is a reversal of a previous revaluation decrease (loss) recognized as an expense in respect of the same asset, in which case the amount of the reversal is recognized as income.

Revaluation decreases (losses) are recognized as expenses except to the extent that the decrease is a reversal of a revaluation increase (gain) that was previously credited to revaluation surplus (via comprehensive income) in respect of the same asset, in which case the amount of the reversal should be recognized in other comprehensive income, thus reducing the amount of the revaluation surplus (IAS 38, paras 85–86).

According to IAS 38, para. 87, the cumulative revaluation surplus 'may' be transferred directly to retained earnings when the surplus is realized. Realization of the surplus may occur through retirement or disposal of the asset or through the process of using up the asset, insofar as the amortization based on the revalued carrying amount exceeds that which would have been calculated on the basis of the asset's historical cost. The transfer from revaluation surplus to retained earnings is not made through the income statement, but directly in the balance sheet, i.e. it does not affect reported earnings in the year the transfer is made.

## Amortization and depreciation

IAS 38 uses the terms *amortization* and *depreciation* interchangeably with reference to intangible assets to refer to the process of systematic allocation of an asset's cost or revalued amount, less any residual value, over its useful life. The residual value should be assumed to be zero, unless:

- either there is a commitment by a third party to purchase the asset at the end of its estimated useful life to the entity (i.e. the period of time over which it is being depreciated), or
- there is an active market for the asset, such that the asset's residual value can be determined by reference to that market and it is probable that the market will exist at the end of asset's estimated useful life to the entity.

An estimate of an asset's residual value is based on the amount recoverable from disposal using prices prevailing at the date of the estimate for the sale of a similar asset that has reached the end of its useful life and has operated under conditions similar to those in which the asset will be used. The residual value is reviewed at least at each financial year end. A change in the asset's residual value is accounted for as a change in an accounting estimate in accordance with IAS 8, *Accounting Policies, Changes in Accounting Estimates and Errors.*

## Useful life

The previous (1998) version of IAS 38 contained a 'rebuttable assumption' that the useful life for an intangible asset could not exceed 20 years, and, in all cases, required amortization. The new version made very significant changes. IAS 38 now requires (paras 88–89) that an entity shall assess whether the useful life of an intangible asset is finite or indefinite and, if finite, the length of, or number of production or similar units constituting, that useful life. An intangible asset shall be regarded by the entity as having an indefinite useful life when, based on an analysis of all the relevant factors, there is no foreseeable limit to the period over which the asset is expected to generate net cash inflows for the entity.

The accounting for an intangible asset is based on its useful life. An intangible asset with a finite useful life is amortized and an intangible asset with an indefinite useful life is not.

Factors that need to be considered in estimating an intangible asset's useful life include the following (IAS 38, paras 90 and 94):

1 The expected usage of the asset by the entity and whether the asset could be efficiently managed by another management team.

2 Typical product life cycles for the asset and public information on estimates of useful lives for similar assets that are used in a similar way.

3 Technical, technological, commercial or other types of obsolescence.

4 The stability of the industry in which the asset operates and changes in the market demand for the outputs of the asset.

5 Expected actions by competitors or potential competitors.

6 The level of maintenance expenditure required to obtain the expected future economic benefits from the asset and the entity's intent and ability to spend such amounts.

7 The entity's period of control over the asset and legal and similar limits on control or use, such as the expiration dates of related leases. If control over the future economic benefits from the asset is achieved though legal rights that have been granted for a finite period, the useful life of the asset should not exceed the duration of the legal rights unless they are renewable and renewal is virtually certain.

8 Whether the asset's useful life is dependent on that of other assets of the entity.

The term 'indefinite' does not mean 'infinite'. The useful life of an intangible asset reflects only that level of future maintenance expenditure required to maintain the asset at its standard of performance assessed at the time of estimating the asset's useful life and the entity's ability and intention to reach such a level. A conclusion that the useful life of an intangible asset is indefinite should not depend on planned future expenditure in excess of that required to maintain the asset at that standard of performance.

**Intangible assets with finite useful lives** The depreciable amount of an intangible asset with a finite useful life shall be allocated on a systematic basis over its useful life. Amortization shall begin when the asset is available for use, i.e. when it is in the location and condition necessary for it to be capable of operating in the manner intended by management. Amortization shall cease at the earliest date that the asset is classified as held for sale (or included in a disposal group that is classified as held for sale) in accordance with IFRS 5, *Non-current Assets Held for Sale and Discontinued Operations* (see Chapter 15), and the date that the asset is derecognized. The amortization method used shall reflect the pattern in which the asset's future economic benefits are expected to be consumed by the entity. If the pattern cannot be reliably determined, the straight line method shall be used. The amortization charge for each period shall be recognized in profit or loss, unless IAS 38 or another Standard permits or requires it to be included in the carrying amount of another asset.

IAS 38 envisages a variety of amortization methods that may be used to allocate systematically the depreciable amount of an intangible asset over the periods making up its useful life. The Standard mentions the straight line, diminishing balance and units of production methods. The straight line method should be used unless the time pattern of consumption of the asset's economic benefits can be determined reliably and clearly indicates that one of the other methods is more suitable. There will rarely, if ever, be persuasive evidence to support a method for intangible assets that is less conservative (that is, results in a lower amount of accumulated depreciation) than the straight line method (IAS 38, paras 97–99).

The amortization period and method should be reviewed at least at each financial year-end and the amortization period should be changed if the expected useful life of the asset is significantly different from previous estimates (IAS 38, para. 104). If the expected time pattern of economic benefits has changed, the amortization method should be changed accordingly. Such changes should be accounted for as changes in accounting estimates under IAS 8 (see Chapter 9).

In addition to all of the above, the requirements of IAS 36, *Impairment of Assets* (discussed in Chapter 15), will apply.

**Intangible assets with indefinite useful lives**  The essential treatment is very simple. Such assets are not depreciated (i.e. shall not be, not need not be). IAS 36 is applied and an impairment test is carried out annually and whenever there is an indication that the intangible asset may be impaired. This will lead to reductions in carrying value to the recoverable amount at the date of the impairment test.

## Retirements and disposals

An intangible asset shall be derecognized:

- on disposal, or
- when no future economic benefits are expected from its use or disposal.

The gain or loss arising from the derecognition of an intangible asset shall be determined as the difference between the net disposal proceeds, if any, and the carrying amount of the asset. It shall be recognized in profit or loss when the asset is derecognized (unless IAS 17, *Leases*, requires otherwise on a sale and leaseback). Gains shall not be classified as revenue. Amortization of an intangible asset with a finite useful life does not cease when the intangible asset is no longer used, unless the asset has been fully depreciated or is classified as held for sale (or included in a disposal group that is classified as held for sale) in accordance with IFRS 5.

## Disclosure

The disclosure requirements are, as usual, long and detailed. Full details of balances, movements over the year and any revaluations or impairment losses are specified.

## ACCOUNTING FOR PURCHASED GOODWILL

As we discussed earlier, purchased goodwill is regulated under IAS by IFRS 3 on business combinations, not by IAS 38 on intangible assets. Nevertheless, the basic issues involved in its treatment are asset/expense questions, not principles of consolidations, and it is appropriate to deal with its treatment here. As already noted, goodwill is defined (IFRS 3, Appendix A) as follows:

> Future economic benefits arising from other assets acquired in a business combination that are not individually identified and separately recognized.

We are now in a position to explore the formal requirements of IFRS 3 in relation to goodwill on acquisition. First, look at Activities 14.2 and 14.3.

## ACTIVITY 14.2

Does goodwill on acquisition meet the IASB's own definition of an asset?

### Activity feedback

*An asset (Framework, para. 4.4) is a resource controlled by the entity as a result of past events and from which future economic benefits are expected to flow. There is certainly a past event and there must logically be an expectation of future economic benefits in the eyes of the management of the acquirer. But is there a 'resource controlled' by the entity? Remember that, by definition, no 'identifiable asset' is involved. The issue is a complicated theoretical one and general opinion seems to be that goodwill on acquisition is certainly not a normal asset, but is at least sufficiently asset-like to be treated as if it was one.*

A variety of ways can be suggested for how goodwill on acquisition might be treated after recognition. Here are seven possible ways:

1 Carry it as an asset and amortize it over its estimated useful life through the profit and loss account.

2 Carry it as an asset and amortize it over its estimated useful life by writing off against reserves.

3 Eliminate it against reserves immediately on acquisition.

4 Retain it in the accounts indefinitely, unless a permanent reduction in its value becomes evident, when impairment is recognized.

5 Charge it as an expense against profits in the period when it is acquired.

6 Show it as a deduction from shareholders' equity (and either amortize it or carry it indefinitely).

7 Revalue it annually to incorporate later non-purchased goodwill.

## ACTIVITY 14.3

Comment on each of these seven possible treatments in relation to rational justification and usefulness.

### Activity feedback

*Here are some thoughts, which you may or may not completely agree with:*

*1  Is a straightforward application of matching the acquisition 'cost' in proportion to the benefit.*

*2  Seems illogical; amortization represents an expense and therefore should appear in the profit and loss account.*

*3  This solves the problem as if the item had never existed. It implies that no asset exists, and that equity must face the 'loss' immediately.*

*4  This is rational if it is accepted that purchased goodwill can be maintained, as a building can.*

*Arguably, however, the reality is that purchased goodwill is gradually being replaced by non-purchased goodwill. It can also be suggested that the costs of maintaining the goodwill are being expensed as they occur and that to charge amortization as well would usually be simple double counting.*

*5  Seems illogical and excessively prudent.*

*6  Also seems illogical, and potentially confusing, being essentially a misrepresentation of either 1 or 4.*

*7  Would be consistent with the trend towards fair value generally, but highly subjective (and inconsistent with legal restrictions in many countries).*

# Goodwill and IFRS 3

Goodwill in IAS GAAP is the difference between the fair value of the purchase consideration given and the aggregate fair values of the identifiable assets and liabilities of the acquiree that are recognized on acquisition, as discussed earlier. What is recognized as goodwill on acquisition is, therefore, a function of the recognition criteria and valuation rules applied to the identifiable assets and liabilities (and notably those in IASs 36, 37, 38, 39 and IFRS 9). As such, it is not itself an identifiable asset or liability but a residual amount. Nevertheless, IAS GAAP require it to be shown as an asset.

Goodwill on acquisition is calculated through the following process (paras 36–37).

The acquirer shall, at the acquisition date, allocate the cost of a business combination by recognizing the acquiree's identifiable assets, liabilities and contingent liabilities that satisfy the recognition criteria in paragraph 37 at their fair values at that date, except for non-current assets (or disposal groups) that are classified as held for sale in accordance with IFRS 5, *Non-current Assets Held for Sales and Discontinued Operations*, which shall be recognized at fair value less costs to sell. Any difference between the cost of the business combination and the acquirer's interest in the net fair value of the identifiable assets, liabilities and contingent liabilities so recognized shall be accounted for as goodwill.

The acquirer shall recognize separately the acquiree's identifiable assets, liabilities and contingent liabilities at the acquisition date, only if they satisfy the following criteria at that date:

- In the case of an asset other than an intangible asset, it is probable that any associated future economic benefits will flow to the acquirer and its fair value can be measured reliably.

- In the case of a liability other than a contingent liability, it is probable that an outflow of resources embodying economic benefits will be required to settle the obligation and its fair value can be measured reliably.

- In the case of an intangible asset or a contingent liability, its fair value can be measured reliably.

It is explicitly recognized that these criteria do 'not preclude' (para. IE 21 to IFRS 3) the recognition of brands as separable identifiable assets.

The excess of cost over the net fair value of the identifiable assets is the goodwill on acquisition figure. The acquirer is required to treat such goodwill as follows (paras 51–52):

The acquirer shall, at the acquisition date:

**(a)** recognize goodwill acquired in a business combination as an asset, and

**(b)** initially measure that goodwill at its cost, being the excess of the cost of the business combination over the acquirer's interest in the net fair value of the identifiable assets, liabilities and contingent liabilities recognized in accordance with para. 36.

Goodwill acquired in a business combination represents a payment made by the acquirer in anticipation of future economic benefits from assets that are not capable of being individually identified and separately recognized. Goodwill acquired in a business combination shall not be amortized. Instead, the acquirer shall test it for impairment annually, or more frequently if events or changes in circumstances indicate that it might be impaired, in accordance with IAS 36, *Impairment of Assets*.

Note that this treatment is exactly consistent with the requirements for identifiable intangible assets with indefinite lives, as discussed earlier in relation to IAS 38.

It is, of course, possible for the calculated goodwill figure to be negative. IFRS 3 studiously avoids calling this negative goodwill, stating that if the acquirer's interest in the net fair value of the identifiable assets, liabilities and contingent liabilities recognized in accordance with para. 36, exceeds the cost of the business combination, the acquirer shall:

- reassess the identification and measurement of the acquiree's identifiable assets, liabilities and contingent liabilities and the measurement of the cost of the combination
- recognize immediately in profit or loss any excess remaining after that reassessment.

It follows that, in future, negative goodwill, under that or any other label, will not appear in IAS group balance sheets. This is a major change. Any negative goodwill brought forward under previous IASB standards is to be derecognized and transferred to retained earnings.

## International developments

Many different methods have been used over the years. The previous IAS requirement was essentially our suggested method 1, with compulsory impairment reviews added on in the case of a useful life over 20 years. The current IAS requirement is essentially our method 4. US GAAP allowed a useful life of up to 40 years until recently. Method 3 was common for many years in the UK and may still be found in a number of European national systems. UK GAAP now allows, in effect, a choice between methods 1 and 4. There is a presumption that useful life will not normally exceed 20 years (requiring method 1); impairment reviews at intervals are specified. A longer useful life or an unlimited life with no annual amortization both require annual impairment reviews. US GAAP has now moved to annual impairment reviews, with amortization prohibited. Harmonization is getting closer, but has not yet been reached.

## REAL WORLD ILLUSTRATION

We give below two extracts from the consolidated financial statements of Ryanair plc for 2012. The first shows clearly that there have been changes over the years in regulation, and Ryanair practice, regarding the calculation of goodwill.

### Business combinations

Business combinations are accounted for using the acquisition method as at the acquisition date, which is the date on which control is transferred to the Company. Control is the power to govern the financial and operating policies of an entity so as to obtain benefits from its activities.

### Acquisitions on or after April 1, 2010

For acquisitions on or after January 1, 2010, the Company measures goodwill at the acquisition date as the fair value of the consideration transferred, plus the recognized amount of any non-controlling interests in the acquiree, less the net recognized amount of the identifiable assets acquired and liabilities assumed.

### Acquisitions between January 1, 2004 and April 1, 2010

For acquisitions between January 1, 2004 and January 1, 2010, goodwill represents the excess of the cost of the acquisition over the Company's interest in the recognized amount of the identifiable assets, liabilities and contingent liabilities of the acquiree.

### Acquisitions prior to January 1, 2004 (date of transition to IFRSs)

As part of its transition to the IFRSs, the Company elected to restate only those business combinations that occurred on or after January 1, 2003. Prior to January 1, 2003, goodwill represented the amount recognized under the Company's previous accounting framework, Irish GAAP.

## REAL WORLD ILLUSTRATION *(Continued)*

The second extract raises some interesting issues which you might like to consider. What is the information content today of this reported figure?

**Intangible assets**

| | At March 31, | | |
| --- | --- | --- | --- |
| | 2012 | 2011 | 2010 |
| | €M | €M | €M |
| Landing rights | 46.8 | 46.8 | 46.8 |

Landing slots were acquired with the acquisition of Buzz Stansted Ltd in April 2003. As these landing slots have no expiry date and are expected to be used in perpetuity, they are considered to be of indefinite life and accordingly are not amortized. The Company also considers that there has been no impairment of the value of these rights to date. The recoverable amount of these rights has been determined on a value-in-use basis, using discounted cash-flow projections for a 20-year period for each route that has an individual landing right. The calculation of value-in-use is most sensitive to the operating margin and discount rate assumptions. Operating margins are based on the existing margins generated from these routes and adjusted for any known trading conditions. The trading environment is subject to both regulatory and competitive pressures that can have a material effect on the operating performance of the business. Foreseeable events, however, are unlikely to result in a change of projections of a significant nature so as to result in the landing rights' carrying amounts exceeding their recoverable amounts. These projections have been discounted using weighted average cost of capital, estimated to be 7.7 per cent for 2012, 7.3 per cent for 2011 and 6.1 per cent for 2010.

Examples of accounting policy choices, and the implications for analysis and interpretation of the financial statements, are also given and discussed in Part Four of this book. See in particular Chapter 32.

## SUMMARY

This chapter, following the exploration of the treatment of tangible long-term assets in Chapter 13, has looked at the treatment of similar intangible assets. We considered in detail the requirements of IAS 38, dealing with separable intangible assets, and of IFRS 3 as regards the treatment of goodwill.

## EXERCISES

*Suggested answers to exercises marked ✓ are to be found on our dedicated CourseMate platform for students.*

*Suggested answers to the remaining exercises are to be found on the Instructor online support resources.*

✓**1**   Is goodwill an asset?

**2**   Identifiable intangible assets should be treated, for all accounting purposes, identically with tangible assets. Discuss.

**3**   Outline five different ways of treating goodwill in financial statements, discussing arguments for and against each one.

**4**   If depreciation is done properly, impairment adjustments will not arise. Discuss.

**5**   CD is a manufacturing entity that runs a number of operations including a bottling plant that bottles carbonated soft drinks. CD has been developing a new bottling process that will allow the bottles to be filled and sealed more efficiently.

The new process took a year to develop. At the start of development, CD estimated that the new process would increase output by 15 per cent with no additional cost (other than the extra bottles and their contents). Development work commenced on 1 May 2005 and was completed on 20 April 2006. Testing at the end of the development confirmed CD's original estimates.

CD incurred expenditure of €180 000 on the above development in 2005/06.

CD plans to install the new process in its bottling plant and start operating the new process from 1 May 2006.

CD's balance sheet date is 30 April.

**Required:**

(i)   Explain the requirements of IAS 38, *Intangible Assets* for the treatment of development costs.

(ii)   Explain how CD should treat its development costs in its financial statements for the year ended 30 April 2006.

# IMPAIRMENT AND DISPOSAL OF ASSETS

# 15

**OBJECTIVES**  After studying this chapter you should be able to:

- describe, apply and appraise the requirements of IAS 36 relating to impairment of assets

- explain what is meant by non-current assets held for sale

- describe how non-current assets held for sale should be recognized and measured in accordance with IFRS

- explain the purpose of issuing information on discontinuing operations, and how such information should be disclosed.

## INTRODUCTION

The previous two chapters have discussed the treatment of various types of non-current assets, and their regular expensing. In this chapter we consider first the question of impairment, i.e. of possible additional irregular write-offs, and second their eventual disposal.

## IMPAIRMENT OF ASSETS

### The problem

Reference to impairment of assets has been made at a number of points in previous chapters. In very simple terms the principle of deferring charges to future periods under the matching principle means, of course, that such deferred charges appear in an intermediate balance sheet as assets.

## ACTIVITY 15.1

If there is a reasonable expectation of future revenues associated with the past expenditure being greater than the deferred expenses, does any other circumstance, such as a low current market value for the asset, lead to a need for immediate write-off down to this lower figure?

*Activity feedback*
*Prudence and the informational needs of lenders with a short-term focus might both suggest an argument for* such an immediate expense charge and reduction in the balance sheet carrying value of the asset (i.e. the deferred expense). However, matching and the informational needs of investors suggest the opposite. Long-term assets should be appraised in a long-term context, it can be argued. The IASB generally takes this second argument.

Very broadly speaking, purchase transactions are recorded in accounting terms first by including the purchased item as an asset at its cost price, then by expensing the item over one or a number of accounting periods according to its usage or consumption pattern. The going concern convention supports this treatment as it explicitly assumes that there will be future operational accounting periods in which present assets can be transferred to expenses.

Strictly, this means that there is no need, at an intermediate stage in this process, to compare the temporary balance sheet number with any form of value – using the word 'value' in its proper sense of monetary benefit to be derived. This would not be in accordance with the prudence convention, however, and would arguably be dangerously misleading to creditors and lenders. Over the years accounting has dealt with the inherent tension and conflict here in a variety of ways, all more or less ad hoc, depending on the accounting issue involved (and often depending also on the country involved).

The IASB has quite properly attempted to provide a general Standard, IAS 36, *Impairment of Assets*, to provide consistency and coherence to this whole matter. The principle of the Standard is clear and simple. First, the carrying amount of an asset is determined in accordance with accounting principles and other relevant International Standards. Second, the 'recoverable amount' of the asset is determined as of that date, being the higher of fair value less costs to sell and the asset's value in use (to the existing entity). If the recoverable amount is lower than the carrying value as recorded, then an impairment loss must be recognized immediately; that is, the carrying value is lowered to the recoverable amount. Otherwise, no impairment loss is required. It is important to emphasize that recoverable amount is a very different concept from fair value and, for non-current assets, will often be significantly higher than fair value. IAS 36 does not require assets within its scope to be recorded at the lower of cost and market or fair value.

The question of which assets IAS 36 does apply to is rather complicated and the following section on scope should be read carefully. Unfortunately, although the principle of IAS 36 is simply stated, the IASB, perhaps influenced by American tradition, found it necessary to specify considerable operational detail in relation to its application. We examine these details later, to the extent that we consider it necessary. However, we are writing a textbook, not a manual for practitioners, and IAS 36 is very much a technical 'how to do it' Standard. It would be unhelpful to attempt to cover all this technical specification here.

A revised version of IAS 36 was effective from 31 March 2004. The only major changes of principle relate to impairment tests for goodwill and are linked with contemporaneous changes introduced by IFRS 3, *Business Combinations* (see Chapter 14).

However, the opportunity was taken to amend and clarify (and make more complex) much of the detailed specification. Further minor changes have since been made.

## Scope and coverage

The essential objective of IAS 36 is to ensure that assets are not carried at a figure greater than their recoverable amount. The Standard itself says nothing about possible or normal methods of arriving at carrying value. The Standard applies whatever the underlying basis of valuation of the asset is.

The Standard begins by saying that it applies to all assets except … and then gives a significant number of exceptions (para. 2). These are generally items that are covered in detail by other International Accounting Standards. Thus, IAS 36 does not apply to:

1 inventories (see IAS 2, *Inventories*, discussed in Chapter 17)
2 assets arising from construction contracts (see IAS 11, *Construction Contracts*, discussed in Chapter 17)
3 deferred tax assets (see IAS 12, *Income Taxes*, discussed in Chapter 21)
4 assets arising from employee benefits (see IAS 19, *Employee Benefits*, discussed in Chapter 22)
5 financial assets that are included in the scope of IFRS 9, *Financial Instruments* (see Chapter 18)
6 investment property that is measured at fair value (see IAS 40, *Investment Property*, discussed in Chapter 13)
7 biological assets related to agricultural activity that are measured at fair value less estimated point-of-sale costs (see IAS 40, *Agriculture*, CourseMate)
8 deferred acquisition costs, and intangible assets, arising from an insurer's contractual rights under insurance contracts within the scope of IFRS 4, *Insurance Contracts* (see Chapter 18)
9 non-current assets (or disposal groups) classified as held for sale in accordance with IFRS 5, *Non-current Assets Held for Sale and Discontinued Operations* (see below).

In relation to point 5, it must be noted that financial assets excluded from IFRS 9 are automatically excluded from the exclusion! Note carefully that the Standard very deliberately describes itself as dealing with impairment of assets, not with impairment of non-current assets. However, it then excludes inventories and construction contracts (IAS 2 and IAS 11) and accounts receivable and cash (both covered by IFRS 9). In many, if not most, businesses, this will mean that all current assets are excluded from consideration under IAS 36. However, the IAS definition of current assets (discussed in Chapter 10) is more generally expressed, and IAS 36 could be applicable to certain current assets in special cases.

## Terminology

IAS 36 gives a number of definitions of key terms. Many of these definitions are inter-related – one term being used in the definition of another (para. 6).

An *impairment loss* is the amount by which the carrying amount of an asset or a cash-generating unit exceeds its recoverable amount.

*Carrying amount* is the amount at which an asset is recognized after deducting any accumulated depreciation (amortization) and accumulated impairment losses thereon.

*Recoverable amount* of an asset or a cash-generating unit is the higher of its fair value less costs of disposal and its value in use.

*Depreciation* (amortization) is the systematic allocation of the depreciable amount of an asset over its useful life.

*Depreciable amount* is the cost of an asset or other amount substituted for cost in the financial statements, less its residual value.

*Useful life* is either:

- the period of time over which an asset is expected to be used by the entity, or
- the number of production or similar units expected to be obtained from the asset by the entity.

*Fair value* is the price that would be received to sell an asset or paid to transfer a liability in an orderly transaction between market participants at the measurement date.

*Costs of disposal* are incremental costs directly attributable to the disposal of an asset or cash-generating unit, excluding finance costs and income tax expense.

*Value in use* is the present value of the future cash flows expected to be derived from an asset or cash-generating unit.

Most of these terms should be fairly easy to understand, but they can be difficult to calculate. Two further definitions are given, as follows.

A *cash-generating unit* is the smallest identifiable group of assets that generates cash inflows that are largely independent of the cash inflows from other assets or groups of assets.

*Corporate assets* are assets other than goodwill that contribute to the future cash flows of both the cash-generating unit under review and other cash-generating units.

When several assets are interrelated in their usage in a way which makes it impossible meaningfully to attribute cash inflows to each individual asset, they are to be considered together as a single cash-generating unit as just defined. In effect, therefore, a cash-generating unit is 'one asset' for the purposes of IAS 36. Corporate assets do not generate their own cash flows, but, as described earlier, are necessary for the generation of cash flows by other units. Special considerations, discussed below, apply to such assets.

## Identifying an asset that may be impaired

It is important to be clear that IAS 36 does not require that the recoverable amount of all assets must be determined annually in order to test for impairment. Rather, it postulates a two-stage process. The first stage is to assess, at each balance sheet date, whether there is any indication that an asset may be impaired. If any such indication exists, the entity should estimate the recoverable amount of the asset.

## ACTIVITY 15.2

Suggest situations that may indicate that an asset has been impaired.

### Activity feedback

*IAS 36 suggests that when assessing whether there is any indication that an asset may be impaired an entity should consider, as a minimum, the following indications (para. 12):*

### External sources of information

**1** *During the period, an asset's market value has declined significantly more than would be expected as a result of the passage of time or normal use.*

**2** *Significant changes with an adverse effect on the entity have taken place during the period or will take place in the near future in the technological, market, economic or legal environment in which the entity operates or in the market to which an asset is dedicated.*

**3** *Market interest rates or other market rates of return on investments have increased during the period and those increases are likely to affect the discount rate used in calculating an asset's value in use and decrease the asset's recoverable amount materially.*

**4** *The carrying amount of the net assets of the reporting entity is more than its market capitalization.*

### Internal sources of information

**1** *Evidence is available of obsolescence or physical damage of an asset.*

**2** *Significant changes with an adverse effect on the entity have taken place during the period or are expected to take place in the near future in the extent to which, or manner in which, an asset is used or is expected to be used. These changes include the asset becoming idle, plans to discontinue or restructure the operation to which an asset belongs, plans to dispose of an asset before the previously expected date and reassessing the useful life of an asset as finite rather than indefinite.*

**3** *Evidence is available from internal reporting that indicates that the economic performance of an asset is, or will be, worse than expected.*

*Several of these considerations require some comment. Items 1 and 2 (under 'External sources of information') are fairly obviously indicators of a possible fall in recoverable amount, relating directly to net selling price and value in use, respectively. In neither case, however, does a low or lower recoverable amount necessarily follow, as recoverable amount is the higher of fair value less costs to sell and value in use. The relevance of item 3 is that value in use, as defined earlier, is the present value of future cash flows. Discounting is thus central to the calculation or recoverable amount and an increase in discount rate may significantly reduce the value in use of an asset, as defined, if the new discount rate is regarded as relevant in the long-term. Item 4, again, is a fairly obvious indicator that something is widely perceived as being wrong somewhere, although not, of course, that every, or any one particular, asset is impaired.*

There are two different formal requirements. The first relates to all assets (para. 9). This is that an entity should assess at each reporting date whether there is any indication that an asset may be impaired. If such an indication exists, the entity should estimate the recoverable amount of the asset. The second is more stringent, but relates only to certain intangible assets. This is that (para. 10):

Irrespective of whether there is any indication of impairment, an entity shall also:

(a) test an intangible asset with an indefinite useful life or an intangible asset not yet available for use for impairment annually by comparing its carrying amount with its recoverable amount. This impairment test may be performed at any time during an annual period, provided it is performed at the same time every year. Different intangible assets may be tested for impairment at different times. However, if such an intangible asset was initially recognized during the current annual period, that intangible asset shall be tested for impairment before the end of the current annual period.

(b) test goodwill acquired in a business combination for impairment annually in accordance with paras 80–99 [as described later].

The concept of materiality applies to the general requirement in para. 9, but not to the specific requirement of para. 10, which, in its defined circumstances, is absolute.

Only if an indication of likely impairment exists do we need, in the general case, to move on to the second stage and actually measure the recoverable amount.

## Measurement of recoverable amount

IAS 36 devotes no fewer than 39 paragraphs to the measurement of recoverable amount, not including another 42 paragraphs on cash-generating units, and sets out detailed computations. Nevertheless, a number of simplifications may be justified. If either fair value less costs of disposal or value in use exceeds the asset's carrying amount, then the other figure need not be determined at all. If fair value less costs of disposal is unobtainable even by reliable estimate because of the absence of an active market, then the recoverable amount can be taken as equal to value in use. Conversely, the recoverable amount may be taken or given by fair value less costs to sell if the nature of the asset, or the nature of its usage by entity is such that value in use is unlikely to differ materially from fair value less costs to sell, which will usually be the case with active and competitive factor markers (i.e. in developed economies).

**Fair value less costs of disposal**  This will often be straightforward to determine, being fair value less any incremental costs that would be directly attributable to the disposal of the asset. Fair value will be determined in accordance with IFRS 13 (see Chapter 8). Costs of disposal, other than those that have already been recognized as liabilities, are deducted in determining net selling price. Examples of such costs are: legal costs, stamp duty and similar transaction taxes, costs of removing the asset and direct incremental costs to bring an asset into condition for its sale. However, termination benefits (as defined in IAS 19, *Employee Benefits*, see Chapter 22), and costs associated with reducing or reorganizing a business after the disposal of an asset, are not direct incremental costs to dispose of the asset (see IAS 37, *Provisions, Contingent Liabilities and Contingent Assets*, discussed in Chapter 20).

**Value in use**  Estimating the value in use in a realistic way is often likely to be rather more difficult. It involves the following steps (para. 31):

1 Estimating the future cash inflows and outflows to be derived from continuing use of the asset and from its ultimate disposal.

2 Applying the appropriate discount rate to these future cash flows. Estimates of future cash flows should include:
   1 projections of cash inflows from the continuing use of the asset, net of projections of cash outflows that are necessarily incurred to generate the cash inflows (including cash outflows to prepare the asset for use) and that can be directly attributed, or allocated on a reasonable and consistent basis, to the asset
   2 net cash flows, if any, to be received (or paid) for the disposal of the asset at the end of its useful life.

Future cash flows should be estimated for the asset in its current condition. It follows that estimates of future cash flows should not include estimated future cash inflows or outflows that are expected to arise from:

1 a future restructuring to which an entity is not yet committed, or

2 future (uncommitted) capital expenditure that will improve or enhance the asset in excess of its originally assessed standard of performance.

The issue of when an entity is 'committed to a future restructuring' is discussed in IAS 37, *Provisions, Contingent Liabilities and Contingent Assets* (see Chapter 20). If it is so committed, then obviously the related cash inflows and outflows are to be included.

The estimate of net cash flows to be received (or paid) for the disposal of an asset at the end of its useful life is determined in a similar way to an asset's fair value less costs to sell, except that, in estimating those net cash flows:

1  an entity uses prices prevailing at the date of the estimate for similar assets that have reached the end of their useful life and that have operated under conditions similar to those in which the asset will be used

2  those prices are adjusted for the effect of both future price increases due to general inflation and specific future price increases (decreases). However, if estimates of future cash flows from the asset's continuing use and the discount rate exclude the effect of general inflation, this effect is also excluded from the estimate of net cash flows on disposal.

**Discount rate**  The key points can be very briefly stated. The discount rate (or rates) should be a pre-tax rate (or rates) that reflect(s) current market assessments of the time value of money and risks specific to the asset (para. 55). The discount rate(s) should not reflect risks for which future cash flow estimates have been adjusted, as this would involve double-counting. The Standard rightly makes no attempt to argue that this process is other than subjective. It does try to suggest a suitable thought process (Appendix A).

As a starting point, the entity may take into account the following rates:

1  the entity's weighted average cost of capital determined using techniques such as the capital asset pricing model

2  the entity's incremental borrowing rate

3  other market borrowing rates.

These rates are adjusted:

1  to reflect the way that the market would assess the specific risks associated with the projected cash flows

2  to exclude risks that are not relevant to the projected cash flows.

Consideration is given to such risks as country risk, currency risk, price risk and cash flow risk. This makes it clear, for example, that the appropriate discount rate may be different for different types of asset or different circumstances within the same entity. What is crucial, above all else except basic rationality and common sense, is that the chosen method should be applied consistently.

## Recognition and measurement of impairment losses

After all the subjectivity, complexity and detail of earlier sections of IAS 36, it is easy to lose sight of the importance of those paragraphs dealing with recognition and measurement of impairment losses. This is the point and purpose of the entire Standard. The Standard requires that if, and only if, the recoverable amount of an asset is less than its carrying amount, the carrying amount of the asset should be reduced to its recoverable amount. That reduction is an impairment loss (para. 59).

An impairment loss should be recognized immediately as an expense in the income statement, unless the asset is carried at revalued amount under another Standard (e.g. under IAS 16, *Property, Plant and Equipment*; see Chapter 13). Any impairment loss of a revalued asset should be treated as a revaluation decrease under the other Standard.

In the general case, if the estimated impairment loss is greater than the carrying value of the relevant asset, the asset is simply reduced to nil, with a corresponding expense. Only if so required by another Standard should a liability be recognized. Common sense indicates, but the Standard feels it necessary to state, that after the impairment loss has been recognized, the depreciation charge for the asset should be adjusted to allocate the revised carrying amount, net of any expected residual value, on a systematic basis over its remaining useful life.

This is all very well when 'an asset' means 'an asset'. But when 'an asset' means 'a cash-generating unit', as discussed earlier, the treatment is not so easy in practice – as the Standard's need for over 40 paragraphs on the topic would suggest. If it is not possible to estimate the recoverable amount of an individual asset, an entity should determine the recoverable amount of the cash-generating unit to which the asset belongs (the asset's cash-generating unit) (para. 66). Identification of an asset's cash-generating unit involves judgement. If the recoverable amount cannot be determined for an individual asset, an entity identifies the lowest aggregation of assets that generate largely independent cash inflows from continuing use.

In other words, an asset's cash-generating unit is the smallest group of assets that includes the asset and that generates cash inflows from continuing use that are largely independent of the cash inflows from other assets or groups of assets.

Perhaps inevitably, the Standard resorts to a series of examples in order to try and indicate more precisely how the analysis of any particular situation should proceed. Common sense and economic substance are perhaps the key watchwords. Thus, if an active market exists for the output produced by an asset or a group of assets, this asset or group of assets should be identified as a cash-generating unit, even if some or all of the output is used internally. If this is the case, management's best estimate of future market prices for the output should be used (para. 70):

1  in determining the value in use of this cash-generating unit, when estimating the future cash inflows that relate to the internal use of the output

2  in determining the value in use of other cash-generating units of the reporting entity, when estimating the future cash outflows that relate to the internal use of the output.

As an indicative illustration, the example given by IAS 36 in relation to this specification follows.

## ILLUSTRATION

A significant raw material used for Plant Y's final production is an intermediate product bought from Plant X of the same entity. X's products are sold to Y at a transfer price that passes all margins to X. Eighty per cent of Y's final production is sold to customers outside the reporting entity. Sixty per cent of X's final production is sold to Y, and the remaining 40 per cent is sold to customers outside the reporting entity.

For each of the following cases, what are the cash-generating units for X and Y?

**Case 1**: X could sell the products it sells to Y in an active market. Internal transfer prices are higher than market prices.

**Case 2**: There is no active market for the products X sells to Y.

*(Continued)*

## ILLUSTRATION    (*Continued*)

### Case 1

X could sell its products on an active market and so generate cash inflows that would be largely independent of the cash inflows from Y. Therefore, it is likely that X is a separate cash-generating unit, although part of its production is used by Y.

It is likely that Y is also a separate cash-generating unit. Y sells 80 per cent of its products to customers outside the reporting entity. Therefore its cash inflows can be considered to be largely independent.

Internal transfer prices do not reflect market prices for X's output. Therefore, in determining value in use of both X and Y, the entity adjusts financial budgets/forecasts to reflect management's best estimate of future arm's length market prices for those of X's products that are used internally (see IAS 36, para. 70).

### Case 2

It is likely that the recoverable amount of each plant cannot be assessed independently from the recoverable amount of the other plant because:

1  The majority of X's production is used internally and could not be sold in an active market. So, cash inflows of X depend on demand for Y's products. Therefore X cannot be considered to generate cash inflows that are largely independent from those of Y.

2  The two plants are managed together.

As a consequence, it is likely that X and Y together is the smallest group of assets that generates cash inflows from continuing use that are largely independent.

Once the cash-generating unit has been defined, the next step is to determine and compare the recoverable amount and carrying amount of that unit. It should go without saying, but the Standard reminds us, that the carrying amount of a cash-generating unit should be determined consistently with the way the recoverable amount of the cash-generating unit is determined.

This means, for example, that the carrying amount of a cash-generating unit includes the carrying amount of only those assets that can be attributed directly or allocated on a reasonable and consistent basis to the cash-generating unit and that will generate the future cash inflows estimated in determining the cash-generating unit's value in use and does not include the carrying amount of any recognized liability, unless the recoverable amount of the cash-generating unit cannot be determined without consideration of this liability. However, the Standard notes that in practice the recoverable amount of a cash-generating unit may be considered either including or excluding assets or liabilities that are not part of the cash-generating unit – for example, a net selling price of a business segment might be determined on the assumption that either the vendor or the purchaser accepts certain obligations. Consistency requires that if the obligation is included in the evaluation of recoverable amount, it is the net carrying value with which this recoverable amount must be compared in determining whether an impairment loss exists.

There are two problems that need special consideration, namely goodwill and corporate assets (as already defined). In essence these two problems are related.

Goodwill, by definition, does not generate cash flows independently from other assets or groups of assets and, therefore, the recoverable amount of goodwill as an individual asset cannot be determined. As a consequence, if there is an indication that goodwill may be impaired, the recoverable amount is determined for the cash-generating unit to which the goodwill belongs. This amount is then compared to the carrying amount of this cash-generating unit and any impairment loss is recognized, attributed first to the goodwill as discussed later.

It is particularly in relation to the treatment of possible impairment of goodwill that the revised version of IAS 36 has been made much more detailed (and therefore, at least apparently, more complex). The previous version of IAS 36 required goodwill acquired in a business combination to be tested for impairment as part of impairment testing of the cash-generating unit(s) to which it related. It employed a 'bottom-up/ top-down' approach under which the goodwill was, in effect, tested for impairment by allocating its carrying amount to each cash-generating unit or smallest group of cash-generating units to which a portion of that carrying amount could be allocated on a reasonable and consistent basis. The Standard now similarly requires goodwill acquired in a business combination to be tested for impairment as part of impairment testing the cash-generating unit(s) to which it relates. However, IAS 36 now clarifies that:

1 The goodwill should, from the acquisition date, be allocated to each of the acquirer's cash-generating units, or groups of cash-generating units, that are expected to benefit from the synergies of the business combination, irrespective of whether other assets or liabilities of the acquiree are assigned to those units or groups of units.

2 Each unit or group of units to which the goodwill is allocated should:

   (a) represent the lowest level within the entity at which the goodwill is monitored for internal management purposes

   (b) not be larger than an operating segment as defined by paragraph 5 of IFRS 8, *Operating Segments*.

3 If the initial allocation of goodwill acquired in a business combination cannot be completed before the end of the annual period in which the business combination occurs, that initial allocation should be completed before the end of the annual period beginning after the acquisition date.

4 When an entity disposes of an operation within a cash-generating unit (group of units) to which goodwill has been allocated, the goodwill associated with that operation should be:

   (a) included in the carrying amount of the operation when determining the gain or loss on disposal

   (b) measured on the basis of the relative values of the operation disposed of and the portion of the cash-generating unit (group of units) retained, unless the entity can demonstrate that some other method better reflects the goodwill associated with the operation disposed of.

5 When an entity reorganizes its reporting structure in a manner that changes the composition of cash-generating units (groups of units) to which goodwill has been allocated, the goodwill should be reallocated to the units (groups of units) affected. This reallocation should be performed using a relative value approach similar to that used when an entity disposes of an operation within a cash- generating unit (group of units), unless the entity can demonstrate that some other method better reflects the goodwill associated with the reorganized units (groups of units).

By way of example, to illustrate point 4 (above), suppose that an entity sells for €100 an operation that was part of a cash-generating unit to which goodwill has been allocated. The goodwill allocated to the unit cannot be identified or associated with an asset group at a level lower than that unit, except arbitrarily. The recoverable amount of the portion of the cash-generating unit retained is €300. Because the goodwill allocated to the cash-generating unit cannot be non-arbitrarily identified or associated with an asset group at a level lower than that unit, the goodwill associated with the operation disposed of is measured on the basis of the relative values of the operation disposed of and the portion of the unit retained. Therefore 25 per cent of the goodwill allocated to the cash-generating unit is included in the carrying amount of the operation that is sold, and 75 per cent is left in the retained portion.

The Standard permits (not requires) the annual impairment test for a cash-generating unit (group of units) to which the goodwill has been allocated to be performed at any time during an annual reporting period, provided that the test is performed at the same time every year and different cash-generating units (groups of units) are tested for impairment at different times. However, if some of the goodwill allocated to a cash-generating unit (group of units) was acquired in a business combination during the current annual period, the Standard requires that unit (group of units) to be tested for impairment before the end of the current period.

The Standard also permits the most recent detailed calculation made in a preceding period of the recoverable amount of a cash-generating unit (group of units) to which goodwill has been allocated to be used in the impairment test for that unit (group of units) in the current period, provided specified criteria are met, as follows:

- The assets and liabilities making up the unit have not changed significantly since the most recent recoverable amount calculation.

- The most recent recoverable amount calculation resulted in an amount that exceeded the carrying amount of the unit by a substantial margin.

- Based on an analysis of events that have occurred and circumstances that have changed since the most recent recoverable amount calculation, the likelihood that a current recoverable amount determination would be less than the current carrying amount of the unit is remote.

Similarly, corporate assets, also by definition, do not generate independent cash flows and, again, recoverable amount is determined by reference to the cash-generating unit to which the corporate asset belongs. In testing a cash-generating unit for impairment, an entity shall identify all the corporate assets that relate to the cash-generating unit under review. If a portion of the carrying amount of a corporate asset can be allocated on a reasonable and consistent basis to that unit, the entity shall compare the carrying amount of the unit, including the portion of the carrying amount of the corporate asset allocated to the unit, with its recoverable amount. Any impairment loss shall be recognized in accordance with para. 104, discussed later. If a portion cannot be allocated on a reasonable and consistent basis to that unit, the entity shall:

1 Compare the carrying amount of the unit, excluding the corporate asset, with its recoverable amount and recognize any impairment loss in accordance with para. 104.

2 Identify the smallest group of cash-generating units that includes the cash-generating unit under review and to which a portion of the carrying amount of the corporate asset can be allocated in a reasonable and consistent basis.

3 Compare the carrying amount of that group of cash-generating units, including the portion of the carrying amount of the corporate asset allocated to that group of units, with the recoverable amount of the group of units. Any impairment loss shall be recognized in accordance with para. 104.

An amazingly lengthy illustrative example (No. 8) is given in an accompaniment to the Standard.

Once the impairment loss for a cash-generating unit has been determined, it has to be deducted from the carrying amounts of specific assets that are part of that unit, in some systematic manner. IAS 36 specifies its requirements with precision (paras 104 and 105).

An impairment loss should be recognized for a cash-generating unit if, and only if, its recoverable amount is less than its carrying amount. The impairment loss should be allocated to reduce the carrying amount of the assets of the unit in the following order:

1 first, to goodwill allocated to the cash-generating unit (if any)

2 then, to the other assets of the unit on a pro rata basis, based on the carrying amount of each asset in the unit.

In allocating an impairment loss the carrying amount of an asset should not be reduced below the *highest of*:

1 its fair value less costs to sell (if determinable)

2 its value in use (if determinable)

3 zero.

The amount of the impairment loss that would otherwise have been allocated to the asset should be allocated to the other assets of the unit on a pro rata basis. A liability should be recognized for any remaining amount of an impairment loss for a cash-generating unit, if, and only if, that is required by other International Accounting Standards.

The effect of this is, first, to eliminate goodwill, but then to ensure that the carrying amount of any individual asset is not reduced so far as to produce a figure not economically relevant to that asset.

**Reversal of an impairment loss** The whole point, in a sense, of impairment losses is that they represent unusual or 'extra' reductions in asset numbers (carrying values) as used in financial statements. If regular depreciation is a downward slope, then an impairment loss is a downward step. The basic cause of this downward step is something unusual and/or extraneous to the asset and its regular accounting treatment. It follows that this cause, this unusual or extraneous factor, may be removed over time. In such a situation, as explained and defined in IAS 36, the original impairment loss must be reversed; *except* for goodwill.

As with impairment losses, we again have a two-stage process. An entity first checks to see whether there is any indication that an impairment loss recognized in earlier years may have decreased significantly. IAS 36 spells out a series of likely indicators (para. 111) that mirror those discussed earlier under 'identifying an asset that may be impaired'.

The formal requirement for reversing impairment losses for an asset other than goodwill (para. 114) is that an impairment loss recognized for an asset in prior years must be reversed if, and only if, there has been a change in the estimates used to determine the asset's recoverable amount since the last impairment loss was recognized. If this is the case, the carrying amount of the asset should be increased to its recoverable amount. That increase is a reversal of an impairment loss. It is important to note that an asset's value in use may become greater than the asset's carrying amount, simply because the present value of future cash inflows increases as they become closer. However, the service potential of the asset has not increased. Therefore, such an impairment loss is not reversed, even if the recoverable amount of the asset becomes higher than its carrying amount.

The reversal of an impairment loss should in no circumstances increase the carrying value of an asset above what it would have been at this balance sheet date if no impairment loss had been recognized in prior years. This means, in particular, that the carrying value of assets subject to depreciation cannot be increased above the figure which the pre-impairment depreciation policy applied to the pre-impairment recoverable amount would have given at this balance sheet date; that is, the amount of the reversal will be less than the amount of the original impairment. The new carrying value forms the basis for a systematic depreciation policy to allocate the carrying value, less estimated residual value if any, over the remaining useful life.

A reversal of an impairment loss for an asset as above should be recognized as income immediately in the income statement, unless the asset is carried at revalued amount under another International Accounting Standard (e.g. under the revaluation model in IAS 16, *Property, Plant and Equipment*; see Chapter 13). Any reversal of an impairment loss on a revalued asset should be treated as a revaluation increase under that other Standard.

A reversal of an impairment loss for a cash-generating unit should be allocated to increase the carrying amount of the assets of the unit on a pro rata basis based on the carrying amount of each asset in the unit and then to goodwill allocated to the cash-generating unit.

In allocating a reversal of an impairment loss for a cash-generating unit, the carrying amount of an asset should not be increased above the lower of:

1 the recoverable amount (if determinable)

2 the carrying amount that would have been determined (net of amortization or depreciation) had no impairment loss been recognized for the asset in prior years.

The amount of the reversal of the impairment loss that would otherwise have been allocated to the asset should be allocated to the other assets of the unit, except for goodwill, on a pro rata basis.

The treatment of a reversal of an impairment loss for goodwill was changed significantly in the revised version of IAS 36 (i.e. with effect from 31 March 2004) as compared with the earlier version. The Standard now completely prohibits the recognition of reversals of impairment losses for goodwill.

The rationale for prohibiting the reversal of impairment losses for goodwill is presented by the IASB as follows. The key point is that IAS 38, Intangible Assets (see Chapter 14), prohibits the recognition of internally-generated goodwill. This prohibition is theoretically debatable, but is undoubtedly widely supported, and is consistent with national laws in many countries including the whole of the EU, following the Fourth Directive.

Given this prohibition, there is still no theoretical problem in arguing, supported by analogy with other assets, that *previously purchased* goodwill that has been subsequently impaired because of a circumstance now reversed should have the impairment loss reversed. However, there is a *practical* problem in distinguishing, numerically as well as conceptually, between a reversal of a previous impairment to previously purchased goodwill on the one hand, and the appearance of new internally generated goodwill, which cannot be recognized, on the other. It is because of this practical impossibility, and the resulting 'danger' of effectively capitalizing internally-generated goodwill that the change to an outright prohibition of the recognition of a reversal of an impairment loss for goodwill has been introduced.

The IASB notes that internally-generated goodwill may in fact be involved at an earlier stage in the whole impairment process, in that purchased goodwill may not be impaired in the first place because its recoverable amount is kept up through the creation of new goodwill to replace the old, but also notes that, again on purely practical grounds, such a position cannot be numerically demonstrated and therefore cannot be prevented.

## Disclosure

The disclosure requirements of IAS 36, like much else in the Standard, are extensive. They are also quite straightforward, requiring detailed numerical, explanatory and background information.

## NON-CURRENT ASSETS HELD FOR SALE AND DISCONTINUED OPERATIONS

The structure or dimension of most companies changes over the years. On the one hand, companies can grow through acquisitions or/and organic growth. On the other hand, companies might also discontinue activities and, as a result, may decrease in size. If a relatively large component of the entity is discontinued then substantial financial disclosure about these activities which are discontinued is required.

It is intuitively likely that assets associated with discontinued operations, or with operations that are approaching a discontinued status, are likely to suffer impairment, and it seems logical to bring such assets, and the IAS 36 impairment Standard, into proximity. Nevertheless, they are technically separate issues and need to be carefully distinguished when considering the detail.

These requirements are part of IFRS 5, *Non-current Assets Held for Sale and Discontinued Operations*. IFRS 5, which was issued in Spring 2004, is one of the first Standards that is a result of the IASB's convergence project. IFRS 5 is meant to close the gap between, on the one hand FASB Statement No. 144, *Accounting for the Impairment or Disposal of Long-lived Assets* (SFAS 144), which was issued in 2001, and on the other the recognition and valuation rules for those assets under IAS/IFRS. SFAS 144 addressed three areas:

1  impairment of long-lived assets to be held and used
2  classification, measurement and presentation of assets held for sale
3  classification and presentation of discontinued operations.

IFRS 5 only deals with the issues mentioned in (2) and (3). With regard to the impairment of long-lived assets to be held and used, the existing differences between the FASB and the IASB were not solved. The difference between US GAAP and IAS/ IFRS is often called a difference between rules-based versus principles-based accounting standards. If one considers IFRS 5 which is a product of the convergence project, one will notice that the criteria for a non-current asset to be defined as 'held for sale' are rather detailed. It is highly likely that the convergence project might move the IAS/IFRS standards away from a purely principles-based accounting system and drive it towards a more rules-based system. Although a substantial convergence is reached for these recognition and measurement items (namely non-current assets held for sale and discontinued operations) differences with SFAS 144 still exist. First, we will present the treatment of non-current assets held for sale under IFRS 5 and, second, we will focus on the information to be reported in relation to discontinuing operations.

# Non-current assets held for sale

**Definition** IFRS 5 presents the definition, the recognition and measurement of non-current assets held for sale. Non-current assets are defined as assets that do not meet the criteria of a current asset. The definition of a current asset is found in IAS 1, para. 66 and is as follows:

An asset shall be classified as current when it satisfies any of the following criteria:

(a) it is expected to be realized in, or is intended for sale or consumption in, the entity's normal operating cycle

(b) it is held primarily for the purpose of being traded

(c) it is expected to be realized within twelve months after the balance sheet date; or

(d) it is cash or the cash equivalent (as defined in IAS 7, *Cash Flow Statements*) unless it is restricted from being exchanged or used to settle a liability for at least twelve months after the balance sheet date.

All other assets are classified as non-current assets.

So, non-current assets include tangible, intangible and financial assets of a long-term nature. IFRS 5 not only considers individual non-current assets, but it also prescribes the definition, the recognition and the valuation rules for disposal groups. In these circumstances, a common example would be the disposal of a subsidiary. The Standard observes that an entity will dispose of a group of assets, possibly with some directly associated liabilities, together in a single transaction (para. 4). The disposal group might include goodwill acquired in a business combination if the group is a cash-generating unit to which goodwill has been allocated or if it is an operation within a cash-generating unit as defined in Appendix A of IFRS 5. In this respect, a disposal group can be a group of cash-generating units, a single cash-generating unit or part of a cash-generating unit.

IFRS 5 states explicitly that the rules of measurement and recognition stipulated in IFRS 5 do not apply to the following assets since they are covered by other Standards: deferred tax assets; assets arising from employee benefits; financial assets within the scope of IFRS 9; non-current assets that are accounted for in accordance with the fair value model in IAS 40, *Investment Property*; non-current assets that are measured at fair value less costs to sell in accordance with IAS 41, *Agriculture*; and contractual rights under insurance contracts as defined in IFRS 4, *Insurance Contracts*.

Essential to the definition of non-current assets held for sale is that the carrying amount of the assets will be recovered principally through sale rather than continuing use in the business (para. 6). Besides these general definitions on the concept of non-current assets held for sale, IFRS 5 goes further into detail by providing more characteristics that need to be fulfilled before a non-current asset can be classified as held for sale. These characteristics are laid down (in paras 7–14) and have a more rules-based character.

With regard to the interpretation of 'held for sale', we summarize the main items of paras 7–14 here.

For an asset (or disposal group) to be classified as held for sale:

- It must be available for immediate sale in its present condition, subject only to terms that are usual and customary for sales of such assets (or disposal groups).
- Its sale must be highly probable, the appropriate level of management must be committed to a plan to sell the asset (or disposal group), and an active programme to locate a buyer and complete the plan must have been initiated.
- The sale should be expected to qualify for recognition as a completed sale within one year from the date of classification. Exception is permitted if the delay is

caused by events or circumstances beyond the entity's control and there is sufficient evidence that the entity remains committed to its plan to sell the asset (or disposal group).

- It must genuinely be sold, not abandoned. The sale transactions, referred to (in paras 7–14) include exchanges of non-current assets for other non-current assets when the exchange has commercial substance in accordance with IAS 16.

## Measurement of non-current assets and disposal groups held for sale

**Measurement on *initial classification* as held for sale** IFRS 5 requires that immediately before the initial classification of an asset (or disposal group) as held for sale, the carrying amount of the asset (or all the assets and liabilities in the group) should be measured in accordance with applicable IFRSs. In other words, an entity should apply its usual accounting policies up until the criteria for classification as held for sale are met.

Thereafter, a non-current asset (or disposal group) classified as held for sale should be measured at the lower of its carrying amount and fair value less costs to sell. According to IFRS 5, the fair value is defined as 'the price that would be received to sell an asset or paid to transfer a liability in an orderly transaction between market participants at the measurement date'. Costs to sell are defined as 'the incremental costs directly attributable to the disposal of an asset (or disposal group), excluding finance costs and income tax expense'. When the sale is expected to occur beyond one year, the costs to sell should be measured at their present value. Any increase in the present value of the costs to sell that arises from the passage of time should be presented in profit or loss as a financing cost. There is no similar requirement to present that element of an increase in fair value that also relates to just the passage of time as finance income.

For the disposal groups, the Standard adopts a portfolio approach. It requires that if a non-current asset within the scope of its measurement requirements is part of a disposal group, the measurement requirements should apply to the group as a whole, so that the group is measured at the lower of its carrying amount and fair value less costs to sell. It will still be necessary to apportion any write down to the underlying assets of the disposal group, but no element is apportioned to items outside the scope of the Standard's measurement provisions.

If a newly acquired asset (or disposal group) meets the criteria to be classified as held for sale (which are subtly different for assets acquired exclusively with a view to subsequent disposal), applying the above requirements will result in the asset (or disposal group) being measured on initial recognition at the lower of its carrying amount had it not been so classified (e.g. cost) and fair value less costs to sell. This means that, if the asset (or disposal group) is acquired as part of a business combination, it will be measured at fair value less costs to sell.

While a non-current asset is classified as held for sale or while it is part of a disposal group classified as held for sale, it should not be depreciated or amortized. Interest and other expenses attributable to the liabilities of a disposal group classified as held for sale should continue to be recognized.

On subsequent remeasurement of a disposal group, the Standard requires that the carrying amounts of any assets and liabilities that are not within the scope of its measurement requirements be remeasured in accordance with applicable IFRSs before the fair value less costs to sell of the disposal group is remeasured.

**Recognition of impairment losses and reversals** The requirement to measure a non-current asset (or disposal group) held for sale at the lower of carrying amount less costs to sell may give rise to a write down in value (impairment loss) and possibly its subsequent reversal. As noted earlier, the first step is to account for any items within the scope of the Standard in the normal way. After that, any excess of carrying value over fair value less costs to sell should be recognized as an impairment.

Any subsequent increase in fair value less costs to sell of an asset up to the cumulative impairment loss previously recognized either in accordance with IFRS 5 or in accordance with IAS 36, *Impairment of Assets*, should be recognized as a gain. In the case of a disposal group, any subsequent increase in fair value less costs to sell should be recognized:

- to the extent that it has not been recognized under another Standard in relation to those assets outside the scope of IFRS 5's measurement requirements
- but not in excess of the cumulative amount of losses previously recognized under IFRS 5 or before that under IAS 36 in respect of the non-current assets in the group that are within the scope of the measurement rule of IFRS 5.

Any impairment loss (or any subsequent gain) recognized for a disposal group should be allocated to the non-current assets in the group that are within the scope of the measurement requirements of IFRS 5. The order allocation should be:

- first, to reduce the carrying amount of any goodwill in the group
- then, to the other assets of the group pro rata on the basis of the carrying amount of each asset in the group.

When assets meet the criteria to be classified as held for sale they have to be presented separately on the balance sheet. In the notes, disclosures have to be made in relation to the facts and circumstances of the sale and the gains or losses recognized after the classification of the non-current assets as 'held for sale'. If assets are no longer used in the operational activities of the firm, they will no longer generate revenues, expenditures and cash. Information on the impact of the disappearance of these items should be presented as information on discontinued operations.

## Discontinued operations

IFRS 5 deals also with the presentation of information on discontinued operations. This type of information disclosure had been regulated already, namely under the superseded IAS 35. IFRS 5 requires the presentation of a single amount on the face of the income statement relating to discontinued operations, with further analysis either on the face of the income statement or in the notes (see Activity 15.3).

### ACTIVITY 15.3

Why do you think financial information about discontinuing operations should be provided to the external user of the financial statements?

#### Activity feedback

*A discontinuing operation is a relatively large component of an entity that is either being disposed of completely or substantially or is being terminated through abandonment or piecemeal sale. The effects of such discontinuation are* *likely to be significant both in their own right and in changing the future results of the remaining components of the entity.*

*Distinguishing between the financial impact of the discontinuing and the continuing operations on the financial situation of an entity will improve the ability of investors, creditors and other users of financial statements to make projections of the entity's cash flows, earnings generating capacity and financial position.*

In order to be useful for decision purposes, the results of an entity need to be presented in a manner that will satisfy the two following objectives. First, the activities and results of the year under review must be reported fully and clearly. Second, readers of the financial statements should be able to understand the implications of the current period results for future periods. This relates to the relevance of accounting information. So the objective of IFRS 5 is to establish a basis for segregating information about a major operation that an entity is discontinuing from information about its continuing operations and to specify minimum disclosures about a discontinuing operation.

**Definition of a discontinued operation** IFRS 5 defines a discontinued operation as:

a component of an entity that either has been disposed of, or is classified as held for sale, and:

(a)  represents a separate major line of business or geographical area of operations

(b)  is part of a single coordinated plan to dispose of a separate major line of business or geographical area of operations, or

(c)  is a subsidiary acquired exclusively with a view to resale.

For the purposes of this definition, a 'component of an entity' is also defined by the Standard as comprising 'operations and cash flows that can be clearly distinguished, operationally and for financial reporting purposes, from the rest of the entity'. In other words, a component of an entity will have been a cash-generating unit or a group of cash-generating units while being held for use.

Business entities frequently close facilities, abandon products or even product lines and change the size of their workforce in response to market forces. Those kinds of termination do not qualify as discontinuing operations but they can occur in connection with a discontinuing operation. A list of such activities which do not qualify as discontinuing operations is presented below:

- gradual or evolutionary phasing out of a product line or class of service
- discontinuing, even if relatively abruptly, several products within an ongoing line of business
- shifting of some production or marketing activities for a particular line of business from one location to another
- closing of a facility to achieve productivity improvements or other cost savings
- selling a subsidiary whose activities are similar to those of the parent or other subsidiaries.

These examples could bring along the recording of impairments or restructuring provisions.

With regard to the presentation of information on those discontinued operations, IFRS 5 stipulates (from para. 33) that an entity shall disclose:

(a)  a single amount on the face of the income statement comprising the total of:

(i)   the post-tax profit or loss of discontinued operations, and

(ii)  the post-tax gain or loss recognized on the measurement to fair value less costs to sell or on the disposal of the assets or disposal group(s) constituting the discontinued operation.

(b) an analysis of the single amount of (a) into:

(i) the revenue, expense and pre-tax profit or loss of discontinued operations and related income tax expense;

(ii) the gain or loss recognized on the measurement to fair value less costs to sell or on the disposal of the assets or disposal group(s) constituting the discontinued operation and related income tax expense.

The analysis may be presented in the notes or on the face of the income statement. If it is presented on the face of the income statement it shall be presented in a section identified as relating to discontinued operations, i.e. separately from continuing operations. The analysis is not required for disposal groups that are newly acquired subsidiaries that meet the criteria to be classified as held for sale on acquisition.

(c) the net cash flow attributable to the operating, investing and financing activities of discontinued operations.

The Standard also makes clear that any gain or loss on the remeasurement of a non-current asset (or disposal group) classified as held for sale that does not meet the definition of a discontinued operation should not be included within these amounts for discontinued operations, but be included in profit or loss from continuing operations.

Further, IFRS 5 requires that these disclosures be re-presented for prior periods presented in the financial statements so that the disclosures relate to all operations that have been discontinued by the balance sheet date for the latest period presented. Accordingly, adjustments to the comparative information as originally reported will be necessary for those disposal groups categorized as discontinued operations.

## ACTIVITY 15.4

Alpha has three segments: pharmaceuticals, chemicals and soft drinks. In 20X3, after an assessment of the corporate strategy for the future, the company decides to concentrate on chemicals and pharmaceuticals.

On 30 September 20X3 the board of directors voted in favour of a disposal plan which would either try to sell off the soft drinks segment as a whole, or, if not successful by the end of 20X3, dispose of the assets of the segment in a piecemeal fashion. An announcement of the plan was made the same day. A month later the company enters into a legally binding sales agreement with one of the major producers of soft drinks in the world. The parties expect the sale to be completed in February 20X4.

The following information for the soft drink segment is available for the financial year 20X3 (figures and transactions are simplified):

| | Book value at 30 September | Recoverable amount at 30 September | Book value/ result at 31 December |
|---|---|---|---|
| Assets | 450 | 400 | 400 |
| Liabilities | 200 | 200 | 200 |
| Revenue | – | – | 300 |
| Operating expenses | – | – | 125 |

An amount of 25 is representing non-cash expenses.

As you are aware, information relating to a discontinuing operation should be presented separately from continuing operations. You should now prepare the information that needs to be disclosed in the financial statements on 31 December 2003. Assume a corporate income tax rate of 30 per cent on the accounting profit for the segment.

Also comment on what other information must be given regarding the discontinuing operation.

### Activity feedback

- As a single amount on the income statement, para. 33 (a): profit for the period from discontinued operations

| | |
|---|---|
| (i) the post-tax result on discontinued operations | 122.5 |
| (ii) the post-tax gain or loss on the measurement of the assets held for sale | 35 |
| Total | 157.5 |

- An analysis of the single amount, para. 33(b)

| | |
|---|---|
| revenue from discontinued operations | 300 |

(Continued)

## ACTIVITY 15.4    (*Continued*)

expenses from discontinued
operations                                           125
(i)   pre-tax result                                 175
(ii)  related income tax expense                     52.5
(iii) the loss on non-current assets
      held for sale                                   50
(iv)  related income tax result                       15

- On the asset side of the balance sheet we should present as a single line item: non-current assets classified as held for sale    400
- Among the liabilities we should disclose as a single line item: liabilities directly associated with non-current assets held for sale    200
- Net cash flow attributable to discontinued operations    200

Note that comparative figures for 20X2 should be restated as well (para. 34). Disclosure requirements (refer to IFRS 5, para. 41):

- A description of the segment soft drinks (also comment on the reason for the disposal).
- Segments in which the discontinuing operation is reported (is a segment in this case).
- The date on which the company announced the plan to discontinue the soft drink segment (also comment on the date when it entered into the binding sales agreement).
- The date when the discontinuance is expected to be completed.

Examples of accounting policy choices, and the implications for analysis and interpretation of the financial statements, are given and discussed in Part Four.

## SUMMARY

This chapter has completed the coverage, begun in Chapter 13, of the accounting treatment of fixed (non-current) assets. We looked in some detail at the issue of impairment of assets in general and of fixed assets in particular, and at the contents of IAS 36. Finally, we explored the requirements of IFRS 5 relating to non-current assets held for sale, and to the reporting of discontinued operations.

## EXERCISES

*Suggested answers to exercises marked ✓ are to be found on our dedicated CourseMate platform for students.*

*Suggested answers to the remaining exercises are to be found on the Instructor online support resources.*

1    If depreciation is done properly, impairment adjustments will not arise. Discuss.

2    What is 'recoverable amount' as the phrase is used in IAS 36? How does it relate to the alternative valuation bases discussed at length in Part One of this book?

✓3    A cash-generating unit was reviewed for impairment at 31 May 20X3 as required by IAS 36, *Impairment of Assets.* The impairment review revealed that the cash-generating unit has a value in use of $25 million and a net realizable value of $23 million.

The carrying values of the net assets of the cash-generating unit immediately prior to the impairment review were as follows:

|                              | $000   |
|------------------------------|--------|
| Goodwill                     | 5 000  |
| Property, plant and equipment | 18 000 |
| Net current assets           | 4 000  |
|                              | 27 000 |

The review indicated that an item of plant (included in the above figure of $18 million) with a carrying value of $1 million had been severely damaged and was virtually worthless.

There was no other evidence of obvious impairment to specific assets.

What is the carrying value of the goodwill relating to the unit immediately after the results of the impairment review have been reflected in accordance with IAS 36?

|   |              |
|---|--------------|
| A | $1 million   |
| B | $2 million   |
| C | $3 million   |
| D | $4 million   |

(CIMA – November 2003)

4    On 31 December 20X1, U purchased 100 per cent of the equity share capital of V, and V became a subsidiary of U on that date. U paid $110 million for the shares, and the fair value of the net assets of V at 31 December 20X1 was $100 million. Goodwill on consolidation is written off over ten years, starting in 20X2. At 31 December 20X2, the balance sheet of V showed the following balances:

|                                | $ million |
|--------------------------------|-----------|
| Property, plant and equipment: |           |
| Land and buildings             | 50        |
| Plant and machinery            | 30        |
| Net current assets             | 15        |
|                                | 95        |

On 31 December 20X2, the directors of U carried out an impairment review in which V was treated as a single cash-generating unit. The recoverable amount of the cash-generating unit at 31 December 20X2 was computed as $96 million. No assets within the cash-generating unit had suffered obvious impairment.

What is the reduction in the consolidated reserves of U as a result of the impairment review of V (not including the normal annual write-off of goodwill)?

|   | $ million  |
|---|------------|
| A | $1 million |
| B | $5 million |
| C | $8 million |
| D | $9 million |

(CIMA – May 2003)

**5** (a) IAS 36, *Impairment of Assets*, was published in June 1998. Its primary objective is to ensure that an asset is not carried on the balance sheet at a value that is greater than its recoverable amount. The Standard does not apply to inventories (including construction contracts). It replaces guidance given in several other International Financial Reporting Standards.

**Required:**

(i) Describe the circumstances where an impairment loss is deemed to have occurred and explain when companies should perform an impairment review of tangible and intangible assets.

(ii) Describe the matters to be considered in assessing whether an asset may be impaired.

(b) Avendus is preparing its financial statements to 30 September 20X3. It has identified the following issues:

(i) Avendus owns and operates an item of plant that had a carrying value of $400 000 and an estimated remaining life of five years. It has just been damaged due to incorrect operation by an employee. It is not economic to repair the plant but it still operates in a limited capacity although it is now no longer expected to last for five years. As the plant is damaged it could only be sold for $50 000. The cost of replacing the plant is $1 million. The plant does not generate cash flows independently and is part of a group of assets that have a carrying value of $5 million and an estimated recoverable amount of $7 million.

**Required:**

Explain how the above item of plant should be treated in the financial statements of Avendus for the year to 30 September 20X3. Your answer should consider the situations where the plant continues to be used and where it would be replaced.

(ii) Avendus owns an investment property which has a remaining useful economic life of five years. The property has a carrying value of $200 000 on 30 September 20X3. It is currently let to Marchant at an annual rental of $50 000 per annum. A surveyor has estimated that Avendus could expect net proceeds of $165 000 from sale of the property. The lease and the rental are due for renegotiation on 1 October 20X3. There is currently a surplus of rental properties and this has affected rental incomes and selling prices considerably. Aware of this, Marchant has offered to rent the property for a further five years, but for an annual rental, payable in advance, of only $40 000. The rental would be payable in full on 1 October each year. The current cost of capital of Avendus is 10 per cent per annum, but current market assessments of a widely expected increase in interest rates means this will soon rise to 12 per cent per annum. Avendus uses the cost method in AS 40, *Investment Property*. The following information can be taken as correct:

| Interest rate | 10% | 12% |
|---|---|---|
| Present value of 4 year annuity | 3.2 | 3.0 |
| Present value of 5 year annuity | 3.8 | 3.6 |

**Required:**

Explain how the above investment property should be treated in the financial statements of Avendus for the year to 30 September 20X3.

Your answer should be supported with numerical calculations.

(iii) Avendus recently acquired a company called Fishright, a small fishing and fish processing company for $2 million. Avendus allocated the purchase consideration as follows:

|                               | $000  |
|-------------------------------|-------|
| Goodwill                      | 240   |
| Fishing quotas                | 400   |
| Fishing boats (2 of equal value) | 1 000 |
| Other fishing equipment       | 100   |
| Fish processing plant         | 200   |
| Net current assets            | 60    |
|                               | 2 000 |

Shortly after the acquisition, one of the fishing boats sank in a storm and this has halved the fishing capacity. Due to this reduction in capacity, the value in use of the fishing business as a going concern is estimated at only $1.2 million. The fishing quotas now represent a greater volume than one boat can fish and it is not possible to replace the lost boat as it was rather old and no equivalent boats are available. However, the fishing quotas are much in demand and could be sold for $600 000. Avendus has been offered $250 000 for the fish processing plant. The net current assets consist of accounts receivable and payable.

**Required:**

Calculate the amounts that would appear in the consolidated financial statements of Avendus in respect of Fishright's assets after accounting for the impairment loss.

(ACCA – December 2003)

**6** Outline the requirements of IFRS 5, *Non-current Assets Held for Sale and Discontinued Operations*.

**7** (a) IAS 36, *Impairment of Assets*, was issued in June 1998 and subsequently amended in March 2004. Its main objective is to prescribe the procedures that should ensure that an entity's assets are included in its balance sheet at no more than their recoverable amounts. Where an asset is carried at an amount in excess of its recoverable amount, it is said to be impaired and IAS 36 requires an impairment loss to be recognized.

**Required:**

(i) Define an impairment loss explaining the relevance of fair value less costs to sell and value in use; and state how frequently assets should be tested for impairment. Note: your answer should NOT describe the possible indicators of an impairment.

(ii) Explain how an impairment loss is accounted for after it has been calculated

(b) The assistant financial controller of the Wilderness group, a public listed company, has identified the matters below which she believes may indicate an impairment to one or more assets:

(i) Wilderness owns and operates an item of plant that cost $640 000 and had accumulated depreciation of $400 000 at 1 October 2004. It is being depreciated at 12½ per cent on cost. On 1 April 2005 (exactly halfway through the year), the plant was damaged when a factory vehicle collided into it. Due to the unavailability of replacement parts, it is not possible to repair the plant, but it still operates, albeit at a reduced capacity. Also, it is expected that as a result of the damage the remaining life of the plant from the date of the damage will be only two years. Based on its reduced capacity, the estimated present value of the plant in use is $150 000. The plant has a current disposal value of $20 000 (which will be nil in two years' time), but Wilderness has been offered a trade-in value of $180 000 against a replacement machine which has a cost of

$1 million (there would be no disposal costs for the replaced plant). Wilderness is reluctant to replace the plant as it is worried about the long-term demand for the product produced by the plant. The trade-in value is only available if the plant is replaced.

**Required:**

Prepare extracts from the balance sheet and income statement of Wilderness in respect of the plant for the year ended 30 September 2005. Your answer should explain how you arrived at your figures.

(ii) On 1 April 2004 Wilderness acquired 100 per cent of the share capital of Mossel, whose only activity is the extraction and sale of spa water. Mossel had been profitable since its acquisition, but bad publicity resulting from several consumers becoming ill due to a contamination of the spa water supply in April 2005 has led to unexpected losses in the last six months. The carrying amounts of Mossel's assets at 30 September 2005 are

|  | $000 |
|---|---|
| Brand (Quencher – see below) | 7 000 |
| Land containing spa | 12 000 |
| Purifying and bottling plant | 8 000 |
| Inventories | 5 000 |
|  | 32 000 |

The source of the contamination was found and it has now ceased.

The company originally sold the bottled water under the brand name of 'Quencher', but because of the contamination it has rebranded its bottled water as 'Phoenix'. After a large advertising campaign, sales are now starting to recover and are approaching previous levels. The value of the brand in the balance sheet is the depreciated amount of the original brand name of 'Quencher'.

The directors have acknowledged that $1.5 million will have to be spent in the first three months of the next accounting period to upgrade the purifying and bottling plant.

Inventories contain some old 'Quencher' bottled water at a cost of $2 million; the remaining inventories are labelled with the new brand 'Phoenix'. Samples of all the bottled water have been tested by the health authority and have been passed as fit to sell. The old bottled water will have to be relabelled at a cost of $250 000, but is then expected to be sold at the normal selling price of (normal) cost plus 50 per cent.

Based on the estimated future cash flows, the directors have estimated that the value in use of Mossel at 30 September 2005, calculated according to the guidance in IAS 36, is $20 million. There is no reliable estimate of the fair value less cost to sell of Mossel.

**Required:**

Calculate the amounts at which the assets of Mossel should appear in the consolidated balance sheet of Wilderness at 30 September 2005. Your answer should explain how you arrive at your figures.

(ACCA – December 2005)

# LEASES

# 16

**OBJECTIVES** After studying this chapter you should be able to:

- explain the issues underlying the accounting treatment of leases

- discuss alternative accounting treatments for leases of various types

- describe, apply and appraise the requirements of IAS 17 in relation to leased assets for lessor and lessee

- understand and contribute to ongoing debates concerning the treatment of leases in financial statements.

## INTRODUCTION

A lease is an agreement that conveys to one party (the lessee) the right to use property, but does not convey legal ownership of that property. It follows that if an asset is defined as something which is legally owned (i.e. that has been acquired in an exchange transaction), then leases will not give rise to an asset in the financial statements of the lessee. It also follows that if nothing has been 'acquired', then nothing is unpaid for; that is, the lease agreement will also not give rise to a liability in the financial statements of the lessee.

If, however, the lease agreement allows the lessee to use the property for all or most of its useful life, requires the lessee to pay total amounts close to and possibly greater than the normal buying price of the item, and requires or assumes that the lessee will look after the item as if the item belonged to it (e.g. insurance, repairs and maintenance), then it is clear that in substance the lessee would be in the same position, both economically and in terms of production and operating capacity, *as if* the lessee actually owned the asset. Furthermore, a contractual requirement to make future payments greater than the net cost of a straightforward purchase of the item means that the lessee is in the same position *as if it* had taken out a loan under agreed regular repayment terms and at an agreed rate of interest. Thus, in such circumstances, the economic substance of the situation is that the lessee has an asset and a liability, although the legal form of the agreement makes it quite clear that the legal ownership of the item remains with the other party (the lessor).

## ACTIVITY 16.1

A company obtains the use of two identical assets costing €100 000 by obtaining one asset on a credit sale agreement and the other on a lease. Assuming fixed assets are only recorded on a company's balance sheet when it has legal ownership, show the adjustments that would be necessary to the company's accounts and identify the problems, if any, with this method of accounting.

### Activity feedback

|  | € |
|---|---|
| Fixed assets | 100 000 |
| Creditors | 100 000 |

Under this method of accounting only one asset would be shown under fixed assets and only the liability to pay for one asset would be shown. The fact that the company has the use of another fixed asset and that they have the liability outstanding for lease payments is not shown and this could be considered misleading to shareholders and to other potential lenders.

If the two assets are obtained in these different ways by two different companies then the difference will be even more obvious. If the assets are being used equally profitably, then one company will appear to be using significantly fewer resources and significantly less finance than the other one to achieve comparable operating activities. This apparent economic (and managerial) efficiency of the company which leases the asset is not logically justified and, in addition, unavoidable obligations are not being recorded as liabilities.

The general principle of substance over form, discussed in Chapter 9, requires that in such circumstances the lessee *does* record an asset and a liability in its balance sheet and also that the lessor records a sale and a debtor in its financial statements.

In broad terms, the whole issue of accounting for leases can be summarized very simply. If a lease agreement essentially gives the parties rights and obligations similar to those arising from a legal purchase, then the accounting proceeds as if it *were* a legal purchase. This gives rise to a fixed asset and an obligation. If, by way of contrast, a lease agreement is, in the context of the particular characteristics of the object in question, essentially a short-term rental, then the accounting treats it as such, giving rise in the books of the lessee to a simple expense, normally allocated on a time basis.

Unfortunately, this simple division masks a considerable amount of practical difficulty. There are problems involved in creating a clear demarcation line between the two situations and a number of particular issues and problems have arisen over the years which IASB and various national Standards have tried to tackle.

## ACTIVITY 16.2

A company signs a lease agreement under which it will pay €2000 at the end of each of years 1–6 inclusive. The purchase cost of the asset concerned is €10 000 and the asset is expected to be worthless after six years. Discuss what the accounting entries in year 1 should be.

| Leasehold asset | | | |
|---|---|---|---|
| 1/1/1 cost | 10 000 | 1 667 depreciation | 31/12/1 |
| Lease liability | | | |
| | | 10 000 | 1/1/1 |
| | | $(2\ 000 - X^i)$ | 31/12/1 |
| Profit and loss | | | |
| 31/12/1 interest | $X^i$ | | |
| 31/12/1 depreciation 1 667 | | | |

### Activity feedback

*In substance, this transaction is clearly a purchase on deferred credit terms. There should be an immediate recording of an asset of €10 000 on day 1, with an equal liability. At the end of year 1, a payment of €2000 is recorded, i.e. a credit. The double-entry for this payment will need to be split two ways. There is a total interest cost of €2000 over the six-year period ((2000 × 6) − 10 000), and some of the €2000 payment at the end of year 1 will be the payment of the interest relating to year 1, say $X^i$. This will be an expense of year 1 and the remainder of this payment, i.e. $(2000 - X^i)$, will be a partial settlement of the liability. There will also be a depreciation charge made at the end of year 1 of €1667, if the straight line basis is used. This gives entries as follows:*

*In year 2 the payment, interest and depreciation entries will be repeated, but the interest expense of $X^{ii}$ should be less than $X^i$, because the liability during year 2 was lower than that during year 1. This follows the basic matching principle by allocating the total interest charge of €2000 over the six years pro rata to the benefit, thus the annual interest charge reduces as the amount borrowed reduces.*

In this chapter we first of all explore the considerable number of definitions given by IAS 17, the key Standard on this issue, and consider the whole issue of the classification of leases into two distinct types – those that are, in substance, creating fixed assets and long-term debt and those that are not. We then look separately at accounting requirements for lessees and lessors. Finally, we look at an actual case study and consider possible future developments. IAS 17 was originally issued in 1982 as *Accounting for Leases,* but was replaced by a new Standard, *Leases,* issued in 1997 but standard from 1 January 1999. A further revision appeared in March 2004, effective for annual periods beginning on or after 1 January 2005, with earlier application encouraged. The main (but limited) objective of this revision was to clarify the classification of a lease of land and buildings and to eliminate accounting alternatives for initial direct costs in the financial statements of lessors. There have been further minor revisions. It is important to note that the measurement and disclosure requirements of IFRS 13, *Fair Value Measurement,* do not apply to IAS 17.

## DEFINITIONS OF IAS 17

- A *lease* is an agreement whereby the lessor conveys to the lessee in return for a payment or series of payments the right to use an asset for an agreed period of time.
- A *finance lease* is a lease that transfers substantially all the risks and rewards incidental to ownership of an asset. Title may or may not eventually be transferred.
- An *operating lease* is a lease other than a finance lease.

The risks of ownership relating to a finance lease are those of breakdown, damage, wear and tear, theft, obsolescence and so on. The rewards of ownership are extracted by using the asset for substantially all its productive usefulness – that is, its economic life – and by receiving its residual value at the time of its disposal.

- *Economic life* is either:
  - the period over which an asset is expected to be economically usable by one or more users, or
  - the number of production or similar units expected to be obtained from the asset by one or more users.
- *Useful life* is the estimated remaining period, from the commencement of the lease term, without limitation by the lease term, over which the economic benefits embodied in the asset are expected to be consumed by the entity.

Note that the useful life relates to the expected situation for the lessee. The economic life relates to the asset, whether or not the current lessee is the only presumed user. Thus, although the useful life can exceed the lease term, the useful life cannot exceed the economic life.

- The *lease term* is the non-cancellable period for which the lessee has contracted to lease the asset together with any further terms for which the lessee has the option to continue to lease the asset, with or without further payment, when, at the inception of the lease, it is reasonably certain that the lessee will exercise the option.
- A *non-cancellable lease* is a lease that is cancellable only in one of the following four circumstances:
  - on the occurrence of some remote contingency
  - with the permission of the lessor
  - if the lessee enters into a new lease for the same or an equivalent asset with the same lessor
  - on payment by the lessee of an additional amount such that, at inception, continuation of the lease is reasonably certain.
- The *inception of the lease* is the earlier of the date of the lease agreement and the date of commitment by the parties to the principal provisions of the lease. As at this date:
  - a lease is classified as either an operating or a finance lease, and
  - in the case of a finance lease, the amounts to be recognized at the commencement of the lease term are determined.
- The *commencement of the lease term* is the date from which the lessee is entitled to exercise its right to use the leased asset. It is the date of initial recognition of the lease (i.e. the recognition of the assets, liabilities, income or expenses resulting from the lease, as appropriate).

One of the major criteria for deciding whether or not a finance lease exists is the total amount, or more accurately the total minimum amount, payable under the lease contract. This leads to a set of related terms, as follows:

- *Minimum lease payments* are the payments over the lease term that the lessee is, or can be, required to make, excluding contingent rent, costs for services and taxes to be paid by and reimbursed to the lessor, together with:
  - in the case of the lessee, any amounts guaranteed by the lessee or by a party related to the lessee, or
  - in the case of the lessor, any residual value guaranteed to the lessor by either:

**1** the lessee

**2** a party related to the lessee, or

**3** a third party unrelated to the lessor that is financially capable of discharging the obligations under the guarantee.

However, if the lessee has an option to purchase the asset at a price that is expected to be sufficiently lower than the fair value at the date when the option becomes exercisable so that, at the inception of the lease, it is reasonably certain to be exercised – that is, a 'bargain purchase option' exists – then the minimum lease payments comprise the minimum payments payable over the lease term and the payment required to exercise this purchase option.

- *Fair value* is the amount for which an asset could be exchanged or a liability settled, between knowledgeable, willing parties in an arm's-length transaction.

- From the viewpoint of the lessee, the *guaranteed residual value* is that part of the residual value which is guaranteed by the lessee or by a party related to the lessee (the amount of the guarantee being the maximum amount that could, in any event, become payable).

- From the viewpoint of the lessor, the *guaranteed residual value* is that part of the residual value which is guaranteed by the lessee or by a third party unrelated to the lessor who is financially capable of discharging the obligations under the guarantee.

- *Unguaranteed residual value* is that portion of the residual value of the leased asset, the realization of which by the lessor is not assured or is guaranteed solely by a party related to the lessor.

- The lessor's *gross investment in the lease* is the aggregate of the minimum lease payments receivable by the lessor under a finance lease and any unguaranteed residual value accruing to the lessor.

- *Net investment in the lease* is the gross investment in the lease discounted at the interest rate implicit in the lease.

- *Unearned finance income* is the difference between:
  - the gross investment in the lease, and
  - the net investment in the lease.

Some of the greatest technical difficulties are caused by the need to, at least theoretically, calculate backwards the interest rates implicitly included in arriving at the total payments under the lease.

- The *interest rate implicit in the lease* is the discount rate that, at the inception of the lease, causes the aggregate present value of (a) the minimum lease payments and (b) the unguaranteed residual value to be equal to the sum of the fair value of the leased asset and any initial direct costs of the lessor.

- The *lessee's incremental borrowing rate of interest* is the rate of interest the lessee would have to pay on a similar lease or, if that is not determinable, the rate that, at the inception of the lease, the lessee would incur to borrow over a similar term, and with a similar security, the funds necessary to purchase the asset.

- *Contingent rent* is that portion of the lease payments that is not fixed in amount but is based on the future amount of a factor that changes other than with the passage of time (e.g. percentage of sales, amount of usage, future price indices, future market rates of interest).

We again emphasize that the definition of fair value in this standard is the old one, not the new one from IFRS 13. The practical implications of this are, frankly, unclear. In its Basis for Conclusions for IFRS 13, at para. BC22, the Board states as follows. 'The IASB concluded that applying the requirements of IFRS 13 might significantly change the classification of leases and the timing of recognizing gains or losses for sale and leaseback transactions. Because there is a project under way to replace IAS 17, the IASB concluded that requiring entities to make potentially significant changes to their accounting systems for the IFRS on fair value measurement and then for the IFRS on lease accounting would be burdensome.' This makes it clear first that the application of IFRS 13 to Lease accounting would have significant effects, and second that those effects are not currently required (or allowed).

## LEASE CLASSIFICATION

As already indicated, the form of words which determines the classification of a lease as either a finance lease or an operating lease is very simple. A lease is classified as a finance lease if it transfers substantially all the risks and rewards incidental to ownership. A lease is classified as an operating lease if it does not transfer substantially all the risks and rewards incidental to ownership. Because the transaction between a lessor and a lessee is based on a lease agreement common to both parties, it is appropriate to use consistent definitions. The application of these definitions to the differing circumstances of the two parties, however, may sometimes result in the same lease being classified differently by lessor and lessee.

The Standard makes no attempt to define 'substantially all'. Some national GAAPs take a much more numerical approach to this question, for example requiring the present value of the minimum lease payments to be 90 per cent or more of the fair value of the asset at the inception of the lease (e.g. the US, Germany). Others, such as the UK, suggest that 90 per cent gives a 'presumption' of a finance lease, but make it clear that the determining factor is 'substantially all', not 90 per cent.

## ACTIVITY 16.3

A lessee leases an asset on a non-cancellable lease contract with a primary term of five years from 1 January 20X1. The rental is €650 per quarter payable in advance. The lessee has the right to continue to lease the asset after the end of the primary period for as long as they wish at a nominal rent. In addition, the lessee is required to pay all maintenance and insurance costs as they arise. The leased asset could have been purchased for cash at the start of the lease for €10 000 and has a useful life of eight years. Calculate the interest rate implicit in the lease.

### Activity feedback
*From the definition of 'interest rate implicit in the lease' we can state that:*

1  *€10 000 (fair value) = the present value at implicit interest rate of 20 quarterly rentals payable in advance of €650.*

2  *The present value of the first rental payable is €650 as it is paid now.*

3  *Thus €9350 = the present value at implicit interest rate of 19 rentals of €650.*

4  *Therefore 9350/650 = 14.385 = present value at implicit interest rate of 19 rentals of €1.*

5  *Using discount tables we can determine the interest rate as 2.95 per cent.*

In principle, IAS 17 and the definitions just given apply to all leases when IAS GAAP is to be followed. However, a number of exceptions are given. IAS 17 does not apply to:

- lease agreements to explore for or use minerals, oils, natural gas and similar non-regenerative resources, or
- licensing agreements for items such as motion pictures, video recordings, plays, manuscripts, patents and copyrights.

Additionally, IAS 17 should not be applied to the measurement by:

- lessees of investment property held under finance leases (see IAS 40, *Investment Property*, Chapter 13)
- lessors of investment property leased out under operating leases (see IAS 40)
- lessees of biological assets held under finance leases (see IAS 41, *Agriculture*, Appendix)
- lessors of biological assets leased out under operating leases (see IAS 41).

What IAS 17 does do is to give a number of examples of situations that 'would normally' (paras 1–5) or that 'could' (paras 6–8) point to a lease being properly classified as a finance lease. These are as follows (paras 10 and 11):

1 The lease transfers ownership of the asset to the lessee by the end of the lease term.

2 The lessee has the option to purchase the asset at a price that is expected to be sufficiently lower than the fair value at the date the option becomes exercisable such that, at the inception of the lease, it is reasonably certain that the option will be exercised (i.e. a bargain purchase option exists).

3 The lease term is for the major part of the economic life of the asset even if title is not transferred.

4 At the inception of the lease, the present value of the minimum lease payments amounts to at least substantially all of the fair value of the leased asset.

5 The leased assets are of a specialized nature such that only the lessee can use them without major modifications being made.

6 If the lessee cancels the lease, the lessor's losses associated with the cancellation are borne by the lessee.

7 Gains or losses from the fluctuation in the fair value of the residual accrue to the lessee (e.g. in the form of a rent rebate equalling most of the residual sales proceeds at the end of the lease).

8 The lessee has the ability to continue the lease for a secondary period at a rent which is substantially lower than market rent (i.e. a bargain rental option).

## ACTIVITY 16.4

Explain briefly in your own words why each of these situations (1–8, above) point towards a finance lease.

### Activity feedback
Our suggested wording is as follows. Because, under situations 1 and 2 the lessee ends up with legal ownership,

the validity of a finance lease classification is obvious. Situation 3 assumes, reasonably enough, that a major part of the economic life (measured in years) must imply transfer of substantially all the risks and rewards of ownership (measured in money). Situation 4 argues that payment of substantially all the purchase price, after

*(Continued)*

## ACTIVITY 16.4    (Continued)

*discounting to present value, must again imply that the substance of the transaction is a purchase on credit terms and situation 5 indicates by definition that only the lessee can derive 'rewards' from possession of the particular items. The remaining three situations (6, 7 and 8), while perhaps less definitive, all clearly point to the likelihood of the lessee being in the in-substance ownership position of deriving the benefits and 'paying the price'.*

The US prescriptive approach is continued in other respects. For example, the US version of situation 3 specifies that for a finance lease the lease term is 75 per cent or more of the economic life of the asset. The UK leasing Standard contains no similar consideration at all, relying on the 'substantially all the risks and rewards' criterion.

Note that the lease classification is to be made at the inception of the lease.

## ACTIVITY 16.5

Costa uses three identical pieces of machinery in its factory. These were all acquired for use on the same date by the following means:

1  Machine 1 rented from Brava at a cost of €250 per month payable in advance and terminable at any time by either party.

2  Machine 2 rented from Blanca at a cost of eight half-yearly payments in advance of €1500.

3  Machine 3 rented from Sol at a cost of six half-yearly payments in advance of €1200.

The cash price of this type of machine is €8000 and its estimated life is four years. Are the three machines rented by operating or finance leases?

### Activity feedback
*Machine 1 is held on an operating lease as there is no transfer of the risks or rewards of ownership. Machine 2 involves a total payment of €12 000. In present value terms this will almost certainly be more than the €8000* *fair value of the asset and therefore clearly more than 'substantially all of the fair value of the leased asset' (see our earlier situation 4). Machine 2 is therefore held on a finance lease. Machine 3 involves a total payment of €7200, the present value of which will be significantly less than €8000, so that situation 4 will not apply. The question is whether or not situation 3 applies – that is, whether or not three years is a 'major part of the economic life' of the machine (which is four years). Under US GAAP, which specifies an arbitrary 75 per cent ratio here, this would be a finance lease under situation 3 (in which circumstance the lease agreement would probably have been changed before signing in order to be a week or two shorter). Under UK GAAP, which focuses more exclusively on situation 4, machine 3 would, on the available information, be an operating lease. Our interpretation of IAS 17 would be that situation 3 does not apply to machine 3, i.e. that this would be treated as an operating lease under IAS GAAP. This example illustrates well the practical difficulties which may arise in lease classification.*

The 2004 revision added a number of detailed requirements relating to leases of land and buildings (paras 14–19). The essential point is that the land and buildings elements of a lease of land and buildings are considered separately for the purposes of lease classification. If title to both elements is expected to pass to the lessee by the end of the lease term, both elements are classified as a finance lease, whether analyzed as one lease or as two leases, unless it is clear from other features that the lease does not transfer substantially all risks and rewards incidental to ownership of one or both elements. When the land has an indefinite economic life, the land element is normally classified as an operating lease unless title is expected to pass to the lessee by the end of the lease term. The buildings element is classified as a finance or operating lease in accordance with the above specifications.

Separate measurement of the land and buildings elements is not required when the lessee's interest in both land and buildings is classified as an investment property in accordance with IAS 40 and the fair value model is adopted. Detailed calculations are required for this assessment only if the classification of one or both elements is otherwise uncertain. In accordance with IAS 40, it is possible for a lessee to classify a property interest held under an operating lease as an investment property. If it does, the property interest is accounted for as if it were a finance lease and, in addition, the fair value model is used for the asset recognized. The lessee should continue to account for the lease as a finance lease, even if a subsequent event changes the nature of the lessee's property interest so that it is no longer classified as investment property.

## ACTIVITY 16.6

Do you think the use of numerical specifications in the finance/operating lease distinction is beneficial?

### Activity feedback

The desirability of creating a precise numerical distinction is very much open to question. It has the obvious surface advantage of apparent objectivity and precision. However, the chosen figure is purely arbitrary. More importantly, the creation of a definitive numerical distinction allows, and arguably encourages, business entities to structure lease contracts so that they fall just marginally below the chosen criterion, even though the whole purpose may quite visibly be, in substance, to finance the 'purchase' of major resources by borrowing. The use of a fixed numerical boundary may substantially reduce subjectivity for the accountant and the auditor, but it may at the same time substantially increase creative accounting and the likelihood of misleading or unfair financial statements.

Yet another attempt to tighten up the requirements for lease capitalization was made by the issue in December 2004 of IFRIC 4, *Determining Whether an Arrangement Contains a Lease*. The interpretation notes that arrangements have developed that do not take the legal form of a lease but convey rights to use assets in return for a payment or series of payments, such as outsourcing arrangements, telecommunication contracts that provide rights to capacity, and take-or-pay and similar contracts in which purchasers must make specified payments, regardless of whether they take delivery of the contracted products or services.

The interpretation specifies that: an arrangement that meets both the following criteria is, or contains, a lease that should be accounted for in accordance with IAS 17:

- Fulfilment of the arrangement depends upon a specific asset. The asset need not be explicitly identified by the contractual provisions of the arrangement. Rather it may be implicitly specified because it is not economically feasible or practical for the supplier to fulfil the arrangement by providing use of alternative assets.

- The arrangement conveys a right to control the use of the underlying asset.

## ACCOUNTING AND REPORTING BY LESSEES – FINANCE LEASES

In the case of finance leases, the substance and financial reality are that the lessee acquires the economic benefits of the use of the leased asset for the major part of its economic life in return for entering into an obligation to pay for that right an amount approximating to the fair value of the asset and the related finance charge.

Lessees should recognize finance leases as assets and liabilities in their balance sheets at amounts equal at the inception of the lease to the fair value of the leased property or, if lower, at the present value of the minimum lease payments (para. 20). In calculating the present value of the minimum lease payments, the discount factor is the interest rate implicit in the lease, if this is practicable to determine; if not, the lessee's incremental borrowing rate should be used. At the inception of the lease, the asset and the liability for the future lease payments are recognized in the balance sheet at the same amounts.

During the lease term, each lease payment should be allocated between a reduction of the obligation and the finance charge so as to produce a constant periodic rate of interest on the remaining balance of the obligation over the amortization period, in the manner illustrated earlier. The asset initially recorded is depreciated in a manner consistent with that used by the lessee for owned assets.

If the circumstances described in situations 1 or 2 earlier are present – that is, a transfer of ownership is clearly foreseeable – then depreciation is usually based on the economic life of the leased asset; otherwise it is based on the shorter of economic life and lease term. Contingent rentals are generally not included in the minimum lease payments and are not accounted for as part of the capitalized lease. They should be charged to expense in the period to which they relate.

## ACTIVITY 16.7

Using the information given in Activity 16.3, assuming the asset has a nil residual value and assuming the asset is leased for a further two years after the primary period, show the accounting entries over the life of the lease required in the lessee's books by IAS 17.

### Activity feedback

The lease falls within the definition of a finance lease, therefore the 'rights in the lease' will be capitalized at fair value of €10 000 and the obligation under the lease of €10 000 will be shown as a liability.

The minimum lease payments amount to 20 × €650 = €13 000, the cash price was €10 000, hence the total finance charge will be €3000.

Remembering that this total finance charge should be allocated to accounting periods during the lease so as to produce a constant periodic rate of charge on the remaining balance of the obligation for each accounting period, then an appropriate method of allocation would be the actuarial method as follows:

| | | € | € |
|---|---|---|---|
| 1.1.XI | Fixed asset | 10 000 | |
| | Creditors (lessor) | | 10 000 |

| Period | Capital sum at start of period € | Rental paid € | Capital sum during period € | Finance charge (2.95% per quarter)* € | Capital sum at end of period € |
|---|---|---|---|---|---|
| 1/X1 | 10 000 | 650 | 9 350 | 276 | 9 626 |
| 2/X1 | 9 626 | 650 | 8 976 | 265 | 9 241 |
| 3/X1 | 9 241 | 650 | 8 591 | 254 | 8 845 |
| 4/X1 | 8 845 | 650 | 8 195 | 242 | 8 437 |
| | | | | 1 037 | |
| 1/X2 | 8 437 | 650 | 7 787 | 230 | 8 017 |
| 2/X2 | 8 017 | 650 | 7 367 | 217 | 7 584 |
| 3/X2 | 7 584 | 650 | 6 934 | 205 | 7 139 |
| 4/X2 | 7 139 | 650 | 6 489 | 191 | 6 680 |
| | | | | 843 | |

*(Continued)*

## ACTIVITY 16.7    (Continued)

| Period | Capital sum at start of period € | Rental paid € | Capital sum during period € | Finance charge (2.95% per quarter)* € | Capital sum at end of period € |
|---|---|---|---|---|---|
| 1/X3 | 6 680 | 650 | 6 030 | 178 | 6 208 |
| 2/X3 | 6 208 | 650 | 5 558 | 164 | 5 722 |
| 3/X3 | 5 722 | 650 | 5 072 | 150 | 5 222 |
| 4/X3 | 5 222 | 650 | 4 572 | 135 | 4 707 |
| | | | | 627 | |
| 1/X4 | 4 707 | 650 | 4 057 | 120 | 4 177 |
| 2/X4 | 4 177 | 650 | 3 527 | 104 | 3 631 |
| 3/X4 | 3 631 | 650 | 2 981 | 88 | 3 069 |
| 4/X4 | 3 069 | 650 | 2 419 | 71 | 2 490 |
| | | | | 383 | |
| 1/X5 | 2 490 | 650 | 1 840 | 54 | 1 894 |
| 2/X5 | 1 894 | 650 | 1 244 | 37 | 1 281 |
| 3/X5 | 1 281 | 650 | 631 | 19 | 650 |
| 4/X5 | 650 | 650 | – | | – |
| | | | | 110 | |
| | | 13 000 | | 3 000 | |

*As calculated using the actuarial method.

We can now apportion the annual rental of €2600 (i.e. 4 × €650) between a finance charge and a capital repayment as follows:

| | Total rental € | Finance charge € | Capital repayments € |
|---|---|---|---|
| X1 | 2 600 | 1 037 | 1 563 |
| X2 | 2 600 | 843 | 1 757 |
| X3 | 2 600 | 627 | 1 973 |
| X4 | 2 600 | 383 | 2 217 |
| X5 | 2 600 | 110 | 2 490 |
| | 13 000 | 3 000 | 10 000 |
| | (a) | (b) | (a)–(b) |

We also need to calculate a depreciation charge. The period for depreciation will be seven years as this is the lesser of economic life (eight years) and lease period (seven years). The annual depreciation charge on a straight line basis is therefore:

$$€10\ 000 \div 7 = €1429$$

The accounting entries in the lessee's books will be as follows, assuming year end as 31 December.
Profit and loss account charges

| | Depreciation | Finance charge | Total |
|---|---|---|---|
| X1 | 1 429 | 1 037 | 2 466 |
| X2 | 1 429 | 843 | 2 272 |
| X3 | 1 429 | 627 | 2 056 |
| X4 | 1 429 | 383 | 1 812 |
| X5 | 1 428 | 110 | 1 538 |
| X6 | 1 428 | – | 1 428 |
| X7 | 1 428 | – | 1 428 |
| | 10 000 | 3 000 | 13 000 |

(Continued)

## ACTIVITY 16.7   (Continued)

*Balance sheet entries*
*Assets held under finance leases*

|  | Cost | | Accumulated depreciation | | Net book value of assets held under finance leases |
|---|---|---|---|---|---|
|  | € |  | € |  | € |
| 31.12.X1 | 10 000 | – | 1 429 | = | 8 571 |
| 31.12.X2 | 10 000 | – | 2 858 | = | 7 142 |
| 31.12.X3 | 10 000 | – | 4 287 | = | 5 713 |
| 31.12.X4 | 10 000 | – | 5 716 | = | 4 284 |
| 31.12.X5 | 10 000 | – | 7 145 | = | 2 855 |
| 31.12.X6 | 10 000 | – | 8 574 | = | 1 426 |
| 31.12.X7 | 10 000 | – | 10 000 | = | – |

*Obligations under finance leases (i.e. the capital element of future rentals payable)*

|  | Obligations under finance leases outstanding at start of year | | Capital repayment | | Obligations under finance leases outstanding at year-end |
|---|---|---|---|---|---|
|  | € |  | € |  | € |
| 31.12.X1 | 10 000 | – | 1 563 | = | 8 437 |
| 31.12.X2 | 8 437 | – | 1 757 | = | 6 680 |
| 31.12.X3 | 6 680 | – | 1 973 | = | 4 707 |
| 31.12.X4 | 4 707 | – | 2 217 | = | 2 490 |
| 31.12.X5 | 2 490 | – | 2 490 | = | – |
| 31.12.X6 |  |  |  |  | – |
| 31.12.X7 |  |  |  |  | – |

## ACCOUNTING AND REPORTING BY LESSEES – OPERATING LEASES

Lease payments under an operating lease should be recognized as an expense in the income statement on a straight line basis over the lease term unless another systematic basis is more representative of the time pattern of the user's benefit (para. 33). Note that the pattern of payment is not relevant. Remember that contingent rent, as defined earlier, is not included in the original calculations. It therefore follows that the rental expense for any year will consist of:

1 the minimum rent under the lease divided equally over the number of years, plus
2 any contingent rent relating to that year.

Now look at Activity 16.8.

## ACTIVITY 16.8

If the lease in Activity 16.6 were to be treated as an operating lease, show the entries in the lessee's books.

| Rental expense | (4 × 650) | 2 600 |  |
|---|---|---|---|
| Creditors | (4 × 650) |  | 2 600 |

### Activity feedback

The only entries in the lessee's books would be the following annual entry:

During the negotiation of a new operating lease or the renewal of an existing one, the lessee may receive

*(Continued)*

## ACTIVITY 16.8    *(Continued)*

incentives to sign the agreement from the lessor. Incentives take many forms, including rent-free periods, reduced rents for a period of time, leasehold improvements on the lessor's account or a cash signing fee. IAS 17 is silent on this matter, but the Standing Interpretations Committee has clarified the position in SIC 15, Incentives in an Operating Lease. *This requires that the benefit of* such incentives be recognized at the inception of the lease and treated as a reduction of rental expense over the term of the lease. The benefit is recognized on a straight line basis, unless another systematic basis is more representative of the time pattern in which benefit is derived from the leased asset.

# ACCOUNTING AND REPORTING BY LESSORS – FINANCE LEASES

As is the case with the financial statements of lessees, the approach is to follow and record the substance of the situation. From the viewpoint of the lessor, the substance is that the lessor has an amount receivable, much of it usually non-current, due from the lessee. In direct relation to the lease contract, the lessor has no other assets or liabilities. The amounts received from the lessee will embrace two elements – a repayment of 'loan' and an interest revenue.

Lessors should recognize assets held under a finance lease in their balance sheets and present them as a receivable at an amount equal to the net investment in the lease (paras 36–41). A lessor aims to allocate finance income over the lease term on a systematic and rational basis. This income allocation is based on a pattern reflecting a constant periodic return on the lessor's net investment outstanding in respect of the finance lease. Lease payments relating to the accounting period, excluding costs for services, are applied against the gross investment in the lease to reduce both the principal and the unearned finance income.

Estimated unguaranteed residual values used in computing the lessor's gross investment in a lease are reviewed regularly. If there has been a reduction in the estimated unguaranteed residual value, the income allocation over the lease term is reviewed and any reduction in respect of amounts already accrued is recognized immediately.

Initial direct costs are often incurred by lessors and include amounts such as commissions, legal fees and internal costs that are incremental and directly attributable to negotiating and arranging a lease. They exclude general overheads such as those incurred by a sales and marketing team. For finance leases other than those involving manufacturer or dealer lessors, initial direct costs are included in the initial measurement of the finance lease receivable and reduce the amount of income recognized over the lease term. The interest rate implicit in the lease is defined in such a way that the initial direct costs are included automatically in the finance lease receivable; there is no need to add them separately. Costs incurred by manufacturer or dealer lessors in connection with negotiating and arranging a lease are excluded from the definition of initial direct costs. As a result, they are excluded from the net investment in the lease and are recognized as an expense when the selling profit is recognized, which for a finance lease is normally at the commencement of the lease term.

An asset under a finance lease that is classified as held for sale (or included in a disposal group that is classified as held for sale) in accordance with IFRS 5, *Noncurrent Assets Held for Sale and Discontinued Operations*, shall be accounted for in accordance with that IFRS (see Chapter 15).

# Finance leasing by manufacturers or dealers

The manufacturer or dealer may be the person who actually provides the asset as well as the finance. A finance lease of an asset by a manufacturer or dealer lessor gives rise to two types of income:

1 The profit or loss equivalent to the profit or loss resulting from an outright sale of the asset being leased, at normal selling prices, reflecting any applicable volume or trade discounts

2 The finance income over the lease term.

The sales revenue recorded at the commencement of a finance lease term by a manufacturer or dealer lessor is the fair value of the asset or, if lower, the present value of the minimum lease payments accruing to the lessor, computed at a commercial rate of interest (para. 44). The cost of sale recognized at the commencement of the lease term is the cost, or carrying amount if different, of the leased property less the present value of the unguaranteed residual value. The difference between the sales revenue and the cost of sale is the selling profit, which is recognized in accordance with the policy followed by the entity for sales which will be consistent with IAS 18 (see Chapter 19).

Manufacturer or dealer lessors sometimes quote artificially low rates of interest in order to attract customers. The use of such a rate would result in an excessive portion of the total income from the transaction being recognized at the time of sale. If artificially low rates of interest are quoted, selling profit must be restricted to that which would apply if a commercial rate of interest were charged. Initial direct costs should be charged as expenses at the inception of the lease.

## ACTIVITY 16.9

A lessor leases out an asset on terms which constitute a finance lease. The primary period is five years commencing 1 July 20X0, and the rental payable is €3000 per annum (in arrears). The lessee has the right to continue the lease after the five-year period referred to for an indefinite period at a nominal rent. The cash price of the asset in question at 1 July 20X0 was €11 372, and the rate of interest implicit in the lease can be calculated to be 10 per cent. Show the entries in the lessor's books.

### Activity feedback

The finance charge is simply the difference between the fair value of the asset (in this case being the cash price of the new asset) and the rental payments over the lease period, i.e. of €15 000 less €11 372 or €3628.

Using the actuarial method with an interest rate of 10 per cent, the allocation of the finance charge will be as follows:

| Year ended 30 June | Balance b/f € | | Finance charge (10%) € | | Rental € | | Balance c/f (in year-end balance sheet) € |
|---|---|---|---|---|---|---|---|
| 20X1 | 11 372 | + | 1 137 | – | (3 000) | = | 9 509 |
| 20X2 | 9 509 | + | 951 | – | (3 000) | = | 7 460 |
| 20X3 | 7 460 | + | 746 | – | (3 000) | = | 5 206 |
| 20X4 | 5 206 | + | 521 | – | (3 000) | = | 2 727 |
| 20X5 | 2 727 | + | 273 | – | (3 000) | = | 0 |
| | | | €3 628 | | €15 000 | | |

(Continued)

## ACTIVITY 16.9    (Continued)

*The relevant extracts from the income statements of the years in question will thus appear as follows:*

|  | 20X1 | 20X2 | 20X3 | 20X4 | 20X5 | Total |
|---|---|---|---|---|---|---|
| Rentals | 3 000 | 3 000 | 3 000 | 3 000 | 3 000 | 15 000 |
| *less* Capital repayments | 1 863 | 2 049 | 2 254 | 2 479 | 2 727 | 11 372 |
| Finance charges | 1 137 | 951 | 746 | 521 | 273 | 3 628 |
| Interest payable | (x) | (x) | (x) | (x) | (x) |  |
| Overheads | (x) | (x) | (x) | (x) | (x) |  |

*The relevant balance sheets will appear as follows:*

| | Year ended June 30 | | | |
|---|---|---|---|---|
| | 20X1 | 20X2 | 20X3 | 20X4 |
| Net investment in finance lease | | | | |
| Current | 2 049 | 2 254 | 2 479 | 2 727 |
| Non-current | 7 460 | 5 206 | 2 727 | – |
| | 9 509 | 7 460 | 5 296 | 2 727 |

# ACCOUNTING AND REPORTING BY LESSORS – OPERATING LEASES

As IAS 17 (para. 49) unsurprisingly says, lessors should present assets subject to operating leases according to the nature of the asset. The asset subject to the operating lease is, in substance as well as in form, a non-current asset of the lessor. Such an asset should be depreciated on a basis consistent with the lessor's policy for similar assets. IAS 16, *Property, Plant and Equipment*, or IAS 38, *Intangible Assets*, will apply (see Chapters 13 and 14). In addition IAS 36, *Impairment of Assets*, will need to be considered (see Chapter 15).

Costs, including depreciation, incurred in earning the lease income are recognized as an expense. Lease income (excluding receipts for services provided such as insurance and maintenance) is recognized in income on a straight line basis over the lease term even if the receipts are not on such a basis, unless another systematic basis is more representative of the time pattern in which use benefit derived from the leased asset is diminished. By definition, no element of selling profit can arise.

Initial direct costs incurred specifically to earn revenues from an operating lease are added to the carrying amount of the leased asset and recognized as an expense over the lease term on the same basis as the lease income.

## Disclosure

The disclosure requirements are extensive for both lessors and lessees. Leases are a form of financial instrument and disclosure requirements relating to financial instruments generally will apply to leases. IAS 17 specifies detailed additional requirements. These include details designed to give a clear indication of the timing of future cash movements and of future expected expense and revenue outcomes.

# SALE AND LEASEBACK TRANSACTIONS

A sale and leaseback transaction involves the sale of an asset by the vendor and the leasing of the same asset back to the vendor. The lease payment and the sale price are usually interdependent as they are negotiated as a package. The accounting treatment of a sale and leaseback transaction depends on the type of lease involved. Again, the principle of substance over form is fundamental.

If the leaseback is an operating lease and the lease payments and the sale price are established at fair value, there has in effect been a normal sale transaction and any profit or loss is recognized immediately. If the sale price is below fair value, any profit or loss should be recognized immediately except that, if the loss is compensated by future lease payments at below market price, it should be deferred and amortized in proportion to the lease payments over the period for which the asset is expected to be used. If the sale price is above fair value, the excess over fair value should be deferred and amortized over the period for which the asset is expected to be used. Also, for operating leases, if the fair value at the time of a sale and leaseback transaction is less than the carrying amount of the asset, a loss equal to the amount of the difference between the carrying amount and fair value should be recognized immediately.

If the leaseback is a finance lease, the transaction is a means whereby the lessor provides finance to the lessee, with the asset as security. For this reason it is not appropriate to regard an excess of sales proceeds over the carrying amount as income because there has, in substance, been no sale. Such excess is deferred and amortized over the lease term. For finance leases, if the fair value at the time of the sale and leaseback transaction is less than the carrying amount of the asset, then no recognition of the difference between the two is necessary (again, because there has in substance not been a sale). However, such a difference might indicate an impairment in accordance with IAS 36, *Impairment of Assets*, which Standard would then be applied (see Chapter 15).

SIC 27 extends the principles of the sale and leaseback discussion earlier to situations of linked multiple transactions in general. The principle of following the substance of the overall situation remains crucial.

# REAL WORLD ILLUSTRATION

The published consolidated financial statements of Euro Disney SCA for the year to 30 September 2000 provided a sharp illustration of how significant the leasing question can be. Broadly speaking, this was a consolidation of the French part of the worldwide Disney organization. It was published in English, but was explicitly stated to follow 'French accounting principles' in the audit report and 'French GAAP' elsewhere. Most of the land and property utilized by Euro Disney is owned, through complicated relationships, by financing companies. Under French GAAP at the time, the leases involved were operating leases and the financing companies are not consolidated. The effect is that major obligations are not revealed. However, a detailed reconciliation is given to US GAAP which, in broad terms, has the same effect as using IAS GAAP as regards the relevant leases.

Four reconciliations are now given.

*Reconciliation of net income (loss)*

| (€ in millions) | 30 September 2000 | 1999 |
|---|---|---|
| Net income, as reported under French GAAP | 38.7 | 23.6 |
| Lease and interest adjustments | (106.0) | (74.5) |
| Other | 1.1 | 1.0 |
| Net loss under US GAAP | (66.2) | (49.9) |

*(Continued)*

## REAL WORLD ILLUSTRATION    *(Continued)*

*Reconciliation of shareholders' equity*

| (€ in millions) | 30 September 2000 | 1999 |
|---|---|---|
| Shareholders' equity, as reported under French GAAP | 1 247.5 | 1 140.8 |
| Cumulative lease and interest adjustments | (1 172.9) | (1 067.0) |
| Effect of revaluing the ORAs and sale/leaseback transactions | 178.1 | 26.7 |
| Other | (14.6) | (15.6) |
| Shareholders' equity under US GAAP | 238.1 | 84.9 |

*Reconciliation of borrowings*

| (€ in millions) | 30 September 2000 | 1999 |
|---|---|---|
| Total borrowings, as reported under French GAAP* | 873.8 | 941.4 |
| Unconsolidated Phase 1 SNCs debt | 1 245.4 | 1 249.6 |
| Lease financing arrangements with TWDC | 236.9 | 236.9 |

| (€ in millions) | 30 September 2000 | 1999 |
|---|---|---|
| Borrowings including unconsolidated Financing Companies | 2 356.1 | 2 427.9 |

| (€ in millions) | 30 September 2000 | 1999 |
|---|---|---|
| US GAAP adjustments to revalue lease financing arrangements and ORAs Total US GAAP borrowings* | (6.3) | (8.5) |

*(excluding accrued interest)

*Balance sheet under US GAAP*

| (€ in millions) | 30 September 2000 | 1999 |
|---|---|---|
| Cash and short-term investments | 452.9 | 347.6 |
| Receivables | 203.2 | 184.6 |
| Fixed assets | 2 493.3 | 2 455.5 |
| Other assets | 169.4 | 161.4 |
| Total assets | 3 318.8 | 3 149.1 |
| Accounts payable and other liabilities | 730.9 | 644.8 |
| Borrowings* | 2 349.8 | 2 419.4 |
| Shareholders' equity | 238.1 | 84.9 |
| Total liabilities and equity | 3 318.8 | 3 149.1 |

*(excluding accrued interest)

Total assets under French GAAP were 2 793.8 for 2000 and 2 518.8 for 1999.

## ACTIVITY 16.10

Calculate the following ratios, within the limits of the given information in the Euro Disney case study: (a) under French GAAP, and (b) under US GAAP, and comment.

$$\frac{\text{net income}}{\text{shareholders' equity}}$$

$$\frac{\text{borrowings}}{\text{equity} + \text{borrowings}}$$

$$\frac{\text{net income}}{\text{total assets}}$$

*Activity feedback*
(a) French GAAP

| | 2000 | 1999 |
|---|---|---|
| $\frac{\text{net income}}{\text{shareholders' equity}}$ | $\frac{38.7}{1247.5} = 3\%$ | $\frac{23.6}{1\,140} = 2\%$ |
| $\frac{\text{borrowings}}{\text{equity} + \text{borrowings}}$ | $\frac{873.8}{873.8 + 1\,247.5} = 41\%$ | $\frac{941.4}{941.4 + 1\,140.8} = 45\%$ |
| $\frac{\text{net income}}{\text{total assets}}$ | $\frac{38.7}{2\,893.8} = 1\%$ | $\frac{23.6}{2\,518.8} = 1\%$ |

*(Continued)*

## ACTIVITY 16.10    (Continued)

(b) US GAAP

$$\frac{\text{net income}}{\text{shareholders' equity}} \qquad \frac{(66.2)}{238.1} = -28\% \qquad \frac{(49.9)}{84.9} = -58\%$$

$$\frac{\text{borrowings}}{\text{equity + borrowings}} \qquad \frac{2\,349.8}{2\,349.8 + 231.8} = 91\% \qquad \frac{2\,419.4}{2\,419.4 + 8.94} = 97\%$$

$$\frac{\text{net income}}{\text{total assets}} \qquad \frac{(66.2)}{3\,318.8} = -2\% \qquad \frac{(49.9)}{3\,149.1} = -2\%$$

*To state the obvious, a very different picture is given. When the substance of the situation is recorded and the contracted (legally as well as economically) liabilities related to the operations are involved, the whole entity is shown to be very highly geared (leveraged), as well as unprofitable. Can both sets of figures be validly regarded as equally fairly presenting the position to readers of the financial statements?*

## Possible future developments

In December 1999 the IASC published a discussion paper on the subject of leases titled 'Leases: Implementation of a New Approach'. The paper had been developed by the G4+1 group. This group consisted of representatives of accounting standard setters from Australia, Canada, New Zealand, the UK and the US working with the IASC (proposing, therefore, that $4 + 1 = 6$!).

The essential, and apparently very radical, proposal was that the arbitrary distinction between operating and finance leases is unsatisfactory and should be abolished, to be replaced by an approach that applies the same regulations for all leases. The IASC noted in the paper that many analysts recast financial statements by applying the same approach to operating and finance leases. G4+1 believed that recognition in a lessee's balance sheet of material assets and liabilities arising from operating leases should take place:

> The general effect of the approach proposed is that the amounts recognized as an asset and a liability by a lessee in respect of a lease of a given item would vary in amount depending on the nature of the lease.

The financial statements would thus reflect the extent to which differing lease arrangements result in financial obligations and provide financial flexibility.

The story of efforts by the IASB, in close cooperation with the FASB, to develop a new standard on accounting for leases is a long, difficult and convoluted one. Suffice to say that the IASB issued an Exposure Draft in August 2010 which proposed that lessees should apply a single model, the 'right-of-use model', to all leases within its scope. In this 2010 ED, the leased asset would have been amortized generally on a straight-line basis, whilst the liability would be amortized using the effective interest rate method. In the income statement, the 2010 ED would have resulted in an accelerated pattern of expense recognition for all leases. However, many constituents indicated that the expense recognition pattern proposed in the 2010 ED did not reflect the economic reality for some types of leases.

In May 2013 the IASB, still working closely with the FASB, issued a revised ED, simply called 'Leases'. This attempts to respond to the criticisms, mentioned above. It introduces a new dividing line, which is likely in itself to generate significant debate, given that one of the project's original objectives was to remove the existing "bright-line" between operating and finance leases, and by implication to have no dividing line at all. The IASB is now proposing two types of leases for expense recognition purposes. Broadly speaking, this revised model results in what is similar to the existing operating lease accounting for property leases, while most equipment leases will be subject to the same front-loaded expense recognition pattern that generated concern in response to the earlier 2010 ED. We thus seem to have an uneasy compromise between conceptual coherence of asset/liability definition, and practical acceptability (there are rumours of heavy lobbying on the FASB by US constituents, and this project is one of the remaining 'convergence' projects between the two Boards). The debates are likely to continue. No effective date is even suggested in the ED, and we would be surprised if earlier than 1 January 2018 is eventually proposed for obligatory adoption. We outline here some key points in the 2013 ED. Changes are still distinctly possible.

The ED establishes the principles that lessees and lessors should apply to report the amount, timing and uncertainty of cash flows arising from a lease.

It will not apply to leases of intangible assets, biological assets, explorations rights and service concessions within the scope of IFRIC 12 *Service Concession Arrangements*. The lessor will be required to split a contract into its respective components, for example a lease including a maintenance contract, using the principles for the allocation of transaction price to performance obligations outlined in the (eventual!) new revenue recognition standard (see Chapter 19). The lease term is the non-cancellable lease term together with renewal option periods where there is significant economic incentive to extend the lease. A contract modification will result in a reassessment of lease assets and liabilities. The difference between the carrying amounts of assets and liabilities under the old lease and the new lease is recognized immediately in profit or loss.

At the commencement date the entity has to classify a lease as either Type A or Type B, where Type A leases normally mean that the underlying asset *is not* property while Type B leases normally mean the underlying asset *is* property.

However, the entity will classify a lease other than a property lease as Type B if:

- the lease term is for an insignificant part of the total economic life of the underlying asset; or
- the present value of the lease payments is insignificant relative to the fair value of the underlying asset at the commencement date of the lease.

Conversely, the entity will classify a property lease as Type A if:

- the lease term is for the major part of the remaining economic life of the underlying asset; or
- the present value of the lease payments accounts for substantially all of the fair value of the underlying asset at the commencement date.

At the commencement date of the lease, the lessee shall discount the lease payments using the rate the lessor charges the lessee, or if that rate is unavailable, the lessee's incremental borrowing rate. The lessee recognizes the present value of lease payments as a liability. At the same time it recognizes a right-of-use asset equal to the lease liability plus:

- any lease payments made to the lessor at or before the commencement date, less any lease incentives received from the lessor; and
- any initial direct costs incurred by the lessee.

After commencement date, the liability is increased by the unwinding of interest and reduced by lease payments made to the lessor. The lease liability is reassessed when there is a change in the expected amount of lease payments. If the remeasurement relates to the current period, the adjustment is reflected directly in profit or loss. Alternatively, the adjustment is recognized in the right-of-use asset provided the adjustment does not result in the right-of-use asset being negative. The right-of-use asset will be subject to impairment.

A lessee will recognize in profit or loss, unless the costs are included in the carrying amount of another asset:

- for Type A leases, the unwinding of the discount on the lease liability as interest and the amortization of the right-of-use asset.
- for Type B leases, the lease payments will be recognized on a straight line basis over the lease term and reflected in profit or loss as a single lease cost. The single lease cost will be allocated to the actual unwinding of interest on the liability and any remaining lease cost is allocated to the amortization of the right-of-use asset. However, the periodic lease cost shall not be less than the periodic unwinding of the discount on the lease liability.
- variable lease payments not included in the lease liability in the period in which the obligation for those payments is incurred.

The lessor model in the ED is broadly similar to current lease accounting.
For Type A leases:

- The lessor will discount the lease payments, as outlined for lessees, using the rate the lessor charges the lessee and recognize this amount as the lease receivable;
- Recognize a residual asset being the sum of the present value of any unguaranteed residual, variable lease payments not included in the lease receivable and an allocation of profit relating to the residual asset;
- Recognize the profit on the portion of the asset leased immediately in profit or loss;
- Recognize the unwinding of interest on the lease receivable and residual asset in profit or loss over the lease term.

A reassessment in the expected lease payments, excluding the impact of credit risk, will be reflected immediately in profit or loss. The interest rate in the lease may be amended during the lease term if certain criteria are met. The lease receivable and residual asset will be subject to impairment.

Income from Type B leases will be recognized in profit or loss on a straight line or other systematic basis over the lease term, similar to current operating lease accounting for lessors. The leased asset will not be derecognized or reclassified but will be depreciated using the principles for owned property, plant and equipment.

## SUMMARY

This chapter has explored the accounting measurement and disclosure problems relating to leases in the financial statements of both lessors and lessees. The requirements of IAS 17 have been explored and illustrated. Finally, suggestions that the distinction between finance and operating leases should be abolished have been considered.

# EXERCISES

*Suggested answers to exercises marked ✓ are to be found on our dedicated CourseMate platform for students.*

*Suggested answers to the remaining exercises are to be found on the Instructor online support resources.*

✓**1**   Explain the theoretical distinction between finance leases and operating leases.

**2**   IAS 17 fails to give a clear definitional distinction between finance and operating leases. Discuss.

**3**   IAS 17 states that a particular lease which is a finance lease for the lessee need not automatically be a finance lease as regards the lessor. Can this make sense?

**4**   The need to account for lease transactions in a useful way proves that the principle of substance over form is essential. Discuss.

**5**   All unavoidable obligations relating to all lease contracts should be shown in the balance sheet of published financial statements. Discuss.

**6**   The following figures have been extracted from the accounting records of Lavalamp on 30 September 20X3:

|  | $000 | $000 |
|---|---|---|
| Sales revenue | | 112 500 |
| Cost of sales (note (i)) | 78 300 | |
| Operating expenses | 11 400 | |
| Lease rentals (note (iii)) | 2 000 | |
| Loan interest paid | 1 000 | |
| Dividends paid | 1 200 | |
| Leasehold (20 years) factory at cost (note (ii)) | 25 000 | |
| Plant and equipment at cost | 34 800 | |
| Depreciation 1 October 20X2 – leasehold | | 6 250 |
| – plant and equipment | | 12 400 |
| Accounts receivable | 25 550 | |
| Inventory – 30 September 20X3 | 21 800 | |
| Cash and bank | | 4 000 |
| Accounts payable | | 7 300 |
| Ordinary shares of $1 each | | 20 000 |
| Share premium | | 10 000 |
| 8% Loan note (issued in 20X0) | | 25 000 |
| Accumulated profits – 1 October 20X2 | | 3 600 |
| | 201 050 | 201 050 |

(i)   Lavalamp has spent $6 million (included in the cost of sales) during the year developing and marketing a new brand of soft drink called Lavaflow. Of this amount, $1 million is for advertising and the remainder is the development costs. A firm of consultants has been reviewing the sales of the new product and based on this, it has valued the brand name of Lavaflow at $10 million and expects the life of the brand to be 10 years. Lavalamp wishes to capitalize the maximum amount of intangible assets permitted under International Financial Reporting Standards.

(ii)   Due to a sharp increase in the values of properties, Lavalamp had its leasehold property revalued on 1 October 20X2 with the intention of restating its carrying value. A firm of surveyors contracted to value the property found that it had suffered some damage which will cost $1.5 million to rectify. They gave a valuation of $24 million for the property on the assumption that the repairs are carried out. Lavalamp has informed Capitalrent, the owner of the property, of the repairs needed. Capitalrent has since sent their own surveyors to inspect the property and have informed Lavalamp that they believe the damage is due to the type of machinery being used in the building and accordingly have requested that Lavalamp pay for the repairs. Lavalamp has taken professional advice on this matter which concluded that the property was not in good condition when it was originally leased, but the use of the plant is making the damage worse. Lavalamp has offered to share the cost of the repairs with Capitalrent, but it has not yet had a reply.

(iii) Included in the income statement charge of $2 million for lease rentals is a payment of $600 000 in respect of a five-year lease of an item of plant (requiring ten payments in total). The payment was made on 1 April 20X3. The fair value of this plant at the date it was leased (1 April 20X3) was $5 million. Information obtained from the finance department confirms that this is a finance lease with an implicit interest rate of 10 per cent per annum. The company depreciates plant used under finance leases on a straight line basis (with time apportionment) over the life of the lease. Other plant is depreciated at 20 per cent per annum on cost. The remaining payments were confirmed as being for operating leases of office equipment.

(iv) A provision for income tax for the year to 30 September 20X3 of $3 470 000 is required.

(v) Lavalamp made and accounted for a rights issue on 1 October 2002 of 1 new share for every 4 held at a price of $1.60 per share. The issue was fully subscribed.

**Required:**
Prepare the financial statements for the year to 30 September 20X3 for Lavalamp in accordance with International Financial Reporting Standards as far as the information permits. They should include:

(a) an income statement

(b) a statement of changes in equity, and

(c) a balance sheet.

Other than for item (ii) above, notes to the financial statements are NOT required, nor is a calculation of earnings per share. Ignore deferred tax.

(ACCA – December 2003)

✓7 (i) Different accounting practices for leases are an area that, without a robust accounting standard, can be used to manipulate a company's financial statements. IAS 17, *Leases,* was revised in 1999 and has as its objective to prescribe the appropriate accounting policies and disclosures for financial and operating leases.

**Required:**
Summarize the effect on the financial statements of a lessee treating a lease as an operating lease as opposed to a finance lease, and describe the factors that normally indicate a lease is a finance lease.

(ii) Gemini leased an item of plant on 1 April 20X1 for a five-year period. Annual rentals in advance were $60 000. The cash price (fair value) of the asset on 1 April 20X1 was $260 000. The company's depreciation policy for this type of plant is 25 per cent per annum on the reducing balance.

**Required:**
Assuming the lease is a finance lease and the interest rate implicit in the lease is 8 per cent, prepare extracts of the financial statements of Gemini for the year to 31 March 20X3.

(ACCA – December 2003)

# INVENTORIES AND CONSTRUCTION CONTRACTS

# 17

OBJECTIVES  After studying this chapter you should be able to:

- explain the composition of inventories

- describe five inventory cost assumptions, i.e. unit cost, first-in, first-out (FIFO), last-in, first-out (LIFO), weighted average and base inventory

- show the effect on annual profit and profit trends of using different inventory cost assumptions

- discuss IAS 2 requirements relating to inventories

- define construction contracts, attributable profit and foreseeable losses

- appraise IAS 11 requirements relating to construction contracts

- calculate amounts to be disclosed in financial statements relating to construction contracts

- identify the disclosure requirements of IAS 2 and IAS 11.

## INTRODUCTION

Inventories, including work in progress, present several problems to the accountant. First, we have to determine the value of the inventories, taking into account that the number of items in inventory changes constantly over time. Second, when inventory items are sold, we need to determine the cost of goods sold and recognize the related revenue. For this purpose we need to determine the revenue recognition (sale) point. The latter issue is solved in the international reporting standards by IAS 18, *Revenue*. In 2008 a revision of IAS 18 began. The new name of the Standard to be issued in the fourth quarter of 2013 (as at Spring of 2013) will be *Revenue From Contracts with Customers*. The new Standard will not only replace the current IAS 18, *Revenue*, but also IAS 11, *Construction Contracts*. More information on the changes the new Standard will entail for the definition, measurement and valuation of contracts with customers are included in Chapter 19 of this book. At the end of this chapter, the most important elements of the exposure draft on 'Revenue from contracts with customers' which apply to construction contracts will be highlighted.

So the valuation of inventories requires care as it is a key determinant of cost of goods sold and therefore in determining net income. Commercial companies purchase goods with the purpose of reselling them to third party customers. Inventories of commercial companies mainly consist of goods purchased for resale. Industrial companies, on the other hand, produce the products which they sell to their customers. Within industrial companies inventories consist of raw materials, work in progress and finished goods. Most industrial companies first produce goods and then face the commercial risk of finding a customer for those products. In a number of cases, however, a contract with the customer in which the revenue is determined has already been negotiated and signed before the start of the production of the goods, according to the specifications agreed with the customer. In these cases, companies do not bear a commercial risk after signing the contract with their customers; their main concern is to keep production costs under control. The latter types of contracts are called construction contracts and are treated in a separate Standard, namely IAS 11, *Construction Contracts*. All other types of inventories are dealt with in IAS 2.

In this chapter we consider first all types of inventories other than construction contracts. We start with a discussion of all methods available for inventory valuation purposes, and thereafter we focus on those methods which are permitted according to IAS 2. Second, we discuss the valuation of construction contracts.

## INVENTORIES

Inventories include:

1 goods or other assets purchased for resale
2 consumable stores
3 raw materials and components purchased for incorporation into products for sale
4 products and services in intermediate stages of completion
5 finished goods.

The 'cost' of each item at each of these stages is the key to determining the costs of goods sold, and the value of inventory still left in the business – the closing inventory. Commercial companies will include in the valuation of the inventory mainly goods purchased for resale. Industrial companies in determining the cost of their inventory need to consider not only the cost of the raw materials, but also the cost of converting raw materials into products and services for sale. Thus, we need to include in our valuation of inventory the following items: costs of purchase and costs of conversion, including both direct and indirect overhead costs.

A moment's reflection will make it obvious that there are practical problems here. 'Direct' items should present no difficulties as figures can be related 'directly' by definition. But overhead allocation necessarily introduces assumptions and approximations: What is the normal level of activity taking one year with another? Can overheads be clearly classified according to function? Which other (non-production) overheads are 'attributable' to the present position and location of an item of inventory? So for any item of inventory that is not still in its original purchased state, it is a problem to determine the cost of a unit or even of a batch. Methods in common use include job, process, batch and standard costing. All include more or less arbitrary overhead allocations. We will elaborate on this issue when we discuss the IASB's definition of costs of conversion included in IAS 2.

Once we have found a figure for the unit cost per product 'in its present location and position', the next difficulty will arise when we have to select an appropriate method for calculating the related cost, where several identical items have been purchased or made at different times and therefore at different unit costs.

Consider the following transactions for company Tradex.

| Purchases: | January | 10 units at €25 each |
| | February | 15 units at €30 each |
| | April | 20 units at €35 each |
| Sales: | March | 15 units at €50 each |
| | May | 18 units at €60 each |

How do we calculate inventory, cost of sales and gross profit? There are several ways of doing this, based on different assumptions as to which unit has been sold or which unit is deemed to have been sold.

## Inventory cost assumptions

Five possibilities are now discussed.

**Unit cost** Here we assume that we know the actual physical units that have moved in or out. Each unit must be individually distinguishable, for example by serial numbers. In these circumstances, we simply add up the recorded costs of those units sold to give cost of sales and of those units left to give stock. This needs no detailed illustration.

**First-in, first-out (FIFO)** Here it is assumed that the units moving out are the ones that have been in the longest (i.e. came in first). The units remaining will therefore be regarded as representing the latest units purchased. Work through the following activity using FIFO method.

## ACTIVITY 17.1

Calculate the cost of sales and gross profit based on FIFO inventory cost assumption from the data for company Tradex.

*Activity feedback*

| | | | € | Cost of sales € |
|---|---|---|---|---|
| January | 10 at €25 | = | 250 | |
| February | 15 at €30 | = | 450 | |
| February total | 25 | | 700 | |
| March | −10 at €25 (Jan.) | = | 250 | |
| | −5 at €30 (Feb.) | = | 150 | 400 |
| March total | 10 | | 300 | |
| April | +20 at €35 | | 700 | |
| April total | 30 | | 1 000 | |
| May | −10 at €30 (Feb.) | = | 300 | |
| | −8 at €35 (Apr.) | = | 280 | 580 |
| May total | 12 at €35 | | 420 | |
| | | | | 980 |

Sales are 750 + 1080 = €1830
Purchases are 250 + 450 + 700
       = €1400

This gives:

| | | € | Cost of sales € |
|---|---|---|---|
| Sales | | | 1 830 |
| Purchases | | 1 400 | |
| Closing inventory | | 420 | |
| Cost of sales | | | 980 |
| Gross profit | | | 850 |

**Last-in, first-out (LIFO)** Here we reverse the assumption. We act as if the units moving out are the ones which came in most recently. The units remaining will therefore be regarded as representing the earliest units purchased. The following activity demonstrates the use of LIFO, so make sure you complete the activity carefully.

## ACTIVITY 17.2

Calculate the cost of sales and gross profit based on LIFO inventory cost assumption using the data for company Tradex.

*Activity feedback*

| | | | € | Cost of sales € |
|---|---|---|---|---|
| January | 10 at €25 | = | 250 | |
| February | 15 at €30 (Feb) | = | 450 | |
| February total | 25 | = | 700 | |
| March | −15 at €30 (Feb.) | = | 450 | 450 |
| March total | 10 | = | 250 | |
| April | +20 at €35 | = | 700 | |
| April total | 30 | | 950 | |
| May | −18 at €35 (Apr.) | = | 630 | 630 |
| May total | 2 at €35 & 10 | = | 320 | |
| | at €25 | | | 1 080 |

This gives:

| | € | € |
|---|---|---|
| Sales | | 1 830 |
| Purchases | 1 400 | |
| Closing inventory | 320 | |
| Cost of sales | | 1 080 |
| Gross profit | | 750 |

**Weighted average** Here we apply the average cost, weighted according to the different proportions at the different cost levels, to the items in inventory. Activity 17.3 shows the fully worked out method, involving continuous calculations. In practice, an average cost of purchases figure is often used rather than an average cost of inventory figure. This approximation reduces the need for calculation to a periodic, maybe even annual, requirement. Try the following activity using weighted average method.

## ACTIVITY 17.3

Calculate the cost of sales and gross profit based on weighted average inventory cost assumption for company Tradex.

### Activity feedback

| | | | € | Cost of sales €|
|---|---|---|---|---|
| January | 10 at €25 | = | 250 | |
| February | 15 at €30 | = | 450 | |
| February total | 25 at €28* | = | 700 | |
| March | −15 at €30 (Feb.) | | 420 | 450 |
| March total | 10 at €28 | = | 280 | |
| April | +20 at €35 | = | 700 | |
| April total | 30 at €32$^{2/3}$** | | 980 | |
| May | −18 at €32$^{2/3}$ | = | 588 | 588 |
| May total | 12 at €32$^{2/3}$ | | 392 | |
| | | | | 1 008 |

This gives:

| | | € | Cost of sales € |
|---|---|---|---|
| Sales | | | 1 830 |
| Purchases | | 1 400 | |
| Closing inventory | | 392 | |
| Cost of sales | | | 1 008 |
| Gross profit | | | 822 |

Working:

$$^{*}28 = \frac{(10 \times 25) + (15 \times 30)}{(10 + 15)}$$

$$^{**}32^{2/3} = \frac{(10 \times 28) + (20 \times 35)}{(10 + 20)}$$

**Base inventory** This approach is based on the argument that a certain minimum level of inventory is necessary in order to remain in business at all. Thus, it can be argued that some of the inventory viewed in the aggregate is not really available for sale and should therefore be regarded as a fixed asset. This minimum level defined by management remains at its original cost and the remainder of the inventory above this level is treated as inventory by one of the other methods. In our example, the minimum level might be ten units.

## ACTIVITY 17.4

Calculate the cost of sales and gross profit based on a minimum inventory level of ten units and using FIFO for company Tradex.

### Activity feedback

January purchase of base stock: 10 at €25 = €250

| | | | € | Cost of sales € |
|---|---|---|---|---|
| February | 15 at €25 | = | 450 | |
| March | 15 at €30 | = | 450 | 450 |
| March total | 0 | | 0 | |
| April | +20 at €35 | = | 700 | |
| April total | 20 | = | 700 | |
| May | −18 at €35 | = | 630 | 630 |
| May total | 2 at €35 | = | 70 | |
| | | | | 1 080 |

This gives:

| | | € | Cost of sales € |
|---|---|---|---|
| Sales | | | 1 830 |
| Purchases | | 1 150 | |
| Closing inventory | | 70 | |
| Cost of sales | | | 1 080 |
| Gross profit | | | 750 |

*In this particular case, the gross profit is the same with this method (base inventory + FIFO) as with LIFO. Can you work out why? This will not generally be the case.*

## Which approach?

So, which approach or approaches are preferable or acceptable?

In selecting a method, management presumably must exercise judgement to ensure that the methods chosen provide the fairest practicable approximation to cost. If standard costs are used to value inventory, they will need to be reviewed frequently to ensure that they bear a reasonable relationship to actual costs incurred during the period. Methods such as base stock and LIFO often result in inventories being stated in the statement of financial position at amounts that bear little relationship to recent cost levels. When this happens, not only can the presentation of current assets be misleading, but there also is potential distortion of subsequent results if inventory levels reduce and out of date costs are drawn into the statement of comprehensive income. However, the method of arriving at cost by applying the FIFO method could be unacceptable in principle because it is not necessarily the same as actual cost and, in times of rising prices, will result in the taking of a profit which has not been realized. To amplify, consider the cost of sales figure for the May sales in the earlier FIFO and LIFO calculations. Is it preferable to match an April cost level against an April revenue (LIFO) or, partially at least, to match a February cost level against an April revenue level (FIFO)? From a statement of financial position viewpoint, however, the criticism of LIFO perhaps makes more sense. The statement of financial position total under both LIFO and base stock is likely to be badly out of date. Applying the latest purchase price level to all units, sometimes called next-in, first-out (NIFO), could also be rejected in principle for the same reason as LIFO.

Before we consider IAS 2 and how it attempts to answer this puzzle, there is another problem to consider. In the activities so far we have virtually been able to match an inventory item with its sale but this is not the general case.

## INVENTORY SYSTEMS

### Periodic systems

Within this system, inventory is determined by a physical count at a specific date. As long as the count is made frequently enough for reporting purposes, it is not necessary to maintain extensive inventory records. The inventory shown in the statement of financial position is determined by the physical count and is priced in accordance with the inventory method used. The net charge between the beginning and ending inventories enters into the computation of costs of goods sold.

### Perpetual system

In a perpetual system, inventory records are maintained and updated continuously as items are purchased and sold. The system has the advantage of providing inventory information on a timely basis, but requires the maintenance of a full set of inventory records. Audit practice will certainly require that a physical check of perpetual inventory records be made periodically.

## IAS REQUIREMENTS FOR INVENTORY

It is now quite clear that the calculation of the appropriate inventory at 'cost' figure is by no means clear-cut. Assumptions in two respects have to be made. First, the determination of the cost of the unit, and, second, the matching of these costs with the items sold. With regard to the first item, IAS 2 states that 'Inventories shall be measured at the lower of cost and net realizable value' (NRV) (para. 9). With regard to the second item, namely the matching issue, IAS 2 allows three of the five methods discussed earlier, namely the unit cost, FIFO and weighted average. In certain circumstances the retail method is allowed. We concentrate, in the sections below, first on the determination of the unit cost of an item in inventory, and afterwards we pay attention to inventory valuation methods allowed by IAS 2. We start the discussion with a review of the scope of IAS 2 and the definitions provided in the Standard for a number of concepts.

## Definitions

In para. 6 of IAS 2, inventories are defined as assets:

(a) held for sale in the ordinary course of the business

(b) in the process of production for such sale, or

(c) in the form of materials or supplies to be consumed in the production process or in the rendering of services.

Excluded from the scope of IAS 2 are construction contracts, financial instruments and biological assets related to agricultural activity and agricultural produce at the point of harvest (dealt with under IAS 41, *Agriculture*; for a discussion of IAS 41, see Course-Mate). With regard to the scope of IAS 2, the text of the Standard (para. 3) mentions further that the Standard does not apply to producers of agricultural and forest products, agricultural produce after harvest, and minerals and mineral products, to the extent that they are measured at NRV in accordance with well-established practices in those industries. Neither does the Standard apply to commodity broker-traders who measure their inventories at fair value less cost to sell. In both cases, changes in fair values are recognized in profit or loss in the period of change.

IAS 2 (para. 6) defines the concepts of NRV and fair value. *Net realizable value* is defined as the estimated selling price in the ordinary course of business less the estimated costs of completion and the estimated costs necessary to make the sale. *Fair value* is defined as the amount for which an asset could be exchanged, or a liability settled, between knowledgeable, willing parties in an arm's-length transaction.

Paragraph 8 of IAS 2 provides a number of examples of items which will be recorded under inventories. For example, merchandise purchased by a retailer and held for resale or land and other property held for resale. They also encompass finished goods produced or work in progress being produced by the entity and include materials and supplies awaiting use in the production process. In the case of a service provider, inventories include the costs of the service for which the entity has not yet recognized the related revenue.

IAS 2 states that inventories must be measured at the lower of cost and NRV. IAS 2 defines (para. 10) the concept of cost of inventories as follows: 'The cost of inventories shall comprise all costs of purchase, costs of conversion and other costs incurred in bringing the inventories to their present location and condition.' The definition of NRV is provided above (see the discussion on the scope of IAS 2). It is obvious that for each separate item of inventory we need to determine both the cost and the NRV.

The separate item point is significant and this is shown in Activity 17.5.

## ACTIVITY 17.5

An entity has three products in its inventory with values as follows:

| Product | Cost | NRV |
|---------|------|-----|
| A | 10 | 12 |
| B | 11 | 15 |
| C | 12 | 9 |
| Total | 33 | 36 |

At what value should the inventory be stated in the statement of financial position in accordance with IAS 2?

**Activity feedback**

*If the inventory is not separated into each type then we would value at the lower of cost of 33 and NRV of 36. The answer is 33. However, IAS 2 requires us to value each type of inventory separately, and therefore the lower in each case is A 10, B 11 and C 9, giving us an inventory valuation of 30.*

In the next section we concentrate on the concept of 'cost of inventory' for industrial companies. In industrial companies, the calculation of the unit cost involves a lot more decisions in order to arrive at the unit cost which can be used for financial reporting purposes.

## Cost of inventory

IAS 2 gives guidance on the costs of the different elements included in the definition of the cost of inventories as follows (see para. 10: 11–18). The cost of inventories should include: all costs of purchase, costs of conversion and other costs incurred in bringing the inventories to their present location and condition. Further amplification of cost is given in para. 11 as follows:

> The costs of purchase of inventories comprise the purchase price, import duties and other taxes (other than those subsequently recoverable by the entity from the taxing authority) and transport, handling and other costs directly attributable to the acquisition of finished goods, materials and services. Trade discounts, rebates and other similar items are deducted in determining the costs of purchase.

It must be noted here that IAS 2 does not permit exchange differences arising directly on the recent acquisition of inventories invoiced in a foreign currency to be included in the costs of purchase of inventories. This change is because the improved IAS 21 has eliminated the allowed alternative treatment of capitalizing certain exchange differences. The cost of purchase applies to the inventories in commercial companies as well as to all materials used in the production process of industrial companies and materials awaiting use in the production process.

The item costs of conversion is explained in paras, 12, 13 and 14 of IAS 2, indicating the associated problems. Costs of conversion include: direct labour, the systematic allocation of fixed production overheads (e.g. depreciation and maintenance charges), and the allocation of variable production overheads (e.g. indirect materials and labour). (Remember here that fixed overheads are those indirect costs of production that remain relatively constant regardless of volume of production, whereas variable overheads are those that vary directly or nearly with volume of production.) IAS 2 prescribes a different allocation procedure for fixed and variable overheads. Variable overheads are allocated to the units produced based on the actual use of production facilities.

The allocation of fixed overheads is based on the normal capacity of production facilities, taking into account the loss of capacity resulting from planned maintenance. However, IAS 2 also proposes two other treatments for the allocation of fixed overhead costs. First, the actual level of production may be used if it approximates normal capacity. Second, in periods of abnormally high production, the amount of fixed overhead allocated to each unit of production is decreased so that, of variable overheads on the actual use of production facilities, inventories are not measured above cost. Where joint products are concerned, a rational basis for allocation of costs of conversion between them needs to be found.

The Standard suggests the use of relative sale value or gross contribution margin as rational and consistent bases. This can be seen as somewhat arbitrary and subjective but is, nevertheless, at least a consistent, if not entirely logical, method for dealing with a difficult issue.

We now focus on the definition of the third element included in the cost of conversion, namely other costs included in the concept 'cost of inventories'. According to para. 15, other costs are included in the inventory only to the extent that they are incurred in bringing the inventories to their present location and condition. Paragraph 16 lists a number of items which are excluded from the cost of inventories and, as a result, they should be recognized as expenses in the period in which they are incurred:

(a) Abnormal amounts of wasted materials, labour and other production costs;

(b) Storage costs, unless those costs are necessary in the production process before a further production stage;

(c) Administrative overheads that do not contribute to bringing inventories to their present location and condition; and

(d) Selling costs.

A good example of storage costs that can be included in the cost of inventory is those involved in the ageing of whisky. As ageing is essential to the production of whisky, whatever storage costs are incurred can be capitalized to the cost of inventory. Work through the following activities carefully.

## ACTIVITY 17.6

Determine the valuation of inventory items A and B from the following data:

|                            | A | B |
|----------------------------|---|---|
| Direct labour charge per item | 2 | 4 |

Fixed production overheads total €50 000 and normal capacity of production is 5200 for product A and 10 200 for product B, but this is reduced by 200 for A and 200 B for planned maintenance. The target of production was 6000 for A and 12 000 for B. Variable production overheads are calculated as €10 000 in total and are to be allocated on a machine hour basis. Each A item takes two hours of machine time and each B one hour.

### Activity feedback

Fixed production overheads will be charged over 5000 A and 10 000 B, as normal capacity is after planned maintenance allowance. The target of production is irrelevant in the calculation unless this high production level is actually achieved, in which case the fixed overheads to each unit will be decreased so as not to measure the item above cost.

|                                                          | A   | B   |
|----------------------------------------------------------|-----|-----|
| Direct labour                                            | 2.0 | 4.0 |
| Fixed overheads (allocated in ratio of 1:2 and on number of items) | 2.0 | 4.0 |
| Variable overheads (0.5 per hour)                        | 1.0 | 0.5 |
|                                                          | 5.0 | 8.5 |

## ACTIVITY 17.7

Calculate the cost of inventories in accordance with IAS 2 using the following data relating to Unipoly Company for the year ended 31 May 20X7.

|  | € |
|---|---|
| Direct materials cost of can opener per unit | 1 |
| Direct labour cost of can opener unit | 1 |
| Other direct costs of can opener unit | 1 |
| Production overheads per year | 600 000 |
| Administration overheads per year | 200 000 |
| Selling overheads per year | 300 000 |
| Interest payments per year | 100 000 |

There were 250 000 units in finished goods at the year-end. You may assume that there were no finished goods at the start of the year and that there was no work in progress. The normal annual level of production is 750 000 can openers, but in the year ended 31 May 20X7 only 450 000 were produced because of a labour dispute.

### Activity feedback

*The direct costs of the inventory are straightforward to calculate as follows:*

|  | € |
|---|---|
| 250 000 units at €1 direct material cost | 250 000 |
| 250 000 units at €1 direct labour cost | 250 000 |
| 250 000 units at direct €1 cost | 250 000 |
|  | 750 000 |

*IAS 2 only permits the inclusion of production overheads in the valuation of inventories and therefore the administration, selling and interest costs (if interest costs meet the requirements identified in IAS 23, Borrowing Costs, see Chapter 13) are not relevant here.*

*To allocate production overhead, the normal production capacity will be used as an allocation basis (600 000/750 000) = €0.8 per unit. In order to calculate the overhead which will be assigned to the inventory, we multiply the overhead cost per unit by the number of units in inventory (0.8 × 250 000 = 200 000). The abnormal costs associated with the labour dispute will be charged as an expense in the period they are incurred. So we arrive at a cost of finished inventory of:*

Cost of finished inventory = €950 000

## ACTIVITY 17.8

Which of the following costs listed below can be included in the cost of inventory in accordance with IAS 2? Reference to paras 9–20 of IAS 2 will help in completing this activity.

Discounts on purchase price
Travel expenses of buyers
Import duties
Transport insurance
Commission and brokerage costs
Storage costs after receiving materials that are
   necessary in the production process
Salaries of sales department
Warranty cost
Research for new products
Audit and tax consultation fees

### Activity feedback

| | |
|---|---|
| Discounts on purchase price | yes |
| Travel expenses of buyers | no |
| Import duties | yes |
| Transport insurance | yes |
| Commission and brokerage costs | yes |
| Storage costs after receiving materials that are necessary in the production process | yes |
| Salaries of sales department | no |
| Warranty cost | no |
| Research for new products | no |
| Audit and tax consultation fees | no |

## Techniques for the measurement of the cost of inventories

For companies producing products and services, IAS 2 permits the use of the standard cost method where normal levels of materials, supplies, labour, efficiency and capacity utilization will be used to calculate a standard cost. These standard costs have to be reviewed regularly if this method is used.

IAS 2 also permits the use of the retail method. The retail method is generally used in the retail industry where there are large numbers of rapidly changing items that have similar margins. The cost of the inventory is determined by reducing the sales value of the inventory by the appropriate gross profit margin. Problems occur with this method when a retailer deals in products of widely differing profit margins or discounts slow moving items.

Once the cost of inventories is determined, the next cost formulas are available to determine the value of the costs of goods sold. In the introduction to this chapter, we explained that five methods or cost formulas are available in order to determine the value of the inventory and the costs of goods sold.

## Cost formulas for the determination of the value of the inventory and the costs of goods sold

IAS 2 distinguishes between interchangeable goods and non-interchangeable goods. Items that are not ordinarily interchangeable and goods or services produced and segregated for specific projects should be assigned by using specific identification of their individual costs (para. 23). This approach equates to the unit cost method described in the introductory section.

For all other types of inventories, IAS 2 advocates the use of FIFO or the weighted average cost formula. We note that IAS 2 does not permit the use of LIFO.

Remember the use of LIFO in a period of rising costs will reduce profits and value inventory on the statement of financial position at older costs, whereas FIFO shows inventory on the statement of financial position at newer costs and what many would regard as a more relevant cost.

The elimination of LIFO, however, does not rule out specific cost methods that reflect inventory flows that are similar to LIFO. For example, when stock bins of coal, cement, etc., are replenished by 'topping up', then LIFO may reflect the actual physical flow of inventories.

When inventories are sold, the carrying amount of those inventories shall be recognized as an expense in the period in which the related revenue is recognized. The closing inventory will appear on the statement of financial position at the lower of cost or NRV.

## Net realizable value

In order to determine the net realizable value (NRV), the company deducts from the selling price in the ordinary course of the business the estimated costs of completion and the estimated costs necessary to make the sale (= marketing, selling and distribution costs). When the cost of the inventory will not be recoverable due to damage, the cost of the inventory will be written down to NRV. The amount of any write-down of inventories to NRV and all losses of inventories shall be recognized as an expense in the period the write-down or loss occurs. The amount of any reversal of any write down of inventories, arising from an increase in the NRV, shall be recognized in the period in which the reversal occurs.

## Disclosure requirements

According to IAS 2, financial statements have to disclose:

- the accounting policies adopted in measuring inventories, including the cost formulas used

- the total carrying amount of inventories and the carrying amount in classifications appropriate to the entity
- the carrying amount of inventories carried at fair value less costs to sell
- the amount of any write-down of inventories recognized as an expense in the period in accordance with para. 34
- the carrying amount of inventories pledged as security for liabilities
- the cost of inventories recognized as an expense during the period
- the amount of any reversal of any write-down that is recognized as a reduction in the amount of inventories recognized as an expense in the period in accordance with para. 34
- the circumstances or events that led to the reversal of a write-down of inventories in accordance with para. 34.

## REAL WORLD ILLUSTRATION

In the 2005 annual report of IBM, the reader is provided with 'critical accounting estimates'. These are estimates requiring degrees of judgement on the application of GAAP. They have this to say on inventories:

The company reviews the market value and demand for its inventory on a quarterly basis to ensure recorded inventory is stated at the lower of cost or market. Inventories at higher risk for write downs or write offs are those in the industries that have lower relative gross margins and that are subject to a higher likelihood of changes in industry cycles. The semiconductor business is one such industry.

Factors that could impact estimated demand and selling prices are the timing and success of future technological innovations, competitor actions, supplier prices and economic trends. To the extent that total inventory losses differ from management estimates by 5 per cent, the company's consolidated net income in 2005 would have improved/declined by an estimated $22 million using 2005 results, depending upon whether the actual results were better/worse, respectively, than expected.

This quite clearly demonstrates that valuation of inventory is not an exact science.

## REAL WORLD ILLUSTRATION

With regard to the valuation rules applied by Adidas in their Consolidated Financial Statements of 2012 (p. 199) we find the following:

Merchandise and finished products are valued at the lower of cost or net realizable value, which is the estimated selling price in the ordinary course of business less the estimated costs of completion and the estimated costs necessary to make the sale. Costs are

determined using a standard valuation method: the 'average cost method'. Costs of finished products include costs of raw materials, direct labour and the components of the manufacturing overheads which can be reasonably attributed. The allocation of overheads is based on the planned average utilization. The net realizable value allowances are computed consistently throughout the Group based on the age and expected future sales of the items on hand.

# CONTRACTS

## Introduction

Construction contracts generally last over a long period of time, certainly longer than one accounting period. Another feature is that the purchase contract for these items is already agreed before production starts. A sales price is determined in the contract.

Such contracts involve all the difficulties discussed earlier in the context of inventories, with one major addition. This is the question of profit allocation over the various accounting periods. If a contract extends over, say, three years, should the contribution to profits be 0 per cent, 0 per cent and 100 per cent, respectively, for the three years? Can we make profits on something before we have finished it? The realization convention might seem to argue against doing so and the old idea of prudence would certainly argue against it too. But would this give a 'fair presentation' of the results for each period? And would it be of any use? All the various users want regular information on business progress. Remember the desirability of timeliness of information. Can we not argue that we can be 'reasonably certain' during the contract, of at least some profit? This discussion has led to two basic methods of dealing with construction contracts: the completed-contract method and the percentage-of-completion (POC) method. This latter requires allocation over accounting periods of the total profit on the contract, while the former delays profit recognition until completion. Try the following activity.

## ACTIVITY 17.9

Zen entity is contracted to Alpha for $2m to construct a building. The following data are available in relation to the contract:

|  | 20X5 | 20X6 | 20X7 |
|---|---|---|---|
| Costs incurred during year | 500 000 | 700 000 | 300 000 |
| Year-end estimate costs to complete | 1 000 000 | 300 000 | |
| Bills raised during year | 400 000 | 700 000 | 900 000 |
| Cash received during year | 200 000 | 500 000 | 1 200 000 |

The contract is completed during 20X7. Show the profit to be included in the accounts under both the POC method and completed-contract method assuming that degree of completion is based on costs incurred.

### Activity feedback

The contract as a whole has the following outcome:

| | |
|---|---|
| Sale price | 2 000 000 |
| Cost of sale (500 + 700 + 300) | 1 500 000 |
| Profit | 500 000 |

20X5 (costs to date × total profit)

$$\frac{-\text{profit previously recognized}}{(\text{Total estimated costs to completion})}$$

20X6 previously recognized profit is 166 667

20X7 previously recognized profit is now 166 667 + 233 333 = 400 000

Under the completed-contract method this profit of 500 000 will not be recognized until 20X7.

Under the POC method, the profit has to be allocated to each accounting year as follows:

$$\frac{500\,000 \times 500\,000 - 0}{1\,500\,000} = 166\,667$$

$$\frac{1\,200\,000 \times 500\,000}{1\,500\,000} - 166\,667 = 233\,333$$

$$\frac{1\,500\,000 \times 500\,000}{1\,500\,000} - 400\,000 = 100\,000$$

In Activity 17.9, the POC was determined on the basis of the proportion of costs already incurred. Having decided on the use of POC method, our next problem is to determine how this profit and indeed any sale, and therefore resulting contract work in progress, should be shown in the accounts. If the contract work in progress is shown as a current asset with its attributable profit, as implied by the POC method, then this is in direct conflict with the requirement to show inventories at cost or NRV, whichever is the lower included in IAS 2. This is why construction contracts for the time being are dealt with in a separate Standard, namely IAS 11. Probably in the second half of 2013, IAS 11 will be replaced by the new standard on revenue from contracts with customers (see Chapter 19). The new standard will become applicable for financial statements prepared after the first of January 2017, but early adoption is permitted. Therefore IAS 11 will still be applied by companies up to 2017, however there is a possibility that some companies will opt for an earlier adoption. The long transition period allows companies to renegotiate their contracts with customers in order to avoid possible negative effects on their financial information (for a further discussion on the management of accounting numbers see Chapters 31 and 32).

## IAS 11

## Definitions

Construction contracts are defined (para. 3) as contracts specifically negotiated for the construction of an asset or a combination of assets that are closely interrelated or interdependent in terms of their design, technology and function of their ultimate purpose or use. IAS 11 distinguishes between two types of construction contracts, namely a fixed price contract and a cost plus contract. The essential difference between the two types of contracts is the way in which the revenue of the transaction is determined.

- *A fixed price contract* is a construction contract in which the contractor agrees to a fixed contract price or a fixed rate per unit of output, which in some cases is subject to cost escalation clauses.
- A *cost plus contract* is a construction contract in which the contractor is reimbursed for allowable or otherwise defined costs, plus a percentage of these costs or a fixed fee.

However, in practice the type of contract is not always so clear-cut and many have characteristics of both types. It is also worth noting that there is no definition given for 'contractor', which appears to be used in a general sense in the Standard.

The Standard also discusses the separability issue. Many contracts can cover the construction of a number of assets and, in these cases, each asset must be treated as a separate contract if:

- separate proposals have been submitted for each asset
- each asset has been subject to separate negotiations and the contractor and customer have been able to accept or reject that part of the contract relating to each asset
- the costs and revenues of each asset can be identified.

Conversely, a group of contracts may in substance be a single construction contract and required to be treated as such when:

- the group of contracts is negotiated as a single package
- the contracts are so clearly interrelated that they are in effect part of a single project with an overall profit margin
- the contracts are performed concurrently or in a continuous sequence.

# Recognition of contract revenue and costs in financial statements

After these definitions and explanations, the Standard finally arrives at the heart of the problem, namely the recognition of the revenues and costs involved in the contract. Contract revenue should comprise (para. 11):

**(a)** the initial amount of revenue agreed in the contract, and

**(b)** variations in contract work claims and incentive payments:

  **(i)** to the extent that it is probable that they will result in revenue, and

  **(ii)** they are capable of being reliably measured.

Contract costs consist of (para. 16):

- costs that relate directly to the specific contract
- costs that are attributable to contract activity in general and can be allocated to the contract
- such other costs as are specifically chargeable to the customer under the terms of the contract.

Thus, in determining appropriate figures for construction contracts, first we calculate the total costs attaching to the contract to date, including appropriate production overheads, which could include borrowing costs. Second, we calculate revenue attributable to the contract to date and therefore attributable profit.

The Standard provides lists of costs that may and may not be charged to a specific contract. Using the Standard, work through the following activity.

## ACTIVITY 17.10

Identify four costs that could be charged to a specific contract and four that may not.

### Activity feedback
Paragraph 17 of the Standard gives a number of items, as follows.
Costs that may be charged are:

- site labour costs
- materials used in construction
- depreciation of assets used on construction
- costs of moving assets to and from the site
- hire charges
- design and technical assistance that is directly related
- estimated costs of rectification and guarantee work, including warranty costs
- claims from third parties
- insurance
- construction overheads.

Costs that may not be charged are:

- general administration costs not specified in the contract
- selling costs
- research and development costs not specified
- depreciation of idle assets not used on a specific contract.

## Amounts to be shown in the financial statements

So far we have discussed all items which need to be taken into account in the valuation process of construction contracts. Next we focus on the amounts which need to be recorded in the statement of financial position and the statement of comprehensive income during the construction period. IAS 11 (para. 22) requires the POC method to be used for the valuation of these contracts as follows:

> When the outcome of a construction contract can be estimated reliably, contract revenue and contract costs associated with the construction contract shall be recognized as revenue and expenses respectively by reference to the stage of completion of the contract activity at the end of the reporting period. An expected loss on the construction contract shall be recognized as an expense immediately in accordance with paragraph 36.

Complete the following activity.

## ACTIVITY 17.11

The following data are available in respect of a construction contract:

| | |
|---|---|
| Costs to date | $2m |
| Total contract revenue expected | $2m |
| Further costs to completion | $0.5m |

How should this contract be treated in the accounts?

### Activity feedback

*The problem here is that the contract is forecast to make a loss of $0.5m and we need to determine how much of this loss should be recognized at the current stage of completion. The POC method might imply we should recognize $2/2.5 \times 0.5 = 0.4$, but prudence would suggest that we should recognize all the foreseeable loss immediately as it becomes apparent. In accordance with IAS 11, we would recognize all the loss of $0.5m.*

The stage of completion of a contract is determined by the method that measures reliably the work performed and this could be:

- proportion that costs incurred for work performed to date bear to total
- estimated costs
- surveys of work performed, or
- completion of a physical proportion of the contract work.

IAS 11 pays a lot of attention to the recognition of the revenues of the construction contracts. In paras 22 and 23, the Standard spells out in detail when revenue can be recognized for a fixed price contract and for a cost plus contract.

In the case of a fixed price contract, the outcome of a construction contract can be estimated reliably when all of the following conditions are satisfied (para. 23):

**(a)** Total contract revenue can be measured reliably.

**(b)** It is probable that the economic benefits associated with the contract will flow to the entity.

**(c)** Both the contract costs to complete the contract and the stage of contract completion at the end of the reporting period can be measured reliably.

**(d)** The contract costs attributable to the contract can be clearly identified and measured reliably so that actual contract costs incurred can be compensated.

In relation to cost plus contracts, the outcome of a construction contract can be estimated reliably when all of the following conditions are satisfied:

**(a)** It is probable that the economic benefits associated with the contract will flow to the entity.

**(b)** The contract costs attributable to the contract, whether or not specifically reimbursable, can be clearly identified and measured reliably.

In Activities 17.12–17.17 we will illustrate the principles laid down in IAS 11 with regard to the recognition and valuation of construction contracts.

IAS 11 also requires that the gross amount due from customers for contract work should be shown as an asset and gross amount due to customers for contract work as a liability. The gross amount due from customers is defined as the net amount of:

> costs incurred + recognized profits
>      – the sum of recognized losses and progress billings

for all contracts in progress for which costs incurred plus recognized profits (less recognized losses) exceeds progress billings.

The gross amount due to customers is defined as the net amount of:

> costs incurred + recognized profits
>      – the sum of recognized losses and progress billings

for all contracts in progress for which progress billings exceed costs incurred plus recognized profits (less recognized losses).

## ILLUSTRATION

An entity is carrying out a contract for F entity. At the end of the first year of the contract the following information is available:

| | |
|---|---|
| Contract revenue | 500 |
| Contract expenses | 450 |
| Billings to entity F | 500 |
| Payments in advance of billings from F | 25 |
| Contract costs incurred | 600 |
| Foreseeable additional losses | 0 |

In accordance with IAS 11, show how this contract would be recorded in the entity's financial statements.

The contract for F currently shows a profit of 500 – 450 = 50 and there is no foreseeable loss.

Thus, in the statement of comprehensive income:

| | |
|---|---|
| Contract revenue | 500 |
| Contract expenses | 450 |
| Profit | 50 |

The gross amount due from customers is costs incurred 600 + recognized profits 50 – (the sum of recognized losses 0 + progress billings 500) = 150.

We must also note that there is a payment in advance by F of 25 and we must record this somewhere.

Therefore, in the statement of financial position:

| | |
|---|---|
| Current assets: | 150 |
| Due from customers' construction contracts | |
| Current liabilities: | 25 |
| Payments in advance construction contracts | |

Now try the following activity.

## ACTIVITY 17.12

The following data are available in respect of a contract for P entity carried out by Q entity at the end of the first year of the contract. Show how the contract should be recorded in the financial statements of Q entity.

| | |
|---|---|
| Contract revenue | 350 |
| Contract expenses | 400 |
| Billings to entity P | 200 |
| Payments in advance of billings by P | 0 |
| Contract costs incurred | 400 |
| Foreseeable additional losses | 60 |

(*Continued*)

## ACTIVITY 17.12    (Continued)

### Activity feedback
There is a loss on this contract of 350 (contract revenue) – 400 (contract expenses to date) – 60 (foreseeable loss) = 110. IAS 11 requires us to recognize the foreseeable loss immediately as an expense and therefore the statement of comprehensive income will be:

| | |
|---|---|
| Contract revenue | 350 |
| Contract expenses | 460 |
| Loss | (110) |

For this contract, contract costs incurred 400 less recognized losses 110 = 290 exceeds progress billings of 200. Therefore, we have an amount due from customers of 290 – 200 = 90.

The statement of financial position will therefore show:

| | |
|---|---|
| Current assets: | |
| Due from customers' construction contracts | 90 |

The following illustration shows the ledger account entries for the contracts of illustration above and Activity 17.12.

## ILLUSTRATION

Remember the data given were:

### Contract P

| | Contract F | Contract P |
|---|---|---|
| Contract revenue | 500 | 350 |
| Contract expenses | 450 | 400 |
| Billings | 500 | 200 |
| Payments in advance of billings | 25 | – |
| Contract costs incurred | 600 | 400 |
| Foreseeable additional losses | – | 60 |

The ledger accounts are shown as follows:

### Contract F

**Contract revenue**

| | | | |
|---|---|---|---|
| Inc 500(2) | | Debtors 500(1) | |

**Contract costs incurred**

| | | | |
|---|---|---|---|
| Costs incurred | 600 | Inc. | 450(3) |
| | | Bal. c/d | 150 |
| | 600 | | 600 |
| Bal. b/d | 150 | | |

This balance is described as amounts due from customers as this will be charged to customers in the future. Paragraph 27 of IAS 11 does allow us to describe these costs as contract work in progress which is what they actually are.

**Income statement**

| | | | |
|---|---|---|---|
| Contract expenses | 450(3) | Contract revenue | 500(2) |
| Profit | 50 | | 150 |

**Debtors**

| | | | |
|---|---|---|---|
| Revenue | 500 | Billing | 500 |

**Billings**

| | | | |
|---|---|---|---|
| Debtor | 500 | Payments | 525 |
| Bal. pays in advance | 25 | | |

### Contract P

**Contract revenue**

| | | | |
|---|---|---|---|
| Inc. | 350(2) | Debtors | 350(1) |

**Contract costs incurred**

| | | | |
|---|---|---|---|
| Costs incur | 400 | P&L | 400(3) |

**Income statement**

| | | | |
|---|---|---|---|
| Contract costs | 400(3) | Contract rev. | 350(2) |
| Prov. for losses | 60(4) | Loss | 110 |

**Debtors**

| | | | |
|---|---|---|---|
| Contract rev. | 350 | Billing | 200 |
| | | Bal. c/d | 150 |
| | 350 | | 350 |
| Bal. b/d | 150 | Prov. loss | 60(5) |
| | | Bal. c/d | 90 |
| | 150 | | 150 |
| Bal. b/d | 90 | | |

Bal. b/d 90 shown as due from customers under current assets (400 – 110 – 200)

**Provision for loss**

| | | | |
|---|---|---|---|
| Debtors | 60(5) | P&L | 60(4) |

(Continued)

## ILLUSTRATION    (*Continued*)

*Notes*

1. Raise the contract revenue.
2. Transfer contract revenue to income statement.
3. Transfer proportion of contract costs incurred to date to income statement or contract expenses.
4. Raise provision for foreseeable losses.
5. Transfer provision to debtors.

The above illustration shows the transfer of balances on the ledger accounts that occurs under the IAS 11 requirements. Now complete the following activities.

## ACTIVITY 17.13

The following data are available in respect of five contracts in progress at the end of year 1 by Gamma Entity. Identify how each contract should be shown in the accounts in accordance with IAS 11.

| | | | Contracts | | | |
|---|---|---|---|---|---|---|
| | A | B | C | D | E | Total |
| Contract revenue recognized in statement of Comprehensive Income | 145 | 520 | 380 | 200 | 55 | 1 300 |
| Contract expenses recognized in statement of Comprehensive Income | 110 | 450 | 350 | 250 | 55 | 1 215 |
| Expected losses | | | | 40 | 30 | 70 |
| Contract costs incurred in period | 110 | 510 | 450 | 250 | 100 | 1 420 |
| Contract costs recognized as contract expenses | 110 | 450 | 350 | 250 | 55 | 1 215 |
| Contract costs relating to future Activity | | 60 | 100 | | 45 | 205 |
| Progress billings | 100 | 520 | 380 | 180 | 55 | 1 235 |
| Payments in advance of billings | | 80 | 20 | | 25 | 125 |

### Activity feedback

*We will explain the treatment of each contract separately.*

### Contract A

*Statement of financial position*

| | |
|---|---|
| Shown as contract revenue | 145 |
| Shown as contract expenses | 110 |
| Gross profit | 35 |

*Statement of financial position*
*The amount to be included in current assets under amounts due from customers calculated as follows: Costs incurred, 110, plus recognized profits, 35, less progress billings, 100 = 45.*

*In this case all the costs incurred to date relate to the contract activity recorded as revenue and are transferred to statement of comprehensive income as contract expenses leaving a zero balance.*

### Contract B

*Statement of comprehensive income*

| | |
|---|---|
| Shown as contract revenue | 520 |
| Shown as contract expenses | 450 |
| Gross profit | 70 |

*Statement of financial position*
*As costs incurred 510 + recognized profits 70 + 580 exceeds progress billings of 520, we have an amount due from customers as follows:*

| | |
|---|---|
| Contract costs incurred to date | 510 |
| Recognized profits | 70 |
| | 580 |
| less Progress billings | 520 |
| Amounts due from customers, current assets | 60 |

*There is also a payment in advance to record under current liabilities of 80.*

### Contract C

| | |
|---|---|
| Contract revenue | 380 |
| Contract expenses | 350 |
| Gross profit | 30 |

*Statement of financial position*
*As with Contract B, as costs incurred = recognized profits exceeds progress billings, there is an amount due from customers to show under current assets as follows:*

(*Continued*)

## ACTIVITY 17.13 *(Continued)*

| | |
|---|---:|
| Contract costs incurred to date | 450 |
| Recognized profits | 30 |
| | 480 |
| *less Progress billings* | 380 |
| Amounts due from customers | 100 |

### Contract D

*Statement of comprehensive income*

| | |
|---|---:|
| Contract revenue | 200 |
| Contract expenses (costs 250 + loss 40) | 290 |
| Gross loss | 90 |

*Statement of financial position*
The amount to be included in current liabilities is calculated as follows:

| | |
|---|---:|
| Contract costs incurred | 250 |
| *less Recognized losses* | 90 |
| | 160 |
| *less Progress billings* | 180 |
| Amount due to customers | 20 |

### Contract E

*Statement of comprehensive income*

| | |
|---|---:|
| Contract revenue | 55 |
| Contract expenses (costs incurred 55 + loss 30) | 85 |
| Gross loss | 30 |

*Statement of financial position*

| | |
|---|---:|
| There is an advance payment – current liabilities | 25 |

As costs incurred less recognized losses exceeds progress billings there is an amount due from customers as follows:

| | |
|---|---:|
| Contract costs incurred | 100 |
| *less Recognized losses* | 30 |
| | 70 |
| *less Progress billings* | 55 |
| Due from customers – current asset | 15 |

*Thus, in total for Contracts A to E, we have:*

| | |
|---|---:|
| Contract revenue (145 + 520 + 380 + 200 + 55) | 1300 |
| Contract expenses (110 + 450 + 350 + 290 + 85) | |
| (note expected losses of 90 included) | 1285 |
| Profit | 15 |
| Payments in advance shown as creditor | 125 |
| (0 + 80 + 20 + 0 + 25) | |
| Payments due from customers shown as current asset (45 + 60 + 100 + 0 + 15) | 220 |
| Payments due to customers shown as liability (Contract D) | 20 |

## ACTIVITY 17.14

The following data is available in respect of two contracts:

| | £000 Contract A | £000 Contract B |
|---|---:|---:|
| Contract revenue recognized | 1 000 | 400 |
| Contract expenses recognized | 600 | 400 |
| Foreseeable additional losses | | 200 |
| Progress billings | 700 | 100 |
| Payments made by customer | 500 | 80 |

Show how the above should be recorded in the financial statements.

### Activity feedback

*Statement of comprehensive income*

| | £000 Total | £000 Contract A | £000 Contract B |
|---|---:|---:|---:|
| Contract revenue | 1 400 | 1 000 | 400 |
| Contract expenses | 1 200 | 600 | 600 |
| | | | (400 + 200 loss) |
| Gross profit | 200 | 400 | (200) |

*Statement of financial position*

| | | | |
|---|---:|---:|---:|
| Gross amount due from customers | 400 | 300 | 100 |
| | | (1000 – 700) | (400 – 100 – 200 loss) |
| Trade receivables | 220 | 200 | 20 |
| | | (700 – 500) | (100 – 80) |

*Note the billings not paid by customers are shown as trade receivables.*

## Changes in estimates of costs

Estimating the stage of completion of a contract relies on estimates of total costs and these may well change throughout the life of the contract. Para. 38 of IAS 11 requires us to treat the changes as a change in accounting estimate in accordance with IAS 8, *Accounting Policies*. The following illustration demonstrates how this works.

### ILLUSTRATION

A construction contract with revenue of £15m is initially estimated to have total costs of £9m and is expected to take four years to complete. In year 2, the costs are re-estimated at £10m, the increased cost being attributed as follows: £0.6m to year 3 and £0.4m to year 4. If we assume the initial costs were attributed as follows, £2m year 1, £2.5m year 2, £3m year 4 and £1.5m year 4, we can calculate the stage of completion of the contract both before and after the re-estimate.

|                        | Year 1 £m | Year 2 £m | Year 3 £m | Year 4 £m |
|------------------------|-----------|-----------|-----------|-----------|
| **Initial estimate**   | 15        | 15        | 15        | 15        |
| Revenue                |           |           |           |           |
| Contract costs to date | 2         | 4.5       | 7.5       | 9         |
| Contract costs to complete | 7     | 4.5       | 1.5       | –         |
|                        | 9         | 9         | 9         | 9         |
| Profit estimate        | 6         | 6         | 6         | 6         |
| % complete             | 22.2%     | 50%       | 83.3%     | 100%      |
| Profit recognized in year | 1.33   | 1.67      | 2         | 1         |

|                        | Year 1 £m | Year 2 £m | Year 3 £m | Year 4 £m |
|------------------------|-----------|-----------|-----------|-----------|
| **Re-estimate**        |           |           |           |           |
| Revenue                | 15        | 15        | 15        | 15        |
| Contract costs to date | 2         | 4.5       | 8.1       | 10        |
| Contract costs to complete | 7     | 5.5       | 1.9       | –         |
|                        | 9         | 10        | 10        | 10        |
| Profit estimate        | 6         | 5         | 5         | 5         |
| % complete             | 22.2%     | 45%       | 81%       | 100%      |
| Profit recognized in year | 1.33   | 0.92      | 1.8       | 0.95      |

Year 2 profit is reduced from £1.67m to £0.92m to take account of the adjustment to the year 1 profit subsequent to the re-estimate. Note that no change is made to the year 1 profit figure in accordance with IAS 8.

## Contract outcome unreliable

So far we have dealt with construction contracts where the outcome can be reliably estimated. For those contracts that cannot be reliably estimated, the Standard requires that revenue should be recognized only to the extent of contract costs incurred that it is probable will be recoverable, and contract costs should be recognized as an expense immediately and therefore no profit will be recognized. If on a contract for which the outcome cannot be reliably estimated total contract costs exceed total contract revenues, then any excess of total contract costs over total contract revenue is recognized as an expense immediately. Complete the following activity.

## ACTIVITY 17.15

An entity is involved in two construction contracts, the outcome of which cannot be assessed with reliability, for which the following data are available:

Contract A   Contract costs incurred 30 000 all probably recoverable.

Contract B   Contract costs incurred 100 000, similar contracts have shown a loss of 15 per cent on contract sales price due to pending legislation affecting the construction. Contract sale price 1m.

   Identify how these two contracts should be treated in the accounts of the entity.

### Activity feedback

| Contract A | Contract revenue (as contract costs can be recovered) | 30 000 |
|---|---|---|
| | Contract costs | 30 000 |
| Contract B | Contract revenue (Note 1) | 0 |
| | Contract costs recognized as expense | 150 000 |

Note 1: *Estimated contract loss is 15 per cent × 1m = 150 000 and therefore total contract costs are 100 000 + 150 000 = 250 000, which exceeds contract revenue 100 000. The excess of total contract costs over total contract revenue, 150 000, is recognized as an expense immediately.*

## Disclosure requirements

These are detailed at paras 39–45 of the Standard and cover such items as:

- amount recognized as revenue in the period
- method used to determine revenue and stage of completion
- aggregate amounts relating to costs and profits recognized, advances received and retentions.

In addition, amounts due to and from customers must be presented as a current asset and liability respectively.

## ACTIVITY 17.16

Using the data from the feedback to Activity 17.13, show as far as possible the disclosure requirements for contracts X and Y in accordance with IAS 11.

### Activity feedback

| | |
|---|---|
| Contract revenue recognized as revenue in period | 850 |
| Contract costs incurred and recognized profits less losses (600 + 400 + 50 − 110) | 940 |
| Advances received | 25 |
| Amounts due from customers (150 + 90) | 240 |

## REAL WORLD ILLUSTRATION

In the financial statements of EADS for the year 2007 (a company active in the air, space and defence transport sectors), we find information on write-downs on their A380 programme.

### Annual Report

Inventories at 31st December 2007 and 2006 consist of the following:

*(Continued)*

## REAL WORLD ILLUSTRATION    *(Continued)*

| (in €m) | 31st December 2007 | 31st December 2006 |
|---|---|---|
| Raw materials and manufacturing supplies | 1 596 | 1 283 |
| Work in progress | 12 253 | 11 260 |
| Finished goods and parts accounted for at lower of cost and net realizable value | 1 217 | 1 224 |
| Advance payments to suppliers | 3 840 | 3 125 |
| Total | 18 906 | 16 892 |

The increase in work in progress of €993 million was mainly driven by the Airbus A380 programme, the A400M programme and the ramp-up at Euro-copter partly compensated by the MBDA quotation change from 50 per cent to 37.5 per cent in the amount of €(318) million. The increase of advance payments provided to suppliers mainly reflects activities in Airbus for supplier funding and in Defence of Euro-fighter Series Production Equipment.

The finished goods and parts for resale before write-down to net realizable value amunt to €1 565 million in 2007 (2006: €1 559 million) and work in progress before write-down to net realizable value amounts to €13 632 million (2006: €12 186 million). Write-downs for finished goods and services are recorded when it becomes probable that total estimated contract costs will exceed total contract revenues. The impairment charges in 2007 and 2006 for work in progress mainly relate to the A380 programme.

In their Financial Statements of 2011 (p. 20) we find information on construction contracts and their valuation among the valuation rules applied for revenue recognition. With regard to construction contracts EADS mentions:

For construction contracts, when the outcome can be estimated reliably, revenues are recognized by reference to POC of the contract activity by applying the estimate at completion method. The stage of completion of a contract may be determined by a variety of ways. Depending on the nature of the contract, revenue is recognized as contractually agreed technical milestones are reached, as units are delivered or as the work progresses. Whenever the outcome of a construction contract cannot be estimated reliably – for example, during the early stages of a contract or when this outcome can no longer be estimated reliably during the course of a contract's completion – all related contract costs that are incurred are immediately expensed and revenues are recognized only to the extent of those costs being recoverable ('early stage method of accounting'). In such specific situations, as soon as the outcome can (again) be estimated reliably, revenue is from that point in time onwards accounted for according to the estimate at completion method, without restating the revenues previously recorded under the early state method of accounting. Changes in profit rates are reflected in current earnings as identified. Contracts are reviewed regularly and in case of probable losses, loss-at-completion provisions is recorded. These loss-at-completion provisions in connection with construction contracts are not discounted.

# FUTURE FOR IAS 11

We mentioned at the start of this chapter that a new standard on revenue recognition, which affects the accounting for construction contracts, would probably be approved in the Autumn of 2013. One of the major changes in the accounting for construction contracts is the fact that revenue should only be recognized when the performance obligation specified in the contract with the customer is satisfied. So satisfaction of the performance obligation becomes the key driver to recognize profits from revenues from contracts with customers. Thus, for some long-term contracts where the completed contract is deemed the main deliverable, no profit would be recognized before that point under the new standard. We outline below the main elements which relate to construction contracts included in the exposure draft on 'Revenue from contracts with customers' (re-ssued ED, November 2011).

In comparison to IAS 11 an important element in the accounting for these construction contracts, is the identification of the performance obligation included in the contract and the determination of the satisfaction of this performance obligation. A performance obligation is defined as a promise in a contract with a customer to transfer a good or service to the customer. If an entity promises to transfer more than one good or service, the entity would account for each promised good or service as a separate performance obligation only if it is distinct. The revenue earned on the contract is determined by the transaction price received from the customer. However revenue is only recognized when the performance obligation determined in the contract is satisfied. With regard to this satisfaction criteria, the IASB distinguishes between satisfaction at a point in time and the satisfaction of performance over time. The basis for recognition is the satisfaction of a performance obligation by transferring a promised good or service to a customer. If an entity does not satisfy a performance obligation over time, the performance obligation is satisfied at a point in time. An entity transfers control of a good or service over time and, hence, satisfies a performance obligation and recognizes revenue over time if at least one of the following two criteria is met:

(a) the entity's performance creates or enhances an asset (for example work in progress) that the customer controls as the asset is created or enhanced; or

(b) the entity's performance does not create an asset with an alternative use to the entity and at least one of the following criteria is met:

   (i) the customer simultaneously receives and consumes the benefits of the entity's performance as the entity performs;

   (ii) another entity would not need to substantially re-perform the work the entity has completed to date if that other entity were to fulfil the remaining obligation to the customer; or

   (iii) the entity has a right to payment for performance completed to date and it expects to fulfil the contract as promised.

The new IAS prescribes criteria to measure the progress towards complete satisfaction of a performance obligation. The ED stipulates that for each separate performance obligation that an entity satisfies over time, the entity shall recognize revenue over time by measuring the progress towards complete satisfaction of that performance obligation. When a performance obligation is satisfied, an entity shall recognize as revenue the amount of the transaction price allocated to that performance obligation. Measurement of progress towards complete satisfaction can be done based on output measures (based on the value to the customers of the goods and services transferred) or on input measures (based on the entity's efforts or inputs to satisfy a performance obligation).

The exact impact of the new recognition principle is at this time difficult to judge.

## SUMMARY

This chapter has defined inventories and construction contracts and identified the accounting requirements for them in accordance with IAS 2 and IAS
11. Valuation of inventories using the unit cost, FIFO, LIFO, weighted average and base inventory are all possible, but all lead to a different profit figure and asset figure. Remember, the improved IAS 2 has now eliminated
the use of LIFO.

It should be clear to you that valuation of inventories is by no means a
straightforward task and it requires management to make several
judgements.

## EXERCISES

*Suggested answers to exercises marked ✓ are to be found on our dedicated CourseMate platform
for students.*

*Suggested answers to the remaining exercises are to be found on the Instructor online support
resources.*

1   P Forte commences business on 1 January buying and selling pianos. He sells two standard
    types, upright and grand, and his transactions for the year are given in the table below.

|  | Upright[1] | | Grand | |
|---|---|---|---|---|
|  | Buy | Sell | Buy | Sell |
| 1 January | 4 at €400 |  | 2 at €600 |  |
| 31 March |  | 1 at €600 |  |  |
| 30 April | 1 at €350 |  | 1 at €700 |  |
| 30 June |  | 1 at €600 |  | 1 at €1 000 |
| 31 July | 2 at €300 |  | 1 at €800 |  |
| 30 September |  | 3 at €500 |  | 2 at €1 100 |
| 30 November | 1 at €250 |  | 1 at €900 |  |

You observe that the cost to P Forte of the pianos is changed on 1 April, 1 July and 1 October
and will not change again until 1 January following.

**Required:**

(a) Prepare a statement showing gross profit and closing inventory valuation separately for
    each type of piano, under each of the following assumptions:

    (i)   FIFO

    (ii)  LIFO

    (iii) weighted average

    (iv)  RC.

(b) At a time of rising prices (i.e. using the grand pianos as an example), comment on the use-
    fulness of each of the methods.

2   Using any information you wish from Exercise 1, illustrate and discuss the effects on the statement of comprehensive income and statement of financial position from using the different cost assumptions available to value closing inventory.

3   Critically appraise the different cost assumptions underlying the valuation of closing inventory.

4   Discuss the solution offered by IAS 2 to the valuation of inventories.

5   IAS 11 uses the percentage-of-completion method for the valuation of construction contracts. Discuss the advantages and disadvantages of this method and appraise whether it results in useful information for users.

✓ 6   Explain the rationale behind the prohibition of the completed-contract method for valuing construction contracts by IAS 11 given that US GAAP permits this option under certain circumstances.

7   The inventory of Base at 30 September 200X was valued at cost €28.5 million. This included €4.5 million of slow-moving stock that Base had been trying to sell to another retailer. The best price Base has been offered for this slow moving stock is €2 million. Identify how Base should record its inventory in its year-end accounts at 30 September 200X.

8   Gear Software, a public limited company, develops and sells computer games software. The revenue of Gear Software for the year ended 31 May 2003 is $5 million, the statement of financial position total is $4 million, and it has 40 employees. There are several elements in the financial statements for the year ended 31 May 2003 on which the directors of Gear require advice.

   (i)   Gear has two cost centres relating to the development and sale of the computer games. The indirect overhead costs attributable to the two cost centres were allocated in the year to 31 May 20X2 in the ratio 60:40 respectively. Also, in that financial year the direct labour costs and attributable overhead costs incurred on the development of original games software were carried forward as work-in-progress and included with the statement of financial position total for inventory of computer games. Inventory of computer games includes directly attributable overheads. In the year to 31 May 20X3, Gear has allocated indirect overhead costs in the ratio 50:50 to the two cost centres and has written the direct labour and overhead costs incurred on the development of the games off to the statement of comprehensive income. Gear has stated that it cannot quantify the effect of this write-off on the current year's statement of comprehensive income. Further, it proposes to show the overhead costs relating to the sale of computer games within distribution costs. In prior years these costs were shown in cost of sales.

   (ii)   In prior years, Gear has charged interest incurred on the construction of computer hardware as part of cost of sales. It now proposes to capitalize such interest and to change the method of depreciation from the straight line method over four years to the reducing balance method at 30 per cent per year. Depreciation will now be charged as cost of sales rather than administrative expenses as in previous years. Gear currently recognizes revenue on contracts in proportion to the progression and activity on the contract. The normal accounting practice within the industrial sector is to recognize revenue when the product is shipped to customers. The effect of any change in accounting policy to bring the company in line with accounting practice in the industrial sector would be to increase revenue for the year by $500 000.

   The directors have requested advice on the changes in accounting practice for inventories and tangible non-current assets that they have proposed.

(ACCA – June 2003)

**9** At 30 September 20X3, Bowtock had included in its draft statement of financial position inventory $250 000 valued at cost. Up to 5 November 20X3, Bowtock had sold $100 000 of this inventory for $150 000. On this date, new government legislation (enacted after the year-end) came into force which meant that the unsold inventory could no longer be marketed and was worthless.

Bowtock is part way through the construction of a housing development. It has prepared its financial statements to 30 September 20X3 in accordance with IAS 11, *Construction Contracts*, and included a proportionate amount of the total estimated profit on this contract. The same legislation, referred to above (in force from 5 November 20X3), now requires modifications to the way the houses within this development have to be built. The cost of these modifications will be $500 000 and will reduce the estimated total profit on the contract by that amount, although the contract is still expected to be profitable.

**Required:**
Assuming the amounts are material, state how the information above should be reflected in the financial statements of Bowtock for the year ended 30 September 20X3.

(ACCA – December 2003)

**10** (i) Linnet is a large public listed company involved in the construction industry. Accounting standards normally require construction contracts to be accounted for using the percentage-(stage)-of-completion basis. However, under certain circumstances they should be accounted for using the completed-contracts basis.

**Required:**
Discuss the principles that underlie each of the two methods and describe the circumstances in which their use is appropriate.

(ii) Linnet is part way through a contract to build a new football stadium at a contracted price of $300 million. Details of the progress of this contract at 1 April 20X3 are shown below:

|  | $ million |
|---|---|
| Cumulative sales revenue invoiced | 150 |
| Cumulative cost of sales to date | 112 |
| Profit to date | 38 |

The following information has been extracted from the accounting records at 31 March 20X4:

|  | $ million |
|---|---|
| Total progress payment received for work certified at 29 February 20X4 | 180 |
| Total costs incurred to date (excluding rectification costs below) | 195 |
| Rectification costs | 17 |

Linnet has received progress payments of 90 per cent of the work certified at 29 February 20X4. Linnet's surveyor has estimated the sales value of the further work completed during March 20X4 as $20 million.

At 31 March 20X4, the estimated remaining costs to complete the contract were $45 million. The rectification costs are the costs incurred in widening access roads to the stadium. This was the result of an error by Linnet's architect when he made his initial drawings. Linnet calculates the percentage of completion of its contracts as the proportion of sales value earned to date compared to the contract price. All estimates can be taken as being reliable.

**Required:**
Prepare extracts of the financial statements for Linnet for the above contract for the year to 31 March 20X4.

(ACCA – June 2004)

11  HS, a contractor, signed a two-year fixed price contract on 31 March 20X8 for $300 000 to build a bridge. Total costs were originally estimated at $240 000. At 31 March 20X9, HS extracted the following figures from its financial records:

|  | $000 |
|---|---|
| Contract value | 300 |
| Costs incurred to date | 170 |
| Estimated costs to complete | 100 |
| Progress payments received | 130 |
| Value of work completed | 165 |

HS calculates the stage of completion of contracts using the value of work completed as a proportion of total contract value.

**Required:**
Calculate the following amounts for the contract that should be shown in HS's financial statements:
- Comprehensive Income statement:
  - Revenue recognized for the year ended 31 March 20X9
  - Profit recognized for the year ended 31 March 20X9.
- Statement of Financial Position:
  - Gross amount due to/from the customer at 31 March 20X9, stating whether it is an asset or liability.

(CIMA P7 – May 2009)

# ACCOUNTING FOR FINANCIAL INSTRUMENTS

## 18

**OBJECTIVES** After studying this chapter you should be able to:

- describe financial instruments

- identify the need to account for them

- outline the history of accounting for financial instruments

- define the scope of IFRS regarding financial instruments

- identify and explain the requirements of the IASB for financial instruments, both current and future

- critically appraise these current and future requirements

- be able to distinguish between financial liabilities and equity

- understand the issues of recognition and derecognition and of measuring different categories of financial assets and liabilities

- identify the need for hedge accounting and understand the basic techniques

- identify and appraise current international accounting requirements for insurance contracts – IFRS 4.

## INTRODUCTION

This chapter is of necessity somewhat complicated as we have to deal with the current Standard in respect of financial instruments, IAS 39, and its replacement, IFRS 9, which is being issued in a piecemeal fashion by the IASB. As at August 2013, IFRS 9 is not complete even though it has been issued, and it is not compulsory on entities until accounting periods beginning on or after 1 January 2015. We will therefore deal with both the current Standard and the future Standard in this chapter.

Financial instruments include such things as swaps (interest rate swaps, credit default swaps, foreign currency swaps) options, and forwards, but also more regular items such as bonds, receivables, loans and shares. They have become more complex over the past 20 years. This complexity has led to difficulties in recognizing, measuring, presenting and disclosure of such instruments in the financial statements of an entity. The real stumbling block in the entire debate on financial instruments is around the issue of whether the financial assets and liabilities involved should be valued at fair value.

This chapter also deals with IFRS 4, *Insurance Contracts*.

## SHORT HISTORY OF ACCOUNTING FOR FINANCIAL INSTRUMENTS

This section is a background section on the long history of regulating the accounting for financial instruments. Discussions still go on and reading this section might confuse you. Don't worry about that: the discussions and developments and changing viewpoints are even confusing to many professionals. You can easily skip this section without having difficulties understanding the rest of the chapter.

### The start of the IASC work

The IASC's work on financial instruments began in 1988 following an OECD symposium on the issue. Even at this early stage, the most difficult issue to deal with concerned the valuation of the instruments and whether this should be at fair value or not. The first Draft Statement of Principle (DSOP) was issued in March 1990 and this advocated fair value measurement for financial assets and liabilities held for trading but not for others. The DSOP was approved by the IASC in November 1990.

In June 1991, ED40 was issued. It advocated a benchmark treatment consisting of fair value for trading items and cost for others, and an allowed alternative of fair value for all items; a compromise solution.

The IASC published a revised ED in 1994 and, after consultation with standard-setting bodies in 20 countries, the IASC decided to split its work on financial instruments into two stages.

### IAS 32, IAS 39 and IFRS 7

The first stage was to deal with presentation and disclosure and the second with recognition and measurement. IAS 32 on presentation and disclosure was published in March 1995. IAS 39, *Financial Instruments: Recognition and Measurement*, was issued in 1998 and revised in 2000, and it was seen as an interim solution to accounting for financial instruments. Its publication was driven by the need for the IASB to have a set of core Standards available for approval by IOSCO by early 1999. The Standard was further revised as part of the improvement project and it is this extant version of 2004 that we consider in this chapter, together with its various amendments up to March 2009.

The complexity of the whole area was further demonstrated by the fact that the IASB decided there was a need to issue guidance on IAS 39 in the form of questions and answers. This guidance was included in a publication from the IASB entitled *Accounting for Financial Instruments – Standards, Interpretations and Implementation Guidance*. Several SICs and IFRICs have also been issued on financial instruments. IAS 32, *Financial Instruments: Disclosure and Presentation*, was, as IAS 39, revised in December 2003, but IAS 32 has now been split into two Standards:

- IAS 32, *Financial Instruments: Presentation*.
- IFRS 7, *Financial Instruments: Disclosures*.

Afterwards, several amendments were made, among which the publication in February 2008 of *Puttable Financial Instruments and Obligations Arising on Liquidation* and in December 2011 on *Offsetting Financial Assets and Financial Liabilities*.

In addition to these changes, there is also a very complex situation as regards the adoption of IAS 39 by the EU. In November 2004, the European Commission adopted what became known as a 'carve-out' version of IAS 39. This 'carve-out' version prohibited the use of the fair value option for financial liabilities. The amendment to IAS 39 in June 2005 has dealt with the fair value option, but there still remain some differences between the full IAS 39 and the 'carve-out' version endorsed by the EU.

# IFRS 9

The IASB has started a project to replace IAS 39 by IFRS 9. The objective of this project is to improve the decision usefulness of financial instruments for users by simplifying the classification and measurement requirements for financial instruments and thereby replace IAS 39.

The project consists of three main phases:

- Phase 1 – Classification and measurement: In November 2009, the IASB published the first part of IFRS 9, *Financial Instruments*, which deals with the classification and measurement of financial assets only. In October 2010, IFRS 9 was expanded to the measurement of financial liabilities and to derecognition of financial assets and liabilities. In December 2010 the IASB deferred the effective date of IFRS 9 to January 2015. An Exposure Draft (ED) on Limited Amendments of IFRS 9 on classification and measurement was published in November 2012.

- Phase 2 – Impairment methodology: An ED was issued in respect of this phase in November 2009 *Financial Instruments: Amortized Cost and Impairment*. A supplement was issued in January 2011 and a revised ED in March 2013 *Financial Instruments: Expected Credit Losses*.

- Phase 3 – Hedge accounting: An ED was issued on *Hedge Accounting* in December 2010. In September 2012 a 'Review draft' of the hedge accounting section of IFRS 9 was published. This Review draft does only discuss general hedge accounting. There is a separate split-off project on macro-hedge accounting.

It is clear from the above overview that it is a real struggle for the IASB to come to a full and definitive version of IFRS 9 as a replacement of IAS 39. Although the first part of IFRS 9 was already published in 2009, the EU has not endorsed this yet. It will probably wait until there is a new complete IFRS 9 before any decision on endorsement will be made.

## Current status

IAS 32 and IFRS 7 are applicable and will not be replaced by IFRS 9. IAS 39 in the old version of 2009 (with some minor amendments afterwards) is still applicable until financial statements 2014. IAS 39 in the current 2013 version does only contain requirements on impairment and hedge accounting, IFRS 9 includes requirements on measurement of assets and liabilities and on derecognition. When IFRS 9 has been further developed, IAS 39 will be removed. An entity applying IFRS may until 2015 choose between the old IAS 39 and the combination of IFRS 9 and the remaining parts of IAS 39. However, all EU entities need to apply the old IAS 39 until the new standards have been endorsed.

In this chapter we will deal with the requirements of IAS 39 which are still current until January 2015 and then cover the requirements of IFRS 9 as it stands at the time of writing. We would advise you to access the IASB's website to ensure you are up-to-date regarding financial instruments, as this is a fast moving topic.

## PROBLEMS IDENTIFIED

### Information available

The growth in the variety of financial instruments available over the past 20 years had given rise to a lack of understanding by users of financial statements of the significance of such instruments on an entity's financial performance, position and cash flows. Many of the instruments were traditionally not recognized in the statement of financial position, and the user was unable to assess the effect of these unless there was adequate presentation and disclosure. In addition, an entity, by the use of financial instruments, can significantly change its financial risk profile resulting in excessive gains or losses depending on whether prices of such instruments move in favour of or against the entity.

### Measurement practice

Measuring financial instruments at historical cost does not always provide the most relevant or consistent information for users. Throughout the programme of work on financial instruments, the view grew that using fair values for such assets and liabilities could provide more relevant information.

However, the use of fair values then raises the question of where the unrealized gain or loss should be reported – in profit or loss or in other comprehensive income (as a change in equity). Historically, the principal driver in the recognition of gains was 'realization', but this may have less relevance in a situation where entities are trading underlying risks. Careful consideration would need to be given to information derived by measuring financial instruments at fair value and recognizing that gain or loss in profit or loss as compared with valuation at historical cost.

## ILLUSTRATION

Entity A enters into an interest swap with B. The notional amount of the swap is €1m, but this amount is not exchanged. A pays interest to B at three-month intervals at 7 per cent, and B pays interest to A at London Interbank Offered Rate (LIBOR). If LIBOR moves above 7 per cent then A gains on the deal, otherwise he loses. On a historical cost basis, no asset or liability would be recorded by either party and interest payments would be shown in profit or loss. It could be the case that at a year-end, if LIBOR has moved to 10 per cent, the fair value of this interest swap is €50 000. If fair value accounting is used then the interest rate swap would be recorded at €50 000 and presumably this gain would be shown in profit or loss. In six months' time the fair value of this swap could have dropped to €10 000 or become negative (when LIBOR is below 7 per cent), and a gain for A is an equivalent loss for B. Which method of accounting for the swap would provide relevant and reliable information to the user? We leave this question for you to debate.

## WHAT IS A FINANCIAL INSTRUMENT?

We start with presenting you with the definitions as applied by the IASB, although it is difficult to understand them immediately when reading. IAS 32 and IAS 39 define a financial instrument as 'a contract that gives rise to a financial asset of one entity and a financial liability or equity instrument of another entity'. A financial asset is

… any asset that is:

**(a)** cash

**(b)** an equity instrument of another entity

**(c)** a contractual right:

   **(i)** to receive cash or another financial asset from another entity;

   **(ii)** to exchange financial instruments or financial liabilities with another entity under conditions that are potentially favourable to the entity.

**(d)** a contract that will or may be settled in the entity's own equity instruments and is:

   **(i)** a non-derivative for which the entity is or may be obliged to receive a variable number of the entity's own equity instruments; or

   **(ii)** a derivative that will or may be settled other than by the exchange of a fixed amount of cash or another financial asset for a fixed number of the entity's own equity instruments. For this purpose the entity's own equity instruments do not include instruments that are themselves contracts for the future receipt or delivery of the equity's own equity instruments.

A financial liability is any liability that is:

**(a)** a contractual obligation:

   **(i)** to deliver cash or another financial asset to another enterprise entity; or

   **(ii)** to exchange financial instruments assets or financial liabilities with another enterprise entity under conditions that are potentially unfavourable to the entity.

**(b)** a contract that will or may be settled in the entity's own equity instruments and is:

   **(i)** a non-derivative for which the entity is or may be obliged to deliver a variable number of the entity's own equity instruments; or

**(ii)** a derivative that will or may be settled other than by the exchange of a fixed amount of cash or another financial asset for a fixed number of the entity's own equity instruments. For this purpose the entity's own equity instruments do not include puttable financial instruments that are classified as equity instruments or instruments that are themselves contracts for the future receipt or delivery of the entity's own equity instruments.

Some elements of the financial asset and liability definition are rather clear, others not. This is especially so for (d) in the financial asset definition and (b) in the financial liability definition. We will defer discussion of these elements to the section of equity versus liability below.

From these definitions we can assert that a financial instrument is the contract, not the asset or liability, and thus we must be clear what is meant by contract, contractual right and obligation. IAS 32 states that 'contract' and 'contractual' refer to an agreement between two or more parties that has clear economic consequences that the parties have little, if any, chance of avoiding, because generally the agreement is enforceable in law. Contracts need not, however, be in writing. Now try the following activity.

## ACTIVITY 18.1

Identify which of the following are financial instruments.

- cash
- gold bullion
- debtors
- creditors
- loans
- bank deposits
- debentures
- a promissory note payable in government bonds
- ordinary shares
- preference shares
- plant and equipment previously bought and paid for by the entity
- pre-payments for goods or services.

### Activity feedback

- *Cash: clearly not a financial instrument, but cash is a financial asset.*
- *Gold bullion: this is a commodity or physical asset as there is no contractual right to receive cash or other financial asset.*
- *Debtors: these are financial assets but not financial instruments as they cannot be described as a contract although they quite possibly arose from a contract.*
- *Creditors; they are, likewise, a financial liability.*
- *Loans: these are financial assets of one entity and liabilities of another but it is debatable whether they are actually a financial instrument as this requires a contract. Presumably there is a contract behind these assets and liabilities and it should be this that is the financial instrument.*
- *Bank deposits: same as for loans.*
- *Debentures: same as for loans.*
- *A promissory note payable in government bonds: this is a financial instrument as the note is the contract that gives the holder the contractual right to receive and the issuer the contractual obligation to deliver government bonds. The bonds themselves are financial assets of one entity and liabilities of another.*
- *Ordinary shares; they can also be regarded as financial instruments if we regard them as a contract that will ultimately result in the entity paying cash to the holder. The Standard defines an equity instrument as any contract that evidences a residual interest in the assets of an entity after deducting all of its liabilities.*
- *Preference shares: same as for ordinary shares.*

*(Continued)*

## ACTIVITY 18.1 *(Continued)*

- Plant and equipment previously bought and paid for by the entity: clearly no financial instruments as there is no contract to settle anything in cash or another financial instrument.

- Pre-payments for goods or services: again, clearly no financial instruments.

This activity is somewhat tortuous given that the Standard uses the terms financial instrument, financial asset and financial liability rather loosely. The Standard tends to confuse the terms financial assets, financial instruments and financial liabilities.

Other examples of financial instruments given in the Standards are derivatives such as financial options, futures and forwards, interest rate swaps and currency swaps. The Standard gives further examples of contracts that do not give rise to financial instruments as they do not involve the transfer of a financial asset. For example, an operating lease for the use of a physical asset can be settled only by the receipt and delivery of services and is therefore not a financial instrument.

However, finance leases are financial instruments as they are contracts which result in a financial asset of one entity and a financial liability of another. (Finance leases are outside the scope of IAS 32 and IAS 39 as they are subject to IAS 17, *Leases*.)

A derivative is defined in the Standards as a financial instrument:

(a) whose value changes in response to the change in a specified interest rate, security price, commodity price, foreign exchange rate, index of prices or rates, a credit rating or credit index or similar variable (underlying)

(b) that requires no initial net investment or little initial net investment relative to other types of contracts that have a similar response to changes in market conditions, and

(c) that is settled at a future date.

Work through the following activity carefully.

## ACTIVITY 18.2

Are the following contracts financial instruments?

1 Entity A enters into both derivatives and an interest rate swap with B, that requires A to pay a fixed rate of 7 per cent and receive a variable amount based on three-month LIBOR. The notional amount of the swap is €1 million but this amount is not exchanged. A pays or receives a net cash amount each quarter based on the difference between 7 per cent and LIBOR.

2 A also enters into a pay fixed, receive variable interest swap with C. The notional amount is for €100m and fixed rate 10 per cent. The variable rate is based on three-month LIBOR. A prepays its fixed interest rate obligation as €100m × 10 per cent × 5 years discounted at market interest rates at inception of the swap.

3 A enters into a contract to pay €10m if X shares increase by 5 per cent or more during a six-month period and to receive €10m if the share price decreases by 5 per cent or more in the same period. No payment is made if the price swing is less than 5 per cent up or down.

*Activity feedback*

1 There is no initial net investment; settlement occurs at a future date and its value changes based on changes in LIBOR, the underlying variable. Therefore, this is a financial instrument as it meets the definition of a derivative.

2 This is also a derivative and therefore a financial instrument, even though there is an initial net investment. The payment of the fixed interest at

*(Continued)*

## ACTIVITY 18.2  (*Continued*)

inception will be regarded as 'little' compared with other similar contracts such as a variable rate bond where the notional amount of €100m would be paid over.

**3** There is no initial net investment, settlement occurs at a future date and the underlying variable is the share price. This is a derivative and therefore a financial instrument.

## DISTINCTION BETWEEN FINANCIAL LIABILITY AND EQUITY

At this stage we need to differentiate between a financial liability and equity. Remember the definition of financial liability. An instrument is a financial liability when:

**(a)** The instrument includes a contractual obligation to deliver cash or another financial asset/liability to another entity or to exchange financial assets or financial liabilities with another entity under conditions that are potentially unfavourable to the issuer.

**(b)** The instrument will or may be settled in the issuer's own equity instruments, where it is:

- a non-derivative that includes a contractual obligation for the issuer to deliver a variable number of its own equity instruments, or
- a derivative that will be settled other than by the issuer exchanging a fixed amount of cash or another financial asset for a fixed number of its own equity instruments. For this purpose the issuer's own equity instruments do not include instruments that have all the features of puttable instruments or instruments that are contracts for the future receipt or delivery of the issuer's own equity instruments.

We will now further discuss (b). The basic idea is that a 'payment' in the form of the entity's own shares (equity instruments) does not result in a liability. However, when the number of shares to be used as payment is variable, this reduces the risk for the holder of the instrument and for that reason the instrument is considered a financial liability.

## ILLUSTRATION

A mandatory convertible bond is issued for an amount of €100 000, with a maturity of one year. Ten per cent interest is accrued to the principal (and not paid). The accrued amount at maturity is €110 000. At the time of issue, the fair value of one share is €1000. At the time of conversion the share price has dropped to €880.

**(1)** At maturity, the bondholder is required to convert the bond into a fixed number of shares. The bond will be converted into 100 shares.

**(2)** At maturity, the bondholder is required to convert the bond into a variable number of shares. The bond will be converted in that number of shares that equals the accrued amount.

In case (1) the bond is classified as equity. In fact, the bondholder, although formally bondholder, already runs the risk as a shareholder. At maturity, the bond with an accrued amount of €110 000 is converted into 100 shares with a total fair value of €88 000.

In case (2) the bond is classified as a liability. At maturity, the bond is converted into 125 shares (110 000/880): the fair value before and after conversion remain the same.

Note that any variability in the number of shares results in the financial instrument being classified as a liability, even if the variability is small and would result in a significant degree of shareholder risk. To avoid interpretation issues the IASB has chosen a rigid distinction.

The other issue in the definition of a financial liability is that of puttable financial instruments. A puttable instrument is a financial instrument that gives the holder the right to put the instrument back to the issuer for cash or another financial asset, or is automatically put back to the issuer on the occurrence of an uncertain future event or the death or retirement of the instrument holder. An example of a puttable instrument is a redeemable, at the option of the holder, share. Based on the general definition, a puttable financial instrument is a financial liability, as the entity may be required to redeem the financial instrument without having the discretion to avoid payment. However, as an exception to the basic principles, puttable a financial instrument that has all the following features can be classed as equity:

- It entitles the holder to a pro-rata share of the entity's net assets in the event of liquidation.
- It is subordinate to all other classes of instruments, i.e. it has no priority under liquidation before others and it does not need to be converted into another instrument before it is subordinate.
- In the subordinate class, all instruments have identical features.
- It does not include an obligation to deliver cash or another financial asset except for the redemption.
- Its cash flows are based substantially on profit or loss attained.

## Compound financial instruments

Some financial instruments can contain both an equity element and a liability element. For example, a bond convertible by the holder into a fixed number of shares of the entity is a compound financial instrument. This is because the instrument comprises a liability to deliver cash or another financial asset on redemption, and a call option granting the holder the right to convert it into a fixed number of shares. IAS 32 requires us to account for the substance of this transaction, both a liability and an equity element, not the legal form. The substance is basically that of issuing a debt instrument with an early settlement provision and warrants to purchase ordinary shares.

IAS 39 tells us how to measure the component parts and we will deal with this in the measurement section.

Now complete Activity 18.3.

### ACTIVITY 18.3

Identify whether the following financial instruments should be classified by the issuer as a liability (debt) or equity in accordance with IFRS.

- A has issued a perpetual preference share redeemable only at A's option. Dividend of 8 per cent is paid annually provided there are sufficient distributable profits.
- B has issued a perpetual convertible bond. Interest of 10 per cent on the bond is paid if a dividend is paid on the ordinary shares of B.

- C issues a perpetual preference share carrying a fixed dividend rate of 5 per cent. If the dividend is deferred then the dividend is accumulated for future payout together with additional interest at 30 per cent.
- D issues specific preference shares to its fund managers. They carry the right to an annual payment based on 25 per cent of realized gains on the fund recorded in the period by D.

*(Continued)*

## ACTIVITY 18.3    (Continued)

### Activity feedback

- A. This is a liability *as management does not have discretion over payment of dividend. The critical feature of a liability, remember, is the existence of an obligation to pay cash or to exchange another instrument under conditions that are potentially unfavourable to the issuer.*

- B. This should be included in equity *as cash is paid over only if a dividend is paid to ordinary shareholders and thus the dividend decision is discretionary.*

- C. *Given the interest obligation on the non-payment of dividend, this must be treated as a liability.*

- D. *Again this is a liability as management have no discretion over the calculation of timing of the amount to be paid.*

(adapted from Accountancy, April 2003, p. 89)

## RECOGNITION AND DERECOGNITION OF FINANCIAL INSTRUMENTS

### Initial recognition

According to the Standard, an entity should only recognize a financial asset or liability on its statement of financial position when it becomes a party to the contractual provisions of the instrument. The Standard then deals with something called 'regular way contracts'.

*Regular way contracts* are those for the purchase or sale of financial assets that require delivery of the assets within the timeframe generally established by regulation or convention in the market concerned. For these contracts, recognition is permitted at either trade date or settlement date but the policy chosen must be applied consistently.

Settlement date accounting, when applied, does, however, require the entity to recognize any change in the fair value of the asset that occurs between the trade and settlement date. This is a somewhat strange requirement given that the financial asset itself is not yet recognized. Regular way contracts actually meet the definition of a derivative as they are forward contracts, but they are not recognized as derivatives because of the short duration of the commitment.

An example of a regular way contract is where a bank makes a loan commitment at a specified rate of interest and then takes a commitment period to enable it to complete its underwriting and to provide time for the borrower to execute the transaction that is the subject of the loan. This commitment period would have to be of a normal duration for such an agreement. The loan, once recognized at either trade date or settlement date, would be carried at amortized cost (see below).

Now complete the activity below.

## ACTIVITY 18.4

On 29 December 20X1 an entity commits to buy a financial asset for €1000 which is its fair value on commitment date (trade date). On 31.12.X1 and 4.1.X2, the settlement date, the fair value of the asset is €1002 and €1003 respectively.

Show the amounts to be recorded for the asset at 29.12.X1, 31.12.X1 and 4.1.X2 using both settlement and trade date accounting and identify where any change in value will be recognized. Assume that the asset is measured at fair value and that all changes in fair value are

(Continued)

## ACTIVITY 18.4 (Continued)

included in profit or loss. Liabilities are measured at (amortized) cost.

### Activity feedback

Table 18.1 explains initial recognition at trade date and Table 18.2 at settlement date.

tled this transaction so the liability still remains and is measured at amortized cost.

3. Settlement date is now reached so the liability is removed, but note that other assets (perhaps cash) would be reduced. There is an additional gain of 1 in profit or loss.

| TABLE 18.1   Trade date accounting | |
|---|---:|
| **Date of balance** | |
| 29.12.X1 (note 1) | |
| Financial asset | 1 000 |
| Liability | (1 000) |
| 31.12.X1 (note 2) | |
| Financial asset | 1 002 |
| Liability | (1 000) |
| P&L | (2) |
| 4.01.X2 (note 3) | |
| Financial asset | 1 003 |
| Liability | |
| P&L | (1) |

| TABLE 18.2   Settlement date accounting | |
|---|---:|
| **Date of balance** | |
| 29.12.X1 | – |
| 31.12.X1 (note 4) | |
| Financial asset | 2 |
| Liability | |
| P&L | (2) |
| 4.01.X2 | |
| Financial asset | 1003 |
| Liability | |
| P&L | (1) |

### Notes:

1. At this stage in the recognition we have both a financial asset that we have purchased and the liability outstanding to pay for this asset.

2. The financial asset is measured at fair value and the change is included in profit and loss. We still haven't set-

4. We need to recognize the change in fair value that has occurred between trade and settlement date even though the full financial asset is not yet recognized.

## Offsetting

A financial asset and a financial liability recognized in the statement of financial position shall be offset, with the net amount presented, when and only when an entity has a legally enforceable right to offset and intends to settle on a net basis or to realize the asset and settle the liability simultaneously. When an entity has the right to receive or pay a single net amount and intends to do so, it has, in effect, only one single financial asset or financial liability. Offsetting is different from derecognition (discussed below) and can never give rise to a recognition of a gain or loss.

## Derecognition

According to IAS 38, para. 17, an entity shall derecognize (remove) a financial asset from the statement of financial position when and only when:

(a) the contractual rights to the cash flows from the financial assets expires; or

(b) it transfers the financial asset as set out in paragraphs 18 and 19 and the transfer qualifies for derecognition in accordance with paragraph 20.

Paras 18 and 19 state that an entity transfers a financial asset if, and only if, it either:

(a) transfers the contractual rights to receive the cash flows of the financial asset; or

(b) retains the contractual rights to receive the cash flows of the financial asset, but assumes a contractual obligation to pay the cash flows to one or more recipients in an arrangement that meets certain conditions: the transferor should become a 'pass-through entity' after the transfer.

A transfer of an asset should qualify for derecognition in accordance with para. 20. Paragraph 20 states that the entity shall evaluate the extent to which it retains the risks and rewards of ownership of the financial asset. In this case:

(a) if the entity transfers substantially all the risks and rewards of ownership of the financial asset, the entity shall derecognize the financial asset and recognize separately as assets or liabilities any rights and obligations created or retained in the transfer;

(b) if the entity retains substantially all the risks and rewards of ownership of the financial asset, the entity shall continue to recognize the financial asset;

(c) if the entity neither transfers nor retains substantially all the risks and rewards of ownership of the financial asset, the entity shall determine whether it has retained control of the financial asset. In this case:

(i) if the entity has not retained control, it shall derecognize the financial asset and recognize separately as assets or liabilities any rights and obligations created or retained in the transfer,

(ii) if the entity has retained control, it shall continue to recognize the financial asset to the extent of its continuing involvement in the financial asset (see paragraph 30).

In summary: the first criterion in judging whether a transfer of an asset results in derecognition is the transfer of substantially all risks and rewards, and when this criterion does not lead to a clear conclusion, the transfer of control is the second criterion.

This area is again complex given that derecognition of a portion of the asset is permitted and there is the possibility of repurchase options or other derivatives being involved. If you work through the following activity you will understand derecognition more clearly.

## ACTIVITY 18.5

In each of the following cases, state (with reasons) whether the financial asset should be derecognized in the books of entity A.

1 A transfers a loan it holds to a bank but stipulates that the bank cannot sell or pledge the loan. (This is to protect the customer to whom the loan was originally made.)

2 A transfers a financial asset to B on terms that stipulate that A can repurchase the asset before the expiry of a specific period at market value at the date of repurchase.

3 A transfers a financial asset to B on terms that stipulate that A must repurchase the asset before the expiry of a specific period and that repurchase is at the value at transfer date plus interest at a fixed rate on that value.

4 A transfers a financial asset to B on terms that stipulate that A can repurchase the asset before the expiry of a specific period and that repurchase is at the value at transfer date plus interest at a fixed rate on that value.

(Continued)

## ACTIVITY 18.5    (Continued)

**5** A transfers a financial asset to B on terms that stipulate that B has a put option and can oblige A to repurchase the asset before the expiry of a specific period and that repurchase is at the value at transfer date plus interest at a fixed rate on that value.

**6** A sells short-term receivables to B and provides a guarantee with that sale to pay for any credit losses that may be incurred on the receivables as a result of the failure of the debtor to pay when due.

### Activity feedback

*1* *Even though the transferee, the bank, cannot sell or pledge the loan, it does receive all other benefits from holding the loan and therefore A would derecognize this financial asset. All significant risks and rewards have been transferred.*

*2* *In this case, the risks and rewards associated with the asset have been transferred to B as he will bear the loss if the market value falls and the gain if it increases. A just has an option to repurchase, not an obligation to do so. The asset will be*

*derecognized by A and recognized when it is repurchased.*

*3* *A does not transfer all significant risks and rewards, as it must repurchase the asset and B just has a lender's return. The significant risks and rewards are retained by A. There is no derecognition.*

*4* *In this case not all significant risks and rewards have been retained, neither have they all been transferred (A still holds the upward risks and rewards, but not the downward risks and rewards). Because A has a repurchase option, A still controls the asset and may therefore not derecognize it.*

*5* *Now B has a put option and as a result A has the downward risks and rewards and not the upward risks and rewards. As B now controls the asset, A would derecognize it, but would provide for the repurchase obligation at fair value.*

*6* *A does not derecognizes these receivables. It has retained all significant risks and rewards, as for short-term receivables credit risk is the only major risk.*

**Derecognition of a financial liability** Derecognition of a financial liability is relatively straightforward. We remove the financial liability from the statement of financial position when the obligation specified in the contract is discharged, cancelled or expires. Occasionally one financial liability will be exchanged for a similar one with the same lender, if the terms of the new agreement are substantially different from the old then the old is derecognized and the new recognized. The problem with this requirement from the Standard, para. 61, is that we need to set boundaries to 'substantially'. The 'Application Guidance' to the Standard at para. 62 states the following: The terms are substantially different if the discounted present value of the cash flows, under the new terms, including any fees paid net of any fees received, is at least 10 per cent different from the discounted present value of the remaining cash flows of the original debt instrument.

**Derecognition accounting treatment** The accounting treatment on derecognition requires the entity to recognize in the net profit or loss for the period the difference between the carrying amount of the asset, or portion, transferred to another party and the sum of the proceeds received or receivable and any prior adjustment to reflect the fair value of that asset that had been reported in other comprehensive income.

Quite often asset derecognition is coupled with the recognition of a new financial asset or liability. When this occurs IAS 39 requires recognition of the new financial asset or liability at fair value and the recognition of a gain or loss on the transaction based on the difference between:

- the proceeds
- the carrying amount of the financial asset sold plus the fair value of any new financial liability assumed, minus the fair value of any new financial asset acquired and

plus or minus any adjustment that had been previously reported in equity to reflect the fair value of that asset.

## ACTIVITY 18.6

In example 6 in Activity 18.5 A is selling short-term receivables to B and providing a guarantee with that sale to pay for any credit losses that may be incurred on the receivables as a result of the failure of the debtor to pay when due. We have concluded that A does not derecognize these receivables as it has retained all significant risks and rewards. Assume that the amount of receivables transferred from A to B is €40 000. The carrying amount of the receivables in the balance sheet of A, taking into account credit risk, is €39 000. At the moment of transfer B pays €34 600, taking into account a fee of €400. All receivables will still be paid to A and A transfers the payments to B. The amount receivables paid is €38 500. Present the journal entries of A at the time of transfer and of the payment of the receivables.

### Activity feedback

*At the time of transfer:*

Dt cash 34 600

Dt fee expense 400 (given the short-term, immediate expensing)

Cr. liability, 35 000

*Payment of receivables:*

Dt cash 38 500

Dt bad debt expenses 500

Cr. Receivables 39 000

+

Dt liability 35 000

Cr. cash 35 000

*The short-term receivables of A would in itself not be recognized by B. B accounts for the cash transfer as a loan receivable that is being redeemed by the cash transfers from A to B. A will of course pay no more than €35 000 to B. The remaining receipts of receivables of €3 500 will be kept by A.*

## CATEGORIES OF FINANCIAL ASSETS AND LIABILITIES

IAS 39 categorizes financial assets in four groups:

- financial assets at fair value through profit or loss
- held-to-maturity investments
- loans and receivables
- available for sale financial assets.

*Financial assets at fair value through profit or loss* include held for trading assets and assets that have been designated in this category upon initial recognition. The asset is held for trading if, regardless of why it was acquired, it is part of a portfolio for which there is evidence of short-term profit taking or was initially acquired for purposes of generating a profit through short-term fluctuations in price or dealer's margins. Derivatives are also held for trading assets, unless they are used for hedging. Financial assets may also be designated in this category upon initial recognition, but only when doing so results in more relevant information (by eliminating accounting mismatches or when the performance of the financial asset is evaluated on a fair value basis). This fair value option is open for any financial asset.

*Held-to-maturity investments* are financial assets with fixed or determinable payments and fixed maturity that an entity has the positive intent and ability to hold to maturity.

*Loans and receivables* originated by the entity are financial assets created by the entity by providing money, goods or services directly to a debtor.

*Available for sale financial assets* is the residual category: assets that are not loans and receivables originated by the entity, held-to-maturity or financial assets at fair value through profit or loss.

There are two groups of financial liabilities:

- Financial liabilities at fair value through profit or loss (under the same conditions as the equivalent asset category)

- Other financial liabilities.

These definitions are very important as the category of financial asset or liability determines the measurement, discussed in the next section.

The following activity will aid your understanding of the issues so far.

## ACTIVITY 18.7

Which categories of financial asset can the following fit into?

1 An investment in a bond acquired with the intent to hold for a long period irrespective of short-term fluctuations in price.

2 A loan issued to a related party with a redeemable on demand option of the entity.

3 Shares held as a temporary investment of cash.

### Activity feedback

1 Held for maturity is the most obvious category. Financial asset at fair value through profit or loss and Available for sale financial assets are possible alternatives.

2 Loans and receivables is the only possible category.

3 If the shares will be held for short-term profit making, the category is Held for trading. However, this does seem to be the case. Then the category is Available for sale.

## MEASUREMENT OF FINANCIAL INSTRUMENTS

At initial recognition, all financial assets and financial liabilities are measured at fair value. Subsequent measurement depends upon the categorization discussed above.

The category 'financial assets at fair value through profit or loss' indicates already the measurement principle: the assets are measured at fair value and remeasurements are recognized in profit or loss. This is also true for financial liabilities at fair value through profit or loss.

Available for sale financial assets are also measured at fair value, but remeasurements are recognized outside profit or loss in other comprehensive income. Upon realization or earlier impairment, the cumulative amounts of remeasurements are recycled to profit or loss. Only when the fair value of the asset cannot be reliably measured, it is measured at cost.

Held-to-maturity investments, loans and receivables, and other financial liabilities are measured at amortized cost using the effective interest method.

IAS 39, *Financial Instruments: Recognition and Measurement*, defines amortized costs and the effective interest method.

*Amortized cost* is the amount at which the financial asset or liability is measured at initial recognition minus principal repayments, plus or minus the cumulative amortization of any difference between the initial amount and the maturity amount, and minus any write-down for impairment or uncollectability.

The *effective interest method* is a method of calculating amortization using the effective rate of a financial asset or liability. The effective interest rate is the rate that exactly discounts the expected stream of future cash payments through maturity or the next market-based repricing date to the current net carrying amount of the financial asset or liability. That computation should include all fees and points paid or received between parties to the contract. The effective interest rate is sometimes termed the level yield to maturity or to next repricing date and is the internal rate of return of the financial asset or liability for that period.

IFRS 13 defines fair value. The fair value concept is discussed in Chapter 8. Remember that fair value is the price that would be received to sell an asset or paid to transfer a liability in an orderly transaction between market participants at the measurement date. The fair value of a fixed-rate bond or loan is generally estimated as the sum of all future cash payments or receipts discounted using prevailing market rate of interest for a similar instrument of an issuer with a similar credit rating.

## ILLUSTRATION

On 1 January 2010, an entity acquires €100 000 par value 9 per cent bonds of Paper Co. priced to yield 10 per cent with a maturity date of 31.12.2014. The value of the bonds on acquisition is:

| | € |
|---|---|
| *Present value of interest payments* | |
| 9% of €100 000 for five years discounted at 10% = 9 000 × 3.79079 (annuity factor at 10% for 5 years): | 34 117 |
| Present value of maturity value = 100 000 × 0.62092 (annuity factor at 10% in 5 years): | 62 092 |
| Fair value (= Market value) | 96 209 |
| Discount from par value is therefore: | 3 791 |
| Par value | 100 000 |
| Thus, the bonds are initially recognized at: | € 96 209 |

Remember that financial instruments should be measured at fair value upon initial recognition.

Subsequent recognition of the bonds each year requires amortization using the effective interest rate method. Thus, we need to amortize the discount from par value over the five years recognizing this together with interest received as interest income.

Table 18.3 shows the carrying amount (amortized cost) (column E) of the instrument each year and the interest income (column A).

## TABLE 18.3  Amortization of bonds

| Year | Interest income CA × 10% A | Cash received B | Discount amortized C | Discount remaining D | Carrying amount (CA) E |
|---|---|---|---|---|---|
| 01.01.10 | | | | 3 791 | 96 209 |
| 31.12.10 | 9 621 | 9 000 | 621 | 3 170 | 96 830 |
| 31.12.11 | 9 683 | 9 000 | 683 | 2 487 | 97 513 |
| 31.12.12 | 9 751 | 9 000 | 751 | 1 736 | 98 264 |
| 31.12.13 | 9 826 | 9 000 | 826 | 910 | 99 090 |
| 31.12.14 | 9 910 | 9 000 | 910 | | 100 000 |

# Impairment

Financial assets measured at (amortized) cost (the categories held to maturity and loans and receivables, as well as the cost exemption in the available for sale category) have to be reviewed for impairment at each statement of financial position date. In determining whether an impairment exists, the IASB applies the 'incurred loss' model: there should be objective evidence of a credit loss event. New proposals (see below) will replace the incurred loss model by an expected loss model. Impairments need to be reversed when the impairment loss has decreased related objectively to an event subsequent to impairment.

For loans and receivables and held-to-maturity investments carried at amortized cost, the impairment loss is measured as the difference between the asset's carrying amount and the present value of future estimated future cash flows using the original effective interest rate as the discount rate. For available for sale assets exceptionally measured at cost the carrying amount should be compared to the present value of estimated future cash flows discounted at the current market rate of return for a similar asset. These impairments may not be reversed.

Also for available for sale financial assets measured at fair value, an impairment test should be made at each reporting date. This will not affect the measurement of the asset, which is at fair value and therefore 'automatically' impaired if applicable, but it may affect the amount included in other comprehensive income that should be recycled to profit or loss. There is an impairment in the situation of a significant decline (for example a fair value that is more than 30 per cent below cost) or prolonged decline (for example a fair value that is lower than cost for more than one year).

---

## ACTIVITY 18.8

Determine the amount of the impairment in each of the following cases:

1  An investment in a three-year bond with an amortized cost of €60 000 has a stated and effective interest rate of 7 per cent. After two years, the creditor of the bond faces serious default risk. The reporting entity expects that it will no longer receive the last year's interest on the bond and it expects to receive only 50 per cent of the principal. Current market interest rates are 10 per cent.

2  An investment in listed shares is an Available for sale financial asset. Acquisition price was €20 000, current market value €12 000. The fair value reserve is – €8000 (ignore taxes).

### Activity feedback

1  *The expected remaining cash flow at the end of year 3 is €30 000. The present value at the original effective tax rate (7 per cent) is €28 037. This will be the new carrying amount. The amount of the impairment is €31 963.*

2  *The amount of €8 000 would normally be considered a significant decline (a decline of more than 30 per cent). As a result, the full amount (€8000) should be recognized as impairment by transferring it to profit or loss (there will no effect on total comprehensive income as the loss will be compensated by an increase in other comprehensive income).*

---

# Compound financial instrument measurement

We previously identified a redeemable bond with an option to convert to a fixed number of ordinary shares as a compound financial instrument. We now need to deal with the measurement of its separate parts.

The Standard tells us to first determine the carrying amount of the liability component by measuring the fair value of a similar liability. The carrying amount of the equity element is then determined by deducting the fair value of the financial liability from the fair value of the compound instrument as a whole. Now complete the following activity.

## ACTIVITY 18.9

On 1 April 20X6, Beta entity issued at par an 8 per cent convertible loan note with a nominal value of £600 000. It is redeemable at par on 31 March 20Y0 or it may be converted into equity shares of Beta on the basis of 100 new shares for each £200 of loan note. An equivalent loan note without the conversion option would have carried an interest rate of 10 per cent. The present value of £1 receivable at the end of each year, based on discount rates of 8 per cent and 10 per cent, are:

| End of year | 8% | 10% |
|---|---|---|
| 1 | 0.9259 | 0.9091 |
| 2 | 0.8573 | 0.8264 |
| 3 | 0.7938 | 0.7513 |
| 4 | 0.7350 | 0.6830 |

Show how the loan note and the interest costs should be presented in the financial statements ended 31 March 20X7 in accordance with IASs.

### Activity feedback

IAS 32 (paras 28–32) requires a convertible loan note to be separated into its equity and liability component. The liability component is equal to the fair value of a similar liability that does not have an equity component. In this example we therefore need to determine the present value at a discount rate of 10 per cent (the comparator) of the future cash flows.

| End of year | Future cash flows | Discount rate 10% | FV |
|---|---|---|---|
| 1 | 48 000 (interest at 8%) | 0.9091 | 43 637 |
| 2 | 48 000 | 0.8264 | 39 667 |
| 3 | 48 000 | 0.7513 | 36 062 |
| 4 | 648 000 (capital + interest) | 0.6830 | 442 584 |
| Liability element | | | 561 950 |
| Equity element | | | 38 050 |
| | | | 600 000 |

Financial statements 31 March 20X7
Statement of financial position

| | |
|---|---|
| Equity – equity option | 38 050 |
| Non-current liabilities – 8% convertible loan note | 570 145 |
| (561 950 + 8 195; see below) | |

### Statement of comprehensive income

Interest costs convertible 10 per cent × 561 950 =
    56 195
Payment: 8 per cent × 600 000 = 48 000
The difference of 8195 is added to the loan note.

Note: the finance costs for the year ending 31 March 20X8 are 10 per cent × 570 145 = 57 014.5. Adding the differences between interest payments and interest costs to the carrying amount of the loan note will result in an amount of 600 000 at the end of year 4.

## HEDGE ACCOUNTING

Hedging is about offsetting the loss or potential loss on one item against the gain or potential gain on another. The loss or gain on the hedging arises from changes in fair values or cash flows. The rules in relation to hedging are complex because IAS 39 does not require all financial instruments to be carried at fair value. Remember, loans and receivables originated by the entity and held-to-maturity as investments are carried at amortized cost. Only financial assets and liabilities held for trading and available for sale, and derivatives, are carried at fair value. Thus, the Standard permits the use of hedging where derivatives are designated as the hedge instrument but only permits non-derivatives to hedge a foreign currency risk. The hedging relationship only qualifies for the special accounting arrangements (for which the term hedge accounting is used) in IAS 39 if (para. 88):

- formal documentation of the detail of the hedge relationship exists indicating the risk to be hedged, the hedged item (the item that is being hedged) and the hedge instrument (the item that is used for realizing the hedge; for all other risks than foreign currency risk this is a derivative)
- the hedge is expected to be highly effective
- in case of hedging a forecast transaction, the forecast transaction is highly probable
- the effectiveness of the hedge can be reliably measured.

Hedged relationships are of three types:

1  *Fair value hedge* where the change in fair value of the asset or liability is hedged.
2  *Cash flow hedge* where the variability to cash flows in the hedged item is hedged.
3  *Foreign currency hedge*, which we consider in Chapter 30.

### Fair value hedges

For fair value hedges the gain or loss from remeasuring the hedging instrument at fair value is recognized immediately in net profit or loss and the gain or loss on the hedged item is also recognized immediately in net profit or loss. Work carefully through the following activity.

### ACTIVITY 18.10

On 1 January 20X0, a fixed 6 per cent interest loan is acquired with a face value and an amortized cost of €100. The loan is measured at amortized cost. Fixed interest loans have a volatile fair value, depending upon the change in market interest rates. To hedge the largest part of the fair value of the loan, the entity acquires an interest rate swap with a nominal amount of €80 where the entity receives 6 per cent interest and pays a variable interest, for instance Euribor + 0.2 per cent. The interest received from the swap is used to pay the interest on the loan. As a result, the entity has swapped a fixed interest loan into a variable interest loan for 80 per cent of the nominal amount.

At 31 December 20X0, due to an increase in market interest rates, the fair value of the interest rate swap is −€4. The fair value is negative, because the entity pays more interest than it receives.

Show the accounting entries if:

1  Hedge accounting is not applied
2  Hedge accounting is applied.

*(Continued)*

## ACTIVITY 18.10 (Continued)

### Activity feedback

1 The derivative would be shown at the fair value of −€4. The change in fair value is included in profit or loss. Also the interest paid for the year (Euribor + 0.2 per cent) is included in profit or loss. The carrying amount of the loan remains unchanged (at amortized cost). Although the derivative is used for hedging fair value volatility, not applying hedge accounting does result in reported volatility (of both the loan and derivative taken together).

2 The derivative would be shown at the fair value of −€4. The change in fair value is again included in profit or loss, as well as the interest paid for the year (Euribor + 0.2 per cent). However, the carrying amount of the loan is now reduced by −€4 (the fair value change of 80 per cent of the loan) and is measured at €96. The reduction is included as a gain in profit or loss. There is no

reported volatility, both the loan and derivative taken together remain measured at €100. In profit or loss on balance only the interest paid is recognized. Note that the loan is not carried at fair value, but at amortized cost plus or minus the fair value changes of the derivative (that only relate to 80 per cent of the loan).

The accounting seems complicated. Why put all compensating value changes in profit and loss and not have a direct adjustment of the carrying amount of the loan? Or even carrying the derivative at cost (= 0)? One reason for this is that the general principle of measuring all derivatives at fair value and recognizing all fair value remeasurements of derivatives in profit or loss is maintained. The other one is that putting all changes in profit or loss would lead to better accounting of ineffectiveness (not all hedging instruments are perfectly effective hedges).

## Cash flow hedges

Cash flow hedge accounting is used when hedging a cash flow risk. This can be both a risk associated with an item recognized in the statement of financial position (such as a loan) and with forecast transactions, like expected future borrowings or expected purchases or sales. A forecast transaction can only be a hedged item when the transaction is highly probable.

Also for cash flow hedges, the derivative should be measured at fair value. However, changes in fair value are not recognized in profit or loss. That portion of the gain or loss on the hedging instrument which is determined to be an effective hedge should be recognized in other comprehensive income, the ineffective portion shall be recognized in profit or loss.

Now complete Activity 18.11.

## ACTIVITY 18.11

Show how the following cash flow hedges should be accounted for.

1 An entity wants to have a two-year fixed rate loan, but the bank only offers a variable rate loan and an interest rate swap. The swap contract requires the entity to pay fixed interest amounts in return for variable interest amounts. The variable interest amounts received will be used to pay the variable interest on the loan. Both the loan and the swap have a nominal amount of €80 000. The fixed rate is 5 per cent, the variable rate is Euribor + 1 per cent.

Immediately after the transactions, Euribor increases from 4 per cent to 5 per cent and remains so until the end of year 2.

2 A production entity has a detailed forecast of the raw materials purchases to be made for the next year. To hedge the price risk, in November 20X3 it has bought two monthly futures (April and June) at fixed raw material prices. For these months the entity expected a purchase of 100 000 units of raw material and the futures are based on that number of units. At reporting date, the fair value of both

(Continued)

## ACTIVITY 18.11    *(Continued)*

futures is – €10 000 each (the raw material price has obviously decreased). At reporting date, the current expectation is that the April purchase will be 80 000 and that the June purchase will be 110 000 units.

### Activity feedback

1  *At the end of year 1, the fair value of the swap, after having swapped the interests for year 1, is €754 (difference between interest to be received in year 2 (6% × 80 000) and interest to be paid in year 2 (5% × 80 000), discounted for one year at 6 per cent. The interest rate swap is measured at the fair value of €754 and this amount is included in other comprehensive income and presented in equity as a separate cash flow hedge reserve. In profit or loss the interest costs are €4000 (5% × €80 000). At the end of year 2, the fair value of the swap, after having swapped the interests for*

year 2, is €0 (a derivative at the end of its lifetime always has a fair value of €0). Interests costs in profit or loss are again €4000, other comprehensive income is – €754. The cash flow hedge reserve is reduced to €0.

2  *The April-future is partly ineffective. As a result, the fair value should be split into the effective part (–€8000) and the ineffective part (–€2000). The effective part is included in other comprehensive income and presented as a cash flow hedge reserve. The ineffective part is included in profit or loss. The June-future is fully effective. There is overhedging (just a part of the purchases are hedged), but overhedging does not result in ineffectiveness of the hedge. Therefore, the full amount of -€10 000 is included in other comprehensive income and presented as a cash flow hedge reserve.*

All of this is quite complicated and requires judgement as to the effectiveness of the hedge at the outset. This 'effectiveness' also needs to be kept under review throughout the life of the hedge and the accounting changed if it is no longer effective. A hedge is normally regarded as effective if expected changes in the hedged item are almost fully offset by changes in the hedging instrument. The actual results need to be in the range of 80 per cent to 125 per cent.

## DISCLOSURE

According to IFRS 7, para. 7, an entity shall disclose information that enables users of its financial statements to evaluate the significance of financial instruments for its financial position and performance. Specific disclosure requirements include:

- carrying amounts of each category of financial assets and financial liabilities
- details regarding financial assets and financial liabilities at fair value through profit or loss
- reclassifications
- details on offsetting financial assets and financial liabilities
- collateral pledged or held
- allowance accounts for credit losses
- defaults and breaches
- amounts of income, expense, gains or losses
- hedge accounting information
- fair value of financial instruments

- qualitative and quantitative information on risk, including credit risk, liquidity risk and market risk
- details on transfers of financial assets.

## THE FUTURE FOR FINANCIAL INSTRUMENTS: IFRS 9

IFRS 9 *Financial Instruments* was issued in November 2009 as part of the first phase of the review of IAS 39 by the IASB. The new Standard is not complete and will not be until the next two phases (i.e. impairment methodology and hedge accounting) and the debate as regards to financial liabilities and derecognition are finished, and the distinction between financial instruments and equity is concluded. Access the IASB website to keep track of developments in these areas.

**IFRS 9, Phase 1** This has made several changes to IAS 39, namely:

- Three categories of financial assets are eliminated (i.e. held-to-maturity, available for sale, and loans and receivables).
- All financial assets are now to be measured at either amortized cost or fair value.
- The condition for measurement at amortized cost is based on the entities' business model.
- Designation at fair value through profit or loss can still be used if this significantly reduces an accounting mismatch.
- Only one impairment method remains in IFRS 9. (This is due to the fact that three categories of financial asset have been eliminated and therefore the impairment method remaining from IAS 39 is that of 'assets at amortized cost'.)
- The classification of financial liabilities remains essentially unchanged, however, there is one essential difference for (non-derivative) financial liabilities measured at fair value through profit or loss (see below).

***Initial recognition of financial assets*** This remains the same as IAS 39.

***Classification*** This is the biggest change area from IAS 39. Financial assets are classified and measured at either *amortized cost* or *fair value*. Amortized cost is used where the asset is held within a business model whose objective is to hold assets in order to collect contractual cash flows, and the contractual terms of the asset give rise on specified dates to cash flows that are solely payments of principal and interest on the principal amount outstanding. However, it is possible for an entity to designate a financial asset as measured at fair value through profit or loss, if doing so eliminates an accounting mismatch. This mismatch can occur when a financial asset is hedged with a financial liability.

If a financial asset does not meet the conditions above, it is classified and measured at fair value. Measuring all financial assets at fair value is not proposed in IFRS 9, as preparers, auditors and regulators were wary of recognizing changes in fair value in the statement of comprehensive income for financial assets that are not held for trading or not managed on a fair value basis. Problems can occur with fair value measurement when it cannot be determined within a narrow range. This reluctance to move to full fair value measurement is also consistent with the views raised in response to the economic crisis in 2008.

The use of the 'business model' is a fundamental building block of IFRS 9 and aligns the accounting with management's intentions for those financial assets. These intentions are not at the level of individual assets.

Paragraph 4.3 of IFRS 9 states that 'interest is consideration for the time value of money and for the credit risk associated with the principal amount outstanding during a particular period of time'. IFRS 9 also gives us further guidance on who determines the business model of an entity in Appendix b 'Application Guidance' para. b4.1: 'the objective of the business model as determined by the entity's key management personnel'. We have to look to IAS 24, Related Party Transactions, for the definition of key management personnel, which is: 'those persons having authority or responsibility for planning, directing, and controlling the activities of the entity directly or indirectly including any director of that entity'. Now complete Activity 18.12 below.

## ACTIVITY 18.12

State whether the following financial assets would be measured at amortized cost or fair value in accordance with IFRS 9.

1  An entity holds investments to collect their contractual cash flows of principal and interest, but would sell an investment in particular circumstances.

2  An entity's business model is to purchase portfolios of loans. If payment on the loan is not made on a timely basis, the entity contacts the debtor by phone, email or post to extract the cash flows.

3  An entity holds bonds in various currencies with stated maturity dates and intends to hold the bonds till maturity. Payments of principal and interest to the entity are linked to the inflation index of the currency in which the loan is issued.

4  An entity holds bonds in various currencies with stated maturity dates and intends to hold the bonds till maturity. Payments of principal and interest to the entity are linked to the bond issuer's net income performance.

5  An entity holds a bond issued by Beta entity with an interest rate of 8 per cent. The bond is redeemable at par or may be converted into Beta equity shares. An equivalent bond without the conversion option would pay an interest rate of 10 per cent.

*Activity feedback*

1  *These investments meet the business model definition, even though some sales may occur, as the main objective is to hold the investments for their contractual cash flows. Measure at amortized cost.*

2  *Again, these purchased loans meet the business model definition and therefore are measured at amortized cost.*

3  *The business model test is clearly met. Also, the cash flows here are solely payments of principal and interest. Linking the interest rate to the currency inflation rate just reflects the real rate of interest in the instrument and therefore they will be measured at amortized cost.*

4  *Again, the business model test is clearly met, but not the 'characteristics of the financial asset test'. The cash flows in this case are not representing the time value of money but the debtor's performance, and thus do not meet the business model definition and therefore will be measured at fair value.*

5  *In any case the cash flows do not only reflect the time value of money and the credit risk. They are also linked to the value of the equity of the issuer. Measure at fair value.*

*Measurement of financial assets* Initially financial debt assets are measured at fair value and thereafter at fair value or amortized cost depending upon its classification using the business model above. All changes to fair value and amortization are recognized through profit or loss. Note here that gains or losses on remeasurement will under IFRS 9 all go through profit or loss, none will go through other comprehensive income. For investments in equity instruments that are not held for trading, however, IFRS 9 permits an entity to make an irrevocable election to present changes in fair value of the investment in the equity instrument in other comprehensive income (as an alternative to profit or loss). There would be no recycling to profit or loss upon impairment or sale of the investment. However, dividends from the investment are recognized in profit or loss.

**Financial liabilities** For (non-derivative) financial liabilities measured at fair value through profit or loss the gains and losses from remeasurement should be included in profit or loss, as in IAS 39, but with the exception that the gain or loss attributable to changes in credit risk should normally be recognized in other comprehensive income. The amounts presented in other comprehensive income are not subsequently recycled to profit or loss. Why is this exception made? Credit risk of a liability is the risk that the liability will not be paid. The credit risk is part of the fair value of the liability. When credit risk increases, the fair value of the liability decreases. Assume Company M issues bonds with a face value and fair value of €100 000 at a fixed rate of 6 per cent. Assume that market interest rates do not change. However, M is having a difficult time and two years later its creditworthiness is lower. If M were to issue a fixed rate bond loan at that moment, it would have to pay 8 per cent. The fair value of the loan has now become less than €100 000 (6 per cent interest and repayment cash flows discounted at 8 per cent). Remember, the 2 per cent interest differential is only due to the change in creditworthiness of M, not to market interest rate changes. When M measures the liabilities at fair value through profit or loss, the decrease in the fair value of the liability will normally be a gain. But that is counterintuitive: the worsening of the credit standing would result in a gain. It is for that reason that this fair value change is included in other comprehensive income, outside profit or loss. However, if such accounting were to create or enlarge an accounting mismatch the credit risk related fair value change would still be recognized in profit or loss.

**Reclassification** If an entity changes its business model for managing financial assets then it will need to reclassify its financial assets. This reclassification is carried out prospectively and previous recognized gains and losses are not restated.

Figure 18.1 summarizes the classification and measurement of financial assets in IFRS 9 for you.

**Exposure draft** This IFRS 9 model of classification and measurement of financial assets might be adapted, following an exposure draft, published in November 2012. The IASB proposes to include a new category for investments in debt: fair value through other comprehensive income (OCI) for those financial assets that contain contractual cash flows that are solely payments of principal and interest and that are held within a business model in which assets are managed *both* in order to collect contractual cash flows and for sale. Under the existing IFRS 9 model, these assets would be classified as fair value through profit or loss, as the business model is not restricted to only collect the interest and repayment cash flows. Some specifics:

- For the applicable financial assets, there is now a choice between this new category and the category of fair value through profit or loss.
- Different from the fair value to OCI option for equity instruments, there is recycling through profit or loss.

## Figure 18.1    Classification and measurement of financial assets

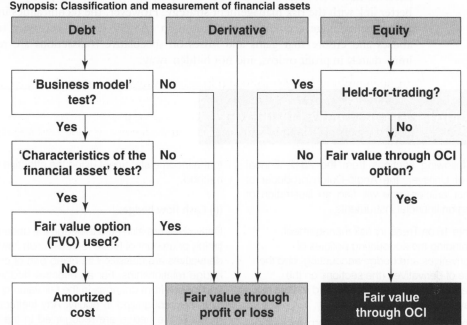

Synopsis: Classification and measurement of financial assets

**IFRS 9, Phase 2 – Impairment** Finding a sound impairment methodology is one of the big challenges of the IASB. The impairment method within IAS 39 is an incurred loss impairment method. This has been heavily criticized, as under this model losses are recognized too late. The IASB is proposing under Phase 2 to move to an impairment method based on expected losses. A first draft of this expected losses model was published in November 2009 and a revised draft in March 2013. The main features of the revised draft are:

- An entity is required to recognize expected credit losses as at the reporting date, independent on the entity first identifying a credit loss event.

- In assessing credit risk and measuring expected credit losses, a broad range of relevant information should be considered, including past events, current conditions and reasonable and supportable forecasts that affect the expected collectability of future cash flows.

- A distinction should be made between (1) financial instruments that have not deteriorated significantly in credit quality since initial recognition or that have low credit risk and (2) other financial instruments. For the financial instruments in the first category, only 12-month expected credit losses are recognized (taking only into account the potential for default in the next 12 months). For the other financial instruments, credit losses are recognized on a lifetime basis.

**IFRS 9, Phase 3 – Hedge accounting** The IASB published an ED on hedge accounting in 2010 and a Review Draft in 2012 to field-test the new proposals. Currently, the rules-based design of the current regulations in IAS 39 are criticized as too complex and arbitrary. Several hedges which are economically sound do not currently qualify for hedge accounting in the financial statements as they do not meet the detailed rules. A move to a principle-based design, which is what the IASB has proposed, would alleviate this. The high-level aim is to simplify hedge accounting and to provide a better link with the risk management strategy. However, the technicalities included in the current hedge accounting regulations in IAS 39 remain necessary to prevent abuses and ensure that gains and losses on speculative transactions are recognized immediately in profit or loss, and not hidden away.

## ANNUAL REPORT 2012 UNILEVER

In the following sections from the 2012 Annual Report of Unilever, the Anglo-Dutch producer of consumer articles, you will find an illustration of reporting on financial instruments:

- Note 16 on Treasury risk management, including the accounting policies of derivatives and hedge accounting, and the use of derivatives (the sections on the management of liquidity risk and market risk have not been reproduced);
- Note 17 on Investment and return, including the accounting policies of financial assets (the sections on financial assets and on the management of credit risk have not been reproduced).

## 16. Treasury risk management

### Derivatives and hedge accounting

Derivatives are measured at fair value with any related transaction costs expensed as incurred. The treatment of changes in the value of derivatives depends on their use as explained below.

#### (i) Fair value hedges

Certain derivatives are held to hedge the risk of changes in value of a specific bond or other loan. In these situations, the Group designates the liability and related derivative to be part of a fair value hedge relationship. The carrying value of the bond is adjusted by the fair value of the risk being hedged, with changes going to the income statement. Gains and losses on the corresponding derivative are also recognized in the income statement. The amounts recognized are offset in the income statement to the extent that the hedge is effective. When the relationship no longer meets the criteria for hedge accounting, the fair value hedge adjustment made to the bond is amortized

to the income statement using the effective interest method.

#### (ii) Cash flow hedges

Derivatives are also held to hedge the uncertainty in timing or amount of future forecast cash flows. Such derivatives are classified as being part of cash flow hedge relationships. For an effective hedge, gains and losses from changes in the fair value of derivatives are recognized in equity. Any ineffective elements of the hedge are recognized in the income statement. If the hedged cash flow relates to a non-financial asset, the amount accumulated in equity is subsequently included within the carrying value of that asset. For other cash flow hedges, amounts deferred in equity are taken to the income statement at the same time as the related cash flow.

When a derivative no longer qualifies for hedge accounting, any cumulative gain or loss remains in equity until the related cash flow occurs. When the cash flow takes place, the cumulative gain or loss is taken to the income statement. If the hedged cash flow is no longer expected to occur, the cumulative gain or loss is taken to the income statement immediately.

#### (iii) Net investment hedges

Certain derivatives are designated as hedges of the currency risk on the Group's investment in foreign subsidiaries. The accounting policy for these arrangements is set out in note 1.

#### (iv) Derivatives for which hedge accounting is not applied

Derivatives not classified as hedges are held in order to hedge certain balance sheet items and commodity exposures. No hedge accounting is applied to these derivatives, which are carried at fair value with changes being recognized in the income statement.

*(Continued)*

The Group is exposed to the following risks that arise from its use of financial instruments, the management of which is described in the following sections:

- liquidity risk (see note 16A);
- market risk (see note 16B); and
- credit risk (see note 17B).

## 16C. Derivatives and hedging

The Group does not use derivative financial instruments for speculative purposes. The uses of derivatives and the related values of derivatives are summarized in the following table:

| | € million Trade and other receivables | € million Other current financial assets | € million Trade payables and other liabilities | € million Current financial liabilities | € million Non-current financial liabilities | € million Total |
|---|---|---|---|---|---|---|
| **31 December 2012** | | | | | | |
| **Foreign exchange derivatives** | | | | | | |
| Fair value hedges | 1 | – | (5) | – | – | (4) |
| Cash flow hedges | 9 | – | (13) | – | – | (4) |
| Hedges of net investments in foreign operations | – | (126)[a] | – | (5) | – | (131) |
| Hedge accounting not applied | 10 | 222 | (16) | (57) | – | 159 |
| **Cross currency swaps** | | | | | | |
| Hedge accounting not applied | – | 38 | – | (30) | (34) | (26) |
| **Interest rate swaps** | | | | | | |
| Fair value hedges | – | 36 | – | – | – | 36 |
| Cash flow hedges | – | – | (146) | – | – | (146) |
| Hedge accounting not applied | – | – | – | – | – | – |
| **Commodity contracts** | | | | | | |
| Cash flow hedges | 3 | – | (22) | – | – | (19) |
| Hedge accounting not applied | – | – | – | – | – | – |
| | 23 | 170 | (202) | (92) | (34) | (135) |
| | **Total assets** | 193 | | **Total liabilities** | (328) | (135) |
| **31 December 2011** | | | | | | |
| **Foreign exchange derivatives** | | | | | | |
| Fair value hedges | 9 | – | (4) | – | – | 5 |
| Cash flow hedges | 22 | – | (19) | – | – | 3 |
| Hedges of net investments in foreign operations | – | 18 | – | (7) | – | 11 |
| Hedge accounting not applied | 22 | 50 | (17) | (92) | – | (37) |
| **Cross currency swaps** | | | | | | |
| Hedge accounting not applied | – | 31 | – | (2) | (23) | 6 |
| **Interest rate swaps** | | | | | | |
| Fair value hedges | – | 109 | – | – | – | 109 |
| Cash flow hedges | – | – | (27) | – | – | (27) |
| Hedge accounting not applied | – | – | – | – | – | – |
| **Commodity contracts** | | | | | | |
| Cash flow hedges | 4 | – | (6) | – | – | (2) |
| Hedge accounting not applied | 1 | – | – | – | – | 1 |
| | 58 | 208 | (73) | (101) | (23) | |
| | **Total assets** | 266 | | **Total liabilities** | (197) | 69 |

[a]The offsetting swaps that are used to hedge concern loans are included in other current financial assets under Hedge accounting not applied.

*(Continued)*

## 17. Investment and return

### Cash and cash equivalents

Cash and cash equivalents in the balance sheet include deposits, investments in money market funds and highly liquid investments. To be classified as cash and cash equivalents, an asset must:

- be readily convertible into cash;
- have an insignificant risk of changes in value; and
- have a maturity period of three months or less at acquisition.

Cash and cash equivalents in the cash flow statement also include bank overdrafts and are recorded at amortized cost.

### Other financial assets

Other financial assets are first recognized on the trade date. At that point they are classified as:

**(i)** held-to-maturity investments;

**(ii)** loans and receivables;

**(iii)** available-for-sale financial assets; or

**(iv)** financial assets at fair value through profit or loss.

#### (i) Held-to-maturity investments

These are assets with set cash flows and fixed maturities which Unilever intends to hold to maturity. They are held at cost plus interest using the effective interest method, less any impairment.

#### (ii) Loans and receivables

These are assets with an established payment profile and which are not listed on a recognized stock exchange. They are initially recognized at fair value, which is usually the original invoice amount plus any directly related transaction costs. Afterwards loans and receivables are carried at amortized cost, less any impairment.

#### (iii) Available-for-sale financial assets

Any financial assets not classified as either loans and receivables or financial assets at fair value through profit or loss are designated as available-for-sale. They are initially recognized at fair value, usually the original invoice amount plus any directly related transaction costs. Afterwards they are measured at fair value with changes being recognized in equity. When the investment is sold or impaired, the accumulated gains and losses are moved from equity to the income statement. Interest and dividends from these assets are recognized in the income statement.

#### (iv) Financial assets at fair value through profit or loss

These are derivatives and assets that are held for trading. Related transaction costs are expensed as incurred. Unless they form part of a hedging relationship, these assets are held at fair value, with changes being recognized in the income statement.

### Impairment of financial assets

Each year the Group assesses whether there is evidence that financial assets are impaired. A significant or prolonged fall in value below the cost of an asset generally indicates that an asset may be impaired. If impaired, financial assets are written down to their estimated recoverable amount. Impairment losses on assets classified as loans and receivables are recognized in profit and loss. When a later event causes the impairment losses to decrease, the reduction in impairment loss is also recognized in profit and loss. Impairment losses on assets classified as available-for-sale are recognized by moving the loss accumulated in equity to the income statement. Any subsequent recovery in value of an available-for-sale debt security is recognized within profit and loss. However, any subsequent recovery in value of an equity security is recognized within equity, and is recorded at amortized cost.

## IFRS 4, *INSURANCE CONTRACTS*

### Introduction

Before the issue of IFRS 4, *Insurance Contracts*, in March 2004, there was no International Accounting Standard to deal with the diverse practices of insurance contract accounting. The IASC had established a steering committee in 1997 to investigate the issues surrounding insurance contracts, but the IASB did not really discuss the matter until 2001. As with many other controversial issues, the IASB has split the project for insurance contracts into two.

*Phase I* (a) to make limited improvements to accounting practices for insurance contracts without requiring major changes that may need to be reversed in *Phase II* (b) to require disclosure that (i) identifies and explains the amounts in an insurer's financial statements arising from insurance contracts and (ii) helps users of those financial statements understand the amount, timing and uncertainty of future cash flows from insurance contracts. Phase I resulted in IFRS 4, which is basically a presentation and disclosure standard.

*Phase II* is concerned with the recognition and measurement of an insurance contract. An ED, *Insurance Contracts*, was published in July 2010. A revised ED is expected in the course of 2013. If adopted, the ED will replace IFRS 4.

The basic issue with an insurance contract is determining the risks and rewards in the contract and who in substance owns them, and in addition how to treat payments received and made within the contract.

## Insurance contract

As defined by IFRS 4, this is a contract under which one party (the insurer) accepts significant insurance risk from another party (the policy holder) by agreeing to compensate the policy holder if a specified uncertain future event (the insured event) adversely affects the policyholder.

Several terms used in the above definition are also defined in IFRS 4:

*Insurance risk:* risk, other than financial risk, transferred from the holder of a contract to the issuer.

*Insured event:* an uncertain future event that is covered by an insurance contract and creates insurance risk.

Risk is the essence of an insurance contract and as such at least one of the following will be uncertain at the inception of the contract:

1 whether an insured event will occur

2 when it will occur

3 how much the insurer will need to pay if it occurs.

For example, insurance against theft or damage to property is an insurance contract as 1 and 2 above are uncertain and the contract will compensate the policy holder for the loss or damage, albeit generally to a limited amount. Life insurance is also deemed an insurance contract under IFRS 4, as, although death is certain, the timing is uncertain. Now complete the following activity.

## ACTIVITY 18.13

Identify which of the following are insurance contracts.

(a) Compensation in cash or kind to contract holders for losses suffered while travelling.

(b) Financial guarantee contract that requires payment even if the holder has not insured a loss on the failure of the debtor to make payments when due.

(c) A contract that requires specified payments to reimburse the holder for a loss it incurs because a specified debtor fails to make payment when due.

(d) A catastrophe bond in which principal interest payments are reduced significantly if a specified triggering event occurs and the triggering event

*(Continued)*

**ACTIVITY 18.13** *(Continued)*

includes a condition that the issuer of the bond suffered a loss.

(e) Loan contract containing a pre-payment fee that is waived if pre-payment results from the borrower's death.

*Activity feedback*

*(a), (c) and (d) are insurance contracts.*

*In (b) there is no specified uncertain future event; the payment is required whatever happens to the debt. Before the contract in (e), the borrower faced no risk corresponding to the prepayment fee, thus no risk has been transferred.*

## Scope

An entity applies IFRS 4 (para. 2) to:

- Insurance contracts that it issues and reinsurance contracts that it holds. A reinsurance contract is defined as an insurance contract issued by one insurer (the reinsurer) to compensate another insurer (the cedant) for losses on one or more contracts issued by the cedant.
- Financial instruments that it issues with a discretionary participation feature.

Excluded from the requirements of IFRS 4 (para. 4) are:

- Product warranties issued directly by a manufacturer, dealer or retailer.
- Employers' assets and liabilities under employee benefit plans.
- Contractual rights or contractual obligations that are contingent on the future use of, or right to use, a non-financial item (e.g. some licence fees, royalties, contingent lease payments and similar items), as well as lessee's residual value guarantee embedded in a finance lease.
- Financial guarantees into which an entity enters or retains on transferring to another party financial assets or financial liabilities within the scope of IAS 39, regardless of whether the financial guarantees are described as financial guarantees, letters of credit or insurance contracts.
- Contingent consideration payable or receivable in a business combination.
- Direct insurance contracts that the entity holds (i.e. direct insurance contracts in which the entity is the policyholder). However, a cedant shall apply this IFRS to reinsurance contracts that it holds.

Now complete the following activity.

**ACTIVITY 18.14**

A sells computer hardware and offers to its customers an extended warranty for a fixed period covering servicing, repairs and maintenance for an annual fixed fee. Is this an insurance contract requiring disclosure under IFRS 4?

*Activity feedback*

*A is accepting significant insurance risks under this contract as neither the number of services that A will be required to perform nor their nature is predetermined, so*

*this does meet the definition of an insurance contract. However, IFRS 4 specifically excludes product warranties issued by a retailer, so this falls outside the scope of IFRS 4. If the extended warranty had been provided by a third party, e.g. a specialist repair firm or even a competing manufacturer or retailer, then the exclusion would not apply and IFRS 4 would need to be applied. The warranty obligation would be accounted for in accordance with IAS 37 (Provisions).*

# Disclosure

IFRS 4 requires disclosure of information that:

1 identifies and explains the amounts in its financial statements arising from insurance contracts

2 helps users to understand the amount, timing and uncertainty of future cash flows from insurance contracts.

Under 1, accounting policies, recognized assets, liabilities, income and expense will be disclosed as well as processes used to determine assumptions within these amounts and the effects of changes in these assumptions. Under 2, terms and conditions of the insurance contract that have a material effect on the cash flows of the insurer, and actual claims compared with previous estimates, will be disclosed.

# Other main features

Other main features of IFRS 4 are that the Standard:

1 exempts an insurer temporarily (until Phase II of the project is complete) from some requirements of other IFRSs;

2 permits an insurer to change its accounting policies, but only if the resulting financial statements would be more relevant but no less reliable or vice versa;

3 permits insurers to introduce an accounting policy that would see the insurance liabilities in each period reflected at market interest rates;

4 does not require the insurer to change its accounting policies even if they are excessively prudent;

5 requires an insurer to unbundle a deposit component (a financial instrument element of the contract) from the insurance component of an insurance contract when certain conditions are met;

6 does no longer allow catastrophe and equalization provisions

7 requires a liability adequacy test at each reporting date.

# Financial guarantee contracts

A financial guarantee contract is defined as a contract that requires the issuer to make specified payments to reimburse the holder for a loss it incurs because a specified debtor fails to make payment when due in accordance with the original or modified terms of a debt instrument. These could also be regarded as insurance contracts. However, IAS 39 states that these financial guarantee contracts are within its scope but permits an issuer to elect to apply either IAS 39 or IFRS 4 on those contracts where it has previously asserted explicitly that it regards such contracts as insurance contracts.

IAS 39 requires that such contracts are initially measured at fair value and subsequently amortized and recorded as income over the period the guarantee applies unless the liability measured in terms of IAS 37 exceeds the carrying amount.

The illustration below should help you understand this.

## ILLUSTRATION

Entity Alpha provides a financial guarantee to a third party entity Beta on 1 January 200X. Under the guarantee, if entity Beta defaults on a specific loan of £10 000 that it has with a bank, Alpha will become liable to repay the loan to the bank excluding interest. The guarantee lasts for five years.

On the date of the guarantee being provided, Beta paid Alpha £500 which it considered to be the fair value of granting the guarantee. In 200Y, the credit market has deteriorated to such a degree that it has become probable that Beta will default on its loan to the bank. How should Alpha account for the guarantee in its accounts in accordance with IAS 39?

On initial recognition, the guarantee must be recognized at fair value, that is £500, thus Alpha will show a financial guarantee liability of £500. Subsequently it will be amortized over its life of five years. Thus, Alpha will credit income with £100 and reduce the liability by £100 for the year ended 31 December 200X.

During 200Y, when the possibility arises that Beta will default on the loan, then Alpha will have to apply IAS 37 to account for the financial guarantee liability. This means Alpha needs to determine the best estimate of the expenditure it would incur if it had to settle the loan. If we assume the best estimate of the liability at 31 December 200Y is £9650 then Alpha will need to charge £9250 as an expense in the statement of comprehensive income and credit the financial guarantee liability account with £9250. The balance on the financial guarantee liability will now be £9650, the amount required to settle the loan.

## Insurance contract – Phase II

The IASB has issued two Exposure Drafts on Insurance Contracts, a first one in 2010 and a second one, as a replacement, in 2013. The Exposure Draft proposes a measurement model that provides information about how insurance contracts contribute to the entity's financial position and performance. The balance sheet amount reflects the expected contract profit from the insurance contract and a current estimate of the amount of future cash flows from the contract, adjusted to reflect the timing and uncertainty relating to those cash flows. The statement of comprehensive income reports an operating results which reflects underwriting experience, the change in uncertainty and the profit from services in the period and, through interest and discount rate changes, both a current and a cost-based view of the cost of financing the insurance contract. It is proposed that any changes in estimates relating to the profits to be earned from an insurance contract are recognized over the remaining coverage period.

The comment period on the Exposure Draft ends in October 2013 and 2014 has been reserved for redeliberations and possibly a final Standard. The IASB expects to allow a period of about three years before the final Standard comes into effect.

## SUMMARY

This has been a complicated chapter. We advise you to carefully read the actual Standards and also keep track on changes to IFRS by accessing the IASB website. Accountants, analysts and many others are struggling with the detail of IAS 39, IFRS 9 and further project work in this area. Until we have the complete version of IFRS 9, its impact cannot be fully measured. IFRS 9 in its complete form will be a Standard that moves accounting beyond the traditional methods and attempts to capture the rights and obligations of complicated financial instruments which in the long-term should provide more useful information to users if it is made understandable to them and less complex than IAS 39. However, from now until 2015, the expected date for compliance with the new IFRS 9, entities can report under

either IAS 39 or IFRS 9 and this will make comparisons between different entity statements even more complex. IFRS 9 contains some very complex rules and regulations for the transition between IAS 39 and IFRS 9 for those who choose early adoption of IFRS 9.

IFRS 4 fills a gap in international accounting standards but it is a stopgap until Phase II of the project on insurance contracts is complete.

As a short summary of the current requirements in IAS 39 we refer to Table 18.4.

## TABLE 18.4   Summary of current major requirements of IAS 39

| Financial instrument | A contract that gives rise to a financial asset of one entity and a financial liability or equity instrument of another entity | | | |
|---|---|---|---|---|
| Distinction between financial liability and equity | A financial liability normally includes a contractual obligation to deliver cash, an equity instrument does not. Compound financial instruments should be split. | | | |
| Recognition and derecognition of financial instruments | Recognition when an entity becomes party to the contractual provisions of the instrument. Derecognition when the contractual rights or obligations expire and when there is a qualified transfer. | | | |
| Categories of financial assets | At fair value through profit or loss | Held-to-maturity | Loans and receivables | Available for sale |
| *Measurement* | *Fair value; changes in profit or loss* | *Amortized cost* | | *Fair value; changes in other comprehensive income (recycling)* |
| *Impairment* | *Not applicable* | *Present value of future cash flows with original effective date as discount rate* | | *Recycling to profit or loss when there is significant or prolonged decline* |
| Categories of financial liabilities | At fair value through profit or loss | | Other | |
| *Measurement* | *Fair value; changes in profit or loss* | | *Amortized cost* | |
| Hedge accounting | Fair value hedge accounting and cash flow hedge accounting. Specific conditions for applying hedge accounting. | | | |
| Disclosure | Extensive significant disclosure requirements | | | |

## EXERCISES

*Suggested answers to exercises marked ✓ are to be found on our dedicated CourseMate platform for students.*

*Suggested answers to the remaining exercises are to be found on the Instructor online support resources.*

✓ **1**   Discuss the problems faced by users of financial reports if financial instruments are kept off statement of financial position.

**2**   What is a financial instrument?

**3**   How does the IASB determine differentiation between financial instruments and other assets and liabilities?

**4**   What is a derivative?

**5**   Discuss the IASB's methodology for the recognition of gains and losses on remeasurement of financial instruments to fair value, and illustrate the effects on the statement of comprehensive income in accordance with IAS 39.

**6**   Appraise the effect of using settlement date accounting as opposed to trade date accounting for regular way contracts.

**7**   Discuss the proposal by the IASB to move to full fair value accounting for financial instruments and identify the effects this move would have on an entity's statement of comprehensive income and statement of financial position.

✓ **8**   It is unrealistic to apply the realization concept to complex financial instruments. Discuss.

**9**   Ambush, a public limited company, is assessing the impact of implementing revised IAS 39, *Financial Instruments: Recognition and Measurement*. The directors realize that significant changes may occur in their accounting treatment of financial instruments and they understand that on initial recognition any financial asset or liability can be designated as one to be measured at fair value through profit or loss (the fair value option). However, there are certain issues that they wish to have explained and these are set out below.

**Required:**
(a)  In a report to the directors of Ambush, outline the following information:
   (i)   How financial assets and liabilities are measured and classified, briefly setting out the accounting method used for each category. (Hedging relationships can be ignored.)
   (ii)  Why the 'fair value option' was initially introduced and why it has caused such concern.

(b)  Ambush loaned $200 000 to Bromwich on 1 December 2003. The effective and stated interest rate for this loan was 8 per cent. Interest is payable by Bromwich at the end of each year and the loan is repayable on 30 November 2007. At 30 November 2005, the directors of Ambush have heard that Bromwich is in financial difficulties and is undergoing a financial reorganization. The directors feel that it is likely that they will only receive $100 000 on 30 November 2007 and no future interest payment. Interest for the year ended 30 November 2005 had been received. The financial year-end of Ambush is 30 November 2005.

**Required:**

(i)  Outline the requirements of IAS 39 as regards the impairment of financial assets.

(ii) Explain the accounting treatment under IAS 39 of the loan to Bromwich in the financial statements of Ambush for the year ended 30 November 2005.

(ACCA 3.5 int. – December 2005)

10  The directors of QRS, a listed entity, have met to discuss the business's medium- to long-term financing requirements. Several possibilities were discussed, including the issue of more shares using a rights issue. In many respects this would be the most desirable option because the entity is already quite highly geared. However, the directors are aware of several recent cases where rights issues have not been successful because share prices are currently quite low and many investors are averse to any kind of investment in shares.

Therefore, the directors have turned their attention to other options. The finance director is on sick leave, and so you, her assistant, have been given the task of responding to the following note from the Chief Executive:

Now that we've had a chance to discuss possible financing arrangements, the directors are in agreement that we should structure our issue of financial instruments in order to be able to classify them as equity rather than debt. Any increase in the gearing ratio would be unacceptable. Therefore, we have provisionally decided to make two issues of financial instruments as follows:

(a)  An issue of non-redeemable preferred shares to raise $4 million. These shares will carry a fixed interest rate of 6 per cent, and because they are shares they can be classified as equity.

(b)  An issue of 6 per cent convertible bonds, issued at par value, to raise $6 million. These bonds will carry a fixed date for conversion in four years' time. Each $100 of debt will be convertible at the holder's option into 120 $1 shares. In our opinion, these bonds can actually be classified as equity immediately, because they are convertible within five years on terms that are favourable to the holder.

Please confirm that these instruments will not increase our gearing ratio should they be issued.

Note: You determine that the market rate available for similar non-convertible bonds is currently 8 per cent.

**Required:**

Explain to the directors the accounting treatment, in respect of debt/equity classification, required by IAS 32, *Financial Instruments: Disclosure and Presentation*, for each of the proposed issues, advising them on the acceptability of classifying the instruments as equity. Your explanation should be accompanied by calculations where appropriate.

(CIMA P8 – Pilot Paper)

11  On 1 February 2007, the directors of AZG decided to enter into a forward foreign exchange contract to buy 6 million florins at a rate of $1 = 3 florins, on 31 January 2010. AZG's year end is 31 March.

Relevant exchange rates were as follows:

1 February 2007 $1 = 3 florins
31 March 2007 $1   = 2.9 florins
31 March 2008 $1   = 2.8 florins

**Required:**

(a) Identify the three characteristics of a derivative financial instrument as defined in IAS 39, *Financial Instruments: Recognition and Measurement.*

(b) Describe the requirements of IAS 39 in respect of the recognition and measurement of derivative financial instruments.

(c) Prepare relevant extracts from AZG's income statement and balance sheet to reflect the forward foreign exchange contract at 31 March 2008, with comparatives. (Note: ignore discounting when measuring the derivative).

(CIMA P8 – May 2008)

**12** *Financial Instrument (a)*

DG acquired 500 000 shares in HJ, a listed entity, for $3.50 per share on 28 May 2009. The costs associated with the purchase were $15 000 and were included in the cost of the investment. The directors plan to realize this investment before the end of 2009. The investment was designated on acquisition as held for trading. There has been no further adjustment made to the investment since the date of purchase. The shares were trading at $3.65 each on 30 June 2009.

*Financial Instrument (b)*

DG purchased a bond with a par value of $5 million on 1 July 2008. The bond carries a 5 per cent coupon, payable annually in arrears and is redeemable on 30 June 2013 at $5.8 million. DG fully intends to hold the bond until the redemption date. The bond was purchased at a 10 per cent discount. The effective interest rate on the bond is 10.26%. The interest due for the year was received and credited to investment income in the income statement.

**Required:**

Explain how financial instruments (a) and (b) should be classified, initially measured and subsequently measured. Prepare any journal entries required to correct the accounting treatment for the year to 30 June 2009.

(CIMA P8 – November 2009)

# REVENUE

# 19

to think revenue with economic entity thinking perhaps with a company that

**OBJECTIVES** After studying this chapter you should be able to:

- define revenue and what type of transactions it arises from

- determine when it should be recognized by an entity

- explain how it should be measured

- critically appraise IAS 18 in relation to revenue recognition and measurement

- identify the disclosure requirements in respect of revenue in accordance with IAS 18

- outline the requirements of the new standard which will replace IAS 18.

## INTRODUCTION

The income statement reports the profit of an entity by matching expenses to revenues, but before we can carry out this matching we need to define revenues and expenses and identify at what point we should recognize them. Many standards that we have already considered are about the expense side of these issues, but as yet we have given very little consideration to the revenue.

Chapter 9 dealt with the general principles in respect of revenue but this chapter will consider them in more detail and also IAS 18, *Revenue*. IAS 18 was originally issued in 1982 and revised in 1993 and is effective for financial statements covering periods beginning on or after 1 January 1995. It is worth noting at this point that neither the USA nor the UK currently has a specific standard on 'revenue'.

## WHAT IS REVENUE?

The *Conceptual Framework for Financial Reporting* defines income as 'increases in economic benefits during the accounting period in the form of inflows or enhancements of assets or decreases of liabilities that result in increases in equity, other than those relating to contributions from equity participants'. It further states that income encompasses both revenues and gains. Revenues are further described as arising 'in the course of the ordinary activities of an entity'. So what is this revenue and how do we distinguish it from other gains?

Revenue is regarded by many as simply the cash that you are paid for selling things and this simple idea also implies exchange – cash for things. We have also carried this idea of exchange through to the balance sheet. Consider the simple exchange of selling an item of inventory for cash – the accounting entries would be to derecognize the item of inventory in the balance sheet and recognize the asset of cash. The asset of cash would qualify as revenue and against this we would match relevant expenses to determine profit. Traditionally we have not regarded the item of inventory as revenue until it is sold or at least until we have exchanged it for another asset, perhaps a debtor. This approach seems to equate revenue with economic activity involving exchange with a customer and ignores other items such as gains on assets that are revalued or carried at current value.

IAS 18 (para. 7) defines revenue as:

> ... the gross inflow of economic benefits during the period arising in the course of the ordinary activities of an entity when those inflows result in increases in equity, other than increases relating to contributions from equity participants.

There are several important notions in this definition:

1 Revenue is the *gross inflow*, i.e. before the deduction of any expenses. We must also presume that this gross inflow is to the entity although it isn't specifically stated in the definition.

2 Revenue results from ordinary activities. This notion distinguishes revenue from other gains. Gains are defined in the Framework as 'other items that meet the definition of income and may, or may not, arise in the ordinary activities of an entity'.

3 Revenue gives rise to an increase in equity.

Now carefully work through Activities 19.1, 19.2 and 19.3.

## ACTIVITY 19.1

An entity receives €100 for the sale of an item of inventory. This amount includes a sales tax at 25 per cent on cost which is payable to the tax authorities. The entity also sells another item of inventory on behalf of an agent for which it only retains a 10 per cent commission charge on sale price. Identify the revenue to the entity in both cases in accordance with the IAS 18 definition.

### Activity feedback
*The first item of inventory only results in an increase in equity of €80. The other €20 is paid directly to the tax authorities and is effectively collected by us on their behalf. The second item of inventory has only generated revenue and subsequent increase in equity to the entity of €10. The other €90 is collected on behalf of the agent.*

## ACTIVITY 19.2

Two entities both sell an item of real estate (cost €1m) for €2m. One entity operates in the chemical industry; the other is a property development company. Identify the revenue for both entities.

### Activity feedback

*For the chemical entity, the income of €2m will be regarded as a gain as the sale of real estate is not regarded as part of the ordinary activities. For the property development company, the income of €2m would be regarded as revenue.*

## ACTIVITY 19.3

The following transactions occur in an accounting period for A entity:

1  1m €1 shares are issued at a premium on nominal value of €2.

2  Property is sold for €2m.

3  The entity deals in the retail of widgets and makes sales of €150 000, 50 per cent of which are on credit.

Identify the revenue for the entity in accordance with IAS 18 for the period.

### Activity feedback

*All these transactions give rise to an increase in equity, but only the last, (3), is regarded as revenue. The share issue (1) is income received from equity participants, and property (2) is not part of the ordinary activities of the entity.*

## FROM WHAT DOES REVENUE ARISE?

So far we have defined revenue as arising from exchange transactions that give rise to gross inflows from ordinary activities. However, exchange transactions, as we have already seen, can take many forms and we need to consider whether all of them or only some give rise to revenue.

Exchange transactions can be viewed as contracts between a seller and a buyer, but would we regard interest received and royalties as part of such an exchange contract and therefore revenue?

Interest received results from the use by another of entity cash or cash equivalent and thus we have an exchange contract that gives rise to an increase in equity, and therefore the interest can be regarded as revenue. Note that when the principal element of the loan is repaid this will not be regarded as revenue as it will not result in an increase in equity, only an asset of cash replacing the debt. Royalties are similar as they are charges for the use of long-term assets of the entity such as copyrights, patents, trademarks and so on. IAS 18 states that revenue arises from three types of transaction and event:

1  the sale of goods

2  the rendering of service

3  the use by others of entity assets yielding interest, royalties and dividends.

There is some revenue that the standard does not deal with. This revenue is generally that which is dealt with by other standards, for example under construction contracts, leases, dividends from associated companies and changes in the fair value of financial assets and liabilities or their disposal (dealt with under financial instruments). Changes in other non-current assets, extraction of mineral ores, insurance contracts of insurance entities, and natural increases in herds, agricultural and forestry products are also outside the scope of IAS 18.

In determining whether or not a sale has been made or a service has been rendered, the standard requires us to determine whether certain conditions have been met before we recognize revenue (see Activity 19.4).

## ACTIVITY 19.4

An entity transfers assets to a customer as follows:

- €2000 of bottles of wine in exchange for €2000 cash, with the option for the customer to return as many of the bottles, unopened, within seven days and claim a refund of the cash paid for each.

- €200 of glasses in exchange for €50 cash where the customer is required to return all glasses within seven days or pay the full price for them.

Identify in each case whether a sale has occurred and therefore whether revenue should be recognized.

### Activity feedback

*The answer here involves us looking at the substance of the transactions and deciding whether the customer, on receipt of the asset, has acquired the associated risks and rewards of the asset.*

*In the case of the wine, it would seem that the customer has received the risks and rewards associated with it but do we recognize all the €2000, or do we only recognize 90 per cent of it, assuming it is normal that 10 per cent is returned. Alternatively, we could delay the recognition of the revenue until the return time has expired.*

*In the case of the glasses, the customer is not acquiring all the risks and rewards associated with them, only a very limited proportion of them. Indeed, the entity retains effective control over them.*

## Sale of goods

IAS 18 identifies several criteria that must be met before revenue can be recognized on sale of goods:

- The entity has transferred to the buyer the significant risks and rewards of ownership of the goods.
- The entity retains neither continuing managerial involvement to the degree usually associated with ownership nor effective control over the goods sold.
- The amount of revenue can be measured reliably.
- It is probable that the economic benefits associated with the transaction will flow to the entity.
- The costs incurred, or to be incurred, in respect of the transaction can be measured reliably.

Now try Activities 19.5 and 19.6.

## ACTIVITY 19.5

Identify, for the following transactions, if and when the risks and rewards associated with the transaction have passed between the parties concerned:

1 A publisher sells books to a retailer on sale or return. If the books are not sold, the retailer returns them to the publisher for a refund. It is impossible

(Continued)

## ACTIVITY 19.5    (Continued)

to estimate reliably how many books will remain unsold.

2  A retailer offers a 12-month guarantee on all its products whereby a customer can return the product for whatever reason and have a full refund. In the normal course of business it has been found that 1 per cent per annum of sales is subject to such refunds.

3  A software house develops a customized finance system for a customer. Title to the software passes to the customer on a given date, but included in the agreement is a three-month warranty period beyond this date to cover the need for any amendments or debugging of the system. It is impossible to estimate the potential for these costs.

4  A piece of machinery is sold by Alpha entity to Beta for €100 000. In addition, Beta is required to pay €75 000 to Alpha for the installation of the machinery. The machinery is inoperable without installation.

5  Alpha sells another machine to Gamma but under an agreement that allows Gamma to return the machine if a contract Gamma is seeking, and for which it needs the machine, is not won. No information is available on the likelihood of Gamma winning the contract.

### Activity feedback

1  *In this example the receipt of revenue to the publisher is dependent on the derivation of revenue by the retailer from the sale of the goods and thus the risks and rewards do not pass until the retailer has sold the books. This would not be regarded as a sale and revenue would only be recognized when the books are sold by the retailer.*

2  *In this case the retailer retains very little risk associated with the products and therefore revenue should be recognized when the sale is made and an accrual made for the expected returns.*

3  *Legal title has passed to the customer but the risks and rewards still remain with the developer until the end of the three-month period. Revenue will not be recognized until the end of the three-month period.*

4  *This sale will not be completed until the installation, which is a material part of the cost, is complete. Revenue will be recognized on completion of installation.*

5  *Revenue cannot be recognized by Alpha until and if Gamma wins the contract.*

## ACTIVITY 19.6

An advertising entity, Choice, contracts to produce an advert about TV1 for it to show on air. The contract entitles Choice to a fee of £100 000 on the first showing of the advert and a repeat fee of £10 000 for each subsequent showing. How should Choice account for the revenue from the contract?

### Activity feedback

IAS 18 requires that revenue should be recognized on a service contract when the revenue flow to the entity is probable and the revenue, the stage of completion of the transaction, and the costs to complete can be reliably measured. The revenue of £100 000 should be recognized by Choice when the advertisement is handed over to TV1. The repeat fees should be recognized as repeats occur, as this is the only time when the revenue can be measured reliably. This contract could also be regarded as comprising of two separate elements (see Activity 19.11) which would give the same answer.

## RECOGNITION

The Standard provides other examples of when to recognize revenue on sale of goods in an appendix. This covers such things as: 'bill and hold' sale (where the buyer accepts the billing for the product but the products are left with the seller until the buyer requests delivery), goods shipped subject to conditions, lay away sales, orders when payment is received in advance, sale and repurchase agreements, sales to intermediate parties, subscription sales, instalment sales and real estate sales. It is worth noting at this stage that the recognition of revenue on sale of goods involves management in a subjective decision, i.e. revenue is recognized when significant risks and rewards have been transferred to the buyer.

**Rendering of services** Criteria for recognition are also required for rendering of services. Consider Activity 19.7 and the two illustrations below.

## ACTIVITY 19.7

Suggest criteria for the recognition of revenue from services rendered.

### Activity feedback
The criteria are quite similar to those for sale of goods.

- *The amount of revenue can be measured reliably.*
- *It is probable that the economic benefits associated with the transaction will flow to the entity.*

- *The stage of completion of the transaction at the balance sheet date can be measured reliably.*
- *The costs incurred for the transaction and the costs to complete the transaction can be measured reliably.*

*The stage of completion criterion is most important here.*

## ILLUSTRATION

Alpha has a contract with Beta to provide daily security services for a period of three years. The contract involves payment by Beta of €10 000 p.a. and commences at Alpha's opening balance sheet date.

At each balance sheet date, Alpha will recognize revenue of €10 000 for the period of three years as this is in line with the performance of the service.

## ILLUSTRATION

A recruitment agency has a contract with Gamma to seek and appoint a new chief executive (CE). The contract is for a period of 18 months. On the appointment of the CE the agency will receive a payment of €25 000.

This revenue will not be recognized by the agency until the service is actually rendered; that is, the CE is

appointed. The specific act of finding the CE is the significant factor that results in revenue and therefore this service would not be recognized on a straight line basis over the period of the contract.

Stage of completion recognition of revenue is often referred to as percentage-of-completion (POC) method (see Chapter 17). The POC can be estimated by one of several methods, but management must choose the most reliable. The methods available are:

- surveys of work performed
- services performed to date as a percentage of total services to be performed
- the proportion that costs incurred to date bear to the estimated total costs of the transaction.

If the revenue cannot be measured reliably for a service then revenue should only be recognized to the extent that costs incurred can be recovered. If the costs cannot be recovered then these are recognized as an expense.

An interestingly problematic issue arises with customer loyalty programmes (popular with, for example, airlines). A 'sale' now involves immediate inflows, but also creates an expected future outflow (of uncertain amount, timing and rate of take-up). Common practice for many years was to recognize the full revenue immediately, and also to recognize an expense (and provision) for the expected costs of supplying the loyalty award.

IFRIC 13, *Customer Loyalty Programmes,* requires an entity that grants loyalty award credits (such as points or travel miles) to customers who buy other goods or services to allocate some of the proceeds of the initial sale to the award credits and recognize these proceeds as revenue only when they have fulfilled their obligations. The amount allocated to the award credits should be measured by reference to their fair value; that is, the amount for which the award credits could be sold separately (which will logically be less than the cost of actually supplying the loyalty award, to allow for expected non-take-up).

If the entity supplies the awards itself, it recognizes the amounts allocated to the award credits as revenue when the credits are redeemed and the entity fulfils its obligation to supply the awards. If a third party supplies the awards, the entity needs to assess first whether it is collecting the amount allocated to the award credits on its own behalf or as an agent for a third party. Also note that a correction to the unrecognized revenue may be needed from time to time to take account of expired unused loyalty rights.

## REAL WORLD ILLUSTRATION

We reproduce below an extract from the accounting policies section of the Financial Statements for the year ended 31 December 2012 of the Air France/KLM Group.

The two sub-groups Air France and KLM have a common frequent flyer programme 'Flying Blue'. This programme enables members to acquire 'miles' as they fly with Air France, KLM or other partner companies. These miles entitle members to a variety of benefits such as free flights with the two companies or other free services with non-flying partners. In accordance with IFRIC 13 'Loyalty programmes', these 'miles' are considered as distinct elements from a sale with multiple elements and one part of the price of the initial sale of the airfare is allocated to these 'miles' and deferred until the Group's commitments relating to these 'miles' have been met. The deferred amount due in relation to the acquisition of miles by members is estimated:

- according to the fair value of the 'miles', defined as the amount at which the benefits can be sold separately;
- after taking into account the redemption rate, corresponding to the probability that the miles will be used by members, using a statistical method.

With regards to the invoicing of other partners in the programme, the margins realized on sales of 'miles' by the sub-groups Air France and KLM to other partners are recorded immediately in the income statement.

The unrecognized revenue, of over two billion euros, appears in the balance sheet as a separately stated current liability.

**Interest, royalties and dividends** The criteria for recognition of these are:

- It is probable that the economic benefits associated with the transaction will flow to the entity.
- The amount of revenue can be measured reliably.

IAS 18 also specifies the period over which these amounts are recognized: 'Interest should be recognized on a time proportion basis that takes into account the effective yield on the asset.' The effective yield is the rate of interest required to discount the stream of future cash receipts expected over the life of the asset to the initial carrying amount of the asset. An example of this is given in Activity 19.8.

## ACTIVITY 19.8

An entity sells a product to another under an agreement that allows for payment to be made by a series of annual instalments of €4000 for four years. The product generally sells for cash at €16 000. The buyer would, under normal circumstances, be able to obtain finance at a cost of 10 per cent per annum. (Note: the buyer is acquiring the product under a 0 per cent financing agreement.) Identify the revenue to be recognized at the outset by the seller and any other accounting entries to be made over the five-year period.

*Activity feedback*
*The revenue must be recognized at fair value which equates to discounting the cash payments made at 10 per cent. The buyer has received the product at a discounted price from normal sale value of €16 000. A corresponding debtor would be raised at the date of sale. As the instalments are received these will be split between the principal amount which reduces the debt and an amount of interest which will be recognized as revenue.*

'Royalties should be recognized on an accrual basis in accordance with the substance of the relevant agreement.' Generally, royalty payments are based on time or sales. If it is time-based then the revenue should be recognized on the same time base. If it is sales-based then revenue is recognized, say, on the budgeted sales with an adjustment to reflect actual sales at the year-end.

'Dividends should be recognized when the shareholder's right to receive payment is established.' This means that the revenue in this case is recognized in accordance with legal form rather than substance.

## HOW SHOULD IT BE MEASURED?

'Revenue is measured at the fair value of the consideration received or receivable' (IAS 18, para. 9). This sounds simple enough. Now that IFRS 13 applies, fair value is the price that would be received to sell an asset or paid to transfer a liability in an orderly transaction between market participants at the measurement date. It follows that in general we would measure the revenue after trade discounts, early payment discounts or volume rebates.

A problem does arise, however, in the case where revenue is not received by the seller for a period of time. In this case, the consideration eventually received, due to the time value of money, will be less than that originally agreed. It is therefore necessary for the nominal amount of revenue to be discounted where there would be a material difference in the amount received due to the time value of money. The question then needing an answer is: 'What discount rate should be used?' The standard answers as follows:

The imputed rate of interest is the more clearly determinable of either:

- the prevailing rate for a similar instrument of an issuer with a similar credit rating, or
- a rate of interest that discounts the nominal amount of the instrument to the current cash sales price of the goods or services.

It is often the case that goods or services are swapped, not for cash but for other goods and/or services. These swaps (barter transactions) can occur of both alike and dissimilar products. We need to determine whether or not these barter transactions should be treated as revenue and, if they are, how that revenue should be measured.

Where the products are alike, which generally occurs for commodities such as milk, gas or oil where suppliers exchange inventories in different locations to fulfil demand, then the exchange is not regarded as one which generates revenue by IAS 18. Where products are dissimilar then, according to IAS 18, revenue is generated and should be measured at the fair value of the goods or services received or, if this cannot be reliably measured, then at the fair value of the goods or services given up. Now work through Activity 19.9.

## ACTIVITY 19.9

Explain the basis of the logic used by IAS 18 in accounting for barter transactions.

### Activity feedback

IAS 18 defines revenue as a gross inflow of economic benefits that should be recognized when an entity has transferred to the buyer the significant risks and rewards of ownership of the goods.

In a barter transaction involving the exchange of oil in Saudi Arabia for oil in Russia, barter of similar products, then the entities involved are not in a substantially different position to that before the exchange, assuming that the barter was a fair exchange. Each will still have the same risks associated with the oil and neither party will actually have been rewarded. There is no revenue because, in substance, there is no sale.

In the situation involving different products then the barter will result in each entity placing itself in a different position in its operating cycle. Each entity has reached the end of the operating cycle in relation to its product and dispensed with the risks and rewards associated with that product. In exchange they have started on the operating cycle in relation to the new product and are now subject to the new risks and rewards associated with it. So, revenue does exist and will be measured by each entity at the fair value of the goods it has received.

In relation to barter transactions involving advertising a specific SIC, SIC 31, *Barter Transactions Involving Advertising Services,* has been issued. The SIC is concerned with the fair value of the revenue and states that:

The revenue in these transactions can only be reliably measured by reference to non-barter transactions that:

- involve advertising similar to the advertising in the barter transaction
- occur frequently
- represent a predominant number of transactions and amount when compared to non-barter transactions to provide advertising that is similar to the advertising in barter transactions
- involve cash and/or another form of consideration (e.g. marketable securities) that has a reliably measurable fair value, and
- do not involve the same counterparty as in the barter transaction.

## Transactions made up of parts

Transactions can often be made up of several components. To identify their substance we will need to unbundle them and recognize the revenue on the separate parts and perhaps at different times.

Now complete Activity 19.10.

---

### ACTIVITY 19.10

An entity sells a product plus a servicing agreement for three years for €15 000. The product without the servicing could be sold at fair value of €9000. At what point should any revenue be recognized?

*Activity feedback*

*At the initial point of sale, €9000 will be recognized as revenue, always assuming all other criteria have been met for recognition. The servicing revenue will be deferred and only be recognized when that service is rendered.*

---

Activity 19.11 involves transactions made up of parts.

In some business sectors multiple element arrangements are increasingly complex. For example, consider your mobile phone package which probably includes a handset sale, pre-paid minutes for calls and texts, message services, discounts and many other special offers and incentives. How do we separate all these things and account for the separate transactions as revenue, as IAS 18 requires?

---

### ACTIVITY 19.11

Silver is a supplier of silver candlesticks. It currently supplies to several retailers but it has recently contracted to supply only to Sable over the next two years. This contract requires a payment, which is non-refundable, from Sable to Silver of £200 000 on signing and an agreement that Sable will pay Silver £30 for each candlestick. The fair value of the candlesticks to retailers is £30. Although Silver cannot sell candlesticks to anyone but Sable, Sable can buy from other suppliers. How should the revenue, i.e. the lump sum of £200 000, and each sale be recognized in Silver's accounts?

*Activity feedback*

*There are two separately identifiable elements in this contract:*

- *The £200 000 which is a payment to Silver for not selling candlesticks to another retailer for two years. However, this cannot be recognized as revenue in full on signing the contract but must be spread over the two-year period.*

- *The sale of each candlestick which will be recognized as each sale is made in accordance with IAS 18.*

---

### ACTIVITY 19.12

In Activity 19.11, if the contract specified that Silver would sell candlesticks to Sable at £20, i.e. £10 less than the fair value sale to retailers, would the recognition of the revenue change?

*Activity feedback*

*The answer is yes as cross-subsidization now exists between the two elements in the contract. The lump sum* of £200 000 now incorporates an element for the discount on fair value. An estimate of the total discount must be made and subtracted from the lump sum; the remainder of the lump sum will then be spread over the two-year period. The discount element will be recognized as each sale is made.

Activity 19.13 should test your understanding of this chapter.

## ACTIVITY 19.13

Identify when the revenue, if indeed there is such, in the following transactions should be recognized.

1 Commitment fees received by an entity to originate or purchase a loan.

2 Advertising media commissions carried out for a client where inflows will be received when the advert is exposed in the media.

3 Tuition fees paid to a training entity.

4 Servicing fees included in the price of a product sold by an entity.

5 An entity sells all its inventory of wine to the bank with the option to repurchase the wine at any time it wishes and at a price that increases by 5 per cent per annum on the original sale price.

### Activity feedback

1 If it is unlikely that a specific loan agreement will be entered into, then the commitment fee will be recognized on a time basis over the commitment period. Otherwise, the commitment fee will be recognized when both parties legally agree to the loan.

2 These will be recognized when the advertisement is seen by the public.

3 Revenue will need to be recognized over the period of tuition.

4 The servicing amount included in the price of the product is separated out and deferred and recognized as revenue over the period of service generally on a straight line basis.

5 In this case it seems apparent that the seller has not transferred the risks and rewards associated with the wine to the bank. In fact, the substance of the transaction is that of a loan guaranteed on the value of the wine. No revenue will be recognized in this case as it is a financing arrangement.

## Disclosure requirements

The disclosure requirements of IAS 18 are quite straightforward and what we would expect. They cover accounting policy adopted to recognize revenue, method of determining stage of completion of services, the amount of significant revenue from sale of goods, rendering of services, interest, royalties and dividends, and the amount of revenue recognized from exchanges of goods or services.

## REAL WORLD ILLUSTRATION

The following is an example of an accounting policy for revenue taken from Vodafone's financial statements for the year ended 31 March 2012.

### Annual Report

#### Revenue

Revenue is recognized to the extent the Group has delivered goods or rendered services under an agreement, the amount of revenue can be measured reliably and it is probable that the economic benefits associated with the transaction will flow to the Group. Revenue is measured at the fair value of the consideration received, exclusive of sales taxes and discounts.

The Group principally obtains revenue from providing the following telecommunication services: access charges, airtime usage, messaging, interconnect fees, data services and information provision, connection fees and equipment sales. Products and services may be sold separately or in bundled packages.

Revenue for access charges, airtime usage and messaging by contract customers is recognized as services are performed, with unbilled revenue resulting from services already provided accrued at the end of each period and unearned revenue from services to be provided in future periods deferred. Revenue from the sale of prepaid credit is deferred until such time as the customer uses the airtime, or the credit expires.

*(Continued)*

## REAL WORLD ILLUSTRATION  *(Continued)*

Revenue from interconnect fees is recognized at the time the services are performed.

Revenue from data services and information provision is recognized when the Group has performed the related service and, depending on the nature of the service, is recognized either at the gross amount billed to the customer or the amount receivable by the Group as commission for facilitating the service.

Customer connection revenue is recognized together with the related equipment revenue to the extent that the aggregate equipment and connection revenue does not exceed the fair value of the equipment delivered to the customer. Any customer connection revenue not recognized together with related equipment revenue is deferred and recognized over the period in which services are expected to be provided to the customer.

Revenue for device sales is recognized when the device is delivered to the end customer and the sale is considered complete. For device sales made to intermediaries, revenue is recognized if the significant risks associated with the device are transferred to the intermediary and the intermediary has no general right of return. If the significant risks are not transferred, revenue recognition is deferred until sale of the device to an end customer by the intermediary or the expiry of the right of return.

In revenue arrangements including more than one deliverable, the arrangements are divided into separate units of accounting. Deliverables are considered separate units of accounting if the following two conditions are met: (1) the deliverable has value to the customer on a stand-alone basis; and (2) there is evidence of the fair value of the item. The arrangement consideration is allocated to each separate unit of accounting based on its relative fair value.

## A REPLACEMENT FOR IAS 18?

The IASB, in conjunction with the FASB, has had a project to revise the requirements for accounting for revenues for a number of years. The project has been proceeding extremely slowly. We reported in our fifth edition about a discussion paper issued in 2008. This was succeeded by an exposure draft in 2010, which received considerable criticism. In November 2011 a second exposure draft was issued. This seems likely to emerge eventually as a new standard, possibly to be numbered IFRS 14. The finalization of the standard is causing much difficulty. It is being conducted as a joint project with the American FASB (which has never before had a general standard on revenues). At the time of writing, the declared intention is to issue a new standard, to replace both IAS 18 and IAS 11, before the end of 2013, for compulsory adoption with effect from 1 January 2017, which seems to be a very long way away, but with early adoption permitted.

Given all the changes, uncertainties, and past and possible future delays, it would be dangerous to assume that the details of this latest exposure draft will remain unaltered. A new standard from the two Boards is promised before the end of 2013, so it can be reliably expected by the end of 2014. Discussions, with votes, involving changes, are still regularly occurring. We give here, however, an outline of the main points of the 2011 exposure draft. Neither we as authors nor you as readers can rely on crystallization of the final details until the standard is finally accepted by the Board(s) and actually published. Two significant features of the proposals are first that the new standard will replace both IAS 18, *Revenues,* and IAS 11, *Construction Contracts,* and second that in some circumstances the recognition of revenue will be significantly delayed as compared with the existing requirements of IAS 18 and IAS 11.

The 'core principle' of the proposals is that an entity should recognize revenue to depict the transfer of promised goods or services to customers in an amount which reflects the consideration to which the entity expects to be entitled in exchange for those goods or services. In order to achieve this principle, an entity should apply all of five designated steps, which are outlined below.

**Step 1**. Identify the contract with a customer. A contract is an agreement between two or more parties which creates enforceable rights and obligations. Each contract will be considered separately regarding steps 2–5 unless specified criteria are met for the combination of contracts.

**Step 2**. Identify the separate performance obligations in the contract. A performance obligation is a promise in a contract with a customer to transfer a good or service to that customer. Distinct goods or services are accounted for separately as different performance obligations. Promised goods or services which are 'not distinct' are combined until the entity identifies a bundle of goods or services which is distinct, thereby creating a single performance obligation. In the real practical world, there is obvious scope for some debate here as to the appropriate treatment. In general, a good or service is distinct if either the entity regularly sells the good or service separately, or the customer can benefit from the good or service either on its own or together with other resources which are readily available to that customer.

**Step 3**. Determine the transaction price. The transaction price is the amount of consideration to which an entity expects to be entitled in exchange for transferring promised goods or services to a customer, excluding amounts collected on behalf of third parties (such as taxes). Note that the amount is the expected entitlement, not the possibly lower expected receipts.

**Step 4**. Allocate the transaction price to the separate performance obligations in the contract. This allocation should be done on a relative stand-alone selling price basis (estimated if necessary).

**Step 5**. Recognize revenue when (or as) the entity satisfies a performance obligation. This is achieved by transferring a promised good or service to a customer. This transfer happens when (or as) the customer obtains control of that good or service.

## ACTIVITY 19.14

Are the proposals for a replacement of IAS 18 significantly different from IAS 18 (and IAS 11)?

### Activity feedback

The essential difference is that the notion of control by the customer has been introduced as a fundamental element. This is likely to significantly delay revenue recognition, particularly in relation to a long-term project or contract. Indeed, the practical effect may well be to in effect revert to something close to the completed contract method for long-term contracts, representing a major change from the substance-based matching principle relating to 'work done', which underlay the older regulations.

But remember that these are still only proposals, and changes have occurred several times before in relation to this project. It is essential that you update yourself with the content of the new standard when you actually study this area. You should also note carefully that unless minds are changed (yet) again, the old requirements of IAS 18 will remain available until 1 January 2017.

## SUMMARY

We have seen throughout this chapter that the recognition of revenue, which is key in the determination of profit of an entity, is dependent on several factors. These factors also require judgements to be made by management, many of which will require subjectivity. Management has to take decisions on:

- what constitutes the ordinary activities of the entity
- whether or not significant risks and rewards of ownership have been transferred to a buyer
- whether the amount of revenue involved can be measured reliably, i.e. can its fair value be determined
- whether it is probable that economic benefits associated with the transaction (sale) will flow to the entity
- whether the costs in respect of the transaction can be measured reliably
- what stage a particular service has reached in its delivery.

We have also seen that revenue is distinguished from income which incorporates gains as well as revenue. Gains are generally seen as being those items that result from activities outside the ordinary activities of the entity, for example gains from the sale of non-current assets or upward revaluations of non-current assets.

All of this ensures that the revenue that is recognized in financial statements is reliable and prudent, but it may not be very relevant in a business world where most production is sold. Currently, we do not recognize gains on stocks of goods for sale but it is arguable that this information would be relevant to users. All we provide them with is information on the cost of the product (or NRV, whichever is the lower), not information on what the asset of stock could be sold for assuming a reasonable marketplace.

IAS 18 is 'principles-based' with few detailed rules. This leaves substantial scope for judgement and interpretation and could lead to a lack of consistency A replacement for IAS 18 is scheduled, after very great argument and delay, to appear before the publication of this book, with adoption mandatory from 1 January 2017.

## EXERCISES

*Suggested answers to exercises marked ✓ are to be found on our dedicated CourseMate platform for students.*

*Suggested answers to the remaining exercises are to be found on the Instructor online support resources.*

✓ **1**    What is revenue? Distinguish it from other gains.

**2**    Useful information is provided to users by restricting the definition of revenue to that arising from ordinary activities only. Discuss.

**3**    IAS 18 is based on substance over form. Discuss.

**4**    Financial reports prepared under IAS 18 are irrelevant and unreliable. Discuss.

**5**   The IAS 18 method of revenue recognition proves that accountants are prudent. Discuss.

**6**   Explain the relationship between revenue recognition and asset valuation.

**7**   Analyze the need to discount deferred inflows to an entity as permitted by IAS 18.

✓ **8**   Recognition of revenue in accordance with IAS 18 is objective. Discuss.

**9**   How does IAS 18 differ from its replacement? Has there been an improvement?

**10**   (a)  Revenue recognition is the process by which companies decide when and how much income should be included in the income statement. It is a topical area of great debate in the accounting profession. The IASB looks at revenue recognition from conceptual and substance points of view. There are occasions where a more traditional approach to revenue recognition does not entirely conform to the IASB guidance; indeed, neither do some International Accounting Standards.

**Required:**

Explain the implications that the IASB's *Framework for the Preparation and Presentation of Financial Statements* (Framework) and the application of substance over form have on the recognition of income. Give examples of how this may conflict with traditional practice and some accounting standards.

(b)  Derringdo sells good supplied by Gungho. The goods are classed as A grade, perfect quality, or B grade, having slight faults. Derringdo sells the A grade goods acting as an agent for Gungho at a fixed price calculated to yield a gross profit margin of 50 per cent. Derringdo receives a commission of 12.5 per cent of the sales it achieves for these goods. The arrangement for B grade goods is that they are sold by Gungho to Derringdo and Derringdo sells them at a gross profit margin of 25 per cent. The following information has been obtained from Derringdo's financial records:

|  |  | $000 |
|---|---|---|
| Inventory held on premises 1 April 2002 | A grade | 2 400 |
|  | B grade | 1 000 |
| Goods from Gungho year to 31 March 2003 | A grade | 18 000 |
|  | B grade | 8 800 |
| Inventory held on premises 31 March 2003 | A grade | 2 000 |
|  | B grade | 1 250 |

**Required:**

Prepare the income statement extracts for Derringdo for the year to 31 March 2003 reflecting the above information.

(ACCA – June 2003)

**11**   Identify when the revenue, if indeed there is any, in the following transactions should be recognized in accordance with IAS 18, *Revenue*.

(a)  Land has been sold by A entity to Connect Housing Association entity for £1m unconditionally and irrevocably with contracts exchanged. £0.6m of the consideration is payable after six months, and £0.4m 12 months after A's year-end. Connect is expecting to build apartments on the land and the project is likely to receive lottery funding, although this is not guaranteed. The uncertainty over the funding is the reason Connect has agreed delayed payment.

(b) B entity rents cars to 'not own fault' accident victims. The rental for such cars is billed to the insurance company of the fault driver. Negotiations then take place between B and the insurance company as to how much of the charge for the rental car will be paid.

(c) Z entity, a broadband network provider, supplies equipment and a maintenance service to its customers at a charge of £216 p.a. The price of the maintenance service is £160 p.a. and the cost of the equipment £80 if purchased separately.

(d) Y entity sells motorboats for £50 000 each. The company also provides moorings at £5000 p.a. to customers. If a customer buys the boat and mooring package together, he is given a 5 per cent discount on the cost of the total package. The normal profit on the boat is 25 per cent and the moorings 50 per cent to Y.

(e) A law firm provides services to defendants on a no-win/no-fee basis. Lawyers' fees are normally charged on a time basis and fees are billed monthly.

(f) A entity sells materials for making doors to two manufacturers, X and Y, who assemble the frames and put glass in the doors. A receives the doors back from X and Y and sells them to a builder for installation in homes. The precise details of the sale of materials to X and Y are as follows:

- X buys the materials at £10 per door from A without any guarantee that A will purchase the assembled doors; X buys materials for assembly from other manufacturers; no price for the purchase of the doors by A is agreed on the sale of materials to X.
- Y buys the materials from A, which cost A £5, at £10 per door; A agrees to buy the finished doors back from Y at £50.

(g) Keepfit plc operates gyms that charge a joining fee of £250. This fee entitles members to life membership. In addition, members pay £6 per session. Non-members can use the gym at £8 per session. Historical records indicate that members use the gym about 50 times per year and that they hold membership for two years.

(h) Lowds plc manufactures and sells caravans. When a customer orders a caravan, an advance payment of 10 per cent of the sale price is required. In most cases orders are taken for caravans that are not yet completed.

(i) A university collects fees from its students at the beginning of the academic year in which the students enrol for the whole of their course. The course may last from one to three years.

12 LMN trades in motor vehicles which are manufactured and supplied by their manufacturer, IJK. Trading between the two entities is subject to a contractual agreement, the principal terms of which are as follows:

- LMN is entitled to hold on its premises up to 80 vehicles supplied by IJK at any one time. LMN is free to specify the ranges and models of vehicle supplied to it. IJK retains legal title to the vehicles until such time as they are sold to a third party by LMN.
- While the vehicles remain on its premises, LMN is required to insure them against loss or damage.
- The price at which vehicles are supplied is determined at the time of delivery; it is not subject to any subsequent alteration.

- When LMN sells a vehicle to a third party it is required to inform IJK within three working days. IJK submits an invoice to LMN at the originally agreed price; the invoice is payable by LMN within 30 days.
- LMN is entitled to use any of the vehicles supplied to it for demonstration purposes and road testing. However, if more than a specified number of kilometres are driven in a vehicle, LMN is required to pay IJK a rental charge.
- LMN has the right to return any vehicle to IJK at any time without incurring a penalty, except for any rental charge incurred in respect of excess kilometres driven.

**Required:**

Discuss the economic substance of the contractual arrangement between the two entities in respect of the recognition of inventory and of sales. Refer where appropriate to IAS 18, *Revenue*.

(CIMA P8 Financial Analysis – 23 May 2006)

**13**  EJ publishes trade magazines and sells them to retailers. EJ has just concluded negotiations with a large supermarket chain for the supply of a large quantity of several of its trade magazines on a regular basis.

EJ has agreed a substantial discount on the following terms:

- The same quantity of each trade magazine will be supplied each month.
- Quantities can only be changed at the end of each six-month period.
- Payment must be made six months in advance.

The supermarket paid $150 000 on 1 September 2007 for six months supply of trade magazines to 29 February 2008. At 31 October 2007, EJ had supplied two months of trade magazines. EJ estimates that the cost of supplying the supermarket each month is $20 000.

**Required:**

(i)   State the criteria in IAS 18, *Revenue,* for income recognition.

(ii)  Explain, with reasons, how EJ should treat the above in its financial statements for the year ended 31 October 2007.

(CIMA P7 Financial Accounting & Tax Principles – 22 November 2007)

**14**  Johan, a public limited company, operates in the telecommunications industry. The industry is capital intensive with heavy investment in licences and network infrastructure. Competition in the sector is fierce and technological advances are a characteristic of the industry. Johan has responded to these factors by offering incentives to customers and, in an attempt to acquire and retain them, Johan purchased a telecom licence on 1 December 2006 for $120 million. The licence has a term of six years and cannot be used until the network assets and infrastructure are ready for use. The related network assets and infrastructure became ready for use on 1 December 2007. Johan could not operate in the country without the licence and is not permitted to sell the licence. Johan expects its subscriber base to grow over the period of the licence, but is disappointed with its market share for the year to 30 November 2008. The licence agreement does not deal with the renewal of the licence, but there is an expectation that the regulator will grant a single renewal for the same period of time as long as certain criteria regarding network build quality and service quality are met. Johan has no experience of the charge that will be made by the regulator for the renewal but other licences have been renewed at a nominal cost. The licence is currently stated at its original cost of $120 million in the statement of financial position under non-current assets.

Johan is considering extending its network and has carried out a feasibility study during the year to 30 November 2008. The design and planning department of Johan identified five possible geographical areas for the extension of its network. The internal costs of this study were $150 000 and the external costs were $100 000 during the year to 30 November 2008. Following the feasibility study, Johan chose a geographical area where it was going to install a base station for the telephone network. The location of the base station was dependent upon getting planning permission. A further independent study has been carried out by third party consultants in an attempt to provide a preferred location in the area as there is a need for the optimal operation of the network in terms of signal quality and coverage. Johan proposes to build a base station on the recommended site on which planning permission has been obtained. The third party consultants have charged $50 000 for the study. Additionally, Johan has paid $300 000 as a single payment together with $60 000 a month to the government of the region for access to the land upon which the base station will be situated. The contract with the government is for a period of 12 years and commenced on 1 November 2008. There is no right of renewal of the contract and legal title to the land remains with the government.

Johan purchases telephone handsets from a manufacturer for $200 each, and sells the handsets direct to customers for $150 if they purchase call credit (call card) in advance on what is called a prepaid phone. The costs of selling the handset are estimated at $1 per set. The customers using a prepaid phone pay $21 for each call card at the purchase date. Call cards expire six months from the date of first sale. There is an average unused call credit of $3 per card after six months and the card is activated when sold.

Johan also sells handsets to dealers for $150 and invoices the dealers for those handsets. The dealer can return the handset up to a service contract being signed by a customer. When the customer signs a service contract, the customer receives the handset free of charge. Johan allows the dealer a commission of $280 on the connection of a customer and the transaction with the dealer is settled net by a payment of $130 by Johan to the dealer being the cost of the handset to the dealer ($150) deducted from the commission ($280). The handset cannot be sold separately by the dealer and the service contract lasts for a 12-month period. Dealers do not sell prepaid phones, and Johan receives monthly revenue from the service contract.

The chief operating officer, a non-accountant, has asked for an explanation of the accounting principles and practices which should be used to account for the above events.

**Required:**

Discuss the principles and practices which should be used in the financial year to 30 November 2008 to account for:

(a) the licences

(b) the costs incurred in extending the network

(c) the purchase of handsets and the recognition of revenue from customers and dealers.

(ACCA P2 int. – December 2008)

# PROVISIONS, CONTINGENT LIABILITIES AND CONTINGENT ASSETS

# 20

**OBJECTIVES**  After studying this chapter you should be able to:

- describe the issues IAS 37 attempts to address

- define provisions and contingencies

- account for provisions and contingencies in accordance with IAS 37

- appraise the recognition and measurement criteria of IAS 37

- describe the presentation requirements in relation to provisions and contingencies

- consider possible changes to IAS 37.

## INTRODUCTION

Financial statements of all entities are prepared at an arbitrary date – the balance sheet date – which is a convenient cut-off point. However, no matter how sophisticated the information systems, judgements still have to be made concerning conditions existing at the balance sheet date with uncertain outcomes. In essence, IAS 37 deals with situations where obligations to or from an entity are uncertain in either existence of event and/or amount of that event. The accounting, or not, for such conditions can have a marked effect on both the balance sheet and income statement of an entity.

## PROBLEMS IDENTIFIED

### ACTIVITY 20.1

PPR entity, a retailer of washing machines, has a year-end of 31 December. During December a washing machine was sold to a customer who carried out the plumbing himself. On 24 December, the washing machine failed to operate correctly, resulting in the customer's house suffering severe damage due to flooding. The customer, together with several relatives, had to spend the festive season in an hotel as his home was uninhabitable. The customer is planning to sue PPR for a considerable amount of damages. Would you, as an accountant for PPR, accrue a loss for the damages pending or not?

*Activity feedback*
*The first question to ask is, is there a liability? A liability is 'a present obligation of the entity arising from past*

*events, the settlement of which is expected to result in an outflow from the entity of resources embodying economic benefits' (Framework, para. 4.4 (b)). The problem here is that the outcome will presumably only be confirmed when the claim for damages is settled. What view should we take of the outcome of this claim? Will we have to pay out damages? If so, how much? Should we assume the claim will be found against the entity and estimate how much that claim will be and accrue in the income statement or not? The decision as to whether we do or not is likely to have a profound effect on profits if the claim is substantial.*

The area of provisions and contingencies has led to substantial creative accounting within accounts and has given rise to the term 'big bath accounting', which is discussed in more detail in Part Four of this book. The following activity illustrates this term.

### ACTIVITY 20.2

An entity with annual expected future profits of €2.5m decides to recognize a provision (on the grounds of prudence) for reorganization costs for future years of €2m in the current year when its expected profits are €4.5m. The reorganization involves decentralization of all activities relating to purchases and sales to the entity's outlying units from the centre.

In the event, the charges for the reorganization are €0.5m next year, €0.5m the following year, and thereafter no further costs arise.

Show the effect of the proposed accounting treatment for the reorganization costs on the profits for the company for the current and future years. Comment on this treatment.

*Activity feedback*

|  | Year 1 | Year 2 | Year 3 | Year 4 |
|---|---|---|---|---|
| Provision b/f | 0.0 | 2.0 | 1.5 | 0.0 |
| Expense | 0.0 | (0.5) | (0.5) | 0.0 |
| Income statement charge | 2.0 | 0.0 | (1.0) | 0.0 |
| Provision c/f | 2.0 | 1.5 | 0.0 | 0.0 |
| Profits | 4.5 | 2.5 | 2.5 | 2.5 |
| Provision charged to income statement | (2.0) | 0.0 | 1.0 | 0.0 |
| Profit after provision | 2.5 | 2.5 | 3.5 | 2.5 |

*The entity has been able to charge the provision for the reorganization against the profits in the first year which were higher than generally expected. In future years the entity has been able to charge €0.5m to the provision instead of the income statement, thus profits in these years have not been*

*reduced. In addition, as all the provision has not been required, the excess provision has been released back to the income statement in year 3 increasing profits to €3.5m. In effect, the entity has taken a 'big bath' in year 1 when it had substantial profits and has protected future years' profits.*

Activities 20.1 and 20.2 show the potential for creativity in the provisions area and therefore the need for a Standard on the issue. If recognition of a provision is further based on the intention to incur expenditure rather than an obligation to do so, then this could create even more creativity in accounting. We could have the situation arising where a provision is provided for the reorganization costs just given, and then if this reorganization is not carried out, the whole provision might be released to next year's profits. The recognition of such a provision does not reflect a change in economic position of the entity, since only an external commitment can affect the financial position at the balance sheet date. Without a complete framework for accounting for and disclosure of provisions, users are not presented with a true and fair view of the state of affairs.

## PROVISIONS, CONTINGENT LIABILITIES AND CONTINGENT ASSETS

IAS 37, issued by the IASB in 1998, updated those parts of IAS 10, *Contingencies and Events Occurring after the Balance Sheet Date* (1974), relating to contingencies, but also issued guidance on provisions which were not covered by IAS 10. IAS 37 effectively bans:

- big bath accounting
- creation of provisions where no obligation to a liability exists, and
- the use of provisions to smooth profits

and required greater disclosure in relation to provisions to aid the user's understanding and present a true and fair view.

### Scope

IAS 37 is to be applied to all entities when accounting for provisions, contingent liabilities and contingent assets except for those items resulting from executory contracts, except where the contract is onerous, and those covered by another IAS. Examples of items covered by another IAS are IAS 11, *Construction Contracts,* and IAS 19, *Retirement Benefits.* Executory contracts also need some explanation. These are contracts where neither party has performed any of its obligations or both parties have partially performed obligations to an equal amount. The Standard does not apply to financial instruments that are within the scope of IFRS 9, *Financial Instruments.*

### ACTIVITY 20.3

Identify an executory contract within entities.

*Activity feedback*
*Such contracts generally cover delivery of future services, for example:*

- *gas, electricity, local taxes*
- *purchase orders*
- *employee contributions in respect of continued employment.*

It is also worth clarifying at this point certain provisions that IAS 37 does not cover. This arises because IAS 37 uses the word 'provisions' to mean a liability of uncertain timing or amount, but in the general language of accounting it is common for the word 'provision' to be applied to:

- provision for depreciation
- provision for doubtful debts
- provision for impairment.

In these cases, the 'provision' is adjusting the carrying amount of the asset; it is not a liability of uncertain timing or amount.

## Objectives

The objectives of IAS 37 are fairly clear and laudable:

> To ensure that appropriate recognition criteria and measurement bases are applied to provisions, contingent liabilities and contingent assets and that sufficient information is disclosed in the notes to the financial statements to enable users to understand their nature, timing and amount.

## Definitions

We have already identified two of these for you (IAS 37, para. 10):

> A *provision* is a 'liability of uncertain timing or amount'.
> A *liability* is a 'present obligation of the entity arising from past events, the settlement of which is expected to result in the outflow from the entity of resources embodying economic benefits'.

One of the key words in the definition of a liability is 'obligation'. So what is an obligation? An obligation can be either legal or constructive:

> A *legal obligation* is an obligation that derives from:
>
> **(a)** contract (through its explicit or implicit terms)
> **(b)** legislation, or
> **(c)** other operation of law.
>
> A contract can become onerous and this occurs when 'the unavoidable costs of meeting the obligations under the contract exceed the economic benefits expected to be received under it'.

(IAS 37, para. 10)

> A *constructive obligation* is an obligation that derives from an entity's actions where:
>
> **(a)** by an established pattern of past practice, published policies or a sufficiently specific current statement, the entity has indicated to other parties that it will accept certain responsibilities; and
> **(b)** as a result the entity has created a valid expectation on the part of those other parties that it will discharge those responsibilities.

(IAS 37, para. 10)

## ACTIVITY 20.4

Identify which of the following is a constructive obligation of the entity.

1 *A*, a leisure entity, causes severe damage to the habitat of wildlife in a country where there is no legal protection for the wildlife. The company has a high profile in the support of wildlife as it makes large contributions to the World Wildlife Fund and campaigns vigorously on its behalf. To rectify the damage to the habitat a charge of €1m is likely.

2 An entity in the oil industry causes severe pollution when one of its tankers grounds off a Pacific island. The entity has avoided costs of cleaning up such contamination in the past and pays little regard to environmental issues.

### Activity feedback

1 *This is a constructive obligation as there is a valid expectation that the entity will clean up the habitat.*

2 *This is not a constructive obligation as no valid expectation has been created by the entity that it will repair the damage to the ocean.*

## ACTIVITY 20.5

Identify in your own words the key differences between a provision and a contingent liability.

### Activity feedback

*Provisions require:*

- *a present obligation arising from a past event*
- *a probable outflow of economic benefits*
- *an evaluation of timing and amount.*

*Contingent liabilities occur when one or more of the conditions for a provision are not met, i.e. either:*

- *a possible obligation from past event exists*
- *and/or an outflow of economic benefits is not probable*
- *and/or a reliable estimate of outflow cannot be made.*

A *contingent liability* is:

- a possible obligation that arises from past events and whose existence will be confirmed only by the occurrence or non-occurrence of one or more uncertain future events not wholly within the control of the entity, or
- a present obligation that arises from past events but is not recognized because:
  - it is not probable that an outflow of resources embodying economic benefits will be required to settle the obligation, or
  - the amount of the obligation cannot be measured with sufficient reliability.

In essence, a contingent liability is a provision where one or more of the three requirements is not met. IAS 37 provides (in an appendix) a useful decision tree to determine whether a provision or contingent liability exists in a given set of circumstances (included here as Figure 20.1).

This is all rather confusing as a provision is in fact a liability which is contingent as its timing or amount is uncertain, but it is called a provision not a contingent liability. A contingent liability as defined by IAS 37 is by its name a liability, but is not recognized as such as it is not charged in the accounts; it is only disclosed.

IAS 37 (para. 10) also defines a contingent asset for us as:

A possible asset that arises from past events and whose existence will be confirmed only by the occurrence or non-occurrence of one or more uncertain future events not wholly within the control of the entity.

**Figure 20.1  Decision tree to determine existence of provision or contingent**

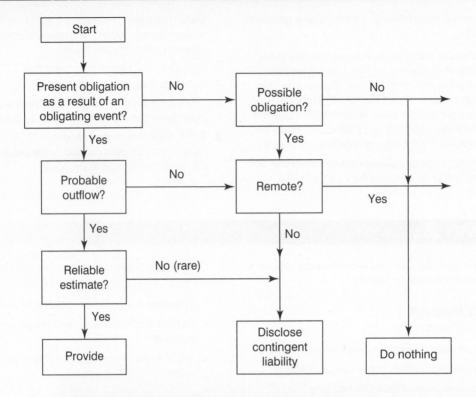

## ACCOUNTING FOR PROVISIONS, CONTINGENT LIABILITIES AND CONTINGENT ASSETS

If the conditions for a provision are met and a reliable estimate can be made of the amount, then this amount will be recognized in the income statement for the year and will be shown as a provision on the balance sheet. A contingent liability is not recognized in the financial statements but it is disclosed as follows:

- a brief description of the nature
- an estimate of its financial effect
- an indication of the uncertainties relating to the amount or timing of outflow
- the possibility of any reimbursement.

A contingent asset is not recognized in the accounts but it is disclosed if the inflow of economic benefits is probable.

You should have noted by now that how we treat future inflow or outflow of economic benefits in the accounts is dependent on how we/management/experts define the words 'probable', 'possible' and 'remote'. IAS 37, in para. 23, states that 'for the purpose of this standard' an outflow is probable, and requires to be recognized, if 'the probability that the event will occur is greater than the probability that it will not'. This explicitly indicates that a 51 per cent likelihood is 'probable'. If not 'probable', a contingent liability is disclosed (as 'possible'), unless the likelihood is 'remote', in which case nothing is reported at all. Neither 'possible' nor 'remote' are defined in the Standard. Remote presumably means very unlikely, and possible is everything above remote but lower than probable.

## ACTIVITY 20.6

Identify how the following items should be treated in the accounts of the entity at year-end 31 December 20X1. All information is at year-end 31 December 20X1 unless stated otherwise.

1 An airline entity is required by law to overhaul its aircraft once every three years. The aircraft were purchased a year ago.

2 An entity has guaranteed a loan taken out by one of its subsidiary entities. In March 20X1, the subsidiary placed itself in liquidation and there would appear to be insufficient funds to repay the loan.

3 An entity catered for a wedding reception in September 20X1. Subsequent to the wedding, several people have died of food poisoning. The entity is disputing liability for the case brought against it by the relatives of the dead and its lawyers advise that it is probable that they will not be found liable.

4 An entity leases a factory under an operating lease. During the year it moves production of its products to a new factory but the old factory lease cannot be cancelled and it cannot be re-let.

5 The government of the country in which an entity operates makes substantial changes to the health and safety legislation under which it must operate. The entity will have to retrain a large proportion of its staff to ensure compliance with the new legislation. No retraining has taken place yet.

6 An entity at the year-end had discounted €600 000 bills of exchange without recourse. At 15 March 20X2, €150 000 were still outstanding and are due to mature in one month's time.

7 No bill has been received for electricity supplied in the last quarter of the year.

### Activity feedback

1 At the current balance sheet date, no obligation to overhaul the aircraft exists independent of the entity's future action. The entity could sell the aircraft to avoid the overhaul cost. This is not a provision, neither is it a contingent liability.

2 The entity has an obligation to fulfil the guarantee given and it appears that an outflow of funds is probable. A provision should be recognized in the accounts.

3 There is no obligation and therefore no provision should be made. It is a contingent liability and a note should be made to the accounts unless the lawyers advise that the probability of any transfer of funds is extremely remote.

4 This is, in fact, an example of an onerous contract. There is a present legal obligation and a provision is required of the unavoidable lease payments in total. Prior to the contract becoming onerous, it would have been treated in accordance with IAS 17, Leases.

5 There is no obligating event as no staff training has taken place yet, and therefore no provision is recognized; neither is there a contingent liability. The entity might need to consider whether there is a possibility it is placing itself in a situation where it will be fined for non-compliance with the new regulations, and, if this is the case (that is, the legislation is already in force), then a provision may need to be made for the fines, if any, that could be imposed.

6 The bills of exchange are without recourse and therefore no liability falls on the entity.

7 This is an accrual as there is very little uncertainty in respect of the timing or the amount due.

There is an example in the Standard of an application to an offshore oilfield. In this example, an entity operating an oilrig has a legal obligation to remove the rig and clean up the site at the end of the oil extraction. The Standard concludes that this cost should be charged as a provision at the outset of the operation. This appears to us to be in direct contrast to the example of the aircraft maintenance at point 1 in Activity 20.6. The oilrig could be sold as easily as the aircraft.

It is a requirement of IAS 37 that provisions be reviewed at each balance sheet date and adjusted where required, and that the expenditure set against a provision is only that in relation to the intent of the provision. Therefore, a provision which we discover is no longer required cannot be used for the offset of other expenditure.

It is often the case that an entity can be reimbursed by another party for some of the expenditure in relation to a provision (e.g. insurance contracts, suppliers' warranties). In these cases, the reimbursement must be treated as a separate asset and indeed only accounted for in the income statement when the reimbursement is virtually certain.

## Measurement of provisions

So far we have been concerned with the recognition of a provision or a contingent liability, but we must also determine an amount. Remember, a provision can only be recognized in the financial statements if a reliable estimate can be made of the amount. If no reliable estimate can be made of the amount, then a contingent liability is disclosed (this will rarely occur).

IAS 37 requires that when determining a reliable estimate this should be 'the best estimate of the expenditure required to settle the present obligation at the balance sheet date' (para. 36). The best estimate is determined by the judgement of management, supplemented by experience of similar transactions and/or reports from independent experts. The emphasis on present obligation in the measurement rule is deliberate and this means that the effect of future events in this measurement must be carefully evaluated. It is only where such future events are expected to occur with some certainty and objectivity that they will be taken account of.

---

### ACTIVITY 20.7

An entity has a present obligation due to a past event to pay €2m to clean up a waste site. It is currently expected that technological developments that are near completion will decrease this cost to €1.5m. It has also been brought to management's attention that some research is underway (but in its infancy) that might reduce these costs further. At what value would the provision for the clean-up costs be shown in the accounts?

*Activity feedback*

*The technological developments appear to have certainty and objectivity to them, but the other research is much less objective and therefore the provision should be shown at €1.5m.*

---

In practice, the decision may not be as clear-cut as we have just indicated. One future event that is not taken account of in measuring a provision is the gain on the expected disposal of a related asset. The Standard states that these gains must be dealt with in accordance with the Standards dealing with the assets concerned. This is presumably because until there is a binding contract to sell the asset, the management can change the decision in respect of the sale. We will deal with this issue again when we look at restructuring and provisions later in this chapter.

The best estimate of a provision can require the use of statistical methods of estimation. This can occur when a provision consists of a large population of items where possible outcomes have various probabilities attached. The method of estimation used in this case is known as 'expected value'.

If the provision relates to a single item or event or a small number of events, then the expected value technique cannot be used. In this case the most 'likely outcome' is used.

## ILLUSTRATION

An entity sells goods under warranty. Past experience indicates that 80 per cent of goods sold will have no defects, 15 per cent will have minor defects and 5 per cent major defects. If minor defects occurred in all goods sold, the cost of rectification would be €5m and for major defects €15m. What is the expected value of the provision to be recorded in the financial statements of the entity at the balance sheet date? The expected value is:

$$80\% \times 0 + 15\% \times 5 + 5\% \times 15 = 1.5m$$

## ACTIVITY 20.8

An entity is facing a substantial legal claim for €5m. The lawyers estimate that there is a 40 per cent chance of successfully defending the claim. At what value should this provision be shown in the accounts?

### Activity feedback

Care needs to be exercised here as the answer is not 60% × €5m. We have to use the most likely outcome technique here. The most likely outcome, 60 per cent chance, is of an unsuccessful defence against the claim, and therefore the best estimate of the provision required is €5m.

## ACTIVITY 20.9

An entity is under warranty to replace a major component in a computer hardware system. The major component costs €0.5m to replace and five of these components are used in the system. Experience shows that there is a 45 per cent chance of only one component failing, a 30 per cent chance of two failing, and a 25 per cent chance of three failures. It has never been known for more than three to fail. What is the value of the provision that should be shown in the accounts of the entity?

### Activity feedback

At first glance the answer to the best estimate would appear to be the costs of one failure, €0.5m, as this is the most likely outcome at 45 per cent occurrence. However, there is a 55 per cent probability that more than one failure would occur, and therefore the best estimate is €1m, that is, of two failures. If the probabilities had been 25 per cent of one failure, 35 per cent of two and 40 per cent of three, then the best estimate would again be €1m (two failures), as there is only a 40 per cent chance of three failures and a 60 per cent chance of fewer than three.

Provisions are measured before the effect of any tax consequences. The tax effect will be shown in accordance with IAS 12, *Income Taxes* (see Chapter 21).

## Measurement at present value

'Where the effect of the time value of money is material, the amount of a provision should be the present value of the expenditure expected to be required to settle the obligation' (IAS 37, para. 45). This requirement of the Standard means that we must discount the expenditures required, and the IAS specifies the discount rate as a pre-tax rate that reflects current market assessments of the time value of money and the risks specific to the liability. If future cash flows are adjusted to take account of risk, then the discount rate used must be risk free and vice versa. This is to ensure that the risk involved in future cash flows is not allowed for twice. The best estimate measurement of the provision is becoming somewhat subjective!

## ACTIVITY 20.10

The information in an earlier Illustration enabled us to calculate the expected value for the provision for warranties. This provision was not discounted, even though it is expected that the time value of money will have a material effect on the provision. What type of discount rate should be applied: risk free or risk adjusted?

*Activity feedback*
*Risk free, as the specific risk has already been accounted for in the information gathered about the number of warranties taken up.*

## ACTIVITY 20.11

An entity identifies a provision for €250 000 at the year-end 31 December 20X1. The outflow of this amount is expected at year-end 20X3. Specific risk associated with this provision has already been taken account of when calculating the best estimate for the provision. A suitable risk-free discount rate to use is identified as 5 per cent.

Show the provision charged in the accounts for the year-ends 20X1, 20X2 and 20X3 assuming no change takes place in the best estimate and any other related entries required.

As at 20X2, the provision is now due for payment in one year's time and therefore will be charged at:

$$250\,000 \times 0.95 = 237\,500$$

As at 20X3, the provision should have been paid at €250 000 and therefore will not be required at the year-end.

*Activity feedback*
As at 20X1, the provision of €250 000 is due for payment in two years' time and therefore will need to be discounted at 5 per cent for a period of two years:

$$250\,000 \times 0.91 = 227\,500$$

The problem inherent in the discounting of provisions is that the carrying amount of the provision increases as the discount unwinds. Where do we account for this unwinding? The IASB view this unwinding as a charge to interest. There is no doubt that this unwinding is a financial item, but whether it should be regarded as an interest charge is debatable.

In Activity 20.11 in year ended 20X2, €10 000 would be charged to interest in the income statement and at year-end 20X3, €12 500.

## SPECIFIC APPLICATION OF RECOGNITION AND MEASUREMENT RULES

IAS 37 identifies three specific applications of recognition and measurement of provisions:

1 *Future operating losses.* These do not meet the definition of a liability as there is no present obligation and thus no liability. The loss will be recognized as it occurs. However, the possibility of future losses should lead management to test assets for impairment.

2 *Onerous contracts.* We discussed these at point 5 in Activity 20.6. IAS 37 requires us to recognize the present obligation under an onerous contract as a provision.

3 *Restructuring.* The issues are presented and discussed in Activity 20.12 which follows.

## ACTIVITY 20.12

The management board of Alex take a decision on 24 March to close down one of its divisions. The board also agrees the detailed plan for closure put forward on 24 March. No further action is taken on the closure and the year-end for Alex is 31 March. What should Alex provide in the accounts in respect of the closure?

### Activity feedback

*The first question to ask is, is there a present obligation (legal or constructive) as a result of a past event? (See Figure 20.1.)*

*The answer is no. The board of Alex can change their mind with regard to the closure. A constructive obligation will exist only when the closure is communicated in detail to employees and customers. A problem does exist here, however, as the point of recognition of the constructive obligation is dependent on a subjective judgement – at what point will the company make a sufficiently specific statement as to the closure? No provision will be made in the accounts as at 31 March.*

*IAS 37 tells us that a constructive obligation to restructure arises only when an entity:*

- *has a detailed formal plan for the restructuring identifying at least:*
  - the business or part of a business concerned
  - the principal locations affected

  - the location, function and approximate number of employees who will be compensated for termination of their services
  - the expenditures that will be undertaken
  - when the plan will be implemented.

- *and restructures by starting to implement that plan or announcing its main features to those affected by it (para. 72).*

*This still leaves us with a subjective judgement to make.*

*In addition, we have to be careful about the expenditure included in a restructuring provision as we cannot include those costs associated with ongoing activities of the entity. Thus, we cannot include retraining or relocation costs of continuing staff, marketing or investment in new systems and distribution networks. We can only include the direct expenditures. Also, remember that gains from expected disposal of assets should not be taken account of when measuring the provision for restructuring.*

## Other applications

In Activity 20.13 there are a further two circumstances outlined for the application of the recognition and measurement rules of IAS 37.

## ACTIVITY 20.13

**1** An entity has for many years made a provision for repair and maintenance of its assets. Should the entity continue to do so under IAS 37?

**2** An entity that operates a chain of retail outlets decides not to insure itself in respect of the risk of minor accidents to its customers, but to self-insure. Based on past experience, it expects to pay €100 000 a year in respect of these accidents. Should provision be made for the amount expected to arise in a normal year?

### Activity feedback

*1 The entity has no constructive or legal obligation for repairs and maintenance as a result of a past event. No provision. Charge the amount of repairs and maintenance to the income statement as actually expensed.*

*2 There is no present obligation as a result of a past event as no event has occurred. No provision. However, as the minor accidents occur the expenditure associated with them will be charged to the income statement.*

## ACTIVITY 20.14

Felix, a commercial port operator, is uncertain how to deal with the following issues in its year-end accounts:

1　Significant one-off refurbishments of operational port assets that are required in the future.

2　A decision has been taken to alter employee conditions by reducing overtime payments from twice the normal rate to 1.5 times at one port. A one-off payment will be made to all employees who accept this change of condition. Employees and unions are aware of the proposed change and have also been informed that if agreement is not given to the proposal other ways will be found to avoid the overtime.

3　Felix has a contract to purchase items at €1 per unit. Current market price of these items is 50c. The items are used in a part of the business that is profitable. The management believes the contract is onerous.

4　Felix purchased four small ports for €100m during the year; however, the Monopolies and Mergers Commission has directed Felix to sell them. No sale has been made by the year-end, but the best estimate of their sale value is €50m.

### Activity feedback

1　There is no present obligation, either legal or obligatory, so no provision or contingent liability is shown.

2　The one-off payment is associated with future work, not current, and therefore no provision should be made.

3　The contract is not onerous as no loss is being made by Felix on these items as they form part of a profitable item.

4　A provision of €50m should be made in the accounts as this is a present obligation due to a past event and a reasonable estimate of the loss can be made.

## Disclosure

The disclosure requirements are fairly extensive but are those you would expect in terms of providing relevant information to users.

## REAL WORLD ILLUSTRATION

The following extract is an example of an accounting policy for provisions and contingencies under the current requirements of IAS 37 taken from Air France group accounts as at 31 December 2011.

### ANNUAL REPORT

### Provisions

The Group recognizes a provision in the balance sheet when the Group has an existing legal or implicit obligation to a third party as a result of a past event, and it is probable that an outflow of economic benefits will be required to settle the obligation. The amounts recorded as provisions are discounted when the effect of the passage of time is material. The effect of the time value of money is presented as a component of financial income. Restructuring provisions are recognized once the Group has established a detailed and formal restructuring plan which has been announced to the parties concerned.

## FOURTH DIRECTIVE AND IAS 37

There was some discrepancy between the original Fourth Directive and IAS 37. The Directive required Member States to ensure that accounts are drawn up in such a way as to take account of all foreseeable and potential losses arising in the financial year

(Article 31(1)(c)(bb)). IAS 37 quite obviously does not do this. Article 31(1)(d) required that charges relating to the financial year irrespective of date of payment must be taken into account, and Article 20 required the creation of a provision to cover charges that are likely to be incurred (or certain) but where amount or timing is uncertain.

Clearly, the Fourth Directive was written at a time when prudence was a key element, even a bias, of financial reporting and since then the underlying concepts of accounting have changed. This inconsistency between the Directive and IAS 37 has now been eliminated by changes in the Directive.

## FUTURE DEVELOPMENTS

In June 2005, the IASB published an exposure draft (ED) to amend IAS 37 as a result of the convergence work with the FASB and also the second phase of the business combinations project. This ED proposed a number of significant amendments (these were outlined in our fourth edition). Some of these were heavily criticized, and the IASB effectively stopped the project for several years. Early in 2010 a working draft of new revised proposals for a replacement Standard was released. Suggested measurement criteria within these revised proposals may be summarized as follows:

(a) The requirement is to measure the amount that the entity would rationally pay on the reporting date to be relieved of the present obligation.

(b) The amount that the entity would rationally pay to be relieved of the present obligation is the lowest of:
   – the present value of the resources required to fulfil the obligation
   – the amount the entity would have to pay to cancel the obligation, and
   – the amount the entity would have to pay to transfer the obligation to that party.

(c) If there is no evidence that the entity could cancel the obligation or transfer it to a third party for a lower amount, the entity measures the liability at the present value of the resources required to fulfil the obligation.

(d) An entity estimates the present value of the resources required to fulfil the obligation using expected present value techniques. The calculations take into account:
   – the outflows of resources expected to be required to fulfil the obligation (the probability-weighted average of the possible outcomes)
   – the time value of money, and
   – if the amount or timing of the outflows is uncertain, any additional amount the entity would rationally pay to be relieved of the risk that the actual cash flows will be different from those expected.

(e) An entity should measure the resource outflows at their value, not cost. If the obligation is to provide a service at a future date, the entity measures the service outflows at the amount it would rationally pay a contractor at the future date to carry out the service on its behalf:
   – if a market exists for such services, the amount is the price that a contractor would charge
   – if no market exists, the entity would estimate the amount.

If adopted, these proposals would represent a very significant change. The 'probability' criterion of IAS 37 would disappear, and be replaced by a fair value measurement of the obligation.

## ACTIVITY 20.15

Rework Activity 20.8 on the assumption that the proposed measurement criteria of 2010 apply.

### Activity feedback

*The answer would be quite different. There is a 60 per cent chance of an obligation of €5m and a 40 per cent* *chance of an obligation of zero. The fair value of this risk (assuming a perfect market) is 60% × €5m + 40% × 0 = €3m.*

Again no progress was made with these 2010 proposals, the joint project between IASB and FASB being abandoned. Late in 2012 the IASB decided to resurrect, as an independent IASB project, the creation of an eventual replacement for IAS 37. Watch this space, but an early definitive replacement should certainly not be expected.

Recent practical examples of the major statements are given in Appendix II to Chapter 32.

## SUMMARY

You should now realize that the area of provisions, contingent liabilities and contingent assets is controversial and requires a great deal of subjective judgement. Many people would argue that IAS 37 lacks prudence in that it does not require the recognition of, and accounting for all, future expenses. We would not argue this as we view prudence as a state of being free from bias, not being overly pessimistic. The issues involved in this chapter have been quite difficult, and Tables 20.1 and 20.2 summarize the position according to IAS 37.

### TABLE 20.1 IAS 37: Summary of provisions and contingent liabilities

| Obligation | Accounting result | Disclosure |
| --- | --- | --- |
| Present obligation that probably requires outflow | Provision recognized | Amounts, nature, uncertainties, assumptions, reimbursements |
| Possible obligation or present obligation that may require outflow | No provision recognized Contingent liability disclosed | Nature, estimate of financial effect, uncertainties, reimbursement |
| Possible obligation or present obligation where outflow remote | | Nil |

### TABLE 20.2 IAS 37: Summary of contingent assets

| Economic benefits | Accounting result | Disclosure |
| --- | --- | --- |
| Inflow virtually certain | Asset rules apply | |
| Inflow probable | No asset recognized Contingent asset disclosed | Nature, financial effect |
| Inflow not probable | | Nil |

# EXERCISES

*Suggested answers to exercises marked ✓ are to be found on our dedicated CourseMate platform for students.*

*Suggested answers to the remaining exercises are to be found on the Instructor online support resources.*

**1** Outline the recommended treatment of provisions, contingent liabilities and contingent assets in accordance with IAS 37, clearly defining and illustrating the meaning of each term.

**2** Identify any other methods of accounting for provisions, contingent liabilities and contingent assets, and discuss why IAS 37 rejects these methods in favour of its recommended treatment.

**3** Discuss the statement that financial reports prepared under IAS 37 provide a 'true and fair view' to users.

**4** Explain the terms:
- big bath accounting
- profit smoothing.

Give an illustration of each.

**5** IAS 37 ensures 'consistency between entities in the recognition and measurement of provisions and contingencies and that sufficient information is disclosed about them to users so that they can understand their effect on current and future results'. Discuss.

**✓ 6** The distinction between a provision and a contingent liability is irrelevant. Discuss.

**7** Describe the accounting arrangements in accordance with IAS 37 for provisions and contingent liabilities. Comment on whether these arrangements provide useful information to users.

**8** Appraise the requirement in IAS 37 to measure a provision at the 'best estimate'.

**✓ 9** Debate the contention that IAS 37 lacks prudence.

**10** (i) In relation to a failed acquisition, a firm of accountants has invoiced Gear for the sum of $300 000. Gear has paid $20 000 in full settlement of the debt and states that this was a reasonable sum for the advice given and is not prepared to pay any further sum. The accountants are pressing for payment of the full amount, but on the advice of its solicitors, Gear is not going to settle the balance outstanding Additionally, Gear is involved in a court case concerning the plagiarism of software. Another games company has accused Gear of copying their games software and currently legal opinion seems to indicate that Gear will lose the case. Management estimates that the most likely outcome will be a payment of costs and royalties to the third party of $1 million in two years' time (approximately). The best case scenario is deemed to be a payment of $500 000 in one year's time and the worst case scenario that of a payment of $2 million in three years' time. These scenarios are based on the amount of the royalty payment and the potential duration and costs of the court case. Management has estimated that the relative likelihood of the above payments are: best case – 30 per cent chance; most likely outcome – 60 per cent chance; and worst case – 10 per cent chance of occurrence. The directors are unsure as to whether any provision for the above amounts should be made in the financial statements.

(ii) In the event of the worst case scenario occurring, the directors of Gear are worried about the viability of their business as the likelihood would be that current liabilities would exceed current assets and it is unlikely that in the interim period there will be sufficient funds generated from operational cash flows

The discount rate for any present value calculations is 5 per cent.

**Required:**

Write a report to the directors of Gear Software explaining the implications of the above information contained in paragraphs (i) and (ii) for the financial statements.

(ACCA – June 2003)

11  IAS 37, *Provisions, Contingent Liabilities and Contingent Assets,* was issued in 1998. The Standard sets out the principles of accounting for these items and clarifies when provisions should and should not be made. Prior to its issue, the inappropriate use of provisions had been an area where companies had been accused of manipulating the financial statements and of creative accounting.

**Required:**

(a) Describe the nature of provisions and the accounting requirements for them contained in IAS 37.

(b) Explain why there is a need for an accounting standard in this area. Illustrate your answer with three practical examples of how the Standard addresses controversial issues.

(c) Bodyline sells sports goods and clothing through a chain of retail outlets. It offers customers a full refund facility for any goods returned within 28 days of their purchase provided they are unused and in their original packaging. In addition, all goods carry a warranty against manufacturing defects for 12 months from their date of purchase. For most goods the manufacturer underwrites this warranty such that Bodyline is credited with the cost of the goods that are returned as faulty. Goods purchased from one manufacturer, Header, are sold to Bodyline at a negotiated discount which is designed to compensate Bodyline for manufacturing defects. No refunds are given by Header, thus Bodyline has to bear the cost of any manufacturing faults of these goods.

Bodyline makes a uniform mark-up on cost of 25 per cent on all goods it sells, except for those supplied from Header on which it makes a mark-up on cost of 40 per cent. Sales of goods manufactured by Header consistently account for 20 per cent of all Bodyline's sales.

Sales in the last 28 days of the trading year to 30 September 2003 were $1 750 000. Past trends reliably indicate that 10 per cent of all goods are returned under the 28-day return facility. These are not faulty goods. Of these, 70 per cent are later resold at the normal selling price and the remaining 30 per cent are sold as 'sale' items at half the normal retail price.

In addition to the above expected returns, an estimated $160 000 (at selling price) of the goods sold during the year will have manufacturing defects and have yet to be returned by customers. Goods returned as faulty have no resale value.

**Required:**

Describe the nature of the above warranty/return facilities and calculate the provision Bodyline is required to make at 30 September 2003:

(i) for goods subject to the 28-day returns policy, and

(ii) for goods that are likely to be faulty.

(d) Rockbuster has recently purchased an item of earth moving plant at a total cost of $24 million. The plant has an estimated life of 10 years with no residual value, however its engine will need replacing after every 5000 hours of use at an estimated cost of $7.5 million. The directors of Rockbuster intend to depreciate the plant at $2.4 million ($24 million/10 years) p.a. and make a provision of $1500 ($7.5 million/5000 hours) per hour of use for the replacement of the engine.

**Required:**
Explain how the plant should be treated in accordance with International Accounting Standards and comment on the directors' proposed treatment.

(ACCA – December 2003)

**12** Nette, a public limited company, manufactures mining equipment and extracts natural gas. The directors are uncertain about the role of the IASB's *Framework for the Preparation and Presentation of Financial Statements* (i.e. the Framework) in corporate reporting. Their view is that accounting is based on the transactions carried out by the company and that these transactions are allocated to the company's accounting period by using the matching and prudence concepts. The argument put forward by the directors is that the Framework does not take into account the business and legal constraints within which companies operate. Further, they have given a situation which has arisen in the current financial statements where they feel that the current accounting practice is inconsistent with the Framework.

**Situation** Nette has recently constructed a natural gas extraction facility and commenced production one year ago (1 June 2003). There is an operating licence given to the company by the government which requires the removal of the facility at the end of its life which is estimated at 20 years. Depreciation is charged on the straight line basis. The cost of the construction of the facility was $200 million and the net present value at 1 June 2003 of the future costs to be incurred in order to return the extraction site to its original condition is estimated at $50 million (using a discount rate of 5 per cent per annum). 80 per cent of these costs relate to the removal of the facility and 20 per cent relate to the rectification of the damage caused through the extraction of the natural gas. The auditors have told the company that a provision for decommissioning has to be set up.

**Required:**
(a) Explain the importance of the Framework to the reporting of corporate performance and whether it takes into account the business and legal constraints placed upon companies.

(b) (i) Explain, with reasons and suitable extracts/computations, the accounting treatment of the above situation in the financial statements for the year ended 31 May 2004

(ii) Discuss whether the treatment of the items appears consistent with the Framework.

(ACCA – June 2004)

**13** NDL drilled a new oil well, which started production on 1 March 2003. The licence granting permission to drill the new oil well included a clause that requires NDL to 'return the land to the state it was in before drilling commenced'.

NDL estimates that the oil well will have a 20-year production life. At the end of that time, the well will be decommissioned and work carried out to reinstate the land. The cost of this decommissioning work is estimated to be $20 million.

**Required:**

As the trainee management accountant, draft a memo to the production manager explaining how NDL must treat the decommissioning costs in its financial statements for the year to 31 March 2003. Your memo should refer to appropriate International Accounting Standards.

(CIMA pilot paper Financial Accounting & Tax Principles)

**14**  U manufactures refrigerators and freezers and sells them with a one-year warranty. It applies the requirements of IAS 37, *Provisions, Contingent Liabilities and Contingent Assets,* to its financial accounts. U has made a provision for future warranty claims each year.

U did not keep accurate records of previous warranty claims so when IAS 37 became effective, it estimated future warranty claims based on an estimated 10 per cent of sales turnover. It also started keeping accurate records of warranty claims.

U has decided to change its method of calculating the provision for warranty claims to the weighted average of the last three years' actual claims paid.

A warranty claim provision of $900 000, calculated on the old basis, has already been entered in the accounts for the year ended 30 September 2004.

| Year to 30 September | 2002 $000 | 2003 $000 | 2004 $000 |
|---|---|---|---|
| Revenue | 7 500 | 8 000 | 9 000 |
| Actual warranty claims paid | 375 | 400 | 325 |

Prepare the accounting entries required in U's year-end accounts to reflect the above change.

(CIMA paper 6B – November 2004)

# INCOME TAXES

# 21

## INTRODUCTION

The amount of tax charged against the profit in any period is an important determinant of the amount attributable to the owners of a company. This amount is determined by the earnings per share. It also obviously has an effect on all other ratios which are calculated after tax. However, the tax charge, calculated according to a country's tax legislation, is not necessarily the same as applying the tax rate to the accounting profits. This difference arises because of the different recognition and measurement rules in tax legislation compared to accounting GAAP. The implications arising from these differences have led to a long, complicated and sometimes badly argued debate over the last three decades or more, both in individual countries and internationally.

## THE EXPENSE QUESTION

The first question to answer is, 'Is tax a business expense?' At first glance your answer might be an unequivocal yes, but it needs further consideration. An expense usually takes the form of an outflow or depletion of assets or incurrences of liabilities during a period from delivering or producing goods, services and so on. Expenses are also discretionary in a sense, i.e. the business could avoid them if it wished. Tax is not a charge for the exchange of goods or services and cannot be avoided by the business. Many see tax not as an expense but as a distribution of income, like distributions to shareholders. This view regards the tax authorities as a stakeholder in the business. If this distribution view of tax were adopted, the rest of this chapter would be irrelevant. Tax is internationally treated as an expense, but the argument for doing so is not very well founded.

## THE DEFERRED TAX PROBLEM

In many countries, the amount of tax payable by a business for a particular period often bears little relationship to the profit as reported by the accountants in the income statement. It is often the case that the tax authorities take the accountant's reported profit figure as their starting point but they make all sorts of adjustments to it in order to determine the amount of taxable income. One of these adjustments can be in respect of depreciation. As we have already seen in Chapter 13, the 'appropriate' charge for depreciation can be a highly uncertain, subjective amount which to many taxation authorities is unacceptable. Additionally, several national governments have felt that by specifying tax allowances (not equivalent to an accountant's depreciation figure) for capital assets against profits, which they can vary from year to year, they can provide incentives to businesses to invest more or to invest in some particular way. The first thing that such tax authorities do to the accountant's profit figure, as calculated and published in the income statement, is to remove all the depreciation entries put in by the accountant. In other words, the depreciation figure, which will have been deducted in arriving at the accountant's profit figure, is simply added back again. (A profit on disposal that will have been added by the accountant will, of course, need to be removed by deduction.) From the resulting figure, the tax authority now deducts whatever the tax allowance for the capital asset is and tax is levied on this taxable profit.

Now consider Activity 21.1, which illustrates the difference between accounting profits and tax authority profits or taxable income.

## ACTIVITY 21.1

An asset attracting 25 per cent tax allowances p.a. costs Deftax Ltd €100 (note that tax allowances apply to the reducing balance of the asset). The asset has an expected life of five years, at the end of which it is estimated it can be sold for €25. In the books of Deftax, the asset is depreciated each year with an amount of €15.

Taxation is payable at the rate of 33 per cent. Calculate the profit after accounting tax as well as taxable income for each year of the expected life of the asset in the knowledge that profit after the accounting tax but before taxes is after a depreciation charge €100 each year.

*(Continued)*

## ACTIVITY 21.1    (*Continued*)

### Activity feedback

In order to determine both values, we first need to distinguish between the depreciation amounts according to accounting GAAP and the depreciation allowances according to the fiscal rules. The depreciation of the asset according to accounting GAAP is €15 per year (€75/5). The fiscal depreciation is a declining amount calculated each year as 25 per cent of the remaining tax base of the asset, whereby the tax base is the amount attributed to that asset for tax purposes. In order to determine the taxable profit, we start from the profit after the accounting tax and add back the depreciation amount according to accounting GAAP. Subsequently, we deduct the tax allowances (depreciation amounts accepted for tax purposes). The outcome is the taxable profit. In the next step, the taxes payable are calculated.

| | Year | | | | |
|---|---|---|---|---|---|
| | 1 | 2 | 3 | 4 | 5 |
| | € | € | € | € | € |
| Accounting profit (after depreciation charge) | 100 | 100 | 100 | 100 | 100 |
| Depreciation | 15 | 15 | 15 | 15 | 15 |
| Tax allowance | −25 | −18 | −14 | −11 | −8 |
| Taxable profit | 90 | 97 | 101 | 104 | 107 |
| Taxes payable | 30 | 32 | 33 | 34 | 36 |

| | Year | | | | |
|---|---|---|---|---|---|
| | 1 | 2 | 3 | 4 | 5 |
| | € | € | € | € | € |
| Profit before tax | 100 | 100 | 100 | 100 | 100 |
| Taxation 33% taxable profit | 30 | 32 | 33 | 34 | 36 |
| Profit after tax | 70 | 68 | 67 | 66 | 64 |
| Profit before tax | 100 | 100 | 100 | 100 | 100 |
| Taxation charge if calculated on accounting profit | 33 | 33 | 33 | 33 | 33 |
| Profit after accounting tax | 67 | 67 | 67 | 67 | 67 |

Activity 21.1 illustrates the difference between profit after accounting tax and taxable profit or taxable income. If the firm uses the taxes payable as tax expense on its income, the profit after tax figures would indicate that in year 2 the performance of the company decreased and continued to do so for the next three years. But have the firm and management been less successful? Arguably not! Over the five-year period the company has made the same accounting profit with the same resources each year (excluding the problems of historical cost here). Thus, the profit after accounting tax figures provides a better guide to performance of the company.

If we look carefully at the activity feedback we note that the total tax charge is €165 over the five-year period using either method. Thus, the use of tax allowances does not alter the total tax due, only the timing of those tax payments. The difference between the depreciation charge in any year and the tax allowance for that year is referred to as the 'timing difference'.

Timing differences are a potential source of differences between accounting profit and taxable profit. IAS 12 (which will be discussed later in this chapter) defines accounting profit as (para. 5) 'profit or loss for a period before deducting tax expense', profit or loss being the excess of revenues minus expenses for the period. The measurement and recognition of the revenues and expenses for the period is determined by the accounting principles. Taxable profit is defined by IAS 12 as 'the profit or loss for the period, determined in accordance with the rules established by the taxation authorities'. An important point in accounting for income taxes is the identification of these differences between accounting profit or income and taxable income. These differences arise from a different treatment of the same transaction by the accounting principles in comparison to the tax principles. Some of these differences are permanent while others are temporary in nature.

**Permanent differences:** A permanent difference between accounting profit and taxable profit arises when the treatment of a transaction by taxation legislation and accounting standards is such that amounts recognized as part of the accounting profit are never recognized as part of the taxable profit or vice versa. A permanent difference need not be recorded and measured and presented on the statement of financial position. A permanent difference only has to be disclosed in the notes to the accounts.

**Temporary differences:** Temporary differences between accounting profit and taxable profit arise when the period in which the revenues and expenses are recognized for accounting purposes is different from the period in which these revenues and expenses are treated as taxable income or as allowable reductions for tax purposes. The existence of temporary differences implies that income tax payable that is calculated on the basis of taxable income will vary in the current period from taxes based on accounting profit, but tax payments will eventually catch up, as illustrated in Activity 21.1.

When we return to Activity 21.1 we notice that the tax allowance has the effect of deferring tax payments in year 1, €3, and year 2, €1, and then collecting these in years 4 (€1) and 5 (€3).

So in future years (4 and 5) we have an eventual payment that relates to years 1 and 2 and arises as a result of the transactions and results of years 1 and 2, and it is therefore arguable that there is a liability created at year 1 (of €3) and increased at year 2 (with €1). We are in effect suggesting that:

1 The tax charge reported on the income statement for years 1 and 2 should really be €33, as this is the amount that must eventually be paid as a result of years 1 and 2 activities.

2 There is a liability of €3 at the end of year 1, in respect of tax related to year 1 but payable in later years (4 and 5) which increases to €4 by the end of year 2.

We can easily allow for both these considerations by creating a liability account, known as a deferred tax account. This is shown below. The amount to be transferred to the credit of the deferred tax account can be formally calculated as follows.

$$\text{Amount} = \text{Tax rate} \times (\text{tax allowances given} - \text{depreciation disallowed})$$

Thus, for year 1:

$$33\% \times (25 - 15) = 3$$
$$33\% \times (18 - 15) = 1$$

| | Year 1 €| 2 €| 3 €| 4 €| 5 €| Total €|
|---|---|---|---|---|---|---|
| Profit before tax | 100 | 100 | 100 | 100 | 100 | 500 |
| Taxation: payable for year | 30 | 32 | 33 | 34 | 36 | 165 |
| Additional charge (credit) to deferred tax account | 3 | 1 | 0 | (1) | (3) | 0 |
| Total tax charge | 33 | 33 | 33 | 33 | 33 | 165 |
| Profit after tax | 67 | 67 | 67 | 67 | 67 | 335 |

The tax expense is the aggregate amount included in the determination of the comprehensive income statement for the period in respect of current tax and deferred tax. As an illustration, we present the journal entries which will be made in years 1 and 4 with regard to income taxes.

*Year 1*

| | | |
|---|---|---|
| Tax expense | 33 | |
| Taxation payable for the year | | 30 |
| Deferred tax liability | | 3 |

*Year 4*

| | | |
|---|---|---|
| Tax expense | 33 | |
| Deferred tax liability | | 1 |
| Taxation payable for the year | | 34 |

The deferred tax account will be credited in years 1 and 2 and debited in years 4 and 5.

*Deferred tax account*

| | € | | € |
|---|---|---|---|
| Balance c/d 31.12.01 | 3 | Appropriation account 31.12.01 | 3 |
| | 3 | | 3 |
| | | Balance b/d 1.1.02 | 3 |
| Balance c/d 31.12.02 | 4 | Approp. acc. 31.12.02 | 1 |
| | 4 | | 4 |
| Balance c/d 31.12.03 | 4 | Balance b/d 1.1.03 | 4 |
| | 4 | | 4 |
| Approp. acc. 31.12.04 | 1 | Balance b/d 1.1.04 | 4 |
| Balance c/d 31.12.04 | 3 | | 4 |
| | 4 | | 4 |
| Approp. acc. 31.12.05 | 3 | Balance b/d 1.1.05 | 3 |
| *For year 4* | | And year 5 | |
| $33\% \times (11 - 15) = -1$ | | $33\% \times (8 - 15) = -3$ | |

## Arguments for deferred tax

From this discussion we can note:

1 The tax charge by including deferred tax is €33 for years 1–5, which provides a profit after tax figure of €67 which reflects the performance of the company.

2 There is a liability balance remaining at the end of each year in respect of tax related to the current or earlier years but not yet paid or due for payment. This, we also suggested, was a desirable outcome.

3 The total position viewed over the five years as a whole remains unaltered. This is to be expected as nothing that we or the tax authorities are doing through tax allowances alters the total tax eventually payable as a result of a year's profits.

All this appears totally logical and in accord with accounting principles. So what is the problem?

# Arguments against deferred tax

A problem occurs with the previous logic if a company buys assets regularly, which is a realistic assumption. Let us demonstrate the problem.

## ACTIVITY 21.2

In addition to the information given in Activity 21.1, Deftax Ltd buys an asset in year 2 for €100, one in year 3 for €120, one in year 4 for €220, and two in year 5 for €250 and €300 respectively. All these assets also have an expected life of five years but, unlike the first asset, all the rest have an expected scrap value of zero. Complete the table in Activity 21.1 using the new information and show the deferred tax account over the five-year period. Comment on the results.

*Year 3:*

| | |
|---|---|
| Asset 1 depreciation | = 15 |
| Asset 2 depreciation | = 20 |
| Asset 3 depreciation 120/5 | = 24 |
| | 59 |

| | |
|---|---|
| Asset 1 tax allowance 25% × (75 − 18) | = 14 |
| Asset 2 tax allowance 25% × (100 − 25) | = 18 |
| Asset 3 tax allowance 25% × 120 | = 30 |
| | 62 |

### Activity feedback

*To help you with the activity, we provide the workings for years 2 and 3 for the calculation of depreciation and capital allowances. Years 4 and 5 follow the same pattern.*

### Workings

*Year 2:*

| | |
|---|---|
| Asset 1 depreciation 75/5 = | 15 |
| Asset 2 depreciation 100/5 = | 20 |
| | 35 |
| Asset 1 tax allowance 25% × 75 = | 18 |
| Asset 2 tax allowance 25% × 100 = | 25 |
| | 43 |

| | Year | | | | |
|---|---|---|---|---|---|
| | 1 | 2 | 3 | 4 | 5 |
| | € | € | € | € | € |
| Accounting profit (after deprec. charged) | 100 | 100 | 100 | 100 | 100 |
| Depreciation | 15 | 35 | 59 | 103 | 213 |
| Tax allowance | 25 | 43 | 62 | 103 | 215 |
| Taxable profit | 90 | 92 | 97 | 100 | 98 |
| Tax charge | 30 | 30 | 32 | 33 | 32 |
| Deferred tax charge | 3 | 3 | 1 | 0 | 1 |
| Total tax | 33 | 33 | 33 | 33 | 33 |
| Profit after tax | 67 | 67 | 67 | 67 | 67 |

| Deferred tax account | | | | |
|---|---|---|---|---|
| Bal. c/d 31.12.01 | 3 | 3 | Appropriation a/c 31.12.01 |
| | 3 | 3 | |
| | | 3 | Bal. b/d 1.1.02 |
| Bal. c/d 31.12.02 | 6 | 3 | Appropriation a/c 31.12.02 |
| | 6 | 6 | |
| | | 6 | Bal. b/d 1.1.03 |
| Bal. c/d 31.12.03 | 7 | 1 | Appropriation a/c 31.12.03 |
| | 7 | 7 | |
| | | 7 | Bal. b/d 1.1.04 |
| Bal. c/d 31.12.04 | 7 | 0 | Appropriation a/c 31.12.04 |
| | 7 | 7 | |
| | | 7 | Bal. b/d 1.1.05 |
| Bal. c/d 31.12.05 | 8 | 1 | Appropriation a/c 31.12.05 |
| | 8 | 8 | |
| | | 8 | Bal. b/d 1.1.06 |

Comparing the tables from Activities 21.1 and 21.2, we see that the total position over the five years is no longer the same. The total tax charge is increased by €8 (165 – 157). This is not surprising as it equals the liability provided for at the end of year 5 on the deferred tax account. The transfer to the deferred tax account can be seen to be the result of an amalgam of positive originating timing differences relating to depreciation. The resultant figure of profit after tax, €67 p.a., reflects the underlying profitability of the company. It does not give an impression of improved profitability because of the effect of tax allowances related to asset acquisitions. Everything appears fine, so where's the problem? The problem is the €8 remaining on the deferred tax account. Does this liability actually exist?

In the long term we can suggest that:

1  If the entity reaches the state where it has a constant volume of fixed assets, merely replacing its existing assets as they wear out and also the price it has to pay for replacement fixed assets does not rise over time, then the balance of liability on the deferred tax account will remain a more or less constant figure.

2  If the entity finds that it is effectively in the position of paying gradually more and more money for fixed assets each year, then the balance of liability on the deferred tax account will gradually rise, apparently without limit.

3  Only if the monetary amount of reinvestment in fixed assets actually falls will the balance of liability on the deferred tax account start to fall.

How likely is each of these three outcomes? In general, 2 will tend to be the most frequent for three reasons:

1  entities have a tendency to expand

2  entities have a tendency to become more capital intensive

3  inflationary pressures tend to cause the amount of money paid for assets to increase over time.

So the most likely outcome, if full provision is to be made for deferred tax in this way, is of a liability figure on the statement of financial position that is apparently ever increasing. But what is a liability? Informally, we can say that it is an amount to be paid out in the future. We have an account representing a liability to the tax authorities. The balance on this account is gradually getting bigger and bigger, and, as far as can reasonably be foreseen, this process is going to continue. Therefore, the liability balance does not seem to be getting paid, neither in the foreseeable future is it likely to be paid. Therefore, it appears that it is not a liability at all within the meaning of the word liability! If the liability account seems all set to keep on growing, is there a probable future sacrifice?

It should be observed that one way of summarizing the two arguments as regards the liability aspect is that we can consider the position for each individual asset or we can consider the position for all assets in the aggregate. In the former case, the tax deferred will all have become payable by the end of the asset's life, so deferred tax provision would seem to be necessary. In the latter case, the aggregate liability is likely to go on increasing so deferred tax provision would seem to be unnecessary.

## Accountants' response

Formally, three approaches have been distinguished:

1  The *flow through approach*, which accounts only for that tax payable in respect of the period in question, i.e. timing differences are ignored.

2  *Full deferral*, which accounts for the full tax effects of timing differences, i.e. tax is shown in the published accounts based on the full accounting profit and the element not immediately payable is recorded as a liability until reversal.

3  *Partial deferral*, which accounts only for those timing differences where reversal is likely to occur in aggregate terms (because, for example, replacement of assets and expansion is expected to exceed depreciation).

These alternatives are discussed and explained in the following activities.

## ACTIVITY 21.3

Should the flow through approach be identified as the method to be used for accounting for tax? Think of the discussion and illustrations in the activities above.

### Activity feedback
Arguments in favour:

- Tax is assessed on taxable profits, not accounting profits. The only liability for tax for the period, therefore, is that accordingly assessed.

- Future years' tax depends on future events and is therefore not a present liability (see definition of liability, Chapter 20).

- Even if current events were giving rise to future tax liabilities, as the tax charge will be based on a complex set of future transactions, it cannot be measured with reliability and therefore should not be recognized.

Arguments against:

- As tax charges can be traced to individual transactions and events, any future tax consequences arising from these should be provided for at the outset.

- Flow through method can understate an entity's liability to tax.

## ACTIVITY 21.4

Should the full deferral method be adopted as the method to be used for accounting for tax? Think of the discussion and illustrations in the activities above.

### Activity feedback
The view can be taken that the amount of tax saving should not appear as a benefit of the year for which it was granted, but should be carried forward and

recredited to the profit and loss account (by way of reduction of the tax charged therein) in the year or years in which there are reversing time differences.

In effect, therefore, the full unreversed element is shown as a liability. Applying this to the circumstances of Deftax Ltd, we arrive at the position in Activity 21.2. Thus, we could well be showing a liability that will never crystallize.

## ACTIVITY 21.5

Should partial deferral be the method adopted for accounting for tax?

### Activity feedback
As we have seen, the one major problem with full deferral is that the balance on the deferred tax account is likely to increase continuously where there is expansion and

replacement at increased prices. If, however, timing differences are regarded in aggregate terms rather than as relating to individual assets, then this could be taken as evidence that the differences were not reversing. In short, is a liability that is never likely to become payable a liability at all? In many businesses, timing differences arising from accelerated capital allowances are of a recurring

*(Continued)*

## ACTIVITY 21.5    (Continued)

*nature and reversing differences are themselves offset, wholly or partially, or are exceeded, by new originating differences thereby giving rise to continuing tax reductions or the indefinite postponement of any liability attributable to the tax benefits received. It is, therefore, appropriate*

*that in the case of accelerated capital allowances, provisions be made for deferred taxation, except insofar as the tax benefit can be expected with reasonable probability to be retained in the future in consequence of recurring timing differences of the same type.*

## ACTIVITY 21.6

On the assumption that the directors of Deftax Ltd foresee no reversal of timing differences for some considerable time and using the information from Activity 21.2, show the impact on tax charges and income figures of the firm using the partial deferral method.

*Activity feedback*

| | Year | | | | |
| --- | --- | --- | --- | --- | --- |
| | *1* | *2* | *3* | *4* | *5* |
| | € | € | € | € | € |
| Profit before tax | 100 | 100 | 100 | 100 | 100 |
| Taxation | 30 | 30 | 32 | 33 | 32 |
| Deferred tax charge | 0 | 0 | 0 | 0 | 0 |
| | 70 | 70 | 68 | 67 | 68 |

Deferred tax calculation

| Year | Originating (O) timing difference | Reversing (R) timing difference | Net timing difference |
| --- | --- | --- | --- |
| 1 | 10 (25 capital allowance – 15 depreciation) | – | 10 (O) |
| 2 | 18 (43 – 35) | – | 8 (O) |
| 3 | 6 (30 – 24) | 3 | 3 (O) |
| 4 | 11 (55 – 44) | 11 | (O) |
| 5 | 28 (138 – 110) | 26 | 2 (O) |
| 6 | Onwards no net reversals | | |

The liability for tax will never crystallize, therefore no provision for deferred tax is required. No net reversal appears ever to be expected.

## Deferral versus liability method

The deferred tax amount is dependent on the tax rate used. When calculating the amount we could either use:

- the tax rate applying when the timing difference originated – deferral method, or
- the tax rate (or the best estimate of it) ruling when the tax will become payable – liability method.

A simple example is used to illustrate the difference.

## ILLUSTRATION

An entity purchases a non-current asset for €5 000 000 on 1.1.X0. It is depreciated on a straight line basis over five years. It attracts tax allowances of €200 000 in X0 and €150 00 in X1. The tax rate in X2 is 30 per cent and X1 is 25 per cent.

|  | X0 | X1 |
|---|---|---|
| Depreciation charge | 100 000 | 100 000 |
| Tax allowance | 200 000 | 150 000 |
| Timing difference | 100 000 | 50 000 |

*Deferred tax provided*

|  | deferral method | | liability method | |
|---|---|---|---|---|
|  | X0 | X1 | X0 | X1 |
|  | 30% | 25% | 30% | 25% |
| Deferred tax charge | 30 000 | 12 500 | 30 000 | 12 500 |
| Deferred tax balance | 30 000 | 42 500 |  | (5 000) |
|  |  |  | 30 000 | 37 500 |

The (5000) in X1 under the liability method adjusts the carry forward of 30 000 to 25 000 which is the timing difference of 100 000 at 25 per cent tax rate. The 37 500 is now the best estimate of the tax payable if the timing differences are reversed, whereas the 42 500 does not represent the best estimate of the likely liability.

## Income statement or balance sheet (statement of financial position) view of deferred tax

When the income statement (IS) view of deferred tax is taken, there is a focus on the difference between the accounting profit and taxable profit. This was the view of deferred tax taken internationally and in the UK and USA until the 1990s. The balance sheet/statement of financial position (BS) view focuses on the difference between the carrying amount of assets and liabilities and their amount in tax terms and forms the basis for current IAS and US GAAP.

In some situations, it makes no difference whether we take an IS or BS view, but in many it does, as the illustration below shows.

The argument for providing deferred tax on this temporary difference (note there is no timing difference) is that it is presumed that the revalued carrying amount of the asset will be recovered through use and will generate taxable income that will be taxable in the future and therefore there is a deferred tax liability. There is a problem with this logic, though, given the definition of a liability as 'a present obligation arising out of a past event'. The future taxable income referred to here is not a past event.

## ILLUSTRATION

An entity buys an asset for €100, depreciated over five years on a straight line basis. Annual depreciation, according to accounting GAAP, is €20 per year. Tax allowances on capital assets are 50 per cent in the first year and tax rate is 30 per cent.

Under the income statement view, known as limiting difference, the deferred tax provided for at the end of the first year is:

| Tax allowance | 50 |
|---|---|
| Depreciation | 20 |
| Timing differences | 30 |
| Deferred tax | 9 |

The balance sheet view, temporary difference, is:

| Net book value (NBV) of asset end year 1 | 80 |
|---|---|
| Tax base (tax written down value) | 50 |
|  | 30 |
| Deferred tax | 9 |

In this example there is no difference between the two methods.

If the asset had been revalued to €200 at the end of year 1, then only the balance sheet calculation would change:

| NBV | 200 |
|---|---|
| Tax base | 50 |
| Temporary differences | 150 |
| Deferred tax | 45 |

## IAS 12 AND TAX

### Introduction

The current version of IAS 12 has major changes from the one first issued in 1979. This original Standard basically allowed deferred tax to be calculated based on any method available – deferral or liability method, full or partial provision – and was based on an income statement approach.

The current IAS 12 is based on a balance sheet approach and the international accounting standard-setter has opted for a full provision method for all temporary, differences. The IASB plans to revise IAS 12 in the future, however no specified timeline has been put forward yet. On its website the IASB (www.ifrs.org/in the standards development section – accessed on 9 March 2013) admits that the IFRS Interpretation Committee and the IASB staff receive many questions on IAS 12, indicating that the standard is sometimes difficult to apply. Income tax is also frequently identified as a source of significant reconciling items for US-listed foreign registrants applying IFRSs. Therefore the IASB and the FASB had already decided in 2002 to undertake a major revision of accounting for tax income. Although, in the October 2009 joint meeting with the FASB, both boards have indicated that they would consider undertaking a fundamental review of accounting for income taxes sometime in the future, the work on income taxes was suspended in 2010 to work on projects with higher priorities. Only limited amendments to IAS 12 were issued in 2010. It is probable that in the future IAS 12 will be substantially revised or replaced by a new standard, however the timeframe of this project is at this time highly uncertain.

### Definitions

The definitions given in IAS 12 (para. 5) are as follows:

- Accounting profit is net profit or loss for a period before deducting tax expense.
- Taxable profit (tax loss) is the profit (loss) for a period, determined in accordance with the rules established by the taxation authorities, upon which income taxes are payable (recoverable).
- Tax expense (tax income) is the aggregate amount included in the determination of net profit or loss for the period in respect of current tax and deferred tax.
- Current tax is the amount of income taxes payable (recoverable) in respect of taxable profit (tax loss) for a period.
- Deferred tax liabilities are the amounts of income taxes payable in future periods in respect of taxable temporary differences.
- Deferred tax assets are the amounts of income taxes recoverable in future period in respect of:
  - **(a)** deductible temporary differences
  - **(b)** the carry forward of unused tax losses, and
  - **(c)** the carry forward of unused tax credits.
- Temporary differences are differences between the carrying amount of an asset or liability in the balance sheet and its tax base. Temporary differences may be either:

**(a)** taxable temporary differences, which are temporary differences that will result in taxable amounts in determining taxable profit (tax loss) of future periods when the carrying amount of the asset or liability is recovered or settled; or

**(b)** deductible temporary differences, which are temporary differences that will result in amounts that are deductible in determining taxable profit (tax loss) of future periods when the carrying amount of the asset or liability is recovered or settled. These lead to deferred tax assets.

• The tax base of an asset or liability is the amount attributed to that asset or liability for tax purposes.

## Tax base

In many cases, the tax base of an asset or liability is fairly obvious.

## ACTIVITY 21.7

An entity buys an asset for €500 000, which it intends to depreciate equally over five years. Under tax legislation, the asset attracts a 50 per cent first-year allowance and then an equal allowance each year over the next four to write the asset down to zero.

What is the tax base of the asset (at the end of each year) and its carrying amount in the statement of financial position?

*Activity feedback*

| | | Tax base | Carrying amount |
|---|---|---|---|
| End year | 1 | 250 000 | 400 000 |
| | 2 | 187 500 | 300 000 |
| | 3 | 125 000 | 200 000 |
| | 4 | 62 500 | 100 000 |
| | 5 | 0 | 0 |

The tax base of an asset is the amount that will be deductible for tax purposes against any taxable economic benefits that will flow to an entity when it recovers the carrying amount of the asset. If those economic benefits will not be taxable then the tax base of the asset is equal to its carrying amount.

## ACTIVITY 21.8

An entity has interest receivable of €200 and dividends receivable of €300 in its statement of financial position (these amounts are thus the carrying amount of the assets). As far as tax legislation that the entity is subject to is concerned, the interest will be taxed in full on a cash basis but the dividends are not taxable. Identify the tax base for the interest receivable and the dividends receivable.

*Activity feedback*
As the interest is taxed in full, there is no deduction from the economic benefit and therefore the tax base is nil.

The benefit of the dividends is not subject to tax and therefore the whole €300 must have been deducted from the economic benefit and thus the tax base of €300. Note the following:

| | Tax base | Carrying amount | Temp. difference |
|---|---|---|---|
| Interest receivable | 0 | 200 | 200 |
| Dividends receivable | 300 | 300 | – |

Thus, deferred tax liability would need to be recognized on the interest but not the dividend receivable.

A similar situation occurs in the case of liabilities where the tax base of a liability is its carrying amount less any amount that will be deductible for tax purposes in respect of that liability in future periods. For example, suppose an entity makes a provision in its accounts for €100 on which tax relief in full will be given when the liability is paid, then:

|  | Tax base | Carrying amount | Temp. difference |
|---|---|---|---|
| Provision | 0 | 100 | 100 |

and a deferred tax asset will be required.

### ACTIVITY 21.9

An entity has a loan of €500 repayable in five years' time. The principal repayment is not deductible for tax purposes. Identify the tax base and therefore the temporary difference.

*Activity feedback*

|  | Tax base | Carrying amount | Temp. difference |
|---|---|---|---|
| Loan | 500 | 500 | 0 |

There are several more examples of tax base calculations in the Standard.

## Current tax liabilities and assets

The requirements of IAS 12 here are quite straightforward (paras 12–13). Unpaid current tax in relation to current or earlier periods is shown as a liability and if the amount paid exceeds the amount due then the excess is recognized as an asset. In addition, where the benefit from a tax loss can be carried back to recover current tax of a previous period, this should also be recognized as an asset.

## Recognition of deferred tax liabilities

A deferred tax liability shall be recognized for all taxable temporary differences, except to the extent that the deferred tax liability arises from:

1 the initial recognition of goodwill, or
2 the initial recognition of an asset or liability in a transaction which is not a business combination and at the time of the transaction affects neither accounting profit nor taxable profit.

We try to explain the reasoning for these two exceptions to the provision of deferred tax using the information you have acquired so far in this chapter.

First, goodwill is an asset and if we assume an earning amount of €1000 then its tax base will be nil which implies a temporary difference of €1000, but if deferred tax is provided on this then the goodwill, which is a function of all the net assets of the acquired business, will change, which will consequently change the deferred tax. This will keep occurring as we try to calculate the deferred tax and thus an exemption is made as the calculation becomes circuitous.

The second exemption can best be understood by an example. Suppose a company buys a current asset for €100 which is not deductible for tax purposes when the asset is sold. Then:

|  | Tax base | Carrying amount | Temp. difference |
|---|---|---|---|
| Asset | Nil | 100 | 100 |

would imply a deferred tax liability should be recognized on the asset. However, the purchase of the asset had created no taxable or accounting income, and therefore no timing difference and thus no need for deferred tax.

Temporary differences are differences between the carrying amount of an asset or a liability in the statement of financial position and its tax base. Temporary differences often occur due to timing differences, i.e. when income or expense is recognized in an accounting profit in a different period to when it is included in taxable profit. Remember the example of depreciation here. There are, however, temporary differences that are not timing differences.

## Temporary differences that are not timing differences

IAS 12 discusses five circumstances where temporary differences arise that are not timing differences. We have already discussed two of these – goodwill and initial recognition of an asset or liability – and, as we saw, this temporary difference does not give rise to deferred tax as IAS 12 exempts them. The other three cases do give rise to deferred tax as we now describe.

**Business combinations** When a combination occurs under the acquisition method, the acquired assets and liabilities are revalued to fair value. However, the tax base of the asset or liability remains at its original figure within the subsidiary. (NB: a group is not a taxable entity.) A temporary difference therefore arises on which a deferred tax liability is recognized.

**Revaluation of assets** Where assets are revalued to fair value there may be a temporary difference. This temporary difference will arise in tax jurisdictions where the tax base of the asset is not adjusted for the revaluation. IAS 12 requires deferred tax to be recognized on this temporary difference. This does seem somewhat illogical. If the tax base of the asset is not adjusted, as there is no tax effect from the revaluation, then how can a liability arise? The IASB justifies the recognition of the liability on the grounds that the asset will generate future taxable income, but this is again debatable as it is difficult to see how future taxable income can equal a past event!

**Investment in subsidiaries, branches, associates and joint ventures** In the case of an entity with these types of investment, the tax base of the investment is generally cost. The carrying amount of the investment, however, changes over time as undistributed profits are built up in the subsidiary, associate and so on, or due to foreign currency translation or when the investment is reduced to its recoverable amount. These changes will give rise to temporary differences and IAS 12 requires deferred tax to be recognized except where:

- the parent, investor or venturer is able to control the timing of the reversal of the difference, and
- it is probable that the difference will not reverse in the foreseeable future.

One circumstance where a parent can control the difference is the declaration of dividends from the subsidiary but the parent could not control the difference in relation to foreign currency translation.

## Recognition of a deferred tax asset

IAS 12 (para. 5) defines a deferred tax asset as the amount of income taxes recoverable in future periods in respect of: (1) deductible temporary differences, (2) the carryforward of unused tax losses and (3) the carryforward of unused tax credits. There are circumstances when a deferred tax asset should not be recognized and these are when it arises from the initial recognition of an asset or liability in a transaction that:

- is not a business combination
- (at the time of the transaction) affects neither accounting profit nor taxable profit (loss).

These mirror the exemptions under deferred tax liability.

---

### ACTIVITY 21.10

An entity has calculated deferred tax assets of €1m which will result in deductions in tax computations for the next three years. Deferred tax liabilities of €0.5m have also been calculated in accordance with IAS 12. Taxable profits, including reversal of deferred tax liabilities, are expected to be €0.2m p.a. over the next three years. How much of the deferred tax asset should be recognized?

*Activity feedback*
*As only €0.6m of the deferred tax asset can be reversed against future taxable profits, this is the only amount that should be recognized.*

---

The amount recognized in the income statement of a period under this approach is the movement in deferred tax from the opening to the closing of the statement of financial position. This difference is recognized in arriving at the net profit and loss for the period, except for tax arising from:

- a transaction or event which is recognized in any accounting period directly in equity, in which case the movement in deferred tax should be accounted for directly in equity, or
- a business combination that is accounted for as an acquisition, in which case the movement in deferred tax is included in the resulting goodwill figure.

## Measurement of deferred tax

IAS 12 requires that deferred tax is measured by reference to tax rates and laws, as enacted or substantively enacted by the balance sheet date that are expected to apply in the periods in which the assets and liabilities to which the deferred tax relates are realized or settled. IAS 12 requires an entity to measure deferred tax relating to an asset depending on whether the entity expects to recover the carrying amount of the asset through use or sale. It can be difficult and subjective to assess whether recovery will be through use or through sale when the asset is measured using the fair value model in IAS 40, *Investment Property*. Therefore IAS 12 provides a practical solution to the problem by introducing a presumption that recovery of the carrying amount will normally be through sale.

## Amount recognized in income statement

So far we have concentrated on the measurement of the deferred tax asset or deferred tax liability in the statement of financial position as this is the approach adopted by IAS 12.

## ACTIVITY 21.11

An entity purchases an asset, cost €50 000, on 1.1.X1. Depreciation is on a straight line basis over its useful life of five years. The taxable allowance for the asset is straight line over four years. On 31.12.X3 the asset is revalued to €45 000, but its useful life and method of depreciation remains unchanged. The revaluation of the asset is irrelevant for tax legislation. Show the charge to the income statement for deferred tax over the life of the asset given tax rate at 30 per cent for all years, and compare it with the situation where there is no revaluation.

### Activity feedback
Revaluation:

| Date | Carrying amount € | Tax base | Temp. difference |
|---|---|---|---|
| 31.12.X1 | 40 000 | 37 500 | 2 500 |
| 31.12.X2 | 30 000 | 25 000 | 5 000 |
| 31.12.X3 | 45 000 | 12 500 | 32 500 |
| 31.12.X4 | 22 500 | 0 | 22 500 |
| 31.12.X5 | 0 | | |

When the asset was revalued, €25 000 would have been transferred to revaluation reserve. The charge against this amount (€25 000) for deferred tax is at 30%

= €7500. Therefore, the net amount credited to revaluation reserve is €17 500 (€25 000 – €7500).

| Deferred tax liability at 30% | Movement in year | IS charge | Equity charge |
|---|---|---|---|
| 750 | 750 | 750 | 0 |
| 1 500 | 750 | 750 | 0 |
| 9 750 | 8 250 | 750 | 7 500 |
| 6 750 | (3 000) | (3 000) | (3 750) |
| 0 | (6 750) | (6 750) | (3 750) |

Transfers from the equity revaluation reserve to retained earnings will be required for the excess depreciation charged over and above historical cost basis net of deferred tax in each of the final two years as follows:

| | |
|---|---|
| Historical cost depreciation charge | 10 000 |
| Revaluation depreciation charge | 22 500 |
| Excess | 12 500 |
| Deferred tax 30% | 3 750 |
| | 8 750 |

and therefore the €3750 will need to be credited to the revaluation reserve in the last two years.
No revaluation:

| Date | Carrying amount | Tax base | Temp. difference | DT liability | Movement in year | Income statement charge |
|---|---|---|---|---|---|---|
| 31.12.X1 | 40 000 | 37 500 | 2 500 | 750 | 750 | 750 |
| 31.12.X2 | 30 000 | 25 000 | 5 000 | 1 500 | 750 | 750 |
| 31.12.X3 | 20 000 | 12 500 | 750 | 2 250 | 750 | 750 |
| 31.12.X4 | 10 000 | 0 | 10 000 | 3 000 | 750 | 750 |
| 31.12.X5 | 0 | – | 0 | 0 | (3 000) | (3 000) |

## ACTIVITY 21.12

An entity purchases shares in another entity, leading to a parent/subsidiary relationship. The fair value of the net assets purchased included a deferred tax liability of €50 000 being temporary differences of €125 000 at 40 per cent. In the accounting year after the purchase it is announced that the tax rate applicable for the following year is to change to 42 per cent. By the end of the accounting year after the year of the purchase, €40 000 of the temporary difference had reversed. Show the deferred tax liability at the end of the accounting year after the year of purchase and state where any changes would be charged.

### Activity feedback
The years are confusing in this activity and it is therefore easier to see the effects using a table.

| Year | Tax rate | Temp. difference | DT liability |
|---|---|---|---|
| Of purchase | 40% | 125 000 | 50 00 |
| After purchase | 40% | 85 000 | 34 000 |
| Next year | 42% | | 35 700 |

If the tax rate change had not been enacted or substantively enacted, the deferred tax liability account would have remained at €34 000, but as the change is known about at the year-end, the deferred tax under the liability method must be accounted for at €35 700 and thus €1700 will be charged to the income statement for the year after the purchase. The charge cannot be debited to any goodwill on the acquisition as it results from a post-acquisition event.

# Presentation and disclosure requirement

IAS 12 is quite prescriptive in the presentation of tax assets and liabilities in the accounts. IAS 12 (para. 79) states that the major components of the tax expenses shall be disclosed separately. These components can include, for example:

- current tax expense (income)
- any adjustments recognized in the period for current tax of prior periods
- the amount of deferred tax expense (income) relating to changes in tax rates or the imposition of new taxes
- the amount of the benefit arising from a previously unrecognized tax loss, tax credit or temporary difference of a prior period that is used to reduce current tax expense
- the amount of the benefit arising from a previously unrecognized tax loss, tax credit or temporary difference of a prior period that is used to reduce deferred tax expense.

The disclosure requirements are extensive and we suggest you read the Standard in detail for these (IAS 12, para. 81). We list a few important disclosures below:

- the following items have to be disclosed separately: (a) the aggregate current and deferred tax relating to items that are charged or credited directly to equity; and (b) the amount of income tax relating to each component of other comprehensive income
- an explanation of the relationship between tax expense (income) and accounting profit in either or both of the following forms (a) a numerical reconciliation between tax expense (income) and the product of accounting profit multiplied by the applicable tax rate(s), disclosing also the basis on which the applicable tax rate(s) is (are) computed; or (b) a numerical reconciliation between the average effective tax rate and the applicable tax rate, disclosing also the basis on which the applicable tax rate is computed
- an explanation of changes in the applicable tax rate(s) compared to the previous accounting period.

In order to illustrate the extensiveness of the disclosure requirements we introduce a real life illustration of AB Nestlé.

## REAL LIFE ILLUSTRATION

The following disclosure is taken from the 2012 financial statements of Nestlé. Note 14 to the statement of financial position and the statement of comprehensive income provides all necessary information to understand Nestlé's accounting for income tax according to IAS 12.

### 14. Taxes

#### 14.1 Taxes recognized in the income statement

| In millions of CHF | 2012 | 2011 |
|---|---|---|
| Components of taxes | | |
| Current taxes[a] | 3 179 | 2 554 |
| Deferred taxes | (229) | (301) |
| Taxes reclassified to other comprehensive income | 501 | 859 |
| **Total taxes** | **3 451** | 3 112 |

*(Continued)*

## REAL LIFE ILLUSTRATION  (*Continued*)

| In millions of CHF | 2012 | 2011 |
|---|---|---|
| Reconciliation of taxes | | |
| Expected tax expense at weighted average applicable tax rate | 3 413 | 3 054 |
| Tax effect of non-deductible or non-taxable items | (206) | (202) |
| Prior years' taxes | (368) | (215) |
| Transfers to unrecognized deferred tax assets | 49 | 83 |
| Transfers from unrecognized deferred tax assets | (13) | (123) |
| Changes in tax rates | (1) | 23 |
| Withholding taxes levied on transfers of income | 374 | 313 |
| Other | 203 | 179 |
| **Total taxes** | **3 451** | 3 112 |

ªCurrent taxes related to prior years represent a tax income of CHF 32 million (2011: tax expense of CHF 35 million).

The expected tax expense at weighted average applicable tax rate is the result from applying the domestic statutory tax rates to profits before taxes of each entity in the country it operates. For the Group, the weighted average applicable tax rate varies from one year to the other depending on the relative weight of the profit of each individual entity in the Group's profit as well as the changes in the statutory tax rates.

### 14.2 Taxes recognized in other comprehensive income

| In millions of CHF | 2012 | 2011 |
|---|---|---|
| Tax effects relating to | | |
| Currency retranslations | 41 | 64 |
| Fair value adjustments on available-for-sale financial instruments | (24) | (29) |
| Fair value adjustments on cash flow hedges | (49) | 159 |
| Actuarial gains/(losses) on defined benefit schemes | 533 | 665 |
| | **501** | 859 |

### 14.3 Reconciliation of deferred taxes by type of temporary differences recognized on the balance sheet

In millions of CHF

| | Property, plant and equipment | Goodwill and intangible assets | Employee benefits | Inventories, receivables, payables and provisions | Unused tax losses and unused tax credits | Other | Total |
|---|---|---|---|---|---|---|---|
| At 1 January 2011 | (1 093) | (1 166) | 1 726 | 837 | 318 | (82) | 540 |
| Currency retranslations | 5 | (12) | (24) | (24) | (15) | 4 | (66) |
| Deferred tax (expense)/income | (223) | (46) | 408 | 10 | 62 | 90 | 301 |
| Modification of the scope of consolidation | (36) | (360) | 10 | 14 | 1 | 12 | (359) |
| At 31 December 2011 | (1 347) | (1 584) | 2 120 | 837 | 366 | 24 | 416 |
| Currency retranslations | 37 | 27 | (65) | (28) | (28) | 2 | (55) |
| Deferred tax (expense)/income | (154) | (91) | 386 | 64 | 57 | (33) | 229 |
| Modification of the scope of consolidation | (11) | (3) | (2) | 17 | – | 36 | 37 |
| At 31 December 2012 | (1 475) | (1 651) | 2 439 | 890 | 395 | 29 | 627 |

(*Continued*)

## REAL LIFE ILLUSTRATION  (*Continued*)

| In millions of CHF | 2012 | 2011 |
|---|---|---|
| Reflected in the balance sheet as follows: | | |
| Deferred tax assets | 2 903 | 2 476 |
| Deferred tax liabilities | (2 276) | (2 060) |
| Net assets | 627 | 416 |

### 14.4 Unrecognized deferred taxes

The deductible temporary differences as well as the unused tax losses and tax credits for which no deferred tax assets are recognized expire as follows:

| In millions of CHF | 2012 | 2011 |
|---|---|---|
| Within one year | 43 | 20 |
| Between one and five years | 317 | 314 |
| More than five years | 1 909 | 1 479 |
| | 2 269 | 1 813 |

At 31 December 2012, the unrecognized deferred tax assets amount to CHF 537 million (2011: CHF 464 million). In addition, the Group has not recognized deferred tax liabilities in respect of unremitted earnings that are considered indefinitely reinvested in foreign subsidiaries. At 31 December 2012, these earnings amount to CHF 15.6 billion (2011: CHF 12.9 billion). They could be subject to withholding and other taxes on remittance.

## Discounting

IAS 12 does not permit the discounting of deferred tax balances with one exception. IAS 12 allows discounting of deferred tax where it relates to a pre-tax amount that is itself discounted. This exception is obvious, as the application of a tax rate to the discounted item will automatically result in a deferred tax charge that is discounted. Deferred tax is defined as a liability and, as payment is sometime in the future, it is obvious that, under the current regime of IAS 12, the amount shown as a liability does not reflect this deferment to the future. Discounting the deferred tax could be seen as an attempt to reflect the fair value, but could also be seen as a method to reflect the time value of money. The IASB is reflecting on discounting, but for the moment it does not permit discounting on deferred tax because:

- reliable calculation is complex and dependent on several factors, not least of which is choice of discount rate, and therefore, if discounting was required, 'reliability' would be questionable
- if discounting is permitted, some entities would discount and others would not, leading to a lack of comparability.

The final activity will test your understanding of the measurement and recognition of deferred taxes.

## ACTIVITY 21.13

In all the following cases identify the amount of deferred tax that should be recognized and by whom.

1 Entity A, which bought a 35 per cent stake in B, sold goods to B costing £20 000 for £30 000. B still holds these goods at the year-end in inventory. A recognizes an adjustment in its consolidated accounts to eliminate its share of the unrealized profit on the goods. A pays tax at 30 per cent and B tax at 40 per cent.

2 Entity C recognizes a liability at its year-end of £50 000 for accrued warranty costs. For tax purposes, the product warranty costs are not deductible until claimed. Tax rate is 30 per cent.

3 Entity D holds an asset with a carrying amount of £100 and a tax base of £60. A tax rate of 20 per cent would apply if the asset were sold and a tax rate of 30 per cent would apply to other income.

### Activity feedback

1 There is a temporary timing difference in respect of A's share of the unrealized profit, i.e. 35% × £10 000 = £3500. This timing difference will reverse in the next 12 months, if we assume that B sells all the goods and therefore a deferred tax asset of £3500 × 30% = £1050 is required. Note that A's tax rate is used here, not B's.

2 The temporary difference in respect of the warranties is £50 000 on which a deferred tax asset of £15 000 should be recognized.

3 If D expects to sell the asset without further use, then a deferred tax liability of 8 (40 × 20%) would be recognized. If it intends to use the asset, a deferred tax liability of 12 (40 × 30%) would be recognized.

## SUMMARY

Within this chapter we have considered the principles of debate on accounting for tax and identified the regulations of IAS 12. We have seen that accounting standard-setting bodies, which all believe that they are issuing standards within a conceptual framework, can view the principles of deferred tax quite differently. Our debate in this chapter has considered deferred tax from a:

- balance sheet or income statement approach
- flow through, partial or full provision method
- deferral or liability method.

We also considered the possibility of discounting deferred tax. We leave you with the question: 'Does the required accounting treatment of taxation in published IAS accounts lead to a true and fair view as required by the Fourth Directive?'

# EXERCISES

*Suggested answers to exercises marked ✓ are to be found on our dedicated CourseMate platform for students.*

*Suggested answers to the remaining exercises are to be found on the Instructor online support resources.*

**1**   Outline the major arguments in favour of always providing for deferred tax where the amounts are material.

**2**   Outline the major arguments in favour of only providing for deferred tax when it is probable that a liability will crystallize.

**3**   Deferred tax should be ignored when preparing financial statements. Discuss.

✓ **4**   Explain and distinguish between:

- the flow through approach
- full deferral
- partial deferral.

✓ **5**   Explain and distinguish between:

- the deferral method
- the liability method.

**6**   Comparability requires that either all entities provide in full for deferred tax or that it is always ignored. Discuss.

✓ **7**   Explain to a non-accountant the difference between the income statement view and the balance sheet view of deferred tax.

**8**   Discounting deferred tax balances would provide useful information to users. Discuss.

**9**   Critically appraise the following statement: 'The required accounting treatment of taxation in published IAS accounts does not lead to a true and fair view as required by the Fourth Directive.'

**10**   (i)   IAS 12, *Income Tax*, details the requirements relating to the accounting treatment of deferred tax.

**Required:**

Explain why it is considered necessary to provide for deferred tax and briefly outline the principles of accounting for deferred tax contained in IAS 12, *Income Tax*.

(ii)   Bowtock purchased an item of plant for $2 000 000 on 1 October 20X0. It had an estimated life of eight years and an estimated residual value of $400 000. The plant is depreciated on straight line basis. The tax authorities do not allow depreciation as a deductible expense. Instead, a tax expense of 40 per cent of the cost of this type of asset can be claimed against income tax in the year of purchase and 20 per cent p.a. (on a reducing balance basis) of its tax base thereafter. The rate of income tax can be taken as 25 per cent.

**Required:**

In respect of the above item of plant, calculate the deferred tax charge/credit in Bowtock's income statement for the year to 30 September 20X3 and the deferred tax balance in the balance sheet at that date.

Note: Work to the nearest $000.

(ACCA – December 2003)

**11** Nette, a public limited company, manufactures mining equipment and extracts natural gas. The directors are uncertain about the role of the IASB's *Framework for the Preparation and Presentation of Financial Statements* (the Framework) in corporate reporting. Their view is that accounting is based on the transactions carried out by the company and these transactions are allocated to the company's accounting period by using the matching and prudence concepts. The argument put forward by the directors is that the Framework does not take into account the business and legal constraints within which companies operate. Further, they have given a situation which has arisen in the current financial statements where they feel that the current accounting practice is inconsistent with the Framework.

**Situation:**

Nette purchased a building on 1 June 20X3 for $10 million. The building qualified for a grant of $2 million which has been treated as a deferred credit in the financial statements. The tax allowances are reduced by the amount of the grant. There are additional temporary differences of $40 million in respect of deferred tax liabilities at the year-end. Also, the company has sold extraction equipment which carries a five-year warranty. The directors have made a provision for the warranty of $4 million at 31 May 20X4 which is deductible for tax when costs are incurred under the warranty. In addition to the warranty provision, the company has unused tax losses of $70 million. The directors of the company are unsure as to whether a provision for deferred taxation is required.

(Assume that the depreciation of the building is straight line over ten years, and tax allowances of 25 per cent on the reducing balance basis can be claimed on the building. Tax is payable at 30 per cent.)

**Required:**

(a) Explain the importance of the 'Framework' to the reporting of corporate performance and whether it takes into account the business and legal constraints placed upon companies.

(b) (i) Explain, with reasons and suitable extracts/computations, the accounting treatment of the above situation in the financial statements for the year ended 31 May 20X4.

　　(ii) Discuss whether the treatment of the items appears consistent with the 'Framework'.

(ACCA – June 2004)

**12** On 1 January 20X3, SPJ had an opening balance of $5000 on its tax account, which represented the balance on the account after settling its tax liability for the previous year. This balance arose from an overestimate of the tax due charged to the previous year's income statement. SPJ has a credit balance on its deferred tax account of $1.6 million at the same date.

SPJ has been advised that it should expect to pay $1 million tax on its trading profits for the year ended 31 December 20X3 and increase its deferred tax account balance by $150 000.

**Required:**

Prepare extracts from the income statement for the year ended 31 December 20X3, balance sheet at that date, and notes to the accounts showing the tax entries required.

(CIMA pilot paper Financial Accounting & Tax Principles)

**13**   The directors of Panel, a public limited company, are reviewing the procedures for the calculation of the deferred tax provision for their company. They are quite surprised at the impact on the provision caused by changes in accounting standards such as IFRS 1, *First Time Adoption of International Financial Reporting Standards,* and IFRS 2, *Share-based Payment.* Panel is adopting International Financial Reporting Standards for the first time as at 31 October 20X5 and the directors are unsure how the deferred tax provision will be calculated in its financial statements ended on that date including the opening provision at 1 November 20X3.

**Required:**

(a)  (i)   Explain how changes in accounting standards are likely to have an impact on the provision for deferred taxation under IAS 12, *Income Taxes.*

(ii)   Describe the basis for the calculation of the provision for deferred taxation on first-time adoption of IFRS including the provision in the opening IFRS balance sheet.

Additionally, the directors wish to know how the provision for deferred taxation would be calculated in the following situations under IAS 12, *Income Taxes:*

(i)   On 1 November 20X3, the company had granted 10m share options worth $40m, subject to a two-year vesting period. Local tax law allows a tax deduction at the exercise date of the intrinsic value of the options. The intrinsic value of the 10m share options at 31 October 20X4 was $16m and at 31 October 20X5 was $46m; the increase in the share price in the year to 31 October 20X5. The directors are unsure how to account for deferred taxation on this transaction for the years ended 31 October 20X4 and 31 October 20X5

(ii)   Panel is leasing plant under a finance lease over a five-year period. The asset was recorded at the present value of the minimum lease payments of $12m at the inception of the lease which was 1 November 20X4. The asset is depreciated on a straight line basis over the five years and has no residual value. The annual lease payments are $3m payable in arrears on 31 October and the effective interest rate is 8 per cent p.a. The directors have not leased an asset under a finance lease before and are unsure as to its treatment for deferred taxation. The company can claim a tax deduction for the annual rental payment as the finance lease does not qualify for tax relief.

(iii)   A wholly owned overseas subsidiary, Pins, a limited liability company, sold goods costing $7m to Panel on 1 September 20X5, and these goods had not been sold by Panel before the year-end. Panel had paid $9m for these goods. The directors do not understand how this transaction should be dealt with in the financial statements of the subsidiary and the group for taxation purposes. Pins pays tax locally at 30 per cent.

(iv)   Nails, a limited liability company, is a wholly owned subsidiary of Panel, and is a cash-generating unit in its own right. The value of the property, plant and equipment of Nails at 31 October 20X5 was $6m and purchased goodwill was $1m before any impairment loss. The company had no other assets or liabilities. An impairment loss of $1.8m had occurred at 31 October 20X5. The tax base of the property, plant and equipment of Nails was $4m as at 31 October 20X5. The directors wish to know how the impairment loss will affect the deferred tax provision for the year. Impairment losses are not an allowable expense for taxation purposes

Assume a tax rate of 30 per cent.

**Required:**

(b) Discuss, with suitable computations, how the situations (i) to (iv) above will impact on the accounting for deferred tax under IAS12, *Income Taxes,* in the group financial statements of Panel.

(ACCA 3.5 int. – December 2005)

**14**　GJ commenced business on 1 October 20X5, and on that date it acquired property, plant and equipment for $220 000. GJ used the straight line method of depreciation. The estimated useful life of the assets was five years and the residual value was estimated at $10 000. GJ's accounting year end is 30 September. All the assets acquired qualified for a first year tax allowance of 50 per cent and then an annual tax allowance of 25 per cent of the reducing balance. On 1 October 20X7, GJ revalued all of its assets; this led to an increase in asset values of $53 000. GJ's applicable tax rate for the year is 25 per cent.

**Required:**

Calculate the amount of the deferred tax provision that GJ should include in its balance sheet at 30 September 20X8, in accordance with IAS 12, *Income Taxes.*

(CIMA P7 – November 2008)

**15**　HF purchased an asset on 1 April 20X7 for $220 000. HF claimed a first year tax allowance of 30 per cent and then an annual 20 per cent writing down allowance, using the reducing balance method. HF depreciates the asset over eight years using straight line depreciation, assuming no residual value. On 1 April 20X8, HF revalued the asset and increased the net book value by $50 000. The asset's useful life was not affected. Assume there are no other temporary differences in the period and a tax rate of 25 per cent p.a.

**Required:**

Calculate the amount of deferred tax movement in the year ended 31 March 20X9 and the deferred tax balance at 31 March 20X9 in accordance with IAS 12, *Income Taxes.*

(CIMA P7 – May 2009)

**16**　On 31 March 20X6, CH had a credit balance brought forward on its deferred tax account of $642 000. There was also a credit balance on its corporate income tax account of $31 000 representing an overestimate of the tax charge for the year ended 31 March 20X5.

CH's taxable profit for the year ended 31 March 20X6 was $946 000. CH's directors estimated the deferred tax provision required at 31 March 20X6 to be $759 000 and the applicable income tax rate for the year to 31 March 20X6 as 22 per cent. Calculate the income tax expense that CH will charge in its income statement for the year ended 31 March 20X6, as required by IAS 12, *Income Taxes.*

(CIMA P7 – May 2006)

# EMPLOYEE BENEFITS

# 22

## INTRODUCTION

In every organization, people are a very important resource. Without a competent and loyal staff of personnel, an entity will usually be unsuccessful. To keep the workforce motivated and loyal, most, if not all, employers provide employees with certain benefits in addition to the wages paid. Employee benefits are usually furnished by the employer in full, but some types of benefits are paid for jointly by the employer and the employee. A benefit package may include: retirement plans; insurance plans, such as hospital, dental, life and disability insurance; stock options; profit-sharing plans; recreational programmes; vacations; and so on.

A number of these employee benefits have a long-term perspective, which implies that elements of uncertainty are involved. As a consequence, accounting for a number of these long-term employee benefits is not that straightforward and of rather a high, technical level.

## ACTIVITY 22.1

If you think of employee benefits, which benefits do you consider to be short-term and which would you regard as long-term?

### Activity feedback

- *Short-term benefits: salaries, paid holiday, bonuses, medical care.*

- *Long-term benefits: medical care after retirement, pension benefits.*

*Equity compensation benefits can be either short-term or long-term depending on the exercise period.*

Most of the employee benefits are dealt with in IAS 19, *Employee Benefits*. One particular type of employee benefit, namely equity compensation or share-based benefits, is dealt with in IFRS 2, *Share-based Payment*. IFRS 2 describes the recognition and valuation rules when an entity undertakes a share-based payment transaction.

As you will notice, the scope of IFRS 2 encompasses all share-based payment transactions made by an entity, not just share-based transactions with employees and top management.

We will first present the definitions, recognition and measurement rules for those employee benefits that fall within the scope of IAS 19. Subsequently we will discuss the accounting treatment of share-based compensation, which is dealt with in IFRS 2.

IAS 19 qualifies as short-term benefits: wages, salaries and social security contributions; paid annual leave and paid sick leave; profit sharing and bonuses (if payable within 12 months of the end of the period); and non-monetary benefits (such as medical care, housing, cars and free or subsidized goods or services) for current employees.

Profit-sharing plans and bonus plans can be long-term or short-term, according to when they are payable (within 12 months or longer). Examples of long-term benefits are: qualified post-employment benefits such as pensions; other retirement benefits; post-employment life insurance; and post-employment medical care. Long-term employee benefits include: long-service leave or sabbatical leave, jubilee or other long-service benefits; and long-term disability benefits.

IAS 19 deals with further termination benefits.

If we discuss the issue of how these benefits should be accounted for then it is important to determine when a company is obliged or required to fulfil these employee benefits. The accounting treatment, which IAS 19 prescribes for employee benefits, is applicable if they result from:

- formal plans or other formal agreements between an entity and individual employees, groups of employees or their representatives
- legislative requirements or from industry arrangements, whereby entities are required to contribute to national, state, industry or other multi-employer plans, or
- informal practices that give rise to a constructive obligation. Informal practices give rise to a constructive obligation where the entity has no realistic alternative but to pay employee benefits. An example of a constructive obligation is where a change in the entity's informal practices would cause unacceptable damage to its relationship with employees.

Accounting for short-term employee benefits is straightforward as these elements do not include many uncertainties. We will look first at those short-term employee benefits. Then we will focus on the long-term employee benefits and, more specifically, on pension benefits.

## ACCOUNTING FOR SHORT-TERM EMPLOYEE BENEFITS

Short-term benefits are salaries, paid leave and bonus plans to be settled wholly before 12 months after the end of the annual reporting period in which the employees render the related services and other benefits payable. With regard to these benefits, the basic valuation rule is as follows: when an employee has rendered service to an entity during an accounting period, the entity should recognize the undiscounted amount of short-term employee benefits expected to be paid in exchange for that service. The benefit will be reported as an expense, unless another International Accounting Standard requires or permits the inclusion of the benefits in the cost of an asset (e.g. see IAS 2, *Inventories*, and IAS 16, *Property, Plant and Equipment*) and as a liability (accrued expense), after deducting any amount already paid. If the amount already paid exceeds the undiscounted amount of the benefits, an entity should recognize that excess as an asset (prepaid expense) to the extent that the prepayment will lead to, for example, a reduction in future payments or a cash refund.

Compensated absences are short-term employee benefits. IAS 19 pays explicit attention to them. Concerning these short-term compensated absences, IAS 19 makes a distinction between accumulating and non-accumulating compensated absences. The difference between the two will result in a different accounting treatment.

## ACTIVITY 22.2

Can you think of some examples of paid absence? Can you distinguish between whether they arise from service rendered in the past (i.e. accumulated absences) or whether they are not related to service rendered at work (i.e. non-accumulated absences)?

### Activity feedback

A typical example of an accumulated compensated absence is absence for vacation (holiday). According to the number of days worked, an employee is entitled to a number of days of paid absence. Examples of non-accumulated absences are sickness leave, maternity and paternity leave and military service.

In the case of accumulating compensated absences, the expected cost of the short-term benefit has to be recognized when the employees render the service that increases their entitlement to future compensated absences.

In the case of non-accumulating compensated absence, the benefit should be recognized when the absence occurs, as in the latter case the absence is not linked to the service rendered by the employees in a period.

## ACCOUNTING FOR PROFIT-SHARING AND BONUS PLANS

The compensation package of many executives, but also of higher and middle management these days, often includes profit-sharing plans or bonus plans. When profit-sharing or bonus plans exist, executives and employees receive a variable amount as compensation on top of their salary. These bonuses can be linked to financial indicators, e.g. accounting numbers such as earnings before interest and taxes (EBIT), return on assets (ROA), return on equity (ROE) or non-financial indicators (e.g. customer satisfaction), or a combination of both.

The obligation to pay an amount to the employees under a profit-sharing or bonus plan results from employee service, not from a transaction with the entity's owners. Therefore, an entity has to recognize the cost of profit-sharing and bonus plans as an expense, not a distribution of net profit (para. 21). The bonus as such qualifies as an obligation. The amount linked to it is dependent on the realized performance in relation to the indicator specified in the profit-sharing or bonus plan.

As a result, the expected cost of profit-sharing and bonus payments should be recognized as an expense and as a liability when, and only when (paras 10 and 17), the entity has a present legal or constructive obligation to make such payments as a result of past events and a reliable estimate of the obligation can be made. A present obligation exists when, and only when, the entity has no realistic alternative but to make the payments.

IAS 19, in itself, unfortunately does not require specific disclosures about short-term benefits; other International Accounting Standards, however, may require disclosures concerning these short-term benefits. For example, where required by IAS 24, *Related Party Disclosures*, an entity has to disclose information about employee benefits for key management personnel, or IAS 1, *Presentation of Financial Statements*, requires that an entity should disclose staff costs.

IAS 19 does not oblige a company to provide information about the formal terms of a bonus or profit-sharing plan to external stakeholders of the company. This information disclosure is left to the voluntary disclosure policy of the firm. Since empirical research related to earnings management found evidence that these bonus plans and profit-sharing plans can create incentives to manage the reported results of a firm, it would be interesting to know the amounts paid out in respect of these plans, but even more interesting to know the indicator (financial or non-financial) which drives the bonus.

This would be useful information for financial analysis purposes (for a further discussion of this item see Chapter 31). Information on the formal terms of the plan (e.g. the indicators to which the bonus is linked) can give the external user of the financial statements an idea concerning the direction in which the results possibly could have been influenced. We might hope that in the wake of the 'accounting scandals of the year 2002', these practices become less common.

## ACCOUNTING FOR EQUITY COMPENSATION BENEFITS

Bonus plans and profit-sharing plans have for a long time been the only widely used instrument to increase compensation of executives and employees. From the beginning of the 1990s, stock-based compensation or share-based payment became very popular. Stock-based compensation can take the form of stock options or gifts of shares for free or at lower than market values. Empirical research on incentives for earnings management also reveals that the existence of stock options might induce management to smooth reported income and to increase income upward in order to boost the share price. These elements are illustrated further in Chapter 31. The instruments that qualify as equity-based compensation are:

**(a)** shares, share options and other equity instruments, issued to directors, senior executives and other employees, and

**(b)** cash payments, the amount of which will depend on the future market price of the reporting entity's shares or other equity instruments, again as part of a remuneration plan.

These instruments, without doubt, have an impact on the result, the financial position and the cash flow of an entity. If a company uses existing shares for the equity-based compensation plans, the company has to buy the shares from existing shareholders. This implies a cost for the company. If a company chooses to issue extra shares (in that case employees can subscribe for new shares), there is a dilutive effect when the options are exercised (see Chapter 25).

Important elements concerning equity-based compensation are the grant date, the exercise date, the exercise price (strike price), the vesting date and vesting requirements. The difference between the exercise price and the market price is the key value driver of warrants/options. Simple methods (intrinsic value) only use this difference for valuation purposes. More sophisticated methods are using valuation methods (for instance, the Black and Scholes (1973) model) which incorporate additional parameters (e.g. volatility).

Relevant accounting valuation issues concerning these benefits are: how to measure the cost of compensation offered by the company to the employees; when to recognize this cost in the profit and loss account; how to account for the financial impact of stock options (e.g. if existing shares are bought, how will they be financed by the company).

Equity-based compensation is a hot topic in accounting regulation. Previous attempts of the United States Financial Accounting Standards Board to prescribe valuation and recognition rules, whereby the cost of the share-based compensation was charged to the profit and loss account, had to be withdrawn under the pressure of the business community. So SFAS 123, *Accounting for Stock-based Compensation*, is one of the exceptional Standards where preparers can make a choice whether or not to include an item on the balance sheet or account for it off balance sheet. However, since Enron, the attitude of the business world is changing. In July 2002, Coca-Cola was the first company to announce that it would recognize the cost of stock-based compensation in its profit and loss account from 2002 on; other companies followed the example of Coca-Cola.

## ACTIVITY 22.3

Look at websites of several companies from different parts of Europe and worldwide and try to find information on stock-based compensation or other elements of compensation. What do you observe?

### Activity feedback

Disclosure on equity-based compensation, and about compensation at large, differs among different countries. In the Anglo-Saxon world, information on compensation has for some time found its way onto the financial statements. Compensation levels of individuals are disclosed in those financial statements. In continental Europe, the presence of the value 'secrecy' (discussed in Chapter 2) probably has an impact on the amount of and the way in which information is disclosed. Further, a diversity of share-based compensation plans is found in the notes to the accounts of companies.

The disclosure of compensation benefits to the external stakeholders of the company is not only determined by accounting regulation. Codes of corporate governance in many countries include disclosure requirements with regard to top management compensation.

The choice left by SFAS 123 with regard to the recognition and measurement of equity-based remuneration instruments is unsatisfactory for the users of financial information. Studies by Bear Stearns and Credit Suisse First Boston, carried out at the start of the twenty-first century, show that if companies belonging to the Standard & Poor's 500 had accounted for their equity-based remuneration investments on the balance sheet with the use of the fair value, the earnings of those companies would have been significantly lower.

One of the first issues the Board, in its new composition, wanted to solve is the recognition and valuation of these equity benefit compensation schemes. At the beginning of 2004, IFRS 2, *Share-based Payment,* was issued. With IFRS 2, the Board has insisted on recognition and measurement of those equity-based remuneration instruments on the balance sheet. A disclosure of these benefits in the notes only and no recognition on the balance sheet was no longer accepted.

The scope of IFRS 2 includes all share-based payment transactions. So IFRS 2 is applicable to more transactions than just equity-based compensation benefits. IFRS 2 defines share-based transactions as those transactions where an entity's equity instruments are transferred by its shareholder to parties that have supplied goods or services to the entity, unless the transfer is clearly for a purpose other than payment for goods or services supplied to the entity. IFRS 2 also applies to transfers of equity instruments of the entity's parent, or equity instruments of another entity in the same group as the entity, to parties that have supplied goods or services to the entity. However, an entity shall not apply this IFRS to transactions in which the entity acquires goods as part of the net assets acquired in a business combination as defined by IFRS 3, *Business Combinations,* in a combination of entities or businesses under common control as defined by IFRS 3, or the contribution of a business in the formation of a joint venture as defined by IAS 31, *Interests in Joint Ventures.* A transaction with an employee (or other party), in his/her capacity as a holder of equity instruments of the entity, is not considered to be a share-based payment transaction and does not fall under the scope of IFRS 2.

IFRS 2 distinguishes with regard to the nature of the share-based payment transactions between three different types of share-based transactions (para. 2):

(a) Equity-settled share-based payment transactions

(b) Cash-settled share-based payment transactions, and

(c) Transactions in which the entity receives or acquires goods or services, and the term of the arrangement provide either the entity or the supplier of those goods or services with a choice of whether the entity settles the transaction in cash (or other assets) or by issuing equity instruments.

In the absence of specifically identifiable goods or services, other circumstances may indicate that goods or services have been (or will be) received, in which case IFRS applies (e.g. a company which provides shares to a charity in order to improve its image of corporate social responsibility). When IFRS 2 was amended in June 2009, special attention was paid to group share-based payment transactions. A share-based payment transaction may be settled by another group entity (or a shareholder of any group entity) on behalf of the entity receiving or acquiring the goods or services. Paragraph 2 also applies to an entity that:

**(a)** receives goods or services when another entity in the same group (or a shareholder of any group entity) has the obligation to settle the share-based payment transaction, or

**(b)** has an obligation to settle a share-based payment transaction when another entity in the same group receives the goods or services.

Paragraph 2 does not apply in group share-based transactions if the transaction is clearly for a purpose other than payment for goods or services supplied to the entity receiving them.

Although the accounting treatment of these three types of share-based payment transaction will be different, the main objective will be that an entity should reflect in its results, and in its financial position, the effects of share-based payment transactions when the goods are obtained and services are received. We will now present and illustrate the definition, recognition and measurement rules of the three types of share-based payment transactions.

## Equity-settled share-based payment transactions

In equity-settled share-based payment transactions, an entity receives goods or services in exchange for equity instruments. For example, an entity acquires equipment from a manufacturer and uses shares as consideration. Another example is a top executive in a company who receives share options or other equity instruments as part of their remuneration schemes.

IFRS 2 (para. 10) states that for these equity-settled share-based payment transactions, the entity shall measure the goods or services received and the corresponding increase in equity, directly, at the fair value of the goods or services received, unless that fair value cannot be estimated reliably. If the entity cannot estimate reliably the fair value of the goods or services received, the entity shall measure their value, and the corresponding increase in equity, indirectly by reference to the fair value of the equity instruments granted (see Activity 22.4).

---

### ACTIVITY 22.4

Consider the two examples just given (the acquisition of the equipment and the compensation of the top executive) and determine which amount will be used under IFRS 2 for the valuation of the transaction in the books of the entity.

#### Activity feedback
*In the case of the equipment, the market value of the equipment will be used to measure, on the one hand, the increase in the fixed assets and, on the other, the increase in equity. In the situation where equity instruments are used as remuneration for services rendered by employees, directors or other senior executives, it is usually not possible to measure directly the services received for particular components of the employee's remuneration package. It might also not be possible to measure the fair value of the total remuneration package*

*independently, without measuring directly the fair value of the equity instruments granted. Furthermore, shares or share options are sometimes granted as part of a bonus arrangement, rather than as a part of the basic remuneration. By granting shares or share options, in addition to other remuneration, the entity is paying additional remuneration to obtain additional benefits. Estimating the fair value of those additional benefits is likely to be difficult. Because of the difficulty of measuring directly the fair value of the services received, the entity shall measure the fair value of the employee services received by reference to the fair value of the equity instruments granted. So the share-based remuneration will be recorded in the books of the company in the following manner. The amount of the fair value of the equity instrument will be debited on an expense remuneration account and credited on an equity account.*

**Determining the fair value of the equity instrument** IFRS 2 distinguishes with regard to the valuation of these equity-settled share-based transactions between two possibilities: first, when the fair value of the goods received and the services rendered can be measured reliably, and, second, when it is not possible to determine this value in a reliable way. In the first situation, the fair value of the goods received or the services rendered is used for the valuation of the transaction. In the second situation, the fair value of the equity instrument will be used for reporting purposes. For example, if an entity grants shares to a charity organization in order to enhance its image, the transaction shall be accounted for according to IFRS 2, and the value of the transaction is the fair value of the equity instruments.

**Grant date** Before focusing further on the recognition and measurement issues of these equity-settled share-based payment transactions, we will explain a number of concepts that play a role in the accounting treatment of these share-based transactions. First, there is the grant date of the share-based payment transaction. This is the date at which the entity and another party (including an employee) agree to a share-based payment arrangement, being when the entity and the other contracting party have a shared understanding of the terms and conditions of the arrangement. At grant date, the entity confers on the other contracting party the right to cash, other assets, or equity instruments of the entity, provided the specified vesting conditions, if any, are met. If that agreement is subject to an approval process (e.g. by shareholders), grant date is the date when that approval is obtained.

**Vesting conditions** In the definition of the grant date, we discover the concept of 'vesting conditions'. These are the conditions that must be satisfied for the counterparty to become entitled to receive cash, other assets or equity instruments of the entity, under a share-based payment arrangement. Vesting conditions include service conditions which require the other party to complete a specified period of service, and performance conditions which require specified performance targets to be met (such as a specified increase in the entity's profit over a specified period of time). Only these two conditions, namely service rendered and performance conditions, need to be considered to determine the vesting conditions.

Vesting conditions shall be taken into account by adjusting the number of equity instruments included in the measurement of the transaction amount so that, ultimately, the amount recognized for goods or services received as consideration for the equity instruments granted shall be based on the number of equity instruments that eventually vest. Hence, on a cumulative basis, no amount is recognized for goods or services if the equity instruments granted do not vest because of failure to satisfy a vesting condition (e.g. the counterparty fails to complete a specified service period, or a performance condition is not satisfied, subject to the requirement of para. 21).

## ILLUSTRATION

A company, Amax, grants 50 share options to each of its 200 employees. If there is no vesting requirement, the employees are entitled to receive these granted options immediately. The fair value of the share option at the grant date is €30. When the equity instruments granted vest immediately, implying that the counterparty is not required to complete a specific period of service before becoming unconditionally entitled to those equity instruments, the entity shall recognize on grant date the services received in full, with a corresponding increase in equity.

In this situation the expense related to these granted share options is:

$$10\,000 \text{ options} \times €30 = €300\,000$$

This amount will be debited on an expense account and credited in an equity account.

## ILLUSTRATION

When company Amax wants to enter its share-based transaction in its books, it needs information on the probability that the employees will remain in service. On the basis of past experience, company Amax estimates that 10 per cent of employees will leave during the three-year period and therefore forfeit their rights to the share options. If we take the example of the share option plan that is only dependent on the vesting condition that the employee remains in service for three years, we will have the following amounts to be entered in the books of company Amax. For this illustration, we assume that after three years the estimates used match exactly with the reality and that the fair value of the option at grant date is €30.

| Year | Calculation |
|------|-------------|
| 1 | 10 000 options × 90% × €30 × 1/3 |
| 2 | (10 000 options × 90% × €30 × 2/3) − 90 000 |
| 3 | (10 000 options × 90% × €30 × 3/3) − 180 000 |

Over the vesting period, an amount of €270 000 has been reported on the profit and loss account as a remuneration expense, and over the same period that amount has been credited to an equity account.

| Amount debited on the expense account | Amount credited on an equity account |
|---------------------------------------|--------------------------------------|
| €90 000 | €90 000 |
| €90 000 | €90 000 |
| €90 000 | €90 000 |

If vesting requirements exist then the grant of the equity instruments is conditional on satisfying specified vesting conditions. For example, a grant of shares or share options to an employee is typically conditional on the employee remaining in the entity's employ for a specified period of time.

Suppose that company Amax still grants 50 share options to each of its 200 employees, but that each grant is conditional on the employee remaining in service over the next three years.

Vesting conditions might also take the form of performance conditions that must be satisfied, such as the entity achieving a specified growth in profit or a specified increase in the entity's share price. Suppose that company Amax grants 50 share options to each of its 200 employees, conditional on the employees remaining in the company for a period of two years. However, the shares will only vest if at the end of year 2 the return on equity of the company has increased by 4 per cent over the vesting period. Company Amax combines a performance condition with a service condition to arrive at the vesting condition.

The entity shall recognize an amount for the goods or services received during the vesting period, based on the best available estimate of the number of equity instruments expected to vest and shall revise that estimate, if necessary, if subsequent information indicates that the number of equity instruments expected to vest differs from previous estimates. On the vesting date, the entity shall revise the estimate to equal the number of equity instruments that ultimately vested. When vesting conditions exist the amount of the services received, measured by the fair value of the equity instruments, is allocated over the vesting period.

After the vesting period, the entity shall not make any subsequent adjustments to its equity.

## Measurement date

The fair value of the equity instruments granted should be determined at the measurement date. IFRS 2 defines the measurement date as the date at which the fair value of the equity instruments is granted. For transactions with employees and others providing similar services, the measurement date is the grant date. For transactions with parties other than employees (and those providing similar services), the measurement date is the date the entity obtains the goods or the counterparty renders service.

If market prices are available, they should be used as fair value of the equity instruments. If market prices are not available, valuation techniques can be used to estimate the fair value of those equity instruments on the measurement date in an at-arm's-length transaction between knowledgeable willing parties. In relation to share options, the Black–Scholes–Merton formula might be used (see Black-Scholes-Wikepedia). When the fair value of the equity instruments cannot be measured reliably, IFRS 2 stipulates that the intrinsic value of the instrument will be used for valuation purposes. The intrinsic value of the equity instrument is defined in the appendix to IFRS 2 as the difference between the fair value of the shares the counterparty has the right to and the price (if any) the counterparty is required to pay for those shares. In many cases, transactions will have an intrinsic value of nil at the date of the grant. Therefore, IFRS 2 requires that all share-based payments measured at intrinsic value be remeasured through profit or loss at each reporting date until the transaction is settled (e.g. the exercise of options granted).

IFRS 2 describes further the recognition and measurement rules on how to deal with modifications to the terms and conditions on which equity instruments were granted, including cancellations and settlements. Discussing these elements in detail would go beyond the purpose of this book.

## Cash-settled share-based payment transactions

For cash-settled share-based payment transactions, the entity shall measure the goods or services acquired and the liability incurred at the fair value of the liability. Until the liability is settled, the entity shall remeasure the fair value of the liability at each reporting date and at the date of settlement, with any changes in fair value recognized in profit or loss for the period.

### ILLUSTRATION

Suppose Amax grants 50 share options to each of its 200 employees, on the condition that the employees remain in service for the next three years. The employees may choose to exercise their options at the end of year 3, year 4 or year 5. The payment will, however, be in cash. The amount of cash to be received will be determined by the value of the option at exercise date. During the first year, eight employees leave the company and the entity estimates that 12 employees will leave the company in the next two years. During year 2, a total of eight employees leave the company and the company estimates that six employees will leave Amax in year 3. In the third year, ten employees leave the company. At the end of year 3, the share options held by the remaining employees vest.

In the third year, 30 employees exercise their options, in the fourth year another 40 employees exercise their options, and in the fifth year the remaining 104 employees exercise their options.

Amax uses the following estimates for the valuation of this cash-settled share-based transaction in its books.

| Year | Fair value | Intrinsic value |
|---|---|---|
| 1 | €10 | |
| 2 | €11 | |
| 3 | €14 | €1 250 |
| 4 | €17 | €1 500 |
| 5 | | €2 000 |

This cash-settled share-based transaction will lead to the following amounts:

| Year | Calculations | Expense | Liability |
|---|---|---|---|
| 1 | $(200 - 20) \times 50 \times €10 \times$ $1/3 = 30\,000$ | 30 000 | 30 000 |
| 2 | $((200 - 22) \times 50 \times €11 \times$ $2/3) - 30\,000 = 35\,266$ | 35 266 | 65 266 |
| 3 | $((200 - 26 - 30) \times 50 \times €14)$ $- 65\,266 = 35\,534 + 30 \times$ $50 \times €12.5 = 18\,750$ | 54 284 | 100 800 |

*(Continued)*

## ILLUSTRATION  *(Continued)*

| Year | Calculations | Expense | Liability |
|------|-------------|---------|-----------|
| 4 | $((144 - 40) \times 50 \times €17) -$ | | |
| | $100\,800 = -12\,400 + 40$ | | |
| | $\times 50 \times €15 = 30\,000$ | 17 600 | 88 400 |
| 5 | $0 \times 88\,400 = -88\,400 + 104$ | | |
| | $\times 50 \times €20 = 104\,000$ | 15 600 | 0 |

The amount in the column 'Expense' represents the remuneration expense for the period and the amount in the column 'Liability' represents the amount on the liability account. In the example of the cash-settled share-based payment transaction presented above, we need to remeasure the liability at its fair value after the vesting date because not all options have been exercised. If all options are exercised at vesting date, no subsequent remeasurements are necessary.

## Share-based payment transactions with cash alternatives

In relation to this third group of share-based payment transactions, a distinction is made between, on the one hand, share-based payment transactions in which the terms of the arrangement provide the counterparty with a choice of settlement and, on the other, share-based payment transactions in which the terms of the arrangement provide the entity with a choice of settlement.

In the first situation where an entity has granted the counterparty the right to choose whether a share-based payment transaction is settled in cash or by issuing equity instruments, the entity has granted a compound financial instrument which includes a debt component (i.e. the counterparty's right to demand payment in cash) and an equity component (i.e. the counterparty's right to demand settlement in equity instruments rather than in cash). For transactions with parties other than employees, in which the fair value of the goods or services received is measured directly, the entity shall measure the equity component of the compound financial instrument as the difference between the fair value of the goods or services received and the fair value of the debt component, at the date when the goods or services are received.

For other transactions, including transactions with employees, the entity shall measure the fair value of the compound financial instrument at the measurement date, taking into account the terms and conditions on which the rights to cash or equity instruments were granted.

For a share-based payment transaction in which the terms of the arrangement provide an entity with the choice of whether to settle in cash or by issuing equity instruments, the entity shall determine whether it has a present obligation to settle in cash and account for the share-based payment transaction accordingly. The entity has a present obligation to settle in cash, if the choice of settlement in equity instruments has no commercial substance (e.g. because the entity is legally prohibited from issuing shares), or the entity has a past practice or a stated policy of settling in cash, or generally settles in cash whenever the counterparty asks for cash settlement.

If the entity has a present obligation to settle in cash, it shall account for the transaction in accordance with the requirements applying to cash-settled share-based payment transactions.

If no such obligation exists, the entity shall account for the transaction in accordance with the requirements applying to equity-settled share-based payment transactions, in paras 10–29. On settlement:

(a) if the entity elects to settle in cash, the cash payment shall be accounted for as the repurchase of an equity interest, i.e. as a deduction from equity, except as noted in (c) below.

**(b)** if the entity elects to settle by issuing equity instruments, no further accounting is required (other than a transfer from one component of equity to another, if necessary), except as noted in (c) below.

**(c)** if the entity elects the settlement alternative with the higher fair value, as at the date of settlement, the entity shall recognize an additional expense for the excess value given, i.e. the difference between the cash paid and the fair value of the equity instruments that would otherwise have been issued, or the difference between the fair value of the equity instruments issued and the amount of cash that would otherwise have been paid, whichever is applicable.

**Group cash-settled share-based payment transactions** In business combinations, employees of subsidiary A might be entitled to share-based compensation whereby they receive shares of the parent entity B. In this situation, subsidiary A accounts for this transaction in its own entity's books according to the principles set out in IFRS 2. For example, in case of an equity-settled share-based payment transaction, the account expenses in relation to employee services of the subsidiary are debited and the equity account of the subsidiary is credited. This credit can be regarded as a capital contribution from the parent, namely entity B in this particular case.

In the parent B's separate financial statements, the parent entity recognizes on the one hand the grant of an equity instrument, and on the other the capital contribution made to its subsidiary. This event will be recorded in the books of the parent entity by debiting the account investment in subsidiary A and by crediting the equity account.

When the consolidated group accounts are prepared, the increase in equity in A's financial statements and the increase in the investment asset in B's separate financial statements are both eliminated upon consolidation.

## ACTIVITY 22.5

A parent entity grants 200 employees of its subsidiary the right to receive 200 shares of the parent entity each, conditional upon the completion of two years' service with the subsidiary entity. The fair value of the shares on grant date is €40 per share. The subsidiary estimates that 90 per cent of the employees will complete the two-year vesting period. This estimate remains the same during the whole vesting period. At the end of the vesting period, 92 per cent of the employees complete the required two years of service.

Account for this transaction in the books of the subsidiary and in the books of the parent entity.

### Activity feedback
*The subsidiary will recognize this share-based payment transaction by debiting an expense account in relation to*
*employee services and crediting an equity account, representing a capital contribution from the parent. The amounts which will be recorded in year 1 and year 2, are presented below:*

*Year 1: 200 employees × 200 shares × 90% estimated vesting × = years × €40 = €720 000*

*Year 2: 200 employees × 200 shares × 92% vesting × 1 year × €40 – €720 000 = €1 472 000 – €720 000 = €752 000*

*The parent entity will increase its investment in its subsidiary by debiting this investment account for €720 000 in year 1 and €752 000 in year 2. The equity account will be credited for €720 000 in year 1 and €752 000 in year 2.*

## Disclosures

Extensive information disclosures about these share-based transactions are required by IFRS 2 (these can be found in the notes to the accounts). In relation to these transactions, an entity shall disclose information that enables users of the financial statement to:

(a)  understand the nature and the extent of share-based payment arrangements that existed during the period

(b)  understand how the fair value of the goods or services received, or the fair value of the equity instruments granted, during the period was determined

(c)  understand the effect of share-based payment transactions on the entity's profit or loss for the period and on its financial position.

These information requirements imply that a detailed description of all share-based payment arrangements have to be disclosed (e.g. the different types of share-based arrangements and their nature and conditions, the number and weighted average exercise price of share options for the outstanding options at the beginning of the period, the ones granted, forfeited, exercised and expired during the period and the ones outstanding at the end of the period, and the ones exercisable at the end of the period), a description of how the fair value is determined, details on the expenses recognized and the liabilities recorded.

## REAL LIFE ILLUSTRATION

To illustrate all the information which needs to be disclosed in relation to share-based payments, we include the information provided by AB Inbev, the largest beer brewer in the world with regard to this item. In note 25 (pages 59–62) all information is included on AB Inbev's share-based payments. This illustration again provides an example of the extensiveness of the disclosure under IFRS.

### 25. Share-Based Payments[1]

Different share and share option programs allow company senior management and members of the Board of Directors to receive or acquire shares of AB InBev or Ambev. AB InBev has three primary share-based compensation plans, the long-term incentive warrant plan ('LTI Warrant Plan'), established in 1999, the share-based compensation plan ('Share-Based Compensation Plan'), established in 2006 and amended as from 2010, and the long-term incentive stock-option plan ('LTI stock-option Plan'), established in 2009. For all option plans, the fair value of share-based payment compensation is estimated at grant date, using a binomial Hull model, modified to reflect the IFRS 2 *Share-based Payment* requirement that assumptions about forfeiture before the end of the vesting period cannot impact the fair value of the option.

Share-based payment transactions resulted in a total expense of 201m US dollar for the year 2012 (including the variable compensation expense settled in shares), as compared to 203m US dollar for the year 2011.

### AB INBEV Share-Based Payment Programs

#### Share-Based Compensation Plan

As from 1 January 2010, the structure of the Share-Based Compensation Plan for certain executives, including the executive board of management and other senior management in the general headquarters, has been modified. From 1 January 2011, the new plan structure applies to all other senior management. Under this plan, the executive board of management and other senior employees will receive their bonus in cash but have the choice to invest some or all of the value of their bonus in AB InBev shares with a five-year vesting period, referred to as bonus shares. The company will match such voluntary investment by granting three matching shares for each bonus share voluntarily invested in, up to a limited total percentage of each participant's bonus. The matching shares are granted in the form of restricted stock units which have a five-year vesting period. Additionally, the holders of the restricted stock units may be entitled to receive from AB InBev additional restricted stock units equal to the dividends declared since the restricted stock units were granted.

During 2012, AB InBev issued 0.7m of matching restricted stock units according to the new Share-Based Compensation Plan, as described above, in relation to the 2011 bonus. These matching restricted stock units are valued at the share price of the day of grant, representing a fair value of approximately 46m US dollar, and cliff vest after five years. During 2011, AB InBev issued 1.1m of matching restricted stock units according to the

[1]Amounts have been converted to US dollar at the average rate of the period.

*(Continued)*

## REAL LIFE ILLUSTRATION  *(Continued)*

new Share-Based Compensation Plan, with an estimated fair value of approximately 62.9m US dollar, in relation to the 2010 bonus.

### LTI Warrant Plan

The company has issued warrants, or rights to subscribe for newly issued shares, under the LTI plan for the benefit of directors and, until 2006, members of the executive board of management and other senior employees. Since 2007, members of the executive board of management and other employees are no longer eligible to receive warrants under the LTI Warrant Plan, but instead receive a portion of their compensation in the form of shares and options granted under the Share-Based Compensation Plan and the LTI Stock-option Plan. Each LTI warrant gives its holder the right to subscribe for one newly issued share. The exercise price of LTI warrants is equal to the average price of the company's shares on the regulated market of Euronext Brussels during the 30 days preceding their issue date. LTI warrants granted in the years prior to 2007 (except for 2003) have a duration of ten years; LTI warrants granted as from 2007 (and in 2003) have a duration of five years. LTI warrants are subject to a vesting period ranging from one to three years.

During 2012, 0.2m warrants were granted to members of the Board of Directors. These warrants vest in equal annual instalments over a three-year period (one third on 1 January of 2014, one third on 1 January 2015 and one third on 1 January 2016) and represent a fair value of approximately 2.5m US dollar. During 2011, 0.2m warrants with a fair value of approximately 3.0m US dollar were granted under this plan.

### LTI Stock-option Plan

As from 1 July 2009, senior employees are eligible for an annual long-term incentive to be paid out in LTI stock options (or, in future, similar share-based instruments), depending on management's assessment of the employee's performance and future potential.

In November 2012 AB InBev issued 4.4m LTI stock options with an estimated fair value of 86m US dollar, whereby 1.2m options relate to American Depositary Shares (ADSs) and 3.2m options to AB InBev shares. In November 2011 AB InBev issued 4.1m LTI stock options with an estimated fair value of 66.2m US dollar, whereby 1.2m options relate to American Depositary Shares (ADSs) and 2.9m options to AB InBev shares.

As from 2010 AB InBev has in place three specific long-term restricted stock unit programs. One program allows for the offer of restricted stock units to certain employees in certain specific circumstances, whereby grants are made at the discretion of the CEO, e.g. to compensate for assignments of expatriates in countries with difficult living conditions. The restricted stock units vest after five years and in case of termination of service before the vesting date, special forfeiture rules apply. In 2012, 0.1m restricted stock units with an estimated fair value of 1.0m US dollar were granted under this program to a selected number of employees. In 2011, 0.1m restricted stock units with an estimated fair value of 2.8m US dollar were granted under this program.

A second program allows for the exceptional offer of restricted stock units to certain employees at the discretion of the Remuneration Committee of AB InBev as a long-term retention incentive for key employees of the company. Employees eligible to receive a grant under this program receive two series of restricted stock units, the first half of the restricted stock units vesting after five years, the second half after ten years. In case of termination of service before the vesting date, special forfeiture rules apply. In December 2012 0.3m restricted stock units with an estimated fair value of 22.7m US dollar were granted under this program to a selected number of employees. In December 2011 0.1m restricted stock units with an estimated fair value of 5.4m US dollar were granted under this program.

A third program allows certain employees to purchase company shares at a discount aimed as a long-term retention incentive for (i) high-potential employees of the company, who are at a mid-manager level ('People bet share purchase program') or (ii) for newly hired employees. The voluntary investment in company shares leads to the grant of 3 matching shares for each share invested. The discount and matching shares are granted in the form of restricted stock units which vest after 5 years. In case of termination before the vesting date, special forfeiture rules apply. In 2012, the company's employees purchased shares under this program for the equivalent of 0.2m US dollar. In 2011, the company's employees purchased shares under this program for the equivalent of 0.2m US dollar.

In order to maintain consistency of benefits granted to executives and to encourage international mobility of executives, an options exchange program has been executed whereby unvested options are exchanged against restricted shares that remain locked-up until 31 December 2018. In 2012, 0.6m unvested options were exchanged against 0.5m restricted shares. In 2011, 2.0m unvested options were exchanged against 1.4m restricted shares. Furthermore, certain options granted

*(Continued)*

## REAL LIFE ILLUSTRATION  *(Continued)*

have been modified whereby the dividend protected feature of these options have been cancelled and replaced by the issuance of options. In 2012 no new options were issued. In 2011 0.6m options were issued, representing the economic value of the dividend protection feature. As there was no change between the fair value of the original award immediately before the modification and the fair value of the modified award immediately after the modification, no additional expense was recorded as a result of the modification.

For further information on share-based payment grants of previous years, please refer to Note 25 *Share-based payments* of the 2011 consolidated financial statements.

The weighted average fair value of the options and assumptions used in applying the AB InBev option pricing model for the 2012 grants of awards described above are as follows:

| Amounts in US dollar unless otherwise indicated[1] | 2012 | 2011 | 2010 |
|---|---|---|---|
| Fair value of options and warrants granted | 19.57 | 14.95 | 14.59 |
| Share price | 86.87 | 57.04 | 51.71 |
| Exercise price | 86.83 | 56.88 | 51.61 |
| Expected volatility | 25% | 26% | 26% |
| Expected dividends | 2.50% | 2.50% | 2.35% |
| Risk-free interest rate | 1.73% | 2.84% | 3.29% |

Expected volatility is based on historical volatility calculated using 2 032 days of historical data. In the determination of the expected volatility, AB InBev is excluding the volatility measured during the period 15 July 2008 until 30 April 2009, in view of the extreme market conditions experienced during that period. The binomial Hull model assumes that all employees would immediately exercise their options if the AB InBev share price is 2.5 times above the exercise price. As a result, no single expected option life applies.

The total number of outstanding AB InBev options and warrants developed as follows:

| Million options and warrants | 2012 | 2011 | 2010 |
|---|---|---|---|
| Options and warrants outstanding at 1 January | 54.4 | 56.1 | 50.8 |
| Options and warrants issued during the year | 4.5 | 4.9 | 9.8 |
| Options and warrants exercised during the year | (3.3) | (4.1) | (1.8) |

| Million options and warrants | 2012 | 2011 | 2010 |
|---|---|---|---|
| Options and warrants forfeited during the year | (2.3) | (2.5) | (2.7) |
| **Options and warrants outstanding at the end of December** | **53.3** | **54.4** | **56.1** |

The range of exercise prices of the outstanding options and warrants is between 10.32 euro (13.62 US dollar) and 66.88 euro (88.24 US dollar) while the weighted average remaining contractual life is 7.93 years.

Of the 53.3m outstanding options and warrants 4.7m are vested at 31 December 2012.

The weighted average exercise price of the AB InBev options and warrants is as follows:

| Amounts in US dollar[1] | 2012 | 2011 | 2010 |
|---|---|---|---|
| Options and warrants outstanding at 1 January | 32.98 | 29.88 | 27.37 |
| Granted during the year | 87.94 | 56.52 | 51.86 |
| Exercised during the year | 31.85 | 23.83 | 25.81 |
| Forfeited during the year | 32.82 | 27.65 | 27.76 |
| Outstanding at the end of December | 38.31 | 32.98 | 29.88 |
| Exercisable at the end of December | 40.65 | 31.91 | 30.71 |

For share options and warrants exercised during 2012 the weighted average share price at the date of exercise was 58.64 euro (77.37 US dollar).

The total number of outstanding AB InBev restricted stock units developed as follows:

| Million restricted stock units | 2012 | 2011 | 2010 |
|---|---|---|---|
| Restricted stock units outstanding at 1 January. | 2.3 | 1.2 | – |
| Restricted stock units issued during the year | 1.1 | 1.2 | 1.2 |
| Restricted stock units exercised during the year | – | – | – |
| Restricted stock units forfeited during the year | (0.1) | (0.1) | – |
| **Restricted stock units outstanding at the end of December** | **3.3** | **2.3** | **1.2** |

---

[1]Amounts have been converted to US dollar at the average rate of the period.

*(Continued)*

## REAL LIFE ILLUSTRATION    (*Continued*)

### AMBEV Share-Based Payment Programs

Since 2005, Ambev has had a plan which is substantially similar to the Share-Based Compensation Plan under which bonuses granted to company employees and management are partially settled in shares. Under the Share-Based Compensation Plan as modified as of 2010, Ambev issued, in March 2012, 1m restricted stock units with an estimated fair value of 24m US dollar. In March 2011, Ambev issued 1.4m restricted stock units with an estimated fair value of 38m US dollar.

As from 2010, senior employees are eligible for an annual long-term incentive to be paid out in Ambev LTI stock options (or, in future, similar share-based instruments), depending on management's assessment of the employee's performance and future potential. In 2012, Ambev granted 3m LTI stock options with an estimated fair value of 43m US dollar. In 2011, Ambev granted 3.1m LTI stock options with an estimated fair value of 37m US dollar.

In order to encourage the mobility of managers, the features of certain options granted in previous years have been modified whereby the dividend protection of these options was cancelled and replaced by the issuance of 0.1m options in 2012 representing the economic value of the dividend protection feature. In 2011, 2.5m options were issued representing the economic value of the dividend protection feature. Since there was no change between the fair value of the original award before the modification and the fair value of the modified award after the modification, no additional expense was recorded as a result of this modification.

The weighted fair value of the options and assumptions used in applying a binomial option pricing model for the 2012 Ambev grants are as follows:

| Amounts in US dollar unless otherwise indicated[1] | 2012 | 2011 | 2010 |
|---|---|---|---|
| Fair value of options granted | 13.64 | 11.98 | 11.24 |
| Share price | 41.72 | 29.65 | 24.09 |
| Exercise price | 41.72 | 24.73 | 24.57 |
| Expected volatility | 33% | 34% | 28% |
| Expected dividends | 0.00% – 5.00% | 0.00% – 5.00% | 2.57% |
| Risk-free interest rate | 2.10% –11.20%[2] | 3.10% –11.89%[2] | 12.24% |

The total number of outstanding Ambev options developed as follows:

| Million options | 2012 | 2011 | 2010 |
|---|---|---|---|
| Options outstanding at 1 January | 29.6 | 26.3 | 20.6 |
| Options issued during the year | 3.1 | 5.6 | 6.6 |
| Options exercised during the year | (2.5) | (1.7) | (0.5) |
| Options forfeited during the year | (1.4) | (0.6) | (0.4) |
| **Options outstanding at the end of December** | **28.8** | **29.6** | **26.3** |

Following the decision of the General Meeting of Shareholders of 17 December 2010, each common and preferred share issued by Ambev was split into 5 shares, without any modification to the amount of the capital stock of Ambev. As a consequence of the split of the Ambev shares with a factor 5, the exercise price and the number of options were adjusted with the intention of preserving the rights of the existing option holders.

The range of exercise prices of the outstanding options is between 11.52 Brazilian real (5.64 US dollar) and 89.20 Brazilian real (43.65 US dollar) while the weighted average remaining contractual life is 8.15 years.

Of the 28.8m outstanding options 5.0m options are vested at 31 December 2012.

The weighted average exercise price of the Ambev options is as follows:

| Amounts in US dollar[1] | 2012 | 2011 | 2010 |
|---|---|---|---|
| Options outstanding at 1 January | 15.92 | 14.83 | 12.46 |
| Granted during the year | 41.95 | 29.37 | 24.57 |
| Exercised during the year | 6.91 | 7.23 | 7.17 |
| Forfeited during the year | 6.82 | 12.66 | 11.59 |
| Outstanding at the end of December | 17.70 | 15.92 | 14.83 |
| Exercisable at the end of December | 9.28 | 7.04 | 7.00 |

For share options exercised during 2012 the weighted average share price at the date of exercise was 78.68 Brazilian real (38.50 US dollar).

The total number of outstanding Ambev restricted stock units developed as follows:

---

[1]Amounts have been converted to US dollar at the average rate of the period.
[2]The weighted average risk-free interest rates refer to granted ADRs and stock options respectively.

(*Continued*)

## REAL LIFE ILLUSTRATION    *(Continued)*

| Million restricted stock units | 2012 | 2011 | 2010 |
|---|---|---|---|
| Restricted stock units outstanding at 1 January | 1.6 | 0.2 | – |
| Restricted stock units issued during the year | 1.0 | 1.4 | 0.2 |
| Restricted stock units exercised during the year | – | – | – |
| Restricted stock units forfeited during the year. | (0.3) | – | – |
| **Restricted stock units outstanding at the end of December** | **2.3** | **1.6** | **0.2** |

During 2012, a limited number of Ambev shareholders who are part of the senior management of AB InBev were given the opportunity to exchange Ambev shares against a total of 0.1m AB InBev shares (1.0m AB InBev shares in 2011) at a discount of 16.7% provided that they stay in service for another five years. The fair value of this transaction amounts to approximately 1.1m US dollar (10m US dollar in 2011) and is expensed over the five years' service period. The fair values of the Ambev and AB InBev shares were determined based on the market price.

## ACCOUNTING FOR LONG-TERM EMPLOYEE BENEFITS: PENSION BENEFITS

The most important long-term employee benefits are pension benefits. Other long-term employee benefits, including long-service leave or sabbatical leave, jubilee or other long-service benefits, long-term disability benefits or medical benefits, are accounted for in a similar manner as pension benefits. Therefore, we will only discuss the recognition and valuation issues related to pension benefits extensively. We will start the discussion by defining the concept of a pension benefit and by an analysis of the impact of a company pension plan on the financial situation of the company.

### Existence of different pension systems

The purpose of a pension is to grant people some money when they are retired. Worldwide, three different types of 'pension systems' can be distinguished, namely state pensions, pensions received from the employer resulting from an employment contract, and individual pension savings plans. So an individual can be entitled to a state pension, on top of that a retirement benefit resulting from his employment contract (if retirement benefits were included), and finally a payment from an individual pension scheme, if the individual has taken the initiative to contribute to an individual savings account. The importance and presence of each type of pension system in a single country is determined by characteristics of the local or national environment.

In some countries state pensions are the major source of income for retired people. In other countries initiatives, such as company pension plans and individual pension schemes, are stimulated by the government and are common practice because of the lower levels of state pensions.

State pensions do not usually create any accounting problems for entities. The companies are collecting the premium from the employees (a deduction from the gross salary) and these amounts, together with employer's contributions (if any), are paid to the government. If the premium due for an accounting period, which will be recorded as an expense, is not equal to the amount transferred to the government, prepaid expenses or accrued expenses can be reported on the balance sheet. According to IAS 19, state pensions should be accounted for as multi-employer plans and these will often have the character of a defined contribution plan (this concept will be defined later on p. 512). The treatment stipulated in IAS 19 concerning state pensions is usually in line with what we have already mentioned.

Individual pension schemes are totally separate from employment contracts, so IAS 19 does not focus on them. IAS 19 deals especially with company pension plans as they have an impact on the financial situation of a company.

## Company pension plans

A company pension plan can be defined as an agreement between an employer and its employees, whereby the former agrees to pay benefits to the latter after their retirement. The terms of the pension plan stipulate the retirement benefit to which an employee is entitled. There are two major categories of pension schemes or pension plans, namely defined benefit plans and defined contribution plans.

**Definition of a pension benefit** In a defined contribution plan, the employer agrees to contribute a specific amount to the pension plan with or without a contribution from the employee. The benefits to be received by the employee at retirement are determined by the contributions transferred to the plan, plus the investment return obtained on those contributions. This implies that an employee will only know the amount which he or she will receive as pension benefit on retirement. The contributions are usually paid into a separate entity (fund or insurance company). Further, the employee bears the risk under this type of pension plan as the amount is, in the end, dependent on the obtained investment return on the amounts contributed and invested.

A defined benefit plan is defined by IAS 19 as all plans other than defined contribution plans. If we want to describe defined benefit plans in somewhat more detail, we would characterize them as those plans where the benefits promised are defined in advance, whereby the amount of pension benefit to be paid depends on the plan's benefit formula. Plans for which the pension benefit formula is based on compensation levels are called pay-related plans. The three most important types of pay-related plans are:

- the *final pay plan,* in which the benefits are calculated as a percentage of the final salary before retirement
- the *final average pay plan,* where the benefits are calculated as a percentage of the average salary of the last three to five years before retirement
- the *career average pay plan,* in which the benefits are related to the average salary someone has earned during his or her career.

In some defined benefit plans, the state pensions are included in the benefit formula. This implies, however, that if the level of state pensions drops, the employer faces a higher cost. Plans whereby the benefit formula is not based on compensation levels are called non-pay-related plans or flat benefit plans. For example, a pension plan whereby the pension benefit is defined as a benefit consisting of contributions plus a guarantee of fixed return is categorized as a defined benefit pension plan and shall be accounted for as such.

**Organization and financing of a company pension plan** Providing retirement benefits to the employees involves many decisions. In addition to a decision about the type of pension benefit promised (defined contribution or defined benefit), decisions regarding the organization and the financing or funding patterns of these benefits also have to be made. The choices made by companies will not only be influenced by company characteristics, but also by characteristics of the national environment. When an employer provides his employees with a defined contribution plan, the finance pattern consists of the contributions, stipulated in the pension plan made to a pension account. The finance pattern and the responsibility of the employer can be determined in a very straightforward way. The pension account in which the funds are accumulated can be administered by the company or by a bank.

A defined benefit plan can be financed through the so-called pay as you go system or through a funding system. Under the pay as you go system the pensions are paid directly from the resources of the company as they fall due. The purpose of a funding system, on the contrary, is to make contributions through the whole employment period of the employee in order to accumulate enough funds to guarantee the pension payments. Usually actuarial cost methods (also called actuarial funding methods) are used to determine the amounts to be financed each period in order to have enough funds to pay the pension benefits when the employees retire.

If pension benefits are financed by means of a funding system, two main types of organizational set-ups are possible: internal funding or external funding. In the case of internal funding, resources are allocated in advance for the provision of benefits, but no separation of these amounts from the other assets of the employer is made. Benefit payments, when due, are made directly by the employer. In some countries, employers are allowed to use those funds accumulated within the entity for financing the operational activities of the entity. In other countries, those funds may be kept in the entity but they have to be invested in certain assets. Very often these plans, financed through internal funding, are called unfunded pension plans in the Anglo-Saxon world. This term might be misleading as it may sound as if no financing arrangements have been made yet, as in the case of the pay as you go system. In fact, internally funded plans is a better way to describe this financing system.

If an employer uses external funding, the resources are accumulated in a separate legal entity (i.e. there is a separate fund). In the Anglo-Saxon world, these plans, which are funded externally, are called funded pension plans. This separate fund may be a unique creation for only one employer or for many employers, or it may be operated by a specialist insurance company running many such schemes. The contract with the insurance company has to stipulate what type of risks and responsibilities are transferred to the insurance company. The terms of this contract are extremely important for accounting purposes as they determine whether insured benefits will be considered a defined contribution type or a defined benefit type.

Para. 46 states in this respect:

An entity may pay insurance premiums to fund a post-employment benefit plan. The entity should treat such a plan as a defined contribution plan unless the entity will have (either directly, or indirectly through the plan) a legal or constructive obligation either:

- to pay the employee benefits directly when they fall due
- or to pay further contributions if the insurer does not pay all future employee benefits relating to employee service in the current and prior periods.

If the entity retains such a legal or constructive obligation, the entity should treat the plan as a defined benefit plan for accounting purposes.

Whether an insured plan qualifies as a defined contribution plan or a defined benefit plan is an extremely important matter, since the way these plans have to be accounted for is totally different. Companies will have a tendency to try to qualify their insured plans as much as possible as defined contribution plans.

Although employers can choose between different types of pension benefit and different ways to organize and finance them, country-specific influences are often encountered. First of all, the importance of the pension benefits granted by the employer versus state pensions differs among countries. In countries like the UK, the USA and the Netherlands, the benefits of company pension plans are a major source of income for retired people. In countries in the south of Europe and also in Belgium and Scandinavian countries, state pensions make up an important part of the income of people after retirement. A wide variety of differences in pension systems are also found on a global basis.

Further, companies may choose between internal funding or external funding. Very often the national environment, however, determines the choice. For example, in the Netherlands and the UK, companies usually fund their pension promises externally. German companies often use internal funding. This practice is responsible for large provisions on the balance sheets of German companies. Very often national legal requirements are the drivers for the observed differences. For example, there might be laws which prohibit internal funding. The possibility of withdrawing funds from an external pension fund in times when surpluses are present will also be dependent on the existing laws of a particular country. In fact, IAS 19 has to take into account all these different possibilities existing worldwide. The IASB has to develop accounting regulations concerning these benefits which can be applied worldwide. IAS 19 is elaborately detailed in order to take into account all of these differences.

Another element which relates to organizational issues is whether an employer joins a multi-employer plan for the organizational and financial aspects in relation to pension benefits, or whether he or she decides to set up the organization and financing as a single-employer plan. In some countries, such as the Netherlands, employers often join multi-employer plans. In relation to multi-employer plans, IAS 19 stipulates that multi-employer plans are defined contribution plans (other than state plans) or defined benefit plans (other than state plans) that:

- pool the assets contributed by various entities that are not under common control
- use those assets to provide benefits to employees of more than one entity, on the basis that contribution and benefit levels are determined without regard to the identity of the entity that employs the employees concerned.

Whether these multi-employer plans are of a defined benefit or a defined contribution type will depend on the terms of the plan.

## ACTIVITY 22.6

How do you think these different types of pension plan affect the financial situation of the sponsoring company, namely the employer?

### Activity feedback

- Pensions represent a cash outflow for the company. The timing of the cash flow will be different according to the funding system which is used by the company: pay as you go system, internal or external funding system and the finance pattern determined by the actuarial funding methods.

- The amount of pension benefits represents a cost for the company. This cost can be reduced

(Continued)

## ACTIVITY 22.6    (*Continued*)

*through advanced funding if positive investment returns are obtained.*

- *When an employee renders service, his/her pension rights accrue. Depending on the terms of the pension plan or the existing company practice, the employer has a legal or constructive obligation.*

*At the time of retirement, the employer owes the employee a certain amount of money. This amount of money is determined in advance in the case of a defined benefit plan or will be dependent on the realized investment return on the amounts contributed to a plan under a defined contribution plan.*

**Impact of company pension plans on the sponsoring company**  In this respect, the concept of vested benefits is important as vested employee benefits are those benefits that are not conditional on future employment. The terms of a pension plan stipulate when pension benefits become vested. Usually an employee has to be in service for a minimum period (e.g. five years) before his pension rights become vested. If the benefits are vested, this means that the employee has earned his/her pension rights independent of whether the employee will stay further with the firm.

From the feedback of Activity 22.6, we have learned that pension benefits do have an impact on the result, cash flow and financial position of a company. Further, we know that pensions and other retirement benefits are a major cost for many entities across many jurisdictions.

As a result, these elements have to be accounted for in the financial statements of the employer. The way these benefits are accounted for will depend largely on the type of pension promise which has been made to the employee, namely a defined contribution into a plan or a promise for a defined benefit at the moment of retirement. Defined contribution plans are much simpler to account for. With regard to the recognition and valuation of pension benefits granted under a defined benefit plan, many technical issues have to be agreed on first.

## Accounting for defined contribution plans

Under a defined contribution plan, the finance pattern and the responsibility of the employer can be determined in a very straightforward way. The amounts to be contributed, according to the terms of the pension plan, should be treated as pension costs for that particular period. If the employer has transferred all the contributions stipulated in the pension plan to a pension scheme, then the employer has fulfilled his pension commitments and no provision has to be shown on the balance sheet.

Paragraphs 51–53 of IAS 19 stipulate reporting and disclosure requirements in relation to a defined contribution plan as follows: when an employee has rendered service to an entity during a period, the entity should recognize the contribution payable to a defined contribution plan in exchange for that service as a liability (accrued expense), after deducting any contribution already paid. If the contribution already paid exceeds the contribution due for service before the balance sheet date, an entity should recognize that excess as an asset (prepaid expense) to the extent that the prepayment will lead to, for example, a reduction in future payments or a cash refund. The contribution payable to a defined contribution plan should also be recorded as an expense, unless another International Accounting Standard requires or permits the inclusion of the contribution in the cost of an asset (see, for example, IAS 2, *Inventories*, and IAS 16, *Property, Plant and Equipment*).

A company should always disclose in the notes the amount recognized as an expense in relation to the defined contribution plans of the company. When a pension plan consists of contributions which guarantee a fixed return, it is considered a defined benefit plan.

## Accounting for defined benefit plans

As mentioned earlier, the pension benefit under this type of plan is determined by the pension plan formula and as such is defined in advance. The formula can be a function of the salary of the beneficiary or another variable.

Until recently, most defined benefit plans determined the benefit to be received as a function of the salary of the employee. In the USA and (gradually) in Europe, cash balance plans are becoming more popular. Cash balance plans are pension plans in which the pension benefit is determined by reference to amounts credited to an employee's account. Those amounts typically comprise in each year a principal amount based on current salary and a specified interest credit. The plan may or may not be funded. If the plan is funded, it may be invested in assets that differ from those which determine the interest credit. On retirement or leaving service (when vesting conditions are met), the employee is entitled to a lump sum equal to the total amount credited to this account.

According to IAS 19, cash balance plans are defined benefit plans. However, they entail specific accounting problems which are not dealt with yet by IAS 19. As a result, the Board will pay attention to these types of plans in the future.

Under a defined benefit scheme, the exact total amount of the benefit is known only at the moment of retirement (in case of a lump sum payment) or when the pensioner dies (in case of annual payments). Only at that moment are all uncertainties gone. The main problem, however, is how to charge this total cost over the subsequent service years of the employee. In many countries actuarial funding methods are used for this accounting allocation problem, and IAS 19 has also opted for this approach by choosing one particular actuarial funding method, namely the projected unit credit method for accounting purposes. Because of the important role of actuarial funding methods in the recognition of pension costs and pension liabilities for accounting purposes, we will pay attention in this section to the function and the mechanisms of those actuarial funding methods (often called by actuaries actuarial cost methods).

**Mechanisms of actuarial funding methods** We will illustrate the purpose and the mechanisms of actuarial funding methods with a numerical example relating to one person, Mr Dupont. This example is highly simplified for pedagogic reasons.

## ACTIVITY 22.7

Assume Mr Dupont enters a pension scheme with a pension formula based on his final salary. The pension benefit he is entitled to receive is defined as follows:

$$Br = k(r - y)Sr$$

where:

$Br$ = pension benefit to be received at retirement

$k$ = % of salary

$r$ = retirement age

$y$ = age at which the employee is entitled to receive benefits

$Sr$ = last salary before retirement

The pension benefit for Mr Dupont is a lump sum payment at retirement. We will further assume $k = 10\%$ and that Mr Dupont enters the company in year 1. His pension benefits are vested from the first moment of employment. The salary levels over the five years of his employment are:

*(Continued)*

## ACTIVITY 22.7   (*Continued*)

Year 1: 100 000

Year 2: 110 000

Year 3: 120 000

Year 4: 140 000

Year 5: 160 000

Calculate the amount of earned pension benefit Mr Dupont is entitled to receive at the end of each year of service rendered.

*Activity feedback*

*The pension benefit Mr Dupont is entitled to increases over the years in the following way:*

Year 1: $B1 = 0.1 \times 1 \times (100\,000) = 10\,000$

Year 2: $B2 = 0.1 \times 2 \times (110\,000) = 22\,000$

Year 3: $B3 = 0.1 \times 3 \times (120\,000) = 36\,000$

Year 4: $B4 = 0.1 \times 4 \times (140\,000) = 56\,000$

Year 5: $B5 = 0.1 \times 5 \times (160\,000) = 80\,000$

Several actuarial cost or funding methods exist to determine the financing or funding pattern for the pension benefits. These different methods will all lead to different funding patterns for the same pension benefit to attain in the end; in the case of Mr Dupont, at the end of year 5. The group of actuarial cost or actuarial funding methods which are most commonly used can be divided in two subgroups, namely *accrued valuation methods* and *projected valuation methods*. The first group, the accrued valuation methods, takes into account only the service rendered to date and the current salary level for the calculation of the amounts to be funded. The amount to be funded in a particular year under this method is equal to the present value of the benefit accrual in that particular year. Only the accrued or earned pension rights are financed under this method. Under the accrued valuation method, expected future salary levels can be taken into account as well as in combination with service already rendered. The accrued benefit valuation method, whereby future salary levels are taken into account, is called the projected unit credit method. This method is chosen by IAS 19 for cost recognition and pension liability valuation purposes.

The second group of actuarial cost methods used by actuaries is called the projected benefit cost methods or projected valuation methods. These actuarial funding methods calculate the total pension benefit an employee will receive on retirement by taking into account the expected service to be rendered over the total service period and the expected salary level at retirement. They allocate that final amount, over the working life of the employee, as a yearly fixed amount or as a fixed percentage of salary.

The main difference in the funding patterns between the two families of actuarial funding methods (accrued valuation methods versus projected valuation methods) is that under the accrued methods, the amounts to be funded at the start of a career of a person are lower than if one were to finance the promised benefit under a projected valuation method, which takes into account from the start the whole expected service period.

Accrued benefit valuation methods use the pension plan formula in order to determine the accrual of pension rights over the years. The amount of accrued benefits at a particular moment can be defined as follows:

$$AB_x = B_x(_{r-x}P_x\,T)V_{r-x}\ddot{a}_r$$

where:

$AB_x$ = actuarial value of accrued benefits at age x

$B_x$ = accrued pension benefits at age x

$_{r-x}P_xT$ = the probability that the employee stays with the firm from age x till retirement
with $P_xT = (1 - q_{mx})(1 - q_{wx})(1 - qd_x)(1 - q_{rx})$

$q_m$ = probability of mortality

$q_w$ = probability of withdrawal from the plan

$q_d$ = probability of disability

$q_r$ = probability of early retirement

$V_{r-x}$ = discount factor from retirement age to age x

$ä_r$ = present value at retirement age of a long life annuity of a single currency unit at the start of each year (needed if the pension benefit will be paid out as an annual payment)

$P_xT$ as such is often called the plan turnover assumption.

**The function of actuarial assumptions** It is clear from the formula just examined that in order to calculate the accrued benefits and the finance patterns related to it, the actuary must make assumptions about a number of variables, such as life expectancy, employee turnover, future salary levels, investment return and so on. These elements are called actuarial assumptions. Some of them are of a demographic nature (e.g. mortality, number of men and women in the plan) others are of an economic nature (e.g. inflation rate, investment return). When these actuarial funding methods are used to determine the finance pattern of the benefits, a company is free to choose the value of these assumptions. When the outcome of the actuarial funding method is used for accounting purposes, IAS 19 (para. 75) stipulates that the actuarial assumptions used should be unbiased and mutually compatible. By the latter, IAS 19 means that actuarial assumptions are mutually compatible if they reflect the economic relationships between factors such as inflation, rates of salary increase, the return on plan assets and discount rates. For example, all assumptions which depend on a particular inflation level (such as assumptions about interest rates and salary and benefit increases) in any given future period assume the same inflation level in that period.

Further, IAS states that financial assumptions should be based on market expectations at the balance sheet date for the period over which the obligations are to be settled (para. 75). The choice of the actuarial assumptions is not immaterial. Minor changes in the assumptions might have substantial impacts on the amounts reported; the assumption with the most material effect is the discount rate (also see the example in Activity 22.13). That is the reason why IAS 19 has paid special attention to the choice of the discount rate (para. 83). The rate used to discount post-employment benefit obligations (both funded and unfunded) should be determined by reference to market yields at the balance sheet date on high-quality corporate bonds. In countries where there is no deep market in such bonds, the market yields (at the balance sheet date) on government bonds should be used. The currency and term of the corporate bonds or government bonds should be consistent with the currency and estimated term of the post-employment benefit obligations.

It is important to state here that the discount rate reflects the time value of money and *not* the actuarial or investment risk.

## ACTIVITY 22.8

Calculate the actuarial value of accrued benefits for Mr Dupont in each of the five years he is in service, based on the service rendered to that date and the current salary level at that time. Assume that the plan turnover assumption is equal to zero and the discount rate is 4 per cent. The pension benefit is paid out as a lump sum at the moment of retirement. The actuarial calculations are made at the end of the year.

### Activity feedback

$AB1 = [0.1 \times (1 \times 100\,000)]/(1.04)^4 = 8\,548$

$AB2 = [0.1 \times (2 \times 110\,000)]/(1.04)^3 = 19\,558$

$AB3 = [0.1 \times (3 \times 120\,000)]/(1.04)^2 = 33\,284$

$AB4 = [0.1 \times (4 \times 140\,000)]/(1.04)^1 = 53\,846$

$AB5 = [0.1 \times (5 \times 160\,000)]/(1.04)^0 = 80\,000$

These actuarial calculations can also be made at the start of each year: the interest factor will then be different. The present value of these accrued benefit obligations increases each year due to the year of extra service rendered by the employee and the interest accrual.

We will now analyze the impact on the amount of accrued benefits in Activity 22.9 when future salary levels are included in the calculations. IAS 19 requires the use of the projected unit credit method for the determination of the pension liability as well as for the determination of a part of the total pension cost. The projected unit credit method takes into account future salary increases.

During the financial crisis in 2008 and also 2009, the yield of government bonds decreased. As a result, there was a lot of critique on the possibility of using the yield of government bonds. The IASB thought of amending this discount rate for measuring employee benefits. The Board considered the responses to the exposure draft issued on this topic in October 2009. The responses indicated that the proposal to use only the yield of corporate bonds raised more complex issues than expected. The Board therefore decided to adhere to its original plan to address measurement issues only in the context of a fundamental review.

## ACTIVITY 22.9

Take into account the expected future salary levels, and calculate the projected benefit obligation (PBO), of Mr Dupont at the end of each year that he is in service. Since we take into account expected future salary levels, we can no longer talk about accrued benefits or amendment earned benefits.

### Activity feedback

$PBO1 = [0.1 \times (1 \times 160\,000)]/(1.04)^4 = 13\,677$

$PBO2 = [0.1 \times (2 \times 160\,000)]/(1.04)^3 = 28\,448$

$PBO3 = [0.1 \times (3 \times 160\,000)]/(1.04)^2 = 44\,379$

$PBO4 = [0.1 \times (4 \times 160\,000)]/(1.04)^1 = 61\,538$

$PBO5 = [0.1 \times (5 \times 160\,000)]/(1.04)^0 = 80\,000$

**Present value of the defined benefit obligation** The present value of the defined benefit obligation, as calculated in Activity 22.9, plays an important role in the valuation of a possible pension liability under IAS 19. The PBO is the starting point for the recognition of a net defined benefit liability (asset) in the statement of financial position of the employer (para. 54).

Paragraph 87 of IAS further stipulates that post-employment benefit obligations should be measured on a basis that reflects:

1 estimated future salary increases that affect the benefits payable

2 the benefits set out in the terms of the plan (or resulting from any constructive obligation that goes beyond those terms) at the end of the reporting period

3  the effect of any limit on the employer's share of the cost of future benefits

4  contributions from employees and third parties that reduce the ultimate cost to the entity of those benefits

5  estimated future changes in the level of any state benefits that affect the benefits payable under a defined benefit plan, if, and only if, either:

6  those changes were enacted before the end of the reporting period;

7  historical data, or other reliable evidence, indicate that those state benefits will change in some predictable manner, for example in line with future changes in general price levels or general salary levels.

As a result of point 5 of para. 87, we notice in practice that when pension plan formulas are renegotiated or new pension plans are set up, the benefits resulting from state pensions are no longer included as a part of the company pension plan benefit formula. Employers clearly want to avoid elements which increase risk and uncertainty.

Now that you are familiar with the workings of actuarial cost methods, we are able to introduce the solution for the determination of the total pension cost and the valuation of pension liabilities and assets which the IASB has opted for. Below is the determination of the defined benefit cost or total pension cost. Thereafter we pay attention to the impact of the pension benefits on the statement of financial position of the employer. However, first we enumerate a number of decisions the Board has taken in relation to pension accounting:

1  Pension accounting will be based primarily on the plan's terms and benefit formula.

2  For accounting purposes, the projected unit credit method will be used.

3  A net defined benefit obligation will be presented on the balance sheet, rather than a consolidation of pension assets and pension liabilities in the financial statements of the employer or the sponsor.

4  Future salary increases will be incorporated in the measurement of the pension liability.

5  The pension plan assets will be measured at fair value.

## Determination of the defined benefit cost in case of a defined benefit plan

The defined benefit cost in a particular year is defined by IAS 19 as the sum of three individual components, namely the service cost, the net interest on the net defined benefit liability (or asset) and the remeasurements of the net defined benefit liability. The former two will be presented on the profit and loss account part of the statement of comprehensive income, whereas the latter will be included in other comprehensive income on the statement of comprehensive income. Two of the three components each consist of a number of subcomponents. The service cost consists of the current service cost, the past service cost and any gains or losses on settlements. The remeasurements of the net defined benefit liability comprises the actuarial gains and losses, the return on plan assets, excluding amounts included in the net interest on the net defined benefit liability (asset) and any change in the effect of the asset ceiling, excluding amounts included in net interest on the net defined benefit liability (asset).

Below we explain all these different items which are included in the defined benefit cost in a particular year.

## The service cost

**Current service cost** As illustrated in Activity 22.9, the current service cost should be calculated with the use of the projected unit credit method. The projected unit credit method attributes the amount to be funded each year on the basis of the plan's benefit formula. These amounts to be funded each year, which result from the projected unit credit method, represent the current service cost. However, if an employee's service in later years will lead to a materially higher level of benefit than in earlier years, an entity should attribute the benefit on a straight line basis:

- from the date when service by the employee first leads to benefits under the plan (whether or not the benefits are conditional on further service)
- until the date when further service by the employee will lead to no material amount of further benefits under the plan, other than from further salary increases.

In those cases, the pension plan formula will no longer determine the cost allocation pattern. In fact, IAS 19 allows in this case an allocation pattern which is more similar to the funding patterns used by the projected valuation methods (see earlier in this chapter).

The PBO in Activity 22.9 increases each year due to the service rendered in each year and the interest accrual on the amount of the PBO at the start of the year. Under IAS 19, the increase due to service rendered is called the current service cost.

### ACTIVITY 22.10

Calculate the current service cost (*CSC*) and the interest accrual for Mr Dupont with the use of the projected unit credit method which takes into account the service rendered to date and the future salary levels. The calculations are made at the end of the year in this example.

#### Activity feedback

|  | Current service cost | Interest accrual | Projected benefit obligation (PBO) |
|---|---|---|---|
| Year 1 | 13 677 | 0 | 13 677 |
| Year 2 | 14 224 | 547 | 28 448 |
| Year 3 | 14 793 | 1 138 | 44 379 |
| Year 4 | 15 384 | 1 775 | 61 538 |
| Year 5 | 16 000 | 2 462 | 80 000 |

*The CSC is determined each year by the increases in earned pension rights according to the pension benefit formula:*

$CSC1 = [0.1 \times (1 \times 160\,000)]/(1{:}04)^4 = 13\,677$
$CSC2 = [0.1 \times (1 \times 160\,000)]/(1{:}04)^3 = 14\,224$
$CSC3 = [0.1 \times (1 \times 160\,000)]/(1{:}04)^2 = 14\,791$
$CSC4 = [0.1 \times (1 \times 160\,000)]/(1{:}04)^1 = 15\,384$
$CSC5 = [0.1 \times (1 \times 160\,000)]/(1{:}04)^0 = 16\,000$

*The interest cost (IC) component is determined as follows:*

$IC1 = 0.04\,(0) = 0$
$IC2 = 0.04\,(13\,677) = \;\;\;547$
$IC3 = 0.04\,(28\,448) = 1\,138$
$IC4 = 0.04\,(44\,379) = 1\,775$
$IC5 = 0.04\,(61\,538) = 2\,462$

**Past service cost** Past service costs arise when an employer grants pension rights for the service rendered prior to the establishment of the pension plan, or when an employer grants an increase in pension benefits also for service rendered in past periods. As a result, the projected benefit obligation will increase. This increase in the amount of the projected benefit obligation resulting from those past service benefits should, on the one hand, be funded or financed and, on the other, be recognized for accounting purposes. The amounts recognized in relation to those past service benefits in a particular year on the income statement are called *past service costs*. IAS 19 defines past service costs as the change in the present value of the defined benefit obligation for employee service in prior periods, resulting from a plan amendment (the introduction or withdrawal of, or changes to, a defined benefit plan) or a curtailment (a significant reduction by the entity in the number of employees covered by the plan).

---

## ACTIVITY 22.11

Assume that from year 4 onwards Mr Dupont is entitled to a pension benefit of 0.15 per cent of his final salary for each year he has been with the firm instead of 0.10 per cent.

The formula of the pension plan of Mr Dupont then becomes:

$$Br = 0.15 \, (r - y) Sr$$

The employer also grants this increase in pension benefits for the first three years of the career of Mr Dupont. We have to remember that the pension rights of Mr Dupont are vested from the start of his employment.

Calculate the new *PBO* at the start of year 4 which takes into account this increase in pension benefits granted for past periods.

### Activity feedback

*PBO start year $4 = 0.15 \, [3 \times (160\,000)] = (1{:}04)^2 = 66\,568$*

*Remember that the PBO at the start of year 4 under the old pension benefit formula was 44 379. This is an increase of the PBO of $22\,189 = (66\,568 - 44\,379)$.*

*In the example of Mr Dupont where these past service benefits are vested, the amount of 22 189 should be recognized immediately as part of the total pension cost in year 4.*

---

## Gains or losses on settlements

A settlement occurs when an entity enters into a transaction that eliminates all further legal or constructive obligation for part or all of the benefits provided under a defined benefit plan, for example when a lump-sum cash payment is made to, or on behalf of, plan participants in exchange for their rights to receive specified post-employment benefits. IAS 19 prescribes that gains and losses on settlements of a defined benefit plan have to be recognized when the settlement occurs. A settlement may arise from an isolated event, such as the closing of a plant, discontinuance of an operation or termination or suspension of a plan. An event is material enough to qualify as a curtailment if the recognition of a settlement gain or loss would have a material effect on the financial statements. Settlements are often linked with a restructuring. Therefore, an entity accounts for a settlement at the same time as for a related restructuring. We notice that it is up to the management to judge whether the effect is material.

Before determining past service cost, or a gain or loss on settlement, the entity shall remeasure net defined benefit liability using the current fair value of plan assets and current actuarial assumptions (including current market interest rates and other current market prices) reflecting the benefits offered under the plan before the plan amendment, curtailment or settlement (para. 99).

We have now defined the three subcomponents of the service cost. The cost item below is presented together with the service cost on the profit and loss account part of the statement of comprehensive income.

## The net interest on the net defined benefit liability (asset)

Based on the data we have available so far, the defined benefit cost for Mr Dupont in the subsequent years would be as shown in Table 22.1.

## TABLE 22.1    Total defined benefit cost

|        | Current service cost | Interest cost component | Total pension cost |
|--------|----------------------|-------------------------|--------------------|
| Year 1 | 13 677 | 0 | 13 677 |
| Year 2 | 14 224 | 547 | 14 771 |
| Year 3 | 14 793 | 1 138 | 15 931 |
| Year 4 | 15 384 | 1 775 | 17 159 |
| Year 5 | 16 000 | 2 462 | 18 642 |

In this example the interest cost component in Activity 22.10 is determined with the use of the discount rate of 4 per cent. IAS 19 calls this interest cost component the net interest on the net defined benefit liability. The interest cost component reflects the time value of money. Para. 123 stipulates that the interest cost component is computed by multiplying the discount rate as determined at the start of the period by the present value of the net defined benefit obligation throughout that period, taking into account any material changes in the obligation. The net interest on the net defined liability (asset) is the change during the period of the net defined liability (asset) that arises from the passage of time. Since the amounts calculated in the activity are calculated at the end of the year, there is no interest cost in the first year. (As we said earlier, this example is simplified for pedagogic reasons.)

The service cost and the net interest on the net defined benefit liability (asset) are reported on the statement of profit and loss, whereas the next part of the total defined benefit cost, namely the remeasurements of the net defined benefit liability (asset) have to be presented in other comprehensive income.

## Remeasurements of the net defined benefit liability (asset)

This part of the defined benefit cost includes three separate items. Two elements, namely the actuarial gains and losses and the return on plan assets, will be discussed below. The third component, namely the change in the effect of the asset ceiling, will be discussed when the recognition of the net defined benefit liability (asset) is discussed.

**Actuarial gains and losses** Actuarial gains and losses arise from two sources. If actuarial assumptions are different from reality, a difference will occur. This difference can be positive or negative. These differences are called experience adjustments in actuarial jargon. If this difference between the actuarial assumption and the reality continues to exist, it could be that the actuarial assumptions used in the actuarial calculations have to be changed. This is a second source of actuarial gains and losses. So, actuarial gains and losses can also result from changes in the actuarial assumptions themselves. A change in the actuarial assumptions used has as a consequence that the future amounts to be funded will be higher or lower. Further, the PBO calculated with the new actuarial assumptions can also be higher or lower than the PBO calculated with the old actuarial assumptions. In the view of an actuary, actuarial gains and losses mean the following: if the PBO (new assumptions) is higher than the PBO (old assumptions) an actuarial loss arises, since the difference is not yet funded and needs to be. In the opposite situation, where PBO (new assumptions) is smaller than the PBO (old assumptions) an actuarial gain arises, since there is now more funded than the present PBO (new assumptions) (see Activity 22.12).

## ACTIVITY 22.12

Assume that at the start of year 4 the discount rate used in the calculations in relation to the pension benefit of Mr Dupont will be changed from 4 per cent to 5 per cent. What will be the impact on the projected benefit obligation at the start of year 4?

PBO at the start of year 4 (new assumptions)
$$= [0.1 \times (3 \times 160\,000)] / (1.05)^2 = 43\,537$$

Remember that the PBO at the start of year 4, using the discount rate of 4%, was PBO4 (old assumptions) 44 379.

### Activity feedback

The PBO at the start of year 4 using a discount rate of 5% is equal to:

In this situation we have an actuarial gain as the PBO calculated with the new assumptions (in this case a new discount rate) is lower than the PBO calculated with the old assumptions. The actuarial gain is 842 (we talk about a gain because the new PBO (43 537) is lower than the old PBO (44 379)).

A major question subsequently arises. How should we account for this actuarial result?

It is obvious that differences between reality and the actuarial assumptions used will occur frequently (e.g. realized salary increases will be higher or lower than estimated salary increases). Since the revision of IAS 19 in 2011, these actuarial gains and losses have to be recognized immediately in other comprehensive income. Before the revision of IAS 19 in 2011, the IASB allowed a so-called corridor approach whereby actuarial gains and losses, which fell within a corridor, needed not be recognized. The amount of actuarial gains and losses falling outside the corridor had to be recognized over a certain period of time. This mechanism was meant to reduce the volatility in the reported pension costs.

**Return on plan assets** This second component of the remeasurements of the defined benefit liability (asset) consists of the return on plan assets, excluding amounts included in the net interest on the net defined liability. Let's illustrate this component with an example. If we take the pension calculations of Mr Dupont in year 3 and year 4, we observe that the current service cost is respectively 14.793 and 15.384, and the interest cost component, which results from the change in the net defined liability (discount rate × defined benefit liability at the start of the period) is 1.138 and 1.775 (see Activity 22.10).

If the return on plan assets would be an amount of 1300 in year 3 and an amount of 1500 in year 4, then the following amounts would be represented as return on plan assets under other comprehensive income: in year 3 (1300 − 1138) = 162 and in year 4 (1500 − 1775) = −275.

The following components would then be included in the accounts of the company

|  | Year 3 | Year 4 |
|---|---|---|
| Profit and loss account |  |  |
| Defined benefit cost | 14 793 | 15 384 |
| Service cost | 1 138 | 1775 |
| Net interest on the net defined liability |  |  |
| Other comprehensive income | 162 | −275 |
| Remeasurement of the defined benefit liability |  |  |

All items making up the defined benefit cost have now been discussed except for one item, namely the effect of the limit in relation to the recognition of a net pension asset or asset ceiling, which will be discussed below.

## Defined benefit liability

After the analysis of the defined benefit cost, we now focus on the possible impact of company pension plans on the statement of financial position of the employer. IAS 19 stipulates that the entity shall report the net defined benefit liability (asset) on the statement of financial position of the employer. The net defined benefit liability (asset) is the deficit or surplus between the present value of the defined benefit obligation less the fair value of the plan assets (if any). The present value of a defined benefit obligation is the present value without deducting any plan assets, of expected future payments required to settle the obligation resulting from employer service in the current and prior periods. The amounts of the PBOs in the activities included in the section on defined benefit costs so far, are equal to this present value of a defined benefit obligation. We have a deficit or a net defined benefit liability when the present value of the defined benefit obligation is larger than the fair value of plan assets. There is a surplus or a net defined benefit asset when the present value of the defined benefit obligation is lower than the fair value of the plan assets. In case of a surplus, the surplus to be reported must never be higher than the so-called asset-ceiling. This asset-ceiling is the present value of any economic benefits available in the form of refunds from the plan or reductions in future contributions to the plan. The present value of these economic benefits should be determined using a discount rate which is calculated by reference to market yields at balance sheet data on high quality bonds.

We observe that a 'net' amount will appear on the statement of financial position and not the total amount of pension liabilities and pension assets.

After the discussion of the measurement of the pension liability, we now turn our attention to the valuation of the pension plan assets.

## Plan assets

Plan assets include (according to the definitions of IAS 19) assets held by a long-term employee benefit fund and qualifying insurance policies. Pension plan assets need to be valued at fair value. On reading the paragraphs on pension plan assets it becomes clear that the market value is regarded as the value. It is stipulated that when no market price is available, the fair value of plan assets is estimated; for example, by discounting expected future cash flows using a discount rate that reflects both the risk associated with the plan assets and maturity, or expected disposal date of those assets (or, if they have no maturity, expected period until the settlement of the related obligation). Further, unpaid contributions due from the reporting entity to the fund, as well as any non-transferable financial instrument issued by the entity and held by the fund, may not be include in the pension plan assets. Plan assets should be reduced further by any liabilities of the fund that do not relate to employee benefits. Where plan assets include qualifying insurance policies that exactly match the amount and the timing of some or all benefits payable under the plan, the fair value of those insurance policies is deemed to be present value of the related obligations.

It is tempting for companies to include future reductions in contributions or refunds in the definition of a defined benefit pension asset in order to decrease the amount of the pension liability to be shown on the balance sheet. Therefore IFRIC 14 was issued. IFRIC 14 addresses the defined benefit pension assets and their minimum funding requirements. If minimum funding requirements exist (depending on the terms of the pension plan and country regulations to improve the security of post-employment benefits), this might limit the ability to reduce future contributions or these minimum funding requirements might give rise to a liability. IFRIC 14 provides guidance as to when refunds or reductions in future contributions can be regarded as available and as a result be included in the definition of a defined benefit pension asset. Therefore it stipulates (para. 7) that:

> An entity shall determine the availability of a refund or a reduction in the future contributions in accordance with the terms and conditions of the plan and any statutory requirements in the jurisdiction of the plan' [(e.g. minimum funding requirements)]. An economic benefit, in the form of a refund or a reduction in future contributions, is available if the entity can realize it at some point during the life of the plan or when the plan liabilities are settled. In particular, such an economic benefit may be available even if it is not realizable immediately at the end of the reporting period.

IAS 19 states further that an entity should determine the present value of defined benefit obligations and the fair value of any plan assets with sufficient regularity that the amounts recognized in the financial statements do not differ materially from the amounts that would be determined at the balance sheet date.

## Disclosure in the notes in relation to pension benefits

On the face of the statement of financial position of the employer, a liability or an asset will be presented. The underlying elements taken into account to determine this net defined benefit liability or asset have to be disclosed in the notes of the financial statements (para. 135). Some extensive disclosures are the result.

An entity shall disclose information that:

(a) explains the characteristics of its defined benefit plans and risks associated with them;

(b) identifies and explains the amounts in its financial statements arising from its defined benefit plans;

(c) describes how its defined benefit plans may affect the amount, timing and uncertainty of the entity's future cash flows.

## REAL LIFE ILLUSTRATION

To illustrate the level of detail which needs to be provided in relation to the pension plan of a company, the information disclosure of Adidas in their annual accounts of 2012 in relation to their pension plan is shown here as an example. In this, textbook IAS 19, as revised in June 2011, is presented. Since application of this revised IAS 19 is only required for financial periods after January 2013, we have to include an illustration on pension disclosures under the measurement and valuation regime of the old IAS 19.

### 24 Pensions and similar obligations

The Group has recognised post-employment benefit obligations arising from defined benefit plans. The benefits are provided pursuant to the legal, fiscal and economic

*(Continued)*

conditions in each respective country and mainly depend on the employees' years of service and remuneration.

*Pensions and similar obligations (€ in millions)*

|  | Dec. 31, 2012 | Dec. 31, 2011 |
|---|---|---|
| Pension liability | 241 | 195 |
| Similar obligations | 10 | 10 |
| **Pensions and similar obligations** | **251** | **205** |

## Defined contribution plans

The total expense for defined contribution plans amounted to € 46 million in 2012 (2011: €36 million).

## Defined benefit plans

Given the diverse Group structure, different defined benefit plans exist, comprising a variety of post-employment benefit arrangements. The Group's major defined benefit plans relate to adidas AG and subsidiaries in the UK and Japan. The defined benefit plans of adidas AG mainly relate to direct pension commitments as well as commitments which relate to the Executive Board and which are managed through a pension fund in combination with a reinsured support fund. The benefit plans generally provide payments in case of death, disability or retirement to former employees and their survivors. The obligations arising from defined benefit plans are partly covered by plan assets. In 2011, the defined benefit plan offered at one of the Japanese subsidiaries of adidas AG was converted into a defined contribution plan, resulting in a plan settlement.

The following tables analyse the defined benefit plans, plan assets, present values of the defined benefit plans, expenses recognised in the consolidated income statement, actuarial assumptions and other information.

*Amounts for defined benefit plans recognised in the consolidated statement of financial position (€ in millions)*

|  | Dec. 31, 2012 | Dec. 31, 2011 |
|---|---|---|
| Present value of funded obligation | 89 | 76 |
| Fair value of plan assets | (76) | (67) |
| **Funded status** | **13** | **9** |
| Present value of unfunded obligation | 228 | 184 |
| Asset ceiling effect | 0 | 1 |
| **Net defined benefit liability** | **241** | **194** |
| Thereof: liability | 241 | 195 |
| Thereof: adidas AG | 196 | 154 |
| Thereof: asset | (0) | (1) |
| Thereof: adidas AG | – | (1) |

The asset ceiling effect arises from a funded defined benefit plan in Germany and is recognised in the consolidated statement of comprehensive income.

The determination of assets and liabilities for defined benefit plans is based upon statistical and actuarial valuations. In particular, the present value of the defined benefit obligation is driven by financial variables (such as the discount rates or future increases in salaries) and demographic variables (such as mortality and employee turnover). The actuarial assumptions may differ significantly from the actual results, i.e. the present value of the actual future performance may differ from the reported present value.

*Actuarial assumptions (in %)*

|  | Dec. 31, 2012 | Dec. 31, 2011 |
|---|---|---|
| Discount rate | 3.5 | 4.3 |
| Expected rate of salary increases | 3.2 | 3.3 |
| Expected pension increases | 2.1 | 2.1 |
| Expected return on plan assets | 4.0 | 4.8 |

The actuarial assumptions as at the balance sheet date are used to determine the defined benefit liability at that date and the pension expense for the upcoming financial year.

The actuarial assumptions for withdrawal and mortality rates are based on statistical information available in the various countries, the latter for Germany on the Heubeck 2005 G mortality tables.

The calculation of the pension liabilities in Germany is based on a discount rate determined using the Mercer Pension Discount Yield Curve (MPDYC) approach which was adjusted in 2012 due to the current market development. Had a discount rate been used which was based on the previous year-end's approach, the defined benefit obligation would have increased by approximately €20 million.

The Group recognises actuarial gains or losses arising in defined benefit plans during the financial year immediately outside the income statement in the consolidated statement of comprehensive income. The actuarial losses recognised in this statement for 2012 amount to €35 million (2011: €13 million). The accumulated actuarial losses recognised amount to €86 million (2011: €51 million).

In 2012, the expected return on plan assets assumption was set separately, by aggregating the expected rate of return for each asset class over the underlying asset allocation, for the various benefit plans. Historical markets were studied and expected

*(Continued)*

## REAL LIFE ILLUSTRATION    *(Continued)*

returns were based on widely accepted capital market principles.

*Pension expenses for defined benefit plans*
*(€ in millions)*

|  | Year ending Dec. 31, 2012 | Year ending Dec. 31, 2011 |
|---|---|---|
| Current service cost | 16 | 12 |
| Interest cost | 11 | 11 |
| Expected return on plan assets | (3) | (4) |
| **Pension expenses for defined benefit plans** | **24** | **19** |

Of the total pension expenses, an amount of €15 million (2011: €13 million) relates to employees of adidas AG. The pension expense is mainly recorded within other operating expenses. The production-related part of the pension expenses is recognised within cost of sales.

*Present value of the defined benefit obligation*
*(€ in millions)*

|  | 2012 | 2011 |
|---|---|---|
| **Present value of the defined benefit obligation as at January 1** | **260** | **237** |
| Currency translation differences | 2 | 3 |
| Current service cost | 16 | 12 |
| Interest cost | 11 | 11 |
| Contribution by plan participants | 0 | 0 |
| Pensions paid | (11) | (10) |
| Actuarial loss | 39 | 10 |
| Plan settlements | 0 | (3) |
| **Present value of the defined benefit obligation as at December 31** | **317** | **260** |

*Fair value of plan assets (€ in millions)*

|  | 2012 | 2011 |
|---|---|---|
| **Fair value of plan assets at January 1** | **67** | **67** |
| Currency translation differences | 2 | 2 |
| Pensions paid | (4) | (3) |
| Contributions by the employer | 4 | 4 |
| Contributions paid by plan participants | 0 | 0 |
| Actuarial gain/loss | 4 | (4) |
| Expected return on plan assets | 3 | 4 |
| Plan settlements | 0 | (3) |
| **Fair value of plan assets at December 31** | **76** | **67** |

Around 85% of the plan assets are related to plan assets in the UK, Germany and Switzerland.

In the UK, the plan assets are held under trust within the pension fund. In Germany, the plan assets are invested in insurance contracts and in a pension fund. The plan assets in Switzerland are held by a pension foundation. In the rest of the world, the plan assets consist predominantly of insurance contracts.

The expected payments for 2013 amount to €11 million. Thereof, €7 million relate to benefits paid directly by the Group companies and €4 million to employer contributions paid into the plan assets. In 2012, the actual return on plan assets was €7 million (2011: €0 million).

*Constitution of plan assets (€ in millions)*

|  | Dec. 31, 2012 | Dec. 31, 2011 |
|---|---|---|
| Equity instruments | 24 | 21 |
| Bonds | 10 | 9 |
| Real estate | 1 | 1 |
| Pension plan reinsurance | 24 | 22 |
| Other assets | 17 | 14 |
| **Fair value of plan assets** | **76** | **67** |

*Historical development (€ in millions)*

|  | Dec. 31, 2012 | Dec. 31, 2011 | Dec. 31, 2010 | Dec. 31, 2009 | Dec. 31, 2008 |
|---|---|---|---|---|---|
| Present value of defined benefit obligation | 317 | 260 | 237 | 207 | 172 |
| Fair value of plan assets | 76 | 67 | 67 | 61 | 53 |
| Thereof: defined benefit assets | 0 | (1) | (1) | (2) | (5) |
| **Deficit in plans** | **241** | **194** | **171** | **148** | **124** |
| Experience adjustments arising on the plan liabilities | (3) | (4) | (1) | (3) | 2 |
| Experience adjustments arising on the plan assets | 4 | (4) | 1 | 3 | (8) |

## Multi-employer plans

In the introductory discussion on pension benefits, the concept of multi-employer plans was introduced. Paragraphs 32 and 33 of IAS 19 define how a multi-employer plan should be accounted for. The terms of the plan will determine whether a multi-employer plan will be classified as a defined benefit plan or a defined contribution plan. Where a multi-employer plan is a defined benefit plan, the company shall account for its proportionate share of the defined benefit obligation, plan assets and costs with the plan in the same way as for any other defined benefit plans. When sufficient information is not available to use defined benefit accounting for a multi-employer plan that is classified as a defined benefit plan, the company might account for the plan as if it were a defined contribution plan. In this situation, the employer has to disclose in the notes to its accounts that the pension plan is in fact a defined benefit plan together with the reason why there is insufficient information to account for the plan as a defined benefit plan. If there is a surplus or a deficit in the plan that may affect the amount of future contributions, information about the surplus or the deficit (basis for the calculation and the implications) should be provided as well.

In the context of a multi-employer plan, a contingent liability (IAS 37) might arise from, for example:

**(a)** actuarial losses relating to other participating entities because each entity that participates in a multi-employer plan shares in the actuarial risks of every other participating entity, or

**(b)** any responsibility under the terms of a plan to finance any shortfall in the plan if other entities cease to participate.

## Defined benefit plans that share risks between various entities under common control

IAS 19 prescribes the accounting treatment of defined benefit plans that share risks between various entities under common control. How these individual entities under common control have to account for promised pension benefit in their separate annual accounts depends on whether or not a contractual agreement or stated policy exists for charging the net defined benefit cost for the plan as a whole to the individual group entities measured in accordance with IAS 19. If such a contract or policy exists, the total pension cost determined according to IAS 19 for the group as a whole, will be split over the individual accounts of the separate entities under common control. If no such policy or contracts exists, then the total pension cost determined in line with IAS 19 will be recognized in the individual statement of the group entity which is the legally sponsoring employer for the plan. The other group entities account only for their contribution to the plan in their individual accounts. Participation in such a plan is a related party transaction for each individual group entity and the necessary disclosures on related party transactions have to be made.

## TERMINATION BENEFITS

### Definition

An entity should recognize termination benefits as a liability and an expense when, and only when, the entity is demonstrably committed to either:

- terminate the employment of an employee or group of employees before the normal retirement date, or
- provide termination benefits as a result of an offer made in order to encourage voluntary redundancy.

So the definition of termination benefits in IAS 19 also includes employee benefits that are payable as a result of an employee's decision to accept voluntary redundancy in exchange for those benefits as well as involuntary determination of the employment. Benefits that are payable in exchange for an employee's decision to accept voluntary redundancy are termination benefits only if they are offered for a short period.

### Recognition

IAS 19 (165) states that an entity shall recognize a liability and expense for termination benefits at the earlier of the following dates:

(a) when the entity can no longer withdraw the offer of those benefits; and (b) when the entity recognizes costs for restructuring that is within the scope of IAS 37 and involves the payment of termination benefits.

IAS 19 recognizes in fact two situations, namely termination benefits payable as a result of an employee's decision to accept an offer of benefits in exchange for the termination of employment; or termination benefits payable as a result of an entity's decision to terminate an employee's employment. The first are in fact voluntary termination benefits that should be recognized when employees accept the entity's offer of those benefits. In the case of an offer made to encourage voluntary redundancy, the measurement of termination benefits should be based on the number of employees expected to accept the offer (para. 140). The latter are termination benefits that should be recognized when an entity is demonstrably committed to a termination. This occurs when the entity has a detailed formal plan for the termination and there is no realistic possibility of withdrawal. The detailed plan should include, as a minimum:

- the location, function, and approximate number of employees whose services are to be terminated
- the termination benefits for each job classification or function
- the time at which the plan will be implemented. Implementation should begin as soon as possible and the period of time to complete implementation should be such that material changes to the plan are not likely.

Where termination benefits fall due more than 12 months after the balance sheet date, the entity shall apply the requirements for other long-term employee benefits, and when termination benefits are expected to be settled wholly before twelve months after the end of the annual reporting period in which the termination benefit is recognized, the entity shall apply the requirements for short-term employee benefits.

## ACCOUNTING BY THE PENSION FUND

When pension benefits are externally funded, the entity to which the amounts are transferred must also prepare financial statements. When the amounts are transferred to an insurance company, the financial statements of the insurance company will give a picture of the financial position of the insurance company.

Financial reporting by pension funds is regulated by IAS 26, *Accounting and Reporting by Retirement Benefit Plans*. The last revision of IAS 26 dates from 1994, which is important to stress, since IAS 19, which focuses on the financial statements of the employer, has been revised twice since then. The financial situation of a pension fund will not be presented in the 'classical' format of financial statements, namely consisting of a balance sheet and an income statement. IAS 26 defines the contents of a pension fund 'report' which should be prepared. Also, in relation to this report, the type of pension benefit (defined contribution or defined benefit) promised plays a role.

When amounts resulting from a defined contribution plan are transferred to a pension fund, the report (para. 13) contains a statement of net assets available for benefits and a description of the funding policy.

When amounts resulting from a defined benefit plan are transferred to a pension fund, the report of the fund should contain either (para. 17):

- a statement that shows:
  - the net assets available for benefits
  - the actuarial present value of promised retirement benefits, distinguishing between vested benefits and non-vested benefits – the resulting excess or deficit
- or a statement of net assets available for benefits including either:
  - a note disclosing the actuarial present value of promised retirement benefits, distinguishing between vested benefits and non-vested benefits, or
  - a reference to this information in an accompanying actuarial report.

If an actuarial valuation has not been prepared at the date of the report, the most recent valuation should be used as a base and the date of the valuation disclosed.

We notice immediately that the concept of defined benefit obligation is not introduced here; IAS 26 only mentions actuarial present value of promised retirement benefits. In order to improve the information value of the annual reports of pension funds, a revision of IAS 26 in line with the vision of IAS 19 would be welcome. It is not certain, however, whether the business world would also welcome a revision in the near future.

## SUMMARY

IAS 19 is considered to be one of the more technical Standards. The same comment applies to IFRS 2, *Share-based Payment*. Pension plans represent assets, liabilities and costs for the sponsoring company. The related amounts are not always easy to determine and the impact on a company may be overlooked. In the acquisition deal of KLM by Air France, the French made a surprising post-acquisition discovery. When the deal was closed and the acquisition price determined, the company management discovered pension surpluses in the pension plan of KLM. This surplus net pension asset could be regarded as an asset of the Air France-KLM group. This meant that Air France had acquired KLM with negative goodwill. The net pension asset was the difference between pension liabilities of €7627 million and pension assets of €8912 million, implying a surplus of €1285 million. To make sure that they accounted for this surplus, which occurred under IAS (KLM had used Dutch GAAP before the acquisition by Air France), Air France-KLM consulted the IASB on its interpretation of IAS 19. This illustrates that pension valuation and pension accounting is not easy. The level of technicality, however, depends on the type of pension promise made.

   Accounting for defined contribution plans is less technical than accounting for defined benefit plans. It has been noticed in recent years that defined contribution plans have become more popular. Could the stricter accounting requirements, which make the uncertainties and the risks involved in a defined benefit plan more visible, have something to do with this?

   In response to calls from preparers and users of financial statements, the IASB is currently conducting a project that will result in significant improvements to pension accounting. The IASB intends to complete this project within the next couple of years. Therefore a fundamental review of all aspects of post-employment benefit accounting is possible in the future.

## EXERCISES

*Suggested answers to exercises marked ✓ are to be found on our dedicated CourseMate platform for students.*

   *Suggested answers to the remaining exercises are to be found on the Instructor online support resources.*

✓ **1**   Company Rebo has five directors who all participate in the following share-based remuneration plan with cash alternatives. The directors have the right to choose between 600 shares or the value of 500 shares paid in cash at vesting date. If the directors opt for the shares, they may not sell them for three years. The only vesting requirement is that the directors should remain three years with the company.

   At the grant date, the entity's share price is €30. At the end of years 1, 2 and 3 the share prices are €33, €36 and €40. The fair value of the share alternative is €28 per share. Calculate the remuneration expense for the equity-based remuneration system of Rebo. Also, indicate which accounts are credited. Further to this, consider both situations, namely that the directors choose the cash alternative and that the directors choose the equity alternative.

✓ **2** IAS 19, *Employee Benefits,* deals, amongst other things with the treatment of post-employment benefits such as pensions and other retirement benefits.

Post-employment benefits are classified as either defined contribution or defined benefit plans.

### Klondike

| | at 31 March 2001 $000 | at 31 March 2002 $000 |
|---|---|---|
| Present value obligation | 1 500 | 1 750 |
| Fair value of plan assets | 1 500 | 1 650 |
| Current service cost – year to 31 March 2002 | | 160 |
| Contributions paid – year to 31 March 2002 | | 85 |
| Benefits paid to employees – year to 31 March 2002 | | 125 |
| Actuarial return on plan assets at 1 April Discount rate for plan liabilities at 1 April 20X1 is 10% | 20X1 is 12% | |

20X1 is 12% Klondike operates a defined benefit post-retirement plan for its employees. The plan is reviewed annually. Klondike's actuaries have provided the information in the table above.

**Required:**

(a) Describe the relevant features and required accounting treatment of defined contribution and defined benefit plans under IAS 19.

(b) Prepare extracts of Klondike's financial statements for the year to 31 March 20X2 in compliance with IAS 19, *Employee Benefits,* insofar as the information permits.

(ACCA – June 2002)

✓ **3** Company Crux grants share options to its employees at 1.1.X1. Each employee will receive ten options if he/she stays with the company for the next three years. At grant date, the turnover percentage of employees is estimated at 20 per cent. The fair value of the option at grant date is €20. The company grants these options to the 100 employees in service at grant date. During the first year four employees leave and the company revises its estimate on employee turnover from 20 per cent to 15 per cent (= 15 employees leaving). During year 2 another four employees leave, the entity revises the estimate to 12 per cent. At the end of the third year, six employees leave the company. The share options of the remaining employees vest at the end of year 3.

Calculate the remuneration expense for years 1, 2 and 3 following from this share option plan. What is the credit side when this expense is recorded in the books of the company?

✓ **4** At the beginning of year 1, an entity grants to 20 senior executives 1000 share options, each based on two conditions. First, the executive has to remain with the entity until the end of year 3. Second, the share options may not be exercised unless the share price has increased from €100 at the beginning of year 1 to above €130 at the end of year 3. If the share price is above €130 at year 3, the share options may be exercised at any time during the next five years.

The entity applies a binomial option-pricing model, which takes into account the possibility that the share price will exceed €130 at the end of year 3 (in this case the share options become exercisable) and the possibility that the share price will not exceed €130 at the end of year 3 (and then the options will be forfeited). It estimates the fair value of the share options with this market condition to be €48 per option.

At the end of year 1, the company estimates the turnover of senior executives at 2 per cent. In the second year, one executive leaves the company but the turnover estimate remains the same. During the third year two executives leave the company. Calculate the remuneration expense for each year in which an expense needs to be recorded. Which account will be credited when the remuneration expense is recorded?

5   An entity grants 100 share appreciation rights to its 200 employees on the condition that they remain with the firm for two years. At the end of these two years, the benefits vest and the employees may exercise the options in the two consecutive years. The benefits will be paid out in cash and the cash amount will be determined by the intrinsic value at the date of exercise. The fair value of the appreciation rights and the intrinsic value of the rights are presented below.

| Year | Fair value | Intrinsic value |
|------|------------|-----------------|
| 1 | 31 | |
| 2 | 36 | 30 |
| 3 | | **40** |

At the end of the first year, ten employees leave the company and the company estimates that in the next year 15 more employees will leave. In year 2, 16 employees leave and 74 employees exercise their share appreciation rights immediately when their benefits vest and the remaining 100 exercise their rights in year 3.

Calculate the remuneration expenses and the amount of the liability to be recognized as a result of these share-based payment transactions.

6   For the determination and recognition of the current service cost and the defined pension liability, one particular actuarial cost method has been chosen, namely the projected unit credit method. This method takes into account expected future salary increases. Comment on this decision. What is your opinion on taking into account these expected salary increases? What arguments could be used in favour of including future salary increases? Are there any arguments against the inclusion of future salary increases?

7   The actuarial assumptions 'discount factor' and 'expected market return' are different elements in the opinion of the IASB, and, as a result, the impact of both assumptions is included separately in the total pension cost. Would the data be less reliable or value relevant if the same value were used for the discount factor and the expected market return? Comment on your opinion.

8   Consider the assumptions 'discount factor' and 'expected market return' again. Take into account the different funding or financing systems (internal and external funding) which companies can use. Does the separate disclosure of the interest cost component and the return on assets increase the information value of the pension data communicated to external users of the financial statements? Discuss.

9   State pension plans are defined in IAS 19 as multi-employer plans. Multi-employer plans can be either of a defined benefit type or of a defined contribution type. Had you been in the

position of the standard setter, would you have included the treatment of the state pension plans in the treatment of the multi-employer plans? Present arguments in favour of your answer.

**10** The following statements relate to accounting for retirement benefits under the provisions of IAS 19, *Employee Benefits.* [The 'net pension asset' is the fair value of plan assets less the present value of plan liabilities.]

(i) Other things being equal, the net pension asset increases when interest rates increase.

(ii) Other things being equal, the net pension asset decreases when share prices fall

(iii) Where the terms of retirement benefits are altered so as to provide immediate additional benefits to retired members, then the cost of the additional benefits should be recognized in the income statement over a period equal to the average life expectancy of the retired members

Which of the statements are true?

A: (i) and (ii) only

B: (i) and (iii) only

C: (ii) and (iii) only

D: All of them

(CIMA – November 2003)

**11** E pays contributions into a post-employment defined benefit plan on behalf of its employees. The balance sheet of the entity at 30 April 2003 showed a net pension liability of $60 million. During the year to 30 April 2004:

- the entity closed down a division and the curtailment of retirement benefits for employees made redundant resulted in a gain of $4 million
- the estimated current service cost was $8 million
- the expected return on assets was $6 million
- the unwinding of the discount on the pension liability was $4 million
- there was no recognition of actuarial gains or losses in the income statement.

The net pension liability at 30 April 2004 was $65 million [before incorporating the actuarial gain or loss for the year].

What is the actuarial gain or loss for the year ended 30 April 2004?

A: A loss of $1 million

B: A gain of $1 million

C: A loss of $3 million

D: A gain of $3 million.

(CIMA – May 2004)

**12** The following information relates to the defined benefits pension scheme of BGA, a listed entity.

The present value of the scheme obligations at 1 November 2006 was $18 360 000, while the fair value of the scheme assets at that date was $17 770 000. During the financial year ended 31 October 2007, a total of $997 000 was paid into the scheme in contributions. Current service cost for the year was calculated at $1 655 000, and actual benefits paid were $1 860 300.

The applicable interest cost for the year was 6.5 per cent and the expected return on plan assets was 9.4 per cent.

The present value of the scheme obligations at 31 October 2007 was calculated as $18 655 500, and the fair value of scheme assets at that date was $18 417 180.

**Required:**

(a) Calculate the actuarial gain or loss on BGA's pension scheme assets and liabilities for the year ended 31 October 2007.

(CIMA – November 2007)

13 JSX, a listed entity, has a defined benefits pension scheme. The following information relates to the pension scheme for the year ended 31 October 20X8:

|  | € |
|---|---|
| Current service cost | 362 000 |
| Contributions to scheme | 550 000 |
| Benefits paid | 662 400 |
| Fair value of scheme assets at 1 November 2007 | 10 660 000 |
| Fair value of scheme assets at 31 October 2008 | 11 204 000 |
| Interest cost in respect of the defined benefit obligation | 730 000 |

The expected return on scheme assets for the year ended 31 October 20X8 was 6.2 per cent.

**Required:**

Calculate the actuarial gain and loss on JSX's pension scheme assets for the year ended 31 October 20X8.

(CIMA P8 – November 2008)

14 LEC operates a benefit pension plan for its employees. The fair value of the plan assets at 1 June 20X8 was $6 200 000. LEC made contributions of $600 000 to the plan in the year to 31 March 20X9 and the expected return on assets has been calculated at $380 000. The pension plan paid out a total of $450 000 in benefits for the period and the fair value of the plan assets at 31 May 20X9 was $6 680 000.

**Required:**

Calculate the actuarial gain or loss in respect of the pension plan assets of LEC's defined benefit pension plan for the year ended 31 March 20X9. Please make clear whether there is a gain or a loss.

(CIMA P8 – November 2009)

15 Kappa is an entity that operates in a sector where the recruitment and retention of high-quality employees is particularly important in order to achieve corporate goals. You are the financial controller of Kappa and you have recently received a memorandum from a member of the board of directors. The memorandum includes the following key issues:

(i) The board is eager to reward employees appropriately, but is aware that large salary payments have an immediate impact on the liquidity and earnings per share of Kappa.

(ii) A more appropriate method of remuneration is to grant key employees share options that will vest at a future date, if the employees comply with specified conditions (e.g. continued employment) or achieve specific performance targets (e.g. completing an assignment to a specified standard or achieving a specified growth in the share price). This would allow employees to exercise the options at an appropriate time for them and would prevent an immediate impact on the liquidity or earnings per share of Kappa at the grant date.

**Required:**

Draft a reply that responds to the observations made by the board. Your reply should focus on the impact on the statement of financial position and income statement of Kappa, rather than the personal tax positions of the employees. Your reply should contain a summary of the appropriate provisions of IFRS 2, *Share-based Payment*.

(ACCA – June 2007)

**16** VB granted share options to its 500 employees on 1 August 20X6. Each employee will receive 1000 share options provided they continue to work for VB for the four years following the grant date. The fair value of the options at the grant date was $1.30 each. In the year ended 31 July 20X7, 20 employees left and another 50 were expected to leave in the following three years. In the year ended 31 July 20X8 18 employees left and a further 30 were expected to leave during the next two years.

**Required:**

Prepare the journal entry to record the charge to VB's income statement for the year ended 31 July 20X8 in respect of the share options, in accordance with IFRS 2 *Share-based Payments*.

(CIMA Financial Management – September 2011)

**17** DF granted 1000 share options to each of its 300 employees on 1 January 20X0, with the condition that they continue to work for DF for 4 years from the grant date. The fair value of each option at the grant date was $5.

Twenty employees left in the year to 31 December 20X0 and at that date another 65 were expected to leave over the next three years. 23 employees left in the year to 31 December 20X1 and at that date another 44 were expected to leave over the next two years.

**Required:**

Calculate the charge to DF's income statement for the year ended 31 December 2011 in respect of the share options and prepare the journal entry to record this.

(CIMA Financial Management – May 2012).

# CHANGING PRICES AND HYPERINFLATIONARY ECONOMIES

# 23

## INTRODUCTION

We spent considerable time on the alternative theoretical and practical possibilities regarding measurement alternatives in Part One, Chapters 4 to 8. It is not necessary to repeat this material or to revisit the thinking behind it. This chapter limits itself to coverage of international regulation on the matter.

## EU FOURTH DIRECTIVE

The majority of the Directive is couched in historical terms, but in Article 33 it does permit Member States to allow and to require a wide variety of alternative methods, provided only that, if such methods are used, information is given in the notes to the accounts suffi-cient for the reader to work out what the balance sheet figures would have been under the historical cost approach. National reactions to this in subsequent national legislation by European countries were broadly what we would expect from our discussion in Chapter 2, i.e. the UK, Ireland and the Netherlands, for example, do allow such variations and most mainland European countries do not. In the summer of 2013 the European Union issued a new Directive to replace the Fourth and Seventh Directives. This appears, or at least intends, to disallow the use of current replacement cost. Remember that a Directive has no effect at entity level until incorporated into the relevant national law.

## IAS GAAP

As we pointed out in Part One, inflation and price increases in the 1970s were much higher in the main developed economies than is the case now.

In 1977 the IASC issued IAS 6, *Accounting Responses to Changing Prices*, which required the disclosure of the effect of any procedures applied to reflect the impact of specific or general price changes. Subsequently the IASC replaced IAS 6 with IAS 15, which required the use of restatement on the basis of either the general price level or current costs when the reporting currency was subject to a significant (but unspeci-fied) degree of inflation. In 1989 the IASC followed an approach similar to that of the FASB, by making IAS 15 optional. In the same year the IASC issued IAS 29, which requires general price-level restatement when the reporting currency is subject to hyperinflation. It is worth noting, however, that IAS GAAP are applied in a number of countries with less developed economies, where significant inflation (but not necessar-ily hyperinflation) may be prevalent. Yet IAS 15 appears to have been little used in practice. It was completely withdrawn with effect from 1 January 2005.

IAS 29, *Financial Reporting in Hyperinflationary Economies*, is another matter. IAS 29 requires that if the functional currency used by an entity is the currency of a hyperinflationary economy, then the entity's financial statements should be restated in units of the same purchasing power, using the measuring unit current at the balance sheet dates (units of current purchasing power). According to IAS 29, para. 37, this restatement should be made using 'a general price index that reflects changes in gen-eral purchasing power' and it is preferable that the same index be used by all entities that report in the currency of the same economy.

The restated financial statements should be presented as the primary financial state-ments and separate presentation of the unrestated financial statements is discouraged. The corresponding figures for the previous period required by IAS 1, *Presentation of Financial Statements* (see Chapter 9), and any information in respect of earlier periods should also be restated in terms of units of current purchasing power at the balance sheet date (IAS 29, paras 7–8). The gain or loss on net monetary position (see later) should be separately disclosed as part of net income (IAS 29, para. 9).

The determination of the functional currency in any particular case, previously dis-cussed in SIC 19, is now covered in the revised IAS 21 (see Chapter 30). It is defined as the currency of the primary economic environment in which the group operates. As a result of these changes, an entity can no longer avoid restatement under IAS 29 by adopting a stable currency, such as the functional currency of its parent, as its own functional currency. The possible implications are well illustrated in the case study on Aeroflot, which follows on p. 525.

IAS 29, para. 3, sets out five characteristics of the economic environment as indicators of hyperinflation, of which the fifth is the most frequently cited:

1  The general population prefers to keep its wealth in non-monetary assets or in a relatively stable foreign currency.

2  The general population regards monetary amounts not in terms of the local currency but in terms of a relatively stable foreign currency.

3  Sales and purchases on credit take place at prices that compensate for the expected loss of purchasing power during the credit period, even when it is short.

4  Interest rates, wages and prices are linked to a price index.

5  The cumulative inflation rate over three years is approaching or exceeds 100 per cent (i.e. the average annual inflation rate over three years is approaching or exceeds $33\frac{1}{3}$ per cent).

The general principles of IAS 29, when applicable, are essentially the current purchasing power (CPP) approach discussed in Chapter 7. Monetary items are not restated because they are already expressed in terms of the monetary units current at the balance sheet date (current purchasing power unit). In the case of monetary items that are linked by agreement to changes in prices such as index-linked bonds and loans, their carrying amounts adjusted in accordance with the agreement are used in the restated balance sheet. Other balance sheet amounts are restated to amounts in units of current purchasing power by applying a general price index, unless they are already carried at amounts in units of current purchasing power, such as current market value or net realizable value (IAS 29, paras 11–14).

For items carried at cost or cost less depreciation, the restated cost or cost less depreciation is determined by applying to the historical costs and accumulated depreciation (if any) the change in a selected general price index from the date of acquisition to the balance sheet date. For items carried at revalued amounts, the revalued amount and accumulated depreciation (if any) are restated by applying the change in the price index from the date of the latest revaluation to the balance sheet date.

If records of the acquisition of property, plant and equipment do not permit the ascertainment or estimation of the acquisition dates, it may be necessary, when the Standard is first applied, to use an independent professional valuation of the items concerned as a basis for their restatement. If no general price index is available to cover the period between acquisition and the balance sheet date, an estimate of the changes in general purchasing power of the reporting currency over that period may be made by using the changes in the exchange rate between the reporting currency and a relatively stable foreign currency (IAS 29, paras 11–18).

The restated amount of a non-monetary item is reduced (in accordance with the appropriate IAS) when it exceeds the amount recoverable from the item's future use, sale or disposal (IAS 29, para. 19). It is not appropriate both to restate capital expenditure (fixed assets) financed by borrowing and to capitalize that part of the borrowing costs that compensates for inflation.

At the beginning of the first period of application of IAS 29, the components of owners' equity are restated by applying a general price index from the dates on which the components were contributed or otherwise arose, except for retained earnings and any revaluation surplus. Any revaluation surplus from prior periods is eliminated and restated retained earnings is the residual amount (balancing figure) in the restated balance sheet. Subsequently, all components of owners' equity are restated by applying a general price index from the beginning of the period (or the date of contribution, if later).

The movements for the period in owners' equity should be disclosed in accordance with IAS 1, *Presentation of Financial Statements* (see Chapter 10) (IAS 29, paras 24–25).

All items in the income statement should be expressed in terms of end of year current purchasing power units. Hence, all income statement amounts need to be restated by applying the change in general price index between the dates at which the amounts were recorded and the balance sheet date. In practice, average index values for sub-periods, such as months, would normally be used, as in the case of average exchange rates used for the translation of foreign currency amounts under IAS 21 (see Chapter 30).

According to IAS 29, para. 27, the gain or loss on the entity's net monetary position may be estimated by applying the change in the general price index to the weighted average for the period of the difference between monetary assets and monetary liabilities.

The gain or loss on the net monetary position should be included in net income. Any adjustment to index-linked assets or liabilities (as mentioned earlier) is offset against the gain or loss on net monetary position. It is suggested that the gain or loss in net monetary position should be presented in the income statement together with interest income and expense and foreign exchange differences related to invested or borrowed funds (IAS 29, paras 27–28).

If an investee, accounted for under the equity method, reports in the currency of a hyperinflationary country, the financial statements of the investee are restated in accordance with IAS 29 in order to calculate the investor's share of its net assets and results of operations (IAS 29, para. 20).

All items in the cash flow statement should be restated in terms of current purchasing power units at the balance sheet date (IAS 29, para. 33). Comparative figures from the previous reporting period and other comparative information that is disclosed in respect of prior periods should be restated in terms of units of current purchasing power at the balance sheet date (IAS 29, para. 34).

These requirements assume an original historical cost set of financial statements. However, IAS 29 also allows for the possibility of 'current cost' financial statements as the basis. Items stated at current cost are already expressed in units of current purchasing power and so are not restated. Other items are restated as described for historical cost balance sheets earlier (IAS 29, para. 29).

The current cost income statement reports items in terms of the purchasing power of the monetary unit at the times when the underlying transactions or events occurred. For example, cost of goods sold and depreciation are recorded at their current costs at the time of consumption. Therefore, all amounts need to be restated into current purchasing power units at the balance sheet date (IAS 29, para. 30). Gain or loss on net monetary position should be calculated and accounted for as already described (IAS 29, para. 31).

A parent that reports in the currency of a hyperinflationary economy may have subsidiaries that also report in currencies of hyperinflationary economies. The financial statements of such subsidiaries should be restated in accordance with IAS 29, as described earlier, before being included in the process of consolidation. In the case of foreign subsidiaries, financial statements (restated, as described earlier, if they are in the currency of a hyperinflationary economy) should be translated into the reporting currency at closing rates as required by IAS 21.

If financial statements with different reporting dates are consolidated, all items, whether monetary or non-monetary, should be restated into units of current purchasing power at the date of the consolidated financial statements (IAS 29, paras 35–36).

When an entity discontinues the preparation and presentation of financial statements in accordance with IAS 29 because the economy of its reporting currency is no longer hyperinflationary, the amounts that are expressed in current purchasing power units as at the end of the previous reporting period should be treated as the basis for the carrying amounts in its subsequent financial statements (IAS 29, para. 38). In other words, these increased numbers are retained as the new 'cost' figure, which in a sense they are not.

The following disclosures should be made:

1 The fact that the financial statements and the comparative figures have been restated for changes in the general purchasing power of the reporting currency and are stated in terms of the unit of purchasing power current at the balance sheet date.

2 Whether the underlying financial statements are based on historical costs or current costs.

3 The identity and level of the general price index used at the balance sheet date and the movement in this index during the current and previous reporting periods (IAS, para. 39).

## Case study

If you have any doubts about technicalities involved in this discussion, you should reread Chapter 7 at this point. Perhaps thankfully, recent examples to illustrate accounting for hyperinflation are scarce. Our case study is not exactly recent, but it is within living memory of the authors, and it is for real! There is no doubt that the Russian airline, Aeroflot, was operating in a hyperinflationary economy according to IAS 29 in the year ended 31 December 1999. The Aeroflot financials quote annual inflation rates for the relevant three years as follows.

| For year ended 31 December | Annual inflation |
|---|---|
| 1999 | 36.70% |
| 1998 | 84.40% |
| 1997 | 11.00% |

However, Aeroflot, among its 'principal accounting policies', reported as follows:

The statutory (i.e. Russian statutory) amounts of non-monetary assets and liabilities have been adjusted to their historical cost denominated in US dollars, the functional currency of the Group (except for certain older assets independently valued in US dollars) so as to present the financial statements in accordance with IAS. The US dollar has been determined as the reporting currency of the Group on the basis that the majority of revenues are denominated in US dollars and settled in US dollars or other foreign currency, the majority of assets and liabilities are denominated in foreign currency, as is a significant portion of operating expenses. Accordingly, these financial statements are presented in US dollars. . . . Since US dollars are not the currency of a hyperinflationary economy, the provisions of IAS 29 have not been applied.

The consolidated statement of operations of Aeroflot for 1999 is shown in Table 23.1. A very significant reduction in the scale of operations is indicated. Revenue in

| TABLE 23.1 | Aeroflot and subsidiaries' consolidated statements of operations, 1999 | |
|---|---|---|
| | Year ended 31 December 1999 | Year ended 31 December 1998 |
| | $ million | $ million |
| Traffic revenue | 865.4 | 1 000.0 |
| Other revenue | 300.8 | 403.1 |
| **Revenue** | **1 166.2** | **1 403.1** |
| Operating costs | (908.9) | (1 103.9) |
| Staff costs | (118.0) | (170.3) |
| Depreciation and amortization expense | (132.0) | (135.1) |
| **Operating costs** | **(1 158.9)** | **(1 409.3)** |
| **Operating income (loss)** | 7.3 | (6.2) |
| Interest expense | (52.2) | (32.2) |
| Interest income | 0.9 | 2.0 |
| Share of income in associated undertakings | 4.6 | 4.4 |
| Foreign exchange and translation loss, net | (6.8) | (18.4) |
| Non-operating income (expenses), net | 40.1 | (25.1) |
| **Loss before taxation and minority interest** | (6.1) | (75.5) |
| Taxation | (52.2) | (134.2) |
| **Loss after taxation** | (58.3) | (209.7) |
| Minority interest | (1.3) | (1.2) |
| **Loss** | **(59.6)** | **(210.9)** |
| **Loss per share** | **($0.05)** | **($0.19)** |

1999 is 17 per cent down on 1998 and operating costs are 18 per cent down. However, the exchange rates for the rouble to the dollar are given in the notes as follows:

| At 31 December | Exchange rate |
|---|---|
| 1997 | $1 = 5.96 r |
| 1998 | $1 = 20.65 r |
| 1999 | $1 = 27.00 r |

Making a rough and simplistic calculation, the average rate of exchange for 1999 can be taken as the mid-point of the beginning and end rates and similarly for 1998. This simplistic calculation gives an average rate for 1999 of 23.82 and for 1998 of 13.31.

## ACTIVITY 23.1

Recalculate the figure for revenues and operating costs from Table 23.1 into historical roubles using the multiplicands given in the illustration and comment on the results.

*Activity feedback*
*The figures are as shown in Table 23.2.*
*Without claiming accuracy for the figures used, it is clear that the trend of activity indicated in nominal*

*(Continued)*

## ACTIVITY 23.1    (Continued)

roubles is the exact opposite of that suggested in the published financials. A significant increase in the scale of operations is now indicated. Also, the result for 1999 in nominal roubles is a profit under these assumptions (albeit small), not a loss. A further refinement of the figures in Table 23.2 is possible. The 1998 figures are expressed (as calculated) in 1998 roubles. Arguably, these should be re-expressed into 1999 roubles for comparison with the reported 1999 figures, i.e. the entire 1998 column in Table 23.2 could be multiplied by 136.7%. This would suggest that in real terms 1998 and 1999 revenues and expenses were not significantly different. Who said that accounting is an exact discipline?

The other question that arises in relation to the Aeroflot example is whether or not the bold claim in the quoted accounting policy that the treatment used, in avoiding IAS 29 adjustments, was in accordance with IAS, is actually correct. The answer is possibly, but, from 1 January 2005, this treatment would definitely not be permitted.

### TABLE 23.2    Aeroflot operating results (recalculated in roubles from Table 23.1)

|  | Year ended 31 December 1999 | Year ended 31 December 1998 |
|---|---|---|
|  | 000 million roubles | 000 million roubles |
| Traffic revenue | 20.614 | 13.310 |
| Other revenue | 7.165 | 5.365 |
| Revenue | 27.779 | 18.675 |
| Operating costs | 21.650 | 14.693 |
| Staff costs | 2.811 | 2.267 |
| Depreciation and amortization | 3.144 | 1.798 |
| Operating costs | 27.605 | 18.758 |
| Operating income (loss) | 0.174 | (0.083) |

## SUMMARY

In this chapter we explored the IAS regulations relating to accounting for inflation, as contained in IAS 29, and related these regulations to the theoretical issues discussed in Part One of this book.

## EXERCISES

*Suggested answers to exercises marked ✓ are to be found on our dedicated CourseMate platform for students.*

*Suggested answers to the remaining exercises are to be found on the Instructor online support resources.*

✓ **1**    Which phenomena is IAS 29 adjusting for when it is applied in the preparation of financial statements?

**2**    The idea that a regular annual inflation rate of 35 per cent requires CPP adjustments, but a regular annual inflation rate of 25 per cent does not, is quite absurd. Discuss.

**3**    Rework a numerical exercise from Chapter 7.

# STATEMENTS OF CASH FLOWS  24

**OBJECTIVES**  After studying this chapter you should be able to:

- identify the need for a statement of cash flows

- describe the difference between funds flow and cash flow

- explain why the IASB found it necessary to require cash flow rather than funds flow statements

- describe the requirements of IAS 7, *Statements of Cash Flow*

- prepare a statement of cash flows

- identify any problems in relation to a statement of cash flows.

## INTRODUCTION

A statement of cash flows, as we will see later, provides additional useful information to users; additional, that is, to the statement of comprehensive income and statement of financial position of an entity. The statement of cash flows emphasizes cash and liquidity rather than revenue, expenses and profit. IAS 7, which was first issued in 1977, originally required a funds flow statement, not a statement of cash flows. IAS 7 was revised in 1992 and now requires a statement of cash flows. Also note that IAS 7's title, before it was changed in 2007 as a result of changes in terminology introduced by IAS 1, was *Cash Flow Statements*. We will also discuss the difference between funds flow and cash flow within this chapter.

## PROFIT VERSUS CASH

The traditional accounting process is an uncertain and complex process. Not only is profit determination complex, it is potentially misleading. In any accounting year there will be a mixture of complete and incomplete transactions. Transactions are complete when they have led to a final cash settlement and these cause no profit measurement difficulties. Considerable problems arise, however, in dealing with incomplete transactions, where the profit or loss figure can only be estimated by means of the accruals concept, whereby revenue and costs are matched with one another so far as their relationship can be established or justifiably assumed and dealt with in the profit and loss account of the period to which they relate.

Thus, the profit for the past year is dependent on the validity of many assumptions about the future. For example, the future life of assets is estimated in order to calculate the depreciation charge for the past year.

The greater the volume of incomplete transactions, the greater the degree of estimation and, accordingly, the greater the risk that investors could turn out to have been misled if actual outcomes deviated from estimates.

To explore the differences between cash flow and profit reporting, consider Activity 24.1 below.

## ACTIVITY 24.1

Two short statements about the same business in the same year follow. Summarize in words what each statement is telling us, and suggest reasons for the differences between them.

| Statement A re: the business | €000 |
|---|---|
| Sales | 410 |
| *less* Cost of sales | 329 |
| | 81 |
| *less* Other expenses | 36 |
| | 45 |
| *less* Depreciation | 13 |
| | 32 |
| *less* Taxation provided | 13 |
| | 19 |
| *less* Dividend provided | 8 |
| Retained | 11 |

| Statement B re: the business | €000 |
|---|---|
| Sales received | 387 |
| *less* Payments for goods for sale | 333 |
| | 54 |
| *less* Other expenses paid | 32 |
| | 22 |
| *less* Capital expenditure | 20 |
| | 2 |
| *less* Taxation paid | 14 |
| | (12) |
| *less* Dividend paid | 7 |
| Increase in borrowing | (19) |

### Activity feedback

*Clearly, statement A is an income statement. It shows the revenues and expenses, calculated on the traditional bases, the taxation charges relating to the year, and the dividends which, it has been decided, should be paid*

*(Continued)*

## ACTIVITY 24.1 *(Continued)*

out to shareholders in relation to that year. It shows a profit and implies (although we do not know the size of the business) a successful year.

Statement B is a statement of cash movement in the year – a summary of the cash book but analyzed into the various reasons the cash has moved. The individual differences between the two statements will be due to

changes in accruals, prepayments and the like. Overall, statement B shows a reduction in the cash resources of the business before the payment of the dividend, and obviously shows an even bigger contraction in the cash resources of the business after the dividend payout in the year. Statement B surely implies an unsuccessful year.

## CASH FLOW REPORTING

People often talk about 'cash flows' or claim to be in favour of 'cash flow statements' or 'cash flow reporting' without being too precise about what they mean. In fact, different people are likely to mean significantly different things, and it is very important that we are able to separate out the various situations and arguments from one another.

At one level, it can be suggested that cash flow reporting – actual and budgeted – should completely replace both the statement of comprehensive income (on whatever basis) and the statement of financial position. The argument for this (ignoring barter situations) is that only cash represents and demonstrates an increase or decrease in the business resources and that this suggests both that only cash should be reported and that only cash need be reported. This argument is surely untenable. Users need information about changes in the command of a business organization over resources, over goods and services, or the power to obtain goods and services.

At a second level, it can be suggested that some form of statement of cash flows on the lines of statement *B* in Activity 24.1 – since it obviously gives information which is potentially useful and which is additional to, and different from, the information in the income statement – should be required as an additional statement in the final reporting package. This is surely logical. Indeed, it is arguable precisely because an income statement for the year is not a good indicator of the cash flow position for the year, and because a statement of cash flows for the year is not a good indicator of the profit and loss position for the year that the argument for including both is so powerful.

However, a weakness of a statement of cash flows, like that in Activity 24.1, is that it is an historical statement, as is a statement of financial position and a statement of comprehensive income. It gives no indication of future cash flows and whether an entity will be able to meet its debts in the future. A forecast statement of cash flows would be required for this.

## FUNDS FLOW OR CASH FLOW?

The funds flow statement, as traditionally prepared for many years, was (conceptually speaking) an extremely odd animal. It tried to adjust away some, but not all, of the accrual adjustments used in the creation of the income statement to start with. Historically, the reason for much of this obscurity was that the funds flow statement, being an additional statement not required by the law, was deliberately designed not to give additional information, but merely to rearrange information already available in a different form. Basically, the funds flow statement concentrated on changes in net current assets rather than cash.

So what is funds flow? Activity 24.2 should illustrate this for you.

## ACTIVITY 24.2

An extract from the balance sheet of A entity as at 31 December 20X9:

| | €000 | €000 |
|---|---|---|
| | 31.12.X9 | 31.12.X8 |
| Inventory | 4 300 | 4 600 |
| Accounts receivable | 2 600 | 1 300 |
| Cash and bank | 1 200 | 2 500 |
| | 8 100 | 8 400 |
| Accounts payable | 6 500 | 7 900 |
| Working capital | 1 600 | 500 |

### Activity feedback

*If we look solely at cash, we could state that A had experienced a decrease in cash of €1 300 000 over the year. Contrariwise, looking at working capital/net current assets provides a much better position; an increase of €1 100 000 over the year. But which figure should users of accounts have regard to when taking decisions?*

## Advantages of cash flow over funds flow

These can be summarized as follows:

- Funds flow data based on movements in working capital can obscure movements relevant to the liquidity and viability of an entity. For example, a significant decrease in cash available may be masked by an increase in inventory or accounts receivable. Entities may, therefore, run out of cash while reporting increases in working capital. Similarly, a decrease in working capital does not necessarily indicate a cash shortage and a danger of failure.

- As cash flow monitoring is a normal feature of business life and not a specialized accounting technique, cash flow is a concept which is more widely understood than are changes in working capital.

- Cash flows can be a direct input into a business valuation model and, therefore, historical cash flows may be relevant in a way not possible for funds flow data.

- A funds flow statement is based largely on the difference between two balance sheets. It reorganizes such data, but does not provide new data. The statement of cash flows may include data not disclosed in a funds flow statement.

So does a statement of cash flows have the relevant characteristics of useful information? Let us see if you can answer Activity 24.3.

## ACTIVITY 24.3

State whether you believe, given your knowledge so far, that cash flow is understandable, relevant, reliable and complete.

### Activity feedback

1 Understandable. *Certainly, cash is a concept that most people understand, whereas accrual*

*accounting takes us a few years to learn and even more years to understand the need for!*

2 Relevant. *Cash certainly is relevant as without it a business cannot operate. Entities may be able to show a healthy profit but have a very poor cash position as they are relying on borrowed funds.*

(*Continued*)

## ACTIVITY 24.3   (Continued)

**3** Reliable. *Cash is the end product of a transaction. It is realized! Whereas funds based on profit require us to estimate a point of realization of revenue prior to receipt of cash and the ultimate realization of cash can be in doubt. Cash is certainly free from bias.*

**4** Complete. *Is anything that is historical information providing a complete picture? A statement of cash flows shows information about the reporting entity's cash flows in the reporting period, but this provides incomplete information for assessing future cash flows. Some cash flows result from transactions that took place in an earlier period and some are expected to result in further cash flows in a future period.*

Looking back to Activity 24.2, where we noted that a healthy funds flow (working capital) of €1m masked a decrease in cash flow of €1.3m, we can see that the selection of funds or cash flow can have a major impact on a user's interpretation of an entity's financial position. It is also worth noting that cash is the 'life blood' of an entity and without it they cannot operate. Cash is also rather a difficult figure to manipulate.

## REQUIREMENTS OF IAS 7

### Scope

The IASB viewed cash flow reporting as so important that there are no exemptions for any entities. No matter what an entity's principal revenue-producing activities might be, they need cash to conduct their operation, to pay their obligations, and to provide returns to their investors; their users need this information as they are interested in how the entity uses and generates cash.

### Generation of cash flows and definitions

Cash flows within an entity can broadly be generated by three activities:

**1** Operating or principal revenue-producing activities, defined by IAS 7 as those activities that are not investing or financing.

**2** Investing activities; the acquisition and disposal of long-term assets and investments not included in cash equivalents.

**3** Financing activities; activities that result in changes in the size and composition of the equity capital and borrowings of the entity.

Some other definitions from IAS 7, for completeness, are:

- *Cash.* Comprises cash on hand and demand deposits.
- *Cash equivalents.* Short-term, highly-liquid investments that are readily convertible to known amounts of cash and which are subject to an insignificant risk of changes in value.

Now complete Activity 24.4.

## ACTIVITY 24.4

Provide examples of cash flows, both inflow and out-flow, from operating, investing and financing activities.

To help we provide an example for each category in Table 24.1. Now extend the table.

### TABLE 24.1  Examples of cash flows

| Operating activities | Investing activities | Financing activities |
| --- | --- | --- |
| Cash receipts from sale of goods and rendering of services | Cash payments to acquire fixed assets | Cash proceeds from issue of shares and other equity instruments |

### Activity feedback

*You may not have identified all the following but the definitive list, as given by IAS 7, is shown in Table 24.2.*

### TABLE 24.2  Definitive list of cash flows as given by IAS 7

| Operating activities | Investing activities | Financing activities |
| --- | --- | --- |
| Cash receipts from sale goods and rendering services | Cash payments to acquire fixed assets | Cash proceeds from issue of shares and other equity instruments |
| Cash receipts from royalties, fees, commissions and other revenue | Cash receipts from sale of fixed assets | Cash payments to owners to acquire or redeem the entity's shares |
| Cash payments to suppliers for goods and services | Cash payments to acquire equity or debt instruments of other entities and interests in joint ventures | Cash proceeds from issuing debentures, loans, notes, bonds, mortgages and other short- or long-term borrowings |
| Cash payments to and on behalf of employees | Cash advances and loans made to other parties | Cash repayments of amounts borrowed |
| Cash payments or refunds of income taxes unless they can be specifically identified with financing or investing activities | Cash receipts from the repayment of advances and loans made to other parties | Cash payments by a lessee for the reduction of the outstanding liability relating to a finance lease |
| Cash receipts and payments from contracts held for dealing or trading purposes | Cash payments for futures, forward contracts, options and swaps except when the contracts are held for dealing or trading purposes or the payments are classified as financing activities | Cash receipts and cash payments of an insurance entity for premiums and claims, annuities and other policy benefits |

The amount of cash flows from operating activities is highly important for users to assess whether enough cash has been generated from this source for the entity to repay loans, make investments in assets and pay dividends. Cash flows under the heading of operating activities are primarily derived from the principal revenue producing activities of the entity.

Separating out the cash flows from investing activities is also seen as important as this provides users with information on investment made in resources that will potentially generate future income and cash flows. Users require information on cash flows within financing activities so that they can predict claims on future cash flows from providers of capital to the entity.

## ACTIVITY 24.5

Identify in which category the following cash flows would be included:

1  An entity purchases a motor vehicle that it intends to sell on to a customer.

2  An entity purchases a motor vehicle that it intends to use as part of its delivery fleet.

3  An entity purchases a motor vehicle using a finance lease.

4  An entity gains the use of a motor vehicle under an operating lease.

5  An entity holds securities for dealing/trading purposes.

6  Interest paid and received and dividends received by an entity.

7  Dividends paid by an entity.

8  An entity purchases a building which it intends to rent to others.

### Activity feedback

1  *This is purchase of an inventory item and is therefore shown under operating activities.*

2  *This is purchase of a fixed asset for the entity and is therefore part of investing activities.*

3  *The entity has acquired the use of a fixed asset, but the cash flow of principal payments will be shown under financing activities. There will be no cash flow under investing activities.*

4  *This time the payments under the operating lease will be treated as cash flows under operating*

*activities, as they are viewed as a normal expense payment of the entity. Note that the motor vehicle, depending on the revenue-producing activities of the entity and how the financing of the motor vehicle is arranged, can be regarded as a cash flow of any of the three categories.*

5  *These are inventory to the dealing house and are therefore part of operating activities as they relate to the principal revenue-producing activities.*

6  *These are usually classified as operating cash flows for a financial institution, but may also be regarded as operating for other entities as they form part of the net profit calculation (IAS 7, para. 33). This paragraph also allows them to be treated as financing – interest paid, or investing – interest and dividends received. The latter alternative seems more sensible to us.*

7  *Dividends paid are obviously financing as they are a cost of obtaining finance. However, IAS 7 allows an alternative categorization under operating activities. This is to enable users to judge the ability of the entity to pay dividends out of operating cash flows. We find this lack of consistency over the treatment of interest and dividends received and paid confusing and it will certainly impair comparability of cash flows between entities where different alternatives have been used.*

8  *This is the purchase of an asset that results in rental income and therefore must be regarded as a cash outflow under operating activities, not investing activities. The rental received will be cash inflow under operating activities.*

## Cash and cash equivalents

The definitions of these are important as cash flows are defined as inflows and outflows of cash and cash equivalents. It should be apparent to you that an investment, dependent on our view of short-term or highly liquid, could be viewed as a cash and cash equivalent, a cash flow item or an investing activity. Bank borrowings are generally viewed, according to IAS 7, as financing activities, but in certain circumstances bank overdrafts can be viewed as part of cash and cash equivalents. These circumstances are where the overdraft forms an integral part of the entity's cash management. Activity 24.6 demonstrates these definitions so make sure you complete it.

## ACTIVITY 24.6

Determine whether the following items are cash, cash equivalents, investing activities or financing.

1  An account held with a bank where withdrawals require 90 days' notice.

2  An account held with a bank where withdrawals require 95 days' notice.

3  An overdraft with the bank which is seen as short-term and part of everyday cash flows of the entity.

4  A loan from the bank for 60 days for a specific purpose.

5  An investment with a bank which has 60 days to maturity, but its final value is subject to significant risk as it is based on the index achievable at that time from a highly fluctuating stock market.

### Activity feedback

1  If you view 90 days as short-term then this is cash equivalent.

2  If you view 95 days as long-term then this would be investing.

3  Cash as part of cash management.

4  Financing as a loan for a specific purpose cannot be viewed as everyday cash management.

5  This investment has a significant risk attached to it in terms of its final value and therefore must be regarded as investing activities.

The decision with regards to 1 and 2 in this activity is clarified by IAS 7 (para. 7) as follows:

An investment normally qualifies as a cash equivalent only when it has a short maturity of, say, three months or less from date of acquisition. It must be readily convertible to a known amount of cash and be subject to an insignificant risk of changes in value.

The decisions required here are quite subjective and it is feasible for one entity to determine an investment as a cash equivalent and for another to determine this as an investing item.

## FORMAT OF CASH FLOW STATEMENT

IAS 7 requires entities to report cash flows during a period in a statement identifying cash flows classified by operating, investing and financing activities. This implies a simple statement as follows:

*Statement of cash flows*
| | |
|---|---|
| Cash flows from operating activities | A |
| Cash flows from investing activities | B |
| Cash flows from financing activities | C |
| Net change in cash and cash equivalents | X |

However, the Standard, in order to provide relevant information to users, requires each of these cash flows to be separated into their constituent parts, i.e.:

1  Gross cash receipts and gross cash payments arising from investing and financing activities. Note here that if a single transaction has cash flows involving financing, investing and operating activities, then the transaction will need to be split into its constituent parts. An example of such a transaction is a finance lease payment where the principal repayment will be disclosed as a cash flow under financing and the interest payment can be disclosed under operating or financing.

2  Gross cash receipts and payments from operating activities or net profit adjusted for effects of a non-cash nature.

3  Cash flows under any of the three sections can be reported net where the cash flows reflect the activities of the customer rather than the entity, or where items are large, maturities short and turnover quick.

4  Cash flows relating to extraordinary items should be identified separately under each category.

5  Cash flows relating to taxes, interest and dividends received and paid, acquisitions and disposals of subsidiaries and other business units.

In addition, the components of cash and cash equivalents are required together with a reconciliation of the amounts in the statement of cash flows, with the equivalent items reported in the statements of financial position.

## Direct or indirect method of determining cash flows

Item 2 in the list above indicates that there are two methods for determining cash flows from operating activities, from cash receipts and payments known as the *direct method*, or from adjusting net profit for non-cash receipts and payments known as the *indirect method*. The Standard prefers the direct method as it 'provides information which may be useful in estimating future cash flows which is not available under the indirect method'. Strangely, the UK ASB requires the indirect method as it does not believe that the benefits to the users of the direct method outweigh the costs of preparing it.

### ACTIVITY 24.7

1  What information would the direct method provide to users that the indirect method would not?

2  Why might the direct method be more costly to prepare than the indirect?

3  How should a non-cash transaction be dealt with in a statement of cash flows?

#### Activity feedback

1  The direct method would identify cash receipts from customers and cash payments to suppliers and employees, whereas the indirect method would only show net profit with its adjustments for depreciation, profit on disposal and changes in working capital, and so on. The actual disclosure of cash receipts and payments enables users to evaluate future cash flows more easily.

2  Entities operate an accounting system that is geared towards accrual accounting. The direct method would require a company to use either an accounting system: (a) which directly records and analyzes the cash flow in relation to each transaction, thus operating two accounting systems; or (b) to adjust sales, costs of sales and other items in the income statement for non-cash items, changes in working capital and other items which relate to investing or financing activities – a time-consuming and costly business. If we take the view that information should be provided that is useful to users – the view of the Framework – then we must support the direct method for the disclosure of operating cash flows.

3  Quite obviously it shouldn't be dealt with as it does not involve a cash flow!

Examples of non-cash transactions given in the Standard are:

• acquisition of assets either by assuming directly related liabilities or by means of a finance lease

• acquisition of an entity by means of an equity issue

• conversion of debt to equity.

All these involve the exchange of a non-cash asset for a non-cash liability, or conversion from one asset or liability to another. These types of transaction will be reported elsewhere in the financial statements.

## ACTIVITY 24.8

From the following information relating to Zen entity, calculate the cash flows from operating activities using both the direct and indirect method.

*Consolidated statement of comprehensive income for the period ended 31 December 20X2*

| | €000 |
|---|---|
| Sales | 30 650 |
| Cost of sales | 26 000 |
| Gross profit | 4 650 |
| Depreciation | (450) |
| Administration and selling expenses | (730) |
| Interest expense | (400) |
| Investment income | 500 |
| Foreign exchange loss | (40) |
| Net profit before taxation | 3 530 |
| Taxes on income | (300) |
| Net profit | 3 230 |

*Consolidated statement of financial position as at 31 December 20X2*

| | 20X2 €000 | €000 | 20X1 €000 | €000 |
|---|---|---|---|---|
| *Assets* | | | | |
| Cash and cash equivalents | | 410 | | 160 |
| Account receivable | | 1 900 | | 1 200 |
| Inventory | | 1 000 | | 1 950 |
| Portfolio investments | | 2 500 | | 2 500 |
| Property, plant and equipment at cost | 3 730 | | 1 910 | |
| Accumulated depreciation | (1 450) | 2 280 | (1 060) | 850 |
| Total assets | | 8 090 | | 6 660 |
| *Liabilities* | | | | |
| Trade payables | | 250 | | 1 890 |
| Interest payable | | 230 | | 100 |
| Income taxes payable | | 400 | | 1 000 |
| Long-term debt | | 2 300 | | 1 040 |
| Total liabilities | | 3 180 | | 4 030 |
| *Shareholders' equity* | | | | |
| Share capital | | 1 500 | | 1 250 |
| Retained earnings | | 3 410 | | 1 380 |
| Total shareholders' equity | | 4 910 | | 2 630 |
| Total liabilities and shareholders' equity | | 8 090 | | 6 660 |

Other information is available as follows:

(a) All the shares of a subsidiary were acquired for €590 000. The fair values of assets acquired and liabilities assumed were as follows:

| | €000 |
|---|---|
| Inventories | 100 |
| Accounts receivable | 100 |
| Cash | 40 |
| Property, plant and equipment | 650 |
| Trade payables | 100 |
| Long-term debt | 200 |

(b) €250 000 was raised from the issue of shares and €250 000 from long-term borrowings.

(c) Interest expense was €400 000, of which €170 000 was paid during the period. €100 000 relating to interest expense of the prior period was also paid during the period.

(d) Dividends paid were €1 200 000.

(e) The liability for tax at the beginning and end of the period was €1 000 000 and €400 000 respectively. During the period, a further €200 000 tax was provided for. Withholding tax on dividends received during the period of €200 000 amounted to €100 000.

(f) During the period, the group acquired property, plant and equipment with an aggregate cost of €1 250 000, of which €900 000 was acquired by means of finance leases. Cash payments of €350 000 were made to purchase property, plant and equipment.

(g) Plant, with original cost of €80 000 and accumulated depreciation of €60 000, was sold for €20 000.

(h) Accounts receivable as at end 31 December 20X2 include €100 000 of interest receivable.

(Adapted from example in Appendix A to IAS 7)

### Activity feedback

*Direct method*
*Cash flow from operations:*

| | |
|---|---|
| Cash receipts from customers (working 1) | 30 150 |
| Cash paid to suppliers and employees (working 2) | (27 420) |
| Cash generated from operations | 2 730 |
| Interest paid (170 + 100 note c) | (270) |
| Income taxes paid (1000 + 200 + 100 − 400) | (900) |
| Cash flow | 1 560 |

*(Continued)*

## ACTIVITY 24.8 (Continued)

*Working 1*

| | | |
|---|---|---|
| Sales – income statement | 30 650 | |
| *add* Opening accounts receivable | 1 200 | |
| *less* Closing accounts receivable | (1 800) | (1 900 – 100 h) |
| *add* Subsidiary accounts receivable | 100 | |
| | 30 150 | |

*Working 2*

| | | |
|---|---|---|
| Cost of sales – income statement | 26 000 | |
| *less* Opening stock | (1 950) | |
| *add* Closing stock | 1 000 | |
| Purchases | 25 050 | |
| *less* Closing trade payables | (250) | |
| *add* Opening trade payables | 1 890 | |
| | 26 690 | |
| Admin and selling expenses | 730 | |
| | 27 420 | |
| Subsidiary trade payables (a) | 100 | |
| *less* Subsidiary inventories (a) | (100) | |
| | 27 420 | |

*(Note: interest and income taxes paid are treated as part of operating activities, dividends paid are not.)*

*Indirect method*

| | | |
|---|---|---|
| Net profit before tax and dividends | 3 530 | |
| *add* Back interest | (100) | |
| Foreign exchange loss | 40 | |
| Depreciation | 450 | |
| | 3 920 | |
| Increase in trade and other receivables | (500) | (700 – 100 subsidiary – 100 interest receivable) |
| Decrease in inventories | 1050 | (950 + 100 subsidiary) |
| Decrease in trade payables | (1 740) | (1 640 + 100 subsidiary) |
| Cash generated from operations | 2 730 | |
| Interest paid | (270) | |
| Income taxes paid | (900) | |
| Net cash flow from operating activities | 1 560 | |

# Cash flows from investing activities

Complete the following activities.

## ACTIVITY 24.9

Now calculate the cash flow from investing activities from the data given in Activity 24.8.

### Activity feedback

*Investing activities cover cash flows in respect of fixed assets, investments in equity or debt, advances and loans to other parties. The balance sheet changes identify any increases/decreases in portfolio investments and property, plant and equipment, and we were also informed about an acquisition of a subsidiary. Therefore:*

| | | |
|---|---|---|
| Cash flow from investing activities | | |
| Acquisition of subsidiary less cash acquired | (550) | (590 – 40) |
| Purchase of property, plant and equipment | (350) | (note f) or (working 1) |
| Proceeds from sale of equipment | 20 | (note g) |
| Dividends received | 200 | (note c) |
| Interest received (investment income – dividends) | 200 | |
| Net cash used in investing activities | (480) | |

| *Working 1* | |
|---|---|
| Opening balance sheet of property, etc., at cost | 1 910 |
| *add* Subsidiary bought | 650 |
| *less* Sale | (80) |
| | 2 480 |
| Closing balance sheet at cost | 3 730 |
| | 1 250 |
| Leased assets so no cash flow | (900) |
| Therefore, assets bought for cash | 350 |

## ACTIVITY 24.10

Now identify the cash flows from financing activities from the data in Activity 24.8.

*Activity feedback*

*Cash flow from financing activities covers proceeds from the issue of shares, loans, etc., and repayments of amounts borrowed.*

*Cash flow from financing activities*

| | | |
|---|---|---|
| Proceeds from issuing shares | 250 | (note b) |
| Proceeds from long-term borrowings | 250 | (note b) |
| Payments of finance lease (working 1) | (90) | |
| Dividends paid | (1 200) | (note d) |
| | (790) | |

Working 1

| | |
|---|---|
| Opening balance sheet long-term debt | 1 040 |
| add Finance lease principal | 900 |
| | 1 940 |
| add Subsidiary long-term loan | 200 |
| | 2 140 |
| New loans | 250 |
| | 2 390 |
| Closing balance sheet long-term debt | 2 300 |
| Therefore, lease principal repaid | 90 |

## Statement of cash flows

If you put the answers of Activities 24.8, 24.9 and 24.10 together and add on cash and cash equivalent changes, you have a full statement of cash flows for the data in Activity 24.8 as follows.

*Direct method cash flow statement*

Cash flow from operating activities

| | | |
|---|---|---|
| Cash receipts from customers (working 1) | 30 150 | |
| Cash paid to suppliers and employees (working 2) | (27 420) | |
| Cash generated from operations | 2 730 | |
| Interest paid (170 + 100 note c) | (270) | |
| Income taxes paid (1 000 + 200 + 100 − 400) | (900) | |
| **Net cash flow from operating activities** | | **1 560** |
| Cash flow from investing activities | | |
| Acquisition of subsidiary less cash acquired | (550) | (590 − 40) |
| Purchase of property, plant and equipment | (350) | (note f) or (working 1) |
| Proceeds from sale of equipment | 20 | (note g) |
| Dividends received | 200 | (note c) |
| Interest received (investment income − dividends) | 200 | |
| Net cash used in investing activities | | (480) |

*Cash flow from financing activities*

| | | |
|---|---|---|
| Proceeds from issuing shares | 250 | (note b) |
| Proceeds from long-term borrowings | 250 | (note b) |
| Payments of finance lease (working 1) | (90) | |
| Dividends paid | (1 200) | (note d) |
| **Net cash used in financing activities** | (790) | |
| **Net increase in cash and cash equivalents** | 290 | |
| Cash and cash equivalents at beginning of period (160–40 f. e. l.) | 120 | |
| Cash and cash equivalents at and period | 410 | |

*Notes to statement of cash flows*

Notes to this cash flow are required in respect of:

- the fair value of assets and liabilities of the subsidiary acquired
- the amount of property, plant and equipment acquired by finance lease
- detailed analysis of the cash equivalents
- segmental cash flows.

IAS 7, Appendix A illustrates these notes.

## PREPARATION OF STATEMENT OF CASH FLOWS

The next activity requires you to prepare a rather more complicated statement of cash flows.

## ACTIVITY 24.11

The balance sheet of Axbrit entity for the year ended 31 March 20X2 is as follows:

| Assets | 20X2 | 20X1 |
|---|---|---|
| Cash and cash equivalents | 27 | 21 |
| Accounts receivable | 15 | 18 |
| Inventory | 25 | 20 |
| Property, plant and equipment at cost | 230 | 160 |
| Accumulated depreciation | (60) | (44) |
| Total assets | 237 | 175 |
| Liabilities | | |
| Trade payables | 47 | 39 |
| Income taxes payable | 16 | 12 |
| Long-term debt | 32 | 30 |
| Total liabilities | 95 | 81 |

| Shareholders' equity | | |
|---|---|---|
| Share capital | 33 | 27 |
| Capital reserves | 30 | 24 |
| Retained earnings | 79 | 43 |
| Total shareholders' equity | 142 | 94 |
| Total liabilities and shareholders' equity | 237 | 175 |

Prepare the statement of cash flows for the year ended 31 March 20X2 given that no property, plant and equipment was sold during the period and that the increase in long-term debt took place on 1 April 20X2 and carried a 10 per cent rate of interest and that dividends paid during the year were €18.

*(Continued)*

## ACTIVITY 24.11    *(Continued)*

### *Activity feedback*

*As we are not given the statement of comprehensive income or any other information to enable us to derive net cash flow from operating activities using the direct method we have to use the indirect method in this example.*

*Indirect method net cash flow from operating activities*

| | | |
|---|---|---|
| Net profit (change in retained earnings + dividends) | | 54 |
| Add interest on long-term loans | 3.2 | |
| Add taxation charge (assume liability at end is charge for period) | 16 | |
| | | 19.2 |
| Net profit before taxation | | 73.2 |
| *add* Depreciation | 16 | |
| Increase in inventories | (5) | |
| Decrease in accounts receivable | 3 | |
| Increase in trade payables | 8 | 22 |
| Cash generated from operations | | 95.2 |

| | | |
|---|---|---|
| Interest paid | | (3.2) |
| Income taxes paid | | (12) |
| Net cash flow investing activities | | 80 |
| Cash flow from investing activities | | |
| Purchase of property, plant and equipment | 70 | |
| Net cash used in investing activities | | (70) |
| Cash flow from financing activities | | |
| Proceeds from issues of shares | 12 | |
| Proceeds from long-term borrowings | 2 | |
| Dividends paid | (18) | |
| Net cash used in financing activities | | (4) |
| Net increase in cash and cash equivalents | | 6 |
| Cash and cash equivalents at beginning of period | | 21 |
| Cash and cash equivalents at end of period | | 27 |

The following activity is a good test of your understanding so far, so complete it before reading the feedback.

## ACTIVITY 24.12

From the statement of comprehensive income and statements of financial position of Thomas Manufacturing entity prepare the statement of cash flows for the year ended 31 December 20X5.

### Thomas Manufacturing statement of comprehensive income for the year ended 31.12.X5

| | € 000 | € 000 |
|---|---|---|
| Sales | | 5 000 |
| Change in inventories | | 500 |
| Own work capitalized | | 150 |
| Other operating income | | 50 |
| Raw materials and consumables | (2 000) | |
| Other external charges | (770) | (2 770) |
| Employee costs | | (1 500) |

| | | |
|---|---|---|
| Depreciation and amortization | | (400) |
| Other operating charges | | (100) |
| | | 930 |
| Income from investments – dividends | | 20 |
| Other interest receivable | | 5 |
| | | 955 |
| Interest payable | | (160) |
| Income before income taxes | | 795 |
| Income taxes | | (317) |
| Income for period | | 478 |
| Dividends paid for the period were €250 000 | | |

*(Continued)*

## ACTIVITY 24.12 (Continued)

Statements of financial position as at 31 12.X4 ... 12.X5

| Cost €000 | Net €000 | | Cost €000 | Deprec. €000 | Net €000 |
|---|---|---|---|---|---|
| | | Non-current assets | | | |
| 200 | 100 | Intangible | 350 | 200 | 150 |
| 1 500 | 800 | Property, plant and equipment | 2 500 | 775 | 1 725 |
| 100 | 100 | Investments | 200 | | 200 |
| 1 800 | 1 000 | | 3 050 | 975 | 2 075 |
| | | Current assets | | | |
| | 1 000 | Inventories | | 1 600 | |
| | 1 000 | Accounts receivable | | 1 200 | |
| | 50 | Investments | | | |
| | 250 | Cash | | 30 | 2 830 |
| | 2 300 | Shareholders' equity | | | 4 905 |
| | 3 300 | | | | |
| | 1 000 | Ordinary shares | | | 1 500 |
| | 200 | Capital reserves | | | 800 |
| | 177 | Retained earnings | | | 405 |
| | 1 377 | | | | 2 705 |
| | | Liabilities | | | |
| | | long term | | | |
| | 980 | Loans | | | 790 |
| | | short-term | | | |
| 600 | | Accounts payable | | 750 | |
| | | Loans | | 257 | |
| 243 | | Taxation | | 274 | |
| | 843 | | | | 1 281 |
| | 100 | Deferred taxes | | | 129 |
| | 923 | | | | 1 200 |
| | 3 300 | | | | 4 905 |

Further information is available as follows:

- As at 1 January X5, freehold land was revalued from €500 000 to €1 000 000.

- During the year ended 31 December X5, plant and equipment costing €300 000, written down to €50 000 at 31 December X4, was sold for €75 000. These book gains and losses were adjusted in to the depreciation charge in the income statement.

- Own work capitalized refers to development work carried forward as an intangible asset.

- Loans with a nominal value of €190 000 were redeemed at par during the year.

- Shares were issued for cash during the year; there were no purchases of the company's own shares.

- The investments shown as current assets at 31 December X4 and not regarded as cash equivalent were sold during the year for €50 000.

### Activity feedback

Indirect statement of cash flows for Thomas Manufacturing:

### Cash flow from operating activities

| | €000 | €000 |
|---|---|---|
| Net profit before tax | | 795 |
| Adjustments for: | | |
| Depreciation (400 + 25 gain adj. on sale into dep.) | 425 | |
| Profit on sale of plant and equipment | (25) | |
| Investment income | (25) | |

(Continued)

## ACTIVITY 24.12   (Continued)

| | €000 | €000 |
|---|---|---|
| Interest expense | 160 | 535 |
| Operating profit before working capital changes | | 1 330 |
| Increase in trade and other receivables | (200) | |
| Increase in inventories | (600) | |
| Increase in trade payables | 150 | (650) |
| Cash generated from operations | | 680 |
| Interest paid | | (160) |
| Income taxes paid (note 1) | | (257) |
| Net cash from operating activities | | 263 |

### Cash flow from investing activities

| | | |
|---|---|---|
| Purchase of intangible fixed assets | (150) | |
| Purchase of property, plant and equipment (note 2) | (800) | |
| Purchase of investments | (100) | |
| Proceeds from sale of investments | 50 | |
| Proceeds from sale of equipment | 75 | |
| Interest received | 5 | |
| Dividends received | 20 | |
| Net cash used in investing activities | | (900) |

### Cash flow from financing activities

| | | |
|---|---|---|
| Proceeds from issues of shares | 600 | |
| Proceeds from long-term borrowings | 257 | |
| Redemption of loans | (190) | |
| Dividends paid | (250) | |
| Net cash from financing activities | | 417 |

### Net decrease in cash and cash equivalents

| | | |
|---|---|---|
| Cash and cash equivalents at beginning of period | | (220) |
| Cash and cash equivalents at end of period | | 250 |
| | | 30 |

**Note 1**

| | €000 |
|---|---|
| Opening balance of taxes (243 + 100) | 343 |
| Add income statement charge (325 − 8) | 317 |
| | 660 |
| Closing balance of taxes (274 + 129) | 403 |
| Therefore taxes paid during the year | 257 |

**Note 2**

| | €000 |
|---|---|
| Opening balance of assets at cost | 1 500 |
| add Revaluation during the year | 500 |
| less Sale at cost | (300) |
| | 1 700 |
| Closing balance at cost | 2 500 |
| Therefore purchase of assets | 800 |

## Disclosure Requirements of IAS 7

As an example of disclosure required in respect of statements of cash flows by IAS 7 we present the statements of cash flow from Samsung included in its financial statements of 2011 (pp. 38–39). Samsung presents for comparative purposes its cash flow information in the Korean currency and in US dollars:

## REAL WORLD ILLUSTRATION

### Consolidate Statements of Cash Flows
*Samsung Electronics Co., Ltd and its subsidiaries*

*(In millions of Korean won, in thousands of US dollars (note 2.27))*
*For the years ended December 31*

| | Notes | 2011 KRW | 2010 KRW | 2011 USD | 2010 USD |
|---|---|---|---|---|---|
| **Cash flows from operating activities** | | | | | |
| Profit for the year | | 13 734 067 | 16 146 525 | 11 908 495 | 14 000 282 |
| Adjustments | 29 | 16 475 605 | 14 088 323 | 14 285 620 | 12 215 662 |
| Changes in operating assets and liabilities | 29 | (4 057 345) | (5 668 035) | (3 518 031) | (4 914 623) |
| Cash flows from operating activities | | 26 152 327 | 24 566 813 | 22 676 084 | 21 301 321 |
| | | | | | *(Continued)* |

# REAL WORLD ILLUSTRATION  (*Continued*)

*(In millions of Korean won, in thousands of US dollars (note 2.27))*
*For the years ended December 31*

| | Notes | 2011 KRW | 2010 KRW | 2011 USD | 2010 USD |
|---|---|---|---|---|---|
| Interest received | | 755 859 | 457 508 | 655 388 | 396 695 |
| Interest paid | | (641 462) | (582 292) | (556 197) | (504 892) |
| Dividend received | | 628 585 | 1 520 037 | 545 032 | 1 317 989 |
| Income tax paid | | (3 977 408) | (2 135 287) | (3 448 719) | (1 851 458) |
| **Net cash generated from operating activities** | | **22 917 901** | **23 826 779** | **19 871 588** | **20 659 655** |
| **Cash flows from investing activities** | | | | | |
| Net decrease (increase) in short-term financial instruments | | 75 666 | (2 991 820) | 65 608 | (2 594 139) |
| Net decrease in short-term available-for-sale financial assets | | 518 479 | 981 599 | 449 561 | 851 122 |
| Proceeds from disposal of long-term available-for-sale financial assets | | 415 096 | 9 207 | 359 920 | 7 983 |
| Acquisition of long-term available-for-sale financial assets | | (419 678) | (414 978) | (363 893) | (359 818) |
| Proceeds from disposal of associates and joint ventures | | 306 804 | 277 907 | 266 023 | 240 967 |
| Acquisition of associates and joint ventures | | (403 538) | (243) | (349 899) | (211) |
| Disposal of property and equipment | | 379 878 | 1 228 007 | 329 384 | 1 064 777 |
| Purchases of property and equipment | | (21 965 678) | (21 619 244) | (19 045 936) | (18 745 551) |
| Disposal of intangible assets | | 9 703 | 16 620 | 8 413 | 14 411 |
| Purchases of intangible assets | | (663 678) | (1 259 895) | (575 460) | (1 092 426) |
| Proceeds from deposits | | 461 454 | 366 304 | 400 116 | 317 614 |
| Payment for deposits | | (594 067) | (420 986) | (515 102) | (365 027) |
| Cash inflows (outflows) from business combination | | (522 740) | 47 549 | (453 256) | 41 229 |
| Cash inflows from disposal of business | | 925 454 | 179 437 | 802 440 | 155 586 |
| Others | | 364 281 | (384 341) | 315 860 | (333 253) |
| **Net cash used in investing activities** | | **(21 112 564)** | **(23 984 877)** | **(18 306 221)** | **(20 796 736)** |
| **Cash flows from financing activities** | | | | | |
| Net proceeds from short-term borrowings | | 977 315 | 868 156 | 847 407 | 752 758 |
| Disposal of treasury stock | | 160 827 | 184 291 | 139 449 | 159 795 |
| Proceeds from debentures and long-term borrowings | | 3 925 406 | 1 137 646 | 3 403 630 | 986 427 |
| Repayment of debentures and long-term borrowings | | (1 145 167) | (304 074) | (992 948) | (263 656) |
| Payment of dividends | | (874 608) | (1 917 637) | (758 353) | (1 662 739) |
| Others | | 65 956 | (120 677) | 57 189 | (104 636) |
| **Net cash provided by (used in) financing activities** | | **3 109 729** | **(152 295)** | **2 696 374** | **(132 051)** |
| **Effect of exchange rate changes on cash and cash equivalents** | | **(14 724)** | **(48 118)** | **(12 767)** | **(41 722)** |
| **Net increase (decrease) in cash and cash equivalents** | | **4 900 342** | **(358 511)** | **4 248 974** | **(310 854)** |
| **Cash and cash equivalents** | | | | | |
| Beginning of the year | | 9 791 419 | 10 149 930 | 8 489 915 | 8 800 769 |
| **End of the year** | | **14 691 761** | **9 791 419** | **12 738 889** | **8 489 915** |

## THE FUTURE

The statement of cash flows is set to be reviewed under the joint project of the IASB/FASB on presentation of financial information in individual statements. Initial discussions are focusing on:

- the need to specify the direct method of calculating cash flows from operations as a requirement
- the need to specify a reconciliation schedule of statements of cash flows to the statement of comprehensive income
- the notion that cash equivalents should not be retained in financial statement presentation
- the need to ensure cohesiveness of financial statements.

### Direct method

As we stated earlier, the IASB prefers the use of the direct method but did not require it in IAS 7 due to the concerns about the cost of preparing a direct method statement of cash flows. It now emerges that there are two approaches to preparing the direct method of cash flows:

- The 'bottom-up' or 'cash ledger' approach (referred to as the 'direct-direct method'). Under this approach, cash receipts and payments are determined by aggregating cash flow amounts from cash ledgers. This is a costly approach.
- The 'top-down' or 'financial statement' approach (referred to as the 'indirect-direct method'). Under this approach, cash receipts and payments are determined by adjusting revenues, expenses, and gains and losses for the change in the related accrual over the period. This approach, it is thought, would be cheaper than the direct-direct method.

### Reconciliation schedule

This would form a new schedule in the financial statements and would be columnar as follows:

| Cash flows | Cash flows not affecting income | Valuation adjustments | All other changes | Comprehensive income |
|---|---|---|---|---|
| A | B | C | D | A – B + C + D |

with a line for each item on the cash flow and comprehensive income statement.

Whether such a complicated reconciliation statement will be of use to users remains to be seen.

## Cohesiveness of financial statements

Within the IASB/FASB joint project on statements of cash flow, the IASB is suggesting that all three statements (i.e. the statement of comprehensive income, the statement of financial position and the statement of cash flows) should use the same section names. The proposed sections are:

*Business* – operating cash flows and investing cash flows

*Financing* – financing asset cash flows and financing liability cash flows

*Income taxes*

*Discontinued operations*

*Equity*

### SUMMARY

Within this chapter we have attempted to show you how to draw up a statement of cash flows using both the direct and indirect method and we highlighted some of the problems associated with it. These problems are:

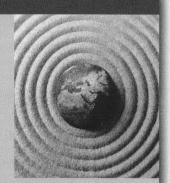

- the arbitrary three-month cut-off for cash equivalents

- the choice of category for interest and dividends

- the difficulty of producing direct cash flows

- the lack of user information in indirect cash flows

- the historical nature of the statement of cash flows.

On the whole, however, the statement of cash flows under IAS 7 is certainly an improvement on the previous funds flow statement and the production of cash flow information provides important information to users. We will deal with the analysis of cash flow statements in Chapter 32.

## EXERCISES

*Suggested answers to exercises marked ✓ are to be found on our dedicated CourseMate platform for students.*

*Suggested answers to the remaining exercises are to be found on the Instructor online support resources.*

1 Comment on the usefulness of both funds flow statements and statements of cash flows to users.

2 Cash is a very difficult figure to fiddle. David Tweedie (former Chairman of the IASB). Discuss.

3 Compare and contrast the direct and indirect method of preparing a statement of cash flows and identify and comment on the reasons why the IASB prefers the direct method.

4 Using the statement of cash flows provided in respect of the Samsung analysis, as far as the information permits, analyze the performance of the group.

✓ 5 Discuss the proposition that a statement of cash flows is more useful to users than an income statement.

6 Differentiate, using illustrative examples where necessary, between cash and cash equivalents.

7 Cash flows should be defined as increases or decreases in cash. Discuss.

8 The following information is available in respect of Barn entity.

*Statement of comprehensive income for the year ended 30 September 20X7*

|  | £m | £m | £m |
|---|---|---|---|
| Gross profit |  |  | 280 |
| Depreciation |  | 60 |  |
| Interest receivable | (10) |  |  |
| Interest payable | 16 | 6 |  |
| Profit on sale of assets |  | (16) |  |
| Impairment of intangibles |  | 40 | 90 |
| Net profit before tax |  |  | 190 |
| Tax |  |  | 80 |
| Net profit after tax |  |  | 110 |
| Dividends paid and proposed |  |  | 80 |
| Retained earnings |  |  | 30 |

*Statements of financial position as at:*

|  | 30.9.X6 £m | 30.9.X7 £m |
|---|---|---|
| **Assets** | | |
| Non-current assets | | |
| Intangibles | 240 | 280 |
| Property, plant and equipment | 640 | 778 |
| | 880 | 1 058 |
| Current assets | | |
| Inventory | 60 | 68 |
| Trade receivables | 48 | 44 |
| Cash and bank | 128 | 144 |
| | 236 | 256 |
| Total assets | 1 116 | 1 314 |
| **Equity and liabilities** | | |
| Equity | | |
| Ordinary share capital | 500 | 600 |
| Share premium | 40 | 60 |
| Retained earnings | 192 | 222 |
| | 732 | 882 |
| Non-current liabilities | 200 | 240 |
| Current liabilities | | |
| Trade payables | 64 | 72 |
| Dividends | 30 | 40 |
| Tax | 90 | 80 |
| | 184 | 192 |
| Total equity and liabilities | 1 116 | 1 314 |

The sale proceeds from the sale of non-current assets was £72m. All interest due has been received and the interest payable has been paid.

**Required:**
(a) Prepare the statement of cash flows for Barn entity for the year ended 30 September 20X7 in accordance with IAS 7, Cash Flow Statements. (Notes to the cash flow statement are not required.)
(b) Identify two limitations of a cash flow statement.

**9** The following information is available in respect of Theta entity.

*Statement of comprehensive income for the year ended 31 December 20X7*

|  | £m | £m | £m |
|---|---|---|---|
| Gross profit |  |  | 420 |
| Depreciation |  | 90 |  |
| Interest receivable | (15) |  |  |
| Interest payable | 24 | 9 |  |
| Profit on sale of assets |  | (24) |  |
| Impairment of intangibles |  | 60 | 135 |
| Net profit before tax |  |  | 285 |
| Tax |  |  | 120 |
| Net profit after tax |  |  | 165 |
| Dividends paid and proposed |  |  | 120 |
| Retained earnings |  |  | 45 |

*Statements of financial position as at:*

|  | 31.12.X6 £m | 31.12.X7 £m |
|---|---|---|
| **Assets** |  |  |
| *Non-current assets* |  |  |
| Intangibles | 360 | 420 |
| Property, plant and equipment | 960 | 1 167 |
|  | 1 320 | 1 587 |
| *Current assets* |  |  |
| Inventory | 90 | 102 |
| Trade receivables | 72 | 66 |
| Cash and bank | 192 | 216 |
|  | 354 | 384 |
| Total assets | 1 674 | 1 971 |
| **Equity and liabilities** |  |  |
| *Equity* |  |  |
| Ordinary share capital | 750 | 900 |
| Share premium | 60 | 90 |
| Retained earnings | 288 | 333 |
|  | 1 098 | 1 323 |
| Non-current liabilities | 300 | 360 |
| Current liabilities |  |  |
| Trade payables | 96 | 108 |
| Dividends | 45 | 60 |

*Statements of financial position as at:*

|  | 31.12.X6 | 31.12.X7 |
|---|---|---|
| **Assets** | £m | £m |
| Tax | 135 | 120 |
|  | 276 | 288 |
| Total equity and liabilities | 1 674 | 1 971 |

The sale proceeds from the sale of non-current assets was £108m. All interest due has been received and the interest payable has been paid.

**Required:**

(a) Prepare the statement of cash flows for Theta entity for the year ended 31 December 20X7 in accordance with IAS 7, Cash Flow Statements. (Notes to the statement of cash flows are not required.)

(b) Identify information that is provided by a statement of cash flows to users that is not provided by a statement of comprehensive income and a statement of financial position.

**10** The following information has been extracted from the draft financial statements of TEX, a manufacturing entity:

*TEX – Income statement for the year ended 30 September 20X3*

|  | $000 |
|---|---|
| Revenue | 15 000 |
| Cost of sales | (9 000) |
| Gross profit | 6 000 |
| Other operating expenses | (2 300) |
|  | 3 700 |
| Finance cost | (124) |
| Profit before tax | 3 576 |
| Income tax expense | (1 040) |
| Dividends | (1 100) |
|  | (1 436) |

*TEX – Balance sheets at 30 September*

|  | 20X3 | | 20X2 | |
|---|---|---|---|---|
|  | $000 | $000 | $000 | $000 |
| **Assets** |  |  |  |  |
| Non-current assets |  | 18 160 |  | 14 500 |
| Current assets: |  |  |  |  |
| Inventories | 1 600 |  | 1 100 |  |
| Trade receivables | 1 500 |  | 800 |  |
| Bank | 150 |  | 1 200 |  |
|  |  | 3 250 |  | 3 100 |
| **Total assets** |  | 21 410 |  | 17 600 |

*TEX – Statement of financial position at 30 September*

| | 20X3 | | | 20X2 |
|---|---|---|---|---|
| | $000 | $000 | $000 | $000 |
| **Assets** | | | | |
| **Equity and liabilities:** | | | | |
| Capital and reserves: | | | | |
| Issued capital | | 10 834 | | 7 815 |
| Accumulated profits | | 5 836 | | 4 400 |
| | | 16 670 | | 12 215 |
| **Non-current liabilities:** | | | | |
| Interest-bearing borrowings | | 1 700 | | 2 900 |
| Deferred tax | | 600 | | 400 |
| | | 2 300 | | 3 300 |
| **Current liabilities:** | | | | |
| Trade payables | 700 | | 800 | |
| Proposed dividend | 700 | | 600 | |
| Tax | 1 040 | | 685 | |
| | | 2 440 | | 2 085 |
| | | 21 410 | | 17 600 |

**Notes**

**Non-current assets:**

| | Property | Plant | Total |
|---|---|---|---|
| | $000 | $000 | $000 |
| *At 30 September 20X2* | | | |
| Cost | 8 400 | 10 800 | 19 200 |
| Depreciation | 13 400 | 3 400 | 4 700 |
| Net book value | 7 100 | 7 400 | 14 500 |
| *At 30 September 20X3* | | | |
| Cost | 11 200 | 134 600 | 24 600 |
| Depreciation | 1 540 | 4 900 | 6 440 |
| Net book value | 9 660 | 8 500 | 18 160 |

(i) Plant disposed of during the year had an original cost of $2 600 000 and accumulated depreciation of $900 000; cash received on disposal was $730 000.

(ii) All additions to non-current assets were purchased for cash.

(iii) Dividends were declared before the balance sheet dates.

**Required:**
Prepare TEX's statement of cash flows and associated notes for the year ended 30 September 20X3, in accordance with IAS 7, *Statements of Cash Flows*.

(CIMA paper, Financial Accounting and Tax Principles – May 2005)

**11**   The financial statements of AG are given below:

*Statement of financial position as at:*

|  | 31 March 20X5 | | 31 March 20X4 | |
|---|---|---|---|---|
|  | $000 | $000 | $000 | $000 |
| **Non-current assets:** | | | | |
| Plant, property and equipment | 4 500 | | 4 800 | |
| Development expenditure | 370 | 4 870 | 400 | 5 200 |
| **Current assets:** | | | | |
| Inventories | 685 | | 575 | |
| Trade receivables | 515 | | 420 | |
| Cash and cash equivalents | 552 | 1 752 | 232 | 1 227 |
| Total assets | | 6 622 | | 6 427 |
| **Equity and liabilities** | | | | |
| **Equity:** | | | | |
| Share capital | 2 600 | | 1 900 | |
| Share premium account | 750 | | 400 | |
| Revaluation reserve | 425 | | 300 | |
| Retained earning | 1 430 | | 1 415 | |
| **Total equity** | | 5 205 | | 4 015 |
| **Non-current liabilities:** | | | | |
| 10% loan notes | 0 | | 1 000 | |
| 5% loan notes | 500 | | 500 | |
| Deferred tax | 250 | | 200 | |
| Total non-current liabilities: | | 750 | | 1 700 |
| **Current liabilities:** | | | | |
| Trade payables | 480 | | 350 | |
| Income tax | 80 | | 190 | |
| Accrued expenses | 107 | | 172 | |
| Total current liabilities: | | 667 | | 712 |
| **Total equity and liabilities** | | 6 622 | | 6 427 |

*Statement of comprehensive income for the year ended 31 March 20X5*

|  | $000 | $000 |
|---|---|---|
| Revenue | | 7 500 |
| Cost of sales | | 4 000 |
| Gross profit | | 3 500 |
| Distribution costs | 900 | |
| Administrative expenses | 2 300 | 3 200 |
| Profit from operations | | 300 |
| Finance costs | | 45 |
| Profit before tax | | 255 |
| Income tax expense | | 140 |
| Profit for the period | | 115 |

**Additional information:**

(i)   On 1 April 20X4, AG issued 1 400 000 $0.50 ordinary shares at a premium of 50 per cent
(ii)   On 1 May 20X4, AG purchased and cancelled all its 10 per cent loan notes at par.
(iii)   Non-current tangible assets include properties which were revalued upwards by $125 000 during the year.
(iv)   Non-current tangible assets disposed of in the year had a net book value of $75 000; cash received on disposal was $98 000. Any gain or loss on disposal has been included under cost of sales.
(v)   Cost of sales includes $80 000 for development expenditure amortized during the year.
(vi)   Depreciation charged for the year was $720 000.
(vii)   The accrued expenses balance includes interest payable of $87 000 at 31 March 20X4 and $12 000 at 31 March 2005.
(viii)   The income tax expenses for the year to 31 March 20X5 is made up as follows

|  | $000 |
|---|---|
| Corporate income tax | 90 |
| Deferred tax | 50 |
|  | 140 |

(ix)   Dividends paid during the year $100 000.

**Required:**
Prepare a statement of cash flows, using the indirect method, for AG for the year ended 31 March 20X5, in accordance with IAS 7, *Statements of Cash Flows*.

(CIMA paper, Financial Accounting and Tax Principles – May 2005)

**12**   The financial statements of CJ for the year to 31 March 20X6 were as follows:

| *Statement of financial position at:* | 31 March 20X6 | | 31 March 20X5 | |
|---|---|---|---|---|
|  | *$000* | *$000* | *$000* | *$000* |
| **Non-current tangible assets:** | | | | |
| Property | 19 160 | | 18 000 | |
| Plant and equipment | 8 500 | | 10 000 | |
| Available for sale investments | 1 500 | | 2 100 | |
|  | | 29 160 | | 30 100 |
| **Current assets:** | | | | |
| Inventory | 2 714 | | 2 500 | |
| Trade receivables | 2 106 | | 1 800 | |
| Cash at bank | 6 553 | | 0 | |
| Cash in hand | 409 | | 320 | |
|  | | 11 782 | | 4 620 |
| **Total assets** | | 40 942 | | 34 720 |
| **Equity and liabilities** | | | | |
| **Equity:** | | | | |
| Ordinary share $0.50 each | 12 000 | | 7 000 | |
| Share premium | 10 000 | | 5 000 | |
| Revaluation reserve | 4 200 | | 2 700 | |
| Retained profit | 3 009 | | 1 510 | |
|  | | 29 209 | | 16 210 |

| Statement of financial position at: | 31 March 20X6 | | 31 March 20X5 | |
|---|---|---|---|---|
| | $000 | $000 | $000 | $000 |
| **Non-current liabilities:** | | | | |
| Interest bearing borrowings | 7 000 | | 13 000 | |
| Provision for deferred tax | 999 | 7 999 | 800 | 13 800 |
| **Current liabilities:** | | | | |
| Bank overdraft | 0 | | 1 200 | |
| Trade and other payables | 1 820 | | 1 700 | |
| Corporate income tax payable | 1 914 | | 1 810 | |
| | | 3 734 | | 4 710 |
| | | 40 942 | | 34 720 |

Statement of comprehensive income for the year to 31 March 20X6

| | $000 |
|---|---|
| Revenue | 31 000 |
| Cost of sales | (19 000) |
| Gross profit | 12 000 |
| Other income | 200 |
| Administrative expenses | (3 900) |
| Distribution costs | (2 600) |
| | 5 700 |
| Finance cost | (1 302) |
| Profit before tax | 4 398 |
| Income tax expense | (2 099) |
| Profit for the period | 2 299 |

**Additional information:**

(i) On 1 April 20X5, CJ issued 10 000 000 $0.50 ordinary shares at a premium of 100 per cent.

(ii) No additional available for sale investments were acquired during the year.

(iii) On 1 July 20X5, CJ repaid $6 000 000 of its interest bearing borrowings

(iv) Properties were revalued by $1 500 000 during the year.

(v) Plant disposed of in the year had a net book value of $95 000; cash received on disposal was $118 000.

(vi) Depreciation charged for the year was properties $2 070 000 and plant and equipment $1 985 000.

(vii) The trade and other payables balance includes interest payable of $650 000 at 31 March 20X5 and $350 000 at 31 March 20X6.

(viii) Dividends paid during the year, $800 000, comprised last year's final dividend plus the current year's interim dividend. CJ's accounting policy is not to accrue proposed dividends.

(ix) Other income comprises:

| | $ |
|---|---|
| Dividends received | 180 000 |
| Gain on disposal of available for sales investments | 20 000 |
| | 200 000 |

Dividends receivable are not accrued

(x) Income tax expense comprises

| | $ |
|---|---|
| Corporate income tax | 1 900 000 |
| Deferred tax | 199 000 |
| | 2 099 000 |

**Required:**
Prepare CJ's statement of cash flow for the year ended 31 March 20X6, in accordance with IAS 7, *Statements of Cash Flows*.

(CIMA paper, Financial Accounting and Tax Principles – May 2006)

13  (a)  Casino is a publicly listed company. Details of its balance sheets as at 31 March 20X5 and 20X4 are shown below together with other relevant information:

*Statement of financial position as at*

|  | 31 March 20X5 | | 31 March 20X4 | |
|---|---|---|---|---|
|  | $m | $m | $m | $m |
| **Non-current assets** (note (i)): |  | 880 |  | 760 |
| Property, plant and equipment |  |  |  |  |
| Intangible assets |  | 400 |  | 510 |
|  |  | 1 280 |  | 1 270 |
| **Current assets:** |  |  |  |  |
| Inventory | 350 |  | 420 |  |
| Trade receivables | 808 |  | 372 |  |
| Interest receivable | 5 |  | 3 |  |
| Short-term deposits | 32 |  | 120 |  |
| Bank | 15 | 1 210 | 75 | 990 |
| **Total assets** |  | 2 490 |  | 2 260 |
| **Share capital and reserves:** |  |  |  |  |
| Ordinary shares of $1 each |  | 300 |  | 200 |
| Reserves |  |  |  |  |
| Share premium | 60 |  | nil |  |
| Revaluation reserve | 112 |  | 45 |  |
| Retained earnings | 1 098 | 1 270 | 1 165 | 1 210 |
|  |  | 1 570 |  | 1 410 |
| **Non-current liabilities:** |  |  |  |  |
| 12% loan note | nil |  | 150 |  |
| 8% variable rate loan note | 160 |  | nil |  |
| Deferred tax | 90 | 250 | 75 | 225 |
| **Current liabilities:** |  |  |  |  |
| Trade payables | 530 |  | 515 |  |
| Bank overdraft | 125 |  | nil |  |
| Taxation | 15 |  | 110 |  |
|  |  | 670 |  | 625 |
| **Total equity and liabilities** |  | 2 490 |  | 2 260 |

The following supporting information is available:

(i) Details relating to the non-current assets are: Property, plant and equipment at:

| | 31 March 20X5 | | | 31 March 20X4 | | |
|---|---|---|---|---|---|---|
| | Cost/ Valuation $m | Depreciation $m | Value Carrying $m | Cost/ Valuation $m | Depreciation $m | Carrying value $m |
| Land and buildings | 600 | 12 | 588 | 500 | 80 | 420 |
| Plant | 440 | 148 | 292 | 445 | 105 | 340 |
| | | | 880 | | | 760 |

Casino revalued the carrying value of its land and buildings by an increase of $70 million on 1 April 20X4. On 31 March 20X5 Casino transferred $3 million from the revaluation reserve to retained earnings representing the realization of the revaluation reserve due to the depreciation of buildings

During the year Casino acquired new plant at a cost of $60 million and sold some old plant for $15 million at a loss of $12 million

There were no acquisitions or disposals of intangible assets.

(ii) The following extract is from the draft income statement for the year to 31 March 20X5:

| | $m | $m |
|---|---|---|
| Operating loss | | (32) |
| Interest receivable | | 12 |
| Finance costs | | (24) |
| Loss before tax | | (44) |
| Income tax repayment claim | 14 | |
| Deferred tax charge | (15) | (1) |
| Loss for the period | | (45) |
| The finance costs are made up of: | | |
| Interest expenses | | (16) |
| Penalty cost for early redemption of fixed rate loan | | (6) |
| Issue costs of variable rate loan | | (2) |
| Issue costs of variable rate loan | | (24) |

(iii) The short-term deposits meet the definition of cash equivalents,

(iv) Dividends of $25 million were paid during the year.

**Required:**

As far as the information permits, prepare a statement of cash flows for Casino for the year to 31 March 20X5 in accordance with IAS 7, *Statements of Cash Flows*.

(b) In recent years many analysts have commented on a growing disillusionment with the usefulness and reliability of the information contained in some companies' income statements.

**Required:**

Discuss the extent to which a company's statement of cash flows may be more useful and reliable than its statement of comprehensive income.

(CIMA paper, Financial Accounting and Tax Principles – June 2005)

14 Extracts from the consolidated financial statements of the EAG Group for the year ended 30 April 20X8 are as follows:

*EAG Group: Consolidated income statement for the year ended 30 April 20X8*

|  | $ million |
|---|---|
| Revenue | 30 750.0 |
| Cost of sales | (26 447.5) |
| Gross profit | 4 302.5 |
| Distribution costs | (523.0) |
| Administrative expenses | (669.4) |
| Finance cost | (510.9) |
| Share of profit of associate | 1.6 |
| Profit on disposal of associate | 3.4 |
| Profit before tax | 2 604.2 |
| Income tax | (723.9) |
| Profit for the period | 1 880.3 |
| Attributable to |  |
| Equity holders of the parent | 1 652.3 |
| Minority interests | 228.0 |
|  | 1 880.3 |

*EAG Group: Statement of financial position at 30 April 20X8*

|  | 20X8 $ million | 20X7 $ million |
|---|---|---|
| **Assets** |  |  |
| **Non-current assets** |  |  |
| Property, plant and equipment | 22 225.1 | 19 332.8 |
| Goodwill | 1 662.7 | 1 865.3 |
| Intangible assets | 306.5 | 372.4 |
| Investment in associate | – | 13.8 |
|  | 24 194.3 | 21 584.3 |
| **Current assets** |  |  |
| Inventories | 5 217.0 | 4 881.0 |
| Trade receivables | 4 633.6 | 4 670.0 |
| Cash | 62.5 | 88.3 |
|  | 9 913.1 | 9 639.3 |
|  | 34 107.4 | 31 223.6 |
| *Equity and liabilities* |  |  |
| **Equity** |  |  |
| Share capital | 4 300.0 | 3 600.0 |
| Retained earnings | 14 643.7 | 12 991.4 |
|  | 18 943.7 | 16 591.4 |
| **Minority interest** | 2 010.5 | 1 870.5 |
| **Non-current liabilities** |  |  |
| Long-term borrowings | 6 133.9 | 6 013.0 |

*EAG Group: Statement of financial position at 30 April 20X8*

|  | 20X8<br>$ million | 20X7<br>$ million |
|---|---|---|
| **Current liabilities** | | |
| Trade payables | 5 579.3 | 5 356.3 |
| Short-term borrowings | 662.4 | 507.7 |
| Income tax | 777.6 | 884.7 |
|  | 7 019.3 | 6 748.7 |
|  | 34 107.4 | 31 223.6 |

## Notes

1. Depreciation of $2 024.7 million was charged in respect of property, plant and equipment in the year ended 30 April 20X8.
2. On 1 January 2008 EAG disposed of the investment in associate for $18 million. The share of profit in the income statement relates to the period from 1 May 20X7 to 31 December 20X7. A dividend was received from the associate on 1 June 20X7. There were no other disposals, and no acquisitions, of investments in the accounting period.
3. Goodwill in one of the group's subsidiaries suffered an impairment during the year. The amount of the impairment was included in cost of sales.
4. The long-term borrowings are measured at amortized cost. The borrowing was taken out on 1 May 20X6, and proceeds of $6 000 million less issue costs of $100 000 were received on that date. Interest of 5 per cent of the principal is paid in arrears each year, and the borrowings will be redeemed five years later on 30 April for $6.55 million. All interest obligations have been met on the due dates. The effective interest rate applicable to the borrowings is 7 per cent. The finance cost in the income statement includes interest in respect of both the long-term and the short-term borrowing. Short-term borrowing comprises overdrafts repayable on demand.
5. Amortization of 25 per cent of the opening balance of intangibles was charged to cost of sales. A manufacturing patent was acquired for a cash payment on 30 April 20X8.
6. An issue of share capital at par was made for cash during the year.
7. Dividends were paid to minority interests during the year, but no dividend was paid to the equity holders of the parent entity.

## Required:

Prepare the consolidated cash flow statement of the EAG Group for the financial year ended 30 April 20X8. The cash flow statement should be presented in accordance with the requirements of IAS 7, *Cash Flow Statements*, and using the indirect method. Notes to the financial statement are NOT required, but full workings should be shown.

(CIMA P8 – May 2008)

**15** The consolidated statement of financial position for MIC as at 31 March 20X9 and its comparative for 20X8 are shown below:

| Assets | 20X9<br>$000 | 20X8<br>$000 |
|---|---|---|
| **Non-current assets** | | |
| Property, plant and equipment | 16 800 | 15 600 |
| Goodwill | 2 900 | 2 400 |
| Investment in associate | 8 000 | 7 800 |

| | 20X9 | 20X8 |
|---|---|---|
| Assets | $000 | $000 |
| **Current assets** | 27 700 | 25 800 |
| Inventories | 11 600 | 12 000 |
| Receivables | 9 400 | 8 200 |
| Held for trading investment | 2 200 | 1 800 |
| Cash and cash equivalents | 1 400 | 4 100 |
| | 24 600 | 26 100 |
| **Total assets** | 52 300 | 51 900 |
| Equity and liabilities | | |
| **Equity attributable to owners of the parent** | | |
| Share capital ($1 ordinary shares) | 12 000 | 10 000 |
| Share premium | 2 800 | — |
| Other reserves | 400 | 400 |
| Retained earnings | 7 300 | 6 300 |
| | 22 500 | 16 700 |
| Non-controlling interest | 6 500 | 6 100 |
| Total equity | 29 000 | 22 800 |
| **Non-current liabilities** | | |
| Long term loans | 14 000 | 18 000 |
| Current liabilities | | |
| Payables | 8 700 | 10 200 |
| Income tax | 600 | 900 |
| | 9 300 | 11 100 |
| **Total liabilities** | 23 300 | 29 100 |
| **Total equity and liabilities** | 52 300 | 51 900 |

The consolidated income statement for MIC for the year ended 31 March 20X9 is shown below:

| | $000 |
|---|---|
| **Revenue** | 12 000 |
| Cost of sales | (8 400) |
| Gross profit | 3 600 |
| Distribution costs | (400) |
| Administrative expenses | (1 260) |
| Finance costs | (450) |
| Share of profit of associate | 500 |
| Profit before tax | 1 990 |
| Income tax expense | (600) |
| PROFIT FOR THE YEAR | 1 390 |
| Attributable to: | |
| Owners of the parent | 1 200 |
| Non-controlling interest | 190 |
| | 1 390 |

## Additional information:

1. There were no disposals of property, plant and equipment in the year. Depreciation charged in arriving at profit totalled $1 800 000.
2. MIC acquired 90 per cent of the ordinary share capital of GH on 1 December 20X8 for a cash consideration of $460 000 plus the issue of 1 million $1 ordinary shares in MIC, which had a deemed value of $3.60 per share at the date of acquisition. The fair values of the net assets acquired were as follows:

|  | $000 |
| --- | --- |
| Property, plant and equipment | 800 |
| Inventories | 2 200 |
| Receivables | 700 |
| Cash and cash equivalents | 200 |
| Payables | (500) |
|  | 3 400 |

   MIC made no other purchases or sales of investments in the year. The group policy is to value the non-controlling interest at acquisition at the proportionate share of the fair value of the net assets.

3. Finance costs include interest on loans and any gains or losses on held for trading investments. All interest due was paid in the year.

## Required:

Prepare the consolidated statement of cash flows for MIC for the year ended 31 March 20X9.

(CIMA F2 – November 2009 Specimen)

# DISCLOSURE ISSUES

# 25

**OBJECTIVES** After studying this chapter, you should be able to:

- explain the purpose of segmental reporting or disclosure of segment information

- describe what is meant by an operating segment

- explain the criteria for the determination of a reportable segment

- describe what is meant by an event after the reporting period

- explain the difference between an adjusting event and a non-adjusting event

- define basic earnings per share

- define diluted earnings per share

- describe the contents and appraise the statement IAS 33 on earnings per share

- describe the main issues of interim financial reporting under IAS 34.

## INTRODUCTION

Most of the standards that we are going to discuss in this chapter have in common that they regulate supplemental information disclosure on top of the data reported in the statement of financial position and the statement of comprehensive income. The aim of the standards discussed in this chapter is the improvement of the information disclosed in the financial statements for decision usefulness. Stakeholders will make economic decisions based on the reported information. The issues to be discussed are segmental reporting (IFRS 8), communication of information on events after the reporting date (IAS 10), the determination of the earnings per share (IAS 33) and interim financial reporting (IAS 34).

## DISCLOSURE OF SEGMENT INFORMATION

The first standard that we will discuss in this chapter is IFRS 8 on the disclosure of segment information.

In the Autumn of 2006, the IASB issued a new Standard on segmental reporting: IFRS 8, *Operating Segments*. IFRS 8 replaces the old IAS 14, *Segmental Reporting*. IFRS 8 is part of the convergence programme with the FASB and its purpose is to achieve convergence in the area of segment reporting with segmental reporting rules under US GAAP. In practice this specific convergence project (see also Chapter 3) implies that IAS 14 is substituted by SFAS 131, *Disclosures about Segments of an Entity and Related Information*, a financial accounting standard of the FASB. As when any standards on segmental reporting are on the agenda of a standard-setter, this Standard has generated a lot of discussion and controversy. When the IASB issued IFRS 8, it made three key decisions in that (1) segments would be identified based on the management perspective; (2) information would be measured on an internal basis; and (3) the line items reported would be those used by the chief operating decision maker (CODM). The IASB is currently undertaking a post-implementation review of IFRS 8. Post-implementation reviews (PIR) are a new element introduced in the due process of international accounting standard setting (see Chapter 3 – adoption of PIR in 2012). The PIR of IFRS 8 is the first major post-implementation review of a Standard undertaken by the IASB. Whether the results of the post implementation review of IFRS 8 will lead to substantial amendments of IFRS 8 is still uncertain at this moment (Summer 2013). During the PIR of IFRS 8, the IASB posted the views of the preparers, investors and other constituents on the website, as well as the results of academic research on IFRS 8. In general, preparers think that the standard works well, while the views of investors are more mixed. Auditors, accounting firms, standard-setters and regulators are generally supportive of the Standard (IFRS – Staff paper: post-implementation review of IFRS 8: operating segments).

### Purpose of the disclosure of segment reporting

Why is disclosure of segment information such a topic of debate?

In order to answer this question, we will first define what segmental reporting means and its purpose. On the statement of financial position and the statement of comprehensive income of a company, aggregated data on sales, expenses, assets and liabilities of a company as a whole are communicated to external parties. For companies active in a single industry, e.g. Pizza Hut, the risk and the volatility of the results disclosed by the company in the statement of comprehensive income are tied to the characteristics of risk and volatility of that specific industry. In this case, external stakeholders are able to make predictions about the future performance of the company based on an assessment of its prior year and current performance and on an assessment of the future evolution of the industry in which the company is active.

Very often, however, companies sell multiple products and are competing in different industries and on different regional markets, e.g. companies such as Nike and Adidas are active in the sport equipment industry and clothing industry and they sell their products worldwide in markets with different levels of purchasing power. A company such as the Scandinavian SAS group is active in the airline industry as well as in the hotel business. The corporate risk and the future performance of these companies or groups is influenced, first, by the individual risks and performance patterns of the different product groups and, second, by the individual risks of the different markets in which they are competing. The risks and volatility of the results of these individual products – or services groups or different markets – can be positively or negatively correlated with each other. If there is a positive correlation between the risks and returns of the individual segments then the risk of the company as a whole is increased and the corporate result will then be highly volatile. If the correlation is negative the corporate risk is reduced. So in order to make predictions about the future performance of multi-business and multinational companies, information on the performance of the individual groups of products or services and the different regional markets is essential.

The provision of that financial information about these different product groups and separate markets is called segmental reporting or disclosure of segment information.

Think of some multinationals or other companies you are familiar with and try to determine whether they are single business or multi-business entities and if they are competing in different markets. What kind of information would you like about them?

Segmental reporting or disclosure of segment information is dealt with in IFRS 8, *Operating Segments*. As mentioned in the introductory paragraph, the key objective of this Standard is to assist the user of financial statements in making judgements about the opportunities and risks facing an entity, by the disclosure of more disaggregated information than that provided in the primary financial statements (meaning the statement of financial position and the statement of comprehensive income of the group).

Information on the result obtained in each segment should be disclosed together with the capital employed in each segment. As the segmental information to be disclosed is more disaggregated, it enables the reader of the financial statements to analyze the financial performance of the entity in the various areas or segments in which it operates. In this respect segmental information increases the value relevance of the accounting information disclosed in the financial statements.

Companies, however, are not very eager to disclose segmental information as these segmental data are of strategic importance. They reveal the profitability of individual markets or business lines. Segmental data not only increase the value relevance of the accounts for investors, but also competitors will make use of those segmental data in their own decision process. As disclosing segmental data is perceived by companies as communicating proprietary information, firms have often tried in the past to provide segmental information of little value relevance. Analysts have consistently criticized the quality and inadequacy of the segment disclosures. Firms often argued that the benefits of informing the capital markets about firm value are smaller than the costs of aiding competitors with the information. The degree of flexibility permitted in segment disclosures was an issue for regulators in the 1980s and the 1990s (Fields,

Lys and Vincent, 2001). In the mid-1990s the American FASB issued a new standard on segment reporting requiring disclosures on segment reporting that are consistent with the firm's internal reporting organization. The IASB now takes a similar approach with IFRS 8, which does not differ from the American standard on segmental reporting.

Before we start with the discussion of the contents of IFRS 8, it is important to stress that IFRS 8 should be applied by those entities whose equity or debt securities are publicly traded and by entities that are in the process of issuing equity or debt securities in public securities markets (IFRS 8, para. 2). Companies that issue voluntarily segmental information in their IAS accounts should also fully comply with IFRS 8 (para. 2). According to IFRS 8 an entity shall disclose information to enable users of its financial statements to evaluate the nature and financial effects of the business activities in which it engages and the economic environments in which it operates.

## Definition of segments

In order to provide guidance on the disclosure of segment information, IFRS 8 starts with a discussion of the concept of an operating segment. The first step towards the disclosure of segmental information is the definition of the different operating segments present in the company. The principle underlying the approach in IFRS 8 is that the process of identifying segments for external reporting purposes begins with the information used by the board of directors and the chief executive officer to evaluate past performance and to make decisions about future allocations of resources. The former IAS 14 had as underlying principles that similar risks and returns were the basis for defining the business and the geographical segments of a company, which would then be the basis for segmental reporting.

Under IFRS 8, segments for which financial information has to be disclosed in the notes are identified on the basis of internal reports that are regularly reviewed by the entity's chief operating decision maker to allocate resources and to evaluate the performance of those segments. Through this management approach of segmental reporting, the user of the financial statements will receive segmental information in the same format and according to the same valuation rules as the management of the company. According to this approach no segments have to be created for external purposes. This certainly facilitates the task of preparers of financial statements. For users of the annual accounts, however, there is a danger that this 'look through the eyes of management' will create an obstacle to the comparability of segment information between different companies. This approach has generated a lot of comment letters from users of financial statements at the stage when Exposure Draft 8 on operating segments was issued.

IFRS 8 (para. 5) provides the following definition for the concept 'operating segment':

An operating segment is a component of an entity:

(a) that engages in business activities from which it may earn revenues and incur expenses (including revenues and expenses relating to transactions with other components of the same entity),

(b) whose operating results are regularly reviewed by the entity's chief operating decision maker to make decisions about resources to be allocated to the segment and assess its performance, and

(c) for which discrete financial information is available.

The above definition implies that internal segments which do not earn revenue, such as corporate headquarters, will not qualify as an operating segment. The term 'chief operating decision maker' identifies a function, not necessarily a manager with a specific title.

Generally, an operating segment has a segment manager who is directly accountable to and maintains regular contact with the chief operating decision maker to discuss operating activities, financial results, forecasts, or plans for the segment. An operating segment can be a business segment or a geographical segment or a combination of both. The post-implementation review of IFRS 8 indicates that preparers have no significant remarks concerning this management approach, investors however have much more mixed reactions. Some investors prefer to have information through the 'eyes of management', whereas other investors mistrust management's intentions and think that segments are reported in such a way as to obscure the entity's true management structure or to mask loss-making activities with individual segments (IFRS Staff paper: post-implementation review: IFRS 8 operating segments, paras 50–53).

The two largest brewers in the world, Anheuser-Bush Inbev (the largest) and Heineken (the second largest) choose geographical segments as operating segments to report. Nestlé chooses a combination of geographical and business segments as operating segments (see Appendix II of Chapter 32) and Unilever opts for only business segments as reportable operating segments (see Appendix III of Chapter 32).

We include the segmental reporting of AB Inbev and Heineken later in this section on segmental reporting.

## Reportable segments

A reportable segment is an operating segment for which segment information is required to be disclosed by the Standard. Only for reportable segments, segment data have to be disclosed in the notes to the statement of financial position and the statement of comprehensive income.

According to IFRS 8 (para. 11) an entity shall report separately information about each operating segment that has been identified or that results from aggregating two or more of those operating segments (for aggregation criteria see para. 12 of IFRS 8), when an operating segment or the aggregation of operating segments exceeds the quantitative thresholds (for a definition of the thresholds see para. 13 of IFRS 8). So once a company knows which segments qualify under the definition of operating segments, a company will focus on the aggregation criteria and work out whether or not operating segments can be combined for reporting purposes. Only information on an operating segment or aggregated segments needs to be disclosed if the segment or aggregated segments exceed a number of quantitative thresholds. So, to sum up, operating segments which comply with the aggregation criteria and meet the quantitative thresholds are externally reportable segments.

When operating segments have similar economic characteristics and subsequently similar long-term financial performance, they might be aggregated. The aggregation criteria are defined as follows (para. 12):

Two or more operating segments may be aggregated into a single operating segment if the segments have similar economic characteristics and if they are similar in the following respects:

(a) the nature of the products and services

(b) the nature of the production processes

(c) the type or class of customer for their product and services

(d) the methods used to distribute their products or provide their services

(e) if applicable, the nature of the regulatory environment, for example banking, insurance or public utilities.

Second, only information on operating segments or aggregated operating segments need to be disclosed if the segment or aggregated segments exceed a number of quantitative thresholds specified in IFRS 8 (para. 13).

An entity shall report separately information about an operating segment that meets any of the following quantitative thresholds:

**(a)** its reported revenue, including both sales to external customers and intersegment sales or transfers, is 10 per cent or more of the combined revenue, internal and external of all operating segments

**(b)** the absolute amount of its reported profit or loss is 10 per cent or more of the greater, in absolute amount, of (i) the combined reported profit of all operating segments that did not report a loss; and (ii) the combined reported loss of all operating segments that reported a loss

**(c)** its assets are 10 per cent or more of the combined assets of all operating segments.

Operating segments that do not meet any of the quantitative thresholds may be considered reportable, and separately disclosed, if management believes that information about the segment would be useful to users of the financial statements.

IFRS 8 specifies further (para. 15) that if the total external revenue reported by operating segments constitutes less than 75 per cent of the entity's revenue, additional operating segments shall be identified as reportable segments (even if they do not meet the quantitative thresholds defined in para. 13) until at least 75 per cent of the entity's revenue is included in reportable segments.

Activity 25.1 illustrates the application of the size criteria or quantitative thresholds in order to determine whether or not an individual segment qualifies to be a reportable segment and whether or not sufficient reportable segments have been distinguished for disclosure in the notes to the accounts.

## ACTIVITY 25.1

The management of a major multinational has identified the following reportable segments:

| | Total segment revenues | Inter-segment revenues | Segment result | Identifiable segment assets |
|---|---|---|---|---|
| Segment A | 750 | | 300 | 800 |
| Segment B | 400 | 40 | −50 | 450 |
| Segment C | 950 | | 250 | 600 |
| Segment D | 500 | 50 | 200 | 900 |
| Segment E | 350 | 35 | 50 | 500 |
| Segment F | 500 | | 150 | 700 |
| Segment G | 550 | | −100 | 750 |
| Segment H | 650 | | 100 | 400 |
| Total segments | 4 650 | 125 | 900 | 5 900 |
| Inter-company eliminations | 125 | | 50 | 150 |
| Consolidated total | 4 525 | | 850 | 4 950 |

## ACTIVITY 25.1  (*Continued*)

1 Assume segments A–H are business segments. Determine which of these business segments would classify as reportable segments.

2 Based on your answer to question 1, determine whether the reportable segments represent sufficient operations (75 per cent threshold test).

### Activity feedback

*1 Reportable segments*

| | Segment revenue[1] >465 10% of 4 650 | Segment result >105 10% of 1 050[2] | Identifiable segment assets >510 10% of 5 100 | Reportable segment |
|---|---|---|---|---|
| Segment A | Yes | Yes | Yes | Yes |
| Segment B | No | No | No | No |
| Segment C | Yes | Yes | Yes | Yes |
| Segment D | Yes | Yes | Yes | Yes |
| Segment E | No | No | No | No |
| Segment F | Yes | Yes | Yes | Yes |
| Segment G | Yes | No | Yes | Yes |
| Segment H | Yes | No | No | Yes |

Notes:

1 The majority of the segment revenue is from external sales in all segments.
2 Combined result of segments in profit 1050; combined result of segments in loss 150; chose the greater in absolute amounts, i.e. 1050.

*2 Number of reportable segments*

*In order to determine the number of reportable segments the threshold of 75 per cent of the external revenue reported by the segments applies. This implies that if the total external revenue reported by the segments constitutes less than 75 of the entity's revenue, additional segments must be identified as reportable segments until at least 75 per cent of the entity's revenue is included in reportable segments.*

*So 75% (4525) = 3394 is the threshold. We will check whether we meet the threshold with individual segments*

*which have passed the size criteria for being an individual reportable segment.*

| | | |
|---|---|---|
| External revenue segment A | = | 750 |
| External revenue segment C | = | 950 |
| External revenue segment D | = | 450 |
| External revenue segment F | = | 500 |
| External revenue segment G | = | 550 |
| External revenue segment H | = | 650 |
| Total | = | 3 850 |

*Even without segment D, the threshold of 75 per cent is met.*

One of the comments received through the PIR of IFRS 8 is that these criteria for determining the individual reportable segments are not always easy to apply. So more guidance could perhaps be expected on these criteria as a result of the comments made during the post-implementation review.

# Disclosure of segmental data

Once the reportable segments are determined, information on these segments must be disclosed in the notes in order to enable users of financial statements to evaluate the nature and financial effects of the business activities in which it engages and the economic environments in which it operates.

First of all some general information has to be provided with regard to the reportable segments (para. 22):

**(a)** factors used to identify the entity's reportable segments, including the basis of organization (for example, whether management has chosen to organize the entity around differences in products and services, geographical areas, regulatory environments, or a combination of factors and whether operating segments have been aggregated), and

**(b)** types of products and services from which each reportable segment derives its revenues.

Second, IFRS 8 states which information needs to be disclosed with regard to each reportable segment. Remember that the internal information communicated and reviewed by the chief operating decision maker is the basis for segmental disclosure. IFRS 8 (para. 23) states that an entity shall report a measure of profit or loss for each reportable segment even if that information is not included in the communication to the chief operating decision maker. With regard to segment assets and segment liabilities, IFRS 8 states that an entity shall report segment assets and segment liabilities for each reportable segment only if such an amount is regularly provided to the chief operating decision maker. The following items need to be disclosed for each reportable segment, if they are also reported to the chief decision maker:

**(a)** revenues from external customers

**(b)** revenues from transactions with other operating segments of the same entity

**(c)** interest revenue

**(d)** interest expense

**(e)** depreciation and amortization

**(f)** material items of income and expense disclosed in accordance with paragraph 86 of IAS 1, *Presentation of Financial Statements*

**(g)** the entity's interest in profit or loss of associates and joint ventures accounted for by the equity method

**(h)** income tax expense or income, and

**(i)** material non-cash items other than depreciation and amortization.

An entity shall report interest revenue separately from interest expense for each reportable segment unless a majority of the segment's revenues are from interest and the chief operating decision maker relies primarily on the net interest revenue to assess the performance of the segment and to make decisions about resources to be allocated to the segment. In that situation, an entity may report that segment's interest revenue net of its interest expense and inform the user of the financial statements about this decision. Further an entity shall disclose the following about each reportable segment whether or not this information is included in the information provided to the chief operating decision maker:

(a) the amount of investment in associates and joint ventures accounted for by the equity method, and

(b) total expenditures for additions to non-current assets other than financial instruments, deferred tax assets, post-employment benefit assets (see the discussion on employee benefits, Chapter 22) and rights arising under insurance contracts.

With regard to disclosure of segmental information, investors communicated in the PIR of IFRS 8 that they were very concerned that companies no longer report certain important line items like depreciation. The fact that only the information disclosed to the chief operating decision maker needs to be disclosed, provides companies the discretion not to disclose important line items.

## Measurement

The measurement of the segment data under IFRS 8 is fundamentally different from the measurement under IAS 14. In contrast with segment data reportable under IAS 14, segment data separated under IFRS 8 do not need to be in compliance with IAS regulations. The amount of each segment item reported shall be the measure reported to the chief operating decision maker for the purposes of making decisions about allocating resources to the segment and assessing its performance. Adjustments and eliminations made in preparing an entity's financial statements and allocations of revenues, expenses, and gains or losses shall be included in determining reported segment profit or loss only if they are included in the measure of the segment's profit or loss that is used by the chief operating decision maker. Similarly, only those assets that are included in the measure of the segment's assets that is used by the chief operating decision maker shall be reported for that segment. If amounts are allocated to reported segment profit or loss or assets, those amounts shall be allocated on a reasonable basis. So segmental data can be valued according to other rules or principles other than IAS/IFRS. This possibility to use internal valuation rules instead of IFRS is another element that might impede comparability of segment data between different companies as the valuation basis of the segment data can be different. The fact that IFRS 8 introduced the possibility of non-IFRS measurement for segmental data, is another major concern for investors and other users of the financial statements. This option reduces greatly the comparability of segmental information between entities.

## Reconciliations

Since there is no obligation for the disclosed segment data to comply with International Accounting Standards the reported totals over all segments might deviate from the figures that appear in the group financial statements which comply with IAS. In order to link the disclosed segment data with the data published in the statement of financial position and the statement of comprehensive income of the entity, the following reconciliations have to be provided:

(a) the total of reportable segments' revenues to the entity's revenue

(b) the total of the reportable segments' measures of profit or loss to the entity's profit or loss before income tax expense or income and discontinued operations; however, if an entity allocates to reportable segments items such as income tax expense or income, the entity may reconcile the total of the segments' measures of profit or loss to the entity's profit or loss after those items

(c) the total of the reportable segments' assets to the entity's assets

(d) the total of the reportable segments' amounts for every other material item of information disclosed to the corresponding amount for the entity; for example, an entity may choose to disclose liabilities for its reportable segments, in which case the entity would reconcile the total of reportable segments' liabilities to the entity's liabilities if the segment liabilities are material.

## Entity-wide disclosures

Besides this requirement to disclose segmental data, IFRS 8 also prescribes the disclosure of entity-wide data. These requirements for entity-wide disclosures also apply to entities that have only one single reportable segment. The IASB is well aware of the fact that some entities' business activities are not organized on the basis of differences in related products and services or differences in geographical areas of operations. In this case such an entity's reportable segments may report revenues from a broad range of essentially different products and services, or more than one of its reportable segments may provide essentially the same products and services. Similarly, an entity's reportable segments may hold assets in different geographical areas and report revenues from customers in different geographical areas, or more than one of its reportable segments may operate in the same geographical area.

In order to ensure that users of financial statements receive at least some information, which they can use for inter-firm comparison and which is understandable in a straightforward way, IFRS 8 states that entities must disclose the following in addition to their segmental data:

1 Information about products and services (revenues from external customers for each product and service or each group of similar products or services).

2 Information about geographical areas:

(a) revenues from external customers:

(i) attributed to the entity's country of domicile and

(ii) attributed to all foreign countries in total from which the entity derives revenues. If revenues from external customers attributed to an individual foreign country are material, those revenues shall be disclosed separately. An entity shall disclose the basis for attributing revenues from external customers to individual countries.

(b) non-current assets other than financial instruments, deferred tax assets, post-employment benefit assets, and rights arising under insurance contracts:

(i) located in the entity's country of domicile and

(ii) located in all foreign countries in total in which the entity holds assets. If assets in an individual foreign country are material, those assets shall be disclosed separately.

The amounts reported in relation to 1 and 2 shall be based on the financial information that is used to produce the entity's financial statements. This implies that this information shall be prepared according to IFRS. If the information is not available in accordance with IFRS and if the cost of producing this information would be excessive, the information can be omitted.

3 Information about major customers. If revenues from transactions with a single external customer amount to 10 per cent or more of an entity's revenues, the

entity shall disclose that fact, the total amount of revenues from each such customer, and the identity of the segment or segments reporting the revenues. The entity need not disclose the identity of a major customer or the amount of revenues that each segment reports from that customer. For the purpose of this IFRS, a group of entities known to a reporting entity to be under common control shall be considered a single customer, and a national government, a local government, or a foreign government shall each be considered a single customer.

These entity-wide disclosures probably compensate for the loss of comparable information on business and geographical segments which was required by IAS 14 but abolished with the introduction of IFRS 8. However, the PIR reveals that entity-wide disclosures are poorly understood and inconsistently applied across entities.

## REAL WORLD ILLUSTRATION

The two largest brewers in the world, Anheuser-Bush Inbev (the largest) and Heineken (the second largest) choose geographical segments as operating segments to report. However, they choose different geographical segments. Comparing the two sets of segmental reporting, what do you learn with regard to the importance of the individual geographic areas for both brewers? Do these brewers use the same line items in their segmental reporting? Does this hinder comparability? What do you know about the measurement used by both brewers for the assets, liabilities, revenues and costs reported in their segmental reporting? Do you find entity-wide disclosures?

In the valuation rules of AB Inbev we find the following information on segmental reporting (p. 35): 'Operating segments are components of the company's business about which separate information is available that is evaluated regularly by management. AB Inbev's operating segment reporting format is geographical because the company's risks and rates of return are affected predominantly by the fact that AB Inbev operates in different geographical areas.' The company's management structure and internal reporting system to the Board of Directors is set up accordingly. A geographical segment is a distinguishable component of the company that is engaged in providing products or services within a particular economic environment, which is subject to risks and return that are different from those of other segments. In accordance with IFRS 8, *Operating Segments*, AB Inbev's reportable geographical segments were determined as North America, Latin America North, Latin America South, Western Europe, Central and Eastern Europe, Asia Pacific and Global Export and Holding Companies. The Company's assets are predominantly located in the same geographical areas as its customers.

Segment results, assets and liabilities include items directly attributable to a segment as well as those that can be allocated on a reasonable basis. Unallocated assets comprise interest bearing loans granted, investment securities, deferred tax assets, income taxes receivable, cash and cash equivalent and derivative assets. Unallocated liabilities comprise equity and non-controlling interest, interest bearing loans, deferred tax liabilities, bank overdrafts, income taxes payable and derivative liabilities. Segment capital expenditure is the total cost incurred during the period to acquire property, plant and equipment, and intangible assets other than goodwill.

### 5. Segment Reporting

Segment information is presented by geographical segments, consistent with the information that is available and evaluated regularly by the chief operating decision maker. AB InBev operates its business through seven zones. Regional and operating company management is responsible for managing performance, underlying risks, and effectiveness of operations. Internally, AB InBev's management uses performance indicators such as normalized profit from operations (normalized EBIT) and normalized EBITDA as measures of segment performance and to make decisions regarding allocation of resources. These measures are reconciled to segment profit in the tables presented (figures may not add up due to rounding).

All figures in the table below are stated in million US dollar, except volume (million hls) and full time equivalents (FTE in units).

| Million US dollar, except volume (million hls) and full time equivalents (FTE in units) | North America 2012 | North America 2011 | Latin America North 2012 | Latin America North 2011 | Latin America South 2012 | Latin America South 2011 | Western Europe 2012 | Western Europe 2011 | Central and Eastern Europe 2012 | Central and Eastern Europe 2011 | Asia Pacific 2012 | Asia Pacific 2011 | Global Export and Holding Companies 2012 | Global Export and Holding Companies 2011 | Consolidated 2012 | Consolidated 2011 |
|---|---|---|---|---|---|---|---|---|---|---|---|---|---|---|---|---|
| **Volume** | **125** | **125** | **126** | **120** | **34** | **34** | **30** | **31** | **23** | **26** | **58** | **56** | **7** | **7** | **403** | **399** |
| **Revenue** | **16 028** | **15 304** | **11 455** | **11 524** | **3 023** | **2 704** | **3 625** | **3 945** | **1 668** | **1 755** | **2 690** | **2 317** | **1 270** | **1 496** | **39 758** | **39 046** |
| Cost of sales | (6 637) | (6 726) | (3 650) | (3 738) | (1 114) | (1 040) | (1 550) | (1 652) | (914) | (984) | (1 565) | (1 319) | (1 018) | (1 174) | (16 447) | (16 634) |
| Distribution expenses | (1 317) | (807) | (1 311) | (1 332) | (263) | (227) | (364) | (409) | (184) | (224) | (235) | (193) | (111) | (120) | (3 785) | (3 313) |
| Sales and marketing expenses | (1 798) | (1 640) | (1 245) | (1 263) | (296) | (272) | (649) | (760) | (400) | (420) | (670) | (588) | (200) | (200) | (5 258) | (5 143) |
| Administrative expenses | (458) | (475) | (600) | (535) | (93) | (85) | (267) | (305) | (113) | (108) | (274) | (221) | (382) | (314) | (2 187) | (2 043) |
| Other operating income/(expenses) | 64 | 54 | 426 | 462 | 4 | 1 | 24 | 37 | 5 | 2 | 121 | 90 | 40 | 48 | 684 | 694 |
| **Normalized profit from operations (EBIT)** | **5 881** | **5 710** | **5 074** | **5 118** | **1 261** | **1 081** | **819** | **856** | **62** | **21** | **67** | **86** | **(400)** | **(264)** | **12 765** | **12 607** |
| Non-recurring items (refer Note 8) | 47 | (188) | (26) | 21 | – | (6) | (2) | (123) | (5) | – | 2 | (9) | (47) | 27 | (32) | (278) |
| **Profit from operations (EBIT)** | **5 928** | **5 521** | **5 049** | **5 139** | **1 261** | **1 076** | **817** | **733** | **57** | **21** | **69** | **77** | **(447)** | **(238)** | **12 733** | **12 329** |
| Net finance cost | (437) | (591) | (362) | (168) | (56) | (60) | (357) | (360) | (117) | (88) | – | 12 | (877) | (1 882) | (2 206) | (3 137) |
| Share of result of associates | 623 | 622 | – | – | 1 | – | 1 | 1 | – | – | – | – | – | – | 624 | 623 |
| **Profit before tax** | **6 114** | **5 552** | **4 687** | **4 971** | **1 205** | **1 016** | **461** | **374** | **(60)** | **(67)** | **69** | **89** | **(1 324)** | **(2 120)** | **11 151** | **9 815** |
| Income tax expense | (1 386) | (1 637) | (491) | (765) | (340) | (289) | (138) | (84) | (13) | 13 | (53) | (42) | 704 | 948 | (1 717) | (1 856) |
| **Profit** | **4 729** | **3 915** | **4 195** | **4 206** | **866** | **727** | **322** | **290** | **(73)** | **(54)** | **16** | **47** | **(621)** | **(1 172)** | **9 434** | **7 959** |
| Normalized EBITDA | 6 706 | 6 573 | 5 801 | 5 814 | 1 432 | 1 254 | 1 155 | 1 225 | 257 | 225 | 396 | 356 | (234) | (90) | 15 511 | 15 357 |
| Non-recurring items (including impairment) | 47 | (188) | (26) | 21 | – | (6) | (2) | (123) | (5) | – | 2 | (9) | (47) | 27 | (32) | (278) |
| Depreciation, amortization and impairment | (824) | (864) | (726) | (696) | (170) | (172) | (336) | (369) | (195) | (204) | (329) | (270) | (166) | (175) | (2 747) | (2 750) |
| Net finance cost | (437) | (591) | (362) | (168) | (56) | (60) | (357) | (360) | (117) | (88) | – | 12 | (877) | (1 882) | (2 206) | (3 137) |
| Share of results of associates | 623 | 622 | – | – | 1 | – | 1 | 1 | – | – | – | – | – | – | 624 | 623 |
| Income tax expense | (1 386) | (1 637) | (491) | (765) | (340) | (289) | (138) | (84) | (13) | 13 | (53) | (42) | 704 | 948 | (1 717) | (1 856) |
| **Profit** | **4 729** | **3 915** | **4 195** | **4 206** | **866** | **727** | **322** | **290** | **(73)** | **(54)** | **16** | **47** | **(621)** | **(1 172)** | **9 434** | **7 959** |
| Normalized EBITDA margin in % | 41.8% | 42.9% | 50.6% | 50.5% | 47.4% | 46.4% | 31.9% | 31.1% | 15.4% | 12.8% | 14.7% | 15.4% | – | – | 39.0% | 39.3% |
| Segment assets | 72 845 | 71 233 | 18 426 | 17 133 | 4 176 | 3 969 | 5 939 | 5 676 | 2 153 | 2 179 | 5 028 | 4 577 | 3 865 | 4 475 | 112 432 | 109 242 |
| Intersegment elimination | | | | | | | | | | | | | | | (5 557) | (3 978) |
| Non-segmented assets | | | | | | | | | | | | | | | 15 746 | 7 163 |
| **Total assets** | | | | | | | | | | | | | | | **122 621** | **112 427** |
| Segment liabilities | 8 292 | 6 762 | 7 383 | 6 004 | 1 627 | 1 232 | 3 751 | 3 009 | 578 | 526 | 2 467 | 1 921 | 2 254 | 3 923 | 26 353 | 23 377 |
| Intersegment elimination | | | | | | | | | | | | | | | (5 557) | (3 978) |
| Non-segmented liabilities | | | | | | | | | | | | | | | 101 825 | 93 028 |
| **Total liabilities** | | | | | | | | | | | | | | | **122 621** | **112 427** |
| Gross capex | 449 | 384 | 1 225 | 1 703 | 287 | 239 | 295 | 300 | 127 | 161 | 786 | 607 | 143 | 279 | 3 313 | 3 673 |
| Additions to/(reversals of) provisions | 13 | 81 | 134 | 82 | 2 | 1 | 3 | 116 | 1 | – | (2) | 11 | (208) | (8) | (57) | 283 |
| FTE. | 17 137 | 17 924 | 37 789 | 33 076 | 8 787 | 8 641 | 8 066 | 7 832 | 9 510 | 10 551 | 34 455 | 36 046 | 1 888 | 2 208 | 117 632 | 116 278 |

*Notes: Net revenue from the beer business amounted to 35 914m US dollar while the net revenue from the non-beer business (soft drinks and other business) accounted for 3 844m US dollar.*

*Net revenue from external customers attributable to AB InBev's country of domicile (Belgium) and non-current assets located in the country of domicile represented 873m US dollar and 1 160m US dollar, respectively.*

## REAL WORLD ILLUSTRATION    (Continued)

We now present the segmental information of the Heineken Group.

## 5. Operating segments

HEINEKEN distinguishes the following six reportable segments:

- Western Europe
- Central and Eastern Europe
- The Americas
- Africa and the Middle East
- Asia Pacific
- Head Office and Other/eliminations.

The first five reportable segments as stated above are the Group's business regions. These business regions are each managed separately by a Regional President. The Regional President is directly accountable for the functioning of the segment's assets, liabilities and results of the region and reports regularly to the Executive Board (the chief operating decision maker) to discuss operating activities, regional forecasts and regional results. The Head Office operating segment falls directly under the responsibility of the Executive Board. For each of the six reportable segments, the Executive Board reviews internal management reports on a monthly basis.

Information regarding the results of each reportable segment is included in the table on the next page. Performance is measured based on EBIT (beia), as included in the internal management reports that are reviewed by

the Executive Board. EBIT (beia) is defined as earnings before interest and taxes and net finance expenses, before exceptional items and amortization of acquisition related intangibles. Exceptional items are defined as items of income and expense of such size, nature or incidence, that in view of management their disclosure is relevant to explain the performance of HEINEKEN for the period. EBIT and EBIT (beia) are not financial measures calculated in accordance with IFRS. EBIT (beia) is used to measure performance as management believes that this measurement is the most relevant in evaluating the results of these segments.

HEINEKEN has multiple distribution models to deliver goods to end customers. There is no reliance on major clients. Deliveries to end consumers are done in some countries via own wholesalers or own pubs, in other markets directly and in some others via third parties. As such, distribution models are country specific and on consolidated level diverse. In addition, these various distribution models are not centrally managed or monitored. Consequently, the Executive Board is not allocating resources and assessing the performance based on business type information and therefore no segment information is provided on business type.

Inter-segment pricing is determined on an arm's-length basis. As net finance expenses and income tax expenses are monitored on a consolidated level (and not on an individual regional basis) and regional presidents are not accountable for that, net finance expenses and income tax expenses are not provided per reportable segment.

### Information about reportable segments

| | Western Europe | | Central and Eastern Europe | | The Americas | | Africa and the Middle East | | Asia Pacific | | Head Office and Other/ eliminations | | Consolidated | |
|---|---|---|---|---|---|---|---|---|---|---|---|---|---|---|
| | 2012 | 2011 | 2012 | 2011 | 2012 | 2011 | 2012 | 2011 | 2012 | 2011 | 2012 | 2011 | 2012 | 2011 |
| **Revenue** | | | | | | | | | | | | | | |
| Third party revenue[1] | 7 140 | 7 158 | 3 255 | 3 209 | 4 507 | 4 002 | 2 639 | 2 223 | 527 | 216 | 315 | 315 | 18 383 | 17 123 |
| Interregional revenue | 645 | 594 | 25 | 20 | 16 | 27 | – | – | – | – | (686) | (641) | – | – |
| **Total revenue** | **7 785** | 7 752 | **3 280** | 3 229 | **4 523** | 4 029 | **2 639** | 2 223 | **527** | 216 | **(371)** | (326) | **18 383** | 17 123 |
| Other income | 13 | 48 | 9 | 7 | 2 | 1 | – | 3 | 1 486 | 5 | – | – | 1 510 | 64 |
| **Results from operating activities** | **739** | 820 | **313** | 318 | **581** | 493 | **613** | 533 | **1 546** | 64 | **(101)** | (13) | **3 691** | 2 215 |
| Net finance expenses | | | | | | | | | | | | | (270) | (430) |
| Share of profit of associates and joint ventures and impairments thereof | 1 | 3 | 24 | 17 | 81 | 77 | 1 | 35 | 109 | 112 | (3) | (4) | 213 | 240 |

(Continued)

## REAL WORLD ILLUSTRATION  *(Continued)*

| | Western Europe 2012 | Western Europe 2011 | Central and Eastern Europe 2012 | Central and Eastern Europe 2011 | The Americas 2012 | The Americas 2011 | Africa and the Middle East 2012 | Africa and the Middle East 2011 | Asia Pacific 2012 | Asia Pacific 2011 | Head Office and Other/ eliminations 2012 | Head Office and Other/ eliminations 2011 | Consolidated 2012 | Consolidated 2011 |
|---|---|---|---|---|---|---|---|---|---|---|---|---|---|---|
| Income tax expenses | | | | | | | | | | | | | (525) | (465) |
| **Profit** | | | | | | | | | | | | | **3 109** | 1 560 |
| Attributable to: | | | | | | | | | | | | | | |
| Equity holders of the Company (net profit) | | | | | | | | | | | | | 2 949 | 1 430 |
| Non-controlling interest | | | | | | | | | | | | | 160 | 130 |
| **EBIT reconciliation** | | | | | | | | | | | | | **3 109** | 1 560 |
| EBIT | 740 | 823 | 337 | 335 | 662 | 570 | 614 | 568 | 1 655 | 176 | (104) | (17) | 3 904 | 2 455 |
| Eia² | 224 | 139 | 12 | 11 | 86 | 85 | 38 | 2 | (1 388) | – | 36 | 5 | (992) | 242 |
| **EBIT (beia)² note 27** | **964** | 962 | **349** | 346 | **748** | 655 | **652** | 570 | **267** | 176 | **(68)** | (12) | **2 912** | 2 697 |
| Beer volumes² | | | | | | | | | | | | | | |
| Consolidated beer volume | 44 288 | 45 380 | 47 269 | 45 377 | 53 124 | 50 497 | 23 289 | 22 029 | 3 742 | 1 309 | – | – | 171 712 | 164 592 |
| Joint Ventures' volume | – | – | 7 578 | 7 303 | 9 611 | 9 663 | 6 002 | 5 706 | 24 297 | 24 410 | (157) | – | 47 331 | 47 082 |
| Licences | 288 | 300 | – | – | 74 | 65 | 1 149 | 1 093 | 675 | 769 | 1 | – | 2 187 | 2 227 |
| Group volume | **44 576** | 45 680 | **54 847** | 52 680 | **62 809** | 60 225 | **30 440** | 28 828 | **28 714** | 26 488 | **(156)** | – | 221 230 | 213 901 |
| Current segment assets | 2 007 | 1 843 | 1 082 | 985 | 1 193 | 1 045 | 959 | 854 | 913 | 91 | (629) | (124) | 5 525 | 4 694 |
| Other non-current segment assets | 8 015 | 8 186 | 3 423 | 3 365 | 5 649 | 5 619 | 2 073 | 1 867 | 7 151 | 2 | 1 619 | 1 143 | 27 930 | 20 182 |
| Investment in associates and joint ventures | 22 | 23 | 196 | 165 | 835 | 711 | 281 | 272 | 534 | 536 | 82 | 57 | 1 950 | 1 764 |
| **Total segment assets** | **10 044** | 10 052 | **4 701** | 4 515 | **7 677** | 7 375 | **3 313** | 2 993 | **8 598** | 629 | **1 072** | 1 076 | **35 405** | 26 640 |
| Unallocated assets | | | | | | | | | | | | | 574 | 487 |
| **Total assets** | | | | | | | | | | | | | **35 979** | 27 127 |
| Segment liabilities | 4 178 | 3 723 | 1 347 | 1 160 | 1 072 | 1 068 | 760 | 653 | 498 | 36 | 238 | 508 | 8 093 | 7 148 |
| Unallocated liabilities | | | | | | | | | | | | | 15 124 | 9 887 |
| Total equity | | | | | | | | | | | | | 12 762 | 10 092 |
| **Total equity and liabilities** | | | | | | | | | | | | | **35 979** | 27 127 |
| Purchase of P, P & E | 260 | 215 | 197 | 170 | 250 | 199 | 395 | 202 | 20 | – | 48 | 14 | 1 170 | 800 |
| Acquisition of goodwill | 7 | – | – | 1 | 36 | 4 | – | 282 | 2 757 | – | 480 | – | 3 280 | 287 |
| Purchases of intangible assets | 26 | 11 | 12 | 9 | 14 | 20 | 2 | – | – | – | 24 | 16 | 78 | 56 |
| Depreciation of P, P & E | (344) | (343) | (247) | (234) | (201) | (183) | (176) | (140) | (11) | – | (38) | (36) | (1 017) | (936) |
| (Impairment) and reversal of impairment of P, P & E | (36) | – | 15 | (2) | (17) | 5 | (8) | (3) | | – | 2 | – | (44) | – |
| Amortization intangible assets | (86) | (100) | (16) | (18) | (103) | (93) | (6) | (6) | (24) | – | (12) | (12) | (247) | (229) |
| (Impairment) and reversal of impairment of intangible assets | (7) | – | – | (3) | – | – | – | | – | | – | | (7) | (3) |

¹Includes other revenue of EUR433 million in 2012 and EUR463 million in 2011.
²Note that these are both non-GAAP measures and therefore unaudited.

## EVENTS AFTER THE REPORTING PERIOD

Financial statements are used mainly for two purposes. First, external stakeholders will use financial statement information in their own decision-making process and, second, financial statements can serve as a basis for control on stewardship. The latter means that management and directors could be held accountable for their policy decisions and actions on the basis of the financial statements.

With regard to the first aim of financial reporting, namely providing useful and reliable information, it is important that external stakeholders get a clear idea about which transactions and their related financial impact are included in the annual accounts and which transactions or events and their related financial impact have not been taken into account in the financial statements. Time passes between the end of the reporting period and the publication of the financial statements to the public. Accounts, no matter how sophisticated the information technology, are never prepared, audited and approved by directors in a few days. Generally there is a time lag of a number of months between the end of the reporting period and the 'signing off' of the accounts by directors. During this period numerous events can occur that may or may not have an influence on the information which is provided, by the final accounts, for users.

## ACTIVITY 25.2

Can you think of activities after the reporting period which might alter the financial picture presented by the financial statements closed at the end of the reporting period?

### Activity feedback

- *The bankruptcy of an important customer.*
- *The levy of import tariffs in an important export market of the company.*
- *The acquisition of a large part of the shares of a company.*
- *A settlement of a court case in which the company is involved.*

The events listed in Activity 25.2 will have an impact on the financial situation of the company and external stakeholders might well change their decisions in relation to the company if they take into account the financial impact of the information becoming available after the reporting period. IAS 10 deals with the communication of the impact of events occurring after the reporting period on the financial situation of the company.

## Definition of events after the reporting period

Paragraph 3 of IAS 10 defines events occurring after the reporting period as those events, both favourable and unfavourable, that occur between the end of the reporting period and the date when the financial statements are authorized for issue. Two types of event can be identified:

- those that provide evidence of conditions that existed at the end of the reporting period (adjusting events after the reporting period)
- those that are indicative of conditions that arose after the end of the reporting period (non-adjusting events after the reporting period).

## Date of authorization for issue

In order to judge the relevance of the information provided through the financial statements it is of extreme importance for the external stakeholders to know when the financial statements have been authorized for issue, as the financial statements do not reflect events after this date. Therefore, para. 17 of IAS 10 states explicitly that an entity should disclose the date on which the financial statements were authorized for issue and who gave that authorization. If the entity's owner or others have the power to amend the financial statements after issuance, the entity should disclose that fact.

### ACTIVITY 25.3

Check the financial statements on several websites of listed companies. Is information disclosure clear on this issue (i.e. date of authorization for issue and who gave the authorization)?

retrievable and it is not obvious where to find that information, especially with regard to the item 'who gave the authorization'.

*Activity feedback*

*As a user of the annual report and the financial statements you will have found out that it is not easily*

An example of such disclosure is found in the 2012 financial statements of Adidas in note 42.

### Date of preparation

The Executive Board of Adidas AG prepared and approved the consolidated financial statements for submission to the Supervisory Board on February 22, 2013. It is the Supervisory Board's task to examine the consolidated financial statements and give their approval and authorization for issue.
Herzogenaurach, February 22, 2013
The Executive Board of Adidas AG

The process involved in authorizing the financial statements for issue will vary depending on the management structure, statutory requirements and procedures followed in preparing and finalizing the financial statements (para. 4). In some cases, an entity is required to submit its financial statements to its shareholders for approval after the financial statements have already been issued. In such cases, the financial statements are authorized for issue on the date of original issuance, not on the date when shareholders approve the financial statements (para. 5). In other cases, the management of an entity is required to issue its financial statements to a supervisory board (made up solely of non-executives) for approval. In such cases, the financial statements are authorized for issue when the management authorizes them for issue to the supervisory board. Care may need to be taken in determining the date of 'authorization' for this purpose. The standard has to allow for a variety of different national systems of corporate governance and of management structure.

IAS 10 makes a distinction between adjusting events after the reporting period and non-adjusting events after the reporting period. For both types of event the financial impact of the events has to be disclosed to the readers of the financial statements, but the disclosure method differs.

## Adjusting events

With regard to adjusting events, an entity should adjust the amounts recognized in its financial statements to reflect adjusting events after the reporting period (para. 8). IAS 10 does not give an explicit definition as guidance for what might be an adjusting event. A list of examples of what the IASB considers to be adjusting events is presented. The following examples should serve as a point of reference for preparers of financial statements (para. 9):

- The settlement after the reporting period of a court case that confirms that an entity had a present obligation at the end of the reporting period. The entity adjusts any provision previously recognized related to this court case in accordance with IAS 37, *Provisions, Contingent Liabilities and Contingent Assets* or recognizes a new provision instead of merely disclosing a contingent liability because the settlement provides additional evidence that would be considered in accordance with para. 16 of IAS 37.

- The receipt of information after the reporting period indicating that an asset was impaired at the end of the reporting period or that the amount of a previously recognized impairment loss for that asset needs to be adjusted. For example:
    - the bankruptcy of a customer which occurs after the end of the reporting period usually confirms that a loss already existed at the end of the reporting period on a trade receivable account and that the entity needs to adjust the carrying amount of the trade receivable account
    - the sale of inventories after the reporting period may give evidence about their net realizable value at the end of the reporting period.

- The determination after the end of the reporting period of the cost of assets purchased or the proceeds from assets sold before the end of the reporting period.

- The determination after the reporting period of the amount of profit-sharing or bonus payments, if the entity had a present legal or constructive obligation at the end of the reporting period to make such payments as a result of events before that date (see IAS 19).

- The discovery of fraud or errors that show that the financial statements were incorrect.

## Non-adjusting events

The name reveals that the amounts related to this type of event after the reporting period should not be recognized in the financial statements themselves, but disclosed in the notes to the accounts. If non-adjusting events after the reporting period are material, non-disclosure could influence the economic decisions of users taken on the basis of the financial statements (para. 21). Accordingly, an entity shall disclose the following for each material category of non-adjusting event after the reporting period in the notes to the accounts:

- the nature of the event
- an estimate of its financial effect, or a statement that such an estimate cannot be made.

Again, examples of non-adjusting events are presented as guidance in IAS 10 (para. 22).

The following are examples of non-adjusting events after the reporting period that would generally result in disclosure:

- a major business acquisition after the reporting period (IFRS 3, *Business Combinations*, requires specific disclosures in such cases) or disposing of a major subsidiary

- announcing a plan to discontinue an operation

- major purchases of assets, classification of assets as held for sale in accordance with IFRS 5, *Non-current Assets Held for Sale and Discontinued Operations*, other disposals of assets or expropriation of major assets by government

- destruction of a major production plant by a fire after the reporting period

- announcing or commencing the implementation of a major restructuring (see IAS 37, *Provisions, Contingent Liabilities and Contingent Assets*)

- major ordinary share transactions and potential ordinary share transactions after the reporting period (IAS 33, *Earnings Per Share*, requires an entity to disclose a description of such transactions, other than when such transactions involve capitalization or bonus issues, share splits or reverse share splits all of which are required to be adjusted under IAS 33)

- abnormally large changes after the reporting period in asset prices or foreign exchange rates

- changes in tax rates or tax laws enacted or announced after the reporting period that have a significant effect on current and deferred tax assets and liabilities (see IAS 12, *Income Taxes*)

- entering into significant commitments or contingent liabilities, for example, by issuing significant guarantees

- commencing major litigation arising solely out of events that occurred after the reporting period.

Since information on not only adjusting but also on non-adjusting events is extremely important for external parties, the disclosure rules on non-adjusting events have become stricter over the years. If an entity receives information after the end of the reporting period about conditions that existed at the end of the reporting date, they are now obliged to adjust disclosures that relate to these conditions, in the light of the new information.

If we study the list of examples of non-adjusting events described in para. 22 of IAS 10, we notice that some events lie within the decision power of the management (e.g. acquisitions, discontinuing operations) and other events are beyond the influence of the management (e.g. fire, change in tax laws). It is interesting to observe that many acquisitions or major investments seem to take place between the end of the reporting period and the signing off of the accounts. By signing the contract after the end of the reporting period, the acquisition becomes a non-adjusting event. If, through the acquisition, control was obtained over another entity, full consolidation of the entity in the group accounts could be avoided and the influence of the liabilities of that entity and goodwill paid on acquisition could be postponed for one year on the group's financial statements.

## REAL WORLD ILLUSTRATION

To illustrate this observation we include the information on events after the reporting period published by Samsung in its Annual Report 2011, note 35 (page 93).

### Annual Report

### 35. Events After the Reporting Period

*A) Merger of Samsung LED*

The merger of Samsung LED with SEC was approved by the Board of Directors on December 26, 2011. The approval of the Board of Directors of the Company replaces shareholders' meeting approval of the acquisition, as the acquisition of Samsung LED is a small and simple merger as defined in the commercial law.

The shareholders of Samsung LED will receive 0.0134934 shares of the Company's common stock for each share of Samsung LED common stock owned on the closing date. The Company transferred its treasury stocks to the shareholders of Samsung LED.

*B) Acquisition of S-LCD*

The Company entered into contracts to acquire remaining issued shares of S-LCD from Sony on December 26, 2011.

The Company acquired shares of S-LCD with a closing date of January 19, 2011.

|  | *(In millions of Korean Won)* |
|---|---|
| Name of the acquired company | S-LCD |
| Purchase price | W 1 067 082 |
| Shares | 329 999 999 shares |
| Percentage of shareholding after acquisition | 100 % |

*C) Spin-off of LCD division*

The Company's Board of Directors approved the spin-off of the Company's LCD division on February 20, 2012. The shareholders will approve the spin-off on March 16, 2012, during the shareholders' meeting

| Category | Details |
|---|---|
| Companies subject to stock split | Samsung Display Corporation[1] |
| Business | LCD |

[1] The name of the newly established company is subject to change according to decision of shareholders' meeting.

150 000 000 shares will be newly issued with par value of W 5000 per shares and be assigned to SEC.

In the following disclosure on events after the reporting period, EADS, active in the air, space and defence industries, communicates in the notes to the financial statements information about contracts signed after the reporting date. EADS also mentions the date when the statements were authorized for issue.

## REAL WORLD ILLUSTRATION

### Events after the Reporting Period

On 29th February 2008, the US Air Force awarded Northrop Grumman Corp., USA a contract for the development and procurement of up to 179 tanker aircraft for approximately $40 billion. This dollar amount includes both priced options for 80 aircraft and unpriced options for another 99 as well as estimated support costs (currently unpriced). The initial contract for the newly named KC-45A, is for the system design and development of four test aircraft for $1.5 billion. The Air Force will be funding this initial tranche over the next three years. EADS North America Inc., USA is the partner to Northrop Grumman Corp., USA on the new tanker contract, with responsibility for assembling airframes and providing completed flight-qualified aircraft and refueling subsystems. The Military Transport Aircraft Division (MTAD) is responsible within the EADS Group for all military derivative programmes based on Airbus platforms, including tankers. Starting in 2011, production of KC-45A airframes will be performed at Airbus' new Mobile, Alabama aerospace centre which will house the Airbus KC-45A final assembly facility.

In addition, EADS Group and Airbus intend to transfer the final assembly of Airbus A330 civilian freighters there. Unsuccessful competitor Boeing announced its imminent intention to file a protest with the General Accounting Office, whose decision would have to be issued within 100 days of the filing as required by law.

*(Continued)*

## REAL WORLD ILLUSTRATION  (*Continued*)

With regard to the plan to sell the Airbus sites in Meaulte, St. Nazaire Ville, Nordenham, Varel, Lau-pheim and Filton and the EADS site in Augsburg, negotiations with selected preferred bidders (Late-coere in France, GKN in the UK and MT Aerospace in Germany) are ongoing. So far, binding agreements have not been reached. Furthermore, the potential divestment of the sites is still subject to EADS' Board of Directors decision.

These Consolidated Financial Statements have been authorized for issuance by the Board of Directors on 10th March 2008.

## Dividends

In the latest revision of IAS 10 the treatment of dividends was dealt with more explicitly. Paragraph 12 states that if dividends to holders of equity instruments (as defined in IAS 32, *Financial Instruments: Disclosure and Presentation*) are declared after the reporting period, an entity shall not recognize those dividends as a liability at the end of the reporting period. In many countries dividends under these circumstances are disclosed as a liability in the national GAAP accounts, the IAS treatment is different.

## The issue of going concern

There is, however, one item which applies to the definition of a non-adjusting event, but which entails an adjustment of the financial statements. We refer to para. 14 of IAS which stipulates that if management determines after the reporting period either that it intends to liquidate the entity or to cease trading, or that it has no realistic alternative but to do so, the financial statements should no longer be prepared on a going concern basis.

This implies that the accounts have to be completely redrawn on a non-going concern basis. The latter has a tremendous impact on the data which will subsequently be presented in the financial statements.

## EARNINGS PER SHARE

Most people or companies buy shares of other companies for investment purposes. Probably only fans of listed football clubs such as Bayern München, Barcelona or Ajax buy shares for purely emotional reasons. An indicator frequently used in the context of evaluating the investment performance of a company is earnings per share (see Chapter 12 and Part 4 of this book). Earnings per share (EPS) is found by dividing profit attributable to the ordinary shareholders by the number of ordinary shares in issue. As an absolute, however, it has no meaning or relevance. Earnings per share becomes relevant in the context of the price/earnings ratio or when the growth rate of the EPS of a company is considered. This will be explained with the following example. If we are told that company A has an EPS of 6c whereas company B has an EPS of 25c, we are unable to compare the performance of the two because we know nothing about their relative size or, more specifically, about the number or value of shares in issue. For the same reasons, the quoted share price of the two companies provides no basis for comparison of the stock market's perceptions of either.

Thus analysts and investors require a basis of comparison and an indicator of confidence in particular companies. Such an indicator is the price/earnings (PE) ratio, which is simply calculated by dividing the share price by the EPS, thereby relating company performance to external perception.

The calculation and use of the PE ratio is illustrated in Activity 25.4, where the PE ratio for company X is calculated to be 7.5 and for company Y, 12.

## ACTIVITY 25.4

In which company would you invest?

| Company | X | Y |
| --- | --- | --- |
| Price per share (a) | 150c | 96c |
| Earnings per share (b) | 20c | 8c |
| PE ratio (a/b) | 7.5 | 12 |

### Activity feedback

Company X has a higher share price and greater EPS, but company Y is expected to perform better in the future. Why? The normal action of supply and demand has bid up the share price of Y relative to current earnings and the market is therefore saying something about its confidence in Y relative to X. Market partici- pants are willing to pay 12 times the EPS to acquire a share in company Y, whereas investors are only willing to pay seven-and-a-half times the EPS to invest in com- pany X. This difference results from an alternative view of the future earnings generating power and prospects of both companies (e.g. markets of company Y repre- sent more growth potential, company Y has more prod- ucts in the early stage of the life cycle of company X). Clearly, a very high PE would indicate such extravagant expectations that there may be some element of risk, but generally a high PE is a good indicator of market support. People are willing to pay more for something they think more highly of.

If the PE ratio is used in this way, being quoted in the financial press and elsewhere, it matters greatly that its derivation is consistent and comparable. There are no problems with the price of the share, but what about the earnings per share?

In this section we will discuss the calculation of the EPS and in Part 4 of the book we further illustrate the use of EPS in the context of the PE ratio. In order to calculate earnings per share, first of all the earnings number has to be defined and, second, the determination of the number of shares to be used in the denominator has to be speci- fied as well. To enhance the comparability of the EPS measure between companies the IASB has issued IAS 33 which deals with the determination of EPS. The IASB is well aware of the fact that IAS 33 mainly improves consistency in the determination of the denominator of the EPS ratio. Companies can still influence their results by using different accounting valuation methods and accounting estimates, as we discuss in Chapter 31.

IAS 33 shall be applied by entities whose ordinary shares or potential ordinary shares are publicly traded and by entities that are in the process of issuing ordinary shares or potential ordinary shares in public securities markets (IAS 33, para. 2). An entity that discloses earnings per share shall calculate and disclose earnings per share in accordance with IAS 33, if they state that their annual accounts comply with IAS/IFRS. This requirement also applies to companies that disclose voluntarily EPS data in their IAS financial statements.

Two types of EPS ratio can be calculated: basic earnings per share (BEPS) and diluted earnings per share (DEPS). The main difference between the two EPS figures is the number of shares they take into account in the denominator. In the calculation of BEPS the outstanding equity share capital during the financial year is taken into consideration. DEPS takes into account, besides the outstanding shares, the existence of securities with no current claim on equity earnings, but which will give rise to such a claim in the future. This information gives potential investors an idea about future changes in the EPS.

As the main objective of IAS 33 is achieving consistency in the determination of the denominator of the EPS ratio, the elements to be included in the denominator should be defined first. Paragraphs 5 and 6 of IAS 33 provide the following definitions:

> *An ordinary share* is an equity instrument that is subordinate to all other classes of equity instruments. Ordinary shares participate in net profit for the period only after other types of shares such as preference shares.
>
> *A potential ordinary* share is a financial instrument or other contract that may entitle its holder to ordinary shares.
>
> *Warrants, options and their equivalents* are financial instruments that give the holder the right to purchase ordinary shares.
>
> *Contingently issuable ordinary shares* are ordinary shares issuable for little or no cash or other consideration upon the satisfaction of certain conditions pursuant to a contingent share agreement, whereby a contingent share agreement is an agreement to issue shares that is dependent on the satisfaction of specified conditions.
>
> *Put options on ordinary shares* are contracts that give the holder the right to sell ordinary shares at a specified price for a given period.
>
> *Dilution* is a reduction in earnings per share or an increase in loss per share resulting from the assumption that convertible securities were converted, that options or warrants were exercised or that ordinary shares were issued upon the satisfaction of certain conditions. As a result of these events the number of outstanding shares will increase.
>
> *Anti-dilution* is an increase in earnings per share or a reduction in loss per share resulting from the assumption that convertible instruments are converted, that options and warrants are exercised, or that ordinary shares are issued upon the satisfaction of specified conditions. As a result of these events the number of outstanding shares will decrease.

Listed companies have to disclose the BEPS and DEPS. We concentrate, first of all, on the BEPS figure and all the issues which might arise in the calculation of this. Later on we discuss the DEPS.

## Basic earnings per share

The basic earnings per share (BEPS) figure represents the amount attributable to the ordinary shareholders by dividing the earnings figure by the weighted average number of ordinary shares outstanding (the denominator) during the period. The calculation of the earnings figure is determined in para. 12. The earnings are equal to the profit and loss attributable to the parent entity. If there are discontinuing operations in a company then the BEPS should also be calculated on the basis of the profit or loss for the period from the continuing operations attributable to the parent entity. If there are no discontinuing operations there is just one BEPS figure. Again, this is to improve the relevance of the information communicated.

The calculation of the earnings included in the numerator shall be the profit or loss adjusted for the after-tax amounts of preference dividends, differences arising on the settlement of preference shares and other similar effects of preference shares classified as equity. The reason is that ordinary shares are not entitled to those elements. The weighted average number of ordinary shares outstanding during the period will figure in the denominator.

---

## ACTIVITY 25.5

The summarized income statement for EPS SA for the year ended 20X6 is as follows:

|  | € | € |
|---|---|---|
| Profit before taxation |  | 1 000 000 |
| Taxation (including deferred adjustment) |  | 400 000 |
|  |  | 600 000 |
| Preference dividend | 50 000 |  |
| Ordinary dividend | 100 000 |  |
|  |  | 150 000 |
|  |  | 450 000 |

The number of ordinary shares in issue is 200 000. Calculate the basic EPS.

### Activity feedback

From the definition of earnings per share:

$$\text{Basic EPS} = \frac{\text{Profit after tax} - \text{Preference dividend}}{\text{Number of ordinary shares}}$$

$$= \frac{600\,000 - 50\,000}{200\,000}$$

$$= €2.75 \text{ per share}$$

---

**Changes in equity share capital during the year** In Activity 25.5 the number of shares in issue is given and remains constant over the financial period. However, in reality, there can be changes in the equity share capital during the financial year under consideration. For the purpose of calculating BEPS, the number of ordinary shares should be the weighted average number of ordinary shares outstanding during the period. This is the number of ordinary shares outstanding at the beginning of the period, adjusted by the number of ordinary shares bought back or issued during the period multiplied by a time-weighting factor. The time-weighting factor is the number of days that the shares are outstanding as a proportion of the total number of days in the period; a reasonable approximation of the weighted average is adequate in many circumstances.

---

## ACTIVITY 25.6

Fullmar plc had issued share capital on 31 December X5 as follows:

> 500 000 preference shares (value €1 each)
> a preference dividend of 7 per cent is attached
> 4 000 000 ordinary shares (value €0.25 each)

Profit after tax for the year ended 31 December X5 was €435 000. On 1 October X5 Fullmar had issued 1 million ordinary shares at full market price (€0.25 each).

Calculate the EPS for Fullmar plc for the year ended 31 December X5.

### Activity feedback

The number of ordinary shares in issue on 1 January X5 was 3 million and 1 million were issued on 1 October X5.

Thus the time weighted average number of ordinary shares in issue for the year was

$$(3\,000\,000 \times 9/12) + (4\,000\,000 \times 3/12) = 3\,250\,000$$

or

$$(3\,000\,000 \times 12/12) + (1\,000\,000 \times 3/12) = 3\,250\,000$$

The earnings for the year attributable to the ordinary shareholders is €435 000 – €35 000 preference dividend = €400 000. Therefore:

$$EPS = \frac{400\,000}{3\,250\,000} \text{ per share}$$

$$= €0.1230 \text{ per share}$$

Note that the 1 million ordinary shares are issued at full market price in this example.

In reality, shares can be issued at a price different from the market price, or shares can be issued without a corresponding change in the resources of the company. Related to this, para. 26 of IAS 33 states that the weighted number of ordinary shares outstanding during the period and for all periods presented shall be adjusted for events, other than the conversion of potential ordinary shares, that have changed the number of ordinary shares outstanding without a corresponding change in resources. Ordinary shares may be issued or the number of ordinary shares outstanding may be reduced, without a corresponding change in resources. Examples include:

- a capitalization or bonus issue (sometimes referred to as a stock dividend)
- a bonus element in any other issue, for example a bonus element in a rights issue to existing shareholders
- a share split
- a reverse share split (consolidation of shares).

In these circumstances the calculation of the EPS in Activity 25.6 needs to be modified. In all those circumstances where these 1 million ordinary shares have been issued at less than market price or for no consideration, the calculations in Activity 25.6 need to take into account this new element. This is illustrated below. A difference will be made between a change in the number of outstanding shares without a change in the resource of the company (e.g. bonus issue and share split) and a change in the number of outstanding shares with a change in the resources of the company, but by which the shares were not issued at market price. We will first illustrate a change in the number of outstanding shares without a change in the resources of the company.

**A bonus issue** In a capitalization or bonus issue or a share split, ordinary shares are issued to existing shareholders for no additional consideration. Therefore, the number of ordinary shares outstanding is increased without an increase in resources. The number of ordinary shares outstanding before the event is adjusted for the proportionate change in the number of ordinary shares outstanding as if the event had occurred at the beginning of the earliest period presented. For example, on a two-for-one bonus issue, the number of ordinary shares that are outstanding before the issue is multiplied by three to obtain the new total number of ordinary shares or by two to obtain the number of additional ordinary shares.

In all these examples more shares have been issued at no 'cost'. The earnings of the business during the year can only be regarded as relating to the shares at the end of the year, i.e. to all the shares including the new ones. No distortion arises, as no resources were passed into the business when the new shares were created.

## ACTIVITY 25.7

Using the same data as in Activity 25.6 but assuming that the shares issued on October X5 were a capitalization issue, calculate the EPS for the year. This means that we now have a bonus issue for no additional consideration, whereby for each three existing shares a new share is issued.

*Activity feedback*

*We now have a capitalization or bonus issue, not a full market price issue of shares, and therefore we assume 4 million shares in issue for the whole of the year. (Note this assumption would be the same no matter at what point during the year the capitalization was made.)*

## ACTIVITY 25.7    (Continued)

*Thus, = 3 000 000 + 1 000 000 = 4 000 000.*

*The number of shares in issue can also be calculated from the following:*

$$3\,000\,000 \times \frac{9}{12} \times \frac{4}{3} + 4\,000\,000 \times \frac{3}{12}$$

$$\text{(bonus factor)}$$

$$EPS = \frac{400\,000}{400\,000} = €0.100 \text{ per share}$$

We need to think about the implications of such changes for meaningful comparison with the prior year's figures. Adjusted earnings per share should be calculated in order to provide meaningful prior year comparative figures. Thus, the EPS figure which relates to year X4 needs to be restarted. This ratio then consists of the earnings of the year (X4) before profit, divided by the new amount of outstanding shares of the current year, namely 4 000 000.

A consolidation of ordinary shares generally reduces the number of ordinary shares outstanding without a corresponding reduction in resources. However, where a share consolidation is combined with a special dividend and the overall effect is a share repurchase at fair value, the reduction in the number of ordinary shares outstanding is the result of a corresponding reduction in resources. The weighted average number of ordinary shares outstanding for the period in which the combined transaction takes place is adjusted for the reduction in the number of ordinary shares from the date the special dividend is recognized.

We will now illustrate the calculation of the EPS when the total number of outstanding shares changes, together with a change in the resources of the company.

**Rights issue at less than full market price**  In a rights issue, the exercise price is often less than the fair value of the shares, for example if Fullmar (see Activity 25.6) had issued the 1 million ordinary shares at a price less than market price. Therefore, such a rights issue includes a bonus element as indicated earlier. The number of ordinary shares to be used in calculating basic earnings per share for all periods before the rights issue is the number of ordinary shares outstanding before the issue, multiplied by the following factor:

$$\frac{\text{Fair value per share immediately before the exercise of rights}}{\text{Theoretical ex-rights value per share}}$$

The theoretical ex-rights value per share is calculated by adding the aggregate fair value of the shares immediately before the exercise of the rights to the proceeds from the exercise of the rights and dividing by the number of shares outstanding after the exercise of the rights or a theoretical ex-rights value per share:

$$\frac{\begin{array}{c}\text{Fair value of all outstanding shares before the exercise of rights} \\ + \text{ total amount received from exercise of rights}\end{array}}{\begin{array}{c}\text{Number of shares outstanding before exercise} \\ + \text{ number of shares issued in the exercise}\end{array}}$$

Where the rights themselves are to be publicly traded separately from the shares before the exercise date, fair value for the purposes of this calculation is established at the close of the last day on which the shares are traded together with the rights.

This is complicated! A rights issue combines the characteristics of a capitalization issue and a full market price issue. New resources are passing into the business so a higher earnings figure, related to these new resources, should be expected. But at the same time there is a bonus element in the new shares, which should be treated like a capitalization issue. To the extent that the rights issue provides new resources, i.e. equates to an issue at full market price, we need to calculate the average number of shares weighted on a time basis. To the extent that the rights issue includes a discount or bonus element we need to increase the number of shares deemed to have been in issue for the whole period. The theoretical ex-rights value per share can be calculated as follows:

- Calculate the total market value of the equity before the rights issue (actual cumulative rights price × number of shares).
- Calculate the total proceeds expected from the right issue (issue price × number of shares).
- Add these two amounts and divide by the total number of shares involved altogether (i.e. by the total number after the rights issue).

We now introduce Activities 25.8 and 25.9 to illustrate the calculations.

## ACTIVITY 25.8

Company TEX wants to raise capital and decides to issue one share for each five outstanding shares. The new shares will be issued at a price of €10. The market value of the shares is €25. The one to five issue takes place on 1 March 20X5 and all shares issued are subscribed. The number of outstanding ordinary shares before the issue was 500. The profit for the year 20X4 is €1600 and the profit for the year 20X5 is €2000. Calculate the EPS for 20X4 and 20X5.

### Activity feedback

The increase in resources of company TEX takes place during the year, namely on 1 March 20X5. The shares are issued at less than market price so this includes a bonus element.

We will first determine the theoretical ex-rights value per share. Using that number we are able to calculate the factor by which we have to multiply the number of outstanding shares before the issue in order to take into account the bonus element included in this issue. Theoretical ex-rights value per share:

$$((€25 \times 500 \text{ shares}) + (€10 \times 100 \text{ shares}))/(500 + 100)$$
$$= €22.5 \text{ per share}$$

Second, we calculate the multiplying factor, i.e. the fair value per share immediately before the exercise of the rights/theoretical ex-rights value per share:

$$€25/€22.5 = 1.11$$

We calculate the EPS for 20X5 and take into account when the issue took place:

$$\text{EPS 20X5} = €2000/((500 \times 1.11 \times 2/12) + (600 \times 10/12)) = €3.37$$

We need to recalculate the EPS for 20X4 = €1 600/ $(500 \times 1.11) = €2.88$.

## ACTIVITY 25.9

Trig plc as at 30 June X5 has €600 000 ordinary shares in issue with a current market value of €2 per share. On 1 July X5 Trig plc makes a four for six rights issue at €1.75 and all rights are taken up. Earnings for the year after tax and preference dividends are €81 579 and the previous year's EPS was declared as 9c. Calculate the EPS figure that should be shown in the financial statements for the year ended 31 December X5.

(Continued)

## ACTIVITY 25.9    (Continued)

### Activity feedback

*We first need to calculate the theoretical ex-rights price of the shares:*

Market value of equity

before rights $= 600\,000 \times €2 = 1\,200\,000$

Proceeds from rights

$$\text{issue} = \frac{400\,000}{1\,000\,000} \times €1.75 = \frac{700\,000}{1\,900\,000}$$

$$\text{Theoretical ex-rights value per share} = \frac{1\,900\,000}{1\,000\,000}$$
$$= 1.90$$

*Second, we calculate the weighted average number of shares:*

$$600\,000 \times \frac{1}{2} \times \frac{2}{1.9} + 1\,000\,000 \times \frac{1}{2} = 815\,789$$
$$\text{(time weighting)} \quad\quad \text{(time weighting)}$$

*Therefore EPS for year ending 31 December*

$$X5 = \frac{8\,157\,900}{815\,789} = 10c \text{ per share}$$

*Third, we need to recalculate the previous year's EPS:*

$$9 \times 1.9/2 = 8.55c \text{ per share}$$

*A reduction has occurred in the previous year's EPS as we have inserted the bonus element of the rights, and we assume that this element has happened for the earlier period reported.*

# Diluted earnings per share

Besides the basic earnings per share, a company must also disclose its diluted earnings per share (DEPS). When there are securities existing at the year-end that will have a claim on equity earnings from some time in the future, then it is clear that at this future time the claim of each currently existing share will, other things being equal, be reduced (or diluted). It is likely to be useful to current shareholders and others to give them a picture of what the EPS would be if this dilution took place. This is done by recalculating the current year's EPS as if the dilution had already occurred.

For the calculation of the numerator of the diluted EPS, the starting amount will be the earnings amount of the BEPS adjusted for the after-tax effect of:

1 any dividends or other items related to dilutive potential ordinary shares deducted in arriving at profit or loss attributable to ordinary equity holders of the parent entity as calculated in accordance with the calculation done for the BEPS

2 any interest recognized in the period related to dilutive potential ordinary shares

3 any other changes in income or expense that would result from the conversion of the dilutive potential ordinary shares.

In the denominator of the DEPS the number of ordinary shares shall be the weighted average number of ordinary shares calculated in accordance with paras 19 and 26 (which relate to the denominator of the BEPS), plus the weighted average number of ordinary shares that would be issued on the conversion of all the dilutive potential ordinary shares into ordinary shares. Dilutive potential ordinary shares shall be deemed to have been converted into ordinary shares at the beginning of the period or, if later, the date of issue of the potential ordinary shares.

Further, it is interesting to note that potential ordinary shares shall be treated as dilutive when, and only when, their conversion to ordinary shares would decrease earnings per share or increase loss per share from continuing operations (para. 41).

This implies that the impact of potential ordinary shares with anti-dilutive effect on EPS is not taken into account when calculating the DEPS. Potential ordinary shares are anti-dilutive when their conversion to ordinary shares would increase earnings per share or decrease loss per share from continuing operations. As a result, an investor will only be informed numerically about the negative impact of potential ordinary shares on the future EPS figure. A positive impact will not be calculated.

We will illustrate the calculation of the DEPS in Activity 25.10.

## ACTIVITY 25.10

The summarized income statement for EPS plc for the year ended 20X1 is as follows:

|  | € | € |
|---|---|---|
| Profit before taxation |  | 1 000 000 |
| Taxation (including deferred adjustment) |  | 400 000 |
|  |  | 600 000 |
| Preference dividend | 50 000 |  |
| Ordinary dividend | 100 000 |  |
|  |  | 150 000 |
|  |  | 450 000 |

The number of ordinary shares in issue is 2 million.

In addition to the 2 million ordinary shares already in issue, however, there exists convertible loan stock of €500 000 bearing interest at 10 per cent. This may be converted into ordinary shares between 20X3 and 20X6 at a rate of one ordinary share for every €2 of loan stock. Corporation tax is taken for convenience as 50 per cent. Calculate the fully diluted EPS.

### Activity feedback

*The fully diluted EPS is found as follows. If the conversion is fully completed then there will be two effects:*

1 *The share capital will increase by 250 000 shares (1 share for every €2 of the €500 000 loan).*

2 *The profit after tax will increase by the interest on the loan no longer payable less the extra tax on this increase. The interest at 10 per cent on €500 000 is €50 000, but the extra tax on this profit increase would be 50 per cent of €50 000, i.e. €25 000.*

*So profit after tax, and therefore 'earnings', will increase by 50 000 – 25 000 = €25 000. Fully diluted EPS will be:*

$$\frac{600\ 000 + 25\ 000 - 50\ 000}{2\ 000\ 000 + 250\ 000}$$
$$= \frac{575\ 000}{2\ 250\ 000}$$
$$= 25.6\text{c per share}$$

*Remember that the fully diluted EPS is a hypothetical calculation. It assumes total conversion into equity participation. The extent to which this assumption is likely in any particular circumstance is irrelevant.*

In determining whether potential ordinary shares are dilutive or anti-dilutive, each issue or series of potential ordinary shares is considered separately rather than in aggregate. The sequence in which potential ordinary shares are considered may affect whether they are dilutive. Therefore, to maximize the dilution of BEPS, each issue or series of potential ordinary shares is considered in sequence from the most dilutive to the least dilutive, i.e. dilutive potential ordinary shares with the lowest 'earning per incremental share' are included in the DEPS calculation before those with a higher earning per incremental share. Options and warrants are generally included first because they do not affect the numerator of the calculation.

IAS 33 considers a number of financial instruments as potentially dilutive and describes their effect on the DEPS figure in the following order:

- options, warrants and equivalent instruments (paras 45–48)
- convertible instruments (paras 42–51)

- contingently issuable shares (paras 52–61)
- purchase options (para. 62)
- written put options (para. 63).

We will illustrate the impact of options on the DEPS figures in Activity 25.11. The impact of convertible instruments on DEPS figures has been illustrated in Activity 25.10.

## ACTIVITY 25.11

Company Capsi realized a profit of 600 000 in the financial year 20X6 which is attributable to the ordinary shareholders. In the year 20X6 300 000 shares are outstanding. The BEPS for company Capsi is €2 (= 600 000/300 000). During the year 20X6 100 000 share options are outstanding of which the exercise price is €10 per share. The market price of the shares of company Capsi was €15 in 20X6. Calculate the DEPS for 20X6.

a part will be issued without consideration. The number of shares considered to be issued at market price will not influence the calculation of the DEPS. The number of shares considered to be issued with no increase in the resources of the company will be assumed to be present from the earliest period which is reported and will have a dilutive effect. So in fact the prior year DEPS should also be adjusted.

### Activity feedback

We will assume that from the number of potentially outstanding shares a part will be issued at market price and

|  | Profit for ordinary shareholders | Number of shares | Earnings per share |
|---|---|---|---|
| Profit 20X6 | 600 000 | | |
| Weighted average number of shares outstanding in 2006 Basic EPS | | 300 000 | |
| Basic EPS | | | 2 |
| Weighted average number of shares under option | | 100 000 | |
| Weighted average number of shares that would have been issued at average market price (100 000 × €10)/€15 | | (66 666) | |
| Diluted EPS | 600 000 | 344 444 | 1.74 |

The latest version of IAS 33 also pays attention to retrospective adjustments. IAS 33 (para. 64) states in this respect that if the number of ordinary or potential ordinary shares outstanding increases as a result of capitalization, bonus issue or share split, or decreases as a result of a reverse share split, the calculation of basic and diluted earnings per share for all periods presented shall be adjusted retrospectively. If these changes occur after the balance sheet date but before the financial statements are authorized for issue, the per share calculations for those and any prior period financial statements presented shall be based on the new number of shares. The fact that per share calculations reflect such changes in the number of shares shall be disclosed. In addition, basic and diluted earnings per share of all periods presented shall be adjusted for the effects of errors and adjustments resulting from changes in accounting policies accounted for retrospectively.

The IASB attaches importance to the EPS figure as it requires in IAS 33 that the basic EPS as well as the diluted EPS should be disclosed on the face of the income statement for the current year as well as for all other years for which information is presented. EPS should be presented for each class of ordinary shares that has a different right to share in net profit for the period. We know that if there are discontinuing operations, two EPS figures have to be disclosed. An entity that reports a discontinuing operation shall disclose the basic and diluted amounts per share for this line item either on the face of the income statement or in the notes to the financial statements. Even if the EPS figure is negative the amounts should be presented.

On the face of the income statement EPS is presented as a single figure. In the notes to the accounts the user of the financial statements can obtain information on the composition of the numerator and the denominator of the basic EPS and the diluted EPS.

It is perhaps useful at this point to look at an example of a calculation of EPS involving more than one type of share issue. The following example (Activity 25.12) appears complicated but only requires a clear thought process and a knowledge of IAS requirements.

## ACTIVITY 25.12

Part of a listed company's consolidated profit and loss account is as follows:

### Chasewater Public Limited Company
### Consolidated P&L account (extract) for the year ended 30 June 20X5

|  | € | € |
|---|---|---|
| Group net profit before taxation | | 500 000 |
| Taxation | | 270 000 |
| Group net profit after taxation | | 230 000 |
| Minority interests in subsidiaries | | 20 000 |
| Attributable to shareholders in Chasewater plc | | 210 000 |
| Extraordinary items (after taxation) | | 11 000 |
| Net profit for year | | 221 000 |
| Dividends (net) | | |
| Preference | 25 000 | |
| Ordinary | 100 000 | |
| | | 125 000 |
| Retained earnings for year | | 96 000 |

Notes:

1   Issued share capital (fully paid), 1 July 20X4: 250 000 10 per cent cumulative preference shares of €1 each and 4 million ordinary shares of 25c each.

2   Loan capital, 1 July 20X4: €500 000 7 per cent convertible debentures (convertible into 200 ordinary shares per €100 debenture, with proportionate increases for subsequent bonus issues and for the bonus element in subsequent rights issues).

3   Changes during the year ended 30 June 20X5:
1 October 20X4 Rights issues of ordinary shares (ranking for dividend 20X4–5): 1 for 4 at €0.90 per share: market price before issue, €1.00.
1 January 20X5 Conversion of €100 000 of 7 per cent convertible debentures.
1 March 20X5 Bonus issue of ordinary shares, 1 for 3.

4   Basic earnings per share for the year ended 30 June 20X4 was 4c.

5   Corporation tax, 52 per cent; income tax basic rate, 30 per cent.

**Required:**

(a)   compute the company's basic earnings per share for the current year and its comparative BEPS for the previous year; and

(b)   compute the company's fully diluted earnings per share for the current year only.

### Activity feedback
*On reading the question you should have noted the following:*

**1**   *a rights issue on 1 October 20X4 of 1 million shares*

**2**   *a conversion of debentures on 1 January 20X5 to 200 000 shares plus the bonus of ordinary shares at 1 for 3 issue.*

*A quantity of convertible debentures still remain in issue. First, we calculate the earnings for the EPS calculation. This is straightforward:*

## ACTIVITY 25.12    (Continued)

| | |
|---|---|
| Profit after tax after extraordinary items | 221 000 |
| *Preference dividend* | 25 000 |
| Earnings for basic EPS calculation | 196 000 |

*Second, as a rights issue has taken place we need to calculate the adjusting factor, i.e.:*

$$\frac{\text{Actual cumulative rights}}{\text{Theoretical ex-rights}} =$$

Market value of equity

before rights = 4 000 000 × €1 = 4 000 000

$$\text{Proceeds of rights issue} = \frac{1\,000\,000}{5\,000\,000} \times 90c = \frac{900\,000}{4\,900\,000}$$

$$\text{Theoretical ex-rights value per share} = \frac{4\,900\,000}{5\,000\,000} = 98c$$

*Adjusting factor = 100/98 (this represents the bonus element of the rights issue).*

*Third, we need to calculate the time weighted average number of shares and remember to include the bonus issue for the whole of the year and multiply the proportion of capital in issue before rights by a factor of 100/98. Note the conversion of debentures on 1 January 20X5 will be to 200 000 × 100/98 shares = 204 082 shares and that the bonus issue will be calculated as follows:*

Number of shares in issue before bonus = 4 000 000 + 1 000 000 rights + 204 082 conversion = 5 204 082

$$\text{Bonus issue at 1 for 3} = \frac{5\,204\,082}{7} = 743\,440$$

Number of shares in issue after bonus = 6 938 776

*Time weighted number of shares =*

$$\left[ 4\,000 \times \frac{3}{2} \times \frac{100}{98} + 5\,000\,0000 \times \frac{3}{12} \times 5\,204\,082 \times \frac{2}{12} \right]$$

$$\frac{4}{3}(\text{bonus factor}) + 6\,938\,776 \times \frac{4}{12}$$

$$= (1\,020\,408.1 + 1\,250\,000 + 867\,347)\frac{4}{3} + 2\,312\,925.3$$

$$= 3\,137\,755.1 \times \frac{4}{3} + 2\,312\,925.3 = 6\,496\,598.6$$

*The fourth, fifth and sixth steps are as follows:*

$$\text{Basic EPS 20X5} = \frac{19\,600\,000}{6\,496\,598.6} = 3.02c$$

$$\text{Revised EPS 20X4} = 4c \times \frac{3}{4}(\text{bonus factor})$$

$$\times \frac{98}{100}(\text{rights factor}) = 2.94c$$

*Fully diluted EPS also needs to be calculated to see if there is a 5 per cent dilution:*

| | € |
|---|---|
| Basic earnings | 196 000 |
| Add back debenture interest assuming full conversion took place at 1 July 20X4 | |

$$\frac{6}{12} \times 7\% \times 500\,000 + 6\frac{6}{12} \times 7\% \times 4\,000\,000 = 31\,500$$

| | |
|---|---|
| Corporate tax adjustment for non-payment of debenture interests | (16 380) |
| Diluted earnings | 211 120 |

*The weighted number of shares will need recalculating assuming all convertible debentures converted on 1 July 20X4, i.e. 1 million shares issued. Note the bonus issue will now be 2 083 333 shares on 1 March 20X5, and the rights issue 1 250 000 shares on 1 October 20X4.*

*Time weighted number of shares:*

$$\left[ 5\,000\,000 \times \frac{3}{12} \times \frac{100}{98} + 6\,250\,000 \times \frac{5}{12} \right] \frac{4}{3} + 833\,333$$

$$\times \frac{4}{12} = 7\,950\,680$$

$$\text{Diluted EPS} = \frac{21\,112\,000c}{7\,950\,680} = 266c$$

## REAL WORLD ILLUSTRATION

The following is an extract from the Annual Accounts of AB Inbev 2012, which illustrates the disclosure on EPS, this important financial figure. The information is disclosed in the second part of note 22 Earnings per share (pages 53–54).

## REAL WORLD ILLUSTRATION    *(Continued)*

### Annual Report

### 22 Earnings per share

The calculation of basic earnings per share is based on the profit attributable to equity holders of AB InBev of 7 243m US dollar (2011: 5 855m US dollar) and a weighted average number of ordinary shares outstanding during the year, calculated as follows:

| Million shares | 2012 | 2011 |
|---|---|---|
| Issued ordinary shares at 1 January, net of treasury shares | 1 598 | 1 593 |
| Effect of shares issued and share buyback programs | 2 | 2 |
| **Weighted average number of ordinary shares at 31 December** | **1 600** | **1 595** |

The calculation of diluted earnings per share is based on the profit attributable to equity holders of AB InBev of 7 243m US dollar (2011: 5 855m US dollar) and a weighted average number of ordinary shares (diluted) outstanding during the year, calculated as follows:

| Million shares | 2012 | 2011 |
|---|---|---|
| Weighted average number of ordinary shares at 31 December | 1600 | 1 595 |
| Effect of share options, warrants and restricted stock units | 28 | 19 |
| **Weighted average number of ordinary shares (diluted) at 31 December** | **1 628** | **1 614** |

The calculation of earnings per share before non-recurring items is based on the profit after tax and before non-recurring items, attributable to equity holders of AB InBev. A reconciliation of profit before non-recurring items, attributable to equity holders of AB InBev to profit attributable to equity holders of AB InBev is calculated as follows:

| Million US dollar | 2012 | 2011 |
|---|---|---|
| Profit before non-recurring items, attributable to equity holders of AB InBev | 7 283 | 6 449 |
| Non-recurring items, after taxes, attributable to equity holders of AB InBev (refer note 8) | (22) | (172) |
| Non-recurring finance cost, after taxes, attributable to equity holders of AB InBev (refer note 8) | (18) | (422) |
| **Profit attributable to equity holders of AB InBev** | **7 243** | **5 855** |

The table below sets out the EPS calculation:

| Million US dollar | 2012 | 2011 |
|---|---|---|
| Profit attributable to equity holders of AB InBev | 7 243 | 5 855 |
| Weighted average number of ordinary shares | 1 600 | 1 595 |
| **Basic EPS** | **4.53** | **3.67** |
| Profit before non-recurring items, attributable to equity holders of AB InBev | 7 283 | 6 449 |
| Weighted average number of ordinary shares | 1 600 | 1 595 |
| **EPS before non-recurring items** | **4.55** | **4.04** |
| Profit attributable to equity holders of AB InBev | 7 243 | 5 855 |
| Weighted average number of ordinary shares (diluted) | 1 628 | 1 614 |
| **Diluted EPS** | **4.45** | **3.63** |
| Profit before non-recurring items, attributable to equity holders of AB InBev | 7 283 | 6 449 |
| Weighted average number of ordinary shares (diluted) | 1 628 | 1 614 |
| **Diluted EPS before non-recurring items** | **4.47** | **4.00** |

The average market value of the company's shares for purposes of calculating the dilutive effect of share options and restricted stock units was based on quoted market prices for the period that the options and restricted stock units were outstanding. 4.9m share options and restricted stock units were anti-dilutive and not included in the calculation of the dilutive effect as at 31 December 2012.

# INTERIM FINANCIAL REPORTING

All the standards discussed in this chapter relate to the disclosure of information with the purpose of enhancing the decision usefulness of the data communicated through the financial statements. Investors, creditors, suppliers, the government and the workforce all make use of data taken from the financial statements. The financial statements are prepared on a yearly basis only. The investors' community, however, appreciates the provision of financial information on a more frequent basis.

Many stock exchanges require half-year interim reports. The US SEC even asks for quarterly interim reports. In Europe, the normal frequency of reporting is biannual. Relatively few European companies follow the North American practice of reporting every quarter. Markets' half-yearly financial reports have to be issued and, where the issuer is required to prepare consolidated accounts, the condensed set of financial statements shall be prepared in accordance with the international accounting standard applicable to the interim financial reporting as adopted pursuant to the procedure provided for under Article 6 of Regulation (EC) No. 1606/2002. This means that half-yearly reports are expected to comply with IAS 34. A company can publish interim financial reports as a result of a requirement by a stock exchange or another regulatory body. The practice of publishing an interim report can also result from a voluntary disclosure decision.

## ACTIVITY 25.13

Look at websites of listed companies and find out how they present their interim financial reports. Do they present other types of financial short-term information?

### Activity feedback
Interim financial reports usually consist of a consolidated statement in a kind of abbreviated format and explanatory notes accompanied by a management report. Besides interim financial statements companies also often disclose on their website operating data on a half-year, quarterly or even monthly basis. If you look at the websites of some major airlines you will even find traffic statistics updated on a monthly basis.

Before we present the contents of IAS 34, we want to underline that IAS does not require companies to publish interim financial reports. Only if an entity reporting under IAS does choose (or is required by other authorities) to issue such interim reports, then IAS prescribes the minimum content of an interim financial report and the principles for recognition and measurement in complete or condensed financial statements for an interim period.

According to accounting theory there are two different theoretical approaches towards interim reporting, namely the 'integral' approach and the 'discrete' approach. The 'integral' approach considers the interim report as part of the yearly financial report. This approach means that in order to prepare the interim reports, preparers will first determine the year totals and subsequently allocate these over the different interim periods.

The discrete approach considers an interim report as being independent from the 12-month financial accounts and will recognize assets, liabilities, expenses and revenue in the period in which they occur.

In principle the IASB has opted for the discrete approach; however, for a number of items we notice the influence of the integral approach.

## Format of interim reports

Concerning the format of the interim report, IAS 34 leaves two options from which management has to choose. As an interim financial report a company can publish either a complete set of financial statements or a set of condensed financial statements for an interim period. The interim period is defined as a financial reporting period shorter than a full financial year. If an entity publishes a complete set of financial statements in its interim financial report, the form and content of those statements should conform to the requirements of IAS 1 for a complete set of financial statements.

If, however, the company chooses for a set of condensed financial statements then the minimum components of the interim financial report are presented in para. 8 of IAS 34, as follows:

- condensed statement of financial position
- condensed statement of comprehensive income
- condensed statement showing either (i) all changes in equity or (ii) changes in equity other than those arising from capital transactions with owners and distributions to owners
- condensed cash flow statement
- selected explanatory notes.

What is meant by 'condensed' is explained further in the Standard: 'Those condensed statements should include, at a minimum, each of the headings and subtotals that were included in its most recent annual financial statements.' Additional line items or notes should be included if their omission would make the condensed interim financial statements misleading. Further basic and diluted earnings per share should be presented on the face of an income statement, complete or condensed, for an interim period.

It is important to stress that IAS 34 starts from the assumption that anyone who reads an entity's interim report will also have access to its most recent annual report. As a result, virtually none of the notes to the annual financial statements is repeated or updated in the interim report. Instead, the interim notes include primarily an explanation of the events and changes that are significant to an understanding of the changes in financial position and performance of the entity since the last annual reporting date. IAS 34 pays explicit attention to the notes accompanying the interim report.

## Notes to the interim reports

Concerning these selected explanatory notes, which are typical for interim reports, para. 16 states which information as a minimum should be included if material and if not disclosed elsewhere in the interim financial report. The information should normally be reported on a financial year-to-date basis. However, the entity should also disclose any events or transactions that are material to an understanding of the current interim period:

- a statement that the same accounting policies and methods of computation are followed in the interim financial statements as compared with the most recent annual financial statements or, if those policies or methods have been changed, a description of the nature and effect of the change
- explanatory comments about the seasonality or cyclicality of interim operations

- the nature and amount of items affecting assets, liabilities, equity, net income or cash flows that are unusual because of their nature, size or incidence
- the nature and amount of changes in estimates of amounts reported in prior interim periods of the current financial year or changes in estimates of amounts reported in prior financial years, if those changes have a material effect in the current interim period
- issuances, repurchases and repayments of debt and equity securities
- dividends paid (aggregate or per share) separately for ordinary shares and other shares
- segment revenue and segment result for business segments or geographical segments, whichever is the entity's primary basis of segment reporting (disclosure of segment data is required in an entity's interim financial report only if IAS 14, *Segment Reporting,* requires that entity to disclose segment data in its annual financial statements)
- material events subsequent to the end of the interim period that have not been reflected in the financial statements for the interim period
- the effect of changes in the composition of the entity during the interim period, including business combinations, acquisition or disposal of subsidiaries and long-term investments, restructurings and discontinued operations. In the case of business combinations, the entity shall disclose the information required to be disclosed under paras 66–73 of IFRS 3, *Business Combinations*
- changes in contingent liabilities or contingent assets since the last annual balance sheet date.

IAS 34 gives the following examples of disclosures required in interim financial reports (para. 17):

- the write-down of inventories to net realizable value and the reversal of such a write-down
- recognition of a loss from the impairment of property, plant and equipment, intangible assets, or other assets, and the reversal of such an impairment loss
- the reversal of any provisions for the costs of restructuring
- acquisitions and disposals of items of property, plant and equipment
- commitments for the purchase of property, plant and equipment
- litigation settlements
- corrections of prior period errors
- any loan default or breach of a loan agreement that has not been remedied on or before the financial reporting date, and
- related party transactions.

Furthermore, individual standards and interpretations also provide guidance regarding disclosures for many of these items.

## Valuation rules for interim reports

IAS 34 stipulates that an entity should apply the same accounting policies in its interim financial report as are applied in its annual financial statements, except for accounting policy changes made after the date of the most recent annual financial statements that are to be reflected in the next annual financial statements.

In many firms, revenues and costs have a seasonal pattern. Think, for example, of firms in the tourism industry or in the ice-cream industry. But in industries where one would not think about seasonal patterns, they may indeed exist, e.g. sale of cars.

With regard to revenue and expense recognition explicit guidance is given on revenues and costs which occur unevenly during the year. Revenues that are received seasonally, cyclically or occasionally within a financial year should not be anticipated or deferred as of an interim date if anticipation or deferral would not be appropriate at the end of the entity's financial year. Costs that are incurred unevenly during an entity's financial year should be anticipated or deferred for interim reporting purposes if, and only if, it is also appropriate to anticipate or defer that type of cost at the end of the financial year.

But, what shall we do with costs and revenues resulting from discretionary decisions by the management? The costs can be allocated evenly over the quarters or they can be changed to a specific quarter only if they have occurred in that specific quarter. Consider again the valuation rules of IAS 34 mentioned earlier. They do not give that much guidance. To overcome this issue the IASB has presented in Appendix B to IAS 34 a list of examples of how to apply the general recognition and measurement principles in relation to interim reports. The examples relate to maintenance, provisions, pensions, intangible assets, year-end bonuses, tax credits and inventories, among other things.

Explicit attention is paid in IAS 34 to the use of accounting estimates. Paragraph 41 stipulates that the measurement procedures to be followed in an interim financial report should be designed to ensure that the resulting information is reliable and that all material financial information that is relevant to an understanding of the financial position or performance of the entity is appropriately disclosed. While measurements in both annual and interim financial reports are often based on reasonable estimates, the preparation of interim financial reports generally will require a greater use of estimation methods than annual financial reports. Again an appendix is used to give more guidance. IAS 34, Appendix C, presents *Examples of the Use of Estimates* (for example, contingencies, pensions, income taxes, provisions, inventories, etc.).

Recently IFRIC No. 10, *Interim Financial Reporting and Impairment,* was issued to resolve a potential conflict between IAS 34 and the requirements of IAS 36 and IAS 39 not to reverse in the subsequent reporting periods impairments on goodwill, on investments in an equity investment classified as available for sale and financial assets covered at cost. In addition, when impairments are recorded in the interim statements, the requirements of IAS 36 and IAS 39 have to be complied with and reversals cannot be recorded in the subsequent (interim) periods.

The frequency of an entity's reporting – annual, half-yearly or quarterly – should not affect the measurement of its annual results. To achieve that objective, measurements for interim reporting purposes are made on a year-to-date basis.

What does this mean?

The requirement to present information on a financial year-to-date basis and to ensure an understanding of the current interim period should be noted carefully. It logically has no effect in the context of half-yearly interim statements, but, if interim statements are issued quarterly, then its implications could be significant. The financial report must satisfy the requirements of providing an understanding of the latest quarter (and its comparatives) and also an understanding of the year-to-date (and its comparatives). For example, a first-quarter report (e.g. 1.1.20X2–31.3.20X2) has to show the data for the three months and comparable figures for the first three months of the previous year (1.1.20X1–31.3.20X1); a third-quarter report has to show the data for the first nine months of the current year (e.g. 1.1.20X2–30.9.20X2) and comparative data for the first nine months of the previous year (1.1.20X1–30.9.20X1) and data of the last three months as well (1.7.20X2–30.9.20X2) and the same period in the previous year (1.7.20X1–30.9.20X1).

In order to help the preparers of interim financial reports, an extensive appendix can be found accompanying IAS 34 in which a large number of examples is given in relation to applying the recognition and measurement principles of IAS to interim financial reports.

With regard to interim reporting the IASB takes a framework-based approach in IAS 34 itself. As such, it seems that the IASB merely sees interim reporting as a frequent version of annual reporting, whereas the business community often uses the interim reports as a signaling device towards the total result of the financial period.

## SUMMARY

In this chapter a set of individual standards has been discussed and illustrated. They all have in common that their purpose is to increase the usefulness of the reported information so that external users of the annual accounts can make better decisions. We remember, however, that although the standards have become stricter over the years, room for judgement is still left and this might threaten the value relevance of the accounting information. However, we must admit that judgement is always inherent to the process of financial reporting.

## EXERCISES

*Suggested answers to exercises marked ✓ are to be found on our dedicated CourseMate platform for students.*

*Suggested answers to the remaining exercises are to be found on the Instructor online support resources.*

✓ **1** Calculate from the following information:

(a) the basic EPS

(b) the fully diluted EPS.

The capital of the company is as follows:

- £500 000 in 7 per cent preference shares of £1 each
- £1 000 000 in ordinary shares of 25p each

- £1 250 000 in 8 per cent convertible unsecured loan stock carrying conversion rights into ordinary shares as follows: on 31 December 120 shares for each £100 nominal of loan stock.

  The P&L account for the year ended 31 December showed:

  (a) profit after all expenses, but before extraordinary items, loan interest and corporation tax £1 200 000. Extraordinary items £100 000 (expense)

  (b) corporation tax is to be taken as 35 per cent of the profits shown in the accounts after all expenses and after loan interest.

✓ **2**  Norman, a public limited company, has three segments which are currently reported in its financial statements. Norman is an international hotel group which reports to management on the basis of region. It does not currently report segmental information under IFRS 8. The results of the regional segments for the year ended 31 May 2008 are as follows:

| Region | Revenue external €m | Revenue internal €m | Segment results Profit/(loss) €m | Segment assets €m | Segment liabilities €m |
|---|---|---|---|---|---|
| European | 200 | 3 | (10) | 300 | 200 |
| South East Asia | 300 | 2 | 60 | 800 | 300 |
| Other regions | 500 | 5 | 105 | 2 000 | 1 400 |

There were no significant intercompany balances in the segment assets and liabilities. The hotels are located in capital cities in the various regions, and the company sets individual performance indicators for each hotel based on its city location.

**Required:**

Discuss the principles in IFRS8, *Operating Segments*, for the determination of a company's reportable operating segments and how these principles would be applied for Normal plc using the information given above.

(ACCA – June 2008)

✓ **3**  As the recently qualified accountant of Aveler plc, a food retailer with financial reporting date 31 December 20X1, you notice the following items occurring before the accounts are approved by the directors:

(a) the sale, during the period from 31 December 20X1 to the date the accounts are approved by the directors, of 1000 tins of baked beans

(b) the purchase, during the period from 31 December 20X1 to the date the accounts are approved by the directors, of 750 tins of baked beans

(c) the incurrence of other expenses, during the period from 31 December 20X1 to the date the accounts are approved by the directors, amounting to €125

(d) notification that a customer who owes the company €10 000 as at 31 December 20X1 has gone into liquidation on 17 January 20X2

(e) a fire on 4 January 20X2 destroys all the stock in one warehouse

(f) the receipt of a letter from the company's insurers stating that it is unclear whether Aveler was actually insured for loss of stock by fire.

Which of these items are relevant to the accounts for the period ending 31 December 20X1?

**4** Outline the circumstances in which events after the reporting date affect the contents of financial statements. In what different ways are those contents affected? Give examples to illustrate your points.

**5** Outline the main difficulties with the disclosure of segmental information and outline possible arguments against the disclosure of segmental information.

**6** In preparing the financial statements for the year ended 31 December 20X5 Alpha plc discovers the following, all of which are material in the context of the company's results:

- Development expenditure that met the required criteria of IAS 38 was previously capitalized and amortized. Alpha now believes that writing off all expenditure on development work would give a fairer presentation of the results.
- A debt that was previously considered to be collectable as at 31 December 20X4 now requires writing off.
- The estimate of costs payable in respect of litigation was €250 000 as at 31 December 20X4. This has now materialized at €280 000.
- The directors of Alpha are of the view that depreciating vehicles by the reducing balance method rather than the straight line method as previously used will present a fairer view of the financial performance of the company.

  How would you treat the information above in preparing the financial statements at the end of 31 December 20X5? The treatment should be in line with IAS/IFRS.

**7** Discuss the advantages and disadvantages of earnings per share as a measure of corporate performance.

**8** The IASB issued IAS 33, *Earnings Per Share*, in 1997 with the objective of determining the principles for the calculation and presentation of earnings per share in order to improve performance comparison. Its main focus is on the denominator of the calculation.

**Required:**
(a) Explain the usefulness of disclosing:

a company's basic earnings per share; (ii) a company's diluted earnings per share.

(b) Below are extracts from the financial statements of Bovine for the year to 31 March 20X3:

Statement of comprehensive income:

| | Continuing operations $000 | Discontinuing operations $000 | Total $000 |
|---|---|---|---|
| Profit (loss) before tax | 1 580 | (200) | 1 380 |
| Tax (charge) relief | (280) | 50 | (230) |
| Profit from the ordinary activities | 1 300 | (150) | 1 150 |
| Extraordinary item as part of continuing operations | | | (120) |
| (net of tax relief of $60) | | | 1 030 |
| Statement of financial position: | | | |
| Ordinary shares of 25 cents each | | | 1 800 |
| 6% Non-redeemable preference shares | | | 500 |

|  | Continuing operations $000 | Discontinuing operations $000 | Total $000 |
|---|---|---|---|
| 10% Convertible preference shares $1 each |  |  | 1 000 |
| Non-current liabilities 8% Convertible loan stock |  |  | 1 500 |

Notes: All shares and loan stocks were in issue prior to the beginning of the current accounting year. The 10 per cent convertible preference shares are convertible to ordinary shares on the basis of three ordinary shares for every five preference shares on 31 March 20X5 at the option of the preference shareholders. The 8 per cent convertible loan stock is redeemable on 31 March 20X5 or can be converted to ordinary shares on the basis of 120 ordinary shares for each $100 of loan stock at the holder's option.

There are also in issue directors' share options for four million ordinary shares. These were issued on 31 March 20X2 and are exercisable on 31 March 20X5 at a price of $1.40 per share. The market price of Bovine's shares can be taken as $2.00 each.

Preference dividends are paid out of taxed profits. Interest on loan stock is an allowable tax reduction. The rate of income tax is 25 per cent.

**Required:**
Calculate Bovine's basic and diluted earnings per share for the year ended 31 March 20X3.

(ACCA – June 2003)

9   IAS 10 deals with the accounting treatment of events occurring after the reporting date.

**Required:**
In assessing the results of a company for the current year, explain why events occurring after the reporting date may be of importance; and describe the circumstances where the financial statements should and should not be adjusted.

During a review of Penchant's draft financial statements (for the year ended 30 September 20X3) in October 20X3, the following matters came to light:

- The company's internal auditors discovered a fraud on one of the company's contracts. A senior employee had accepted an inducement of $200 000 for awarding the construction of roadways on one of the company's contracts to a particular subcontractor. Investigations showed that the price of the subcontracting was $1 million higher than another comparable tender offer. At 30 September 20X3 the contract was approximately 50 per cent complete.
- An earthquake occurred on 10 October 20X3. It caused damage to an in progress contract that it is estimated will cost $500 000 to rectify.
- At 30 September 20X3 the company's head office premises were included in the draft financial statements at a value of $12 million. A building surveyor's report showed that they had fallen in value by $2 million. This was due partly to the discovery of ground subsidence and partly to a general fall of 10 per cent in property prices caused by a sharp unexpected rise in interest rates announced in October 20X3.

–   In October 20X3 there was a sharp fall in the value of a foreign currency. Penchant was owed a substantial amount for the final instalment of a completed contract whose price was fixed in that currency. The estimated loss due to the fall in the exchange rate has been translated at $250 000.

    Note: you may assume the above figures are material.

**Required:**

For each of the items above, explain how Penchant should treat them under International Financial Reporting Standards.

(ACCA – December 2003)

**10**   Classify the events below as adjusting events or non-adjusting events according to IAS 10:

(a)  shortly after the financial reporting date a survey of an item of property, plant and equipment revealed significant structural problems with the asset

(b)  a lawsuit alleging damages suffered from an accident that occurred after the financial reporting date

(c)  a bankruptcy of a customer that occurs after the financial reporting date

(d)  at year-end, management has the intention to decide upon the implementation of a restructuring plan. After the financial reporting date, but prior to the issuance date of the company's financial statements, management approves and announces the plan.

**11**   Hamlet, a publicly listed company, is preparing its financial statements to 30 September 20X4. In previous years it has chosen to write off all of its development expenditure even where management have been confident that the related projects would be profitable. The company is aware that development expenditure meeting the definition of an intangible asset in IAS 38, *Intangible Assets*, should be capitalized. In the near future Hamlet intends to prepare its financial statements under International Financial Reporting Standards and as a step towards this, the management of Hamlet are to change their accounting policy for development expenditure for the current year to comply with IAS 38. Reproduced below are details of Hamlet's development expenditure for the relevant years. For the purpose of implementing the new policy management consider four years to be an appropriate amortization period for all development expenditure. Amortization should commence in the year following initial capitalization.

|  |  | $million |
| --- | --- | --- |
| Amounts written off in year to 30 September: | 20 X 0 | 500 |
|  | 20 X 1 | 400 |
|  | 20 X 2 | 900 |
|  | 20 X 3 | 640 |
|  | 20 X 4 | 720 |

No development expenditure occurred in any year prior to 30 September 20X0. The accumulated profit of Hamlet at 1 October 20X2 was $2500 million. You may assume that the above development expenditure meets the definition of a recognizable intangible asset in IAS 38.

**Required:**

(a) Describe the circumstances in which companies are permitted to change their accounting policies under International Financial Reporting Standards and discuss what constitutes a change of accounting policy.

(b) Prepare extracts of Hamlet's statement of comprehensive income and statement of financial position for the year to 30 September 20X4 together with comparative figures to reflect the change in accounting policy in respect of development expenditure; and calculate the restated accumulated profits at 1 October 20X2.

    Hamlet uses the benchmark treatment in IAS 8, *Net Profit or Loss for the Period, Fundamental Errors and Changes in Accounting Policies*. Ignore deferred tax.

(ACCA – December 2003)

12   AB had 10 million $0.50 ordinary shares in issue at 1 January 20X7. On 1 August 20X7 AB issued 2 million $0.5 ordinary shares at a premium of $0.30. Throughout the year AB had in issue $2 million 7 per cent convertible bonds redeemable in 20X9. The terms of the instrument allow the bondholders to convert every $100 of bonds held to 50 ordinary shares of $0.50. AB's profit available to ordinary shareholders was $3 million for the year ended 31 December 20X7. AB pays tax at 30 per cent.

**Required:**

Calculate the basic and diluted earnings per share for AB for the year ended 31 December 20X7.

(CIMA P8 – May 2009)

13   GA had 5 million $1 ordinary shares in issue at 1 May 20X8. On 30 September 20X8 GA issued a further 2 million $1 ordinary shares at par. Profit before tax for the year ended 30 April 20X9 was $650 000 and the related income tax charge was $210 000.

**Required:**

Calculate the basis earnings per share for GA for the period to 30 April 20X9.

(CIMA P8 – November 2009)

14   AGZ is a listed entity. You are a member of the team drafting its financial statements for the year ended 31 August 2008.

    Extracts from the draft income statement, including comparative figures, are shown below:

|  | 2008 $million | 2007 $million |
|---|---|---|
| Profit before tax | 276.4 | 262.7 |
| Income tax expense | 85.0 | 80.0 |
| Profit for the period | 191.4 | 182.7 |

    At the beginning of the financial year, on 1 September 2007, AGZ had 750 million ordinary shares of 50¢ in issue. At that date the market price of one ordinary share was 87.6¢.

    On 1 December 2007, AGZ made a bonus issue of one new ordinary 50¢ share for every three held.

    In 2006, AGZ issued $75 million convertible bonds. Each unit of $100 of bonds in issue will be convertible at the holder's option into 200 ordinary 50¢ shares on 31 August 2012. The interest expense relating to the liability element of the bonds for the year ended 31 August

2008 was $6.3 million (2007 – $6.2 million). The tax effect related to the interest expense was $2.0 million (2007 – $1.8 million).

There were no other changes affecting or potentially affecting the number of ordinary shares in issue in either the 2008 or 2007 financial years.

**Required:**
(a)  Calculate earnings per share and diluted earnings per share for the year ended 31 August 2008, including the comparative figures.

Explain the reason for the treatment of the bonus shares as required by IAS 33, *Earnings Per Share*.

(CIMA P8 – November 2008)

15  BJS, a listed entity, had a weighted average of 27 million ordinary shares in issue during its financial year ended 31 August 20X6. It was also financed throughout the year by an issue of 12 per cent convertible bonds with a par value of $50 million. The bonds are convertible at the option of the holders at the rate of 12 new ordinary shares for every $100 of bonds at par value. The tax rate applicable to BJS was 30 per cent during the financial year. The profit attributable to ordinary shareholders for the year ended 31 August 20X6 was $100 million. Calculate earnings per share, and diluted earnings per share, for BJS for the year ended 31 August 20X6.

(CIMA – November 2006)

16  A quote from a colleague: ' I never look at the operating segment information in a set of financial statements when I am making investment decisions – it's just lots and lots of numbers I won't understand. It must cost entities a significant amount of money to produce the information, which must outweigh the benefits it provides'.

**Required:**
(a)  Discuss the benefits that could be gained by investors from reviewing the operating segment disclosures when making future decisions on investment.
(b)  Discuss the limitations of using operating segment information when making investment decisions.
(c)  Discuss how the requirements of IFRS 8 Operating Segments assist entities in minimizing the costs of producing these disclosures.

(CIMA Financial Management – March 2012)

17  Which one of the following is not included in the definition of an operating segment in accordance with IFRS 8 *Operating Segments*?
(a)  A component of an entity that earns the majority of its revenue from sales to external customers.
(b)  A component of an entity that engages in business activities from which it may earn revenues and incur expenses.
(c)  A component of an entity whose operating results are regularly reviewed by the entity's chief operating decision maker, to make decisions about resource allocations and assess performance.
(d)  A component of an entity for which discrete financial information is available.

(CIMA Financial Operations – November 2010)

**18** According to IFRS 8, *Operating Segments*, which two of the following apply to reportable segments?

(a) The results of the segment must be prepared using the same accounting policies as are used for the financial statements.

(b) A reportable segment is a component of the entity whose operating results are regularly reviewed by the entity's chief operating decision maker in order to make decisions about resource allocations.

(c) Information for reportable segments is required to be prepared based on products and geographical areas.

(d) A reportable segment is every segment that accounts for 10 per cent or more of the sales revenue.

    1   (a) and (b)

    2   (a) and (c)

    3   (b) and (c)

    4   (b) and (d)

(CIMA Financial Operations – May 2011)

**19** Which one of the following would be classified by WDC as a non-adjusting event according to IAS 10, *Events After the Reporting Period?* WDC's year end is 30 September 20X1.

(a) WDC was notified on 5 November 20X1 that one of its customers was insolvent and was unlikely to repay any of its debts. The balance outstanding at 30 September 2011 was $42 000.

(b) On 30 September WDC had an outstanding court action against it. WDC had made a provision in its financial statements for the year ended 30 September 20X1 for damages awarded it of $22 000. On 29 October 20X1 the court awarded damages of $18 000.

(c) On October 20X1 a serious fire occurred in WDC's main production centre and severely damaged the production faculty.

(d) The year end inventory balance included $50 000 of goods from a discontinued product line. On 1 November 2011 these goods were sold for a net total of $20 000.

(CIMA Financial Operations – November 2011)

# PART THREE

## CONSOLIDATED ACCOUNTS AND THE MULTINATIONAL

In this part we look in some detail at the preparation of financial statements for several entities that could be regarded as a group. Such statements are known as consolidated financial statements and the techniques for preparing them are complicated and require detailed regulations. The preparation of consolidated accounts is covered in four chapters. The first, Chapter 26, discusses the accounting for business combinations, where an acquirer obtains control over an acquiree. After acquisition, the acquirer becomes a parent and the acquiree a subsidiary. In Chapter 27 the requirements and techniques of consolidated financial statements are discussed, where the parent and its subsidiaries are presented as one economic entity. The third, Chapter 28, is a chapter that we would encourage you to study, but is not essential if all you wish to gain from this text is 'How to prepare consolidated financial statements'. This chapter presents some alternative methods of preparing consolidated accounts. The fourth, Chapter 29, deals with other relationships between entities, including associates and joint ventures, and how we should display those relationships within financial statements.

Many groups of entities operate in different countries and, therefore, different currencies, so we need rules and regulations for conversion from one currency to another before we can prepare the consolidated financial statements. We also need to consider the accounting for the relatively simple operation of receiving or making payments in a foreign currency. The accounting for this may not be as easy as it first appears. These foreign currency issues are discussed in Chapter 30.

At the end of this part we invite you to form your own opinion as to whether the information provided by consolidated accounts and in respect of foreign entities and different currency transactions is helpful to users.

# BUSINESS COMBINATIONS 26

> **OBJECTIVES** After studying this chapter you should be able to:
>
> - understand a business combination and how to account for it
>
> - understand the accounting for goodwill
>
> - be able to determine goodwill in more complex situations, such as non-controlling interests and step-acquisitions
>
> - know how to account for disposals, both with and without loss of control
>
> - know the basic requirements of IFRS 3, *Business Combinations*.

## INTRODUCTION

Most people are familiar from their daily newspapers with such words as 'takeover' and 'merger'. In this chapter we will discuss the issues that arise when a takeover or merger, for which we use the word 'business combination', takes place.

IFRS 3, *Business Combinations*, defines a business combination as a 'transaction or other event in which an acquirer obtains control of one or more businesses'. It further defines a business as an 'integrated set of activities and assets that is capable of being conducted and managed for the purpose of providing a return in the form of dividends, lower costs or other economic benefits directly to investors or other owners, members or participants'. The result of nearly all business combinations is that one entity, the acquirer, obtains control of one or more other businesses, the acquiree (IFRS 3, para. 4). This is usually realized by acquiring the shares in the acquiree from the former shareholders.

## Control

The concept of 'control' is essential in this respect. An acquirer or investor controls an acquiree or investee when it is exposed, or has rights, to variable returns from its involvement with the investee and has the ability to affect those returns through its power over the investee (IFRS 10, para. 5). The essential features are the existence of power and the use of this power to affect the (variable) returns. We will discuss the concept of control further in the next chapter.

For the investor that controls we use the term 'parent', for the investee that is being controlled we use the term 'subsidiary'. In discussing business combinations in this chapter we will use the terms acquirer and acquiree, as this indicates the process of acquisition; after acquisition the acquirer becomes the parent and the acquiree the subsidiary. The parent will then prepare consolidated financial statements, bringing the figures of parent and subsidiary together. Preparing consolidated financial statements is the subject of Chapter 27.

## ACCOUNTING FOR THE BUSINESS COMBINATION: THE BASICS

IFRS 3 requires an entity to account for each business combination by applying the acquisition method (or purchase method). Applying the acquisition method requires:

- identifying the acquirer
- determining the acquisition date
- recognizing and measuring the identifiable assets acquired and the liabilities assumed
- accounting for goodwill.

## Identifying the acquirer

In a business combination, control is obtained for the first time. We need to identify who is the acquirer and who the acquiree. This acquirer is not always easy to identify but the standard tells us that we have to identify one and that usually there are indications available to us. For example (IFRS 3, paras B14–15):

- If the combination is effected by primarily transferring cash or other assets or by incurring liabilities, the acquirer is usually the entity that transfers the cash or other assets or incurs liabilities.
- The acquirer is usually the entity whose owners as a group retain or receive the largest portion of the voting rights to the combined entity.
- If the business combination results in the management of one of the combining entities being able to dominate the selection of the management team of the

resulting combined entity, the entity whose management is able to dominate is usually the acquirer.

- The acquirer is usually the entity whose owners have the ability to elect or appoint or remove a majority of the members of the governing body of the combined entity.

Note the use of the word 'usually' in the examples.

The Standard also states that a new entity formed to effect a business combination is not necessarily the acquirer. If a new entity is formed to issue equity interests to effect a business combination, one of the combining entities that existed before the business combination shall be identified as the acquirer. The new entity is then considered to be created by, and an extension of, the acquirer.

## Determining the acquisition date

The acquisition date is the date on which the acquirer obtains control of the acquiree (IFRS 3, para. 8). This is generally the so-called closing date: the date on which the acquirer legally transfers the consideration, acquires the assets and assumes the liabilities of the acquiree. However, the acquirer might obtain control on a date that is either earlier or later than the closing date.

## Recognizing and measuring the identifiable assets acquired and the liabilities assumed

IFRS 3 requires us to allocate the cost of the combination (the acquisition price or purchase price) by recognizing the assets, liabilities and contingent liabilities at their fair values. The purchase price is the fair value of the consideration without including acquisition costs. The difference between the purchase price and the fair value of the net assets (assets minus liabilities) is recognized as goodwill. This is commonly known as the purchase price allocation or PPA. Note that it is necessary to determine the fair values of the assets and liabilities and that the acquirer cannot determine the amount of goodwill on the basis of the book values in the financial statements of the acquiree. In identifying the assets and liabilities at fair value, the acquirer might identify intangible assets in accordance with IAS 38 that had not been recognized on the balance sheet of the acquiree. This will be the case for internally generated intangible assets such as brands and customer lists. As we have seen in Chapter 14, these may not be recognized in the balance sheet as they are internally generated. However, from the perspective of the acquirer, these intangibles are acquired and therefore need to be recognized at fair value.

Activity 26.1 shows how to account for an acquisition and how to determine goodwill.

## ACTIVITY 26.1

H bought 100 per cent of the shares of S at a purchase price of €650 000. The book value of the net assets of S at the acquisition date according to the balance sheet of S was €400 000. The fair value of the net assets of S at the acquisition date were €600 000. Calculate the goodwill on consolidation in accordance with IFRS 3.

*Activity feedback*

| | |
|---|---|
| Purchase price | 650 000 |
| Net assets at fair value | 600 000 |
| Goodwill | 50 000 |

The purchase price or consideration can be in different forms. Activity 26.2 answers this question so you should complete it before reading the answer.

## ACTIVITY 26.2

Identify three forms of consideration that could be given in a business combination.

### Activity feedback
The consideration given can include:

- cash
- other assets
- a business or subsidiary of the acquirer
- ordinary or preference equity instruments of the acquirer
- options or warrants.

## REAL WORLD ILLUSTRATION

### Business combinations at DSM

Business combinations are accounted for using the acquisition method. The cost of an acquisition is measured as the aggregate of the consideration transferred, including liabilities incurred toward the former owners, measured at acquisition date fair value, and the amount of any non-controlling interest in the acquiree. Acquisition costs incurred are expensed.

As of the acquisition date identifiable assets acquired, liabilities assumed and any non-controlling interest in the acquiree are recognized separately from goodwill. Identifiable assets acquired and the liabilities assumed are measured at acquisition date fair value. For each business combination, DSM elects whether it measures the non-controlling interest in the acquiree at fair value or at the proportionate share of the acquiree's identifiable net assets.

(From: DSM, Integrated Annual Report 2012, p. 140)

## Accounting for goodwill

As stated above, goodwill is the difference between the purchase price and the fair value of the net assets. Why would acquirers pay more than the fair value of the assets and liabilities? In other words, why would the fair value of the shares in the entity acquired be higher than the fair value of the underlying assets and liabilities? The fair value of the shares will normally be determined by reference to the present value of the cash flows from the entity. This present value is normally not fully reflected in assets and liabilities and can be related to 'intangibles' like work force, reputation, innovative capacity, market power, etc., intangibles that are not specifically identifiable and measurable and are therefore not reflected in the balance sheet. Furthermore, an acquirer might want to pay goodwill because of synergy possibilities between the entity acquired and the already existing business.

IFRS 3 requires that after initial recognition the business combination goodwill should be measured at cost less any accumulated impairment losses. Thus, this goodwill is not amortized but tested for impairment. This impairment test is carried out in accordance with IAS 36, *Impairment of Assets*.

Previously IFRS did permit amortization of business combination goodwill. Whether the new accounting method results in a more robust view of goodwill on the statement of financial position depends on the robustness of the impairment reviews. The rationale for carrying goodwill on the statement of financial position of the combined business at its impaired cost as opposed to amortizing that goodwill through the profit or loss account is outlined in the IASB's Basis for Conclusions to IFRS 3. The Board initially considered three possible treatments for goodwill arising on a business combination:

**(a)** straight line amortization but with an impairment test whenever there was an indication that the goodwill might be impaired

**(b)** non-amortization but with an impairment test annually or more frequently if events or changes in circumstances indicated that the goodwill was impaired

**(c)** permitting entities a choice between (a) and (b).

Point (c) was soon discounted in the deliberations as permitting such choices impairs the usefulness to users, as both comparability and reliability are diminished. However, many respondents to the Exposure Draft supported method (a) as the acquired goodwill can be considered to be consumed over time and replaced with internal goodwill. This would be consistent with the general prohibition in IFRS to capitalize internal goodwill. These respondents felt that straight line amortization over an arbitrary period, given that the pattern of use and useful life of goodwill is difficult to predict, with impairment tests was a reasonable balance between conceptual soundness and operational issues. In other words, (a) was the pragmatic solution. However, the Board was not impressed with pragmatism, being doubtful of the benefits of amortizing acquired goodwill but not recognizing internal goodwill. They felt that the amortization was unhelpful, as, unlike a tangible fixed asset, goodwill does not have a finite physical utility life. Thus the Board decided that (b) was the way forward; as long as a rigorous and operational impairment test could be devised (see IAS 36, Chapter 14) then more useful information would be provided to users by the use of (b). Whatever method we use to account for acquired or inherent goodwill in the financial statements, has a very large impact on the net assets and profit or loss recorded for the year. If users are not aware of this fact the decisions they make from using the information given could be flawed.

Both IFRS SME and the Accounting Directive of the European Union do require method (a) and are therefore in conflict with IFRS.

Goodwill is not necessarily a positive amount. The fair value of the net assets might be higher than the purchase price. In that case the acquirer obtains control in the acquiree company at a discounted price (i.e. as opposed to at a premium). The standard refers to this as a 'bargain purchase'. In practice, this is not so far-fetched as it might at first sight appear, in that an acquiring entity may for various reasons (e.g. empire building) be quite willing to purchase an entity with a recent history of trading losses, together with a forecast future of losses. This discount on the purchase price at the date of acquisition may be thus thought of as compensation for anticipated future losses to the acquiring group. One might also reasonably assume that in the medium-term future the group would hope to turn this subsidiary into profitability.

If negative goodwill is identified then IFRS 3 requires the acquirer to reassess the calculation of the fair values of the net assets and to then recognize the negative goodwill that still exists in profit or loss. (See Chapter 14 for goodwill in more detail.)

## REAL WORLD ILLUSTRATION

Goodwill represents the excess of the cost of an acquisition over DSM's share in the net fair value of the identifiable assets and liabilities of an acquired subsidiary, joint venture or associate.

Goodwill paid on acquisition of subsidiaries and joint ventures is included in intangible assets. Goodwill paid on acquisition of associates is included in the carrying amount of these associates. Goodwill is not amortized but tested for impairment annually and when there are indications that the carrying amount may exceed the recoverable amount. A gain or loss on the disposal of an entity includes the carrying amount of goodwill relating to the entity sold.

(From: DSM, Integrated Annual Report 2012, p. 141)

In Activity 26.1 we already calculated goodwill. The following activity contains some further goodwill questions.

---

## ACTIVITY 26.3

1 H acquired 100 per cent of the net assets of S at a fair value of €1 000 000. The net book value of H's net assets was €900 000 and fair value €1 040 000. Identify the value of goodwill.

2 Refer to Activity 26.1. The goodwill was calculated at €50 000 at acquisition date. Assume that the useful life of acquired goodwill is considered to be 10 years. What would be the amount of goodwill after one year?

*Activity feedback*

1 Purchase price      1 000 000
Fair value of the net assets acquired      1 040 000
Negative goodwill on acquisition      40 000

2 *It depends. There is no amortization, so the goodwill is not reduced during its useful life. If there is no impairment, then the goodwill would still be €50 000. If the recoverable amount is lower, this will reduce the amount of goodwill recorded (see Chapter 14).*

---

# SPECIFIC ISSUES ON ACCOUNTING FOR THE BUSINESS COMBINATION

## Non-controlling interests

Until now we have silently assumed that the acquirer buys 100 per cent of all the shares of the acquiree. This is not necessary in order to obtain control. An acquirer might also buy, for instance, 80 per cent of the shares. An acquirer then still has control over 100 per cent of all the assets and liabilities of the acquiree, but its economic share in equity and results is only 80 per cent. When acquiring 80 per cent there is also a so-called 'non-controlling interest' of 20 per cent in the acquiree. The usual expression in the past for a non-controlling interest has been a minority interest, but, as we shall further explain in the next chapter, an entity can have control in another entity without having the majority of the shares. For that reason, the term non-controlling interest is more appropriate.

Why is a discussion of the non-controlling interest of importance in discussing business combinations? After all, if we acquire 80 per cent of the shares, the purchase price is based on 80 per cent of the shares and from an economical perspective we only have 80 per cent of the net assets. This is true and is one way of looking at it. Upon consolidation, when the parent consolidates the assets and liabilities for 100 per cent, as we will discuss in the next chapter, a non-controlling interest will be recognized, but this will not affect goodwill. This is how we have accounted for business combinations for some time.

But IFRS 3 allows two views on the measurement of non-controlling interests and related goodwill. Non-controlling interests in the acquiree are required to be measured at either:

1 the non-controlling interest's proportionate share of the acquiree's identifiable net assets at fair value (the view above), or

2 fair value (the new and preferred view).

The second view implies that the purchase price allocation will not be based on the purchase price that the acquirer paid, but on the purchase price that the acquirer would have paid when it acquired 100 per cent of the shares. The goodwill is then also determined on a 100 per cent basis, including the goodwill that is allocated to the non-controlling interest. Thus, depending upon which method is chosen, to value the non-controlling interest will result in different figures in the consolidated financial statements in respect of the non-controlling interest and goodwill.

Activity 26.4 illustrates the accounting for a business combination with a non-controlling interest.

## ACTIVITY 26.4

H bought 80 per cent of the shares of S at a purchase price of €640 000. The fair value of the net assets of S at the acquisition date was €700 000. If H had acquired 100 per cent of the shares of S the purchase price would have been €790 000. The fair value of the non-controlling interest is therefore €150 000 (€790 000 − €640 000). Note that the fair value of the non-controlling interest is not proportional to that of the controlling interest: the price of 80 per cent of the shares is more than four times the price of 20 per cent of the shares. This can be explained by the so-called control premium, the additional value of obtaining control of S. Now calculate the goodwill on consolidation in accordance with IFRS 3, according to both alternatives.

*Or:*

| | |
|---|---:|
| Purchase price | 640 000 |
| Non-controlling interests (20% × 700 000) | 140 000 |
| | 780 000 |
| Net assets at fair value | 700 000 |
| Goodwill | 80 000 |

Alternative 2:

| | |
|---|---:|
| Purchase price (on the basis of 100%) | 790 000 |
| Net assets at fair value | 700 000 |
| Goodwill | 90 000 |

*Or:*

| | |
|---|---:|
| Purchase price | 640 000 |
| Non-controlling interests (at fair value) | 150 000 |
| | 790 000 |
| Net assets at fair value | 700 000 |
| Goodwill | 90 000 |

### Activity feedback

Alternative 1:

| | € |
|---|---:|
| Purchase price | 640 000 |
| Net assets at fair value (80%×700 000) | 560 000 |
| Goodwill | 80 000 |

Determining the fair value of the non-controlling interest can be difficult if there isn't a ready market in the shares. Furthermore, from the acquirer's perspective it is somewhat hypothetical to account as if 100 per cent of all the shares have been bought, while the real acquisition was only for 80 per cent.

In Chapter 28 we will discuss this issue further when we discuss the different concepts that lie behind the two alternatives.

## Business combination achieved in stages

An acquirer sometimes obtains control of an acquiree in which it already holds some of the equity shares. For example, immediately prior to the parent obtaining control of the subsidiary it may have held a 35 per cent non-controlling interest. If the parent then acquires another 30 per cent which gives it control then we have a business combination achieved in stages. IFRS 3 requires us to remeasure the previously held equity interest at its acquisition date fair value recognizing the resulting gain or loss in profit or loss. The purchase consideration is now the aggregate of the fair value of the non-controlling interest previously held, plus the consideration given for the new purchase to obtain control. The goodwill will be calculated by comparing this total consideration to the fair value of the controlling interest in net assets. Now try Activity 26.5.

---

## ACTIVITY 26.5

H entity holds 30 per cent of the voting shares of S entity which it purchased several years ago at a cost of €250 000. As at 31 December 201X, H purchased a further 50 per cent of S for a consideration of €600 000. The fair value of S's net assets at 31 December 201X is €1 000 000. It is estimated that H paid a control premium of €50 000. Identify the amount to be included in profit and loss, the amount of goodwill, and the non-controlling interest to be included in the consolidated financial statements of H as at 31 December 201X. In calculating goodwill, we will measure the non-controlling interest at the proportionate share of the acquiree's identifiable net assets at fair value (alternative 1 above).

### Activity feedback

First we need to value the original holding at fair value. On the information we have available we must assume that the fair value of the original holding can be calculated by reference to the consideration paid for the new 40 per cent holding after disregarding the control premium.

| | |
|---|---:|
| Control premium: | 50 000 |
| Consideration for 50% without premium | 550 000 |
| Fair value of whole of S using consideration | |
| (550 000 × 100/50) | 1 100 000 |
| Fair value of 30% original holding | |
| (30% × 1 100 000) | 330 000 |
| Original cost of 30% holding | 250 000 |
| Gain on holding (330 000 − 250 000) | |
| transferred to profit and loss | 80 000 |
| Calculation of goodwill: | |
| Consideration for 80% in S: | |
| 330 000 + 600 000 | 930 000 |
| Fair value of net assets (80% × 1 000 000) | 800 000 |
| Goodwill on consolidation | 130 000 |
| Non-controlling interest (20% × 1 000 000) | 200 000 |

## Subsequent remeasurement of amounts in a business combination

It is not always possible to have a definitive purchase price calculation when drawing up the financial statements. This will especially be the case when acquisitions have been made towards year-end. IFRS 3 allows to include provisional amounts in the consolidation process. IFRS 3 identifies a measurement period within which adjustments can be made to these provisional amounts to ensure compliance with IFRS 3 requirements. The measurement period cannot exceed one year from the date of acquisition and ends when the acquirer receives the information it was seeking about facts and circumstances that existed as of the acquisition date that would change the provisional figures, or the acquirer learns that more information is not obtainable. Adjustments should be made retrospectively as from the acquisition date. When adjusting the provisional figures the acquirer needs to ensure that only adjustments pertinent to the circumstances at acquisition are included. Now attempt the following activity.

---

## ACTIVITY 26.6

H entity acquired the whole of the voting shares of S entity on 31 December 201X. When preparing the consolidated financial statements on 31 December 201X, H included provisional figures for the fair value of some of S's non-current assets and liabilities. As at 31 March 201X+1 the following information was available on these non-current assets and liabilities:

| Non-current asset/(liability) | Provisional fair value 31 December 201X | Fair value 31 March 201X+1 or sale proceeds |
|---|---:|---:|
| | € | € |
| Building 1 | 500 000 | 650 000 |
| Building 2 | 350 000 | 400 000 |
| Plant and equipment | 90 000 | 85 500 |
| (Liability to pay damages on accident) | 250 000 | 300 000 |

## ACTIVITY 26.6    (Continued)

Building 1 was sold on 10 January 200X+1. Building 2 was sold on 31 March 200X+1. The higher sales price of building 2 is caused by an increase during the two months from 1 February 200X+1.

Plant and equipment is depreciated on a straight line basis and has an expected remaining life of five years and no residual value.

The damages are finally agreed with the third party involved as at 31 March 200X+1.

Identify the assets/liabilities that would require remeasurement in the consolidated financial statements as at the acquisition date.

### Activity feedback

*Building 1 will be adjusted in the consolidated statements at acquisition date from €500 000 to €650 000 as*

*the sale value on 10 January is likely to reflect the fair value as at 31 December 200X.*

*Building 2 will not be adjusted assuming that the increase in value is due to the period between February and end-March 200X+1.*

*Plant and equipment will not be adjusted as the fall in value reflects the depreciation charged for that three-month period (90 000 / 60 = 1500 depreciation per month, so 4500 for three months).*

*The damages will be adjusted to €300 000 as the final settlement figure provides evidence of the liability at acquisition date.*

*The two remeasurements will reduce goodwill on consolidation by €100 000.*

## Contingent consideration

Acquisition agreements often provide for adjustment to the acquisition price of an acquisition dependent on future events. In terms of IFRS 3 this is a contingent consideration: the consideration (acquisition price) is contingent upon future events. These future events can be:

- the results of the acquiree's operations exceeding or falling short of an agreed level
- the market price of securities issued as part of the purchase consideration being made.

These contingent considerations are sometimes indicated as 'earn out liabilities'. Changes in the acquisition price resulting from a contingent consideration are not measurement adjustments as discussed above. At the acquisition date, the acquirer should determine the fair value of the contingent consideration. When the contingent consideration is classified as equity (for instance a contingent consideration in the form of shares) there is no remeasurement and the subsequent settlement shall be accounted for within equity. When the contingent consideration is classified as a liability it will be remeasured to its best estimate at every balance sheet date. Remeasurements will be accounted for in profit and loss.

## ACTIVITY 26.7

Should possible subsequent adjustments to the acquisition price of an acquisition be ignored at the date of acquisition or should a reasonable estimate of the probable effect be made?

### Activity feedback

*Accounting judgements concerned with probability and reliable estimates elsewhere should have led you to the*

*conclusion that we should make a reasonable estimate of the purchase consideration including these future events based on the adjustment being probable and measurement reliable.*

## ACTIVITY 26.8

Entity A acquired all the issued share capital of entity B when the fair value of B's net assets was €500 000. The cost of the acquisition was €600 000 but included a proviso that an additional payment needed to be made when earnings of B were 10 per cent above the previous year; the consideration would be increased by €100 000 for each percentage point above 10 per cent. A considers that there is a 60 per cent chance that earnings levels will not be above the 10 per cent increase, a 30 per cent chance that the increase will be 11 per cent (additional payment of €100 000), and a 10 per cent chance that the increase will be 12 per cent (additional payment of €200 000); including the time value of money, A calculates the fair value of the earn out liability to be €45 000. In addition, A guaranteed the market price of the securities issued to B's shareholders on the acquisition for six months. The acquisition date was 1 October 201X and consolidated financial statements were drawn up as at 31 December 201X.

In the year ended 31 December 201X+1 it was noted that B's earnings were 11 per cent in excess of the previous year and that the market price of the securities had fallen by €25 000.

Identify the goodwill on acquisition and adjustments necessary in the consolidated financial statements as at 31 December 200X+1.

*Activity feedback*

| | |
|---|---:|
| Purchase consideration (fixed) | 600 000 |
| Contingent consideration | 45 000 |
| Total purchase consideration | 645 000 |
| Fair value of net assets | 500 000 |
| Goodwill | 145 000 |

*Subsequent events create an increase in the earn-out liability of €55 000 to €100 000. This increase will be shown in profit and loss and does not affect the purchase consideration and goodwill.*

*The fall in the market price of the securities will be dealt with by a further issue of securities by A to B. The increase in securities will reduce the premium or increase the discount on the initial issue; it will also not affect the purchase consideration.*

*It is important to note that the initial estimate of fair value determines the amount of goodwill.*

## Transactions with the non-controlling shareholder

A parent that already has control can buy shares of the non-controlling shareholder. This is not a business combination as there is no change in control. IFRS 10.23 requires these transactions to be accounted for as equity transactions. It is not allowed to recognize an additional amount of goodwill on the new shares acquired.

A parent can also sell shares to other parties and remain in control. These transactions are also accounted for in equity and do not result in a profit or loss.

## ACTIVITY 26.9

The value of a subsidiary's net assets at 31 March 201X is €400 000. At this date the parent, which held a 100 per cent share in the subsidiary, disposes of 40 per cent for €200 000. On the original acquisition of the subsidiary, goodwill of €80 000 arose. This goodwill has not subsequently been impaired and is in addition to the net assets of €400 000. How should the parent account for this transaction?

*Activity feedback*

| | |
|---|---:|
| Consideration received | 200 000 |
| Share of net assets disposed (including goodwill (40% × (400 000 + 80 000)) | 192 000 |
| 'Profit' on disposal to be recognized in equity | 8 000 |

*If, for example, the goodwill had been impaired to €60 000, then the impairment loss would have been recognized in previous profit and loss accounts. The 'profit' on disposal, assuming no change in the proceeds, would then have been calculated as follows:*

| | |
|---|---:|
| Consideration received | 200 000 |
| Share of net assets disposed (including goodwill (40% × (400 000 + 60 000)) | 184 000 |
| 'Profit' on disposal to be recognized in equity | 16 000 |

## LOSS OF CONTROL

In this section we discuss the opposite of a business combination: the loss of control.
A parent can lose control of a subsidiary by, for example:

- selling part of its ownership such that it is left with less than 50 per cent
- the subsidiary becoming subject to control of a government, court administrator or regulator
- the subsidiary becoming subject to some other contractual agreement that results in another investor gaining control.

In the most simple situation, an entity sells all the shares of the subsidiary. The former parent will then derecognize the assets including any goodwill and liabilities of the subsidiary at their carrying amounts at the date when control is lost. The difference with the fair value of the consideration received is recorded as a gain on sale.

When the former parent still retains an interest in the former subsidiary, IFRS 10, para. 25, requires that the remaining investment is revalued at fair value with the difference being accounted for in profit and loss. This in fact means that the transaction is accounted for as if all the shares held had been sold and a new investment had been acquired at fair value.

## ACTIVITY 26.10

We use a slightly different fact pattern than in Activity 26.9.

The value of a subsidiary's net assets at 31 March 201X is €400 000. At this date the parent, which held a 100 per cent share in the subsidiary, disposes of 70 per cent for €420 000. On the original acquisition of the subsidiary, goodwill of €80 000 arose. This goodwill has not subsequently been impaired and is in addition to the net assets of €400 000. The fair value of the remaining 30 per cent is estimated to be €150 000 (this is not proportional to the fair value of the 70 per cent interest as the 70 per cent interest contains a control premium). How should the parent account for this transaction?

*Activity feedback*

| | |
|---|---:|
| Consideration received | 420 000 |
| Share of net assets disposed (including goodwill (70% × (400 000 + 80 000)) | 336 000 |
| Profit on shares sold | 84 000 |
| Fair value of remaining shares | 150 000 |
| Book value of remaining shares (30% × (400 000 + 80 000)) | 144 000 |
| Profit on shares held | 6 000 |
| Total profit (included in profit and loss account) | 90 000 |

## DISCLOSURE REQUIREMENTS OF IFRS 3

IFRS 3 requires such disclosures that 'enable users of financial statements to evaluate the nature and financial effect of business combinations' (para. 59). Disclosure is required as follows:

- names and descriptions of combining entities
- acquisition date
- percentage of voting equity instruments acquired
- primary reason for the business combination and a description of how the acquirer obtained control of the acquiree

- cost of the combination and the components of the cost
- details of operations disposed of due to the combination
- details of fair values of assets, liabilities and contingent liabilities acquired
- amount of any negative goodwill in a bargain purchase and a description of reasons why the transaction resulted in a gain
- amount of acquiree's profit or loss since the acquisition date included in the acquirer's profit or loss
- a reconciliation of the carrying amount of goodwill at the beginning and end of the reporting period.

You can read the full disclosure requirements in Appendix B of IFRS 3.

## REAL WORLD ILLUSTRATION

### Acquisitions 2012

On 22 June 2012 DSM obtained control of Kensey Nash Corporation by acquiring 100 per cent of the shares. From that date onwards the financial statements of Kensey Nash have been consolidated by DSM and reported in the segment Innovation Center. The acquisition will strengthen and complement DSM's biomedical business, one of the Emerging Business Areas of DSM. Kensey Nash is a US-based, technology-driven biomedical company, primarily focused on regenerative medicine utilizing its proprietary collagen and synthetic polymer technology. Kensey Nash has annual sales of approximately US$90 million and employs about 325 people. In accordance with IFRS 3 the purchase price of Kensey Nash needs to be allocated to identifiable assets and liabilities acquired. Goodwill paid for the acquisition of Kensey Nash amounted to €128 million. The goodwill primarily resulted from the skills and knowledge of the workforce, sales synergies in relation to the opportunities for cross-selling and certain fixed cost synergies that are unique to DSM.

On 18 July 2012 DSM obtained control of Ocean Nutrition Canada (ONC) by acquiring 100 per cent of the shares. From that date onwards the financial statements of ONC are consolidated by DSM and reported in the Nutrition segment. The acquisition expands DSM's Nutritional Lipids growth platform. ONC is a leader in fish-oil derived Omega-3 fatty acids for dietary supplements, highly complementary to DSM's acquisition of Martek in 2011. ONC has annual sales of approximately CAD 190 million and employs about 415 people. In accordance with IFRS 3 the purchase price of ONC needs to be allocated to identifiable assets and liabilities acquired. Goodwill paid for the acquisition of ONC amounted to €238 million. The goodwill primarily resulted from the skills and knowledge of the workforce, sales synergies in relation to the opportunities for cross-selling and certain operating and variable cost synergies that are unique to DSM.

On 18 December 2012 DSM obtained control of Fortitech, Inc. by acquiring 100 per cent of the shares. From that date onwards the financial statements of Fortitech are consolidated by DSM and reported in the Nutrition segment. The acquisition strengthens DSM's Human Nutrition and Health business, by expanding the company's value chain presence and adding additional capabilities. Fortitech has annual sales of approximately US$ 270 million and employs about 520 people. In accordance with IFRS 3 the purchase price of Fortitech needs to be allocated to identifiable assets and liabilities acquired. This so-called purchase price allocation together with the conversion of the financial statements to IFRS has not been completed and therefore the consolidation is based on the unadjusted balance sheet of Fortitech. Once the purchase price allocation is completed the value of assets and liabilities will be adjusted and the final goodwill will be determined. Sales and profit of Fortitech in the period between the acquisition and the end of the year 2012 were immaterial for DSM as a result of the limited number of working days that remained and the impact of the holiday period. Up to one year from the acquisition date the initial accounting for business combinations needs to be adjusted to reflect additional information that has been received about facts and circumstances that existed at the acquisition date and would have affected the measurement of amounts recognized as of that date. As a result of such adjustments the values of assets and liabilities recognized may change in the one year period from the acquisition date.

*(Continued)*

## REAL WORLD ILLUSTRATION    *(Continued)*

The impact of all acquisitions made in 2012 on DSM's consolidated balance sheet, at the date of acquisition, is summarized in the following table.

| 2012 | Kensey Nash | | Ocean Nutrition | | Fortitech, Inc. | | Other acquisitions | | Total | |
|---|---|---|---|---|---|---|---|---|---|---|
| Assets | Book value | Fair value | Book value | Fair value | Book value | Fair value | Book value | Fair value | Book value | Fair value |
| Intangible assets | 18 | 136 | – | 114 | 1 | 1 | – | 35 | 19 | 286 |
| Property, plant and equipment | 45 | 55 | 57 | 63 | 53 | 53 | 30 | 33 | 185 | 204 |
| Other non-current assets | 3 | 2 | – | – | 4 | 4 | – | – | 7 | 6 |
| Inventories | 12 | 16 | 35 | 47 | 38 | 38 | 14 | 16 | 99 | 117 |
| Receivables | 25 | 12 | 41 | 49 | 29 | 29 | 8 | 8 | 103 | 98 |
| Cash and cash equivalents | 29 | 29 | 10 | 10 | 8 | 8 | – | – | 47 | 47 |
| **Total assets** | **132** | **250** | **143** | **283** | **133** | **133** | **52** | **92** | **460** | **758** |
| Non-controlling interests | – | – | – | – | – | – | – | – | – | – |
| Liabilities | | | | | | | | | | |
| Non-current liabilities | 5 | 39 | 5 | 48 | 5 | 5 | – | 1 | 15 | 93 |
| Current liabilities | 71 | 72 | 84 | 84 | 46 | 46 | 5 | 5 | 206 | 207 |
| **Non-controlling interests and liabilities** | **76** | **111** | **89** | **132** | **51** | **51** | **5** | **6** | **221** | **300** |
| **Net assets** | **56** | **139** | **54** | **151** | **82** | **82** | **47** | **86** | **239** | **458** |
| Acquisition price (in cash) | | 216 | | 390 | | 474 | | 120 | | 1 200 |
| Acquisition price (payable) | | 51 | | (1) | | 13 | | 2 | | 65 |
| **Consideration** | | **267** | | **389** | | **487** | | **122** | | **1 265** |
| **Goodwill** | | **128** | | **238** | | **405** | | **36** | | **807** |

The acquisition of Kensey Nash contributed €35 million to net sales in 2012. If the acquisition had occurred on 1 January 2012, additional net sales would have been approximately €67 million. The acquisition contributed €14 million to EBITDA. Kensey Nash related exceptional items amounted to €8 before tax (see note 6: Exceptional items).

The acquisition of ONC contributed €60 million to net sales in 2012. If the acquisition had occurred on 1 January 2012, additional net sales would have been approximately €131 million. The acquisition contributed €15 million to EBITDA. ONC related exceptional items amounted to €20 before tax (see note 6: Exceptional items).

Other acquisitions comprise Verenium, Cilpaz & Laba, the cultures and enzymes business of Cargill and Oatwell.

Together, the acquisitions in 2012 contributed €103 million to net sales. If all acquisitions had occurred on 1 January 2012, additional net sales would have been approximately €253 million (excluding Fortitech). The acquisitions in 2012 contributed €26 million to EBITDA; this would have been approximately €53 million (excluding Fortitech) if they had all occurred on 1 January 2012.

(From: DSM, Integrated Annual Report 2012, pp. 155–156)

## SUMMARY

In this chapter we have dealt with accounting for business combinations. All business combinations are accounted for by applying the acquisition method. The acquirer is the entity that obtains control in the acquiree. The acquisition date is the date that control is obtained. At that date the purchase price is allocated to assets, liabilities and contingent liabilities (all to be measured at fair value) and the remaining amount is goodwill. Under IFRS, goodwill is not amortized but only tested for impairment. Goodwill might be negative, in which case the amount is recognized in profit and loss.

In case of acquiring less than 100 per cent of the shares, there will be a non-controlling interest. A business combination can be achieved in stages. The previously held equity interest will then be remeasured at its acquisition date fair value, recognizing the remeasurement in profit and loss. A business combination can also be provisional, in which case the fair values of assets and liabilities might be subsequently remeasured, effecting goodwill if the remeasurement is within a year after the acquisition. Changes in contingent considerations do not affect goodwill, but are accounted for in profit and loss.

All transactions with the non-controlling shareholder, without changing the existence of control, are accounted for in equity. If, however, there is a loss of control, the gain or losses are recognized in profit and loss, including the gain to fair value remeasurement of the remaining investment.

IFRS 3 requires extensive disclosures.

After the business combination, the acquirer will be the parent company and the acquiree the subsidiary company. The parent will prepare consolidated accounts, which is the topic of the next chapter.

You will find a limited number of exercises at the end of this chapter. There are many more exercises at the end of Chapter 27, many of them integrating the subjects of business combinations and consolidated financial statements.

## EXERCISES

*Suggested answers to exercises marked ✓ are to be found on our dedicated CourseMate platform for students.*

*Suggested answers to the remaining exercises are to be found on the Instructor online support resources.*

1   On 30 June 2004, *C* purchased 75 per cent of the equity shares of *D* for $16 million. The statement of financial position of *D* showed net assets of $14 million. This was before taking account of the following items:

   • The market value of *D*'s properties at 30 June 2004 (included in the statement of financial position of *D* at a carrying value of $8 million) was $10 million.

   • On 30 June 2004, *D* was in the process of negotiating an insurance claim in respect of inventory that was damaged before that date. The claim was for $1 million and, although nothing has yet been received, the directors of *D* are confident that the claim will be successful.

   What is the goodwill on consolidation that will appear in the consolidated statement of financial position of *C* at 30 June 2004?

   (CIMA paper – November 2004)

**2**   Barking, an unlisted company, operates in the house building and commercial property investment development sector. The sector has seen an upturn in activity during recent years and the directors have been considering future plans with a view to determining their impact on the financial statements for the financial year to 30 November 20X4.

(a) Barking wishes to obtain a stock exchange listing in the year to 30 November 20X4. It is to be acquired by Ash, a significantly smaller listed company in a share for share exchange whereby Barking will receive sufficient voting shares of Ash to control the new group. Due to the relative values of the companies, Barking will become the majority shareholder with 80 per cent of the enlarged capital of Ash. The executive management of the new group will be that of Barking.

As part of the purchase consideration, Ash will issue zero dividend preference shares of $1 to the shareholders of Barking on 30 June 20X4. These will be redeemed on 1 January 20X5 at $1.10 per share. Additionally Ash will issue convertible interest free loan notes. The loan notes are unlikely to be repaid on 30 November 20X5 (the redemption date) as the conversion terms are very favourable. The management of Ash have excluded the redemption of the loan notes from their cash flow projections. The loan notes are to be included in long-term liabilities in the statement of financial position of Ash. As part of the business combination Ash will change its name to Barking Inc.

(b) The acquisition will also have other planned effects on the company. Barking operates a defined benefit pension scheme. On acquisition the scheme will be frozen and replaced by a group defined contribution scheme, and as a result no additional benefits in the old scheme will accrue to the employees. Ash's employees are also in a defined benefit scheme which has been classified as a multi-employer plan but it is currently impossible to identify its share of the underlying assets and liabilities in the scheme. After acquisition, Ash's employees will be transferred to the group's defined contribution scheme, with the previous scheme being frozen.

(c) As a result of the acquisition the company will change the way in which it recognizes sales of residential properties. It used to treat such properties as sold when the building work was substantially complete, defined as being when the roof and internal walls had been completed. The new policy will be to recognize a sale when a refundable deposit for the sale of the property has been received and the building work is physically complete. Legal costs incurred on the sale of the property are currently capitalized and shown as current assets until the sale of the property has occurred. Further, it has been decided by the directors that as at 30 November 20X4, the financial year-end, some properties held as trading properties of both companies will be moved from the trading portfolio to the investment portfolio of the holding company, and carried at fair value.

(d) The directors intend to carry out an impairment review as at 30 November 20X4 in order to ascertain whether the carrying amount of goodwill and other non-current assets can be supported by their value in use. The plan is to produce cash flow projections up to 20X4 with an average discount rate of 15 per cent being used in the calculations. The ten-year period is to be used as it reflects fairly the long-term nature of the assets being assessed. Any subsequent impairment loss is to be charged against the statement of comprehensive income.

**Required:**

Draft a report to the directors of Barking, setting out the financial reporting implications of the above plans for the financial statements for the year to 30 November 20X4.

(ACCA – December 2003)

**3**    *HA* acquired 100 per cent of *SB*'s equity shares on 1 April 2010 for $185 000. The values of *SB*'s assets at that date were:

|  | Book value | Fair value |
|---|---|---|
|  | $000 | $000 |
| Property | 100 | 115 |
| Plant and equipment | 75 | 70 |

On 1 April 2010 all other assets and liabilities had a fair value approximately equal to their book value.

*SB*'s equity at 1 April 2010 was:

|  | $000 |
|---|---|
| $1 equity shares | 150 |
| Share premium | 15 |
| Retained earnings | (22) |

Calculate the goodwill arising on the acquisition of *SB*.

(CIMA – May 2011)

# CONSOLIDATED FINANCIAL STATEMENTS  **27**

**OBJECTIVES**  After studying this chapter you should be able to:

- outline the need for consolidated financial statements

- prepare consolidated financial statements in accordance with IFRS

- understand and apply the mechanics of preparing consolidated financial statements.

## INTRODUCTION

In the last chapter we discussed accounting for business combinations, where an acquirer acquires an acquiree. After acquisition, the acquirer is a parent and the acquiree is a subsidiary. Both parent and subsidiary need to draw up their financial statements of the legal entity. But this gives just a limited view of what happens in the group, the parent and the subsidiary together. Remember that the parent exercises control over the subsidiary, so it also exercises control over all the assets and liabilities in the subsidiary. A user of financial statements would be interested in financial statements where all assets and liabilities and all revenues and costs that are under the control of the parent are reflected. This is the reason why a parent not only prepares its own legal entity set of financial statements but also consolidated financial statements, financial statements of a parent and all its subsidiaries.

In this chapter we will discuss the issues that arise in preparing consolidated accounts.

## CONTROL

We refer back to Chapter 26 where we discussed the concept of control. A parent exercises control over a subsidiary. Control means that a parent is exposed, or has rights, to variable returns from its involvement with the subsidiary and has the ability to affect those returns through its power over the subsidiary (IFRS 10, para. 5). So the three essential elements for an investor (parent) are:

• power over the investee (subsidiary)

• exposure, or rights, to variable returns from its involvement with the investee

• the ability to use its power over the investee to affect the amount of the investor's returns.

An investor has power over the investee when the investor has existing rights that give it the current ability to direct the relevant activities of the investee. Power arises from rights, such as voting rights attached to shares. Power can also result from one or more contractual arrangements.

An investor is exposed, or has rights to, variable returns from its involvement with the investee when the investor's returns from its involvement have the potential to vary as a result of the investee's performance. The investor's returns can be positive, negative or both positive and negative.

For control to exist, the investor must have the ability to use its power to affect the returns. If an investor is an agent, and not a principal, it has delegated decision rights and it acts on behalf and for the benefit of another party. Such an investor would not have control over the investee.

IFRS 10 introduces the concept of de facto control. Even if an investor does not have the majority of the voting rights, the existing voting rights might give the investor the power to direct the relevant activities unilaterally. This will normally be the case when the investor has more voting rights than other investors and other investors act independently. As an example, given in IFRS 10, para. B43, assume that an investor has 48 per cent of the voting rights, while the remaining voting rights are held by thousands of shareholders, none individually holding more than 1 per cent of the voting rights. Further assume that none of the shareholders has any arrangement to consult any of the others or make collective decisions. In this situation the conclusion would be that the 48 per cent investor has (de facto) control.

Another issue in determining control is potential voting rights. For example, take investors A and B, both having an interest in entity C. A has 10 per cent of the voting rights, B has 90 per cent. Based on this scenario alone, B would have control. However, A and B have contracted a substantive call option for A, giving A the current unconditional right to acquire 45 per cent of the shares in C held by B at fair value. As a result, A controls C while it can at any time direct the relevant activities of C (by using the call option and then having 55 per cent of the voting rights).

## ACTIVITY 27.1

Identify in each of the following circumstances whether B is a subsidiary of A, i.e. whether A exercises control over B.

**1** A owns 40 per cent of the voting rights of B and has an agreement with a shareholder who holds a further 15 per cent of the voting rights that enables him to vote for these shares as well.

**2** A owns 42 per cent of the voting rights of B but also has an agreement to govern the financial and operating policies of B.

**3** A owns 35 per cent of the voting rights of B and also has the power to appoint or remove five of the nine members of the board of directors.

**4** A owns 33 per cent of the voting rights of B and 100 per cent of the voting rights of C which in turn holds 20 per cent of the voting rights of B.

### Activity feedback
*In cases 1, 2 and 3, A clearly controls the decisions of B and therefore B is a subsidiary of A.*

*Case 4 is also an example of a subsidiary relationship and Figure 27.1 should show this more clearly. A controls C and therefore also 20 per cent of B which together with its own 33 per cent holding gives it control over 53 per cent of B. This is an example of a mixed group.*

## Figure 27.1 A subsidiary relationship

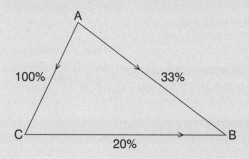

## ACTIVITY 27.2

We explore mixed groups a little further in this activity. In the examples given identify the parent–subsidiary relationships:

**1** H owns 75 per cent of the voting shares of S, which in turn owns 40 per cent of the voting shares of S1. H also owns directly 15 per cent of the voting shares of S1.

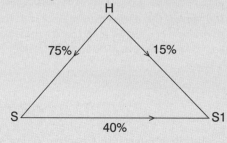

**2** H owns 100 per cent of the voting shares of S, which in turn owns 30 per cent of S1. H also owns 75 per cent of S2 which in turn owns 25 per cent of S1.

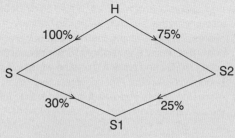

(Continued)

## ACTIVITY 27.2   (Continued)

**3** H owns 60 per cent of the voting shares of S which in turn owns 20 per cent of the voting shares of S1. H also owns directly 20 per cent of the voting shares of S1.

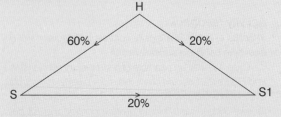

### Activity feedback

#### Example 1

- S is a subsidiary of H (75 per cent ownership), S1 is not a subsidiary of S (assuming no information in respect of dominant influence).

- H directly owns 75% × 40% of S1 + 15% of S1 = 30% + 15% = 45% which would imply no subsidiary relationship.

- However, H controls S and thus controls 40% of S1 plus 15%.

- Therefore, S1 is a subsidiary of H and will be consolidated with a non-controlling interest of 55%.

#### Example 2

- S and S2 are subsidiaries of H. S1 requires further analysis.

- H directly owns 100% × 30% + 75% × 25% of S1 = 30% + 18.75% = 48.75% only.

- However, H controls 30% + 25% = 55%.

- Thus, S1 is also a subsidiary of H and will be consolidated with a non-controlling interest of 51.25%.

#### Example 3

- S is a subsidiary of H.

- H owns 60% × 20% + 20% of S1 = 32% of S1.

- H controls 20% + 20% of S1 = 40%.

- Thus, S1 is not a subsidiary of H (assuming no indication of dominant influence) and will not be consolidated.

## ACTIVITY 27.3

**1** H currently holds 48 per cent of the shares of S. H does not have the power to govern the policies of S, nor the power to remove members of the board, nor the power to cast the majority of votes at meetings. The remaining 52 per cent of S's shares are held by four investors that all have 13 per cent of the shares. Is S a subsidiary of H?

**2** Entities A and B currently own 55 per cent and 45 per cent respectively of the ordinary voting right shares of entity C. Entity B also holds debt instruments that are convertible into ordinary shares of entity C at any time. If the debt were converted, entity B would hold 70 per cent of the voting shares and entity A's holding would become 30 per cent. The conversion would require entity B to borrow additional funds to make the conversion payment. Is C a subsidiary of A, B or neither?

### Activity feedback

**1** The question is whether H has de facto control in S. In this situation, the four investors can easily organize themselves and together outnumber H. So this would not be a case of de facto control. However, if the 52 per cent shares were divided equally among about 30 shareholders, there could be more reason to conclude that H controls S and that S therefore is a subsidiary of H. There is a high degree of judgement involved in determining whether de facto control exists.

**2** The conversion rights owned by B give B the power to set the operating and financial policies of C. Therefore C is a subsidiary of B not of A. This is an example of potential voting rights. The fact that additional funds have to be borrowed is not relevant.

## Non-controlling interest

We have discussed the concept of non-controlling interest in Chapter 26. Put simply, non-controlling interest is that part of the subsidiary that the holding (parent) entity does not own. This non-controlling interest is usually less than 50 per cent but can, as in example 2 of Activity 27.2, be more than 50 per cent if ownership does not define the control. This is the reason why the phrase 'non-controlling interest' is better than 'minority interest', as the non-controlling interest does not necessarily reflect a minority of the shares.

## NEED FOR CONSOLIDATED ACCOUNTS

If we examine the separate accounts of two entities, H and S, where H holds 55 per cent of the ordinary voting shares of S, then we will find the following information available to us. We will refer to H as the 'holding' enterprise, S as the 'subsidiary' and when considering both entities together we will regard them as a 'group'.

In H's statement of financial position the shareholding (interest) in S will simply appear as an investment recorded at its cost of acquisition, historical cost. IFRS allows to measure the investment at fair value, but, as this option is seldom used for investments in subsidiaries, we will not discuss that measurement option any further. So our assumption is that the investment is recorded at historical cost. However, as with other assets in a statement of financial position, the use of historical cost as the basis of valuation would not normally give the shareholders of H any indication of the value of the subsidiary or the underlying assets and liabilities.

In relation to the holding entity's statement of comprehensive income (or statement of profit and loss) the only reference to the subsidiary would be 'dividends received from S' (assuming there were any) and, of course, this would give no indication of the subsidiary's profitability.

As far as the group is concerned, the holding entity's financial statements give no meaningful information about the group's activities, hence it would be useful to find a way to prepare information about the related activities of H and S in a consolidated (combined) format.

This is where the need for group accounts arises: to provide useful information to shareholders and other users of the holding entity's financial statements about the group as a whole.

IFRS 10, para. 19 requires a parent to prepare consolidated financial statements using uniform accounting policies for like transactions and other events in similar circumstances. Consolidated accounts combine assets, liabilities, equity, income, expenses and cash flows of the parent with those of its subsidiaries as being a single economic entity.

IFRS 10, para. 4a, however, exempts a parent from presenting consolidated financial statements if it meets all the following conditions:

- the parent is a wholly owned or partly owned subsidiary of another entity
- the parent's debt or equity instruments are not traded in a public market or the parent is not in the process of issuing any class of instruments in a public market
- the ultimate or any intermediate parent produces consolidated statements available for public use that comply with IFRS.

## PREPARATION OF CONSOLIDATED STATEMENTS OF FINANCIAL POSITION

In this section we will discuss the preparation of consolidated statements of financial position, and, in the next section, preparation of consolidated statements of comprehensive income. In preparing the consolidated accounts we will discuss in detail the need for eliminating intercompany relationships. The principles discussed are in line with the requirements of IFRS 10.

### Consolidated statement of financial position at the date of acquisition

So far we have identified a need for group accounts to show useful information to users. But what would be useful information to these users? We can presume that they will need to know the total assets and liabilities of the subsidiary that they control, together with the parent's own assets and liabilities. From this we can assume that we will add all the assets and liabilities of the parent and subsidiary together. If we do this we will then need to eliminate the investment from the parent statement of financial position (as we have included the net assets) and add in the goodwill on acquisition. If we haven't acquired the whole of the subsidiary there will also be a non-controlling interest and we will need to include this in the group statement of financial position or we will not balance. The following example demonstrates the consolidation process where there is no non-controlling interest, i.e. 100 per cent ownership. This example prepares a consolidated statement at the date of the acquisition of the subsidiary.

## Example 27.1

The statements of financial position of H and S as at 31 December 201X are as follows:

|  | H<br>€ | S<br>€ |
|---|---|---|
| Property, plant and equipment | 140 000 | 45 000 |
| Investment in S | 75 000 | |
| Net current assets | 20 000 | 15 000 |
|  | 235 000 | 60 000 |
| Share capital | 150 000 | 50 000 |
| Reserves | 85 000 | 10 000 |
|  | 235 000 | 60 000 |

H acquired the whole of the share capital of S for €75 000 cash on 31 December 201X. The fair value of S's net assets at this date were €67 000. Prepare the consolidated statement of financial position of H group as at 31 December 201X.

To do this consolidation there are several steps:

1  Calculate the goodwill.

2  Revalue the net assets of the subsidiary S to fair value.

3  Consolidate H and S.

| 1 | Purchase price | 75 000 |
|---|---|---|
| | Fair value of net assets acquired | 67 000 |
| | Goodwill | 8 000 |
| 2 | S revalued statement of financial position | |
| | Net assets | 67 000 |
| | Share capital | 50 000 |
| | Reserves | 10 000 |
| | Revaluation reserve | 7 000 |
| | | 67 000 |
| 3 | Group consolidated statement of financial position | |
| | Net assets (140 000 + 20 000 + 67 000) | 227 000 |
| | Goodwill on acquisition | 8 000 |
| | | 235 000 |
| | Share capital | 150 000 |
| | Reserves | 85 000 |
| | | 235 000 |

Note that the share capital of S and the reserves from S at the date of acquisition, including the revaluation reserve, do not appear in the consolidated statement of financial position. This is because they have been replaced with the net assets acquired and the goodwill value.

The following example shows the preparation of the group consolidated statement of financial position when there is less than 100 per cent ownership. We determine the non-controlling interest on the basis of the proportion in the fair value of the net assets acquired.

## Example 27.2

The statements of financial position of A and B as at 31 December 201X are as follows:

| | A<br>€ | B<br>€ |
|---|---|---|
| Net assets | 403 000 | 87 000 |
| Investment in B | 72 000 | – |
| | 475 000 | 87 000 |
| Share capital | 350 000 | 60 000 |
| Reserves | 125 000 | 27 000 |
| | 475 000 | 87 000 |

A bought 75 per cent of S as at 31 December 201X for a purchase price of €72 000 and the value of the net assets bought equaled fair value.

| 1 | Purchase price | 72 000 |
|---|---|---|
| | Fair value of net assets acquired (75% × 87.000) | 65 250 |
| | Goodwill | 6 750 |

| 2 | Group consolidated statement of financial position | |
|---|---|---|
| | Net assets (403 000 + 87 000) | 490 000 |
| | Goodwill | 6 750 |
| | | 496 750 |
| | Share capital | 350 000 |
| | Reserves | 125 000 |
| | Equity attributable to the shareholders of H | 475 000 |
| | Non-controlling interest (25% × 87 000) | 21 750 |
| | Total equity | 496 750 |

Now try Activity 27.4.

## ACTIVITY 27.4

The statements of financial position of H and S at the date H acquired 1 000 000 shares of S with a nominal value of €0,10 per share, at a fair value of €120 000 for cash (the transaction has not yet been entered) are as follows:

| | H €000 | S €000 |
|---|---|---|
| Land and buildings | 650 | 105 |
| Plant and equipment | 110 | 21 |
| Net current assets | 163 | 11 |
| | 923 | 137 |
| Share capital €1 shares | 800 | |
| Share capital €0,10 shares | | 125 |
| Reserves | 123 | 12 |
| | 923 | 137 |

The fair value of S's net assets at the date of acquisition was €142 000 (€108 000 land and buildings, €22 000 plant and equipment, €12 000 net current assets).

Prepare the consolidated statement of financial position of H group as at 31 December 201X after the acquisition.

### Activity feedback

*Remember first to amend H's statement of financial position for the purchase of the shares in S. This will require* an entry 'investment in S €120 000' and net current assets will be reduced to €43 000 for the cash payment.

H acquired 1 000 000 shares of €0,10 (€100 000) from a total of €125 000 million, i.e. 80 per cent ownership.

Consolidated statement of financial position of H group as at 31 December 201X

| 1 | Purchase price | 120 000 |
|---|---|---|
| | Fair value of net assets acquired (80% × 142.000) | 113 600 |
| | Goodwill | 6 400 |
| 2 | Group consolidated statement of financial position | |
| | Net assets (923 000 – 120 000 + 142 000) | 945 000 |
| | Goodwill | 6 400 |
| | | 951 400 |
| | Share capital | 800 000 |
| | Reserves | 123 000 |
| | Equity attributable to the shareholders of H | 923 000 |
| | Non-controlling interest (20% × 142 000) | 28 400 |
| | Total equity | 951 400 |

## Consolidated statement of financial position later than date of acquisition

We obviously have to prepare consolidated accounts subsequent to the date of acquisition and as long as we know the fair value of the assets acquired and the cost of that acquisition this is quite easy. We can only include the parent share of the reserves post acquisition in the consolidation. The following example shows you how to prepare a consolidated statement of financial position later than the date of acquisition where there is a 100 per cent ownership.

## Example 27.3

H entity purchased 100 per cent of the equity share capital of S for cash at 31 December year 1 at a price of €2 per share when the balance on S entity's reserves stood at €4000.

The consolidation is required to be made at 31 December year 2 at which point the individual statements of financial position of the two entities are as follows:

|  | H | S |
|---|---|---|
| Property, plant and equipment | 75 000 | 13 000 |
| Investment in S | 20 000 | – |
| Current assets | 23 000 | 4 000 |
|  | 118 000 | 17 000 |
| Share capital €1 | 60 000 | 10 000 |
| Reserves | 58 000 | 7 000 |
|  | 118 000 | 17 000 |

No further shares have been issued by S during year 2.

| | |
|---|---|
| Purchase price | 20 000 |
| Fair value of net assets acquired: | |
| 10 000 (shares) + 4000 (pre-acquisition reserves) | 14 000 |
| Goodwill | 6 000 |

Consolidated statement of financial position for H group as at 31 December year 2

| | |
|---|---|
| Property plant and equipment | 88 000 |
| Current assets | 27 000 |
| Goodwill | 6 000 |
| | 121 000 |
| Share capital | 60 000 |
| Reserves (58 000 + (7000 − 4000)) | 61 000 |
| | 121 000 |

Now try Activity 27.5 but note that in this activity there is also a non-controlling interest.

## ACTIVITY 27.5

H entity purchased 80 per cent of the equity share capital of S Ltd for cash at 31 December year 1 at a price of €1.50 per share, when the balance on S entity's reserves stood at €2 000.

The consolidation is required to be made at 31 December year 2, at which point the individual statements of financial position of the two entities are as follows:

(*Continued*)

## ACTIVITY 27.5 (Continued)

| | €<br>H | €<br>S |
|---|---|---|
| Property, plant and equipment | 60 000 | 5 000 |
| Investment in S entity | 9 600 | – |
| Current assets | 35 000 | 6 000 |
| | 104 600 | 11 000 |
| Represented by shares of €1 | 40 000 | 8 000 |
| Reserves | 64 600 | 3 000 |
| | 104 600 | 11 000 |

*Notes:*

| | | |
|---|---|---|
| 1 | Cost of investment in S entity | 9 600 |
| | Acquired ordinary shares at 31 December | |
| | year 1 (80 per cent × 8000) | 6 400 |
| | Acquired reserves at 31 December = | |
| | (being 80% of balance of €2000 on | |
| | reserves of S entity at 31 December | |
| | year 1) | 1 600 |
| | Total (80% × 10 000) | 8 000 |
| | Goodwill on acquisition | 1 600 |
| 2 | Reserves of H entity at 31 December | |
| | year 2 | 64 600 |
| | Reserves of S entity accruing to | |
| | group since date of acquisition | |
| | to 31 December year 2 = | |
| | (3000 – 2000) × 80% | 800 |
| | | 65 400 |

### Activity feedback

The consolidated statement of financial position as at 31 December year 2 would then be as follows:

| | € |
|---|---|
| Property plant and equipment | 65 000 |
| Current assets | 41 000 |
| Goodwill (note 1) | 1 600 |
| | 107 600 |
| Represented by shares of €1 | 40 000 |
| Group reserves (note 2) | 65 400 |
| | 105 400 |
| Non-controlling interest (note 3) | 2 200 |
| | 107 600 |

| | | |
|---|---|---|
| 3 | Share capital as 31 December year 2 of S | |
| | entity accruing to non-controlling | |
| | interests (20% × 8000) | 1 600 |
| | Reserves at 31 December year 2 of S | |
| | entity accruing to non-controlling | |
| | interests (20% × 3000) | 600 |
| | Total (20% × 11 000) | 2 200 |

## Inter-company trading and the elimination of unrealized profits

When one member of a group, S, buys goods from an external supplier at a price (say) of €100, and sells those goods to a fellow group entity, S1, at a price of €140, then S can legitimately show a profit of €40 in its own statement of comprehensive income. However, on consolidation of the accounts of S and S1 it should be recognized that this sale from S to S1 could not give rise to a profit as far as the group statement of comprehensive income is concerned, as the sale is in effect an internal group transfer. In order for the group to realize a profit on sale, the sale must be made to a customer outside the group. Now complete the following activity.

## ACTIVITY 27.6

Entity A owns 75 per cent of the shares in entity B, bought when the reserves of B were €200 000. The individual statements of financial position of A and B as at 30 June 201X are given below. During the year B has sold goods to A at a profit margin of 25 per cent on cost. €50 000 of these goods lie in A's closing stock as at 30 June 201X.

*(Continued)*

## ACTIVITY 27.6 (Continued)

|  | A €000 | B €000 |  | €000 |
|---|---|---|---|---|
| **Assets** |  |  | **Liabilities** |  |
| Land and plant | 1 000 | 200 | Creditors | 46 |
| Stock | 600 | 400 |  | 2 434 |
| Debtors | 200 | 40 | Represented by: |  |
| Investment in B | 275 | – | Shares of €1 | 1 000 |
|  | 2 075 | 640 | Reserves (note 3) | 1 280.5 |
| **Liabilities** |  |  |  | 2 280.5 |
| Creditors | 30 | 16 | Non-controlling interests (note 4) | 153.5 |
|  | 2 045 | 624 |  | 2 434 |
| Represented by |  |  |  |  |
| Shares of €1 | 1 000 | 100 |  |  |
| Reserves | 1 045 | 524 |  |  |
|  | 2 045 | 624 |  |  |

Prepare the consolidated statement of financial position as at 30 June 201X.

### Activity feedback

Consolidated statement of financial position as at 30 June 201X:

| | €000 |
|---|---|
| **Assets** | |
| Goodwill (note 1) | 50 |
| Land and plant | 1 200 |
| Stock (1 000 – 10) (note 2) | 990 |
| Debtors | 240 |
| | 2 480 |

*Notes*

| | | | |
|---|---|---|---|
| 1 | Cost of investment in B | | 275 |
| | *Less* ordinary shares acquired | 75 | |
| | Reserves acquired (75% × 200) | 150 | 225 |
| | | | 50 |
| 2 | Goods in A stock delivered by B: | | 50 |
| | Profit margin included: | | |
| | (50 – 50/1.25) | | 10 |
| 3 | Reserves A | | 1 045 |
| | Reserves post-acquisition B | | |
| | 75% (524 – 10 – 200) | | 235.5 |
| | | | 1 280.5 |
| 4 | Non-controlling interest | | |
| | 25% ordinary shares | | 25 |
| | 25% reserves = 25% × (524 – 10) | | 128.5 |
| | | | 153.5 |

## Reconciliation of inter-company balances

It is commonplace for entities within a group to shuffle liquidity and stocks between themselves as and when required and indeed this is one of the advantages of a group structure. Obviously with reference to such transactions, the indebtedness to/from member entities will need to be recorded in the individual entities' books of account as appropriate. Hence, each entity will carry balances within the group. In relation to the group's position as regards the outside world, these balances are internal balances and will, therefore, be shown in the group statement of financial position. They are, in fact, cancelled on consolidation across the individual statement of financial positions of group members. If, for example, a subsidiary borrows money from its parent, this will be a financial asset in the individual accounts of the parent and a financial liability in the individual accounts of the subsidiary. On consolidation, these balances are eliminated.

Occasionally, however, it is not possible to cancel out such inter-entity balances, and this may often be due to transfer of goods or cash between group entities straddling the financial year-end. A consolidation adjustment is required at the year-end to adjust for goods or cash in transit between two entities before we can carry out the consolidation of accounts. The adjustment assumes that we account for the transit item as though it had reached its destination. It is important to note that these adjustments we are making here only affect the consolidated accounts; we make no adjustment for these inter-entity balances to the individual accounts of each entity.

## ACTIVITY 27.7

The financial year-end of two entities A and B within the same group is 31 December. On 29 December A despatched goods to B to the invoice value of €40 000 and charges B's ledger account accordingly. B does not receive either goods or invoice until 4 January. Prepare the consolidation adjustment on B's books and note any other adjustment that may be required on consolidation.

### Activity feedback
The adjustment will bring the goods into B's books as at 31 December.

| B ledger books | Dr | Cr |
|---|---|---|
| Goods in transit | €40 000 | |
| A current account | | €40 000 |

On consolidation the respective inter-company balances in the current accounts which are now in agreement will cancel out.

However, we must remember that this stock of €40 000 in transit will contain an element of unrealized profit and this will need eliminating on consolidation.

## Consistency of reporting dates and accounting policies within the group

Generally, the financial statement of a parent and its subsidiaries will be drawn up to the same date to enable easy preparation of consolidated financial statements. However, sometimes it is impracticable to do this and consolidation can take place using the accounts prepared to different dates provided the difference is no greater than a specified number of months, for example three months. Activity 27.8 will test your understanding of the preparation of consolidated statements of financial position for a parent and its subsidiary where there are several adjustments to make before consolidation can take place.

## ACTIVITY 27.8

On 1 October 2010 H entity acquired two million of S entity's ordinary shares paying £4.50 per share. At the date of acquisition the retained earnings of S were £4 200 000. The draft statements of financial position of the two entities as at 30 September 2012 were as follows:

| | H £000 | S £000 |
|---|---|---|
| **Assets** | | |
| Non-current assets | | |
| Land | 11 000 | 6 000 |
| Plant and equipment | 10 225 | 5 110 |
| Investment in S | 9 000 | |
| | 30 225 | 11 110 |

| | H £000 | S £000 |
|---|---|---|
| Current assets | | |
| Inventory | 4 925 | 3 295 |
| Trade receivables | 5 710 | 1 915 |
| Cash | 495 | |
| | 11 130 | 5 210 |
| **Total assets** | 41 355 | 16 320 |
| **Equity and liabilities** | | |
| Equity | | |
| Ordinary shares £1 | 5 000 | 2 500 |
| Retained earnings | 25 920 | 8 290 |
| | 30 920 | 10 790 |

(Continued)

## ACTIVITY 27.8 (Continued)

| | H £000 | S £000 |
|---|---|---|
| Non-current liabilities | | |
| 10% loans | 6 000 | 2 000 |
| Current liabilities | | |
| Trade payables | 3 200 | 2 255 |
| Bank overdraft | | 285 |
| Tax | 1 235 | 990 |
| | 4 435 | 3 530 |
| **Total equity and liabilities** | 41 355 | 16 320 |

Extracts from the statement of comprehensive income of S entity before inter-group adjustments for the year ended 30 September 2012 are:

| | £000s |
|---|---|
| Profit before tax | 2 700 |
| Taxation | 800 |
| Profit after tax | 1 900 |

The following information is also relevant:

1 During the year S sold goods to H for £0.9m. S adds a 20 per cent mark-up on cost to all its sales. Goods with a transfer price of £240 000 were included in H's inventory as at 30 September 2012.

2 The fair values of S's land and plant and equipment at the date of acquisition were £1m and £2m respectively in excess of the carrying values. S's statement of financial position has not taken account of these fair values. Group depreciation policy is land not depreciated, plant and equipment depreciated 10 per cent per annum on fair value.

3 An impairment review has been carried out on the consolidated goodwill as at 30 September 2012 and it has been found that the goodwill has been impaired by £400 000 during the year.

**Required**

Prepare the consolidated statement of financial position of H group as at 30 September 2012. Deferred taxes may be neglected.

*Activity feedback*

| Purchase of 80%: (2 million/2.5 million) | |
|---|---|
| Purchase price (2 million × 4.50) | 9 000 |
| Fair value of net assets acquired (80% × | |
| (2500 + 4200 + 3000 revaluation) | 7 760 |
| Goodwill | 1 240 |

*Consolidated statement of financial position for H group as at 30 September 2012*

| | £000s |
|---|---|
| **Assets** | |
| Non-current assets | |
| Land (11 000 + 6000 + 1000) | 18 000 |
| Plant and equipment (10 225 + 5110 + 2000 | |
| − 400 (10% × 2 million × 2 years) | |
| depreciation) | 16 935 |
| Intangible assets (1240 goodwill − 400 | |
| impairment) | 840 |
| | 35 775 |
| Current assets | |
| Inventory (4925 + 3295 − 40 unrealized | |
| profit; 240/120 × 100 = 200 cost for S) | 8 180 |
| Trade receivables (5710 + 1915) | 7 625 |
| Cash | 495 |
| | 16 300 |
| **Total assets** | 52 075 |
| **Equity and liabilities** | |
| Equity | |
| Ordinary share capital | 5 000 |
| Retained earnings (25 920 + (8290 − 4200 | |
| pre acq. − 400 dep. − 40 unrealized profit) | |
| 80% − 400 impairment) | 28 440 |
| | 33 440 |
| Non-controlling interest (20% (10 790 − 400 − | |
| 40 + 3000 revaluation)) | 2 670 |
| Non-current liabilities | |
| 10% loans (6 000 + 2 000) | 8 000 |
| Current liabilities | |
| Trade payables (3200 + 2255) | 5 455 |
| Bank overdraft | 285 |
| Tax (1235 + 990) | 2 225 |
| | 7 965 |
| **Total equity and liabilities** | 52 075 |

## Summary so far

We can usefully refresh our memory of group accounts and work through a full example at this point (Activity 27.9), using rules we have identified so far.

## ACTIVITY 27.9

The statements of financial position of Alexander and Britton on 30 June 20X1 were as follows:

| | Alexander | | Britton | |
|---|---|---|---|---|
| **Fixed assets** | | | | |
| Land and | | | | |
| buildings | 108 000 | | 64 000 | |
| *less* | | | | |
| Depreciation | 20 000 | 88 000 | 32 000 | 32 000 |
| Plant and | | | | |
| machinery | 65 000 | | 43 000 | |
| *less* | | | | |
| Depreciation | 25 000 | 40 000 | 29 000 | 14 000 |
| | | 128 000 | | 46 000 |
| **Investments** | | | | |
| Shares in Britton | | 35 000 | | |
| **Current assets** | | | | |
| Inventory | 25 000 | | 27 000 | |
| Trade | | | | |
| receivables | 48 000 | | 21 000 | |
| Bank | 22 000 | | 6 000 | |
| | 95 000 | | 54 000 | |
| **Current** | | | | |
| **liabilities** | | | | |
| Trade payables | 112 000 | | 34 000 | |
| **Net current** | | | | |
| **assets** | | (17 000) | | 20 000 |
| | | 146 000 | | 66 000 |
| **Equity** | | | | |
| Ordinary €1 | | | | |
| share | | 100 000 | | 50 000 |
| Retained | | | | |
| earnings | | 46 000 | | 16 000 |
| | | 146 000 | | 66 000 |

1 Alexander acquired 37 500 shares in Britton several years ago when there was a debit balance on the retained earnings of €3000.

2 During the year ended 30 June 20X1 Alexander purchased a machine from Britton for €5000 which had yielded a profit on selling price of 30 per cent to that company. Depreciation on the machine had been charged in the accounts at 20 per cent on cost.

3 Britton purchases goods from Alexander providing Alexander with a gross profit on invoice price of 33 1/3 per cent. On 30 June 20X1 the stock of Britton included an amount of €8000 being goods purchased from Alexander for €9000 (Britton has reduced the goods to its lower net realizable value with an amount of €1000).

Prepare the consolidated statement of financial position of Alexander and its subsidiary as at 30 June 20X1.

### Activity feedback

Purchase of 75%: (37 500/ 50 000)

| | |
|---|---|
| Purchase price | 35 000 |
| Fair value of net assets acquired | |
| (75% × (50 − 3) | 35 250 |
| Negative goodwill | 250 |
| Adjustments | |
| Inter-group transfer of machine – | |
| unrealized profit | |
| (30% × 5000) | 1 500 |
| Excess depreciation charged | |
| 20% × 1500 | 300 |
| Britton's accounts unrealized | |
| profit | 1 200 |
| Inter-group stock transfer – | |
| unrealized profit 33 1/3% × | |
| €9000 | 3 000 |
| Impairment made by Britton | 1 000 |
| Net reduction of value | 2 000 |

**Consolidated statement of financial position as at 30 June 20X1**

| **Fixed assets** | | |
|---|---|---|
| Land and buildings (88 000 + 32 000) | | 120 000 |
| Plant and machinery (40 000 + 14 000 − 1200) | | 52 800 |
| | | 172 800 |
| **Current assets** | | |
| Inventory (25 000 + 27 000 − 2000) | 50 000 | |
| Trade receivables (48 000 + 21 000) | 69 000 | |
| Bank (22 000 + 6000) | 28 000 | |
| | 147 000 | |

*(Continued)*

## ACTIVITY 27.9  (Continued)

| Consolidated statement of financial position as at 30 June 20X1 | | | Note 1 | |
|---|---|---|---|---|
| **Current liabilities** | | | Retained earnings of Alexander | 46 000 |
| Trade payables (112 000 + 34 000) | | 146 000 | Unrealized profit on stock | (2 000) |
| **Net current assets** | | 1 000 | Post-acquisition profits of Britton: 75% (16 000 (retained earnings 30.6.X1) + 3000 (debit balance at acq. date) – 1 200 (unrealized profit on sale of machine)) | |
| | | 173 800 | | |
| **Equity** | | | | |
| Ordinary €1 shares | | 100 000 | | |
| Retained earnings (note 1) | | 57 600 | | 13 350 |
| | | 157 600 | | |
| Non-controlling interest | | | Negative goodwill | 250 |
| (25% (66 000 – 1200) | | 16 200 | | 57 600 |
| | | 173 800 | | |

# Preparation of consolidated accounts involving more than one subsidiary

These are relatively straightforward if you remember the rules already explained. The following example shows how consolidations of more than one subsidiary are made.

## Example 27.4

H entity purchased 80 per cent of the equity share capital of S1 for cash at 31 December year 1 at a price of €7000 when the balance on S1's reserves stood at €4000. H also purchased 70 per cent of the equity share capital of S2 for cash at 31 December year 1 at a price of €12 000 when the balance on S2's reserves stood at €8000. The individual statements of financial position of the three entities at 31 December year 2 when the consolidation is required to be made are as follows:

|  | H | S1 | S2 |
|---|---|---|---|
| Current assets | 15 000 | 3 000 | 10 000 |
| Investment in S1 | 7 000 | | |
| Investment in S2 | 12 000 | | |
| Plant and machinery | 30 000 | 8 000 | 14 000 |
| | 64 000 | 11 000 | 24 000 |
| Share capital €1 | 40 000 | 4 000 | 8 000 |
| Reserves | 24 000 | 7 000 | 16 000 |
| | 64 000 | 11 000 | 24 000 |

Net assets of S1 and S2 at acquisition date are assumed to be at fair value.

| Purchase S1 | |
|---|---|
| Purchase price | 7 000 |
| Fair value of net assets acquired (80% × (4000 + 4000) | 6 400 |
| Goodwill | 600 |
| Non-controlling interest (20% × 11 000) | 2 200 |
| Post-acquisition reserves accruing to group (80% × (7000 – 4000)) | 2 400 |

Purchase S2

| | |
|---|---:|
| Purchase price | 12 000 |
| Fair value of net assets acquired $(70\% \times (8000 + 8000))$ | 11 200 |
| Goodwill | 800 |
| Non-controlling interest $(30\% \times 24\ 000)$ | 7 200 |
| Post-acquisition reserves accruing to group $(70\% \times (16\ 000 - 8000))$ | 5 600 |

Consolidated statement of financial position as at 31 December year 2

| | |
|---|---:|
| Current assets | 28 000 |
| Plant and machinery | 52 000 |
| Goodwill $(600 + 800)$ | 1 400 |
| | **81 400** |
| Share capital | 40 000 |
| Reserves $(24\ 000 + 2400 + 5600)$ | 32 000 |
| Non-controlling interests $(2200 + 7200)$ | 9 400 |
| | **81 400** |

We include an activity here (Activity 27.10) of a consolidation involving several companies to test your understanding and application of the techniques of consolidation.

## ACTIVITY 27.10

A plc acquired 5m €1 shares of B Ltd five years ago when the reserves of B stood at £6m. B Ltd acquired 2.25m €1 shares in C Ltd four years ago when the accumulated reserves of C were €0.5m. A plc also acquired 3m €1 shares of D Ltd two years ago when D's reserves were €0.3m. At the date of acquisition the net book value of all assets equated to fair value. There has been no issue of shares in any of these companies throughout the five-year period. The statements of financial position of the group companies as at 31.12.201X are:

| | A | B | C | D |
|---|---:|---:|---:|---:|
| | €m | €m | €m | €m |
| Fixed assets | 45 | 5 | 1.5 | 2 |
| Investment in B | 16 | – | – | – |
| Investment in C | – | 4.5 | – | – |
| Investment in D | 4 | – | – | – |
| Net current assets | 32 | 18 | 2.5 | 1 |
| | 97 | 27.5 | 4 | 3 |
| Share capital | 18 | 7.5 | 3 | 4 |
| Reserves | 79 | 20 | 1 | (1) |
| | 97 | 27.5 | 4 | 3 |

Prepare the consolidated statement of financial position of A group as at 31.12.201X.

### Activity feedback

B and D are subsidiaries of A with controlling interests of 66.6 per cent (5m/7.5m) and 75 per cent (3m/4m)

respectively. C is a subsidiary of B at an ownership of 75 per cent (2.25m/3m) but as B is a subsidiary of A then C is also a subsidiary of A at a controlling interest of 50 per cent (the economic interest of A in C is 66.6% × 75% = 50%, the remaining 50 per cent being the non-controlling interest). Figure 27.2 aids understanding here.

The goodwill calculations at acquisition are:

| | B | C | D | Total |
|---|---:|---:|---:|---:|
| | €m | €m | €m | €m |
| Purchase price | 16 | 4.5 | 4 | |
| Shares bought | 5 | 2.25 | 3 | |
| Reserves bought | 4 | 0.375 | 0.225 | |
| | 9 | 2.625 | 3.225 | |
| Goodwill | 7 | 1.875 | 0.775 | |
| Group share (note 1) | 7 | 1.25 | 0.775 | 9.025 |
| Non-controlling interest calculations: | | | | |
| Total net assets | 23 | 4 | 3 | |
| NCI% share | 33.3 | 50 | 25 | |
| NCI | | 7.67 | 2 | 0.75 | 10.42 |

Note 1 Goodwill for 100 per cent for B and D (directly held by A); Goodwill for C is directly held by B (for 100 per cent); share of A in B is 66.6 per cent (× 1.875 = 1.25).

(Continued)

## ACTIVITY 27.10    (Continued)

**Consolidated statement of financial position**

| | €m | | €m |
|---|---|---|---|
| | | Share capital | 18 |
| Goodwill | 9.025 | Reserves [79 + (20 – 6)2/3 + (1 – 0.5) | |
| Fixed assets | 53.5 | 1/2 + (–1 – 0.3)3/4] | 87.605 |
| Net current assets | 53.5 | Non-controlling interest | 10.42 |
| | 116.025 | | 116.025 |

## Figure 27.2    Subsidiaries and controlling interest

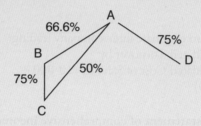

# PREPARATION OF CONSOLIDATED STATEMENT OF COMPREHENSIVE INCOME

The principles of preparation of a consolidated statement of comprehensive income are the same as those for the statement of financial position. Thus we will add together each individual line from the statement of comprehensive income deducting inter-entity transactions as we go. At some point we will need to deduct the profit attributable to the non-controlling interest. A simple example demonstrates the preparation of a consolidated statement of comprehensive income.

## Example 27.5

The individual statements of comprehensive income of High and Low as at 31 December 201X are as follows:

| | *High* | *Low* |
|---|---|---|
| Turnover | 100 000 | 50 000 |
| Cost of sales | 75 000 | 30 000 |
| Gross profit | 25 000 | 20 000 |
| Distribution expenses | 4 000 | 3 000 |
| Administration expenses | 7 000 | 8 000 |
| | 14 000 | 9 000 |
| | | |
| Investment income: Dividends received | 2 250 | |
| | 16 250 | |
| Taxation | 7 000 | 3 000 |
| Net income/Comprehensive income | 9 250 | 6 000 |

The share capital of Low consists of 100 000 €1 shares of which High bought 75 000 on 1 January 201X for €90 000. The fair value of Low's assets at date of acquisition equated to net book values and the only reserves existing when High bought in were retained profits of €4000. During the year High sold goods to Low for €12 000 which included a profit of €2000. As at 31.12.1X 40 per cent of these goods still remain in Low's stocks. The dividends paid and proposed by Low are all paid out of current profits.

First, we need to identify the goodwill on acquisition:

| | | |
|---|---:|---:|
| Purchase price | | 90 000 |
| Bought 75% of Low's shares (100 000) | 75 000 | |
| Bought 75% of Low's retained profits (4000) | 3 000 | |
| | | 78 000 |
| Goodwill | | 12 000 |

Next, we need to eliminate inter-company trading:

| | |
|---|---:|
| Reduce consolidated Turnover by | 12 000 |
| Reduce consolidated Cost of Sales by (10 000 + 60% × 2000) | 11 200 |

### Consolidated statement of comprehensive income for the year ended 31.12.0X

| | | |
|---|---:|---:|
| Turnover (150 000 – 12 000) | | 138 000 |
| Cost of sales (105 000 – 11 200) | | 93 800 |
| | | 44 200 |
| Distribution expenses | 7 000 | |
| Administration expenses | 15 000 | 22 000 |
| | | 22 200 |
| Taxation | | 10 000 |
| Consolidated comprehensive income on ordinary activities after tax | | 12 200 |
| Attributable to non-controlling interest (25% × 6000 (= Low's profit after tax)) | | 1 500 |
| Attributable to shareholders of High | | 10 700 |

Note that all allocation of profits to the non-controlling interest for the year takes place after calculating consolidated earnings after tax and that the inter-entity transactions in relation to Low's dividends paid to High is eliminated.

Note also that the total of income and expenditure for the parent and the subsidiary is included in the consolidated statement of comprehensive income. This is in accordance with the inclusion of the total of assets and liabilities in the consolidated statement of financial position. IFRS requires to present the division of consolidated comprehensive income to shareholders of the parent and to the non-controlling interest.

The final activity of this chapter, Activity 27.11, requires you to prepare both a consolidated statement of financial position and a consolidated statement of comprehensive income.

## ACTIVITY 27.11

The summarized statements for the year ended 30 June 2013 for A, B and C entities are as follows:

**Statements of comprehensive income for the year ended 30 June 2013**

|  | A | B | C |
|---|---|---|---|
|  | £000 | £000 | £000 |
| Revenue (Turnover) | 15 000 | 8 000 | 6 000 |
| Cost of sales | (7 200) | (4 300) | (4 100) |
|  | 7 800 | 3 700 | 1 900 |
| Expenses | (3 300) | (2 100) | (1 100) |
| Profit before tax | 4 500 | 1 600 | 800 |
| Tax | (1 400) | (650) | (260) |
| Profit for the year | 3 100 | 950 | 540 |

**Statements of financial position as at 30 June 2013**

|  | A | B | C |
|---|---|---|---|
| **ASSETS** |  |  |  |
| NON-CURRENT ASSETS |  |  |  |
| (fixed assets) |  |  |  |
| Property, plant and |  |  |  |
| equipment | 2 652 | 1 810 | 1 300 |
| Investment in B | 1 302 |  |  |
| Investment in C | 1 256 |  |  |
|  | 5 210 | 1 810 | 1 300 |
| CURRENT ASSETS |  |  |  |
| Inventory | 630 | 460 | 320 |
| Trade receivables | 560 | 370 | 280 |
| Cash | 160 | – | 90 |
|  | 1 350 | 830 | 690 |
| **TOTAL ASSETS** | 6 560 | 2 640 | 1 990 |
| **EQUITY AND LIABILITIES** |  |  |  |
| **EQUITY** |  |  |  |
| Ordinary shares | 1 600 | 850 | 900 |
| Share premium | 100 | 50 | 300 |
| Retained earnings | 3 850 | 1 210 | 360 |
|  | 5 550 | 2 110 | 1 560 |
| NON-CURRENT |  |  |  |
| LIABILITIES |  |  |  |
| Loans | 450 | 170 | 110 |
| CURRENT LIABILITIES |  |  |  |
| Trade payables | 470 | 280 | 300 |
| Bank overdraft | – | 70 | – |
| Tax | 90 | 10 | 20 |
|  | 560 | 360 | 320 |
| **TOTAL EQUITY AND LIABILITIES** | 6 560 | 2 640 | 1 990 |

The following information is also available:

(i)   A acquired a 70 per cent share in B and an 80 per cent share in C on 1 July 2012. The fair values of B's assets at that date equalled those shown on the statement of financial position. At acquisition date the fair value of C's property was £500 000 in excess of the statement of financial position value. A, B and C all depreciate their property, plant and equipment on the same basis. Property is depreciated on a straight line basis over 50 years.

(ii)  As at 30 June 2013 the fair value of the consolidated goodwill was reviewed and found to have a value 5 per cent less than its carrying value at the consolidation date. This impairment is to be accounted for in the consolidated accounts.

(iii) Inter-group sales (A to B) in the period from 1 July 2012 to 30 June 2013 are £3 100 000 on which A made a profit of 15 per cent on selling price. Of these goods £500 000 (at selling price from A to B) are still in B's closing inventory (stock) amount.

Prepare the consolidated statement of comprehensive income for the year ended 30 June 2013 and the consolidated statement of financial position as at that date for the group.

### Activity feedback

|  | £000 |
|---|---|
| *Acquisition of B* |  |
| Purchase price | 1 302 |
| Ordinary shares 70% × 850 | 595 |
| Share premium 70% × 50 | 35 |
| Retained earnings at acquisition date |  |
| (1210 – 950 post-acq. profit) × 70% | 182 |
|  | 812 |
| Goodwill on acquisition | 490 |
| Impairment on review 5% | (24.5) |
| Goodwill on 30/6/2013 | 465.5 |
| Non-controlling interest |  |
| Ordinary shares 30% × 850 | 255 |
| Share premium 30% × 50 | 15 |
| Attributable to NCI from retained earnings |  |
| 30% × 1210 | 363 |
|  | 633 |

(Continued)

## ACTIVITY 27.11 (Continued)

|  | £000 |
|---|---|
| Acquisition of C |  |
| Purchase price | 1 256 |
| Ordinary shares 80% × 900 | 720 |
| Share premium 80% × 300 | 240 |
| Fair value adjustment 500 × 80% | 400 |
| Retained earnings at acquisition date |  |
| (360 – 540 post-acq. profit) × 80% | (144) |
|  | 1 216 |
| Goodwill on acquisition | 40 |
| Impairment on review 5% | (2) |
| Goodwill on 30/6/2013 | 38 |
| Non-controlling interest |  |
| Ordinary shares 20% × 900 | 180 |
| Share premium 20% × 300 | 60 |
| Attributable to NCI from retained earnings |  |
| 20% × 360 | 72 |
| 20% fair value adjustment of 500 | 100 |
| Depreciation charge on fair value 10 × 20% | (2) |
|  | 410 |
| Total goodwill before impairment (490 + 40) | 530 |
| Total impairment at 5% | 26.5 |
| Total goodwill after impairment (465.5 + 38) | 503.5 |
| Total non-controlling interest (633 + 410) | 1 043 |

Depreciation required on fair value of
property 500/50 =10

Inter-group sales reduce consolidated
revenue by 3100, and reduce
consolidated cost of sales by
(85% × 3100 + 390) = 3025
Unrealized profit: 3100 – 3025 = 75
[Total profit on sale: 15% × 3100 = 465;
realized 15% × 2600 = 390; unrealized
15% × 500 = 75).

### Consolidated statement of comprehensive income for the year ended 30 June 2013

| | | £000 |
|---|---|---|
| Revenue | 15 000 + 8000 | |
| | + 6000 – 3100 | 25 900 |
| Cost of sales | 7200 + 4300 | |
| | + 4100 – 3025 | (12 575) |
| | | 13 325 |
| Expenses | 3300 + 2100 | |
| | + 1100 + dep. 10 | (6 510) |
| Goodwill | | |
| impairment | 26.5 | (26.5) |
| | | (6 536.5) |
| Profit before tax | | 6 788.5 |

(*Continued*)

### Consolidated statement of comprehensive income for the year ended 30 June 2013

| | | £000 |
|---|---|---|
| Taxation | 1400 + 650 + 260 | (2 310) |
| Consolidated | | |
| comprehensive | | |
| income | | 4 478.5 |
| Attributable to NCI | | |
| 30% × 950 + 20% × (540 – 10) | | 391 |
| Attributable to | | |
| shareholders of A | | 4 087.5 |

### Consolidated statement of financial position as at 30 June 2013

| | | £000 |
|---|---|---|
| Non-current assets | | |
| Property, plant and | 2652 + 1810 | |
| equipment | + 1300 + 500 – 10 | 6 252 |
| Goodwill | | 503.5 |
| | | 6 755.5 |
| Current assets | | |
| Inventory | 630 + 460 + 320 | |
| | – 75 | 1 335 |
| Trade receivables | 560 + 370 + 280 | 1 210 |
| Cash | 160 + 90 | 250 |
| | | 2 795 |
| Total assets | | 9 550.5 |
| Equity and | | |
| liabilities | | |
| Equity | | |
| Ordinary shares | | 1 600 |
| Share premium | | 100 |
| Retained earnings | 3850 – 3100 | |
| | + 4087.5 | 4 837.5 |
| | | 6 537.5 |
| Non-controlling | | |
| interest | | 1 043 |
| Total equity | | 7 580.5 |
| Non-current | | |
| liabilities | | |
| Loans | 450 + 170 + 110 | 730 |
| Current liabilities | | |
| Trade payables | 470 + 280 + 300 | 1 050 |
| Bank overdraft | | 70 |
| Taxation | 90 + 10 + 20 | 120 |
| | | 1 240 |
| Total equity and | | |
| liabilities | | 9 550.5 |

## SUMMARY

In this chapter we have dealt with the preparation of consolidated state- ments of financial position and consolidated statements of comprehensive income. We first investigated the control concept a little further. The essen- tial elements of control are: power of the investor (parent) over the investee (subsidiary); exposure or rights to variable returns from the involvement with the investee; and the ability to use the power to affect the returns. We dis- cussed the need for consolidated accounts and have given many examples and activities in preparing them, both at and after the date of acquisition. Specific issues are the inter-company trading and the elimination of unreal- ized profits, the reconciliation of intercompany balances, and the consis- tency of reporting dates and accounting policies within the group. This was a rather technical chapter. The many exercises at the end of this current chapter will provide you with plenty of practice in preparing consolidated group financial statements.

## EXERCISES

*Suggested answers to exercises marked ✓ are to be found on our dedicated CourseMate platform for students.*

*Suggested answers to the remaining exercises are to be found on the Instructor online support resources.*

1   What is 'control' as used in relation to consolidated financial statements?

2   Construct (using appropriate assumptions) a mixed group structure bringing together a holding entity, a subsidiary and a sub-subsidiary.

3   The preparation of consolidated financial statements provides useful information to users. Discuss.

4   Appraise the need for consolidated accounts.

5   *D* has owned 80 per cent of the equity shares of *E* since 1 January 1996. *E* has owned 60 per cent of the equity shares of *F* since 1 January 1994. The accumulated profits of *F* at the latest statement of financial position date, 31 December 2003, stood at $30m. The accumulated profits of *F* stood at $12m on 1 January 1994 and $14m on 1 January 1996.

    Ignoring goodwill, what will be included in the consolidated accumulated profits of *D* at 31 December 2003 in respect of *F*?

6   At 1 April 20X3 *S* held 80 000 of the 100 000 issued ordinary shares of *T*. The acquisition of *T* took place on 1 April 20X2 and goodwill on acquisition was recorded at $120 000. The directors of *S* have agreed that the goodwill on acquisition has been impaired by $36 000 as at 1 October 20X3. On 1 October 20X3, *S* disposes of $20 000 shares in *T* for $125 000. At that date *T*'s total net assets are $400 000.

    Calculate the consolidated profit and loss before tax on disposal of the shares.

**7** As well as its investment in T (see question 6) S also held 75 per cent of the shares of U. U sells goods to S. During the year ending 31 March 20X4, U sells goods to S for $100 000. The cost of the goods to U is $80 000. At the year end S's inventories include $16 000 of goods purchased from U.

Calculate the adjustment required in respect of unrealized profit, and describe the accounting treatment of the adjustment in the consolidated statement of comprehensive income and the consolidated statement of financial position.

**8** Parentis, a public listed company, acquired 600m equity shares in Offspring on 1 April 2006. The purchase consideration was made up of:
  – a share exchange of one share in Parentis for two shares in Offspring
  – the issue of $100 10 per cent loan note for every 500 shares acquired; and
  – a deferred cash payment of 11 cents per share acquired payable on 1 April 2007.

Parentis has only recorded the issue of the loan notes. The value of each Parentis share at the date of acquisition was 75 cents and Parentis has a cost of capital of 10 per cent per annum.

The statements of financial position of the two companies at 31 March 2007 are shown below:

|  | Parentis $m | Parentis $m | Offspring $m | Offspring $m |
|---|---|---|---|---|
| Assets |  |  |  |  |
| Property, plant and equipment (note (i)) | 640 |  | 340 |  |
| Investments | 120 |  | nil |  |
| Intellectual property (note (ii)) | nil |  | 30 |  |
|  | 760 |  | 370 |  |
| Current assets |  |  |  |  |
| Inventory (note (iii)) | 76 |  | 22 |  |
| Trade receivables (note (iii)) | 84 |  | 44 |  |
| Bank | nil | 160 | 4 | 70 |
| Total assets |  | 920 |  | 440 |
| Equity and liabilities |  |  |  |  |
| Equity shares of 25 cents each |  | 300 |  | 200 |
| Retained earnings 1 April 2006 | 210 |  | 120 |  |
| Year ended 31 March 2007 | 90 | 300 | 20 | 140 |
|  |  | 600 |  | 340 |
| Non-current liabilities 10% loan notes |  | 120 |  | 20 |
| Current liabilities |  |  |  |  |
| Trade payables (note (iii)) | 130 |  | 57 |  |
| Current tax payable | 45 |  | 23 |  |
| Overdraft | 25 | 200 | nil | 80 |
| Total equity and liabilities |  | 920 |  | 440 |

The following information is relevant:

(i) At the date of acquisition the fair values of Offspring's net assets were approximately equal to their carrying amounts with the exception of its properties. These properties had a fair value of $40m in excess of their carrying amounts which would create additional depreciation of $2m in the post-acquisition period to 31 March 2007. The fair values have not been reflected in Offspring's statement of financial position.

(ii) The intellectual property is a system of encryption designed for Internet use. Offspring has been advised that government legislation (passed since acquisition) has now made this type of encryption illegal. Offspring will receive $10m in compensation from the government.

(iii) Offspring sold Parentis goods for $15m in the post-acquisition period. $5m of these goods are included in the inventory of Parentis at 31 March 2007. The profit made by Offspring on these sales was $6m. Offspring's trade payable account (in the records of Parentis) of $7m does not agree with Parentis's trade receivable account (in the records of Offspring) due to cash in transit of $4m paid by Parentis.

(iv) Due to the impact of the above legislation, Parentis has concluded that the consolidated goodwill has been impaired by $27m.

**Required:**
Prepare the consolidated statement of financial position of Parentis as at 31 March 2007.

(ACCA 2 int. – June 2007)

9 Ejoy, a public limited company, has acquired two subsidiaries. The details of the acquisitions are as follows:

| Company | Date of acquisition | Ordinary share capital $m | Reserves at acquisition $m | Fair value of net assets at acquisition $m | Cost of investment $m | Ordinary share capital of $1 acquired $m |
|---|---|---|---|---|---|---|
| Zbay | 1 June 2004 | 200 | 170 | 600 | 520 | 160 |
| Tbay | 1 December 2005 | 120 | 80 | 310 | 216 | 72 |

The draft statements of comprehensive income for the year ended 31 May 2006 are:

| | Ejoy $m | Zbay $m | Tbay $m |
|---|---|---|---|
| Revenue | 2 500 | 1 500 | 800 |
| Cost of sales | (1 800) | (1 200) | (600) |
| Gross profit | 700 | 300 | 200 |
| Other income | 70 | 10 | – |
| Distribution costs | (130) | (120) | (70) |
| Administrative expenses | (100) | (90) | (60) |
| Finance costs | (50) | (40) | (20) |
| Profit before tax | 490 | 60 | 50 |
| Income tax expense | (200) | (26) | (20) |
| Profit for the period | 290 | 34 | 30 |
| Profit for year 31 May 2005 | 190 | 20 | 15 |

The following information is relevant to the preparation of the group financial statements

(i) Tbay was acquired exclusively with a view to sale and at 31 May 2006 meets the criteria of disposal group. The fair value of Tbay at 31 May 2006 is $300m and the estimated selling of the shareholding in Tbay are $5m.

(ii) Ejoy entered into a joint venture with another company on 31 May 2006. The joint venture is a company and Ejoy has contributed assets at fair value of $20m (carrying value $14). Each party will hold five million ordinary shares of $1 in the joint venture. The gain on the disposal of the assets ($6m) to the joint venture has been included in 'other income'

(iii) On acquisition, the financial statements of Tbay included a large cash balance. Immediately after acquisition Tbay paid a dividend of $40m. The receipt of the dividend is included in the statement of comprehensive income of Ejoy. Since the acquisition of Zbay there have been no further dividend payments by these companies.

(iv) Zbay has a loan asset which is being carried at $60m in the draft financial statements year ended 31 May 2006. The loan's effective interest rate is 6 per cent. On 1 June 2005 the company felt that because of the borrower's financial problems, it would receive $20m in approximately two years time, on 31 May 2007. At 31 May 2006, the company still expects to receive the same amount on the same date. The loan asset is classified as 'loans and receivables'.

(v) On 1 June 2005, Ejoy purchased a five-year bond with a principal amount of $50m and an interest rate of 5 per cent which was the current market rate. The bond is classified as an 'available for sale' financial asset. Because of the size of the investment, Ejoy has entered into a floating interest rate swap. Ejoy has designated the swap as a fair value hedge of the bond. At 31 May 2006 interest rates were 6 per cent. As a result, the fair value of the bond has decreased to $48. Ejoy has received $0.5m in net interest payments on the swap at 31 May 2006 and the fair value hedge has been 100 per cent effective in the period. No entries have been made in the statement of comprehensive income to account for the bond or the hedge.

(vi) No impairment of the goodwill arising on the acquisition of Zbay had occurred at 1 June 2005. The recoverable amount of Zbay was $630m and that of Tbay was $290m at 31 May 2006. Impairment losses on goodwill are charged to cost of sales.

(vii) Assume that profits accrue evenly throughout the year and ignore any taxation effects.

**Required:**

Prepare a consolidated statement of comprehensive income for the Ejoy Group for the year ended 31 May 2006 in accordance with International Financial Reporting Standards.

(ACCA 3.5 int. – June 2006)

**10** The statements of comprehensive income for *AB*, *CD* and *EF* for the year ended 31 May 2009 are shown below:

|  | AB | CD | EF |
|---|---|---|---|
|  | $000 | $000 | $000 |
| **Revenue** | 6 000 | 3 000 | 1 000 |
| Cost of sales | (4 800) | (2 400) | (800) |
| Gross profit | 1 200 | 600 | 200 |
| Distribution costs | (64) | (32) | (10) |

|  | AB $000 | CD $000 | EF $000 |
|---|---|---|---|
| Administrative expenses | (336) | (168) | (52) |
| Finance costs | (30) | (15) | (5) |
| **Profit before tax** | 770 | 385 | 133 |
| Income tax expense | (204) | (102) | (33) |
| **PROFIT FOR THE YEAR** | 566 | 283 | 100 |
| **Other comprehensive income:** | 200 | 100 | 30 |
| **Revaluation of property** |  |  |  |
| Tax effect of revaluation | (42) | (21) | (6) |
| **Other comprehensive income for the year, net of tax** | 158 | 79 | 24 |
| **TOTAL COMPREHENSIVE INCOME FOR THE YEAR** | 724 | 362 | 124 |

### Additional information:

AB operates a defined benefit pension plan for its employees. At the year end, there is an actuarial loss of $52 000 on the pension plan liabilities and an actuarial gain of $40 000 on pension plan assets. These amounts are not reflected in the above statements. In accordance with the amendment to IAS 19, *Employee Benefits*, AB recognizes actuarial gains and losses from the defined benefit plan in other comprehensive income in the period that they occur.

AB holds a 15 per cent investment in XY which is designated as available for sale. The fair value of this investment at 31 May 2009 was $106 000. The investment is currently recorded in the financial statements at $92 000.

AB owns 80 per cent of the ordinary share capital of CD and exercises control over its operating and financial policies. AB owns 30 per cent of the ordinary share capital of EF and exerts significant influence over its operating and financial policies.

### Required:

Prepare the consolidated statement of comprehensive income for the AB Group, taking account of the information provided in the notes above. Ignore any further taxation effects of notes 1 and 2.

(CIMA F2 – November 2009 Specimen)

11 Below are the summarized balance sheets for three companies as at 31 March 2009:

|  | Pacemaker £m | £m | Syclop £m | £m | Vardine £m | £m |
|---|---|---|---|---|---|---|
| *Fixed assets* |  |  |  |  |  |  |
| Tangible |  | 520 |  | 280 |  | 240 |
| Investments |  | 345 |  | 40 |  | nil |
|  |  | 865 |  | 320 |  | 240 |
| Current assets |  |  |  |  |  |  |
| Stock | 142 |  | 160 |  | 120 |  |
| Debtors | 95 |  | 88 |  | 50 |  |
| Cash and bank | 8 |  | 22 |  | 10 |  |
|  | 245 |  | 270 |  | 180 |  |
| Creditors: amounts falling due within one year | (200) |  | (165) |  | (80) |  |
| Net current assets |  | 45 |  | 105 |  | 100 |
| Creditors: amounts falling due after more than one year |  |  |  |  |  |  |

|                          | Pacemaker | | Syclop | | Vardine | |
|--------------------------|-----------|--------|--------|--------|---------|--------|
|                          | £m        | £m     | £m     | £m     | £m      | £m     |
| Fixed assets             |           |        |        |        |         |        |
| 10% loan notes           |           | (180)  |        | (20)   |         | (nil)  |
| Net assets               |           | 730    |        | 405    |         | 340    |
| Capital reserves         |           |        |        |        |         |        |
| Equity shares of £1 each |           | 500    |        | 145    |         | 100    |
| Share premium            | 100       |        | nil    |        | nil     |        |
| Profit and loss account  | 130       | 230    | 260    | 260    | 240     | 240    |
|                          |           | 730    |        | 405    |         | 340    |

**Notes:**

Pacemaker is a public listed company that acquired the following investments:

(i)   Investment in Syclop

On 1 April 2007 Pacemaker acquired 116 million shares in Syclop for an immediate cash payment of £210m and issued at par one 10 per cent £100 loan note for every 200 shares acquired. Syclop's profit and loss account reserve at the date of acquisition was £120m.

(ii)  Investment in Vardine

On 1 October 2008 Pacemaker acquired 30 million shares in Vardine in exchange for 75 million of its own shares. The market value of Pacemaker's shares at the date of this share exchange was £1.60 each. Pacemaker has not yet recorded the investment in Vardine.

(iii) Pacemaker's other investments, and those of Syclop, are available-for-sale investments which are carried at their fair values as at 31 March 2008. The fair values of these investments at 31 March 2009 are £82m and £37m respectively.

Other relevant information:

(iv)  At the date of acquisition Syclop owned a recently built property that was carried at its (depreciated) construction cost of £62m. The fair value of this property at the date of acquisition was £82m and it had an estimated remaining life of 20 years.

For many years Syclop has been selling some of its products under the brand name of 'Kyklop'. At the date of acquisition the directors of Pacemaker valued this brand at £25m with a remaining life of 10 years. The brand is not included in Syclop's balance sheet.

The fair values of all other identifiable assets and liabilities of Syclop were equal to their carrying values at the date of acquisition.

(v)   The stock of Syclop at 31 March 2009 includes goods supplied by Pacemaker for £56m (at selling price from Pacemaker). Pacemaker adds a mark-up of 40 per cent on cost when selling goods to Syclop. There are no intra-group debtors or creditors at 31 March 2009.

(vi)  Vardine's profit is subject to seasonal variation. Its profit for the year ended 31 March 2009 was £100m.

£20m of this profit was made from 1 April 2008 to 30 September 2008.

(vii) None of the companies have paid any dividends for many years.

(viii) The goodwill of Syclop has an estimated life of five years. The goodwill of Vardine has an indefinite life and it has not been impaired.

**Required:**
Prepare the consolidated balance sheet of Pacemaker as at 31 March 2009.

(ACCA – June 2009)

12  On 1 April 2009 Pandar purchased 80 per cent of the equity shares in Salva. The acquisition was through a share exchange of three shares in Pandar for every five shares in Salva. The market prices of Pandar's and Salva's shares at 1 April 2009 were £6 and £3.20 per share respectively.

On the same date Pandar acquired 40 per cent of the equity shares in Ambra paying £2 per share.

The summarized profit and loss accounts for the three companies for the year ended 30 September 2009 are:

|  | Pandar £'000 | Salva £'000 | Ambra £'000 |
|---|---|---|---|
| Turnover | 210 000 | 150 000 | 50 000 |
| Cost of sales | (126 000) | (100 000) | (40 000) |
| Gross profit | 84 000 | 50 000 | 10 000 |
| Distribution costs | (11 200) | 7 000 | (5 000) |
| Administrative expenses | (18 300) | 9 000 | (11 000) |
| Investment income (interest and dividends) | 9 500 |  |  |
| Finance costs | (1 800) | (3 000) | nil |
| Profit (loss) before tax | 62 200 | 31 000 | (6 000) |
| Corporation tax (expense) relief | (15 000) | (10 000) | 1 000 |
| Proft (loss) for the year | 47 200 | 21 000 | (5 000) |

The following information for the equity of the companies at 30 September 2009 is available:

|  | Pandar | Salva | Ambra |
|---|---|---|---|
| Equity shares of £1 each | 200 000 | 120 000 | 40 000 |
| Share premium | 300 000 | nil | nil |
| Profit and loss account – 1 October 2008 | 40 000 | 152 000 | 15 000 |
| Profit (loss) for the year ended 30 September 2009 | 47 200 | 21 000 | (5 000) |
| Dividends paid (26 September 2009) | nil | (8 000) | nil |

The following information is relevant:

(i)  The fair values of the net assets of Salva at the date of acquisition were equal to their carrying amounts with the exception of an item of plant which had a carrying amount of £12m and a fair value of £17m. This plant had a remaining life of five years (straight-line depreciation) at the date of acquisition of Salva.

In addition Salva owns the registration of a popular Internet domain name. The registration, which had a negligible cost, has a five year remaining life (at the date of acquisition); however, it is renewable indefinitely at a nominal cost. At the date of acquisition the domain name was valued by a specialist company at £20m.

The fair values of the plant and the domain name have not been reflected in Salva's financial statements.

No fair value adjustments were required on the acquisition of the investment in Ambra.

(ii) Immediately after its acquisition of Salva, Pandar invested £50m in an 8 per cent loan note from Salva. All interest accruing to 30 September 2009 had been accounted for by both companies. Salva also has other loans in issue at 30 September 2009.

(iii) Pandar has credited the whole of the dividend it received from Salva to investment income.

(iv) After the acquisition, Pandar sold goods to Salva for £15m on which Pandar made a gross profit of 20 per cent.

Salva had one third of these goods still in its stock at 30 September 2009. There are no intra-group current account balances at 30 September 2009.

(v) The goodwill of Salva has an indefinite life; the goodwill of Ambra has a five year life. There have been no impairment losses to goodwill at 30 September 2009. All depreciation/amortization is charged to cost of sales.

(vi) All items in the above profit and loss accounts are deemed to accrue evenly over the year unless otherwise indicated.

**Required:**

(a)

(i) Calculate the goodwill arising on the acquisition of Salva at 1 April 2009.

(ii) Calculate the carrying amount of the investment in Ambra to be included within the consolidated balance sheet as at 30 September 2009.

(b) Prepare the consolidated profit and loss account for the Pandar Group for the year ended 30 September 2009.

(ACCA – December 2009)

13    On 1 April 2009 Picant acquired 75 per cent of Sander's equity shares in a share exchange of three shares in Picant for every two shares in Sander. The market prices of Picant's and Sander's shares at the date of acquisition were £3.20 and £4.50 respectively.

In addition to this Picant agreed to pay a further amount on 1 April 2010 that was contingent upon the post-acquisition performance of Sander. At the date of acquisition Picant assessed the fair value of this contingent consideration at £4.2m, but by 31 March 2010 it was clear that the actual amount to be paid would be only £2.7m (ignore discounting). Picant has recorded the share exchange and provided for the initial estimate of £4.2m for the contingent consideration.

On 1 October 2009 Picant also acquired 40 per cent of the equity shares of Adler paying £4 in cash per acquired share and issuing at par one £100 7% loan note for every 50 acquired shares in Adler. This consideration has also been recorded by Picant. Picant has no other investments.

The summarized balance sheets of the three companies at 31 March 2010 are:

|  | Picant £'000 | Sander £'000 | Adler £'000 |
|---|---|---|---|
| Fixed assets |  |  |  |
| Tangible fixed assets | 37 500 | 24 500 | 21 000 |
| Investments | 45 000 | nil | nil |
|  | 82 500 | 24 500 | 21 000 |

| | Picant £'000 | Sander £'000 | Adler £'000 |
|---|---|---|---|
| Current assets | | | |
| Stock | 10 000 | 9 000 | 5 000 |
| Debtors | 6 500 | 1 500 | 3 000 |
| | 16 500 | 10 500 | 8 000 |
| Creditors: amounts falling due within one year | | | |
| Contingent consideration | (4 200) | nil | nil |
| Other current liabilities | (8 300) | (7 500) | (3 000) |
| | (12 500) | (7 500) | (3 000) |
| Creditors: amounts falling due after more than one year | | | |
| 7% loan notes | (14 500) | (2 000) | (nil) |
| | 72 000 | 25 500 | 26 000 |
| Capital and reserves | | | |
| Equity shares of £1 each | 25 000 | 8 000 | 5 000 |
| Share premium | 19 800 | nil | nil |
| Profit and loss account | | | |
| – at 1 April 2009 | 16 200 | 16 500 | 15 000 |
| – for the year ended 31 March 2020 | 11 000 | 1 000 | 6 000 |
| | 72 000 | 25 500 | 26 000 |

The following information is relevant:

(i) At the date of acquisition the fair values of Sander's tangible fixed assets were equal to their carrying amounts with the exception of Sander's factory which had a fair value of £2m above its carrying amount. Sander has not adjusted the carrying amount of the factory as a result of the fair value exercise. This requires additional annual depreciation of £100 000 in the consolidated financial statements in the post-acquisition period.

Also at the date of acquisition, Sander had an intangible asset of £500 000 for software in its balance sheet.

Picant's directors believed the software to have no recoverable value at the date of acquisition and Sander wrote it off shortly after its acquisition.

(ii) At 31 March 2010, Picant's current account with Sander was £3.4m (debit). This did not agree with the equivalent balance in Sander's books due to some goods-in-transit invoiced at £1.8m that were sent by Picant on 28 March 2010, but had not been received by Sander until after the year end. Picant sold these goods at cost plus 50 per cent.

(iii) All goodwill is amortized over a five-year life. There was no impairment to the investment in the associate or to consolidated goodwill at 31 March 2010.

(iv) Assume all profits accrue evenly through the year.

**Required:**

(a) Prepare the consolidated balance sheet for Picant as at 31 March 2010.

(b) Picant has been approached by a potential new customer, Trilby, to supply it with a sub-stantial quantity of goods on three months credit terms. Picant is concerned at the risk that such a large order represents in the current difficult economic climate, especially as Picant's normal credit terms are only one month's credit. To support its application for credit, Trilby has sent Picant a copy of Tradhat's most recent audited consolidated financial statements. Trilby is a wholly-owned subsidiary within the Tradhat group. Tradhat's consolidated financial statements show a strong balance sheet including healthy liquidity ratios.

**Required:**
Comment on the importance that Picant should attach to Tradhat's consolidated financial statements when deciding on whether to grant credit terms to Trilby.

(ACCA – June 2010)

**14**    On 1 June 2010, Premier acquired 80 per cent of the equity share capital of Sanford. The consideration consisted of two elements: a share exchange of three shares in Premier for every five acquired shares in Sanford and the issue of a £100 6% loan note for every 500 shares acquired in Sanford. The share issue has not yet been recorded by Premier, but the issue of the loan notes has been recorded. At the date of acquisition shares in Premier had a market value of £5 each.

The summarized draft financial statements of both companies are:

*Profit and loss accounts for the year ended 30 September 2010*

|  | Premier £'000 | Sanford £'000 |
|---|---|---|
| Turnover | 92 500 | 45 000 |
| Cost of sales | (70 500) | (36 000) |
| Gross profit | 22 000 | 9 000 |
| Distribution costs | (2 500) | (1 200) |
| Administrative expenses | (5 500) | (2 400) |
| Finance costs | (100) | nil |
| Profit before tax | 13 900 | 5 400 |
| Corporation tax | (3 900) | (1 500) |
| Profit for the year | 10 000 | 3 900 |

*Balance sheets as at 30 September 2010*

|  | Premier £'000 | Sanford £'000 |
|---|---|---|
| Fixed assets |  |  |
| Tangible fixed assets | 25 000 | 13 900 |
| Investments | 1 800 | nil |
|  | 26 800 | 13 900 |
| Current assets | 12 500 | 2 400 |
| Creditors: amounts falling due within one year: | 10 000 | (6 800) |
| Creditors: amounts falling due after more than one year: |  |  |
| 6% loan notes | (3 000) | nil |
|  | 26 300 | 9 500 |
| Capital and reserves |  |  |
| Equity shares of £1 each | 12 000 | 5 000 |
| Land revaluation reserve – 30 September 2009 (note (i)) | 1 500 | nil |
| Other equity reserve – 30 September 2009 (note (iv)) | 500 | nil |
| Profit and loss account | 12 300 | 4 500 |
|  | 26 300 | 9 500 |

The following information is relevant:

(i) At the date of acquisition, the fair values of Sanford's assets were equal to their carrying amounts with the exception of its property. This had a fair value of £1.2m below its carrying amount. This would lead to a reduction of the depreciation charge (in cost of sales) of £50 000 in the post-acquisition period. Sanford has not incorporated this value change into its own financial statements.

Premier's group policy is to revalue all properties to current value at each year-end. On 30 September 2010, the value of Sanford's property was unchanged from its value at acquisition, but the land element of Premier's property had increased in value by £500 000, although this has not yet been recorded by Premier.

(ii) Sales from Sanford to Premier throughout the year ended 30 September 2010 had consistently been £1m per month. Sanford made a mark-up on cost of 25 per cent on these sales. Premier had £2m of stock (at cost to Premier) that had been supplied in the post-acquisition period by Sanford as at 30 September 2010.

(iii) Premier had a trade creditor balance owing to Sanford of £350 000 as at 30 September 2010. This agreed with the corresponding trade debtor in Sanford's books.

(iv) Premier's investments include some available-for-sale investments that have increased in value by £300 000 during the year. The other equity reserve relates to these investments and is based on their value as at 30 September 2009. There were no acquisitions or disposals of any of these investments during the year ended 30 September 2010.

(v) Consolidated goodwill is amortized over a five-year life. Goodwill has not been impaired as at 30 September 2010.

**Required:**
(a) Prepare the consolidated profit and loss account for Premier for the year ended 30 September 2010.
(b) Prepare the consolidated balance sheet for Premier as at 30 September 2010

(ACCA – December 2010)

# ALTERNATIVE CONCEPTS ON CONSOLIDATION AND BUSINESS COMBINATIONS

# 28

## INTRODUCTION

In Chapters 26 and 27 we discussed the accounting for business combinations and the preparation of consolidated financial statements along the lines of IFRS requirements. In this chapter we will discuss alternative concepts that lie behind preparing consolidated financial statements and accounting for business combinations.

Alternative concepts on consolidation are:

- the parent concept
- the entity concept
- proportional consolidation.

These concepts also influence the determination of goodwill on a business combination, within the acquisition accounting method discussed in Chapter 26. Alternatives to acquisition accounting discussed in this chapter are:

- pooling of interests accounting
- carry over accounting.

Finally, we will discuss equity accounting, a method that is applicable in acquiring shares in other entities without obtaining control but obtaining significant influence or joint control.

## THE PARENT CONCEPT

With the parent concept (or parent entity concept or proprietary concept) of accounting, the assumption is made that the consolidated financial statements are being prepared to be primarily of use by the shareholders of the controlling parent entity. The non-controlling interests are credited with their share of the net tangible assets of the subsidiary. This non-controlling shareholding can then be reflected as a quasi-liability: it is not part of equity (as equity is only the amount that belongs to the shareholders of the parent), but it can be labelled part of group equity. Furthermore, applying the parent concept results in a net income determination excluding the amount that is attributable to the non-controlling interest. In preparing consolidated financial statements, IFRS does not apply the parent concept.

## ACTIVITY 28.1

Take a look again at Activity 27.11. What would be the amount of net comprehensive income and of equity applying the parent concept?

### Activity feedback

Applying the parent concept would result in an amount of net comprehensive income of £4087.5, being only the net income that is attributable to the shareholders of A. The amount attributable to the non-controlling interest (£391) would be considered an element of expenses.

In the consolidated statement of financial position, the equity would be £6537.5. The amount of £7580.5 might be labelled as group equity.

The parent concept also has its consequences in accounting for business combinations, especially the determination of goodwill upon acquisition. In Chapter 26 we discussed the two alternatives that currently exist in IFRS 3 for measuring the non-controlling interest in the acquiree:

- at the proportionate share of the acquiree's identifiable net assets at fair value
- at fair value.

The goodwill resulting from the first alternative is the goodwill that is paid by the parent in acquiring control and therefore is the goodwill amount that fits within the parent concept. In applying the second alternative, full goodwill would be determined, which fits within the entity concept (see below). As IFRS does not apply the parent concept in preparing consolidated accounts, it seems inconsistent that applying this concept in determining goodwill is acceptable. This inconsistency was not what the IASB had wanted; in an earlier draft only the full goodwill determination was required. However, this proposal met fierce opposition in Europe, where the parent concept had previously been the dominant concept. For this reason, with the fear of non-endorsement by the European Union, the IASB decided to allow two alternatives. However, the parent concept is not allowed in determining equity and net profit in the consolidated accounts. Also the accounting for transactions with the non-controlling shareholder, all to be accounted for within equity, does not fit within the parent concept (applying the parent concept would result in an additional amount of goodwill when the parent would acquire the non-controlling interest).

In all examples and activities in Chapters 26 and 27 we have used the parent concept alternative, showing only the goodwill allocated to the parent company. The reason for this is that the large majority of European entities apply this method of determining goodwill.

Sometimes a distinction is made within the parent concept in determining the non-controlling interest at acquisition:

- the non-controlling interest is determined on the basis of the fair values of the assets and liabilities at the acquisition date: this is the method discussed above
- the non-controlling interest is determined on the basis of the book values of the assets and liabilities at the acquisition date; in this situation there is no revaluation of assets and liabilities at the time of acquisition.

The latter method is sometimes referred to as *the* parent concept and the first as the parent concept extension method. We use the term parent concept for the first alternative. The second alternative is an easy one from a pragmatic point of view, but is no longer applied or permitted and will therefore not be discussed any further.

## THE ENTITY CONCEPT

The entity concept (or group entity concept) views the group as a unit and makes no distinction between shareholders. The difference between the parent and entity concept only occurs where there is less than 100 per cent purchase of the shares of an entity. In preparing consolidated financial statements according to IFRS the entity concept prevails. This means that non-controlling interests are part of equity and net comprehensive income includes the net income that is attributable to non-controlling interests. The use of the entity concept has been extensively illustrated in the examples and activities in Chapters 26 and 27.

In accounting for business combinations, IFRS 3 applies the entity concept, with the one exception that we indicated above: goodwill might be determined on the basis of the parent concept, based on the goodwill acquired by the parent and not the goodwill of the group as a whole (non-controlling interests are then calculated on the basis of the share in the fair value of the net assets acquired and not at fair value).

## PROPORTIONAL CONSOLIDATION

The method of consolidation that is in line with IFRS and that has been discussed in the foregoing chapters is that of full consolidation. This means that, even if a parent does not have 100 per cent of the shares, it still consolidates 100 per cent of the net assets as the parent has control of 100 per cent of the net assets. The economic interest is not decisive, it is the fact of having control. This results in a non-controlling interest. When an entity has an economic interest of 80 per cent and has control, it consolidates 100 per cent of the net assets and recognizes a non-controlling interest for 20 per cent of the net assets.

An alternative might be to apply the consolidation on the basis of the economic interest. This is what we call proportional consolidation: consolidation to the proportion of the shares held. In this case there is no non-controlling interest.

Proportional consolidation is not acceptable by the IASB in a parent–subsidiary relationship. It is, however, a traditional option in accounting for joint ventures. Taking into account the recent new standard IFRS 11, proportional consolidation will no longer be allowed. However, for some specific joint arrangements the comparable method of proportional accounting will be applicable. This will be further discussed in the next chapter.

## COMPARISON OF THE THREE CONCEPTS OF CONSOLIDATION

Work through the following activity carefully.

## ACTIVITY 28.2

A buys 80 per cent of B for cash €2200 when net assets of B have a fair value of €2000 and net book value is €1500. The fair value of 100 per cent of B is €2700 (this is not proportional to the price for 80 per cent because of the control premium). The fair value of the non-controlling interest is €500 (€2700 – €2200). A's statement of financial position at the date of acquisition was:

|  | € |
| --- | --- |
| Net assets (including investment in B) | 5 000 |
| Share capital | 4 000 |
| Reserves | 1 000 |
|  | 5 000 |

Compare and contrast the information provided in the consolidated statement of financial position of A group using the three concepts discussed – parent concept, entity concept and proportional consolidation.

### Activity feedback

Table 28.1 gives an overview.

Table 28.1 shows that the consistent figures throughout the three methods are only those of share capital and reserves of the holding company. The net assets change depending on how much of the fair value of the net assets each method considers attributable to

the group. The proportional consolidation method excludes all reference to the portion of assets owned by the non-controlling interest whereas the parent and entity concepts assume that the group might not own all of the subsidiary's assets but it certainly controls them. The parent concept only incorporates the net book value of the portion of assets owned by the non-controlling interest, it disregards the fair value of this portion. The goodwill under the entity concept includes what could be regarded as the non-controlling interest goodwill. The non-controlling interest is shown at either 25 per cent of the fair value of net assets excluding goodwill (parent concept) or 25 per cent of the net assets at fair value including goodwill (entity concept). The proportional method of course makes no reference to a non-controlling interest.

Applying the parent concept and proportional consolidation equity is 5000 (excluding the non-controlling interest), the entity concept results in an equity of 5500. IFRS applies the entity concept, but allows two alternatives, resulting in an equity of 5400 or 5500; the alternative with an equity of 5400 is a mixture between the entity concept (non-controlling interests are part of equity) and the parent concept (the amount of the non-controlling interests).

(Continued)

## ACTIVITY 28.2    (Continued)

### TABLE 28.1    Information on statements of financial positions (three concepts)

| | Parent concept | Entity concept | Proportional consolidation |
|---|---|---|---|
| Net assets (1) (2) | 4 800 | 4 800 | 4 400 |
| Goodwill (3) (4) | 600 | 700 | 600 |
| | 5 400 | 5 500 | 5 000 |
| Share capital | 4 000 | 4 000 | 4 000 |
| Reserves | 1 000 | 1 000 | 1 000 |
| Equity | 5 000 | | 5 000 |
| Non-controlling interest (5) (6) | 400 | 500 | |
| Equity | | 5 500 | |

(1)  Net assets (parent concept, entity concept): 5000 – 2200 (investment in B) + 2000 (assets B) = 4800
(2)  Net assets (proportional consolidation): 5000 – 2200 + 1600 (80% × 2000) = 4400
(3)  Goodwill (parent concept, proportional consolidation): 2200 (purchase price) – 1600 (80% × 2000) = 600
(4)  Goodwill (entity concept): 2700 – 2000 = 700
(5)  Non-controlling interest (parent concept): 20% × 2000 = 400
(6)  Non-controlling interest (entity concept): 500 (fair value, including allocated goodwill of 100).

## ALTERNATIVE METHODS IN ACCOUNTING FOR BUSINESS COMBINATIONS

In Chapter 26 we discussed the accounting for business combinations and identified one method prescribed: acquisition accounting (or purchase accounting). We will now discuss two alternative methods: pooling of interests accounting and carry over accounting.

### Pooling of interests accounting

Prior to the issue of IFRS 3, IAS 22, which now no longer exists, identified another method of accounting for a business combination: the pooling of interests method (alternative name: 'merger accounting'). According to this method the assets and liabilities entities would be combined on the basis of their book values. This method was required in a situation of a 'uniting of interests'. IAS 22 defined this as follows:

> A uniting of interests is a business combination in which the shareholders of the combining enterprises combine control over the whole, or effectively the whole, of their assets and operations to achieve a continuing mutual sharing in the risks and benefits attaching to the combined entity such that neither party can be identified as an acquirer.

Many respondents to the IASB on the issue of business combinations believe such uniting of interests (or true mergers) still occur, even if only rarely, and that it will be impossible in such cases to identify an acquirer as required by IFRS 3. IFRS 3 has now eliminated the use of pooling of interests accounting method because:

- it has virtually eliminated the idea that true mergers do occur
- in no circumstances, according to the Board, does the pooling of interests method provide superior information to that provided by the acquisition method.

The Basis for Conclusions to IFRS 3 does conclude that if true mergers exist, which it doubts, then a better accounting method to use for them could be the 'fresh start method'. This method requires both entities in the business combination to value all assets at fair value. However, the IASB also disregarded the fresh start method and has no plans to debate it.

Pooling of interest accounting is, however, not fully ruled-out for IFRS-appliers. Transactions under common control (internal reorganizations within a group) are out of the scope of IFRS 3 and, in practice, pooling of interests accounting (or carry over accounting, see below), is applied in these situations, even if the internal reorganization is not a true merger from the perspective of the entities involved.

## Differences between acquisition accounting and pooling of interests accounting

The main differences between the two methods can be examined under the headings of

1 Acquisition date
2 Goodwill
3 Share premium (paid-in surplus)
4 Reserves.

**Acquisition date** Applying pooling of interests accounting does not involve the identification of an acquisition date, as with acquisition accounting. There is no acquisition, and therefore no acquisition date. In fact there is a new reporting entity and the consolidated financial statements are presented as if the new reporting entity had always existed. Not only are all combined figures presented as from the first date of the statutory year, also comparative figures are presented as if the merger had been effected in that comparative year.

**Goodwill** With a merger, there is no change in ownership and we merely have a pooling of resources. A consolidated statement of financial position produced for a merger situation will simply combine the existing statements of financial position, and the assets will therefore remain at the book values at which they appear in the original statements of financial position of the separate entities. That is to say, no goodwill is recognized in the new statement of financial position (since none is in fact acquired).

However, with acquisition accounting the net assets of the entity acquired will be revalued as at the date of acquisition and, of course, the difference between the purchase consideration and this asset revaluation will give rise to goodwill (premium) on acquisition.

**Share premium** With an acquisition where an entity issues shares to acquire another entity the cost of the investment is recorded in the acquirer's statement of financial position and, of course, any shares issued in consideration are recorded at fair value, i.e. nominal value plus share premium created. However, with a merger situation, shares issued in the share-for-share exchange involved are recorded at nominal value, i.e. no share premium is created.

**Reserves** Applying acquisition accounting results in reserves that are equal to those of the acquirer before the acquisition. However, pooling of interests accounting will result in reserves that are the sum of the reserves of the acquirer and the acquiree.

It is obvious when one considers these differences why pooling of interests accounting was popular. Following from this, it can be seen that with pooling of interests accounting the statement of financial position of the new entity does not carry a goodwill figure that might have to be impaired against income (and had to be amortized during the period that IAS 22 was applicable). Also the revaluation to fair value of assets would lead to higher depreciation amounts. However, the benefit of presenting higher earnings comes with a lower equity. It is appropriate here to consider an example of the application of pooling of interests accounting and also to contrast it with acquisition accounting (see Activity 28.3).

## ACTIVITY 28.3

Two companies, A and M, have the following respective statements of financial position as at 31 December 201X:

| | A | M |
| --- | --- | --- |
| | € | € |
| Ordinary shares (€1) | 9 000 | 6 000 |
| Earned surplus | 2 000 | 3 000 |
| | 11 000 | 9 000 |
| Represented by | | |
| Net current assets | 5 000 | 2 000 |
| Plant and machinery | 6 000 | 7 000 |
| | 11 000 | 9 000 |

A acquired the whole of the share capital of M on the basis of a one-for-one share exchange as at the given date, at which point the market values of their respective shares were:

| A | €4 |
| M | €4 |

The fair values of M's tangible assets as at 31 December 201X were:

| | € |
| Plant and machinery | 8 000 |
| Net current assets | 2 500 |

Prepare the consolidated statement of financial position for A using both acquisition method (as per Chapter 26) and the pooling of interests method.

### Activity feedback
Consolidated statement of financial position as at 31 December 201X:

| | Acquisition accounting | | Pooling of interests accounting |
| --- | --- | --- | --- |
| Share capital ($1) | 15 000 | (note 1) | 15 000 |
| Share premium (paid-in surplus) | 18 000 | (note 2) | – |
| Reserves | 2 000 | (note 3) | 5 000 |
| | 35 000 | | 20 000 |
| Represented by: | | | |
| Net current assets | 7 500 | (note 4) | 7 000 |
| Plant and machinery | 14 000 | (note 4) | 13 000 |
| Goodwill on acquisition | 13 500 | (note 4) | – |
| | 35 000 | | 20 000 |

*Notes*
1 Based on a one-for-one exchange, A will need to issue a further 6 000 €1 shares (i.e. 9000 + 6000 = 15 000).
2 Issued at a price of €4 per share the share premium on the issue of A shares for acquisition accounting purposes will be €3 per share (i.e. 6000 × €3 = €18 000).
3 For acquisition accounting purposes (but not for merger accounting) the reserves of M of €3 000 as at the date of acquisition will be frozen.
4 Cost of investment

| (i.e. 6000 shares at €4 each) | 24 000 |
| less *Fair value of net assets* acquired (i.e. €8000 + 2500) | (10 500) |
| | 13 500 |

*(Continued)*

## ACTIVITY 28.3 (Continued)

*Despite the simplicity of this example the differences are amply illustrated:*

**1** *Under acquisition accounting a share premium account arises.*

**2** *Under pooling of interests accounting the reserves of M are part of the reserves of A.*

**3** *For acquisition accounting the assets of M are recorded at fair values, whereas for pooling of interests accounting purposes book values prevail.*

### Carry over accounting

An alternative for applying pooling of interests accounting in mergers and acquisition under common control is carry over accounting. This method is in between acquisition accounting and pooling of interests accounting. Carry over accounting requires identifying an acquisition date, but at this date the business combination is accounted for by combining the entities at their book values, so without revaluation to fair values and without recognizing goodwill. Comparative numbers are not restated, as would be the case in applying pooling of interests accounting.

## ACTIVITY 28.4

Refer back to Activity 28.3. Now assume that A and M are both subsidiaries within a group. The financial position on 31 December 201X is as given in Activity 28.3. The acquisition date is 31 December 201X. During 201X, before the acquisition date, A made a profit of €100, M made a profit of €90. What would be the comprehensive income for A for 201X when applying the following methods:

- Acquisition accounting
- Pooling of interests accounting
- Carry over accounting?

### Activity feedback
*For both acquisition accounting and carry over accounting the acquisition date is important. As the acquisition date was 31 December 201X, no profit of M would be accounted for by A. So A would report a comprehensive income of €100. Pooling of interests accounting implies that A and M would always have been combined. Therefore, the profit of A and M are added together, and the profit of A, being the sole shareholder of B, would be €190. The comparative figures of A and M would also be combined, both in the statement of financial position and in the statement of comprehensive income.*

*After the acquisition, carry over accounting would result in the same statement of financial position as pooling of interests accounting.*

## EQUITY ACCOUNTING

In a business combination one entity obtains control over another entity, resulting in a parent–subsidiary relationship. An entity can also buy shares in another entity without obtaining control, for instance obtaining significant influence or even joint control (control together with another entity). Significant influence normally exists when 20–50 per cent of the shares have been acquired. The entity in which the significant interest exists is named an 'associate'. In this situation the equity method of accounting might be applicable.

A fuller discussion of the equity accounting method and its use for dealing with associated entities is given in the next chapter (Chapter 29), together with a consideration of IAS 28 and IAS 31. In this chapter we limit ourselves to an introductory example.

## ILLUSTRATION

On 31 December 2012 A entity acquired 1200 ordinary shares in B entity (4000 ordinary shares) at a cost of €3 per share. B's net assets at 31 December 2012 had a book value (and fair value) of €5600.

The statement of financial positions of A and B as at 31 December 2013 are as follows:

|  | A | B |
|---|---|---|
|  | € | € |
| Net current assets | 2 000 | 3 600 |
| Property, plant and equipment | 30 000 | 6 400 |
| Investment in B | 3 600 | – |
|  | 35 600 | 10 000 |
| Ordinary shares €1 | 16 000 | 4 000 |
| Reserves | 19 600 | 2 600 |
|  | 35 600 | 6 600 |

A is required to issue consolidated financial statements and decides to apply equity accounting to its investment in B.

First, we need to identify the goodwill in the investment as we did for acquisition accounting.

|  | € |
|---|---|
| Cost of investment | 3 600 |
| Purchased 30% of B's net assets | 1 680 (30% × 5 600) |
| Goodwill | 1 920 |

Net assets of B at 31 December 2013 are €6600, so the net income of B during 2013 was €1000. The share of A in the income of B is 30% × €1000 = 300.

Consolidated statement of financial position of A entity 31 December 2013 using equity accounting for B:

|  | € |
|---|---|
| Net current assets | 2 000 |
| Property, plant and equipment | 30 000 |
| Investment in B 1920 (goodwill) + (30% × 6600) |  |
|  | 3 900 |
|  | 35 900 |
| Ordinary shares €1 | 16 000 |
| Reserves (19 600 + 300 share of B since purchase) | 19 900 |
|  | 35 900 |

## SUMMARY

In this chapter we discussed alternative concepts that lie behind preparing consolidated financial statements and accounting for business combinations.

Alternative concepts on consolidation are:

- the parent concept: consolidated financial statements are being prepared from the perspective of the shareholders of the parent, resulting in an equity that excludes non-controlling interests

- the entity concept: this concept views the group as a unit and makes no distinction between shareholders; equity includes non-controlling interests

- proportional consolidation: consolidated financial statements are prepared on the basis of the economic share in the assets and liabilities and non-controlling interests are not accounted for.

In accounting for business combinations, alternatives to acquisition accounting discussed in this chapter are:

- pooling of interests accounting: assets and liabilities are combined on the basis of book values, assuming that the new reporting entity had always existed (comparative amounts are adjusted)

- carry over accounting: assets and liabilities are combined on the basis of book values, but at acquisition date.

Finally, we discussed the basics of equity accounting, a method that is applicable in acquiring shares in other entities without obtaining control but with obtaining significant influence or joint control.

## EXERCISES

*Suggested answers to exercises marked ✓ are to be found on our dedicated CourseMate platform for students.*

*Suggested answers to the remaining exercises are to be found on the Instructor online support resources.*

1   Appraise the effects on a group's financial statements of the use of merger accounting as opposed to acquisition accounting in order to account for business combinations.

✓ 2   Identify the essence of proportional consolidation and equity accounting and explain when each can be used in the preparation of consolidated financial statements in accordance with IAS GAAP.

# ACCOUNTING FOR ASSOCIATES, JOINT ARRANGEMENTS AND RELATED PARTY DISCLOSURES

**29**

By George Georgiou, University of Birmingham, UK

## OBJECTIVES  After studying this chapter you should be able to:

- identify an associate and a joint venture

- identify the need to disclose related party transactions

- consider the mechanics of accounting for an associate and a joint venture

- explain the requirements of IAS 24, *Related Party Disclosures*

- explain the requirements of IAS 28, *Investments in Associates and Joint Ventures*

- explain the requirements of IFRS 11, *Joint Arrangements.*

## INTRODUCTION

So far within this section we have dealt primarily with the provision of information to users in respect of a holding in a subsidiary entity. However, one entity may have a holding in another that does not give it control but does mean it has significant influence over the net assets of that entity. This chapter considers the appropriate methods to account for holdings/relationships where control is not achieved such that useful information is provided to users.

## EQUITY ACCOUNTING AND ASSOCIATES

We gave you an example of equity accounting in Chapter 28. It will be useful (via Activity 29.1) for you to look back at the illustration we provided.

### ACTIVITY 29.1

Using the illustration at the end of Chapter 28 identify the main differences in the preparation of a consolidated statement of financial position using equity accounting as opposed to acquisition accounting.

*Activity feedback*
*The illustration shows us that equity accounting consolidates entity B as a one-line addition and not by including*

*the fair value of the net assets of B at each individual line of the statement of financial position. This one line consolidation, however, does show us more than the original cost of the investment in B as it includes the goodwill and A's share of the earnings of B since it made the investment.*

## IAS 28, *INVESTMENTS IN ASSOCIATES*

IAS 28 was originally issued in 1989 and amended in 1994, 1998, 1999, 2000 and 2011. IAS 28's main objective was to reduce alternatives in the application of the equity method, not to consider the fundamental approach of using the equity method to account for associates.

### IAS 28 definitions

From Activity 29.1 we could define the *equity method* of accounting as a method by which the investment is initially recognized at cost and adjusted thereafter for the post-acquisition change in the investor's share of the net assets of the investee. The profit or loss of the investor includes the investor's share of the profit or loss of the investee. This is, in fact, how IAS 28 defines it.

The equity method in consolidated financial statements provides the user of the statements with much more information than recording the investment at cost and accounting for any distributions from the investee. The user is able to see his share of the results of the investment and calculate more useful ratios.

*An associate* is defined by IAS 28 as an entity, including an unincorporated entity such as a partnership, over which the investor has significant influence and that is neither a subsidiary nor an interest in a joint venture (para. 2).

*Significant influence* is defined as the power to participate in the financial and operating policy decisions of the investee but is not control or joint control over those policies.

Significant influence is amplified in IAS 28 as a situation where the investor holds, directly or indirectly through subsidiaries, 20 per cent or more of the voting power of the investee and that if such a situation exists significant influence will be presumed unless it can be clearly evidenced otherwise and vice versa.

Significant influence is usually evidenced by:

- representation on the board of directors or equivalent governing body of the investee
- participation in policy making processes

- material transactions between the investor and the investee
- interchange of managerial personnel
- provision of essential technical information.

Complete the following activity.

---

## ACTIVITY 29.2

Identify whether an associate relationship exists in the following examples in accordance with IAS 28.

**1** Entity A owns 20 per cent of entity B and appoints one out of the seven directors. The remaining shares are held equally by two entities that both appoint three of the seven directors. A board meeting is quorate if four directors attend. In the event of tied decisions the chair of the board who is appointed by one of the other entities has a casting vote.

**2** Entity A owns 15 per cent of B and appoints two of six directors to the board. Each director has one vote at meetings and the chair who is from entity A has a casting vote. The other four directors do not represent a shareholding of more than 5 per cent.

**3** Entity A manufactures gadgets for retailer B. B designs the gadgets and normally 90 per cent of A's sales are made to B. B owns 12 per cent of the shares of A.

**4** Entity A has a 16 per cent holding in B. B retails software packages developed by A who holds the licence to the software. B retails no other software packages.

### Activity feedback

*1 Entity A has very little influence in entity B, as at any board meeting he will be outvoted. B is not an associate of A.*

*2 In this case although entity A holds less than 20 per cent, A has significant influence given his voting rights on the board, 33.3 per cent, and his chair casting vote.*

*3 Although B only holds 12 per cent of the shares B exerts significant influence as A is reliant on B for the continuation of the business. A is an associate of B.*

*4 B is dependent on A for technical information and therefore B is an associate of A.*

---

## Example of accounting policy for associate – Vodafone

An associate is an entity over which the Group has significant influence and that is neither a subsidiary nor an interest in a joint venture. Significant influence is the power to participate in the financial and operating policy decisions of the investee but is not control or joint control over those policies.

The results and assets and liabilities of associates are incorporated in the consolidated financial statements using the equity method of accounting. Under the equity method, investments in associates are carried in the consolidated balance sheet at cost as adjusted for post-acquisition changes in the Group's share of the net assets of the associate, less any impairment in the value of the investment. Losses of an associate in excess of the Group's interest in that associate are not recognized. Additional losses are provided for, and a liability is recognized, only to the extent that the Group has incurred legal or constructive obligations or made payments on behalf of the associate.

Any excess of the cost of acquisition over the Group's share of the net fair value of the identifiable assets, liabilities and contingent liabilities of the associate recognized at the date of acquisition is recognized as goodwill. The goodwill is included within the carrying amount of the investment.

The licences of the Group's associated undertaking in the US, Verizon Wireless, are indefinite lived assets as they are subject to perfunctory renewal. Accordingly, they are not subject to amortization but are tested annually for impairment, or when indicators exist that the carrying value is not receivable.

## Exemptions from the use of equity method

An investment in an associate shall be accounted for using the equity method except when:

**(a)** the investment is classified as held for sale in accordance with IFRS 5, *Non-current Assets Held for Sale and Discontinued Operations*;

**(b)** the investment is held by, or is held indirectly through, an entity that is a venture capital organization, or a mutual fund, unit trust and similar entities including investment-linked insurance funds, the entity may elect to measure investments in those associates at fair value through profit or loss in accordance with IFRS 9 (IAS 28, para. 18);

**(c)** *all of the following apply:*
- the investor is a wholly owned subsidiary, or is a partially owned subsidiary of another entity and its other owners, including those not otherwise entitled to vote, have been informed about, and do not object to, the investor not applying the equity method;
- the investor's debt or equity instruments are not traded in a public market (a domestic or foreign stock exchange or an over-the-counter market, including local and regional markets);
- the investor did not file, nor is it in the process of filing, its financial statements with a securities commission or other regulatory organization, for the purpose of issuing any class of instruments in a public market; and
- the ultimate or an intermediate parent of the investor produces consolidated financial statements available for public use that comply with International Financial Reporting Standards.

(IAS 28, para. 17)

## Goodwill in equity accounting

In accordance with IAS 28, goodwill, if positive, is included in the carrying amount of the investment. (Under a previous version of IAS 28 the goodwill was amortized but remember amortization of goodwill is no longer permitted under IFRS.) The goodwill, unlike that in the case of a subsidiary, is not identified separately or subject to a separate impairment test. The investment in its entirety is tested for impairment. To do this test, in accordance with IAS 36, the recoverable amount of the investment, which is the higher of value in use and fair value less costs to sell, is compared with its carrying amount whenever there is an indication of impairment as prescribed by IAS 39. If the goodwill on the purchase of the associate is negative then this is excluded from the carrying amount of the investment and is included as income in the determination of the investor's share of the associate's profit or loss in the period in which the investment is acquired.

## ILLUSTRATION

If the cost of the investment in the illustration at the end of Chapter 28 is €1500 and the reserves of the parent €17 500 then the identified goodwill would be as follows:

|  | € |
|---|---|
| Cost of investment | 1 500 |
| Purchased 30% of net assets of €5600 | 1 680 |
| Negative goodwill | (180) |

The statement of financial position would be as follows:

|  | € | € |
|---|---|---|
| Net current assets |  | 2 000 |
| Property, plant and equipment |  | 30 000 |
| Investment in B – cost | 1 500 |  |
| – share of earnings since purchase |  |  |
| 30% (10 000 – 5600) | 1 320 |  |
| – exclusion of goodwill | 180 | 3 000 |
|  |  | 35 000 |
| Capital shares |  | 16 000 |
| Reserves | 17 500 |  |
| Reserves since purchase | 1 320 |  |
| Negative goodwill | 180 | 19 000 |
|  |  | 35 000 |

## Accounting treatment of losses

Equity accounting requires that the investment in the associate is originally stated at cost and subsequently adjusted for the post-acquisition share of the investor company in the profits or losses of the associate. However, IAS 28, para. 38, specifies that:

> If an entity's share of losses of an associate or a joint venture equals or exceeds its interest in the associate or joint venture, the entity discontinues recognizing its share of further losses. The interest in an associate or a joint venture is the carrying amount of the investment in the associate or joint venture determined using the equity method together with any long-term interests that, in substance, form part of the entity's net investment in the associate or joint venture.

It is interesting that the interest in the associate includes long-term interests of the investor company in the associate entity. For example, an item for which settlement is neither planned nor likely to occur in the foreseeable future is, in substance, an extension of the entity's investment in that associate. Such items may include preference shares and long-term receivables or loans but do not include trade receivables, trade payables or any long-term receivables for which adequate collateral exists, such as secured loans. The question, of course, is what happens once the investor company discontinues the use of the equity method. If there are such interests, losses recognized under the equity method in excess of the investor's investment in ordinary shares are applied to the other components of the investor's interest in the associate in the reverse order of their seniority (i.e. prior to liquidation). After the interest in the associate is reduced to zero, IAS 28, para. 39, states that additional losses are recognized by a provision (liability) only to the extent that the investor has incurred legal or constructive obligations or made payments on behalf of the associate. If this is not the case the investor simply keeps a record of its share of losses without recognizing them. If the associate subsequently reports profits, the investor resumes recognizing its share of these profits only after its share of the profits equals the share of losses not recognized (IAS 30, para. 39).

The following activity illustrates this issue.

## ACTIVITY 29.3

Demosthenes plc purchased 30 per cent of Marina Inc. for €3000 on 31.12.X5. During the following three years (X6, X7 and X8), Marina Inc. had a loss of €11 000, a profit of €400 and a profit of €700 respectively.

**Required**

How would Demosthenes plc account for its investment in Marina Inc. in its accounts for 31.12.X6, 31.12.X7 and 31.12.X8? Assume that Demosthenes' interest in Marina Inc. is the carrying amount of the investment using the equity method.

### Activity feedback

|  | 31.12.X6 | 31.12.X7 | 31.12.X8 |
|---|---|---|---|
| *Income statement* |  |  |  |
| Share of Marina's gains/(losses) | (3 000) | zero | 30 |
| *Balance sheet* |  |  |  |
| Investment in Marina | zero | zero | 30 |
| *Memorandum records* |  |  |  |
| Marina's profit/(losses) | (11 000) | 400 | 700 |
| Share of profit/(losses) | (3 300) | 120 | 210 |
| Recognized profit/(loss) | (3 000) | zero | 30 |
| Unrecognized loss | (300) | (180) | zero |

For the year ended 31.12.X6, Demosthenes' share of Marina's loss is €3300 (30% × €11 000) which exceeds its investment of €3000 in Marina by €300. Therefore, Demosthenes will recognize a loss of €3000 (which is equal to its investment) and reduce its investment to zero. At the same time Demosthenes would keep a record of the unrecognized loss of €300. Note that we assume that Demosthenes did not incur any legal or constructive obligations or made payments on behalf of the associate, so there is no need to make any provisions with respect to Marina's loss.

For 31.12.X7, Demosthenes' share of Marina's profit is €120 (30% × €400). Demosthenes will not recognize this profit as it is lower than the unrecognized loss of €300 and it will continue to keep the investment at zero. However, it will reduce the unrecognized loss to €180 (€300 – €120).

For 31.12.X8, Demosthenes' share of profit is €210 (30% × €700). Demosthenes will recognize, however, only €30 (€210 less unrecognized loss of €180). Its investment in Marina will also be stated at €30.

## Disclosure requirements for associates

These are identified in paras 20–23 of IFRS 12 and require the entity to disclose:

**(a)** the nature, extent and financial effects of its interests in joint arrangements and associates.

This includes requirements to disclose for each associate that is material to the entity: their name and the nature of activities; their principal place of business; proportion of ownership held in them by the entity; summarized financial information, such as: assets, liabilities, revenues, profit and loss from continuing operations, and comprehensive income; aggregate financial information for all associates that on their own are immaterial to the entity (IFRS 12, paras 21–22).

**(b)** the nature of, and changes in, the risks associated with its interests in associates.

This includes a requirement to disclose contingent liabilities (as specified in IAS 37) incurred relating to its interests in associates (including its share of contingent liabilities incurred jointly with other investors' significant influence over, the associates), separately from the amount of other contingent liabilities (IFRS 12, para. 23).

The example below is taken from Vodafone's financial statements for the year ended 31 March 2012. These disclosures were made before the 2011 revision of IAS 28 but, as you will see, cover most of what the amended IAS 28 requires.

## ANNUAL REPORT

### 14. Investments in associates

At 31 March 2012, the Company had the following principal associates carrying on businesses which affect the profits and assets of the Group. The Company's principal associates all have share capital consisting solely of ordinary shares, unless otherwise stated, and are all indirectly held. The country of incorporation or registration of all associated undertakings is also their principal place of operation.

| Name | Principal activity | Country of incorporation or registration | Percentage[1] of shareholdings |
|---|---|---|---|
| Cellco Partnership[2] | Network operator | US | 45.0 |
| Safaricom Limited[3] [4] | Network operator | Kenya | 40.0 |

Notes:
1  Effective ownership percentages of Vodafone Group plc at 31 March 2010, rounded to the nearest tenth of one per cent.
2  Cellco Partnership trades under the name Verizon Wireless.
3  The Group also holds two non-voting shares.
4  At 31 March 2012, the fair value of Safaricom Limited was KES 51 billion (£386m) based on the closing quoted share price on the Nairobi stock exchange.

The Group's share of the aggregated financial information of equity accounted associated undertakings is set out below.

| | 2012 £m | 2011 £m | 2012 £m |
|---|---|---|---|
| Share of revenue in associates | 20 601 | 24 213 | 23 288 |
| Share of result in associates | 4 963 | 5 059 | 4 742 |
| Share of discontinued operations in operations in associates | | 18 | 93 |

| | 2012 £m | 2011 £m |
|---|---|---|
| Non-current assets | 38 788 | 45 466 |
| Current assets | 3 764 | 5 588 |
| **Share of total assets** | **42 552** | **51 034** |
| Non-current liabilities | 3 990 | 5 719 |
| Current liabilities | 2 888 | 6 656 |
| Non-controlling interests | 566 | 554 |
| Share of total liabilities and minority interests | | |
| **Non-controlling interests** | **7 444** | **12 292** |
| **Share of equity shareholders' funds in associates** | **35 108** | **38 105** |

*(Continued)*

## 15. Other investments

Non-current other investments comprise the following, all of which are classified as available-for-sale, with the exception of public debt and other debt and bonds, which are classified as loans and receivables, and cash held in restricted deposits:

|  | 2012 £m | 2011 £m |
|---|---|---|
| **Included within non-current assets:** |  |  |
| Listed securities: |  |  |
| Equity securities | 1 | 1 |
| Unlisted securities: |  |  |
| Equity securities | 671 | 967 |
| Public debt and bonds | 54 | 3 |
| Other debt and bonds | 65 | 72 |
| Cash held in restricted deposits | – | 338 |
|  | **791** | **1 381** |

Unlisted equity securities include a 26 per cent interest in Bharti Infotel Private Limited. Unlisted equity investments are recorded at fair value where appropriate, or at cost if their fair value cannot be reliably measured as there is no active market from which their fair values can be derived.

In the year ended 31 March 2011 the Group sold its 3.2 per cent interest in China Mobile for £4264m generating a £3019m income statement gain, including income statement recognition of foreign exchange rate gains previously recognized in equity.

For public debt and bonds, other debt and bonds and cash held in restricted deposits, the carrying amount approximates fair value.

## IFRS 11, *JOINT ARRANGEMENTS*

### Introduction

So far we have defined investment in another entity as either a subsidiary relationship, an associate relationship or a simple trade investment.

There is one other type of investment we need to consider and that is a joint arrangement. The IASB issued a standard on such arrangements in 1990, IAS 31, *Interests in Joint Ventures*, and has continued to update it since then. In May 2011, however, it replaced IAS 31 with IFRS 11, *Joint Arrangements*.

### Definitions

A joint arrangement is an arrangement of which two or more parties have joint control (IFRS 11, para. 4).

'*Joint control* is the contractually agreed sharing of control of an arrangement, which exists only when decisions about the relevant activities require the unanimous consent of the parties sharing control' (IFRS 11, para. 7). The definition of 'control' is the same as in IFRS 10.

A joint arrangement is dependent on a contractual agreement, usually in writing. This agreement will cover several issues such as duration of the activity, reporting obligations, appointment of the governing body of the entity, capital contributions by the parties involved and the sharing of income, expenses or results. The contract will establish joint control by all ventures involved and will ensure that no one party can control the activity. Quite often though one party may be appointed as the operator or manager of the joint arrangement but he will still have to act within the financial and operating policies agreed by all parties involved. If this is not the case and one party can act unilaterally then the arrangement is not a 'joint arrangement' (see Activity 29.4).

## ACTIVITY 29.4

Serp Company, a building firm, is involved in the following arrangements with other building entities:

- An interest in a project Castle Residential with Locking entity and Crawford entity. The project involves the renovation of the castle building to provide resident accommodation. The participants have equal shares in the project and are to share profits equally. Invoices are sent to Cork entity, which has contracted with the venturers for the work by each of the participants for their work done.
- A 30 per cent interest in Alpha entity to the board of which Serp appoints two directors.
- A 70 per cent interest in Beta entity.
- An equal interest with X entity in Gamma.
- The consent of Serp and X is required to all decisions on financial and operating policies of Gamma essential to activities, economic performance and financial position.
- A 3 per cent interest in Wimp entity.
- A 22 per cent interest in Alpine entity which is seen as a short-term investment.

- An interest in Delta entity. Serp, Delta and Condo are to share equally in the income, expenses and results of Delta and they have each contributed the same capital. Condo has the power to vary the financial and operating policies of Delta as it sees fit.

Identify what type of relationship each of these arrangements is, as far as SERP is concerned, based on our discussions so far.

### Activity feedback
Castle Residential is a joint arrangement as the parties have joint control.

Alpha is an associate as we can presume significant influence from two directors.

Beta is a subsidiary if we assume 70 per cent interest implies 70 per cent voting rights.

Gamma is a joint arrangement as it is jointly controlled by Serp and X.

Wimp and Alpine are simple investments as the former investment does not demonstrate any significant influence and the latter is for a short-term.

Delta is actually a subsidiary of Condo, not of Serp, and thus Serp will only account for the results of Condo as a trade investment.

## Types of joint arrangement

A joint arrangement can take many different forms both legally and in substance but IFRS 11 categorizes them into two groups:

- joint operations
- joint ventures.

The classification of joint arrangements into these two categories depends on the rights and obligations of the parties involved.

*Joint operations* are joint arrangements where the parties that have joint control of the arrangement, known as the *joint operators*, have rights to the assets, and obligations for the liabilities, relating to the arrangement.

*Joint ventures* are joint arrangements where the parties that have joint control of the arrangement, known as the *joint venturers*, have rights to the **net assets** of the arrangement.

From the above definitions it becomes clear that the critical point in assessing whether the arrangement is a joint operation or a joint venture is the determination of the rights and obligations of the parties involved in relation to the joint arrangement. The first step in assessing these rights and obligations is to determine whether the joint arrangement is structured through a separate vehicle, such as the establishment of a corporation or partnership. If this is not the case then the joint arrangement is a joint operation. For example, two companies may enter into an agreement to operate an asset together and share any resulting output.

If the joint arrangement is structured through the establishment of a separate entity then the arrangement may either be a joint operation or a joint venture. The determinant factor in assessing this is the controlling parties' rights to the assets, and obligations for the liabilities, relating to the arrangement that is held in the separate vehicle (para. B20). IFRS 11 specifies that in order to assess these rights and obligations the following need to be examined:

**(i)** the legal form of the separate vehicle (see paras B22–B24);

**(ii)** the terms of the contractual arrangement (see paras B25–B28); and

**(iii)** when relevant, other facts and circumstances (see paras B29–B33).

## The legal form of the separate vehicle

The scrutiny of the legal form of the separate vehicle is the first step in determining the nature of the arrangement. For example, the legal form may not establish a separation between the parties involved and the separate vehicle. This will be the case if the separate vehicle is a partnership that has unlimited liability. In this case the parties involved have rights to the assets and obligations for the liabilities of the partnership which means that the arrangement will be deemed to be a joint operation.

On the other hand, if the separate vehicle is a UK corporation then this means that from a legal point of view there is a separation between the investors and the assets/liabilities of the vehicle. This, however, is not sufficient to establish from an accounting point of view whether the arrangement is a joint operation or a joint venture. For this purpose we need to examine the terms of the arrangement and any other facts.

## Assessing the terms of the contractual arrangement

Irrespective of the legal form of the separate vehicle the arrangement may include contractual terms that give to the parties involved rights and obligations relating to the assets and the liabilities of the separate vehicle. IFRS 11 provides a number of examples of such terms: i) The parties share all interests (e.g. rights, title or ownership) in the assets relating to the arrangement in a specified proportion; ii) The parties share all liabilities, obligations, costs and expenses in a specified proportion; iii) The parties are jointly and severally liable for the obligations of the arrangement; iv) The parties are liable for claims raised by third parties. The inclusion of any of these terms will indicate that the arrangement is a joint operation, regardless of the legal form of the separate vehicle. The absence, however, of such terms does not guarantee that the arrangement is a joint venture as other facts may still indicate that the arrangement is a joint operation. This is examined next.

## Assessing other facts and circumstances

Besides terms included in the arrangement, certain facts and circumstances may also give the parties involved rights to the assets, and obligations for the liabilities, of the arrangement that the legal form of the entity does not confer. IFRS 11 specifies two criteria in assessing whether this might be the case: i) whether the joint arrangement primarily aims to provide the parties with an output (i.e. the parties have rights to substantially all of the economic benefits of the assets); and ii) whether the arrangement depends on the parties on a continuous basis for settling its liabilities.

If both of these criteria are met then the joint arrangement is a joint operation as the rights to the assets and obligation for the liabilities are given to the parties involved.

---

### ACTIVITY 29.5

A, B and C jointly establish a corporation Z over which they have joint control. There are no contractual terms that give A, B and C rights to the assets or obligations for the liabilities of Z. A, B and C agree that they will each purchase a third of all the output produced by Z. The price of the output sold to A, B and C is set by A, B and C, and Z cannot sell output to third parties unless A, B and C approve it. Is Z a joint venture or a joint operation?

#### Activity feedback

Z is a corporation which indicates a separation of the three controlling parties and the assets and liabilities of Z. In addition no contractual terms exist to negate this separation. Both of these factors might indicate that Z is a joint venture. However, they are not sufficient to conclusively establish that Z is a joint venture. Facts and other circumstances also need to be considered. Z is dependent on the three parties to sell and set the price for its output. Furthermore, in order to sell output to third parties Z needs the approval of A, B and C. Therefore, from every perspective Z is dependent on A, B and C which have all of the economic benefits of Z's assets. The three parties are also effectively responsible for its liabilities given that they buy all of Z's output which cannot be sold to other parties. These facts indicate that the joint arrangement is a joint operation, not a joint venture.

Now if Z was allowed to sell to other parties then this would have changed the nature of the situation. A, B and C would not have had all of the economic benefits and clearly not assume the liabilities of Z. Therefore, Z would have been a joint venture: A, B and C would have rights to the net assets of Z, not rights to assets and obligations to its liabilities.

---

## ACCOUNTING FOR JOINT ARRANGEMENTS

### Accounting for joint operations and joint ventures

The determination of whether a joint arrangement is a joint operation or a joint venture is important as the accounting for these two types of entities is different. This is discussed next.

**Joint operations** FRS 11 (para. 21) requires that a joint operator 'accounts for the assets, liabilities, revenues and expenses relating to its involvement in a joint operation in accordance with the relevant IFRSs'. So the interest of the joint operator in a joint operation is not accounted for as an investment in another entity. Instead each asset and liability (and related income and expenses) to which the joint operator has contractual rights are accounted using applicable IFRSs. For example, assume that parties A and B entered into a joint operation to manufacture a product together. Party A has purchased and provided to the operation the machinery required. Party A will then recognize this machinery as part of its property, plant and equipment under IAS 10 (like any other tangible asset that it owns).

**Joint ventures** In contrast to the treatment of a joint operation, a joint venturer recognizes its interest in a joint venture as an investment and accounts for that investment using the equity method in accordance with IAS 28, *Investments in Associates and Joint Ventures* (IFRS 11, para. 24). Therefore, the accounting treatment of joint ventures and associate entities (discussed in an earlier section of this chapter) is the same. It is noteworthy that under the previous standard, IAS 31, a joint venturer had the choice to use either proportional consolidation (as described in Chapter 27) or the equity method.

## ACTIVITY 29.6

X entity acquired 600 $1 common shares in Y entity at a price of $1.50 per share on 31 December 20X1 at which point the statement of comprehensive income of Y had a credit balance of $2000. The respective statement of financial positions of X and Y as at 31 December 20X2 are summarized here:

|  | X $ | Y $ |
|---|---|---|
| Net current assets | 1 000 | 1 800 |
| Property plant and equipment | 15 000 | 3 200 |
| Investment in Y | 900 | – |
|  | 16 900 | 5 000 |
| Common shares $1 | 8 000 | 2 000 |
| Reserves | 8 900 | 3 000 |
|  | 16 900 | 5 000 |

   X is required to prepare consolidated financial statements as it has several subsidiaries for the year ended 31 December 20X2. You are required to draft the initial consolidated statement of financial position of the group as at December 20X2 before the inclusion of the subsidiaries but after the inclusion of Y assuming, first, that the investment in Y is a joint venture. How would your answer change if Y was an associate of X?

*Activity feedback*
*Y as a joint venture and as an associate using the accounting treatment required by IFRS 11:*

|  | € |
|---|---|
| Net current assets | 1 000 |
| Property, plant and equipment | 15 000 |
| Investment in Y (see note 1) | 1 200 |
|  | 17 200 |
| Common shares € 1 | 8 000 |
| Reserves (see note 2) | 9 200 |
|  | 17 200 |

| Note 1: Investment in Y | € | Note 2: Reserve calculation | € |
|---|---|---|---|
| Cost of investment | 900 | X reserves | 8 900 |
| Share of Y's post-acquisition profit | | 30% of Y post-acquisition | 300 |
| 30% × 1 000 | 300 | (1 000) | 9 200 |
|  | 1 200 | | |

## Transactions between a venturer and a joint venture

The standard which deals with this issue is IAS 28, which treats transactions between an entity and its associates and transactions between an entity and its joint ventures in the same manner. When a venturer contributes or sells assets to a joint venture (referred to as 'downstream' transactions), recognition of any proportion of a gain or loss from the transaction should reflect the substance of the transaction.

The assets are retained by the joint venture and provided the venturer has transferred the significant risks and rewards of ownership, the venturer should recognize only that portion of the gain or loss, which is attributable to the interests of the other venturers. The same rule applies to 'upstream transactions', transactions in which the joint venture sells or contributes assets to the investor entity, i.e. gains or losses are recognized only to the extent of the unrelated investors' interests in the joint venture (IAS 28, para. 28).

A different rule, however, applies for downstream and upstream transactions when there is evidence of a reduction in the net realizable value of the assets involved or of an impairment loss of those assets. In the case of downstream transactions those losses shall be recognized in full by the investor, whilst in the case of upstream transactions the investor shall recognize its share in those losses (IAS 28, para. 29).

Complete the activity below.

## ACTIVITY 29.7

A joint venture, Gamma entity, is set up between A, B, and C entities. All venturers share equally in the joint venture. After establishment of the joint venture A sells to Gamma for cash some items of equipment, carrying value in A's books €1m, for €1.6m.

Show the adjustments to be made in A's consolidated financial statements in respect of the above transaction.

### Activity feedback

In A's individual statements the transaction will have been recorded as a sale of equipment thus:

| | |
|---|---|
| Dr Cash | 1.6m |
| Cr Equipment | 1m |
| Cr Statement of comprehensive incomes – gain on sale | 0.6m |

*The gain on sale of 0.6m, in accordance with IAS 28, should only be recognized in the consolidated financial statements as that part which is attributable to the other venturers. Thus only 2/3 × 0.6m = €0.4m should be recognized.*

*Under the equity method the following adjustments will be required.*

| | |
|---|---|
| Cr Investments in JV | 0.2 |
| Dr Statement of comprehensive income | 0.2 |

## Disclosure in respect of joint ventures

IFRS 11 does not include any disclosure requirements. These are included in IFRS 12, and are almost identical to those for associates (IFRS 12, paras 20–23) that we outlined earlier in this chapter.

The following is an example of disclosure of joint ventures from Vodafone's financial statements for the year ended 31 March 2012.

## ANNUAL REPORT

## 13. Investments in joint ventures

### Principal joint ventures

At 31 March 2012, the Company had the following joint ventures carrying on businesses which affect the profits and assets of the Group. Unless otherwise stated the Company's principal joint ventures all have share capital consisting solely of ordinary shares, which are indirectly held, and the country of incorporation or registration is also their principal place of operation.

| Name | Principal activity | Country of incorporation or registration | Percentage shareholdings [1] | |
|---|---|---|---|---|
| Indus Towers Limited | Network infrastructure | India | 35.5 | [2] |
| Vodafone Hutchison Australia Pty Limited [3] | Network operator | Australia | 50.0 | |
| Vodafone Fiji Limited | Network operator | Fiji | 49.0 | [4] |
| Vodafone Omnitel N.V.[5] | Network operator | Netherlands | 76.9 | [6] |

Notes:

1  Effective ownership percentages of Vodafone Group plc at 31 March 2012, rounded to the nearest tenth of one per cent.

2  42 per cent of Indust Towers Limited is held by Vodafone India Limited ('VIL') in which, as discussed in note 12, footnote 4, the Group had a 64.4 per cent interest through wholly owned subsidiaries and a further 20.1 per cent indirectly through less than 50 per cent owned entities.

3  Vodafone Hutchison Austrialia Pty Limited has a year end of 31 December.

4  The Group holds substantive participating rights held by the non-controlling shareholder provide that shareholder with a veto right over the significant financial and operating policies of Vodafone Fiji Limited and which ensure it is able to exercise joint control over Vodafone Fiji Limited with the majority shareholder.

5  The principal place of operation of Vodafone Omnitel N.V. is Italy.

6  The Group considered the existence of substantive participating rights held by the non-controlling shareholder provide that shareholder with a veto right over the significant financial and operating policies of Vodafone Omnitel N.V., and determined that, as a result of these rights, the Group does not have control over the financial and operating policies of Vodafone Omnitel N.V., despite the Group's 76.9 per cent ownership interest.

### Effect of proportionate consolidation of joint ventures

The following table presents, on a condensed basis, the effect on the consolidated financial statements of including joint ventures using proportionate consolidation. The results of Vodacom Group Limited are included until 18 May 2009 when it became a subsidiary. The results of Australia are included from 9 June 2009 following its merger with Hutchison 3G Australia. The results of Polkomtel are included until its disposal on 9 November 2011.

(Continued)

|                                                    | 2012<br>£m | 2011<br>£m | 2010<br>£m |
|----------------------------------------------------|---------|---------|---------|
| Revenue                                            | 7 436   | 7 849   | 7 896   |
| Cost of sales                                      | (4 483) | (4 200) | (4 216) |
| Gross profit                                       | 2 953   | 3 649   | 3 680   |
| Selling, distribution and administrative expenses  | (1 231) | (1 624) | (1 369) |
| Impairment losses                                  | (2 450) | (1 050) | –(12)   |
| Operating profit                                   | (432)   | 975     | 2 299   |
| Net financing costs                                | (141)   | (146)   | (152)   |
| Profit before tax                                  | (573)   | 829     | 2 147   |
| Income tax expense                                 | (552)   | (608)   | (655)   |
| Profit for the financial year                      | (1 125) | 221     | 1 492   |

|                                                 | 2012<br>£m | 2011<br>£m |
|-------------------------------------------------|---------|---------|
| Non-current assets                              | 15 707  | 19 043  |
| Current assets                                  | 911     | 1 908   |
| Total assets                                    | 16 186  | 20 951  |
| Total shareholders' funds and total equity      | 12 574  | 16 389  |
| Non-current liabilities                         | 1 721   | 1 887   |
| Current liabilities                             | 2 323   | 2 675   |
| Total liabilities                               | 4 044   | 4 562   |
| Total equity and liabilities                    | 16 618  | 20 951  |

Note that the company has used proportionate consolidation, which is a method that it will not be able to use once it has implemented IFRS 11. The following is the statement of Vodafone's accounting policy on joint ventures, which describes the use of proportionate consolidation.

# RELATED PARTY DISCLOSURES

So far in this chapter we have dealt with accounting for business combinations, subsidiaries, associates and joint ventures. However, what we have not considered is that the parties in these business combinations often enter into transactions with each other that unrelated parties would not undertake. For example:

- Assets and liabilities may be transferred between parties at values above or below market value.

- One party may make a loan to another at a beneficial interest rate or without taking into account the full risk involved.

- Services carried out by one party for another may be charged for at a reduced rate.

When working through the accounting techniques for business combinations we learnt that such transactions required eliminating in the group consolidated accounts.

However, one of our basic assumptions within accounting is that transactions are carried out at arm's length between independent parties. If they are not, then users of financial statements will be misled if they are not provided with information in respect of these related party transactions. However, if we wish to give such information to users we need to have uniformity of information provided by enterprises and to clearly define when parties are related. This issue is dealt with by IASB in IAS 24 first issued in July 1984 and most recently updated in December 2009.

## Related party issue

IAS 24 in its consideration of the related party issue maintains that related party relationships could have an effect on the financial position and operating results of the reporting enterprise and that this effect can occur even if no transactions have taken place.

### ACTIVITY 29.8

Identify a related party situation where:

- A transaction occurs that affects the financial position and operating results of the reporting enterprise.

- A situation where no transaction occurs but an effect is still felt on the financial position and operating results of the reporting enterprise.

*Others are agency arrangements, leasing arrangements, licence agreements, guarantees and collaterals, management contracts and transfer of research and development.*

- *Such a situation could be where a subsidiary may terminate relations with a trading partner on acquisition by the parent of a fellow subsidiary engaged in the same trade as the former partner. Another such situation would be where a subsidiary, once acquired, is instructed by its parent not to engage in certain activities, e.g. research and development.*

#### Activity feedback

- *There are several situations you could have identified here and three of them we identified for you above.*

## IAS 24 definitions

*Related party*: a person or entity that is related to the entity that is preparing its financial statements (referred to as the 'reporting entity') [IAS 24.9].

**(a)** A person or a close member of that person's family is related to a reporting entity if that person:

   **(i)** has control or joint control over the reporting entity;

   **(ii)** has significant influence over the reporting entity; or

   **(iii)** is a member of the key management personnel of the reporting entity or of a parent of the reporting entity.

**(b)** An entity is related to a reporting entity if any of the following conditions applies:

   **(i)** The entity and the reporting entity are members of the same group (which means that each parent, subsidiary and fellow subsidiary is related to the others).

   **(ii)** One entity is an associate or joint venture of the other entity (or an associate or joint venture of a member of a group of which the other entity is a member).

**(iii)** Both entities are joint ventures of the same third party.

**(iv)** One entity is a joint venture of a third entity and the other entity is an associate of the third entity.

**(v)** The entity is a post-employment defined benefit plan for the benefit of employees of either the reporting entity or an entity related to the reporting entity. If the reporting entity is itself such a plan, the sponsoring employers are also related to the reporting entity.

**(vi)** The entity is controlled or jointly controlled by a person identified in (a).

**(vii)** A person identified in (a)(i) has significant influence over the entity or is a member of the key management personnel of the entity (or of a parent of the entity).

*Close members of the family of a person* are those family members who may be expected to influence, or be influenced by, that person in their dealings with the entity and include:

**(a)** that person's children and spouse or domestic partner;

**(b)** children of that person's spouse or domestic partner; and

**(c)** dependants of that person or that person's spouse or domestic partner.

*Compensation* includes all employee benefits (as defined in IAS 19, *Employee Benefits*) including employee benefits to which IFRS 2, *Share-based Payment,* applies. Employee benefits are all forms of consideration paid, in exchange for services rendered to the entity. It also includes such consideration paid on behalf of a parent of the entity in respect of the entity.
Compensation includes:

**(a)** short-term employee benefits, such as wages, salaries, and social security contributions, paid annual leave and paid sick leave, profit sharing and bonuses (if payable within 12 months of the end of the period) and non-monetary benefits (such as medical care, housing, cars and free or subsidized goods or services) for current employees;

**(b)** post-employment benefits such as pensions, other retirement benefits, post-employment life insurance and post-employment medical care;

**(c)** other long-term employee benefits, including long-service leave or sabbatical leave, jubilee or other long-service benefits, long-term disability benefits and, if they are not payable wholly within 12 months after the end of the period, profit-sharing, bonuses and deferred compensation;

**(d)** termination benefits; and

**(e)** share-based payments.

*Related party transaction* is a transfer of resources, services or obligations between related parties, regardless of whether a price is charged.

*Control* and *significant influence* are as defined in IFRS 10 and IAS 28.

## Disclosure requirements of IAS 24

This breaks down into two areas:

1 Where no transactions have occurred between the parties but control exists. In this case the relationship must be disclosed so that the user can form a view about the effect of the relationship on the reporting enterprise.

2 Where transactions have occurred between related parties. In this case the nature of the relationship, the types of transactions and elements of the transactions necessary for an understanding of the financial statements must be disclosed.

Complete the following activity.

### ACTIVITY 29.9

Identify those elements of a related party transaction that you believe should be disclosed so as to provide an understanding of the financial statements.

*Activity feedback*
You probably identified:

- name of related party
- volumes and amounts involved in the transactions

- amounts and volumes outstanding at the statement of financial position date
- amounts written off in respect of debts due from the related party
- pricing policies
- transfer of a major asset at a reduced price
- those where a free service was given.

IAS 24 requires disclosure of four elements:

- amount of the transactions
- amount of outstanding balances
- provision for doubtful debts
- expense recognized during the period in respect of bad or doubtful debts together with the name of the entity's parent and key management personnel compensation in total and for each of:
  - short-term employee benefits
  - post-employment benefits
  - other long-term benefits
  - termination benefits
  - share-based payment.

The following is an example of disclosure for related party transactions taken from Vodafone's financial statements for the year ended 31 March 2009.

## ANNUAL REPORT

## 31. Related party transactions

The Group's related parties are its joint ventures (see note 13), associates (see note 14), pension schemes, directors and Executive Committee members. Group contributions to pension schemes are disclosed in note 23. Compensation paid to the Company's Board and members of the Executive Committee is disclosed in note 30.

### Transactions with joint ventures and associates

Related party transactions can arise with the Group's joint ventures and associates primarily comprise fees for the use of products and services including network airtime and access charges, and cash pooling arrangements.

No related party transactions have been entered into during the year which might reasonably affect any decisions made by the users of these consolidated financial statements except as disclosed below. Transactions between the Company and its joint ventures are not material to the extent that they have not been eliminated through proportionate consolidation or disclosed below.

|  | 2012 £m | 2011 £m | 2010 £m |
|---|---|---|---|
| Sales of goods and services to associates | 195 | 327 | 281 |
| Purchase of goods and services from associates | 107 | 171 | 159 |
| Purchase of goods and services from joint ventures[1] | 207 | 206 | 194 |
| Net interest receivable from joint ventures [1] | (7) | (14) | (44) |
| Trade balances owed |  |  |  |
| by associates | 15 | 52 | 24 |
| to associates | 18 | 23 | 17 |
| by joint ventures | 9 | 27 | 27 |
| to joint ventures | 89 | 67 | 40 |
| Other balances owed by joint ventures [1] | 365 | 176 | 751 |

Notes

1   Amounts arise through Vodafone Hutchison Australia and Indus Towers and represent amounts not eliminated on consolidation. Interest is paid in line with market rates. Amounts owed by and owed to associates are disclosed within notes 17 and 25. Dividends received from associates are disclosed in the consolidated statement of cash flows.

### Transactions with directors other than compensation

During the three years ended 31 March 2012, and as of 21 May 2012, neither any director nor any other executive officer, nor any associate of any director or any other executive officer, was indebted to the Company.

During the three years ended 31 March 2012, the Company has not been a party to any other material transaction, or proposed transactions, in which any member of the key management personnel (including directors, any other executive officer, senior manager, any spouse or relative of any of the foregoing or any relative of such spouse), had or was to have a director indirect material interest.

# SUMMARY OF ACCOUNTING METHODS FOR ASSOCIATES AND JOINT ARRANGEMENTS

Previously we dealt with the accounting treatment required for subsidiary entities. This chapter considered the accounting for associate entities and joint arrangements (joint ventures and joint operations). The following activity illustrates further the accounting treatment for subsidiaries, associates and joint arrangements.

## ACTIVITY 29.10

The following information is available with respect to Demos plc and its group of companies for the year ended 31 March 20X8. The income statements are as follows:

|  | Demos €000 | Veta €000 | Alpha €000 | Sigma €000 |
|---|---|---|---|---|
| Revenue | 9 000 | 6 000 | 15 000 | 10 000 |
| Cost of sales | 3 900 | 2 200 | 8 000 | 5 000 |
| Gross profit | 5 100 | 3 800 | 7 000 | 5 000 |
| Administration and distribution | 900 | 1 200 | 2 100 | 1 100 |
| Operating profit | 4 200 | 2 600 | 4 900 | 3 900 |
| Dividends received | 50 |  |  |  |
| Interest payable | 150 | 170 |  | 1 100 |
| Profit before tax | 4 100 | 2 430 | 4 900 | 2 800 |
| Taxation | 1 750 | 1 100 | 2 100 | 1 100 |
| Profit after tax | 2 350 | 1 330 | 2 800 | 1 700 |

The balance sheets of the group companies as at 31 March 20X8 were as follows:

|  | Demos €000 | Veta €000 | Alpha €000 | Sigma €000 |
|---|---|---|---|---|
| Property, plant and equipment | 16 500 | 10 130 | 30 000 | 27 500 |
| Investments in: |  |  |  |  |
| Sigma | 12 000 |  |  |  |
| Veta | 2 500 |  |  |  |
| Alpha | 5 700 |  |  |  |
| Brum | 5 000 |  |  |  |
| Current assets | 3 200 | 1 000 | 4 000 | 2 500 |
| Total assets | 44 900 | 11 130 | 34 000 | 30 000 |
| Current liabilities | 2 900 | 800 | 2 700 | 900 |
| Long-term liabilities | 2 200 | 4 000 | 7 500 | 9 000 |
| Total liabilities | 5 100 | 4 800 | 10 200 | 9 900 |
| Net assets | 39 800 | 6 330 | 23 800 | 20 100 |
| Share capital | 10 000 | 5 000 | 4 000 | 8 000 |
| Retained profits | 29 800 | 1 330 | 19 800 | 12 100 |
| Shareholders' equity | 39 800 | 6 330 | 23 800 | 20 100 |

### Additional information

1 Demos plc and SwissCo SA have an equal interest in Veta which they account for as a joint venture. On 31.3.X7 in the consolidated balance sheet of Demos plc, Veta was stated at €2 500 000.

2 Demos plc purchased 30 per cent of Alpha on 31.3.X4 for €5 700 000. On that date the retained profit of Alpha were €14 000 000. Demos plc treats Alpha as an associate company.

3 Demos plc purchased 70 per cent of the shares of Sigma for €12 000 000 when the net assets of Sigma were €15 000 000.

4 Investment in Brum represents a held for trading investment, the value of which has not changed from the previous year.

### Required

Prepare the consolidated financial statements for the Demos group for the year ended 31.3.X8.

### Activity feedback

1 *Consolidated income statement for the year ended 31.3.X8.*

|  | €000 |  |
|---|---|---|
| Revenue | 19 000 | (9 000+10 000) |
| Cost of sales | 8 900 | (3 900+5 000) |
| Gross profit | 10 100 |  |
| Administration and distribution | 2 000 | (900 + 1 100) |
| Operating profit | 8 100 |  |
| Dividends received | 50 |  |
| Interest payable | 1 250 | (150 + 1 100) |
| Share of Alpha's net profit | 840 | (30% × 2 800) |
| Share of Veta's net profit | 665 | (50% × 1 330) |
| Profit before tax | 8 405 |  |
| Taxation | 2 850 | (1 750 + 1 100) |
| Profit for the financial year | 5 555 |  |
| Attributable to: |  |  |
| Equity shareholders | 5 045 |  |
| Non-controlling interests | 510 |  |

(Continued)

## ACTIVITY 29.10   (Continued)

*The subsidiary Sigma is fully consolidated; while the equity method of accounting is used to account for the net profit of the associate Alpha and the joint venture Veta. Therefore Demos reports its share of the net profit of Alpha (30% × 2 800) and Veta (50% × 1 330).*

**2** *Consolidated balance sheet as at 31.3.X8.*

|  | €'000 |  |
|---|---|---|
| Property, plant and equipment | 44 000 | (16 500 + 27 500) |
| Goodwill | 1 500 | Note 1 |
| Investments in: |  |  |
| Veta | 3 165 | Note 2 |
| Alpha | 7 440 | Note 3 |
| Brum | 5 000 |  |
| Current assets | 5 700 | (3 200 + 2 500) |
| Total assets | 66 805 |  |
| Currents liabilities | 3 800 | (2 900 + 900) |
| Long-term liabilities | 11 200 | (2 200 + 9 000) |
| Total liabilities | 15 000 |  |
| Net assets | 51 805 |  |
| Share capital | 10 000 | Demos' capital |
| Retained profits | 35 775 | Note 4 |
| Non-controlling interests | 6 030 | Note 5 |
| Shareholders' equity | 51 805 |  |

### Note 1. Goodwill relating to Sigma

| | |
|---|---|
| Cost of investment | 12 000 |
| *Less* 70% of Sigma's net assets (15 000) | 10 500 |
| | 1 500 |

*See Chapter 28 for alternative method of calculating goodwill and non-controlling interests.*

### Note 2. Investment in Joint Venture Veta

| | |
|---|---|
| Value stated at 31.3.X7 in consolidated BS | 2 500 |
| Share of profit for the year (50% × 1100) | 665 |
| | 3 165 |

### Note 3. Investment in Associate Alpha

| | | |
|---|---|---|
| Cost of investment | | 5 700 |
| *Add* Share of post-acquisition profits: | | |
| Retained profits at 31.3.X8 | 19 800 | |
| *Less*: Retained profits at acquisition | 14 000 | |
| Post-acquisition profits | 5 800 | |
| Demos' share (30%) | 30% | 1 740 |
| | | 7 440 |

### Note 4. Retained Profits

| | |
|---|---|
| Demos' retained profits | 29 800 |
| Share of Sigma's post-acquisition profits (70% × 5 100) | 3 570 |
| Share of Alpha's retained profit (30% × 5 800) | 1 740 |
| Share of Veta's profit for the year (50% × 1 330) | 665 |
| | 35 775 |

### Note 5. Non-controlling interests

| | |
|---|---|
| Share in net assets of Sigma (30% × 20 100) | 6 030 |

## SUMMARY

Previous chapters explored the financial reporting requirements for subsidiary entities, which are entities over which a holding company has control. This chapter has considered the IFRS requirements for two different types of intercompany investments. First, associate entities, which are entities over which the holding company has significance influence but not control or joint control. Second, joint arrangements where two or more parties have joint control of the arrangement. There are two types of joint arrangements: joint ventures and joint operations. A joint arrangement is a joint operation when the parties have rights to the assets, and obligations for the liabilities. If not, the joint arrangement is a joint venture. In addition, this chapter considered the disclosures required for related party transactions.

## EXERCISES

*Suggested answers to exercises marked ✓ are to be found on our dedicated CourseMate platform for students.*

*Suggested answers to the remaining exercises are to be found on the Instructor online support resources.*

**1** Define a subsidiary, associate and related party entity.

**2** Identify how a subsidiary, associate and related party will be dealt with in the financial statements of a group.

**3** Using any information you can find in respect of 'Enron' discuss the following statement: *If Enron had prepared its financial statements using IAS GAAP instead of US GAAP it would have had to account for special purpose entities differently.*

✓ **4** The following draft statement of financial positions relate to Largo, a public limited company, Fusion, a public limited company and Spine, a public limited company, as at 30 November 20X3.

|  | Largo $m | Fusion $m | Spine $m |
|---|---|---|---|
| Non-current assets |  |  |  |
| Tangible non-current assets | 329 | 185 | 64 |
| Investment in Fusion | 150 |  |  |
| Investment in Spine | 30 | 50 |  |
| Investment in Micro | 11 |  |  |
|  | 520 | 235 | 564 |
| Current assets | 120 | 58 | 40 |
|  | 640 | 293 | 104 |
| Capital and reserves |  |  |  |
| Called up ordinary share capital of $1 | 460 | 110 | 50 |
| Share premium account | 30 | 20 | 10 |

| | Largo $m | Fusion $m | Spine $m |
|---|---|---|---|
| Accumulated reserves | 120 | 138 | 35 |
| | 610 | 268 | 95 |
| Non-current liabilities – deferred tax | 20 | 20 | 5 |
| Current liabilities | 10 | 5 | 4 |
| | 640 | 293 | 104 |

The following information is relevant to the preparation of the group financial statements:

(i) Largo acquired 90 per cent of the ordinary share capital of Fusion and 26 per cent of the ordinary share capital of Spine on 1 December 20X2 in a share for share exchange when the accumulated reserves were Fusion $136m and Spine $30m. The fair value of the net assets at 1 December 20X2 was Largo $650m, Fusion $330m and Spine $128m. Any increase in the consolidated fair value of the net assets over the carrying value is deemed to be attributable to property held by the companies. There had been no new issue of shares since 1 December 20X2.

(ii) In arriving at the fair value of net assets acquired at 1 December 20X2, Largo has not accounted for the deferred tax arising on the increase in the value of the property of both Fusion and Spine. The deferred tax arising on the fair valuation of the property was Fusion $15m and Spine $9m.

(iii) Fusion had acquired a 60 per cent holding in Spine on 1 December 19X9 for a consideration of $50m when the accumulated reserve of Spine was $10m. The fair value of the net assets at that date was $80m with the increase in fair value attributable to property held by the companies. Property is depreciated within the group at 5 per cent per annum.

(iv) The directors of Largo wish to account for the business combination as a uniting of interests. On 1 December 20X2, before the share exchange, the market capitalization of the companies was: $644m, Largo; $310m, Fusion; and $310m, Spine. The number of employees of Largo was 50 per cent more than the combined total of the employees of both Fusion and Spine. The new Board of Directors will comprise ten directors, seven of whom will be nominated by Largo. As a result of the directors' wish to use the pooling accounting method, the cost of the investment in Fusion and Spine, shown in the financial statements of Largo, is simply the nominal value of the share capital issued. The directors feel that pooling accounting is appropriate as former institutional shareholders of Fusion own a substantial amount of equity in the new business combination with the result that Largo cannot dominate the new business combination because of their influence over the management of the new entity.

(v) Largo purchased a 40 per cent interest in Micro, a limited liability investment company on 1 December 20X2. The only asset of the company is a portfolio of investments which is held for trading purposes. The stake in Micro was purchased for cash for $11m. The carrying value of the net assets of Micro on 1 December 20X2 was $18m and their fair value was $20m. On 30 November 20X3, the fair value of the net assets was $24m. Largo exercises significant influence over Micro. Micro values the portfolio on a 'mark to market' basis.

(vi) Fusion has included a brand name in its tangible non-current assets at the cost of $9m. The brand earnings can be separately identified and could be sold separately from the rest of the business. The fair value of the brand at 30 November 20X3 was $7m. The fair value of the brand at the time of Fusion's acquisition by Largo was $9m.

**Required:**
Prepare the consolidated statement of financial position of the Largo Group at the year ended 30 November 20X3 in accordance with International Financial Reporting Standards, explaining the reasons why pooling of interests accounting would not be used for the business combination.

(ACCA – December 2003)

5   The following statements refer to a situation where an investing entity K seeks to exert control or influence over another entity L. Assume that K is required to prepare consolidated accounts because of other investments.

   (a)  If K owns more than 20 per cent, but less than 50 per cent of the equity shares in L, then L is bound to be an associate of K.

   (b)  If K controls the operating and financial policies of L, then L cannot be an associate of K.

   (c)  If L is an associate of K, then any amounts payable by L to K are not eliminated when preparing the consolidated statement of financial position of K.

   Which of the statements are true?

     (i)   (a) and (b) only

     (ii)  (b) only

     (iii) (b) and (c) only

     (iv)  (a) and (c) only.

6   Disclosure of related party transactions in financial statements provides no useful information to users. Discuss.

7   Explain what a special purpose entity is and identify how the IASB requires these to be accounted for.

8   Hosterling purchased the following equity investments:

   On 1 October 2005: 80 per cent of the issued share capital of Sunlee. The acquisition was through a share exchange of three shares in Hosterling for every five shares in Sunlee. The market price of Hosterling's shares at 1 October 2005 was $5 per share.

   On 1 July 2006: 6 million shares in Amber paying $3 per share in cash and issuing to Amber's shareholders 6 per cent (actual and effective rate) loan notes on the basis of $100 loan note for every 100 shares acquired.

   The summarized statement of comprehensive incomes for the three companies for the year ended 30 September 2006 are:

|  | Hosterling $000 | Sunlee $000 | Amber $000 |
|---|---|---|---|
| Revenue | 105 000 | 62 000 | 50 000 |
| Cost of sales | (68 000) | (36 500) | (61 000) |
| Gross profit/(loss) | 3 700 | 25 500 | (11 000) |
| Other income (note (i)) | 400 | nil | nil |
| Distribution costs | (4 000) | (2 500) | (4 500) |
| Administrative expenses | (7 500) | (7 000) | (8 500) |
| Finance costs | (1 200) | (900) | nil |
| Profit/(loss) before tax | 24 700 | 15 600 | (24 000) |
| Income tax (expense)/credit | (8 700) | (2 600) | 4 000 |
| Profit/(loss) for the period | 16 000 | 13 000 | (20 000) |

The following information is relevant:

(i) The other income is a dividend received from Sunlee on 31 March 2006.

(ii) The details of Sunlee's and Amber's share capital and reserves at 1 October 2005 were:

| | Sunlee $000 | Amber $000 |
|---|---|---|
| Equity shares of $1 each | 20 000 | 15 000 |
| Retained earnings | 18 000 | 35 000 |

(iii) A fair value exercise was carried out at the date of acquisition of Sunlee with the following results:

| | Carrying amount $000 | Fair value $000 | Remaining life (straight line) |
|---|---|---|---|
| Intellectual property | 18 000 | 22 000 | Still in development |
| Land | 1 700 | 20 000 | Not applicable |
| Plant | 30 000 | 35 000 | Five years |

The fair values have not been reflected in Sunlee's financial statements.

Plant depreciation is included in cost of sales.

No fair value adjustments were required on the acquisition of Amber.

(iv) In the year ended 30 September 2006 Hosterling sold goods to Sunlee at a selling price of $18m. Hosterling made a profit of cost plus 25 per cent on these sales. $7.5m (at cost to Sunlee) of these goods were still in the inventories of Sunlee at 30 September 2006.

(v) Impairment tests for both Sunlee and Amber were conducted on 30 September 2006. They concluded that the goodwill of Sunlee should be written down by $1.6m and, due to its losses since acquisition, the investment in Amber was worth $21.5m.

(vi) All trading profits and losses are deemed to accrue evenly throughout the year.

**Required:**

(a) Calculate the goodwill arising on the acquisition of Sunlee at 1 October 2005.

(b) Calculate the carrying amount of the investment in Amber at 30 September 2006 under the equity method prior to the impairment test.

(c) Prepare the consolidated statement of comprehensive income for the Hosterling Group for the year ended 30 September 2006.

(ACCA 2.5 int. – December 2006)

✓ **9** (a) Hapsburg, a public listed company, acquired the following investments:

● On 1 April 2003, 24 million shares in Sundial. This was by way of an immediate share exchange of two shares in Hapsburg for every three shares in Sundial plus a cash payment of $1 per Sundial share payable on 1 April 2006. The market price of Hapsburg's shares on 1 April 2003 was $2 each.

● On 1 October 2003, 6 million shares in Aspen paying an immediate $2.50 in cash for each share.

Based on Hapsburg's cost of capital (taken as 10 per cent per annum), $1 receivable in three years' time can be taken to have a present value of $0.75.

Hapsburg has not yet recorded the acquisition of Sundial but it has recorded the investment in Aspen.

The summarized statement of financial positions at 31 March 2004 is:

| | Hapsburg | | Sundial | | Aspen | |
|---|---|---|---|---|---|---|
| | $000 | $000 | $000 | $000 | $000 | $000 |
| Non-current assets | | | | | | |
| Property, plant and equipment | | 41 000 | | 34 800 | | 37 700 |
| Investments | | 15 000 | | 3 000 | | nil |
| | | 56 000 | | 37 800 | | 37 700 |
| Current assets | | | | | | |
| Inventory | 9 900 | | 4 800 | | 7 900 | |
| Trade and other receivables | 13 600 | | 8 600 | | 14 400 | |
| Cash | 1 200 | 24 700 | 3 800 | 17 230 | nil | 22 300 |
| Total assets | | 80 700 | | 55 000 | | 60 000 |
| Equity and liabilities | | | | | | |
| Capital and reserves | | | | | | |
| Ordinary shares $1 each | | 20 000 | | 30 000 | | 20 000 |
| Reserves: | | | | | | |
| Share premium | 8 000 | | 2 000 | | nil | |
| Accumulated profits | 10 600 | 18 600 | 8 500 | 10 500 | 8 000 | 8 000 |
| | | 38 600 | | 40 500 | | 28 000 |
| Non-current liabilities | | | | | | |
| 10% loan note | | 16 000 | | 4 200 | | 12 000 |
| Current liabilities | | | | | | |
| Trade and other payables | 16 500 | | 6 900 | | 13 600 | |
| Bank overdraft | nil | | nil | | 4 500 | |
| Taxation | 9 600 | 26 100 | 3 400 | 10 300 | 1 900 | 40 000 |
| Total equity and liabilities | | 80 700 | | 55 000 | | 60 000 |

The following information is relevant:

(i) Below is a summary of the results of a fair value exercise Sundial carried out; date of acquisition:

| Asset | Carrying value at acquisition $000 | Fair value at acquisition $000 | Notes |
|---|---|---|---|
| Plant | 10 000 | 15 000 | Remaining life at acquisition four years |
| Investments | 3 000 | 4 500 | No change in value since acquisition |

The book values of the net assets of Aspen at the date of acquisition were considered to be a reasonable approximation to their fair values.

(ii) The profits of Sundial and Aspen for the year to 31 March 20X4, as reported in their entity financial statements, were $4.5m and $6m respectively. No dividends have been paid by any of the companies during the year. All profits are deemed to accrue evenly throughout the year.

(iii) In January 20X4 Aspen sold goods to Hapsburg at a selling price of $4m. These goods had cost Aspen $2.4m.

    Hapsburg had $2.5m (at cost to Hapsburg) of these goods still in inventory at 31 March 20X4.

(iv) All depreciation is charged on a straight-line basis.

**Required:**

Prepare the consolidated statement of financial position of Hapsburg as at 31 March 20X4 in accordance with current IASs.

(b) Some commentators have criticized the use of equity accounting on the basis that it can be used as a form of off-statement of financial position financing.

**Required:**

Explain the reasoning behind the use of equity accounting and discuss the above comment.

(ACCA – June 2004)

**10**    Jay, a public limited company, has acquired the following shareholdings in Gee and Hem, both public limited companies.

| Date of acquisition | Holding acquired | Fair value of net assets $m | Purchase consideration $m |
|---|---|---|---|
| **Gee** | | | |
| 1 June 2003 | 30% | 40 | 15 |
| 1 June 2004 | 50% | 50 | 30 |
| **Hem** | | | |
| 1 June 2004 | 25% | 32 | 12 |

The following statement of financial positions relate to Jay, Gee and Hem at 31 May 2005:

| | Jay $m | Gee $m | Hem $m |
|---|---|---|---|
| Tangible non-current assets | 300 | 40 | 30 |
| Investment in Gee | 48 | | |
| Investment in Hem | 22 | | |
| Current assets | 100 | 20 | 15 |
| Total assets | 470 | 60 | 45 |
| Share capital of $1 | 100 | 10 | 6 |
| Share premium account | 50 | 20 | 14 |
| Revaluation reserve | 15 | | |
| Retained earnings | 135 | 16 | 10 |
| Total equity | 300 | 46 | 30 |
| Non-current liabilities | 60 | 4 | 3 |
| Current liabilities | 110 | 10 | 12 |
| Total equity and liabilities | 470 | 60 | 45 |

The following information is relevant to the preparation of the group financial statements of the Jay Group:

(a) Gee and Hem have not issued any new share capital since the acquisition of the share-holdings by Jay. The excess of the fair value of the net assets of Gee and Hem over their carrying amounts at the dates of acquisition is due to an increase in the value of Gee's non-depreciable land of $10m at 1 June 2003 and a further increase of $4m at 1 June 2004, and Hem's non-depreciable land of $6m at 1 June 2004. There has been no change in the value of non-depreciable land since 1 June 2004. Before obtaining control of Gee, Jay did not have significant influence over Gee but has significant influence over Hem. Jay has accounted for the investment in Gee at market value with changes in value being recorded in profit or loss. The market price of the shares of Gee at 31 May 2005 had risen to $6 per share as there was speculation regarding a takeover bid.

(b) On 1 June 2004, Jay sold goods costing $13m to Gee for $19m. Gee has used the goods in constructing a machine which began service on 1 December 2004. Additionally, on 31 May 2005, Jay purchased a portfolio of investments from Hem at a cost of $10m on which Hem had made a profit of $2m. These investments have been incorrectly included in Jay's statement of financial position under the heading 'Investment in Hem'.

(c) Jay sold some machinery with a carrying value of $5m on 28 February 2005 for $8m. The terms of the contract, which was legally binding from 28 February 2005, was that the pur-chaser would pay an initial deposit of $2m followed by two instalments of $3.5m (including total interest of $1m) payable on 31 May 2005 and 2006. The purchaser was in financial difficulties at the year-end and subsequently went into liquidation on 10 June 2005. No payment is expected from the liquidator. The deposit had been received on 28 February 2005 but the first instalment was not received. The terms of the agreement were such that Jay maintained title to the machinery until the first instalment was paid. The machinery was still physically held by Jay and the machinery had been treated as sold in the financial statements. The amount outstanding of $6m is included in current assets and no interest has been accrued in the financial statements.

(d) Gee is considered to be a cash-generating unit in its own right. At 31 May 2005, Jay has determined that the recoverable amount of Gee is $64m and that of Hem is $68m.

(e) Group policy is to depreciate plant and equipment on the reducing balance basis over ten years. Depreciation is calculated on a time-apportionment basis.

(f) There are no inter-company amounts outstanding at 31 May 2005.

**Required:**
Prepare the consolidated statement of financial position of the Jay Group as at 31 May 2005 in accordance with International Financial Reporting Standards.

(ACCA 3.5 int. – June 2005)

11  On 1 June 2005, Egin, a public limited company, was formed out of the reorganization of a group of companies with foreign operations. The directors require advice on the disclosure of related party information but are reluctant to disclose information as they feel that such transactions are a normal feature of business and need not be disclosed.

Under the new group structure, Egin owns 80 per cent of Briars, 60 per cent of Doye, and 30 per cent of Eye. Egin exercises significant influence over Eye. The directors of Egin are also directors of Briars and Doye but only one director of Egin sits on the management board of Eye. The management board of Eye comprises five directors. Originally the group comprised five companies but the fifth company, Tang, which was a 70 per cent subsidiary of Egin, was sold on 31 January 2006. There were no transactions between Tang and the Egin Group during the year to 31 May 2006. 30 per cent of the shares of Egin are owned by another company, Atomic, which exerts significant influence over Egin. The remaining 40 per cent of the shares of Doye are owned by Spade.

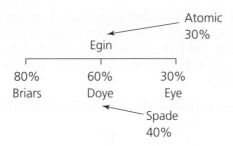

During the current financial year to 31 May 2006, Doye has sold a significant amount of plant and equipment to Spade at the normal selling price for such items. The directors of Egin have proposed that where related party relationships are determined and sales are at normal selling price, any disclosures will state that prices charged to related parties are made on an arm's-length basis.

The directors are unsure how to treat certain transactions relating to their foreign subsidiary, Briars. Egin purchased 80 per cent of the ordinary share capital of Briars on 1 June 2005 for €50m when its net assets were fair valued at €45m. At 31 May 2006, it is established that goodwill is impaired by €3m. Additionally, at the date of acquisition, Egin had made an interest free loan to Briars of $10m. The loan is to be repaid on 31 May 2007. An equivalent loan would normally carry an interest rate of 6 per cent taking into account Briars' credit rating. The exchange rates were as follows:

|  | Euros to $ |
| --- | --- |
| 1 June 2005 | 2.0 |
| 31 May 2006 | 2.5 |
| Average rate of year | 2.3 |

Financial liabilities of the Group are normally measured at amortized cost.

One of the directors of Briars, who is not on the management board of Egin, owns the whole of the share capital of a company, Blue, that sells goods at market price to Briars. The director is in charge of the production at Briars and also acts as a consultant to the management board of the group.

**Required:**

(i)　Discuss why it is important to disclose related party transactions, explaining the criteria which determine a related party relationship.

(ii)　Describe the nature of any related party relationships and transactions which exist:

- within the Egin Group including Tang
- between Spade and the Egin Group
- between Atomic and the Egin Group

commenting on whether transactions should be described as being at 'arm's length'.

(ACCA 3.5 int. – June 2006)

**12** AC is a listed entity that has made several investments in recent years, including investments in BD and CF. The financial assistant of AC has prepared the accounts of AC for the year ended 31 December 2008. The financial assistant is unsure of how the investments should be accounted for and is not sufficiently experienced to prepare the consolidated financial statements for the AC group.

The summarized balance sheets of *AC, BD* and *CF* are given below.

| | *AC*<br>*$000* | *BD*<br>*$000* | *CF*<br>*$000* |
|---|---|---|---|
| *Summarized balance sheets* | | | |
| **Assets** | | | |
| **Non-current assets** | | | |
| Property, plant and equipment | 25 700 | 28 000 | 15 000 |
| Investments | 34 300 | – | – |
| **Current assets** | 17 000 | 14 000 | 6 000 |
| | 77 000 | 42 000 | 21 000 |
| **Equity and liabilities** | | | |
| **Equity** | | | |
| Share capital ($1 ordinary shares) | 30 000 | 20 000 | 8 000 |
| Revaluation reserve | 3 000 | 1 000 | 1 000 |
| Other reserves | 1 000 | – | – |
| Retained earnings | 22 000 | 9 000 | 9 000 |
| | 56 000 | 30 000 | 18 000 |
| **Non-current liabilities** | 6 000 | 4 000 | – |
| **Current liabilities** | 15 000 | 8 000 | 3 000 |
| | 77 000 | 42 000 | 21 000 |

**Investments**

AC acquired 14m $1 ordinary shares in BD on 1 March 2003 for $18m. At the date of acquisition BD had retained earnings of $3m and a balance of $1m on revaluation reserve.

On 1 July 2008, AC acquired a further 20 per cent stake in BD for $7m. BD made profits of $1.6m in the year to 31 December 2008 and profits are assumed to accrue evenly throughout the year.

AC acquired 40 per cent of the $1 ordinary share capital of CF on 1 February 2005 at a cost of $7m. The retained earnings of CF at the date of acquisition totalled $6m.

The remaining investment relates to an available for sale investment. The investment has a market value of $2·6m at 31 December 2008. The financial assistant was unsure of how this investment should be treated, so the investment is included at its original cost.

CF revalued a property during the year resulting in a revaluation gain of $1m. There were no other revaluations of property, plant and equipment in the year for the other entities in the group. All revaluations to date relate to land, which is not depreciated in accordance with group policy.

During the period, AC sold goods to CF with a sales value of $800 000. Half of the goods remain in inventories at the year end. AC made 25 per cent profit margin on all sales to CF.

An impairment review was performed in the period and it was estimated that the goodwill arising on the acquisition of CF was impaired by 30 per cent.

**Required:**

(a) Explain how each of the three investments held by AC should be accounted for in the consolidated financial statements.

(b) Prepare the consolidated balance sheet of the AC group as at 31 December 2008.

(CIMA P8 – May 2009)

# FOREIGN CURRENCY TRANSLATION

# 30

**OBJECTIVES**  After studying this chapter you should be able to:

- explain the necessity for foreign currency conversion and translation

- understand and apply the techniques of currency translation

- understand the concepts of functional currency and presentation currency

- describe the IFRS regulations in respect of foreign currency transactions

- describe the IFRS regulations in respect of translating foreign entities

- explain the basics of hedging foreign currency exposure and the application of hedge accounting

- understand specific issues as extending the net investment, translating goodwill, accounting for disposals, translating into currencies of hyperinflationary economies, and the IFRS disclosure requirements.

## INTRODUCTION

Business is increasingly international. Whenever a business has any dealings abroad, it will be involved in 'foreign' currencies. Since an entity generally keeps its accounting records and prepares its accounting reports in its own 'home' currency, figures expressed in foreign money units need to be re-expressed in 'home' units or whatever the reporting currency is. If foreign currency exchange rates remain absolutely constant, i.e. if the value of one currency in terms of the other does not change, then no difficulties arise. But this is rarely the case and, as we all know, exchange rates can and do fluctuate very considerably over relatively short periods of time.

## CURRENCY CONVERSION

Currency conversion is required when a foreign currency transaction is completed within an accounting period. A transaction, foreign or otherwise, can be regarded as comprising two events:

- the purchase or sale of an asset or the incurring of an expense or item of income
- the receipt or payment of monies for these assets, expenses or items of income.

These events need to be recorded in an entity's books as they occur (see Activity 30.1).

## ACTIVITY 30.1

A UK entity sells goods to a Swiss entity on 1 May 20X2 for SWFr750 000. Payment is received on 1 August 20X2.

Exchange rate 1 May 20X2 is £1 = SWFr3.5544.

1 August 20X2 is £1 = SWFr3.7081.

The year-end for the entity is 30 September 20X2 and the reporting currency is the British pound sterling. Record this transaction in the entity's books and name the balance on the accounts receivable account.

### Activity feedback

*Remembering the transaction comprises two events, we need to record the sale of goods immediately, but we must record the event in £s not SWFrs.*

*Both the sales and the account receivables are recorded for an amount of £211 006 (750 000 / 3.5544; exchange rate on 1 May 20X2).*

*When payment is received on 1 August X2 it will be in the form of SWFr750 000 which we must convert to sterling at the exchange rate at the time = 750 000 / 3.7081 = £202 260.*
*This event will be recorded as:*

|  | £ | £ |
|---|---|---|
| Dr. Cash | 202 260 | |
| Cr. Accounts receivable | | 202 260 |

*Thus, there will be a balance on the accounts receivable account of £8746, which is obviously a loss on exchange and will need to be reported in profit or loss.*
*Similarly, if the exchange rate had decreased from May to August a profit on exchange would have occurred which again would be reported as profit on ordinary activities.*

## CURRENCY TRANSLATION

Activity 30.1 involved a transaction that was completed by the year-end but we need to consider how to deal with foreign transactions that are not completed by the year-end (see Activity 30.2.)

## ACTIVITY 30.2

Let us assume in Activity 30.1 that the entity's year-end is 30 June 20X2 when the exchange rate is £1 = SWFr3.6573. Record this transaction in the entity's books.

### Activity feedback

The initial sale will be recorded as before but at the year-end 30 June 20X2 the accounts receivable account will show a balance of £211 006. This balance is not correct because if the debt was paid at this date we would receive SWFr750 000 = £205 069 which is the value of the debt at 30 June 20X2. Thus we translate the accounts receivable account at the year-end at the exchange rate ruling, which is known as the spot rate, at a given date. The exchange difference of £5937 (£205 069 – £211 006) is the loss on exchange identified as at 30 June X2, which will be debited to profit or loss within the statement of comprehensive income:

|                        | £     | £     |
|------------------------|-------|-------|
| Dr. Exchange loss      | 5 937 |       |
| Cr. Accounts receivable |       | 5 937 |

When the debt is finally paid on 1 August 20X2 a further loss of £2809 is identified for the next year. Notice the total loss of £8746 is now split over the two years.

The currency translation follows the idea of prudence as we are taking account of the loss as soon as we are aware of it. However, what would we have done if on 30 June 20X2 the exchange rate was £1 = SWFr3.4973?

This time at the year-end the debtor would translate as 750 000 / 3.4973 = £214 451 giving a profit on exchange of £3445 and on 1 August 20X2 when the debt is finally settled a loss of £12 191. The gain of £3445 is an unrealized gain and prudence might suggest that we should not recognize this gain. But let us see what IAS 21 says on this issue.

## IAS 21 REQUIREMENTS FOR ENTITY'S FOREIGN CURRENCY TRANSACTIONS

The Standard was issued in 1983, revised in 1993 and revised again under the improvement project 2004. Several small amendments have been made since. IAS 21 states in para. 28:

Exchange differences arising on the settlement of monetary items or on translating monetary items at rates different from those at which they were translated on initial recognition during the period, or in previous financial statements, shall be recognized in profit or loss in the period in which they arise (...)

Further, para. 29 goes on to state:

When monetary items arise from a foreign currency transaction and there is a change in the exchange rate between the transaction date and the date of settlement, an exchange difference results. When the transaction is settled within the same accounting period as that in which it occurred, all the exchange difference is recognized in that period. However, when the transaction is settled in a subsequent accounting period, the exchange difference recognized in each period up to the period of settlement is determined by the change in exchange rates during each period.

Thus, the IAS is telling us to recognize an unrealized gain in the accounts (in the activity this was £3445). This treatment can be justified on the grounds that:

- where exchange gains arise on short-term monetary items their ultimate cash realization can normally be assessed with reasonable certainty and they are therefore realized in accordance with realization conventions
- it provides symmetry with losses.

Now attempt the following activity.

## ACTIVITY 30.3

An entity, Axel, purchases an asset for €12 000 from a foreign entity on 1.3.X2 when the exchange rate between the two currencies involved was 1FC = €2. The currency in which Axel holds its accounts is FCs. At the statement of financial position date of Axel, 30.6.X2, the exchange rate is 1FC = €1.50. Show the entries by Axel to record this transaction initially and those required at the statement of financial position date.

*Activity feedback*

*On 1.3.X2:*

| | | |
|---|---|---|
| Dr. Asset | 6 000 | |
| Cr. Accounts payable | | 6 000 |

*On 30.6.X2*

| | | |
|---|---|---|
| Dr. Exchange loss | 2 000 | |
| Cr. Accounts payable | | 2 000 |

*The balance of accounts payable is FC000 (12.000 / 1.5).*

In Activity 30.3, only the monetary item, accounts payable, has been reported using the closing rate at the statement of financial position date. Under the requirements of IAS 21 only foreign currency monetary items should be reported using the closing rate; non-monetary items which are carried at historical cost denominated in a foreign currency should be reported using the exchange rate at the date of acquisition or, if the fair value is used, the exchange rate prevalent when the fair value was determined. Therefore, the book value of the asset is not adapted when exchange rates change.

## Loans

Transactions can also involve the origination of a loan. IAS 21 defines monetary items as 'units of currency held and assets and liabilities to be received or paid in fixed or determinable number of units of currency' (para. 8). Thus a loan will be translated as any other monetary item at closing rate and the exchange gain or loss credited or charged to income. We might question the rationale for taking the unrealized exchange gain on the loan at the statement of financial position date to profit here but it at least provides consistent symmetrical treatment with the loss which is equally unrealized.

## Functional currency

In a situation where an entity has many transactions in foreign currencies, the question may arise in which currency the entity would do its accounting. One might think of the local currency in the country where the company is situated, but that is not necessarily the case.

IAS 21 uses the concept of functional currency. The functional currency is the currency of the primary economic environment in which the entity operates. An entity should translate all transactions into its functional currency. All other currencies than the functional currency are foreign currencies. An entity that is situated in the Netherlands, with the euro as its local currency, might have the US dollar as its functional currency, for instance when the entity is working in the oil and gas industry that is predominantly dollar-based. For this entity, the euro would be a foreign currency. All transactions in euros need to be translated into US dollars.

When determining its functional currency an entity has to consider the guidance in accordance with IAS 21, paras 9–14. There is a certain hierarchy in determining the functional currency.

Firstly, the primary economic environment in which an entity operates is normally the one in which it primarily generates and expends cash. An entity considers the following factors in determining its functional currency:

**(a)** the currency

   **(i)**  that mainly influences sales prices for goods and services; and

   **(ii)** of the country whose competitive forces and regulations mainly determine the sales prices of its goods and services;

**(b)** the currency that mainly influences labour, material and other costs of providing goods or services.

Secondly, the following factors may also provide evidence of an entity's functional currency:

- the currency in which funds from financing activities are generated
- the currency in which receipts from operating activities are usually retained.

To summarize: first the currency of sales and costs, and second the currency of assets and liabilities.

Each individual reporting entity, including all foreign entities or foreign operations (a subsidiary, associate, joint arrangement or branch of the reporting entity) should determine its own functional currency. Only individual entities can have a functional currency. A group does not have a functional currency. IAS 21 gives some additional factors to consider in determining the functional currency of a foreign operation. The specific question is whether the foreign operation determines its own functional currency based on sales, costs, assets and liabilities (as indicated above) or whether this foreign operation is so much close to the reporting entity that its functional currency should be the same as that of the reporting entity. Factors to be taken into account are:

- Whether the activities of the foreign operation are carried out as an extension of the reporting entity, rather than being carried out with a significant degree of autonomy. An example of the former is when the foreign operation only sells goods imported from the reporting entity and remits the proceeds to it. An example of the latter is when the operation accumulates cash and other monetary items, incurs expenses, generates income and arranges borrowings, all substantially in its local currency.
- Whether transactions with the reporting entity are a high or low proportion of the foreign operation's activities.
- Whether cash flows from the activities of the foreign operation directly affect the cash flows of the reporting entity and are readily available for remittance to it.

- Whether cash flows from the activities of the foreign operation are sufficient to service existing and normally expected debt obligations without funds being made available by the reporting entity.

When the above indicators are mixed and the functional currency is not obvious, management uses its judgement to determine the functional currency that most faithfully represents the economic effects of the underlying transactions, events and conditions.

Once determined, the functional currency is not changed unless the factors just outlined change.

We provide below some examples where determination of an entity's functional currency is less than apparent.

## Example 30.1

For each of the following determine the functional currency:

1 An entity operating in France owns several buildings in Paris that are rented to foreign companies, mostly US companies. The lease contracts are determined in US dollars and payment can be made in either US dollars or euros.

   We have a mixed situation here and therefore need to consider the factors outlined in IAS 21:

   - The local circumstances in Paris determine the rental yields thus indicating the euro as functional currency.
   - Lease payments denominated and could be paid in US dollars indicates the dollar as the functional currency.
   - Presumably labour and other expenses are paid in euros indicating the euro as the functional currency.

   Overall it is the euro that would appear to most faithfully represent the economic effects of the entity and therefore should be taken as the functional currency.

2 A US entity has a foreign subsidiary located in Greece. The Greek subsidiary imports a product manufactured by its parent, paying in dollars, which it sells throughout Greece with selling prices denominated in euros and determined primarily by local competition. The subsidiary's long-term financing is primarily in the form of dollar loans from its parent and distribution of its profits is under parental control. Proceeds of the subsidiary are remitted to the parent on a regular basis.

   Again we have a mixed situation and need to consider the factors outlined in IAS 21:

   - The currency mainly influencing sales prices is the euro.
   - The currency mainly influencing labour and other expenses is again presumably the euro except that purchases of inventory are made in US dollars.
   - The currency in which funds from financing activities are generated is the dollar and the subsidiary has little autonomy, merely acting as an agent in Greece for the parent.

   Although sales are made in euros, the Greek subsidiary is a foreign entity that seems closely linked to its parent and on balance the functional currency is the dollar, being the functional currency of the parent.

An entity entering into a foreign currency transaction records that transaction initially by applying to the foreign currency amount the spot exchange rate between the functional currency and the foreign currency at the date of the transaction. This is what we did in Activity 30.3.

IAS 21 does allow a change in an entity's functional currency. However, this can only happen where there is a change in the underlying transactions, events and conditions. This could occur when there is a change in the currency that mainly influences the sale prices of goods and services.

In accordance with para. 37 of IAS 21, the change in the functional currency is accounted for prospectively. An entity translates all items into the new functional currency using the exchange rate at the date of the change. The resulting translated amounts for non-monetary items are treated as their historical cost.

# IAS 21 REQUIREMENTS FOR TRANSLATING FOREIGN OPERATIONS FOR CONSOLIDATION PURPOSES

In a group each entity has determined its own functional currency. Different foreign operations (subsidiaries, associates, joint arrangements and branches of the reporting entity) should, for consolidation purposes, all be translated into one currency. This currency is the presentation currency. So the presentation currency is the currency in which the financial statements are presented.

Also, for individual financial statements for each entity, the presentation currency can be different from the functional currency. The reason for this can be the shareholder, for instance a Dutch entity having the euro as its functional currency uses the yen as its presentation currency because it is a subsidiary of a Japanese parent.

However, in most cases, translating from functional currencies into a presentation currency will happen when preparing consolidated accounts, and this is what we will focus on.

## Translating from functional to presentation currency

According to IAS 21, the translation from functional to presentation currency occurs as follows:

1 assets and liabilities for each statement of financial position presented shall be translated at the closing rate at the date of that statement of financial position

2 income and expenses for each statement of comprehensive income shall be translated at exchange rates at the date of the transactions; it is possible to use average rates here

3 all resulting exchange differences shall be recognized in other comprehensive income (OCI, therefore outside profit or loss). This is different from translating transactions into the functional currency, as all the resulting exchange differences are then presented as profit or loss. The cumulative exchange differences presented in other comprehensive income are presented as a separate component of equity.

Look at Activity 30.4.

## ACTIVITY 30.4

The statement of financial position of Zhou Ltd at 31.12.X4 is as follows:

|  | FCs | FCs |
|---|---|---|
| Share capital |  | 300 |
| Retained profits |  | 100 |
|  |  | 400 |
| Equipment at cost | 350 |  |
| less Depreciation | 50 | 300 |
| Inventory | 80 |  |
| Net monetary current assets | 60 | 140 |
| Long-term loans |  | (40) |
|  |  | 400 |

The presentation currency for Zhou Ltd is Crowns (CRs) and as at:

|  | FCs to CRs |
|---|---|
| 1 January X4 | 5 |
| Average for the year to 31 December X4 | 4.5 |
| 31 December X4 | 4.2 |

Statement of comprehensive income for the year ended 31.12.X4 is as follows:

|  | FCs |
|---|---|
| Sales | 600 |
| less Cost of sales | 400 |
| Gross profit | 200 |
| less Depreciation | (50) |
| less other expenses | (50) |
| Net profit | 100 |

Translate the financial statements of Zhou Ltd into the presentation currency from the functional currency and show clearly where any exchange difference is recognized.

### Activity feedback

Statement of financial position as at 31.12.X4

|  | Rate | CRs | CRs |
|---|---|---|---|
| Share capital | 5 | 60 |  |
| Retained profits (1) |  | 21.4 |  |
| Currency translation reserve (2) |  | 13.8 | 95.2 |
| Equipment at cost | 4.2 | 83.3 |  |
| less Depreciation | 4.2 | 11.9 | 71.4 |
| Inventory | 4.2 | 19 |  |
| Net monetary current assets | 4.2 | 14.3 |  |
| Long-term loans | 4.2 | (9.5) | 23.8 |
|  |  |  | 95.2 |

Statement of comprehensive income for the year ended 31.12.X4

|  | Rate | CRs | CRs |
|---|---|---|---|
| Sales | 4.5 |  | 133.3 |
| less Cost of sales | 4.5 |  | 88.9 |
| Gross profit |  |  | 44.4 |
| Depreciation | 4.2 | 11.9 |  |
| Other expenses | 4.5 | 11.1 | 23 |
| Net profit |  |  | 21.4 |
| Other comprehensive income (2) |  |  | 13.8 |
| Total comprehensive income |  |  | 35.2 |

1  Retained profits was FC100, being equal to the profit of X4 (opening amount was 0). Translated retained profit is the net profit in the statement of comprehensive income.
2  The opening amount of the currency translation reserve was zero. The exchange difference for the year is the amount required to balance the statements. This exchange difference is also included as other comprehensive income. The amount of 13.8 can be directly calculated as follows:

– exchange difference on opening balance of assets and liabilities (being 300, the amount of share capital, as the opening balance of retained earnings and currency translation reserve were 0): (300 / 4.2 =) 71.4 / (300 / 5 =) 60 = 11.4, plus the difference between translating net profit at closing rate and net profit as translated: (100 / 4.2 =) 23.8 – 21.4 = 2.4.

## ALTERNATIVE TRANSLATION METHODS FOR FINANCIAL STATEMENTS OF FOREIGN OPERATIONS

We have discussed above the IFRS requirements on translation of financial statements of foreign entities. Translating assets and liabilities at closing rate is required by

IAS 21, but it is just one of the alternative options that have traditionally been identified. In this section we will explore some of these alternatives.

When translating any particular item we can take two basic possible views:

1  We can use the exchange rate ruling when the item was created (historical rate).

2  We can use the exchange rate ruling when the item is being reported (current or closing rate).

Since we can apply this choice to each item in the financial statements one at a time, it is clear that many different combinations are possible. Four that have been suggested are now outlined.

## Single rate (closing rate)

This is based on the idea that the holding entity has a net investment in the foreign operation and that what is at risk from currency fluctuations is this net financial investment. All assets, liabilities, revenues and expenses will be translated at the closing (statement of financial position date) rate. Exchange differences will arise if the closing rate differs from the previous year's closing rate or from the date when the transaction occurred. This is the method IAS 21 requires.

## Mixed rate (current/non-current)

Here, current assets and liabilities would be translated at the closing rate, whereas fixed assets and non-current liabilities would be translated at the rate ruling when the item was established (i.e. current items are translated at current rates and fixed items are translated at fixed rates).

## Mixed rate (monetary/non-monetary)

This proposal would translate monetary assets and liabilities at the closing rate and all non-monetary assets and liabilities at the rate ruling when the item was established. There is an analogy here with the arguments for current purchasing power accounting. Monetary items are automatically expressed in current monetary units, so use the current rate for them, and non-monetary items are expressed in out-of-date monetary units, so use the out-of-date rate for them.

## Mixed rate (temporal)

This is based on the idea that the foreign operations are simply a part of the group that is the reporting entity. Some of the individual assets and liabilities of the group just 'happen' to be abroad. The valuation basis used to value the assets and liabilities determines the appropriate exchange rate. Those assets recorded on a historical cost basis would be translated at the historical rate – the rate ruling when the item was established. Assets recorded on a current value basis would be translated at the current (closing) rate. Revenues and expenses should theoretically be translated at the rate ruling on the date when the amount shown in the accounts was established, i.e. assuming an even spread of trading at the average rate for the year.

It is important to avoid the assumption that the temporal method means using historical exchange rates. The words temporal and historical are sometimes, quite wrongly, used interchangeably in this context. 'Temporal' means literally 'at the time', i.e. consistent with the underlying valuation basis. So the temporal method does mean using historical exchange rates when applied to historical cost accounts. But the temporal method means using current exchange rates when applied to current value accounts. This would broadly reduce the temporal method to the single rate method.

The temporal method is in fact prescribed by IAS 21 for translating transactions and events into the functional currency, before translating the functional currency into the presentation currency at closing rate.

Tables 30.1 and 30.2 provide a useful summary of the IAS 21 requirements using both the temporal method and the closing rate method.

### TABLE 30.1  Financial statements of a foreign operation translated into the functional currency (temporal method)

| Item | Translation rate |
| --- | --- |
| Cost and depreciation of property, plant and equipment and intangible assets | Rate at date of acquisition or fair valuation date |
| Inventories | Rate when cost incurred |
| Monetary items | Closing rate |
| Income and expense items | Rate at date of transaction or average rate for the period if rates do not fluctuate significantly |
| Exchange differences | Profit and loss |

### TABLE 30.2  Financial statements of a foreign operation translating from the functional currency into the presentation currency (closing rate method)

| Item | Translation rate |
| --- | --- |
| All assets and liabilities whether monetary or non-monetary | Closing rate |
| Income and expense items | Rate at date of transaction or average rates for the period if rates do not fluctuate significantly |
| Exchange differences | Other comprehensive income |

Activity 30.5 shows the differences between the two methods, so complete it carefully.

## ACTIVITY 30.5

Home established a 100 per cent ownership of Away on 1 January year 8 by subscribing to €25 000 of shares in cash when the exchange rate was 12 CU (currency unit) to the €. Away raised a long-term loan of 100 000 CU locally on 1 January year 8 and immediately purchased equipment costing 350 000 CU, which was expected to last ten years with no residual value. It was to be depreciated under the straight line method. The accounts of Away in CU for year 8 follow, during which the relevant exchange rates were:

|  | CU to € |
| --- | --- |
| 1 January | 12 |
| Average for year | 11 |
| Average for period in which closing inventory acquired | 10.5 |
| 31 December | 10 |

Statement of comprehensive income for year 8

|  | CU |
| --- | --- |
| Sales | 450 000 |
| less Cost of sales | (360 000) |
| Gross profit | 90 000 |
| less Depreciation | (35 000) |
| Other expenses | (15 000) |
| Net profit | 40 000 |

Statement of financial position as at 31 December year 8

|  |  |
| --- | --- |
| Share capital | 300 000 |
| Retained profits (1) | 40 000 |
|  | 340 000 |
| Equipment at cost | 350 000 |
| less Depreciation | 35 000 |
|  | 315 000 |
| Inventory | 105 000 |
| Net monetary current assets | 20 000 |
| less Long-term loans | (100 000) |
|  | 340 000 |

1   Balance of the opening retained earnings was zero, so this amount represents the net profit for the year.

Translate the accounts for the foreign operation using both the closing rate and temporal method and identify what to do with the exchange differences.

### Activity feedback

| Statement of comprehensive income for year 8 | Rate | Closing | Temporal | Rate |
| --- | --- | --- | --- | --- |
| Sales | 11 | 40 909 | 40 909 | 11 |
| less Cost of sales | 11 | 32 727 | 32 727 | 11 |
| Gross profit |  | 8 182 | 8 182 |  |
| less Depreciation | 10 | (3 500) | (2 917) | 12 |
| Other expenses | 11 | (1 364) | (1 364) | 11 |
| Net profit (excluding exchange differences) |  | 3 318 | 3 901 |  |

| Statement of financial position as at 31 December year 8 |  | Closing | Temporal | Rate |
| --- | --- | --- | --- | --- |
| Share capital |  | 25 000 | 25 000 |  |
| Retained profits (= net profit) |  | 3 318 | 3 901 |  |
|  |  | 28 318 | 28 901 |  |
| Equipment at cost |  | 28 318 | 28 901 |  |
| less Depreciation | 10 | 35 000 | 2 167 | 12 |
|  | 10 | 31 500 | 2 917 | 12 |
|  |  | 31 500 | 26 250 |  |
| Inventory | 10 | 10 500 | 10 500 | 10.5 |
| Net monetary current assets | 10 | 2 000 | 2 000 | 10 |
| less Long-term loans | 10 | (10 000) | (10 000) | 10 |
|  |  | 34 000 | 28 250 |  |
| Exchange difference (balance) |  | (5 682) | 651 |  |
|  |  | 28 318 | 28 901 |  |

(Continued)

## ACTIVITY 30.5   *(Continued)*

*The share capital figure in the closing rate method (as in the temporal method) is translated at the original rate to highlight the exchange differences.*

*The exchange difference, a loss, of €651 under the temporal method should be charged to the profit and loss for the current year. Both the net profit and retained earnings, including the exchange difference, are therefore 3250, resulting in an equity of 28 250.*

*Had the exchange difference been a gain it would have been credited to profit or loss in accordance with IAS 21.*

*Under the closing rate method, the issue is more complex. Differences have arisen in respect of each type of statement of financial position item because the opening balances (representing the net investment in the overseas subsidiary by the holding company) have been retranslated back into € at the closing rate. The total gain of €5682 can be broken down as in Table 30.3.*

### TABLE 30.3   Retranslation at closing rate

| Item | Opening rate | Opening rate | Difference |
|------|-------------|-------------|-----------|
| Opening fixed assets | 350 000/10 | 350 000/12 | CU 5 834 credit |
| Opening net current assets | 50 000/10 | 50 000/12 | CU   833 credit |
| Opening long-term loans | 100 000/10 | 100 000/12 | CU 1 667 debit |
| Net profit | 40 000/10 = 4 000 | 40 000/average = 3 318 | CU   682 credit |

*IAS 21 requires that this gain is taken to other comprehensive income and presented as a separate component of equity (for instance named Translation reserve). Total comprehensive income therefore is €9000 (net profit €3318 + other comprehensive income €5682). Total equity is €34 000.*

*Summarized:*

|  | Temporal method | Closing rate method |
|--|-----------------|---------------------|
| Net profit | 3 250 | 3 318 |
| Total comprehensive income | 3 250 | 9 000 |
| Equity | 28 250 | 34 000 |

*Alternative calculation:*

- *exchange difference on opening balance of assets and liabilities: 300 000 / 10 – 300 000 / 12 = 5 000 credit, plus*
- *difference between translating net profit at closing rate and net profit as translated: 682 credit (see above)*

We finish this section with two related activities to demonstrate consolidation of a foreign subsidiary.

## ACTIVITY 30.6

A UK entity Bei (with the £ as presentation currency) has a wholly owned US subsidiary Jing (with the $ as functional currency) which was acquired for US$1 000 000 on 31 December 20X1. The fair value of the net assets at the date of acquisition was US$800 000 giving rise to goodwill on acquisition of $200 000.

Exchange rates were as follows:

| | |
|--|--|
| 31 December 20X1 | £1 = US$2.0 |
| Average rate during year | £1 = US$1.65 |
| 31 December 20X2 | £1 = US$1.5 |

*(Continued)*

## ACTIVITY 30.6  (Continued)

During the year Jing paid a dividend of $28 000 when the exchange rate was £1 = US$1.75. The summarized financial statements for Jing were as follows:

Jing statement of profit or loss for the year ended 31 December 20X2

|  | $000 |
|---|---|
| Operating profit | 270 |
| Interest paid | (30) |
| Profit before tax | 240 |
| Tax | (60) |
| Profit after tax | 180 |

Jing statement of financial position as at 31 December

|  | 20X2 | 20X1 |
|---|---|---|
|  | $000 | $000 |
| Non-current assets at cost | 510 | 450 |
| Depreciation | (196) | (90) |
|  | 314 | 360 |
| Current assets |  |  |
| Inventory | 348 | 252 |
| Trade receivables | 420 | 290 |
| Cash | 480 | 420 |
|  | 1 248 | 962 |

Jing statement of financial position as at 31 December

|  | 20X2 | 20X1 |
|---|---|---|
|  | $000 | $000 |
| Current liabilities |  |  |
| Trade payables | (250) | (226) |
| Tax | (60) | (36) |
|  | (310) | (262) |
| Net current assets | 938 | 700 |
| Loans | (300) | (260) |
| Net assets | 952 | 800 |
| Share capital | 400 | 400 |
| Retained profits (1) | 552 | 400 |
|  | 952 | 800 |

1  Retained profits 20X2: $400 (pre-acquisition profit) + $180 (profit for the year) minus $28 (dividend).

Translate the financial statements of Jing prior to consolidation with Bei the holding entity. Calculate the exchange differences to be included in other comprehensive income, including the exchange difference on goodwill.

### Activity feedback

Jing's financial statements need to be translated into the presentation currency before consolidation, thus we need to use the closing rate method. Therefore statement of comprehensive income items will be translated at the average rate of 1.65 and all assets and liabilities at the closing rate of 1.5 for 20X2, 2.0 for 20X1.

Jing statement of profit or loss for the year ended 31 December 20X2

|  | $000 |  | £000 |
|---|---|---|---|
| Operating profit | 270 | 1.65 | 163.7 |
| Interest paid | (30) | 1.65 | (18.2) |
| Profit before tax | 240 |  | 145.5 |
| Tax | (60) | 1.65 | (36.4) |
| Profit after tax | 180 | 1.65 | 109.1 |

Jing statement of financial position as at 31 December

|  | 20X2 | 1.5 | 20X1 | 2.0 |
|---|---|---|---|---|
|  | $000 | $000 | $000 | $000 |
| Non-current assets at cost | 510 | 340 | 450 | 225 |
| Depreciation | (196) | (130.7) | (90) | (45) |
|  | 314 | 209.3 | 360 | 180 |
| Current assets |  |  |  |  |
| Inventory | 348 | 232 | 252 | 126 |
| Trade receivables | 420 | 280 | 290 | 145 |
| Cash | 480 | 320 | 420 | 210 |
|  | 1248 | 832 | 962 | 481 |

(Continued)

## ACTIVITY 30.6   (*Continued*)

*Jing statement of financial position as at 31 December (continued)*

|  | 20X2 $000 | 1.5 $000 | 20X1 $000 | 2.0 $000 |
|---|---|---|---|---|
| Current liabilities |  |  |  |  |
| Trade payables | (250) | (166.7) | (226) | (113) |
| Tax | (60) | (40) | (36) | (18) |
|  | (310) | (206.7) | (262) | (131) |
| Net current assets | 938 | 625.3 | 700 | 350 |
|  |  |  |  |  |
| Loans | (300) | (200) | (260) | (913) |
| Net assets | 952 | 634.6 | 800 | 400 |
| Share capital | 400 | 200 (1) | 400 | 200 |
| Retained profits | 552 | 434.6 | 400 | 200 |
|  | 952 | 634.6 | 800 | 400 |

*Share capital remains translated at the original rate (2.0).*

*The retained profit figure of £434 600 includes an exchange difference to be identified separately as follows:*

– *exchange difference on opening balance of assets and liabilities: 800 / 1.5 – 800 / 2.0 = 133.3 credit, plus*

– *difference between translating net profit at closing rate and net profit at average rate: 180 / 1.5 – 180 / 1.65 = 10.9 credit, plus*

– *difference between translating dividend paid at closing rate and at the rate at the moment of*

*payment: 28 / 1.5 – 28 / 1.75 = 2.7 debit (this is a debit as dividend payments is a reduction of retained earnings)*

– *total: £141 500 credit (gain)*

*From the perspective of Bei there is another exchange difference: on goodwill. Assuming no impairment, this exchange difference is £33.333 (200 000 / 1.5 – 200 000 / 2); this is a gain.*

*The total exchange difference of £ 174 833 is a separate component of equity in the consolidated accounts of Bei (Translation reserve), see Activity 30.7.*

## ACTIVITY 30.7

This activity is a follow up of Activity 30.6.

*Summarized statement of financial position of Bei 31 December 20X2*

|  | 20X2 | 20X1 |
|---|---|---|
| Investment in subsidiary (1m @ 2.0 date of acquisition) | 500 | 500 |
| Cash | 416 | 400 |
|  | 916 | 900 |
| Share capital | 900 | 900 |
| Retained profits (dividend received 28 @ 1.75 date of translation) | 16 | |
|  | 916 | 900 |

Note that the statement of financial position of Bei uses the temporal method to translate the dividend and investment in subsidiary as we are translating these to the functional currency (£).

Given the feedback of Activity 30.6, complete the consolidation for 20X2.

### Activity feedback

*Consolidated statement of profit and loss 31 December 20X2*

| | |
|---|---|
| Operating profit of Jing | 163.7 |
| Operating profit of Bei | 16 |
|  | 179.7 |
| Elimination of inter-entity dividend | (16) |
|  | 163.7 |
| Interest paid | (18.2) |
|  | 145.5 |
| Tax | (36.4) |
|  | 109.1 |

*(Continued)*

## ACTIVITY 30.7    *(Continued)*

*Consolidated statement of financial position as at 31 December 20X2*

| | |
|---|---:|
| Goodwill | 133.3 |
| Non-current assets | 209.3 |
| | 342.6 |
| Current assets | |
| Inventory | 232 |
| Trade receivables | 280 |
| Cash (416 + 320) | 736 |
| | 1 248 |
| Current liabilities | |
| Trade payables | (166.7) |
| Tax | (40) |
| | 206.7 |

*Consolidated statement of financial position as at 31 December 20X2*

| | |
|---|---:|
| Net current assets | 1 041.3 |
| Loan | (200) |
| | 1 183.9 |
| Share capital | 900 |
| Retained profits | 109.1 |
| Translation reserve | 174.8 |
| | 1 183.9 |

*The exchange differences for 20X2 of £174 833 are recognized as other comprehensive income. Total comprehensive income 20X2 is £283 933 (£109.100 + £174 833).*

# HEDGE ACCOUNTING

An entity that has transactions or monetary positions in a foreign currency (all currencies other than the functional currency) is exposed to foreign currency risk. We have seen that exchange differences arising from translating the foreign currency monetary positions into the functional currency will affect profit or loss. An entity can protect itself from the exchange risk by, for instance, buying derivatives such as foreign currency swaps, options or forwards. The hedge accounting for these financial instruments has been discussed in Chapter 18.

Another form of exchange risk is a result of translating the financial statements of foreign entities from their functional currency into a different presentation currency. These exchange differences do not directly affect profit or loss (although this might happen on disposal, see below), but they have impact on other comprehensive income and equity. Although there are no direct cash flow consequences, unless profit is paid out by way of dividend, an entity might have good reasons to protect itself also against these accounting translation differences. One good reason might be to limit the volatility of equity.

One way of hedging the exposure position of the investment (share in equity) in a foreign operation is to raise loans in a foreign country denominated in the functional currency of the foreign operation. From the point of view of the home (investing) entity it has:

- an asset, exposed to an exchange risk
- a liability also exposed to an exchange risk.

Because the exchange risk of the liability compensates the exchange risk of the asset, this is a form of hedging. Normally, in the consolidated financial statements the exchange differences on the asset (the net investment = assets minus liabilities of the investee, translated at closing rate) would be recognized in other comprehensive income (outside profit or loss), but the exchange difference of the loan from the foreign currency to the functional currency (being a transaction of the investing entity) would be recorded in profit or loss. As an exception, IAS 21 requires us to classify as other comprehensive income those exchange differences arising on a foreign currency liability where that liability is used as a 'hedge'.

Interestingly, IAS 21 does not deal with hedge accounting for foreign currency items in much detail and we have to refer to IAS 39 for further guidance. The criteria in IAS 39 used to identify a hedge are as follows:

- At the inception of the hedge there is a formal document to support classification as a hedge.
- The hedge is expected to be highly effective.
- A forecasted transaction which is the subject of the hedge must be highly probable.
- The effectiveness of the hedge can be reliably measured.
- The hedge was assessed on an ongoing basis and determined actually to have been highly effective throughout the financial reporting period.

For a further discussion on hedge accounting refer to Chapter 18.
Now complete the following activity.

## ACTIVITY 30.8

An entity whose year-end is 31 March, and which prepares its accounts in £ sterling, takes out two loans on 1 August, one for €50 000 and one for $30 000, when the exchange rates were £1 = €1.80 and £1 = $1.60. The $ loan is used to make an equity investment of $30 000 at £1 = $1.60. At the same time another equity investment is the purchase of 100 000 Australian dollars (A$): £1 = A$1.9. How would this be shown in the entity's books at the year-end when £1 = €1.86 = $1.5 = A$1.95 given the reporting currency is £?

### Activity feedback
Initially, when the loans and investments are taken up they will need to be recorded in the books in £s as follows:

- Loan €: £27 778 (50 000 / 1.8) credit
- Loan $: £18 750 (30 000 / 1.6) credit
- Investment $: £18 750 (30 000 / 1.6) debit
- Investment A$: £52 632 (100 000 / 1.9) debit

In the consolidated financial statements long-term monetary items, i.e. the € loan and the $ loan, will be translated at year-end exchange rates (closing rates), as well as the investments (either the consolidated assets and liabilities of the investments or the investments in associates applying the equity method). Normally, all exchange differences on the loans will be recognized in profit or loss and exchange differences on the investments will be recognized in other comprehensive income. In this case, however, when the investing entity applies hedge accounting documenting that the $ investment is hedged with the $ loan, the exchange difference on the loan avoids profit and loss and is included in other comprehensive income.

At year end:

- Loan €: £26 882 (50 000 / 1.86) credit; exchange gain £896 in profit and loss
- Loan $: £20 000 (30 000 / 1.5) credit; exchange loss £1250 in other comprehensive income
- Investment $: £20 000 (30 000 / 1.5) debit; exchange gain £1250 in other comprehensive income
- Investment A$: £51 282 (100 000 / 1.95) debit; exchange loss £1350 in other comprehensive income.

## SOME OTHER ISSUES

In this section we deal with a few other issues:

- Extending the net investment
- Goodwill and fair value adjustments
- Disposal of a foreign entity
- Hyperinflationary economies
- Disclosure requirements

We have concluded in this chapter that exchange differences on accounting for transactions and events in foreign currencies into the functional currency are recognized in profit or loss while exchange differences that arise on consolidating foreign entities in the presentation currency are recognized in other comprehensive income. As discussed, an exception to this is hedge accounting. There is one more exception: in addition to investing in the equity of the foreign entity, a parent may also give a long-term or permanent loan in the functional currency of the foreign entity. Such a loan would be considered a part of the parent's net investment in the foreign entity: the exchange differences on this loan will also be recognized in other comprehensive income and not in profit or loss. The same holds for the reverse situation, where a foreign entity gives a loan in its functional currency to the parent: this would reduce the net investment and the exchange differences on this borrowing would also be recognized in other comprehensive income.

Goodwill and fair value adjustments are recognized by the acquirer in a business combination (see Chapter 26). They are not pushed down to the acquiree/subsidiary in their financial statements. However, for translating foreign entities from their functional currency to the presentation currency all goodwill and fair value adjustments are treated as assets and liabilities of the foreign operation. Thus they shall be expressed in the functional currency of the foreign operation and shall be translated at closing rate.

Disposal of a foreign entity is dealt with in accordance with para. 48 of IAS 21. On the disposal of a foreign operation, the cumulative amount of the exchange differences deferred in the separate component of equity relating to that foreign operation should be recognized in profit or loss. As a result, in profit or loss both the gain or loss on disposal and all exchange differences recognized in other comprehensive income (both on the investment and on the loans used for hedging) are recognized. This has no effect on total comprehensive income, as these realized exchange differences have already been recognized in other comprehensive income as part of the total comprehensive income. This is what we call 'recycling': the amount included in other comprehensive income in earlier years is now recycled to profit and loss. The exchange gain (or loss) recognized in profit and loss will be fully compensated by the loss (or gain) recognized in other comprehensive income.

IFRS has some specific requirements for those entities reporting in a currency of a hyperinflationary economy. The financial statements of such a foreign entity have to be dealt with in accordance with IAS 29 before the requirements of IAS 21 are applied. IAS 29 requires (in para. 8) that:

> The financial statements of an entity whose functional currency is the currency of a hyperinflationary economy, whether they are based on a historical cost approach or a current cost approach, should be stated in terms of the

measuring unit current at the statement of financial position date. The corresponding figures for the previous period required by IAS 1, *Presentation of Financial Statements*, and any information in respect of earlier periods should also be stated in terms of the measuring unit current at the statement of financial position date.

Paragraph 9 goes on to state: 'The gain or loss on the net monetary position should be included in profit or loss and separately disclosed.'

This means that, before translating transactions and events into the functional currency, the effects of general inflation should be taken into account by using a stable current measuring unit. We will not further discuss the techniques for this 'restate–translate' procedure.

Paragraphs 51–57 of IAS 21 require certain disclosures, among others:

- The amount of exchange differences recognized in profit or loss
- The amount of exchange differences recognized in other comprehensive income
- The amount of the separate component of equity (Translation reserve), and a reconciliation between the beginning and the end of the period
- The functional currency of the parent and the presentation currency of the parent and the group and the reason why they are different, if so.

## ANNUAL REPORT

### Heineken Consolidated Statement of Comprehensive Income

| | Note | 2012 | 2011 |
|---|---|---|---|
| **For the year ended 31 December** | | | |
| *In millions of EUR* | | | |
| **Profit** | | **3 109** | **1 560** |
| **Other comprehensive income:** | | | |
| Foreign currency translation differences for foreign operations | 24 | 45 | (493) |
| Effective portion of change in fair value of cash flow hedges | 24 | 14 | (21) |
| Effective portion of cash flow hedges transferred to profit or loss | 24 | 41 | (11) |
| Ineffective portion of cash flow hedges (transferred to profit or loss) | 24 | – | – |
| Net change in fair value available-for-sale investments | 24 | 135 | 71 |
| Net change in fair value available-for-sale investments transferred to profit or loss | 24 | (148) | (1) |
| Actuarial gains and losses | 24/28 | (439) | (93) |
| Share of other comprehensive income of associates/joint ventures | 24 | (1) | (5) |
| **Other comprehensive income, net of tax** | **24** | **(353)** | **(553)** |
| **Total comprehensive income** | | **2 756** | **1 007** |
| Attributable to: | | | |
| Equity holders of the Company | | 2 608 | 884 |
| Non-controlling interests | | 148 | 123 |
| **Total comprehensive income** | | **2 756** | **1 007** |

*(Continued)*

# Consolidated Statement of Changes in Equity

| In millions of EUR | Note | Share capital | Share Premium | Translation reserve | Hedging reserve | Fair value reserve | Other legal reserves | Reserve for own shares | ASDI | Retained earnings | Equity attributable to equity holders of the Company | Non-controlling interests | Total equity |
|---|---|---|---|---|---|---|---|---|---|---|---|---|---|
| **Balance as at 1 January 2011** | | **922** | **2 701** | **(93)** | **(27)** | **90** | **899** | **(55)** | **666** | **4 829** | **9 932** | **288** | **10 220** |
| Other comprehensive income | 12/24 | – | – | (482) | (42) | 69 | – | – | – | (91) | (546) | (7) | (553) |
| Profit | | – | – | – | – | – | 253 | – | – | 1 177 | 1 430 | 130 | 1 560 |
| **Total comprehensive income** | | **–** | **–** | **(482)** | **(42)** | **69** | **253** | **–** | **–** | **1 086** | **884** | **123** | **1 007** |
| Transfer to retained earnings | | – | – | – | – | – | (126) | – | – | 126 | – | – | – |
| Dividends to shareholders | | – | – | – | – | – | – | – | – | (474) | (474) | (97) | (571) |
| Purchase/reissuance own/non-controlling shares | | – | – | – | – | – | – | (687) | – | – | (687) | (1) | (688) |
| Allotted Share Delivery Instrument | | – | – | – | – | – | – | 694 | (666) | (28) | – | – | – |
| Own shares delivered | | – | – | – | – | – | – | 5 | – | (5) | – | – | – |
| Share-based payments | | – | – | – | – | – | – | – | – | 11 | 11 | – | 11 |
| Share purchase mandate | | – | – | – | – | – | – | – | – | 96 | 96 | – | 96 |
| Acquisition of non-controlling interests without a change in control | | – | – | – | – | – | – | – | – | (21) | (21) | (1) | (22) |
| Disposal of interests without a change in control | | – | – | – | – | – | – | – | – | 33 | 33 | 6 | 39 |
| **Balance as at 31 December 2011** | | **922** | **2 701** | **(575)** | **(69)** | **159** | **1 026** | **(43)** | **–** | **5 653** | **9 774** | **318** | **10 092** |

(Continued)

| In millions of EUR | Note | Share capital | Share Premium | Translation reserve | Hedging reserve | Fair value reserve | Other legal reserves | Reserve for own shares | Retained earnings | Equity attributable to equity holders of the Company | Non-controlling interests | Total equity |
|---|---|---|---|---|---|---|---|---|---|---|---|---|
| **Balance as at 1 January 2012** | | **922** | **2 701** | **(575)** | **(69)** | **159** | **1 026** | **(43)** | **5 653** | **9 774** | **318** | **10 092** |
| Other comprehensive income | 12/24 | – | – | 48 | 58 | (9) | 4 | – | (442) | (341) | (12) | (353) |
| Profit | | – | – | – | – | – | 222 | – | 2 727 | 2 949 | 160 | 3 109 |
| **Total comprehensive income** | | **–** | **–** | **48** | **58** | **(9)** | **226** | **–** | **2 285** | **2 608** | **148** | **2 756** |
| Transfer to retained earnings | | – | – | – | – | – | (473) | – | 473 | – | – | – |
| Dividends to shareholders | | – | – | – | – | – | – | – | (494) | (494) | (110) | (604) |
| Purchase/reissuance own/non-controlling shares | | | | | | | | | | | | |
| Own shares delivered | | – | – | – | – | – | – | 17 | (17) | – | – | – |
| Share-based payments | | – | – | – | – | – | – | – | 15 | 15 | – | 15 |
| Share purchase mandate | | – | – | – | – | – | – | – | – | – | – | – |
| Acquisition of non-controlling interests without a change in control | | – | – | – | – | – | – | – | (212) | (212) | 715 | 503 |
| Disposal of interests without a change in control | | – | – | – | – | – | – | – | – | – | – | – |
| **Balance as at 31 December 2012** | | **922** | **2 701** | **(527)** | **(11)** | **150** | **779** | **(26)** | **7 703** | **11 691** | **1 071** | **12 762** |

(Continued)

## (b) Foreign currency

### (i) Foreign currency transactions

Transactions in foreign currencies are translated to the respective functional currencies of HEINEKEN entities at the exchange rates at the dates of the transactions. Monetary assets and liabilities denominated in foreign currencies at the reporting date are retranslated to the functional currency at the exchange rate at that date. The foreign currency gain or loss arising on monetary items is the difference between amortized cost in the functional currency at the beginning of the period, adjusted for effective interest and payments during the period, and the amortized cost in foreign currency translated at the exchange rate at the end of the reporting period.

Non-monetary assets and liabilities denominated in foreign currencies that are measured at fair value are retranslated to the functional currency at the exchange rate at the date that the fair value was determined.

Non-monetary items in a foreign currency that are measured in terms of historical cost are translated using the exchange rate at the date of the transaction. Foreign currency differences arising on retranslation are recognized in profit or loss, except for differences arising on the retranslation of available-for-sale (equity) investments and foreign currency differences arising on the retranslation of a financial liability designated as a hedge of a net investment, which are recognized in other comprehensive income.

Non-monetary assets and liabilities denominated in foreign currencies that are measured at cost remain translated into the functional currency at historical exchange rates.

### (ii) Foreign operations

The assets and liabilities of foreign operations, including goodwill and fair value adjustments arising on acquisition, are translated to euro at exchange rates at the reporting date. The income and expenses of foreign operations, excluding foreign operations in hyperinflationary economies, are translated to euro at exchange rates approximating the exchange rates ruling at the dates of the transactions. Group entities, with a functional currency being the currency of a hyperinflationary economy, first restate their financial statements in accordance with IAS 29, *Financial Reporting in Hyperinflationary Economies* (see 'Reporting in hyperinflationary economies' below). The related income, costs and balance sheet amounts are translated at the foreign exchange rate ruling at the balance sheet date.

Foreign currency differences are recognized in other comprehensive income and are presented within equity in the translation reserve. However, if the operation is a non-wholly-owned subsidiary, then the relevant proportionate share of the translation difference is allocated to the non-controlling interests. When a foreign operation is disposed of such that control, significant influence or joint control is lost, the cumulative amount in the translation reserve related to that foreign operation is reclassified to profit or loss as part of the gain or loss on disposal. When HEINEKEN disposes of only part of its interest in a subsidiary that includes a foreign operation while retaining control, the relevant proportion of the cumulative amount is reattributed to non-controlling interests. When HEINEKEN disposes of only part of its investment in an associate or joint venture that includes a foreign operation while retaining significant influence or joint control, the relevant proportion of the cumulative amount is reclassified to profit or loss.

Foreign exchange gains and losses arising from a monetary item receivable from or payable to a foreign operation, the settlement of which is neither planned nor likely in the foreseeable future, are considered to form part of a net investment in a foreign operation and are recognized in other comprehensive income, and are presented within equity in the translation reserve.

*(Continued)*

## 3. Significant accounting policies

The following exchange rates, for the most important countries in which HEINEKEN has operations, were used while preparing these consolidated financial statements:

| In EUR | Year-end 2012 | Year-end 2011 | Average 2012 | Average 2011 |
|---|---|---|---|---|
| BRL | 0.3699 | 0.4139 | 0.3987 | 0.4298 |
| GBP | 1.2253 | 1.1972 | 1.2332 | 1.1522 |
| MXN | 0.0582 | 0.0554 | 0.0592 | 0.0578 |
| NGN | 0.0049 | 0.0049 | 0.0050 | 0.0047 |
| PLN | 0.2455 | 0.2243 | 0.2390 | 0.2427 |
| RUB | 0.0248 | 0.0239 | 0.0250 | 0.0245 |
| SGD | 0.6207 | 0.5946 | 0.6229 | 0.5718 |
| VND in 1000 | 0.0364 | 0.0367 | 0.0373 | 0.0348 |
| USD | 0.7579 | 0.7729 | 0.7783 | 0.7184 |

### (iii) Reporting in hyperinflationary economies

When the economy of a country in which we operate is deemed hyperinflationary and the functional currency of a Group entity is the currency of that hyperinflationary economy, the financial statements of such Group entities are adjusted so that they are stated in terms of the measuring unit current at the end of the reporting period. This involves restatement of income and expenses to reflect changes in the general price index from the start of the reporting period and, restatement of non-monetary items in the balance sheet, such as P, P & E to reflect current purchasing power as at the period end using a general price index from the date when they were first recognized. Comparative amounts are not adjusted. Any differences arising were recorded in equity on adoption.

### (iv) Hedge of net investments in foreign operations

Foreign currency differences arising on the retranslation of a financial liability designated as a hedge of a net investment in a foreign operation are recognized in other comprehensive income to the extent that the hedge is effective and regardless of whether the net investment is held directly or through an intermediate parent. These differences are presented within equity in the translation reserve. To the extent that the hedge is ineffective, such differences are recognized in profit or loss. When the hedged part of a net investment is disposed of, the relevant amount in the translation reserve is transferred to profit or loss as part of the profit or loss on disposal.

## 12. Net finance income and expenses

### Recognized in profit or loss

| In millions of EUR_ | 2012 | 2011 |
|---|---|---|
| **Interest income** | **62** | **70** |
| **Interest expenses** | **(551)** | **(494)** |
| Dividend income on available-for-sale investments | 2 | 2 |
| Dividend income on investments held for trading | 23 | 11 |
| Net gain/(loss) on disposal of available-for-sale investments | 192 | 1 |
| Net change in fair value of derivatives | (7) | 96 |
| Net foreign exchange gain/(loss) | 15 | (107) |
| Impairment losses on available-for-sale investments | – | – |
| Unwinding discount on provisions | (7) | (7) |
| Other net financial income/(expenses) | 1 | (2) |
| **Other net finance income/(expenses)** | **219** | **(6)** |
| **Net finance income/(expenses)_** | **(270)** | **(430)** |

*(Continued)*

Included in other net finance income on the line Net gain/(loss) on disposal of available-for-sale investments are the sale of our 9.3 per cent minority shareholding in Cerveceria Nacional Dominicana S.A. in the Dominican Republic leading to a gain on disposal of the available-for-sale investment of pre-tax EUR175 million and the revaluation of HEINEKEN's existing 22.5 per cent interest in Brasserie d'Haiti of EUR20 million.

## Recognized in other comprehensive income

| In millions of EUR_ | 2012 | 2011 |
|---|---|---|
| Foreign currency translation differences for foreign operations | 45 | (493) |
| Effective portion of changes in fair value of cash flow hedges | 14 | (21) |
| Effective portion of cash flow hedges transferred to profit or loss | 41 | (11) |
| Ineffective portion of cash flow hedges transferred to profit or loss | – | – |
| Net change in fair value of available-for-sale investments | 135 | 71 |
| Net change in fair value available-for-sale investments transferred to profit or loss | (148) | (1) |
| Actuarial (gains) and losses | (439) | (93) |
| Share of other comprehensive income of associates/joint ventures | (1) | (5) |
| | (353) | (553) |
| Recognized in: | – | – |
| Fair value reserve | (9) | 69 |
| Hedging reserve | 58 | (42) |
| Translation reserve | 48 | (482) |
| Other | (450) | (98) |
| | (353) | (553) |

## 24. Income tax on other comprehensive income

| In millions of EUR | Amount before tax | Tax | 2012 Amount net of tax | Amount before tax | Tax | 2011 Amount net of tax |
|---|---|---|---|---|---|---|
| **Other comprehensive income** | | | | | | |
| Foreign currency translation differences for foreign operations | 67 | (22) | 45 | (504) | 11 | (493) |
| Effective portion of changes in fair value of cash flow hedge | 16 | (2) | 14 | (31) | 10 | (21) |
| Effective portion of cash flow hedges transferred to profit or loss | 57 | (16) | 41 | (14) | 3 | (11) |
| Ineffective portion of cash flow hedges transferred to profit or loss | – | – | – | – | – | – |
| Net change in fair value available-for-sale investments | 203 | (68) | 135 | 71 | – | 71 |
| Net change in fair value available-for-sale investments transferred to profit or loss | (192) | 44 | (148) | (1) | – | (1) |
| Actuarial gains and losses | (562) | 123 | (439) | (109) | 16 | (93) |
| Share of other comprehensive income of associates/joint ventures | (1) | – | (1) | (5) | – | (5) |
| **Total other comprehensive income** | **(412)** | **59** | **(353)** | **(593)** | **40** | **(553)** |

The difference between the income tax on other comprehensive income and the deferred tax reported in equity (note 18) can be explained by current tax on other comprehensive income.

## SUMMARY

Foreign currency translation is a fascinating topic but not an easy one to grasp. It is difficult to get to grips with the logic of applying one set of rules to translation to functional currency and another to presentation currency. Remember:

- Within a group, each individual entity should determine its functional currency. The functional currency is the currency of the primary economic environment in which the entity operates.

- An entity should translate all transactions into its functional currency. For individual entity transactions non-monetary items are translated at originating exchange rate but monetary items at closing rate if not settled. Thus unrealized gains and losses due to foreign currency fluctuations will be taken to profit or loss generally as part of ordinary activities. This is the temporal method.

- Foreign entities translating to presentation currency use the closing rate for statement of financial position and average rate (generally) for statement of comprehensive income. This usually occurs when there is a need to prepare consolidated financial statements. Exchange differences are taken to other comprehensive income.

- In a few specific cases exchange differences on transactions are not taken to profit or loss, but are recognized on other comprehensive income: Loans to hedge the net investment and extensions or reductions of the net investment by intercompany borrowings.

- Goodwill and fair value adjustments are treated as assets and liabilities of the foreign operation and need to be translated at closing rates.

- Upon disposal of a foreign entity, the cumulative exchange differences will be included in profit or loss.

- Foreign operations in hyperinflationary economies have to be stated in the measuring unit current at the statement of financial position date before translation.

## EXERCISES

*Suggested answers to exercises marked ✓ are to be found on our dedicated CourseMate platform for students.*

  *Suggested answers to the remaining exercises are to be found on the Instructor online support resources.*

**1**  Explain the differences in treatment and the effect of translating financial statements using the temporal and closing rate method.

**2**  Identify the circumstances under which IAS 21 permits the use of the closing rate method and the temporal method for translation of financial statements.

✓ **3**  Should exchange differences appear in the statement of comprehensive income of an entity or be charged direct to reserves? State the reasons for your answer.

**4**  What is the difference between foreign currency conversion and foreign currency translation?

✓ **5**  Critically appraise the concepts on which the closing rate and temporal methods are based and discuss the factors that will be taken into account by a group choosing between the two methods.

**6**    What is 'hedge accounting'? Identify the requirements of IAS 21 in accounting for hedges.

**7**    The statement of comprehensive incomes for Home and its wholly owned subsidiary Foreign for the year ended 31 July 2006 are shown below:

|  | Home | Foreign |
|---|---|---|
|  | $000 | Crowns 000 |
| Revenue | 3 000 | 650 |
| Cost of sales | (2 400) | (550) |
| Gross profit | 600 | 100 |
| Distribution costs | (32) | (41) |
| Administrative expenses | (168) | (87) |
| Finance costs | (15) | (10) |
| Profit (Loss) before tax | 385 | (38) |
| Income tax | (102) | 10 |
| Profit (Loss) for the period | 283 | (28) |

Notes

1    The presentation currency of the group is the $ and Foreign's functional currency is the Crown.

2    Home acquired 100 per cent of the ordinary share capital of Foreign on 1 August 2004 for 204 000 Crowns. Foreign's share capital at that date comprised 1000 ordinary shares of 1 Crown each, and its reserves were 180 000 Crowns. In view of its subsidiary's losses, Home's directors conducted an impairment review of the goodwill at 31 July 2006. They concluded that the goodwill had lost 20 per cent of its value during the year (before taking exchange differences into account). The impairment should be reflected in the consolidated financial statements for the year ended 31 July 2006.

3    On 1 June 2006, Home purchased an item of plant for 32 000 Florins. At the year end, the payable amount had not yet been settled. No exchange gain or loss in respect of this item is reflected in Home's statement of comprehensive income above.

4    Exchange rates are as follows:

| On 1 August 2004: | 1.7 Crowns = $1 |
|---|---|
| On 31 July 2006: | 2.2 Crowns = $1 |
| Average rate for year ended 31 July 2006: | 2.4 Crowns = $1 |
| On 1 June 2006: | 1.5 Florins = $1 |
| On 31 July 2006: | 1.6 Florins = $1 |

**Required:**

Prepare the consolidated statement of comprehensive income for the Home group for the year ended 31 July 2006. (Work to the nearest $100.)

**8**    Memo, a public limited company, owns 75 per cent of the ordinary share capital of Random, a public limited company which is situated in a foreign country. Memo acquired Random on 1 May 2003 for 120m Crowns (CR) when the retained profits of Random were 80m Crowns. Random has not revalued its assets or issued any share capital since its acquisition by Memo. The following financial statements relate to Memo and Random:

## Statement of financial positions at 30 April 2004

|  | Memo $m | Random CRm |
|---|---|---|
| Tangible non-current assets | 297 | 146 |
| Investment in Random | 48 | – |
| Loan to Random | 5 | – |
| Current assets | 355 | 102 |
|  | 705 | 248 |

**Capital and reserves**

|  | Memo $m | Random CRm |
|---|---|---|
| Ordinary shares of $1/1CR | 60 | 32 |
| Share premium account | 50 | 20 |
| Accumulated profit | 360 | 95 |
|  | 470 | 147 |
| Non current liabilities | 30 | 41 |
| Current liabilities | 205 | 60 |
|  | **705** | **248** |

## Statement of comprehensive incomes for year ended 30 April 2004

|  | Memo $m | Random CRm |
|---|---|---|
| Revenue | 200 | 142 |
| Cost of sales | (120) | (96) |
| Gross profit | 80 | 46 |
| Distribution and administrative expenses | (30) | (20) |
| Operating profit | 50 | 26 |
| Interest receivable | 4 | – |
| Interest payable | – | (2) |
| Profit before taxation | 54 | 24 |
| Income tax expense | (20) | (9) |
| Profit after taxation | 34 | 15 |

The following information is relevant to the preparation of the consolidated financial statements of Memo:

(a) The directors wish to treat goodwill in accordance with recent proposals as a foreign currency asset. Goodwill has been subjected to an impairment review as at 30 April 2004 and is deemed to be impaired by $2m.

(b) During the financial year Random has purchased raw materials from Memo and denominated the purchase in crowns in its financial records. The details of the transaction are set out below:

|  | Date of transaction | Purchase price $m | Profit percentage on selling price |
|---|---|---|---|
| Raw materials | 1 February 2004 | 6 | 20% |

At the year-end, half of the raw materials purchased were still in the inventory of Random. The inter-company transactions have not been eliminated from the financial statements and the goods were recorded by Random at the exchange rate ruling on 1 February 2004. A payment of $6m was made to Memo when the exchange rate was 2.2 Crowns to $1. Any exchange gain or loss arising on the transaction is still held in the current liabilities of Random.

(c)  Memo had made an interest free loan to Random of $5m on 1 May 2003. The loan was repaid on 30 May 2004. Random had included the loan in non-current liabilities and had recorded it at the exchange rate at 1 May 2003.

(d)  The fair value of the net assets of Random at the date of acquisition is to be assumed to be the same as the carrying value.

(e)  Random operates with a significant degree of autonomy in its business operations.

(f)  The following exchange rates are relevant to the financial statements:

|  | Crown to $ |
|---|---|
| 30 April/1 May 2003 | 2.5 |
| 1 November 2003 | 2.6 |
| 1 February 2004 | 2 |
| 30 April 2004 | 2.1 |
| Average rate for year to 30 April 2004 | 2 |

(g)  Memo has paid a dividend of $8m during the financial year and this is not included in the statement of comprehensive income.

**Required:**
Prepare a consolidated statement of comprehensive income for the year ended 30 April 2004 and a consolidated statement of financial position at that date in accordance with International Financial Reporting Standards. (Round calculations to the nearest $100 000.)

(ACCA – June 2004)

9  Small was incorporated in 1985 and prior to its acquisition by Big had built up its own customer base and local supplier network. This was not disturbed when Small became a subsidiary of Big as the directors of Big were anxious that the local expertise of the management of Small should be utilized as much as possible. Therefore all the day-to-day operational decisions regarding Small continued to be made by the existing management, with the directors of Big exercising 'arm's-length' strategic control.

The statement of financial positions of Big and Small at 31 March 2003 is given below. The statement of financial position of Small is prepared in florins, the functional currency for Small.

|  | Big $000 | $000 | Small FL000 | FL000 |
|---|---|---|---|---|
| **Non-current assets:** | | | | |
| Property, plant and equipment | 60 000 | | 80 000 | |
| Investments | 9 500 | 69 500 | | 80 000 |
| **Current assets:** | | | | |
| Inventories | 30 000 | | 40 000 | |
| Trade receivables | 25 000 | | 32 000 | |
| Cash | 3 000 | 58 000 | 4 000 | 76 000 |
|  | | 127 500 | | 156 000 |
| **Issued capital and reserves:** | | | | |
| Called up share capital (50 cents/ ½ florin shares) | | 30 000 | | 40 000 |
| Revaluation reserve | | 15 000 | | – |
| Accumulated profits | | 34 000 | | 44 000 |
|  | | 79 500 | | 84 000 |
| **Non-current liabilities:** | | | | |
| Interest-bearing borrowings | 15 000 | | 30 000 | |
| Deferred tax | 5 000 | | 9 000 | |
|  | | 20 000 | | 39 000 |
| **Current liabilities:** | | | | |
| Trade payables | 12 000 | | 15 000 | |
| Tax | 16 000 | 28 000 | 18 000 | 33 000 |
|  | | 127 500 | | 156 000 |

## Notes to the statement of financial positions
### Note 1 – Investment by Big in Small
On 1 April 1997, Big purchased 60 million shares in Small for 57m florins. The accumulated profits of Small showed a balance of 20m florins at that date. The accounting policies of Small are the same as those of Big except that Big revalues its land, whereas Small carries its land at historical cost. Small's land had been purchased on 1 April 1994. On 1 April 1997, the fair value of the land of Small was 6m florins higher than its carrying value in the individual financial statements of that entity. By 31 March 2003, the difference between fair value and carrying value had risen to 11m florins. Apart from this accounting policy difference, no other fair value adjustments were necessary when initially consolidating Small as a subsidiary.

### Note 2 – Intra-group trading
On 6 March 2003, Big sold goods to Small at an invoiced price of $6 000 000, making a profit of 25 per cent on cost. Small recorded these goods in inventory and payables using an exchange rate of 5 florins to $1 (there were minimal fluctuations between the two currencies in the month of March 2003). The goods remained in the inventory of Small at 31 March 2003 but on 29 March 2003, Small sent Big a cheque for 30m florins to clear its payable. Big received and recorded this cash on 3 April 2003.

## Note 3 – Exchange rates

| Date | Exchange rate (florins to $1) |
|---|---|
| 1 April 1994 | 7 |
| 1 April 1997 | 6 |
| 31 March 2002 | 5.5 |
| 31 March 2003 | 5 |
| Weighted average for the year to 31 March 2003 | 5.2 |
| Weighted average for the dates of acquisition of closing inventory | 5.1 |

### Required:

Translate the statement of financial position of Small at 31 March 2003 into $s and prepare the consolidated statement of financial position of the Big Group at 31 March 2003.

(CIMA – May 2003)

**10** Little was incorporated over 20 years ago, operating as an independent entity for 15 years until 1998 when it was taken over by Large. Large's directors decided that the local expertise of Little's management should be utilized as far as possible, and since the takeover they have allowed the subsidiary to operate independently, maintaining its existing supplier and customer bases. Large exercises 'arm's length' strategic control, but takes no part in day-to-day operational decisions.

The statement of financial positions of Large and Little at 31 March 2004 is given below. The statement of financial position of Little is prepared in francos (F), its reporting currency.

| | Large $000 | $000 | Litte F000 | F000 |
|---|---|---|---|---|
| **Non-current assets:** | | | | |
| Property, plant and equipment | 63 000 | | 80 000 | |
| Investments | 12 000 | 75 000 | – | 80 000 |
| **Current assets:** | | | | |
| Inventories | 25 000 | | 30 000 | |
| Trade receivables | 20 000 | | 28 000 | |
| Cash | 6 000 | 51 000 | 5 000 | 63 000 |
| | | 126 500 | | 143 000 |
| **Issued capital and reserves:** | | | | |
| Called up share capital (50 cents/1 Franco shares) | | 30 000 | | 40 000 |
| Revaluation reserve | | – | | 6 000 |
| Accumulated profits | | 35 000 | | 34 000 |
| | | 65 000 | | 80 000 |

|  | Large $000 | $000 | Litte F000 | F000 |
|---|---|---|---|---|
| **Non-current liabilties:** |  |  |  |  |
| Interest-bearing borrowings | 20 000 |  | 25 000 |  |
| Deferred tax | 6 000 | 26 000 | 10 000 | 35 000 |
| **Current liabilties:** |  |  |  |  |
| Trade payables | 25 000 |  | 20 000 |  |
| Tax | 7 000 |  | 8 000 |  |
| Bank overdraft | 3 000 | 35 000 | – | 28 000 |
|  |  | 126 000 |  | 143 000 |

### Notes to the statement of financial positions
### Note 1 – Investment by Large in Little
On 1 April 19X8 Large purchased 36 000 shares in Little for 72m francos. The accumulated profis of Little at that date were 26m francos. Large's accounting policy in respect of goodwill on acquisition is to amortize it on a straight line basis over five years.

### Note 2 – Intra-group trading
Little sells goods to Large, charging a mark-up of one-third on production cost. At 31 March 20X4, Large held $1m (at cost to Large) of goods purchased from Little in its inventories. The goods were purchased during March 20X4 and were recorded by Large using an exchange rate of $1 = 5 francos. (There were minimal fluctuations between the two currencies during March 20X3.) At 31 March 20X3, Large's inventories included no goods purchased from Little. On 29 March 20X4, Large sent Little a cheque for $1m to clear the intra-group payable. Little received and recorded this cash on 3 April 20X4.

### Note 3 – Accounting policies
The accounting policies of the two companies are the same, except that the directors of Little have decided to adopt a policy of revaluation of property, whereas Large includes all property in its statement of financial position at depreciated historical cost. Until 1 April 20X3, Little operated from rented warehouse premises. On that date, the entity purchased a leasehold building for 25m francos, taking out a long-term loan to finance the purchase. The building's estimated useful life at 1 April 20X3 was 25 years, with an estimated residual value of nil, and the directors decided to adopt a policy of straight line depreciation. The building was professionally revalued at 30m francos on 31 March 20X4, and the directors have included the revalued amount in the statement of financial position.[1]

### Note 4 – Exchange rates

| Date | Exchange rate (francos to $1) |
|---|---|
| 1 April 19W8 | 6.0 |
| 31 March 20X3 | 5.5 |
| 31 March 20X4 | 5.0 |
| Weighted average for the year to 31 March 20X4 | 5.2 |
| Weighted average for the dates of acquisition of closing inventory | 5.1 |

[1]Depreciation during the year ended 31.3.X4 was calculated on the historical cost. No other property was owned by Little during the year.

**Required:**

(a) Explain (with reference to relevant accounting standards to support your argument) how the financial statements (statement of financial position and statement of comprehensive income) of Little should be translated into $s for the consolidation of Large and Little.

(b) Translate the statement of financial position of Little at 31 March 20X4 into $s and prepare the consolidated statement of financial position of the Large group at 31 March 20X4.

*Note:* Ignore any deferred tax implications of the property revaluation and the intra-group trading.

11    On 1 November 2003, DX invested in 100 per cent of the share capital of EY, a new entity incorporated on that date. EY's operations are located in a foreign country where the currency is the Franc. DX has no other subsidiaries.

The summary financial statements of the two entities at their 31 October 2008 year-end were as follows:

**Summary income statements for the year ended 31 October 2008**

|  | DX $000 | EY Franc 000 |
| --- | --- | --- |
| **Revenue** | 3 600 | 1 200 |
| Cost of sales, other expenses and income tax | (2 800) | (1 000) |
| **Profit for the period** | 800 | 200 |

**Summary statements of changes in equity for the year ended 31 October 2008**

|  | DX $000 | EY Franc 000 |
| --- | --- | --- |
| Brought forward at 1 November 2007 | 5 225 | 1 500 |
| Profit for the period | 800 | 200 |
| Dividends | (200) | – |
| Carried forward at 31 October 2008 | 5 825 | 1 700 |

**Summary balance sheets at 31 October 2008**

|  | DX $000 | EY Franc 000 |
| --- | --- | --- |
| Property plant and equipment | 5 000 | 1 500 |
| Investment in EY | 25 | – |
| Current assets | 4 400 | 2 000 |
|  | 9 425 | 3 500 |
| Share capital | 1 000 | 50 |
| Retained earnings | 4 825 | 1 650 |
| Current liabilities | 3 600 | 1 800 |
|  | 9 425 | 3 500 |

Relevant exchange rates were as follows:

1 November 2003 1$ = 2.0 francs

31 October 2007 1$ = 2.3 francs

31 October 2008 1$ = 2.7 francs

Average rate for year ended 31 October 2008 1$ = 2.6 francs

**Required:**

(a) Explain the meaning of the term 'functional currency' as used by IAS 21, *The Effects of Changes in Foreign Exchange Rates,* and identify THREE factors that an entity should consider in determining its functional currency.

(b) Prepare:

(i)   the summary consolidated income statement for the year ended 31 October 2008;

(ii)  the summary consolidated balance sheet at 31 October 2008.

(c) Prepare the summary consolidated statement of changes in equity for the year to 31 October 2008 and a calculation that shows how the exchange gain or loss for the year has arisen.

(Work to the nearest $.)

(CIMA P8 – November 2008)

# PART FOUR
# FINANCIAL ANALYSIS

In Part One we focused on what financial reporting is all about – what it is trying to achieve and how the accountant sets about achieving it. Parts Two and Three presented the standards that have been created to govern financial reporting. In those three parts, a preparer's approach to financial reporting was taken as we describe the mechanisms, principles and rules through which financial information is provided to users. In Part Four, a user's approach is followed. In this part we analyze how different stakeholders of a company can use the information provided in the annual accounts to gain some insight as to the reporting entity's stability, performance, future prospects or whatever else may interest them.

# INTERPRETATION OF FINANCIAL STATEMENTS

# 31

**OBJECTIVES** After studying this chapter you should be able to:

- explain how industry analysis can be useful in the context of financial analysis

- explain why knowledge of the corporate strategy is important for financial analysis

- describe the different incentives for annual accounts management

- describe the different variables which enlarge the accounting discretion of management

- identify the practices which are used for annual accounts management purposes

- explain the purpose of entity analysis

- describe what is meant by quality of disclosure

- describe what is meant by accounting quality.

## INTRODUCTION

Financial statements provide valuable information for different stakeholders. In Chapters 1 and 12 we identified the users of accounting information and their differing needs. In Chapter 12 we introduced the basics of ratio analysis. In Part Four of the book, we elaborate further on the topic of financial analysis. The following activity provides a useful piece of revision.

## ACTIVITY 31.1

Identify the users of accounting information and their needs/objectives.

### Activity feedback

- Investors/owners *Is the money invested in the business making a suitable return for them or could it earn more if invested elsewhere? Is the business a safe investment; that is, is it likely to become insolvent/bankrupt? Should the investors invest more money in the business?*

- Suppliers *Is the business able to pay for the goods bought on credit? Will the business continue to be a recipient of the goods the supplier produces?*

- Customers *Is the business able to supply the goods the customer requires and when it requires them? Will the business continue in operation so that guarantees on goods purchased will be met?*

- Lenders *Is there adequate security for the loan made? Does the business make a sufficient profit*

and have enough cash available to make the necessary payments to the lender of interest and capital?

- Employee *Does the business make sufficient profit and have enough cash available to make the necessary payments to the employees? Will the business continue in operation at its current level so that the employee has secure employment?*

- Government *For example, to calculate taxation due or to aid decision making in respect of the economy as a whole of a country.*

- Public *The majority of their needs are in respect of employment, pollution and health and safety, which are not particularly, as yet, provided by financial statements.*

*A prime source of information for all these economic decision makers are the financial statements published by the company.*

Since the financial statements serve as a means of communication with the external stakeholders of a firm, they may sometimes be 'managed' to convey a certain message to the outside world. As well as the financial statements, the whole annual report together with interim statements and other releases of financial information and non-financial information, are subject to this phenomenon of 'manipulation' or 'misrepresentation'. Therefore, it is extremely important for users of financial accounting information to be able to 'undo' this manipulation and to uncover the underlying economic performance of the firm. Economic decision makers must therefore be aware of the incentives a company may have to influence the annual accounts, of the available discretion management enjoys to pursue these incentives and of the means they have available for this purpose.

Knowledge about 'annual accounts management' is as important as a sound knowledge about the techniques of financial analysis in order to understand and judge properly the information provided through the annual accounts. In Part Four we discuss both elements in depth. The topic of 'annual accounts management' will be discussed in this chapter. The techniques of financial analysis (e.g. trend analysis, common size financial statements, ratio analysis and cash flow analysis) are presented and illustrated in Chapter 32.

Financial statements are a source of information about a company since they present a picture of the economic performance of a firm. This economic performance, however, is determined to a large extent by the adopted business strategy or strategies of a firm and by the economic and industrial environment in which a firm is operating. As a result, accounting numbers are a reflection of the strategy adopted and of the industry environment in which the firm operates. Therefore, it is worthwhile gaining a clear insight into the industry and business characteristics of a company before starting with the analysis of its financial statements. Studying the economic and industrial environment of a company together with its strategy is often called 'industry analysis' in textbooks on financial and corporate reporting and analysis.

## INDUSTRY ANALYSIS

In order to determine whether a company is, in fact, able to repay its debt or whether it is making a reasonable profit or is worthwhile to invest in, we need to compare the performance of the company with a benchmark. Besides gaining insight into how a firm's strategy and its business environment have an impact on the data in the annual accounts, industry analysis also provides benchmarking data to financial analysts and all other users of accounting information. For example, boards of directors judge the performance of the top management of the company by comparing the company's performance with the performance of competitors in the same industry. Industry analysis provides benchmarks against which the current performance, the financial status and the investment potential of a particular company can be compared. However, we need to take great care in carrying out this benchmarking so that we do not invalidate the results. In setting benchmarks against which we can compare a company, we must remain aware of the limitations of this comparison. This item will be further elaborated in the next chapter.

## ACTIVITY 31.2

Within the scope of industry analysis, data from other businesses in the same industry or industry averages could be used for comparative or benchmarking purposes in order to evaluate the economic and financial situation of a company. What could be their limitations?

### Activity feedback
- Other businesses *Uses – is our business performing as well? Limitations – businesses may not be truly comparable with regard to size and type, e.g. grocery sole trader compared to supermarket; manufacturer compared to retailer. Further external factors may affect one business, e.g. a lengthy strike. Accounting*

*standards and accounting policies on which accounting information is prepared may be different, e.g. inventory valuations, depreciation, historical cost or revalued amount, treatment of research and development, treatment of goodwill.*

- Industry averages *Industry averages have uses and limitations very similar to those of other businesses. Additionally, an average is simply a figure which takes account of the best but also of the worst.*

*Activity 31.3 repeats information from Chapter 12, but it is included here in a slightly different format for pedagogical reasons.*

Each of the four benchmarks identified is commonly used in assessing business status, performance and potential, but interpretation of accounts is highly subjective and requires skilled judgement, bearing in mind the limitations of these benchmarks.

In the next two sections a brief overview of the elements to be considered in the context of industry analysis will be presented.

## Analysis of the business environment

As different elements of the business and the economic environment of a company have an impact on the revenue and costs levels of the firm, we may state that the competitive environment determines to a certain extent the profit potential of a company. An important element with regard to industry profitability is the level of competition in an industry. This level of competition is influenced by the type of competition, the barriers to entry, the production capacity available in the industry, the existing relationships, agreements and alliances.

The degree of competition in an industry determines to a large extent the price which can be charged for the products or services to the customer. The competition can be perfect competition, monopoly or any form in between. Firms in a monopoly position with no substitutes for their products or services can charge higher prices than firms in a situation of perfect competition with a high number of substitutes and high price elasticity of demand. The danger of substitute products can be avoided if firms are able to differentiate their products or services. This possibility will be determined by the existing switching costs.

The level of price competition in an industry is also a function of the cost structure which is related to the technology used and the existence of economies of scale. If the ratio fixed to variable costs is high, firms have a tendency to engage in price wars in order to fully utilize the production capacity they have invested in. Many economic textbooks mention the airline industry as a typical example of an industry where such a policy is often applied. However, if we analyze more closely the value chain of an airline company then this observation (= high fixed costs) relates only to the transport activities in the value chain of the airline. Other activities in the value chain (such as reservations and sales, catering, handling) have a higher proportion of variable costs in their total cost structure. Therefore, price wars intended to fill up the empty seats in the airplanes will increase costs in the other activity areas of the value chain of an airline, where costs are much more variable.

Another element which characterizes the competitive environment of a firm is the presence of high or low barriers to entry. In industries with low barriers to entry the pricing of existing firms within that industry is more constrained and so is the potential for abnormal profits. Barriers to entry could be created through the technology used, the access to channels of distribution, the supplier relationships and the existence of excess capacity.

A further important aspect of industry analysis is the study of the relation of the input and output market of a firm. As input market we distinguish the labour market, the capital market and the suppliers' market. The power relations in these different markets and the scarcity of the resources determine to a large extent the price a company has to pay for those inputs. For example, in times of economic prosperity the bargaining power of airline pilots with regard to their salaries is much higher than in times of economic downturn, when there is labour-related overcapacity in the airline industry.

The power relations with the buyers in the output market of the firm determine to a large extent the margin which a company can earn. If 80 per cent of the turnover of company X is bought by company Y, then the bargaining position with regard to a price increase on the goods delivered to Y of company X is very weak.

Regulation, or its absence, further characterizes the environment in which a firm operates. Regulation includes, among other things, government regulations, legal requirements and taxation.

The environment of the firm consists mainly of factors that are beyond the control of the management. The only way to avoid certain environmental characteristics is often to switch to another industry or another country. Such changes, however, are not always obvious.

## Analysis of the business strategy and corporate strategy

**Business strategy** The management of a firm will choose what type of business to be in by taking into account environmental and industry characteristics, together with an analysis of strengths and weaknesses of the company. The next step is to decide in which manner the firm is going to compete with other firms within the same industry. This implies choices with regard to the products or services and their characteristics which will be offered, with regard to the type of customers to attract and with regard to how these products or services will be produced. The firm's business strategy is the strategy that managers choose to achieve a competitive advantage. Several typologies to define strategy exist. The most well known is that of Porter. He defines two generic competitive strategies, namely a low-cost strategy and a differentiation strategy (Porter, 1985). Cost leadership can be achieved through economies of scale and scope, economies of learning, efficient production, simpler product design, lower input costs, cost control and leaner organizational processes. A firm following a low-cost strategy in the automobile industry is Hyundai. In the airline business Ryanair, EasyJet and Southwest airlines are important low-cost airlines. Until now they have been successful in their strategy through a combination of several elements such as lower input costs (lower wage levels), efficient production (higher asset utilization through reduced setup time, so more flights a day can be operated), different organizational processes (ticket sales only through the Internet), the use of secondary airports, negotiations with airport authorities whereby costs (landing fees) which had normally a fixed character (= paid per type of plane landed) were given a variable character (= passenger landed) and simpler product design (only transport is offered and passengers need to pay for the extras, e.g. food and drinks and luggage).

A firm following a differentiation strategy seeks to sell a unique product or service. Uniqueness can be achieved through superior customer service, product design and product features, brand loyalty, distribution network or technology. Mercedes Benz or BMW follow a differentiator strategy in the automobile sector. Whether a firm can develop or sustain cost leadership or differentiation depends on the organization of the value chain. 'The value chain is defined as the sequence of business functions in which utility [usefulness] is added to the products or services of an organization' (Horngren *et al.*, 2002, p. 8). These functions are research and development, design of products, services or processes, production, marketing, distribution and customer service. The activities in the value chain of a low-cost competitor will be organized differently from the activities in the value chain of a differentiator.

Firm profitability will be influenced not only by the chosen strategy but also by structural cost drivers such as scale, scope, experience, technology, complexity, executional cost drivers such as workforce involvement, total quality management, capacity utilization, plant layout efficiency, product configuration, linkages with suppliers or customers (Shank and Govindarajan, 1992) and operational cost drivers which are cost drivers specific to activities in the value chain. Although these mentioned cost drivers are usually firm-specific, certain drivers can be distinguished for an industry as a whole.

Research into the cost drivers in the airline industry (Banker and Johnston, 1993) revealed the existence of two different types of cost driver – those related to actual outputs and those related to output capacity. Actual outputs are the number of passengers carried or tons of cargo handled. The number of passengers is the cost driver for handling and catering. Fuel consumption and labour hours for scheduled flight crews and attendants vary more with aircraft size, seating capacity, distance and other characteristics of flights and aircrafts than with the actual number of passengers carried or tons of cargo handled. The cost of aircraft maintenance varies more with the number of flights, hours flown and characteristics of the aircraft such as number of engines than with actual outputs such as number of passengers carried. Executional cost drivers in the airline business are elements such as density of the network and hub concentration.

So, value chain analysis provides insights into how activities in and outside the company are organized and how value is created through these activities for the customer. In the context of value chain analysis, it is important to assess the resources available to a company: physical (i.e. location, equipment), and human and financial resources, together with intangibles (brands, know how). A benchmarking of a company's resources and activities with the resources and activities of a competitor, provides insights into the competitive strength of a company.

Value chain analysis can be taken one step further and be executed on the level of the industry as a whole. SAS presents in its Annual Report an overview of the value chain of the aviation industry:

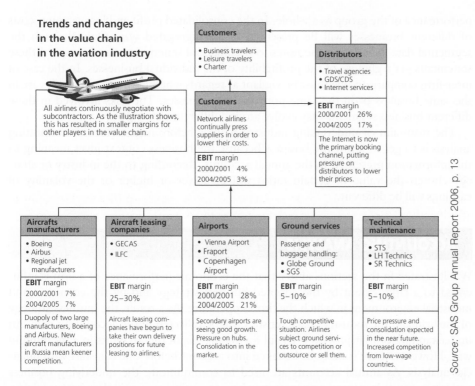

**Trends and changes in the value chain in the aviation industry**

All airlines continuously negotiate with subcontractors. As the illustration shows, this has resulted in smaller margins for other players in the value chain.

**Customers**
- Business travelers
- Leisure travelers
- Charter

**Distributors**
- Travel agencies
- GDS/CDS
- Internet services

**EBIT** margin
2000/2001  26%
2004/2005  17%

The Internet is now the primary booking channel, putting pressure on distributors to lower their prices.

**Customers**

Network airlines continually press suppliers in order to lower their costs.

**EBIT** margin
2000/2001  4%
2004/2005  3%

| Aircrafts manufacturers | Aircraft leasing companies | Airports | Ground services | Technical maintenance |
|---|---|---|---|---|
| • Boeing<br>• Airbus<br>• Regional jet manufacturers | • GECAS<br>• ILFC | • Vienna Airport<br>• Fraport<br>• Copenhagen Airport | Passenger and baggage handling:<br>• Globe Ground<br>• SGS | • STS<br>• LH Technics<br>• SR Technics |
| **EBIT** margin<br>2000/2001  7%<br>2004/2005  7% | **EBIT** margin<br>25–30% | **EBIT** margin<br>2000/2001  28%<br>2004/2005  21% | **EBIT** margin<br>5–10% | **EBIT** margin<br>5–10% |
| Duopoly of two large manufacturers, Boeing and Airbus. New aircraft manufacturers in Russia mean keener competition. | Aircraft leasing companies have begun to take their own delivery positions for future leasing to airlines. | Secondary airports are seeing good growth. Pressure on hubs. Consolidation in the market. | Tough competitive situation. Airlines subject ground services to competition or outsource or sell them. | Price pressure and consolidation expected in the near future. Increased competition from low-wage countries. |

*Source:* SAS Group Annual Report 2006, p. 13

The accounting numbers of a company will be influenced not only by decisions taken with regard to its own competitive position, but also by evolutions in the industry value chain in which the company is active. In order to judge the performance or financial position of a firm properly, its value chain should be compared with the value chain of competitors and the industry value chain.

**Corporate strategy** Some firms operate in only one industry but others are competitive in several.

## ACTIVITY 31.4

Think of companies such as Unilever, Walt Disney Corporation, McDonald's and BMW. In how many businesses are they competitive?

*Activity feedback*

*Single industry:*
McDonald's (fast food)

BMW (car manufacture)

*Multiple businesses:*
Unilever (food, cleansing agents, skincare products)

Walt Disney Corporation (movies, TV channel, theme parks, real estate).

At corporate level the management can choose to be active only in one business or to operate in multiple businesses. Corporate strategy decisions focus on where corporate resources will be invested. Business strategy decisions are concerned with how to compete in defined product markets. Some companies prosper by competing in one industry whereas others operate successfully in different industries.

For financial analysis purposes it is important to know whether a company is a multi-business company, in which case, the consolidated annual accounts reflect the performance of the group as a whole. In the consolidated profit and loss account, costs of different businesses will be presented in an aggregated way. Only through the segmental data included in the notes to the financial statements can the user of these statements get a glimpse of the profitability of the individual businesses. In the case of inter-firm comparison one must be vigilant as regards whether or not companies are in the same business or in the same portfolio of businesses. The risks involved in these different business segments may evolve around different patterns.

The main aim of undertaking industry analysis before one starts with accounting analysis is to get to know the business because the business context gives meaning to the information presented in the annual accounts. According to the industry or strategy chosen the value of certain ratios will be lower or higher or the volatility of earnings will be different.

## ACCOUNTING ANALYSIS

We illustrated in the sections above that the economic performance of a firm is influenced to a large extent by the adopted business strategy and by the economic and industrial environment in which the firm is operating. As a result, the business strategy of the firm and the industry characteristics will be reflected in the accounting data. An understanding of that process is useful for an analysis of the accounts in a meaningful way. However, there is more to be taken into account before one can start with financial analysis. As annual accounts are used to communicate the underlying business reality to outside investors, managers may have incentives to manipulate investors' perceptions or the perception of other stakeholders and to present the performance and financial position of the firm more positively than in actuality. Managers may choose accounting and disclosure policies that make it more difficult for external users of financial statements to understand the true economic performance of the business.

Besides adopting a business strategy, the management can also adopt what is called an 'accounting reporting strategy'. Management may employ a number of accounting methods and accounting estimates – real decisions such that the performance represented through the published accounting numbers deviates from the underlying economic performance. This toolkit of methods, estimates and real decisions used to influence the accounting numbers according to the accounting strategy is used by top management with or without approval from the board of directors. The purpose of accounting analysis is to try to detect what the incentives, opportunities and mechanisms are to misrepresent the financial situation and the performance of a company and to provide an indication as to whether there is a possibility that the underlying economic performance might be different from the performance presented through the accounting numbers.

We now proceed with the discussion of the different elements of accounting analysis. First we analyze the incentives and opportunities management has to influence the accounting numbers. Second we concentrate on the mechanisms (accounting method choice, accounting estimate choice, real transactions) management can use to influence the accounting numbers and which are determined by the amount of accounting flexibility available. This knowledge about the incentives, opportunities and mechanisms available to influence the accounting numbers will enable the external user of the annual accounts to detect more easily the underlying economic performance of the firm and will allow the user to make a more reliable judgement about the underlying economic performance and financial position of that firm.

# Accounting analysis: incentives to manage the annual accounts

The management of a company can have different incentives to manage the accounting numbers which present the performance and the financial position. Academic research into earnings management has shown that earnings management incentives result from the external and internal contracts governing the firm. This stream of research is inspired mainly by the agency paradigm. Among the external contracts governing the firm, we can distinguish between contracts with shareholders, debt holders and the government and other regulatory authorities. The most important internal contract of the firm is that with top management. Academic research provides evidence that incentives to manage accounting numbers are embedded in all contracts. Research into earnings management or financial misrepresentation uses several definitions to describe the phenomenon. We cite two of these definitions here:

> Earnings management is a purposeful intervention in the external financial reporting process, with the intent of obtaining some private gain (as opposed to, say, merely facilitating the neutral operation of the process).

> (Schipper, 1989, p. 92)

> Earnings management occurs when managers use judgement in financial reporting and in structuring transactions to alter financial reports to either mislead some stakeholders about the underlying economic performance of the company, or to influence contractual outcomes that depend on reported accounting numbers.

> (Healy and Wahlen, 1999, p. 368)

In the sections below we make a pedagogical presentation of these incentives towards earnings management, taking into account the contract from which they originate.

## Incentives driven by the contract with shareholders

In the accounting literature there is ample evidence of different characteristics of accounting numbers, which are viewed favourably by current and potential shareholders. Shareholders will appreciate those accounting numbers and react with high share prices and a lower cost of capital. High share prices are beneficial for the company, such as when an initial public offering (IPO) is planned, but also for top management, such as when they have stock options. These characteristics of accounting numbers and disclosure are small loss avoidance (Burghstahler and Dichev, 1997; Burghstahler and Eames, 2006); recurrent and increasing stream of earnings (Barth *et al.*, 1995; DeAngelo *et al.*, 1996; Bloomfield, 2008); low earnings volatility (Trueman and Titman, 1988; Hand, 1989; Bartov, 1993; Hunt *et al.*, 1995); meeting earnings targets or benchmarks (DeGeorge *et al.*, 1999; Kasznik, 1999; Pope *et al.*, 2007; Koonce and Lipe, 2010; Baginski *et al.*, 2011; Cao and Narayanamoorthy, 2011); and reducing information asymmetry through increased voluntary and mandatory disclosure (Healy and Palepu, 1993; Botosan, 1997; Sengupta, 1998; Healy *et al.*, 1999; Leuz and Verrechia, 2000; Bailey *et al.*, 2006; Rogers and Van Buskirk, 2009).

**Small loss avoidance behaviour** It has been noticed that companies tend to avoid small losses and prefer instead to report small profits. Earnings management research has provided evidence for this practice which the research calls 'small loss avoidance'. DeGeorge *et al.* (1999) and Burgstahler and Dichev (1997) present evidence that managers of US firms use accounting discretion to avoid reporting small losses. Small losses are more likely to lie within the bounds of insiders' reporting discretion and, consequently, can be avoided through earnings management. This implies, further, that if a loss cannot be avoided by accounting decisions, companies have a tendency to go for a one-time big loss, which is known as 'big bath accounting'.

**Recurrent and increasing stream of earnings** In periods preceding a capital increase (i.e. pre-IPO period) the management of the company might be tempted to produce a steady stream of increasing earnings over the years. In this situation, earnings are not only smoothed and reported as less volatile but an upward trend of the results is also shown. Some recent studies show that earnings are managed prior to or around IPOs (Friedlan, 1994; Neil *et al.*, 1995) or seasoned equity offerings (Shivakumar, 1998; Rangan, 1998).

**Low earnings volatility** Investors and analysts evaluate an investment in a firm as more risky when the reported results are volatile. This volatility has an impact on the market price of the shares. A higher risk perception means a lower share price. Thus, managers may have an incentive to influence the perception of the capital market with regard to the volatility of the business.

**Meeting earnings targets and benchmarks** The first earnings target a company must achieve in order to be appreciated by the capital market is to meet the previous year's earnings. In addition, top management usually present targets to the capital markets (e.g. in presentations made to financial analysts) which include an improvement in relation to prior periods. When a company does not meet these targets, the company faces a drop in share price (unless the whole industry is facing the same situation). Therefore, the management of a company will always try to meet the target it has put forward. Further, top management must also make sure that they do not perform below the industry average, since the latter is a benchmark used by current and potential shareholders.

## Incentives driven by debt contracts: accounting-based debt covenants

Very often the terms of a lending agreement involve debt covenants which are specified as accounting ratios and may not be violated. A violation of these debt covenants might entail an increase of the interest rate applied to a loan or an immediate repayment of that loan or extra collateral. So managers have an incentive to choose those accounting methods and estimates which reduce the violation of the debt covenant (Sweeney, 1994; Easton *et al.*, 2009; Nikolaev, 2010; Jiang, 2010). Sweeney found further that firms approaching default respond with income increasing accounting changes. Using actual debt covenant violations, DeFond and Jiambalvo (1994) found support for earnings management by managers of firms with debt covenant violations.

It is not compulsory under most GAAP systems to disclose information about debt covenants. The following example taken from the annual accounts of Barry-Callebaut (the largest manufacturer worldwide of cocoa and chocolate products) in the year 2002/2003 is the result of a voluntary disclosure decision made by the firm:

> The term and revolving facilities agreement also contains certain financial covenants, including, amongst others, a maximum senior leverage ratio, a minimum interest cover ratio and a minimum solvency ratio, next to a number of potentially restrictive undertakings limiting or preventing specific business transactions.

> (Note 13, financial statements 2002/2003, p. 96)

As can be seen below, cash flow figures are included in Euro Disney SCA's information on debt covenants:

> The Group's debt agreements include covenants between the Group and the lenders, which were significantly modified as a result of the restructuring. The renegotiated covenants continue to include restrictions on additional indebtedness and capital expenditures, the provision of certain financial information and compliance with the financial covenant based upon the ratios of certain actual and forecasted cash flows (as defined in our bank agreements) to the Group's debt service payment requirements. Compliance with the latter does not begin until fiscal year 2006.

> (Euro Disney SCA Annual Report 2005, p. 25)

**Contracts with governments and regulatory authorities** Tax authorities use accounting data in order to determine the tax base of a company. Accounting methods might be chosen with a tax effect in mind. Especially in continental Europe (e.g. Germany, Belgium, France) there is a strong link between the reported income in the individual accounts of the company and the tax income.

Regulatory agencies may use accounting data to evaluate regulatory policies (e.g. import tariffs, anti-trust actions). Empirical evidence can be found that earnings management is induced by political or regulatory processes (Key, 1997; Guenther et al., 1997).

Articles in company laws with regard to dividend payments, companies in distress and bankruptcy conditions often refer to ratios in the individual or group accounts of a company which may or may not be exceeded or violated. This results in an incentive to manage these ratios if there is a risk that ratios may be violated.

## Incentives driven by employment contracts

In relation to these contracts with top management there is the implicit incentive that top managers want to keep their jobs. Research results do indeed indicate that top managers are dismissed when their firms perform below the average industry performance (Pourciau, 1993; Godfrey et al., 2003). Therefore top management has an incentive to publish a performance which equals the industry average performance.

Alongside such implicit incentives, contracts with top management often also include explicit incentives to manage the accounting numbers.

**Management compensation** Top management compensation often consists of three individual components: a base salary, a bonus plan linked to a certain indicator, and shares or share options. When the bonus plans of top management are linked to reported profits, there is an incentive to choose those accounting methods and accounting estimates which make the company exceed the profit targets stipulated in their compensation contract. This finding not only holds for top management compensation but also for lower-level managers compensated on the basis of accounting numbers. Linking compensation to accounting numbers does not only create incentives for managing those numbers. Jensen and Murphy (1990) claim that paying executives on the basis of accounting profits rather than on changes in shareholder wealth not only generates incentives to manipulate the accounting system but also generates incentives to ignore projects with large net present values in favour of less valuable projects with larger immediate accounting profits.

In his seminal paper in this area, Healy (1985) found support for earnings management by managers of firms with bonus plans linked to accounting numbers. Healy shows that ceilings (i.e. the upper earnings found in the bonus scheme) in compensation contracts have a predictable effect on accounting accruals. Similar studies revealing a positive association between executives' incentives and the presence of earnings management followed after Healy's seminal paper (Cheng and Warfield, 2005; Erickson *et al.*, 2006; Efendi *et al.*, 2007; Jones and Wu, 2010).

Due to this possible negative effect of accounting numbers-based compensation other forms of management compensation emerged. Stock option plans became very popular and 'stock-based performance measures' are often argued to be superior to accounting-based performance measures. However, short-term behaviour of the management might arise when the exercise period of the options is short.

In order to avoid short-termism, bonuses with a long-term perspective can be introduced and combined with a stock option plan that is in alignment with shareholders' interest, in order to stimulate top management behaviour.

## REAL WORLD ILLUSTRATION

Below we illustrate the different components from the remuneration scheme applied by Unilever in relation to their top executives (Unilever Annual Report and Accounts 2012, pp. 64–67). In a transparent way, Unilever communicates the different components of its remuneration policy.

### At a Glance . . .

The key elements of the remuneration for Executive Directors are:

- fixed elements base salary and fixed allowance
- linked to short-term performance annual bonus
- linked to long-term performance MCIP and GSIP.

The following section sets out Unilever's 2013 remuneration policy which remains unchanged from previous years.

## REAL WORLD ILLUSTRATION (Continued)

| Element | Purpose and link to strategy | Operation | Opportunity | Performance metrics | Changes made to policy | Supporting information |
|---|---|---|---|---|---|---|
| **Base salary** | Supports the recruitment and retention of Executive Directors of the calibre required to implement our strategy. | Set by the Boards on the recommendation of the Committee and generally reviewed once a year against three reference points:<br><br>i. peers in other global companies of a similar financial size (market capitalization and turnover) and complexity to Unilever, taking into consideration factors such as the number of employees, human capital complexity and international nature of the business*;<br><br>ii. the individual's skills, experience and performance; and<br><br>iii. pay and conditions across the wider organization.<br><br>Base salaries may be reviewed more often than annually in exceptional circumstances.<br>Base salary changes are usually effective from 1 January. | Unilever's policy is to set the reference point for all Executive Director salaries at around median against an appropriate peer group and then to set individual base salary levels at an appropriate level relative to that reference point by taking into consideration the individual's skills, experience and performance.<br>The Boards, on the proposal of the Committee, apply that approach to manage the base salary levels of the Executive Directors. | n/a | None | For 2013, base salaries for Executive Directors are:<br><br>• CEO £1 010 000<br>• CFO £714 000 |
| **Fixed allowance** | Provides a competitive alternative to the provision of itemized benefits and pension. Simplifies the package. Delinks increases in benefits and allowances from increases in base salary.<br>Paid in cash. | The fixed allowance is reviewed periodically by the Committee against market benchmarks based on other companies of a similar size and complexity in line with the approach to base salary.<br>Changes in the fixed allowance are usually effective from 1 January. | Unilever's policy is to set the reference point for fixed allowances at or below median against an appropriate peer group and then to make as few variations as possible based on individual circumstances.<br>The Boards, on the proposal of the Committee, apply that approach to manage the fixed allowances of the Executive Directors. | n/a | None | For 2013, fixed allowances for Executive Directors are:<br><br>• CEO £250 000<br>• CFO £300 000<br>For the CFO, this includes housing allowance, which is being phased out to nil in 2015. At current rates the CFO's fixed allowance will be reduced to £260 000 per annum in 2014 and to £220 000 per annum in 2015. |
| **Other benefits plus pension** | Provides certain benefits on a cost-effective basis. | Provision of death, disability and medical insurance cover and actual tax return preparation costs.<br>Unilever will also pay the CEO's social security obligation in the CEO's country of residence to protect him against the difference | Social security obligation in CEO's country of residence dependent on earnings in year.<br>Conditional supplemental pension accrual capped from 2012 onwards at 12% of the lower of | n/a | None | For 2013, the accrual for the CEO's conditional supplemental pension will be capped at £117 123.<br>For details of benefits provided during 2012 see page 77. |

## REAL WORLD ILLUSTRATION (Continued)

| Element | Purpose and link to strategy | Operation | Opportunity | Performance metrics | Changes made to policy | Supporting information |
|---|---|---|---|---|---|---|
| | | between the employee social security obligations in his country of residence versus the UK. In line with the commitments made to the CEO upon recruitment, he also receives a conditional supplemental pension accrual to compensate him for the arrangement forfeited on leaving his previous employer. This supplemental pension accrual is conditional on the CEO remaining in employment with Unilever to age 60 and subsequently retiring from active service or his death or total disability prior to retirement. | actual base salary or 2011 base salary (£920 000) plus 3% pa. | | | |
| Annual bonus | The annual bonus has been designed to support our business strategy and the ongoing enhancement of shareholder value through a focus on the delivery of annual financial, strategic and operational objectives. | Unilever targets set annually to ensure they are appropriately stretching for the delivery of threshold, target and maximum performance. Payouts, determined by the Committee, depend on actual performance against targets, the quality of results and performance against personal performance goals. Annual bonuses may be subject to 'clawback' in the event of a significant downward revision of the financial results of the Group. Unless otherwise determined by the Committee, Executive Directors are required to invest at least 25% of their annual bonus into the MCIP (see page 66). | Target bonus opportunities (as percentage of base salary) are: <br>• CEO 120% <br>• other Executive Directors 100% <br>Maximum bonus opportunities (as percentage of base salary) are: <br>• CEO 200% <br>• other Executive Directors 50% | Annual bonus awards are based on: actual performance against Unilever targets, the quality of results and performance against personal performance goals. Performance metrics are selected to support the annual business strategy and the enhancement of shareholder value. Unilever targets and personal performance goals for the Executive Directors are set by the Committee on an annual basis and may be changed as appropriate. | None | For 2013 bonuses, financial performance will be assessed against the following metrics: <br>• underlying sales growth (1/3); <br>• underlying volume growth (1/3); and <br>• core operating margin improvement (1/3). <br>In determining annual bonus awards the Committee also assesses the delivery against personal performance goals and the quality of performance; in terms of both business results and leadership, including corporate social responsibility and progress against the delivery of USLP goals. |
| Management Co-Investment Plan (MCIP) The key terms of the MCIP were approved by shareholders at the 2010 AGM. | The MCIP encourages senior management to shift their focus firmly towards the sustained delivery of high performance results over the longer term by requiring them to invest at least 25% of | Executive Directors are required to buy Unilever's shares out of their after-tax annual bonus. They must invest at least 25% and may invest up to 60% of the value of their gross annual bonus in Unilever's shares (investment shares) and receive a corresponding number of performance-related shares | Vesting of the matching shares ranges between 0% and 150% of the grant level, dependent on actual performance against long-term MCIP targets. As such, the maximum award of matching shares for the CEO and CFO (as a percentage of base salary), assuming a maximum | The Committee sets three-year performance targets for each MCIP matching share award and may change these for future awards as the Committee considers appropriate. | None | Performance metrics for 2013 awards which are measured over the three-year period 2013–2015 are described under the GSIP on page 67. The Committee considers that using the same performance metrics across both the MCIP and GSIP is appropriate, as the performance metrics used reflect our key strategic |

| Element | Purpose and link to strategy | Operation | Maximum | Performance metrics | |
|---|---|---|---|---|---|
| *(MCIP – continued)* | their annual bonus in Unilever's shares and hold those shares for at least 3 years. These shares can earn additional matching shares to the extent that long-term performance targets are met. | (matching shares), which will vest only after three years subject to:<br>• Unilever's performance against long-term MCIP targets over the next three years;<br>• continued employment; and<br>• maintenance of the underlying investment shares.<br>Awards under the MCIP may be subject to 'clawback' in the event of a significant downward revision of the financial results of the Group. Awards under the MCIP are subject to 'ultimate remedy' whereby the Committee may adjust awards where the result is considered unfair | bonus, maximum deferral under the MCIP and maximum performance under the MCIP, would be 180% of base salary and 135% of base salary respectively. | Performance metrics are linked to Unilever's clearly stated growth ambition and our long-term business strategy. | None<br><br>goals and maintain the alignment of our incentive plans to delivering our clearly stated growth ambition. Given that we use four different performance metrics, the Committee believes that the proportion of remuneration linked to each performance condition is not excessive. |
| **Global Share Incentive Plan (GSIP)**<br>The key terms of the GSIP were approved by shareholders at the 2007 AGM. | The GSIP incentivizes Executive Directors to achieve Unilever's clearly stated growth ambition by delivering sustained high performance and sustainable returns for shareholders over the longer term. | Awards of shares are made annually with vesting conditional on Unilever's performance against long-term targets over the next three years.<br>Awards under the GSIP may be subject to 'clawback' in the event of a significant downward revision of the financial results of the Group. Awards under the GSIP are subject to 'ultimate remedy' whereby the Committee may adjust awards where the result is considered unfair | Target awards of conditional shares under the GSIP each year (as a percentage of base salary) are limited to:<br>• CEO – 200%<br>• other Executive Directors – 178%<br>The vesting range for awards of conditional shares is between 0% and 200% of the grant level. Accordingly the maximum award of shares under the GSIP are (as a percentage of base salary):<br>• CEO – 400%<br>• other Executive Directors – 356% | The Committee set three-year performance targets for each conditional GSIP award and may change these for future awards as the Committee considers appropriate. Performance metrics are linked to Unilever's clearly stated growth ambition and its long-term business strategy. | Awards made in 2013 are subject to four equally weighted long-term performance metrics over the three-year period 2013–2015:<br>• underlying sales growth;<br>• core operating margin improvement;<br>• cumulative operating cash flow; and<br>• relative total shareholder return.<br>For the three business focused metrics, 25% of awards vest for threshold performance and 200% for the GSIP (150% for the MCIP) vest for maximum performance.<br>Against the TSR comparator group, comprising 19 other companies (20 including Unilever), 60% vests if Unilever is ranked 10th (which is 53rd percentile performance against this group), 100% vests if Unilever is ranked 7th and 200% for the GSIP (150% for the MCIP) vests if Unilever is ranked 3rd or above.<br>Further details of the TSR comparator group are set out on page 73.<br>When determining the level of vesting the Committee also considers the underlying performance of the business to ensure the payouts are appropriate |

The higher the influence of the bonus and the stock option plan in the total compensation of managers, the stronger the incentive towards earnings management and towards influencing the accounting numbers of the company in such a way that the capital market reacts with an increase in the share price. Despite the expectations that stock option plans would align shareholders' interests with the interest of management, research evidence is now available which shows that stock option plans also induce top management towards earnings management. This information about top management compensation structure can be found in the notes of the annual accounts or in the corporate governance information disclosed by the company.

**Incentives at the time of executive turnover** Annual accounts management by top executives may be observed when executive changes take place within companies. Executive changes can be forced or voluntary (e.g. retirement). The outgoing CEO or executive team as well as the incoming CEO or executive team can have incentives to influence the accounts. Research on CEO turnover and annual accounts management distinguishes between CEO turnover in troubled firms and CEO turnover in non-troubled firms. Dechow and Sloan (1991) investigated the hypothesis that CEOs, in their final years of office (before retirement), manage discretionary investment expenditures to improve short-term earnings performance (for example, spending less on R&D). LaSalle et al. (1993) reported evidence that is consistent with the hypothesis that new CEOs exploit their accounting discretion to blame their predecessors for poor performance, establish a lower benchmark for subsequent performance evaluation and relieve future earnings of charges that would otherwise have to be made. Murphy and Zimmerman (1993) and Godfrey et al. (2003) also found evidence that incoming CEOs of poorly performing firms took 'big baths'.

However, it is important to stress that reduced profits or losses when a new CEO or new management team comes in could also be the result of the 'income borrowing behaviour' of the former CEO. The outgoing CEO could have improved his performance through accounting decisions in the immediate years before the turnover which increases the reported results, or through income-smoothing behaviour above sustainable levels for several years. So, the outgoing CEO in this case has increased the reported income by using accounting practices which borrow income from the future. In these circumstances, the new CEO will be faced with less profit or even a loss due to the reversal effect of the practices used by his predecessor (this is discussed later).

The new incoming top management team is often tempted to undertake big bath accounting. In their first year in office, compensation will not be tied greatly to the results of the company. In later years, however, compensation will be tied to the performance of the company. Through this 'big bath' a new CEO is able to front-load costs and secure himself higher profits in the years to follow.

Big bath accounting, which is observed not only in terms of executive turnover, will be explained below.

**Big bath accounting to manage future earnings** Setting the objective to maximize the loss is referred to in the literature as big bath accounting. Of course, there are limits to the loss one can present to the stakeholders without influencing their actions. Big bath accounting may occur under any of the following three circumstances:

First of all, big bath accounting can occur in case of a (one-time) heavy loss that cannot be avoided by income maximizing accounting interventions (see small loss avoidance). Faced with such a situation the firm's management may choose to maximize the loss in the current accounting period. In years of economic downturn, this practice is often observed.

Secondly, big bath accounting can occur when the annual accounts are cleaned up before or after an acquisition, a merger or other form of business cooperation. Big bath accounting usually implies the frontloading of costs through large asset write downs and increases in provisions (restructuring provisions are extremely popular for this purpose) in order to enhance the future performance of the firm. In the financial year where 'a bath is taken' a substantial loss is reported; however, in the following years performance will rise, partly due to reduced depreciation charges or a decrease of provisions.

Thirdly, big bath accounting may occur at the time of executive handover, especially when the prior CEO was dismissed for poor performance (for a discussion on this see the prior section). This practice has received increasing levels of criticism over recent years. The reinforcement of the conditions for creating restructuring provisions under IAS 37 is a result of those practices. The extract below from the speech of Schuetze, chief accountant of the SEC, refers to the practice of big bath accounting and the methods used to achieve this accounting strategy:

## Cookie jar reserves

One of the accounting 'hot spots' that we are considering this morning is accounting for restructuring charges and restructuring reserves. A better title would be accounting for general reserves, contingency reserves, rainy day reserves or cookie jar reserves.

Accounting for so-called restructurings has become an art form. Some companies like the idea so much that they establish restructuring reserves every year. Why not? Analysts seem to like the idea of recognizing as a liability today, a budget of expenditures planned for the next year or next several years in downsizing, right-sizing or improving operations and portraying that amount as a special, below-the-line charge in the current period's income statement. This year's earnings are happily reported in press releases as 'before charges'. CNBC analysts and commentators talk about earnings 'before charges'. The financial press talks about earnings before 'special charges'. (Funny, no one talks about earnings before credits-only charges.) It's as if special charges are not real. Out of sight, out of mind . . .

The occasion of a merger also spawns the wholesale establishment of restructuring or merger reserves. The ingredients of the merger reserves and merger charges look like the makings of a sausage. In the Enforcement Division, I have seen all manner and kind of things that ordinarily would be charged to operating earnings instead being charged 'below the line'. Write-offs of the carrying amounts of bad receivables. Write-offs of cost of obsolete inventory. Writedowns of plant and equipment costs, which, miraculously at the date of the merger, become non-recoverable, whereas those same costs were considered recoverable the day before the merger. Write-offs of previously capitalized costs such as goodwill, which all of a sudden are not recoverable because of a merger. Adjustments to bring warranty liabilities up to snuff. Adjustments to bring claim liabilities in line with management's new view of settling or litigating cases. Adjustments to bring environmental liabilities up to snuff or in line with management's new view of the manner in which the company's obligations to comply with EPA will be satisfied. Recognition of liabilities to pay for future services by investment bankers, accountants and lawyers. Recognition of liabilities for officers' special bonuses. Recognition of liabilities for moving people. For training people. For training people not yet hired. For retraining people. Recognition of liabilities for moving costs and refurbishing costs. Recognition of liabilities for new software that may be acquired or written, for ultimate sale to others. Or some liabilities that go by the title 'other'.

It is no wonder that investors and analysts are complaining about the credibility of the numbers.

*Source*: Speech by Walter P. Schuetze, Chief Accountant, Enforcement Division, US Securities and Exchange Commission, 22 April 1999. http://www.sec.gov/news/speech/speecharchive/1999/spch276.htm

## Other incentives to manage accounting numbers

**Competitive pressures** Data from the annual accounts might be useful for the competition. Especially in a situation where one company is obliged to disclose more proprietary information due to national GAAP requirements, companies have a tendency either to avoid this disclosure or to decrease the quality of disclosure. For example, segmental data will be disclosed on a more aggregated level or high recurring profits might be topped off to avoid entry in the industry by new firms.

**Union negotiations** Facing forthcoming union negotiations the management might have an incentive to decrease the net result of the company. Strong company profits might incite the unions to ask for a salary increase. These incentives will be more present in companies, industries or countries with strong labour union power.

If we consider the incentives listed we can see that some of them are recurring and others are non-recurring incentives to manage the accounts.

### ACTIVITY 31.5

Which of the incentives listed above could be classified as 'recurring' and which could be classified as 'non-recurring'?

*Activity feedback*
*Recurring incentives could be reducing earnings volatility for listed companies and efforts to sustain share*

*prices when stock options are granted. Further, regulatory incentives can be recurring if, for example, a company is located in a country where there is a link between tax income and accounting income. Non-recurring incentives could be present in the situation of an individual public offering, a merger or acquisition or an executive turnover.*

In research related to earnings management, the notion of implicit contracts is introduced. Contracts can be between the firm and its customers, suppliers, short-term creditors, employees, capital providers and other stakeholders. Bowen *et al.* (1995) and Kasanen *et al.* (1996) find evidence that implicit contracts induce earnings management.

In the previous section we discussed the incentives to manage the accounting numbers embedded in the contracts governing the firm. According to the type of incentive, a different reporting strategy and as a result a different type of annual accounts management, will be used. For example, if a firm is involved in union negotiations the aim will be the decrease of the reported profits in the period before the negotiations. Because each company is subject to a different set of contracts, the incentives for accounting numbers management and the resulting reporting strategies will also differ among companies. Although general checklists to detect earnings management are available (see Nelson *et al.*, 2003; Penman, 2003), the toolbox used by corporate management will be unique to each company.

## ACTIVITY 31.6

Consider some of the different types of incentives presented earlier to manage the annual accounts. What type of accounting strategy would be appropriate for these different types of incentives?

### Activity feedback
- *Capital market considerations.*
  - Risk perception *The accounting strategy of the firm would be to engage in earnings management with the purpose of presenting earnings or results which are less volatile than the underlying economic results that the firm has obtained. In this situation income smoothing would be pursued and this practice would be a 'recurring activity'. In periods with 'high' economic income, profits would be topped off and in periods with 'lower' income increasing measures would be used.*
  - Prepare for an initial public offering *In this case the accounting strategy could consist of showing a good performance over the years before the IPO and an improvement of the balance sheet structure. Different types of annual accounts management might be combined into the overall reporting strategy: income smoothing in order to influence the perceived risk of the company, balance sheet management to improve the structure of the balance sheet; and increasing the result upwards over a time period before the IPO.*

- Tax incentives *In countries where there is a link between accounting income and taxable income, the accounting strategy is to decrease the reported profit in order to reduce taxable profit. This type of management will be recurring as long as the company exists.*

- Compensation contracts *In the case of stock options, an increasing share price is desired. The reporting strategy could consist of income smoothing practices, undertaken to reduce the perceived risk of the company, and further income increasing measures might be used as well. Bonus plans with ceilings might entail one-time earnings management upwards to the ceiling or one-time earnings management below the ceiling.*

Discussing the incentives to manage the accounting numbers, it is worthwhile mentioning that, although a distinction is made between earnings management and balance sheet management or management of the statement of financial position, the impact of the methods used for those purposes are not isolated to the statement of comprehensive income or the statement of financial position alone. In reality, earnings management also has an indirect impact on certain items of the statement of financial position. For example, an accounting method change with regard to depreciation (change from declining method to straight line method) will influence not only the depreciation expense on the statement of comprehensive income, but also the reported book value of the assets on the statement of financial position. The same indirect effect can be observed when a company decides to manage the statement of financial position. If a company wants to improve the debt/equity ratio through switching from owned assets to assets acquired under operational leasing contracts, not only the liability structure of the statement of financial position will be altered, the character of the costs involved will change as well. A large part of the costs related to the use of the asset will switch from depreciation costs to rental costs. For financial analysis purposes the former are regarded as non-cash costs whereas the latter are considered as cash costs.

The case 'the story of Sabena and the airline industry' is included in the appendix to this chapter. This case illustrates the different steps in accounting analysis and includes activities to test your knowledge of these steps.

## ACCOUNTING ANALYSIS: THE AVAILABLE ACCOUNTING DISCRETION

Accounting analysis tries to detect whether management has not only the incentives to manage the numbers but also the capability to influence the accounting numbers. In order to detect this capability to influence the numbers, it is necessary to gain insight into the elements which enlarge the accounting discretion of top management. Accounting discretion is first of all influenced by the type of GAAP a company applies. Second, research results indicate that certain company characteristics, board of directors' characteristics, auditors' characteristics and characteristics of the institutional environment all influence the accounting discretion available to top management. We enumerate below the most important findings of these research streams in order to facilitate a judgement on the available accounting discretion.

### Impact of the quality of accounting standards used

Accounting analysis involves an evaluation of the accounting flexibility available to the management of a company. This accounting flexibility is, to a large extent, determined by the type of GAAP which is applied. Some GAAP systems allow more valuation choices for one item than others. According to the GAAP applied, the same transactions or operations can be accounted for in a different way, but according to the GAAP applied the flexibility for judgement available to management might be greater.

Preparing financial statements implies complying with the regulation which governs financial reporting (generally accepted accounting principles, e.g. US GAAP, IAS/IFRS, UK GAAP, German GAAP, Japanese GAAP). However, since most GAAP are not a rigid set of principles, the management of a company has a certain flexibility with regard to the choice of valuation methods and accounting estimates to use. The level of flexibility will depend on the GAAP being applied. Accounting standards that are characterized by more flexibility allow managers more easily to report income in those financial periods when managers have incentives to present better results. These types of accounting standards are called low quality accounting standards. High-quality GAAP are recognized as leaving less room for the kind of accounting flexibility which allows management to report the results in the period they wish them to appear in the profit and loss account.

The aim of the IASB (Foundation Constitution, part A, para. 2) is 'to develop in the public interest, a single set of high-quality, understandable and enforceable global accounting standards that require high-quality, transparent and comparable information in financial statements and other financial reporting to help participants in the world's capital markets and other users make economic decisions'. As a result, we observe over recent years that the flexibility in the IAS/IFRS has decreased. In most standards, the allowable treatment has been removed, leaving only the prior benchmark treatment in place (e.g. with IAS 8 the prospective application of accounting method or policy changes was deleted from the Standard). Since more countries and more regulatory authorities require listed groups to comply with IFRS, it is somewhat easier for users to compare the difference in available accounting flexibility among listed companies. For non-listed companies, and especially SMEs, differences in accounting flexibility are to a large extent influenced by the national GAAP they use.

In their Annual Report, the corporate management of Adidas explained in their own words what the change from a low-quality GAAP to higher-quality GAAP meant for them when they complied for the first time with IFRS:

## REAL WORLD ILLUSTRATION

### 3 Framework for Accounting Policies in accordance with IFRS and Explanation of Major Differences compared with German Accounting Policies

The major differences between the accounting policies and consolidation methods according to IFRS and German law as set out in § 292a section 2 No. 4b of the German Commercial Code (HGB) are outlined below.

#### a) Framework for Accounting Policies in Accordance with IFRS

The accounting policies of entities in accordance with IFRS are based on the objective of providing investors with decision-relevant information.

Based on the assumption that decision-relevant information should be provided to investors, it follows that accounting policies should be aimed at showing an entity's operating results, rather than determining the amount of distributable profits, whilst bearing in mind the need for protection of creditors.

As a rule, accounting policies in accordance with IFRS have a lower level of prudence than German accounting policies, which leads to the following major differences:

- Minimization of possibilities for establishing and releasing hidden reserves.

- The consistency requirement (recognition, valuation, classification, consolidation) is to be strictly followed; changes in accounting policies are only permitted if it can be proven that the change leads to an improvement in the fair presentation of the financial statements.

- Economic substance has precedence over legal form. The principle of substance over form has a stronger influence in accounting policies in accordance with IFRS than in German GAAP.

(Adidas Annual Report 2004, p. 138)

Empirical research has provided evidence that companies that use the so-called 'low-quality' accounting standards have more flexibility to manage the accounting numbers and as a result more earnings management occurs (Leuz *et al.*, 2003) (see also Chapter 2). These low-quality standards are found in countries with a code law system and a creditor orientation in financial reporting. However, we also learned in Chapter 2 that 'high-quality' accounting standards on their own are no guarantee for 'high-quality' financial reporting. The institutional environment (shareholder protection, degree of enforcement of accounting standards and risk of litigation) plays a significant role in the quality of financial reporting in a country.

That standard's quality is no guarantee of reporting quality implies that it is not sufficient just to check whether or not a company is using high-quality accounting standards to be able to evaluate the accounting flexibility available to management. Since these research results indicate that the application quality might differ among countries, it is necessary also to consider the institutional environment before obtaining a complete picture of the available accounting quality and sources of discretion.

## Institutional characteristics

Many authors classify the quality of GAAP to be applied in a jurisdiction as an institutional characteristic. We discuss the quality of GAAP as a separate point above. In this section we concentrate on those institutional characteristics which do influence accounting quality. In international comparative analysis on accounting quality of published accounting information, the data show that the degree of investor protection (LaPorta *et al.*, 1997, 1998), the risk of litigation (Ball *et al.*, 2000; Leuz and Verrechia, 2000) and the degree of enforcement (Hope, 2003) all create opportunities for earnings management (Bushman and Piotroski, 2006; Djankov *et al.*, 2008; Leuz, 2010). In countries with low investor protection, low risk of litigation and low degree of enforcement, the accounting quality of published financial information will be low. This implies that the annual accounts could represent less faithfully the underlying economic situation of a company. A switch to a higher-quality GAAP does not automatically imply that the annual accounts represent better accounting quality (see references to Chapter 2).

Next to institutional characteristics, firm specific variables do influence the accounting discretion available to management. Academic research reveals three important variables, namely, the ownership structure, the governance characteristics and the audit quality.

## Company characteristics

Research results provide evidence that the degree of ownership concentration affects the nature of contracting and demonstrate that accounting information quality declines as ownership concentration increases (Donnelly and Lynch, 2002; Fan and Wong, 2002; Ajinkya *et al.*, 2005; Fan, 2007; Jaggi *et al.*, 2009). Further, due to improved visibility, and more dispersed ownership and listing requirements, the quality of earnings of listed companies is found to be higher than in non-listed companies, especially in those countries where securities regulators have sufficient qualified staff and the legal power to enforce full compliance with the domestic accounting standards or the accounting standards accepted for listing. The amount of accounting flexibility will be less.

## Board Characteristics

Governance research has focused extensively on the question of whether or not certain board characteristics are indicators of weaker board monitoring. Research results do indicate that board monitoring becomes weaker when the chairman of the board is also the CEO of the company; when the majority of board members are internal company members or directors with family or economic ties to the company; when there are interlocking directorships; and where no audit committee exists. It is important to note in relation to the research results on company characteristics, audit quality and board characteristics mentioned above that they represent the behaviour of the 'average' firm. They may give an indication in an individual case, but they have no absolute power of prediction in a particular case (Boyd, 1994; Beasley, 1996; Peasnell *et al.*, 2001, 2005; Klein, 2002; Brown and Caylor (2006); Adams and Ferreira, 2007; Jaggi *et al.*, 2009).

## Audit quality

The quality of the auditors has a direct impact on the available accounting discretion of the management. Research results so far have provided evidence that the presence of the big four auditors seems to constrain earnings management (Johnson *et al.*, 2002; Carcello and Nagy, 2004; Bedard and Johnstone, 2004; Maijoor and Vanstraelen, 2006; Rusmin, 2010). Not only does external auditing of high-quality constrain earnings management, so does internal control of high quality (Doyle *et al.*, 2007).

The first steps of accounting analysis consist of investigating whether incentives for annual accounts management are present and whether top management has sufficient accounting discretion in order to pursue a reporting strategy of influencing the accounting numbers in line with these incentives. The incentives towards financial misrepresentation are driven by the external and internal contracts governing the firm. The available discretion to do so is created by the quality of the GAAP applied, the institutional, ownership, governance and audit characteristics. In the next steps of accounting analysis, we focus our attention on the choices available to management to influence the accounting numbers.

## Accounting analysis: Methods of accounting numbers management

In most articles and textbooks, the practices, choices or methods used for annual accounts management are usually divided into three broad categories, namely accounting method choice, accounting estimate choices and real decisions (operating decisions, financing decisions or investment decisions).

Accounting method choice and accounting estimate choice are accounting decisions with no direct first order effect on cash flows (Jiambalvo, 1996). An indirect influence could be present when the amount of taxes payable is affected. This happens in countries where taxable income is based on accounting income. However, when real earnings management is used, there is a direct impact on the cash flow.

Real choices are decisions to structure transactions in certain ways and real production and investment decisions to achieve a desired accounting outcome. The uses of accounting methods and accounting estimates are called methods of accounting earnings management. In the past, academic research has mainly focused on accounting earnings management (see Armstrong *et al.*, 2010 and Kothari *et al.*, 2010). The presence of earnings management is detected by proxies for earnings management, such as total accruals, working capital accruals, discretionary accruals or performance-matched accruals.

Academic research into real earnings management started later than research into accruals management, but the number of articles on this issue is increasing (Wayne *et al.*, 2004; Roychowdhury, 2006; Gunny, 2010). In practice, a company can pick a single element to manage the accounts but most often a portfolio of elements is used, whereby accounting and real earnings management are combined (Graham *et al.*, 2005; Cohen *et al.*, 2008; Cohen and Zarowin, 2010; Zang, 2012). The management of balance sheet numbers has received far less research attention.

Besides these three main instruments, other mechanisms can be used to manage the impression of the reader of the financial statements towards one more favourable about the performance and the financial position of the company. In this respect Francis (2001) lists the following elements which can be used for accounting numbers management or impression management: timing of adoption of new Standards;

choices about display (number of statements, layout of statement); aggregation decisions; classification decisions and disclosure decisions.

We now discuss the three main categories of earnings management. The case in the appendix to this chapter illustrates how a portfolio of methods was used to influence the accounting numbers of Sabena.

**Accounting method choice** An accounting method choice is present when there are several possible valuation methods for the same item under the GAAP which has to be applied for the preparation of the annual accounts. Some examples are listed here which could be categorized under the heading accounting method choice:

- choice of depreciation method (e.g. declining method, straight line or accelerated method)
- choice of inventory valuation (LIFO, FIFO or weighted average)
- choice whether or not to capitalize certain expenditures (e.g. R&D, software, advertising)
- choice with regard to the valuation base (historical cost versus fair value).

With regard to accounting method choice the possibility of influencing the accounts can be limited by the accounting standard setter. A standard setter can always remove options from the available set of accounting valuation methods. Accounting method choice is not the most popular item to be used for annual accounts management purposes as the visibility of those choices is perceived as rather high. If one applies an accounting method change, the impact on the results of the company and the equity should be disclosed in the notes (for further discussion see the section on quality of disclosure). IAS 8 presented the accounting treatment of accounting method changes and the necessary information disclosure in relation to such a change. The aim of IAS 8 is to enhance comparability in a situation of an accounting method change.

Different accounting methods available might hinder the comparability of financial information published under different GAAP regimes. But also under IFRS different choices are possible. We refer here to Activity 32.10 in the next chapter, where two large multinationals both following IFRS choose different valuation methods for their agricultural products. The user of the annual accounts should take this into account when comparing the figures.

**Accounting estimates** For the preparation of the financial statements accounting decisions relate not only to the choice of valuation methods to be applied but also to the accounting estimates to be used for valuation purposes. The use of accounting estimates for annual accounts management purposes is often preferred by management above accounting method changes because they are less visible and less costly than changes in accounting methods. Below, a few items of the financial statements are presented in which accounting estimates play a role.

*Bad debt allowances:* Research has revealed that this type of accrual is often used for management purposes (e.g. McNichols and Wilson, 1988). A change in the amount of bad debt allowance is often not visible as this amount is netted off from the receivables. The use of bad debt allowances is one of the oldest methods practised for earnings management purposes. Influencing the amount of bad debt allowance is a typical example of accounts management.

*Inventory.* Related to inventories there is, first of all, the accounting method choice (FIFO, LIFO, weighted average). Secondly, in many GAAP systems there are requirements to use full costing for inventory valuation purposes for industrial companies. In this case, overhead should be allocated to the production. Many standards on inventory valuation require that the allocation of the overhead be based on the company's normal level of activity. Companies in distress are sometimes tempted to allocate part of the unused capacity to the products instead of charging that amount to the P&L account. As a result, these costs related to the unused capacity will be carried forward through the inventory to 'hopefully' more favourable financial years.

For contracts which are valued with the use of the 'percentage of completion method', judgement can be exercised in determining the exact percentage of completion as well as the costs still to incur on the contract.

*Provisions:* Provisions are a very popular balance sheet item for managing earnings. Provisions are used for smoothing purposes as well as for one time increases or decreases of the results. External analysts should always investigate the reasons why provisions are created. Sometimes they have the character of amounts set aside for intentional use later on. This use of provisions for the increase of reported profit when 'economic profit' is lower is also called rainy day accounting. Low-quality GAAP offers more possibilities for creating provisions for earnings management purposes but still possibilities exist under high quality GAAP.

*Choice of the residual value and the useful life:* In order to determine the depreciable amount of property, plant and equipment, management must estimate the residual value and the useful life of this property, plant and equipment. The residual value and the useful life of a PPE will be estimated taking into account the expected usage of the asset, the expected physical wear and tear and the technical and commercial obsolescence. Higher or lower residual values and shorter or longer useful lives will influence the annual depreciable amounts reported on the profit and loss account and the book values recorded on the balance sheet or statement of financial position.

Even in the same industry, when firms are complying with IFRS, differences in estimates can occur. If we compare, for example, the useful lives and the residual values Lufthansa and Ryanair take into account in order to calculate the depreciable amounts, we notice differences.

Lufthansa (Annual Report 2009, p. 158): new aircraft are depreciated over a period of twelve years to a residual value of 15 per cent.

Ryanair (Annual Report 2009/2010, p. 136): aircraft are depreciated on a straight line basis over their estimated useful lives to estimated residual values. The company's estimate of the recoverable amount of aircraft residual values is 15 per cent of market value and the useful life is determined at 23 years from date of manufacture.

We notice that although the estimates for the residual values are equal, the depreciable amounts will be much higher in the first 15 years of life of an aircraft in the books of Lufthansa than of Ryanair for the same aircraft. When airlines have portfolios of aircraft of different ages these differences will diminish after a while.

*Impairment:* The IASB has introduced impairment to move financial reporting from a historical cost basis to a fair value basis (see Chapter 13). An asset is impaired when an entity will not be able to recover that asset's balance sheet carrying value, either through using it or selling it. Although IAS 36 made the criteria to determine the carrying value more explicit, there is still room for judgement (see Chapter 13).

**Real transactions** Companies are constantly engaged in operating, financing and investment transactions. These real transactions, however, can also be used for annual accounts management purposes. Common examples are the deferral of transactions to future periods, such as purchases or R&D. In some cases, the choice of a particular transaction (e.g. financing through a finance lease or operating lease) is not neutral with regard to the impact on the annual accounts. As a result, the choice of operating, investment and financing decisions might be influenced or even determined by accounting valuation or presentation issues. Sometimes, real transactions are only undertaken with the purpose of annual accounts management. A common example is the sale of assets with a gain on disposal. This has an immediate favourable effect on the result of that year (except for certain sale and leaseback transactions; see Chapter 15). The possibility of creating profit through a sale of assets depends to a large extent on the valuation principles which are applied in the company or are required by the GAAP to which the company complies. In a historical cost environment the possibilities for these one-time big gains are much larger than in an environment dominated by fair value valuation. The impact of these one-time gains could even be enhanced by combining the real transactions (sale of asset) with a large write-down or impairment the year before the sale. Influencing the earnings through a sale of assets with gains on disposal is easier for companies that are part of a group. In these cases, not at arm's length prices can be realized on these transactions.

Off-balance sheet leasing can be undertaken in order to improve the solvency ratios of the company. Under IFRS the future payments of the operating lease contract have to be disclosed in the notes. The user of the annual accounts can adjust the on-balance sheet debt with the amounts of off-balance sheet debt (see Part II of Sabena case in appendix to Chapter 32). However, not all real methods of accounting numbers management are visible. The accounting numbers of consolidated accounts can be influenced to a large extent by not including companies one controls in the consolidation scope. These techniques are more difficult to detect since the user of the annual accounts is not aware of the substance of the relationships between the different companies. In order to illustrate these practices, we now present a section on entity analysis.

## ENTITY ANALYSIS

In Part Three of this textbook on consolidated or group accounts we saw that results of the individual accounts can be influenced through intra-group sales. If there is a relationship of control these results are eliminated in the group accounts in the consolidation process. This means, however, that it is important to look into the different relationships one company might have with other companies and how this relationship is accounted for. There are different kinds of relationship between an investor company and the company it has invested in. These different kinds of relationship need different accounting treatments. The following treatments are laid down in all GAAP: control (the investee is consolidated), significant influence (equity method) and no influence (valuation at cost).

When there is a control relationship, there is always the possibility of transferring profits from one company to the other by means of transfer prices for goods and services transferred between group members. These intra-group profits are eliminated when all companies over which a holding company has control are fully consolidated.

In case of a significant influence in a company, but without control, the undertaking is accounted for by the equity method. In situations where there is control but the undertaking is accounted for by the equity method, the accounts of both parties involved do not present a true picture of the underlying relationship and position of the group.

The 'real' nature of the relationship should be considered and compared with the accounting treatment applied in the annual accounts. Sometimes it might be that the accounting treatment does not comply with the underlying relationship. As an external analyst it is extremely useful to know why there is this difference and what the impact on the published accounts is. Especially under rules-based GAAP, companies can set up separate entities using legal constructions in such a way that the legal form of the relationship does not comply with the definition of control embedded in the GAAP used by the controlling company. In these circumstances, a change in the accounting standards might turn an associated company into a subsidiary for reporting purposes. We will elaborate this item further at the end of this section.

Through the following activity we will illustrate the impact on the annual accounts of the investor according to the accounting method applied: full consolidation or equity method. This activity illustrates further the reporting procedures presented in Part 3.

We notice that if the transactions with associated entities are accounted for in a correct manner the impact on the net result of the investor company is the same as under full consolidation. The only difference concerning the profit and loss account relates to the lines where the result is eliminated (see Activities 31.7 and 31.8). The operating result under the equity method is always 10 000, in the case of consolidation the loss or profit made by B on the sale is reflected in the operating result. Although the net result is the same under both the equity method and full consolidation, the amounts representing the operating revenue and the operating result are different. This might have an impact on ratios calculated where sales or operating results are included in the nominator or denominator. (See Chapter 32 for more information on ratio analysis.) The main difference with regard to full consolidation or equity relates mainly to the statement of financial position. The amount of debt is much higher in the case of full consideration.

## ACTIVITY 31.7

Company A owns 45 per cent of the shares of company B; company A bought the shares on 1.1.X. Company A sells goods or services to company B. Company B sells the goods or services further to their clients. The beginning statements of financial position of the individual accounts of company A and B follow. Assume that company A sells a product to company B, at year-end 31.12.X company B has sold all products to third parties. The cost of the products for company A amounts to €40 000. Company A sells the products to company B for €50 000. In the first situation company B is able to realize a turnover of €56 000 with the sale of the products to its customers. In the second situation company B realizes only a turnover of €42 000. This sale of products is the only activity for company A and B in the year X.

*Statement of financial position*

| | Company A 1.1.X | Company B 1.1.X |
|---|---|---|
| Financial assets | 45 000 | |
| Other assets | 755 000 | 400 000 |
| Total assets | 800 000 | 400 000 |
| Equity | 300 000 | 100 000 |
| Liabilities | 500 000 | 300 000 |
| Total equity + liabilities | 800 000 | 400 000 |

*(Continued)*

## ACTIVITY 31.7   (*Continued*)

Consider, for both situations, the impact on the statement of comprehensive income for company B. Take further into account the regulation on accounting for associated entities and consider the impact on the statement of comprehensive income of company A, the investor, if the shareholding in B is accounted for under the equity method. When solving this activity bear in mind what you learned about the equity method and accounting for associated companies in earlier chapters of this book.

### Activity feedback

*Situation 1: Company B is able to sell the products for €56 000*

| | Individual accounts, company A | Individual accounts, company B | Group accounts, company A |
|---|---|---|---|
| **Statement of financial position** | | | |
| Financial assets | 45 000 | | 47 700 |
| Other assets | 765 000 | 406 000 | 765 000 |
| Total assets | 810 000 | 406 000 | 812 700 |
| Equity | 310 000 | 106 000 | 312 700 |
| Liabilities | 500 000 | 300 000 | 500 000 |
| Equity + liabilities | 810 000 | 406 000 | 812 700 |
| **Income statement** | | | |
| Operating Revenue | 50 000 | 56 000 | 50 000 |
| Operating costs | 40 000 | 50 000 | 40 000 |
| Operating results | 10 000 | 6 000 | 10 000 |
| Results from associated undertakings | | | 2 700 |
| Net result | 10 000 | 6 000 | 12 700 |

*Situation 2: Company B sells the products for €42 000*

| | Individual accounts, company A | Individual accounts, company B | Group accounts, company A |
|---|---|---|---|
| **Statement of financial position** | | | |
| Financial assets | 45 000 | | 41 400 |
| Other assets | 765 000 | 392 000 | 765 000 |
| Total assets | 810 000 | 392 000 | 806 400 |
| Equity | 310 000 | 92 000 | 306 400 |
| Liabilities | 500 000 | 300 000 | 500 000 |
| Equity – liabilities | 810 000 | 392 000 | 806 400 |
| **Income statement** | | | |
| Operating revenue | 50 000 | 42 000 | 50 000 |
| Operating costs | 40 000 | 50 000 | 40 000 |
| Operating results | 10 000 | (8 000) | 10 000 |
| Results from associated undertakings | | | (3 600) |
| Net result | 10 000 | (8 000) | 6 400 |

## ACTIVITY 31.8

Assume that there are underlying contracts between the management of company A and the shareholders of company B in which agreements are made that company A has the power to control the operating and financing activities of company B. Remember what you learned about consolidation in Part Three. Consider also the definition of control in IFRS 3 and the accounting method prescribed in IAS 27. How should company A now account for company B and what would be the difference with the situation presented under Activity 30.7?

### Activity feedback

*Company A would now have to consolidate company B. The consolidated accounts of the group AB would present the following picture.*

(*Continued*)

## ACTIVITY 31.8    (Continued)

| | B sold the products for €56 000 | B sold the products for €42 000 | | B sold the products for €56 000 | B sold the products for €42 000 |
|---|---|---|---|---|---|
| **Consolidated statement of financial position** | | | **Consolidated statement of comprehensive income** | | |
| Total assets | 1 171 000 | 1 157 000 | Operating revenue | 56 000 | 42 000 |
| Equity (capital – reserves) | 300 000 | 300 000 | Operating costs | 40 000 | 40 000 |
| Results of the year | 12 700 | 6 400 | Net result | 16 000 | 2 000 |
| Minority interests | 58 300 | 50 600 | Share of minority interests | (3 300) | 4 400 |
| Liabilities | 800 000 | 800 000 | Net result for the group | 12 700 | 6 400 |
| Total equity and liabilities | 1 171 000 | 1 157 000 | | | |

A further element with regard to entity analysis is the question of whether all entities with which a company has a link have been included in the consolidated accounts and are properly accounted for (consolidated, equity method or valued at cost according to the relation). In this context the creation of special purpose entities is important.

In the last decades of the twentieth century SPVs were created, at the start mainly for lease purposes and, later on, for other reasons (e.g. increasing revenue). Feng *et al.* (2009) provided empirical evidence of the use of special purpose vehicles for earnings management purposes during the period 1997–2004.

The entity analysis performed should take into account whether or not all special purpose entities set up by a company are included or left out from the consolidation process. However, there can be differences in the GAAP which is applied. It is said that the SPEs which Enron had created and which they could exclude from consolidation under US GAAP would have been consolidated if Enron had applied IAS/IFRS. In the wake of the accounting scandals, the FASB looked into these issues. In January 2003, the FASB issued FASB Interpretation no. 46, *Consolidation of Variable Interest Entities – VIE (FIN 46)*, and amended it in October 2003. Variable interest entities are entities that lack sufficient equity to finance their activities without additional financial support from other parties or whose equity holders lack adequate decision-making ability based on the criteria set forth in that Interpretation. Economic criteria such as 'lack of sufficient equity to finance the activities' or 'lack of decision-making ability' now dominate the decision whether or not to consolidate an entity in the group accounts.

Due to this change in the standards on variable interest entities, the Walt Disney Company had to include its two theme parks, Euro Disney in France and Hong Kong Disneyland, in its group accounts with the use of the full consolidation method. Up until 2003 both theme parks were included in the group accounts of the Walt Disney Company with the use of the equity method. With regard to the investment Euro Disney, the economic situation of Euro Disney and its relationship with the Walt Disney Company are now presented in Activity 31.9.

## ACTIVITY 31.9

When you read the following information, taken from Note 2 of the annual accounts of the Walt Disney Company (TWDC), consider the characteristics of a variable interest entity. Which elements embedded in FIN 46 do you recognize in the relationship between the Walt Disney Company and Euro Disney?

The Walt Disney Company holds 39 per cent of the capital of Euro Disney SCA, but Euro Disney SCA is managed by Euro Disney SA, which is an indirect 99 per cent owned subsidiary of the Walt Disney Company. Further, in connection with a financial restructuring of Euro Disney in 1994, Euro Disney Associe's SNC, a wholly owned affiliate of the Walt Disney Company, entered into a lease arrangement with a financing company with a non-cancellable term of 12 years related to substantially all of the Disneyland Park assets and then entered into a 12-year sub-lease agreement with Euro Disney on substantially the same terms. At the conclusion of the sub-lease term, Euro Disney will have the option of assuming Disney SNC's rights and obligations under the lease for a payment of $90m over the ensuing 15 months. If Euro Disney does not exercise its option, Disney SNC may purchase the assets, continue to lease the assets or elect to terminate the lease. In the event the lease is terminated, Disney SNC would be obligated to make a termination payment to the lessor equal to 75 per cent of the lessor's then outstanding debt related to the Disneyland Park assets, which payment would be approximately $1.3 billion. Disney SNC would then have the right to sell or lease the assets on behalf of the lessor to satisfy the remaining debt, with any excess proceeds payable to Disney SNC. Euro Disney's financial difficulties, notwithstanding, the company believes it is unlikely that Disney SNC would be required to pay the 75 per cent lease termination payment as the company currently expects that in order for Euro Disney to continue its business it will either exercise its assumption option in 2006 or that the assumption of the lease by Euro Disney will otherwise be provided for in the resolution to Euro Disney's financial situation.

(Note 2 of the annual accounts of TWDC, 2003)

### Activity feedback

*We distinguish the lack of management power. Euro Disney is, in fact, managed by a subsidiary of the Walt Disney Company. Further we notice that due to the weak financial situation of Euro Disney from the start, a subsidiary of the Walt Disney Company bears the financial risks in relation to the lease agreements Euro Disney has with the lessor of the assets. Euro Disney SNC is obliged to fulfil the commitments towards the lessor if Euro Disney SCA is not able to pay the lessor.*

*Although the economic situation and the legal situation of the relationship between the Walt Disney Company and Euro Disney did not change from 2003 to 2004, the accounting method the Walt Disney Company will use to account for its investment in Paris will be different. This change in method is a result of a change in accounting standards. In Note 2 of its annual accounts the Walt Disney Company informs its readers about the impact of the change in accounting method (from equity method to full consolidation method for Euro Disney and Hong Kong Disneyland) on the figures of the income statement and the statement of financial position of the Walt Disney Company. This information, included in Note 2 of the annual report of TWDC 2003, is presented on the next page.*

As discussed in Note 2 of the annual accounts of TWDC 2003, the implementation of FIN 46 will likely require the Walt Disney Company to consolidate both Euro Disney and Hong Kong Disneyland for financial reporting purposes in the first quarter of fiscal 2004. The figures labelled 'as adjusted' present consolidated results of operations and financial position for the Walt Disney Company as of and for the year ended 30 September 2003 as if Euro Disney and Hong Kong Disneyland had been consolidated based on our current analysis and understanding of FIN 46.

Now take a look of Activity 31.10.

| | As reported $000 | Euro Disney $000 | Hong Kong Disneyland $000 | Adjustments $000 | As adjusted $000 |
|---|---|---|---|---|---|
| **Results of Operations** | | | | | |
| Revenues | $ 27 061 | $ 1 077 | $ 5 | $ (10) | $ 28 133 |
| Cost and expenses | (25 360) | (1 032) | (7) | 9 | (25 360) |
| Amortisation of intangibles assets | (18) | – | – | – | (18) |
| Gain on sale of business | 16 | – | – | – | 16 |
| Net interest expense | (793) | (101) | – | – | (894) |
| Equity in the income of investees | 334 | – | – | 24 | 358 |
| Restructuring and impairment charges | (16) | – | – | – | (16) |
| Income before income taxes, minority interest and the cumulative effect of accounting change | 2 254 | (56) | (2) | 23 | 2 219 |
| Income taxes | (789) | – | – | 13 | (776) |
| Minority interests | (127) | – | – | 22 | (105) |
| Cumulative effect of accounting change | (71) | – | – | – | (71) |
| Net income/(loss) | $ 1 267 | $ (56) | $ (2) | $ 58 | $ 1 267 |
| **Statement of financial position:** | | | | | |
| Cash and cash equivalents | $ 1 583 | $ 103 | $ 76 | $ | $ 1 762 |
| Other current assets | 6 731 | 191 | 9 | (9) | 6 922 |
| Total current assets | 8 314 | 294 | 85 | (9) | 8 684 |
| Investments | 1 849 | – | – | (623) | 1 226 |
| Fixed assets | 12 678 | 2 951 | 524 | – | 16 153 |
| Intangible assets | 2 786 | – | – | – | 2 786 |
| Goodwill | 16 966 | – | – | – | 16 966 |
| Other assets | 7 395 | 128 | 9 | – | 7 532 |
| Total assets | $ 49 988 | $ 3 373 | $ 618 | $ (632) | $ 53 347 |
| Current portion of borrowings[1] | $ 2 457 | $ 2 528 | $ – | $ (388) | 4 597 |
| Other current liabilities | 6 212 | 487 | 61 | (85) | 6 675 |
| Total current liabilities | 8 669 | 3 015 | 61 | (473) | 11 272 |
| Borrowings | 10 643 | – | 237 | – | 10 880 |
| Deferred income taxes | 2 712 | – | – | – | 2 712 |
| Other long-term liabilities | 3 745 | 289 | – | (71) | 3 963 |
| Minority interests | 428 | – | – | 301 | 729 |
| Shareholders' equity | 23 791 | 69 | 320 | (389) | 23 791 |
| Total liabilities and shareholders' equity | $ 49 988 | $ 3 373 | $ 618 | $ (632) | $ 53 347 |

[1]All of Euro Disney's borrowings are classified as current as they are subject to acceleration if a long-term solution to Euro Disney's financing needs is not achieved by March 31, 2004.

## ACTIVITY 31.10

Lufthansa acquired 49 per cent of the shares of the Swiss company Air Trust AG in late 2005. Air Trust AG owns 100 per cent of the shares of the airline SWISS, the combination of the bankrupt airline Swissair and Crossair.

The other shareholder of the company Air Trust AG is the Swiss Almea Foundation which holds 51 per cent of the shares. A direct takeover of SWISS in 2005–2006 is not possible because the traffic rights of SWISS might lose

(Continued)

## ACTIVITY 31.10    *(Continued)*

their value. (See extract below from Lufthansa Annual Report 2005, p. 55):

> The traffic rights of SWISS are based on bilateral agreements with the target countries and are tied to Switzerland as the home location. In the wake of a direct takeover of Swiss by Lufthansa these traffic rights would lose their value. That is why the full integration of SWISS will occur only after talks have been held with the target countries in which the traffic rights are to be secured. This process is progressing well. It is unlikely, however, that the negotiations will be concluded before the end of 2006.
>
> On 3 May 2005, Lufthansa acquired 11 per cent of the shares in AirTrust AG at a price of TCHF 11. The purpose of this company is to purchase and hold shares of Swiss International Air Lines AG. Following approval by the EU commission and the US antitrust enforcement agency, the share in AirTrust AG was increased by 38 per cent at a price of TCHF 38 to in total 49 per cent on 27 July 2005. The remaining 51 per cent will be acquired as soon as negotiations with regard to securing air traffic rights have been concluded and the respective arrangements provided. AirTrust AG is treated as a special purpose entity under SIC 12 fully consolidated in the consolidated financial statements. Since the purchase price was equal to the acquired equity share, the transaction has not resulted in any goodwill.
>
> Balance sheet of Air Trust AG immediately before and after the acquisition date:

| | 1.7.2005 TCHF |
|---|---|
| Assets | |
| Liquid funds | 100 |
| Equity and liabilities | |
| Equity | 100 |

> After 27 July 2005, AirTrust AG successively acquired shares from Swiss International Air Lines AG, which purchase was financed by loans from Deutsche Lufthansa AG. As at 31 December 2005,

> AirTrust AG held 99.4 per cent of the SWISS shares. However, it does not exercise any controlling influence because it has no representative in the administrative board of Swiss International Air Lines AG and no other means of control. The majority of the members of the administrative board is provided by Almea Shiftung, with two of the five seats being currently assigned to Deutsche Lufthansa AG. Swiss International Airlines AG is, therefore, accounted for at equity in the consolidated financial statements. The profit contribution of AirTrust AG including this investment in Swiss International Airlines AG accounted for under the equity method amounted to in total €292m in financial year 2005. The result includes income of €291m from the excess balance of the assets and liabilities of Swiss International Air Lines AG acquired through Air Trust AG and measured at fair value over the acquisition cost of such shares. Even with complete inclusion in the group of consolidated companies as from the beginning of financial year 2005, the profit contribution would be unchanged.

(Lufthansa Annual Report 2006, pp. 82–83)

The comment about the profit contribution not being influenced by the choice between the equity method and full consolidation is correct. However, what would change if Lufthansa would fully consolidate SWISS into its accounts?

### Activity feedback
*The external debt of SWISS would increase the debt figure of the Lufthansa Group. Further, minority interests (51 per cent in this case) would have to be recognized. Intrafirm transactions would have to be eliminated. This might change the amounts of revenues and expenses, but would not affect the net result of the group (see also the example of the Walt Disney Company).*

*Lufthansa acquired the remaining 51 per cent of the shares of SWISS in 2007 and SWISS is now fully consolidated in the annual accounts of Lufthansa from 2007 onwards.*

At the end of the discussion on annual accounts management practices it is important to highlight that most methods of annual accounts management have what is called a *reversal effect*. Reversal means that income increasing accounting interventions in the current period lead to a decrease in income in future periods and vice versa. In fact, many of the methods applied involve only inter-temporal shifts in accounting income. In the literature accounting method choices are often labelled as having a reversal effect (declining depreciation will have lower profits in the beginning than the straight line method, but after a certain moment in the life span of the asset the situation reverses), whereas a real transaction is often labelled as having a one-time effect. However, all three practices (accounting method changes, accounting estimates and real transactions) might entail reversing effects. If one sells, for example, a fuel hedge contract to have an increase in profits in the year the contract is sold, the company will probably suffer from higher fuel prices in the period thereafter. So the sale of the contract is not limited to a one time effect.

An element that might differ between the different methods for annual accounts management is the timing of the reversal effect.

---

### ACTIVITY 31.11

Think of some methods to be used for annual accounts management purposes with a short reversal time and some with a longer reversal time.

#### Activity feedback

A change in accounting methods or estimates in the area of the working capital of a firm might have a short reversal period, e.g. a switch from one inventory valuation method to another, a change in the estimates of bad debt allowances.

Working capital accruals reverse in the short-term as these elements are short-term assets and liabilities. This implies that if the results fall short the year after, additional earnings influence practices must be used if one does not want the result to drop. The reversal period in relation to non-working capital items is longer. For example, the gain realized on sale and leaseback transactions is spread out over the life span of the leased asset.

---

Bowen *et al.* (1995) found that management in general chooses accounting interventions with a long-term positive effect on accounting income. However, if the compensation scheme of the management had short-term perspectives, practices with shorter reversal periods were used. Not including a company in the group accounts, although one controls the company, influences the accounting numbers on a permanent basis. We do not see a reversal with regard to these consolidation choices.

So, for financial analysis purposes it is not only important to understand the accounting flexibility which is available, but it is also necessary to know which valuation rules, estimates and other mechanisms are chosen in the presentation of the annual accounts. In order to get an idea about these elements the quality of disclosure in the financial statements is an important determinant of the visibility of these accounting interventions. Unfortunately, the level of disclosure differs among companies.

## Quality of disclosure

When management provides the necessary disclosures in the notes to the balance sheet or the statement of financial position, profit and loss account or the statement of comprehensive income and cash flow statement, it facilitates the analysis of the business reality of the company by external parties. Financial statements are meant to inform the stakeholders of the firm about the result, the cash flow and the financial position of the firm. In principle, the published figures should represent the underlying economic situation of the firm. However, due to the flexibility that exists in the accounting standards to be applied and the incentives top executives face towards earnings management, a situation might be created in which the published figures in the financial statements do not translate the underlying economic condition of the firm. Although companies must provide a minimum level of disclosure as required by the GAAP they are complying with, the management team can always make more voluntary disclosures. Disclosure quality refers to the compliance of a company to all the disclosures required by the GAAP and to the informativeness of the voluntary disclosures which are presented in the annual report. So disclosure quality and the level of disclosure can also be extended to the narrative part of the annual report. This will be discussed further in Chapter 32. Empirical and analytical accounting research has paid attention to disclosure practices. Most empirical research studies provide evidence that an increase in disclosure leads to lower costs of capital due to the reduction in information asymmetry (e.g. Leuz and Verrechia, 2000). The analytical research, however, indicates that there is an optimal level of disclosure for a company.

Disclosure quality is an important benchmark when inter-firm comparisons are made and it relates to several aspects. Some examples of disclosure quality will now be illustrated.

**Description of accounting methods and accounting estimates** So far we have learned that the choice of accounting valuation methods and accounting estimates can influence the reported income and the statement of financial position structure. Adequate disclosure in the notes on the methods and the estimates used might enable external analysts to get an idea of the impact of the choice and to reconcile earnings of different firms when executing a comparative financial analysis of companies. Further, a company can also explain why a particular choice has been made. If we compare the different airlines we notice that the level of explanation with regard to, for example, how frequent flyer obligations are accounted for, differs. Frequent flyer programmes could create obligations for an airline. However, the obligation is dependent on several terms of the contract between the airline and the customer. On top of that several ways exist to account for these obligations: the incremental cost approach whereby the costs are charged to P&L when passengers make use of the bonus miles or the revenue minus approach, whereby part of the revenue of the ticket sale is deferred to the moment the passenger makes use of the bonus miles (a provision is then created). We illustrate these differences with extracts of the notes of three airlines both applying IFRS.

In the notes containing the description of the accounting policies of Sabena we find the following brief disclosure (Annual Report 2000, p. 50, n. 5.7):

> Appropriate provisions are also made for liabilities arising from mileages accrued via the Qualiflyer frequent flyer programme. These provisions are equal to the costs to be incurred as such credits are redeemed.

In the accounts of British Airways, the programmes themselves are described together with the way they are accounted for:

## REAL WORLD ILLUSTRATION

### Revenue recognition Mileage programmes

The Group operates two principal loyalty programmes. The airline frequent flyer programme operates through the airline's 'Executive Club' and allows frequent travellers to accumulate 'BA Miles' mileage credits which entitle them to a choice of various awards, primarily free travel. The estimated direct incremental cost of providing free redemption service, including British Airways' flights, in exchange for redemption of miles earned by members of the Group's 'Executive Club' is accrued as members of the scheme accumulated mileage. These costs are charged to selling costs.

*(Continued)*

## REAL WORLD ILLUSTRATION    *(Continued)*

In addition, 'BA Miles' are sold to commercial partners to use in promotional activity. The fair value of the miles sold is deferred and recognized as revenue on redemption of the miles by the participants to whom the miles are issued. The incremental cost of providing free redemption services is recognized when the miles are redeemed.

The Group also operates the AIRMILES scheme, operated by the Company's wholly-owned subsidiary Airmiles Travel Promotions Limited. The scheme allows companies to purchase miles for use in their own promotional activities. Miles can be redeemed for a range of benefits, including flights on British Airways and other carriers. The fair value of the miles sold is deferred and recognized as revenue on redemption of the miles by the participants to whom the miles are issued. The incremental cost of providing free redemption services is recognized when the miles are redeemed.

(British Airways Annual Report 2005/2006, p. 61)

In the financial statements of the Emirates Group (2011) we find the information regarding the accounting for the frequent flyer programme under note 3 'critical accounting estimates and judgements.'

## REAL WORLD ILLUSTRATION

### Frequent flyer programme

Emirates accounts for award credits as a separately identifiable component of the sales transaction in which they are granted. The consideration in respect of the initial sale is allocated to award credits based on their fair value and is accounted as a liability (deferred revenue) in the consolidated statement of financial position.

Estimation techniques are used to determine the fair value of mile credits and reflect the weighted average of a number of factors, i.e. fare per sector, flight upgrades and partner rewards. A rolling 12-month historical trend forms the basis of the calculations. Adjustments to the fair value of miles are also made for miles not expected to be redeemed by members and the extent to which the demand for an award cannot be met for the dates requested.

A level of judgement is exercised by management due to the diversity of inputs that go into determining the fair value of miles. It is also difficult to present the sensitivity of a change in value of one or set of the inputs given the complexity of the workings (Emirates Group).

**Explanation of significant changes in accounting methods and accounting estimates**
Accounting method changes hinder external users of the financial statements in comparing the income and the statement of financial position structures over the years. Adequate disclosure of the new accounting method applied and the impact on comparability could facilitate the analysis. Changes in accounting methods, estimates and presentation can occur because of a voluntary decision of management or because of a change in accounting regulation. The impact of these changes on the accounting numbers needs to be disclosed, otherwise inter-period and inter-firm comparability of firm information is hindered. An example of disclosure in relation to an accounting method change is provided in Activity 31.9 on the Walt Disney Company.

## APPENDIX

## Case: The story of Sabena and the airline industry – Part I

The purpose of this case study is to illustrate the different elements of accounting analysis through a real life example. Sabena was the Belgian national flag carrier which was declared bankrupt in 2001. We use the data of Sabena and the different competitor airlines of those periods for accounting analysis purposes. Although the real life case happened before the introduction of IFRS, all items discussed in this case are still possible today. Therefore this case is still relevant for pedagogic purposes. In Part I of this case in this chapter we concentrate on the incentives towards accounting numbers management embedded in the contract of the firm, the discretion available, the accounting choices made to present the financial statements and the quality of disclosure. In Chapter 32, we use the data of Sabena again to illustrate the techniques of financial analysis.

In relation to the airline Sabena, data from the last ten years of its existence (1991–2001) will be used. Within the time span covered the analysis will mainly focus on the period 1995–2001 during which Sabena was linked to the SAir Group. The SAir Group was the majority shareholder of the airline Swissair which also ceased to exist at the beginning of 2002. If we need to compare the performance of Sabena and the Swissair/SAir Group with the other airlines, then we use the financial statements of the years 1999, 2000 and 2001. A short overview of the last ten years of the existence of Sabena is presented in Activity 31.12.

## ACTIVITY 31.12

When reading the information below about Sabena, keep in mind the overview of the academic literature on the existing incentives towards accounting numbers management. Which elements from the literature could possibly be related to this company?

Sabena, Belgium's national flag carrier, was founded in 1923. Sabena was a state-owned entity, characterized by a weak financial performance for as long as it existed. Due to the deregulation of the airline industry which would gradually take place in the European Union from the beginning of the 1990s, airlines were investigating all forms of cooperation and alliances with each other. It was already clear at that time that it would be extremely difficult for Sabena to survive on its own. In order to make Sabena an attractive bride for a partnership a major restructuring had taken place in 1991. Subsequently Sabena entered in 1992 into cooperation with Air France. The French partner acquired 37 per cent of the shares of Sabena. The partnership with Air France came to an end two years later in 1994. Mid-1995 Swissair acquired a large minority holding of 49.5 per cent in the capital of Sabena. Together with the investment in the share capital of Sabena, a loan of 151m CHF was granted by Swissair

to the Belgian government, which remained the majority shareholder with 50.5 per cent of the shares. The loan to the Belgian government entitled Swissair at that time to raise its equity holding in Sabena from 49.5 per cent to 62.25 per cent later on.

The shareholder agreement signed by the two shareholders (SAir and the Belgian government) included, among other things, the following items. The articles of the shareholders' and masters' agreement stipulated that the managing director (CEO) be appointed at the suggestion of both shareholders (Belgian state and SAir). Further, the articles stipulated that the other members of the management committee of Sabena could be appointed or dismissed by the board of directors on the proposal of the managing director.

In February 1996 one of the top executives of the SAir Group became President and CEO of Sabena. From the management team in place at Sabena at the beginning of 1996 only one person remained on the board of the management team at the time of the bankruptcy in 2001. In this short time frame many management positions

*(Continued)*

## ACTIVITY 31.12  *(Continued)*

were occupied by several persons; the position of chief financial officer changed hands three times in those five years.

Sabena was the first airline in which the SAir Group took a substantial minority shareholding. The acquisition of this substantial minority shareholding (49.5 per cent) fitted into the new strategy of Swissair. Their new corporate strategy was presented in their Annual Report 1996 (p. 1):

Swissair has moved from its traditional structure as an airline to become a corporate group that conducts airline-related activities in addition to actual airline operations. The new group structure, named the SAir Group will underscore the diversity of the new corporation.

Together with this new corporate strategy, a new CEO, a former controller from within the company, was appointed in the SAir group. The strategy of the business segment airlines of the SAir Group was to obtain a market share of 20 per cent in Europe (Luchinger, 2003, p. 210). This strategy, called the 'hunter' strategy would be pursued by taking substantial minority shareholdings in EU airlines. Sabena was the first and later on French (AOM, Air Litoral), German (LTU), Italian (Volare) and Portuguese Airlines (Portugalia, TAP) followed. As Switzerland was not a member of the EU, acquiring a majority shareholding in the EU airlines would result in these airlines becoming non-EU airlines.

The acquisition of minority holdings by SAir in other airlines was beneficial not only for obtaining a market share of 20 per cent but also for the so-called second pillar of the SAir Group, namely the airline-related business segments (e.g. catering, ground handling, technics, logistics, information systems). Illustrations of this practice can be found in several annual reports of the SAir Group. The following evidence is found on p. 18 of the 1996 SAir Group Annual Report:

Atraxis' first year as an independent information technology company was very challenging ... Several reservations and handling systems were delivered to third-party customers and made operational, including the complete migration of the Sabena booking and handling system.

Further:

On December 16, Swisscargo and Sabena signed an agreement whereby Swisscargo's distribution network would market the entire freight capacity of Sabena's fleet of aircraft as of January 1, 1997.

Swisscargo thereby enlarged its freight capacity by almost one quarter and is taking full advantage of the chance to create a cargo hub in Brussels.

(SAir Group 1997 Annual Report, p. 20)

In the notes to the annual accounts of the SAir Group of 1997 we find the following explanation concerning the operating revenues: 'Results for 1997 also include the assumption by Swisscargo of Sabena's cargo business, which increased the relevant operating revenue item by CHF160m.' It is interesting to note here that the so-called 'assumption' of the cargo business of Sabena by SAir is, in fact, a non-event in the annual report of Sabena. In the annual reports of Sabena the titles in the narrative part switch from cargo to cargo handling and in the five-year overview of summary airline operating statistics the statistics relating to cargo are replaced by the words 'assumed by SAir'. The growth in the airline-related activities came from acquisitions and from providing services to the Qualiflyer Group, which included all the airlines in which SAir hold substantial shareholdings. (SAir Group Annual Report 2000, p. 4): 'Group companies active in the airline-related businesses generated added revenue by performing maintenance, catering, IT and cargo services for Qualiflyer Group airlines.'

Whereas Sabena had only two shareholders (the Belgian Government 50.5 per cent and the SAir Group 49.5 per cent), the SAir Group was listed with dispersed ownership. Even employees held shares in SAir as we learn from the notes to the annual accounts of the SAir Group (e.g. note 4 of the Annual Report of the SAir Group of 1998, p. 19): 'The SAir Group also issues shares to its personnel. These shares carry dividend and voting rights, but cannot be sold for three years after their issuance.' As in many large listed groups stock options were also granted to staff members.

At the end of 1996 both SAir and Sabena were headed by new CEOs who had committed themselves to growth and profitability. With regard to Sabena, evidence of this commitment to profitability can be found in the consecutive annual reports of 1995, 1996 and 1997:

Our collaboration with Swissair, the strengthening of our balance sheet achieved in 1995 and the commercial growth witnessed over the last three years are all strong building blocks which enable us to achieve our objective of profitability from 1998.

(Sabena Annual Report 1995)

*(Continued)*

## ACTIVITY 31.12    (*Continued*)

A year of transition for Sabena, 1996 was hallmarked by the creation of a new management team headed by a new CEO. The Horizon '98 plan points the way to a return to profitability in 1998.

(Sabena Annual Report 1996, p. 5)

Sabena succeeded in 1997 in reaping the first benefits of the Horizon '98 programme in the drive to balance the books and make the airline profitable again. . . . [p. 9] The aim of all these measures (Horizon '98 plan) is to return Sabena to profitability in 1998.

(Sabena Annual Report 1997, p. 5)

In 1998 Sabena 'showed' the promised profit. Figure 31.1 shows the operating result and the net result of Sabena NV over the period 1991–2000 and the 1998 figures are, indeed, in the black.

Sabena NV represents the holding company of the Sabena Group but at the same time it is also the airline. The revenue of Sabena NV makes up 90 per cent of the revenue of the Sabena Group and the total assets of Sabena NV represent 85 per cent of the total assets of the Sabena Group. For this reason it makes sense to look at the behaviour of the individual accounts of Sabena NV. These individual accounts are prepared according to Belgian GAAP for the whole time frame. The results of 1998 were commented on by the board of directors in the Annual Report as follows:

The main reason why the year has been such a turning point is because we have managed to re-establish our profitability. The efforts made to cut costs, to increase productivity and to occupy more aircraft seats, have clearly borne fruit . . . . In summary we can state that,

## Figure 31.1    Ten-year overview of the operating and net result of Sabena NV

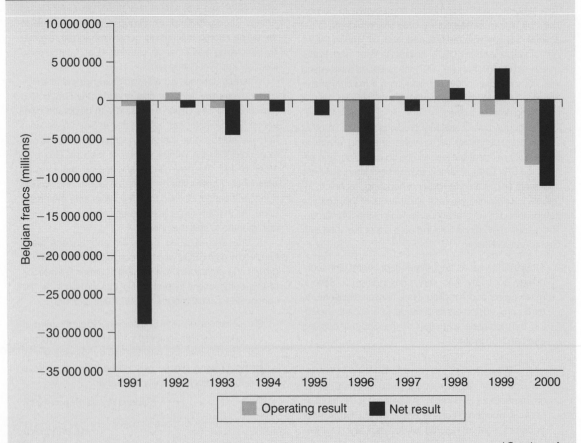

(*Continued*)

## ACTIVITY 31.12    (*Continued*)

this year, Sabena has finalized the groundwork done in 1996 and 1997 within the framework of the 'Horizon '98 Plan'. Its task is now to ensure profitable growth based on continued restraint in matters of expenditure.

The fact that in 1997, and especially 1998, the economic climate was very favourable for the airline industry was not mentioned as a possible explanation for the positive figures. In line with the growth strategy of the SAir Group the board of directors of Sabena took the decision in 1997 to renew and expand the fleet in the coming years. To fill this extra seat capacity offered on the market Sabena engaged heavily in price competition. The number of passengers indeed grew as we will see later, but the mix of passengers was very unfavourable. In the main, it was economy class passengers who were attracted, among them many transfer passengers. These transfer passengers create extra variable costs (handling, etc.) and are therefore not very profitable for an airline. The percentage of business class passengers decreased especially from 2000 on, the year when the sale of the tickets for both airlines (Swissair and Sabena) was for the first time carried out for a period of 12 months through the newly created Airline Management Partnership (AMP) between the two airlines.

The results for the Sabena Group over the same time frame show a rather similar pattern, except for 1992 and

1999 (group accounts are only available from 1992 on) (see Figure 31.2). In those years the results of the individual accounts of Sabena NV were positively influenced by gains on intra-group sale of assets (for example, in 1999, the creation of a new 100 per cent owned subsidiary Sabena Technics NV which would be responsible for maintenance, repair and overhaul of planes). These intra-group results are, of course, eliminated in the process of consolidation (see Part 3 consolidated or group accounts).

From 1999 on the group accounts of Sabena were prepared with the use of IAS. The group loss of 1999 was explained in the message of the board of directors as follows:

1999 turned into another year of strong growth for the Sabena Group in spite of an ever more demanding competitive climate. It was a year that saw us exceed the 10-million passenger mark. But the unexpected increase in certain costs, particularly in the price of fuel, lowered operating results. Because of certain extraordinary transactions, amongst which the sale of Equant shares, the net results of the Sabena Group show a slight profit. Nonetheless, the Board has decided to absorb into the 1999 figures part of the restructuring costs linked to the Airline Management Project (AMP).

## Figure 31.2    Overview of the operating and net result of the Sabena Group

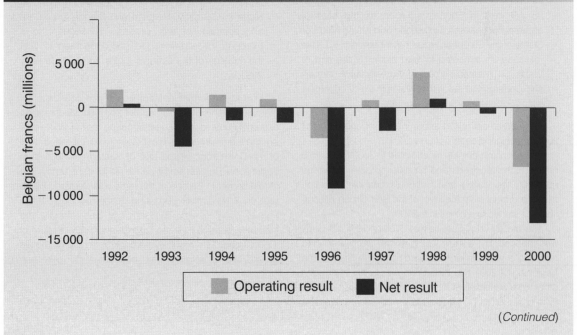

(*Continued*)

## ACTIVITY 31.12 *(Continued)*

The message of the board of directors reported further on the start of AMP and what it meant for Swissair and Sabena:

As initially provided in the 1995 agreements, the two airline companies have decided to combine their commercial activities by the formation of a partnership.

The divisions of the two companies have been restructured and spread over two administrative headquarters: Brussels for Marketing, Product and Sales, Zurich for the Management of the network and support functions. Because of the permanency of this new agreement, the Board of Directors asked the two main shareholders of Sabena, being the Belgian State and the SAir Group, for an agreement on matters pertaining to the future shareholding structure.

It is obvious from the description in the annual report that the creation of AMP would have an impact on the structure of the Sabena Group and perhaps on the SAir Group as well. Employees from the SAir Group and from Sabena were transferred to AMP. Concerning the impact on costs and revenues, the annual report remains vague.

The agreement between the shareholders on the future shareholding structure, talked about in the report of 1999, was described in the annual report of Sabena of 2000 as follows (Annual Report 2000, p. 3):

Two principal events distinguished the year 2000: the agreement between the shareholders under which the SAir Group would take a majority holding of 85 per cent in Sabena as soon as the bilateral agreements between Switzerland and the 15 Member States of the European Union have been ratified. This ratification is expected to take place by the end of 2001 .... The establishment of the AMP as a partnership under British law with affiliates in every country in which Sabena and Swissair operate.

The agreement talked about in the Sabena report of 2000, was signed on 25 January 2001.

The economic climate deteriorated in 2000 (economic crises, high fuel prices and an unfavourable exchange rate with the dollar) and Sabena's financial situation became dramatic. At the level of the SAir Group difficulties also started to emerge mid-2000.

The 'old' CEO left Sabena mid-2000 and the company was headed by a new CEO whom the Swiss had recruited a year earlier from a competitor airline. At the beginning of 2001 two CEO changes shortly after each other were witnessed at the top of the SAir Group as well. Both new CEOs got the task to turn the tide and restore

profitability. In both annual reports the reader is informed about how each company will proceed in achieving this target. Sabena Annual Report 2000:

In order to improve the result sharply in the short term, the 'Blue Sky' restructuring programme was launched .... The Board of Directors will give every priority in 2001 to redressing the performance of the Group and to signing sustainable partnerships.

SAir Group Annual Report, Message from the new Chairman, p. 5:

Our main priority is to reorganize the Group's airline sector, the first pillar of the dual strategy, and restore it to a sound financial condition . . .. The SAir logistics, SAir services and SAir relations divisions, forming the second pillar of our dual strategy, have either met or surpassed their performance targets.

The reorganization of the airline segment at the SAir Group meant that the 'hunter' strategy was abandoned in 2001. SAir Group Annual Report 2000, p. 4:

Beginning in 1995 the Group began to follow a strategy of acquiring minority holdings in foreign airlines.... The Board realized that the depth of the resources required to implement the chosen strategy, in terms of time, capital and management capacity, was greater than the Group could provide. The lack of ample financial resources to pursue additional acquisitions and to carry out the required refinancing plans in Germany, Belgium and France forced the abandonment of this strategy. Subsequent to a thorough investigation, the Board decided to shift the strategy of the Group's airline sector in January 2001.

Due to the further deterioration of the economic climate, the events of 11 September 2001, social unrest, an extremely unfavourable cost structure due to prior management decisions and, last but not least, the withdrawal of the SAir Group at the end of September 2001 from Sabena, the Belgian airline had to file for bankruptcy. The oldest carrier in Europe at that time was declared bankrupt on 7 November 2001 and ceased to exist, at the age of 78 years old. Thousands of jobs (directly and indirectly) were lost (some estimates suggest a figure of 17 000) and, as a result of the bankruptcy the economic growth rate of Belgium was reduced by 0.2 per cent.

*(Continued)*

## ACTIVITY 31.12 *(Continued)*

In Switzerland too, many people lost their jobs due to the serious financial problems at the SAir Group.

### *Activity feedback*

- *Sabena was looking for a partner at the beginning of the 1990s, the annual accounts had to look attractive. Accumulated losses from the years before were cleaned up in a major restructuring.*

- *There is evidence of implicit contracts on the part of the board of directors of Sabena towards profit. The texts of the board of directors in the annual reports of 1995, 1996 and 1997 contain implicit contracts which make a promise for profitability from 1998 on.*

- *Two CEO changes are observed: one in 1996 and the other in 2000. However, there is a difference between the first CEO change and the second. The CEO coming on board in 1996 had the goal of pursuing growth and profitability. The CEO of the new millennium was facing a company in distress.*

- *Regulatory aspects could also play a role.*

*Taxes: In Belgium, there is a strong link between reported accounting income in the individual accounts and the income which is used to determine taxable profit.*

*Regulatory aspects: Although there has been deregulation since the beginning of the 1990s, the airline business is still a highly regulated industry.*

So far we have discussed the incentives present to possibly influence the accounting numbers. If we consider the academic research on the variables which influence the accounting discretion available to management, we observe that Sabena uses Belgian GAAP for its individual accounts. The group accounts are prepared according to Belgian GAAP until 1998 and from 1999 onwards Sabena issues group accounts in compliance with IFRS. Sabena is characterized by a concentrated ownership and Belgium is a code law country. In the next part of the case, we focus on the methods used to influence accounting numbers.

**Accounting choices** In this section we illustrate several choices which influenced the accounting numbers published.

An example of rainy day accounting can be found in the annual accounts of Sabena in the time frame 1991 to 1995. A substantial amount of provisions were created in the annual accounts of 1991 before the cooperation with Air France. These provisions were then released until 1996 when a new management team headed by a Swiss CEO had taken over. The gradual release of these provisions reduced the negative reported results over that period.

Provisions, however, can also be used to 'frontload' costs, frontloading meaning bringing future costs to the current period. The purpose is to enhance the profitability in future periods. This frontloading of costs by increasing provisions was encountered in the first years of the cooperation between Sabena and the SAir Group. Evidence of this practice is found in the following annual report:

> The group result for 1995 remained in the red to the tune of BEF 1.620m. This includes an exceptional provision of BEF 1.090m for the renewal of the fleet ... [p. 22]. Following the decision by the Board of Directors to make exceptional provisions of BEF 1.090m to effect a rapid standardization of the long haul fleet, consolidated results in 1995 showed a net loss of BEF 1.620m BEF.

(Sabena Annual Report 1995, p. 5)

## ACTIVITY 31.13

Is this provision created in 1995 in accordance with conceptual frameworks governing financial reporting?

*Activity feedback*

*This provision does not really match with definitions and concepts found in the conceptual frameworks.*

More provisions follow in the financial year 1996:

The Board of Directors has decided to set off the exceptional charges in 1996 against major reductions in values and provisions designed to ease the fleet harmonization and modernization process. The total amount of money involved in the reduction of values and provisions for the fleet (A310–B747) is BEF 1531m.

(Sabena Annual Report 1996, p. 9)

The evolution of the provisions over the period 1991–2000 in the annual accounts of Sabena is presented in Figure 31.3.

High-quality standards are characterized by their stringent rules for the creation and the use of provisions. A provision for the renewal of the fleet, would under strict compliance with IAS/IFRS, not have been possible. So these practices are more easy to apply for managers when they use low-quality accounting standards. However, if managers are operating in countries with weak shareholder protection and low risk of litigation it might be tempting to use this type of earnings management even when high-quality accounting standards are used for the preparation of the financial statements. Due to the low risk of litigation the costs of non-compliance with accounting standards are low. The latter is referred to in the literature as GAAP-application quality.

## Figure 31.3 Evolution of provision of Sabena NV

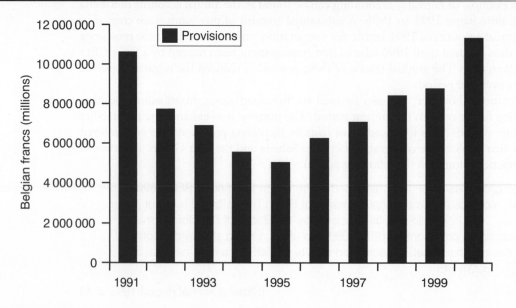

*Impairment of assets:* Through impairment of assets, costs in the current period increase and the remaining book value is lower. As a result, future depreciation costs will be lower. Sabena recorded, beside the creation of provisions for fleet renewal, impairment of assets on the aircraft present in their fleet as we saw in the extract of the Annual Report of 1996 (p. 9), cited earlier. Large impairments of assets also occurred in 1997:

> The board of directors decided actively to pursue the recovery plan to redress the accounts of Sabena and its subsidiaries in order to provide them with the maximum resources for the future. Within Sabena, the pursuit of this recovery plan was mainly reflected in the value reductions made to aircraft, above all in the case of the 2 Boeing 747s.
>
> (Sabena Annual Report 1997, p. 9)

These aircraft were later the subject of sale and leaseback transactions. The surplus realized at the moment of the sale of the aircraft was spread over the leasing period of those planes in 1998 and in 1999. As a result the impact of the leasing costs of those planes on the profit and loss account was softened in those years. Here we observe a combination of an accrual accounting decision (recording of impairments) followed by a real transaction (sale and leaseback of a plane). The impact of these one-time gains could even be enhanced by combining the real transactions (sale of asset) with a large write-down or impairment before the year of sale. This practice was applied by Sabena. The airplanes on which large impairments had been recorded were sold. A number of those planes were leased back for a short time period. The profits realized on those planes were deducted from the rental costs for the years 1998 and 1999; as a result the operating costs for the airline were lower in 1998 and 1999.

Gains or losses realized on the sale of assets always have an influence on the individual accounts of the entity that undertakes the transaction. However, if the sale is realized within a group, these intra-group sales with gains or losses have no influence on the group accounts. In circumstances in which individual accounts are used for regulatory, tax or legal purposes, one must be vigilant for these intra-group profits. The profit reported in 1999 in the individual accounts of Sabena NV was mainly created through the transfer of assets from Sabena NV to a newly created subsidiary Sabena Technics NV. It had no effect on the result in the group accounts.

It is clear that not all changes in accounting estimates, accounting method changes and real transactions are induced by earnings management motives or balance sheet management motives. It is important for an analyst to consider all possible explanations for these changes or transactions when they occur.

**The different steps in accounting analysis** In Figure 31.1 we presented the net results of Sabena NV over the years 1991–2000 and in Figure 31.2 the results of the Sabena Group over the years 1992–2000. In this section we link together all the information we have collected so far on Sabena and re-analyze the evolution of the reported results. The aim of this illustration is to analyze the accounting and reporting strategy and to get an idea of the underlying economic result.

In 1991 big bath accounting was practised in order to enhance the future of Sabena. Figure 31.1 clearly illustrates this. In 1992 the cooperation with Air France started. The figure presents the operating result and the net result of the individual accounts of Sabena NV over the period 1992–2000. Figure 31.2 presents the consolidated results of the Sabena Group over the same period. In Figure 31.4 the important company events are mentioned.

In the first time frame, namely the cooperation with Air France, the results fluctuate almost within a more narrow band-width. The results were kept within that band-width partly due to the release of provisions over those years (see Figure 31.3). In 1992 the individual accounts were positively influenced due to the sale of the charter activities to another entity, namely Sabena Leasing NV, which is also part of the Sabena group. This intra-group sale was only beneficial for the individual accounts of Sabena, in the group accounts this intra-group profit was eliminated.

At the start of the second time frame, namely the cooperation with the SAir Group, especially in 1996, the financial year where the new CEO comes in, the results drop sharply. The subsequent messages of the board of directors even provide information on the goal they were pursuing and on the methods they were using to obtain the goal. The accounting strategy was making it possible for Sabena to show profit from 1998 on. The subsequent messages of the board of directors could be regarded as

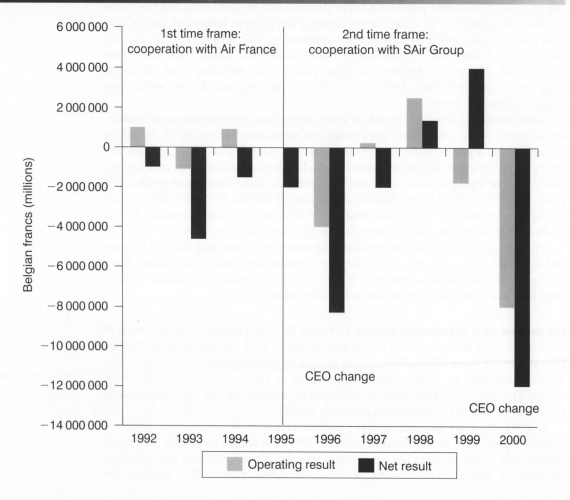

Figure 31.4   Net and operating result of Sabena NV, 1992–2000

implicit contracts for profitability from 1998 on. For example (Sabena Annual Report 1997, p. 30):

> In 1997 the Sabena Group's exceptional result was influenced, as it had been in 1996, by the implementation of the balance sheet recovery plan with the intention that certain factors should no longer have an adverse effect on the profit and loss account in the coming years.

The two time frames can also be distinguished if we represent the exceptional costs and exceptional revenues in a graphical way (Figure 31.5). During the cooperation with Air France it is a rather stable pattern. From 1996 to 1999 we observe a gradual increase of exceptional revenue. In 2000 a new CEO comes in.

If we return to the second time frame in Figure 31.4 we might state that the front-loading of costs, a favourable economic climate and gains on disposal of assets resulted in the 'promised' profit in 1998 in the individual accounts as well as in the consolidated accounts. The gain in the number of planes (mainly Boeings) acquired under a sale and leaseback agreement also favourably influenced the result of 1999, as part of the gain was carried forward. In 1999 the group results were negative again (see Figure 31.2); the individual accounts, however, showed a good profit figure of 4 billion BEF through intra-group sales as explained earlier. The 'reported' results of Sabena looked fair in 1998, although whether the underlying economic performance had also improved could not yet be judged. This would only become clear after a few years, since Sabena had practised to some extent what is called big bath accounting in the years before 1998. Many stakeholders involved considered this reported profit as a major breakthrough. In many textbooks, however, warnings with regard to big bath accounting can be found. For example, Penman (2001, p. 601):

> This intertemporal shifting of income means that earnings quality is not only doubtful in the year of the manipulation but also in subsequent years when borrowing or saving of income 'comes home to roost'.

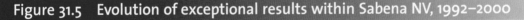

**Figure 31.5  Evolution of exceptional results within Sabena NV, 1992–2000**

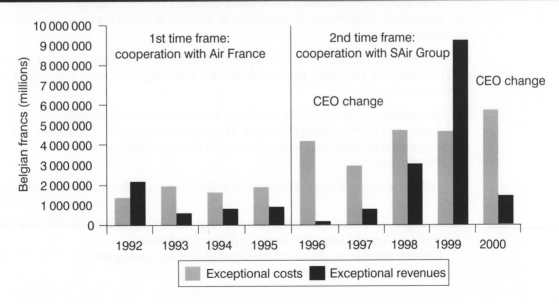

It is important to note here that the board of directors of Sabena had made in their messages the necessary disclosures, so that external parties who had taken the time to look at the annual reports of prior years, knew they had to judge the results of 1998 with the necessary caution.

Due to the elements mentioned in the introduction of this case on Sabena – unfavourable economic climate, rising costs due to prior management decisions, extensive and expensive fleet renewal and to a lesser extent rather expensive outsourcing of activities (evidence of the latter can be found in interviews given by the management of Sabena to the press and by declarations of the members of the management before the parliamentary investigation committee in Belgium), high fuel prices, unfavourable exchange rate with the dollar – but also due to the reversal effect of certain of the accounting methods used, the results of 2000 collapsed.

**Quality of disclosure** The last part of the accounting analysis is a focus on the quality of disclosure. An example which relates to quality of disclosure is the level of compliance with disclosures required by GAAP and the extra-voluntary disclosure provided on that item. With regard to related parties a separate disclosure has to be made under several GAAP, e.g. IAS/IFRS (see Chapter 30). If we compare the item 'related party disclosures' between the annual accounts of the SAir Group and Sabena we observe differences, even though both airlines prepare their annual accounts using IAS/IFRS at the turn of the century.

SAir limits the explicit note on related parties to note 29 'Transactions with board members and key shareholders'. Board members and key shareholders are indeed third parties, however; we know that the airlines in which SAir holds a substantial minority shareholding qualify as related parties due to the way they are accounted for in the books of SAir, namely by using the equity method. Information on those third parties is distributed over several different items in the notes of the financial statements of the SAir Group (SAir Annual Report 2000, p. 33). For example n. 12, p. 21 on the accounts receivable includes elements which classify in fact as related party disclosures:

> Trade accounts receivable: of which CHF 66m due from associated undertakings, other accounts receivable: of which CHF 12m due from associated undertakings, current loans: of which CHF 13m due from associated undertakings.

Related party information is also found in the notes on lease payments (see Chapter 32). Sabena, on the other hand, included the following disclosure with regard to related parties:

> No transactions were effected with Board members, affiliated companies or key shareholders in the course of the year. There are no receivables or liabilities outstanding between the Sabena Group and its Board members or key shareholders.
>
> (Sabena Annual Report 2000, note 28 Transactions with Board members and key shareholders, p. 67)

Given the information available between SAir and Sabena, this disclosure does not represent the actual relationship between the two companies.

Through this case we illustrated the steps taken in accounting analysis.

## SUMMARY

The purpose of financial statements is to provide to external parties information on the performance and the financial position of a company. At the same time, however, financial statements are viewed by the management of a company as a means of communication to the outside world. Sometimes, tension may arise to publish a result somewhat different from the underlying economic result. In this situation, the company will influence the published accounting numbers. The aim of this chapter was first to illustrate how industrial, economic and company characteristics (i.e. organization of the value chain) have an impact on the accounting numbers. Second, in the part of this chapter on accounting analysis we discussed how users of annual accounts might be able to determine if the annual accounts are possibly managed on the one hand by analyzing the incentives present towards earnings management and the circumstances influencing the available accounting discretion to top management and on the other hand by investigating the choices made by top management to prepare the annual accounts. The purpose of accounting analysis is to get an idea of the underlying economic result and financial position and only this information is useful or value relevant for decision-making purposes.

It is important to remember, however, that each toolkit for manipulation (accounting methods, accounting estimates and real decisions) is unique to the needs and the environment of each individual company. So each accounting analysis will be unique.

## EXERCISES

*Suggested answers to exercises marked ✓ are to be found on our dedicated CourseMate platform for students.*

*Suggested answers to the remaining exercises are to be found on the Instructor online support resources.*

**1** Identify as many examples as possible where the choice of accounting policy could significantly affect the analysis and interpretation of published financial statements.

**2** The summarized statement of financial positions of three businesses in the same industry are shown below for 200X.

|  | A £000 | B £000 | C £000 |
|---|---|---|---|
| Intangibles | 100 | – | 10 |
| Tangible fixed assets | 886 | 582 | 580 |
| Current assets | 920 | 580 | 950 |
| Current liabilities | (470) | (252) | (486) |
|  | 1 436 | 910 | 1 054 |
| Long-term liabilities | (100) | (20) | (50) |
|  | 1 336 | 890 | 1 004 |
| Share capital | 200 | 40 | 300 |
| Revaluation reserve | 80 |  |  |
| Retained profits | 1 056 | 850 | 704 |
|  | 1 336 | 890 | 1 004 |

The operating profit and sales for the three companies for the years in question were:

| | | | |
|---|---|---|---|
| Operating profit | 282 | 194 | 148 |
| Sales | 2 100 | 1 500 | 1 750 |

The companies had different treatments for the intangibles. Company A is amortizing this at £10 000 per annum and company C at £2000 per annum. Company B has written off goodwill of £40 000 to retained profits in the year. Included in the depreciation expense of company A is an extra £4000 over and above the historical cost depreciation caused by an earlier revaluation of its premises.

Appraise the financial performance and stability of each of these three companies within the limits of the information given.

3   If you consider companies such as McDonald's, Kentucky Fried Chicken, Burger King, etc., what are the value drivers in their industry? What are the critical factors in their industrial environment? Comment on these. Subsequently, contrast your findings with an analysis of the value drivers of companies such as Boeing and Airbus. What do you observe? How will these different industry characteristics and value drivers have an impact on the financial statements of these companies? You might look up their annual reports on their websites for inspiration.

4   Identify as many examples as possible where the choice of accounting methods, accounting estimates or even real transactions could significantly affect the analysis and interpretation of the financial statements. Comment on how these choices affect the financial statements.

5   Consider again the examples you have listed in answering question 3. Relate these findings to the national GAAP of your own country. Does the national GAAP in your country allow accounting flexibility on many of the items listed?

6   Compare the accounting flexibility of the national GAAP in your own country with the flexibility in IAS/IFRS. Which of the two systems allows less flexibility to the preparer of the financial statements?

7   Would the information provided through financial statements improve if you could eliminate accounting flexibility from the standards?

8   You, as an accountant, are asked by your financial director to choose suitable companies to compare your own company with. Explain, in a report to her, what would influence your choice and how you would adjust for differing accounting policies, if any.

# TECHNIQUES OF FINANCIAL ANALYSIS

# 32

OBJECTIVES After studying this chapter you should be able to:

- identify potential red flags that obstruct comparability of financial accounting data

- perform the following types of analysis and appraise the results:
  - trend analysis
  - common size analysis
  - ratio analysis
  - segmental analysis
  - cash flow analysis.

## INTRODUCTION

The purpose of financial analysis is to evaluate the performance and the financial position of a firm given the strategy of the firm, the economic and industrial environment in which the company is competitive, the level of accounting flexibility influenced by the quality of GAAP applied, and the incentives and opportunities present towards earnings management. Several techniques of financial analysis exist. The best known technique is that of ratio analysis, in which items of the balance sheet or the statement of financial position and profit and loss account or statement of comprehensive income are related to each other. This technique was introduced to you in Chapter 12. In order to review the elements discussed in Chapter 12, we start with the activities below.

## ACTIVITY 32.1

Using the annual accounts of a company, which ratios would you calculate in order to evaluate the performance and the financial position of the firm?

### Activity feedback
*Any reader of this text who has some introduction to this topic will come up with ratios such as:*

- *current assets/current liabilities to judge the ability of a company to repay its debt in the short-term*
- *debt/equity to evaluate the financial risk of a company in the long-term*
- *results/equity to decide whether or not the investments are used in a profitable way.*

## ACTIVITY 32.2

Can you judge the financial situation of a company properly, based only on the ratios of one particular year? Why or why not?

### Activity feedback
*First of all, there is no external benchmark to compare the performance of the firm with, for example, a competitor in the same industry. Second, judging the performance of a firm based on the results of a particular year or even two years is not that meaningful. Information from one or two years is too short a time frame on which to build an internal benchmark.*

*Think of the case of Sabena in the appendix to Chapter 31. Had you been given only the annual accounts of 1998 or even 1998 and 1999, would you have been able to make a proper judgement on the economic and financial situation of Sabena? The answer is simply, 'no'. The profits of 1998 and the figures of 1999 tell a different story if the data from 1995, and more especially 1996 and 1997, are added.*

In order to evaluate the performance of a firm in a meaningful way a comparison is needed with firms in the industry, with the past performance of the firm itself or with an absolute benchmark. In ratio analysis, however, no absolute benchmarks exist, except maybe that profitability should be above the weighted average cost of capital. But even that absolute benchmark in some industries is not always fulfilled.

From the illustrations in the activities thus far it becomes clear that the performance of a firm should be judged in a relevant time frame and against some industry benchmarks. The analysis of the performance or the financial position of the firm over time is called horizontal analysis or trend analysis. The comparison with the performance or financial position of other companies or a whole industry is done by vertical analysis or common size analysis. Before trend analysis and vertical analysis can be undertaken, it is necessary to check that there are no elements present which would disturb the comparison over time and between companies. The elements of industry analysis and accounting analysis (both discussed in Chapter 31) should be kept in mind here.

In the following section we illustrate these pitfalls related to comparability.

## ACTIVITY 32.3

Which elements can you think of that would disturb the comparison of firm performance over time or between companies?

*Activity feedback*
- *Changes in the structure of the company through a merger, acquisition or creation of new subsidiaries*

- *differences in valuation methods or accounting estimates applied*
- *differences in presentation*
- *different time spans.*

## ELEMENTS OF NON-COMPARABILITY IN FINANCIAL STATEMENTS

Activity 32.3 listed some red flags that should be checked before one starts analyzing the performance and the financial position of a company.

## Changes with regard to the time span of the financial year

Companies might decide to change the time span of a particular year for several reasons. We can observe this practice if a company suffers from a huge loss (e.g. trading losses on financial contracts), the company may decide to extend the financial year from 12 months to 15 months by changing the reporting date. As a result, this huge loss is then compensated by profits of 15 months instead of 12.

Companies can also create very short financial years in which huge losses or restructurings are accounted for. An example can be found in the annual accounts of the 1991 financial year of Sabena. For the purpose of big bath accounting, the financial year 1991 of Sabena, the Belgian flag carrier which went bankrupt in 2001, was split into two financial years. The first financial year covered three months (1.1.1991–31.3.1991). The second financial year of 1991 covered the other nine months (1.4.1991–31.12.1991). The bath was located in the first annual report of 1991, the second annual report of 1991 showed a profit.

| *Financial year* | *1.1.1991–31.3.1991*<br>*in 000 BEF* | *1.4.1991–31.12.1991*<br>*in 000 BEF* |
|---|---|---|
| Operating profit/(loss) | (2 808 673) | 2 161 465 |
| Net profit/(loss) | (30 230 650) | 1 132 000 |

The comparative figures in the annual accounts of 1992 were those of the second annual report of 1991. For the purpose of the case of Sabena included in the appendices of Chapter 31 and this chapter, Sabena's two financial years of 1991 have been combined to obtain results for a 12-month period for comparative purposes.

## Different balance sheet dates

Companies use different closing dates for their financial statements. Even within the same industry, differences can be observed. For example, in the airline business the following dates are used as balance sheet dates by the different airlines:

31 March: Ryanair

31 September: easyJet

31 December: Lufthansa, Air France-KLM and IAG (= International Airline Group: British Airways and Iberia)

If we compare the annual accounts of the two low-cost carriers for the financial year with closing dates in 2001 (see analysis in Appendix I to this chapter), we have to take into account that easyJet closed its financial statements after the 11 September terrorist attacks on the World Trade Center in New York and the Pentagon in Washington, DC by terrorists; and Ryanair and British Airways had done so before that event. The same applies to other events affecting the airlines, e.g. SARS and closing airspaces due to events of nature (volcanic eruptions) or events of human origin (terrorist attack).

## Changes in company structure

Over the years companies merge, acquire other companies or parts of other companies or restructure activities into different separate legal business entities. If a company is involved in mergers or acquisitions, observed growth is often not organic growth but rather growth through acquisition. This should be considered in a different way. Often companies disclose in the notes to the accounts the main drivers of the growth.

For example, the SAir Group, to which the airline Swissair belonged, grew mainly through acquisitions in the last years of the twentieth century. In Note 1 of the annual report of SAir (financial year 2000) information is provided on the causes of the growth in revenue:

> The increase of 24.8 per cent in operating revenue from 1999 to 2000 can be split up in 48 per cent growth through acquisition, 14 per cent positive impact of currency movements and 38 per cent resulting from organic growth.
>
> (SAir, Annual Accounts 2000, p. 14, n.1)

These changes in company structures are especially hindering for trend analysis. Some company restructurings can create an impression of decline, although in reality part of the activities have been moved to a separate entity. When operations are discontinued due to a restructuring of activities, shareholders need information on the share of these discontinued activities in the results, the financial position and the cash flow of the group. IFRS 5 stipulates that in case of discontinued activities the impact should be disclosed to the reader of the accounts. The main objective is to ensure comparability for the reader of the annual accounts. This information message is important for financial analysts and investors, who estimate a company's future revenue generating power on the basis of revenues from continuing operations and more specifically from the recurring profit from continuing operations.

Companies that merge or are involved in acquisition have increasing absolute numbers for revenue, earnings before interest and taxes (EBIT) results and total assets. These firms often like to stress this increase in absolute amounts of revenue, EBIT and results, without putting in the spotlight the fact that the increase derives mainly from acquisition. Impression management is often observed in these circumstances; fortunately we also observe companies that disclose the origin of the increase in these absolute figures in a transparent way. For example, Nestlé uses a construct called RIG, which is equal to 'real internal growth'. In this figure the impact of acquisitions, mergers or spin-offs are eliminated, together with the impact of inflation and price changes.

## Accounting method changes and accounting estimate changes

All GAAP have the consistency principle in their standards: companies are supposed to apply the same accounting policies from one period to the next. The purpose of this consistency principle is enhancing comparability between financial statements over time. However, in practice, changes are observed and the user of the financial statements should take them into account. In the notes to the accounts the impact of the changes have to be discussed (see Chapter 9 for discussion of IAS 8); it will depend, however, on the quality of disclosure whether or not the user of the accounts is able to judge the impact of the change on the performance and the financial position of the company.

## A change in GAAP applied

Companies not only change accounting methods or estimates over the years, they sometimes switch from one set of accounting regulation or standards to another set of standards. This is a one-time change that might have a serious impact on the results and on the balance sheet of the company. When new standards are issued by standard setters and companies have some flexibility to choose the period of first-time adoption of the new standard, comparability will be threatened. In times where standard setters issue a lot of new standards, comparability over the years becomes an issue. It is even more important when companies can choose the first period of adoption of the new standard.

## REAL WORLD ILLUSTRATION

The illustration below indicates how Unilever informs the readers of its annual accounts with regard to changes in the standards applied (Unilever Annual Report and Accounts 2012, 1. Accounting information and policies – recent accounting developments, p. 91).

### 1. Accounting information and policies

#### Critical accounting estimates and judgements

The preparation of financial statements requires management to make judgements, estimates and assumptions in the application of accounting policies that affect the reported amounts of assets, liabilities, income and expenses. Actual results may differ from these estimates. Estimates and judgements are continuously evaluated and are based on historical experience and other factors, including expectations of future events that are believed to be reasonable. Revisions to accounting estimates are recognized in the period in which the estimate is revised and in any future period affected.

Information about critical judgements in applying accounting policies, as well as estimates and assumptions that have the most significant risk of causing a material adjustment to the carrying amounts of assets and liabilities within the next financial year, are included in the following notes:

- separate presentation of items in the income statement – note 3;

- measurement of defined benefit obligations – note 4B;

- key assumptions used in discounted cash flow projections – note 9;

- utilization of tax losses and recognition of other deferred tax assets – note 6B;

- likelihood of occurrence of provisions and contingencies, including tax investigations and audits – notes 19 and 20; and

*(Continued)*

## REAL WORLD ILLUSTRATION 32.1 *(Continued)*

- measurement of consideration and assets and liabilities acquired as part of business combinations – note 21.

### Recent accounting developments
#### *Adopted by the Group*
The following amended standards are relevant to the Group and have been adopted for the first time in these financial statements, with no material impact:

- IFRS 7 'Financial Instruments: Disclosures (Amendment)'.

- IAS 12 'Income Taxes (Amendment) – Deferred Taxes: Recovery of Underlying Assets'.

#### *Not adopted by the Group*
The Group is currently assessing the impact of the following new standards and amendments that are not yet effective.

The Group does not currently believe adoption of these standards would have a material impact on the consolidated results or financial position of the Group. All of the following new standards and amendments are effective from 1 January 2013 unless otherwise stated. Standards have not yet been endorsed by the EU unless otherwise stated:

- IAS 19 'Employee benefits (Revised)' changes a number of disclosure requirements for post-employment arrangements and restricts the accounting options available for defined benefit pension plans. The return on pension plan assets and finance charge will be replaced by a net interest expense or income, calculated by applying the liability discount rate to the net defined benefit asset or liability. The Group expects this change will result in an increase in finance costs of €150m in 2012 (€179m in 2011) with a corresponding increase in actuarial gains or losses on pension schemes before tax when restated under the new standard. The revised standard has been endorsed by the EU.

- IFRS 13 'Fair value measurement' explains how to measure fair value and enhances fair value disclosures. The standard does not significantly change the measurement of fair value but codifies it in one place. This standard has been endorsed by the EU.

- IFRS 9 'Financial instruments', replaces the current classification and measurement models for financial assets with two classification categories: amortized cost and fair value. Classification is driven by the business model for managing the assets and the contractual cash flow characteristics. Financial liabilities are not affected by the changes. Effective from 1 January 2015.

- Amendments to IAS 1 'Presentation of items of other comprehensive income' will result in items of other comprehensive income that may be reclassified to profit or loss being presented separately from items that would never be reclassified. Endorsed by the EU and effective from 1 July 2012.

- Amendments to IAS 32 'Financial instruments: Presentation' (effective from 1 January 2014) and IFRS 7 'Financial instruments: Disclosures' provide additional guidance on when financial assets and liabilities may be offset. These standards have been endorsed by the EU.

- Amendments to IFRS 10 'Consolidated financial statements', IFRS 11 Joint arrangements' and IFRS 12 'Disclosure of interests in other entities' on transition guidance.

- Amendments to IAS 1 'Presentation of Financial Statements' clarifies comparative information requirements.

- Amendments to IAS 16 'Property, plant and equipment' explains that servicing equipment is not classified as inventory when used for more than one period.

- Amendments to IAS 32 'Financial Instruments: Presentation' clarifies that the treatment of tax on distributions and equity transaction costs must follow IAS 12 'Income taxes'.

- Amendments to IAS 34 'Interim Financial Reporting' aligns the disclosure required for segment assets and liabilities in interim financial statements with IFRS 8 'Operating segments'.

The EU has endorsed the following standards, which will be mandatory from 1 January 2014 with early application permitted. This is a year later than the adoption dates in the standards themselves, which require that entities complying with IFRS as issued by the IASB apply them from 1 January 2013. The Group will adopt these standards from 1 January 2013, which is a year early from an EU perspective. The impact of the standards on the

*(Continued)*

## REAL WORLD ILLUSTRATION 32.1   *(Continued)*

consolidated results or financial position of the Group will not be material.

- IFRS 10 'Consolidated financial statements' replaces current guidance on control and consolidation. The core principle that a consolidated entity presents a parent and its subsidiaries as if they were a single entity remains unchanged, as do the mechanics of consolidation.

- IFRS 11 Joint arrangements' requires joint arrangements to be accounted for as a joint operation or as a joint venture depending on the rights and obligations of each party to the

arrangement. Equity accounting for joint ventures, already used by Unilever, will become mandatory.

- IFRS 12 'Disclosure of interests in other entities' requires enhanced disclosures of the nature, risks and financial effects associated with the Group's interests in subsidiaries, associates, joint arrangements and unconsolidated structured entities.

- IAS 27 'Separate financial statements (Revised)'. The standard is revised to reflect the issue of IFRS 10.

- IAS 28 'Investments in associates and joint ventures (Revised)'. The standard is revised to reflect the issue of IFRS 11.

## Differences in presentation

With regard to differences in presentation we observe two main issues. First of all, the contents of 'similar' items used in the annual accounts can be different. Secondly, different companies use different ways of presentation, classification, aggregation and layout. Standardized formats for balance sheet or statement of financial position and profit and loss accounts or statement of comprehensive income facilitate comparison. In practice, however, companies use different formats and layouts. Several GAAP require a minimum layout with which companies have to comply (see Chapters 9 and 10 for the discussion of the layout of the balance sheet or statement of financial position and the income statement under the Fourth and Seventh EU Directive and IFRS). IAS prescribes only a minimum layout for the statement of financial position and the statement of comprehensive income, which allows substantial room for company-specific choices with regard to the layout.

If we compare the statements of comprehensive income of Nestlé and Unilever (see Appendices II and III to this chapter), we observe a different approach. Although both companies choose a statement of comprehensive income in two parts (first part the profit and loss account and second part the elements charged directly to equity) there are still a lot of differences.

## ACTIVITY 32.4

Go to Appendices II and III of this chapter and look at the total assets, total debt and equity of Nestlé and Unilever.

### Activity feedback
When you look at both statements of financial position, you will notice that the layout and presentation chosen by both companies is different. With regard to income, we notice that Nestlé provides more information on the different components of operating costs on the face of the income statement than Unilever does. Unilever provides a breakdown of operating costs, but it does so in the notes to the accounts. It is up to the user to collect

this information from the notes and to create comparable information.

Corrections of this type can only be executed if one is analyzing a small number of companies; however, in large-scale analyses (e.g. for large industry analyses or for academic research) these corrections are often not made. So we observe that differences have not vanished with the compulsory introduction of IAS. One might wonder how these differences are taken into account by companies constructing databases like Worldscope, Amadcus, Osiris, Datastream etc.. These databases are extensively used for academic research purposes.

## TREND ANALYSIS OR HORIZONTAL ANALYSIS

Benchmarks are necessary to make a sound judgement about the performance of a company. With the use of trend analysis we compare the performance of the firm with its own history. In annual reports we often find change statistics comparing the figures of two consecutive years. However, some caution is needed when using this published information (see Activity 32.5).

## ACTIVITY 32.5

Table 32.1 presents percentages of change between 1999 and 2000 published in the Sabena Annual Report 2000, p. 9. Is a reported increase always positive?

*Activity feedback*
*If negative amounts are involved, care should be taken with the presented statistics. The change in net result and the change in treasury position is not favourable at all, although it is presented as a positive change figure.*

## TABLE 32.1    Sabena Group consolidated: key figures, 2000/1999

|  | *1999 (million EUR)* | *2000 (million EUR)* | *% 2000/1999* |
|---|---|---|---|
| Turnover | 2 228 | 2 436 | 9.3 |
| Operating result | 15 | (163) | −1 208.7 |
| Net result | (14) | (325) | 2 226.1 |
| Operating cash flow | 138 | (51) | −137.1 |
| Cash flow net result | 124 | (108) | −187.1 |
| Changes in treasury position | (80) | (225) | 182.1 |
| Balance sheet total | 2 471 | 2 358 | −4.6 |
| Equity | 223 | (97) | −143.3 |
| Ratio long-term debt/equity | 5.0 | 10.9 | 118.0 |

*Source:* Sabena Annual Report 2000, p. 9.

With trend analysis or horizontal analysis we analyze how financial statement items have changed over time. According to the literature, a five-year time frame is necessary; longer periods, for example ten years, are also possible, although the number of elements which disturb comparison only increases over such a long period. For the purpose of trend analysis a base year is chosen and all the financial statement items are then expressed as an index relative to the base year. Therefore, the choice of the base year is relatively important, as the performance over the years to follow is bench marked to this base year.

If trend analysis is applied on the items of the profit and loss account or the statement of comprehensive income, the focus lies on the evolution of the revenue or turnover and the costs related to it. Whether or not the relation between the evolution of the sales and the costs should be linear, depends on the industry characteristics. From the section on industry analysis we know that for the airline industry only catering and handling costs are somewhat variable and are a function of the number of passengers transported. The other costs related to the air transport are a function of the output capacity of the airline which is measured as available seat kilometre or available ton kilometre. We illustrate trend analysis on the basis of the evolution of the operating revenue and operating costs of Ryanair and easyJet in Tables 32.2 and 32.3. We have chosen Ryanair and easyJet for this comparative trend analysis and not Lufthansa or Air France KLM, because the segment analysis of these companies informs us that only easyJet and Ryanair have comparable activities, since those two airlines have no other major activity-lines besides passenger transport (see further in the section on segment analysis). In addition we need to mention that only those items are included in the horizontal analyses, which are to a large extent comparable.

### TABLE 32.2   Horizontal analysis, Ryanair, 2007–2011 (financial reporting date is 31 March)

| | Horizontal analysis (%) | | | | |
| --- | --- | --- | --- | --- | --- |
| | 2007 | 2008 | 2009 | 2010 | 2011 |
| Operating revenue | 100 | 121 | 132 | 134 | 162 |
| Operating expenses | 100 | 123 | 161 | 147 | 1 781 |
| Fuel and oil costs | 100 | 114 | 181 | 129 | 177 |
| Staff costs | 100 | 126 | 137 | 148 | 166 |
| Depreciation | 100 | 123 | 178 | 164 | 194 |
| Aircraft rentals | 100 | 125 | 134 | 164 | 167 |
| Maintenance, materials and repairs | 100 | 135 | 159 | 205 | 223 |
| Marketing and distribution costs | 100 | 584 | 638 | 608 | 649 |
| Airport and handling charges | 100 | 145 | 162 | 168 | 180 |
| Operating profit – continuing operations | 100 | 114 | 20 | 85 | 103 |

*Source:* Data taken from the Annual Reports of Ryanair.

If we analyze the data and focus on the growth rate of turnover in comparison to the growth of the operating costs, we notice that some costs grow faster.

If we analyze the different cost components, we notice that both low-cost carriers seem to be able to keep the increase in staff costs in line with revenue growth. Fuel and oil is supposed to be a variable cost, following the growth of the airlines in terms of routes and flights offered. Although fuel costs are a function of distance flown and the number of takeoffs, the steep increase in fuel costs does not necessarily mean that the increase is only due to more offered flights. The fuel cost component is also a function of the kerosene price and fluctuations in the dollar currency. From 2000 the kerosene price started to rise again and airlines were facing higher fuel costs for the same flights offered. The impact could be postponed for a period if the airline had been able to hedge against these fuel price increases. Costs related to output capacity (e.g. depreciation, amortization and aircraft leasing) fluctuate not only with the number of planes in the fleet, but also with regard to the age of the fleet. Finally, we notice that for both airlines marketing costs increase rapidly. As an external user of financial statements one must always keep in mind that competitors also watch evolutions of costs (trend analysis) and breakdown of those costs (common size analysis). Anecdotal evidence exists that smoothing around certain levels for certain cost items is practised

TABLE 32.3 Horizontal analysis, easyJet, 2007–2011 (financial reporting date is 30 September)

| | Horizontal analysis (%) | | | | |
| --- | --- | --- | --- | --- | --- |
| | 2007 | 2008 | 2009 | 2010 | 2011 |
| Operating revenue | 100 | 131 | 148 | 165 | 192 |
| Operating expenses | 100 | 140 | 162 | 172 | 196 |
| Fuel and oil costs | 100 | 167 | 190 | 172 | 216 |
| Staff | 100 | 129 | 150 | 165 | 199 |
| Depreciation | 100 | 133 | 166 | 216 | 249 |
| Aircraft leasing | 100 | 120 | 126 | 126 | 118 |
| Maintenance, materials and repairs Engineering and other aircraft costs | 100 | 150 | 165 | 180 | 182 |
| Airport and ground handling, costs | 100 | 132 | 160 | 174 | 200 |
| Marketing and selling costs | 100 | 122 | 124 | 242 | 268 |
| Operating profit – before non-recurring items | 100 | 53 | 35 | 101 | 156 |

*Source:* Data taken from the Annual Reports of easyJet.

in several industries. Consumers also keep an eye on the annual accounts. For example, which airline in the world would publish a profit and loss account showing decreasing costs with regard to maintenance if the fleet capacity remains constant or increases?

## COMMON SIZE ANALYSIS

The benchmark to compare the performance of a firm within trend analysis is its own past performance. In common size analysis the benchmarking element is the performance of other firms, usually taken from the same industry. For the purpose of external benchmarking the size effect needs to be eliminated, and this is done by expressing the items of the profit and loss account as percentage of sales and the items of the balance sheet in percentages of total assets.

Table 32.4 presents the common size analysis of the operating costs of Ryanair and easyJet. We observe that staff costs represent a similar proportion of operational cost of both airlines. We notice, however, that airport and handling costs are much lower for Ryanair. This is probably due to the fact that Ryanair uses more secondary airports than easyJet. Although both low-cost carriers spend a lot on marketing costs, Ryanair exceeds easyJet by far. In the end Ryanair realizes on €100 sales an operational profit of €13.4, whereas easyJet realizes with €100 an operational profit of €7.7.

Through common size balance sheets we are able to compare, on the one hand, the financing structure of different companies and, on the other, where they have invested these resources. So balance sheet data provide information on the financing and the investment policy of a company. The items on the balance sheets of Lufthansa, the International Airways Group (IAG), Air France-KLM and Ryanair will now be

### TABLE 32.4 Common size analysis of the operational profit of easyJet and Ryanair (2007/2011)

|  | Ryanair % | easyJet % |
|---|---|---|
| Sales | 100 | 100 |
| Operating expenses | 86 | 92 |
| – staff | 10.3 | 11.7 |
| – fuel and oil costs | 33.8 | 26.5 |
| – airport and ground handling costs | 13.5 | 26.7 |
| – depreciation | 7.6 | 2.4 |
| – rental costs/leasing costs | 2.6 | 3.1 |
| – maintenance costs | 2.6 | 2.9 |
| – marketing costs | 4.2 | 2.9 |
| Operating profit | 13.4 | 7.79 |

*Source:* Data taken from the Annual Report of easyJet and Ryanair.

reformulated or regrouped so that the headings include similar items which are comparable (Table 32.5).

Studying the way in which those companies are financed we notice that IAG, Air France-KLM and Lufthansa are more financed through external debt than Ryanair.

### TABLE 32.5 Common size analysis of group balance sheet %

|  | IAG | Ryanair | Air France-KLM | Lufthansa |
|---|---|---|---|---|
|  | 31 Dec. 2011 | 31 March 2012 | 31 Dec. 2011 | 31 Dec. 2011 |
| Total non-current assets | 70.17 | 56.93 | 76.54 | 66.33 |
| Intangible assets | 8.72 | 5.19 | 4.39 | 5.61 |
| Tangible assets | 48.51 | 54.71 | 46.65 | 51.81 |
| Financial assets | 3.38 | 4.26 | 8.92 | 8.49 |
| Pension assets | 6.66 | – | 11.78 | – |
| Total current assets | 29.82 | 43.06 | 23.46 | 33.76 |
| Inventory | 2.02 | 0.03 | 2.14 | 2.21 |
| Liquid assets | 10.00 | 39.05 | 8.36 | 3.16 |
| Other current assets | 17.70 | 1.30 | 12.96 | 28.30 |
| Total assets | 100.00 | 100.00 | 100.00 | 100.00 |
| Total equity | 28.70 | 36.75 | 22.31 | 28.65 |
| Total non-current liabilities | 38.16 | 43.10 | 44.21 | 36.52 |
| Provisions and pension liabilities | 7.70 | 1.14 | 7.54 | 9.77 |
| Other non-current liabilities | 30.46 | 41.9 | 36.66 | 26.75 |
| Total current liabilities | 33.05 | 20.14 | 33.48 | 34.84 |
| Total equity and liabilities | 100.00 | 100.00 | 100.00 | 100.00 |

*Source:* Annual reports of the International Airline Group (IAG = British Airways and Iberia), Air France/KLM, Lufthansa and Ryanair.

A substantial part of their long-term debt is made up of provisions. Further we observe that these traditional airlines use more short-term debt than Ryanair.

With regard to the asset side, we notice that Ryanair has a lot of liquid assets. The recent acquisition attempts are probably a way to invest this cash (Spring 2013). As expected intuitively, we see that an airline's resources are to a large extent invested in tangible assets. For Air France-KLM a net pension asset on the Dutch pension plans represents about 11 of the total assets of the group. We have to mention that this common size analysis is carried out on the group accounts of those companies. Whether the groups have similar structures will be discussed later in the section on segment analysis.

Corporate strategic decisions determine the different business lines in which a company is active. The consolidated group accounts represent the overall performance of the different industries or businesses in which a company competes. Segmental information provides an overview of the different businesses and the proportion of each business unit in the total revenue and the results before interest and taxes (EBIT). A discussion on segmental reporting under IAS can be found in Chapter 25. In the next section we illustrate how the use of segmental data could shed extra light on the analysis of the group's profit and loss account and balance sheet included in the group accounts.

## SEGMENTAL ANALYSIS

Segmental reporting informs the user of the group accounts on the breakdown of the total revenue over the different business segments. For an evaluation of the breakdown of the operational costs in the common size analysis (see Tables 32.4 and 32.5) in a more meaningful way, the segmental data included in the accounts also need to be considered.

We learn from the segmental data that the business lines in which the airline companies are active, differ. Only easyJet and Ryanair are almost exclusively active in the area of passenger transport. As well as passenger transport, the other airline companies such as Lufthansa and Air France-KLM are also active in the area of aircraft maintenance, and Lufthansa are also active in catering and IT. Therefore the operating cost items in the income statement of Lufthansa and Air France-KLM are aggregated figures of different activities. For this reason we only used easyJet and Ryanair for a comparative horizontal analysis because these airlines have been only active in passenger transport over that period of time (see trend analysis or horizontal analysis). An analysis of the segmental data shows that the results of the business lines 'maintenance of aircraft' are less volatile than the results in the business line 'passenger transport'.

In the section on ratio analysis below, we compare the performance and financial position of Unilever and Nestlé. Although both companies are active in consumer business, the question of whether they are fully comparable needs to be raised (go to Appendix II and Appendix III at the end of this chapter and check their operating segments). If one consults the segmental data in the notes to the accounts of both companies, we notice that the information provided on the reportable segments is not comparable. Unilever opts for a geographical breakdown, whereas Nestlé combines geographical with product-based segments. The entity-wide disclosures on products provide some data useful to gaining insight into the differences between the companies. We notice that a substantial part of Unilever's turnover does not result from food and beverages, but from personal care and home care products. Nestlé's turnover results mainly from food and beverages, apart from pharmaceutical products. A comparison of like things would focus on a comparison of the food and beverages activities of Nestlé and Unilever. In the section on ratio analysis, we compare the aggregated information disclosed in the annual accounts.

After the IASB issued IFRS 8, the inter-firm comparability of segmental data declined; since IFRS 8 the valuation rules for the presentation of segmental data can be the internal valuation rules instead of IFRSs. Under IAS 14, the predecessor of IFRS 8, the segmental data had to be valued according to the IFRSs used for the preparation of the annual accounts. Segmental information disclosed under IAS 14 could therefore be used by external stakeholders for comparative analysis. Further, because the reportable segments follow the internal reporting documents (see Chapter 25 on IFRS 8, segmental disclosure) we end up with a segment which can only be used with great difficulty for inter-firm comparisons. The loss of this comparable information explains to a large extent why users of financial statements wrote so many comment letters when the exposure draft 'operating segments' was issued for comment by the IASB and why this topic generates a lot of attention in the post-implementation review.

Segmental reporting data may also be subject to manipulation. When a company plans for an IPO on a particular segment, there is an incentive to present increasing non-volatile results for that segment. On the other hand, if a company considers segmental data as proprietary data, which it does not want to disclose to the competition, then an incentive for manipulation will arise as well.

## RATIO ANALYSIS

Financial statements identify a multitude of figures for us, for example profit before tax, gross profit, total of fixed assets, net current assets. As already mentioned these figures do not mean very much unless we can compare them with something else. In previous sections of this chapter on techniques of financial analysis we have benchmarked the whole statement of financial position and statement of comprehensive income of a company against its own historical data (trend analysis) or against the data of other companies (common size profit and loss account and common size balance sheets) in order to be able to evaluate the overall performance. In Chapter 12 we discussed the technique of ratio analysis. This technique enables us to focus on specific questions concerning the financial situation of the company. We repeat the issues analyzed in Chapter 12 here again in broader context:

- Can the business meet its financial commitments? Can the business pay its debt? Is it liquid (financial status)?

- How successful is the business? Is it making a reasonable profit? Is it utilizing its assets to the fullest? Is it, in fact, profitable and efficient?

- Is the business a suitable investment for shareholders or would returns be greater if they invested elsewhere? Is it a good investment?

Items of the statement of comprehensive income or the statement of financial position related to these questions will be combined in a ratio to provide useful information to the user of the accounts for his or her decision making.

With ratios we relate certain items of the statement of financial position and the statement of comprehensive income to each other in order to evaluate the financial status, performance or investment potential of a business.

Before starting with ratio analysis, one must always check the pitfalls which may hinder the comparability of financial statement data. We have discussed these pitfalls to a large extent in the first part of this chapter so we will not repeat them here. Besides data from the airline industry, in this section on ratio analysis we will also use data from the annual accounts of several groups which specialize in consumer goods, namely Nestlé and Unilever. The main objective in including these accounts is to illustrate the different ratios which might be calculated on the basis of these financial statements rather than compare the financial situation of the two multinationals, which have as similarities that they are recognizable worldwide and are active in consumer goods. Nestlé is active in the following business segments: beverages, milk products, nutrition and ice cream, prepared dishes, cooking aids, pet care, chocolate, confectionery and biscuits and pharmaceutical products. Unilever is active in the following business segments: savoury and dressings, spread and cooking products, beverages, ice cream and frozen products, foods and home and personal care products.

In Appendices II and III to this chapter, we include the balance sheet, comprehensive statement of income, cash flow statement and statement of changes in equity of both companies. With respect to Unilever we also provide an extract of the notes in which information on the breakdown of the operating costs is provided. We observe that both companies still use the term 'balance sheet' to describe the presentation of their assets and liabilities and equity at year-end (financial statements 2012). IAS 1 now calls this statement the 'statement of financial position', but companies are still allowed to use the term 'balance sheet'. Both companies use for the presentation of the statement of comprehensive income the option of presenting the profit or the loss of the year in one statement. Next they add a second statement in which all revenues and costs that are charged directly to equity are presented. The amount of total comprehensive income represents the total of all costs and revenues which have been charged to equity in a direct way (through the statement of comprehensive income) or an indirect way (through the income statement). So far all profitability ratios calculated and EPS figures take only the result into account which is charged to equity through the income statement. When you carry out the activities, please notice the differences in presentation between both companies.

We start with a discussion of the ratios which are helpful in assessing the following questions:

- How successful is the business?
- Is it making a reasonable profit?
- Is it utilizing its assets to the fullest?
- Is it in fact profitable and efficient?

We will pay attention to the characteristics of IAS accounts.

## RATIO ANALYSIS AND THE IAS ACCOUNTS

The IASB foresees a minimum content for the balance sheet or statement of financial position and the statement of comprehensive income.

In some countries domestic GAAP prescribes extensive detailed layouts of the balance sheet and profit and loss account. The IASB did not opt for such an approach. When you look at the profit and loss account of Nestlé and compare it with the layout and the contents of the profit and loss account of Unilever, you will understand the consequence of the IASB's choice. With the approach of the IASB the preparer of the annual accounts has more freedom with regard to presentation. In these circumstances, classification and presentation decisions may be used to create a certain impression. The user, however, is left with the task of reorganizing the information presented in order to try to achieve some comparability, before even ratio analysis or any other financial technique can be applied.

The issue of comparability relates not only to items on the face of the statement of financial position or the statement of comprehensive income, which are presented under different headings, but also to items which are presented by one company in the notes where the other companies opt for a disclosure on the face of the statement of financial position.

In some countries the national GAAP prescribe the use of a specified layout with a specified number of items which must appear on the statement of financial position and the statement of comprehensive income. If an item is not present or does not apply to the company, the preparer must insert a zero or the words 'not available'. In relation to the IAS solution companies can disclose a certain item under another line item and hide the information from the public by not presenting that specific single line item on the face of the statement of financial position or the statement of comprehensive income. Under the IAS a number of items must be recognized in the equity account without influencing the profit or loss reported on the income statement. In relation to other items (e.g. actuarial gains and losses and past service costs in relation to pension plans) companies have a choice. Comparing performance ratios between companies, we need to consider the choices made by companies.

## IASB mixed valuation model

In the early years the IASC opted for the historical cost model. In recent years the fair value approach gained more ground, especially in the later IASs and the new IFRS. Adaptations were also made to early IASs in order to allow for revaluations of asset items. As a result, companies often have a choice between the historical cost model or the fair value model. A user of the accounts must be aware of the difference. Ideally, a company would provide the two values (historical cost and fair value) so that users of the accounts could carry out a reconciliation of the asset values in order to improve comparability. For example, if we analyze the balance sheet of Unilever, we notice the presence of biological assets.

### ACTIVITY 32.6

After consulting IAS 41, *Agricultural Products*, on Course-Mate, discover which valuation model the IASB prefers for biological assets and agricultural products.

*Activity feedback*
*IAS 41 prefers the fair value model for agricultural products and biological assets, though the historical cost method is allowed.*

If we consult the notes of the annual accounts of Unilever we notice that Unilever applies the fair value method:

The fair value of tea bushes older than 10 years is based on the market price of the estimated recoverable tea leaf volumes, net of harvest costs. The fair value of palm trees older than 8 years is based on the market price of the estimated recoverable palm oil volumes, net of harvest costs. The fair value of immature tea bushes and oil palm trees is based on the present value of the net cash flows expected to be generated by the plants at maturity.

(Unilever Annual Report 2005, p. 102, n. 12)

If we analyze the balance sheet of LVMH (Louis Vuitton Moet Hennessy – a company active in the wine and spirits segment, the jewellery and watches segment, and fashion and leather goods) we do not observe biological assets, although IAS 1 requires them to be mentioned as a single line item on the face of the balance sheet. The notes of the accounts, however, inform us that the group has biological assets, but that they are valued according to the historical cost model and that they are included in the single line item 'property, plant and equipment':

> Vines, for champagnes, cognacs and other wines produced by the Group, are considered as biological assets as defined in IAS 41 *Agriculture*. As their valuation at market value differs little from that recognized at historical cost, no revaluation is undertaken for these assets.

> (LVMH Annual Report 2005, p. 76, n. 1.10)

## Performance of the firm

Ratios which try to give a picture of a firm's profitability combine the result of a firm with the investments made for the generation of that result. The two most common ratios are return on equity (ROE) and return on assets (ROA).

$$\text{Return on equity (ROE)} = \text{Profit/Equity}$$

The profit figure used in this ratio can be before or after tax. In the case of group accounts one has to make sure that if the minority interests are not added up to the equity of the group, the share in the profit of the company of the minority interests should be excluded from the profit in the numerator as well. Besides ROE another widely used profitability ratio is ROA:

$$\text{Return on assets (ROA)} = (\text{Profit before tax} + \text{Interest})/\text{Total assets}$$

Instead of using the total assets in the denominator, net total assets can be used. The net assets are equal to the equity of the company and the long-term debts. This ratio is also often called return on capital employed (ROCE) or return of net total assets:

$$\text{Return on capital employed (ROCE)} = (\text{Profit before tax} + \text{Long-term interest})$$
$$/(\text{Equity} + \text{Long-term debt})$$

Applicable to the calculation of all performance ratios, ROA, ROE and ROCE, is the question of which investment base with which one should compare the result: investment base at the beginning of the year or an average equity base. In practice, very often the equity base at the end of the year is taken. If one has data available only for one year, then in that case there is not much of a choice.

In order to determine whether the obtained profitability is sufficient or excellent, one needs a benchmark. Suitable benchmarks for these ratios, besides the already known time series data and competitor or industry data, could be the proceeds of an investment in risk-free loans. The latter could answer the question: would the owners be better off selling the business and placing the proceeds in a bank deposit account?

## ACTIVITY 32.7

Calculate the ROA and the ROE of Nestlé and Unilever. Evaluate what the difference between the outcome of the ratios will be according to the different investment bases used [investment base at the beginning of the year ($= t - 1$) and investment base at the end of the year ($= t$)]. Compare also the difference of an ROE, whereby minority interests are included with an ROE with minority interests ($= MI$) are not included. We calculate the ROE after tax.

### Activity feedback

| | Nestlé | | Unilever | |
|---|---|---|---|---|
| $ROA_{t-1}$ | $\dfrac{14\ 042}{1\ 114\ 091}$ | 12.30% | $\dfrac{7\ 209}{47\ 512}$ | 15.17% |
| $ROA_t$ | $\dfrac{14\ 042}{126\ 229}$ | 11.12% | $\dfrac{7\ 209}{46\ 166}$ | 15.61% |
| $ROE_t$ | $\dfrac{11\ 060}{58\ 274}$ | 18.97% | $\dfrac{4\ 948}{14\ 293}$ | 34.61% |
| $ROE_t$ with MI | $\dfrac{11\ 060}{62\ 604}$ | 17.60% | $\dfrac{4\ 948}{15\ 716}$ | 31.48% |
| $ROE_t$ without MI | $\dfrac{10\ 611}{60\ 947}$ | 17.40% | $\dfrac{4\ 480}{15\ 159}$ | 29.55% |

If we compare the profitability ratios of the two companies, we notice that the ROAs are much closer to each other than the ROE. So on the operating side the companies perform in a rather similar way. The difference with regard to ROE is caused by the higher leverage of Unilever (see Activity 32.14) and therefore Unilever is able to realize a larger improvement between ROA and ROE than Nestlé. The leverage of a firm is the result of a financing decision taken by top management on the use of different financial sources by the company (equity versus debt). However, this positive effect of higher ROE has as a consequence as well that Unilever scores higher on the ratios presenting financial risk (see later in this section). When a company is making profit then ROA and ROE are always lower if the investment base at the end of the year is taken.

The return on total assets can be calculated at corporate level, if the information is available on the level of the operating segments through segmental disclosure, the profitability of the reportable segments can be calculated as well.

If we take total comprehensive income of both companies and calculate ROA and ROE using total assets and total equity at the end of the reporting period, we end up with the figures below:

| | *Nestlé* | *Unilever* |
|---|---|---|
| ROA | $10\ 021/126\ 229 = 7.9$ | $4\ 389/46\ 166 = 9.50$ |
| ROE | $9\ 430/62\ 604 = 15.06$ | $3\ 863/15\ 159 = 25.48$ |

For both companies the other comprehensive income is negative. The most important items for both companies are the losses on pension schemes and the foreign currency translations. Given the volatility in these other comprehensive income items (see prior year figures of Nestlé and Unilever), we have to be very cautious in using this information.

To retrieve information on operating decisions and investment decisions, the profitability ratio ROA can be broken down further by relating results to sales and sales to the investment base:

$$\text{Return on assets} = \frac{\text{Profit}}{\text{Total sales}} \times \frac{\text{Total sales}}{\text{Assets}}$$

The first ratio (profit/total sales) is called the profit margin ratio which expresses the result in a currency generated by each currency unit of sales. This ratio focuses on profitability and is a result of the operating decisions taken in the company. The second ratio (total sales/assets) focuses on efficiency and provides information on investment decisions and how efficiently these investments are used.

An analysis of the different cost components in relation to the sales figures could reveal interesting differences between companies. If costs are classified in the profit and loss account according to their function, then the following ratios could be calculated:

- cost of sales/sales
- marketing and sales costs/sales
- distribution cost/sales
- administrative cost/sales.

## ACTIVITY 32.8

### Recent accounting developments

Which 'profit' is the most meaningful to be combined with sales in the ratio (profit/total sales)? Look at the statement of comprehensive income of Unilever and Nestlé.

### Activity feedback

There is the choice between the operating result and the net result of the company. The operating result is related directly to the sales, whereas the net result is also influenced by financing activities. So the most obvious choice is the operating result. If the net result is used, then the combination with the asset turnover (total sales/assets) results in the ROA figure again.

## ACTIVITY 32.9

Calculate the ratios for Nestlé and Unilever.

### Activity feedback

| | Nestlé | | Unilever | |
|---|---|---|---|---|
| Profit margin | $\dfrac{13\ 451}{92\ 186}$ | 14.59% | $\dfrac{6\ 683}{51\ 324}$ | 13.02% |
| Asset turnover | $\dfrac{92\ 186}{126\ 229}$ | 0.73 | $\dfrac{51\ 324}{46\ 166}$ | 1.11% |

Although Nestlé and Unilever arrive at similar ROAs, there are small underlying differences. The product margins of Nestlé are slightly higher than those of Unilever. Nestlé's turnover of total assets is somewhat lower than Unilever's turnover.

In the section on industry analysis in Chapter 31 we discussed factors influencing the pricing policy of a company and those influencing the cost levels. Sales price levels and cost levels together determine the profit margin.

## ACTIVITY 32.10

Try to calculate the ratios for cost of sales/sales, marketing and sales cost/sales, distribution cost/sales and administrative cost/sales for the two groups. What do you observe? Nestlé discloses these cost items on the face of the income statement. With regard to Unilever, however, these items are disclosed in the notes. Note 3 of the accounts of Unilever reveals that the selling and administrative costs are €13 632. The marketing costs are included in the item 'other operating costs'. Note 3 reveals that other operating costs includes the following item 'Advertising and promotion' = €6763.

### Activity feedback
The layouts of the profit and loss accounts are different and for Unilever the information is not on the face of the profit and loss account, but is to be found in the notes. The two companies make a different subdivision so that the individual components cannot be compared. For comparative purposes we have added up distribution costs, marketing costs and selling and administrative costs:

|  | Nestlé | Unilever |
|---|---|---|
| Cost of goods sold/sales | 52.50% | 59.82% |
| Marketing, sales, distribution and administrative costs\sales | 30.21% | 32.92% |

The figures confirm what is generally known: these companies spent a lot of money on marketing and sales costs.

The information obtained from these ratios which relate the different cost components to the sales figure can also be obtained from a common size analysis of the profit and loss account. See, for example, the common size analysis of the operating cost items of the airlines in Table 32.4.

The next group of ratios to be examined concentrates on the investment decisions and how effectively these assets in which the firm has invested are used. The performance of a firm is influenced not only by the profit margin obtained on its products or services but also by the effectiveness of its operations. The turnover of assets can be regarded as an efficiency ratio, but it is one of a very general nature. Long-term as well as short-term assets are included in the overall ratio total sales/total assets. With regard to efficiency, the short-term elements are the centre of attention, although in some industries the efficient use of the long-term assets is much more crucial.

The following ratios focus on the turnover of short-term assets.

**Turnover of inventory** The turnover of inventory is calculated as the 'cost of goods sold/inventory'. The average inventory level is used as denominator. The turnover of the inventory could also be expressed in days, the ratio then becomes ((average inventory/cost of goods sold) × 365). (See Activity 32.11.)

Using the same ratio structure the turnover of trade receivables and trade payables can be calculated, and the average collection or payment period. The following ratios provide that information (and see Activity 32.12):

- sales/trade receivables
- (trade receivables/sales) × 365
- purchases/trade payables
- (trade payables/purchases) × 365.

Not only efficiency influences the outcome of these ratios. They could be influenced by industry characteristics. Average collection periods are often determined by industry practice. Also country influences can play a role.

The ratios concerning the trade payables can only be calculated if information on the purchases is provided in the annual accounts.

## ACTIVITY 32.11

Calculate the inventory turnover and the number of inventory days for the two companies.

### Activity feedback

| | Nestlé | | Unilever | |
|---|---|---|---|---|
| Inventory turnover | $\dfrac{48\ 398}{9\ 125}$ | 5.30 | $\dfrac{30\ 703}{4\ 436}$ | 6.92 |
| Number of inventory days | | 68 days | | 52 days |

These companies are very close to each other. One must be cautious since a higher turnover rate could be due either to more efficient inventory management or to the perishable nature of the products.

## ACTIVITY 32.12

Calculate the trade receivable turnover and the collection period for Nestlé and Unilever.

### Activity feedback

| | Nestlé | | Unilever | |
|---|---|---|---|---|
| Trade receivables turnover | $\dfrac{92\ 186}{13\ 404}$ | 6.87 | $\dfrac{51\ 324}{4\ 436}$ | 11.56 |
| Collection period | | 53 days | | 31 days |

Nestlé uses in its presentation for financial analysts the concept of 'cash conversion cycle', which consists of the collection period plus the number of days in inventory minus the days of credit granted by suppliers. In order to calculate the last item, it uses cost of goods sold in the denominator, whereas more correctly it should use the amount purchased. The figure they present in this presentation is lower than the figure we arrive at. We notice that Unilever is able to collect its receivables earlier than Nestlé.

The value obtained for the ratios presented will differ between industries (e.g. a steel company versus a wholesale company), and the usefulness of the ratios will also differ according to the industry.

**Industry-specific ratios** The ratio cost of goods sold/sales is more meaningful for companies active in consumer and industrial goods than for companies in a service industry such as insurance companies and banks. Some industries have their own specific ratios (such as banks, insurance companies, airlines) which characterize the key drivers of performance in that specific industry. For the airline industry such ratios are, for example, unit revenue or yield which represent the average amount of traffic revenue per RPK/RPM or RTK/RTM. In this ratio revenue passenger kilometres/miles (RPK/M) is defined as the number of paying passengers multiplied by the distance they are flown in kilometres/miles. Revenue tonne kilometres/miles (RTK/M) is defined as the number of tonnes of paid traffic (passengers, freight and mail) multiplied by the distance this traffic is flown in kilometres or miles.

These operating statistics or industry-specific key ratios are disclosed by companies on a voluntary basis. Industry practice is usually the driving force for this type of disclosure. This implies that the level of disclosure of these industry-specific ratios differs significantly between companies. The issue of quality of disclosure, which was discussed in Chapter 31, is relevant in this context. Further it is essential to keep in mind that these operating statistics or ratios are presented in the non-audited part of the annual report. A proper comparison between companies based on these voluntary disclosed industry ratios is therefore not always possible and should be executed with great caution as it concerns non-audited data.

## Financial status

In order to judge the financial situation of a firm, the external stakeholders want answers to questions such as: Can the business meet its financial commitments? Can the business pay its debt? Is it liquid? External stakeholders need information on the financial status of a company. It is essential for a business to be able to pay its debts as and when they fall due, otherwise its chances of remaining in operation become remote. For that purpose there is a need to analyze the assets available to the company to meet its liabilities. This can be done in the short-, medium- and long-term.

**Short-term financial status or the liquidity of a firm** If we analyze the assets available in order to meet the short-term liabilities of the firm, we focus on the structure of the working capital of a company, namely the relation between current assets and current liabilities. The acid test ratio or quick ratio and the current ratio can be used for this purpose (see Activity 32.13).

$$\text{Current ratio} = \text{Current assets}/\text{Current liabilities}$$
$$\text{Acid test ratio} = (\text{Current assets} - \text{Inventory}) = \text{Current liabilities}$$

An analysis of the short-term liquidity uncovers a company's ability to pay or satisfy all short-term obligations as they fall due. The acid test ratio is a more conservative indicator of the short-term liquidity risk than the current ratio.

If one calculates the current liabilities on the basis of IAS financial statements, one always needs to check whether long-term borrowings due within 12 months have not been mentioned under the amount of long-term liabilities. For the calculation of the above ratios we have taken the amounts of current liabilities mentioned on the face of the balance sheet. If a company fully complies with IAS 1 and it includes this amount of long-term borrowing due within 12 months under the long-term debt, then this implies that there is already a refinance agreement for those amounts (IAS 1) and as such those amounts are not 'economically speaking' due within 12 months.

Current assets are supposed to be converted into cash in the current operating cycle of the company. The higher the ratio the more resources a company has available to repay the short-term debts. In the acid test or quick ratio the inventory is excluded from the current assets as it is the least convertible item of the group. It is often observed that companies in distress keep production levels constant although their sales drop. If these companies use a full cost approach for inventory valuation purposes then they are able to capitalize a part of their overhead in a growing inventory amount. The IAS/IFRS only allow the full cost approach for inventory valuation purposes (see Chapter 17). This improves the comparability among the data published by firms complying with IAS/IFRS.

## ACTIVITY 32.13

Calculate both current and acid test ratios for Nestlé and Unilever.

### Activity feedback

|  | Nestlé |  | Unilever |  |
|---|---|---|---|---|
| Current ratio | $\frac{35\ 205}{38\ 753}$ | 0.90 | $\frac{12\ 147}{15\ 815}$ | 0.76 |
| Acid test ratio | $\frac{26\ 080}{38\ 753}$ | 0.67 | $\frac{7\ 711}{15\ 815}$ | 0.48 |

Both companies have a current ratio lower than one. This implies that the suppliers of those companies are important providers of financial resources to those companies.

It is difficult to set absolute benchmarks for short-term liquidity ratios, the level of the ratio is highly dependent on industry characteristics. So only companies from the same industry can serve as an appropriate benchmark for judgement of the liquidity.

**Long-term financial status** The long-term financial status of a company refers to the ability of a company to meet its debt in the long run. A key element in this respect is the capital structure of the firm. Companies have two main sources of funds, namely debt and equity. Each has different well known characteristics (e.g. fixed versus variable rewards, fixed repayment schedules versus repayment when the company liquidates). The financial risk or financial strength of a company is measured by ratios which relate debt to equity. The most commonly used ratio worldwide in this respect is the debt/equity ratio. A high debt/equity ratio implies higher financial risk, since a higher ratio points at higher interest charges and a wider exposure to possible interest changes. Further, debt needs to be repaid often at a fixed date irrespective of whether or not the company has sufficient funds available.

Several alterations can be made to the numerator and the denominator of this ratio in relation to the focus of the analysis, e.g. Debt/(Equity + Debt), Long-term Debt/Equity.

Further, the debt/equity ratio could be influenced by national or institutional differences (see Chapter 2). In countries with a shareholder orientation the debt/equity ratio will be lower than in countries with a credit orientation. Information on the financial risk of a company can be provided by the ratios but also by a common size analysis of the statement of financial position structure (see the section on common size analysis in this chapter) or by trend analysis with ratios as input data. Ratio analysis and common size analysis are complementary techniques of analysis rather than substitutes.

## ACTIVITY 32.14

Calculate debt/equity ratios for the two companies.

### Activity feedback

| | Nestlé | | Unilver | |
|---|---|---|---|---|
| Debt/equity | $\frac{63\ 625}{62\ 604}$ | 1.01 | $\frac{30\ 450}{15\ 716}$ | 1.93 |
| Debt/equity + debt | $\frac{63\ 625}{126\ 229}$ | 0.50 | $\frac{30\ 450}{46\ 166}$ | 0.65 |
| Long-term debt/equity | $\frac{24\ 872}{62\ 604}$ | 0.39 | $\frac{15\ 716}{46\ 166}$ | 0.93 |
| Equity/debt + equity | | 0.49 | | 0.34 |

Unilever is more financed through external debt, whereas Nestlé is financed to a large extent by equity. Half of the debt of Unilever is short-term debt. Through this high leverage Unilever is able to increase its ROE substantially, as its ROA is above its cost of debt. However, this high leverage also implies that Unilever faces a higher financial risk than Nestlé. In order to know if it is a relatively high risk one needs to compare Unilever's data with all companies in the same industry.

The debt/equity ratio is often used in debt covenants. In Chapter 31 we discussed how a threat of a possible violation of the debt covenants could lead to annual accounts management. A ratio which tries to circumvent the effect of these practices of annual accounts management is the interest cover ratio. This ratio indicates the safety margin between profit and interest charges or the ratio shows how many times operating profit covers net financial expenses:

Interest cover ratio = Profit before interest and taxation / Net interest costs

## ACTIVITY 32.15

Calculate the interest cover ratio for the two companies.

### Activity feedback

| | Nestlé | | Unilever | |
|---|---|---|---|---|
| Interest cover ratio | $\frac{13\ 451}{591}$ | 22.75 | $\frac{7\ 209}{526}$ | 13.703 |

Nestlé has a higher safety margin than Unilever and this is no surprise, since Unilever has a higher leverage. For the calculation of the net interest cost of Unilever, we eliminated the impact of the pension costs recorded under the finance costs on the income statement of Unilever.

The financial risk of a company is directly linked to the capital structure of a company. A company with a high proportion of debt financing is highly leveraged.

High financial leverage implies high risk. To get an idea about the leverage of the firm the debt/equity ratio is often used. Financial leverage influences the financial risk of a company and further it has an impact on the relation between ROE and ROA. Whether or not ROE is bigger than ROA depends on two elements. First, the leverage of the company and second, the difference between ROA and the interest cost of the firm. The latter is often called the spread. If the obtained ROA is higher than the interest cost, a company can increase the level of ROE compared to ROA by switching from equity financing to debt financing. If, however, ROA is lower than the interest cost of the firm, the relation works in the opposite way. ROE will be lower than ROA and the difference will increase with higher leverage.

Up to now in this section on ratio analysis we have used ratios taken from other companies as benchmarks. Another possibility is to benchmark a ratio against its own historical performance within the same firm. In this type of analysis, trend analysis is combined with ratio analysis. The red flags of comparability should also be taken into account when interpreting the data.

In Appendix I to this chapter, we include a trend analysis and common size analysis using the ratios of a company instead of the original absolute amounts. We perform this analysis in order to discuss the financial situation of Sabena.

## Investment perspective

Potential investors in a company use different sets of information in order to decide whether or not to buy shares of a certain company. The question on their mind is whether the company is a worthwhile investment. When investors possess shares in a company they continuously assess their investment. The decision to be taken is a 'hold' or 'sell' decision.

Although for these 'buy' or 'sell' decisions the ratios on the profitability, efficiency and financial status of a company provide useful information, specific ratios are developed with regard to this investment decision. These ratios focus on those elements which are specifically relevant for shareholders, namely the return obtained on their investment. This return can take the form of dividends or capital appreciation.

In Chapter 12 we presented a number of different ratios which could be used by investors to evaluate the profit potential of their investment. These ratios concentrated on the dividend performance of these companies (net dividend and dividend cover ratio), on the earnings potential of the investment (earnings per share) and on the evolution of the share price of those companies (price earnings ratio). The earnings per share ratio and the price earnings ratio have been discussed in Chapter 25.

These investment ratios are usually included and discussed in reports of financial analysts or reports of industry analysts. Investors and potential investors use the information contained in those reports to make buy, hold or sell decisions.

In order to illustrate these investor ratios, we present the EPS and ROE of the four airlines based on their financial statements of 2005 and compare these with the price/earnings ratio (PE ratio taken from Davy European Transport and Leisure Report 2006; see Ryanair website).

|  | *BEPS* | *DEPS* | *PE* | *ROE* |
|---|---|---|---|---|
| Air France/KLM | 3.25€ | 3.25€ | 11.6 | 11% |
| British Airways | 40.4p | 39.8p | 10 | 24% |
| Lufthansa | 0.95€ | 0.95€ | 23 | 10.4% |
| Ryanair | 40.00€ | 39.74€ | 20 | 15.3% |

What did these figures mean at that time?

At the time the report was made, the market wanted to pay 20 times the EPS of Ryanair and Lufthansa, whereas investors wanted to pay only ten times the EPS of Air France-KLM and British Airways. Further we observe that there is not exactly a link between ROE and PE. This is because in the PE ratio much more information is included than in ROE, which is a historical measure. The appraisal by the investors of opportunities for the company, and the way in which the top management of the company can react to threats and opportunities in the market, all influence the share price and, as a result, the PE ratio. On the other hand, the 10 PE value of British Airways and Air France-KLM could also mean that these companies were undervalued at the time of the report.

Companies try to influence the share price not only by providing those accounting numbers to the market which the market appreciates (see Chapter 31), but also by providing information to the market outside the financial statements. This information is non-audited and therefore can be more subject to impression management. Conference calls and financial analysts' presentations have become a 'classical' means of communicating with the investor community, as well as putting information on the website of the company. Very often the company management translates the accounting numbers into new numbers which suit their message better. They create their own ratios, such as 'like for like sales', 'profit before one time expenditures, before goodwill and impairment', and many others. All the ratios presented by companies in their financial analysts' presentations and as key figures in the annual reports must be regarded with caution. Very often these are figures taken from the annual accounts but corrected for negative elements; those corrections are never presented as corrections but as improvements of the figures of the annual accounts.

In the following sections we are going to analyze a number of new measures created for shareholders in order to measure the value of the company.

**Shareholder value and total shareholder return** These ratios could be labelled as the more 'traditional' ones to use for assessing the attractiveness of an investment in certain shares. In the 1980s the concept of shareholder value emerged. Total shareholder return represents the change in capital value of a company over a one-year period, plus dividends, expressed as a plus or minus percentage of the opening value.

The concept of 'total shareholder return' is used by Unilever, as described in the following extract from the company's 2009 Annual Report (p. 46):

## REAL WORLD ILLUSTRATION

### Total Shareholder Return (TSR)

TSR measures the returns received by a shareholder, capturing both the increase in share price and the value of dividend income (assuming dividends are re-invested). Unilever's TSR performance is compared with a peer group of competitors over a three-year rolling performance period. This period is sensitive enough to reflect changes but long enough to smooth out short-term volatility. The return is expressed in US dollars, based on the equivalent US dollar share price for NV and PLC. US dollars were chosen to facilitate comparison with companies in Unilever's chosen reference group. The choice of currency affects the absolute TSR but not the relative ranking.

Unilever's TSR target is to be in the top third of a reference group including 20 other international consumer goods companies on a three-year rolling basis. At the end of 2008 we were positioned 9th, and at the end of 2009 the ranking was 5th. In 2009, the following companies formed the peer group of comparator companies:

*(Continued)*

**REAL WORLD ILLUSTRATION 32.2** *(Continued)*

| | | |
|---|---|---|
| Avon | Heinz | Orkla |
| Beiersdorf | Kao | Pepsico |
| Cadbury | Kimberly–Clark | Procter & Gamble |
| Clorox | Kraft | Reckitt Benckiser |
| Coca-Cola | Lion | Sara Lee |
| Colgate | L'Oreal | Shiseido |
| Danone | Nestlé | |

Unilever's position relative to the TSR reference group:

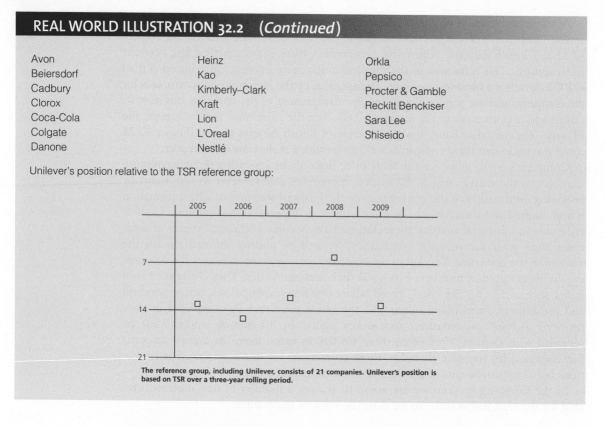

The reference group, including Unilever, consists of 21 companies. Unilever's position is based on TSR over a three-year rolling period.

The founding father of the concept of shareholder value was Rappaport (1998) and the idea behind the concept was that the future stream of forecast earnings would be a much better starting point to evaluate the future economic potential of a firm. Future cash flows are often used as a proxy for future earnings. Various metrics were developed in the wake of this shareholder value approach. Within the set of 'new' ratios two groups can be distinguished, namely one group of metrics which is developed around the economic value added concept and, second, a group of ratios which focuses on the future cash flows of a firm.

Some of these new metrics have really been developed recently, while others have been around for years under another name. Those that have been around for years have been relabelled after minor modifications to the existing metric. The most well known is the EVA concept which builds on the residual income concept and has been trademarked by Stern Stewart & Co.:

> The foundations for these new performance measures are residual income and internal rate of return (IRR) concepts developed in the 1950s and 1960s. Stern Stewart & Co's trademarked 'economic value added' however is the firm's proprietary adaptation of residual income.
>
> (Ittner and Larcker, 2001)

In essence, economic value added is created when the net operating profit after tax is higher than the company's cost of capital (including debt and equity). Stern Stewart suggest several corrections to the different items of the concept in order to undo accounting distortions resulting from accrual accounting.

EVA is a single-period measure and in order to be useful for financial analysis it should be judged against prior year data. Further, EVA is a monetary measure which is less useful for inter-firm comparison. These shortcomings for external analysis are not surprising since EVA was developed in the first place as a management tool for driving the value creation within the firm. A firm can increase its economic value added through the following actions:

- increasing the net operating profit after tax by operational measures which could increase revenues, decrease costs or both
- reducing the cost of capital by changing the financing structure of the company
- improving the utilization of the capital employed.

The second group of 'new' ratios represents multi-period metrics which are built on cash flow information. The most well-known metric is the cash flow return on investment (CFROI). This concept is developed by the Boston Consulting Group and represents an economic measure of a company's performance that reflects the average underlying IRR on all existing investment projects. The CFROI can be defined as annual gross cash flow relative to the invested capital of the business unit.

Based on a simplified CFROI rate the Boston Consulting Group developed a residual income measure, which is called cash value added (CVA). CVA is the spread between CFROI and the real cost of capital, multiplied with the investment in fixed assets plus working capital.

We learn from the annual report of Lufthansa, financial year 2012 (pp. 30–32) that CVA is their central financial performance indicator. An illustration of Lufthansa's interpretation of value-based management is reproduced here.

## REAL WORLD ILLUSTRATION

Since 2011, the renewed LH-Performance programmes have run for four years. More information on the share programmes is available at www.lufthansagroup.com/investor-relations.

### Results 'LH-Performance'

|  | End of programme | Outperformance as of 31.12.2012 in % | Performance as of 31.12.2012 in % |
| --- | --- | --- | --- |
| LH-Performance 2012 | 2016 | 2 | 18 |
| LH-Performance 2011 | 2015 | 4 | 26 |
| LH-Performance 2010 | 2013 | 19 | −2 |
| LH-Performance 2009 | 2012 | 18 | −3 |

**No changes to the structure and volume of Executive and Supervisory Board remuneration in the reporting year (Remuneration report in accordance with Section 315 Paragraph 2 No. 4 HGB)**

The structure of Executive Board remuneration introduced in 2011 is intended to achieve a roughly equal balance between the two components 'fixed annual salary' and 'variable annual bonus and remuneration with a long-term incentive effect and risk characteristics'. It has been ensured that the variable remuneration components are overwhelmingly based on a period of several years. They are subject to a satisfactory operating result and a significant minimum performance or outperformance of the Lufthansa share.

*(Continued)*

## REAL WORLD ILLUSTRATION 32.3 *(Continued)*

For the financial year 2012, the members of the Supervisory Board were paid a fixed sum of EUR 50 000 for an ordinary member, plus a variable bonus dependent on net profit for the period, whereby the total remuneration of an ordinary member of the Supervisory Board was capped at EUR 100 000. In accordance with the resolution adopted at the Annual General Meeting on 8 May 2012, the remuneration of Supervisory Board members is to be switched to an exclusively fixed sum of EUR 80 000 for an ordinary member with effect from the financial year 2013. The detailed remuneration report and amounts paid to the individual members of the Executive and Supervisory Boards can be found in the Notes to the consolidated financial statements, '**Note 50' from p. 193**.

### Value-based management and targets

#### Sustainable increase in Company value is the ultimate objective

Since 1999, the Lufthansa Group has applied a value-based management system to lead and manage the Group. This approach is an integral part of all planning, management and controlling processes. The demands made of the Company by investors and lenders in terms of sustainable capital appreciation are firmly embedded in the whole system of corporate management. The objective is to create sustainable value across economic cycles. The achievement of value creation targets is reviewed on a regular basis and the results are incorporated into our internal and external reporting. The value-based management system is also linked to performance-related pay. Details can be found in the section '**Performance-related pay for managers is linked to the Company's performance' from p. 29**

#### Value contribution is measured by CVA

The Lufthansa Group uses CVA as its main performance indicator. CVA is based on the return expectations of all investors and lenders and measures the value contribution generated in the reporting period by each individual business segment and by the Group as a whole.

The CVA is an absolute residual amount, which is calculated as the difference between the cash flow generated in a given year and the minimum cash flow required to increase the value of the Company. If the cash flow generated is higher than the minimum required cash flow, the value creation is expressed by a positive CVA. The individual parameters are calculated as follows.

The minimum required cash flow is the sum of the required return on capital employed, the capital recovery rate and the flat tax rate. The capital base is defined as the total of non-current and current assets less interest-free liabilities. It is measured at historic cost. This makes value calculation and generation independent of the depreciation and amortization applied. The required return on capital is calculated using the weighted average costs of debt and equity for the Lufthansa Group and for the individual operating segments (weighted average cost of capital – WACC).

The WACC for the 2012 financial year is determined by the parameters shown in the following table:

#### Return on capital 2012

| in % | |
|---|---|
| Risk-free market interest rate | 3.2 |
| Market risk premium | 5.1 |
| Beta factor | 1.1 |
| Proportion of equity | 50.0 |
| Proportion of debt | 50.0 |
| **Cost of equity** | **8.8** |
| **Cost of debt** | **3.6** |

These parameters are reviewed every year and updated as required for the following year's corporate planning and performance measurement. Short-term fluctuations are smoothed in order to ensure the long-term character of the concept. In the course of the regular review of the individual parameters of CVA, it became apparent that, given consistently low interest rates and further falls in the risk premium for shareholders' equity, it was necessary to adjust the WACC. In the following financial year 2013, a WACC of 6.2 per cent is used for the Lufthansa Group.

On the basis of the financial strategy, a target capital structure of 50 per cent equity at market value and 50 per cent debt is used to calculate the WACC for both the Group and the business segments. The different segment risks are factored in by means of individual costs of equity, and therefore total costs of capital. In this way, the Lufthansa Group ensures that the allocation of capital to projects in the business segments is adjusted for risk. The following table illustrates the required return on

## REAL WORLD ILLUSTRATION 32.3    (Continued)

capital for the Lufthansa Group and its individual business segments:

### Cost of capital (WACC) for the Group and the business segments

| in % | 2012 | 2011 | 2010 | 2009 | 2008 |
|---|---|---|---|---|---|
| Group | 7.0 | 7.0 | 7.9 | 7.9 | 7.9 |
| Passenger Airline Group | 7.0 | 7.0 | 7.9 | 7.9 | 7.9 |
| Logistics | 7.2 | 7.2 | 8.2 | 8.2 | 8.2 |
| MRO | 6.7 | 6.7 | 7.6 | 7.6 | 7.6 |
| Catering | 7.0 | 7.0 | 7.9 | 7.9 | 7.9 |
| IT Services | 6.7 | 6.7 | 7.6 | 7.6 | 7.6 |

The minimum required cash flow includes what is known as capital recovery, in order to reflect the depletion of the Company's non-current assets in the production process. This is derived from total depreciable non-current assets and represents the amount that needs to be put by every year and invested at a rate equivalent to the WACC in order to recoup the amount of the purchase costs by the end of the asset's useful life. Finally, the expected tax payment is added by applying a surcharge of currently 0.6 per cent of the capital base. The resulting minimum required cash flow for the year 2012 came to EUR 3.0bn (previous year: EUR 3.0bn).

### Reconciliation EBITDA$^{plus}$

| in €m | 2012 | 2011 |
|---|---|---|
| **Operating result** | **524** | **820** |
| Depreciation and amortization | 1 722 | 1 663 |
| Result from disposal of property, plant and equipment | 53 | 29 |
| Income from reversal of provisions | 162 | 163 |
| Impairment losses on intangible assets and property, plant and equipment | −137 | −76 |
| Change in pension provisions before interests | 132 | 138 |
| **Operating EBITDA$^{plus}$** | **2 456** | **2 737** |
| Pro rata pre-tax results of non-consolidated equity investments | 124 | 168 |
| Interest income | 141 | 177 |
| Result from disposal of financial assets | 642 | −30 |
| **Financial EBITDA$^{plus}$** | **907** | **315** |
| **EBITDA$^{plus}$** | **3 363** | **3 052** |

In the Lufthansa Group, the cash flow effectively generated is represented by EBITDA$^{plus}$, which is made up of an operating and a financial component. The operating component of EBITDA$^{plus}$ is derived from the operating result by adjusting it for non-cash items. These are principally depreciation and amortization, income from the write-back of provisions and net changes in pension provisions. Then the financial component of EBITDA$^{plus}$ is added, comprising pro rata pre-tax earnings of non-consolidated equity investments, net interest income and earnings contributions from the disposal of financial investments. This ensures that EBITDA$^{plus}$ includes all significant cash-relevant items. In the reporting year, the Lufthansa Group's EBITDA$^{plus}$ came to EUR 3.4bn (previous year: EUR 3.1bn).

In order to obtain the CVA the minimum required cash flow is then deducted from EBITDA$^{plus}$.

### Calculation of cash value added (CVA) 2012

| in €m | | |
|---|---|---|
| Cash flow (EBITDA$^{plus}$) | | 3 363 |
| (operating result + reconciliation items) | | |
| Minimum required cash flow | 2 988 | |
| (capital base × cost of capital) + (depreciable capital base × capital recovery rate) | | |
| | **CVA** | **375** |

### The Lufthansa Group generated a value contribution of EUR 375m in 2012

In the financial year 2012, the Lufthansa Group generated a positive CVA of EUR 375m. The reason for the substantial increase compared with the previous year

(Continued)

## REAL WORLD ILLUSTRATION 32.3  (*Continued*)

was a significantly positive earnings effect from the disposal of financial investments, which resulted from the transfer and sale of shares in Amadeus IT Holding S.A. Further information can be found in the chapter '**Earnings position' on p. 47.**

### Value creation (CVA) of the Lufthansa Group and the business segments

| in €m | 2012 | 2011 | 2010 | 2009 | 2008 |
|---|---|---|---|---|---|
| Group | 375 | 99 | 71 | −858 | 654 |
| Passenger Airline Group | −340 | −122 | −198 | −691 | 346 |
| Logistics | 65 | 202 | 233 | −264 | 71 |
| MRO | 241 | 152 | 172 | 164 | 188 |
| Catering | 39 | −25 | −28 | −68 | −17 |
| IT Services | 7 | 23 | −23 | 3 | 29 |

Experience shows that it is difficult to give a forecast for future value creation. The current macroeconomic outlook makes achieving a positive CVA in 2013 look ambitious. The Lufthansa Group nevertheless stands by its intention of generating sustainable value across economic cycles. In the last ten years, for example, the Lufthansa Group has generated a positive aggregate value of EUR 2.2bn.

We have a number of additional financial targets in addition to value creation that are described more closely in the following section and in the section '**Financial strategy' from p. 35**.

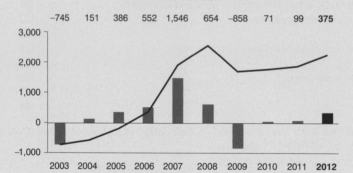

**Performance of Lufthansa Group of the last ten years**
Cash value added in €m

| −745 | 151 | 386 | 552 | 1,546 | 654 | −858 | 71 | 99 | **375** |

■ Annual CVA  — Cumulative CVA

## Limitations of ratio analysis

The limitations of ratio analysis also apply to analysis of financial statements in general. We have already discussed items such as changes in environment, absence of comparable data, different accounting policies, which may limit the usefulness of the information resulting from ratio analysis, horizontal analysis or common size analysis. In this section we point out a few more limitations.

**Non-monetary factors** Non-monetary factors are not reflected in financial statements. Thus, such factors as the quality of the product or service are not reflected, neither is whether labour relations are good or bad. In the section on disclosure of non-financial data we will see how companies are trying to overcome this lack of information. More and more non-financial indicators of performance are introduced in the annual reports.

**Historical cost accounting** The historical nature of accounts must always be borne in mind as our interpretation of the business is based on this historical information, but this may not be the best guide as to the future performance, financial status and investment potential. However, with recent evolutions in IAS/IFRS and US GAAP the impact of historical cost accounting might diminish in the coming years.

## ACTIVITY 32.16

The following sales figures are available for David plc:

| X0 | X1 |
|---|---|
| £000 | £000 |
| 700 | 800 |

The price of goods sold has been subject to an increase of 10 per cent at the beginning of X1. What is the magnitude of the increase in the volume of trade?

*Activity feedback*
*Sales have increased by £100 000 from X0 to X1 but £70 000 of this is due to the price increase, inflation in the price of goods sold. Volume of sales has only increased by £30 000, that is 4 per cent not 14 per cent.*

**Short-term fluctuations** Ratio analysis does not identify short-term fluctuations within one year in assets and liabilities as our appraisal is based on a balance sheet which provides values of assets and liabilities as at a point in time. By using these year-end figures we may, for example, present a better view of liquidity than has been the case throughout the year.

**Changes in the value of money** We all know how inflation can affect the value of the euro, pound, dollar or yen in our pocket and this is no different for a business. In fact, inflation and price changes could render the whole of our ratio analysis invalid. Short-term fluctuations are better reflected in interim reports.

## Multivariate analysis

The ratio analysis we have considered so far is of a univariate type. This is where one ratio is considered at a time and then all ratios, once calculated, are assessed together and the analyst makes a considered judgement on the state of the entity. By way of contrast, multivariate analysis combines some of the ratios together in a specified manner by applying weightings to each of the ratios. The result is an index number that is compared to previous years, other companies and industrial averages. Multivariate analysis has been widely used in predicting corporate failure. In 1968, Altman combined five ratios to produce what he named a Z score:

$$Z = 0.012X1 + 0.014X2 + 0.033X3 + 0.006X4 + 0.999X5$$

X1 = Working capital/Total assets

X2 = Retained earnings/Total assets

X3 = Earnings before interest and tax/Total assets

X4 = Market capitalization/Book value of debt

X5 = Sales/Total assets

In his seminal article (Altman, 1968), companies with Z scores above 2.99 had not failed whereas those companies with a Z score below 1.81 had. His research was undertaken in the manufacturing sector of the United States. In the context of this type of multivariate analysis it is important to remember that results of such multivariate analyses in relation to the economic health of a company must be used with extreme caution. The results of these multivariate analyses are only valid for companies located in the same region, active in the same industry and existing more or less in the same time period. The reason for this limited application is that national environments influence reporting practices (see Chapter 2), that the economic climate constantly changes and that the value of the ratios is influenced by industry characteristics.

Another internationally well-known model is that of Taffler. This group carried out similar work in the UK but they have not published the details of this as it is used as a working model and they need to retain the commercial interest. What we do know about the model are the ratios included:

$$Z = c_0 + c_1 X1 + c_2 X2 + c_3 X3 + c_4 X4$$

$X1$ = Profit before tax/Current assets

$X2$ = Current assets/Current liabilities

$X3$ = Current liabilities/Total assets

$X4$ = Length of time which the company can continue to finance its operations using its own assets with no revenue inflow.

The usefulness of these models is, unfortunately, still often limited to the region from which the company data were taken for the estimation procedure. Our view is that the use of several ratios with additional information (such as trend, common size, industry and accounting analysis) and a good deal of common sense should enable you to make a reasonable assessment of a company's financial status, performance, potential and position in the market. The multivariate models used the individual ratios as input without making a proper assessment on the quality of the data and typical characteristics of the data.

## DISCLOSURE OF NON-FINANCIAL DATA

The current company performance as well as the long-term company performance is influenced by several factors which are called in the literature drivers of performance or drivers of value creation. These drivers relate to elements such as customer satisfaction, internal organization of the business processes, the quality and service of the products or the innovation capability of the firm. In the last two decades of the twentieth century these drivers of performance started to play a much more prominent role in the management control systems of companies. Internal performance evaluation systems within companies are now built around financial as well as non-financial performance indicators. Many of these indicators are chosen because they are the drivers of future value creation. The most well-known scorecard in which financial indicators are combined with non-financial indicators is the balanced scorecard, a normative concept developed by Kaplan and Norton (1992).

Since elements such as customer satisfaction, innovative capabilities and organizational efficiency are key drivers of performance in the long run, information on these value drivers or performance drivers is also interesting for external users of annual accounts. These indicators might help external users to forecast future performance.

Over recent years we observe that companies which have this information on non-financial indicators available in their internal management information systems also include them in their annual reports. This information on non-financial key drivers for success is always included in the narrative or descriptive part of the annual report and is therefore non-audited.

Since these non-financial data became integrated in a number of annual reports, the academic community started to research the information content of this non-financial information. The focus of the research relates to the information contents of non-financial data and to the predictive value of the data or what is called the value relevance of the data (e.g. Amir and Lev, 1996; Ittner and Larcker, 2001). Research results so far show that non-financial data are complementary to financial data and the value relevance of financial accounting data continues. Further (using customer satisfaction data) Ittner and Larcker obtained evidence that non-financial data have predictive value, but the relation is non-linear.

In Chapter 11 the communication of additional information to the statement of financial position, the statement of comprehensive income, the changes in equity and the notes to the accounts are discussed. Most popular these days are additional statements on corporate social responsibility, sustainability and the environmental policy of the company, product information and market growth. Very often this information is bundled in a sustainability report. These additional reports contain interesting information to relate to the annual report. However, one must keep in mind that this information is non-audited. In order to provide some guidance on this extra information the IASB has paid attention to the disclosure of management information to the annual accounts with its ED on Management Commentary, which will lead to a guidance on this issue in the near future.

Listed companies provide a lot of information on their websites. Interesting data can be found in the presentations made to financial analysts which companies usually post on their website among other information for investors. However, one has to bear in mind that the information provided is non-audited and that companies often use pro-forma financial data in those presentations. In these pro-forma financial data, companies undo the impact of some accounting standards and use their own valuation rules.

## CASH FLOW STATEMENT

The cash flow statement, its preparation and its contents have been discussed in Chapter 24. Cash flow information helps the external user to get an idea of whether or not a company is able to generate net positive cash flows. To be able to sort out the different origins of cash, the cash flows are divided into three groups in the cash flow statement, namely cash flow from operating activities, cash flow from investment activities and cash flow from financing activities.

Studying cash flow data, users of this statement want to know, in the first place, if a company can generate cash from its operations. In the second place, the analyst will try to find out whether this internally generated cash is sufficient to finance the investments of the company or whether the firm needs to rely on external borrowing or an equity increase. The relations between the three components of the cash flow will differ according to the financial situation of the company. The cash flow patterns in a fast growing company will differ from those of a company in distress. In companies in distress the cash flow generated from operating activities is often negative. This negative cash flow can be compensated through a disposal of assets and borrowing extra funds from creditors or a capital increase. Fast growing companies might generate a positive operational cash flow or even a negative cash flow. In most cases the operational cash flow is not enough to finance growth. Therefore these fast growers have to rely on additional external financing either from creditors or an increase in capital from the shareholders. These parties will provide the necessary funds since the prospects of a fast grower look much more promising than the prospects of companies in distress. However, cash flow patterns are not always that predictable. If we analyze the cash flow statement of Sabena the year before bankruptcy we still find a positive operating cash flow; however, the remainder of the picture is not that positive (see the case in Appendix I to this chapter).

Although one might have the impression that the comparability issue is less important with cash flow data, one still has to be alert for differences. For example, dividends, taxation and interests can be presented differently among companies. Further, one has to be sure that the bottom line represents an increase or decrease in cash and cash equivalents available in the company. Sometimes the bottom line is working capital movements.

Based on cash flow information a number of ratios providing insights on a company's liquidity position can be calculated. They are complementary to the current ratio, the acid test ratio and the solvency ratios. First of all, one can substitute the current assets in the nominator of the current ratio through the figure 'cash flow from operations'. Through this substitution one avoids the convertibility-to-cash problem of current assets. The current ratio then becomes:

Cash flow to short-term debt: Cash flow from operations / current liabilities

Similar to the cash flow to short-term debt ratio, one can calculate the cash flow to debt ratio. This ratio calculates the coverage of the repayment of the debt (interest expenses or other costs are not taken into account in this calculation) by the current cash flow of the company.

Cash flow to debt: Cash flow from operations / total debt

The interest cover ratio has the earnings before interest and taxes (EBIT) in the nominator. This amount is influenced by accruals items. As an alternative one can calculate this interest cover ratio by substituting EBIT through cash flow from operations.

Interest cover ratio (cash) = cash flow from operations / net finance expense

A ratio which shows the proportion of investments a company is able to fund through its own operations, is the ratio below:

Capital expenditure ratio = cash flow from operations / investments

This ratio provides an idea of a firm's long-term risk.

## ACTIVITY 32.17

Calculate these ratios based on the cash flow information included in the statements of cash flow of Nestlé and Unilever.

### Activity feedback

|  | Nestlé<br>In million € | Unilever<br>In million € |
| --- | --- | --- |
| Cash flow to short-term debt | 15 772 / 38 753 = 0.40 | 6 836 / 15 815 = 0.43 |
| Cash flow to debt | 15 772 / 63 625 = 0.24 | 6 836 / 30 450 = 0.22 |
| Interest cover ratio (cash) | 15 772/ 519 = 26.68 | 6 836 / 526 = 12.99 |
| Capital expenditure ratio | 15 772 934 / 5 368 = 2.93 | 6 836 / 1 975 = 4.46 |

From Chapter 31 we know that information provided through the statement of financial position and the statement of comprehensive income might be biased or distorted through annual accounts management (accounting method choices, changes in accounting estimates or real transactions). It is believed that in situations where large accruals are recorded, cash flow information gives a more reliable picture of the performance of the firm than the result reported in the profit and loss account. However, the usefulness of cash flow information in general and in relation to undoing the effect of accrual accounting varies from firm to firm (empirical evidence can be found in Dechow, 1994). Cash flow figures can be influenced by real decisions. Further, clarification and presentation decisions can be made in order to provide the impressions of a healthy operating cash flow. So in order to make a proper assessment about the economic situation and performance of a company, data from the balance sheet, profit and loss account, the notes and the cash flow statement should always be combined. This is often called the cash flow check. With the discussion of the analysis of the cash flow statement the most important techniques of financial analysis have been discussed.

# APPENDIX I

## Case: The story of Sabena – Part II

In the second part of the case of Sabena, we illustrate a number of techniques discussed in Chapter 32.

Based on the available data, we undertake a common size analysis on a number of items of the profit and loss account of all airlines included in the case. This common size analysis will be used to illustrate a number of elements which are of importance in comparing performances of different companies. From a number of airlines in Europe we have taken those cost items which are comparable and used them in a common size profit and loss account with regard to operating revenue, some operating costs and operating result. Since the following illustrations and those further on in this chapter serve to illustrate how one gains more insight into the financial situation of Sabena, we present the figures for the year 2000 for all airlines involved in the case. We still have to remember that British Airways and Ryanair use UK GAAP, KLM uses Dutch GAAP and all the others use IAS/IFRS (see Table 32.6). Although since then IFRS has become compulsory for listed companies, many of the items discussed still happen under IFRS. They also apply to the majority of non-listed companies in the world.

## TABLE 32.6   Common size analysis of operating revenue and operating cost components (%)

|  | BA | Lufthansa | SAS | AA | KLM | Ryanair | SAir | Sabena |
|---|---|---|---|---|---|---|---|---|
| Operating revenue | 100 | 100 | 100 | 100 | 100 | 100 | 100 | 100 |
| Operating costs | 95.90 | 93.47 | 96.78 | 100.69 | 96.02 | 76.61 | 96.28 | 105.75 |
| Fuel | 11.88 | 9.13 | 8.33 | 11.38 | 14.91 | 13.02 | 6.35 | 10.74 |
| Staff | 25.61 | 22.08 | 31.40 | 18.76 | 27.07 | 12.56 | 27.77 | 22.17 |
| Depreciation | 7.71 | 6.23 | 4.61 | 12.88 | 6.16 | 12.14 | 6.11 | 4.75 |
| Lease cost | 2.38 | 0.38 | 3.99 | 1.66 | 4.89 | 1.49 | 5.47 | 13.89 |
| Other | 48.32 | 55.66 | 8.45 | 56.01 | 45.99 | 37.40 | 50.59 | 54.19 |
| Operating result | 4.10 | 6.53 | 3.22 | −0.69 | 3.98 | 23.39 | 3.72 | −5.75 |

*Source:* Austrian Airlines Annual Report 2000, British Airways Annual Report 2000/2001, KLM Annual Report 2000/2001, Lufthansa Annual Report 2000, Ryanair Annual Report 2000/2001, Sabena Annual Report 2000, SAir Annual Report 2000, and SAS Annual Report 2000.

## ACTIVITY 32.18

What kinds of difference do you notice? Can you think of an explanation, taking into account all the elements which have been discussed already concerning airlines?

*Activity feedback*
*Ryanair has substantially lower staff costs than the other companies. Further, the lease costs differ among the air-*

*lines. However, the lease costs which refer to operating lease contracts should always be considered in combination with depreciation and amortization costs.*

Airlines which own a large percentage of their fleet or operate their fleet under financial lease agreements have higher depreciation costs than airlines leasing most of their aircraft under operating lease contracts. The quality of disclosure with regard to the item owned aircraft, aircraft under financial lease or aircraft under operating lease differs among the airlines. Some comparative data are presented with regard to this item. Some airlines disclose in the narrative part of the annual accounts the breakdown of their fleet according to the way it is financed. A few examples are listed in Table 32.7.

## TABLE 32.7  Information on fleet capacity of British Airways, KLM, Lufthansa and Sabena

|  | Aircraft owned | Financial leading | On balance sheet | Operational leasing | Total |
|---|---|---|---|---|---|
| Lufthansa | 273 (82%) | 49 (15%) | 322 (97%) | 9 (3%) | 331 (100%) |
| KLM | 87 (41%) | 78 (37%) | 165 (77%) | 48 (23%) | 213 (100%) |
| Sabena | 8 (9%) | 32 (37%) | 40 (46%) | 47 (54%) | 87 (100%) |
| British Airways |  |  | 226 (67%) | 112 (33%) | 338 (100%) |

*Source:* British Airways Annual Report 2000/2001, KLM Annual Report 2000/2001, Lufthansa Annual Report 2000 and Sabena Annual Report 2000.

We learn from this comparative analysis that Lufthansa is the only carrier which owned at that time a large part of its fleet. Whether or not a plane is accounted for as a financial lease or an operating lease depends not only on the contract, but also on the GAAP applied. To illustrate the impact we present an historical overview of the composition of the fleet and the way it is accounted for in Table 32.8. The data included in Table 32.8 will be used again later in this case.

The fuel cost expressed as a percentage of operating revenue differs drastically among these companies. We know already that distance flown, number of take-offs and kerosene price has an influence, but that alone does not explain the differences.

## TABLE 32.8    Aircraft operated by the Sabena Group

| Year | Aircraft owned | | Aircraft under financial leasing | | Aircraft under operational leasing | | Total |
|---|---|---|---|---|---|---|---|
| 1993 | 33 | 49.25% | 15 | 22.39% | 19 | 28.36% | 67 |
| 1994 | 27 | 38.57% | 19 | 27.14% | 24 | 34.29% | 70 |
| 1995 | 26 | 33.77% | 19 | 24.68% | 32 | 41.56% | 77 |
| 1996 | 38 | 48.72% | 8 | 10.26% | 32 | 41.03% | 78 |
| 1997 | 35 | 50.00% | 4 | 5.71% | 31 | 44.29% | 70 |
| 1998 | 10 | 13.51% | 3 | 4.05% | 61 | 82.43% | 74 |
| 1999 | 8 | 9.76% | 31 | 37.80% | 43 | 52.44% | 82 |
| 2000 | 8 | 9.20% | 32 | 36.78% | 47 | 54.02% | 87 |

*Source:* Sabena Annual Reports 1993–2000.

**Segmental analysis** A comparative analysis between airline activities (passengers and freight and mail) versus airline-related activities reveals that SAS, Lufthansa but especially the SAir Group have diversified activities (Table 32.9).

## ACTIVITY 32.19

Can you think of another explanation for the observed differences in the cost structures of the airlines?

### Activity feedback
When we compare British Airways and Ryanair at 31 March 2001 these companies are almost 100 per cent airlines, with very few other activities at that time. The group accounts of SAS, however, not only present reve-

nues and costs from the airline business, but also include the costs and the revenues stemming from their hotel business. Further, Lufthansa and SAir have, besides their airlines, other airline-related businesses such as catering, ground handling, IT, etc. This explains the lower percentage of fuel costs in relation to operating revenue, whereas British Airways and Ryanair were not active in these airline-related businesses at that time.

## TABLE 32.9    Breakdown of total group revenue over different business segments (%)

| | Passenger traffic | Freight and mail | Other (technics, ground handling, catering, etc.) |
|---|---|---|---|
| Ryanair | 88 | | 12 |
| British Airways | 84 | 6 | 10 |
| SAS | 70 | 5 | 25 |
| Lufthansa | 61 | 14 | 25 |
| KLM | 65 | 17 | 18 |
| Austrian Airlines | 75 | 6 | 19 |
| SAir Group | 41 | 10 | 49 |
| Sabena | 85 | Assumed by SAir in 1997 | 15 |

*Source:* Financial statements of 2000, Austrian Airlines, 2000, British Airways and KLM, 2000/2001, Lufthansa, 2000, Ryanair, 2000/2001, Sabena, SAir, and SAS, 2000.

The data of the SAir Group do not come as a surprise, as their corporate strategy since 1996 is their so-called two pillar strategy. Growth in the so-called second pillar is among acquisitions and organic growth also obtained by integrating the airline-related activities of the airlines in which they acquire a substantial minority shareholding into the SAir Group. If we analyze the annual report of Sabena of 1994, we observe that before the cooperation with SAir (Sabena Annual Report 1994, p. 6) passenger traffic made up 75.1 per cent of total revenue, cargo and other airline-related activities amounted to 25 per cent of the total revenue. These proportions had been changing up to 2000. So we learn from the Sabena Annual Report 2000, p. 24, that in 2000 the catering activities were further integrated and outsourced to Gate Gourmet, the catering company from the SAir Group.

The analysis of the segmental disclosure of a company can shed light on the corporate strategy of the group and on the importance of the different business or geographical segments of the group. In Table 32.10 the horizontal analysis of the different business segments of the SAir Group is presented (the analysis is based not on total revenue, which includes inter-segment revenue, but on external revenue).

## TABLE 32.10　Horizontal analysis of different business segments of the SAir Group (%)

|  | 1997 | 1998 | 1999 | 2000 |
|---|---|---|---|---|
| External revenue | 100 | 107.02 | 123.17 | 153.74 |
| SAirlines | 100 | 106.54 | 116.37 | 130.40 |
| SAir Services | 100 | 120.37 | 147.00 | 243.86 |
| SAir Logistics | 100 | 105.18 | 110.61 | 141.77 |
| SAir Relations | 100 | 104.61 | 131.79 | 170.58 |
| SAir Group | 100 | 2 700 | 2 400 | 8 200 |

Source: SAir Group Annual Report of 1997, 1998, 1999, 2000.

Focusing on the business segment airlines of the SAir Group we learn from their annual report that for the years 1998, 1999 and 2000 the revenue and earnings before interest and taxes (EBIT) of the leasing activities of their company, Flightlease, are combined with the revenue and EBIT of the airlines Swissair, Crossair and Balair into one business segment airline.

## ACTIVITY 32.20

Leasing and airline activities are combined into one business segment, 'Airlines', in the financial years 1999 and 2000 (Table 32.10). What do you think of this approach?

### Activity feedback

Earlier in the chapter we mentioned that depreciation and rental and lease costs should always be considered together in order to determine the impact of the airplane capacity costs on the results. According to the financing policy chosen (financial leasing, operational leasing or owned and financed through equity or loans) the depreciation and rental costs will be higher or lower. In 1998 Swissair sold and leased back a large part of its fleet. The leasing company, Flightlease, was involved in these transactions. In order to make EBIT and other data of the SAirlines (Swissair,

Crossair and Balair) comparable with other airlines, the leasing activities were added to the business segment airlines. That was the explanation given by financial analysts.

This argument would have been acceptable had Flightlease been responsible only for the leasing activities of Swissair, Crossair and Balair, the airlines in which the SAir Group was the majority shareholder. However, Flightlease also leases planes to associated entities such as Sabena and its subsidiary, Sobelair, LTU and several other airlines. Taking that information into account the argument is less acceptable. In the notes to the annual accounts of SAir we find with regard to leased assets the following information (SAIR Annual Accounts 2000, p. 30, n. 26) 'Future lease income from aircraft lease agreements amounts to CHF 1.6 billion and will stem largely from associated undertakings.'

**Trend analysis** In the following section, we apply trend analysis and common size analysis on the operating revenue and operating cost data of Sabena NV over the last ten years (1991–2000) of its existence. We use the individual accounts of Sabena NV because they have been prepared according to Belgian GAAP for the whole time frame of the analysis, whereas the group accounts were published in Belgian GAAP up to 1998 and from 1999 according to IAS. As already mentioned, Sabena NV represents the airline and accounts for 90 per cent of the revenue of the Sabena Group. In the data presented, comparability is enhanced by adding the cost and revenue data of Sabena Technics (the subsidiary created in 1999) to the data of Sabena NV after correction for inter-segment revenue (more explanation on this item will follow after this trend and common size analysis). Many elements resulting from the accounting strategy of Sabena (see subsequent reports of the board of directors, discussed in Chapter 31), were reported as exceptional costs and exceptional revenue, so the operating revenue and operating costs reported relate to the operating activities. The evolution of some airline operating statistics is also presented.

## ACTIVITY 32.21

Taking into account the information given about Sabena in Chapter 31, the discussion on trend analysis, common size analysis and segmental analysis, what evolutions do you observe in Tables 32.11 and 32.12? What explanations can you give? What extra information would you like to have in order to make a better judgement?

## TABLE 32.11  Horizontal analysis of the operating result of Sabena NV and Sabena Technics (%)

| Sabena + Technics | 1991 | 1992 | 1993 | 1994 | 1995 | 1996 | 1997 | 1998 | 1999 | 2000 |
|---|---|---|---|---|---|---|---|---|---|---|
| Operating revenue | 100.00 | 98.24 | 100.99 | 108.86 | 112.82 | 115.24 | 132.98 | 162.43 | 170.83 | 192.92 |
| Mat. cons | 100.00 | 90.96 | 102.68 | 105.23 | 94.94 | 107.78 | 71.51 | 71.84 | 80.75 | 113.58 |
| Serv. goods | 100.00 | 99.81 | 112.49 | 121.94 | 133.11 | 145.49 | 192.05 | 247.31 | 278.48 | 346.18 |
| Personnel cost | 100.00 | 92.81 | 86.09 | 86.08 | 93.75 | 100.87 | 99.73 | 108.32 | 118.26 | 116.35 |
| Dep. fix assets | 100.00 | 117.11 | 115.97 | 118.36 | 118.02 | 118.17 | 111.48 | 112.54 | 84.36 | 105.16 |
| Current assets | 100.00 | 33.33 | 8.89 | 8.92 | 3.62 | 10.66 | −36.65 | 15.65 | −7.02 | −33.40 |
| Provisions | 100.00 | 88.30 | 6.88 | 29.63 | −27.62 | 2.60 | −33.90 | 0.66 | 57.50 | 68.22 |
| Other | 100.00 | 88.42 | 81.07 | 72.06 | 55.70 | 110.21 | 98.41 | 132.60 | 138.52 | 128.85 |
| Operating cost | 100.00 | 95.33 | 101.71 | 106.02 | 111.45 | 121.44 | 130.79 | 156.08 | 171.21 | 205.54 |
| Operating result | 100.00 | −140.97 | 160.05 | −125.10 | −0.42 | 625.45 | −47.75 | −359.65 | 202.21 | 1231.30 |
| Activity data | 1991 | 1992 | 1993 | 1994 | 1995 | 1996 | 1997 | 1998 | 1999 | 2000 |
| Actual production | | | | | | | | | | |
| passengers | 100.00 | 104.11 | 120.96 | 141.20 | 165.69 | 171.41 | 227.69 | 289.86 | 332.46 | 362.19 |
| hours | 100.00 | 104.74 | 118.31 | 126.41 | 142.99 | 164.98 | 170.88 | 208.46 | 239.94 | 258.51 |
| km | 100.00 | 104.15 | 117.54 | 126.69 | 143.57 | 162.00 | 166.11 | 209.33 | 243.61 | 263.82 |

*Source:* Sabena Annual Reports 1991–2000.

*(Continued)*

## ACTIVITY 32.21 (Continued)

### TABLE 32.12 Vertical analysis of the operating result of Sabena NV + Sabena Technics NV (%)

| Sabena + Technics | 1991 | 1992 | 1993 | 1994 | 1995 | 1996 | 1997 | 1998 | 1999 | 2000 |
|---|---|---|---|---|---|---|---|---|---|---|
| Operating revenue | 100.00 | 100.00 | 100.00 | 100.00 | 100.00 | 100.00 | 100.00 | 100.00 | 100.00 | 100.00 |
| Mat. cons | 23.61 | 21.86 | 24.01 | 22.83 | 19.87 | 22.08 | 12.70 | 10.44 | 11.16 | 13.90 |
| Serv. goods | 40.44 | 41.09 | 45.05 | 45.30 | 47.71 | 51.06 | 58.40 | 61.57 | 65.93 | 72.57 |
| Personnel cost | 32.66 | 30.85 | 27.84 | 27.82 | 27.13 | 28.58 | 24.49 | 21.78 | 22.61 | 19.69 |
| Dep. fix assets | 4.39 | 5.23 | 5.04 | 4.77 | 4.59 | 4.50 | 3.68 | 3.04 | 2.17 | 2.39 |
| Current assets | 1.64 | 0.56 | -0.14 | 0.13 | 0.05 | 0.15 | -0.45 | 0.16 | -0.07 | -0.28 |
| Provisions | -1.86 | -1.67 | -0.13 | -0.51 | 0.46 | -0.04 | 0.47 | -0.01 | -0.63 | -0.66 |
| Other | 0.35 | 0.32 | 0.28 | 0.23 | 0.17 | 0.34 | 0.26 | 0.29 | 0.29 | 0.24 |
| Operating cost | 101.23 | 98.23 | 101.95 | 98.59 | 100.00 | 106.68 | 99.56 | 97.28 | 101.46 | 107.85 |
| Operating result | -1.23 | 1.77 | -1.95 | 1.41 | 0.00 | -6.68 | 0.44 | 2.72 | -1.46 | -7.85 |

*Source:* Sabena and Sabena Technics NV Annual Reports 1991–2000.

### Activity feedback

*Most meaningful is to focus the analysis on those operating cost components which are less influenced by accrual accounting decisions. Operating cost items such as changes in values in current assets and provisions will therefore be left out of this analysis.*

*Taking into account all the data presented so far on Sabena in Chapters 31 and 32, we know that there have been at least three 'events' which had an impact on the structure of Sabena NV in that period, namely the 'assumption' of cargo by the SAir Group, the creation of Sabena Technics NV and the creation of the Airline Management Partnership. Only with regard to the creation of Sabena Technics can the external user of the annual accounts judge the impact as Sabena Technics is fully consolidated in the group accounts and its individual accounts are published. The impact of the assumption of the cargo business by SAir on the operating revenue and the operating costs of Sabena is not clear for an external user of the annual accounts. We only know from the annual report of SAir that their group operating revenue increased positively as a result of the assumption of Sabena's cargo business. The impact of this assumption on the revenues and costs of Sabena is not disclosed. This hinders further the compara-*

*bility of the airline statistics over time. So more information on the impact of the 'assumption' of the cargo business by SAir would be welcome.*

*That the creation of the Airline Management Partnership (AMP) will have an impact on the operating revenues and operating costs of Sabena is clear. Personnel costs, for example, decrease in 2000 as a number of employees of Sabena are transferred to the AMP. The same happens at the level of the SAir Group, employees from SAir are also transferred to the AMP. Evaluating the impact of the AMP on the situation of Sabena is rendered more difficult for the external analysts as the AMP was organized under the legal form of a partnership located in the UK. One of the characteristics of a partnership under the European Directives is that the financial statements do not have to be made public.*

*Further we learn from the annual report of SAir [see Chapter 31, extract SAir Annual Report 1999, financial statements (p. 19) and financial statements year 2000 (p. 17)] that in 1998 and in 1999 shares which could be sold after three years were given to personnel and share options were also granted to staff members. It would be interesting to know how many of the AMP employees own shares of the SAir Group.*

We will now turn to the evolution of the individual operating cost items.

In this ten-year period the two time frames (namely the cooperation with Air France and the cooperation with the SAir Group) clearly step out of the data. Different patterns can be observed from 1991 to 1995 and from 1996 until 2000. In the first time frame, the cooperation with Air France, there is a smooth growth of operating revenue. The different operating cost categories follow more or less at the same pace. The vertical analysis shows that the proportion of each cost component in total revenue remains stable in the first half of the last decade of the twentieth century. In the second time frame when the SAir Group took a substantial minority shareholding (49.5 per cent) in Sabena, the growth rate increased. The aim of SAir was to acquire, together with its associated undertakings, a market share of 20 per cent in Europe. Those airline operating statistics, which are comparable over the ten-year timespan show an enormous increase in the last years of the twentieth century. This was a result of the fleet expansion. From Table 32.10 we learn that there is an enormous increase in the fleet capacity in the year 1999. From Chapter 31 we know that Sabena tried to fill up the increased seat capacity by price reductions. This policy did result in a growing number of passengers carried, but most of the extra passengers were economy class. These passengers increase the rather variable costs such as handling and catering, which represent activities which had to be bought for a large part from the airline-related segments or the second pillar of the SAir Group in the last years of the existence of Sabena. As a result of this policy, the trend pattern of the cost components and the proportion of each cost component in the total revenue lost their stability in the second half of the 1990s.

The decrease in the component 'materials and consumables' until 1998 can be explained by the policy of outsourcing, but also by the favourable fuel prices and the favourable exchange rate to the dollar. An unfavourable change in these last two years at the end of the twentieth century explains the steep rise in component materials and consumables costs.

Due to the outsourcing of activities, the component 'services and other goods' rose, but that is not the sole explanation. The steep rise in this component in the last two years is also due to the enormous fleet expansion of Sabena, financed through operating lease contracts. The impact of this fleet expansion on the costs of 1999 was somewhat softened as the realized gains on the sale of planes were offset with the lease costs. In 2000 this effect disappeared to a large extent and the costs of the fleet expansion now hit the profit and loss account with their full impact. (The impact of this fleet expansion on the finance structure of Sabena is illustrated in the section on ratio analysis.) The personnel cost decreases in 2000; this could be due to the creation of the AMP, but we cannot be completely sure of this as the only information received about AMP is that: 'The partnership constituted a complete merger of the commercial departments of Sabena and Swissair ... From the economic aspect of achieving savings, AMP realized a reduction in expenditure for the two airlines of around EUR 100m per annum' (Sabena Annual Report 2000, p. 14).

Depreciation costs remain rather stable over the ten-year period. This is due to the fact that capacity cost for the aeroplanes switch from depreciation to lease costs over the years (Sabena NV used Belgian GAAP). The increase from 1999 to 2000 can be explained by the increase in book values of the fixed assets transferred from Sabena NV to Sabena Technics NV together with the goodwill created in the course of the creation of this subsidiary. This results in higher depreciation costs.

Further care should be taken in evaluating the trend data of the operating result. As the base year had a negative operating result, years with a positive operating result get a negative sign. Years with a negative operating result have a positive sign.

**Comparability in trend analysis** The creation of the subsidiary Sabena Technics NV shows how one has to be aware of changes in the company structure, which hinder comparability. The accounts of the airline Sabena NV seem to suggest a decline in total operating revenue from 1998 to 1999 (see Table 32.13).

TABLE 32.13 Operating revenue and some operating cost items of Sabena NV (%)

|  | 1998 | 1999 | 2000 |
|---|---|---|---|
| Operating revenue | 100 | 97.51 | 110.88 |
| Materials and consumables | 100 | 92.04 | 139.11 |
| Services and goods delivered | 100 | 111.68 | 139.02 |
| Personnel cost | 100 | 91.24 | 88.38 |
| Depreciation fixed assets | 100 | 50.58 | 46.16 |

Source: Sabena NV Annual Reports, 1998, 1999 and 2000.

In reality, however, the activities of maintenance and repair were, in 1999, separated into Sabena Technics NV. In order to make a proper comparison over three years we need a constant entity structure. If we add up the data of Sabena Technics NV with those of Sabena NV and correct for intra-group transactions then (data taken from the segmental information in the group accounts) we get a picture which shows growth. In Table 32.14 we present the evolution of the total operating revenue and some operating cost items of Sabena NV, whereby the necessary corrections are made to obtain a constant entity.

TABLE 32.14 Operating revenue and some operating cost items of Sabena NV totalled with operating revenue and operating cost items of Sabena Technics NV (%)

|  | 1998 | 1999 | 2000 |
|---|---|---|---|
| Operating revenue | 100 | 105.17 | 118.77 |
| Materials and consumables | 100 | 112.41 | 158.11 |
| Services and goods delivered | 100 | 112.61 | 139.98 |
| Personnel cost | 100 | 109.18 | 107.42 |
| Depreciation fixed assets | 100 | 74.96 | 93.44 |

Source: Sabena NV Annual Reports 1998, 1999 and 2000 and Sabena Technics NV Annual Reports 1999 and 2000.

Although we have now managed to keep the entity of analysis constant, the influence of the changes in book value of the assets is not eliminated. With the transfer of assets from Sabena NV to Sabena Technics NV, the book value of those assets was increased as well. As a result the depreciation costs rise.

As Sabena Technics was a 100 per cent subsidiary of Sabena NV the accounts of the Sabena Group were not influenced by this restructuring. The increase in book value of the assets now remaining with Sabena Technics has no influence on the group accounts, because this increase is eliminated in the consolidation process.

**Ratio analysis** As an illustration of a trend analysis performed on ratios we will analyze the evolution of the debt/equity ratio of the Sabena Group over the years 1992–2000. The trend analysis of the debt/equity ratio clearly reveals an increasing financial risk over the years towards the final stage of bankruptcy. Before we start with the analysis of the data, the pitfalls of comparability need to be checked. If we check for comparability over time, we notice the following elements. With regard to the Sabena Group as a whole no major structural changes have taken place over the time frame considered except for the year 2000 when the Airline Management Partnership was created. Further, we have noticed some structural changes within the group (e.g. 1992 the sale of the charter company Sobelair from Sabena NV to Sabena Leasing, 1999 the creation of a new subsidiary Sabena Technics NV). These within-group structural changes have no influence on the overall group structure. A second element which needs to be taken into account in the period of analysis (1992–2000) is the change of the applied GAAP. Up to 1998 the annual group accounts complied with Belgian GAAP. From 1999 on the group accounts were published using IAS/IFRS. The group accounts of 1999 include comparative data on 1998 which were also prepared with the use of IAS/IFRS.

In Table 32.15 the evolution of the debt/equity ratio of the Sabena group is presented. For the year 1998 the debt/equity ratio is calculated twice, once with data originating from the Belgian GAAP group accounts (D/E = 6.31) published in 1998 and then with the comparative data included in the IAS group accounts data (D/E = 8.49) of 1999.

We notice that when in 1998 Belgian GAAP data are used the debt/equity ratio is lower. The higher ratios under IAS are due to the fact that a number of lease contracts which could be accounted for as operating lease contracts under Belgian GAAP qualified under IAS/IFRS as finance lease contracts. Since from 1995 on we could find in the notes to the annual accounts information on future operating lease payments, we have added up these future operating lease payments with the debt included on the face of the balance sheet. Using this amount (balance sheet debt + off-balance sheet debt relating to operating lease contracts) in the numerator, we have calculated a ratio which we have labelled the 'extended' debt/equity ratio.

The 'Belgian' debt/equity ratio fluctuates around six until 1998. The improvement of the ratio in 1995 was due to a capital increase, the positive effect of which did not last very long. Due to the accounting strategy followed by the board of directors, which was communicated in the annual report of 1996, equity decreased substantially. The debt/equity ratio shows an increase in financial risk only from 1999 (or 1998 with IAS accounts) on. The 'extended' debt/equity ratio revealed the deterioration of the financial situation of the Sabena Group much sooner.

The evolution of the 'extended' debt/equity ratio shows clearly that from the start of the cooperation with the SAir Group in 1995 the financial risk increased each year. In 1997 the situation has become critical; in 2000 both ratios (debt/equity and 'extended' debt/equity) point to a dramatic situation. The extreme deterioration of the debt/equity ratio in 2000 is caused by two elements. First of all the huge losses of 2000 take the equity into the red. The second cause of the steeply rising ratios is the increasing lease commitments due to the fleet expansion.

## TABLE 32.15    Evolution of the debt situation of the Sabena Group, 1992–2000

| | 1992 | 1993 | 1994 | 1995 | 1996 | 1997 | 1998 | 1999 | 2000 |
|---|---|---|---|---|---|---|---|---|---|
| Debt/equity IAS switch in 1999 | 5.87 | 7.28 | 6.10 | 3.14 | 5.42 | 6.23 | 6.31 | 9.68 | −26.92 |
| Debt/equity IAS switch in 1998 | | | | | | | 8.49 | 9.68 | −26.92 |
| 'Extended' debt/Equity (*) | | | | 3.99 | 6.7 | 9.28 | 9.17 | 13.21 | −42.73 |

*Balance sheet debt + off balance sheet debt relating to operating lease contracts.
*Source:* Group accounts of Sabena 1992–2000.

**Cash flow analysis** As a last item in this case study, we look at the cash flow information published by Sabena and the SAirgroup.

Looking into the details of the operating cash flow of Sabena (Table 32.16) we notice that the loss in 2000 is almost offset by non-cash expenses which were recorded in the profit and loss account. The operating cash flow turns positive in the end through a rather substantial decrease in working capital, especially if we compare the movement in working capital with the previous year (1999). Further, the company keeps investing, however external funds from creditors are not used to finance these investments. The cash flow from financing activities has turned negative and represents substantial cash outflows. Finally, looking at the bottom line of the cash flow, we notice that the company suffers from a substantial decrease in liquid assets in the year 2000.

With regard to the cash flow check, if we analyze the profit and loss account of the SAir Group for the year 2000 in combination with the cash flow statement of the same group we notice indeed that cash flows are less influenced by accruals.

According to the report of the new incoming CEO, the financial difficulties at the SAir group necessitated the following measures:

## TABLE 32.16 Consolidated cash flow statement of the Sabena Group, 1999 and 2000

|  | 1999 in million euros | 2000 in million euros |
|---|---|---|
| Net result for the year | (10) | (323) |
| Minority interests | (3) | (2) |
| Depreciation of intangible, tangible fixed and financial assets | 127 | 128 |
| Profits/losses realized sustained on assets sales | (30) | (14) |
| Taxation | 1 | 2 |
| Other corrections and value adjustments | 115 | 204 |
| **Cash flow operations before changes in working capital** | **200** | **(5)** |
| Changes in working capital excluding disposable funds | 123 | 330 |
| Interest paid | (56) | (34) |
| Taxes paid | (1) | (11) |
| Interest received | 14 | 19 |
| Dividends received |  |  |
| Decrease in liabilities | (82) | (129) |
| Total | (124) | (155) |
| **Net cash inflow operating activities (A)** | **199** | **170** |
| Investments in tangible fixed and financial assets | (315) | (143) |
| Proceeds from sales of tangible fixed assets | 169 | 40 |
| **Net cash inflow from investment activities (B)** | **(146)** | **(102)** |
| **Net cash inflow from financing activities (C)** | **(99)** | **(202)** |
| **Net decrease/increase in disposable funds (A+ B + C)** | **(46)** | **(134)** |
| Cash and cash equivalents at beginning of year | 324 | 278 |
| Decrease/increase in disposable funds | (46) | (134) |
| Adjustments for foreign currency translations on opening | (1) |  |
| **Cash and cash equivalents at year-end** | **278** | **143** |

*Source:* Sabena Group Accounts 2000.

The realignment of our Group's overall business thrust requires corrective action in balance sheet terms, with the charging of extensive depreciation and provisions to the 2000 results. This will enable the Swissair Group to focus on its new corporate objectives free of the financial burdens of the past.

(SAir Group Annual Report 2000, p. 5)

The financial year 2000 ended for the SAir Group with a loss of 2885m CHF whereas the year 1999 ended with a profit of 273m CHF. Looking at the cash flow statements of 1999 and 2000 (Table 32.17) we notice in both years positive cash flows from operating activities and an increase in cash and cash equivalents at the bottom line of the cash flow statement.

## TABLE 32.17   Cash flow and result information of SAir, 1999–2000

| CHF million | 1999 | 2000 |
| --- | --- | --- |
| Net result | 273 | (2 885) |
| Cash flow from operations | 1 423 | 1 191 |

## APPENDIX II

## The financial statements of Nestlé

From the financial statements of 2012

## Consolidated income statement for the year ended 31 December 2012

| In millions of CHF | Notes | 2012 | 2011 |
|---|---|---|---|
| Sales | 3 | 92 186 | 83 642 |
| Other revenue | | 138 | 128 |
| Cost of goods sold | | (48 398) | (44 127) |
| Distribution expenses | | (8 167) | (7 602) |
| Marketing and administration expenses | | (19 688) | (17 395) |
| Research and development costs | | (1 544) | (1 423) |
| Other trading income | 4 | 141 | 51 |
| Other trading expenses | 4 | (656) | (736) |
| **Trading operating profit** | **3** | **14 012** | **12 538** |
| Other operating income | 4 | 146 | 112 |
| Other operating expenses | 4 | (226) | (179) |
| **Operating profit** | | **13 932** | **12 471** |
| Financial income | 13 | 110 | 115 |
| Financial expense | 13 | (591) | (536) |
| **Profit before taxes and associates** | | **13 451** | **12 050** |
| Taxes | 14 | (3 451) | (3 112) |
| Share of results of associates | 15 | 1 060 | 866 |
| **Profit for the year** | | **11 060** | **9 804** |
| of which attributable to non-controlling interests | | 449 | 317 |
| of which attributable to shareholders of the parent (net profit) | | 10 611 | 9 487 |
| **As percentages of sales** | | | |
| Trading operating profit | | 15.2% | 15.0% |
| Profit for the year attributable to shareholders of the parent (net profit) | | 11.5% | 11.3% |
| **Earnings per share** (in CHF) | | | |
| Basic earnings per share | 16 | 3.33 | 2.97 |
| Diluted earnings per share | 16 | 3.32 | 2.96 |

# Consolidated statement of comprehensive income for the year ended 31 December 2012

| In millions of CHF | Notes | 2012 | 2011 |
|---|---|---|---|
| **Profit for the year recognized in the income statement** | | **11 060** | **9 804** |
| Currency retranslations | | (1 052) | (1 166) |
| Fair value adjustments on available-for-sale financial instruments | | | |
| – Unrealized results | | 309 | (199) |
| – Recognition of realized results in the income statement | | 16 | 7 |
| Fair value adjustments on cash flow hedges | | | |
| – Recognized in hedging reserve | | (110) | (423) |
| – Removed from hedging reserve | | 272 | (42) |
| Actuarial gains/(losses) on defined benefit schemes | 10 | (2 063) | (2 503) |
| Share of other comprehensive income of associates | 15 | 497 | 456 |
| Taxes | 14 | 501 | 859 |
| **Other comprehensive income for the year** | **18** | **(1 630)** | **(3 011)** |
| **Total comprehensive income for the year** | | **9 430** | **6 793** |
| of which attributable to non-controlling interests | | 393 | 284 |
| of which attributable to shareholders of the parent | | 9 037 | 6 509 |

# Consolidated balance sheet as at 31 December 2012 before appropriations

| In millions of CHF | Notes | 2012 | 2011 |
|---|---|---|---|
| **Assets** | | | |
| **Current assets** | | | |
| Cash and cash equivalents | 13/17 | 5 840 | 4 938 |
| Short-term investments | 13 | 3 585 | 3 050 |
| Inventories | 5 | 9 125 | 9 255 |
| Trade and other receivables | 6/13 | 13 404 | 13 340 |
| Prepayments and accrued income | | 844 | 900 |
| Derivative assets | 13 | 586 | 731 |
| Current income tax assets | | 1 028 | 1 094 |
| Assets held for sale | 2 | 793 | 16 |
| **Total current assets** | | **35 205** | **33 324** |
| **Non-current assests** | | | |
| Property, plant and equipment | 7 | 26 903 | 23 971 |
| Goodwill | 8 | 32 615 | 29 008 |
| Intangible assets | 9 | 13 643 | 9 356 |
| Investments in associates | 15 | 9 846 | 8 629 |
| Financial assets | 13 | 5 003 | 7 161 |
| Employee benefits assets | 10 | 84 | 127 |
| Current income tax assets | | 27 | 39 |

| In millions of CHF | Notes | 2012 | 2011 |
|---|---|---|---|
| Deferred tax assets | 14 | 2 903 | 2 476 |
| **Total non-current assets** | | **91 024** | **80 767** |
| **Total assets** | | **126 229** | **114 091** |
| **Liabilities and equity** | | | |
| **Current liabilities** | | | |
| Financial dept | 13 | 18 568 | 16 100 |
| Trade and other payables | 13 | 14 456 | 13 584 |
| Accruals and deferred income | | 3 229 | 2 909 |
| Provisions | 12 | 441 | 576 |
| Derivative liabilities | 13 | 428 | 646 |
| Current income tax liabilities | | 1 631 | 1 417 |
| Liabilities directly associated with assets held for sale | | 1 | – |
| **Total current liabilities** | | **38 753** | **35 232** |
| **Non-current liabilities** | | | |
| Financial debt | 13 | 9 009 | 6 207 |
| Employee benefits liabilities | 10 | 8 554 | 7 105 |
| Provisions | 12 | 2 842 | 3 094 |
| Deferred tax liabilities | 14 | 2 276 | 2 060 |
| Other payables | 13 | 2 191 | 2 119 |
| **Total non-current liabilities** | | **24 872** | **20 585** |
| **Total liabilities** | | **63 625** | **55 817** |
| Equity | 18 | | |
| Share capital | | 322 | 330 |
| Treasury shares | | (2 078) | (6 722) |
| Translation reserve | | (17 923) | (16 927) |
| Retained earnings and other reserves | | 80 626 | 80 116 |
| **Total equity attributable to shareholders of the parent** | | **60 947** | **56 797** |
| Non-controlling interests | | 1 657 | 1 477 |
| **Total equity** | | **62 604** | **58 274** |
| **Total liabilities and equity** | | **126 229** | **114 091** |

# 3. Analyses by segment

## 3.1 Operating segments

### Revenue and results

*In millions of CHF*                                                                                                            *2012*

| | Sales[a] | Trading operating profit | Net other trading income/(expenses)* | of which impairment of assets other than goodwill | of which restructuring costs | Impairment of goodwill |
|---|---|---|---|---|---|---|
| Zone Europe | 15 385 | 2 417 | (88) | (40) | (40) | – |
| Zone Americas | 28 927 | 5 380 | (248) | (13) | 15 | – |
| Zone Asia, Oceania and Africa | 18 912 | 3 587 | (10) | 9 | (19) | – |
| Nestlé Waters | 7 174 | 636 | (41) | (20) | (15) | (1) |
| Nestlé Nutrition | 7 858 | 1 511 | (31) | (3) | (6) | (12) |
| Other[b] | 13 930 | 2 393 | (80) | (6) | (30) | (1) |
| Unallocated items[c] | | (1 912) | (17) | (2) | – | – |
| **Total** | **92 186** | **14 012** | **(515)** | **(75)** | **(95)** | **(14)** |

*Included in trading operating profit.

*In millions of CHF*                                                                                                            *2011*

| | Sales[a] | Trading operating profit | Net other trading income/(expenses)* | of which impairment of assets other than goodwill | of which restructuring costs | Impairment of goodwill |
|---|---|---|---|---|---|---|
| Zone Europe | 15 243 | 2 372 | (169) | (66) | (43) | – |
| Zone Americas | 26 756 | 4 922 | (273) | (18) | (21) | – |
| Zone Asia, Oceania and Africa | 15 291 | 2 892 | (74) | (31) | (12) | (9) |
| Nestlé Waters | 6 520 | 520 | (19) | (8) | (1) | (5) |
| Nestlé Nutrition | 7 233 | 1 443 | (36) | (18) | (9) | – |
| Other[b] | 12 599 | 2 119 | (78) | (9) | (14) | (2) |
| Unallocated items[c] | | (1 730) | (36) | – | – | – |
| **Total** | **83 642** | **12 538** | **(685)** | **(150)** | **(100)** | **(16)** |

*Included in trading operating profit.
[a]Inter-egment sales are not significant.
[b]Mainly Nespresso, Nestlé Professional, Nestlé Health Science, Food and Beverages Joint Ventures and Pharma Joint Ventures managed on a worldwide basis.
[c]Refer to the Segment reporting section of Note 1 – Accounting policies for the definition of unallocated items.

Refer to Note 3.3 for the reconciliation from trading operating profit before taxes and associates.

## Assets and other information

| In millions of CHF | | | | | 2012 |
|---|---|---|---|---|---|
| | Segment assets | of which goodwill and intangible assets | Capital additions | of which capital expenditure | Depreciation and amortization of segment assets |
| Zone Europe | 11 804 | 2 251 | 1 038 | 1 019 | (534) |
| Zone Americas | 22 652 | 9 555 | 1 162 | 1 088 | (878) |
| Zone Asia, Oceania and Africa | 14 353 | 4 465 | 1 692 | 1 556 | (537) |
| Nestlé Waters | 6 369 | 1 654 | 424 | 407 | (491) |
| Nestlé Nutrition | 24 118 | 15 123 | 10 276 | 426 | (174) |
| Other[a] | 11 157 | 4 392 | 705 | 638 | (491) |
| Unallocated items[b] | 11 209 | 8 818 | 234 | 234 | (45) |
| Inter-segment eliminations | (2 146) | | | | |
| **Total segments** | **99 516** | **46 258** | **15 531** | **5 368** | **(3 150)** |
| Non-segment assets | 26 713 | | | | |
| **Total** | **126 229** | | | | |

| In millions of CHF | | | | | 2011 |
|---|---|---|---|---|---|
| | Segment assets | of which goodwill and intangible assets | Capital additions | of which capital expenditure | Depreciation and amortization of segment assets |
| Zone Europe | 11 561 | 2 304 | 971 | 871 | (574) |
| Zone Americas | 23 081 | 9 831 | 1 267 | 1 102 | (783) |
| Zone Asia, Oceania and Africa | 13 806 | 4 561 | 4 819 | 1 142 | (441) |
| Nestlé Waters | 6 602 | 1 720 | 594 | 407 | (474) |
| Nestlé Nutrition | 12 848 | 6 486 | 590 | 477 | (198) |
| Other[a] | 10 936 | 4 438 | 1 595 | 537 | (338) |
| Unallocated items[b] | 11 117 | 9 024 | 254 | 243 | (117) |
| Inter-segment eliminations | (2 140) | | | | |
| **Total segments** | **87 811** | **38 364** | **10 090** | **4 779** | **(2 925)** |
| Non-segment assets | 26 280 | | | | |
| **Total** | **114 091** | | | | |

[a]Mainly Nespresso, Nestlé Professional, Nestlé Health Science, Food and Beverages Joint Ventures and Pharma Joint Ventures managed on a worldwide basis.
[b]Refer to the Segment reporting section of Note 1 – Accounting policies for the definition of unallocated items.

## 3.2 Products

### Revenue and results

*In millions of CHF*                                                                    *2012*

|  | Sales | Trading operating profit | Net other trading income/(expenses)* | of which impairment of assets other than goodwill | of which restructuring costs | Impairment of goodwill |
|---|---|---|---|---|---|---|
| Powdered and liquid beverages | 20 038 | 4 502 | (101) | (8) | (35) | – |
| Water | 7 178 | 636 | (41) | (20) | (16) | (1) |
| Milk products and ice cream | 18 564 | 2 799 | (148) | (12) | (15) | – |
| Nutrition and HealthCare | 10 676 | 1 958 | (50) | (3) | (10) | (11) |
| Prepared dishes and cooking aids | 14 432 | 2 041 | (62) | (13) | (15) | (1) |
| Confectionery | 10 438 | 1 782 | (92) | (15) | (16) | – |
| PetCare | 10 810 | 2 206 | (4) | (2) | 12 | – |
| Unallocated items[a] |  | (1 912) | (17) | (2) | – | (1) |
| **Total** | **92 816** | **14 012** | **(515)** | **(75)** | **(95)** | **(14)** |

*Included in trading operating profit.

*In millions of CHF*                                                                    *2011*

|  | Sales | Trading operating profit | Net other trading income/(expenses)* | of which impairment of assets other than goodwill | of which restructuring costs | Impairment of goodwill |
|---|---|---|---|---|---|---|
| Powdered and liquid beverages | 18 204 | 4 129 | (151) | (35) | (40) | (2) |
| Water | 6 526 | 520 | (19) | (8) | (1) | (5) |
| Milk products and ice cream | 16 406 | 2 251 | (211) | (37) | (25) | (5) |
| Nutrition and HealthCare | 9 744 | 1 820 | (55) | (20) | (16) | – |
| Prepared dishes and cooking aids | 13 933 | 2 016 | (69) | (18) | (9) | – |
| Confectionery | 9 065 | 1 524 | (136) | (30) | (11) | (4) |
| PetCare | 9 764 | 2 008 | (8) | (2) | 2 | – |
| Unallocated items[a] |  | (1 730) | (36) | – | – | – |
| **Total** | **83 642** | **12 538** | **(685)** | **(150)** | **(100)** | **(16)** |

*Included in trading operating profit.
[a]Refer to the segment reporting section of Note 1 – Accounting policies for the definition of unallocated items.

Refer to Note 3.3 for the reconciliation from trading operating profit before taxes and associates.

## Assets and liabilities

| In millions of CHF | Assets | of which goodwill and intangible assets | Liabilities |
|---|---|---|---|
| | | | 2012 |
| Powdered and liquid beverages | 10 704 | 403 | 4 335 |
| Water | 6 654 | 1 693 | 1 848 |
| Milk products and ice cream | 15 998 | 5 544 | 3 864 |
| Nutrition and HealthCare | 20 644 | 12 135 | 3 450 |
| Prepared dishes and cooking aids | 13 523 | 6 463 | 2 750 |
| Confectionery | 8 352 | 2 104 | 2 345 |
| PetCare | 14 001 | 9 252 | 1 656 |
| Unallocated items[a] and intra–group eliminations | 719 | 2 151 | (3 099) |
| **Total** | **90 595** | **39 745** | **17 149** |

| In millions of CHF | Assets | of which goodwill and intangible assets | Liabilities |
|---|---|---|---|
| | | | 2011 |
| Powdered and liquid beverages | 9 770 | 393 | 3 872 |
| Water | 6 640 | 1 678 | 1 747 |
| Milk products and ice cream | 13 496 | 4 397 | 3 456 |
| Nutrition and HealthCare | 16 837 | 9 762 | 2 959 |
| Prepared dishes and cooking aids | 12 922 | 6 308 | 2 703 |
| Confectionery | 6 482 | 1 023 | 2 034 |
| PetCare | 13 569 | 9 141 | 1 514 |
| Unallocated items[a] and intra–group eliminations | 911 | 2 184 | (2 614) |
| **Total** | **80 627** | **34 886** | **15 671** |

[a]Refer to the segment reporting section of Note 1 – Accounting policies for the definition of unallocated items.

**3.3 Reconciliation from trading operating profit to profit before taxes and associates**

| In millions of CHF | 2012 | 2011 |
|---|---|---|
| Trading operating profit | 14 012 | 12 538 |
| Impairment of goodwill | (14) | (16) |
| Net other operating income/(expenses) excluding | | |
|   impairment of goodwill | (66) | (51) |
| **Operating profit** | **13 932** | **12 471** |
| Net financing cost | (481) | (421) |
| **Profit before taxes and associates** | **13 451** | **12 050** |

**3.4 Customers** There is no single customer amounting to 10% or more of Group's revenues.

**3.5 Geography (top ten countries and Switzerland)**

| In millions of CHF | 2012 | | 2011 | |
|---|---|---|---|---|
| | Sales | Non-current assets[a] | Sales[b] | Non-current assets[a] |
| USA | 23 712 | 16 483 | 21 539 | 17 115 |
| France | 5 691 | 1 781 | 5 634 | 1 722 |
| Brazil | 5 348 | 1 211 | 5 375 | 1 242 |
| Greater China region | 5 158 | 5 112 | 2 500 | 4 298 |
| Germany | 3 270 | 1 430 | 3 338 | 1 356 |
| Mexico | 3 246 | 686 | 2961 | 596 |
| United Kingdom | 2 935 | 1 058 | 2 675 | 877 |
| Italy | 2 219 | 875 | 2 273 | 895 |
| Canada | 2 182 | 644 | 2 078 | 452 |
| Australia | 2 151 | 985 | 2 106 | 1 080 |
| Switzerland[c] | 1 518 | 2 925 | 1 503 | 2 636 |
| Rest of the world and | | | | |
|   unallocated items | 34 756 | 39 971 | 31 660 | 30 066 |
| **Total** | **92 186** | **73 161** | **83 642** | **62 335** |

[a]Relate to property plant and equipment intangible assets and goodwill.
[b]While the total 2011 comparative sales are unchanged the split by country has been restated based on an improved methology to identify more precisely customer country location.
[c]Country of domicile of Nestlé S.A.

The analysis of sales by geographic area is stated by customer location.

## APPENDIX III

# The financial statements of the Unilever Group 2012

## Consolidated income statement for the year ended 31 December

|  | € million 2012 | € million 2011 | € million 2010 |
|---|---|---|---|
| **Turnover** 2 | **51 324** | 46 467 | 44 262 |
| **Operating profit** 2 | **6 989** | 6 433 | 6 339 |
| After (charging)/crediting non-core items 3 | **(73)** | 144 | 308 |
| Net finance costs 5 | **(397)** | (377) | (394) |
| Finance income | **136** | 92 | 77 |
| Finance costs | **(526)** | (540) | (491) |
| Pensions and similar obligations | **(7)** | 71 | 20 |
| Share of net profit/(loss) of joint ventures and associates 11 | **105** | 113 | 111 |
| Other income/(loss) from non-current investments 11 | **(14)** | 76 | 76 |
| **Profit before taxation** | **6 683** | 6 245 | 6 132 |
| Taxation 6A | **(1 735)** | (1 622) | (1 534) |
| **Net profit** | **4 948** | 4 623 | 4 598 |
| Attributable to: |  |  |  |
| Non-controlling interests | **468** | 371 | 354 |
| Shareholders' equity | **4 480** | 4 252 | 4 244 |
| **Combined earnings per share** 7 |  |  |  |
| Basic earnings per share (€) | **1.58** | 1.51 | 1.51 |
| Diluted earnings per share (€) | **1.54** | 1.46 | 1.46 |

References in the consolidated income statement, consolidated statement of comprehensive income, consolidated statement of changes in equity, consolidated balance sheet and consolidated cash flow statement relate to notes on pages 90 to 131, which form an integral part of the consolidated financial statements.

# Consolidated statement of comprehensive income for the year ended 31 December

| | € million 2012 | € million 2011 | € million 2010 |
|---|---|---|---|
| Fair value gains/(losses) on financial instruments net of tax: | | | |
| On cash flow hedges | (141) | (148) | 41 |
| On available-for-sale financial assets | 16 | (20) | 2 |
| Actuarial gains/(losses) on pension schemes net of tax | (644) | (1 243) | 105 |
| Currency retranslation gains/(losses) net of tax[a] | (316) | (703) | 460 |
| **Other comprehensive income** 6C | (1 085) | (2 114) | 608 |
| Net profit | 4 948 | 4 623 | 4 598 |
| **Total comprehensive income** 15 | 3 863 | 2 509 | 5 206 |
| Attributable to: | | | |
| Non-controlling interests | 444 | 314 | 412 |
| Shareholders' equity | 3 419 | 2 195 | 4 794 |

[a]Includes fair value gains/(losses) on net investment hedges of €(160) million (2011: €45 million; 2010: €107 million).

# Consolidated balance sheet as at 31 December

| | € million 2012 | € million 2011 |
|---|---|---|
| **Assets** | | |
| **Non-current assets** | | |
| Goodwill 9 | **14 619** | 14 896 |
| Intangible assets 9 | **7 099** | 7 017 |
| Property, plant and equipment 10 | **9 445** | 8 774 |
| Pension asset for funded schemes in surplus 4B | **672** | 1 003 |
| Deferred tax assets 6B | **1 113** | 421 |
| Financial assets 17A | **535** | 478 |
| Other non-current assets 11 | **536** | 632 |
| | **34 019** | 33 221 |
| **Current assets** | | |
| Inventories 12 | **4 436** | 4 601 |
| Trade and other current receivables 13 | **4 436** | 4 513 |
| Current tax assets | **217** | 219 |
| Cash and cash equivalents 17A | **2 465** | 3 484 |
| Other financial assets 17A | **401** | 1 453 |
| Non-current assets held for sale 22 | **192** | 21 |
| | **12 147** | 14 291 |
| **Total assets** | **46 166** | 47 512 |
| **Liabilities** | | |
| **Current liabilities** | | |
| Financial liabilities 15C | **2 656** | 5 840 |
| Trade payables and other current liabilities 14 | **11 668** | 10 971 |
| Current tax liabilities | **1 129** | 725 |
| Provisions 19 | **361** | 393 |
| Liabilities associated with assets held for sale 22 | **1** | — |

|                                                      | € million 2012 | € million 2011 |
|------------------------------------------------------|---------------:|---------------:|
|                                                      | 15 815         | 17 929         |
| **Non-current liabilities**                          |                |                |
| Financial liabilities 15C                            | 7 565          | 7 878          |
| Non-current tax liabilities                          | 100            | 258            |
| Pensions and post-retirement healthcare liabilities: |                |                |
| Funded schemes in deficit 4B                         | 2 291          | 2 295          |
| Unfunded schemes 4B                                  | 2 040          | 1 911          |
| Provisions 19                                        | 846            | 908            |
| Deferred tax liabilities 6B                          | 1 393          | 1 125          |
| Other non-current liabilities 14                     | 400            | 287            |
|                                                      | 14 635         | 14 662         |
| **Total liabilities**                                | 30 450         | 32 591         |
| **Equity**                                           |                |                |
| **Shareholders' equity**                             |                |                |
| Called up share capital 15A                          | 484            | 484            |
| Share premium 15B                                    | 140            | 137            |
| Other reserves 15B                                   | (6 196)        | (6 004)        |
| Retained profit 15B                                  | 20 731         | 19 676         |
| **Shareholders' equity**                             | 15 159         | 14 293         |
| Non-controlling interests 15B                        | 557            | 628            |
| **Total equity**                                     | 15 716         | 14 921         |
| **Total liabilities and equity**                     | 46 166         | 47 512         |

These financial statements have been approved by the Directors.
**The Board of Directors**
5 March 2013

## 2. Segment information

*Segmental reporting* The Group has revised its operating segments to align with the new structure under which the business is managed. From 2012, operating segment information is provided based on four product areas rather than geographical regions. The four product areas are:

**Personal care** – including sales of skincare and haircare products, deodorants and oral care products.

**Foods** – including sales of soups, bouillons, sauces, snacks, mayonnaise, salad dressings, margarines and spreads.

**Refreshment** – including sales of ice cream, tea-based beverages, weight-management products and nutritionally enhanced staples sold in developing markets.

**Home care** – including sales of home care products, such as laundry tablets, powders and liquids, soap bars and a wide range of cleaning products.

*Revenue recognition* Turnover comprises sales of goods after the deduction of discounts, sales taxes and estimated returns. It does not include sales between group companies. Discounts given by Unilever include rebates, price reductions and incentives given to customers, promotional couponing and trade communication costs.

Turnover is recognized when the risks and rewards of the underlying products have been substantially transferred to the customer. Depending on individual customer terms, this can be at the time of despatch, delivery or upon formal customer acceptance.

**Core operating profit** From 2012 the Group refers to core operating profit which means operating profit before the impact of non-core items (refer to note 3 for explanation of non-core items).

| 2012 | € million Personal care | € million Foods | € million Refreshment | € million Home care | € million Total |
|---|---|---|---|---|---|
| Turnover | 18 097 | 14 444 | 9 726 | 9 057 | 51 324 |
| Operating profit Non-core items 3 | 2 928 160 | 2 605 (73) | 911 | 545 (14) | 6 989 73 |
| Core operating profit | 3 088 | 2 532 | 911 | 531 | 7 062 |
| Share of net profit/(loss) of joint ventures and associates | 1 | 5 | 99 | – | 105 |
| Depreciation and amortization | 336 | 311 | 340 | 212 | 1 199 |
| Impairment and other non-cash charges[a] | 189 | 141 | 106 | 128 | 564 |

The home countries of the Unilever Group are the Netherlands and the United Kingdom. Turnover and non-current assets[b] for these two countries combined, the USA and Brazil (being the two largest countries outside the home countries) and all other countries are:

| 2012 | € million Netherlands/ United Kingdom | € million USA | € million Brazil | € million All other countries | € million Total |
|---|---|---|---|---|---|
| Turnover | 3 980 | 7 834 | 3 813 | 35 697 | 51 324 |
| Non-current assets[b] | 3 353 | 8 670 | 2 235 | 17 441 | 31 699 |

No other country had turnover or non-current assets (as shown above) greater than 10 per cent of the Group total.

*Additional information by geographies* Although the Group's operations are managed by product area, we provide additional information based on geographies. The analysis of turnover by geographical area is stated on the basis of origin. Sales between geographical areas are carried out at arm's length and were not material.

| 2012 | € million<br>Asia/<br>AMET/<br>RUB[c] | € million<br>The<br>Americas | € million<br>Europe | € million<br>Total |
|---|---|---|---|---|
| Turnover | 20 357 | 17 088 | 13 879 | 51 324 |
| Operating profit non-<br>core items | 2 637 | 2 433 | 1 919 | 6 989 |
| | 30 | (13) | 56 | 73 |
| Core operating profit | 2 667 | 2 420 | 1 975 | 7 062 |
| Share of net profit/<br>(loss) of joint<br>ventures and<br>associates | (2) | 68 | 39 | 105 |

## 3. Gross profit and operating costs

*Research and market support costs* Expenditure on research and market support, such as advertising, is charged to the income statement as incurred.

| | € million<br>2012 | € million<br>2011 | € million<br>2010 |
|---|---|---|---|
| Turnover | 51 324 | 46 467 | 44 262 |
| Cost of sales | (30 703) | (27 930) | (25 890) |
| Gross profit | 20 621 | 18 537 | 18 372 |
| Selling and<br>administrative<br>expenses | (13 632) | (12 104) | (12 033) |
| Operating profit | 6 989 | 6 433 | 6 339 |

*Other* Other items within operating costs include:

| | € million<br>2012 | € million<br>2011 | € million<br>2010 |
|---|---|---|---|
| Staff costs 4 | (6 291) | (5 345) | (5 599) |
| Distribution costs | (3 264) | (3 080) | (3 015) |
| Raw and packaging materials and goods<br>    purchased for resale | (20 998) | (19 253) | (17 636) |
| Amortization of finite-life intangible assets and<br>    software 9 | (213) | (191) | (174) |
| Depreciation of property, plant and equipment 10 | (986) | (838) | (819) |
| Advertising and promotions | (6 763) | (6 069) | (6 064) |
| Research and development | (1 003) | (1 009) | (928) |
| Exchange gains/(losses): | (118) | (9) | 7 |
|     On underlying transactions | (96) | (45) | (36) |
|     On covering forward contracts | (22) | 36 | 43 |
| Lease rentals: | (558) | (452) | (465) |
|     Minimum operating lease payments | (558) | (456) | (465) |
|     Contingent operating lease payments | (8) | (3) | (4) |
|     *Less* Sub-lease income relating to operating<br>    lease agreements | 8 | 7 | 4 |

## SUMMARY

External parties use financial statement data to obtain information on several aspects of a company, e.g. is the company liquid, can the company repay its debt, is the company performing well? Several techniques exist to extract information from the financial statements in order to answer those questions. One purpose of this chapter was to explain and illustrate these techniques (trend analysis, common size analysis, ratio analysis, segmental analysis and cash flow analysis). A common characteristic of all these techniques is that benchmarks (internal and external) with which to compare the company data are needed in order to have information value for decision purposes. A necessary condition for benchmarking is the comparability of data. As a result, the second purpose of this chapter was to point out and illustrate several pitfalls which might hinder the comparability of financial accounting data. If accounting analysis is combined with several techniques of financial analysis, external parties should be able to judge the performance and the financial position of a company in a proper perspective.

## EXERCISES

*Suggested answers to exercises marked ✓ are to be found on our dedicated CourseMate platform for students.*

*Suggested answers to the remaining exercises are to be found on the Instructor online support resources.*

1   You are the management accountant of Expand, a company incorporated in Dollarland. The company is seeking to grow by acquisition and has identified two potential investment opportunities. One of these, Hone, is also a company incorporated in Dollarland. The other, Over, is a company incorporated in Francland.

   You have been presented with financial information relating to both companies. The financial information is extracted from their published financial statements. In both cases, the financial statements conform to domestic accounting standards. The financial statements of Hone were drawn up in $s while those of Over were drawn up in Francs. The information relating to Over has been expressed in $s by taking the figures in Francs and dividing by 1.55 – the $/Franc exchange rate at 31 December 20X1. The financial information is given below.

**Income statements**

| Year ended | 31 March 20X2 | 31 March 20X1 | 31 December 20X1 | 31 December 20X0 |
|---|---|---|---|---|
| | $ million | $ million | $ million | $ million |
| Revenue | 600 | 550 | 620 | 560 |
| Cost of sales | (300) | (250) | (320) | (260) |
| Gross profit | 300 | 300 | 300 | 300 |
| Other operating expenses | (120) | (105) | (90) | (85) |
| Profit from operations | 180 | 195 | 210 | 215 |
| Finance cost | (20) | (18) | (22) | (20) |

### Income statements

| Year ended | Hone 31 March 20X2 $ million | Hone 31 March 20X1 $ million | Over 31 December 20X1 $ million | Over 31 December 20X0 $ million |
|---|---|---|---|---|
| Profit before tax | 160 | 177 | 188 | 195 |
| Income tax expense | (50) | (55) | (78) | (90) |
| Net profit for the period | 110 | 122 | 110 | 105 |

### Statements of changes in equity

| Year ended | Hone 31 March 20X2 $ million | Hone 31 March 20X1 $ million | Over 31 December 20X1 $ million | Over 31 December 2000 $ million |
|---|---|---|---|---|
| Balance brought forward | 470 | 418 | 265 | 240 |
| Net profit for the period | 110 | 122 | 110 | 105 |
| Dividends | (70) | (70) | (80) | (80) |
| Balance carried forward | 510 | 470 | 295 | 265 |

### Statements of changes in equity

| | Hone 31 March 20X2 $ million | Hone 31 March 20X1 $ million | Over 31 December 20X1 $ million | Over 31 December 20X0 $ million |
|---|---|---|---|---|
| Non-current assets | 600 | 570 | 455 | 440 |
| Inventories | 60 | 50 | 55 | 50 |
| Trade receivables | 80 | 75 | 90 | 80 |
| Cash | 10 | 20 | 15 | 15 |
| | 750 | 715 | 615 | 585 |
| Issued share capital | 150 | 150 | 110 | 110 |
| Reserves | 360 | 320 | 185 | 155 |
| | 510 | 470 | 295 | 265 |
| Interest-bearing borrowings | 150 | 150 | 240 | 240 |
| Current liabilities | 90 | 95 | 80 | 80 |
| | 750 | 715 | 615 | 585 |

Expand is more concerned with the profitability of potential investment opportunities than with liquidity. You have been asked to review the financial statements of Hone and Over with this concern in mind.

### Required:

(a) Prepare a short report to the directors of Expand that, based on the financial information provided, assesses the relative profitability of Hone and Over.

(b) Discuss the validity of using this financial information as a basis to compare the profitability of the two companies.

(CIMA – May 2001)

✓ **2**    It has been suggested that cash is king and that readers of a company's accounts should pay more attention to information concerning its cash flows and balances than to its profits and other assets. It is argued that cash is more difficult to manipulate than profit and that cash flows are more important.

**Required:**
(a)  Explain whether you agree with the suggestion that cash flows and balances are more difficult to manipulate than profit and non-cash assets.

(b)  Explain why it might be dangerous to concentrate on cash to the exclusion of profit when analyzing a set of financial statements.

(CIMA, adapted)

**3**    Look up the financial statements of two companies competing in the same industry in your country. Calculate their return on equity (ROE). First, try to explain the difference observed with the use of ratio analysis. Subsequently, add trend analysis, common size analysis, segmental analysis and cash flow analysis to it. What extra information do these supplemental analyses give you? If you were to carry out an industry analysis, would this give you extra information on top of it?

**4**    Look up the PE ratios of several airlines; what do you observe? How does the market value the prospects of each of these companies? Do the underlying financial statements confirm the market appreciation? Or do you observe conflicts?

**5**    Question 4 can be repeated for listed companies in several industries. Do you observe industry differences?

**6**    In which industries would you expect inventory turnover to be lower, in which industries would you expect this ratio to be higher? Comment on this (discuss this in relation to asset turnover also).

**7**    In which industries would you expect profit margins to be lower, in which industries would you expect this ratio to be higher?

**8**    Heavy Goods plc carries on business as a manufacturer of tractors. In 20X4 the company was looking for acquisitions and carrying out investigations into a number of possible targets. One of these was a competitor, Modern Tractors plc. The company's acquisition strategy was to acquire companies that were vulnerable to a takeover and in which there was an opportunity to improve asset management and profitability.

The chief accountant of Heavy Goods plc has instructed his assistant to calculate ratios from the financial statements of Modern Tractors plc for the past three years and to prepare a report based on these ratios and the industry average ratios that have been provided by the trade association. The ratios prepared by the assistant accountant and the industry averages for 20X4 are set out as follows.

**Required:**

You are required to write a full appraisal and report.

| | 20X2 | 20X3 | 20X4 | 20X4 |
|---|---|---|---|---|
| | *Industry average (%)* | | | |
| Sales growth | 30.00 | 40.00 | 9.52 | 8.25 |
| Sales/total assets | 1.83 | 2.05 | 1.60 | 2.43 |
| Sales/net fixed assets | 2.94 | 3.59 | 2.74 | 16.85 |
| Sales/working capital | −21.43 | −140.00 | 38.33 | 10.81 |
| Sales/debtors | 37.50 | 70.00 | 92.00 | 16.00 |
| Gross profit/sales | 18.67 | 22.62 | 19.57 | 23.92 |
| Profit before tax/sales | 8.00 | 17.62 | 11.74 | 4.06 |
| Profit before interest/interest | 6.45 | 26.57 | 14.50 | 4.95 |
| Profit after tax/total assets | 9.76 | 27.80 | 13.24 | 8.97 |
| Profit after tax/equity | 57.14 | 75.00 | 39.58 | 28.90 |
| Net fixed assets/total assets | 62.20 | 57.07 | 58.54 | 19.12 |
| Net fixed assets/equity | 3.64 | 1.54 | 1.75 | 0.58 |
| Equity/total assets | 18.29 | 37.07 | 33.45 | 32.96 |
| Total liabilities/total assets | 81.71 | 62.93 | 66.55 | 69.00 |
| Total liabilities/equity | 4.47 | 1.70 | 1.99 | 2.40 |
| Long-term debt/total assets | 36.59 | 18.54 | 29.27 | 19.00 |
| Current liabilities/total assets | 45.12 | 44.39 | 37.28 | 50.00 |
| Current assets/current liabilities | 0.84 | 0.97 | 1.11 | 1.63 |
| (Current assets − stock)/current liabilities | 0.43 | 0.54 | 0.72 | 0.58 |
| Stock/total assets | 17.07 | 18.54 | 14.63 | 41.90 |
| Cost of sales/stock | 8.71 | 8.55 | 8.81 | 4.29 |
| Cost of sales/creditors | 6.10 | 6.25 | 6.17 | 12.87 |
| Debtors/total assets | 4.88 | 2.93 | 1.70 | 18.40 |
| Cash/total assets | 15.85 | 21.46 | 25.08 | 9.60 |

Note: Total assets = (fixed assets at net book value + current assets) and net fixed assets = fixed assets at net book value.

(ACCA, adapted)

**9** Seville plc is a rapidly expanding trading and manufacturing company. It is currently seeking to extend its product range in new markets. To achieve this growth it needs to raise €800 000. The directors are considering two sources of funds:

(i) A rights issue at €2.00 per share. The shares are trading at €2.50 (2000 €2.20) per share.

(ii) A bank loan at an interest rate of 15 per cent and repayable by instalments after two years. The bank would want to secure the loan with a charge over the company's property.

The following are extracts from the draft financial statements.

## Seville plc Draft income statement extract year ended 31.12.X1

|  | 20X0 €000 | 20X1 €000 |
|---|---|---|
| Turnover | 1 967 | 1 991 |
| Operating profit | 636 | 698 |
| Interest payable | (45) | (55) |
| Profit before taxation | 591 | 643 |
| Taxation | (150) | (140) |
| Profit after taxation | 441 | 503 |
| Extraordinary item | (90) | – |
| Profit for the year | 361 | 453 |
| *Fixed assets* |  |  |
| tangible | 1 132 | 1 504 |
| intangible | 247 | 298 |
| Draft balance sheet | 1 379 | 1 802 |
| *Current assets* |  |  |
| stocks | 684 | 679 |
| debtors | 471 | 511 |
| cash in hand and at bank | 80 | 117 |
| *Creditors: due within one year* |  |  |
| trade | (336) | (308) |
| taxation | (140) | (190) |
| dividends | (80) | (80) |
| *Creditors: due after more than one year* |  |  |
| 10% debentures, repayable 2004 | (450) | (450) |
| finance lease | – | (100) |
|  | 1 608 | 1 981 |
| *Capital and reserves* |  |  |
| ordinary share capital €1 shares | 800 | 800 |
| revaluation reserve | 144 | 144 |
| profit and loss | 664 | 1 037 |
|  | 1 608 | 1 981 |

*Operating profit*

Operating profit has been arrived at after charging or crediting the following:

|  | 20X0 €000 | 20X1 €000 |
|---|---|---|
| Depreciation | 110 | 150 |
| Gain on disposal of property (as part of a sale and leaseback transaction) | – | 95 |

Notes: *Extraordinary item* The extraordinary loss consists of reorganization costs in a branch where a reduction in activity involved various measures including redundancies. Attributable tax credit is €38 000.

*Deferred taxation* Deferred taxation has not been provided because it is not considered probable that a liability will crystallize. If deferred taxation had been provided in full then a liability for the year of €7 000 would have arisen (2000 €8 000).

*Contingent liability* There is a contingent liability of €85 000 (2000 €80 000) in respect of bills of exchange discounted with bankers.

Further investigation has revealed that stock includes items subject to reservation of title of €40 000 and obsolete or slow moving items of €28 000 (2000 €28 000).

An age analysis of debtors has revealed that debts overdue by more than one year amount to €40 000 (2000 €40 000).

The auditors are yet to report and there is some discussion as to the classification of the gain on disposal and the reorganization costs.

The directors forecast that the new funds will generate an operating profit of €300 000, and that the 20X1 operating profit will be repeated. If new shares are issued the dividend will increase to €150 000.

### Required:

Prepare a full report on progress, strengths and weaknesses, supported by ratio analysis.

(ACCA, adapted)

10  Recycle plc is a listed company which recycles toxic chemical waste products. The waste products are sent to Recycle plc from all around the world. You are an accountant (not employed by Recycle plc) who is accustomed to providing advice concerning the performance of companies, on the basis of data which are available from their published financial statements. Extracts from the financial statements of Recycle plc for the two years ended 30 September 20X7 are as follows:

### Statements of comprehensive income – year ended 30 September

|  | 20X7 | 20X6 |
|---|---|---|
|  | €m | €m |
| Turnover | 3 000 | 2 800 |
| Cost of sales | (1 600) | (1 300) |
| Gross profit | 1 400 | 1 500 |
| Other operating expenses | (800) | (600) |
| Operating profit | 600 | 900 |
| Interest payable | (200) | (100) |
| Profit before taxation | 400 | 800 |
| Taxation | (150) | (250) |
| Profit after taxation | 250 | 550 |
| Proposed dividend | (200) | (200) |
| Retained profit | 50 | 350 |
| Retained profit b/fwd | 900 | 550 |
| Retained profit c/fwd | 950 | 900 |

### Statements of financial position at 30 September

|  | 20X7 | | 20X6 | |
|---|---|---|---|---|
|  | €m | €m | €m | €m |
| Tangible fixed assets | | 4 100 | | 3 800 |
| Current assets: | | | | |
| Stocks | 500 | | 350 | |
| Debtors | 1 000 | | 800 | |
| Cash in hand | 50 | | 50 | |
|  | 1 550 | | 1 200 | |
| Current liabilities: | | | | |
| Trade creditors | 600 | | 600 | |
| Taxation payable | 150 | | 250 | |
| Proposed dividend | 200 | | 200 | |

**Statements of financial position at 30 September**

|  | 20X7 | | 20X6 | |
|---|---|---|---|---|
|  | €m | €m | €m | €m |
| Bank overdraft | 750 | | 50 | |
|  | 1 700 | | 1 100 | |
| Net current (liabilities)/assets | | (150) | | 100 |
| Long-term loans (repayable 2009) | | (1 000) | | (1 000) |
|  | | 2 950 | | 2 900 |
| Capital and reserves: | | | | |
| Called-up share capital (€1 shares) | | 2 000 | | 2 000 |
| Profit and loss account | | 950 | | 900 |
|  | | 2 950 | | 2 900 |

You ascertain that depreciation of tangible fixed assets for the year ended 30 September 20X7 was €1200m. Disposals of fixed assets during the year ended 30 September 20X7 were negligible. You are approached by two individuals.

A is a private investigator who is considering purchasing shares in Recycle plc. A considers that Recycle plc has performed well in 20X7 compared with 2006 because turnover has risen and the dividend to shareholders has been maintained.

B is resident in the area immediately surrounding the premises of Recycle plc and is interested in the contribution made by Recycle plc to the general well-being of the community. B is also concerned about the potential environmental effect of the recycling of chemical waste. B is uncertain how the published financial statements of Recycle plc might be of assistance in addressing social and environmental matters.

**Required:**

Write a full report addressed to A, supported by appropriate ratios.

(CIMA, adapted)

11   H plc manufactures vehicle parts. The company sells its products to a number of independent distributors who resell the goods to garages and other retail outlets in their areas. H plc has a policy of having only one distributor in any given geographical area. Distributors are selected mainly on the basis of financial viability. H plc is keen to avoid the disruption of sales and loss of credibility associated with the collapse of a distributor. The company is currently trying to choose between two companies which have applied to be its sole distributor in Geetown, a new sales area.

The applicants have supplied the following information:

|  | Applicant X | | | Applicant Y | | |
|---|---|---|---|---|---|---|
|  | 20X3 | 20X4 | 20X5 | 20X3 | 20X4 | 20X5 |
| Sales (£000) | 1 280 | 1 600 | 2 000 | 1 805 | 1 900 | 2 000 |
| Gross profit % | 22 | 20 | 18 | 23 | 22 | 24 |
| Return on capital employed % | 8 | 12 | 16 | 14 | 15 | 16 |
| Current ratio | 1.7:1 | 1.9:1 | 2.1:1 | 1.7:1 | 1.65:1 | 1.7:1 |
| Quick ratio | 1.4:1 | 1.1:1 | 0.9:1 | 0.9:1 | 0.9:1 | 0.9:1 |
| Gearing % | 15 | 21 | 28 | 29 | 30 | 27 |

**Requirements:**

(a) Explain why trends in accounting ratios could provide a more useful insight than the latest figures taken on their own.

(b) Using the information provided above, explain which of the companies appears to be the safer choice for the role of distributor.

(CIMA, adapted)

**12** Arizona plc has carried on business for a number of years as a retailer of a wide variety of do-it-yourself goods. The company operates from a number of stores around the United Kingdom. In recent years, the company has found it necessary to provide credit facilities to its customers in order to achieve growth in turnover. As a result of this decision, the liability to the company's bankers has increased substantially.

The statutory accounts of the company for the year ended 31 March 20X8 have recently been published, and extracts are provided below, together with comparative figures for the previous two years.

**Statement of comprehensive income for the years ended 31 March**

|  | 20X6 | 20X7 | 20X8 |
|---|---|---|---|
|  | £m | £m | £m |
| Turnover | 1 850 | 2 200 | 2 500 |
| Cost of sales | (1 250) | (1 500) | (1 750) |
| Gross profit | 600 | 700 | 750 |
| Other operating costs | (550) | (640) | (700) |
| Operating profit | 50 | 60 | 50 |
| Interest from credit sales | 45 | 60 | 90 |
| Interest payable | (25) | (60) | (110) |
| Profit before taxation | 70 | 60 | 30 |
| Taxation | (23) | (20) | (10) |
| Profit after taxation | 47 | 40 | 20 |
| Dividends | (30) | (30) | (20) |
| Retained profit | 17 | 10 | – |

**Statement of financial position at 31 March**

|  | 20X6 | 20X7 | 20X8 |
|---|---|---|---|
|  | £m | £m | £m |
| Tangible fixed assets | 278 | 290 | 322 |
| Stocks | 400 | 540 | 620 |
| Debtors | 492 | 550 | 633 |
| Cash | 12 | 12 | 15 |
| Trade creditors | (270) | (270) | (280) |
| Taxation | (20) | (20) | (8) |
| Proposed dividends | (30) | (30) | (20) |
| Bank overdraft | (320) | (520) | (610) |
| Debentures | (200) | (200) | (320) |
|  | 342 | 352 | 352 |

**Statement of financial position at 31 March**

|  | 20X6 £m | 20X7 £m | 20X8 £m |
|---|---|---|---|
| Share capital | 90 | 90 | 90 |
| Reserves | 252 | 262 | 262 |
|  | 342 | 352 | 352 |

## Other information:
- Depreciation charged for the three years was as follows:

| Year ended 31 March | 20X6 £m | 20X7 £m | 20X8 £m |
|---|---|---|---|
|  | 55 | 60 | 70 |

- The debentures are secured by a floating charge over the assets of Arizona plc. Their repayment is due on 31 March 20X8.
- The bank overdraft is unsecured. The bank has set a limit of £630m on the overdraft.
- Over the past three years, the level of credit sales has been:

| Year ended 31 March | 20X6 £m | 20X7 £m | 20X8 £m |
|---|---|---|---|
|  | 213 | 263 | 375 |

Given the steady increase in the bank overdraft which has taken place in recent years, the company has recently written to its bankers to request an increase in the limit. The request was received by the bank on 15 May 20X8, two weeks after the 20X8 statutory accounts were published.

You are an accountant employed by the bankers of Arizona plc. The bank is concerned at the steep escalation in the level of the company's overdraft and your regional manager has asked for a report on the financial performance of Arizona plc for the last three years.

**Required:**
Write a report to your regional manager which analyzes the financial performance of Arizona plc for the period covered by the financial statements.

Your report may take any form you wish, but should specifically address the particular concern of the bank regarding the rapidly increasing overdraft. Therefore, your report should identify aspects of poor performance which could have contributed to the increase in the overdraft.

(CIMA)

13 You are an investment analyst. A client of yours, Mr A, owns 3.5 per cent of the share capital of Price. Price is a listed company and prepares financial statements in accordance with International Accounting Standards. The company supplies machinery to agricultural businesses. The year-end of Price is 31 July and the financial statements for the year ended 31 July 20X1 were approved by the directors on 30 September 20X1. Following approval, copies of the financial statements were sent to all shareholders in readiness for the annual general meeting which is due to be held on 30 November 20X1. Extracts from these financial statements are given below:

**Statement of comprehensive income – year ended 31 July**

|  | 20X1 $000 | 20X0 $000 |
|---|---|---|
| Revenue | 54 000 | 51 000 |
| Cost of sales | (42 000) | (40 000) |
| Gross profit | 12 000 | 11 000 |
| Other operating expenses | (6 300) | (6 000) |
| Profit from operations | 5 700 | 5 000 |
| Finance cost | (1 600) | (1 000) |
| Profit before tax | 4 100 | 4 000 |
| Income tax expense | (1 200) | (1 200) |
| Net profit for the period | 2 900 | 2 800 |

**Statement of financial position at 31 July**

|  | 20X1 $000 | 20X1 $000 | 20X0 $000 | 20X0 $000 |
|---|---|---|---|---|
| **Non-current assets:** |  |  |  |  |
| Property plant and equipment |  | 44 200 |  | 32 000 |
| **Current assets:** |  |  |  |  |
| Inventories | 8 700 |  | 7 500 |  |
| Receivables | 13 000 |  | 12 000 |  |
| Cash and cash equivalents | 200 |  | 1 500 |  |
|  |  | 21 900 |  | 21 000 |
|  |  | 66 100 |  | 53 000 |
| **Capital and reserves:** |  |  |  |  |
| Issued share capital |  | 20 000 |  | 20 000 |
| Reserves |  | 20 300 |  | 14 000 |
|  |  | 40 300 |  | 34 000 |
| **Non-current liabilities** |  | 15 400 |  | 10 000 |
| **Current liabilities:** |  |  |  |  |
| Trade payables | 8 000 |  | 7 800 |  |
| Tax | 1 200 |  | 1 200 |  |
| Bank overdraft | 1 200 |  | Nil |  |
|  |  | 10 400 |  | 9 000 |
|  |  | 66 100 |  | 53 000 |

*Statement of changes in equity*

|  | $000 |
|---|---|
| Balance at 31 July 20X0 | 34 000 |
| Surplus on revaluation of properties | 5 000 |
| Net profit for the period | 2 900 |
| Dividends | (1 600) |
| Balance at 31 July 20X1 | 40 300 |

**Extracts from notes to the financial statements finance cost – year ended 31 July**

|  | 20X1 | 20X0 |
|---|---|---|
|  | $000 | $000 |
| On 10% interest-bearing borrowings | 1 000 | 1 000 |
| On zero-rate bonds | 400 | Nil |
| On bank overdraft | 200 | Nil |
|  | 1 600 | 1 600 |

*Non-current liabilities at 31 July*

|  | 20X1 | 20X0 |
|---|---|---|
| 10% borrowings repayable 31 July 20X6 | 10 000 | 10 000 |
| Zero-rate bonds | 5 400 | Nil |
|  | 15 400 | 10 000 |

The zero-rate bonds were issued for proceeds of $5m on 1 August 20X0. The lenders are not entitled to interest during their period of issue. The bonds are repayable on 31 July 20X4 for a total of $6 802 450. The bonds are quoted on a recognized stock exchange. However, the company intends to hold the bonds until they mature and then repay them.

**Revaluation of properties:** This is the first time the company has revalued any of its properties.

**Depreciation of non-current assets:** Depreciation of non-current assets for the year totalled $4m (2000 – $3m).

Your client always attends the annual general meeting of the company and likes to put questions to the directors regarding the financial statements. However, he is not a financial specialist and does not wish to look foolish by asking inappropriate questions. Mr A intends to ask the following three questions and seeks your advice based on the information provided. The points he wishes to make are as follows:

**Point 1:** Why, when the company has made almost the same profit as last year and has borrowed more money through a bond issue, has the company got a bank overdraft of $1.2m at the end of the year when there was a positive balance of $1.5m in the bank at the end of the previous year? This looks wrong to me.

**Point 2:** The company has a revaluation surplus of $5m included in the statement of changes in equity. I have never understood this statement. Surely surpluses are shown in the income statement. Perhaps our accountants are unaware of the correct accounting treatment?

**Point 3:** I don't understand the treatment of the zero-rate bonds. The notes tell me that these were issued for $5m and no interest was paid to the investors. The accounts show a finance cost of $400 000 and a balance owing of $5.4m. Is this an error? On the other hand, perhaps the $5.4m is the fair value of the bonds? I feel sure an International Accounting Standard has been issued that requires companies to value their borrowings at fair value.

**Required:**
Prepare a reply to Mr A that evaluates the issues he has raised in the three points and provides appropriate advice. You should support your advice with references to International Accounting Standards.

(CIMA – November 2001)

**14** You are the Management Accountant of Drax. The entity prepares financial statements to 31 March each year. Earnings per share is regarded as a key performance indicator and the executive directors receive a bonus if the earnings per share exceeds a given target figure. Good corporate governance is ensured by the appointment of a number of non-executive directors, who rigorously scrutinize the financial statements each year to ensure that the earnings per share figure has been correctly computed.

Drax has recently appointed a new non-executive director who seeks your advice regarding the financial statements for the year ended 31 March 20X3. Extracts from these financial statements (excluding the comparative figures) are given below. The financial statements comply with relevant Accounting Standards in all material respects.

**STATEMENTS OF FINANCIAL PERFORMANCE**
**Income statement – year ended 31 March 20X3**

|  | Continuing operations $ million | Discontinuing operations $ million | Total $ million |
|---|---|---|---|
| Revenue | 1 000 | 100 | 1 100 |
| Cost of sales | (520) | (70) | (590) |
| Gross profit | 480 | 30 | 510 |
| Other operating expenses | (200) | (40) | (240) |
| Profit from operations | 280 | (10) | 270 |
| Loss on disposal of discontinuing operations (note 1) | – | (30) | (30) |
| Profit before finance costs | 280 | (40) | 240 |
| Finance costs |  |  | (55) |
| Profit before tax |  |  | 185 |
| Income tax expense |  |  | (55) |
| Profit after tax |  |  | 130 |
| Minority interests |  |  | (45) |
| Group profit for the period |  |  | 85 |

**Earnings per equity share 59.13 cents**

**Statement of changes in equity – year ended 31 March 20X3**

|  | $ million | $ million |
|---|---|---|
| Balance at 1 April 20X2 |  | 270 |
| Profit for the financial year |  | 85 |
| Unrealized surplus on the revaluation of properties |  | 22 |
| Currency translation differences on foreign currency net investments | 12 |  |
| Less exchange losses on related foreign currency loans | (9) |  |
| Dividends (all equity) |  | (50) |
| Issue of share capital (note 2) |  | 60 |
| Balance at 31 March 20X3 |  | 390 |

## NOTES TO THE FINANCIAL STATEMENTS:

### Note 1

During the year Drax disposed of a subsidiary. The loss on disposal shown in the income statement consists of two elements:

Disposal proceeds less related net assets less related goodwill   $45 million **loss**

Gain on curtailment of retirement benefits relating to disposal   $15 million **profit**.

### Note 2

At the start of the period, Drax had 120m $1 equity shares in issue. Drax had no non-equity shares. On 1 July 20X2, Drax made a rights issue to existing shareholders of one share for every four held at $2 per share. The market value of each share immediately before the rights issue was $2.50.

### Note 3

Defined benefit pension plan

|  | At 31 March 20X3 $ million | At 31 March 20X2 $ million |
|---|---|---|
| Present value of funded obligations | 500 | 4 500 |
| Fair value of plan assets | (2 600) | (2 700) |
| Unrecognized actuarial losses | (380) | (350) |
| Net liability in balance sheet | 2 020 | 1 450 |

The new non-executive director has sent you a list of questions to which he requires answers:

(a) Please show how the earnings per share figure has been computed.

(b) I am a non-executive director for another entity operating in the same industry as Drax with roughly the same revenue and with very similar unit costs of raw materials. The nominal value of the shares of this other entity is $1 yet its earnings per share is quite different from that of Drax. How can this be?

(c) I am very suspicious about some of the figures in the statement of changes in equity and in the pension plan liability. It would seem to me that exchange losses on loans and actuarial losses relating to the pension plan should be in the income statement. Are the executive directors trying to maximize the earnings per share for their own ends?

(d) I don't understand how the 'gain on curtailment of retirement benefits' is a gain that goes to the income statement. Shouldn't it be treated in the same way as the actuarial losses that seem to be included in the balance sheet figure for the pension plan liability?

**Required:**

Prepare a reply to the questions the non-executive director has raised. You should refer to the provisions of relevant Accounting Standards where appropriate. Assume that the non-executive director has a reasonable general knowledge of business but that he is not familiar with the detail of Accounting Standards.

(CIMA – May 2003)

**15**    You are the accountant of Acquirer. Your entity has the strategy of growth by acquisition and your directors have identified an entity, Target, which they wish to investigate with a view to launching a takeover bid. Your directors consider that the directors of Target will contest any bid and will not be very cooperative in providing background information on the entity. Therefore, relevant financial information is likely to be restricted to the publicly available financial statements.

Your directors have asked you to compute key financial ratios from the latest financial statements of Target [for the year ended 30 November 20X2] and compare the ratios with those for other entities in a similar sector. Accordingly, you have selected ten broadly similar entities and have presented the directors with the following calculations:

| Ratio | Basis of calculation | Ratio for Target | Spread of ratios for comparative entities | | |
|---|---|---|---|---|---|
| | | | Highest | Average | Lowest |
| Gross profit margin | $\dfrac{\text{Gross profit}}{\text{Revenue}}$ | 42% | 44% | 38% | 33% |
| Operating profit margin | $\dfrac{\text{Profit from operations}}{\text{Revenue}}$ | 29% | 37% | 30% | 26% |
| Return on total capital | $\dfrac{\text{Profit from operations}}{\text{Total capital}}$ | 73% | 92.5% | 69% | 52% |
| Interest cover | $\dfrac{\text{Profit from operations}}{\text{Finance cost}}$ | 1.8 times | 2.5 times | 1.6 times | 1.6 times |
| Gearing | $\dfrac{\text{Debt capital}}{\text{Total capital}}$ | 52% | 56% | 40% | 28% |
| Dividend cover | $\dfrac{\text{Profit after tax}}{\text{Dividend}}$ | 5.2 times | 5 times | 4 times | 3 times |
| Turn of inventory | $\dfrac{\text{Cost of sales}}{\text{Closing inventory}}$ | 4.4 times | 4 times | 4 times | 3.2 times |
| Receivables days | $\dfrac{\text{Trade receivables}}{\text{1 day's sales revenue}}$ | 51 days | 81 days | 62 days | 49 days |

**Required:**

(a) Using the ratios provided, write a report that compares the financial performance and position of Target to the other entities in the survey. Where an issue arises that reflects particularly favourably or unfavourably on Target, you should assess its relevance to a potential acquirer.

(b) Identify any reservations you have regarding the extent to which the ratios provided can contribute to an acquisition decision by the directors of Acquirer. You should highlight the extent to which the financial statements themselves might help you to overcome the reservations you have identified.

(CIMA – November 2003)

**16** BHG is a successful listed entity that designs and markets specialist business software. BHG's directors have decided to adopt a policy of expansion into overseas territories through the acquisition of similar software businesses possessing established shares of their domestic markets. BHG's aim is to obtain control, or at the minimum, significant influence (represented by at least 40 per cent of issued share capital) of investee entities. Target investee entities are likely to be listed entities in their own countries, but the acquisition of unlisted entities is not ruled out.

You are a senior accountant in BHG, and you have been asked by the Chief Financial Officer (CFO) to establish a set of key accounting ratios for use in:

(i)   the initial appraisal of potential acquisitions;

(ii)  ongoing appraisal following acquisitions.

The ratios will be used as part of a suite of quantitative and non-quantitative measurements to compare businesses with each other. The CFO has suggested that it would be appropriate to identify no more than five to seven key financial ratios.

One of your assistants has suggested a list of five key accounting ratios as suitable for both initial and ongoing appraisal and comparison. She has provided reasons to support the case for their inclusion as key ratios.

1   Earnings per share: 'one of the most important investor ratios, widely used by all classes of investor to assess business performance'.

2   Dividend yield: 'this ratio provides a very useful measurement that allows comparison with yields from other equity and non-equity investments'.

3   Gearing: 'this is of critical importance in determining the level of risk of an equity investment'.

4   Gross profit margin: 'allows investors to assess business performance, and is of particular use over several accounting periods within the same organization. It is also very useful for comparing performances between businesses'.

5   Asset turnover ratios: 'allow the investor to compare the intensity of asset usage between businesses, and overtime'.

**Required:**

(a) Discuss the extent to which each of the five suggested accounting ratios is likely to be useful to BHG for both initial and ongoing appraisal and comparison, and the extent to which your assistant's assessments of the value of the ratios are justified.

(b) Explain the problems and limitations of accounting ratio analysis in making inter-firm and international comparisons.

(CIMA – May 2008)

**17** ST, UV and WX are listed entities operating in the same business sector. At 31 October 20X6, their PE ratios were reported as follows:

ST 16.2

UV 12.7

WX 8.4

Which ONE of the following statements about these PE ratios is correct?

The PE ratios suggest that:

(a) ST is regarded by the market as the riskiest of the three entities.

(b) ST has the highest earnings per share of the three entities.

(c) UV represents the safest investment because its PE lies approximately mid-way between the other two.

(d) WX's share price may be relatively lower than that of ST and UV because of an adverse effect such as a profit warning.

(CIMA – May 2006)

# REFERENCES

## Chapter 2

Alexander, D. and Nobes, C. (2004) *Financial Accounting: An International Introduction*, 2nd edn, Harlow, Pearson Education.

Ali, A. and Hwang, L.-S. (2000) 'Country-specific factors related to financial reporting and the value relevance of accounting data', *Journal of Accounting Research* 38(1):1–21.

American Accounting Association (1977) *Accounting Review* 52(4 supp.).

Armstrong, C., Barth, M., Jagolinzer, A. and Riedl, E. (2010) 'Market reaction to the adoption of IFRS in Europe', *Accounting Review* 85(1):31–61.

Ball, R., Kothari, S.P. and Robin, A. (2000) 'The effect of international institutional factors on properties of accounting earnings', *Journal of Accounting and Economics* 29(1):1–51.

Ball, R. and Shivakumar, L. (2002) 'Earning quality in UK private firms', Working paper, London Business School.

Barth, M., Landsman, W. and Lang, M. (2008) 'International accounting standards and accounting quality', *Journal of Accounting Research* 46(3):467–98.

Basu, S. (1997) 'The conservatism principle and the asymmetric timeliness of earnings', *Journal of Accounting and Economics* 24(1):3–37.

Beuselinck, C. Joos, P., Khurana, L. and Van der Meulen, S. (2009) 'Mandatory IFRS reporting and stock price informativeness' SSRN-*eLibrary*.

Beuselinck, C., Joos, P., Khurana, L. and Van der Meulen, S. (2010) 'Mandatory adoption of IFRS and analysts' forecasts information properties', SSRN-*eLibrary*

Botosan, C. and Plumlee, M. (2002) 'A re-examination of disclosure level and the expected cost of equity capital', *Journal of Accounting Research* 40(1):21–40.

Burghstahler, D.C., Hail, L. and Leuz, C. (2006) 'The importance of reporting incentives: Earnings management in European private and public firms', *Accounting Review* 81(5):983–1016.

Bushman, R. and Piotroski, J. (2006) 'Financial reporting incentives for conservative accounting: The influence of legal and political institutions', *Journal of Accounting and Economics* 42:107–48.

Byard, D., Li, Y. and Yu, Y. (2011) 'The effect of mandatory EFRS adoption on financial analysts' information environment', *Journal of Accounting Research* 49(1):69–96.

Chaney, P., Faccio, M. and Parsley, D. (2011) 'The quality of accounting information in politically connected firms', *Journal of Accounting and Economics* 51:58–76.

Christensen, H., Hail, L. and Leuz, C. (2012), 'Mandatory IFRS reporting and changes in enforcement', SSRN-*eLibrary*.

da Costa, R.C., Bourgeois, J.C. and Lawson, W.M. (1978) 'A classification of international financial accounting practices', *International Journal of Accounting (Education and Research)* 8(7):73–85.

Daimler-Benz (1989–94) Annual Reports.

d'Arcy, A. (2001) 'Accounting classification and the international harmonization debate – an empirical investigation', *Accounting, Organizations and Society* 26:327–49.

Daske, H., Hail, L., Leuz, C. and Verdi, R. (2008) 'Mandatory IFRS reporting around the world: Early evidence on the economic consequences', *Journal of Accounting Research* 46(5):1085–142.

Fama, E. and Jensen, M. (1983) 'Separation of ownership and control', *Journal of Law and Economics* 26(2): 301–25.

Florou, A. and Pope, P. (2012) 'Mandatory IFRS adoption and investor asset allocation decisions', *The Accounting Review* 87(6):1993–2025.

Frank, W.G. (1979) 'An empirical analysis of international accounting principles', *Journal of Accounting Research* 17(2):593–605.

Gebhardt, G. and Novotny-Farkas, Z. (2011), 'Mandatory IFRS adoption and accounting quality of European banks', *Journal of Business Finance and Accounting* 38(3–4):289–333.

Gray, S. (1988) 'Towards a theory of cultural influence on the development of accounting systems internationally', *Abacus* March.

Guenther, D. and Young, D. (2000) 'The association between financial accounting measures and real economic activity: A multinational study', *Journal of Accounting and Economics* 29(1):53–72.

Hatfield, H.R (1966) 'Some variations in accounting practices in England, France, Germany, and the United States', *Journal of Accounting Research* 4(2):169–82.

Hofstede, G. (1984) *Culture's Consequences: International Differences in Work-related Values*, Beverly Hills, CA, Sage.

Hope, O.K. (2003a) 'Disclosure practices, enforcement of accounting standards, and analysts' forecast accuracy:

An international study', *Journal of Accounting Research* 41(2):235–72.

Hope, O.K. (2003b) 'Firm-level disclosures and the relative roles of culture and legal origin', *Journal of International Financial Management and Accounting* 14(3):218–48.

Horton, J., Serafeim, G. and Serafeim, I. (2012) 'Does mandatory IFRS adoption improve the information environment', *Contemporary Accounting Research* 30(1):388–423.

Jackson, H. and Roe, M. (2009) 'Public and private enforcement of securities laws: Resource-based evidence', *Journal of Financial Economics* 93:207–38.

Jiao, T., Koning, M., Mertens, G. and Rosenboom, P. (2012) 'Mandatory IFRS adoption and its impact on analysts' forecasts', *International Review of Financial Analysis.* 2(1):343–71.

Kvaal, E. and Nobes, C. (2011) 'IFRS policy changes and the continuation of national patterns of IFRS practice', *European Accounting Review* 21(2):56–63.

Kvaal, E. and Nobes, C. (2012) 'IFRS policy changes and the continuation of National Patterns of IFRS Practice', *European Accounting Review* 21(2):343–371.

Lambert, R. and Larcker, D. (1987) 'An analysis of the use of accounting and market measures of performance in executive compensation contracts', *Journal of Accounting Research* 25(supp.):85–125.

Lambert, R., Leuz, C. and Verrecchia, R. (2007) 'Accounting information, disclosure, and the cost of capital', *Journal of Accounting Research* 45(2):385–420.

Landsman, W., Maydew, E. and Thornock, J. (2011) 'The information content of annual earnings announcements and mandatory adoption of IFRS', *Journal of Accounting and Economics* 53(1–2):34–54.

Lang, M., Maffet, M. and Owens, E. (2012) 'Earnings comovement and accounting comparability: The effects of mandatory IFRS adoption', *SSRN e-library*.

La Porta, R., Lopez-de-Silanes, F., Shleifer, A. and Vishny, R. (1997) 'Legal determinants of external finance', *Journal of Finance* 52(3):1131–50.

La Porta, R., Lopez-de-Silanes, F., Shleifer, A. and Vishny, R. (1998) 'Law and finance', *Journal of Political Economy* 106(6):1113–55.

Leuz, C. (2010) 'Different approaches to corporate reporting regulation: How jurisdictions differ and why?', *Accounting and Business Research* 40(3):229–56.

Leuz, C., Nanda, D. and Wysocki, P. (2003) 'Earnings management and investor protection: An international comparison', *Journal of Financial Economics* 69(3):505–27.

Leuz, C. and Verrecchia, R.E. (2000) 'The economic consequences of increased disclosure', *Journal of Accounting Research* 38(3 supp.):91–124.

Mey, A. (1966) 'Theodore Limperg and his theory of values and costs', *Abacus* 2(1):3–23.

Mueller, G.G. (1967) *International Accounting*, New York, Macmillan.

Nair, R.D. and Frank, W.G. (1980) 'The impact of disclosure and measurement on international accounting classifications', *Accounting Review* 55(3):426–50.

Nobes, C.W. (1980) 'International classification of accounting systems', unpublished paper.

Nobes, C.W. and Parker, R. (2003) *Comparative International Accounting,* 7th edn, London, Prentice Hall.

Ordelheide, D. and KPMG (eds) (2001) *Transnational Accounting,* 2nd edn, London, Palgrave.

Penman, S.H. and Zhang, X.-J. (2002) 'Accounting conservatism, the quality of earnings, and stock returns', *Accounting Review* 77(2):237–64.

Pope, P. and McLeay, S. (2011) 'The European IFRS experiment: Objectives, research challenges and some early evidence', *Accounting and Business Research* 41(3):233–266.

Pope, P. and Walker, M. (1999) 'International differences in the timeliness, conservatism, and classification of earnings', *Journal of Accounting Research* 37(3 supp.):53–87.

Schipper, K. (2000) 'Accounting research and the potential use of international accounting standards for cross-border securities listings', *British Accounting Review* 32(3):243–56.

Schmalenbach, E. (1927) 'Der Kontenrahmen', *Zeitschrift fur betriebswirtschaftliche Forschung* 21:385–402.

Seidler, L.J. (1967) 'International accounting – the ultimate theory course', *Accounting Review* 42(4):775–81.

Tarca, A. (2012) 'Report to the Trustees of the IFRS Foundation: Appendix – The case for Global Accounting Standards: Arguments and evidence', *Staff paper prepared by the IFRS Foundation Staff – 22 October 2012*, 68–84.

# Chapter 3

IFRS Foundation and IASB (2010) 'Who we are and what we do', London, IFRS.

Schipper, K. (2005) 'The introduction of international accounting standards in Europe: Implications for international convergence', *European Accounting Review* 14(1):101–26.

# Chapter 4

Edwards, E.O. and Bell, P.W. (1961) *The Theory and Measurement of Business Income,* Berkeley, CA, University of California Press.

Fisher, I. (1930) *The Theory of Interest,* New York, Macmillan. (Reprinted as 'Income and capital', in Parker and Harcourt, 1969.)

Hicks, J. (1946) *Value and Capital: An Inquiry Into Some Fundamental Principles of Economic Theory,* 2nd edn, Oxford, Clarendon Press. (Reprinted as 'Income' in Parker and Harcourt, 1969.)

# Chapter 5

Edwards, E.O. and Bell, P.W. (1961) *The Theory and Measurement of Business Income,* Berkeley, CA, University of California Press.

# Chapter 6

Edwards, E.O. and Bell, P.W. (1961) *The Theory and Measurement of Business Income,* Berkeley, CA, University of California Press.

# Chapter 7

Bonbright, J.C. (1937) *The Valuation of Property,* New York, McGraw-Hill.
Mey, A. (1966) 'Theodore Limperg and his theory of values and costs', *Abacus* 2(1):3–23.
Sandilands Report (1975) *Inflation Accounting Committee,* MND 6225, London, HMSO.
Schmalenbach, E. (1959) *Dynamic Accounting,* London, Gee & Co.
Sweeney, H.W. (1936) *Stabilized Accounting,* New York, Harper & Bros.

# Chapter 8

Edwards, E.O. and Bell, P.W. (1961) *The Theory and Measurement of Business Income,* Berkeley, CA, University of California Press.

# Chapter 9

Ball, R. and Brown, P. (1968) 'An empirical evaluation of accounting income numbers', *Journal of Accounting Research* (Autumn):159–78.
Beaver, W. (1968) 'The information content of annual earnings announcements', *Journal of Accounting Research* (Supplement):67–92.
Hail, L., Leuz, C. and Wysocki, P. (2010) 'Global convergence and the potential adoption of IFRS by the US (Part I): Conceptual underpinnings and economic analysis', *Accounting Horizons* 24(3):355–94.
Hendriksen, E.S. (1977) *Accounting Theory,* 3rd edn, Homewood, IL: R.D. Irwin.
Jensen, M.C. and Meckling, W.H. (1976) 'The theory of the firm: Managerial behavior, agency costs and ownership structure', *Journal of Financial Economics* 3:305–60.
Kahneman, D. and Tversky, A. (1972) 'Subjective probability: A judgment of representativeness', *Cognitive Psychology* 3:430–54.
Kahneman, D. and Tversky, A. (1973) 'On the psychology of prediction', *Psychological Review* 80:237–51.

Kahneman, D. and Tversky, A. (1979) 'Prospect theory: An analysis of decisions under risk', *Econometrica* 47:313–27.
La Porta, R., Lopez-de-Silanes, F., Shleifer, A. and Vishny, R.W. (1997) 'Legal determinants of external finance', *Journal of Finance* 52(3):1131–50.
Leuz, C. (2010) 'Different approaches to corporate reporting regulation: How jurisdictions differ and why', *Accounting and Business Research* 40(3):229–56.
Nobes, C. (1998) 'Towards a general model of the reasons for international differences in financial reporting', *Abacus* 34(2):162–87.
Odean, T. (1998) 'Are investors reluctant to realize their losses?', *Journal of Finance* 53(5):1775–98.
Riahi-Belkaoui, A. (2004) *Accounting Theory,* 5th edn, USA: South-Western, Cengage Learning.
Ryan, B., Scapens, R.W. and Theobald, M. (2002) *Research Method and Methodology in Finance and Accounting* 2nd edn, Thomson, London.
Scott, D.R. (1940) 'The accounting exchange: Selling accounting short', *The Accounting Review* 15(4):507–9.
Shefrin, H. (2000) *Beyond Greed and Fear: Understanding Behavioral Finance and the Psychology of Investing,* Boston, MA.: Harvard Business School Press.
Shiller, R.J. (2000) *Irrational Exuberance,* Princeton, N.J., Princeton University Press.
Shiller, R.J. (2003) 'From efficient markets theory to behavioral finance', *Journal of Economic Perspectives* 17(1):83–104.
Shleifer, A. (2000) *Inefficient Markets,* Oxford: Oxford University Press.
Simon, H.A. (1979) 'Rational decision making in business organizations', *American Economic Review* 69(4):493–513.
Smith, M. (2011) *Research Methods in Accounting,* 2nd edn, London: Sage.
Statman, M. and Shefrin H. (1985) 'The disposition to sell winners too early and ride losers too long: Theory and evidence', *Journal of Finance* 40(3):777–90.
Staubus, G.J. (1959) 'The residual equity point of view in accounting', *The Accounting Review* 34(1):3–13.
Staubus, G.J. (1961) *A Theory of Accounting to Investors.* Berkeley, CA: University of California Press.
Thaler, R.H. (1999) 'Mental accounting matters', *Journal of Behavioural Decision Making* 12:183–206.
Van Mourik, C. (2014a) 'Methodology in financial accounting theory', in Van Mourik, C. and Walton P. eds, *The Routledge Companion to Accounting, Reporting and Regulation,* Abingdon, Routledge.
Van Mourik, C. (2014b) 'Fundamental issues in financial accounting and reporting theory', in Van Mourik, C. and Walton P. eds, *The Routledge Companion to Accounting, Reporting and Regulation,* Abingdon, Routledge.
Watts, R.L. and Zimmerman, J.L. (1978) 'Towards a positive theory of the determination of accounting standards', *The Accounting Review* 53(1):112–34.

Watts, R.L. and Zimmerman, J.L. (1979) 'The demand for and supply of accounting theories: The market for excuses', *The Accounting Review* 54(2):273–305.

Williams, P.F. (2002) 'Accounting and the moral order: Justice, accounting and legitimate moral authority', *Accounting in the Public Interest*, 2:1–21.

Williams, P.F. (2006) 'Accounting for economic reality: Whose reality? Which justice?', *Accounting in the Public Interest* 6:37–44.

Yu, S.C. (1976) *The Structure of Accounting Theory*. Gainesville, FL: University Presses of Florida.

## Chapter 10

Cearns, K. and the G4 + 1 standard setters (1999) Reporting Financial Performance: Proposals for Change (G4 + 1 Position Paper). http://www.frc.org.uk/Our-Work/Publications/ASB/Reporting-Financial-Performance-Proposals-for-Chan.aspx (accessed 11 March 2013).

## Chapter 11

Accounting Standards Steering Committee (1975) *The Corporate Report,* London.

Adams, R. (1994) 'Ready for a greening', *Accountancy Age* (5):May.

Berle, A.A. and Means, G.C. (1932) *The Modern Corporation and Private Property*, New York: Macmillan.

Cadbury Committee (1992) *Financial Aspects of Corporate Governance* (The Cadbury Report), London, Gee.

Carroll, A.B. (1991) 'The pyramid of corporate social responsibility: Toward the moral management of organizational stakeholders', *Business Horizons* 34(4):39–48.

European Commision (2011) A Renewed Strategy 2011–14 for Corporate Social Responsibility. COM (2011) 681. http://eur-lex.europa.eu/LexUriServ/LexUriServ.do?uri=COM:2011:0681:FIN:EN:PDF (accessed 4 June 2013).

FRC (2012) *The UK Corporate Governance Code*. Financial Reporting Council, September.

Freeman, R.E. (1984) *Strategic Management: A Stakeholder Approach*. Boston, MA: Pitman.

Friedman, M. (1970) 'The social responsibility of business is to increase its profits', *New York Times Magazine*, 13 September.

Greenbury Committee (1995) *Directors' Remuneration: Report of a Study Group Chaired by Sir Richard Greenbury* (The Greenbury Report), London, Gee.

Hampel Committee (1998) *Committee on Corporate Governance: Final Report* (The Hampel Report), London, Gee.

Hicks, J.R (1946) *Value and Capital*, 2nd edn, Oxford, Oxford University Press.

Higgs Committee (2003) *Review of the Role and Effectiveness of Non-executive Directors* (The Higgs Report), London, DTI.

OECD (1999) *OECD Principles of Corporate Goverance*. Organization of Economic Cooperation and Development, Paris.

OECD (2004) *OECD Principles of Corporate Goverance*. Organization of Economic Cooperation and Development, Paris.

O'Rourke, D. (2004) 'Opportunities and Obstacles for Corporate Social Responsibility Reporting in Developing Countries'. The World Bank, March 2004. http://nature.berkeley.edu/orourke/PDF/CSR-Reporting.pdf (accessed 4 June 2013).

Smith, A. (1776) *The Wealth of Nations*, London, Stathan and Cadell.

Turnbull Committee (1999) *Internal Control: Guidance for Directors on the Combined Code* (The Turnbull Report), London, Institute of Chartered Accountants in England & Wales.

## Chapter 16

IASC (1999) *Leases: Implementation of a New Approach*, London, IASC.

## Chapter 17

IASC (2011) *Revenue Recognition in Contracts with Customers*, London, IASC.

## Chapter 22

Black, F. and Scholes, M. (1973) 'The pricing of options and corporate liabilities', *Journal of Political Economy* 81(3):637–54.

## Chapter 25

Fields, T., Lys, T. and Vincent, L. (2001) 'Empirical research on accounting choice', *Journal of Accounting and Economics* 31(1–3):255–307.

## Chapter 31

Adams, R. and Ferreira, D. (2007) 'A theory of friendly boards', *Journal of Finance* 62(1):217–50.

Ajinka, B., Bhojraj, S. and Sengupta, P. (2005) 'The association between outside directors, institutional investors and the properties of management earnings forecasts', *Journal of Accounting Research* 43(3):343–76.

Armstrong, C., Barth, M., Jagolinzer, A. and Riedl, E. (2010) 'Market reaction to events surrounding the adoption of IFRS in Europe', *The Accounting Review* 85(1):31–61.

Baginski, S., Hassell, J. and Wieland, M. (2011) 'An examination of the effects of management earnings forecast form and explanations on financial analyst forecast revisions', *Advances in Accounting* 27(1):17–25.

Bailey, W., Karolyi, G. and Salva, D. (2006) ' The economic consequences of increased disclosure: Evidence from international cross-listings', *Journal of Financial Economics* 81(1):175–213.

Ball, R., Kothari, S.P. and Robin, A. (2000) 'The effect of international institutional factors on properties of accounting earnings', *Journal of Accounting and Economics* 29(1):1–51.

Banker, R. and Johnston, H. (1993) 'An empirical study of cost drivers in the US airline industry', *Accounting Review* 68(3):576–601.

Barth, M., Elliot, J. and Finn, M. (1995) 'Market rewards associated with increasing earnings patterns', Working paper, Cornell University.

Bartov, E. (1993) 'The timing of asset sales and earnings manipulation', *Accounting Review* 68:840–55.

Beasley, M.S. (1996) 'An empirical analysis of the relation between the board of director composition and financial statement fraud', *Accounting Review* 71(4):443–65.

Bedard, J. and Johnstone, K. (2004), 'Earnings management risk, corporate governance risk, and auditors planning and pricing decisions', *The Accounting Review* 79(2):277–304.

Bloomfield, R. (2008). 'Discussion of annual report readability, current earnings, and earnings persistence', *Journal of Accounting and Economics* 45(2–3):248–52.

Botosan, C.A. (1997) 'Disclosure level and the cost of equity capital', *Accounting Review* 72(3):323–49.

Bowen, RM., DuCharme, L. and Shores, D. (1995) 'Stakeholders' implicit claims and accounting method choice', *Journal of Accounting and Economics* 20(3):255–95.

Boyd, B.K. (1994) 'Board control and CEO compensation', *Strategic Management Journal* 15(5):335–44.

Brown, L. and Caylor, M. (2006) 'Corporate governance and firm valuation', *Journal of Accounting and Public Policy* 25(4):409–34.

Burgstahler, D. and Eames, M. (2006) 'Management of earnings and analysts' forecasts to achieve zero and small positive earnings surprises', *Journal of Business Finance and Accounting* 35(5):633–52.

Burgstahler, D. and Dichev, I. (1997) 'Earnings management to avoid earnings decreases and losses', *Journal of Accounting and Economics* 24(1):99–126.

Bushman, R. and Piotroski, J. (2006) 'Financial reporting incentives for conservative accounting: The influence of legal and political institutions', *Journal of Accounting and Economics* 42:107–148.

Cao, Z. and Narayanamoorthy, G. (2011) 'The effect of litigation risk on management earnings forecasts', *Contemporary Accounting Research* 28(1):125–73.

Carcello, J. and Nagy, A. (2004) 'Audit firm tenure and fraudulent financial reporting', *Auditing: A Journal of Practice and Theory* 23(2):55–69.

Cheng, J. and Warfield, T. (2005) 'Equity incentives and earnings management', *The Accounting Review* 80(2):441–476.

Cohen, D., Dey, A. and Lys, T. (2008) 'Real and accrual based earnings management in the pre and post Sarbanes Oxley periods', *The Accounting Review* 83(3):757–87.

Cohen, D. and Zarowin, P. (2010) 'Accrual-based and real earnings management activities around seasoned equity offerings', *Journal of Accounting and Economics* 50(1):2–19.

DeAngelo, H., DeAngelo, L. and Skinner, D. (1996) 'Reversal of fortune: Dividend signaling and the disappearance of sustained earnings growth', *Journal of Financial Economics* 40(3):341–71

Dechow, P.M. and Sloan, R.G. (1991) 'Executive incentives and the horizon problem: An empirical investigation', *Journal of Accounting and Economics* 14(1):51–89.

DeFond, M.L. and Jiambalvo, J. (1994) 'Debt covenant violation and manipulation of accruals', *Journal of Accounting and Economics* 17(1–2):145–76.

DeGeorge, F., Patel, J. and Zeckhauser, R. (1999) 'Earnings management to exceed thresholds', *Journal of Business* 72(1):1–33.

Djankov, S., La Porta, R., Lopez-de-Silanes, F. and Shleifer, A. (2008) 'The law and economics of self-dealing', *Journal of Financial Economics* 88:430–65.

Donnelly, R and Lynch, C. (2002) 'The ownership structure of UK firms and the informativeness of accounting earnings', *Accounting and Business Research* 32(4):245–57.

Doyle, J., Ge, W. and McVay, S. (2007) 'Accruals quality and internal control over financial reporting', *The Accounting Review* 82(5):1141–70.

Easton, P.D., Monahan, S.J. and Vasvari, F.P. (2009) 'Initial evidence on the role of accounting earnings in the bond market', *Journal of Accounting Research* 47(3):721–66.

Efendi, J., Srivastava, A. and Swanson, E. (2007) 'Why do corporate managers misstate financial statements? The role of option compensation and other factors', *Journal of Financial Economics* 85(3):667–708.

Erickson, M., Hanlon, M. and Maydew, E. (2006) 'Is there a link between executive equity incentives and accounting fraud?' *Journal of Accounting Research*, 44(1):113–43.

Fan, Q. (2007) 'Earnings management and ownership retention for initial public offering firms: theory and evidence', *The Accounting Review* 82(1):1–27.

Fan, J.P.H. and Wong, T.J. (2002) 'Corporate ownership structure and the informativeness of accounting earnings in East Asia', *Journal of Accounting and Economics* 33(3):401–25.

Feng, M., Gramlich, J. and Gupta, S. (2009) 'Special purpose vehicles: empirical evidence on determinants and earnings management', *Accounting Review* 84(6):1833–76.

Francis, J. (2001) 'Discussion of empirical research on accounting choice', *Journal of Accounting and Economics* 31(1–3):309–19.

Friedlan, J.M. (1994) 'Accounting choices of issuers of initial public offerings', *Contemporary Accounting Research* 11(1):1–31.

Godfrey, J., Mather, P. and Ramsey, A. (2003) 'Earnings and impression management in financial reports: The case of CEO changes', *Abacus* 39(1):95–123.

Graham, J., Harvey, C. and Rajgopal, S. (2005) 'The economic implications of corporate financial reporting', *Journal of Accounting and Economics* 40(1–3):3–75.

Guenther, D., Maydew, E. and Nutter, S. (1997) 'Financial reporting, tax costs and book-tax conformity', *Journal of Accounting and Economics* 2(3)3:225–48.

Gunny, K. (2010) 'The relationship between earnings management using real activities manipulation and future performance: evidence from meeting earnings benchmarks', *Contemporary Accounting Research* 27(3):855–88.

Hand, J.R.M. (1989) 'Did firms undertake debt-equity swaps for an accounting paper profit or true financial gain?', *Accounting Review* 64(4):587–623.

Healy, P.M. (1985) 'The effect of bonus schemes on accounting decisions', *Journal of Accounting and Economics* 7(1–3):85–107.

Healy, P.M., Hutton, A. and Palepu, K.G. (1999) 'Stock performance and intermediation changes surrounding sustained increases in disclosure', *Contemporary Accounting Research* 16(3):485–520.

Healy, P.M. and Palepu, K.G. (1993) 'The effect of firms' financial disclosure strategies on stock prices', *Accounting Horizons* 7(1):1–11.

Healy, P.M. and Wahlen, J.M. (1999) 'A review of the earnings management literature and its implications for standard setting', *Accounting Horizons* 13(4):365–83.

Hope, O.K. (2003) 'Disclosure practices, enforcement of accounting standards and analysts' forecast accuracy: An international study', *Journal of Accounting Research* 41(2):235–72.

Horngren, C.T., Bhimani, A., Datar, S.M. and Foster, G. (2002) *Management and Cost Accounting*, 2nd edn, London, Financial Times-Prentice Hall.

Hunt, A., Moyer, S.E. and Shevlin, T. (1995) 'Earnings volatility, earnings management, and equity value', Working paper, University of Washington.

Jaggi, B., Leung, S. and Gul, F. (2009) 'Family control, board independence and earnings management: Evidence based on Hong Kong firms', *Journal of Accounting and Economic Policy* 28(4):281–300.

Jensen, M.C. and Murphy, K.J. (1990) 'Performance pay and top-management incentives', *Journal of Political Economy* 98(2):225–64.

Jiambalvo, J. (1996) 'Discussion of: "Causes and consequences of earnings manipulation: An analysis of firms subject to enforcement actions by the SEC"', *Contemporary Accounting Research* 13(1):37–47.

Jiang, J. (2010) 'Beating earnings benchmarks and the cost of debt', *The Accounting Review* 83(2):377–416.

Johnson, V., Khurana, I. and Reynolds, J. (2002), 'Audit-firm tenure and the quality of financial reports', *Contemporary Accounting Research* 19(3):637–60.

Jones, R. and Wu, Y. (2010) 'Executive compensation, earnings management and shareholder litigation', *Review of Quantitative Finance and Accounting* 35(1):1–20.

Kasanen, E., Kinnunen, J. and Niskanen, J. (1996) 'Dividend-based earnings management: Empirical evidence from Finland', *Journal of Accounting and Economics* 22(1–3):283–312.

Kasznik, R. (1999) 'On the association between voluntary disclosure and earnings management', *Journal of Accounting Research* 37(1):57–81.

Kasznik, R. and McNichols, M. (2002) 'Does meeting earnings expectations matter? Evidence from analyst forecast revisions and share prices', *Journal of Accounting Research* 40(3):727–59.

Key, K.G. (1997) 'Political cost incentives for earning management in the cable television industry', *Journal of Accounting and Economics* 23(3):309–37.

Klein, A. (2002) 'Audit committee, board of director characteristics and earnings management', *Journal of Accounting and Economics* 33(3):375–400.

Koonce, L. and Lipe, M. (2010) 'Earnings trend and performance relative to benchmarks: How consistency influences their joint use', *Journal of Accounting Research* 48(4):859–84.

Kothari, S, Ramana, K. and Skinner, D. (2010) 'Implications for GAAP from an analysis of positive accounting research in accounting', *Journal of Accounting and Economics* 50:246–86.

LaPorta, R., Lopez-de-Silanes, F., Shleifer, A. and Vishny, R (1997) 'Legal determinants of external finance', *Journal of Finance* 52(3):1131–50.

LaPorta, R., Lopez-de-Silanes, F., Shleifer, A. and Vishny, R (1998) 'Law and finance', *Journal of Political Economy* 106(6):1113–55.

LaSalle, R.E., Jones, S.K. and Jain, R. (1993) 'The association between executive succession and discretionary accounting changes: Earning management or different perspectives?', *Journal of Business Finance and Accounting* 20(5):653–71.

Leuz, C. (2010) 'Different approaches to corporate reporting regulation: How jurisdictions differ and why?', *Accounting and Business Research* 40(3):229–56.

Leuz, C., Nanda, D. and Wysocki, P.D. (2003) 'Earning's management and inventor protection: An international comparison', *Journal of Financial Economics* 69(3):505–27.

Leuz, C. and Verrechia, RE. (2000) 'The economic consequences of increased disclosure', *Journal of Accounting Research* 38 (supp.):91–124.

Luchinger, R. (2003) *Swissair: L'histoire secrete de la debacle,* Lausanne, Editions Bilan.

Maijoor, S. and Vanstraelen, A. (2006) 'Earnings management within Europe: The effects of member state audit environment, audit firm quality and international capital markets', *Accounting and Business Research* 36(1):33–52.

McNichols, M. and Wilson, G.P. (1988) 'Evidence of earnings management from the provision for bad debts', *Journal of Accounting Research* 26(3 supp.):1–31.

Murphy, K.J. and Zimmerman, J.L. (1993) 'Financial performance surrounding CEO turnover', *Journal of Accounting and Economics* 16(1–3):273–315.

Nelson, M.W., Elliott, J.A. and Tarpley, R.L. (2003) 'How are earnings managed? Examples from auditors', *Accounting Horizons* 17(supp.):17–35.

Neil, J.D., Pourciau, S.G. and Schaefer, T.F. (1995) 'Accounting method choice and IPO valuation', *Accounting Horizons* 9(3):68–80.

Nikolaev, V.V. (2010) 'Debt covenants and accounting conservatism', *Journal of Accounting Research* 48(1):51–89.

Peasnell, K.V., Pope, P.F. and Young, S. (2001) 'The characteristics of firms subject to adverse rulings by the Financial Reporting Review Panel', *Accounting and Business Research* 31(4):291–311.

Peasnell, K.V., Pope, P.F. and Young, S. (2005), 'Board monitoring and earnings management: Do outside directors influence abnormal accruals?', *Journal of Business Finance and Accounting* 32(7/8):1246–311.

Penman, S.H. (2001) *Financial Statement Analysis and Security Valuation,* Boston, MA, McGraw-Hill/Irwin.

Penman, S.H. (2003) *Financial Statement Analysis and Security Valuation,* 2nd edn, Boston, MA, McGraw-Hill.

Pope, P., Gore, P. and Singh, A. (2007) 'Earnings management and the distribution of earnings relative to targets: UK evidence', *Accounting and Business Research* 37(2):151–166.

Porter, M.E. (1985) *Competitive Advantage: Creating and Sustaining Superior Performance,* New York, Free Press.

Pourciau, S. (1993) 'Earnings management and non-routine executive changes', *Journal of Accounting and Economics* 16(1–3):317–36.

Rangan, S. (1998) 'Earnings management and the performance of seasoned equity offerings', *Journal of Financial Economics* 50(1):101–22.

Rogers, J. and Van Buskirk, A. (2009) 'Shareholder litigation and changes in disclosure behavior', *Journal of Accounting and Economics* 47(1-2):136–56.

Roychowdhury, S. (2006) 'Earnings management through real activities manipulation', *Journal of Accounting and Economics* 42(3):335–70.

Rusmin, R. (2010), 'Auditor quality and earnings management: Signaporean evidence', *Managerial Auditing Journal* 25(7):618–38.

Schipper, K. (1989) 'Commentary earnings management', *Accounting Horizons* 3(4):91–102.

Sengupta, P. (1998) 'Corporate disclosure quality and the cost of debt', *Accounting Review* 73(4):459–74.

Shank, J.K. and Govindarajan, V. (1992) 'Strategic cost management and the value chain', *Journal of Cost Management* Winter:5–21.

Shivakumar, L. (1998) 'Market reaction to seasoned equity offering announcements and earnings management', Working paper, London Business School.

Sweeney, A.P. (1994) 'Debt-covenant violations and managers' accounting responses', *Journal of Accounting and Economics* 17(3):281–308.

Trueman, B. and Titman, S. (1988) 'An explanation for accounting income smoothing', *Journal of Accounting Research* 26(3):127–39.

Wayne, T.B., Herrmann, D.R. and Inoue, T. (2004) 'Earnings management through affiliated transactions', *Journal of International Accounting Research* 3(2):1–25.

Zang, A. (2012), 'Evidence on the tradeoff between real manipulation and accruals manipulation', *The Accounting Review* 87(2):675–703.

## Chapter 32

Altman, E.I. (1968) 'Financial ratios, discriminant analysis and the prediction of corporate bankruptcy', *Journal of Finance* 23(4):589–609.

Amir, E. and Lev, B. (1996) 'Value-relevance of nonfinancial information: The wireless communications industry', *Journal of Accounting and Economics* 22 (1–3):3–30.

Dechow, P.M. (1994) 'Accounting earnings and cash flows as measures of firm performance: the role of accounting accruals', *Journal of Accounting and Economics* 18(1): 3–42.

Ittner, C.D. and Larcker, D.F. (2001) 'Assessing empirical research in managerial accounting: A value-based management perspective', *Journal of Accounting and Economics* 32(1–3):349–411.

Kaplan, R. and Norton, D. (1992) 'The balanced scorecard: Measures that drive performance', *Harvard Business Review* (Jan–Feb):71–9.

Rappaport, A. (1998) *Creating Shareholder Value: A Guide for Managers and Investors,* New York, Free Press.

# INDEX

# CREDIT LINES FOR THIRD PARTY ITEMS WHICH REQUIRED PERMISSIONS CLEARANCE